INTERNATIONAL MARKETING MANAGEMENT

Houghton Mifflin Company ■ **Boston**

Dallas   Geneva, Illinois   Palo Alto   Princeton, New Jersey

INTERNATIONAL MARKETING MANAGEMENT

STRATEGIES AND CASES

Jean-Pierre Jeannet

Babson College, Wellesley, Massachusetts
IMEDE, Lausanne, Switzerland

Hubert D. Hennessey

Babson College, Wellesley, Massachusetts

To Our Students

Printed in the U.S.A.

Library of Congress Catalog Card Number: 87-80430

ISBN: 0-395-35675-X

DFGHIJ-H-99876543210

CONTENTS

PREFACE

Over the past ten years, we have taught international marketing extensively in a number of institutions, both in the United States and abroad. The field of international marketing has changed significantly in the 1980s, with a whole range of new concepts and materials having evolved. Most recently, international marketing has been revolutionized by the concept of globalization. However, we found that existing educational materials usually lacked key features that were important for effective teaching in this growing field. As we began to create our own material piece by piece and case by case, it seemed appropriate to proceed with a book. The final product has benefited immensely from constant material testing, rewriting, review, and reformulation. The result is what we believe to be the first major textbook that fully incorporates the global point of view in international marketing.

In approaching our task, we were guided by the view that most firms need to become increasingly sophisticated in their international expansion. As the international marketplace becomes more competitive, firms, regardless of their origin, need to enhance their managerial resources so that they can cope better with these new requirements.

In the past, most instructors and practitioners in the field believed that the key to effective international marketing was a sensitivity to foreign cultures. As a result, much of the educational material concentrated on building an understanding of foreign cultures. Today's environment has changed, however. Although a thorough cultural understanding is still necessary for success in international marketing, many companies and their management have found that an emphasis on strategy is just as important for success abroad. Companies fail not only for cultural reasons but increasingly for strategic reasons. Many companies also do not live up to their potential abroad because management does not see the importance of competing in international markets. It is for these reasons that we have devoted much of our material to the strategic aspects of international marketing, including environmental considerations such as culture in our discussion of international marketing decisions.

Based on our view that international marketing effectiveness requires a strategic understanding, we have chosen a decidedly managerial approach to the field. Issues are tackled from the manager's point of view and concepts are included that help students address specific international marketing issues. Also, the conceptual material consistently emphasizes a global point of view of international marketing. A global point of view requires the integration of all relevant trends, facts, and markets into an overall framework that allows managers to consider many different markets simultaneously rather than on a country by country basis.

The text has been written for students of international marketing both in the United States and abroad. It is designed for use at undergraduate, graduate, and executive programs. However, the text is written in such a way that even experienced practitioners will be able to profit from its conceptual approach. Much of the material used in this text has been extensively class tested with these target audiences, allowing us to enhance both its usefulness and relevancy as a teaching tool.

The book has a number of features that we believe will substantially enhance students' learning experiences. A part opening model visually organizes the subject matter into a "roadmap" leading the reader to each part of the book. Part and chapter overviews also integrate the various topics to be discussed and highlight important issues. Each chapter concludes with a series of thought-provoking questions designed to help students assimilate the chapter material.

The text contains numerous examples of international marketing situations faced by actual U.S. and foreign organizations. Particular attention has been focused on Japan, an increasingly important trading partner and competitor for many international firms. The authors have been fortunate to have taught and conducted research in Japan, which has added to the insights and examples provided.

A key feature of this book is its collection of cases. Based on real international marketing problems, these fourteen cases represent a rich collection of typical issues faced by managers. All cases have been classroom tested, represent many different types of industries and countries, and allow the students to experience some actual international marketing issues. Pedagogically, they are intended to help the students move from understanding pure concepts to practicing international marketing. The cases are up-to-date and comprehensive, thus allowing for lively and productive discussions in class.

ACKNOWLEDGEMENTS

To write a completely new textbook in international marketing is a major undertaking that could not have been completed without the active support and help of a great many people.

We are indebted to our institutions, Babson College and IMEDE International Management Development Institute, for their support. Babson College generously supported us in the manuscript preparation stage. Norman Govoni, our Chairman, patiently encouraged our work and was always available with helpful advice based upon his own extensive experience in publishing text books. Our marketing colleagues at Babson offered great encouragement and advice throughout the book. The Babson Board of Research financially supported several research projects that aided this book. At IMEDE, we are particularly indebted to Dean Derek Abell who supported our case research and allowed us to use IMEDE case materials. This book was greatly enhanced by our ability to test important concepts in an international setting with both graduate students and experienced executives.

The content of the cases would not have been possible without the generous participation of a number of companies and executives: Rune Glimenius and David Webster at Alfa-Laval; Ernst Thomke and Franz Sprecher from SMH (Swatch and Tissot cases); Ian Souter at Nestlé; Paul Green at New England Nuclear; Mr. Nakamoto of American Hospital Supply—Japan; Hansruedi Bieri at Bieri Pumps; Dieter Hanusek and Juerg Opprecht at Soudronic; John Sweeney at Puritan-Bennett; and Harold Todd, Masahiro Horita, and Brian Taylor at Nippon Vicks K.K. These executives and others who prefer to remain anonymous gave generously of their time so that other practicing as well as future managers could learn from their own experiences.

To turn the collected material and data into readable form we always could count on a number of students, graduate assistants, and research associates. Babson students Gary Silva, Peter Mark, David Rittenhouse, Maricel Blum, and John Bleh wrote parts of the cases used in this text. Kim Koehler researched material for a number of chapters. Susan Nye, who served both as graduate assistant at Babson College and as research associate at IMEDE, and Barbara Priovolos wrote several of the cases at IMEDE. And finally, we would like to thank Professor John Marthinsen, Professor of Economics and International Business at Babson College, for having contributed Chapter 2.

Throughout the development of this book, a number of reviewers have made important contributions. These reviews were extremely important in the revision and improvement of the text. We especially thank

Pradeep Rau
University of Delaware

L. Trankiem
California State University

William Cunningham
Southwest Missouri State

Michael Steiner
University of Wisconsin

Samuel Rabino
Northeastern University

Charles de Mortanges
University of New Hampshire

Joseph Miller
Indiana University at
Bloomington

Alex Christofides
Ohio State University

Kate Gillespie
University of Texas

Aubrey Mendelow
Dusquesne University

John L. Hazard
Michigan State University

H. Ralph Jones
Miami University

Jean Boddewyn
CUNY-Bernard M. Baruch
College

Susan Douglas
New York University

James McCullough
   The University of Arizona

Zahir A. Quraeshi
   Western Michigan State

G. P. Lauter
   The George Washington
   University

A. H. Kizilbash
   Northern Illinois University

Attila Yaprak
   Wayne State University

B. G. Bizzell
   Stephen F. Austin University

Adel I. El-Ansary
   The George Washington
   University

Joseph L. Massie
   University of Kentucky

Phillip D. White
   University of Colorado

We are grateful to our publisher, Houghton Mifflin Company, for having had the confidence in us to underwrite the development of this book. Over time we had the pleasure of working with a number of their editors who have seen this project through to its completion. We thank them for their patience, their encouragement, and their professionalism in supporting our writing efforts. Houghton Mifflin has also provided us with a first-class staff in turning the manuscript into its final form. The marketing, production, art, editorial, permission, and manufacturing staffs have substantially added to the quality of this finished book.

A number of people have been instrumental in the preparation of the manuscript of this book. We would like to thank our department secretaries Marion Powers, Charlotte Cobb, and Joan Brawley who have typed earlier versions of the manuscript. Connie Stumpf and her staff (Vickie Del Bono, Anne Duffy, Kim Wells, Joanne Solomon) helped with the preparation of the final draft. Their efforts and their willingness to deal with our numerous revisions are most appreciated. We have also benefited from the editing experience of Frances Dalton, Martha Lanning, John Bleh, and Bob Eastman who revised and improved the manuscript during earlier stages of its development.

We would like to thank our wives, Patricia and Ellen, For the last four years, they have had to see us spend many evenings and weekends on the development of the manuscript and they have encouraged us during the normal ups and downs that are inherent in such a project.

Finally, we extend our greatest gratitude to our students at Babson College and IMEDE International Management Development Institute for their constant help and inspiration. Their interest in international marketing issues inspired us to undertake and complete this project. Therefore we are happy to dedicate this book to our students.

J.P.J.
H.D.H.

INTERNATIONAL MARKETING MANAGEMENT

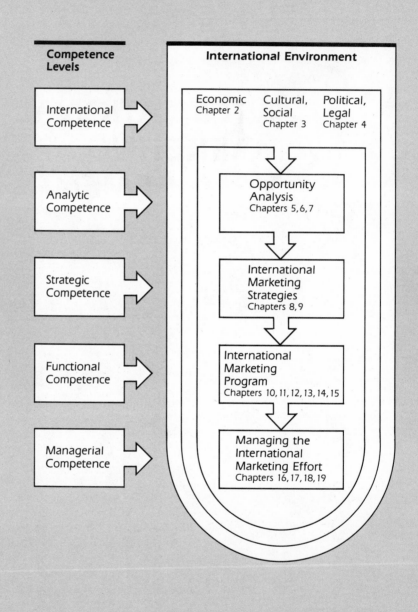

Competence Levels

International Competence

Analytic Competence

Strategic Competence

Functional Competence

Managerial Competence

International Environment

Economic
Chapter 2

Cultural, Social
Chapter 3

Political, Legal
Chapter 4

Opportunity Analysis
Chapters 5, 6, 7

International Marketing Strategies
Chapters 8, 9

International Marketing Program
Chapters 10, 11, 12, 13, 14, 15

Managing the International Marketing Effort
Chapters 16, 17, 18, 19

PART 1

INTRODUCTION

1 ◼ INTERNATIONAL MARKETING: AN OVERVIEW

In this first section of the text, we provide an introduction to the field of international marketing. An overview of the most important international marketing decisions is given, and the major problems encountered by international firms are highlighted. This section also will provide you with an introduction to the text itself and the conceptual framework we used to develop the book. Understanding this plan should assist you in quickly integrating concepts into an overall framework for international marketing; it should also make it easier for you to appreciate the complexities of international marketing.

1.

INTERNATIONAL MARKETING: AN OVERVIEW

This first chapter will introduce you to the field of international marketing. We concentrate first on the scope of international marketing, using several examples to illustrate that it is a broad process encompassing many firms and a wide range of activities. We then present definitions that will relate international marketing to other fields of study. In the next section, we examine the differences between domestic and international marketing and explain why domestic companies often have difficulty marketing abroad. The chapter continues with a description of the major participants in international marketing. We also provide an explanation of why mastering international marketing skills can be valuable to your future career. A conceptual outline of the book concludes the chapter.

THE SCOPE OF INTERNATIONAL MARKETING

It is generally understood that a company like Boeing, the world's largest commercial airline manufacturer and one of the leading exporters of the United States, engages in international marketing when it sells its airplanes to airlines across the globe.[1] Likewise, Ford Motor Company, which operates large manufacturing plants in several countries, engages in international marketing even though a major part of its output is sold in the country where it is manufactured.

Today, however, the scope of international marketing has broadened and includes many other business activities. The activities of large U.S. department store chains, such as K mart and Bloomingdale's, include a substantial element

---

1. "Smoother Sailing Overseas," *Business Week,* April 18, 1986, p. 289.

of importing. When these stores search for new products abroad to sell in the United States, they practice another form of international marketing. A whole range of service industries are involved in international marketing; many large advertising firms, banks, investment bankers, public accounting firms, consulting companies, hotel chains, and airlines now market their services worldwide.

International marketing encompasses some activities that only indirectly result in international transactions. A new breed of international marketer is illustrated by Carl Sontheimer, a retired engineer who in the mid-1970s was looking for a retirement activity. He visited a food fair in France and came across a food processor not yet found in the United States.[2] He redesigned the machine, and it became a best seller in the United States under the Cuisinart brand name. By looking for new ideas outside his home market, Sontheimer was practicing a different type of international marketing—one that has become a growth industry.

When Clark Equipment Company, a United States–based manufacturer of construction machinery, acquired Euclid, another U.S. firm, the idea was to add Euclid's heavy construction trucks to Clark's front-end loaders to improve Clark's position with its dealers in the United States. Many of these dealers had been approached by Komatsu, the leading Japanese construction equipment company and only second to Caterpillar worldwide. By adding Euclid trucks to its product line, Clark expected to check Komatsu's expansion in the United States.[3] Consequently, what appeared like a domestic market move was actually aimed at a potential foreign competitor. Such competitive decisions are as much a part of international marketing as any examples cited earlier.

Definitions of International Marketing and International Marketing Management

Having examined the scope of international marketing, we are now able to define it more accurately. Any definition has to be built, however, on basic definitions of marketing and marketing management, with an added explanation of the international dimension. We understand *marketing* as the performance of business activities directing the flow of products and services from producer to consumer. A successful performance of the marketing function by a firm is contingent upon the adoption of the marketing concept, consisting of (a) a customer orientation, (b) an integrated marketing organization, and (c) customer satisfaction.[4] *Marketing management* is the execution of a company's marketing operation. Management responsibilities consist of planning, organizing, and controlling the marketing program of the firm. To accomplish this job, marketing

---

2. "From France, The Cuisinart," *The New York Times,* July 31, 1977.

3. "Clark Equipment Buys Subsidiary of Daimler-Benz," *The Wall Street Journal,* January 6, 1984, p. 6.

4. Philip Kotler, *Marketing Management,* 5th ed. (Englewood Cliffs, N.J.: Prentice-Hall, 1984), p. 4.

FIGURE 1.1 International Marketing

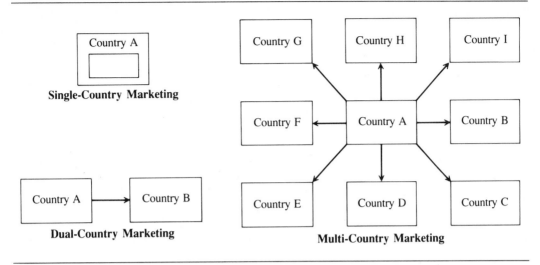

Single-Country Marketing

Dual-Country Marketing

Multi-Country Marketing

management is assigned decision-making authority over product strategy, communication strategy, distribution strategy, and pricing strategy. The combination of these four aspects of marketing is referred to as the marketing mix.

For international marketing management, the basic aims of marketing and the responsibilities described above remain unchanged. What is different is the execution of these activities in more than one country. Consequently, we define *international marketing management* as *the performance of marketing activities across two or more countries*. We are now moving from single-country decisions to multi-country decisions. As shown in Figure 1.1, in some situations, only one or two countries are involved; in other situations, dozens of countries are involved simultaneously.

A U.S. firm exporting products to Mexico is engaged in a marketing effort across two countries: the United States and Mexico. Another U.S. firm operating a subsidiary in Mexico that manufactures and markets locally under the direction of the U.S. head office is also engaged in international marketing to the extent that the head office staff directs and supervises this effort. Consequently, international marketing does not always require the physical movement of products across national borders. International marketing occurs whenever marketing decisions are made that encompass two or more countries.

Relationships with Other Fields of Study

The field of international marketing is related to other fields of study. In its broadest terms, international marketing is a subset of *international business,* which is defined as the performance of all business functions across national

FIGURE 1.2 International Marketing and Related Fields of Study

boundaries. International business includes all functional areas such as international production, international financial management, and international marketing (see Figure 1.2).

International trade theory, which explains why nations trade with each other, is a related concept. This theory is aimed at understanding product flows between countries, either in the form of exports or imports. A U.S. corporation exporting machinery to Japan would find its transactions recorded as an export in the United States whereas the same transaction would be treated as an import in Japan. In this situation, international marketing and international trade are concerned with the same phenomenon.

Should the same U.S. company produce its machinery in Japan and sell locally, however, there would be no exchange of goods between the two countries. Consequently, there would be no recognized international trading activity. However, as we have seen earlier, the U.S. company's decision to build machinery in Japan and sell it there would still be considered an international marketing decision. We can therefore conclude that international marketing goes beyond strict definitions of international trading and includes a wider range of activities.

International marketing should not be confused with *foreign marketing* which consists of marketing activities carried out by foreign firms within their own countries. Marketing by Brazilian firms in Brazil is therefore defined as foreign marketing and is not the principle focus of this book. However, Brazilian firms engaged in marketing their products in the United States are engaged in international marketing and are subject to the same concepts and principles as are U.S. firms marketing in Brazil.

DIFFERENCES BETWEEN INTERNATIONAL AND DOMESTIC MARKETING

Companies marketing products or services abroad have always had to deal with a wider range of issues than those encountered by domestic firms. The following section will give some insight into the special difficulties encountered in the international market.

Using a Domestic Strategy Abroad: Risk or Opportunity?

When a company uses an initial marketing strategy abroad, its success or failure depends greatly upon the market where it is used. In 1977, Apple Computer Company began distribution of its personal computer in Japan. At that time there were no other personal computer products on the market. However, by 1985 Apple still had only a very small market share, and the company had failed to achieve any significant market penetration. Initially, Apple left all marketing to Japanese distributors and provided little or no support. Japanese competitors and IBM had begun to market Japanese-language machines. The Apple could only be used by Japanese who understood English very well, which limited its market to a small group. It was only years later that Apple brought in a team of technicians from its head office to adapt products to the Japanese language and built a subsidiary staff with local managers. At this point, it will be an uphill battle to expand sales beyond the estimated 10,000 units in a market believed to be about 1.2 million units.[5]

Although Apple did poorly in Japan, it operated very successfully in France. There, Apple became the leader in personal computers, reaching sales of $94 million in 1984 and expecting sales of $128 million in 1985. In France, Apple used many of the high-visibility promotions begun in the United States by adapting them to the French environment. Promotional activities included sponsoring film festivals and selling Apple jogging suits, decals, and duffel bags. Each year an "Apple Expo" was held in Paris. Apple did extremely well by focusing on in-home businesses and independent professionals, such as doctors and lawyers,

---

5. "Apple Loser in Japan Computer Market, Tries to Recoup by Redesigning Its Models," *The Wall Street Journal,* June 21, 1985, p. 30.

achieving a market share of 35 percent in 1984 compared to 27 percent for IBM.[6]

In the two examples described above, Apple tried to duplicate a marketing strategy that had proven successful in its home market. In Japan it failed, whereas in France it succeeded, with Apple achieving a higher market share than in its home market. We don't mean to imply that companies risk failure each time they expand an initial marketing strategy across the globe. Coca-Cola, Pepsi Cola, and Eastman Kodak have found that the same basic strategy can be employed in many countries.[7] What is the reason that some companies meet success and others fail?

DETERMINING INTERNATIONAL MARKETING STRATEGIES: FACTORS LIMITING STANDARDIZATION[8]

From an international marketing manager's point of view, the most cost-effective method to market products or services worldwide is to use the same program in every country, provided environmental conditions favor such an approach. However invariably, as we have seen in the previous section, local market characteristics exist that require some form of adaptation to local realities. One of the challenges of international marketing is to determine the extent of standardization for any given local market. To do this, the international marketing manager must become aware of any factors that would limit standardization. Factors limiting standardization can be categorized into four major groups: market characteristics, industry conditions, marketing institutions, and legal restrictions (see Table 1.1).

Market Characteristics

Market characteristics can have a profound effect on international marketing strategy. The physical environment of any country—determined by its climate, product use conditions, and population size—often forces marketers to adjust products to local conditions. Many cars in Canada come equipped with a built-in heating system that is connected to an electrical outlet to keep the engine from freezing while turned off. In warmer climates, cars are not equipped with such a heating unit but are more likely to require air conditioning. The product use conditions for washing machines in Europe differ from country to country. In

---

6. "Can Apple Transplant Its Sexy French Marketing?" *Business Week,* June 10, 1985, p. 10.

7. Theodore Levitt, "The Globalization of Markets," *Harvard Business Review,* May–June 1983, pp. 92–102.

8. This section draws heavily on Robert D. Buzzell's classical article, "Can You Standardize Multinational Marketing?" *Harvard Business Review,* vol. 36, November–December 1968, pp. 102–113.

Germany, manufacturers have been forced to add built-in heaters because home-makers prefer to boil the water during the regular washing cycle and use a cold-water fill. British homemakers prefer to fill washing machines with hot water directly from a house boiler, making a built-in heating unit unnecessary.[9] A country's *population* will affect the market size in terms of volume, allowing for lower prices in larger markets. Market size or expected sales volume greatly affect channel strategy. Company-owned manufacturing and distribution are often possible in larger markets, whereas independent distributors are often used in smaller countries.

Macroeconomic factors also greatly affect international marketing strategy. The income level, or gross national product (GNP) per capita, varies widely among nations—from below $100 for some of the world's poorest nations to above $10,000 for rich countries such as Kuwait, Sweden, and the United States. Depending on income level, countries have been categorized according to stages of economic development, ranging from a pre-industrial stage to full economic maturity.[10] As can be expected, marketing environments will differ considerably according to income level. If the population's level of technical skill is low, a marketer might be forced to simplify product design to suit the local market. Pricing may be affected to the extent that countries with lower income levels show higher price elasticities for many products compared to developed countries. Furthermore, convenient access to credit is often restricted to buyers in developing countries, impacting negatively on the sale of capital goods and consumer durables. Exchange rate fluctuations distort prices among countries for many products that otherwise might sell at similar prices. This leads to the problem of cross shipping products to take advantage of price gaps. With specialization among channel members differing widely among various countries, depending on macroeconomic factors, companies often find themselves forced to adjust channel policies to compensate for the absence of the middleman they normally rely on in their home country. Wage levels and the availability of manpower may influence a company to choose a different approach for its sales-force. Since the motivation to purchase some products depends on a country's income level, advertising and promotion strategy may have to be adjusted for such changes.

Cultural and social factors are less predictable influences on the marketing environment, and they have often frustrated many international marketers. Customs and traditions have the greatest effect on product categories when a country's population has had prior experience with a given product category. INCAP, an agency supported by several central American governments and located in Guatemala, developed a low cost, high protein beverage in the form of *atole* (thin gruel), a popular drink customarily consumed hot by Guatemalans. This same product was rejected by consumers in neighboring El Salvador be-

9. See *"Hoover (A),"* Harvard Business School, Harvard Case Clearing House, 9-582-102.
10. W. W. Rostow, *The Stages of Economic Growth* (London: Cambridge University Press, 1960).

TABLE 1.1 Factors Limiting Standardization in Different Marketing Mix Areas

	Product Design	Pricing	Distribution Channels
Market Characteristics			
PHYSICAL ENVIRONMENT:	Climate Product use conditions	Market size	Market size
MACROECONOMIC FACTORS:	Level of technical skill Income level Labor costs in relation to capital costs	Income level Availability of credit Exchange rates	Specializing among channel members Customer mobility
CULTURAL AND SOCIAL FACTORS:	Customs and traditions Attitudes toward foreign goods	Attitude toward bargaining Attitude toward credit	Consumer shopping patterns
Industry Conditions			
STAGE OF PRODUCT LIFE CYCLE IN EACH MARKET:	Extent of product differentiation	Elasticity of demand	Availability of outlets
COMPETITION:	Quality technological level of competition	Prices of substitutes Local costs	Competitors' control of channels
Marketing Institutions			
DISTRIBUTION SYSTEMS:		Prevailing margins	Number and types available
ADVERTISING MEDIA AND AGENCIES:			
Legal Restrictions	Product standards Patent laws Tariffs and taxes	Tariffs and taxes Antitrust laws Resale price maintenance Restrictions on sales of products in certain outlets	Ability to "force" distribution Resale price maintenance

Source: Reprinted by permission of the Harvard Business Review. An exhibit adapted from "Can you Standardize Multinational Marketing?" by R. D. Buzzell (November–December 1968). Copyright © 1968 by the President and Fellows of Harvard College. All rights reserved.

TABLE 1.1 continued

	Sales Force	*Advertising and Promotion*
Market Characteristics		
PHYSICAL ENVIRONMENT:	Market size Dispersion of customers	
MACROECONOMIC FACTORS:	Wage levels Availability of manpower	Purchase motivation
CULTURAL AND SOCIAL FACTORS:	Attitudes toward selling	Language literacy symbolism
Industry Conditions		
STAGE OF PRODUCT LIFE CYCLE IN EACH MARKET:	Need for missionary and sales effort	Awareness or prior experience with product
COMPETITION:	Competitors' sales forces	Competitive advertising messages and budgets
Marketing Institutions		
DISTRIBUTION SYSTEMS:	Number, types, and dispersion of outlets, channel patterns	Extent of self-service Desirability of private brands
ADVERTISING MEDIA AND AGENCIES:	Effectiveness of pull strategy	Media availability, cost, overlaps
Legal Restrictions	Employment restrictions	Trademark laws
	Specific restrictions on selling	Specific restrictions on messages

cause the product would thicken when it was cool, which was the way El Salvadorians usually consumed *atole*.[11] Another hurdle in international marketing is language, which has become a major focus for international marketers. There are many examples of poor translations of promotional material. Pepsi Cola once used a literal translation of its popular U.S. campaign theme "Come Alive with Pepsi" in Germany without realizing that *come alive* in German meant "come alive out of the grave."[12]

Industry Conditions

Industry conditions often vary by country since products frequently are in varying stages of the product life cycle. New product introduction in a country without prior experience might affect the extent of product differentiation since only one or two versions of the product might be introduced initially. Also, a company might find itself in a situation where limited awareness or prior experience of a country will require a considerable missionary sales effort and primary demand stimulation, whereas in more mature markets the promotional strategy is likely to concentrate on brand differentiation. The level of local competition can be expected to vary substantially by country. The higher the technological level of the competition, the more an international company must improve the quality level of its products. The varying prices of local substitutes or low local production costs can be expected to influence pricing policy. In countries where competitors control channels and maintain a strong sales force, the strategy of a multinational company might differ significantly from that in a country where the company holds a competitive advantage.

Marketing Institutions

For historic and economic reasons, marketing institutions have assumed different forms in different countries. Practices in distribution systems often entail different margins for the same product, requiring a change in company pricing strategy. Availability of outlets is also likely to vary by country. Mass merchandisers such as supermarkets, discount stores, and department stores are widely available in the United States and other industrialized countries but are largely absent in less developed nations in Southern Europe, Latin America, and other parts of the world. Such variations may lead to considerably different distribution strategies. Likewise, advertising agencies and media are not equally accessible in all countries; and the absence of mass media channels in some countries makes a "pull" strategy less effective.

---

11. Gordon E. Mircale, *The Quaker Oats Company (A)*, 1966.
12. David A. Ricks, *Big Business Blunders: Mistakes in Multinational Marketing* (Homewood, Ill.: Dow Jones—Irwin, 1983), p. 84.

Legal Restrictions

Legal restrictions also require consideration for the development of an international marketing strategy. Product standards issued by local governments must be observed. To the extent that they differ from one country to another, unified product design often becomes an impossibility. Tariffs and taxes may require adjustments in pricing to the extent that a product can no longer be sold on a high-volume basis. Specific restrictions may also be problematic. In Europe, restrictions on advertising make it impossible to mention a competitor's name, despite the fact that such an approach may be an integral part of the advertising strategy in the United States.

To carry out the international marketing task successfully, international managers have to be cognizant of all the factors that influence the local marketing environment. Frequently, they need to target special marketing programs for each country.

MAJOR ACTORS IN INTERNATIONAL MARKETING

Several types of companies are major participants in international marketing. Among the leaders are multinational corporations (MNCs), exporters, importers, and service companies. These firms may be engaged in manufacturing consumer or industrial goods, in trading, or in the performance of a full range of services. What all participants have in common is a need to deal with the complexities of the international marketplace.

Multinational Corporations

Multinational corporations (MNCs) are companies that manufacture and market products or services in several countries. Typically an MNC operates a number of plants abroad and markets products through a large network of fully owned subsidiaries.

Although the United States is home to the largest number of MNCs, the first multinationals were of European origin and included firms such as Nobel and Alfa-Laval of Sweden, Unilever of the United Kingdom, Royal Dutch/Shell of the Netherlands, and Nestlé of Switzerland. Some of the first U.S. companies to go multinational included Singer, which opened its first subsidiary in England in 1870, and NCR, Remington, Burroughs, Otis, and Westinghouse.[13] Most of these companies possessed valuable patents that they wanted to protect from

---

13. Mira Wilkins, *The Emergence of Multinational Enterprise: American Business Abroad from the Colonial Era to 1974* (Cambridge, Mass.: Harvard University Press, 1970), pp. 37–45.

competition abroad. To cash in on their technological advantage, they opened branch plants in many European countries.

Today, the majority of large, U.S., *Fortune* 500 firms are multinational corporations, and most others have at least some international business involvement. Among the leaders are Exxon, Dow Chemical and Gillette, with more than half of their sales generated abroad.[14] The ranks of MNCs have been swelled by a large number of European and Asian firms. *Fortune*'s list of the largest foreign corporations included 77 from the United Kingdom, 32 from Canada, 36 from France, 55 from West Germany, 20 from Sweden, 12 from Switzerland, and 10 from Italy. Interestingly, many of the *Fortune* firms were from countries outside of Europe and North America. There were 147 from Japan, 10 from South Korea, 7 from Brazil, and 5 from India. Only a few years ago, the list was made up largely of European and Canadian companies.[15]

One of the newcomers to the field of international business, Daewoo from Korea, is an excellent example of a company that has risen to a strong international position in just a few years. The company is a large conglomerate active in a number of fields. Daewoo Heavy Industries (DHI) produces products such as diesel engines, fork lift trucks, excavators, machine tools, and precision machines. Exports rose from less than 10 percent of sales in 1983 to almost one-third of sales in 1986. The company has a number of licensing agreements with foreign firms such as Caterpillar of the United States for whom DHI is becoming a major producer.[16] Another rapidly growing division is Daewoo Telecom, which designed and engineered a personal computer sold in the United States as the Leading Edge Model D. It is one of the best-selling, IBM-compatible personal computers on the market.[17] The interest of foreign MNCs in the U.S. market continues to grow. Perrier, the French bottled-water company, acquired Poland Spring, Calistoga, Oasis Water, Zephyr Hill, and most recently Arrowhead, all local brands. The company is committed to the U.S. market, secure of its size and expected growth.[18] Table 1.2 shows that foreign investment in the United States has grown rapidly in the past few years. It appears that competition from international firms is likely to increase over time, and some of the strongest competitors for established MNCs are likely to be newcomers from developing countries.

Service Companies

The early MNCs were largely manufacturers of industrial equipment and consumer products. Many of the newer MNCs are service companies. Commercial

---

14. "Smoother Sailing Overseas," p. 289.
15. "The 500 Largest Industrial Corporations Outside the U.S.," *Fortune,* August 4, 1986, p. 201.
16. "Daewoo Gets Ready to Play World Role," *Financial Times,* May 9, 1986, p. 23.
17. "Foreign Clones Spark a Mid-Life Crisis," *Financial Times,* June 9, 1986, p. 28.
18. "Perrier's Unquenchable U.S. Thirst," *Business Week,* June 29, 1987, p. 46.

TABLE 1.2 Foreign Investment in the United States in 1980 and 1985 (in U.S. Billions of Dollars)

	1980	1985		1980	1985
By Industry			*By Country*		
Manufacturing	33.0	60.8	Britain	14.1	43.8
Petroleum	12.2	28.1	Netherlands	19.1	36.1
Wholesale trade	11.5	27.5	Japan	4.7	19.1
Real estate	6.1	18.6	Canada	12.1	16.7
Banking	4.6	11.5	W. Germany	7.6	14.4
Insurance	6.1	11.0	Switzerland	5.0	11.0
Retail Trade	3.6	6.7	France	3.7	6.3
Finance	1.3	4.7	Kuwait	0.3	4.0
Mining	1.3	4.0	Australia	0.3	2.7
Other	3.2	10.0	Sweden	1.7	2.4

Source: Data from U.S. Department of Commerce, as published in ''The Selling Off of America,'' *Fortune,* December 22, 1986. © 1986 Time Inc. All rights reserved.

banks, investment bankers, and brokers have turned themselves into multinational service networks. Airlines and hotel companies have gained multinational status. Less noticeable are the multinational networks of public accounting firms, consulting companies, advertising agencies, and a host of other service-related industries. This multinationalization of the service sector has not been restricted to the United States but has been mirrored in many other countries as well.

Examples of U.S. service companies with international involvement abound. McDonald's now gets close to 20 percent of its revenues from foreign operations, and almost 40 percent of its new outlets are foreign.[19] With some 7,000 restaurants in the United States and tough competition from other domestic chains, McDonald's expects most of its future growth to come from abroad. Kentucky Fried Chicken, operating about 1,700 restaurants outside the United States, is McDonald's strongest competitor abroad. American brokerage firms have also looked for new opportunities abroad. As the Japanese financial markets became increasingly deregulated, U.S. brokers such as Merrill Lynch, Goldman, Sachs, and others have set up operations in Tokyo. Many of these companies had set up networks in Europe earlier.[20] Even U.S. hospitals are getting involved in international business. International Health Systems was formed as a go-between for foreign patients and U.S. hospitals. The company

19. ''McWorld?'' *Business Week,* October 13, 1986, p. 78.
20. ''U.S. Brokers Expand in Japan,'' *The New York Times,* February 7, 1984.

has signed up several hospitals, mostly those affiliated with medical schools. United States health services are interested in boosting foreign hospital admissions, which account for only about 3 to 5 percent of all admissions. Foreign patients tend to be wealthy and can pay cash for all services.[21] Foreign sales are also important to the U.S. entertainment industry. Warner Communications, a major producer of movies, markets its products internationally.[22] And with U.S. construction and real estate development markets going through a difficult period of time, some U.S. developers have become active in growth markets such as London.[23]

Exporters

Exporters are firms that market products abroad but produce largely in their home country. Most large exporters have evolved into multinational companies. However, multinational companies, by shipping products between subsidiaries, have maintained some of the largest export operations. Of the largest exporters in the United States, Boeing, McDonnell Douglas, and the aircraft unit of United Technologies produce in the United States.[24] Other leading exporters can be found among mineral, agricultural, and forestry companies. Many U.S. companies that follow a strict export-only policy are smaller firms. Some may have foreign subsidiaries devoted only to marketing and sales. Even some of the foreign subsidiaries operating in the U.S. market can become exporters. Honda Motor Co. has been exporting the Gold Wing 1,200cc motorcycle from its U.S. plant since 1980. After selling it in fourteen overseas markets, Honda started to ship these motorcycles to Japan in 1987.[25]

Importers

As described earlier, importing is as much an international marketing decision as exporting. Companies that neither export nor have multinational status may still participate in international marketing through their importing operations. Many of the largest U.S. retail chains maintain import departments that are in contact with suppliers in many overseas countries. Other major importers are MNCs which source products from their own plants abroad or from other clients.

21. "Hospitals Woo Rich Patients from Abroad," *The Wall Street Journal*, November 6, 1984.

22. *The New York Times*, September 14, 1986.

23. "The Latest American Export: Office Developers Go Abroad," *The Wall Street Journal*, October 23, 1985, p. 35.

24. "Smoother Sailing Overseas," p. 289.

25. "Honda Will Ship to Japan Motorcycles Made in the U.S.," *The Wall Street Journal*, July 3, 1987, p. 25.

Among the largest U.S. importers are oil companies and subsidiaries of foreign MNCs, particularly those of European and Japanese origin.

For the purpose of this text, we will use *international company* or *international firm* as umbrella terms that may include MNCs, exporters, importers, and service companies.

THE IMPORTANCE OF INTERNATIONAL MARKETING

International marketing is a very broad activity, and it is expanding rapidly. As we discussed earlier, international trade is one of the important components of international marketing. Between 1973 and 1986, total world trade was estimated to have grown from about $574 billion to $2,110 billion.[26] Some 55 percent of this volume was in manufactured products compared to about 43 percent in primary products.[27] Table 1.3 compares world exports of manufactured products in the years 1973, 1980, 1981, and 1985. The table shows a clear upward trend in the world trade of manufactured goods. Most of this world trade was concentrated in heavy machinery, transport equipment, motor vehicles, specialized machinery, and office and telecommunications equipment. And this did not include the local business of foreign-owned subsidiaries.

World trade in services—in shipping, insurance, banking, and other service-related industries—increased to $448 billion in 1980 and now accounts for about 25 percent of total world trade. Service trade is referred to as "invisible trade" because the traded goods are abstract and difficult to quantify. Major components of service trade are investment income with 33 percent, transport with 23 percent, and travel with 19 percent. The U.S. Department of Commerce has estimated the foreign business of U.S. service industries at about $144 billion in exports and $122 billion in imports.[28] This invisible sector of total world trade is expanding quickly and is expected to grow at a faster rate than world trade in manufactured goods and commodities. For 1984, revised export figures for services were estimated at $69 billion to $91 billion, accounting for about 25% of U.S. exports.[29]

A substantial portion of international marketing operations does not get recorded in international trade statistics. In particular, MNC overseas sales of locally manufactured and locally sold products are not included in world trade figures. Consequently, total volume in international marketing far exceeds the

26. "The Uruguay Round of Multinational Trade Negotiations," *Japan Economic Institute Report* (Washington, D.C.: Japan Economic Institute, June 12, 1987), p. 2.

27. "Statistical Trends: World Trade," *Financial Times*, April 25, 1983, p. 5.

28. "Services—The Star of U.S. Trade," *The New York Times*, September 14, 1986, p. 74.

29. "Services Are 25% of Total Y.S. Exports, But They Create Few Jobs, Study Says," *The Wall Street Journal*, July 2, 1987, p. 6.

TABLE 1.3 World Exports of Manufactured Products (U.S. billions of dollars)

	1973	1980	1981	1985
Iron and steel	28.5	76.2	74.0	69.3
Chemicals	41.9	153.0	148.5	163.4
Other semi-manufacturers	29.0	92.7	88.5	86.4
Engineering products	188.0	593.0	615.0	682.0
Specialized industry machinery	52.5	159.0	160.5	150.6
Office and telecommunications equipment	17.2	59.6	62.0	97.9
Road motor vehicles	41.0	127.4	129.5	158.3
Other machinery/transportation equipment	62.0	198.7	211.0	216.3
Household appliances	15.3	48.3	52.0	58.9
Textiles	23.4	55.4	53.5	55.4
Clothing	12.6	40.2	41.0	49.2
Other consumer goods	24.3	83.7	82.5	91.6
Total manufactures	347.5	1,094.1	1,103.0	1,197.3
Percent of world exports	60%	55%	56%	62%

Source: Data from *GATT International Trade 1981/1982,* as published in *Financial Times,* April 25, 1983, p. 5. 1985 data from *GATT International Trade 1985/1986,* p. 157.

volume of $1,915 billion for total world trade in 1984. The U.S. Department of Commerce estimated that the 1981 income of foreign affiliates of U.S. service firms amounted to about $100 billion, compared with export earnings of $40 billion for the same year (see Table 1.4).[30] Although no detailed statistics are available, this pattern suggests that the overall volume of international marketing amounts to a multiple of world trade volume.

Why Companies Become Involved in International Marketing

Companies become involved in international markets for a variety of reasons. Some firms simply respond to orders from abroad without any organized efforts of their own. But most companies take a more active role because they have determined that it is to their advantage to pursue foreign business export volume on an incremental basis. The profitability of a company can increase when fixed manufacturing costs are already committed and additional economies of scale are achieved.

30. "GATT Stage Set for Reagan to Break Down Services Trade Bars," *Financial Times,* November 22, 1982, p. 3.

TABLE 1.4 Estimated Foreign Business of U.S. Service Industries (Exports from the U.S. and Income of Overseas Affiliates)

	1977 (in millions)	1981 (in millions)
Total receipts for exports	$23,295	$ 40,520
Travel	6,150	12,168
Passenger fares	1,366	2,991
Other transportation	7,264	12,168
Fees and royalties from affiliated foreigners	3,793	5,867
Fees and royalties from unaffiliated foreigners	920	1,386
Other private services	3,802	5,940
Total income of foreign affiliates	69,220	99,953
Oil and gas field services	3,251	6,454
Petroleum tanker operations	8,249	9,576
Pipeline transmission, oil and gas	1,570	1,823
Finance (except banking), insurance, and real estate	14,884	20,703
Banking	2,205	4,290
Construction	10,141	20,889
Wholesale and retail trade	2,950	5,196
Transportation and communication	13,412	15,570
Hotels and lodging	1,550	1,799
Advertising	1,448	1,583
Motion pictures and TV tape and film	1,063	1,234
Engineering, architecture, surveying	3,207	4,695
Accounting	433	503
Other personal and business services	4,857	5,638
Total, exports plus affiliates' income	92,515	140,473

Source: Data from the U.S. Department of Commerce, as published in *Financial Times*, November 22, 1982, p. 3. Reprinted by permission.

Companies pursue growth in other countries after their domestic market has reached maturity. United States manufacturers of pet food have found that many European markets offer more growth opportunity than the United States. In some markets, such as France and the Netherlands, growth has reached 30 percent or more.[31] In other countries, such as Spain and Italy, pet foods are not widely accepted but major growth is anticipated in the near future.

31. "U.S. Multinationals Find a Growth Area Feeding Europe's Pets," *Financial Times*, October 20, 1982, p. 22.

Companies move into foreign markets to get additional volume. H. J. Heinz, the United States–based food producer, achieved about one third of its sales abroad, mostly in Europe, Australia, and New Zealand.[32] However, the company's entire sales of more than $3 billion were achieved with only 15 percent of the world's population. As a result, Heinz is aggressively looking for opportunities in Third-World countries, with the goal of increasing sales in those areas to $1 billion by 1990.

When a company's customers move overseas, many firms follow suit. Major U.S. banks have shifted to serve their U.S. clients in key financial centers around the world by opening branches. United States advertising agencies have created networks to serve the interests of their multinational clients. As some Japanese manufacturers opened plants in the United States, many of their component suppliers followed and built operations nearby. Not following these clients would have meant a loss of business.

Companies also enter the international arena for purely defensive purposes. Those that are concerned about foreign competition, in particular certain U.S. companies, have launched businesses in Japan to check the advance of Japanese competitors. Others such as Olivetti of Italy entered the United States to learn from the most advanced market in the office equipment industry. Whether companies participate for the pursuit of new opportunities or for any other reason, most have been able to enhance their overall competitiveness as a result of pursuing foreign ventures.

Why Study International Marketing?

You have probably asked yourself why you should study international marketing. You also may have wondered about the value of this knowledge in your future career. While it is not very likely that many university graduates find an entry-level position in international marketing, it is nevertheless a fact that each year United States–based international companies hire large numbers of marketing professionals. Since many of these firms are becoming increasingly internationalized, competence in international marketing will become even more important in the future—and many marketing executives will be pursuing international marketing as a career. Career opportunities exist with a large number of exporters; and candidates will require international marketing skills. Furthermore, each year many university graduates are hired for the marketing efforts of foreign-based MNCs in the United States. These companies are also looking for international competence within their managerial ranks.

With the U.S. service sector becoming increasingly internationalized, many graduates joining service industries have found themselves confronted with in-

32. "Heinz Sets Out to Expand in Africa and Asia, Seeking New Markets, Sources of Materials," *The Wall Street Journal,* September 27, 1983.

ternational opportunities at early stages of their careers. Today, consulting engineers, bankers, brokers, and public accountants are all in need of international marketing skills to compete in a rapidly changing environment. Consequently, a solid understanding and appreciation of international marketing will benefit the careers of most business students, regardless of the field or industry they might enter.

A Need for More Globetrotters

Compared to other industrialized nations, the United States severely lacks a sufficient number of international marketing professionals. The professionals and the firms actively participating in international marketing through exporting, importing, or production abroad have been called globetrotters.[33] Globetrotters, as active participants in international marketing, play a key role in the success of international firms. In this competitive business, the United States has seen its share of world exports steadily decline. In 1953, the United States accounted for 19 percent of total world exports, more than twice the share of second-ranked United Kingdom with about 8 percent. At that time, Japan accounted for only 2 percent of world exports. In 1984, the U.S. share had decreased to 12 percent, whereas Japan and Germany shared second place with about 8 percent each.[34]

There are other indications that the United States is lagging behind other countries in globetrotting. From 1870 to 1970, the United States almost always reported a positive trade balance, exporting more goods than importing. This began to change in the 1970s, and despite the large increase in earnings of the service industry, the overall balance of trade has turned substantially negative by about $120 billion (see Figure 1.3).[35] It has been estimated that a trade deficit of this size has cost the United States several million jobs. Although many reasons for this lagging performance lie beyond the control of individual companies, there is much that company management can do to redress the imbalance. Foreign companies fight much harder than U.S. firms to retain foreign markets. Because the foreign firms' domestic markets are usually smaller than the U.S. market, foreign firms are more motivated than U.S. firms to succeed abroad.

Despite this problem, foreign trade or international marketing is still not given enough attention by large sectors of United States society. Whereas university graduates in other countries learn one or more foreign languages as a matter of course, U.S. graduates usually have no foreign language competence. About 50,000 Japanese business professionals work in New York, all with a good

---

33. Hans Thorelli and Helmut Becker, *International Marketing Strategy,* rev. ed. (New York: Pergamon Press, 1980), p. 14.

34. *The Economist,* January 18, 1986, p. 91.

35. "US Economy Grows Ever More Vulnerable to Foreign Influences," *The Wall Street Journal,* October 27, 1986, pp. 1, 16.

FIGURE 1.3 U.S. Trade Deficit 1973–1986

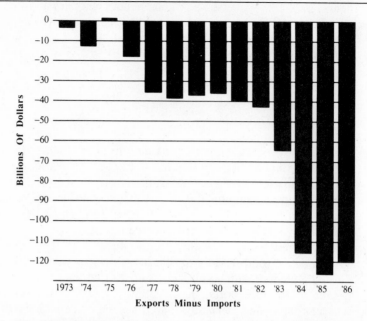

Exports Minus Imports

Source: Reprinted from the August 29, 1983 issue of *Business Week* by special permission, © 1983 by McGraw-Hill, Inc. 1973–1983 data from Commerce Department, Data Resources Inc.; 1984–1986 data from the United Nations, *World Economic Survey 1986;* p. 46.

understanding of English. Only about 500 U.S. business professionals working in Tokyo have a good command of the Japanese language. Although it is too simplistic to associate foreign language capabilities with effective globetrotting, this comparison nevertheless serves as an indicator of interest in international business.

A Need for More Globe Watchers

Few of us can avoid the impact of international competition today. Many of our domestic industries have fallen upon hard times. Foreign competition has made enormous inroads in the manufacture of apparel, textiles, shoes, electronic equipment, and steel. As a result, these industries have become internationalized (see Figure 1.4). Although foreign competition for many consumer goods has been evident for years, inroads by foreign firms in investment good industries have been equally spectacular. By 1985, imports accounted for 20 percent of the U.S. market for industrial goods.[36] The U.S. machine tool industry found

36. "America's War on Imports," *Fortune Magazine,* August 19, 1985, pp. 26–29.

FIGURE 1.4 Internationalization of Selected Industries

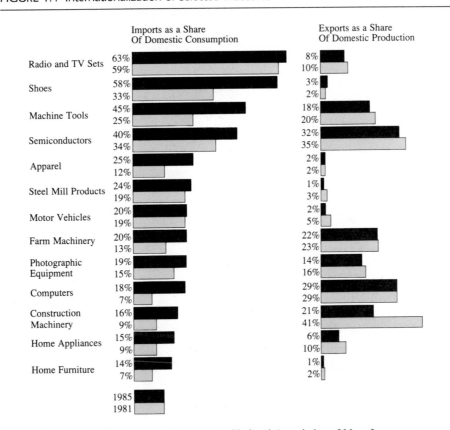

Source: Data from U.S. Commerce Department, National Association of Manufacturers, as published in The Wall Street Journal, October 27, 1986. Reprinted by permission of The Wall Street Journal, © Dow Jones & Company, Inc. 1986. All rights reserved.

it had to appeal to the U.S. government for help because imported machine tools increased their share of domestic consumption from 25 percent in 1982 to 55 percent in 1986.[37] Management of companies competing with foreign firms requires globe watching skill: an ability to judge the next move of foreign competitors by observing them abroad, in order to be better prepared to compete at home.

Import competition has been rising even in industries that used to be reserved largely for domestic companies. In the dry-soup market, Japanese firms now account for 9 percent of U.S. volume, a relatively recent development. Nissin Foods USA, the U.S. subsidiary of a Japanese company, has opened up its second automated processing plant less than 70 miles from Campbell Soups,

---

37. "Cost-Cutting Will Still Be the Watchword," Business Week, January 12, 1987.

the leading U.S. firm.[38] In 1983, processed food imports by the United States exceeded processed food exports for the first time. The paper industry, long protected from foreign competition, has had to deal with increased competitiveness of foreign firms. Foreign firms have made significant inroads in the manufacture of coated paper, such as that used in magazines, as the value of the U.S. dollar made foreign sourced products increasingly cost competitive. Paper manufacturers from such countries as Brazil, Chile, and South Africa have established a strong presence in the U.S. market.[39]

Even the service industry is not immune from foreign competition. For decades, Nielson, the leading U.S. marketing research company, enjoyed a near-monopoly in the rating of television programs. Now it is facing serious competition from a newcomer from the United Kingdom, AGB. This U.K. company gained a competitive edge with its "people reader," which allows the company to record viewership automatically in each connected T.V. set. Nielsen still relies on selected viewers to record what they watch in diaries.[40]

United States retailers also have new competition. Aside from foreign investors buying up existing U.S. retailing companies, new firms with novel approaches have entered the country. One of the most recent arrivals is Sweden-based IKEA, which features inexpensive, easy-to-assemble Scandinavian furniture. IKEA has built its first store in Philadelphia, selling flat-packed furniture that customers can cart away by themselves and assemble at home. IKEA already operated a chain of more than 70 stores in many European countries, earning sales of more than $1 billion.[41]

Certainly, managers everywhere will be called upon to react to economic developments in many parts of the world. In this new economic world—where international business involves not only the exporting or importing of products but also the transfer of marketing ideas and practices—more and more companies will be asking managers to become globe watchers.

William Litwin serves as an excellent example of how astute globe watching can be converted into a profitable business. In 1975, in the midst of the oil crisis, Litwin observed a Japanese-made kerosene stove on the boat of a relative. With the intent of selling such a stove through his own country store, he visited its manufacturer in Japan. After some days of negotiation, he was allowed to represent the Japanese company in the U.S. on an exclusive basis for an initial one year period, and later for an indeterminate period. Litwin sold the kerosene stove through a newly founded company, Kero-Sun. Kero-Sun accounted for about one-third of the three million kerosene stoves sold in the United States in 1981, and volume quickly grew to more than $100 million in 1982.[42]

---

38. "U.S. Food Firms Face More Imports and Rise in Foreign Plants Here," *The Wall Street Journal,* November 18, 1986, p. 1.

39. "Foreign Rivals Worry Paper Companies," *The New York Times,* November 10, 1986, p. 105.

40. "AGB Breaks into U.S. Networks," *Financial Times,* October 16, 1986, p. 16.

41. "Shopping Swedish Style Comes to the U.S." *Fortune Magazine,* January 20, 1986, p. 63.

42. "Hotter Competition for the Heater Leader," *Fortune,* March 8, 1982, pp. 93–95.

THE ORGANIZATION OF THIS BOOK

This text is structured around the basic requirements for making sound international marketing decisions. It takes into account the need to develop several types of competencies to analyze international marketing issues. The international marketer must be able to deal with decision areas on various complexity levels. We will first discuss each of these three dimensions of the international marketing task before we discuss the outline for this text.

Competencies

To compete successfully in today's international marketplace, companies and their management must master certain areas of competence. *International competence* is needed to perform in the international economy. It includes a knowledge of the dynamics of world economy, of major national markets, and of social and cultural environments. *Analytic competence* is needed to pull together a vast array of information and data and to assemble relevant facts. *Strategic competence* helps executives focus on the strategic or long-term requirements of their firms as opposed to short-term, opportunistic decisions. An international marketer must also possess *functional competence,* or a thorough background in all areas of marketing. Finally, *managerial competence* is the ability to implement programs and organize effectively on an international scale.

Managers with domestic responsibility will also need analytic, strategic, functional, and managerial competence. They do not need international competence. Consequently, we can isolate one component that sets the international executive apart from his or her domestic counterpart.

Decision Areas

Successful international marketing requires the ability to make decisions not typically faced by single-country firms. These decision groupings include environmental analysis, opportunity analysis, international marketing strategies, international marketing programs, and international marketing management. Managers continuously must assess foreign environments and perform *environmental analyses* relevant to their business. In a second step, managers need to do an *opportunity analysis* that will tell them which products to pursue in which markets. Once opportunities have been identified, *international marketing strategies* are designed to define long-term efforts of the firm. The company then may design *international marketing programs* to determine the marketing mix. Finally, international marketing must *manage the international marketing effort,* which requires attention to planning, personnel, and organization.

Our five levels of competence are closely related to the five major international marketing decision areas described above. International competence is needed to perform an environmental analysis. Analytic competence is the basis for opportunity analysis. Sound international marketing strategies are based upon strategic competence. To design international marketing programs one needs functional competence. Finally, managerial competence is needed for managing the international marketing effort.

Chapter Organization

This text is organized around the flow of decisions as depicted in Figure 1.5. The five decision areas are treated in several chapters which delineate the respective competence levels most appropriate for each decision area.

Part 1, which includes Chapter 1, provides an overview of international marketing and its challenges today.

Part 2, Chapters 2 through 4, deals with the international environment. In order to build international competence, special emphasis is given to the economic, cultural, social, political, and legal forces companies must contend with to be successful.

Part 3, Chapters 5 through 7, concentrates on the opportunity analysis. Chapters in this section highlight international markets or countries, international buyers, and the research or analysis necessary to pinpoint opportunities abroad.

Chapters 8 and 9, forming Part 4, deal with strategic issues. Chapter 8 introduces the elements of global strategy. Chapter 9 describes how companies can enter markets they have decided to target.

Part 5, consisting of Chapters 10 through 15, aims at developing the competence to design international marketing programs consistent with a global strategy. The chapters in this section cover product strategies, product development, pricing, channel management, communications, and advertising.

The chapter material concludes with Part 6, Chapters 16 through 19. Here the emphasis is on building managerial competence in an international environment. Chapters 16 through 19 deal with issues of organization, controlling, and financing international marketing operations, and also with the technical aspects of the export and import trade process.

The final section of the book includes international marketing cases that will allow you to practice the concepts developed in the text. These cases feature a wide range of complexity levels and address different decision areas of the international marketing process. They are all based on real situations, although the names of some of the companies are disguised.

FIGURE 1.5 International Marketing Management

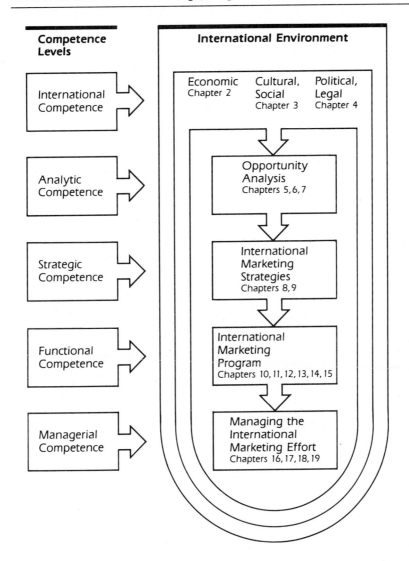

CONCLUSIONS

As a separate activity of business, international marketing is of great importance to individual companies, to countries, and to prospective managers. With markets and industries becoming increasingly internationalized, most companies have to become active participants in international marketing. The competitive positions of most companies, both abroad and in their domestic markets, rests on their ability to succeed in international marketing. At the same time, the economies of entire countries rest on the international marketing skills of its managers. The standard of living of many people will depend on how well local industry does in the international market place. These forces will place a premium on executive talent that is able to direct marketing operations from an international perspective. It is clear that many business professionals will need to understand the international dimension if they are to progress in their careers.

When it comes to a trained cadre of professional international marketing executives, the United States has typically lagged behind other countries. The U.S. market is so large that domestic problems tend to overshadow international marketing opportunities. As a result, most U.S. executives develop their careers largely in a domestic setting and have little direct exposure to foreign markets. Executives in foreign countries are more apt to have travelled abroad and tend to speak one or two foreign languages. Their ability to understand international complexities is thus more developed than it is in their U.S. counterparts. All of this gives many foreign firms a considerable edge in competing for international dominance.

Although the need to develop an international competence may be clear, the circumstances that determine successful marketing practices for foreign markets are far less clear. The foreign marketing environment is characterized by a wide range of variables not typically encountered by domestic firms. This makes the job of international marketing extremely difficult. However, despite the complexities involved, there are concepts and analytic tools that can help international marketers. By learning to use these concepts and tools, you can enhance your own international competence—you will be able to contribute to the marketing operations of a wide range of firms, both domestic and foreign.

Questions for Discussion

1. Explain the scope of international marketing.
2. How and why does international marketing differ from domestic marketing?
3. Which do you think would be the most relevant factors limiting international marketing standardization of yogurts, automobiles, and desk-top personal computers?
4. How does international marketing as a field relate to your future career in business? How would you expect to come in contact with international marketing activities?

5. Why are so many U.S. industries facing import competition?
6. Investigate one or two U.S. firms that do well abroad and analyze why they are successful.
7. Explain the major roles of multinational corporations (MNCs) and other types of firms in international marketing and how they participate in this activity.
8. What do you think are the essential skills of successful "globetrotting"?
9. Which are the important skills for successful "globe watching"?
10. List ten items most important to you that you hope to be able to understand or accomplish by reading this book.

For Further Reading

Cavusgil, S. Tamer, and John R. Nevin. "State-of-the-Art in International Marketing: An Assessment." In *Review of Marketing 1981*. Ed. Ben W. Enis and Kenneth J. Loering. Chicago: American Marketing Association, 1981, pp. 195–216.

Davidson, William H. *Global Strategic Management*. New York: John Wiley and Sons, 1982.

Kaynak, Erdener, ed. *Global Perspectives in Marketing*. New York: Praeger, 1985.

Kotler, Philip." "Global Standardization—Courting Danger." *The Journal of Consumer Marketing* (Spring 1986), pp. 13–15.

Levitt, Theodore. "The Globalization of Markets. *Harvard Business Review* (May–June 1983), pp. 92–102.

Porter, Michael E. "The Strategic Role of International Marketing. *The Journal of Consumer Marketing* (Spring 1986), pp. 17–21.

Pugel, Thomas A. "Foreign Trade and U.S. Market Performance." *Journal of Industrial Economics* (December 1980), pp. 18–23.

Ricks, David A., and Michael R. Czinkota. "International Business: An Examination of the Corporate Viewpoint." *Journal of International Business Studies* (Fall 1979), pp. 97–100.

Simon-Miller, Françoise. "World Marketing: Going Global or Acting Local? Five Expert Viewpoints." *The Journal of Consumer Marketing* (Spring 1986), pp. 5–7.

Wiklund, Erik. *International Marketing Strategies*. New York: McGraw-Hill, 1987.

Wind, Yoram, and Howard Perlmutter. "On the Identification of Frontier Issues in Multinational Marketing." *Columbia Journal of World Business* (Winter 1977), pp. 131–139.

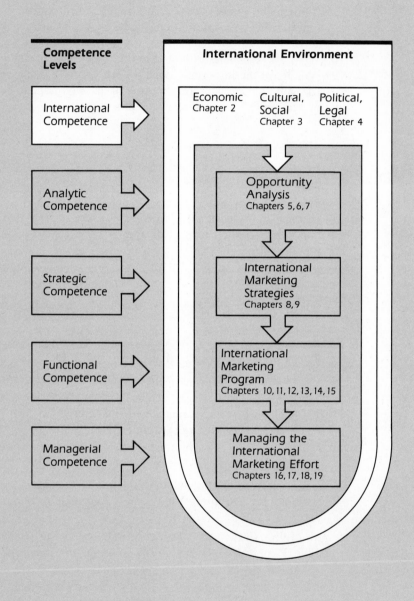

PART 2

THE INTERNATIONAL MARKETING ENVIRONMENT

2 ■ ECONOMIC FORCES

3 ■ CULTURAL AND SOCIAL FORCES

4 ■ POLITICAL AND LEGAL FORCES

This section of the book will introduce you to the environmental factors that influence international marketing decisions. Throughout this section, we maintain an analytical emphasis so that general concepts can be applied from country to country. Rather than simply describe a large number of environmental differences, we focus on several approaches companies have adopted to cope with these differences. Our aim is to maintain a managerial point of view throughout the section.

In Chapter 2, we explain the nature of the various economic forces that shape developments within individual countries as well as within the international economy. Chapter 3 describes the social and cultural influences that shape the local marketing environment. Finally, in Chapter 4, we discuss the political and legal forces affecting international firms, focusing on how companies cope with these forces.

2.

THE INTERNATIONAL ECONOMY

Billions of dollars worth of goods and services are traded between nations every day. Businesses establish operations and borrow in locations throughout the world. Financial investors purchase stocks and bonds expeditiously on United States, European, and Asian markets. Banks lend and arbitrage currencies worldwide. It is only when these transactions are interrupted or threatened that the true scope and significance of the international economy is appreciated.

This chapter introduces you to important aspects of world trade and finance. We begin by focusing on nations' international transactions as summarized by their balances of payments. From that base, we explain the workings of the foreign exchange market and the causes of exchange rate movements. Finally, we discuss comparative advantage as the basis for international trade, highlight the sources of nations' competitive advantage, and describe trade protectionism.

INTERNATIONAL TRADE: AN OVERVIEW

Few individuals in the world are totally self-sufficient. Why should they be? Restricting consumption to self-made goods would lower living standards by narrowing the range and reducing the quality of goods we consume. For these same reasons, there are few nations with economies independent from the rest of the world. It would be difficult to find a national leader both willing and able to impose such an economic hardship on domestic residents.

Foreign goods play a central and significant role in virtually all nations' living standards. But, as Table 2.1 shows, there appears to exist considerable variation among countries in their relative reliance on foreign trade. Imports are less than 15 percent of the gross national products (GNP) of Japan, Mexico, and

TABLE 2.1 Imports as a Percent of GNP for Selected Nations, 1985 (Figures in Billions of Units of Domestic Currency)

	Currency	*GNP*	*Imports*	*Imports/GNP*
Industrial Nations				
Australia	Australian dollars	223.1	43.3	19%
Belgium	Belgian francs	4,777.0	3,473.0	73%
Canada	Canadian dollars	461.8	122.8	27%
West Germany	German marks	1,847.0	574.7	31%
Japan	Yen	317,252.0	40,163.0	13%
The Netherlands	Guilders	414.0	245.1	59%
Norway	Kroner	488.8	195.6	40%
United States	U.S. dollars	3,998.1	398.6	10%
Switzerland	Swiss francs	241.5	88.0	36%
Developing Nations				
Greece	Drachmas	4,493.3	1,513.5	34%
Mexico*	Mexican pesos	27,029.6	2,775.3	10%
Pakistan	Rupees	515.6	101.1	20%
Rumania	Lei	845.6	160.8	19%
Saudi Arabia*	Riyals	359.1	175.9	48%
South Africa	Rands	133.1	31.8	24%
Venezuela	Bolivars	357.3	65.1	18%

* Figures reflect 1984 data due to unavailability of 1985 information.

Source: International Monetary Fund, *International Financial Statistics: Yearbook,* Volume XL, Number 6, June 1987. Reprinted by permission of the International Monetary Fund.

the United States, whereas nations like the Netherlands and Belgium have import-to-GNP ratios of 59 percent or more.

Even in countries that seemingly have no great reliance on imports (such as the United States), foreign goods and services play more than just a marginal role. For instance, Peter Johnson, a student, was awakened this morning by his Sony clock radio. After showering, he put on an Italian-made jacket while listening to the latest release by British singer, Sting. At breakfast, he had a cup of Brazilian coffee, a bowl of cereal made from American-grown wheat, and a Colombian banana. A quick glance at his Swiss Tissot watch showed him that he would have to hurry if he wanted to be on time for his first class. He drove to campus in a Toyota Camry, stopping on the way to fill the tank with gas from OPEC oil. Once in class, he rushed to take a seat with the other students, 30 percent of whom were foreign.

The figures given in Table 2.1 are useful for identifying nations' international dependence, but they should be taken only as rough indicators. If there were a disruption of international trade, there is little doubt that the United States would be harmed much less than the Netherlands. But how about Japan? Japan is a nation with relatively few natural resources. It survives by importing raw materials, processing them, and then re-exporting the finished products. Japan's import-to-GNP ratio is small (indicating a lack of reliance on foreign trade) only because its exports are so large—making its GNP large. Therefore, this country would be one of the major victims of trade curtailment.

Although the focus, so far, has been on world trade in goods and services, other transactions play an equally important role. International investments, foreign borrowing and lending, as well as grants-in-aid are essential to nations' health and well-being. Because all international transactions play such a significant role, much effort is devoted to recording and analyzing them. The next section will show how this recording is done and how the results are analyzed.

BALANCE OF PAYMENTS

Newspapers, magazines and nightly T.V. news programs are filled with stories relating to aspects of international business. Oftentimes, media coverage centers on the implications of a nation's trade deficit/surplus or on the economic consequences of an undervalued/overvalued currency. What are trade deficits? What factors will cause a currency's international value to change? The first step in answering these questions is to gain a clear understanding of the contents and meaning of a nation's balance of payments.

The balance of payments is an accounting record of the transactions between the residents of one country and the residents of the rest of the world over a given period of time.[1] It resembles a company's sources-and-uses-of-funds statement. Transactions in which domestic residents either purchase assets (goods and services) from abroad or reduce foreign liabilities are considered uses (outflows) of funds because payments abroad must be made. Similarly, transactions in which domestic residents either sell assets to foreign residents or increase their liabilities to foreigners are sources (inflows) of funds because payments from abroad are received.

Listed in Table 2.2 are the principal parts of the balance of payments statement; the current account, the capital account, and the official transactions account. There are three items under the Current Account. The Goods category states the monetary values of a nation's international transactions in physical goods. The Services category shows the values of a wide variety of transactions

---

1. An excellent source of historical and internationally comparable data can be found in the *Balance of Payments Yearbook* published yearly by the International Monetary Fund.

TABLE 2.2 Balance of Payments

	Uses of Funds	Sources of Funds
Current Account		
1. Goods	Imports	Exports
2. Services	Imports	Exports
3. Unilateral transfers	Paid abroad	From abroad
Capital Account		
1. Short-term investment	Made abroad	From abroad
2. Long-term investments	Made abroad	From abroad
a. Portfolio investment		
b. Direct investment		
Official Transactions Account		
1. Official reserve changes	Gained	Lost

such as transportation services, consulting, travel, passenger fares, fees, royalties, rent, and investment income. Finally, Unilateral Transfers include all transactions for which there is no quid pro quo (i.e., gifts). Private remittances, personal gifts, philanthropic donations, relief, and aid are included within this account.

The Capital Account category is divided into two parts on the basis of time. Short-term transactions refer to maturities less than or equal to one year and long-term transactions refer to maturities longer than one year. Purchases of Treasury bills, certificates of deposit, foreign exchange, and commercial paper are typical short-term investments. Long-term investments are separated further into portfolio investments and direct investments.

In general, portfolio investments imply that no ownership rights are held by the purchaser over the foreign investment. Debt securities such as notes and bonds would be included under this heading. Direct investments are long-term ownership interests, such as business capital outlays in foreign subsidiaries and branches. Stock purchases are included as well, but only if such ownership entails substantial control over the foreign company. Countries differ in the percentage of total outstanding stock an individual must hold in order for an investment to be considered a direct investment in their balance of payments statements. The International Monetary Fund reports that these values range from 10 percent, for widely dispersed holdings, to 25 percent.[2]

2. International Monetary Fund, *Balance of Payments Manual,* 4th ed. (Washington D.C.; International Monetary Fund, 1977), pp. 137–138.

Because it is recorded in double-entry bookkeeping form, the balance of payments as a whole must always have its inflows (sources of funds) equal all its outflows (uses of funds). Therefore, the concept of a deficit or surplus refers only to selected parts of the entire statement. A deficit occurs when the particular outflows (i.e., uses of funds) exceed the particular inflows (i.e., sources of funds). A surplus occurs when the inflows considered exceed the corresponding outflows. In this sense, a nation's surplus or deficit is similar to that of an individual, government, or business. If we spend more than we earn, we are in a deficit position. If we earn more than we spend, we are running a surplus.

Balance of Payments Measures

Three balance of payments measures are considered to be important by many businesspersons, government officials, and economists. These are the balance on merchandise trade, the balance on goods and services, and the balance on current account.[3] The balance on merchandise trade is the narrowest measure because it considers only internationally traded goods. For this reason, critics feel that it is of the least practical value. They argue that the balance on merchandise trade is a vestigial remnant of the seventeenth century mercantilist conviction that if one country gained from trade, the other lost.[4] In those war-torn times, domestic economic policies were geared toward ensuring that exports exceeded imports. In so doing, domestic jobs were provided and the excess funds (usually precious metals) earned through the surpluses could be used to support armies and navies for imperialist expansions—or to defend against them. However, if jobs are the goal, there seems to be little point in separating goods from services. Both activities give jobs to willing workers.

Defenders of the measure feel that jobs connected to physical goods are more important than service-oriented jobs; and therefore, the balance on merchandise trade is a useful economic indicator. They contend that if an international disruption occurred, it would be better to live in a country with textile factories, steel mills, farms, and electronics firms rather than in a country with a labor force of insurance clerks, computer consultants, and tourist guides.

The balance on goods and services has a direct link to most national income accounting systems. It is reported in the national income and national product statements as "net exports." If this figure is positive, a net transfer of resources is taking place from the surplus nation to the debtor nations. Many analysts feel that if the balance is negative, it is an indication that a nation is not living within

---

3. The classic discussion of balance of payments is found in James Meade, *The Balance of Payments* (London: Oxford University Press, 1951).

4. Examples of mercantilist thought can be found in Thomas Mun, "England's Treasure by Foreign Trade," in *Early English Tracts in Commerce,* ed. John McCullock (Norwich: Jarrold and Sons, 1952). See also Joseph Schumpeter, *History of Economic Analysis* (New York: Oxford University Press, 1954).

its means. To have such a deficit position, the country would have to be a net borrower of foreign funds or a net recipient of foreign aid.

The most widely used measure of a nation's international payments position is the balance-on-current-account statement. As with the balance-on-goods-and-services statement, it shows whether a nation is living within or beyond its means. Because it includes unilateral transfers, deficits (in the absence of government intervention) must be financed by international borrowing or by selling foreign investments. Therefore, the measure is considered to be a reflection of the change in a nation's financial claims on other countries.

Exchange Rates

The purchase of a foreign good or service can be thought of as involving two sequential transactions—the purchase of the foreign currency followed by the purchase of the foreign item itself. If the cost of buying either the foreign currency or the foreign item rises, the price to the importer increases. A ratio that measures the value of one currency in terms of another currency is called an *exchange rate*. With it, one is able to compare domestic and foreign prices.

When a currency rises in value, it is said to *appreciate*. If it falls in value, it is said to *depreciate*. Therefore, a change in the value of the U.S. dollar exchange rate from 0.65 British pounds to 0.70 British pounds is an appreciation of the dollar and a depreciation of the pound. After all, the dollar now commands more pounds while a greater number of pounds must be spent to purchase one dollar.

The Foreign Exchange Market

Unlike major stock markets where trading is done on central exchanges (e.g., the New York Stock Exchange and the London Stock Exchange), foreign exchange transactions are handled on an over-the-counter market—largely by phone, teletype, and telex. Private and commercial customers, as well as banks, brokers and central banks conduct millions of transactions on this worldwide market daily.

As Figure 2.1 shows, the foreign exchange market has a hierarchical structure. Private customers deal mainly with banks in the retail market, and banks stand ready to either buy or sell foreign exchange as long as a free and active market for the currency exists.

Not all banks participate directly in the foreign exchange market. In the United States, a bank must have a substantial volume of international business to justify setting up a foreign exchange department. Thus, most small financial intermediaries handle customers' business through their correspondent banks.

Banks that have foreign exchange departments trade with private commercial customers on the retail market; but they also deal with other banks (domestic or foreign) and brokers on the wholesale market. Generally, these wholesale

FIGURE 2.1 Structure of the Foreign Exchange Market

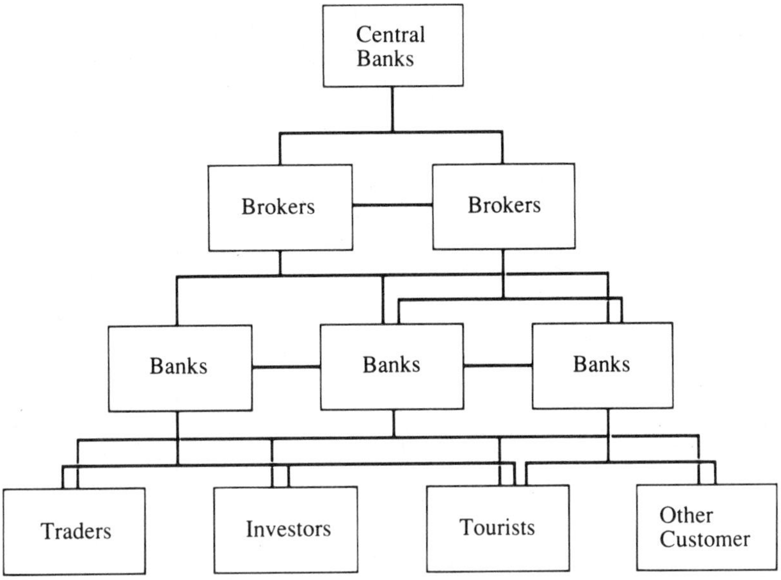

transactions are for amounts of one million dollars or more. Many of these trades are made on the basis of verbal agreements and it is only some days later that written documentation is formally exchanged.

The foreign exchange market is probably as close as one can get to the economists' proverbial ideal of pure competition. There are many buyers and sellers, no one buyer or seller can influence the price, the product is homogeneous, there is relatively free entry into and exit from the market and there is virtually perfect worldwide information. If prices among banks differed by even a fraction of a cent, arbitragers would immediately step in for the profits they could earn risk-free. Through telex machines, telephone calls, and voice boxes that lead directly into other banks'/brokers' trading rooms, participants keep abreast of the market. Positions are opened and closed minute-by-minute, and the pace of activity in a foreign exchange dealing room can be quite frantic.

Central banks play a key role in the foreign exchange markets because they are the ultimate controllers of domestic money supplies. When they enter the market to directly influence the exchange rate value, they deal mainly with brokers and large money market banks. Their trading is not done to make a profit but to attain some macroeconomic goal, such as altering the exchange rate value, reducing inflation, or changing domestic interest rates. In general, even if central banks do not intervene in the foreign exchange markets, their actions influence exchange rate values because large increases in a nation's money supply will increase its inflation rate and lower the international value of its currency.

Causes of Exchange Rate Movements

Exchange rates are among the most closely watched and politically sensitive economic variables. Regardless of which way the rates move, some groups are hurt while other groups are helped. If a currency's value rises, domestic businesses will find it more difficult to compete internationally and the domestic unemployment rate may rise. If the value of the currency falls, foreign goods become more expensive and the cost of living increases. What are the causes of these exchange rate movements and to what extent can governments influence them?

Market exchange rates are determined by the forces of supply and demand. The greater the supply of a currency to the foreign exchange market or the lesser its demand, the lower will be its international value. Similarly, the greater the demand for a currency in the foreign exchange market or the lower its supply, the higher will be its international value. Therefore, to predict movements in a currency's international value, one must identify the participants whose transactions affect these supply and demand forces and determine which factors will cause them to change their behavior.

Identifying the international participants is a relatively easy matter since they have been implicitly mentioned already in the discussion of the balance of payments. Recall that the balance of payments is nothing more than a summary of a nation's international transactions. In the Current Account and the Capital Account, traders, speculators, and investors are the major players. To this list, we will add government participants. The following sections will show how these groups act and react to overlapping market signals.

Traders

International trade in goods and services is influenced mainly by changes in relative international prices and relative income levels. If, for example, the U.S. inflation rate exceeds that of West Germany, then U.S. goods will become progressively more expensive than West German goods. Consequently, U.S. consumers will begin to demand more of these foreign goods, thereby increasing the supply of dollars to the foreign exchange market (i.e., increasing the demand for German marks). For the same reason, West German consumers will reduce their demand for dollars (i.e., reduce their supply of marks) as they purchase fewer U.S. goods. Therefore, relatively high inflation in the U.S. will cause the international value of the dollar to fall and the value of other currencies to rise.

Consumption is constrained by income, the ability to borrow, and the availability of credit. This is true both for individuals and nations. However, when speaking of a country's income, gross national product (GNP) is the most widely used measure. An increase in GNP will give the citizens of a nation the wherewithal to purchase more goods and services. Since many of the newly purchased goods are likely to be foreign, increases in GNP will raise the demand for foreign products and therefore raise the demand for foreign currencies. If, for example, the U.S. growth rate exceeds that of West Germany, there will be a net increase in the demand for German marks and a lowering of the dollar's international value.[5]

Speculators

Speculators buy and sell currencies in anticipation of changing future values. If there were a widespread expectation that the Japanese yen would rise in relative value to the dollar, speculators would try to purchase yen now (i.e., sell dollars) in anticipation of that change. As the demand for yen increased in the spot market and the supply of yen for dollars fell, the yen's exchange rate value would rise. Similarly, as the supply of dollars increased and the demand for them decreased, the international value of the dollar relative to yen would fall. Consequently, spot market rates are very much influenced by future expectations.

Investors

One of the main factors influencing investors' decisions is the differential between international interest rates. If, for example, Italian interest rates were greater than U.S. interest rates (adjusted for such things as risk, taxability, and maturity), then investors would have an incentive to place their funds where they earned the highest return—in Italy. The supply of dollars in the foreign exchange market would rise (as U.S. investors purchased Italian securities) and the demand for dollars would fall (as Italians purchase domestic rather than U.S. securities). The effect of these investments would be to lower the value of the dollar relative to the lira.

As important as relative interest rates are to the international investment decision, expected changes in exchange rates are equally important. There can be a substantial difference between the interest rate at which funds are placed in foreign investments and the net return after repatriation. The gains made on higher foreign interest rates can be partially or fully offset by changes in a currency's value. This risk might be eliminated by contracting on the forward exchange market; but in general the forward rates are arbitraged to the point where these rates completely offset the interest rate advantage. This is why relative inflation rates reappear as an important determinant of international transactions. A relatively high domestic inflation rate is one of the major causes

---

5. For an alternative point of view, see Jacob A. Frenkel and Harry Johnson, "The Monetary Approach to the Balance of Payments: Essential Concepts and Historical Origins" in *The Monetary Approach to the Balance of Payments*, ed. J.A. Frenkel and H.G. Johnson (Toronto: University of Toronto Press, 1976).

of a depreciation in the exchange value of a currency.[6] Therefore, a high inflation rate implies that the currency carries high nominal interest rates, an expensive spot exchange value, and a relatively cheap forward exchange rate value.

Governments

Governments enter foreign exchange markets in a variety of ways, ranging from the international purchase of goods and services to the granting of foreign aid. Perhaps the most pronounced impact governments have is as discretionary interveners in foreign exchange markets. Suppose the United States and Japan agreed to lower the dollar's value relative to yen. To do so, dollars would have to be supplied—and yen demanded—in the foreign exchange markets.

For the United States, this would mean putting upward pressure on the domestic money supply as newly created dollars were exchanged for circulating Japanese yen. For Japan, this type of intervention would mean putting downward pressure on its money supply as dollar reserves were used to take yen off the market. Because governments have such strong and direct controls over domestic money supplies, subsequent changes in other economic variables (e.g., inflation and interest rates) will result from this activity.

INTERNATIONAL AGENCIES FOR PROMOTING ECONOMIC AND MONETARY STABILITY

Stability in the international economy is a prerequisite for worldwide peace and prosperity. It was for this reason that at the end of World War II, a group of thirty countries met at Bretton Woods, a small ski resort in New Hampshire, and formed both the International Monetary Fund and the World Bank (the International Bank for Reconstruction and Development). With headquarters in Washington D.C., these two agencies have played, and continue to play, major roles in the international scene. Although they have accomplished many notable achievements, perhaps their most important contribution has been to initiate forums for summit discussions of controversial financial topics.

---

6. The Purchasing Power Parity theory explains that exchange rates can be predicted by estimating relative international inflation rates. See Gustav Cassel, *The World's Monetary Problems* (London; Constable, 1921); Jacob A. Frenkel, "Purchasing Power Parity: Doctrinal Perspective and Evidence from the 1920s," *Journal of International Economics,* vol. 8, May 1978; and Jacob A. Frenkel, "The Collapse of Purchasing Power Parity During the 1970s," *European Economic Review,* vol. 16, May 1981.

International Monetary Fund

The major goals of the International Monetary Fund (IMF) are to promote orderly and stable foreign exchange markets, maintain free convertibility among the currencies of member nations, reduce international impediments to trade, and provide liquidity to counteract temporary balance of payments disequilibria. While the IMF has no legal powers to enforce its decisions, strong and subtle pressures can be brought to bear on noncomplying nations.

In the early years following its creation, the IMF focused its attention on restoring currency convertibility among members and ensuring that adequate liquidity existed for countries experiencing balance of payments difficulties. Free convertibility was regained by 1958, but the liquidity issue was a much more difficult problem to solve. International trade expanded rapidly over the post-war period, but international reserves in both dollars and gold grew less rapidly. To increase the amount of international liquidity and to take some of the pressure off these reserve assets, the IMF in 1970 began issuing Special Drawing Rights (SDRs) to member nations. These SDRs (mutual book credits) gave nations the right to purchase foreign currencies; and with these currencies, they could finance temporary balance of payments deficits.

In 1973, major trading nations abandoned the fixed exchange rate system set up at Bretton Woods in 1944. As a result, the need for increases in world liquidity to finance balance of payments deficits was reduced substantially. Today, the IMF has taken on some different tasks and has a somewhat new image. Prior to the 1970s, the agency funded operations with contributions from member nations, but this changed as the IMF began selling some of its gold reserves and banking part of the capital gain. In the 1980s, the IMF took another step away from the past by borrowing in the private capital markets.

Over the past decade, the IMF has begun to extend longer term credits to the developing nations, rather than only short-term balance of payments aid. To qualify for such loans, the Fund may require that countries take drastic economic steps, such as reducing tariff barriers, making businesses independent, curbing domestic inflation, and cutting government expenditures. While many nations have resented such intervention, banks worldwide have used the IMF as a screening device for their private loans to many developing countries. If countries qualify for IMF loans, they are considered for private credit.

World Bank (International Bank for Reconstruction and Development)

The World Bank along with its sister organizations, the International Finance Corporation and the International Development Association, give long-term loans mainly to developing nations. In this sense, these three institutions are like merchant bankers (i.e., suppliers of capital) for the developing nations.

The World Bank acts as an intermediary between the private capital markets and the developing nations. It makes long-term loans (usually 15 or 25 years) carrying rates that reflect prevailing market conditions. By virtue of its AAA credit rating, the bank is able to borrow private funds at relatively low market rates and pass the savings off to the developing nations. However, because it must borrow to obtain capital and is not funded by members' contributions, the World Bank must raise lending rates when its costs (i.e., market interest rates) rise.

The International Finance Corporation (IFC) provides risk capital to fledgling companies in developing nations. For its investments, the IFC acquires stocks or bonds in the newly established businesses. After the company becomes solvent, the IFC tries to sell these securities on the domestic capital markets and to reinvest the receipts into other projects worldwide.

The International Development Association lends what may be termed *soft money* to developing nations. Funds used for these loans do not come directly from the private capital markets but are donated by member nations—meaning that they are usually taxpayer financed. Loan maturities are for fifty years and a grace period may be granted on all payments for up to ten years. Moreover, the interest that IDA charges to debtor nations is only 0.75 percent above the agency's cost of funds.

Together these agencies have tried to encourage entrepreneurial endeavors in underdeveloped parts of the world. Their loans have focused on areas that promote domestic industry and employment. The idea is age old: "If you give a starving man a fish, you will feed him for a day. If you teach him how to fish, you will feed him for a lifetime."

THE BASIS FOR TRADE: ABSOLUTE VERSUS COMPARATIVE ADVANTAGE

Internationally traded goods and services rank among the largest categories in most nations' balance of payments. Because jobs and standards of living seem to be so closely tied to these inflows and outflows, there is much debate about why particular countries find their competitive advantages in certain goods and not others, whereas other countries have different advantages and disadvantages.

Over the past twenty years, not only has there been a dramatic rise in the volume of trade, but numerous changes have been made in its patterns as well. Countries that once exported vast amounts of steel, such as the United States, are now net importers of the metal. Other nations such as Japan, once known for their inexpensive, handmade products, now compete internationally in high-tech products. What caused these trade pattern changes? Why do countries that are able to produce virtually any product choose to specialize in only certain goods? Where do international cost advantages originate? In the twenty-first century, will we still think of South Korea and China as having their greatest advantage in handmade goods, or are they the Japans and Taiwans of the future?

Absolute Advantage

While there are many variables that might be listed as the primary determinants of international trade, productivity differences rank high on the list. Take, for example, two countries—Spain and West Germany. Suppose the average Spanish worker can produce either 400 machines or 1,600 pounds of tomatoes in one year. Over the same time period, the average West German worker can produce either 500 machines or 500 pounds of tomatoes. (This information is summarized in Table 2.3.) In this case, West German workers can produce more machinery, absolutely, than Spanish workers; whereas Spanish workers can produce more tomatoes, absolutely, than their West German counterparts.

Given these figures, Spain is the obvious low-cost producer of tomatoes and should export them to West Germany. Similarly, West Germany is the low-cost producer of machines and should export them to Spain.[7]

We should not conclude from the previous example that absolute differences in production capabilities are necessary for trade to occur. Consider the same two countries—Spain and West Germany. Now, assume that the average Spanish worker can produce either 200 machines or 800 pounds of tomatoes each year whereas the average West German worker can produce either 500 machines or 1,000 pounds of tomatoes (see Table 2.4). West Germany has an absolute advantage in both goods, and it appears as though only Spain would benefit from trade. But the basis for mutually advantageous trade is present, even here. The reason lies in the concept of comparative advantage.

Comparative Advantage

Comparative advantage measures a product's cost of production, not in monetary terms but in terms of the foregone opportunity to produce something else. It focuses on tradeoffs. To illustrate, the production of machines means that resources cannot be devoted to the production of tomatoes. In West Germany, the worker who produces 500 machines will not be able to grow 1,000 pounds of tomatoes. Alternatively, if we standardize, the cost can be stated as follows: each 1 pound of tomatoes costs 0.5 machines; or 1 machine costs 2 pounds of tomatoes. In Spain, producing 200 machines forces the sacrifice of 800 pounds of tomatoes. Alternatively, this means that 1 pound of tomatoes costs 0.25 machines; or 1 machine costs 4 pounds of tomatoes (see Table 2.5).[8]

---

7. The concept of absolute advantage can be found in Adam Smith, *The Wealth of Nations* (New York: Modern Library, 1937). (Originally published in 1776).

8. David Ricardo, "Principles of Political Economy and Taxation" in *The Works and Correspondence of David Ricardo*, ed. Pierro Sraffa and Maurice H. Dobb (Cambridge, England: The University Press, 1951–1955), ch. 7.

TABLE 2.3 Worker Productivity: Example 1

	Machinery	Tomatoes
Spain	400	1,600
West Germany	500	500

TABLE 2.4 Worker Productivity: Example 2

	Machinery	Tomatoes
Spain	200	800
West Germany	500	1,000

From the example given above, it can be seen that even though Spain has an absolute disadvantage in both commodities, it still has a comparative advantage in tomatoes. For Spain, the cost of producing one pound of tomatoes is 0.25 machines while for West Germany, the cost is 0.5 machines. Similarly, even though West Germany has an absolute advantage in both products, it has a comparative cost advantage only in machines. It costs West Germany only 2 pounds of tomatoes to produce one machine while in Spain the cost is 4 pounds of tomatoes.

The last step in the discussion of the comparative advantage concept is to choose a mutually advantageous trading ratio and to show how it can benefit both countries. Any trading ratio between 1 machine = 2 pounds of tomatoes (Spain's domestic trading ratio) and 1 machine = 4 pounds of tomatoes (West Germany's domestic trading ratio) will benefit both nations (see Table 2.6). Suppose we choose 1 machine = 3 pounds tomatoes. Since West Germany will be exporting machinery, it gains by getting 3 pounds of tomatoes rather than the 2 pounds it would have produced domestically. Likewise, because Spain will be exporting tomatoes, it gains because 1 machine can be imported for the sacrifice of only 3 pounds, rather than 4 pounds, of tomatoes.

Sources of Comparative Advantage

The discussion of comparative advantage illustrates that relative rather than absolute differences in productivity can form a determining basis for international trade. Although the concept of comparative advantage provides a powerful tool for explaining the rationale for mutually advantageous trade, it gives little

TABLE 2.5 Opportunity Costs of Production

Spain	West Germany
1 machine costs 4 pounds of tomatoes	1 machine costs 2 pounds of tomatoes
1 pound of tomatoes costs 0.25 machines	1 pound of tomatoes costs 0.50 machines

TABLE 2.6 Mutually Advantageous Trading Ratios

Tomatoes	Machines
1 pound tomatoes = 0.50 machines	1 machine = 4 pounds tomatoes
↕	↕
1 pound tomatoes = 0.25 machines	1 machine = 2 pounds tomatoes

insight into the source of the relative productivity differences. Specifically, why does a country find its comparative advantage in one particular good or service rather than another product? Is it by chance that the United States is a net exporter of aircrafts, machinery, and chemicals but a net importer of steel, textiles, and consumer electronic products? Or can we find some systematic explanations for this pattern?

The answers to these questions are of more than just academic concern because they have an impact on the standard of living and livelihood of millions of people. The importance of understanding productivity differences is especially apparent in countries where trade barriers (e.g., tariffs and quotas) are about to be either erected or dismantled. For instance, during the formative years of the European Common Market, discussions centered on the economic disruptions that would occur when Germany, Italy, and France dropped their tariff barriers and permitted free trade among them. These issues have resurfaced each time a new country (e.g., Greece, Spain, and Portugal) has applied for membership to the European Community. They were hotly debated in 1982 when the Reagan Administration proposed trade liberalization measures for Latin American countries in the Caribbean Basin Initiative. Similarly, they were at the center of the three hundred or more trade protection bills awaiting action before the U.S. Congress in 1986.

Many theories have been advanced to explain the composition of international trade, but only three of them have gained a widespread following: the Labor Productivity theory, the Factor Proportions theory, and the Product Life Cycle theory. Each of these explanations provides some insight into this issue.

The Labor Productivity Theory

The oldest, and perhaps simplest, explanation of the source of comparative advantage focuses on international differences in labor productivity. The reasoning is as follows. If it takes the average Japanese worker less time to produce a good than it takes his or her counterpart in France, then Japan should have a competitive advantage in producing this commodity. The savings in labor should be reflected in the relative costs that determine international trade. Therefore, under this theory, the key to understanding comparative advantage is in determining why labor productivities among nations differ.[9]

The strength of this theory lies in its appeal to common sense and in its ability to be tested empirically. Over the years, numerous studies have shown a strong correlation between trade flows and labor productivity.[10] The theory's major problem is that it gives no insight into *why* the labor in one country should be more productive than it is elsewhere. Moreover, it seems to imply that labor is the only important input used in producing goods—surely, it is not. The production process also requires capital, natural resources, and the entrepreneur. On all of these counts, the Factor Proportions theory gives some clarification.

The Factor Proportions Theory[11]

The Factor Proportions theory provides another common-sense explanation for the patterns of international trade. It rests on two very realistic assumptions and a deductive conclusion. First, it assumes that different products have different relative input requirements. For example, both machinery and textiles require capital and labor in their production processes, but relatively more capital is needed for each unit of labor in the production of machinery than in the production of textiles.

The second assumption is that, just as commodities differ in their relative input requirements, countries differ in their relative resource endowments. Many of the Asian, African, and Latin American countries are distinguished by their large and growing populations. In comparison to the more developed countries (e.g., United States, West Germany, and Switzerland), these na-

---

9. The Labor Theory of Value can be found in the works of both Adam Smith and David Ricardo. See Smith, *The Wealth of Nations,* and *The Works and Correspondence of David Ricardo,* ed. Sraffa and Dobb.

10. See Eli Heckscher, "The Effect of Foreign Trade on the Distribution of Income," *Economisk Tidskrift,* vol. 21, 1919; Bertil Ohlin, *Interregional and International Trade* (Cambridge, Mass.: Harvard University Press, 1933).

11. The factor proportions theory can be found in G.D.A. MacDougal, "British and American Exports: A Study Suggested by the Theory of Comparative Costs," *Economic Journal,* December 1951 and September 1952; Bela Balassa, "An Empirical Demonstration of Classical Comparative Cost Theory," *Review of Economics and Statistics,* August 1963; Robert M. Stern, "British and American Productivity and Comparative Costs in International Trade," *Oxford Economic Papers,* October 1962.

tions employ far less capital per worker. Consequently, the Factor Proportions theory predicts that countries with high labor-to-capital ratios will have relatively cheap labor and therefore will be able to produce and export labor-intensive goods. Similarly, nations relatively rich in capital will be able to export capital-intensive goods.

The logic in this theory is compelling. By couching international trade in terms of both relative resource endowments and relative commodity requirements, it provides an explanation for a vast array of international transactions. Using it, one is able to explain some of the obvious trade flows in primary products. For example, South Africa trades gold and Canada trades nickel because these resources exist in highest relative abundance. The theory also helps to explain why the United States produces machinery, aircraft, and chemicals (both capital and education-intensive), but imports steel, textiles, and shoes (both more labor intensive and low-skill oriented).

If the Factor Proportions theory is correct, then a country wishing to change its comparative advantage would have to focus (over time) on modifying its relative, rather than absolute, resource endowments. Such a task might be more difficult than simply changing the absolute amount of a single resource, but certainly not impossible. Japan, for example, once the producer of low-quality, labor-intensive goods, has been able to change its relative resource endowment by educating its population and devoting considerable resources to obtaining capital. Today, it is an industrial giant and has gained the reputation of being one of the economic miracles of the twentieth century.

Although the Factor Proportions theory has been useful in explaining international trade patterns (both at any time and over time), a third explanation, the Product Life Cycle theory, more effectively deals with certain types of products. This theory is dynamic in nature and stresses both technology changes and variations in production input requirements. It is mainly concerned with high technology products that have been invented and produced by industrial countries.

The Product Life Cycle Theory

The patterns of international trade shift like grains of sand. Perhaps, it is inevitable. For example, the United States once enjoyed a substantial international comparative advantage in steel, radios, televisions, semiconductors, electronic products, and motion pictures; but this advantage has slipped away. Why did this shift occur? Some might argue that it was due to management errors or inefficiencies, and they may be partly correct. However, another explanation, the Product Life Cycle theory, demonstrates that changes in comparative advantage will be inevitable with many high technology products.[12]

---

12. The product life cycle theory can be found in Raymond Vernon, "International Investment and International Trade in the Product Cycle," *Quarterly Journal of Economics,* May 1966; W. Gruber, D. Mehta, and R. Vernon, "The R&D Factor in International Trade and Investment of United States Industries," *Journal of Political Economy,* February 1967.

This theory focuses on the role of technology, economies of scale, transportation costs, and changing input requirements. To best explain it, imagine a hypothetical, high-tech product being introduced by a Boston-based firm. In the early stages of production, success is uncertain. Mass production is difficult because the market has not been developed and experimentation with the product's design and production process are needed. Moreover, highly skilled engineers and other technical support must be used to assist in design changes. As a result, production facilities are located near the market they serve and only the richest domestic markets are targeted for product introduction.

Once the market is identified and developed, exports to high-income foreign countries (e.g., United Kingdom, West Germany, and Switzerland) begin. With these increased sales come the cost-saving gains associated with large-scale production. While competition may begin at this stage, the cost advantages bestowed by patents, trade secrecy, and the product's novelty are sufficient to keep most of this competition at bay.

As time passes, the product and its process become more standardized. There is no longer a need for highly skilled labor to make product modifications. Furthermore, since the market has been already developed, a significant barrier to entry is reduced. As a result, in the foreign markets where the product has been introduced, import-competing firms are created. They survive initially because they do not have to pay the relatively large transportation costs borne by the United States–based company. They are often given tariff protection by their respective governments as well. These two cost advantages are sufficient to offset the economies of scale enjoyed by the initiating (U.S.) firm. At first, foreign competitors sell exclusively within their own markets. Since these imitators must bear similar transportation costs and face the same tariff barriers as the U.S. firm, sales to third countries are difficult.

Once production volume increases, these foreign competitors begin to enjoy cost-saving economies of scale. Using their domestic markets as a base, they expand into new foreign markets. Gradually, they take on a larger share of the world market, and competition becomes most intense in Third-World countries. Although foreign producers may now have certain advantages over the United States, they still have not made significant inroads into the U.S. market, but this final phase of the cycle is not long in coming.

With further standardization of the production process and with the market better defined, production gravitates toward nations with the cheapest relative labor costs or with the greatest relative abundance of needed resources (just as the Factor Proportions theory would predict). At this point, the inventor country (the United States) becomes a net importer, unless a new innovation or invention can set off another wave of the production/consumption cycle.

This dynamic theory of trade implies that comparative advantage in high technology goods may, in the early stages of production, be transitory. For industrial nations, such as the United States or West Germany, this is important because it means that a strong export position in these products can only be achieved by a high rate of new product invention and innovation or a slow rate of product imitation. In either case, the end results are the same. Comparative advantage weakens over time.

INTERNATIONAL TRADE: DOES IT DESERVE SPECIAL TREATMENT?

The principles of comparative advantage can be applied to any type of trade—international, intranational or interpersonal. But if this is true, why is there so much concern about the international sector? Few residents of Massachusetts complain about the jobs that Pennsylvania, California, or Michigan factories take away from the New England area. Is the problem that people perceive international trade as an "us against them" situation while they perceive domestic trade as "us against us"? Or are there legitimate differences when one goes beyond the national borders?[13]

There seem to be some obvious factors one can point to in differentiating international from intranational trade. Varying currencies, languages, traditions, and cultures are just a few examples. But how significant are they? Switzerland, a developed, but relatively small Western European country, has four official languages—German, French, Italian, and Romansch—and an assortment of widely differing dialects. The country is divided into 26 cantons and in most respects, each canton wields more authority than does the national government. The result is a nation where rules and regulations vary canton by canton. In regards to its currency, Switzerland is bordered by West Germany, France, Austria, Italy, and Lichtenstein. While the Swiss franc is the national currency, many merchants throughout the country accept payment in any of these neighboring currencies. What factors distinguish foreign from domestic trade in Switzerland? It seems that there are few, if any, distinguishing characteristics. Certainly, the ones listed above are more apparent than real. If, in general, this is true, then international trade becomes nothing more than a simple subset of broader trade issues.

PROTECTIONISM AND TRADE RESTRICTIONS

Economists have spent considerable time identifying and quantifying the net gains from free international trade. In large part, the benefits are obvious. After all, trade by its very nature involves a voluntary exchange of assets between two parties. In the absence of coercion, the motives behind this exchange must be for

---

13. See Lester Thurow, *The Zero Sum Society: Distribution and the Possibilities for Economic Change* (New York: Basic Books, 1980).

mutual benefit. The controversy surfaces when domestic producers are considered. Foreign imports seem to take business away from domestic firms and to increase the domestic unemployment rate.[14]

Free trade, like all competitive or technological changes, creates and destroys. It gives and it takes away. By increasing competition, it lowers the price of the imported goods and raises the demand for efficiently produced domestic goods. In these newly stimulated export industries, sales will increase, profits will rise, and stock prices will climb. Clearly, consumers of the imported good and producers of the exported good are benefited by these new conditions. However, it is equally clear that there are groups that are harmed as well. Domestic producers of the import-competing good are one of the most visible groups. They experience noticeable declines in market share, falling profits, and deteriorating stock prices.

It is a fact of life that there are both beneficiaries and victims from free trade, just as there are when virtually any change is made. For instance, if someone were to discover a way for people to grow three or four sets of teeth in a lifetime, most people would benefit from this discovery. Nevertheless, there exists a group of people—dentists, oral surgeons, and periodontists—who would be hurt. Should this invention be withheld from the market because this group is hurt? The true test of a discovery is not whether or not victims exist, but whether the benefits outweigh the inevitable losses.[15]

Herein lies the major reason for protectionist legislation. The victims of free trade are highly visible and their losses quantifiable. Governments use protectionism as a means of lessening the harm done to this easily identifiable group. The individuals who are helped by free trade tend to be dispersed throughout the nation rather than concentrated in one particular region. Moreover, their monetary gain is only a fraction of the total purchase price of the commodity.

Protectionist legislation tends to be in the form of either tariffs, quotas, or qualitative trade restrictions. The following sections describe these barriers and their economic effects.

Tariffs

Tariffs are taxes on goods moving across an economic or political boundary. They can be imposed on imports, exports, or on goods in transit through a country on their way to some other destination. In the United States, export tariffs are constitutionally prohibited, but in other parts of the world they are

---

14. For details on the arguments against protectionism, see Robert Z. Lawrence and Robert E. Litan, "Why Protectionism Doesn't Pay," *Harvard Business Review*, May–June 1987, pp. 60–67.
15. Leland Yeager and David G. Tuerck, *Foreign Trade and U.S. Policy* (New York: Praeger Publishers, 1976), pp. 1–11, 40–88.

quite common. Of course, the most common type of tariff is the import tariff, and it is on this kind that we will focus our attention.

Import tariffs have a dual economic effect. First, they tend to raise the price of imported goods and thereby protect domestic industries from foreign competition. Second, they generate tax revenues for the governments imposing them. It is important to recognize this duality because, oftentimes, the situations resulting from the tariffs are quite different from what was originally intended. Moreover, regardless of what the goals are (e.g., increasing tax revenue or raising employment), tariffs may not be the most direct or effective means of attaining them.

Today, most nations impose import duties for the purpose of protecting domestic manufacturers. In some cases (as when they are imposed on expensive-to-store agricultural products), foreign sellers will lower their prices to offset any tariff increase. The net effect is for the consumer-paid price to differ only slightly, if at all, from the pre-tariff level. Consequently, the nation has greater tariff revenues but little additional protection for the domestic producers.

When tariffs do raise the price of the imported good, consumers of the imported good are disadvantaged whereas the import-competing industries are helped. Quite often, another unintended group is hampered as well. This group is made up of domestic producers (e.g., automobile manufacturers) that use the imported good (e.g., steel) in their production processes. Tariffs permit foreign businesses to acquire these material inputs at the cheaper international price. Therefore, restrictive duties may put domestic companies at a competitive disadvantage.[16] Occasionally, this unintended side effect leads to subsequent layers of tariff protection to compensate for the higher prices.

Quotas

Quotas are physical limits on the *amount* of goods that can be imported into a country. Unlike tariffs that restrict trade by directly increasing prices, quotas increase prices by directly restricting trade. Naturally, to have such an effect, imports must be restricted to levels below the free trade level.

For domestic producers, quotas are a much surer means of protection. Once the limit has been reached, imports cease to enter the domestic market regardless of whether foreign exporters lower their prices. Consumers have the most to lose with the imposition of quotas. Not only are their product choices limited and prices increased, but the goods that are imported carry the highest profit margins. Restrictions on imported automobiles, for instance, will bring in more luxury models with high-cost accessories.

16. W. Max Corden, "The Structure of a Tariff System and the Effective Protective Rate," *Journal of Political Economy*, vol. 74, June 1966, pp. 221–237.

Like tariffs, quotas have both revenue and protection effects. The protection effects are the most apparent since trade is unequivocally being curtailed. The revenue effects are less obvious. When a government imposes arbitrary restrictions on imported goods, companies vie for the right to conduct this limited trade. One source estimated that the net effects of the U.S. quota system on product categories such as apparel or steel cost U.S. consumers about $10 billion in 1985. Quotas protect foreign companies from competition among themselves and also tend to limit the impact on prices set by U.S. firms that can be assured a certain volume.[17] One option is for the government to auction these rights to the highest bidder. In this way, the government gains revenues similar to those earned under a tariff.[18] However, if these rights are given away (as has been done in the United States on occasion), the revenue that was earned by the government is reported as windfall profits by the domestic importers and foreign exporters.

Orderly Marketing Arrangements and Voluntary Export Restrictions

Over the years, certain words in our vocabulary have become associated with a strongly objectionable mental image. One such word is *depression*. In the years immediately prior to the 1930s, economic downturns were called *depressions*, but now they are called *recessions*. Why is this? The answer, in large part, is due to the strong psychological associations the word *depression* has to the Great Depression. Because no president or Congress would want to be considered responsible for such a grave situation, the new term, *recession*, was coined. Now, the downturns are the same, but the name to describe them has changed.[19]

In the same sense, the word *quota* has come to be associated with the most selfish of protectionist legislation. There can be strong political and economic repercussions associated with such unilateral, beggar-thy-neighbor policies. To avoid these problems, the new terms, *orderly marketing arrangement* and *voluntary export restriction* have been invented.[20] In general, an orderly marketing arrangement is an agreement between countries to share markets by limiting foreign export sales. Usually, they have a set duration and provide for some annual increase in foreign sales to the domestic market. Korea and Taiwan are two countries that have negotiated orderly marketing agreements with the United States. Korea has pledged a number of steps to keep the U.S. trade deficit with that country to $7 billion in 1987. Taiwan has granted more liberal-

17. "Tariffs Aren't Great, But Quotas Are Worse," *Business Week,* March 16, 1987, p. 64.

18. Monica Langley, "The Idea of Auctioning Import Rights Appeals to Lawmakers Faced with Trade, Budget Gaps," *The Wall Street Journal,* February 6, 1987, p. 44.

19. See John K. Galbraith, *Money: Whence It Came, Where It Went* (Boston: Houghton Mifflin, 1975).

20. See Kent Jones, *Politics Versus Economics in World Steel Trade* (London: George Allen & Unwin, 1986).

ized trade concessions, including a currency appreciation, to keep its trade surplus with the United States from passing $18 billion in 1987.[21]

The euphemistic terms are intended to give the impression of fairness. After all, who can be against anything that is orderly or voluntary? But when one scratches beneath the surface of these so-called negotiated settlements, a different image appears. First, the negotiations are initiated by the importing country with the implicit threat that, unless concessions are made, stronger unilateral sanctions will be imposed. They are really neither orderly nor voluntary. They are quotas in the guise of negotiated agreements.

The Trade Act of 1974 gave presidents of the United States the right to negotiate orderly marketing arrangements rather than unilaterally impose tariffs or quotas.[22] Since then, the United States has negotiated various agreements. One such arrangement forced Japan to restrict its yearly exports to the United States to 1.68 million automobiles each year. From 1981 to 1984, these limitations cost U.S. consumers an estimated $15.7 billion in additional automobile expenses.[23]

Commodity Agreements

In theory, the purpose of a commodity agreement is to stabilize market prices over an extended period of time. Agricultural goods and mining resources are the products chosen most often for these agreements. This is because their supplies are inflexible in the short-run and because their demands can be both volatile and price insensitive. The agreement can be made either exclusively by only producers of the good or between the major buyers and sellers.

Producer agreements ordinarily restrict or control output by means of production quotas. Ideally, production limits should be increased in years when market demand is high and reduced when market demand is low. In this manner, the roller coaster, up-and-down movement of prices might be avoided.

Commodity agreements between buyers and sellers generally operate through a stabilization agency. The agency buys up surplus production in years when prices are likely to decline and then supplies the market from its stockpile when prices are likely to rise. In general, these agreements do not last very long. Members too often try to set prices at levels that are unrealistically high. The result is that the stabilization agency's stockpile grows from year to year and the costs associated with buying and storing these products soar.[24]

21. "Where Sanctions Against Japan Are Really Working," *Business Week,* May 11, 1987, p. 61.

22. Trade Act of 1974, sec. 301.

23. U.S. International Trade Commission, *The Internationalization of the Automobile Industry and Its Effects on the U.S. Automobile Industry,* U.S. ITC Publication 1712 (Washington D.C., 1985), p. xiv.

24. A recent example is the International Tin Agreement that collapsed in late 1985. See "Death Rattle of an Old Tin Market?" *The Economist,* December 2, 1985, pp. 81–82.

Under the producer agreements, unity tends to be strongest when demand is strong; but as market strength weakens, so does the will to abide by the output restrictions. Voluntary export limits require that members restrict their production for the well-being of the organization. But each participant in the agreement is aware that, as a single seller, more output could be sold if there were a way to circumvent or evade the export quotas. Consequently, it is common to see illegal actions and price concessions when markets decline.

Formal and Administrative Nontariff Trade Barriers

The final category of trade restrictions is perhaps the most problematic and certainly the least quantifiable. As Table 2.7 (sections D, E, and F) shows, there is a virtual potpourri of rules and taxes that impede international trade. Not all of these barriers are discriminatory and protectionist. Restrictions dealing with public health and safety are certainly legitimate. But the line between social well-being and protection is a fine one.

At what point do consular fees, import restrictions, packaging regulations, performance requirements, licensing rules, and government procurement procedures discriminate against foreign producers? Is a French tax on automobile horsepower targeted against powerful U.S. cars or is it simply a tax on inefficiency and pollution? Are U.S. automobile safety standards unfair to West German, Japanese, and other foreign car manufacturers? Does a French ban on advertising bourbon and Scotch (but not cognac) serve the public's best interest?

Sometimes, nontariff barriers can have considerable impact on foreign competition. For decades, West German authorities forbade the sale of beer in Germany unless it was brewed from barley malt, hops, yeast, and water. If any other additives were used, which was common elsewhere, German authorities denied foreign brewers the right to label their products as beer. Only recently has the law been struck down by the European Court of Justice.[25]

The General Agreement on Tariffs and Trade—The GATT

Because of the deleterious effects of protectionism, most painfully felt during the 1930s Great Depression, twenty-three nations banded together in 1947 to form the General Agreement on Tariffs and Trade (or the GATT). Over its thirty-year life, the GATT has been a major forum for the liberalization and promotion of nondiscriminatory international trade between participating nations. Liberalization is promoted through periodic trade rounds or negotiations. Nondiscrimination is encouraged by the use of most-favored-nation clauses. These require that

25. "EC Claims Victory as Court Overturns Germany's Age-Old Ban on Beer Imports," *The Wall Street Journal,* March 13, 1987, p. 29.

TABLE 2.7 Nontariff Trade Barriers

Formal Trade Restrictions	*Administrative Trade Restrictions*
A. NONTARIFF IMPORT RESTRICTIONS (PRICE-RELATED MEASURES) Surcharges at border Port and statistical taxes Nondiscriminatory excise taxes and registration charges Nondiscriminatory excise taxes and registration charges Discriminatory excise taxes, government insurance requirements Nondiscriminatory turnover taxes Discriminatory turnover taxes Import deposit Variable levies Consular fees Stamp taxes Various special taxes and surcharges B. QUANTITATIVE RESTRICTIONS AND SIMILAR SPECIFIC TRADE LIMITATIONS (QUANTITY-RELATED MEASURES) Licensing regulations Ceilings and quotas Embargoes Export restrictions and prohibitions Foreign exchange and other monetary or financial controls Government price setting and surveillance Purchase and performance requirements Restrictive business conditions Discriminatory bilateral arrangements Discriminatory regulations regarding countries of origin International cartels Orderly marketing agreements Various related regulations C. DISCRIMINATORY FREIGHT RATES (FLAG PROTECTIONISM)	D. STATE PARTICIPATION IN TRADE Subsidies and other government support Government trade, government monopolies, and granting of concessions or licenses Laws and ordinances discouraging imports Problems relating to general government policy Government procurement Tax relief, granting of credit and guarantees Boycott E. TECHNICAL NORMS, STANDARDS AND CONSUMER PROTECTION REGULATIONS Health and safety regulations Pharmaceutical control regulations Product design regulations Industrial standards Size and weight regulations Packing and labeling regulations Package marking regulations Regulations pertaining to use Regulations for the protection of intellectual property Trademark regulations F. CUSTOMS PROCESSING AND OTHER ADMINISTRATIVE REGULATIONS Antidumping policy Customs calculation bases Formalities required by consular officials Certification regulations Administrative obstacles Merchandise classification Regulations regarding sample shipments, return shipments, and re-exports Countervailing duties and taxes Appeal law Emergency law

Source: Beatrice Bondy, *Protectionism: Challenge of the Eighties* (Zurich, Union Bank of Switzerland, 1983), p. 19. Reprinted by permission.

each nation extend to all members the same trade concessions it extends to its most-favored trading partner. Through this provision, trade restrictions have been effectively reduced and price distortions have been minimized.

Although the GATT's most notable gains have been in reducing tariff and quota barriers on certain goods, it has helped as well to simplify and homogenize trade documentation procedures, reduce qualitative trade barriers, curtail dumping (i.e., selling abroad at a cost less than the cost of production),[26] and discourage government subsidies.

ECONOMIC INTEGRATION AS A MEANS OF PROMOTING TRADE

There is little argument that free trade bestows net gains on trading nations—especially in the long run. The problem is that with so many entrenched vested interest groups, it is difficult to change trading rules from where they are to where they ought to be. Reducing protectionist legislation would cause considerable short-term dislocations, putting much economic and political pressure on a nation's power structure.

As a partial step in the trade liberalization process, countries have begun to move toward limited forms of economic integration. While the degree of economic integration can vary considerably from one organization to another, four major types of integration can be identified: free trade areas, customs unions, common markets, and monetary unions. Some of these concepts will be covered in greater detail in Chapter 5.

Free Trade Areas

The simplest form of integration is a free trade area. Within a *free trade area* nations agree to drop trade barriers among themselves, but each nation is permitted to maintain independent trade relations with nongroup countries. There is little attempt, at this level, to coordinate such things as domestic tax rates, environmental regulations, and commercial codes; and generally, such areas do not permit resources (i.e., labor and capital) to flow freely across national borders. Moreover, because each country has autonomy over its money supply,

---

26. Economists prefer to define *dumping* as selling below the variable cost per unit because only in such cases is the decision uneconomical.

exchange rates can fluctuate relative to both member and nonmember countries. Examples of free trade areas are the Latin American Free Trade Area and the European Free Trade Area.

Customs Unions

Customs unions, a more advanced form of economic integration, possess the characteristics of a free trade area, but with the added feature of a common external tariff/trade barrier for the member nations. Individual countries relinquish the right to set their nongroup trade agreements independently. Rather, a supranational policy-making committee makes these decisions. An historic example of a customs union was the 1834 German Zollverein that was composed of several German states and paved the way for the eventual uniting of Germany in 1870.

Common Markets

The third level of economic integration is a common market. Here, countries have all the characteristics of a customs union, but in addition, the organization encourages resources (i.e., labor and capital) to flow freely among the member nations. For example, if jobs are plentiful in West Germany but scarce in Italy, workers can move from Italy to West Germany without having to worry about severe immigration restrictions. In a common market, there is usually an attempt to coordinate tax codes, social welfare systems and other legislation that influences resource allocation. Finally, while each nation still has the right to print and coin its own money, exchange rates among nations are oftentimes fixed or permitted to fluctuate only within a narrow band. The most notable example of a common market is the European Economic Community (EEC). Established in 1957, the EEC has been an active organization for trade liberalization and continues to increase its membership size.

Monetary Unions

The highest form of economic integration is a monetary union. A *monetary union* is a common market in which member countries no longer regulate their own currencies. Rather, member country currencies are replaced by a common currency regulated by a supranational central bank. To date, no good examples of a monetary union exist, even though some of the initiators of the European Common Market had envisioned this as an ultimate step for its members.

Trade Creation and Trade Diversion[27]

On the surface, it would seem that any form of economic integration would move the world closer to the free trade ideal, but that may not be true. When nations drop trade barriers among themselves, but maintain a common external barrier, both harmful and beneficial effects can result, and the net effect is unclear. Beneficial effects, called *trade creation,* occur when member nations increase their production of efficiently produced goods and begin consuming lower priced goods from the participant nations. Negative effects, called *trade diversion,* occur when nations, because of the common external trade barriers, begin to consume intraunion goods when nonunion goods are cheaper. Only if the trade creation effects exceed the trade diversion effects is the integration effort considered a move toward freer trade.

Determining, a priori, whether there will be net beneficial effects can be difficult. Such factors as the similarities or differences in member nations' range of potentially tradable goods, the level of preunion protection, and the number of participating countries are involved. If there are large differences in the types of tradable goods (e.g., one country produces bananas while the other produces automobiles), the chances are that the pretrade level of trade protection was already low and not much will be gained by forming a union. If there is a sizable overlap in the range of tradable goods (e.g., both nations produce industrial-type goods, such as automobiles), competition will cause prices to fall and quality to improve as efficient intraunion producers begin selling in their newly expanded markets.

With regard to the number of countries participating in the economic integration effort, the larger the number forming the union, the greater the chances that trade creation will outweigh trade diversion. In the extreme case where all nations in the world participate, trade diversion could not occur. Trade would always flow from the lowest-cost producer.

Perhaps the most beneficial effects of economic integration are the dynamic ones. Economists usually couch their analyses in a setting where they are able to quantify the amount of trade creation and trade diversion that should occur. While these calculations are useful, they fail to catch all the beneficial effects that occur, over time, after trade restrictions have been liberalized. Members may find a homogenizing influence at work—a higher tolerance of cultural differences, larger markets, a reduced willingness to raise protectionist barriers every time unemployment rises, and a more rapid adoption of new technologies.

---

27. See Jacob Viner, *The Customs Union Issue* (New York: The Carnegie Endowment for International Peace, 1953); James Meade, *The Theory of Customs Unions* (Amsterdam: North Holland, 1955); and Dennis Swann, *The Economics of the Common Market* (Baltimore: John Hopkins University Press, 1975).

CONCLUSIONS

Nations of the world are linked by a multidimensional network of economic, social, and political ties. In the future, these connections will become even more important and more complex. As they do, countries will find themselves richer but more vulnerable to foreign disturbances, and this vulnerability increasingly will cast issues surrounding international trade and finance into the political arena.

Economics teaches that any change in rules or in financial circumstances will help some groups while hurting other groups. Therefore, it is important to understand that papers are written and speeches are made from particular points of view. Exchange-rate movements, tariffs, quotas, and customs unions can be viewed as alternative means of achieving economic goals. The real issue is not whether the changes will take place, but rather which of these means provides the most benefits with the fewest costs.

This chapter was written to describe the fundamentals of international trade and finance. With an understanding of these fundamentals, you will be able not only to comprehend the technical issues raised by the media but to formulate your own views on these subjects as well. Through such understanding will come an ability both to analyze international economic events and to critically evaluate the proliferation of articles that are being written in the area.

Questions for Discussion

1. If a nation has a balance on merchandise trade deficit, can it be said that the nation has a weak currency in the international markets as well?
2. Regarding question 1, examine both the balance of payments statistics and the foreign exchange rate statistics presented in the International Monetary Fund's *International Financial Statistics*. What link, if any, do you see between Switzerland's balance on merchandise trade and the value of the Swiss franc over the past five years?
3. Calculate your individual balance of payments over the past month. What was your balance on merchandise trade, balance on goods and services and your current account balance?
4. Exchange rate changes have been called a ''double-edged sword'' because they hurt some sectors of the nation while helping other sectors. Explain why this is true.
5. If interest rates in the United Kingdom rise while those in West Germany remain unchanged, explain what pressure this will put on the spot and forward British pound per the German mark exchange rate.
6. Suppose the U.S. Federal Reserve reduces the rate of growth of the money supply causing the U.S. inflation rate to fall, interest rates to rise, and

economic growth to decline. What impact will these economic changes have on the actions of the participants in the foreign exchange market?

7. The concept of *comparative advantage* is one of the most powerful in all of economic theory (both at the domestic level and the international level). Explain why this is true. What does the concept show? What are its implications for international and intranational trade?

8. Suppose that Brazil can produce with an equal amount of resources either 100 units of steel or 10 computers. At the same time, West Germany can produce either 150 units of steel or 10 computers. Explain which nation has a comparative advantage in the production of computers. Choose a mutually advantageous trading ratio, and explain why this ratio increases the welfare of both nations.

9. In April 1987, President Reagan imposed a tariff on goods imported into the U.S. made with Japanese semiconductors. Explain which groups in the U.S. were helped by this action and which groups were hurt by this action. Explain why a tax on semiconductors (themselves) would have actually lowered the level of protection given to U.S. computer manufacturers. Do you believe this action was evidence of good economic thinking?

10. In terms of their economic effects on a nation's economy, explain the similarities and differences between tariffs and quotas.

11. Based on each of the following distinct and separate cases, explain which trade theory best describes the trading pattern cited. Briefly explain why you chose the theory you did.

    a. The opening of trade between the United States and China has resulted in the importation of textiles and other hand-made craftwork by the United States from China and the exportation of machinery and steel from the United States to China.

    b. Currently, the United States is a major importer of televisions from Japan. It once was a major exporter of televisions to Japan.

For Further Reading

Drucker, Peter F. "Economics Erases National Boundaries." Excerpt from *Managing in Turbulent Times* by Peter F. Drucker. New York: Harper and Row, 1979.

"Europe Drives a Hole Through Those American Sanctions." *The Economist,* (August 28, 1982), p. 15.

Kindleberger, Charles P., and Peter H. Lindert. *International Economics.* 7th ed. Homewood, Ill.: Irwin, 1984.

Nevin, John J. "Doorstop for Free Trade." *Harvard Business Review,* (March–April 1983), p. 91.

Rabino, Samuel. "An Attitudinal Evaluation of an Export Incentive Program: The Case of Disc." *Columbia Journal of World Trade,* (Spring 1980), p. 61.

Root, Franklin R. *International Trade and Investment.* 5th ed. Cincinnati: Southwestern, 1984.

Rostow, W. W. *The Stages of Economic Growth.* 2nd ed. Cambridge: The University Press, 1971.

Wells, Louis T., Jr. "A Product Life Cycle for International Trade?" *Journal of Marketing,* (July 1968), pp. 1–6.

3.

CULTURAL AND SOCIAL FORCES

In Chapter 1, we explained that the complexities of international marketing are partially caused by societal and cultural forces. In this chapter, we describe some of these cultural and societal influences in more detail. However, since it is not possible to list all of them—or even to fully describe the major cultures of the world—some of the more salient forces are highlighted. Figure 3.1 shows the components of culture that are described in this chapter. We also provide an analytical framework that will suggest to the international marketing practitioner what he or she might look for. Thus, rather than suggesting all the possible cultural or societal factors that might affect international marketers, we concentrate on the analytical processes they can use to identify and monitor any of the large number of cultural influences encountered around the globe.

A DEFINITION OF CULTURE

Anthropology, the study of man, is a discipline that focuses on the understanding of human behavior. Cultural anthropology examines all human behaviors that have been learned, including social, linguistic, and family behaviors.[1] Culture includes the entire heritage of a society transmitted by word, literature, or any other form. It includes all traditions, habits, religion, art, and language. When a child is born in a certain country of the world he or she has the same essential need for food, shelter, and clothing as any child born anywhere else in the world.

---

1. Charles Winick, "Anthropology's Contributions to Marketing," *Journal of Marketing,* July 1961, p. 54.

FIGURE 3.1 Cultural Analysis

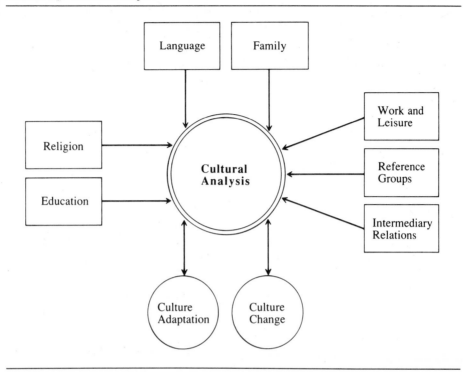

But the child will begin to develop desires for nonessential things. The development and priority of these wants are based on messages from family and peers—and thus are a result of culture. Culture is the human aspect of a person's environment; it consists of beliefs, morals, customs, and habits learned from others.

Cultural Influences on Marketing

The function of marketing is to earn profits by satisfying human wants and needs. In order to understand and influence consumers' wants and needs, marketers must understand their culture, especially in an international environment. Figure 3.2 is a diagram of how culture affects human behavior. As the figure shows, culture is embedded in elements of the society such as religion, language, history, and education. These elements of the society give direct and indirect messages to consumers about the selection of goods and services. Culture answers these questions for example: Is tea or coffee the preferred drink? Is black or white worn at a funeral? What type of food is eaten for breakfast?

FIGURE 3.2 Cultural Influences on Buyer Behavior

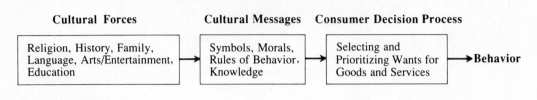

The effect of culture was illustrated in a survey that was conducted in six European countries (with similar per capita income) to determine preferences in consumer durables. Households having an automatic clothes washer ranged from 67 percent in Italy to 25 percent in the United Kingdom. The use of freezers ranged from 31 percent in West Germany to 13 percent in France. Household ownership of vacuum cleaners ranged from 99 percent in the Netherlands to 29 percent in Italy.[2] Behaviors in these countries were different based on cultural preferences with regard to methods of cleaning, the use of fresh foods, etc. Understanding the cultural will help marketers to understand consumer behavior and the need for products and services.

Isolating Cultural Influences

One of the most difficult tasks for international marketers is assessing the cultural influences affecting their operations. In the actual marketplace there are always several factors working simultaneously, and it is extremely difficult to isolate any one of them. Frequently, *cultural differences* has been the general term assigned to any noticeable differences between countries. However, when environmental factors differ, what is termed *cultural* may in fact be attributable to other factors. Quite often, when countries with both economic and cultural differences are compared, the differences are credited solely to the varying cultural systems. The analyst should be aware that though many of the differences are culturally based, other environmental factors, such as the level of economic development, political system, or legal system, could also be responsible for the differences. (These other aspects of the environment affecting consumer behavior will be discussed in Chapters 4 and 5.)

---

2. *Consumer Europe* (London: Euromonitor Publications, 1976), p. 36.

LANGUAGE

Language is a key component of culture because most of a society's culture finds its way into the spoken language. Thus, in many ways language embodies the culture of the society. Knowing the language of a society can become the key to understanding its culture. But language is not merely a collection of words or terms. Language expresses the thinking pattern of a culture—and to some extent even forms the thinking. Linguists have found that cultures with more primitive languages or a limited range of expression are more likely to be limited in their thought patterns. Many languages cannot accommodate modern technological or business concepts, forcing the cultural elite to work in a different language.

Forms of Address

The English language has one form of address: all persons are addressed with the pronoun *you*. Not so in many other languages. In the Germanic and Romance languages there are always two forms, the personal and formal address. In Japanese there are even three. Depending on status, a Japanese person will speak differently to a superior, a colleague, or a subordinate. And there are different forms for male and female in many expressions. These differences in language represent different ways of interacting. English, particularly as it is spoken in the United States, is much less formal than Japanese. Consequently, knowing the Japanese language would give a foreigner a good understanding of the cultural mores regarding social status and authority. Of course, one can develop a cultural understanding or empathy by learning about a culture. However, learning a foreign language in itself can substantially develop cultural empathy.

Overcoming the Language Barrier

International marketing communications are heavily affected by the existence of different languages. Advertising has to be adjusted to each language, and personal contacts are made difficult by a widely existing language barrier. To overcome this language barrier, businesspeople all over the world have relied on three approaches: direct translation of written material, interpreters, or acquiring foreign language skills.

Translations are made for a wide range of documents, including sales literature, catalogues, advertising, and contracts. Though this increases the initial costs of entering a market, few companies can conduct their business over the long run without translating material into the language of their customers. If a company does not have a local subsidiary, competent translation agencies are available in most countries. Some companies even route their foreign correspondence through a translation firm, thus communicating with the foreign client on all matters in their own language. This often increases the likelihood of concluding a deal.

The use of translators is usually restricted to higher level executives because of their high costs. Traveling with executives and attending meetings, translators perform a very useful function where a complete language barrier exists. They are best used for a limited time only and cannot realistically overcome long-term communication problems.

Both translation services and translators depend on translating one foreign language into another. Experience shows that this also involves risks.[3] In many situations it is almost impossible to translate fully a given meaning into a second language. When the original idea, or thought, is not part of the second culture, the translation may be meaningless. Brand names have been particularly affected by this, since they are not normally translated. Consequently, a company may get into difficulty with the use of a product name in a foreign country even though its advertising message is fully translated. General Motors' experience with its Nova model is typical here. Though it could easily be pronounced in Spanish, the literal meaning is *no va,* or "does not go." That was certainly not the right attribute for a car.[4] Today, companies tend to carefully choose product names in advance to ensure that the meaning in all major languages is neutral and/or positive. They also want to make sure that the name can be easily pronounced. Language differences may have caused many blunders during the period of rapid business expansion after World War II; but careful translations have now reduced the number of international marketing mistakes. However, the language barrier still remains, and companies that do more to overcome this barrier frequently achieve better results.

Another approach to the problem is to learn a foreign language. United States citizens in general have been remiss in learning foreign languages, whereas citizens of other nations have invested much time and effort in language study. Although international business is increasingly being transacted in English, it should not be assumed that all foreign executives speak it. Furthermore, few executives speak English well enough to have serious business discussions, and even fewer can communicate fluently in written English. As a result, native English-speaking executives should not use the excuse that their counterparts speak English anyway. True, it is difficult to select a suitable language to learn. Some languages, such as Japanese or German, are spoken in only one geographic area, whereas others such as Spanish or French are spoken in many countries. But if marketers really believe in the saying that "you have to speak the language of your customer," then there is every advantage in finding a way

3. David A. Ricks, *Big Business Blunders: Mistakes in Multinational Marketing* (Homewood, Ill.: Dow Jones-Irwin, 1983) pp. 75–95.
4. Ibid., p. 83.

to communicate in the client's native language. If one considers the value of developing cultural empathy through learning a foreign language, an argument can be made that learning any language will develop such cultural skills. Looking at foreign languages from that point of view would allow the student to approach the learning as a developmental skill that can be applied in many ways. In a sense, by learning one foreign language, the student can learn to appreciate all other cultures that are different.

We can now draw two major conclusions about the impact of language on international marketing. First, a firm must adjust its communication program and design communications to include the languages used by its customers. Second, the firm must be aware that a foreign language may contain different thinking patterns or indicate varying motivations on the part of prospective clients. This is much more difficult. To the extent that such differences occur, the simple mechanical translation of messages will not suffice. Instead, the company may have to change the entire marketing message to reflect the different cultural patterns.

RELIGION

Many businesspeople ignore the influence religion might have on the marketing environment. But even in the United States, religion has had a profound impact, although we are not aware of it on a daily basis. Historically, the religious tradition in the United States, based upon Christianity and Judaism, emphasized hard work, thriftiness, and a simple lifestyle. These religious values have certainly altered over time; many of our modern marketing activities would not exist if these older values persisted. Thrift, for instance, presumes that a person will save hard-earned wages and will use these savings for purchases later on. Today ample credit facilities exist to supplement or even supplant savings. Hard work is no longer the raison d'etre for many U.S. consumers; more time and energy are given to leisure activities. The simple lifestyle has given way to conspicuous consumption. This latter development also affects purchasing and consumption patterns.

Christian Traditions

There still are, however, religious customs that remain a major factor in marketing today, both here and abroad. Christmas is one Christian tradition that, at least in respect to consumption, remains an important event for many consumer goods industries. Retailers traditionally have their largest sales around that time. Christmas can be used as an illustration of substantial differences even among largely Christian societies. A large United States–based retailer of consumer electronics found out the hard way about these differences when it opened its first retail outlet in the Netherlands. The company planned the opening to coincide with the start of the Christmas selling season, as this would allow the firm to show a profit in the first year, and advertising space was bought accordingly in late November and December. The results were less than satisfactory, however, because major gift giving in Holland takes place not around December 25, Christmas Day, but on St. Nicholas Day, December 6, the Dutch traditional day of gift giving. Thus, the opening of the U.S. company's retail operation was late and missed the major buying season.

Many other variations surrounding Christmas gift giving can be found. In France, it is traditional to exchange gifts on January 6, often called "Little Christmas." Also different are the personages who bring the gifts. In the United States, as in the United Kingdom, Santa Claus brings the Christmas gifts; but in German-speaking countries, gifts are brought by an angel representing the Christ Child. In German areas, Santa Claus or St. Nicholas comes on December 6 to bring small gifts and food to those children who behaved. All of these examples show that local variations of religious traditions can have a substantial impact on international marketing activities.

Islam

Religion's impact on international marketing becomes more apparent when the observer compares one religion to another. It is beyond the scope of this text to give a complete description of all world religions with specific implications for marketing. However, by using one non-Christian religion, Islam, some of the potential impact can be documented. We've chosen Islam in view of its growing influence in many countries.

With about 767 million followers, Islam is the religion of 20 percent of the world's population.[5] Islam was established by the prophet Mohammed in Mecca in A.D. 610. Thirteen years later, when Mohammed had to flee to nearby Medina, he established the first Islamic city-state.[6] By his death in 632, the holy book of Islam, the *Koran,* had been completely revealed. It is believed to contain God's own words. The *Koran* was supplemented by the *Hadith* and *Sunna* which contain the reported words and actions of the prophet Mohammed. These works contain the primary sources of guidance for all Muslims on all aspects of life.

With the expansion of the Islamic state, additional guidance was needed; and as a result the *Sharia,* or legal system, emerged. Based on the *Koran,* the *Sharia* gives details of required duties and outlines all types of human interac-

5. Mushtaq Luqmani, Zahir Quraeshi, and Linda Delene, "Marketing in Islamic Countries: A Viewpoint," *MSU Business Topics,* Summer 1980, p. 17.

6. Muhammad Abdul-Rauf, "The Ten Commandments of Islamic Economics," *Across the Board,* August 1979, p. 7.

tions. It essentially constitutes what elsewhere would be considered criminal, personal, and commercial law. These Islamic guidelines cover all aspects of human life and categorize human behavior as obligatory, merely desirable, forbidden, merely undesirable, or neutral. The principal goal is to guide human beings in their quest for salvation because the basic purpose of human existence is to serve God. Divine guidance is to be accepted as given; and it is believed to meet both the spiritual and psychological needs of the individual, making him or her a better social being. The nonritual divine guidance covers, among other areas, the economic activities of society. This latter guidance offers people a wide range of choices while protecting them from evil. A set of basic values restricts economic action and should not be violated or transgressed.

The Islamic value system, as it relates to economic activities, requires a commitment to God and a constant awareness of God's presence even while engaged in material work. Wealth is considered a favor of God to be appreciated; it cannot be regarded as a final goal. Wealth is to be used to satisfy basic needs in moderation. With the real ownership of wealth belonging to God, man is considered only a temporary trustee. Material advancement thus does not entail higher status or merit. In Islam all people are created equal and have the right of life, the right of liberty, the right of ownership, the right of dignity, and the right of education. For the true Muslim, the achievement of goals is both a result of individual efforts and also a blessing from God. A Muslim should therefore not neglect the duty of working hard to earn a living.

In their work, Muslims are required to uphold the Islamic virtues of truth, honesty, respect for the rights of others, pursuit of moderation, sacrifice, and hard work. Moderation applies to virtually all situations. The resulting Islamic welfare economy is based upon the bond of universal brotherhood in which the individuals, while pursuing their own good, avoid wrongdoing to others. In their economic pursuits, true Muslims not only have their own material needs in mind but accept their social obligations and thereby improve their own position with God. The Islamic culture has many specific implications for international marketers. A summary of these implications is shown in Table 3.1.

The prohibition of usury has led to quite different practices with respect to lending in Arab societies.[7] Since this law prohibits interest payments, special Islamic banks were formed. These banks maintain three types of accounts: nonprofit accounts with a very small minimum deposit and the right of immediate withdrawal without notice, profit-sharing deposit accounts, and social services funds. These banks do not charge a fixed rate of interest on loans. Instead, the "interest payment" is levied according to the profits derived from the funds employed. The depositors thus get earnings on their deposits depending on the amount of profits earned by the bank. Such Islamic banks now exist in many countries, particularly Egypt, Saudi Arabia, Kuwait, Sudan, Dubai, and Jordan. In Pakistan, where the population is 97 percent Moslem, the Murree Brewery

---

7. Ibid., pp. 15–16.

TABLE 3.1 Marketing in an Islamic Framework

Elements	Implications for Marketing
I. *Fundamental Islamic Concepts*	
A. Unity. (Concept of centrality, oneness of God, harmony in life.)	Product standardization, mass media techniques, central balance, unity in advertising copy and layout, strong brand loyalties, a smaller evoked size set, loyalty to company, opportunities for brand-extension strategies.
B. Legitimacy. (Fair dealings, reasonable level of profits.)	Less formal product warranties, need for institutional advertising and/or advocacy advertising, especially by foreign firms, and a switch from profit maximizing to a profit satisficing strategy.
C. Zakaat. (2.5 percent per annum compulsory tax binding on all classified as "not poor.")	Use of "excessive" profits, if any, for charitable acts; corporate donations for charity, institutional advertising.
D. Usury. (Cannot charge interest on loans. A general interpretation of this law defines "excessive interest" charged on loans as not permissible.)	Avoid direct use of credit as a marketing tool; establish a consumer policy of paying cash for low value products; for high value products, offer discounts for cash payments and raise prices of products on an installment basis; sometimes possible to conduct interest transactions between local/foreign firm in other non-Islamic countries; banks in some Islamic countries take equity in financing ventures, sharing resultant profits (and losses).
E. Supremacy of human life. (Compared to other forms of life, objects, human life is of supreme importance.)	Pet food and/or products less important; avoid use of statues, busts—interpreted as forms of idolatry; symbols in advertising and/or promotion should reflect high human values; use floral designs and artwork in advertising as representation of aesthetic values.
F. Community. (All Muslims should strive to achieve universal brotherhood—with allegiance to the "one God." One way of expressing community is the required pilgrimage to Mecca for all Muslims at least once in their lifetime, if able to do so.)	Formation of an Islamic Economic Community—development of an "Islamic consumer" served with Islamic-oriented products and services, for example, "kosher" meat packages, gifts exchanged at Muslim festivals, and so forth; development of community services—need for marketing or nonprofit organizations and skills.
G. Equality of peoples.	Participative communication systems; roles and authority structures may be rigidly defined but accessibility at any level relatively easy.
H. Abstinence. (During the month of Ramadan, Muslims are required to fast without food or drink from the first streak of dawn to sunset—a reminder to those who are more fortunate to be kind to the less fortunate and as an exercise in self-control.)	Products that are nutritious, cool, and digested easily can be formulated for Sehr and Iftar (beginning and end of the fast).

TABLE 3.1 Marketing in an Islamic Framework *(cont.)*

Elements	Implications for Marketing
Consumption of alcohol and pork is forbidden; so is gambling.	Opportunities for developing nonalcoholic items and beverages (for example, soft drinks, ice cream, milk shakes, fruit juices) and nonchance social games, such as Scrabble; food products should use vegetable or beef shortening.
I. Environmentalism. (The universe created by God was pure. Consequently, the land, air, and water should be held as sacred elements.)	Anticipate environmental, antipollution acts; opportunities for companies involved in maintaining a clean environment; easier acceptance of pollution-control devices in the community (for example, recent efforts in Turkey have been well received by the local communities).
J. Worship. (Five times a day; timing of prayers varies.)	Need to take into account the variability and shift in prayer timings in planning sales calls, work schedules, business hours, customer traffic, and so forth.
II. *Islamic Culture*	
A. Obligation to family and tribal traditions.	Importance of respected members in the family or tribe as opinion leaders; word-of-mouth communication, customer referrals may be critical; social or clan allegiances, affiliations, and associations may be possible surrogates for reference groups; advertising home-oriented products stressing family roles may be highly effective, for example, electronic games.
B. Obligations toward parents are sacred.	The image of functional products could be enhanced with advertisements that stress parental advice or approval; even with children's products, there should be less emphasis on children as decision makers.
C. Obligation to extend hospitality to both insiders and outsiders.	Product designs that are symbols of hospitality, outwardly open in expression; rate of new product acceptance may be accelerated and eased by appeals based on community.
D. Obligation to conform to codes of sexual conduct and social interaction. These may include the following:	
1. Modest dress for women in public.	More colorful clothing and accessories are worn by women at home; so promotion of products for use in private homes could be more intimate—such audiences could be reached effectively through women's magazines; avoid use of immodest exposure and sexual implications in public settings.
2. Separation of male and female audiences (in some cases).	Access to female consumers can often be gained only through women as selling agents, salespersons, catalogs, home demonstrations, and women's specialty shops.
E. Obligations to religious occasions. (For example, there are two major religious observances that are celebrated—Eid-ul-Fitr, Eid-ul-Adha.)	Tied to purchase of new shoes, clothing, sweets, and preparation of food items for family reunions, Muslim gatherings. There has been a practice of giving money in place of gifts. Increasingly, however, a shift is taking place to more gift giving; due to lunar calendar, dates are not fixed.

Source: Mushtaq Luqmani, Zahir A. Quraeshi, and Linda Delene, ''Marketing in Islamic Countries: A Viewpoint,'' *MSU Business Topics,* Summer 1980, pp. 20–21. Reprinted by permission.

Company operates at only 27 percent of capacity. Only non-Moslems and visitors can purchase alcohol; and they are limited to six bottles of beer and one bottle of liquor each month. Moslems caught with alcohol are subject to flogging.[8]

The influence of Islamic habits on business even outside the Islamic world was demonstrated in the construction of a new luxury hotel in Paris. The hotel, a renovated building near the center of Paris, was selected partially for the reason that some of the rooms face Mecca. Decorated in the latest interior style, some rooms are equipped with buttons that bring down shades with engraved minarets on them. According to the hotel management, one-third of the hotel guests are expected to come from the Middle East.[9]

Certainly, international marketers require a keen awareness of how religion can influence business. They need to search actively for any such possible influences even when the influences are not very apparent. Developing an initial awareness of the impact religion has on one's own culture is often very helpful in developing cultural sensitivity.

EDUCATION

Though the educational system of a country largely reflects its own culture and heritage, education can have a major impact on how receptive consumers are to foreign marketing techniques. Education shapes people's outlooks, desires, and motivation. To the extent that educational systems differ by country, we can expect differences among consumers. However, education not only affects potential consumers, it also shapes potential employees for foreign companies and for the business community overall. This will influence business practices and competitive behavior.

Executives who have been educated in one country are frequently poorly informed about educational systems elsewhere. In this section, we will indicate some of the major differences in educational systems throughout the world and explain their impact on international marketing.

Levels of Participation

In the United States, although compulsory education ends at age 16, virtually all students who obtain a high school diploma stay in school until age 18 (see Table 3.2). While at high school, some 25 percent take vocational training courses.

---

8. "Teetotaling but Tolerant, Pakistan Lets Its Only Brewery Totter Along," *The Wall Street Journal,* April 14, 1987, p. 28.
9. "Nouveaux-riches Elysees," *The Economist,* February 27, 1982, p. 66.

TABLE 3.2 Educational Statistics of Selected Countries (in Percentages)

Countries	Participation in Secondary Education	Literacy Rates
United States	95	99
Canada	102	99
United Kingdom	86	99
Germany	74	99
France	90	99
Italy	74	93
Netherlands	102	99
Spain	89	97
Yugoslavia	82	90.5
Sweden	83	99
Japan	95	99
Korea	94	90
Australia	94	98.5
India	34	36
Mexico	55	88.1
Brazil	35	76
Venezuela	45	85.6
Afghanistan	8	12
Israel	74	88*/70†
Egypt	58	40
Nigeria	29	25–30
Kenya	19	47
South Africa	76	100**/50††
Tunisia	36	62

* Jews   ** whites
† Arabs   †† blacks

Source: UNESCO, *1985 Statistical Yearbook*, pp. 111-17–111-68; *The World Fact Book 1986* (Washington, D.C.: CIA, June 1986), pp. 1–270. Reprinted by permission.

After high school, students either go on to college or find a job. About half of the high school graduates go on to some type of college.

This pattern is not shared by all countries. The large majority of students in Europe go to school only until age 16; then they join some kind of apprenticeship program. This is particularly the case for Germany, where formal apprenticeship programs exist for about 450 job categories. These programs are under tight government supervision and typically last three years. They include on-the-job training, with one day a week of full-time school. About two-thirds of young

Germans enter such a program after compulsory full-time education.[10] During their first year they can expect to earn about 25 percent of the wages earned by a fully trained craftsman in their field. Only about 30 percent of the young Germans finish university schooling.

In Great Britain the majority of young people take a job directly in industry and receive informal on-the-job training. In Japan, as in the United States, apprenticeships attract only a small percentage of the youth. In both the United States and Japan, companies provide a substantial amount of in-house training. Some comparative statistics are contained in Figure 3.3.

Participation in secondary education will affect literacy levels and economic development. Even with similar levels of participation in secondary education, the attitudes of some countries about the quantity and quality of education differ. For example, Japanese high school students attend class 240 days per year whereas U.S. students attend class 180 days per year. Also, only 35 percent of Japanese high school seniors spend less than five hours per week on homework, but as many as 76 percent of U.S. students spend less than 5 hours on homework each week.[11]

Literacy and Economic Development

The extent of education affects marketing on two levels. First there is the problem of literacy. In societies where the average level of participation in the educational process is low, one typically finds a low level of literacy (see Table 3.2). This not only affects the people's earning potential, and thus their level of consumption, but also determines the communication options for marketing programs, as we will see in Chapters 14 and 15. A second concern is how much young people earn. In countries like Germany, where many of the youth have considerable earnings by age 20, the value or potential of the youth market is quite different from that in the United States, where a substantial number of youths do not enter the job market until age 21 or 22.

Recent studies by The Organization for Economic Cooperation and Development have found a definite link between the percentage of 16 year olds staying in school beyond the minimum leaving age and a country's economic well being. Countries like Japan, Holland, West Germany, Austria, and the United States get a high return on their educational expenses since so many young people stay in school, either in traditional or vocational schools. Portugal, Spain, Britain,

---

10. "School's Out," *The Economist,* December 12, 1981, p. 91.
11. "High Schools in U.S. Lack Drive of Japan's But Show Spontaneity," *The Wall Street Journal,* March 10, 1987, p. 20.

FIGURE 3.3 Percentage Distribution of Young People After Compulsory Education

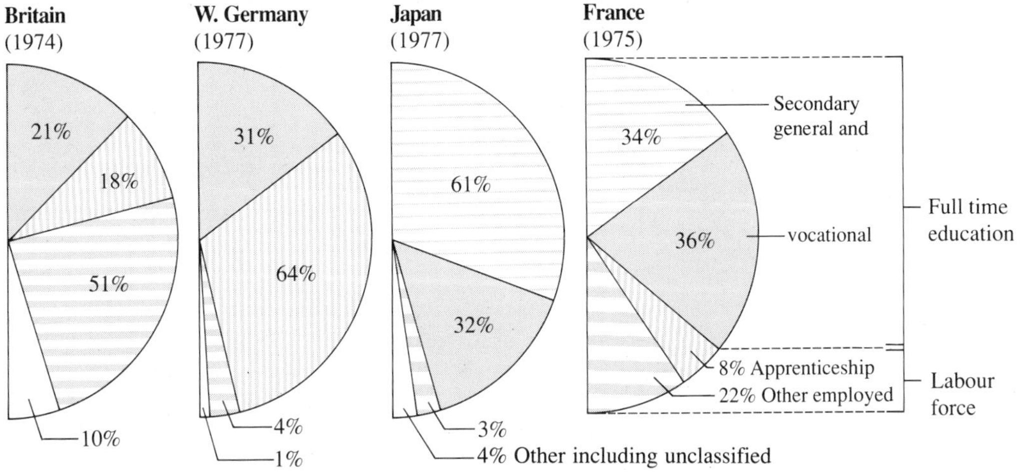

| Britain (1974) | W. Germany (1977) | Japan (1977) | France (1975) |

Britain (1974): 21%, 18%, 51%, 10%

W. Germany (1977): 31%, 64%, 4%, 1%

Japan (1977): 61%, 32%, 3%, 4% Other including unclassified

France (1975): 34% — Secondary general and, 36% — vocational — Full time education, 8% Apprenticeship, 22% Other employed — Labour force

Source: The Economist, December 12, 1981, p. 91. © 1981 The Economist, distributed by Special Features. Reprinted by permission.

and New Zealand get a poor return on their educational expenses because so few young people continue their education.[12]

The educational system also affects the type of employees and executive talent. The typical career path of a U.S. executive involves a four-year-college program and, in many cases, a post-degree, Masters in Business Administration (MBA) program. This type of executive education is rare outside the United States. Top management talent may have university degrees in other fields. For example, law is among the more popular degrees. In many areas of the world, it might be impossible to hire university graduates. In the United States, the sales organizations of many large companies are staffed strictly with university graduates. In many other countries, sales as a profession has a lower status; and it is probably very difficult to attract university graduates.

Different countries have substantially different ideas about education in general, and management education in particular. In general, though differences exist between countries, traditional European education emphasizes the mastery of a subject through knowledge acquisition. In contrast, the U.S. approach emphasizes analytic ability and an understanding of concepts. Students passing through the two educational systems will probably develop different thinking patterns and attitudes. It requires a considerable amount of cultural sensitivity

12. "The Wealth of Nations," The Economist, December 20, 1986, p. 101.

for an international manager to understand these differences and to make the best use of the human resources that are available.

THE FAMILY

The role of the family varies greatly between cultures, as do the roles that the various family members play. Across cultures, we find differences in family sizes, in the employment of women, and in many other factors that are of great interest to marketers. Particularly since the family is a primary reference group and has always been considered an important determinant of purchasing behavior, these differences are of interest.[13] Companies familiar with family interactions in Western society cannot assume that they will find the same patterns elsewhere. For example, the Chinese value family above individuals or even country. People have strong ties with family members. Within a family an individual has no rights or property—expenses are shared.[14] Therefore, product advertising appeals must focus on family benefits, not individual benefits.

One development centers around the nature of the nuclear family. The term *nuclear family* is used with reference to the immediate family group—father, mother, and children living together.[15] In the United States, and to some degree in Western Europe as well, we have found strong trends toward the dissolution of the traditional nuclear family.[16] As a result of an increasing divorce rate, the "typical" family of father, mother, and children living in one dwelling is rapidly becoming a thing of the past or "atypical." Furthermore, families are smaller than they used to be due to the drop in fertility rates. Also, an increasing number of women are working outside the home. (See Table 3.3.) These circumstances have substantially changed purchasing patterns, especially among U.S. families.

Marketers who have only dealt with U.S. consumers should not expect to find the same type of family structure elsewhere. In many societies, the role of the male as head of household is more pronounced; and in some cultures (as in Asia or Latin America), the differences tend to be substantial. This male dominance coincides with a lower rate of participation by women in the labor force outside the home. On the average, this results in a lower family income, since double wage earners increase the average family incomes. The number of children per family also shows substantial variations by country or culture. In many Eastern European countries and in Germany, one child per family is fast ap-

---

13. J. Barry Mason and Hazel F. Ezell, *Marketing Principles and Strategy* (Plano, Tex.: Business Publications, 1987), p. 266.

14. Ester Lee Yao, "Cultivating Guan-xi (Personal Relationships) with Chinese Partners," *Business Marketing*, January 1987, p. 64.

15. John C. Mowen, *Consumer Behavior* (New York: Macmillan, 1987), p. 399.

16. Fabian Linder, "The Nuclear Family Is Splitting," *Across the Board*, July 1980, p. 52.

TABLE 3.3 Family Statistics of Selected Countries

Country	Fertility Rates[1]	Average Size of Household[2]	Active Women as a Percent of Total Female Population[5]
United States	61.0	2.7	41.8
Canada	55.5	3.1	54.3*
United Kingdom	52.8	2.7	37.4
Germany	40.1	2.4[3]	35.3
France	62.5	2.9	34.8
Italy	46.5	3.0	28.2
Netherlands	46.2	2.5[4]	35.9*
Spain	73.1	3.5[3]	16.5
Yugoslavia	64.2	N/A	32.9
Sweden	47.1	2.4	68.0
Japan	49.2	3.2	38.6
Korea	82.0	4.5	29.3
Australia	62.2	3.1	45.7
India	136.7	N/A	19.8
Mexico	99.8	5.5[3]	18.2
Brazil	94.0	4.9	26.6*
Venezuela	138.8	5.8[4]	18.7
Afghanistan	232.5	6.2	4.9
Israel	104.5	3.8	26.2
Egypt	160.7	5.2	12.5
Nigeria	N/A	N/A	20.6
Kenya	N/A	N/A	N/A
South Africa	N/A	N/A	22.8
Tunisia	151.9	5.5[4]	11.5

* Data is for women 15 years and older only.
N/A = Not Available.

Source: [1] Adapted from *1984 Demographic Yearbook*, 36th Edition, Copyright United Nations 1984; [2] *1982 Demographic Yearbook*, 34th Issue, Copyright, United Nations 1982; [3] *Statistical Yearbook 1982/1983*; [4] *Compendium of Human Settlement Statistics*; [5] Data is for different years 1980–1985 and from different sources, such as census, household surveys, official estimates, and so on. See *1986 Year Book of Labor Statistics* (Geneva: International Labor Office). Copyright © 1987, International Labor Organization, Geneva.

proaching the rule, whereas families in many developing countries are still large by Western standards. Different views with regard to appropriate family size are partially reflected in the practice of birth control. As can be seen in Figure 3.4, countries with higher income levels show a much greater tendency to use family planning methods.

So far we have discussed only the nuclear family. However for many cultures, the extended family—including those relatives such as grandparents, in-laws, aunts, uncles, etc.—is of considerable importance. In the United States, older parents usually live alone, either in individually owned housing, in special housing for the elderly, or in nursing homes (for those who can no longer care for themselves). In countries with lower income levels and in rural areas, the extended family still plays a major role, further increasing the size of the average household.

Because the family plays such an important role as a consumption unit, marketers need to understand family roles and composition as they differ from country to country. At this point we are not so much concerned with the demographic aspects, though they will concern us as we discuss the various market opportunities in Chapters 5 and 6. Here, the primary emphasis is on the roles the individual family members play, their respective influence on each other, and the society's expectation as to what role each family member ought to play. Such an understanding is crucial for the marketing of consumer products and tends to affect both communication policy and product policy.

WORK AND LEISURE

The attitudes a society holds toward work have been documented to have a substantial impact on a society's or culture's economic performance. David McClelland has maintained that it is not a country's external resources that determine its economic rise, but its level of entrepreneurial spirit to exploit existing resources.[17] What was found to be crucial was the orientation or attitudes toward achievement and work. Cultures with a high level of achievement motivation were found to show a faster rise in economic development than those with low achievement motivation.

A well-known German sociologist, Max Weber, investigated the relationship between attitudes toward work and religion. In his famous work published in 1904, *The Protestant Ethic and The Spirit of Capitalism,* Weber was one of the first to speculate on the influence of religion on the work ethic by demonstrating

---

17. David C. McClelland and David G. Winter, *Motivating Economic Achievement* (New York: Free Press, 1969).

FIGURE 3.4 Birth Control Use and per Capita Income (Data from Married Women Aged 15–49*)

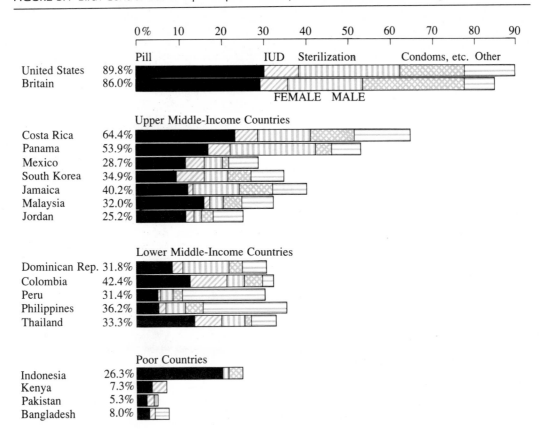

* Except in America (aged 15–44), Britain (16–49), and Costa Rica and Panama (20–49)

Source: "Whatever Happened to New Methods of Birth Control?" *The Economist,* May 30, 1981, p. 86. ©
1981 The Economist, distributed by Special Features. Reprinted by permission.

differences between Protestant and Catholic attitudes toward work. McClelland
later expanded Weber's theory to cover all religions and found that economies
with a more Protestant orientation exceeded economies with a Catholic orientation in per capita income. McClelland ascribed this to the Protestant, particularly
Calvinist, belief that man did not necessarily receive salvation from God through
work, but that success in work could be viewed as an indication of God's grace.
Consequently, accumulating wealth was not viewed as a shameful activity that
needed to be hidden. Traditional Catholic doctrine viewed money making in
more negative terms. It was Weber's theory that this difference in attitude to-

ward wealth caused Protestant societies to outperform Catholic societies in economic terms.

Religion thus appears to be a prime influence on attitudes toward work. Observers have theorized that the Shinto religion encourages the Japanese people to have a strong patriotic attitude which is in part responsible for Japan's excellent economic performance.[18] The low rate of economic performance in some developing countries is thus attributed in part to their different attitudes toward work as dictated by their religions.

A discussion on work will usually lead to a discussion of its opposite—leisure. Different societies have different views about the amount of leisure time that is acceptable. In most economically developed countries, particularly where work has become a routine activity, leisure has become a major aspect of life. In such countries the development of the leisure industries is an indication that leisure can be as intensely consumed as any other product. In Western European countries it is typical for employees and management alike to receive three to five weeks of vacation time and to embark upon trips away from home. In Japan, official vacations may reach the same number of weeks, but employees only take a portion of it. In the United States vacations are shorter, and people tend to use up their allotted time off. These differences in the usage of leisure time to some degree reflect differences in attitudes toward work.

REFERENCE GROUPS

The impact of reference groups on buying behavior has been documented by many writers in marketing.[19] Past experience clearly indicates that the concept of reference group influence applies to many cultures. Differences can be found in the types of relevant reference groups and in the nature of their influence on individual consumers.

Peer Groups

The account of a U.S. journalist traveling in the U.S.S.R. gives an excellent illustration of the different types of peer reference groups found abroad. The journalist became curious about the fact that many young people in Russia were

---

18. Vern Terpstra, *International Marketing* (New York: Dryden Press, 1987), p. 101.
19. Leon G. Schiffman and Leslie Lazar Kanuk, *Consumer Behavior,* 3rd ed., (Englewood Cliffs, N.J.: Prentice-Hall, 1987), p. 374.

wearing the same type of blue jeans and T-shirts that young people wore in the United States. In fact, some of these items had been acquired at very high prices on the black market. The reporter concluded, after several personal conversations, that the people who wore this type of clothing were seen as having a sense of fashion-mindedness, and they derived high status within their social groups. In contrast, U.S. consumers who wore blue jeans and T-shirts normally conveyed a sense of informality and casualness about their appearance. Indeed, the U.S. consumers wanted just the opposite of what Russian consumers wanted. Consequently, we can observe the influence of different reference groups on the same product category, as they induce consumption but satisfy different purposes. International marketers are well advised to ensure that communication programs based on specific reference groups are consistent with the cultural and social environment of that reference group in the foreign market.

Role Models

Famous sports personalities have traditionally been used as a way to exploit the reference group concept. The idea is to use the prestige of accomplished athletes to promote certain products. However, not all sports are equally popular in all parts of the world. The U.S. interest in baseball is shared only by certain Latin American and Asian nations, and not at all in Europe. On the other hand, soccer dominates only in Europe and Latin America, and not in the United States. Some sports such as tennis or golf have an international following but do not attract large parts of the population. Consequently, it might be difficult to find a sports personality who is equally recognized around the world.

There are some reference groups of U.S. origin that appear to have substantial universal appeal. The "American way of life" is one phenomenon that might explain the success of many U.S. consumer products elsewhere. Though not always clearly defined, it does represent an attraction to large groups of people in most countries. What might be considered American might in fact only be a cover for a modern or high-income lifestyle. Consequently, foreign consumers aspire to a high level of economic status as exemplified by the U.S. lifestyle, or the commonly held image of such a life. In any case, some companies have successfully capitalized on this lifestyle, and Americans have become a reference group for numerous products in markets abroad.

Another U.S. symbol with international appeal is the American cowboy of the "Wild West." An image of a cowboy on a horse triggers substantially similar reactions in most countries, even where the cultural background is otherwise diverse. The cowboy might very well be one of the few commonly shared symbols around the world and might account for the success of the well-known Philip-Morris Marlboro campaign featuring western scenes.

Country Image

The success of the U.S. company Levi Strauss in foreign markets can partially be credited to the penchant of foreign consumers for western-style clothing. Texas Boot Co., a division of U.S. Shoe Corp., found a growing market for boots in Europe by emphasizing leisure and sportswear shoes.[20] Other U.S. firms have had more difficulty, partially because of the image foreign consumers have of shoes manufactured in the United States. Market research revealed that French manufacturers were viewed as leading in high-fashion women's shoes, whereas Italian companies dominated the market for light-weight men's shoes. Europeans viewed shoes manufactured in the United States as stiff, heavy, boxy, and lacking in a variety of styles. United States manufacturers took the lead only with western boots. Once a strong image exists, it is extremely difficult to change a prevailing view.

On an international level, countries can assume the position of a reference group. Over time, various countries, or the residents of various countries, have become known for achievements in some aspects of life, culture, or industry. Other countries thus may attach a special quality to the behavior of these consumers or to products that originated in these countries. When the German beer, Beck, was touted in the United States as "the German beer that is number one in Germany," the idea was to capitalize on the image of German beer drinkers as being the most discriminating. BSN-Gervais, Danone, the French company that brewed Kronenbourg, was attempting to take on Heineken, the leading import into the United States, by claiming "Europeans like Heineken, but they love Kronenbourg." This campaign tried to take advantage of the fact that Kronenbourg was the largest selling bottled beer in Europe. BSN decided not to emphasize French Alsace as the origin of the beer. Since the brand name Kronenbourg sounded German to most U.S. consumers, the company was banking on the positive image of German beers in general.[21]

The U.S. brewer Anheuser-Busch faced a different problem when entering the European market. Anheuser-Busch marketed its beer as the beer brewed with "high-country barley" from Wyoming, using the German voice used in John Wayne films as the narrator. The same Western theme was used in France, where Busch beer was advertised as "the beer of the men of the West." Because the United States was not recognized by Europeans as a major beer-brewing country, the company took advantage of already existing images familiar to European consumers.[22]

20. "An Export Foothold for U.S. Made Shoes," *Business Week,* Sept. 4, 1978, p. 74.

21. "Big Battle Is Brewing As French Beer Aims to Topple Heineken," *The Wall Street Journal,* February 22, 1980, p. 24.

22. "Anheuser Tries Light Beer Again," *Business Week,* June 29, 1981, p. 140.

The perfume industry, for decades dominated by French firms, has been greatly affected by the "Made in Paris" phenomenon. Consumers all over the world have come to admire and expect more of perfumes made by French companies. American firms have tried to overcome this handicap with aggressive marketing policies and the creation of new products based upon market research and new insights into perfume-making chemistry. Still, it has proved to be very difficult to enter this high-prestige market, and some U.S. cosmetic leaders have not been able to duplicate their domestic success abroad. To overcome the "Made in Paris" mystique, foreign companies have acquired French cosmetic firms. Pfizer acquired Coty in 1964, and later Revlon acquired Balmain and Raphael. American Cyanamid purchased the Pierre Cardin brand. Foreign firms are now said to control about 25 percent of the French perfume market.[23]

Shiseido, the leading Japanese cosmetics firm, avoided a direct attack on the top French firms by primarily emphasizing skin care products. Traditionally, Japanese cosmetics have emphasized skin care, whereas Western cosmetics have concentrated on fragrances and make-up. When Shiseido entered the German market, the company's message was that Japanese women had concentrated on skin care for generations, thus establishing that the Japanese were experts in skin care products.[24] After various cosmetic firms campaigned heavily against the French industry, some two dozen French firms formed a trade group designed to enhance their image worldwide. Under the name "Prestige de la Parfumerie Francaise," the group planned over several years to spend several million French francs to hold onto the German market, the most important export market for French cosmetics and perfumes.[25]

Research has shown that buyers attach certain values to "Made in XYZ" labels. Akira Nagashima tested the opinions of Japanese and U.S. businesspersons on their attitudes with respect to "Made in the U.S.A." versus "Made in Japan" or "Made in Europe." Some 93 percent of the U.S. businesspeople said they would select a "Made in the U.S.A." product first whereas only 3 percent of the Japanese gave "Made in the U.S.A." their first choice. This negative attitude on the part of Japanese businesspeople can probably be explained.[26] A later study found that 70 percent of the Japanese business leaders surveyed were concerned about building factories in the United States because of their doubts

23. "Die Parfumeurs unter Konkurrenzdruck," (The Perfume Companies Under Pressure), *Neue Zürcher Zeitung,* March 21–22, 1981, p. 17.

24. Ibid.

25. Ibid.

26. Akira Nagashima, "A Comparison of Japanese and U.S. Attitudes Toward Foreign Products," *Journal of Marketing,* vol. 34, January 1970, p. 73.

about the "quality of labor."[27] Actually these Japanese businesspersons expressed a concern about the quality of U.S. products in general; the quality of labor was only a subelement. A survey conducted by the American Society for Quality Control of 7,000 heads of households in the United States found that about 75 percent believed foreign products were equal to or better than U.S. made products.[28]

Belarus, a Russian tractor company selling in the United States, was fighting the strongly established shoddy image of Russian goods in the U.S. market. It sold its tractors at prices that were about 10 percent below the leading U.S. models but had been able to sell only 4,000 between 1975 and 1980. Though the buyers of Belarus tractors appeared satisfied with the product, the "Made in Russia" label presented an enormous handicap for the company.[29] This experience, and that of other companies, indicates that a company has to consider the possible impact of its "Made in XYZ" label on the image of its products. While a company or product image might be within the control of the MNC, country images might have to be accepted as given. Where the country has a positive image, the origin of the product or company can be exploited. In other cases, the MNC might be advised to select a strategy that plays down the origin of the product. As international cosmetic firms have demonstrated in France, a positive country label can be obtained by opening operations in a particular country known for its achievements in a certain industry.

THE CHALLENGE OF CULTURAL CHANGE

Sometimes, what may appear to be a cultural difference may in fact be due to other influences, particularly economic influences. These other influences are subject to considerable change over short periods of time. Some examples follow.

Although Kellogg has sold Kellogg's Corn Flakes in France since 1935, it has only recently penetrated the breakfast market. The slow growth of corn flake demand was related to two aspects of French culinary habits. First, the French did not eat corn; 80 percent of the corn harvested in France was fed to pigs and chickens.[30] Second, of those who ate cereal for breakfast, 40 percent poured on

---

27. "To Japan 'Made in the U.S.' Means Products Aren't the Very Best," *The Wall Street Journal,* February 19, 1981, p. 34.

28. "American-Made Products Get Poor Ratings in Poll," *The Wall Street Journal,* December 10, 1980, p. 20.

29. "This Tractor is Russian. It's Stalled," *The Wall Street Journal,* March 9, 1980, p. 1F.

30. "While Americans take to Croissants, Kellogg Pushes Corn Flakes on France," *The Wall Street Journal,* November 11, 1986, p. 40.

warm milk, which didn't do much for the crunchiness or taste of corn flakes. To overcome these cultural biases, Kellogg put instructions on its Corn Flakes boxes and radically boosted television advertising with "Tony le Tigre." The average French person ate 10 ounces of cereal in 1985; and Kellogg expected consumption to increase by 25 percent each year until 1990. However, Corn Flakes consumption in France had a long way to go to reach the average consumption of 9 pounds in the United States, 12 pounds in England, and 13 pounds in Australia.[31]

The United States–based MNC, Pillsbury, for some time dominated the refrigerated dough business in the United States. Expansion into Germany was very successful despite a long tradition of homemakers making their own dough for baked products or buying these products at local bakeries. Germans, who had always eaten rolls for breakfast, found that small bakers were initially stopping deliveries and later closing up shop in large numbers due to economic pressures. The innovation of refrigerated dough, developed for German tastes, thus reached the market at a crucial time when economic problems were overcoming the traditional suppliers of dough and baked products.[32]

Perrier, the French producer of bottled mineral spring water, successfully launched its product in the United States despite this market's practice of consuming soft drinks, beer, or tap water instead.[31] United States per capita consumption of bottled water was less than one liter compared to 55 liters each in France and Italy. Despite these cultural hurdles, the French company started a major push in 1976 and increased its annual volume from 3 million to 200 million bottles in 1979, achieving a one percent share of the U.S. soft drink market. Though these figures may not indicate a large volume, they nevertheless indicated a considerable change in U.S. consumption habits.[33]

American fast-food chains have been particularly successful in Japan. In fact, most of the new restaurant concepts in Japan came from the United States. Some concepts, such as home delivery for pizza, were difficult to adopt in a city such as Tokyo where street names or consecutive numbers on houses are nonexistent. However, Japanese consumers have readily accepted new American restaurant forms because they tend to have a great interest in the U.S. lifestyle.[34]

A more dramatic change was triggered by technological innovation. The Japanese have now shifted from using hand-operated abacuses to operating hand-held electronic calculators. Though abacus production declined only from

31. Ibid.

32. Barrows Mussey, "Pillsbury Hits Big Jackpot with German Refrigerator Dough," *Advertising Age,* May 19, 1975, p. 34.

33. "Perrier Sales Lose Momentum as Hard Times Hit U.S. Market," *Business Standard,* July 4, 1980, p. 3.

34. "Family in Japan Plays Big Role in Importing Fast Food from U.S.," *The Wall Street Journal,* March 3, 1987, p. 11.

3.1 million in 1965 to 2 million in 1978, Japanese calculator sales rose from 4,000 to 42.3 million over the same period. Within a few years, the way mathematical operations were carried out by an entire nation had been fundamentally changed.[35]

There are many challenges for marketers seeking to change cultural habits. The New Zealand Meat Board, the world's largest exporter of lamb, traced its inability to penetrate important markets to consumer resistance to the strong flavor and odor of lamb meat. Following several years of research, government scientists found the natural cause of this taste and developed a special grain diet for lambs before slaughter. This solution was considered for some markets only; traditional lamb-purchasing areas such as the United Kingdom, the Mediterranean, and Middle East countries would prefer the stronger taste.[36]

In Brazil, multinational beverage companies made huge investments in vineyards in the hope of changing wine-drinking patterns. Annual per capita wine consumption in Brazil amounted to only one half-gallon. By contrast, neighboring Argentina had a consumption of 23 gallons. Even a modest increase in per capita consumption within a population of 120 million will represent a substantial volume increase.[37]

Lotus Development Corporation, the largest software company in the world, had recently entered the Japanese market, but it did not expect the landslide acceptance it achieved in the United States. According to the president of Lotus Development—Japan, "You can't push Japanese management people to use the keyboard. . . . The Japanese way of working is totally different."[38] In Japanese offices it was unusual to see anyone but a secretary working on a personal computer. Lotus advertisements showed a group of samurai warriors around another warrior holding a floppy disk. As Lotus hoped to start the office productivity revolution in Japan, their new president in Tokyo expected it would be successful with the young managers.

The companies in these examples have viewed the absence or low-level of consumption as an indication of potential for growth, rather than as a given cultural trait not subject to change. Many companies have not pursued this goal. International marketers must determine whether observed differences are actually permanent or subject to influence, either by the company itself or by other societal trends.

35. "Japan's Abacus Makers Begin to Breathe Easier a Decade After the Advent of Electronic Calculators," *The Wall Street Journal,* September 14, 1979, p. 44.

36. "New Zealand Hopes to Aid Lamb Exports in Bid to Cut Meat's Odor, Strong Flavor," *The Wall Street Journal,* September 13, 1976, p. 38.

37. "Multinationals Push to Turn Brazilians into Wine Drinkers," *The Wall Street Journal,* April 8, 1980, p. 19.

38. "Can Lotus Make Japanese Executives Love PC's?" *The New York Times,* November 30, 1986, p. 6F.

ADAPTING TO CULTURAL DIFFERENCES

Some companies have made special efforts to adapt their products or services to various cultural environments. Nowhere are these strategies as apparent as in Japan, where foreign companies have to compete in an economically developed market with greatly differing cultural patterns. One critical cultural trait of the Japanese is to resist outside influence. Such resistance is not met by foreign companies alone. New Japanese companies face the same barrier. To overcome such resistance, United States–based Procter & Gamble obtained access to the Japanese distribution channel by first buying into and later acquiring a Japanese soap manufacturer, Nippon Sunhome. The acquired company's existing sales-force provided the needed link to the wholesale distribution channel. P&G could exploit the personal contacts that Nippon Sunhome's salesforce had built up over time.[39]

Some companies found that their products needed special adaptations to the cultural requirement of the Japanese market. General Mills, in its attempt to penetrate the Japanese cake mix market, was looking for a mix that could be baked without the traditional electric oven present in most American or European homes. The company developed a cake mix that could be prepared in an electric rice cooker. However, the product turned out to be unsuccessful because Japanese homemakers believed the cake mix might contaminate the purity of their rice flavor.[40] Levi Strauss was another company that had to find a unique strategy for Japan. To compete against Japanese companies, Levi Strauss attempted to establish its product as the most authentic by using film clips of old John Wayne movies in its commercials. The jeans, however, were made in Japan to satisfy the tighter fit desired by Japanese consumers. To gain the cooperation of local retailers, the company delivered weekly and offered free training courses to help store managers run their business more efficiently.[41]

American Express had to devise a unique strategy in Japan to overcome the Japanese preference for paying in cash. Though there were about 70 million credit cards in circulation in Japan in 1980, they were rarely used. Annual charges averaged $400 compared to $1,500 in the United States. The Japanese appeared embarrassed if they could not pay in cash when out for dinner. For company entertainment, top executives frequently had their bills sent to the company; and junior executives obtained a cash advance before taking out clients. Research showed that Japanese businesspersons wanted primarily cash and security when traveling abroad. As a result, American Express offered a card that, in addition to normal charges, allowed customers to draw $2,200 in cash each month. This adaptation to Japanese requirements expanded the American Express credit card business in Japan.[42]

---

39. "Inside Japan's 'Open' Market," *Fortune*, October 5, 1981, p. 124.
40. Ibid., p. 122.
41. Ibid., p. 126.
42. Ibid., p. 127.

INTERMEDIARY RELATIONS

The most common roles found in almost any marketing system are wholesalers, retailers, and salespeople. We find that these roles are played differently in each country. Frequently the differences are due to culture, though there may be other influences that might cause different role behavior.

Again, Japan offers some excellent examples of unique role expectations. In the late 1950s, Sony experienced market resistance in a few prefectures in northeastern Japan. Sales appeared to have reached a plateau. The national product manager happened to come across a salesperson's field report indicating that one retailer had determined through an experiment that National Panasonic radios outperformed Sony's. Upon further checking, the product manager found that the experiment had been conducted in a washing machine! Informed that the experiment outcome depended on how the radio was placed in the washing machine, the product manager flew out to the store together with the local salesperson and the Research and Development engineer. The store owner was honored to receive such distinguished guests, and he gladly repeated the experiment for the company engineer. The retailer, already impressed by the Sony executive visit, appeared very impressed with the Sony radio performance. The product manager knew that in a few days a large retailer meeting was to take place in the region. He also knew that the Sony experiment would become common knowledge among retailers. The experiment brought Sony closer to many retailers, and sales increased by about 20 percent.[43] This example demonstrates how executives, salespeople, and retailers relate to one another in Japan. The personal visit showed care and sincerity on the part of the large company. On purely analytical grounds, the solution adopted by the Japanese product manager was emotionally oriented and might not make much sense. However, the mutual expectations that participants in a marketing system have of one another are not the same for all countries.

CULTURAL ANALYSIS FOR INTERNATIONAL MARKETING

We do not feel it is sufficient to describe cultural differences by citing only past experiences of companies. Clearly, we could never cover all of the possible mistakes or cultural differences that MNCs might experience abroad. Consequently, we have restricted ourselves to a few examples indicating the kind of problems MNCs face. However, because it is impossible to predict all the possi-

---

43. Masaaki Imai, "Emotional Aspect Figures Larger in Resolving Problems in Japan," *The Japan Economic Journal,* March 27, 1979, p. 12.

ble problems that can be encountered abroad, it becomes necessary to provide some analytical framework to deal with cultural differences.

In a classic article, James E. Lee exposed the natural tendency among executives to fall prey to a self-reference criterion. Lee defines the *self-reference criterion* as an "unconscious reference to one's own cultural values."[44] How does this work? Within each culture, we have come to expect certain truths or basic facts. These facts have become part of our experience and are therefore rarely challenged. As we continue our experience in one culture only, there are few occasions when such inherent beliefs can be exposed. The self-reference criterion also helps us under new circumstances. Whenever we face an unknown situation, we have an inherent tendency to fall back upon prior experience to solve the new problem. There is one substantial handicap to this automatic reflex: if the new situation takes place in a different cultural environment, then the self-reference criterion might invoke past experience that is not applicable.

To avoid the trap of the self-reference criterion habit, Lee suggests that executives approach problems using a four-step analysis. In the first step, the problem is to be defined in terms of the executive's home cultural traits, habits, or norms. Here the analyst can invoke the self-reference criterion. In a second step, the problem is to be defined in terms of the foreign cultural traits, habits, or norms. Value judgements should be avoided at this step. In the third step, the executive is to isolate the personal biases relating to the problem and determine if or how they complicate the problem. And finally, in the fourth step, the problem is to be redefined without the self-reference criterion influence in a search for the optimum solution. Consequently, the four-step approach is designed to avoid culture-bound thinking on the part of executives or companies. (We will further develop this approach in Chapter 7, where a model to analyze the entire international environment is presented.)

Businesspeople moving to another culture will experience stress and tension, often called culture shock. When an individual enters a different culture, he or she must learn to cope with a vast array of new cultural cues and expectations as well as to identify which old ones no longer work.

The authors of a book titled *Managing Cultural Differences* offer the following ten tips to deflate the stress and tension of cultural shock.

- Be culturally prepared.
- Learn local communication complexities.
- Mix with the host and nationals.
- Be creative and experimental.
- Be culturally sensitive.
- Recognize complexities in host cultures.
- Perceive one's self as a culture bearer.

44. James E. Lee, "Cultural Analysis in Overseas Operations," *Harvard Business Review*, March–April 1966, pp. 106–114.

- Be patient, understanding, and accepting of one's self and hosts.
- Be most realistic in expectations.
- Accept the challenge of intercultural experiences.[45]

CONCLUSIONS

In this chapter, we introduced you to the wide variety of possible cultural and social influences present in international marketing operations. What we've presented here represents only the tip of the iceberg, a very small fraction of all the potential factors.

It is essential for international marketers to avoid a cultural bias, or the self-reference criterion, when dealing with business operations in more than one culture. As the president of a large industrial company in Osaka, Japan, recently explained to one of the authors, our cultures are 80 percent identical and 20 percent different. The successful businessperson is the one who can identify the differences and deal with them. This is of course a very difficult task, and few executives ever reach the stage where they can claim to be completely sensitive to cultural differences. The analytical concepts presented at the end of the chapter can help you to deal with cultural differences. These concepts will be refined further in Chapter 7.

Questions for Discussion

1. Explain the difference between the wants and needs people are born with and the wants and needs that are learned through culture?
2. What process can a marketer use to be sure that an advertisement or brochure gives the desired message in an unfamiliar language?
3. If you were marketing automobiles to a predominantly Islamic population, how would it differ from marketing to a predominantly Christian population?
4. How would the education systems in the United States, Japan, England, and West Germany affect the marketing of banking services to young adults aged 16–22.
5. What aspects of the culture would influence the marketing of women designer blue jeans in a number of different countries. How would these cultural influences affect magazine advertising?
6. The country of origin of a product is said to influence consumer demand.

---

45. Philip R. Harris and Robert T. Moran, *Managing Cultural Differences*, 2nd ed. (Houston: Gulf Publishing, 1987), pp. 212–215.

Why are specific products preferred from certain countries? (France—perfumes, Japan—electronics, Germany—beer)

7. When entering a new market, how can you "learn" the culture?

For Further Reading

Douglas, Susan, and Bernard Dubois, "Looking at the Cultural Environment for International Marketing Opportunities." *Columbia Journal of World Business* (Winter 1977), p. 102.

Douglas, Susan P. "Cross-National Comparisons and Consumer Stereotypes: A Case Study of Working and Nonworking Wives in the U.S. and France." *The Journal of Consumer Research* (June 1976), pp. 12–20.

Geert, Hofstede. "National Cultures Revisited." *Asia-Pacific Journal of Management* (September 1984), pp. 22–29.

Graham, John L. "The Influence of Culture on Business Negotiations." *Journal of International Business Studies,* (Spring 1985), pp. 81–96.

Hall, Edward T. *Beyond Culture,* Garden City, New York: Anchor Press, 1976.

Harris, D. George. "How National Cultures Shape Management Styles." *Management Review* (July 1982), pp. 58–61.

Harris, Philip R., and Robert T. Moran. *Managing Cultural Differences.* 2nd ed. Houston: Gulf Publishing, 1987.

Pizam, Abraham, and Arie Reichel, "Cultural Determinants of Managerial Behavior." *Management International Review.* No. 2, (1977), p. 66.

Redding, S. G. "Cultural Effects on the Marketing Process in Southeast Asia." *Journal of Market Research Society* (April 1982), pp. 86–98.

Reynolds, John I. "Developing Policy Responses to Cultural Differences." *Business Horizons* (August 1978), pp. 30, 31.

Terpstra, Vern, and Kenneth David. *The Cultural Environment of International Business.* 2nd ed. Cincinnati: Southwestern, 1985.

4.

POLITICAL AND LEGAL FORCES

International marketing executives, by the very nature of their jobs, must inter-face with a multitude of political and legal systems that substantially complicate their tasks. The purpose of this chapter is to identify these political and legal forces. A conceptual framework will be provided to assist the reader in identify-ing the relevant political and legal factors as they pertain to each situation. Figure 4.1 maps out the elements covered in the chapter and shows the relation-ships between them.

Dealing simultaneously with several political and legal systems makes the job of an international marketing executive extremely complex. Because of these factors, many problems exist that increase the levels of risk that exist in the international marketplace. MNCs have learned to cope with such complexities by developing methods and risk reduction strategies. Toward the end of this chapter, the nature of these strategies will be explained.

The first part of this chapter deals primarily with political factors, and the second part is devoted to legal aspects of international marketing. The emphasis will be on the regulations or laws that affect the international marketing busi-ness transactions conducted by today's MNCs. It is difficult to separate political from legal forces since many laws are actually politically inspired or motivated. Nevertheless, some separation of the two areas was made to allow for a better organization of the subject matter.

HOST COUNTRY POLITICAL FORCES

The rapidly changing nature of the international political scene is evident to anyone who regularly reads, listens to, or watches the various news media.

FIGURE 4.1 Analyzing Political Forces

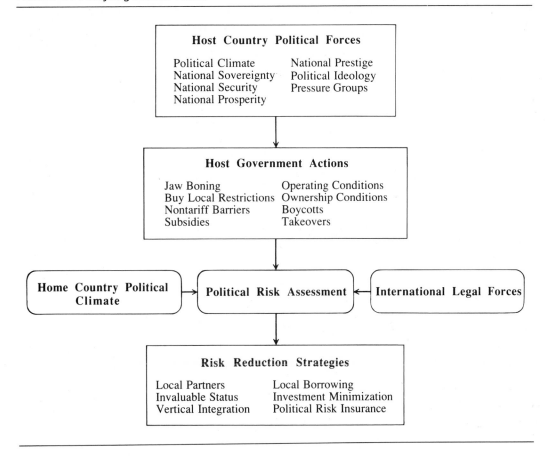

Political upheavals, revolutions, or changes in government policy occur daily and can have an enormous effect on international business. As governments change, opportunities for new business might be lost or, just as often, newly gained. For the executive, this means constant adjustments to maximize new opportunities and minimize losses.

The principal actors in the political arena, besides the MNC, are the host country governments, home country governments, and transnational bodies or agencies. The respective interactions of these three groups result in a given political climate that may positively or negatively affect the operations of the MNC. The difficulty for the MNC stems from the fact that the firm is simultaneously subject to all three, often conflicting influences; whereas a strictly domestic corporation has to deal with only one, namely the home country political climate. The situation is further complicated by the fact that MNCs maintain operations in scores of countries—meaning that companies must be able to simultaneously manage many sets of political relationships. In the following sections of this chapter, we will discuss the host country political climate, the home country political climate, and transnational legal forces that regulate international trade. We also focus on political risk assessment and analyze the types of risk reduction strategies that might be employed to manage in such a complex world.

Political Climate

Any country that contains an operational unit (manufacturing, finance, sales office, etc.) of the MNC can be defined as a host country. By definition, MNCs deal with many different host countries, each with their own political climate. In each country, the political climate is largely determined by the way the various participants, or actors, interact with each other. It is influenced by the actions of the host-country government and local special interest groups, as well as by the prevailing political philosophy. Stable political climates are those where the presently existing relationships among the key actors are not expected to change. Conversely, political climates are termed unstable when the nature of the interactions or their outcomes are unpredictable. Though the political climate of a country could be analyzed with respect to various segments of society, for the purpose of this text we restrict ourselves to those aspects that relate to the business sectors.

Governments

Governments of host countries are key actors in the political arena. In most cases they either initiate or implement political actions that then impact on the operation of foreign companies operating within their jurisdictions. Today there are about 150 nations accepted as full members at the United Nations, a number that should give some indication as to the large number of independent countries that exist at this time. Although each government may give the impression of acting as a single and homogeneous force, governments in most countries represent a collection of various, at times conflicting, interests. Governments are sharply influenced by the prevailing political philosophy, existing local pressure groups or special interest groups, and the government's own self-interest. All of these factors lead to government actions that international companies must not only recognize but also actively incorporate into their national marketing strategies. What is of prime importance then is the ability to understand the rationale behind government actions.

Understanding governmental behavior only makes sense if there is a rational basis for leaders' actions and decisions. As many political scientists have pointed out, these actions usually flow from the government's interpretation of its own self-interest. This self-interest, often called national interest, may be expected to differ from nation to nation, but it typically includes the following goals:

1. *Self-preservation.* This is the prime goal of any entity, including states or governments.
2. *Security.* To the extent possible, each entity seeks to maximize the opportunity for continued existence and to minimize threats from the outside.
3. *Prosperity.* Improved living conditions for a country's citizens is an important and constant concern.
4. *Prestige.* Most governments or countries seek this either as an end in itself or to help reach other objectives.
5. *Ideology.* Governments frequently protect or promote an ideology in combination with other goals.[1]

The interaction of governments with MNCs can be understood through a basic appreciation of their national interest. The goals cited above are frequently the source of governmental actions either encouraging or limiting the business activities of MNCs. Many MNC executives erroneously believe that such limiting actions will mostly occur in developing countries. On the contrary, there are as many examples of restrictive government actions in the most developed countries, which indicates the universal nature of this type of governmental behavior. Such restrictive behavior most often occurs when a government perceives the attainment of its own goals threatened by the activities or existence of a body beyond its total control, namely the foreign subsidiary of a foreign MNC.

National Sovereignty and the Goal of Self-preservation

A country's self-preservation is most threatened when its national sovereignty is at stake. Sovereignty gives a nation complete control within a given geographic area, including the ability to pass laws and regulations and the power to use necessary reinforcement. Governments or countries frequently view the existence of sovereignty as a key to reaching the goal of self-preservation. Though sovereignty may, of course, be threatened by a number of factors, it is the relationship between a government's attempt to protect its sovereignty and the MNC's policies to achieve its own goals that are of prime interest to us.

Due to the fact that subsidiaries, or branch offices, of MNCs are substantially controlled or influenced by decisions made in headquarters beyond the physical or legal control of the host government, such foreign companies are frequently viewed as a danger to the host country's national sovereignty. (It is important to recognize in this context that perceptions on the part of host countries are typically more important than actual facts.)

---

1. Vern Terpstra, *The Cultural Environment of International Business* (Cincinnati: South-Western, 1978), p. 225. That section of this book was actually written by Stephen J. Kobrin.

One of the best examples of a conflict between a local government and the MNCs' local units took place in Canada. Due to its long border with the United States, Canada had become a popular market for subsidiaries of U.S. MNCs. Through local operations, these MNCs could circumvent the tariff barrier erected decades ago. It is a fact that there were more foreign MNCs operating in Canada than in any other country in the world. Most of these MNCs were of U.S. origin. For such important industry segments as food, chemicals, refining, automobiles, and textiles, foreign MNCs controlled more than 50 percent of the assets. In the crucial energy segment, foreign MNCs controlled about 70 percent.[2]

To redress this imbalance in key industries, Canada's government has passed a number of laws and instituted some new regulations that are aimed at reasserting control over Canada's industry. Now, the Foreign Investment Review Agency (FIRA) must accept any change in ownership of foreign subsidiaries or the opening of new investments in Canada.[3]

Canada's attempt to limit foreign control of its industry showed significant results in several key economic sectors. As a result, the application of the law has been relaxed. However, this was also partially in response to a ruling of the General Agreements on Tariffs and Trade (GATT), of which Canada is a member, that some of Canada's policies were in violation of GATT rules.[4] Recall that the GATT, originally signed after World War II, is an agreement of the member nations to reduce tariffs and solve trade disputes.

As many emerging nations attempt to control their own political and economic destiny, attempts to restrict foreign MNCs will increase. Governments tend to focus on industries dominated by a large number of foreign-based MNCs. Targeting these large foreign units can become a cause célèbre for the entire nation. Large industrial complexes like mines, telephone companies, or steel works are much more likely to be affected by this than smaller companies out of the public eye. Often the periods of tight control of MNCs are followed by periods of liberalization, reflecting the need for a long-term perspective.

The Need for National Security

It is natural for a government to strive to protect its country's borders from outside forces. Typically, the military establishment becomes a country's principal tool to prevent outside interference. Consequently, many concerns about national security have to do with a country's armed forces or related agencies. Other areas sensitive to the national security are aspects of a country's infrastructure, its essential resources, utilities, and the supply of crucial raw mate-

---

2. "Trudeau's War on U.S. Business," *Fortune,* April 6, 1981, pp. 74–82.
3. Ibid.
4. "Canada Eases Curbs on Foreign Investment," *Financial Times,* February 7, 1984, p. 5.

rials, particularly oil. To ensure their security, host governments tend to strive for control of these sensitive areas and resist any influence foreign firms may gain over such companies or agencies.

Examples of such government influence abound. The U.S. government, for one, does not typically purchase military material from foreign controlled firms, even if they have subsidiaries in the United States. Other foreign governments give preference to their own arms industry to achieve a certain measure of independence from outside interference. For example, the Japan Defense Agency planned to have Mitsubishi Heavy Industries build a new jet fighter with home-grown technology rather than buy an existing one from General Dynamics or McDonnell Douglas in the United States. Although Japan was being pressured by the Reagan administration to buy from the United States, Japanese officials felt that if they continued to rely of foreign technology, Japan's defense capability would be diminished.[5]

Fostering National Prosperity

A key goal for governments is to ensure the material prosperity of its citizens. Prosperity is usually expressed in national income or GNP, and comparisons between countries are frequently made with respect to per capita income or GNP per capita figures. However prosperity is measured, most governments strive to provide full employment and an increasing standard of living. Part of this goal is to enact an economic policy that will stimulate the economic output of businesses active within its borders. MNCs can assume an important role inasmuch as they add to a host country's GNP and thus enhance its income. However, any action that runs contrary to the host government's goals, though it may be in the best interest of the MNC, will likely cause a conflict between the foreign MNC and the host country government. Furthermore, a host country may take actions that unilaterally favor local industry over foreign competitors to protect its own standard of living and prosperity.

For many countries, a high level of imports represents a drain on their monetary resources and lost opportunities to expand their own industrial base. Under such circumstances, a host country may move towards a restriction of imports beyond the imposition of tariffs or customs duties. It puts up what are called nontariff barriers. Both the Italian and French governments have protected their local automobile industries from Japanese competition by using nontariff barriers. The Italian government has for many years restricted the import of Japanese automobiles to a total of 2,000 units annually. The French government, through selective use of import licenses, has limited Japanese producers to only 3 percent of the market. As these examples have shown, govern-

5. "U.S. Urges Japan to Import Jet Fighter Rather Than Develop One Domestically," *The Wall Street Journal*, March 16, 1987, p. 19.

ment actions can frequently close an otherwise attractive market to an MNC.

Most host governments try to enhance a nation's prosperity by increasing its exports. To do this, some governments have sponsored export-credit arrangements combined with some form of political risk insurance. (Some other methods of increasing exports are described in more detail in Chapters 18 and 19.) Particularly in Europe, heads of governments often engage in state visits to encourage major export transactions. Political observers often have pointed out that both the French president or the German chancellor spend a substantial amount of their state visits on business and trade affairs, more so than is typically the case for the president of the United States. Attracting MNCs with a high export potential to open up operations in their countries is of critical interest to host governments. Frequently, such MNCs can expect special treatment or subsidies. The Irish government established the Irish Development Agency whose principal aim is to attract MNCs with export potential to Ireland. Companies can expect tax-free status for many years and low-interest loans to finance capital expenditures. In some cases, host governments can even request a certain export quota before an MNC will receive the permission to build a local operation.

The host government's export policy is of interest to MNCs considering to locate operations in a particular country. By collecting information on a government's policies or orientation, an MNC can make an optimal choice that might give it access to benefits not available in some other countries.

Enhancing Prestige

The pursuit of prestige can take many forms. It doesn't always take the form of industrial achievements. Whereas the governments of some countries may choose the support of sports teams or individual athletes as a matter of national prestige, other host governments influence the business climate for the same reason. Having a national airline operating from their country can give rise to national prestige. Other particularly developed countries would like to see their industries achieve leadership in certain technologies such as telecommunications, electronics, robotics, or aerospace.

A host government trying to enhance its country's prestige will frequently encourage local or national companies at the expense of a foreign MNC. One example was the French government's intervention on behalf of the vineyard Chateau Margaux. On the grounds that it would damage national prestige to do otherwise, the Bordeaux winery was sold to a French supermarket chain despite the fact that a U.S. buyer had offered a higher price.[6]

---

6. "France's Erratic Policies on Investments by Foreigners Confuse Many U.S. Firms," *The Wall Street Journal,* April 7, 1980, p. 24.

In the future, MNCs will need to develop a keen sense for what constitutes national prestige as perceived by host governments. Businesspersons cannot expect that host governments will have an explicit policy on such issues. Instead, MNCs will have to derive from a series of overt or covert government actions some notions on national prestige. Once an MNC has a clear definition or idea of what prestige constitutes for a host government, it can avoid policies that are in direct conflict with government intentions or aspirations and emphasize those actions that tend to enhance the host country's prestige.

Political Ideologies

Many governments are attached to a certain political philosophy. For example, the United States promotes capitalism and the Soviet Union promotes communism. Because of its political ideology, a government may engage in actions that go beyond immediate security needs—greatly affecting the political climate of the country.

A strong ideology can permeate the domestic market of a host country. Governments with a strong Marxist leaning do not encourage private ownership, thus precluding MNCs from either keeping their operations or opening new subsidiaries. Aside from the previously mentioned ideologies of capitalism and communism, some form of social-democratic ideology is encountered in many countries. Loosely united under the umbrella of a London-based organization, Socialist International, member countries express the desire to replace capitalism by a "system in which the public interest takes precedence over the interest of private profit."[7] In general, this translates into a commitment to maintain high employment, to allow some form of employee influence over corporate decisions, to encourage redistribution of wealth, and to take the initiative in economic policy through publicly communicated long-range plans.

For a foreign-based MNC to be welcomed in such an environment requires an ability to adapt and accept the prevailing political philosophy. Invariably, it means accepting some power sharing with local entities. This might be more difficult for U.S. MNCs than for MNCs whose home country subscribes to the same political ideology.

Host Country Pressure Groups

Host country governments are not the only actors influencing the political climate and thus affecting the operations of foreign MNCs. There are other groups that have a stake in the treatment of MNCs or in political and economic deci-

---

7. "The Social Democratic Design for Europe's Economy," *Business Week,* December 22, 1975, p. 24.

sions that indirectly affect foreign businesses. In most instances, they cannot act unilaterally. Thus, they try to pressure either the host government or the foreign businesses to conform to their views. Such pressure groups exist in most countries and may be made up of ad hoc groups or permanently structured associations. Political parties are a common pressure group, though they frequently cannot exert much influence outside the government. Parties generally associated with a leftist point of view frequently advocate policies restricting MNCs. Under extreme circumstances, political splinter groups can even use terrorism as a tactic, as was the case in Latin American countries during the 1970s. Foreign businessmen or heads of MNCs' subsidiaries were frequently abducted. Deaths have been rare; but often the executives were released for ransom and/or when the desired changes in operating procedures were made.

Some of the most potent pressure groups are found, however, among the local business community itself. These are local industry associations and occasionally local unions. When local companies get into trouble due to foreign competition, they frequently petition their government to help by placing restrictions on the foreign competitors. In the United States, industry groups have in the past attempted to block some imports in textiles, shoes, consumer electronics, and steel. In most of these cases the U.S. government did not implement the full demands of these pressure groups. In the case of the steel industry, the U.S. government enforced a trigger-price mechanism that was geared toward keeping out foreign steel sold at dumping prices. (These import restrictions are described in more detail in Chapter 19.)

HOST GOVERNMENT ACTIONS

In the previous section, we focused on various governmental concerns and the underlying motivations for certain political actions. In this section, we will analyze some of the typical policies host governments may choose to control foreign-based businesses. The relationships between the underlying motivations and the chosen policies will also be discussed. The host governments' policies are presented in order of their severity, from the least to the most severe.

Jaw Boning

When governments intervene in the business process in an informal way, often without a legal basis, this is termed *jaw boning*. Governments use this type of intervention to prevent an action that, though legal, is perceived to be contrary to their own interests or goals. The effectiveness of jaw boning lies in the possibility of stronger action at a later time should the "culprit" not fall into line.

The British government pressured Japanese automobile manufacturers to accept a limit on their exports to the United Kingdom. They wanted Japanese imports to account for no more than 11 percent of the total U.K. passenger car market. The market share of Japanese commercial vehicles rose from only 7 percent to over 15 percent between 1979 and 1981.[8] This substantially hurt the local producers, primarily Ford and BL. As a result, the British government called in representatives of the Japanese manufacturers to negotiate about a ceiling for both passenger and commercial vehicles.[9]

The leverage of host governments comes from the fact that foreign MNCs depend on permits and approvals issued by host governments. Such favored treatment might be at risk if a company proceeds against the expressed wishes of the host government despite the fact that no laws were violated.

"Buy Local" Restrictions

Since governments are important customers of industry in virtually every country, they can use this purchasing power to favor certain suppliers. Frequently, local companies are favored over foreign imports. An industry that is particularly subject to such local favoritism is the telecommunications industry because telephone companies are state run in most countries. For foreign MNCs, the case of Japan's Nippon Telegraph & Telephone Public Corp. (NTT) was particularly problematic. For years, NTT granted contracts exclusively to a few local suppliers, virtually shutting out foreign-based MNCs. Pressures from foreign governments led to international agreements under the umbrella of GATT, and other international organizations have established new rules that tend to prevent direct government intervention except for cases of national security and a few other exemptions. This has also opened up opportunities for foreign firms with Japan's NTT.[10]

Nontariff Barriers

Under this heading we can include any government action that is not an official custom tariff but that nevertheless inhibits the free flow of products between countries. (See Table 2.7 for a detailed listing.) These barriers may not necessarily add to landed costs but are more likely to result in a limitation on product flows. To a large extent nontariff barriers are used by governments to keep imports from freely entering the home market. There are many types of measures that may be taken. A common one is import restrictions or quotas. The Brazilian government introduced strong action to stem the flow of imports in

---

8. "Trucks: If You Can't Beat Them, Block Them," *The Economist,* November 28, 1981, p. 80.
9. Ibid.
10. "Japan: Why the U.S. Still Has Not Cracked NTT," *Business Week,* January 11, 1982; and "High-Technology Gateway," *Business Week,* August 9, 1982, p. 40.

1976. As part of a plan to limit imports to only 20 percent of the previous year's total, fiscal incentives and tax exemptions on capital goods were abolished. Payments of 360 days in advance for imports with the Central Bank added to their costs. While such measures have an immediate effect, companies that depend on imports for part of their supplies were suddenly forced to develop local sources.[11]

The Ministry of Posts and Telecommunications in Japan recently excluded Motorola from the bulk of the Japanese car phone market by only giving them a license for Western Japan, excluding Tokyo. The car phone market in Tokyo was awarded to the giant Nippon Telegraph and Telephone and Teleway Japan (18 percent owned by Toyota).[12]

Subsidies

Government subsidies represent free gifts that host governments make available with the intention that the overall benefits to the economy by far exceed such grants. They are a popular instrument used to both encourage exports or to attract MNCs to a certain country. In a study compiled by the U.S. Department of Commerce, 26 percent of U.S. MNC subsidiaries abroad were reported to have received investment incentives while another 20 percent were offered tax breaks. Incentives vary by countries. Seventy percent of U.S. subsidiaries in Ireland are receiving incentives. In South Korea, 53 percent received incentives; and around 40 percent received incentives in Israel, Taiwan, and Brazil. Developed countries such as Britain, Spain, Sweden, and Australia granted incentives to about one-third of U.S. subsidiaries operating there. The figure for Japan was only 9 percent.[13] All of these actions were intended to attract operations to their countries with the expectation of higher employment and exports.

Governments may also use direct or indirect subsidies to encourage industries that will be major exporters. Exporters have multiple benefits, since they provide employment as well as increase revenue into the country through export sales. An example of a direct subsidy would be a government that agrees to pay $1.00 for each pair of shoes to help a local producer compete more effectively in foreign markets. GATT agreements outlaw direct export subsidies but do not usually prohibit indirect subsidies. An indirect subsidy is the result of a subsidy on a component of the exported product. For example, a government may provide a subsidy on the canvas used to manufacture tents, which are exported.

11. "Brazil: Tough Import Controls Shake-Up Business," *Business Week,* January 12, 1976, p. 38.

12. "Curbs in Japan on Motorola's Car Phones Worsen Dispute with U.S. over Access," *The Wall Street Journal,* March 5, 1987, p. 33.

13. *The Economist,* December 12, 1981, p. 73.

Operating Conditions

Host country governments have a direct influence on the operations of a foreign subsidiary when they impose specific conditions on the company's operations. According to a report issued by the U.S. Department of Commerce, such conditions are becoming more common. Of the 23,641 U.S. subsidiaries operating abroad in 1977, 14 percent had to accept at least one type of operating restriction. Such conditions imposed typically included a pledge about the share of jobs going to local nationals. There were fewer conditions imposed on the amount of sales exported. Performance pledges were most common in Latin America, however, where typically one-third to one-half of operating U.S. subsidiaries had made any pledges.[14]

Even Canada imposed conditions on U.S. subsidiaries through its Foreign Investment and Review Agency, FIRA. When Apple Computer, Inc. applied to enter the Canadian market it won an approval by pledging to build a factory in Canada, to share data on potential clients with Canadian companies, and by promising to use Canada's Telidon videotex technology worldwide in home information products.[15] Similarly, the U.S. media concern, Gannett Co., won approval to acquire a Canadian outdoor advertising company, Mediacom Inc., only after the U.S. company agreed to source newsprint for a planned national U.S. newspaper from Canada. Gannett was also required to sell its laser printing technology, which had cost Gannett $14 million to develop, to a Canadian company for the sum of one dollar.[16]

Ownership Conditions

Host governments sometimes pursue the policy of requiring that local nationals become part owners of the foreign company. These governments believe that this would guarantee fair contributions to the local economy. The restrictions can range from an outright prohibition of full foreign ownership, as is the case in primarily communist countries in Eastern Europe, to selective policies aimed at key industries.

One country that has used ownership conditions extensively is India. India's Foreign Exchange Regulation Act of 1973 stipulates that foreign ownership may not exceed 40 percent unless the foreign firm or Indian company belongs to a key industry, manufacturing materials such as chemicals, turbines, machinery, tractors, or fertilizers. Additional exceptions could be granted for companies that exported more than 60 percent of their output or that have incorporated high

---

14. "Bait for Multinationals," *The Economist,* December 12, 1981, p. 73.
15. "Canada Widens Its Grip on U.S. Investment," *Business Week,* November 23, 1981, p. 43.
16. Ibid.

technologies. For companies that qualify for such exemptions, the maximum percentage may, however, not exceed 74 percent.[17] Since 1976 there exists an intermediate solution that allows foreign ownership of maximum 51 percent as long as 60 percent of sales take place in key industries or high technology with an export content of 10 percent.[18]

Indian policies caused some companies, such as Coca-Cola Company and International Business Machines Corp., to leave in 1978. However, later changes in the government have brought a softening of India's stance and the country is again courting firms that can contribute new technologies.[19]

Boycotts

The previously discussed policies are aimed at restricting or limiting the freedom of action of foreign firms. Boycotts, however, tend to completely shut out some companies from a given market. Typically, politically motivated boycotts tend to be directed at companies of certain origin or companies that have engaged in transactions with political enemies.

One of the most publicized boycott campaigns was the boycott waged by some Arab countries against firms that had engaged in business beyond simple export transactions with Israel. The boycott was administered by the Arab League, a group that had been in existence since 1945 and included about twenty member countries. Boycott lists were sent from the group's offices to member countries who then decided whether they wanted to enforce it. Though no complete and official list seemed to exist, it was estimated that some 1800 names were on the list, both company names and brand names. About 1,500 of these names were American firms or products. One U.S. company on the list was Ford Motor Company, which supplied an Israeli car assembler with flat-packed cars for local assembly. Xerox was placed on the list after having financed a documentary on Israel. And Coca-Cola Company was added to the boycott list for having licensed an Israeli bottler. The embargo did not always include all Arab League member nations. Coca-Cola was represented in Algeria, Tunisia, and Morocco. The actual enforcement was, therefore, quite selective and differed by industry. Manufacturers of military hardware sold equally to both Israel and Arab countries. Hilton maintained hotels in both Israel and Arab countries, just as IBM was in a position to do business with both camps.[20]

---

17. "Auslandskapital in Indien Unerwunscht" (Foreign Investors Declared Undesirable in India), *Neue Zucher Zeitung,* March 8, 1978, p. 21.
18. Ibid.
19. "India: Reviving the Welcome for U.S. Business," *Business Week,* March 1, 1982, p. 31.
20. "That Curious Barrier on the Arab Frontiers," *Fortune,* July 1975, p. 82.

Takeovers

No action a host government can take is more drastic than a takeover. Broadly defined, takeovers are any actions that a host government initiates resulting in a loss of ownership or direct control by the foreign MNC. There are, of course, several types of takeovers.[21] *Expropriation* is used to describe a formal, or legal, taking over of an operation with or without the payment of compensation. *Confiscation* is an expropriation without any compensation. The term *domestication* is used to describe the limiting of certain economic activities to local citizens; this means a takeover by either expropriation, confiscation, or forced sales. Governments may domesticate industry by imposing one of the following requirements: transfer of partial ownership to nationals, promotion of nationals to higher levels of management, and purchase of raw materials or components produced locally. If the MNC cannot meet these requirements, it may be forced to sell its operations in that country.

Several studies have been made to suggest that takeovers are becoming more frequent and are a major threat to MNCs operating abroad. In a study compiled by Hawkins, Mintz, and Provissiero, a total of 170 foreign takeovers of U.S. subsidiaries were registered for the period 1946 to 1973. Comparing these findings with the total of 23,282 U.S. subsidiaries operating outside the U.S. gives us a takeover rate of about 0.6 percent. Though this is a small percentage, it is important to note that takeover rates varied substantially by region: 6.4 percent for Africa, 2.2 percent for Latin America, 3.0 percent for the Middle East, and 1.3 percent for Asia. In absolute numbers, three Latin American countries accounted for over one-third of these takeovers: Argentina, 13; Chile, 36; and Peru, 14. Only 38 countries had takeovers, with the vast majority having had none at all.[22] These statistics were supported by a broader survey of all countries by the United Nations in which 875 takeovers were identified for the 1960–1974 period.[23] Ten countries had accounted for two-thirds of all takeovers, and 50 countries registered none at all.

The takeovers of U.S. subsidiaries were most frequently associated with a change in government, typically a move to the left. More recently, the propor-

---

21. Richard D. Robinson, *International Business Management* (New York: Dryden, 1973), p. 374.

22. See Franklin R. Root, "The Expropriation of American Companies," *Nationalization, Expropriation, and Other Takings of the United States and Certain Foreign Property Since 1960* (Washington: U.S. Department of State, Bureau of Intelligence and Research, Research Study RECS-14, November 30, 1971); *Business Horizons,* April 1968, p. 69; John F. Truit, "Expropriation of Private Foreign Investment: A Framework to Consider the Post World War II Experience of British and American Investors," Ph.D. thesis, Graduate School of Business, Indiana University, 1969, revised and published as *Expropriation of Private Investment,* International Business Research Series No. 3, Indiana University, 1974; *Permanent Sovereignty over Natural Resources,* Report of the Economic and Social Council to the Secretary-General (A/9716), New York, United Nations, 1974; and Robert G. Hawkins, Norman Mintz, and Michael Provissiero, "Government Takeovers of U.S. Foreign Affiliates," *Journal of International Business Studies,* Spring 1976, pp. 3–16.

23. Ibid.

TABLE 4.1 Host Government Goal and Policy Actions

	Self-preservation	Security	Prosperity	Prestige	Ideology
Actions					
Jaw Boning	X	X	X	X	X
"Buy Local"	X	X	X		
Nontariff Barriers	X		X		
Subsidies	X		X		
Operating Restrictions	X	X	X		
Ownership Conditions		X			
Boycotts					X
Takeovers					

X: Likelihood of using given action to accomplish certain goals

tion of takeovers of manufacturing operations has increased. Hawkins, Mintz, and Provissiero classified the majority of the takeovers in their survey as expropriations.[24]

Though all of these above cited reports covered periods up to 1974, takeovers have happened since then in consistently large numbers. Takeovers more recently took place in Iran and Nicaragua; and some are even taking place in France where the French subsidiary of ITT has been slated for nationalization.[25] How MNCs can deal with such risks in the future will be dealt with in a later segment of this chapter.

This section on host government actions was intended to illustrate how host governments can impact on the local operations of MNCs. The section before this concentrated more on the motivations behind these governmental actions. Table 4.1 is a chart identifying and relating certain policy actions to the underlying goals discussed in this chapter. Though any combination of goal and action is possible, past history tends to suggest that certain actions are more often associated with specific goals.

HOME COUNTRY POLITICAL FORCES

Managers of MNCs need not only be concerned about political developments abroad. Many developments take place at home that can have great impact on

---

24. Hawkins et al., "Government Takeovers of U.S. Foreign Affiliates," pp. 3–16.
25. "Nationalization Without Tears," *The Economist,* December 19, 1981, p. 77.

what an MNC can do internationally. The political development in an MNC home country tends to affect either the role of MNCs in general or, as is more often the case, some particular aspects of their operations. Consequently, restrictions can be placed on MNCs not only by host countries but by home countries as well. An astute international manager must therefore be able to monitor political developments both at home and abroad.

This section of the chapter will emphasize home country policies and actions directed at MNCs. Some of these actions are unique and have only recently come into existence to any large extent.

Home Country Actions

Home countries are essentially guided by the same six interests described earlier in this chapter: national sovereignty, national security, prosperity, prestige, ideology, and power. In general, a home country government wishes to have its country's MNCs accept its national priorities. As a result, home country governments at times look towards MNCs to help them achieve political goals. They may engage in any or all the actions outlined earlier: jaw boning, nontariff barriers, subsidies, operating restrictions, etc.

How then do home country policies differ? In the past, home country governments have tried to prevent companies from doing business on ideological, political, or national security grounds. At worst, this can result in an embargo on trade with a certain country. Following the unilateral declaration of independence of Rhodesia from the British Empire under white minority rule, most nations followed the United Nations resolutions and embargoed trade with Rhodesia, thus prohibiting companies located within their borders to engage in any business with Rhodesian firms. This embargo was lifted when black majority rule was won under a new government in what is now called Zimbabwe. Many black African nations embargo any trade with South Africa, and Arab countries prohibit any trade between their countries and Israel.

Home Country Pressure Groups

The kind of pressures that MNCs are subject to in their home countries are frequently different from the types of pressures brought to bear on them abroad. In many ways, MNCs had to deal with special interest groups abroad for a long time. But the type of special interest groups found domestically have only come into existence over the last ten to fifteen years. Such groups are usually well organized, tend to get extensive media coverage, and have succeeded in catching many companies unprepared. While part of their actions has always been geared toward mobilizing support to get the home country government to sponsor specific regulations favorable to their point of view, they have also managed to place companies directly under pressure.

MNCs can come under pressure for two major reasons: (1) for the choice of their markets and (2) for their methods of business. The recent controversy surrounding the involvement of MNCs in South Africa is a typical example of this first type of pressure. Most citizens of Western countries abhor the political system and race separation in South Africa. They have attacked MNCs for their tacit approval of the system in working under South African regulations. The controversy spread to several countries but was particularly debated in the United States. Civil Rights groups and church groups began to show up at annual meetings. During IBM's 1975 annual meeting in Pittsburgh, some shareholders had proposed that IBM completely halt its activities in South Africa.[26] Following a fifty-minute debate, the proposal was voted down by a large margin. But the public debate persisted and other companies started to be drawn into the controversy. Then, in 1976, riots broke out in Soweto near Johannesburg. These developments prompted a dozen U.S. MNCs in 1977 to accept a code established by the Reverend Dr. Leon Sullivan from Philadelphia, who also happened to be a member of the board at General Motors.[27] The Sullivan Principles covered six basic areas:

- Nonsegregation of races in all eating, comfort, and work facilities
- Equal and fair employment practices
- Equal pay for comparable work
- Training programs to prepare blacks and other nonwhites for supervisory, administrative, clerical, and technical jobs in substantial numbers
- More blacks and other nonwhites in management and supervisory positions
- Improving employees' lives outside the work environment in such areas as housing, transportation, scheduling, recreation, and health.[28]

Many of the about 350 U.S. companies active in South Africa eventually joined in signing the Sullivan Principles despite the fact that its implementation in many ways was in violation of official South African laws and labor regulations. In mid-1987, Reverend Sullivan changed his position and recommended complete divesture rather than his original principles.

When political troubles in South Africa intensified, some of the U.S. companies decided to reduce their involvement. Among those who decided to disinvest were Ford Motor Company, Coca-Cola, PepsiCo, and Perkin-Elmer.[29] A total of fifty-five U.S. companies have closed or sold their South African operations since 1984.[30] The South African controversy is particularly interesting because it

---

26. *The New York Times,* April 29, 1975.

27. "The Case for Doing Business in South Africa," *Fortune,* June 19, 1978, p. 70.

28. Ibid.

29. "U.S. Companies Are Pulling Out—But Apartheid Is Likely to Stay," *Business Week,* June 24, 1985.

30. "Out of Africa? Well, Not Really," *The New York Times,* August 17, 1986, p. 4F.

marked one of the first instances in which the behavior of MNCs was prescribed not by the host country but by political pressures at home.

A second source of controversy involves the business practices of MNCs in three areas: product strategies, promotion practices, and pricing practices. Product strategies would include the decision to cease marketing a certain product (such as pesticides or pharmaceuticals), usually for safety reasons. Promotional practices include the way the products are advertised or pushed through distribution channels. Pricing practices refer to the policy of charging higher or unfair prices.

The infant formula controversy involved participants from many countries and serves as a good example of the kind of pressure sometimes placed on MNCs. Infant formula was being sold all over the world as a substitute and/or supplement for breast-feeding. Though even the producers of infant formula agreed that breast-feeding was superior to bottle-feeding, changes started to take place in Western society decades ago that brought about the decline of infant breast-feeding. Following World War II, several MNCs expanded their infant formula productions in Third-World countries where birth rates were much higher than in the West. Companies that had intended their products to be helpful found themselves embroiled in controversy. Critics blasted the product, saying it was unsafe under Third-World conditions. Because the formula had to be mixed with water, the critics charged that the sanitary conditions and contaminated water in developing countries led to many deaths. As a result, the critics requested an immediate stop to all promotional activities, such as nurses visiting mothers and the distribution of free samples. Nestlé Company, as one of the leading infant-formula manufacturers, became the target of a boycott by consumer action groups in the United States and elsewhere. Under the leadership of INFACT, the Infant Formula Action Coalition, a consumer boycott of all Nestlé products was organized to force the company to change its marketing practices.[31] The constant public pressure resulted in the development of a code sponsored by the World Health Organization (WHO). This code, accepted by the Thirty-fourth WHO General Assembly in 1981 (with the sole dissenting vote from the United States), primarily covered the methods used to market infant formula. Producers and distributors could not give away any free samples, had to avoid contact with consumers, and were not allowed to do any promotion geared toward the general public. The code was subject to voluntary participation by the WHO member governments.[32] The effect of this controversy was that new regulations, or codes, eventually became part of the legal system. Thus, today's executive must be prepared to deal with issues in home markets that might not be echoed abroad.

---

31. "The Corporation Haters," *Fortune,* June 16, 1980, p. 126.

32. For a detailed background on the infant-formula issue, see "Nestlé and the Infant Food Controversy" (A) and (B), by Christopher Gale, George Taucher, and Michael Pearce, *IMEDE,* Lausanne, Switzerland, and University of Western Ontario, London, Ontario, Canada.

CHANGES IN THE POLITICAL CLIMATE

The presence of political risk means that a foreign company could lose part or all of its investment in another country due to some political actions on the part of either the host country government or other pressure groups. The previous sections have detailed the various elements of political risk by describing the actors, their motivation, and their available options to participate and determine the political climate of a country. As we emphasized in the section on takeovers, the political climate of a country is hardly ever static. Instead, key decisions are often made during sudden and radical changes in the political climate of a host country. Sudden changes of power, especially when the new leadership is committed to a leftist economic and political philosophy, have frequently lead to hostile political climates and takeovers. Such changes in government can happen as a result of open elections or unexpected coup d'états or revolutions.

The fall of the Iranian shah in 1980 is a typical example of a sudden change that caught many MNCs by surprise. The impact on U.S. business included a total of 3,848 claims—and a full 518 were for more than $250,000. The claims are being settled by The Hague Tribunal, which is dispersing funds from one billion dollars of Iranian assets, which were set aside after the release of the American diplomats who had been held hostage for 14 months. The largest single settlement was $49.8 million paid to R. J. Reynolds.[33] The damage was not only to U.S. MNCs. Many MNCs operating from Europe and Japan were forced to close either all or parts of their operations. The following war between Iran and Iraq further limited the attractiveness of the area and caused additional losses to foreign investors.

Even during periods of war and civil unrest, business goes on. In 1979, U.S. investment in El Salvador reached $150 million in U.S. dollars. By 1984, this was reduced to about $50 million.[36] Many U.S. firms quit the country as it became embroiled in a bitter civil war that saw many of their executives kidnapped or held hostage. But despite these trying circumstances, AVX Corp.'s local subsidiary assembling electronic components was rated better than the company's other eight foreign plants. Operations were maintained by changing shifts to allow workers to be home during hours of high risk. Texas Instruments responded by consolidating its two operations into one and by hiring a full-time professional security force.[34]

Of particular concern to companies operating in various parts of the world is the increasing international terrorism. A U.S. business organization published figures that placed the number of worldwide terrorist incidents at 572 in 1975, 728

---

33. "Slow Progress on Iran Claims," *The New York Times,* November 14, 1984, pp. D1, D5.

34. "U.S. Corporations Are Hoping for a More Stable Environment After Today's Elections," *The New York Times,* March 25, 1984, p. 6.

TABLE 4.2 International Terrorist Incidents Against U.S.
Citizens and Property, 1979–83

	1979	*1980*	*1981*	*1982*	*1983*
Total Incidents	236	272	257	401	393
U.S. CASUAL-TIES:					
Killed	15	9	7	7	274*
Wounded	22	19	41	12	118*

* Includes Beirut bombings

Source: Office for Combatting Terrorism, U.S. State Department, as
published in, "U.S. Readies Anti-Terrorism Policy," *The Wall Street
Journal,* March 12, 1984, p. 32. Reprinted by permission of *The Wall
Street Journal,* © Dow Jones & Company, Inc. 1984. All rights reserved.

in 1976, 1,255 in 1977 and 1,500 in 1978.[35] In 1979 the attacks continued to
increase. About 75 percent of terrorist activities during the 1970s occurred in just
fourteen countries. The countries where U.S. business came under attack most
frequently were, other than the United States, Argentina, Italy, Colombia, and
Puerto Rico. A full 55 percent of the U.S. citizens kidnapped overseas have been
businesspersons. Companies have replied by hiring special security personnel,
purchasing kidnap insurance, and employing specialized firms to negotiate with
terrorists in case of a kidnapping. Ransom demands have been rising with
amounts in excess of one million dollars becoming more frequent.[36] The number
of U.S. casualties caused by international terrorism is shown in Table 4.2. According to Risks International, a Virginia firm that monitors terrorism, the number of terrorist incidents has been growing at 12 to 15 percent each year. In 1984,
there were 21 terrorist attacks on American businesses and executives resulting
in 28 deaths, 64 injuries, and $22 million in property damages.[37]

A major concern for MNCs is the financial aspect of investment. Changes in
the political climate and financial structure of a country can result in policies that
can make a profitable operation unprofitable. Edward Roberts, the manager of
International Credit at Union Carbide reports, "The big problem we're facing
now is not with expropriation of assets, but rather with the ability to repatriate
funds for material we shipped in."[38] American Motors' joint venture in China,
Beijing Jeep Corporation, was shut down for seven weeks in 1986 due to Chinese

35. *Overseas Business Trends,* Rhode Island Hospital Trust National Bank, February, 1980.
36. "Terrorism: Why Business Is Now a Prime Target," *International Management Europe,* p. 20.
37. "Business Copes with Terrorism," *Fortune,* January 6, 1986, p. 47.
38. "Real-Life Risky Business," *Business Marketing,* vol. 72, January 1987, p. 50.

government restrictions on joint venture foreign purchases. Beijing Jeep imports 90 percent of its parts to assemble the Jeep Cherokee, but it could not get enough hard currency due to the new regulations. The problem was eventually resolved when AMC agreed to start using more locally produced parts.[39]

Faced with such a changing political climate, what can companies do? Internationally active companies have reacted on two fronts. First, they have started to perfect their own intelligence system to prevent situations where they get caught unaware. Secondly, they have developed several risk reducing business strategies that will help to limit the exposure, or losses, should a sudden change occur. The following sections will concentrate on these two solutions.

POLITICAL RISK ASSESSMENT

Because more than 60 percent of United States–based MNCs have suffered some type of politically motivated damage between 1975 and 1980, many companies have established systems to systematically analyze political risk.[40] One piece of evidence that political risk assessment is becoming of age is the formation of the Association of Political Risk Analysts (APRA) in 1981 with about 200 members.[41] For a company to establish an effective political risk assessment (PRA) system, it has to decide first on the objectives of the system. Another aspect concerns the internal organization, or the assignment of responsibility within the company. Finally, some agreement will have to be reached on how the analysis is to be done.

The Objectives of Political Risk Assessment

Potential risks have been described in detail in the earlier parts of this chapter. Of course, companies everywhere would like to know about impending governmental instabilities so that no new investments would be placed in those countries. But even more important is the monitoring of existing operations and their political environment. Particularly with existing operations, not much is gained by knowing in advance of potential changes in the political climate unless such advanced knowledge can also be used for future action. As a result, political risk assessment is slowly moving from predicting events to developing strategies to help companies cope with changes.[42] But first, political risk assessment has to

39. Ibid., p. 52.

40. "More Firms Are Hiring Own Political Analysts to Limit Risks Abroad," *The Wall Street Journal,* March 30, 1981, p. 17.

41. Bob Donath, "Handicapping and Hedging the Foreign Investment," *Industrial Marketing Management,* February 1981, p. 56.

42. "The Post-Shah Surge in Political-Risk Studies," *Business Week* December 1, 1980, p. 69.

deal with the potential political changes. The questions to be answered by such an analysis are Should we enter a particular country? Should we stay in a particular country? and What can we do with our operations in country X given that development Y can occur?

The Organization of Political Risk Assessment

Although Professor Root found little evidence of systematic political risk assessment in a study he conducted in 1968, more than half of the large United States–based MNCs surveyed by the Conference Board indicated that company internal groups were reviewing the political climate of both newly proposed and current operations. In companies that did not have any formalized systems for political risk assessment, top executives tended to obtain first-hand information through direct contact by travelling and talking with other businesspeople.[43]

This informal and unstructured approach once spelled trouble for a U.S. company. Eaton, a diversified U.S. manufacturer, built a plant in Southern Normandy, France, that was notorious for its troublesome communist unions.[44] If the company had known about the labor situation, it would never have built there, of course. As a result of this and other unsatisfactory experiences, Eaton established a group of full-time political analysts at its headquarters that included former government employees with an extensive background in political risk assessment. Other companies with a full-time corporate staff are Gulf Oil, General Motors, American Can, TRW, and General Electric.[45]

The way Gulf Oil was able to make use of its political risk assessment serves as an example of the power of correct information. Gulf's small team of analysts warned of the Iranian shah's probable fall several months before it was generally anticipated. The same group supported an exploration venture in Pakistan despite the Soviet invasion of Afghanistan that had just taken place. More risky was Gulf's decision to proceed with its operations in Angola. Prior to the civil war in Angola, Gulf's analyst foresaw that a Marxist group would emerge as the most powerful force among the three factions vying for control of the country. Gulf managers felt, however, that the Marxist government would provide both a stable and reasonable government, so they decided to invest. Angola has since become one of Gulf's most important overseas production sources.[46]

Rather than rely on a centralized corporate staff, some companies prefer to delegate political risk assessment responsibility to executives or analysts located

---

43. Franklin Root, "U.S. Business Abroad and Political Risks," *MSU Business Topics*, Winter 1968, pp. 73–80; and Stephen J. Kobrin, et al., "The Assessment and Evaluation of Noneconomic Environments by American Firms: A Preliminary Report," *Journal of International Business Studies*, Spring/Summer 1980, pp. 32–47.

44. "The Multinationals Get Smarter About Political Risks", *Fortune*, March 24, 1980, p. 88.

45. "The Post-Shah Surge in Political-Risk Studies," p. 69.

46. "The Multinationals Get Smarter," p. 87.

in the particular region. Exxon and Xerox both use their subsidiary and regional managers as a major source. The use of distinguished foreign policy advisors is practiced by another group. Bechtel, the large California-based engineering company, made use of the services of Richard Helms, a former CIA director and U.S. ambassador in Iran. Henry Kissinger, a former U.S. Secretary of State, has advised Merck; Goldman, Sachs; and the Chase Manhattan Bank. General Motors and Caterpillar have also maintained outside advisory panels.[47]

Information Needs

Though expropriations and takeovers have been a major problem for MNCs in the past, companies now view other political actions as actually more dangerous. Delayed payments or restrictions on profit repatriation was viewed as the major problem in a study done by a U.S. consulting firm, Heidrick & Struggles, Inc.[48] This was confirmed by research done by the Conference Board (see Table 4.3). An executive of General Motors even went so far as to state that his firm was more concerned about "indigenization," or required local content, leading General Motors away from general political risk studies to studies of the country's regulatory processes.[49]

Professor Root, one of the first academics to take an interest in political risk assessment, suggested that MNCs look for answers to six broad key questions:

1. How stable is the host country's political system?
2. How strong is the host government's commitment to specific rules of the game, such as ownership or contractual rights, given its ideology and power position?
3. How long is the government likely to remain in power?
4. If the present government is succeeded, how would the specific rules of the game change?
5. What would be the effects of any expected changes in the specific rules of the game?
6. In light of those effects, what decisions and actions should be taken now?[50]

Another approach used by Lawrence Bloom, an independent consultant on political risk, concentrated on viewing each country in terms of its political issues and the major political actors. The analysis was to determine which one of these actors would have the greatest influence with respect to important decisions.[51]

---

47. Ibid.
48. "More Firms Are Hiring Own Political Analysts to Limit Risks Abroad," p. 1.
49. "The Post-Shah Surge in Political-Risk Studies, p. 69.
50. Donath, "Handicapping and Hedging the Foreign Investment," *Industrial Marketing Management,* p. 57. Copyright 1981 by Elsevier Science Publishing Co., Inc.
51. "The Multinationals Get Smarter," p. 98.

TABLE 4.3 Most Important Aspects of the Overseas
Environment*

	Percent of Respondents
Political stability	79.5
Foreign investment climate	79.5
Profit remittances and exchange controls	69.4
Taxation	51.4
Expropriation	28.4
Political part attitudes toward foreign investors	24.2
Labor strikes and unrest	21.1
Administrative procedures	15.8
Public sector industrial activities	13.2
Public image of the firm	5.3

* Respondents were asked to select four.

Source: Stephen J. Kobrin, John Basek, Stephen Blank, Joseph La Pa-
lombara, "The Assessment and Evaluation of Noneconomic Environments by American Firms: A Preliminary Report," *Journal of International Business Studies,* Spring/Summer 1980, p. 41. Reprinted by permission.

One of the most common approaches in political risk assessment is the use
of "risk indices" available from specialized country risk assessment services. A
survey of 59 companies located in nine countries found that 76 percent used
outside risk evaluation services, such as BERI, S.A., Business International,
The Economist Intelligence Unit, or Frost & Sullivan.[52] Business International
(BI) surveyed about 70 countries twice each year.[53] BI correspondents and other
specialists rated the countries on 55 topics, each carrying a specific weight for an
index. The countries were then ranked according to risk probability and operating conditions. The report also included discount factors to be applied to projects
in various countries.

Another well-known service is available from Frost & Sullivan (F&S).[54] The
research company ranks individual "actors" according to the nature and importance of their opinions on specific issues in any given country. The results for a
1980–1981 survey are contained in Figure 4.2. The figure charts 61 countries
according to their likelihood of restricting business activities and their relative
political stability.

52. F. T. Haner with John S. Ewing, *Country Risk Assessment* (New York: Praeger, 1985), p. 170.
53. "The Post-Shah Surge," p. 69.
54. Donath, "Handicapping and Hedging the Foreign Investment," p. 57.

FIGURE 4.2 Sixty-One Countries Classified by Instability and Restrictions on Business

Political Instability	Restrictions On Business: High	Restrictions On Business: Medium	Restrictions On Business: Low
High	El Salvador Iran Zaire	Philippines	Bolivia
Medium	Libya Kenya Nicaragua Nigeria Zambia	Argentina Dominican Republic Canada Ecuador, Egypt Indonesia Morocco, Pakistan Panama, Peru Portugal Tunisia Turkey Yugoslavia	Brazil Columbia India, Italy Israel South Africa Spain Thailand Uruguay Zimbabwe
Low	China	Algeria Greece Mexico Saudi Arabia Venezuela	Australia Austria Chile, Denmark Finland, France Ireland Japan Kuwait Maylasia Netherlands New Zealand Norway Singapore South Korea Sweden, Taiwan United Kingdom United States West Germany

Source: Reprinted by permission of the publisher from "Handicapping and Hedging the Foreign Investment" by Bob Donath, *Industrial Marketing Management,* vol. 66, no. 2, p. 58. Copyright 1981 by Elsevier Science Publishing Co., Inc.

Motorola would often use consultants to determine political risk. For example, in 1987 Motorola used consultants to evaluate the investment risk for a facility in a Southeast Asian country. A far East business information service reported on how other businesses were responding to the political climate. Another consultant analyzed financial risks. An academic analyzed factors relating to operating costs.[55]

Though quite a few companies are using their own computerized models, among them American Can and United Technologies, few analysts would be willing to depend strictly on indices or numbers for their assessment. Professor Stover used the "product life cycle" theory to describe risk probability for MNCs. MNCs have most bargaining chips on their side when the initial investment is made. As markets become established, this bargaining power tends to shift in favor of the host government.[56] Other variations depend on the nature of the technology used by the local subsidiary. In any case, companies are advised to look beyond the overall climate and make project-specific assessments.

What MNCs do with their assessment depends on the data they collect. Exxon, for one, integrated its political assessment with its financial plans. In cases where Exxon expects a higher political risk, the company may add 1 to 5 percent to its required return on investment.[57] The political risk assessment should also help the company to stay out of a certain country when it is necessary. However the collected data should be carefully differentiated so that the best decision can be made. Recall Gulf's decision to go into Angola despite the Marxist government there.

RISK REDUCTION STRATEGIES

Determining or assessing political risk should not be an end in itself. The key to political risk assessment is its integration of risk-reducing strategies that eventually enable companies to enter a market or remain in business. Many MNCs have experimented with different forms of ownership arrangements, production, and financing that were geared towards reducing political risk to an acceptable minimum. We will enlarge upon these alternatives with a discussion of the tools managers can use to deal with political risk rather than leave a market or refuse to enter one.[58]

---

55. "How MNCs Are Aligning Country-Risk Assessment with Bottom-Line Concerns," *Business International Weekly Report to Managers of Worldwide Organizations,* June 1, 1987, pp. 169–170.
56. Ibid.
57. "The Multinationals Get Smarter," p. 88.
58. The following sections are adapted from *Insurance Decisions,* published by the CIGNA companies, Philadelphia. Reprinted by permission.

Local Partners

To rely on local partners with excellent contacts to the host country governing elite is a strategy that has been used effectively by many companies. This may range from placing local nationals on the boards of foreign subsidiaries to accepting a substantial capital participation from local investors. According to a survey done for a U.S. research organization, The Conference Board, some 40 percent of U.S. companies with sales in excess of $100 million engaged in some type of joint ventures with local partners. About half of these companies claimed that their joint ventures were just as profitable as fully-owned subsidiaries, and 12 percent viewed their joint ventures even more profitable.[59] Though many host countries require some form of local participation as a condition for entering their market, there are many firms that do so voluntarily. Diamond Shamrock, a United States–based MNC, built its chemical plant in South Korea with the help of a local partner to get more favorable operating conditions.[60] Another company that relies heavily on local joint ventures is Cabot Corp., a leading manufacturer of carbon black.

Invaluable Status

Achieving a status of indispensability is an effective strategy for firms that have exclusive access to high technology or specific products. Such companies keep research and development out of the reach of their politically vulnerable subsidiaries and, at the same time, enhance their bargaining power with host governments by emphasizing their contributions to the economy. When Texas Instruments wanted to open an operation in Japan more than twenty years ago, the company was able to resist pressures to take on a local partner due to its advanced technology. This occurred at a time when any other foreign MNC was forced to accept local partners.[61] The appearance of being irreplaceable obviously helps reduce political risk.

Vertical Integration

MNCs that maintain specialized plants in various countries, each dependent on each other, are expected to incur fewer political risks than firms with fully integrated and independent plants in each country. A firm practicing this form of distributed sourcing can offer economies of scale to a local operation. This can

---

59. Donath, "Handicapping and Hedging the Foreign Investment," p. 61.
60. "More Firms Are Hiring Own Poltiical Analysts," p. 17.
61. Yves L. Doz and C. K. Prahalad, "How MNCs Cope with Host Government Intervention," *Harvard Business Review,* March–April 1980, p. 152.

become crucial for success in many industries. If a host government were to take over such a plant, its output level would be spread over too many units, products, or components, thus rendering the local company uncompetitive due to a cost disadvantage. Further risk can be reduced by having at least two units engage in the same operation to prevent the MNC itself from becoming hostage to overspecialization. Unless multiple sourcing exists, a MNC could be virtually shut down if only one of its plants were affected negatively.

Local Borrowing

One of the reasons why Cabot Corp. prefers local partners is that they are then able to borrow locally instead of bringing foreign exchange to a host country.[62] Financing local operations from indigenous banks and maintaining a high level of local accounts payables maximizes the negative effect on the local economy if adverse political actions were taken. Typically, host governments don't expropriate themselves, and they would be hesitant to cause problems for their local financial institutions. Local borrowing, however, is not always possible due to restrictions placed on foreign companies who might otherwise crowd local companies out of the credit markets.

Minimizing Fixed Investments

Political risk of course is always related to the amount of capital at risk. Given equal political risk, an alternative with comparably lower exposed capital amounts would be preferable. A company could decide to lease facilities instead of buying them, or they could rely more on outside suppliers provided they exist. In any case, MNCs should keep exposed assets to a minimum to limit damage due to political risk.

Political Risk Insurance

As a last recourse, MNCs can purchase insurance to cover their political risk. According to a survey of U.S. companies with sizable foreign investments conducted in 1979, only about 30 percent had insurance against expropriation, 20 percent against inconvertibility of currency, and even less than that carried insurance against contract repudiation. With the political developments of Iran and Nicaragua in rapid succession and the assassinations of President Park of

---

62. "The Multinationals Get Smarter," p. 98.

Korea and President Sadat of Egypt all taking place between 1979 and 1981, many companies have begun to change their attitudes on risk insurance.

United States–based companies have two sources for such insurance: government insurance or private insurance. The Overseas Private Investment Corporation (OPIC) was formed in 1969 by the U.S. government to facilitate the participation of private U.S. firms in the development of less developed countries. OPIC offers three kinds of political risk insurance in one hundred developing countries. The agency covers losses caused by currency inconvertibility, expropriation, and bellicose actions such as war and revolution. Because "developing countries are all in hock up to their ears, about 98 percent of our clients buy currency inconvertibility coverage," says Robert L. Jordan, OPIC's director of public affairs.[63] To obtain coverage for an investment, a corporation must demonstrate that the project satisfies both U.S. foreign policy objectives and the aspirations of the host country. This includes an examination of the employment effect, balance of payments impact, environments, and human rights among many other factors. United States companies paid an estimated $100 million for political risk insurance in 1980.[64] Of that total, about one-third was spent on OPIC coverage and another third on Foreign Credit Insurance coverage, a service that insures accounts receivables. The rest was spent on private insurance carriers. Worldwide, MNCs were estimated to have spent some $600 million on political risk premiums.

Although some companies did have insurance against political risks, others did not. Among those that did was Cabot Corp. who used initially joint-venture partners and local borrowings to reduce its own investment. Cabot's own capital contribution was insured, just as it was elsewhere. Thus, the firm's investment of $3 million in its Iran venture was well covered by insurance. Earlier, Cabot had been able to recoup its losses both in Argentina and Colombia.[65] Starrett Housing Corp., a company with little foreign experience, got involved in Iran in 1975 with the help of some local partners who were closely connected to the shah. The company had to leave Iran, leaving the residential construction unfinished. To cover its investment of $38 million, the company relied on an Iranian bank closely linked with the shah's business interests. Starrett decided against OPIC insurance due to price considerations. It now has turned out rather difficult to collect against Starrett's letter of guarantee since the local bank's management changed during the Iranian revolution.[66] The price of risk insurance depends, of course, on the country. Rates range from as low as 0.5 percent for the best areas to about 3 percent for risky countries, and they can go as high as 9 percent for high risks. The average risk premium paid around 1980 was closer to 1 percent of contract value.

63. Kate Bertrand, "Real-Life Risky Business," *Business Marketing,* vol. 72, January 1987, p. 53.
64. "Insuring Against Risk Abroad," *Business Week,* September 14, 1981, p. 62.
65. "The Multinationals Get Smarter," p. 98.
66. Ibid., p. 95.

INTERNATIONAL LEGAL FORCES

In many ways, the legal framework of nations is the result of a particular political philosophy or ideology. Just as each country has its own political climate, so does the legal system change from country to country. Internationally active companies thus find themselves in a situation where they have to conform to more than one legal system. Although this is complex enough, the difficulty of determining whose laws apply in some cases adds further to an already complex environment.

Here we will discuss some of the current major legal challenges that require adjustment and consideration at the corporate level. In later chapters, we will present the specific legal requirements covering certain aspects of the international marketing program. Such material has been added to the chapters on pricing, advertising, and export mechanics, among others.

Of particular interest to us in this chapter are the laws pertaining to commercial behavior, such as laws against bribery and laws regulating competition and product liability. We will also discuss the emergence of international courts.

Laws Against Bribery and Corrupt Practices

Though bribery in international business has been known to exist for years, the publicity surrounding some bribery scandals in the early 1970s has caused a public furor about the practice in the United States. For example, in 1975 the United States–based MNC, United Brands, was accused of paying a bribe of $1.25 million in 1974 to a high government official in Honduras later identified as that country's president.[67] The bribe had been paid to obtain a reduction of an export tax levied by Honduras on each box of bananas. United Brands was a major banana exporter that marketed its products worldwide under the Chiquita label. Despite the public outcry about the affair that resulted in the replacement of the Honduran president, United Brands' only violation of U.S. laws was the failure to have reported the payments by concealing them in the books of its subsidiaries.[68] As a result of these revelations, scores of U.S. companies voluntarily declare such payments to the SEC. According to some sources, more than 300 U.S. corporations voluntarily declared illicit payments.

The flood of declarations triggered a new federal law, The Foreign Corrupt Practices Act of 1977, intended to stop the payments of bribes. Though the act covered the whole range of record keeping and control activities of a company both in the U.S. and abroad, its best known section specifically prohibited U.S. companies, their subsidiaries, and representatives from making payments to

---

67. "Honduran Bribery," *Time,* April 21, 1975, p. 74.
68. "Honduras: A Genuine Banana Coup," *Time,* May 5, 1975, p. 29.

high ranking foreign government officials or political parties. Specifically, the FCPA stated: "Prohibited are the use of an instrumentality of interstate commerce (such as the telephone or the mails) in the furtherance of a payment or even an offer to pay 'anything of value,' directly or indirectly, to any foreign official with discretion or to any foreign political party or foreign political candidate, if the purpose of the payment is the 'corrupt' one of getting the recipient to act (or to refrain from acting) in such a way as to assist the company in obtaining or retaining business for or with or directing business to any person." This portion of the FCPA applied to all U.S. concerns and was not exclusively limited to companies subject to SEC jurisdiction.[69] The penalties for violation can be very stiff: an executive who violates the FCPA may be imprisoned for up to five years and fined up to $10,000. The company involved may be fined up to one million dollars. Though the law prohibits outright bribery, small facilitating payments are not outlawed as long as they are made to government clerks without any policy-making responsibility.

One of the principal reasons that payoffs continue is the different treatment of bribery by various governments. Contrary to U.S. law, the German government considers payoffs legal as long as they are made outside Germany. Furthermore, any such payments are tax deductible. As a result, many United States–based MNCs consider themselves at a disadvantage when competing for business in certain parts of the world where kickbacks are common. Some efforts have been made to help U.S. companies distinguish illegal from legal payments. Under a new procedure, the continual division of the U.S. Justice Department reviews proposed transactions and lets the companies know about the legal consequences.[70] There is little likelihood that other governments would come around to accepting the U.S. positions. Europeans and Japanese view such payments as a cost of business.

To avoid any conflict with the law, some U.S. companies have developed their own guidelines. DuPont Co. had adopted its own code of ethics before the FCPA became law in 1977; and, according to company officials, it is said to be even more stringent.[71] Other companies that have spelled out in detail what employees can or cannot do include General Motors and Lockheed Corp.[72] Companies with a clear technological lead such as IBM typically don't have to make payoffs to sell their products.[73] And one official at a U.S. aircraft company stated that since the passing of the FCPA in 1977 the requests for payoffs were down by 80 percent.[74]

69. Hurd Baruch, "The Foreign Corrupt Practices Act," *Harvard Business Review*, January–February 1979, p. 44.

70. "U.S. Outlines its Review of Foreign Payments," *The New York Times*, March 25, 1980, p. D1.

71. *The Wall Street Journal*, August 2, 1979.

72. "Misinterpreting the Antibribery Law," *Business Week*, September 3, 1979, p. 150.

73. "The Global Costs of Bribery," *Business Week*, March 15, 1976, p. 22.

74. *The Wall Street Journal*, August 2, 1979, p. 19.

Rejection of a request for a payoff often puts the executive in a difficult position. One strategy is to transform the private payoff into a public gift of funds for a hospital, services for the public good, or jobs for the unemployed. These actions may satisfy the request for funds while not violating the provisions of the FCPA.[75]

Laws Regulating Competitive Behavior

Many countries have adopted laws that govern the competitive behavior of their firms. In some cases, as for the European Community (EC), supranational bodies enforce their own laws. Unfortunately for MNCs, these anti-trust laws are frequently contradictory or differently enforced, adding great complexity to the job of the international executive. The United States, with its long-standing tradition of anti-trust enforcement, has had considerable impact on the multinational operations of U.S. MNCs and increasingly on those of foreign-based MNCs operating in the United States.

But foreign MNCs entering the U.S. market may also have to deal with U.S. anti-trust legislation. When Bic Corp., the U.S. subsidiary of the French firm Bic, offered to buy American Safety Razor Co., the U.S. government insisted that the brand names Personna, Flicker, and Gem would have to be sold within two years. Unable to agree on the wording of the deal, the French company withdrew the offer to acquire ASR.[76]

In other countries, anti-trust legislation may be enforced differently than in the United States. Though each member country of the EC has some anti-trust laws, the Common Market Commission, which functions to some extent as a government, enforces its anti-trust legislation on a European level. Starting rather slowly, enforcement and convictions increased in the early 1970s to reach about twenty convictions each year.[77] According to the EC agreement, companies are not allowed to abuse the dominant market position in either the entire EC territory or a significant part of it. Several large MNCs have been convicted for various violations in the areas of pricing, distribution policies, or mergers. One of the firms under investigation was International Business Machines Corp., which came under attack for some of its marketing practices.[78] Several U.S. and European computer firms selling plug-compatible equipment for IBM customers complained to the European Commission that IBM suddenly changed its selling practices. IBM had been restricting operating information on how to connect

---

75. Jeffrey A. Fadiman, "A Travelers Guide to Gifts and Bribes," *Harvard Business Review*, July–August 1986, pp. 122–136.

76. "Why BIC Dropped Its U.S. Razor Deal," *Business Week*, March 7, 1977, p. 23.

77. "Trustbusting in Europe," *The New York Times*, January 18, 1976, p. 17.

78. "The Brussels Threat to IBM," *The Economist*, February 6, 1982, p. 47.

computer units and had been inducing its clients to buy only IBM software by refusing to price memories and software separately from the overall cost of a computer. The case was settled in 1984 and IBM was required to publish within four months of a new product announcement any information required by competitors to develop compatible equipment.[79]

Product Liability

Though there are regulations or laws that directly affect all aspects of international marketing, regulations on product liability are included here because of their enormous impact on all firms. Specific regulatory acts, or laws, pertaining to other aspects of the marketing mix, namely pricing, distribution, and promotion, have been included in other chapters.

Regulations on product liability are relatively recent and started first in the United States. Other countries have laws on product liability as well; and one of the major problems for international marketers involves the differences in laws in different countries or regions. In the United States, product liability is viewed in the broadest sense, or along the lines of strict liability. For a product sold in defective condition that becomes unreasonably dangerous for the user, both producer and distributor can become liable.

While U.S. firms have adjusted to the legal situation in the United States, foreign companies have had substantial difficulties in doing so. European firms, which due to their less stringent laws carried very low insurance coverage, were suddenly hurt by escalating premiums. One British cookie manufacturer that paid $28,000 in worldwide product liability insurance in 1976, saw its premium raised to $110,000 in 1977 just for the portion of its U.S. business that accounted for only 5 percent of the company's sales. Another British concern producing machine tools saw its premiums escalate by a factor of 15 between 1974 and 1977 as a result of some suits brought against it in the United States. For foreign firms with a very small U.S. business it might become worthwhile to stop exports to the U.S. rather than pay the insurance premiums. Other firms may absorb the risk themselves.[80]

But product liability laws have changed in Europe as well. In the mid-1970s, the European Commission proposed a set of regulations that was to supercede each member country's laws. Traditionally, the individual country laws had been rather lax by U.S. standards. The new regulations have been described as even tougher than those in the United States.[81] In the United States, the plaintiff must prove that the product was defective at the time it left the producer's hand,

79. "The Road is Clear for IBM's Probe into Europe," *Business Week*, August 20, 1984, p. 44.
80. "Europe: A Liability Threat to U.S. Bound Exports," *Business Week*, March 14, 1977, p. 42.
81. "Common Market Nations Likely To Adopt Harsher Product-Liability Codes for Firms," *The Wall Street Journal*, March 3, 1977.

whereas under the EC guidelines it is the manufacturer who must prove that the product was not defective when it left his control. Nevertheless, there are differences due to the different legal and social systems. In the EC, trials will be decided by judges and not common jurors. And the existing extensive welfare system will automatically absorb many of the medical costs that are subject to litigation in the United States. Furthermore, it is typical for the loser in a court judgment in Europe to bear the legal costs. In the case of product liability cases, if a company were found to owe damages to a plaintiff, then it would also have to pay the plaintiff's legal costs according to typical fee standards. This differs substantially from the U.S. system in which a winning plaintiff's lawyer typically is compensated through a predetermined percentage of the awarded damages, a practice that in the eyes of many experts has raised award damages and, as a result, liability insurance costs.

The rapid spread of product liability litigation, however, forces companies with international operations to carefully review their potential liabilities and to acquire appropriate insurance policies. Although an international marketing manager cannot be expected to know all the respective rules and regulations, executives must nevertheless anticipate potential exposure and, by asking themselves the appropriate questions, make sure that their firms consider all possible aspects.

Patents and Trademarks

Patents and trademarks are used to protect products, processes, and symbols. Patents and trademarks are issued by each individual country, so marketers must register every product in every country they intend to trade in. The International Convention for the Protection of Industrial Property, honored by forty-five countries, gives all nationals the same privileges when applying for patents and trademarks. Also, the agreement gives patent coverage for one year after the trademark or patent is applied for in one country, thus limiting pirating of the product in other countries.

Pirating products has become a significant problem in the 1980s affecting computers, watches, designer clothes, and industrial products. The International Trade Commission estimated that in 1982 the cost of pirating was $5.5 billion for U.S. business.[82] Patents, trademarks, and pirating will be discussed in more detail in Chapter 10.

International Court Judgments

One of the great difficulties with international law is the determination of which law applies where. In the United States, state courts will enforce each other's

---

82. "Intellectual Property: Foreign Pirates Worry U.S. Firms," *C&EN,* September 1, 1986, p. 9.

judgments automatically. This is normally not the case with international judgments. One exception, however, judgments within the European Community. A French court will uphold a decision of a German court and can enforce it even though the legal basis for the judgment might be different. How far this can go is illustrated by a suit filed in Austria against Jean-Claude Killy, the former French skiing champion.[83] According to both German and Austrian law, anyone who has any amount of personal property, however small, in those countries can leave himself or herself open for a suit. When Jean-Claude Killy left a pair of shorts once in an Austrian ski resort, that was sufficient to be sued in an Austrian court. Such a judgment would have to be enforced by other European courts that could attach property. In the case of a U.S. firm, it could mean that a judgment against it in Italy, for example, could be enforced against property the firm owns in Germany. To avoid being subject to often much stricter European law, the U.S. government concluded a treaty with the British government to recognize each other's court judgments. As a consequence, U.K. courts will not have to enforce EC judgments against U.S. firms made in other EC member states.[84]

The International Court in The Hague, Netherlands, will render judgments on international business disputes, but its judgments are not automatically binding to the parties involved. The European Court, situated in Luxembourg, renders judgments that are only binding in the EC member states. To deal with this lack of a generally accepted and binding court, companies frequently use a predetermined format of arbitration panels. They may consist of specially appointed representatives, or the firms may use panels available from the International Chamber of Commerce. In any event, companies are advised to include in major contracts specific rules of how they expect to solve contract disputes. A simple dependence on national courts is often insufficient.

CONCLUSIONS

In this chapter we have outlined the major political and regulatory forces facing MNCs. Our approach was not so much to identify and list all possible influences or actions that might impact on international marketing operations. Instead, we have provided only a sample of potential acts. It is up to executives with international responsibility to devise structures and systems that systematically deal with these environmental influences. What is important in this context is to recognize that companies can adopt risk reduction strategies to compensate for some of these risks, but certainly not for all of them. For effective international marketing management, executives will have to become forward looking, anticipate potential adversary or even positive changes in the environment, and not wait until they occur. To accomplish such a task, a systematic monitoring sys-

83. "Court Judgments Go International," *Business Week,* February 1977, p. 50.
84. Ibid.

tem that encompasses both political and legal developments will become necessary.

Questions for Discussion

1. The telecommunications industry in Japan has traditionally been tightly controlled, with very little non-Japanese equipment allowed. What aspects of Japan's political forces may have influenced this control over the Japanese telecommunications market?
2. In 1987, Japan began to open its telecommunications market, especially to United States and European firms. How did political forces influence this change?
3. How could a country develop its own expertise in a product that is primarily imported; for example, automobiles in Egypt?
4. With executives in a variety of different countries, what strategies can be used to protect against terrorist activities?
5. What are the different methods that a company can develop/obtain political risk assessment information?
6. John Deere has decided to enter the tractor market in Central America. What strategies could it use to reduce the possible affect of political risk?
7. While attempting to deliver a large computer system (selling price $1.4 million) to a foreign government, the Minister of Transportation advises that a fee of $20,000 is required to assure proper coordination of the custom clearance delivery process. What would you do?

For Further Reading

Behrman, Jack N., J. J. Boddewyn, and Ashok Kapoor. *International Business-Government Communications*. Lexington, Mass.: D.C. Heath, 1975.

Bradley, David G. "Managing Against Expropriation." *Harvard Business Review* (July–August 1977), pp. 75–83.

Cao, A. O. "Nontariff Barriers to U.S. Manufactured Exports." *Columbia Journal of World Business* (Summer 1980), p. 95.

Davidow, Joel. "Multinationals, Host Governments and Regulation of Restrictive Business Practices." *Columbia Journal of World Business* (Summer 1980), pp. 14–19.

Graham, John L. "The Foreign Corrupt Practices Act." *Journal of International Business Studies* (Winter 1984), pp. 107–121.

Kaikati, Jack G. "The Export Trading Company Act." *California Management Review* (Fall 1984), pp. 59–69.

Kaikati, Jack G., and Wayne A. Label. "American Bribery Legislation: An Obstacle to International Marketing." *Journal of Marketing* (Fall 1980), pp. 38–43.

Kobrin, Stephen J. "Assessing Political Risk Overseas." *The Wharton Magazine* (Winter 1981/1982), pp. 25–31.

Kobrin, Stephen J. "Political Risk." *Journal of International Business Studies* (Spring–Summer 1979), pp. 67–80.

Kobrin, Stephen J. "Why Does Political Instability Result in Increased Investment Risk? *Columbia Journal of World Business* (Fall 1978), pp. 113–22.

Shapiro, Alan C. "Managing Political Risk: A Policy Approach." *Columbia Journal of World Business* (Fall 1981), pp. 63–70.

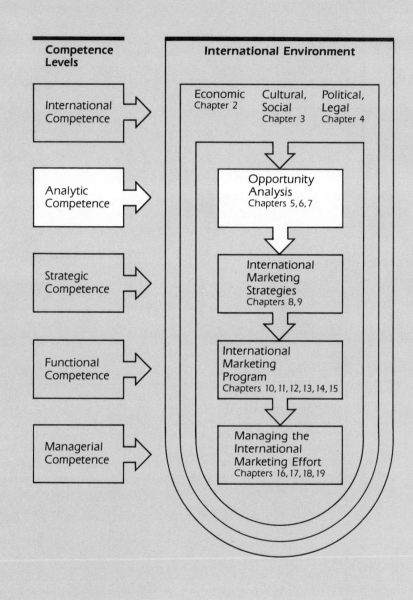

PART 3
OPPORTUNITY ANALYSIS

5 ▪ INTERNATIONAL MARKETS

6 ▪ INTERNATIONAL BUYERS

7 ▪ INTERNATIONAL MARKETING RESEARCH

Although the global marketplace is large, with more than 150 countries or territories, international marketers are constantly looking for the most appropriate markets and the best opportunities for their firms. Analyzing, classifying, and selecting opportunities for future business is an important aspect of international marketing management. In Part 3, we concentrate on the skills necessary to do this job well.

Chapter 5 provides analytic concepts to analyze opportunities within countries and groups of countries. In Chapter 6, we discuss the major market segments within each country's consumer, industrial, and government sectors and analyze the differences in these segments from market to market. In the final chapter of this section, Chapter 7, we cover the methods by which companies collect market data, and we discuss ways to analyze this market research data for decision making.

We have given this section a largely analytic focus. Our aim in doing this has been to encourage analytic competence, which is so necessary for success in international marketing.

5.
INTERNATIONAL MARKETS

An important aspect of international marketing is the assessment of market opportunities. Every time a company decides to expand into foreign markets it must systematically evaluate possible markets to identify the country or group of countries with the greatest opportunities. This process of evaluating worldwide opportunities is complicated for a number of reasons. First, there are some 150 countries in the world; obviously, it is difficult to examine all these opportunities. Second, due to the number of countries and resource limitations, the initial screening process is usually limited to the analysis of published data. Third, many possible markets are small, with little data available about specific consumer, business, or government needs.

In this chapter, which is diagrammed in Figure 5.1, we first discuss the process for selecting markets. Then, to illustrate the screening process, we present a detailed example of how this process would be used to select a market for dialysis equipment. In the final sections of the chapter, we discuss the rationale for grouping countries together and present the market groups in existence around the world today.

SCREENING INTERNATIONAL MARKETING OPPORTUNITIES

The assessment of international marketing opportunities is a screening process that involves gathering relevant information on each country and filtering out the less desirable countries. A model for selecting foreign markets is shown in Figure 5.2. The model includes a series of four filters to screen out countries. It is necessary to break the process down into a series of steps due to the large

FIGURE 5.1 International Markets

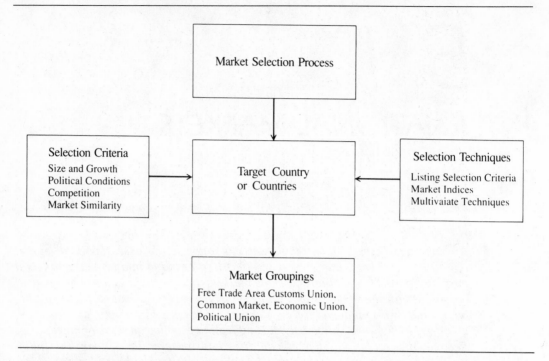

number of market opportunities. Although a firm does not want to miss a potential opportunity, it is not possible to conduct extensive market research studies in every one of the 150 countries of the world. The screening process is used to identify good prospects. Two common errors of country screening are (1) ignoring countries that offer good potential for the company's generic products and (2) spending too much time investigating countries that are poor prospects.[1] The screening process thus allows a firm to quickly focus efforts on a few of the most promising market opportunities by using only published secondary sources available in most business libraries.[2]

The first stage of the selection process uses macro variables to discriminate between countries that represent basic opportunities and countries with little or no opportunity or with excessive risk. Macro variables describe the total market in terms of economic activity, social forces, and political structure. Well-documented economic, social, geographic, and political information is used in this filter. Often macro economic statistics indicate that the country is too small, as described by the gross national (or domestic) product. Possibly the gross na-

---

1. Franklin R. Root, *Entry Strategies for International Markets* (Lexington, Mass.: Lexington Books, 1987), p. 33.
2. See Susan P. Douglas and C. Samuel Craig, *International Marketing Research* (Englewood Cliffs, N.J.: Prentice-Hall, 1983), pp. 306–325 for a detailed listing of secondary sources of information.

FIGURE 5.2 A Model for Selecting Foreign Markets

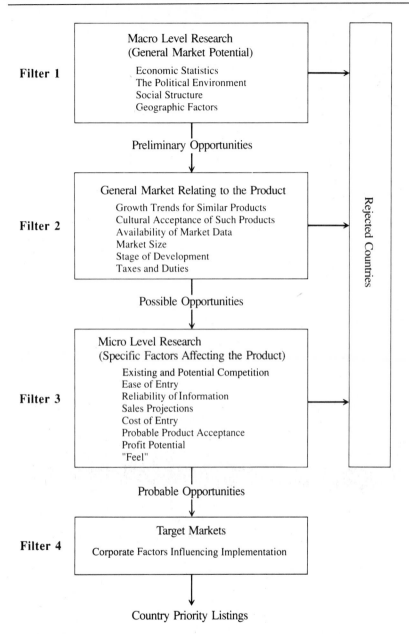

Source: R. Wayne Walvoord, "Export Market Research," *Global Trade Magazine,* May 1980, p. 83. Reprinted by permission.

tional product seems large enough, but the personal disposable income per household may be too low. Political instability can also be used to remove a country from the set of possible opportunities.

In the second stage of the selection process variables are used which indicate the potential market size and acceptance of the product or similar products. Often proxy variables are used in this screening process. A proxy variable is a similar or related product which indicates a demand for your product. For example, if you are attempting to measure the potential market size and receptivity for satellite television reception equipment, possible proxy variables may be the number of televisions per household, total sales of VCRs, or total sales of microwave ovens. The number of televisions and VCRs would indicate the potential for home entertainment and the sales of microwave ovens would indicate a propensity to use advanced technologies in place of traditional appliance technology. The year-to-year growth rates and the total sales of similar or proxy products are excellent predictors of market size and growth. Other factors in the second stage of the selection process can also be used to screen out countries, such as the stage of economic development, taxes and duty requirements. If you do not plan to manufacture locally, a high import duty may eliminate a country from consideration in the second stage of the screening process.

The third stage of the screening process focuses on micro-level considerations such as competitors, ease of entry, cost of entry, and profit potential. Micro-level factors will influence the success or failure of a specific product in a market. At this stage of the screening process marketers may only be considering a small number of countries, so it is feasible to get more detailed, up-to-date information from the U.S. Department of Commerce, the U.S. State Department, and from other companies currently operating in that country. The focus of the screening process switches from total market size to profitability. For example, based on the current and potential competitors, how much would you need to invest to gain a particular market share? Given the cost of entry and the expected sales, what is the expected profit? This stage of the analysis focuses on the quantitative profit expected; but many subjective judgments are made to arrive at the expected profit.

The fourth stage of the screening process is an evaluation and rank ordering of the potential target countries based on corporate resources, objectives, and strategies. For example, although South Africa may have the same expected potential as Venezuela, Venezuela may be given a higher priority since successful entry into Venezuela could later be followed by entry into Colombia and Bolivia.

Criteria for Selecting Target Countries

The process of selecting target countries through the four stage screening process in Figure 5.1 requires that the companies identify the criteria to be used to

TABLE 5.1 Macro Indicators of Market Size

GEOGRAPHIC INDICATORS
  Size of the country, in terms of geographic area
  Climatic conditions
  Topographical characteristics

DEMOGRAPHIC CHARACTERISTICS
  Total population
  Population growth rate
  Age distribution of the population
  Degree of population density

ECONOMIC CHARACTERISTICS
  Total gross national product
  Per capita gross national product
  Per capita income (also income growth rate)
  Personal or household disposable income
  Income distribution

---

differentiate desirable countries from less desirable countries. Research on international investment decisions has shown that the four critical factors affecting market selection are market size and growth, political conditions, competition, and market similarity.[3] The following portion of the chapter will explain each of these factors and their use in the market selection process.

Market Size and Growth

It is obvious that the potential market size and growth would be an important factor in selecting markets. The larger the potential demand for a product in a country the more attractive it will be to a company.[4]

Measures of market size and growth can be on both a macro and a micro basis. On a macro basis, it may be determined that the country needs a minimum set of potential resources to be worth further consideration. Table 5.1 shows a summary of potential macro indicators of market size.

There are a variety of readily available statistics that are macro indicators of market size. If you are screening countries for a firm that sells microwave ovens,

---

3. William H. Davidson, "Market Similarity and Market Selection: Implications for International Market Strategy," *Journal of Business Research,* vol. 11, December 1983, pp. 439–456.
4. R. B. Stobaugh, Jr., "How to Analyze Foreign Investment Climates," *Harvard Business Review,* September–October 1969, pp. 100–107.

TABLE 5.2 Micro Indicators of Market Size

Radios	Hotel beds
Televisions	Telephones
Cinema seats	Tourist arrivals
Scientists and engineers	Passenger cars
Hospitals	Civil airline passengers
Hospital beds	Steel production
Physicians	Rice production
Alcoholic liquor consumption	Number of farms
Coffee consumption	Land under cultivation
Gasoline consumption	Electricity consumption

you may decide not to consider any country with a personal disposable income per household of less than $10,000 per year. The logic of this criterion would be that if the average household has less than $10,000, the potential for a luxury item like a microwave oven would not be great. However, a single statistic can sometimes be deceptive. For example, a country may have an average household income of $8,000, but there may be one million households with an income of over $10,000. These one million households would be potential buyers of microwaves.

The macro indicators of market potential and growth are usually used in the first stage of the screening process, because the data are readily available and can be used to quickly eliminate countries with little or no potential demand. However, because the macro indicators of market size are general and crude, in the second stage of the screening process it is recommended that micro indicators of market potential be used. Micro indicators usually indicate actual consumption of a company's product or a similar product. Table 5.2 shows an example of micro indicators of market size.

These micro indicators can be used to estimate market size. The number of households with televisions indicates the potential market size for televisions, if every household purchased a new television. Depending on the life of the average television in use, one could estimate the annual demand. Although the actual consumption statistics may not be available for a certain product category, often the consumption of similar or substitute products are used as proxy variables. For example, in determining the market size for surgical sutures, marketers may use the number of hospital beds or doctors as a proxy variable. The number of farms may indicate the potential demand for tractors.

The macro and micro indicators of market size allow the marketer to determine or infer the potential market size. Next the marketer needs to evaluate the risk associated with each market opportunity.

TABLE 5.3 Indicators of Political Risk

Probability of nationalization	Percent of the voters in the Communist party
Bureaucratic delays	Restrictions on capital movement
Number of expropriations	Government intervention
Number of riots or assassinations	Limits on foreign ownership
Political executions	Soviet economic aid
Number of Socialist seats in the legislature	Soldier/civilian ratio

Political Conditions

The impact of a host country's political condition on market selection is described in studies by Stephan J. Kobrin and Franklin R. Root.[5] The influence of the host country's political environment was described in detail in Chapter 4. Though political risk tends to be more subjective than the quantitative indicators of market size, it is equally important. For example, the revolution in Iran in 1978 resulted in the exposure of over one billion dollars in U.S. assets.

Any company can be hurt by political risk, from limitations on the number of foreign company officials, limits on the amount of profits paid to the parent company, or outright takeovers. There are a number of indicators that can be used to assess political risk.[6] Table 5.3 shows some indicators of political risk that may be used in country selection.

Historically, extractive industries such as oil and mining have been susceptible to the political risk of expropriation. More recently, the financial, insurance, communication, and transportation industries have been targets of expropriation. As shown in Table 5.3, many aspects of political risk assessment can be analyzed based on historical data. Unfortunately, historical indicators are not always that accurate, since political conditions can change radically with a new government. As we mentioned in Chapter 4, some companies have in-house staff to assess political risk. American Can, United Technologies, and Borg Warner are three such companies.[7] We also noted some of the syndicated services that rate the political risk of most countries in the world. Major sources of informa-

5. S. J. Kobrin, "The Environmental Determinants of Foreign Direct Manufacturing Investment: An Ex-Post Empirical Analysis," *Journal of Business Studies,* Fall–Winter 1976, pp. 29–42; F. R. Root, "U.S. Business Abroad and Political Risks," *MSU Business Topics,* Winter 1968, pp. 73–80.

6. R. Rummel and David Heenan, "How Multinationals Analyze Political Risk," *Harvard Business Review,* January–February 1978, pp. 67–76.

7. Susan P. Douglas and C. Samuel Craig, *International Marketing Research* (Englewood Cliffs, N.J.: Prentice-Hall, 1983), pp. 83–84.

tion are the World Political Risk Forecast by Frost & Sullivan; Business International Rating of 57 Countries; Business Environment Risk Index and Political Risk Index of BERI, Ltd.; and the Economist Intelligence Unit. In addition to these major sources of information, many multinational companies often consult banks, accounting firms, and domestic government agencies for political risk information.[8]

Competition

The number, size, and quality of the competition in a particular country will affect a firm's ability to enter and compete profitably.[9] In general, it is more difficult to determine the competitive structure of foreign countries than it is to determine the market size or political risk. Because of the difficulty of obtaining information, competitive analysis is usually done in the last stages of the screening process when a small number of countries are being considered.

Some secondary sources are available that describe the competitive nature of a marketplace. The Findex Directory publishes a listing of the most readily available research reports. These reports tend to concentrate on North America and Europe, but there are some reports available on Japan, the Middle East, and South America. These research reports usually cost between $500 and $5,000, with the average report being about $1,200. In some cases, there may not be a research report covering a specific country or product category, or it may be too expensive. Another good source of information is the U.S. government. The U.S. Department of Commerce and the U.S. State Department may be able to provide information on the competitive situation. Also, in almost every country, the U.S. embassy will employ a commercial attaché whose main function is to assist U.S. companies entering that foreign marketplace. Embassies of the foreign country being investigated may also be able to help marketers in their analysis. For example, in investigating the competition for farm implements in Spain, you could call or write the Spanish embassy in Washington, D.C. and ask for a list of manufacturers of farm implements in Spain.

Other sources of competitive information vary widely depending on the size of the country and the product. Many of the larger countries have Chambers of Commerce or other in-country organizations that may be able to assist potential investors. For example, if you were investigating the Japanese market for elec-

---

8. F. T. Haner with John S. Ewing, *Country Risk Assessment* (New York: Praeger, 1985), p. 171.
9. Igal Ayal and Zif Jehiel, "Competitive Market Choice Strategies in International Marketing," *Columbia Journal of World Business,* Fall 1978, pp. 72–81.

tronic measuring devices, the following groups could assist you in determining the competitive structure of the market in Japan:

- U.S. Chamber of Commerce in Japan
- Japan External Trade Organization (JETRO)
- American Electronics Association in Japan
- Japan Electronic Industry Development Association
- Electronic Industries Association of Japan
- Japan Electronic Measuring Instrument Manufacturers Association

The final and usually most expensive way to assess the market is to go to the country and interview potential customers and competitors to determine the size and strength of the competition.

Market Similarity

A recently published study provides strong evidence that market similarity can be used for country selection. A study of 954 product introductions by 57 U.S. firms found a significant correlation between market selection and market similarity.[10]

The concept of market similarity is simple. A firm tends to select countries based on their similarity to the home market. Therefore, when a company decides to enter foreign markets, it will enter the markets first that are most similar. For example, a U.S. firm would enter Canada, Australia, and the United Kingdom before entering less similar markets like Spain, South Korea, or India. Measures of similarity are (1) aggregate production and transportation, (2) personal consumption, (3) trade, and (4) health and education.[11]

As shown in Table 5.4, the selection of foreign markets tends to follow similarity very closely. Although language similarities were not measured in the study, it's worth noting that the top three markets all use the same language. Using market similarity as a selection variable is relatively simple. One could use the similarity ranking shown in Table 5.4, update it with the most recent economic data, or develop other criteria for determining similarity.

The premise behind the selection of similar markets is the desire of a company to minimize risk in the face of uncertainty. Entering a market that has the same language, a similar distribution system, and similar customers is less difficult than entering a market in which all these variables are different.

10. William H. Davidson, "Market Similarity and Market Selection: Implications for International Market Strategy," *Journal of Business Research*, vol. 11, December 1983, pp. 439–456.
11. Ibid.

TABLE 5.4 Similarity to the United States and Position in the Entry Sequence

	Similarity to the United States	Position in Investment Sequence
Canada	1	2
Australia	2	3
United Kingdom	3	1
West Germany	4	6
France	5	4
Belgium	6	10
Italy	7	9
Japan	8	5
Netherlands	9	12
Argentina	10	15
Mexico	11	8
Spain	12	13
India	13	16
Brazil	14	7
South Africa	15	14
Philippines	16	17
South Korea	17	18
Colombia	18	11

Source: Reprinted by permission of the publisher from "Market Similarity and Market Selection: Implications for International Market Strategy" by William H. Davidson, *Journal of Business Research*, vol. 11, no. 4, p. 446. Copyright 1983 by Elsevier Science Publishing Co., Inc.

TECHNIQUES OF MAKING MARKET SELECTION DECISIONS

The framework for making market selection decisions usually follows the systematic screening process shown in Figure 5.2. There are different techniques that can be used to accomplish the screening processes. These techniques vary from simple listings of selection criteria to complex combinations of different criteria into an index. These techniques will be discussed individually.

Listing of Selection Criteria

The simplest way to screen countries is to develop a set of criteria that are required as a minimum for a country to move through the stages of the screening

TABLE 5.5 Screening Process to Target Countries for Kidney Dialysis Equipment

FILTER 1: Macro-Level Research

Gross domestic product over $15 billion

Gross domestic product per capita over $1,500

FILTER 2: General Market Factors Relating to the Product

Less than 200 people per hospital bed

Less than 1,000 people per doctor

Government expenditures for the health care over $100 million

Government expenditures for health care per capita over $20

FILTER 3: Micro Level Factors Specific to the Product

Kidney-related deaths over 1,000

Patient use of dialysis equipment— Over 40 percent growth in treated population

FILTER 4: Final Screening of Target Markets

Number of competitors

Political stability

process. To illustrate the screening methodology, we have outlined the screening process that could be used by a manufacturer of kidney dialysis equipment (see Table 5.5).

The minimum cut-off number for each criterion would be established by management. As we move through the screening process, the criteria become more specific. The following text will give the rationale for each of the screening criteria and cut-off point.

Macro Level Gross National Product

Introduction of dialysis equipment in a new market requires a significant support function including salespeople, service people, replacement parts inventory, and an assured continuous supply of dialyzers, dialysate fluid, needles, tubing, and so on. Developing countries lack the technical infrastructure to support such high-level technology. Therefore, management might decide only to consider countries having a minimum size of U.S. $15 billion GNP, thus excluding many of the developing economies of the world from consideration. Also, dialysis requires substantial government support. A tradeoff then develops between acceptable expenditures for dialysis and acceptable kidney-related death rates. GDP per capita is an indicator of the level at which this tradeoff will occur. The lower the GDP per capita, the lower the expected government expenditure for dialysis equipment, given other pressing societal needs such as food, shelter, and so on. Therefore, the GDP per capita over U.S. $1,500 would be set as a minimum. These economic factors would limit the market to twenty-eight countries in the world, excluding North America. These are the following:

| All of Europe except Hungary,
    Iceland, Ireland, Luxembourg
U.S.S.R.
New Zealand | South Africa
Brazil
Venezuela
Australia | Iran
Argentina
Iraq |

General Market Factors Related to the Product—Medical Concentration

Hemodialysis is a sophisticated procedure that requires medical personnel with advanced training. In order for a country to support advanced medical equipment, it will require a high level of medical specialization. Higher levels of medical concentration will allow doctors the luxury of specialization in a field such as nephrology (the study of kidneys).

Management might determine that a population of less than 1,000 per doctor and a population of less than 200 per hospital bed indicate that medical personnel would be able to achieve the level of specialization needed to support a hemodialysis program. This second step of the screening process would eliminate only Iran, Iraq, Brazil, and Venezuela. As would be expected, the majority of countries with high GNP and GNP per capita have a high level of medical concentration.

Public health expenditures show the government's contribution to the medical care of its citizens—a factor of obvious importance in hemodialysis. Management might believe that countries that do not invest substantially in the health care of their population would generally tend not to be interested in making an even more substantial investment in a hemodialysis program. Thus, countries that did not have a minimum of U.S. $20 expenditure per capita or U.S. $100 million in total expenditures for health care would be eliminated from consideration. This would exclude Austria, Portugal, Yugoslavia, the U.S.S.R., and South Africa from the analysis. Thus, nineteen countries would have the ability to purchase and satisfactorily support dialysis equipment. Dialysis programs were already under way in most of these countries.

The third stage of the screening process will identify which countries will provide the best opportunities for the sale of kidney dialysis machines.

Micro-Level Factors Specific to the Product

Management might decide that there are two micro-level factors to consider: (1) the number of kidney-related deaths and (2) the growth rate of the treated patient population.

1. *Kidney-Related Deaths*. The number of deaths due to kidney failure is a good indicator of the number of people in each country who could have used dialysis equipment. The company only would be interested in countries with a minimum of 1,000 deaths per year due to kidney-related causes. A lower death rate indicates that the country has little need for dialysis equipment or

that the market is currently being well-served by competitive equipment. The Netherlands, Argentina, Norway, Switzerland, and Sweden would be eliminated from analysis on these grounds.

2. *Growth Rate of the Treated Patient Population.* Analysis of the growth rate of the kidney treatment population demonstrates a growth in potential demand. Newly opened markets, with the greatest growth potential are the best targets for a new supplier of dialysis equipment. These are the countries in which the treated patient population continues to grow at a minimum of 40 percent per year. This criterion would exclude all but the following: Italy, with 75.1 percent; Greece, with 63.4 percent; and Spain, with 60.1 percent. Competition in all three of these markets is substantially less than in the United States, Japan, and the remainder of Western Europe.

Final Screening of Target Markets

The screening process has identified three target countries. To select one of these countries, an analysis of the competition and political stability would be conducted. Discussions with the five major suppliers of dialysis equipment might indicate that Italy already has two local suppliers. Greece is being served by the four major European suppliers. Spain has a strong preference for U.S. equipment and is served only by one supplier. An evaluation of the political environment in each country would indicate that Greece has a stable government. Italy's government continues to be unstable as evidenced by recent changes in the ruling coalition. Spain is making a transition to a stable democracy.

After evaluating the data, management would most likely select Spain for the initial market entry. The final decision would be based on the following review of each market.

Greece would be discounted as a potential market for the following reasons:

1. There is significant competition from other companies.
2. The corporate income tax is higher than that of Spain.
3. Products are subject to a "turnover" tax.
4. There is a high inflation rate.

Similarly, Italy would be discounted for these reasons:

1. Continual government turnover and terrorist actions make the business environment unstable.
2. There is extensive foreign as well as local competition.
3. The projected growth for dialysis equipment is slower than it was in Spain.
4. Products are subject to a 14 percent value-added tax.
5. There is an extremely high inflation rate.

Spain would be chosen for the following reasons:

1. The political outlook is stable. It appears that the transition to democracy will continue.

2. There is aggressive government support for health care.
3. There is a very high growth rate predicted for kidney equipment (23%).
4. Competition at this time is minimal.
5. There is no value-added tax.
6. Government subsidies for home use of dialysis equipment would stimulate demand.
7. The inflation rate is lower than in Italy or Greece.
8. U.S. products and firms have a good reputation in the country.

Market Indices for Country Selection

Another technique for analyzing country selection criteria is to develop indices that combine statistical data and allow the marketer to look at a large number of variables quickly. For example, Business International has published market indicators for the past twenty-five years which allow managers to quickly compare country opportunities. There are three indices which Business International publishes: market size, market growth, and market intensity.

Market size is the measure of total potential based on the total population (double-weighted), urban population, private consumption expenditure, steel consumption, cement and electricity production, and ownership of telephones, cars and televisions. Market growth is an indicator of the rate of increase in the size of the market. The growth is determined based on an average of several indicators over five years: population, steel consumption, cement and electricity production, ownership of passenger cars, trucks, buses, televisions, and telephones. The market intensity index measures the richness of a market or the concentration of the purchasing power. The average world intensity is designated as 1.0 and each country is calculated in proportion to the average world intensity. The intensity is calculated for each market by averaging the per capita consumption of steel, ownership of telephones and televisions, and the production of cement and electricity levels, private consumption expenditure (double-weight), ownership of passenger cars (double-weight), and the proportion of urban population (double-weight). Figure 5.3 shows the largest twenty-two countries and their percentage of the world market. The size of the circle represents the relative market size.

Customized Weighted Multivariate Technique

Every company has particular needs and interests when selecting market opportunities. They relate to the product line, the corporate strategy and objectives, and the normal entry strategy. For example, a company that usually builds a new plant in each country would be more sensitive to the political risk variable than a company that exports. Larger companies normally will develop a screening and monitoring system that includes a large number of variables weighted specifically for that firm.

FIGURE 5.3 Business International Market Indices: Size, Growth, and Intensity of the Twenty-two Largest Markets

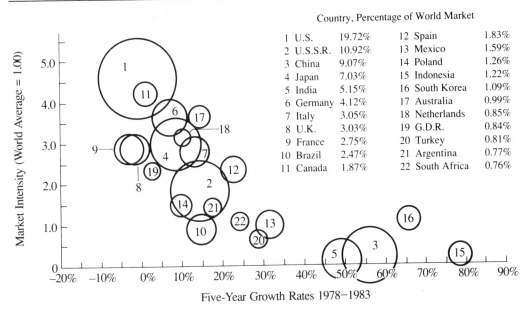

Country, Percentage of World Market

1	U.S.	19.72%	12	Spain	1.83%
2	U.S.S.R.	10.92%	13	Mexico	1.59%
3	China	9.07%	14	Poland	1.26%
4	Japan	7.03%	15	Indonesia	1.22%
5	India	5.15%	16	South Korea	1.09%
6	Germany	4.12%	17	Australia	0.99%
7	Italy	3.05%	18	Netherlands	0.85%
8	U.K.	3.03%	19	G.D.R.	0.84%
9	France	2.75%	20	Turkey	0.81%
10	Brazil	2.47%	21	Argentina	0.77%
11	Canada	1.87%	22	South Africa	0.76%

Source: "Indicators of Market Size for 117 Countries," *Business International*, 1986 edition. Reprinted by permission.

American Can had developed a system called PRISM which reduces two hundred variables collected from various data sources to an index of economic desirability and an index of risk payback. The information collected includes the macro indicators of investment climate, such as per capita income, market size, and inflation, as well as indicators of the quality of the infrastructure, such as capital availability, bureaucratic delays, and enforceability of contracts. Table 5.6 shows the factors that are included in the American Can system.[12]

Notice the difference in the importance of each factor in the scales. The variables are weighted based on their importance to management with particular emphasis given to items that would mean a short-term change in the investment climate. A number of factors are used in both the payback (risk) index and the desirability index. Political stability is most important in the payback index, weighted three times more important than the next item. In the desirability index, quality of the infrastructure and availability of financing were the two most important factors.

In all of the screening systems we have discussed, the industrialized West-

---

12. Susan P. Douglas and C. Samuel Craig, *International Marketing Research* (Englewood Cliffs, N.J.: Prentice-Hall, 1983), pp. 289–292.

TABLE 5.6 American Can Company's Relative Factor Weights for Major Indexes

Payback Index	Percentage	Desirability Index	Percentage
Political stability	26.0	Quality of infrastructure	13.6
Political freedom	7.0	Availability of financing	10.1
Civil liberties	7.0	Labor situation	9.1
Quality of infrastructure	6.7	Market growth	8.6
Nationalization probability	6.3	Currency convertibility	6.6
Desire for foreign investment	5.6	Per capita income	7.1
Bureaucratic delays	5.4	Market size	7.1
Market size and growth	4.4	Inflation	6.8
Inflation	3.6	Physical quality of life	6.0
Labor situation	3.5	Bureaucratic delays—Red tape	5.1
Currency stability	3.3	Enforceability of contracts	4.4
Balance of payments	3.3	Balance of payments	3.4
Likelihood of internal disorder	3.2	Currency history	3.2
Availability of financing	2.4	Corporate tax level	2.2
Restrictions on capital movements	2.3	Local management	2.0
Enforceability of contracts	1.8	Cultural interaction	1.7
Government intervention	1.5	Reserves imports ratio	1.3
Limits on foreign ownership	1.4	Government intervention	0.8
Cultural interaction	1.4		
Limits on expansion	1.1		
Local management and partners	1.0		
Physical quality of life	1.0		
Corporate tax level	0.8		

Source: Susan P. Douglas and C. Samuel Craig, *International Marketing Research* (Englewood Cliffs, N.J.: Prentice-Hall, 1983), pp. 289–292. Reprinted by permission of American National Can Company.

ern nations will rate the highest due to consumer buying power. To determine the desirability of a country relative to its economic development, American Can plots the scale against per capita consumer spending as shown in Figure 5.4. Countries whose desirability index is substantially above that of other countries at the same level of economic development are considered bright prospects.

Similar results can be achieved by use of cluster analysis, a multivariate statistical method. The analysis is particularly helpful in reducing a large amount of information to the most meaningful dimensions. An excellent example is the work performed by Sethi and Curry.[13] These authors collected 56 macroeco-

13. S. Prakash Sethi and David Curry, "Variable and Object Clustering of Cross-Cultural Data: Some Implications for Comparative Research and Policy Formulation," in *Multinational Business Operation*, ed. S. Prakash Sethi and Jagdish N. Sheth (Pacific Palisades, Calif.: Goodyear Publishing, 1973), Vol. III, pp. 31–61.

FIGURE 5.4 Economic Desirability Based on PRISM

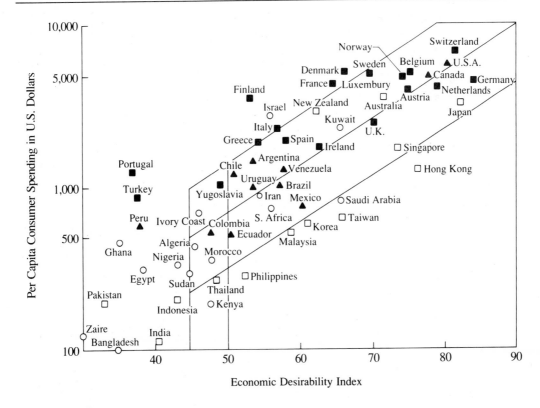

■ Europe

▲ Western Hemisphere

○ Mideast/Africa

□ Asia

Source: Susan P. Douglas and C. Samuel Craig, *International Marketing Research* (Englewood Cliffs, N.J.: Prentice-Hall, 1983), pp. 289–292. Reprinted by permission of American National Can Company.

nomic variables about 93 countries in order to group countries in subclusters according to their environmental similarities. First, the 56 variables were factored to reduce the data to the following group of six major variables:

1. Aggregate production and transportation
2. Affluence and lifestyles
3. Purchasing power of money
4. International trade
5. Economic advancement, higher education, and political heterogeneity
6. Nutrition and movie entertainment

Using the clustering technique, the scores of the 93 countries were simultaneously analyzed for similarities along these six dimensions. There were finally six country groupings and a small cluster of unique countries that did not easily fit any of the six clusters: Belgium, Spain, Japan, and the United States. In general, the results closely paralleled what an analyst would expect from grouping countries on a judgmental basis. This suggests that environmental statistics can in fact be used as a guide in grouping countries. Also, judgments about market potential can be made by inference or other methods as long as the country being analyzed is similar and data is available. This type of analysis of course becomes most meaningful if performed with specific product- or company-related variables, such as the success factors described earlier. The analyst would be able to work with more homogeneous country clusters where results are more transferable. Just as important is the general concept of the analysis and its approach. In many circumstances, managers do not have immediate access to a cluster analysis. Instead the method should be viewed as a conceptual guide that can be approximated by an individual analyst performing research without the help of any mechanical or electronic devices. In other words, managers charged with marketing products or services on a global scale should always mentally perform an analysis approaching the conceptual framework of the cluster analysis. As we will see in later chapters, there are numerous decisions that hinge on a correct assessment of a firm's market potential for its products in selected target countries.

GROUPING INTERNATIONAL MARKETS

There are many ways to group international markets. The chapters on the political, economic, and cultural environments demonstrated that the interaction between these variables cause each country to be unique, therefore making it difficult to group countries together. Despite these difficulties, it is often necessary to group countries together to be considered as a single market or as a group of similar markets. In this segment of the chapter, we will explore the rationale for grouping markets and the various ways that marketers can group countries together.

Rationale for Grouping Markets

The two principles that often drive the need for larger market groupings are critical mass and economies of scale. *Critical mass,* a term used in physics and military strategy, indicates that a minimum amount of effort is necessary before any impact will be achieved. *Economies of scale* is a term used in production situations; it means that greater levels of production result in lower costs per unit, which obviously increases profitability.

The costs of marketing products within a group of countries are lower for three reasons. First, the potential volume to be sold in many countries is too small to support a full marketing effort. Second, the geographic proximity makes it easy to travel from one country to another often in two hours or less. Third, the barriers to entry are often the same in countries with an economic grouping, for example, the European Community. Finally, in pursuing countries with markets similar to the home market, a company gains leverage with existing marketing programs.

Marketing Activities Influenced by Grouping

The major activities used to enter a new market are market research, product development or product modification, distribution, and promotion. Each of these activities can be influenced by economies of scale and critical mass. The following section of the chapter will show how each of these four activities relate to country groupings.[14]

Market Research

In the screening process, marketers use many secondary sources of market information, which are readily available. As stated previously, these secondary sources are acceptable for selecting target countries, but they are not sufficient to develop a marketing strategy to penetrate a specific market. Before entering a new market, the company will need to invest in the acquisition of knowledge about the specific aspects of marketing the product in each country. Normally the following questions must be answered:

1. Who makes the purchase decisions?
2. What decision criteria do consumers use to select the product?
3. How must the product be modified?
4. What are the channels of distribution?
5. What are the competitive price levels?

These and many other questions must be answered before the first product can be shipped. The cost of this knowledge will often be higher than domestic market research due to the distance to travel, cultural differences, and language differences. Given the sizable investment required to obtain this market knowledge, there are economies of scale if two or more countries can be included in the same market research study.

---

14. Vern Terpstra, "Critical Mass and International Marketing Strategy," *Journal of Academy of Marketing Sciences,* Summer 1983.

Product Development/Product Modification

The development of new products and the modifications of current products require a large investment. Given the cost, there are obvious economies of scale when these costs are spread over a number of markets. This is particularly true if the markets are similar, so that the same modified product can be sold in a number of markets. For example, Procter & Gamble's Head & Shoulders Dandruff Shampoo is manufactured in a single European plant; however, the company takes advantage of European Community regulations by selling the product throughout Europe with a "Euro-bottle" label in eight languages.[15]

Distribution

The distribution aspect of marketing is particularly important in serving international markets. In the case of exporting, the marketer is faced with all the mechanics of getting the product from the domestic market to the foreign market, which includes documentations, insurance, and financial arrangements. Also, the shipping rates will vary, depending on the size of the shipment. Less than carload size orders will be at a higher price per pound than full carloads. The mechanics and shipping aspects of exporting are influenced by economies of scale and critical mass. If one only plans to ship a small amount each month to a South American country, it may not be worth the effort. Without a critical mass of business, it is not worth the effort of learning the mechanics and processing the paperwork. Also, if you do not have sufficient volumes to ship, transportation costs will escalate.

The distribution systems within foreign markets also are influenced by the number of markets served. Many distributors and dealers in foreign markets handle numerous markets. For example Caps Gemini, a large software firm, has operations in every European country. Given the multicountry nature of many distributors, it is usually beneficial to enter a group of similar markets through the same distribution channels.

Promotion

A major task of the international marketer is promotion, which includes advertising and personal selling. Advertising is used as a communications device to give customers a message about a product via television, radio, or print media. In many parts of the world these three forms of communication cross country boundaries; for example, a message on West German television would be heard

---

15. "Unilever Aims to Bolster Lines in US" *The Wall Street Journal* June 19, 1987, p. 6.

in Switzerland. For this reason there may be economies of scale in grouping two or more markets together when entering a new area.

Selling is a very important part of the promotional process, which almost always requires an in-country sales force. Establishing and managing a sales force is a large fixed cost expense that lends itself to economies of scale. Spreading the cost of a sales office, rent, secretarial staff, sales support, sales managers, and sometimes the salesperson, over two or three countries can be very cost-effective.

GROWTH OF FORMAL MARKET GROUPS

Countries have used the concept of market groupings for centuries. The British Commonwealth preference system linked the markets of the United Kingdom, Canada, Australia, New Zealand, India, and former colonies in Africa, Asia, and the Middle East. The growth of market groups since World War II was encouraged by the success of the European Economic Community, now called the European Community (EC). A market group is created when two or more countries agree to reduce trade and tariff barriers between themselves, therefore creating a trade unit.

Successful trade units or market groups are based on favorable economic, political, or geographic factors. A country will agree to join a trade unit based on one or more of the above factors, *if* the expected benefits of becoming part of the trade unit exceed the disadvantages and loss of sovereignty caused by joining the group.

Economic Factors

The major benefit of every market group is usually economic. Member countries of the group experience reduced or eliminated tariffs and duties that stimulate trade between member countries. They also have common tariff barriers against firms from nonmember countries. Joining together with other countries gives members a greater economic security, reducing the impact of competition from member countries and increasing the group's strength against foreign competitors. For example, when the United States planned to impose tariffs on French cheese, Italian wine, Greek olives, and Danish ham, the twelve-nation European Economic Community was ready to retaliate with tariffs on U.S. wheat, rice, and corn.[16]

Consumers benefit from the reduced trade barriers through lower prices. Economies that are complementary rather than directly competitive tend to

---

16. "A Duty to Pay for Government Items," *Insight,* January 26, 1987, p. 46.

FIGURE 5.5 Forms of International Integration

	Removal of Internal Tariffs	Common External Tariffs	Free Flow of Capital and Labor	Harmonization of Economic Policy	Political Integration
Free Trade Area	■				
Customs Union	■	■			
Common Market	■	■	■		
Economic Union	■	■	■	■	
Political Union	■	■	■	■	■

Source: Ruel K. Kahler and Roland L. Kramer, *International Marketing*, 5th ed., p. 343. Reprinted by permission of South-Western Publishing Company.

make better members of a market group. Most of the problems within the European Community have revolved around agricultural products; member countries are threatened by products from other member countries, such as eggs, milk, and chicken.

Political Factors

In most countries, the political system and its ideology are dominant environmental forces. The political system usually reflects the aspirations of the nation. It's easy to see, then, why market groups are made up of countries with similar political aspirations. A major impetus for the original formation of the European Community was the need for a unified entity to protect against the political threat of the U.S.S.R.

Geographic Factors

Countries that share common borders tend to function better in a market group for the simple fact that it is easier to move goods back and forth across the truck and railroad systems. Also, countries that share boundaries have experienced each other's cultures and probably have had a history of trade.

Types of Market Groups

There are five different types of market groups: the free trade area, customs union, common market, economic union and political union. A country may enter an agreement with another country or group of countries using one of these five types of groups. The level of integration and cooperation between countries will depend on the type of group they form. Figure 5.5 shows which aspects of international integration are included in each type of agreement.

Major Market Groups

Market agreements that formed the major market groups are shown in Table 5.7. The next sections will describe these market groups and the agreements that brought them together. The sections are divided according to geographic area.

Europe

Europe has three major market groups: the European Community (EC), the European Free Trade Association (EFTA), and the Council for Mutual Economic Assistance (COMECON).

The European Community (EC), originally called the European Common Market when it was established in 1958, is a true common market. The EC has grown from the original six countries to twelve countries, and there is the possible addition of other countries in the future. The EC also has preferential trade agreements with the European Free Trade Association, and a number of Caribbean, Pacific, and African countries. The EC has increased its role over time through the establishment of the European Parliament, The Court of Justice, and the creation of the European Currency Unit. Because of this increased economic and monetary power, some argue that the EC has become an economic union. The EC has fostered a great deal of public and private cross-border cooperation, which resulted in Airbus and many other multicountry alliances. Some executives are beginning to refer to the European Marketplace as Europe Inc., reflecting its development into a unified entity.[17]

The European Free Trade Association (EFTA) was created in 1959 by countries that did not join the EC. The EFTA, consisting of six countries, operates as a free trade area and has a free trade agreement with the EC.

The Council for Mutual Economic Assistance (COMECON) was formed in 1949 as a political union of ten Eastern European communist countries. Because these ten countries are tightly controlled by the Soviet Union, the COMECON operates as a political group. Economic integration is difficult in centrally con-

---

17. Business International, ''Europe Inc—No Longer a Fantasy,'' *Executive Focus/Europe*, June 22, 1987, p. 1.

TABLE 5.7 Summary of Market Agreements

	Member Countries	Population (in millions)	GNP (billions of U.S. dollars)	GNP per Capita (U.S. dollars)	Exports to United States (millions of U.S. dollars)	Imports from United States (millions of U.S. dollars)
EUROPEAN AGREEMENTS						
European Community (EC) (Customs Union)	Belgium	9.8	83.2	8,450	3,398	3,170
	Luxembourg	.4	4.9	13,380		1,075
	Denmark	5.1	57.3	11,240	1,754	8,161
	France	54.9	526.6	9,550	8,432	10,982
	Germany	61.1	667.9	10,940	19,047	1,692
	Ireland	3.6	17.3	4,840	1,017	5,396
	Italy	56.9	371.1	6,520	9,697	12,767
	United Kingdom	56.5	474.2	8,390	15,122	742
	Portugal	10.2	20.1	1,970	525	3,265
	Spain	38.7	168.8	4,360	2,434	5,359
	the Netherlands	14.4	132.9	9,180	3,590	321
	Greece	9.9	35.2	3,550	371	
	Total	321.5	2,559.5	7,961	65,387	52,930
European Free Trade Association (EFTA) (Free Trade Area)	Austria	7.5	69.1	9,160	798	773
	Iceland	.2	2.6	10,720	220	62
	Norway	4.1	57.6	13,890	1,015	1,134
	Sweden	8.3	99.1	11,890	3,541	2,391
	Switzerland	6.4	105.2	16,380	2,860	1,799
	Finland	4.9	53.5	10,800	859	718
	Total	31.4	387.1	12,328	9,293	7,619
Council for Mutual Economic Assistance (COMECON) (Political Union)	Cuba	10.1	12.3*	1,218	—	1
	Bulgaria	8.9	214.5*	2,753	36	114
	Czechoslovakia	15.5	76.4*	4,929	78	69
	East Germany	16.7	60.8*	3,941	93	80

Hungary	10.7	15.9*	1,529	197	245
Mongolia	1.9	1.3*	684	NA	NA
Poland	37.3	61.1*	1,638	226	262
Romania	22.9	39.8*	1,738	865	208
U.S.S.R.	277.6	698.8*	2,517	403	2,665
Vietnam	61.6	NA	NA	—	22
Total	463.2	990.9	2,467	1,898	3,666
AFRICAN AGREEMENTS					
Afro-Malagasy Economic Union (Economic Union)					
Cameroon	10.1	8.3	810	308	68
Central African Republic	2.5	.7	270	1	1
Chad	5.0	.5*	110*	1	28
Congo-Brazzaville	1.8	1.9	1,020	587	13
Benin	4.0	1.1	270	1	74
Gabon	1.0	3.3	3,340	476	100
Ivory Coast	9.8*	6.0*	610*	507	77
Mali	7.5	1.1	140	6	33
Mauritania	1.6*	.7*	450*	1	29
Niger	6.4	1.3	200	9	14
Total	49.7	24.9	501	1,897	473
East Africa Customs Union (Customs Union)					
Ethiopia	42.2	4.6	110	42	223
Kenya	20.4	6.0	290	91	106
Sudan	21.9	7.4	330	8	270
Tanzania	22.2	5.8	270	5	36
Uganda	15.5	3.2	230	108	5
Zambia	6.6	2.6	400	54	60
Total	128.8	29.6	230	308	700
West African Economic Community (WAEC) (Common Market)					
Ivory Coast	9.8*	6.0*	610*	507	77
Mali	7.5	1.1	140	6	33
Mauritania	1.6*	.7*	450*	1	29
Niger	6.4	1.3	200	9	14

TABLE 5.7 continued

Member Countries	Population (in millions)	GNP (billions of U.S. dollars)	GNP per Capita (U.S. dollars)	Exports to United States (millions of U.S. dollars)	Imports from United States (millions of U.S. dollars)
Senegal	6.6	2.4	370	5	67
Burkina Faso	7.8	1.1	140	1	30
Total	39.7	12.6	317	529	250
Maghreb Economic Community (Common Market)					
Algeria	21.8	55.2	2,530	2,206	473
Libya	3.6	27.0	7,500	43	342
Morocco	21.9	13.4	610	30	210
Tunisia	7.1	8.7	1,220	112	148
Total	54.4	104.3	1,917	391	1,173
Casablanca Group (Free Trade Area)					
Egypt	47.1	32.2	680	77	2,555
Ghana	12.7	5.0	390	86	59
Guinea	6.0	2.0	320	127	56
Morocco	21.9	13.4	610	30	210
Total	87.7	52.6	600	320	2,880
Economic Community of West African States (ECOWAS) (Customs Union)					
Benin	4.0	1.1	270	1	74
Cape Verde	0.3	0.1	430	—	—
The Gambia	0.7	0.2	230	1	12
Ghana	12.7	5.0	390	86	59
Guinea	6.0	2.0	320	127	56
Guinea-Bissau	0.9	0.1	170	—	—
Ivory Coast	9.8*	6.0*	610*	507	77
Liberia	2.2	1.0	470	94	80
Mali	7.5	1.1	140	6	33
Mauritania	1.6*	0.7*	450*	1	29
Niger	6.4	1.3	200	9	14
Nigeria	99.7	75.9	760	2,826	743
Senegal	6.6	2.4	370	5	67

Country					
Sierra Leone	3.7	1.4	370	17	7
Togo	3.0	.8	250	11	17
Burkina Faso	7.8	1.1	140	1	30
Total	172.9	100.2	579	3,692	1,298

LATIN AMERICAN AGREEMENTS

Latin American Integration Association (LAIA) (Free Trade Area)

Country					
Argentina	30.5	65.1	2,130	1,073	740
Bolivia	6.3	3.9	470	92	132
Brazil	135.5	222.0	1,640	6,801	3,105
Chile	11.9	17.3	1,440	850	651
Colombia	28.4	37.6	1,320	15	83
Ecuador	9.4	10.8	1,160	1,637	575
Mexico	78.8	163.8	2,080	15,029	11,132
Paraguay	3.4	3.2	940	4	35
Peru	18.6	17.8	960	1,047	496
Uruguay	3.0	5.0	1,660	519	71
Venezuela	17.3	53.8	3,110	6,209	3,399
Total	343.1	600.3	1,750	33,276	20,419

Central American Common Market (Common Market)

Country					
Costa Rica	2.6	3.3	1,290	442	396
El Salvador	5.6	3.9	710	376	490
Guatemala	7.7	9.9	1,240	407	445
Honduras	4.4	3.2	730	393	339
Nicaragua	3.3	2.8	850	45	46
Total	23.6	23.1	980	1,663	1,716

Andean Common Market (ANCOM) (Common Market)

Country					
Bolivia	6.3	3.9	470	92	132
Colombia	28.4	37.6	1,320	15	83
Ecuador	9.4	10.8	1,160	1,637	575
Peru	18.6	17.8	960	1,047	496
Venezuela	17.3	53.8	3,110	6,209	3,399
Total	80.0	123.9	1,549	9,000	4,685

TABLE 5.7 continued

Member Countries	Population (in millions)	GNP (billions of U.S. dollars)	GNP per Capita (U.S. dollars)	Exports to United States (millions of U.S. dollars)	Imports from United States (millions of U.S. dollars)
Caribbean Community and Common Market (CARICOM) (Common Market)					
Antigua and Barbuda	0.08	0.16	2,030	—	—
Barbados	0.25	1.18	4,680	182	251
Belize	0.16	0.18	1,130	45	62
Dominica	0.08	0.09	1,160	—	—
Grenada	0.09	0.09	970	—	—
Guyana	0.81	0.46	570	49	48
Jamaica	2.23	2.09	940	192	484
Montserrat	0.01	NA	NA	—	—
Trinidad & Tobago	1.2	7.14	6,010	1,376	600
St. Kitts-Nevis-Anguilla	0.04	0.07	1,520	—	—
St. Lucia	0.16	0.13	1,210	—	—
St. Vincent	0.12	0.10	840	—	—
Total	5.23	11.69	2,235	1,844	1,445
ASIAN AGREEMENTS					
Arab Common Market (ACM) (Common Market)					
Egypt	47.1	32.2	680	77	2,555
Iraq	15.6	NA	NA	446	470
Jordan	3.5	4.0	1,560	10	404
Syria	10.5	17.1	1,630	1	89
Kuwait	1.7	24.7	14,270	180	606
Total	78.4	78.0	1,242	714	4,124
Regional Cooperation for Development (RDC) (Ad hoc arrangement)					
Iran	45.2	NA	NA	693	81
Pakistan	94.9	36.2	380	274	822
Turkey	49.4	56.1	1,130	589	1,424
Total	189.5	92.6	640	1,556	2,327

Association of South East Asian Nations (ASEAN) (Free Trade Area)					
Indonesia	162.2	86.6	530	4,168	1,341
Malaysia	15.6	31.9	2,050	1,970	1,881
Singapore	2.6	19.0	7,420	4,830	3,988
Philippines	54.7	32.6	600	1,658	1,344
Thailand	51.0	42.1	830	1,402	1,052
Total	286.1	212.5	743	14,028	9,606
Other Major Countries					
Australia	15.8	171.2	10,840	2,344	5,249
Canada	25.4	347.3	13,670	68,283	54,617
China	1041.1	318.9	310	2,336	5,199
Hong Kong	5.4	33.8	6,220	9,301	2,815
India	765.1	194.8	250	2,253	1,806
Israel	4.2	21.1	4,920	2,072	1,701
Japan	120.5	1,366	11,330	66,684	26,099
New Zealand	3.2	23.7	7,310	820	957
Saudi Arabia	11.5	102.1	8,860	1,843	4,922
South Africa	32.4	65.3	2,010	1,455	1,416
United States	238.8	3,915	16,400	—	—
Yugoslavia	23.1	47.9	2,070	463	778

* 1984 data. All other data is 1985 data.

Source: Adapted from *Direction of Trade and Statistics Yearbook* (Washington, D.C.: International Monetary Fund, 1986); and *The World Bank Atlas 1987.* Reprinted by permission.

trolled economies because a free market does not exist. In COMECON countries most trade is done through official foreign trade organizations that handle almost all importing and exporting.[18] Mr. Gorbachev plans to change the structure of COMECON countries. The planning commission in Czechoslovakia has decided to remove numerous businesses from the central planning process and reduce subsidies and production targets.[19]

Africa

The continent of Africa has seven major market agreements in force: Afro-Malagasy Economic Union, East Africa Customs Union, Maghreb Economic Community, Casablanca Group, Economic Community of West African States, West African Economic Community, and Customs and Economic Union of Central Africa. The success of the EC has prompted African countries to get together to form these groups. Unfortunately, however, the groups have had little success in promoting trade and economic progress because most African nations are small with limited economic infrastructure to produce goods.

Latin America

There are four major market agreements in Latin America: Andean Common Market, Central American Common Market, Caribbean Community and Common Market, and Latin American Integration Association. Latin America faces a number of problems which make it difficult to achieve significant economic integration and cooperation between countries. The low level of economic activity, political turmoil, and the extreme differences in economic development from country to country are stumbling blocks to the success of these market agreements.

Middle and Far East

There are three market agreements in the Middle and Far East: Arab Common Market, Regional Cooperation for Economic Development, Association of South East Asian Nations. The Arab Common Market was formed in 1964 by Egypt, Iraq, Kuwait, Jordan, and Syria. Progress has been achieved toward the development of free trade and eliminations of tariffs between member countries. Equalization of external tariff is expected in the future. The Regional Coopera-

---

18. "East-West Trade—A Breath of Competition," *Financial Times*, January 10, 1986, p. 15.
19. "Social Contract: Life Is Good in Czechoslovakia, But the Ration of Salami Implies Submission to State," *The Wall Street Journal*, July 13, 1987, p. 13.

tive for Economic Development (RCD) was formed in 1964 between Iran, Pakistan, and Turkey. The RCD was originally established to provide hydroelectric power and future economic development. The revolution in Iran has stopped any progress on reducing trade barriers for the RCD.

The Association of South East Asian Nations (ASEAN), formed in 1977, includes Indonesia, Malaysia, Singapore, the Philippines, and Thailand. All the ASEAN countries, except Singapore, have an abundance of labor and a developing economy. ASEAN is seeking closer economic integration and cooperation between the member countries. ASEAN is economically the fastest growing area of the world.

CONCLUSIONS

The world marketplace is large and complex. The international company needs to systematically evaluate the entire world market on a regular basis to be sure that company assets are directed toward the countries with the best opportunities. The basis for an evaluation of countries should be a comparative analysis of different countries. Certain countries may be unsuitable because of their unstable political situation, and other countries may have little potential because their population is small and/or the per capita income is low. The screening process gives the firm information about market size, competition, trade regulations, and distribution systems that will become the basis for the development of a market strategy.

The nature of the world marketplace has changed as a result of the development of major regional market groups. The economic integration of a number of countries offers great opportunities to MNCs. Many national markets that are too small individually become significant when combined with other countries. By locating production facilities in one country of a market group, the MNC has access to the other markets with little or no trade restrictions. The market groups also increase competition. Local producers who for years completely dominated their national markets due to tariff protection now face competition from many other member countries.

The development of these market groups can also have negative effects on international marketers. If a company is unable or unwilling to build a manufacturing plant in a certain market group, it may be unprofitable to export to that market. There are often more regulations within market groups, making it more complicated and expensive to move goods from one country to another. Also, the market group does not necessarily reduce the complexity of the consumer and cultural differences. For example, while West Germany and Spain are both in the EC, the marketing programs, products, and strategies for success in each market will probably be different.

The success of market groups formed after World War II, particularly the EC, indicates that market groups will continue to grow in the future. International marketers need to monitor the development of new groups and any changes in the structure of current groups, since changes within market groups will result in changes in market size and competition.

Questions for Discussion

1. Searching for the best international opportunity often requires an analysis of all the countries of the world. How will the initial screening differ from the final screening of possible countries to enter?
2. If you were evaluating opportunities for caviar, but found that no countries had data on caviar consumption, what other indicators of market size would you use to evaluate the size of each country's market?
3. Using Figure 5.2, how would you compare the potential for caviar consumption in Germany, India, and S. Korea?
4. In the sale of hair shampoo, what are the advantages of grouping countries together rather than marketing to each country individually?
5. What are the differences between a free trade area, a customs union, and a common market? If you were marketing to a grouping of countries but only had a manufacturing plant in one of the countries, which of the three types of agreements would you prefer?
6. What are the reasons for the growth in the establishment of country groupings?

For Further Reading

"A Common Market of Sorts." *The Economist* (February 19, 1983), p. 25.

Auguier, Antoine A. *French Industry's Reaction to the European Common Market*. New York: Garland, 1984.

Behrman, Jack N. "Transnational Corporations in the New Economic Order." *Journal of International Business Studies* (Spring/Summer, 1981), pp. 29–42.

Cracco, Etienne, and Guy Robert. "*The Uncommon Common Market.*" In Ronald C. Curhan, *1974 Combined Proceedings*. Chicago: American Marketing Association, 1975.

Dichter, Ernest. "The World Customer." *Harvard Business Review* (July – August 1962), pp. 119–121.

"Here Come the Multinationals of the Third World." *The Economist* (July 23, 1983), p. 55.

Lasserre, Philippe. "The New Industrializing Countries of Asia: Perspectives and Opportunities." *Long Range Planning* (June 1981), pp. 36–43.

Lipsey, R. "The Theory of Customs Unions: A General Survey." *Economic Journal*, 70 (1960), pp. 496–513.

Luqman, Mushtag, A. Quraeshi, and Linda Delene. "Marketing in Islamic Countries." *MSU Business Topics*, No. 3 (1980), pp. 17–26.

Sethi, S. Prakash. "Comparative Cluster Analysis for World Markets." *Journal of Marketing Research* (August 1971), pp. 348–354.

Sethi, S. Prakash, and Richard H. Holton, "Review of Comparative Analysis for International Marketing." *Journal of Marketing Records* (November 1969), pp. 502, 503.

Staude, Gavin. "Marketing to the African Segment of the South African Market." *European Journal of Marketing*, No. 6 (1978), pp. 400–412.

6.
INTERNATIONAL BUYERS

If all buyers around the world acted in the same way, then international market-ing would not be as challenging or difficult as it is. If all buyers were the same, international marketers could use the same marketing program to meet their needs. However, buyers are different—and there are major variations from country to country, often even within countries. Also, the international buyer can be a consumer, a business, or a government; and each differs from market to market as a result of distinct economic, cultural, social, and political struc-tures. The international marketing manager's job is further complicated by the interaction of these dimensions in an ever-changing context. Whereas the pre-vious sections analyzed the impact of the cultural, economic, and political struc-tures, this chapter synthesizes these systems and demonstrates how they relate to buyer behavior patterns.

It is important for the international marketer to identify the similarities and differences in international buyers. These similarities and differences will dictate the need for product modifications and adaptations. Also, the marketing strat-egy will need to be modified to be successful with different sets of consumers. Figure 6.1 summarizes the chapter and shows the various aspects of each type of buyer discussed.

THE PURCHASE DECISION PROCESS

All buyers go through a similar process to select a product or service for pur-chase, which is shown in Figure 6.2. While this may be a simplified view of a complicated process, it is easy to see that the process is heavily influenced by the economy, social class, family, and taste. While the process will be similar from

FIGURE 6.1 International Buyers

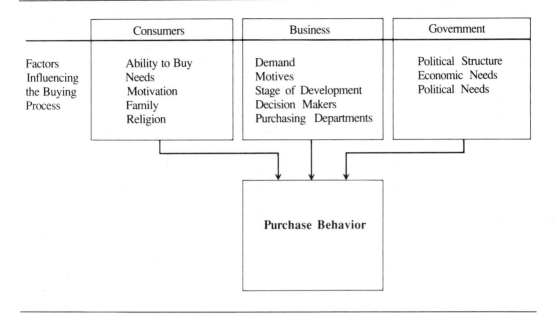

country to country, the final purchase decision will vary because of the differences in the social, economic, and cultural systems. International buyers differ
in what they buy, why they buy, who makes the purchase decision, how they
buy, when they buy, and where they buy. This chapter will provide a framework
to evaluate the buying process for consumers, businesses, and governments.

ANALYZING THE INTERNATIONAL BUYER

In every marketing situation it is important to understand potential buyers and
the process they use to select one product over another. Most of the elements of
a marketing program are designed to influence the buyer to choose one product
versus a competitor's product. Figure 6.3 summarizes a process that can be used
to analyze the buyer.

In the case of each type of buyer—consumer, business or government—the
marketer must be able to identify who the buyers are, what is the size of the
potential market and how do they make a purchase decision. For example, in
purchasing automobiles in Italy, who usually makes the decision, the husband or
wife? When a Japanese company purchases a computer system, what type of
people are involved? Is price more important than the reputation of the computer
manufacturer? When a young man in Germany decides to open a savings account, what information sources does he use to select a bank?

Having set a framework for understanding international buyers, we will
examine each type of buyer—consumers, business, and government.

FIGURE 6.2 Purchase Decision Process

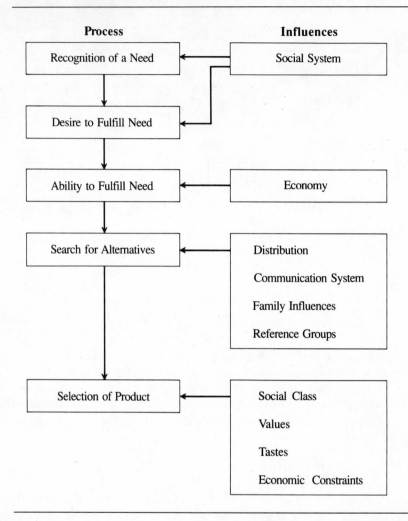

CONSUMERS

Consumers around the world have many similar needs. All people must eat, drink, and be sheltered from the elements. Once these basic needs are met, consumers will seek to improve their standard of living with a more comfortable environment, more leisure, and increased social status. While basic needs and the desire for an improved standard of living are universal throughout the world, people's ability to achieve these objectives is not universal. The economic, political, and social structure of countries affects the ability and method con-

FIGURE 6.3 International Buyer Analysis Process

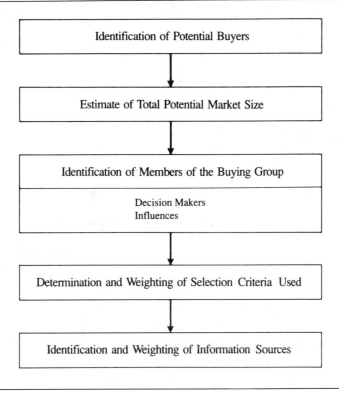

sumers use to fulfill needs. To understand a consumer market, one must examine four aspects of consumer behavior:

1. The ability of people to buy
2. Consumer needs
3. Buying motives
4. The buying process

Figure 6.4 illustrates consumer buying behavior in terms of these four aspects.

Ability to Buy

In order for a consumer to purchase a product, he or she must have the ability to buy. The medium of exchange in most societies is a country's form of currency. The ability to buy a product is affected by the amount of wealth a country possesses and the distribution of the wealth. As shown in Figure 6.4, a country accumulates wealth by the sale of goods to other countries (exports) and the sale of goods within the country. These inflows of money are offset by the outflows of money to pay for necessary imports.

TABLE 6.1 Selected Data on Consumer Buying Power (In U.S. Dollars)

	GNP (In billions)	GNP/Capita (In billions)
United States	3,663	11,338
United Kingdom	426	7,640
France	490	8,890
Japan	1,233	10,200
Sweden	96	11,510
Kuwait	22	13,620
Colombia	29	1,430
Egypt	40	466
Zaire	5	200
India	193	240
Kenya	4.5	280

Source: The World Fact Book, Directorate of Intelligence of the CIA, 1986. Reprinted by permission.

A very important indicator of total consumer potential is gross national product (GNP) because it indicates the value of production in a country, which is a crude indicator of market size. The GNP per capita shows the value of production per consumer, which is a crude indicator of potential per consumer. The per capita national income is better than the GNP, as a measure of gross consumer purchasing power, because it eliminates capital consumption and business taxes which are not part of personal income. As shown in Table 6.1, GNP and GNP per capita can vary significantly from country to country.

The total wealth in a country is an important indicator of market potential. With a GNP per capita of U.S. $10,200 in Japan and U.S. $11,510 in Sweden, it is expected the demand for automobiles would be greater than in Zaire or Egypt with GNP per capita below U.S. $300.

The accumulated income (GNP) is thus divided among the members of a society as shown in Figure 6.4. The distribution of wealth in a country is a function of the following:

National Economy

- How much of GNP goes to fund the government
- How much of GNP is used to pay for imports
- How the remaining wealth is distributed

Income Distribution

- The distribution of company ownership
- Labor rates versus management rates
- Social structure

FIGURE 6.4 Consumer Buying Behavior

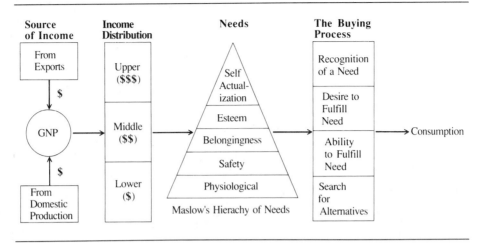

The government has a major influence on the distribution of wealth. A large government will take a large share of the wealth through taxes or ownership of industries. The government also sets policies and laws to regulate the distribution of wealth. For example, a graduated income tax with a 60 to 90 percent tax on high levels of income and no taxes on low levels of income will help to evenly distribute the income. The revenue that remains in the private sector will be distributed to workers, managers and owners of the industries. Low labor wages and unemployment will tend to increase the size of the lower income class. Concentration of business ownership in a few families will decrease the size of the upper class. The social structure of the country can also affect income distribution. For example, in Japan where an emphasis is placed on group versus individual needs, 95 percent of the population reports that they are in the middle class.

Table 6.2 compares the distribution of family income in the United States, the United Kingdom, and India. The United States has a large middle class whereas the greatest portion of India's population is in the lower income class. The rate of change in economic levels also affects the ability to buy. It is harder for an Indian to move from the lower to the middle class than it is for a U.S. citizen because of the caste structure which makes upward mobility very difficult. The amount a consumer has to spend is not solely accounted for by disposable income; it also reflects the availability and use of consumer financing. The United States is becoming a cashless society and many purchases are financed through private credit organizations, such as banks, finance companies, store financing, automobile credit, and so on. Cultural attitudes can affect the use of credit. The West German avoids credit, so only 15 to 20 percent of retail purchases are made using credit, while 80 percent of U.S. purchases are paid for with credit cards.[1] Governments also subsidize spending through social pro-

---

1. "Frugal Foreigners," *The Wall Street Journal,* December 17, 1986, pp. 1, 14.

TABLE 6.2 Percent Distribution of Family Income

Household Income*	United States	United Kingdom	India
Under $5,000	7.9	18.2	99.0
$5,000 to $9,999	13.2	35.1	1.0
$10,000 to $14,999	12.2	29.8	—
$15,000 to $19,999	11.4	7.9	—
$20,000 to $24,999	10.4	5.1	—
$25,000 to $34,999	16.9	2.9	—
$35,000 to $49,999	15.3	0.8	—
$50,000 and over	12.8	0.2	—

* All figures show gross income.

Source: Statistical Abstract of the United States, 1986 (106th) Edition (Washington, D.C.: U.S. Bureau of the Census, 1985), p. 445; *Annual Abstract of Statistics, 1987 Edition* (London: Board of Inland Revenue, 1987), p. 258; *Household Income and Its Disposition* (New Delhi: National Council of Applied Economic Research, 1980), p. 243.

grams such as unemployment income and national health care. Long-term demographics can also affect income distribution. For example, in 1980 11.2 percent of the U.S. population was over 65 years old versus 15.5 percent in West Germany and 9.0 percent in Japan. The number of people over 65 will change radically over the next 30 years. In 2010, 13.8 percent of the U.S. population will be over 65 compared to 20.7 percent in West Germany and 18.2 percent in Japan.[2]

Consumer Needs

Money is spent to fulfill basic human needs. An appropriate framework in determining needs was developed by Abraham Maslow. Maslow's Hierarchy of Needs model explains that humans will tend to satisfy lower-level needs, such as the physiological need for food, clothing, and shelter, before attempting to satisfy higher-level needs such as safety, belongingness, or esteem (see Figure 6.4). Figure 6.5 illustrates Maslow's theory in terms of the consumption patterns within different countries. The figure shows that the structure of consumption for each country varies depending on the income per capita. A developing country with a small GNP, such as Kenya, spends over 80 percent on food whereas a developed country, such as the United States, spends only 20 percent.

---

2. Japan Economic Institute, "Projected Demographic Changes in the Major Industrial Countries," *The Japan Economic Report,* March 27, 1987, p. 5.

FIGURE 6.5 Structure of Consumption of Selected Countries

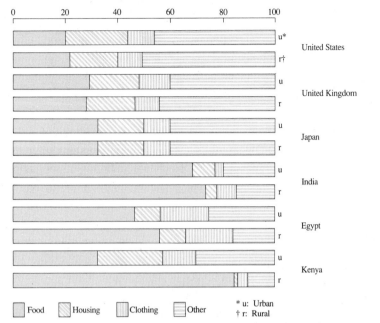

Source: *Household Income and Expenditure Statistics: 1968–1976,* No. 3 (Geneva: International Labor Organization, 1979). Reprinted by permission.

Consumers will be affected by the economic strength of the country and the distribution of income to potential consumers. As shown in Figure 6.5, as consumers have less funds available for purchases, they will spend more (as a percentage of total spending) on lower-level needs such as food and shelter.

While it is possible to generalize about the order of consumer purchases based on Maslow's hierarchy of needs, the patterns may vary by country. For example, a study of the purchase behavior in the United Kingdom revealed that stoves are purchased first, vacuum cleaners second, and washing machines third. What is most interesting is that 76 percent of the households did not buy a refrigerator until having purchased a stove, vacuum, and washing machine.[3]

Buyer Motivation

Although the ability to buy is influenced by a variety of economic elements, it is easier to identify and qualify than the motivation to buy. As mentioned earlier,

---

3. Graham F. Pyatt, *Priority Patterns and the Demand for Household Durable Goods* (New York: Cambridge University Press, 1964).

FIGURE 6.6 Environmental Influences on Consumer Behavior

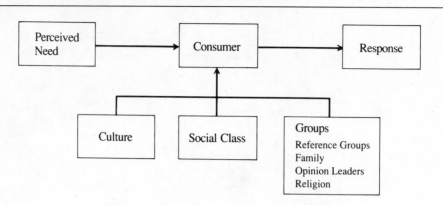

all consumers have some similarities as members of the human race. Unfortunately, however, buyer behavior is not uniform among all humans. Buyer behavior is learned, primarily from the culture. As a marketer moves from culture to culture (within and between countries), buyer behavior will differ.

Consumer behavior is a complex process in any culture. Figure 6.6 shows the environmental influences that affect a consumer during the buying process. All of these factors will vary from country to country.

As we discussed in Chapter 3, culture refers to widely shared norms or patterns of behavior within a large group of people.[4] These norms can directly affect product usage. For example, mothers in Brazil feel that only they can properly prepare foods for their babies, and they are therefore reluctant to buy processed foods. This cultural norm in Brazil caused difficulty for Gerber Products despite the fact that their products were selling well in other Latin American countries.[5] Social class is a grouping of consumers based on income, education, and occupation. Consumers in the same social class tend to have similar purchase patterns. The perceived class structure and the distribution of income will affect purchase behavior.

Consumers belong to a variety of different groups which also influence purchase behavior. For example, in Moslem countries it is difficult to sell insurance because religious leaders claim it is a form of usury and gambling, both of which are explicitly prohibited in the *Koran*.[6]

---

4. Henry Assael, *Consumer Behavior and Marketing Action,* 3rd ed. (Boston: Kent, 1987), p. 15.
5. Ann Helmings, "Culture Shocks," *Advertising Age,* May 17, 1982, p. M-9.
6. D. E. Allen, "Anthropological Insights into Consumer Behavior," *European Journal of Marketing,* vol. 5, Summer 1971, p. 54.

Family Structure

The structure of the family and the roles assigned to each member play an important part in determining who makes a decision and who does the influencing. Table 6.3 shows the results of a study that examined and compared decision-making roles in families from the United States and Venezuela. Nine products/services were picked and each family within the survey was asked to identify which member made the decision with respect to purchasing the product. The overriding contrast between the two samples was the role of the husband. More joint decisions regarding major purchases were made in the United States than in Venezuela. In all purchase decisions, except groceries and savings, the Venezuelan husband made more decisions than the U.S. husband. Families in the United States make more joint decisions than Venezuelan families.

International marketers must be aware that variations in family purchasing roles may exist in foreign markets due to the social and cultural differences. Marketing strategy may change based on the respective role of family members. For example, a U.S. manufacturer of appliances or furniture may find it advisable to incorporate the husband into their Venezuelan marketing strategy to a larger extent than in the United States.

Family structure, particularly the number of two-parent families (versus single-parent families), will also affect the level of household income. Also, families with two working parents will have a higher level of pooled income than single-parent or one-working-parent families. The pooling of incomes will positively influence the demand for consumer durables and luxury goods.

Religion

As we noted in Chapter 3, religion affects behavior patterns by establishing moral codes and taboos. What, when, and how consumers buy is a function of their religion. Traditional Catholics don't eat meat on Fridays during Lent and Orthodox Jews are forbidden to eat pork. The Christian sabbath is on Sunday, Jewish sabbath on Saturday, and the Moslem sabbath on Friday. Religion influences the attitudes and beliefs of people with regard to interests, work, leisure, family size, family relationships, and so on. Many of these influences affect the type of products people purchase, why they buy them, even the newspapers they read. For example, in some countries if too much attention is given to the body in advertisements, the product may be rejected as immoral.

Educational Systems

Formal education involves public or private schools or institutions where learning takes place in a structured environment. The literacy rate is the standard

TABLE 6.3 Mean Number of Purchase Decisions by Product Type

Product	United States	Venezuela
Groceries		
Husband	.23	.23
Joint	.60	.69
Wife	3.20	3.08
Furniture		
Husband	.41	1.16
Joint	3.41	2.71
Wife	2.23	2.16
Major Appliances		
Husband	.98	1.97
Joint	3.21	2.10
Wife	.85	.93
Life Insurance		
Husband	2.65	3.38
Joint	1.23	.55
Wife	.15	.05
Automobiles		
Husband	2.59	4.16
Joint	3.06	1.42
Wife	.41	.40
Vacation		
Husband	1.00	1.51
Joint	3.68	3.18
Wife	.40	.41
Savings		
Husband	1.00	1.07
Joint	1.61	1.60
Wife	.44	.34
Housing		
Husband	.34	.87
Joint	2.47	1.82
Wife	.34	.39
Doctor		
Husband	.03	.10
Joint	.35	.42
Wife	.62	.49

Source: Robert T. Green and Isabella Cunningham, "Family Purchasing Roles in Two Countries, *Journal of International Business Studies,* Spring/Summer 1980, p. 95. Reprinted by permission.

measurement used to assess the extent and success of educational systems, and it normally varies directly with economic development.

In Europe and Japan the literacy rate exceeds 90 percent (see Table 3.3), whereas in many developing countries it runs as low as 15 percent. Low levels of literacy affect marketers in two ways: first, it reduces the market for products which require reading, such as books and magazines; second, it reduces the effectiveness of advertising.

Education includes the process of transmitting skills, ideas, attitudes, and knowledge. The educational process in effect transmits the existing culture and traditions to the next generation. Often, the goals of an educational system will include broader political goals, such as India's programs to improve agriculture and reduce the birth rate.

The international marketer is impacted by the educational system of the markets he or she serves. The educational system will determine the nature of the consumer market and the kinds of marketing personnel available. Some of the major implications of dealing with poorer educational systems follow:

1. If consumers are largely illiterate, advertising programs and package labels will need to be adapted.
2. If girls and women are largely excluded from formal education, marketing programs will differ greatly from those aimed at U.S. females.
3. Conducting marketing research can be difficult, both in communicating with consumers and in getting qualified researchers.
4. Products that are complex or need written instructions may need to be modified to meet the educational attainments of members in the channel.
5. Relations with, and cooperation from, the distribution channel will depend partly on the educational and skill levels of the market.
6. The nature and quality of marketing support services, such as advertising agencies, will depend on how well the educational system prepares people for such occupations.[7]

Consumption Patterns

It is difficult to generalize about consumer behavior in each country of the world and for every product category, but consumption patterns vary considerably. The differences in consumption patterns are caused by consumers' ability to buy and their motivation to buy. Table 6.4 shows consumption patterns for a number of food items in selected countries.

The differences from country to country are tremendous. In Korea, India, and Nigeria the meat consumption per day is 20 grams or less, whereas it is over 200 grams in the United States, Canada, Germany, France, and Australia. These

---

7. Vern, Terpstra, *International Marketing,* 4th ed. (Chicago: Dryden Press, 1987), p. 96.

TABLE 6.4 Consumption Patterns in Selected Countries

	Milk (kilograms/ capita)	Coffee (kilograms/ capita)	Meat Consumption (grams/day)	Sugar (kilograms/ capita)
United States	122.5	4.4	304	44.7
Canada	111.2	4.2	272	46.8
United Kingdom	145.1	2.4	197	NA
Germany	108.1	7.4	220	NA
France	88.8	5.5	241	NA
Italy	80.3	4.4	166	NA
Netherlands	97.1	9.7	185	NA
Spain	103.2	3.4	150	28.7
Yugoslavia	95.9	2.3	102	31.9
Sweden	160.2	11.6	151	40.9
Japan	36.4	2.2	64	25.0
Korea	16.0	NA	19	12.2
Australia	105.4	2.2	285	55.1
India	19.0	NA	4	8.2
Mexico	94.2	NA	61	43.9
Brazil	79.2	NA	85	45.4
Venezuela	88.3	NA	115	51.9
Israel	190.7	NA	34	24.2
Nigeria	3.5	NA	20	8.7
Kenya	69.1	NA	43	19.9
South Africa	82.3	NA	105	37.7

NA = Not Available.

Source: Data on milk reprinted by permission of Euromonitor Publications, Ltd., from *European Marketing Data Statistics 1987/1988* and *International Marketing Data Statistics* 1987/1988; other columns reprinted by permission of the International Coffee Organization, International Sugar Organization, and the Food & Agriculture Organization Commission, from their 1985 Annual Reports.

statistics are critical to an exporter of beef. Consider the difference in market size caused by consumers who use over 50 kilograms of sugar each year (Australia, Venezuela) versus the consumers who use less than 10 kilograms (India, Nigeria).

The consumption patterns for wine vary tremendously from country to country. For example, in France the average consumption is 90 litres per person versus 8 litres in the United States or Britain as shown in Figure 6.7.

The high consumption of wine in Europe versus the United States is offset by the high consumption of soft drinks. The average American drinks five times

FIGURE 6.7 Wine Consumption for Selected Countries

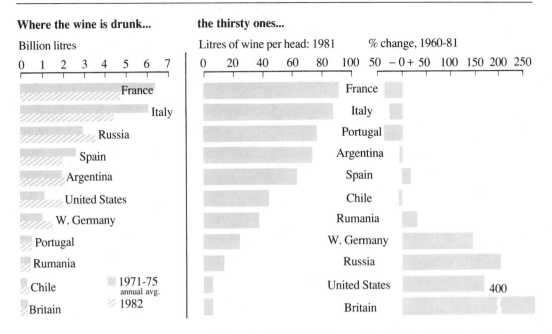

Source: The Economist, December 24, 1983, p. 6. © 1983 The Economist, distributed by Special Features. Reprinted by permission.

as many soft drinks as a Frenchman, three times as many as an Italian, and two-and-one-half times as many as a German.[8]

Different customs and attitudes in foreign countries will affect product usage rates. See Table 6.5 for the results of a survey in a number of different countries regarding housecleaning, children, and deodorant.

These differences in attitudes will influence the marketing strategy. An advertising campaign that depicts a floor cleaner as a timesaving device in the United States may need to be changed or modified for Italian homemakers, showing how the cleaner gives the cleanest floor and receives the highest praise. Advertising messages that deodorant is a social requirement are accepted in the United States but may be overlooked in Australia. The difference in attitudes

8. *Beverage Industry Annual Manual* (Cleveland: Harcourt, Brace, Jovanovich Publications, 1987), p. 16.

TABLE 6.5 Cross-cultural Attitudes Toward Housecleaning, Children, and Deodorants

"A house should be dusted and polished three times a week."	"My children are the most important thing in my life."	"Everyone should use a deodorant."
Agreement Rate	Agreement Rate	Agreement Rate
86% Italy	86% Germany	89% U.S.A.
59% U.K.	84% Italy/French Canada	81% French Canada
55% France	74% Denmark	77% English Canada
53% Spain	73% France	71% U.K.
45% Germany	71% U.S.A.	69% Italy
33% Australia	67% Spain	59% France
25% U.S.A.	57% U.K.	53% Australia
	56% English Canada	
	53% South Africa	
	48% Australia	

Source: Joseph T. Plummer, "Consumer Focus in Cross-National Research," *Journal of Advertising,* vol. 6, Spring 1977, pp. 10–11. Reprinted by permission.

also affect consumption. In France and Great Britain the annual consumption of deodorants is about $3.75 per person versus $7.85 in the United States.[9]

The patterns of consumption also vary with services. For example, about 15 percent of the world's countries have 95 percent of the telephones. As shown in Figure 6.8, the United States, Europe and Japan represent only 27 percent of the world's population but have 87 percent of the 508 million telephones. The United Nations has established a fund to speed up the adoption of telephones around the world. Studies by the Brookings Institute, the University of Texas, Stanford University, the University of Cairo, and Massachusetts Institute of Technology indicate that telephones have significant economic benefits to the consumer in excess of the cost and contribute to a rise in per capita income. For example, The World Bank reported that when Sri Lankan farmers received telephones, prices of produce increased from 55 percent of Colombo prices to 85 percent.[10]

BUSINESS MARKETS

Business buyers around the world are much more predictable than consumers because they are more influenced by the economic considerations of cost and

9. "Unilever Aims to Bolster Lives in U.S.," *The Wall Street Journal,* June 19, 1987, p. 6.
10. "Third World Telephones," *The Economist,* December 17, 1983, pp. 82–85.

FIGURE 6.8 World Telephone Market

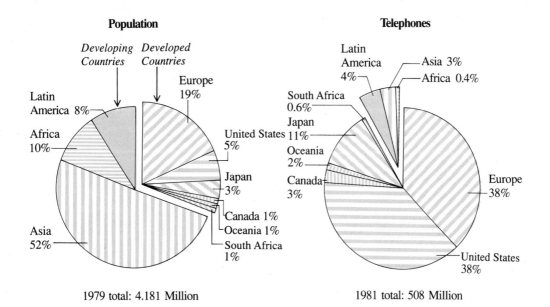

Population

Developing Countries
Developed Countries
Europe 19%
Latin America 8%
Africa 10%
United States 5%
Japan 3%
Asia 52%
Canada 1%
Oceania 1%
South Africa 1%

1979 total: 4.181 Million

Telephones

Latin America 4%
Asia 3%
Africa 0.4%
South Africa 0.6%
Japan 11%
Oceania 2%
Canada 3%
Europe 38%
United States 38%

1981 total: 508 Million

Source: The Economist, December 17, 1983, page 82. © 1983 The Economist, distributed by Special Features. Reprinted by permission.

less by social or cultural factors. For example, a purchasing agent in Japan who is purchasing specialty steel for his company will attempt to get the best possible product at the lowest cost, which is similar to how a purchasing agent in the United States or West Germany would act. The criteria that business buyers use will be much the same around the world. However, the buying process used by business buyers and the negotiation process will be influenced by local culture and will vary from country to country. The terms *business buyer* and *industrial buyer* are used interchangeably in this chapter, although business buyers normally include all types of businesses, whereas industrial buyers are limited to manufacturing businesses.

Characteristics of Industrial Markets

Buying Motives

Industrial buying is less affected by such cultural factors as social roles, religion, and language than is consumer buying. The purchasing agent, regardless of his or her background, will be primarily influenced by the use of the product, its cost, and delivery.

TABLE 6.6 Average Labor Cost in Manufacturing for Selected Countries

	Year	Rate in National Currency[a]	Rate/Month in U.S. Dollars[b]
United States	1985	($) 12.97/hr.[c]	2075.
United Kingdom	1984	(£) 5.10/hr.	1085.
Germany, Fed. Rep.	1984	(M.) 31.72/hr.	1783.
France	1984	(fr.) 84.35/hr.	1544.
Italy	1981	(l.) 9210/hr.	1296.
Netherlands	1984	(gld.) 34.41/hr.	1716.
Sweden	1985	(k.) 84.20/hr.[c]	1566.
Japan	1984	(Y) 355,780/mo.	1498.
Korea, Rep. of	1985	(won) 384,160/mo.	442.
Philippines	1983	(p.) 15,868/yr.[c]	119.
Mexico	1985	(p.) 1476,400/yr.[c]	479.
Venezuela	1983	(b.) 58,919/yr.	1143.
Swaziland	1982	(lil.) 4990/yr.[c]	384.
Tunisia	1980	(d.) 1440/yr.[c]	49.

Note: Due to the different years and exchange rate effects, this data is not comparable from country to country.

Source: (a) 1986 Year Book of Labour Statistics, 46th Issue, (Geneva, Switzerland: International Labour Office), Table 22 pp. 793–795. © 1987 International Labour Organization, Geneva, Switzerland; (b) Average exchange rates for the appropriate year were from International Financial Statistics Yearbook 1986, (Washington, D.C.: International Monetary Fund), pp. 176–731. Reprinted by permission; (c) These countries report compensation of employees rather than labor cost, which is reported by the other countries.

Industrial products, such as raw materials or machinery, are sold to businesses to be used in a manufacturing process to produce other goods. Given that the objective of the manufacturer is to maximize profit, the critical buying criterion will focus on the performance of the product purchased versus its cost. This is called the *cost-performance criterion,* and it is used along with other buying criteria such as service, dependability, knowledge of the selling company, and so on.

Because the cost-performance criterion is critical, the economic situation in the purchasing country will affect the decision process. Cost performance is a function of the local cost of labor and the scale of operation. As can be seen in Table 6.6, which lists manufacturing labor cost averages in selected countries, wage levels vary from country to country. Thus, selling an industrial robot that replaces three workers in the manufacturing of a certain product would be more easily justified in the United States or Japan, where monthly wages average $1,000 for each worker, than it would be in India or Zaire where labor cost is less than $30 for each worker each month.

Labor costs play a key role in the level and type of manufacturing. Countries with a surplus of labor normally have lower labor costs, as supply exceeds demand. These lower pay rates result in a certain type of manufacturing which is labor intensive. Therefore, they will be less apt to purchase sophisticated automatic machinery because the same job can get done with the cheaper labor. China's main objective, for example, is to import technology that optimizes their vast population. Companies wishing to export to labor intensive countries must be aware that labor-saving measures might not be appreciated or readily applied. On the other hand, highly developed countries with a high labor rate are prime targets for automated manufacturing equipment. The United States has relatively high labor rate or $13.52/hour; and there are a number of other countries with high rates, such as West Germany ($16.74), Switzerland ($16.63), Denmark ($14.04), France ($12.40), and Japan ($11.48).[11] These countries have begun to see an emergence of service industries, which require human labor instead of machines. Labor in these areas is expensive, for a great deal of expertise is needed. Thus, a country normally moves from labor-intensive industry to capital-intensive and then to technical-intensive industry.

Stage of Economic Development

The nature of the industrial structure varies from country to country. The size and type of industry in a country depends on the level of economic development. While it is dangerous to generalize about countries, the level of economic development is a good indicator of the types of industrial products a country will need and the sophistication of its industrial infrastructure.

Each country basically goes through five stages of economic development and each stage relates to the extent of production capability (see Table 6.7). The stage of economic development is a function of the cost of labor, technical capability of the buyers, scale of operations, interest rates, and level of product sophistication.

It is difficult to use the stages of economic development as a device to segment markets because many countries are in a state of change and can overlap two stages at a time. Also the level of development may not be a good indicator for all product lines. For example, a Third-World country in the first stage may purchase advanced technology like telecommunication satellites, computer systems, or nuclear power to speed up their industrialization.[12]

The international marketer must adjust the product offerings to the stage of economic development in potential markets. For example, if a company manufactures buses for sale to countries in all stages of economic development, the product line may vary from high quality luxury buses for countries in advanced

---

11. Business International, "Germany Leads European Labor Cost League," *Business Europe, Fortnightly Managers Monitor,* June 15, 1987, p. 2.

12. Norman W. McGuiness and Blair Little, "The Influence of Product Characteristics on the Export Performance of New Industrial Products," *Journal of Marketing,* Spring 1981, pp. 110–122.

TABLE 6.7 Stages of Economic Development

STAGE 1. THE TRADITIONAL SOCIETY

One with limited production functions, primarily agricultural. The level of productivity in manufacture as in agriculture is limited by the inaccessibility of modern science, its applications, and its frame of mind.

STAGE 2. THE PRECONDITIONS FOR TAKE-OFF

Societies in transition toward modernization. Some investment in infrastructure occurs and there is a widening scope of internal and external commerce. Some modern manufacturing appears but the society is still mainly characterized by the old social structure and values.

STAGE 3. THE TAKE-OFF

Resistance to change lessens and the forces for economic growth come to dominate the society. Industries expand rapidly, requiring new investment. New techniques spread in agriculture as well as industry.

STAGE 4. THE DRIVE TO MATURITY

Continuing growth extends modern technology over the whole range of economic activity. The make-up of the economy changes unceasingly as technique improves, new industries grow and older ones level off. The economy extends its range into more complex technologies.

STAGE 5. THE AGE OF HIGH MASS CONSUMPTION

The leading sectors shift toward durable consumers' goods and services. The structure of the working force changes with more employed in offices or in skilled factory jobs. The extension of modern technology as an objective is joined with a desire to improve social welfare and security.

Source: Walt W. Rostow, *The Stages of Economic Growth,* 2nd ed. Copyright © 1971 by Cambridge University Press. Reprinted by permission.

stages of development to small, simple buses that offer basic transportation at a minimal price for countries in the early stages of development.

The Buying Process

Industrial buying is a complex process that includes a number of different people. The people involved in the buying process are members of the *buying center.*[13] The size of the buying center can vary from one person to fifty people depending on the complexity of the buying company, the importance of the decision, and the value of the purchase. It is not unusual to encounter groups of

---

13. Frederick E. Webster, Jr. and Yorman Wind, *Organizational Buying Behavior* (Englewood Cliffs, N.J.: Prentice-Hall, 1972), p. 6.

fifteen to twenty individuals involved in the purchase process.[14] One of the major tasks of a marketer is to determine who is involved in the purchase process so that communications through the mail, media, or salesperson can be directed at the appropriate people in the company. The people involved in the buying process can be described by the role they play. The most common roles follow:

> *Initiators.* Persons who first recognize or anticipate a problem that may be solved by buying a good or service.
>
> *Gatekeepers.* Persons who control information or access, or both, to decision makers.
>
> *Influencers.* Persons who have some positive or negative input into what is to be bought.
>
> *Deciders.* Persons who actually say yes or no to a contemplated purchase.
>
> *Purchasers.* Persons who process the paperwork and place the order.
>
> *Users.* Persons who ultimately will use the product or service being bought.[15]

The different members of the buying center can be found in companies throughout the world. Although the objective of purchasing the best value at the lowest cost may be universal, the composition of the buying center and the interactions between members of the buying center will vary by country.

Decision Making by Industrial Buyers

In the international marketplace it is often difficult to identify the members of the buying center and their role in the buying process. Often the success of a company will be dependent on the salesperson's ability to identify the key individuals, determine their role, and communicate the appropriate information to them. Less-developed countries may not have well-developed staff functions, such as engineering or purchasing, so purchase decisions may be made by a line manager, such as a production manager or plant manager. In Japan, where companies are organized with a great deal of attention given to age and seniority, the decision maker may appear to be a senior-level, older person, but the real decision may be made by a younger, lower-level manager. These differences in the decision process from country to country are very important to the international marketer.

Around the world, purchasing is often a separate function. Efficient purchasing consists of the efficient use of production resources. Developing countries

---

14. G. Van Der Most, "Purchasing Process: Researching Influences Is Basic to Marketing Planning," *Industrial Marketing,* October 1976, p. 120.

15. Thomas V. Bonoma, "Major Sales: Who Really Does the Buying?" *Harvard Business Review,* vol. 60, May–June 1982, p. 113.

and industrialized countries with a small domestic market must purchase goods and services from other countries. The efficient use of these foreign sources of supply is critical for profitability.[16] The level of purchasing expertise and efficiency varies from country to country, and it will change over time. Two elements that influence the purchasing process are the organizational factors related to purchasing and the decision-making process.

A good example of the way in which organizational factors influence the purchasing process can be found by reviewing the buying decisions in Indian organizations. In a study conducted in 1960, four Indian firms were analyzed in detail to determine how organizational factors influenced purchasing patterns. The study revealed the following:

- A lack of professionalism on the part of persons involved in the purchasing process
- A lack of centralization and integration of functions as a profit center
- Secondary status of the people involved in the purchasing process
- Lack of involvement of the purchasing personnel in important inventory management functions[17]

A recent study disclosed changes in the above buying patterns. The buying systems are now more streamlined, the purchasers have more responsibility and authority, advanced planning is being implemented, faster decision making and continuous feedback from suppliers is taking place. Most importantly, what this study illustrated was that the purchasing trends in India mirror the United States patterns of the 1950s. This thirty-year lag enables marketing managers to better understand present processes and anticipate future trends.[18]

The international marketer must also be aware that the process of decision making varies in different countries. It is important to know who the decision maker will be, what the relationship is between the decision maker and the other members of management, and what process is used to make decisions. Table 6.8 summarizes the corporate decision-making styles of managers in the United States, Japan, Mexico, and the Middle Eastern countries. As shown in the table, the decision process is somewhat different in each country. For example, in the United States and Japan, subordinates and other managers are likely to be involved in a major purchase decision, whereas in Mexico or the Middle East the decision will be made at a high level with little or no subordinate input. Understanding these differences will help the marketer to be successful in different markets.

16. Lars Hallen, "International Purchasing in a Small Country: An Exploratory Study of Five Swedish Firms," *Journal of International Business Studies,* Winter 1982, p. 99.

17. Sarin Sharad, "Buying Decision in Four Indian Organizations," *Industrial Marketing Management,* vol. 11, February 1982, pp. 25–37.

18. Ibid.

TABLE 6.8 Contrasts in Managers' Decision-Making Styles

	U.S. Firms	Japanese Firms	Mexican Firms	Middle Eastern Firms
Delegation of authority	Yes. Believed to be essential in increasing subordinates' capabilities	Yes. Subordinate development is a primary management function; worker suggestions for improvement are sought and accepted	No. Authoritarian style reflects manager's individualism; subordinate development is not manager's responsibility	No. Authority rests at the top; delegation depends on personal relationship
Participation in decision making	Yes. Subordinates contribute to decisions; believed to improve motivation and performance	Yes. Subordinates participate in and initiate decisions; consensus of all employees is sought	No. May indicate to subordinates that manager is unsure of own job; maintaining social distance is important	No. Chain of command is rigidly followed
Importance of planning	High. Problem solving is valued, planning is a tool for decision making emphasis on short-term planning	High. Planning is valued, more emphasis on long-term planning	Low. Plans appear to restrict the manager's personal expression	Low. Ad hoc planning
Emphasis in communication style	Direct and frank	Polite, respectful; patience in difficult topics	Maintenance of pleasant relations; avoidance of difficult issues	Tone depends on position, power, or family influence
Commitment to firm's objectives	Doing well for the firm is an essential component of career success	Firm's and manager's goals are one and the same; manager identifies with firm	Career success is based on personal relations with superiors	Reluctance to take risks inherent in decision making; success dependent on contacts and being of the "right" social position

Sources: Adapted from Eugene C. McCann, "Anglo-American and Mexican Management Philosophies," *MSU Business Topics,* Summer 1970, pp. 28–37. Reprinted by permission; William Ouchi, *Theory Z: How American Business Can Meet the Japanese Challenge,* Reading, Mass.: Addison-Wesley, © 1981, p. 58. Reprinted with permission; M. L. Dadawy, "Styles of Mideastern Manager," Reprinted/condensed from the *California Management Review,* Vol. 22, no. 3. © 1980 by The Regents of the University of California. By permission of The Regents.

Factors Influencing International Purchasing

In many situations a buyer will have the choice of purchasing a domestic product/service or a foreign product/service. The buyer's perceptions of product quality may be influenced by the product's country of origin, feelings of nationalism, and the firm's competence with international transactions. Although it is assumed that industrial buyers will be completely rational and purchase products based on concrete decision criteria such as price, quality, and performance, research has shown that professional purchasers are also influenced by the country of origin even when all other variables are held constant.[19] The international marketer must recognize the country of origin stereotypes and use this information when developing a marketing strategy. Highly nationalistic countries will tend to encourage economic self-sufficiency even at the expense of economic efficiency, which will have a negative effect on the international marketer. A study of purchasing behavior by Swedish companies found that buyers preferred to deal with domestic suppliers but would use foreign suppliers when necessary.[20] The study also found that the purchasing firm's competence for international business is positively related to the use of international suppliers. International purchasers will generally have broad market knowledge, an ability to handle foreign cultural patterns, and a knowledge of international trade techniques.[21] Given the results of this analysis, the international marketer should pay close attention to the level of nationalism in a country, the country of origin stereotypes, and the competence of purchasing function to deal with international suppliers.

GOVERNMENT MARKETS

A large number of international business transactions involve governments. For example, 80 percent of all international trade of agricultural products is handled by governments. The U.S. government buys more goods and services than any other government, business, industry, or organization in the world.[22] Selling to governments can be both time consuming and frustrating. However governments are large purchasers and contracting with them can provide enormous returns.

---

19. Phillip D. White and Edward W. Cundiff, "Assessing the Quality of Industrial Products," *Journal of Marketing,* January 1978, pp. 80–86.

20. Hallen, "International Purchasing in a Small Country: An Exploratory Study of Five Swedish Firms," pp. 99–111.

21. Ibid.

22. *Selling to the Government Markets: Local, State, Federal* (Cleveland: Government Product News, 1975), p. 2.

The size of government purchases depends upon the economic or political orientation of the country. In highly developed, free-market countries, the government has less of a role than in state-controlled markets, like the U.S.S.R., where all buying is under direct control of the state. Less-developed countries lack the economic infrastructure to facilitate private companies, thus governments play a major role in overseeing the purchase of foreign products. The amount of government purchases is also a function of state-owned operations. For example, in the United States, the only government-owned operation is the postal system, whereas in India, the government owns the postal, telecommunications, electric, gas, oil, coal, railway, airline, and shipbuilding industries.

The Buying Process

Governmental buying processes tend to be highly bureaucratic. In order to sell to the U.S. Department of Defense, a firm has to get on a bidding list for each branch of the armed forces. These bidding lists are issued on an annual basis; thus, if a firm is not able to get the bid, it must wait a full year to try again.

Governments make it harder for a foreign firm to sell to them; many place their own domestic firms ahead of foreign operations. Also, negotiating with foreign governments can be a very formal process. Understanding cultural differences is essential to not overstep boundaries.

Government procurement processes vary from country to country. The following sections describe purchasing processes in Belgium, China, and socialist countries.

Marketing to the Belgian Government[23]

In Belgium, 90 percent of all public contracts are awarded to the lowest bidder. The remaining 10 percent are granted through "invitation to tender," where factors other than price are taken into consideration. These other factors may include the company's financial viability, technical competence, and post-sale service. Central government supplies, excluding data processing and telecommunications, must be bought through the Central Supplies Office. Regional, local, and quasi-governmental bodies, such as Sabena Airlines, purchase supplies independently. Here are several recommendations to companies that would like to sell to the Belgian government:

- Manufacture in Belgium. Preference is given to a local supplier if other things are equal.

---

23. The information in this section has been drawn from Business International, "How to Sell to Belgium's Public Sector," *Business Europe,* October 2, 1981, pp. 314–315.

- Develop a European image. A strong EC image has favored companies such as Siemens and Philips.
- Use the appropriate language. Although both Flemish and French are officially accepted, ask which is preferred in the department that is accepting the bid.
- Emphasize the recruitment of labor following the winning of a contract. Companies are favored if they will employ Belgian people.
- When new technology is involved, get in at the beginning. It is often difficult and expensive for the government to change to a different technology at a later date.
- Whenever possible, use local contractors. The Belgian government would like a bidder to use as many local contractors as possible.

Obviously, bidding for Belgian government work would be particularly difficult for suppliers with no local participation of subcontractors or manufacturing in Belgium or the EC. However, every government market will have some limitations.

Marketing to the Chinese Government

Before 1978, China had a simple system where all purchasing was delegated by the Ministry of Foreign Trade to the large state trading companies. Negotiations took place at the biannual Canton Trade Fair between the state trading companies and the importers.[24] There was minimal, if any, contact with the respective province end-user, and after-sale service was nonexistent.[25]

By 1979, this structure was decentralized, giving the authority for importing to the various ministries. Most of these ministries established their own trading companies. Also major factories were given authority to deal directly with foreigners. This means that foreign businesses can now deal with either a trading corporation of one of the ministries or with the end-user. Also, the power to conduct trade has been granted to provinces and municipalities.

Although businesspersons have a wider range of contacts than they did in the 1950s, they must make sure that the project they are interested in is being handled by the correct organization. Provinces are still not given carte blanche in what they can do, and they are generally placed under some sort of financial limit.[26] Thus, although contact is easier, coordination between contacts is

---

24. Judith Lubman, "The Helps and Hindrances of Decentralization," *Financial Times,* October 19, 1983, p. IX—China Section.

25. Adam Williams, "Picking a Way Through the Maze," *Financial Times,* October 19, 1983, p. IX—China Section.

26. Ibid.

FIGURE 6.9 The Trade Ministry and Its Subsidiary Import Export Corporations

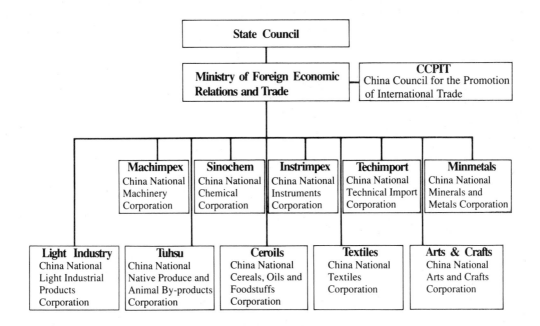

Source: Adam Williams, ''Picking a Way Through the Maze,'' *Financial Times,* October 19, 1983, p. IX—China Section. Reprinted by permission.

harder. Figure 6.9 shows the various Chinese government organizations that are responsible for developing trade. As can be seen in the figure, some ministries may conflict with one another. For example, the China National Electronics Import Export Corporation may conflict with the China National Investments Corporation.

The Chinese government has given the international marketer numerous government organizations to negotiate with on a national and provincial level. The businessperson approaching China today must be aware of these increased options, alert to the potential confusion between central and provincial organizations, and pick his or her contacts very carefully.

Although most governments purchase airplanes, office supplies, and military equipment, even the sale of products such as Avon facial cream and Heinz baby food must be negotiated with the Chinese government. After three years of negotiation, Avon reached an agreement to sell one of its 700 products in Chinese department stores.[27] H. J. Heinz recently signed a joint venture agreement with the General Corporation of Agriculture, Industry, and Commerce to build a baby-food factory in Guanghou. The president and CEO of Heinz stated, "This is a tremendous growth opportunity . . . the U.S. produces 3.5 million babies per year. China produces 16 million."[28] After two years of negotiation with the Ministry of Light Industry, Coca-Cola Company reached an agreement for Coke to be sold in China.[29]

Authorities offer the following suggestions for marketing to the Chinese government:

- Before going to China, conduct research with other companies, the Department of Commerce, and other consultants to determine the correct Chinese organization to approach.
- If possible bring your own translator.
- Be patient. The Chinese as negotiators are not in a hurry. Chinese negotiators want to show their superiors they are shrewd negotiators.
- Physical distribution is a critical limitation in China. The road system is poor; the airlines are used to transport people not cargo; and the national rail and water transportation systems are for bulk food, coal, and building materials. Be sure to discuss the transportation and distribution of your product in China with your trading partner.
- Repatriation of profits is extremely difficult since China has a limited supply of hard currency. Products, agreements, and joint ventures that will increase China's exports will help improve the likelihood of getting profits out of the country.
- Plan for the excessively high cost of doing business in China. In 1984, it cost $250,000 per year to maintain a manager in Peking.
- Recognize the importance of good *guanxi* (connections). The trade representative in the U.S. Embassy can help you establish relationships with people who can help with all the difficulties of doing business in China, such as getting a hotel room, arranging travel, getting to the correct ministry, and so on.[30]

Marketing to Socialist Countries

Comecon countries (Cuba, Bulgaria, Czechoslovakia, East Germany, Hungary, Mongolia, Poland, Romania, the U.S.S.R., and Vietnam) share common political and economic ideals. Although these countries offer a vast market, dealing

27. "Avon Adds China to Its List of Foreign Markets," *Marketing News,* October 15, 1982, p. 1.

28. "Heinz, China Agree on Baby Food Plant," *The Wall Street Journal,* September 4, 1984, p. 5.

29. Joseph O. Eastlack, Jr. and Roberta Lucker, "Is China Moving from Marx to Mastercard?" *Journal of Consumer Marketing,* vol. 3, Summer 1986, p. 9.

30. Ibid., pp. 14–17.

with these countries is extremely difficult. The underlying problem stems from their economic and political orientations, which oppose Western philosophies and promote self-sufficiency. Firms used to dealing in the free markets have established basic marketing strategies that cannot be readily applied to the socialist market.

Understanding the basic differences and how they impact upon specific marketing functions is the first step to developing a comprehensive strategy. Free-world practitioners must understand the peculiarities of the Comecon countries and the resulting effect on marketing in these countries.

Some of the effects of the socialist system on the traditional marketing mix follow: Promotion is planned by central planning authority. The objective is to produce a sufficient number of products within the constraints of the system. Products are generic, with little differentiation, and overall product quality is average to poor. For example, little attention is given to the color or style of clothes. Pricing is not related to supply and demand, but rather to the product's social desirability. Products that are desirable are subsidized, whereas luxury items are heavily taxed.[31]

The role of promotion in socialist countries is to educate the consumer not to increase product sales. In fact, advertising will sometimes be used to reduce the demand for a product. Since supply is believed to create its own demand in a socialist economy, there is little need for sales efforts or high levels of retail service. The customer is suppose to seek out the product without advertising or sales efforts.

Another aspect in dealing with Eastern European countries is that of countertrade.[32] *Countertrade* involves East-West transactions whereby the Eastern buyer is able to pay in part or wholly in locally produced goods. Some forms of countertrade include barter, compensation, product buy back, or counterpurchase. The concept of countertrade and the difficulties of dealing with it are discussed in Chapter 18.

Economic and Political Needs of Governments

Firms involved in selling to foreign governments must not only have an understanding of the political and economic structures, they must also evaluate a country's industrial trends vis-à-vis the national system. Factors to be considered involve what the government's responsibility is to industry; what the gov-

---

31. Charles S. Mayer, "Marketing in Eastern European Socialist Countries," *University of Michigan Business Review,* vol. 28, January 1976, pp. 16–17.

32. Joseph Mandato, Thomas J. Skula, and Kenneth L. Wyse, "Counterpurchase Sales in the German Democratic Republic," *Columbia Journal of World Business,* Spring 1978, pp. 87–89.

ernment priorities are; national defense; high-tech, industrial efficiency; and financial self-sufficiency. The level of economic development involves not only the GNP but the state of production. China, for example, is pushing for modernization but does not want production techniques at the expense of its large labor pool. The desire to lessen unemployment is a major interest to most countries. Governments are also confronted with balance of payments problems. Trade deficits—importing more than exporting—will affect the position of a country's currency with respect to foreign currencies. The more the government imports, the more expensive the products become because the government must use more foreign exchange.

Governments tend to protect their domestic industry to reduce high unemployment and GNP deficits. Whether products are for consumer, industrial, or government use, protection in the form of tariffs, subsidiaries, and quotas are levied if domestic industries are threatened. Because the government looks out for its domestic companies, they will stay clear of those product/services where a restriction is imposed.

Protection of domestic products/services extends beyond that imposed by the foreign governments. The threat of reducing national security has governments of domestic firms employing restrictions on various products. The transfer of technology such as nuclear plants, computers, telecommunications or military weapons is usually restricted so that these critical technologies do not get in the wrong hands.

CONCLUSIONS

If a marketer wants to succeed, he or she must know who the potential buyer is and how this buyer will make the decision to purchase. Consumers can be radically different from country to country because of their ability to buy and their cultural preferences.

The largest business markets for U.S. goods are in countries that have a sophisticated industrial infrastructure, such as Canada, Japan, West Germany, and England. These countries have a large industrial base, a financial basis and a transportation network. These countries are large importers and exporters of goods and services.

Developing countries offer a different type of market opportunity. They have specific economic needs that must be met with limited financial resources. In these situations the government is likely to get involved in the purchase process, offering concessions to get the correct product or agreement. In many cases the government will be the decision maker.

As a marketer evaluates different consumer, business, and government market opportunities, he or she must be aware of the nature of the differences between countries.

Questions for Discussion

1. What are the critical factors that will influence a consumer's ability to purchase a product such as a stereo system?
2. Given the data on family decision making in the United States and Venezuela in Table 6.2, how would the marketing of automobiles be different in the two countries?
3. What causes the large difference in sugar consumption per person (shown in Table 6.4) in the United States, Korea, India, and Venezuela?
4. If you were marketing typewriters worldwide, how would the stages of economic development influence the marketing mix?
5. Would the buying process be more similar from country to country for deodorant or delivery vans? Why?
6. If selling a product like nuclear power plants, which are purchased mostly by governments, how would a marketer prepare to sell to Belgium, Egypt, or Mexico? What process should be used to understand the government buying process in each of these countries?

For Further Readings

Bonoma, Thomas, and Benson Shapiro. *Segmenting the Industrial Market.* Lexington, Mass.: D.C. Heath, 1983.

Dichter, Ernest. "The World Customer." *Harvard Business Review* (July-August 1962), pp. 119–121.

Guthery, Dennis Alan. "Income and Social Class as Indicators of Buyer Behavior in an Advanced LDC: A Case Study of Durable Good Purchases in Porto Alegre, Brazil." A Paper presented at the Academy of International Business Annual Meeting, Washington, D.C., 1982.

Moriarty, Rowland T. *Industrial Buying Behavior.* Lexington, Mass.: D.C. Heath, 1983.

Poser, Gunter, and Zoher Shipchandler. "Impact of Inflation on Consumer Life Style." *European Journal of Marketing,* 13, No. 3 (1979), pp. 103–112.

Shipchandler, Zoher. "Change in Demand for Consumer Goods in International Markets," *International Marketing.* 2nd ed. Ed. Subhash Jain and Lewis Tooker, Jr. Boston: Kent, 1986.

Shipchandler, Zoher. "Keeping Down with the Joneses: Stagflation and Buyer Behavior." *Business Horizons,* 25, No. 6 (1982), pp. 32–38.

Tillinghast, Charles C. Jr. "Competing Against State-Owned Enterprises." Paper presented at the Academy of International Business Annual Meeting, Las Vegas, June 1979.

Vernon, Ivan R. "The International Aspects of State Owned Enterprises." *Journal of International Business Studies* (Winter 1979), pp. 7–15.

7.
INTERNATIONAL MARKETING RESEARCH

In the previous chapters, we introduced you to a variety of consumers, markets, and environments. The main purpose of this chapter is to provide a framework for analyzing these variables and for collecting the appropriate data for such analysis. Figure 7.1 provides an overview of international market research.

Although this chapter is written around research issues in an international environment, the emphasis is managerial rather than technical. Throughout the chapter, the focus is on how companies can obtain useful and accurate information that will help them make some of the strategic and marketing program decisions described in our later chapters.

SCOPE OF INTERNATIONAL MARKETING RESEARCH

The international marketing research function is to provide adequate data and cogent analysis for effective decision making on a global scale. In contrast to the marketing research with a domestic focus, the international researcher will face a multitude of environments and a scarcity of relevant data. In many cases, this requires more flexibility, resourcefulness, and ingenuity on the part of the researcher to overcome the numerous obstacles encountered in carrying out the research task.

The analytical research techniques practiced by domestic businesses also apply to international marketing projects. The key difference is in the complexity of assignments as additional variables are dealt with. International marketers have to judge the comparability of their data across a large number of markets. They frequently are faced with making decisions based upon very limited data. As a result, international marketing research can aptly be described as making

FIGURE 7.1 International Marketing Research and Analysis

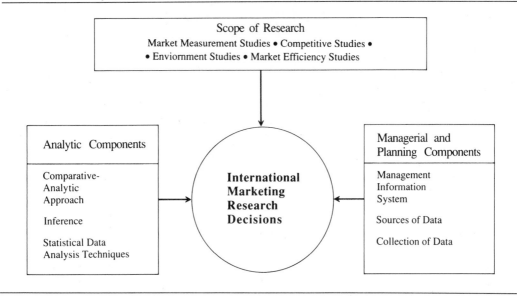

the best out of limited resources. Traditionally, marketing research has been charged with four broad areas of responsibility:

1. *Market Measurement Studies*. One of the most frequent tasks of researchers is to determine the size of a market or its potential as well as a firm's sales potential. Included in this area are sales forecasts for a given product in a given country. A firm's expected sales for a product in a given country is also an important input into the development of an international marketing plan.

2. *Competitive Studies*. To provide insights about competitors, both domestic and foreign, is an important assignment for the international marketing researcher. The researcher must study the general competitive behavior of industries in the various markets within which the firm will compete.

3. *Environmental Studies*. Given the added environmental complexity of international marketing, managers need factual and timely input on the international environment—particularly relating to the economic, political, and legal elements of the international marketing environment.

4. *Marketing Efficiency Studies*. Marketing efficiency studies deal with the efficiency of the marketing mix and the desirable allocation of budgets to cover the many marketing tasks that need to be performed. On an international level, firms may want to explore the best or most effective marketing mix for certain countries. Included would be studies on price elasticities, channel effectiveness, and advertising effectiveness.

TABLE 7.1 Tactical International Marketing Decisions Requiring Marketing Research

Marketing Mix Decision	Type of Research
Product policy decision	Focus groups and qualitative research to generate ideas for new products
	Survey research to evaluate new product ideas
	Concept testing, test marketing
	Product benefit and attitude research
	Product formulation and feature testing
Pricing decisions	Price sensitivity studies
Distribution decisions	Survey of shopping patterns and behavior
	Consumer attitudes to different store types
	Survey of distributor attitudes and policies
Advertising decisions	Advertising pretesting
	Advertising posttesting, recall scores
	Surveys of media habits
Sales promotion decisions	Surveys of response to alternative types of promotion
Sales force decisions	Tests of alternative sales presentations

Source: Susan P. Douglas and C. Samuel Craig, *International Marketing Research,* © 1983, p. 32. Reprinted by permission of Prentice-Hall, Inc., Englewood Cliffs, New Jersey.

International market research is used to make both strategic and tactical decisions. Strategic decisions would include the selection of what markets to enter, how to enter the markets (exporting licensing, joint venture), and where to locate production facilities. Tactical decisions are decisions about the specific marketing mix to be used in a country. Table 7.1 shows the various types of tactical marketing decisions and the types of research used to collect the necessary data.

New product development and/or product adaptation will require product benefit research and product testing to meet environmental conditions, customer tastes, and competitive constraints. Advertising, sales promotion, and sales force decisions will all require data from the local market in the form of testing. The type of information required is often the same as that required in domestic marketing research, but the process is more complex due to the variety of cultures and environments.

IMPORTANCE OF INTERNATIONAL MARKET RESEARCH

The complexity of the international marketplace, the extreme differences from country to country, and the frequent lack of familiarity with foreign markets accentuate the importance of international market research. Before making market entry, product position, or market mix decisions, accurate information is required about the market size, market needs, competition, and so on. Market research provides the necessary information to avoid costly mistakes of poor strategies or lost opportunities.

Market research can guide product development for a foreign market. Based on a research study conducted in the United States, one U.S. firm introduced a new cake mix in England. Believing that homemakers wanted to feel that they participated in the preparation of the cake, the U.S. marketers devised a mix that required homemakers to add an egg. Given the success in the U.S. market, the marketers confidently introduced the product in England. The product failed, however, because the British did not like the fancy American cakes. They preferred cakes that were tough and spongy and could accompany afternoon tea. The technique of having homemakers add an egg to the mix did not eliminate basic taste and style differences.[1]

CHALLENGES IN PLANNING INTERNATIONAL RESEARCH

International market researchers are facing five principal challenges:

1. Complexity of research design
2. Lack of secondary data
3. Costs of collecting primary data
4. Coordination of research and data collection across countries
5. Difficulty of establishing comparability and equivalence[2]

Deciding on the proper unit of analysis is a principal factor behind the added complexity for international research design. When defining a company's target market, the researcher will have to select from possible target countries or from among clearly identified segments to be found in all countries. For many countries, this research will have to be conducted with a lack of secondary data. Few countries publish such a wealth of information as the United States and thus

1. David A. Ricks, *Big Business Blunders: Mistakes in Multinational Marketing* (Homewood, Ill.: Dow Jones—Irwin, 1983), pp. 129–130.
2. Susan P. Douglas and C. Samuel Craig, *International Marketing Research* (Englewood Cliffs, N.J.: Prentice Hall, 1983), pp. 16–19.

researchers are forced either to spend considerable resources finding such data or to accept secondary data when it is available. In many countries, the cost of collecting primary data is substantially higher than in a competitive market such as the United States. This is particularly the case for developing countries, which is why the secondary data is not always reliable. Consequently, researchers will have to make tradeoffs between the need for more accurate data and the limited resources available to accomplish the tasks.

Because companies can ill afford for each subsidiary to obtain its own expensive primary data, coordination of research and data collection across many countries becomes necessary. Companies that can successfully manage this task will be in a situation to avoid costly duplication of research. The borrowing of research results from one country to another is hindered by the general difficulty of establishing comparability and equivalence among various research data. Full comparability can only be achieved when identical procedures are used. A recent study found that, even with the same scales measuring the same attributes of products, different cultures will exhibit different degrees of reliability due to different levels of awareness, knowledge, and familiarity.[3] With research capabilities differing from country to country, international market research administration becomes a real challenge.

A CONCEPTUAL FRAMEWORK FOR INTERNATIONAL MARKET RESEARCH: THE COMPARATIVE ANALYTIC APPROACH

In the first part of this chapter we discussed the scope of market research situations and the difficulties encountered in conducting research. Although an understanding of the difficulties of collecting information for foreign markets will help to increase the quality of information obtained, an overall conceptual framework is necessary to provide the analyst with the relevant questions to ask. Consequently, this section of the chapter is focused on building a framework that can guide international marketing managers in formulating market research studies.

Pioneered by T. A. Hagler in the late 1950s, comparative research actually lead to the establishment of international marketing as a discipline.[4] Comparative marketing focuses on the entire marketing system; but this macro approach becomes less important as specific problems at the company level need to be

---

3. Ravi Parameswaran and Attila Yaprak, "A Cross-National Comparison of Consumer Research Measures," *Journal of International Business Studies,* Spring 1987, p. 45.

4. Jean Boddeyn, "A Framework for Comparative Marketing Research," *Journal of Marketing Research,* May 1966, pp. 149–153; and *Comparative Management and Marketing.* (Glenview, Ill.: Scott, Foresman, 1969).

FIGURE 7.2 Comparative Approach

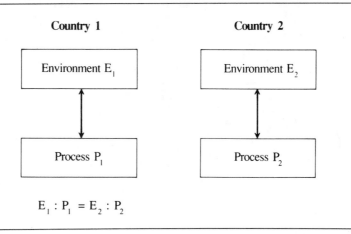

$$E_1 : P_1 = E_2 : P_2$$

analyzed. However, the comparative approach can be adapted to specific micromarketing problems.

Marketing as a Function of the Environment

The comparative marketing analysis emphasizes the study of the marketing process in its relationship to the prevailing environment. Marketing is not viewed as an independent process separated from environmental influences. Instead, the marketing process (P) is viewed as a direct function of environment (E), or $(P) = f(E)$. Under changed environmental conditions, the existing marketing processes are also expected to change. As shown in Figure 7.2, in a dual-country analysis employing the comparative approach, the marketing environment (E_1) in Country 1 is investigated with respect to its causal effect on the marketing process (P_1). The resulting functional relationship is transferred to a second country whose environment (E_2) may be known but whose marketing process (P_2) will be assessed based upon the earlier developed functional relationships $P_1 = f(E_1)$. The resulting analysis can be represented as:

$$P_1: E_1 = P_2: E_2$$

where P_2 is the unknown. The marketing process (P) can also be referred to as the marketing mix.

This macro-level approach can be extended to the managerial level, as illustrated in Figure 7.3.[5] Let us assume the possible transfer of a marketing mix

5. Jean-Pierre Jeannet, "International Marketing Analysis: A Comparative-Analytic Approach," Working Paper, 1981.

FIGURE 7.3 Managerial Approach to Comparative Analysis

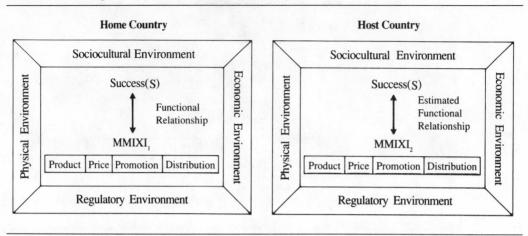

($MMIX_1$) from the home country to the host country. The unknown is the required nature of the marketing mix ($MMIX_2$) as a function of the new environment (E_2). The comparative approach is based upon an assessment of the existing relationship between the present program ($MMIX_1$) and the environment (E_1).

The results of such an analytic assessment are then transferred into the environment (E_2) of the host country whose environmental conditions are known, or have been researched, by the analyst. The unknown component, the desired marketing mix ($MMIX_2$), will therefore be estimated based upon the known functional relationship $MMIX_1 = f(E_1)$, with E_2 given, or $MMIX_2 = f(E_2)$.

An Example: McDonald's

We can illustrate this concept by using an example familiar to most of us. McDonald's has reached a tremendous success in the United States (the home country) by way of an aggressive and well structured marketing mix ($MMIX_1$). The elements may be described as follows:

Product/Service Design. A standardized product of high and consistent quality emphasizing speed of service and long opening hours.

Price. A low price policy.

Distribution. Placing restaurants in areas where customers primarily live—suburban and urban locations.

Promotion. A strong advertising campaign focused on the consumer, particularly young people, via heavy use of TV.

With this $MMIX_1$ as described above, McDonald's has been extremely success-ful in the United States. In the early 1970s, several foreign countries were tar-geted for possible expansion and an assessment had to be made as to the best approach for McDonald's to pursue. The traditional approach would view suc-cess (S_1) as a function of McDonald's effective marketing strategy ($MMIX_1$) or as a direct result of the company's own efforts. The comparative-analytic ap-proach advanced here, however, views McDonald's success as a function of a given set of marketing mix variables ($MMIX_1$) that were effective only due to the home country environment (E_1). This view places a key emphasis on the envi-ronmental variables that allowed McDonald's marketing mix to become suc-cessful.

$$S_1 = f(MMIX_1)$$

$$MMIX = f(E_1)$$

The difference between the two approaches is important. The comparative-analytic view sees McDonald's primarily as having been able to take advantage of an existing opportunity (E_1), whereas the traditional approach views Mc-Donald's success primarily as a direct result of its own efforts.

Viewing The Marketing Mix (MMIX) as a Function of the Environment

Viewing the marketing mix as a function of the existing environment emphasizes an environmental view of the marketing process.[6] The emphasis is now on the existing environment that enables a given marketing mix to be successful. That view is of great importance, since success is no longer defined as unilateral or solely a function of the marketing mix. By looking at $MMIX_1$ in the home coun-try, underlying environmental factors (E_1) are uncovered that enable success. Thus the company is viewed as taking advantage of a given opportunity rather than creating one by its own actions. The first step is to look at the environmen-tal factors.

Understanding the Components of the Marketing Environment

The critical environmental variables may be grouped into four major categories: physical, social, economic, and regulatory.

---

6. Robert Bartels, "Are Domestic and International Marketing Dissimilar?" *Journal of Marketing*, July 1968, pp. 56–61.

Physical Environmental Variables

Included in this category are the physical constraints with respect to the conditions of the product's use or the physical properties of the particular market. These are population, population density, geographic area, climate, and the physical conditions of the product's use (surroundings, space and size requirements, etc.). Variables such as population have an effect on the absolute size of any target market and, similar to climate, tend to be subject to little change over time. The physical use conditions relate to a product's function in any given environment. As a result, we are viewing consumption of the product and/or service as a *physical event* directly influenced by physical environmental variables that have to be recognized to determine a marketing mix.

Turning again to the McDonald's example several variables from the physical environment have contributed toward McDonald's success in the United States. An important influence on McDonald's distribution or location policies was the concentration of the U.S. population in suburbia. Opening 4,000 units in the United States was possible due to the absolute size of the population, which is about 220 million people. It is important to recognize that the market size is often finite, and that any country with a different population would, of course, not offer the same opportunities, everything being equal. The physical use conditions of McDonald's are less restrictive because they are directly shaped by the firm's policies and the building of outlets. The situation is different in cases where consumers take products home for consumption and are restricted by their own physical environments, such as the size of apartments or kitchens.

Social Environmental Variables

This category includes all relevant factors from the social and cultural background of any given marketing environment, including the following: cultural background (race, religion, customs, habits, and languages); the educational system; and social structure (the individual's roles, family structure, social classes, and reference groups).

As we've mentioned before, the social environment is a primary influence on the role expectations of buyers and sellers, regardless of the differences in the physical environment. Since the social environment does not change rapidly over time, many domestic marketers can lose sight of the fact that they've subconsciously chosen a marketing mix that incorporates many social values. Defining the social forces that impact on a marketing mix is the first step in shedding the cultural bias that affects so many managers unknowingly.

In the case of McDonald's, there were several social and cultural forces that greatly affected its success. For one, the value that U.S. society placed on time favored the consumption of meals with minimum time effort. Saving time, in fact, created the desire for meals purchased outside the home on an unplanned or impulse basis. The result was a burgeoning demand for low-priced food that was available any time and that could be purchased with minimum shopping effort. Another important factor was the prevailing family structure in the United States and the trend towards a youth-oriented culture. In the 1960s and 1970s, the decision making role had been changed to such an extent that often children would make the selection of a place to eat. McDonald's special emphasis on children and teenagers as advertising targets has been successful largely because the strategy capitalized on these existing social trends.

The changing role of the wife in the typical U.S. household has resulted in an ever-increasing number of women accepting employment outside the household. Whether this resulted in a lower valuation of the home-cooked meal in a social sense is debatable; nevertheless, it greatly increased the acceptability of eating meals outside the home as compared to home-cooked meals.

Not to be underestimated is the habit or heritage of the hamburger itself. Truly, the hamburger represents a long-standing tradition of the U.S. food and restaurant scene, and hamburger made up the daily meal of many Americans before McDonald's arrived on the scene. It is fair to state, then, that the product's success stemmed to a considerable degree from the selection of an already existing and widely popular product. Aside from the type of service, the product did not represent an innovation. Of course, there are other reasons for dining out, and U.S. customers often make other choices. But the social and cultural influences to a large extent prepared the ground for the success of an operation such as McDonald's.

What is important then is to isolate the salient social and cultural variables impacting on the success of a company's products or services. The combined sociocultural variables create the *sociocultural event* that becomes an essential part of the consumption and use of any product or service. Understanding the nature of the sociocultural event in the home country as the starting point for analyzing the respective variables in the host country is the basis of the comparative-analytic model.

Economic Environmental Variables

Under this category we include all aspects of the economic environment, both on a macro- and micro-level, such as GNP, GNP per capita, price levels, income distribution, and prices of competitive products and services.

Economic considerations impact on most consumption or buying decisions. Typically income or price related, they by no means completely dominate marketing behavior but certainly exert a considerable influence on buyers. To the extent that income levels of consumers differ from country to country, the trade-offs consumers make in order to maximize economic satisfaction are different. Different price levels for products also cause changes in buying behavior even under a constant income level. The international marketer must isolate the specific income and price variables to arrive at a given combination, termed the *economic event,* that impacts on the success of a given product or service. The analytic-comparative model suggests that the elements and nature of the economic event with regards to a foreign market can largely be found by first investigating the relevant factors in a company's home market.

For McDonald's, a significant variable of the economic environment was the income level of the U.S. population and the resulting disposable income available for frequent visits to fast-food restaurants. It is still more expensive to frequent a fast-food outlet than to prepare an equivalent meal at home; consequently, the success of fast-food outlets does not so much stem from their price advantage over food purchased in stores. Instead, it was the *relative price advantage* of fast-food restaurants compared to the more traditional or simple diner type restaurants that ensured their tremendous success. Consuming a meal at a place such as McDonald's becomes an economic event to the extent that economic variables are introduced into the consumer's decision making process affecting the particular product or service choice.

Regulatory Environmental Variables

The regulatory environment includes all actions of governments or agencies influencing business transactions such as commercial law or codes, consumer protection laws, product liability laws, regulatory agencies (e.g., FDA, CAB, ICC, etc.), local regulations, and zoning laws.

Regulations tend not to stimulate needs or demands for services and products. Instead, they act in an *enabling manner* (or disabling, depending on point of view) by restricting choices for the multinational corporation or prescribing the nature of its marketing effort. Companies have to be aware of the particular regulations that make an existing marketing program effective since such an approach may not be duplicated in other countries, even if it were desirable from a business point of view.

The possible effect of the regulatory environment can be illustrated by turning to our example. Certainly, the use of TV advertising to reach children was one of the reasons for McDonald's success in the United States. But in many other countries, particularly those in Europe, such advertising is banned outright. On an operational level, it may be difficult to get teenage help in some countries or impossible to keep operating during hours customary in the United States. Since the United States has in many ways a more liberal regulatory environment, U.S. MNCs often face the situation in which operations cannot be carried out in the accustomed fashion. This is true even when the target customers in other countries would respond positively to U.S. methods or practices and the relevant physical, economic, and social events indicate that their use would be beneficial.

Analyzing Environmental Variables

The importance of these environmental variables has been emphasized by previous writers with respect to international marketing. Robert Bartels has highlighted physical, social, and economic variables in his environmental marketing concept.[7] Robert Buzzell included a similar set of variables in his analysis of elements that may prevent a standardization of marketing programs across several countries.[8] Furthermore, Warren Keegan has concentrated on the same variables as influencing extension versus adaptation decisions for product design or communications strategy.[9] What is different about the comparative-analytic approach is its focus on the situational and its method of selecting the salient environmental variables that may affect the product's and/or service's success in any country. Since the selected environmental variables are the ones most clearly related to a product's and/or service's success in the home country, they can be referred to as *success factors*.

Traditionally, marketers have viewed success factors as variables under marketing management's control. With the comparative-analytic approach, success factors are treated as a function of the environment, which means that success becomes recognized as a function of a given scenario of outside factors not always subject to management's control. Typically, marketing programs succeed because managements take advantage of opportunities or positive constellations of success factors. Therefore, we are "allowed" to be successful provided we spot the opportunity. This reversed view results in a greater appreciation of the role that environmental variables play in marketing and also tends to avoid traditional tendencies to overestimate the impact of management's own actions in the marketplace.

The comparative-analytical approach provides a methodology for marketers to analyze their success in current markets as a function of the marketing mix and the environment. It also provides an approach for isolating the critical environmental variables. These variables become the focus of the international market research process. In the McDonald's example, the variables we analyzed were population, population density, the family structure, role of the mother, income levels, and the availability of advertising media to reach children.

THE INTERNATIONAL MARKET RESEARCH PROCESS

Although conducting market research internationally usually adds to the complexity of the research task, the basic approach remains the same for domestic and international assignments. International or domestic market research is a four step process consisting of the following:

7. Ibid.

8. Robert D. Buzzell, "Can You Standardize Multinational Marketing?" *Harvard Business Review,* November–December 1968, pp. 102–113.

9. Warren J. Keegan, "Multinational Product Planning: Strategic Alternatives," *Journal of Marketing,* January 1969, p. 58.

1. Problem definition and developing the research objectives
2. Determination of the sources of information
3. Collection of the data from secondary and/or primary sources
4. Analysis of the data and presentation of the results

While these four steps in the process will be the same for both international and domestic research, problems in implementation will occur because of cultural and economic differences from country to country.

Problem Definition and Development of Research Objectives

In any market research project, the most important task is to define what information you are after. This process, which can take weeks or months, determines the choice of methodologies, the types of people you wish to interview, and the appropriate time frame in which to conduct your research.[10]

Problems may not be the same in different countries or cultures. This may reflect differences in socioeconomic conditions, levels of economic development, cultural forces, or the competitive market structure.[11] For example, bicycles in a developed country may be competing with other recreational goods, such as skis, baseball gloves, or exercise equipment; whereas in a developing country, they may be a major form of basic transportation competing with small cars, mopeds, and scooters.

The comparative-analytic approach can be used to isolate the critical environmental variables in the home market. These variables should be included in the problem definition and research objectives.

Determination of Sources of Data

For each assignment, researchers may choose to base their analysis on primary data (data collected specifically for this assignment) or use secondary data (already collected and available data). Since costs tend to be much higher for research based upon primary data, researchers usually exhaust secondary data first. Often also called desk research or library research, this approach depends on the availability of material and its reliability. Secondary sources may include government publications, trade journals, and data from international agencies or service establishments such as banks or advertisement agencies. Although a substantial body of data exists from the most advanced industrial nations, secondary data are less available for developing countries. Not every country pub-

10. Michael Brizz, "How to Learn What Japanese Buyers Really Want," *Business Marketing,* January 1987, p. 72.
11. Douglas and Craig, *International Marketing Research,* pp. 16–19.

lishes a census, and some published data are not to be considered reliable. For example, in Nigeria, the total population is of such political importance that published census data are generally believed to be highly suspect. For reasons such as this, MNCs sometimes have to proceed with the collection of primary data in developing countries at a much earlier stage than in the most industrialized nations.

Data Collection

The collection of data from secondary sources includes the task of calling, writing, or visiting the potential secondary sources. Often, one source will lead to another source until you find the information desired or determine that the information does not exist.

Collecting Secondary Data

For any marketing research problem, the analysis of secondary data should be a first step. Although not available for all variables, often data is available from public and private sources at a fraction of the cost for obtaining primary data. It would be impractical to include a listing of all the secondary data sources available on international markets, but some secondary data sources would be banks, consulates, embassies, foreign chambers of commerce, libraries with foreign information sections, foreign magazines, public accounting firms, security brokers, and state development offices in foreign countries. A good business library and the local U.S. Department of Commerce are always good places to start a search for secondary data. Table 7.2 lists some of the major sources of published secondary data.

Four problems exist with secondary data: (1) the lack of necessary data, (2) accuracy of the data, (3) comparability of the data, and (4) the age of the data. In some cases, no data have been collected. For example, outside of the United States, there is little data on the number of retailers, wholesalers, and distributors. In Ethiopia and Chad no population statistics are available. The accuracy of the data varies from country to country, with the data from highly industrialized nations likely to be more accurate than that from developing countries.[12] This is a result of the mechanism for collecting data. In industrialized nations, relatively reliable procedures are used for national accounting and for collecting population and industry statistics. In developing countries, where a major portion of the population is illiterate, the data may be based on estimates or rudimentary procedures. Furthermore, data may not be directly comparable from country to country. The population statistics in the United States are collected every ten years,

---

12. Ibid., p. 79.

TABLE 7.2 Major Sources of Secondary Data

U.S. DEPT. OF COMMERCE

Foreign Trade Report (U.S. exports by commodity and by country)

Global Market Surveys (Global market research on targeted industries)

Country Market Surveys (Detailed reports on promising countries covering 15 industries)

Business America (Magazine presenting domestic and international business news)

Overseas Marketing Report (Prepared for all countries, includes trade forecasts, regulations, and market profiles)

INTERNATIONAL MONETARY FUND

International Financial Statistics (Monthly report on exchange rates, inflation, deflation, country liquidity, etc.)

NATIONAL TECHNICAL INFORMATION SERVICES

Market Share Reports (Reports the size of 88 markets and identifies export opportunities)

UNITED NATIONS

Yearbook of Industrial Statistics (Statistics for minerals, manufactured goods, electricity, and gas)

Statistical Yearbook (Population, production, education, trade, wages)

Demographic Yearbook (Population, income, marriages, deaths, literacy)

WORLD BANK

Country Economic Reports (Macroeconomic and industry trends)

World Development Report (Population, investment, balance of reports, defense expenditures)

BUSINESS INTERNATIONAL

Business International Data Base (Economic indicators, GNP, wages, foreign trade, production, and consumption)

EUROMONITOR PUBLICATIONS

European Marketing Data and Statistics (Population, employment, production, trade, standard of living, consumption, housing communication)

PREDICASTS

Worldcasts (Economics, production, utilities)

THE ECONOMIST

E.I.U. World Outlook (Forecasts of trends for 160 countries)

Marketing in Europe (Product markets in Europe—food, clothing, furniture, household goods, appliances)

whereas population statistics in Bolivia are collected every twenty-five years. Also, countries may calculate the same statistic different ways. For example, Gross Domestic Product (GDP) may include the income of national companies in foreign countries in some cases and not in others. Finally, the age of the data is a constant problem. Population statistics are usually two to five years old. Industrial production statistics can be one to two years old. With different growth rates, it is difficult to use older data to make decisions.

To test the quality of secondary data, marketers should investigate the following:

1. When was the data collected?
2. How was the data collected?
3. What is the expected level of accuracy?
4. Who collected the data, and for what purpose was it collected?

If secondary data is not available or usable, the marketer will need to collect primary data.

Collecting Primary Data

Once secondary sources of information have been exhausted, the next step is to collect primary data that will meet the specific information requirements for making the management decision. Sources of primary data will be the people in the target country who would purchase or influence the purchase of products. These are consumers, businesses, or governments. Collecting the appropriate data will require the development of a process to do so. The collection of primary data involves the process of developing a research instrument, selecting a sample, collecting the data, and analyzing results. These steps are the same in domestic and multinational environments. The process of collecting data in different cultures creates a number of challenges for the international marketer. These challenges include comparability of data, willingness of the potential respondent to participate, and the ability of the respondent to understand and communicate.

Comparability of data is important irrespective of whether research is conducted in a single-country or multi-country context. Research conducted in a single country may be used at a later date to compare with the results of research in another country.[13] For example, if a product is tested in France and is successful, the company may decide to test the Italian market. The test used for the Italian market must be comparable with the test in the French market to assess the possible outcome in Italy.

A second challenge in research is the willingness of the potential respondent. For example in many cultures a man would consider it inappropriate to discuss

---

13. Douglas and Craig, *International Marketing Research*, p. 132.

his shaving habits with anyone, but especially with a female interviewer. Problems of unwillingness to participate can be resolved with careful planning. For example, in some cultures, it may be necessary to enlist the aid of a local person to gain cooperation.

Another challenge in survey research is the translation from one language to another. Translation equivalence is important, first to assure that the respondents understand the question and second to assure that the researcher understands the response. Idiomatic expressions and colloquialisms are often translated incorrectly. For example, the French translation of a *full* airplane became a *pregnant* airplane and in German a *"Body by Fisher"* became a *corpse by Fisher*.[14] In a recent case, Braniff found its translation of *to be seated in leather* became *to be seated naked* in Spanish.[15] In order to avoid these translation errors, experts suggest the technique of back-translation.[16] First, the questionnaire is translated from the home language into the language of the country where it will be used by a bilingual who is a native speaker of the foreign country. Then, this version is translated back to the home language by a bilingual who is a native speaker of the home language. Another translation technique is parallel translation, in which two or more translators translate the questionnaire. The results are compared, and differences are discussed and resolved.

Data can be collected by mail, telephone, or face-to-face. The technique for collecting the data will vary by country. In Japan, it is recommended that personal, face-to-face discussion be used instead of telephone or mail questionnaires.[17] Although personal interviews are expensive and time consuming, the Japanese preference for face-to-face contact suggests that personal interviews will yield better information than data collected by mail or telephone. In fact, many Japanese managers are skeptical about Western-style market research. Senior and middle managers will often go into the field and speak directly with consumers and distributors. This technique of collecting information called "soft-data," though less rigorous than large scale consumer studies, gives the manager a real feel for the market and the consumers.[18]

Sample Selection

After developing the instrument and converting it to the appropriate language, the researcher will determine the appropriate sample design. Due to its advan-

14. Ricks, *Big Business Blunders,* p. 83.

15. "Braniff, Inc.'s Spanish Ad Bears Cause for Laughter," *The Wall Street Journal,* February 9, 1987, p. 5.

16. R. Brislin, "Back-Translation for Cross-Cultural Research," *Journal of Cross Cultural Psychology,* vol. 1, 1970, pp. 185–216.

17. Brizz, "How to Learn What Japanese Buyers Really Want," p. 72.

18. Johny K. Johansson and Ikujiro Nonaka, "Market Research the Japanese Way," *Harvard Business Review,* May–June 1987, pp. 16–22.

tage of predicting the margin of error, researchers generally prefer to use probability sampling. The great power of a probability sample lies in the possibility of predicting the corresponding errors: (1) sampling errors or the chance of not receiving a true sample of the group investigated; (2) response errors or the deviation of responses from the facts due to either incorrect recall or unwillingness to tell the truth; and (3) nonresponse errors or uncertainty of the views held by members of the sample that were never reached.[19] For these reasons, probability samples are generally preferred by researchers.

In many foreign countries, however, the existing market infrastructure and the lack of available data or information substantially interferes with the attempts to use probability samples. Sampling of larger populations requires the availability of detailed census data, called *census tracks*, and maps from which probability samples could be drawn. Where such data is available it is often out of date. Thus stratification is prevented.[20] Further difficulties arise from inadequate transportation that may prevent field workers from actually reaching selected census tracks in some areas of the country. Sampling is particularly difficult in countries having several spoken languages because it is impractical to carry out a nationwide survey.

Due to the special circumstances of international sampling, Charles Mayer has defined three additional errors over and above those previously described.[21] Mayer suggested that the total error should be evaluated using a technique called the Error Ratio Decomposition (ERD). Included in the total error are (a) definitional errors, (b) instrument errors, and (c) frame errors.

The *definitional error* is caused by the different ways a research problem may be defined in each country. Conceptual equivalence cannot be automatically assumed because different countries view products in different conceptual terms; bicycles and motorcycles, for example, are viewed as means of transportation in one country and as leisure vehicles in another. When a research project is carried out in several countries, care must be taken to assure definitional equivalence with respect to the product or service considered. In Japan, for instance, noncarbonated fruit drinks are consumed with great frequency as alternatives to soft drinks. In doing a soft drink study in Japan, fruit drinks would have to be included in the list of alternatives, while the same would not necessarily be true in the United States. Consequently, researchers must be careful to consider and define the products in relation to competing products, as they may vary from country to country. Temporal equivalence may be hard to achieve

19. Paul E. Green and Donald S. Tull, *Research for Marketing Decisions*, 4th ed. (Englewood Cliffs, N.J.: Prentice-Hall, 1978), pp. 111–112.

20. W. Boyd Harper, Jr., Ronald E. Frank, William F. Massy, and Mostafa Zoheir, "On the Use of Marketing Research in the Emerging Economies," *Journal of Marketing Research*, vol. 1, November 1964, pp. 20–23.

21. Charles S. Mayer, "Multinational Marketing Research: Methodological Problems," in *International Marketing Strategy*, ed. Hans Thorelli and Helmut Becker (New York: Pergamon Press, 1980), pp. 162–171.

because time lags may exist between research in the various countries causing additional errors. And finally, market structure equivalence, another source of definitional error, may be caused due to differing market sizes, penetration rates, channel structures, or competition. In a survey conducted in Europe, French and German consumers were reported to have consumed more spaghetti than Italian consumers. This result was caused by asking about the consumption of branded spaghetti only, the typical method of marketing spaghetti in France and Germany. In Italy, most spaghetti was consumed in loose and unbranded form, causing a response that would have to be interpreted with great care.[22]

Instrument error may be caused by either the instrument chosen for data collection or the interviewer involved. The absence of linguistic equivalence is one cause, but this can be achieved through careful translation of the instrument. Also, the participants' perceptions of each other may be different from country to country, making it difficult to reach contextual equivalence. This is particularly the case where perceptions of the social status of either the interviewer or the respondent vary substantially among countries. Particularly important is to achieve instrumental equivalence. Researchers have to be aware that some survey instruments may not work equally well across countries. Telephone interviews are not reliable where a substantial portion of the society does not own a telephone. In some countries, mail service is so unreliable that other methods of surveying or data collection have to be used. And finally, response-style equivalence may be difficult to reach because the social conventions in some countries tend to produce more nay-sayers or yea-sayers.

Frame errors are caused by the selection of samples from different sources or lists in each country. Since the same census track data may not be available elsewhere, other public data may be used as a basis to randomly select respondents. Though the sample may be properly arrived at for each country, comparability could be endangered due to the frame error.

INTERNATIONAL MARKETING RESEARCH TECHNIQUES

There are a variety of analytic techniques that can be used in international market research. These techniques may be used in domestic market research, but they are often modified to deal with the complexities of international markets.

Demand Analysis

Demand for products or services can be measured at two levels: aggregate demand for an entire market or country and company demand as represented by

---

22. Ibid., p. 166.

FIGURE 7.4 Market Potential and Sales Potential Filter

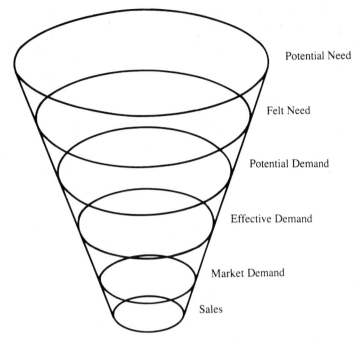

Potential Need

Felt Need

Potential Demand

Effective Demand

Market Demand

Sales

Source: Richard D. Robinson, *Internationalization of Business,* 2nd ed. (Chicago: The Dryden Press, 1984), p. 36. Copyright 1984 CBS College Publishing. Reprinted by permission of Holt, Rinehart & Winston.

actual sales. The former is generally termed the *market potential* whereas the latter is referred to as *sales potential*. A very useful concept developed by Richard Robinson views both market and sales potential as a filtering process (see Figure 7.4). According to Robinson, demand or potential demand can be measured at six successive levels, the last and final level representing actual sales by the firm.[23] The six levels of demand are explained as follows.

Potential Need

The potential need for a product or service is primarily determined by the demographic and physical characteristics of a country. The determinant factors are a country's population, climate, geography, natural resources, land use, life ex-

23. Richard D. Robinson, *Internationalization of Business* 2nd ed. (Chicago: The Dryden Press, 1984), p. 36.

pectancy, and other factors that we have termed part of the physical environment.

The potential need could only be realized if all consumers in a country used a product to the fullest extent regardless of social, cultural, or economic barriers. This represents the ideal case that may never be actually reached. Of course, the country's consumers would not purchase the product if there were no need. Therefore, the researcher has to pose the question: Is there a potential need, either now or in the future?

Felt Need

Though a potential need as defined above may exist to the uninvolved observer, one should not assume that everyone in a market actually feels a need for the product or service under investigation. Different life-styles may cause some consumers not to feel a need for a product. For instance, a farmer in a developing country who drives his produce to a local market in an animal-drawn cart has a potential use for a pick-up truck but may himself not feel the need for one. Thus, the felt need is substantially influenced by the cultural and social environment, including the amount of exposure the consumers or buyers have to modern communications. The key question for the researcher is to evaluate the extent to which the potential need is culturally and socially appropriate among the target customers.

Potential Demand

The felt need represents the aggregate desire of a target population to purchase a product. However, the lack of sufficient income may prevent some of the customers from actually purchasing the product or service. The result is potential demand or the total amount the market would be ready to absorb. The economic variables preventing the realization of sales are generally beyond the control of any individual company. For example, the average income per household may seem to indicate a large demand for washing machines, but the distribution of income is skewed so that 10 percent of the population has 90 percent of the wealth. To identify if potential demand is blocked, a firm must look at income distribution data.

Effective Demand

Though potential demand may exist, regulatory factors may prevent prospective customers from being able to satisfy their demand. Included are regulations on imports, tariffs, and foreign exchange; specific regulations on product standards with respect to safety, health, pollution; legal aspects such as patents, copyrights, trademarks; fiscal controls such as taxes, subsidies, or rationing and allocations; economic regulations including price controls and wage controls; political regulations including restrictions on buying foreign goods, the role of the government in the economy, and the power of the government to impose controls.

The presence of any of the above cited factors can cause the potential demand to be reduced to a lower level, in other words, to effective demand. Marketing research should, therefore, uncover the extent to which regulatory factors are present and determine the possible actions a firm might take to avoid some of the impact on demand.

Market Demand

The extent to which the effective demand can be realized depends substantially on the marketing infrastructure available to competing firms in a country. The degree to which a country's transportation system has been developed is important as well as its efficiency in terms of cost to users. Additional services marketers use regularly are storage facilities, banking facilities (particularly for consumer credit), available wholesale and retail structure, and advertising infrastructure. The absence of a fully developed marketing infrastructure would cause market demand to be substantially below effective demand. Marketing research will have to determine the effectiveness of the present marketing system and locate the presence of any inhibiting factors.

Sales Potential

The actual sales volume that a company will realize in any country is essentially determined by its competitive offering vis-à-vis other firms who also compete for a share of the same market. The resulting market share is determined by the relative effectiveness of the company's marketing mix. In determining a company's sales potential the researcher will have to assess whether the company can meet the competition in terms of product quality and features, price, distribution, and promotion. The assessment should result in an estimate of the company's market share, given the assumptions about the company's mode of entry (see Chapter 9) and marketing strategy (see Chapter 8).[24]

The difficulty, of course, is the determination of the various demand levels and the collection of the facts that can be used to determine actual potential and sales forecasts. Let's look at a situation in which a company is investigating a market that already has had experience with the product to be introduced. In

---

24. Franklin R. Root, *Entry Strategies for International Markets* (Lexington, Mass.: Lexington Book, 1987) p. 41.

such a case, the research effort is aimed at uncovering the data on present sales, usage, or production to arrive at the market demand (see Figure 7.4). Consequently, this is primarily an effort in collecting data from secondary information sources or commissioning professional marketing research through independent agencies when necessary.

Analysis by Inference

Available data from secondary sources are frequently of an aggregate nature and do not satisfy the specific needs of a firm focusing on just one product at a time. A company must usually assess market size based on very limited data on foreign markets. In such cases, market *assessment by inference* becomes a necessity. This technique uses available facts about related products or other foreign markets as a basis for inferring the necessary information for the market under analysis. Market assessment by inference is a low cost method that is analysis based and should take place before a company engages in any primary data collection at a substantial cost. Inferences can be made based upon related products, related markets' sales, and related environmental factors.

Inferences based upon related products. Few products are consumed or used alone without any ties to other prior purchases or products in use. Such relationships exist, for example, between replacement tires and automobiles on the road and electricity consumption and the use of appliances. In some situations, it may be possible to obtain data on related products and uses as a basis for inferred usage of the particular product to be marketed. From experience in other similar markets, the analyst is able to apply usage ratios that can provide for low cost estimates. For example, the analyst can determine the number of replacement tires needed per X automobiles on the road. A clear understanding of usage patterns can be gained from performing a comparative analysis as described earlier.

Inferences based upon related markets' size. Quite frequently, if market size data are available for other countries, use can be made of this information to derive estimates for the particular country under investigation. For example, consider that market size is known for the United States and estimates are required for Canada, a country with a comparable economic system and consumption patterns. Statistics for the United States could be scaled down by the relative size of either GNP, population, or other factors to about one-tenth of U.S. figures. Similar relationships exist in Europe where the known market size of one country can provide a basis for an inference about a related country. Of course, the results are not exact, but they provide a basis for further analysis. The cost and time lag for collecting primary market data often forces the analyst to use the inference approach.

Inferences based upon related environmental factors. A more comprehensive analysis can be provided following a full comparative analysis as outlined previously. After collecting data on the relevant environmental variables for a given product, an inference may be made on the market potential. The estimate's reliability would depend on the type of data available on the success factors. Actual data on success factors are of course preferable to inferences based upon the demand structure in a related market. Reed Moyer described a series of additional methods suited for forecasting purposes which often involve the use of historic data.[25] Some of these methods are described below in abbreviated form.

Analysis of Demand Patterns. By analyzing industrial growth patterns for various countries, insights can be gained into the relationship of consumption patterns to industrial growth. Relationships can be plotted between gross domestic product per capita, GNP per capita, and the percent of total manufacturing production accounted for by major industries. During earlier growth stages with corresponding low per capita incomes, manufacturing tends to center on necessities such as food, beverages, textiles, and light manufacturing. With growing incomes, the role of these industries tends to decline and heavy industry assumes a greater importance. By analyzing such manufacturing patterns, forecasts for various product groups can be made for countries at lower income levels since they often repeat the growth patterns of more developed economies. Similar trends can be observed for a country's import composition. With increasing industrialization, countries develop similar patterns only modified by a country's own natural resources. Energy-poor countries must import increasing quantities of energy as industrialization proceeds, whereas energy-rich countries can embark on an industrialization path without significant energy imports. Industrialized countries import relatively more food products and industrial materials than manufactured goods, which are more important for the less industrialized countries. Understanding these relationships can help the analyst in determining future trends for a country's economy and may help determine future market potential and sales prospects.

Multiple Factor Indexes

This technique has already been successfully used by domestic marketers. It entails the use of proxies to estimate demand if the situation should prevent the direct computation of a product's market potential. A multiple factor measures potential indirectly, using proxy variables that intuition or statistical analysis reveal to be closely correlated to the potential for the product under review.

A good example for such an approach is Ford Motor Company's analysis for its overseas tractor business.[26] To evaluate the attractiveness of its various

25. Reed Moyer, "International Market Analysis," *Journal of Marketing Research,* vol. 5, November 1968, pp. 353–360.

26. Gilbert D. Harrell, and Richard O. Kiefer, "Multinational Strategic Market Portfolios," *MSU Business Topics,* Winter 1981, pp. 5–15.

FIGURE 7.5 Key-Country Matrix

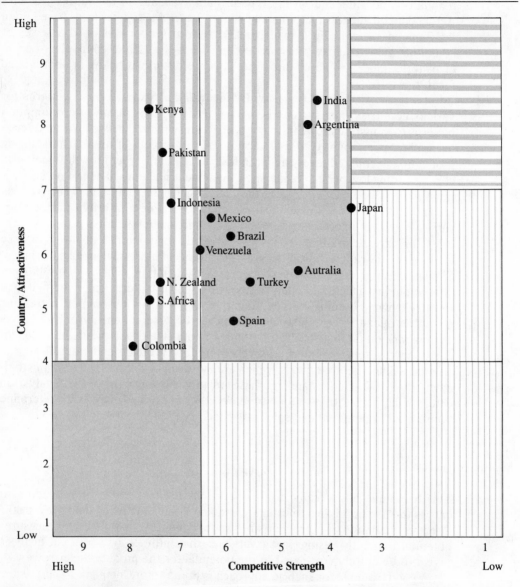

Gilbert D. Harrell and Richard O. Kieter, "Multinational Strategic Market Portfolios," MSU Business Topics, Winter 1981, p. 13. Reprinted by permission.

overseas markets, the company developed a scale and rated each country based on country attractiveness and competitive strength. These two dimensions were measured based on the following:

Country Attractiveness	*Competitive Strength*
1. Market size	1. Market share
2. Market growth rate	2. Product fit
3. Government Regulations	3. Contribution margin
Price controls	Profit per unit
Nontariff barrier	Profit percentage, net of dealer
Local content	cost
4. Economic and Political Stability	4. Market Support
Inflation	Quality of distribution system
Trade balance	Advertising versus competition
Political stability	

These items were evaluated by Ford executives and rated on a ten-point scale for each item. The items are combined based on the relative weight of each item to determine the coordinates of the X and Y axis. Figure 7.5 illustrates Ford's use of the market evaluation system for Ford's key countries. The weights are indicative of the firm's effort to rank markets via multiple factor indexes.

Competitive Studies

As every marketer knows, the results in the marketplace do not only depend on researching buyer characteristics and meeting buyer needs. To a considerable extent, success in the marketplace is influenced by a firm's competition. Companies competing on an international level have to be particularly careful with monitoring competition since some of the competing firms will most likely be located abroad thus creating additional difficulties in keeping abreast of the latest developments.

First, a company will have to determine who its competitors are. The domestic market will certainly provide some input here. However, it is of great importance to include any foreign company that either presently is or might become a competitor in the future. For many firms, the constellation of competitors will most likely change over time. One U.S. company, Caterpillar, could consider other domestic competitors its major competitors both domestically and abroad. More recently, the Japanese firm Komatsu has established itself as the second largest firm for earthmoving equipment, forcing Caterpillar to concentrate more resources on this new competitor.[27] Included in a company's monitoring system should therefore be *all* major competitors, both domestic and foreign. The monitoring should not be restricted to activity in the competitors' domestic market only but must include competitors' moves anywhere in the

---

27. "Komatsu on the Track of Cat," *Fortune*, September 20, 1981, pp. 164–174.

TABLE 7.3 Monitoring Competition: Facts to be Collected

OVERALL COMPANY STATISTICS
Sales and market share profits
Balance sheet
Capital expenditures
Number of employees
Production capacity
Research and development capability

MARKETING OPERATIONS
Types of products (quality, performance, features)
Service and/or warranty granted
Prices and pricing strategy
Advertising strategy and budgets
Size and type of sales force
Distribution system (includes entry strategy)
Delivery schedules (also spare parts)
Sales territory (geographic)

FUTURE INTENTIONS
New product developments
Current test markets
Scheduled plant capacity expansions
Planned capital expenditures
Planned entry into new markets/countries

COMPETITIVE BEHAVIOR
Pricing behavior
Reaction to competitive moves, past and expected

world. Many foreign firms first innovate in their home markets, expanding abroad only when the initial debugging of the product has been completed. A U.S. firm would therefore lose valuable time if, say, a Japanese competitor's action would only be picked up upon entry of the U.S. market. Any monitoring system needs to be structured in such a way as to ensure that competitors' actions will be spotted wherever they tend to occur first. Komatsu, Caterpillar's major competitor worldwide, subscribed to the *Journal Star,* the major daily newspaper in Caterpillar's hometown, Peoria, Illinois. Also important are the actions taken by subsidiaries because they might signal future moves elsewhere in a MNC's global network of subsidiaries.

Table 7.3 contains a list of the type of information a company might collect on its competitors. Aside from the general business statistics, a competitor's profitability might shed some light on the capacity to pursue new business in the future. Learning about others' marketing operations will allow the investigating company to assess, among other things, the market share to be gained in any given market. Whenever major actions are planned, it is extremely helpful to know what the likely reaction of competitive firms will be and to include them in a company's contingency planning. And, of course, monitoring a competitor's new products or expansion programs might give early hints on future competitive threats.

There are numerous ways to monitor competitor's activities. Thorough study of trade or industry journals is an obvious starting point. Also, frequent visits can be made to major trade fairs where competitors exhibit their products. At one such recent fair in Texas, engineers of Caterpillar were seen measuring Komatsu equipment.[28] Other important information can be gathered from the company's foreign subsidiaries located in the home markets of major competitors. The Italian office equipment manufacturer Olivetti assigned a major intelligence function to its U.S. subsidiary because of the subsidiary's direct access to competitive products in the U.S. marketplace. A different approach was adopted by the Japanese pharmaceutical company Esei who opened a liaison office in Switzerland, home base to several of the world's leading pharmaceutical companies. To keep track of a firm's competitors is an important international research function. The effort is most effectively performed on a permanent basis rather than ad hoc. To achieve the status of a permanent monitoring operation, responsibilities need to be assigned to personnel well placed to carry out this important activity.

Environmental Studies

Frequently it becomes necessary to study the international environment beyond the customary monitoring function that most international executives perform. Of particular interest are the economic, physical, sociocultural, and political environments.

When focusing on the economic environment, the primary interest will be on the economic activity in target countries. Major economic indicators are GNP growth, interest levels, industrial output, employment levels, and the monetary policy of the country under investigation. Studies focusing on one country are frequently undertaken when a major decision regarding that country has to be made. This could include a move to enter the country or to significantly increase the firm's presence in that market through large new investments.

Also frequently studied are the international economy and the role of the various supranational organizations, as these affect the business climate for multinational firms. For example, it is important for companies active in Europe to learn about the possible impact or likelihood of new regulations or decisions of the European Community. Frequently, reviews of such agencies or groups are ordered when a major move is imminent and information is needed on the potential impact of these decisions.

---

28. Ibid.

Since the physical environment tends to be the most stable aspect of the foreign marketing environment, such studies are frequently made for major market entry decisions or when the introduction of a new product requires a special analysis of that particular aspect of the environment. Included within the physical environment are population and related statistics on growth, age composition, birthrates, and life expectancy, as well as data on the climate and geography of a country.

Of particular interest is the sociocultural environment already described in some detail in Chapter 3. The salient factors include social classes, family life, lifestyles, role expectations of the sexes, reference groups, religion, education, language, customs, and traditions. Market researchers have classified these statistics as psychographics. The primary interest to the MNC is the potential effect of these variables on the sale of its products. Since the sociocultural environment is also unlikely to change over the short run, and since changes that do occur tend to be of a more gradual nature, such studies are most likely ordered when a major marketing decision in the local market is contemplated. As MNCs gain experience in any given country, its staff and local organization accumulate considerable data on the social and cultural situation that can be tapped whenever needed. A full study of these environmental variables is therefore most useful when the MNC does not already have a base in that country and past experience is limited.

Frequently management will investigate the regulatory environment of a given country because those influences can substantially affect marketing operations anywhere. Today, regulatory influences can originate both with national and supranational organizations. National bodies tend to influence the marketing scene within the borders of one country only whereas supranational agencies have a reach beyond any individual country. National regulations may include particular rulings affecting all businesses, such as product liability laws, or could be targeted at individual industries only. In the United States, the latter type would include regulatory agencies such as the U.S. Food and Drug Administration (FDA) or the Civil Aeronautics Board (CAB). Examples of supranational regulations are those issued by the European Community (EC) with respect to business within the member nations or the United Nations' Center for Transnational Corporations that has issued a nonbinding code of conduct for MNCs.

Regulatory trends can be of great importance to MNCs and may even lead to new opportunities. It is generally accepted by most observers that U.S. safety and emission control regulations for passenger automobiles are the most stringent to be found anywhere in the world. Recognizing this fact, the French Peugeot Company has maintained a small beachhead in the U.S. market, even with a small and insignificant sales volume, primarily to gain the experience of engineering cars under these stringent conditions. The company felt that this experience could be usefully applied elsewhere as other countries adopted similar regulations. Consequently, a MNC would not only monitor the regulatory environment to adopt products and marketing operations to meet with local success. In addition, firms might find it useful to keep informed about the latest regulations regarding their business in countries that have preceded other countries with pertinent legislation even if they may not conduct any business there.

Market Efficiency Studies

Spending substantial sums on marketing operations worldwide, MNCs are, of course, interested in finding out if their funds are spent in the most efficient manner. Studies on domestic marketing efficiencies may have been conducted routinely. Recently MNCs have attempted to investigate the most efficient resource allocation for foreign markets. One such example has been conducted by the World Bank and was reported by Charles Ramond.[29]

The data bank was established by the World Bank in 1970 to assist major manufacturers of consumer goods who had their major sales and earnings outside the United States. One such company was interested in an analysis of its major marketing expenditure variables in thirty-two target countries where most of the firm's business originated. Despite the extensive data bank available, the firm selected only seventeen descriptor variables that appeared most important to the firm's business success (see Table 7.4).

The unnamed MNC made available ten marketing expenditure variables (independent variables labelled *A* through *J*) and one payoff variable (the dependent variable). Linear regression aimed at estimating payoff as a function of the independent variables indicated that variable *F* accounted for 73 percent of the variance, and variable *C* accounted for another 19 percent. But since this analysis included all thirty-two countries, differences among countries or country clusters would not become apparent. Consequently, payoffs were regressed separately for each identifiable group or cluster of countries that had first to be determined.

The thirty-two countries were initially classified by their seventeen descriptor variables using the clustering technique as statistical analysis. The results were three major clusters of countries: rich European and Far Eastern countries, poor Asian and Latin American countries, and richer Latin American countries (see Table 7.5).

The initial analysis confirmed that the same descriptor variables did not relate equally in rich and poor countries. The following results were obtained by using the technique of multiple linear regression for the principal clusters one and two:

Cluster 1: 15 rich European and Far Eastern countries:

$$\text{Payoff} = 16(\text{population } 25\text{–}34) - 38(\text{population } 15\text{–}24) + 2(\text{passenger cars in use}) + 44(\text{population } 10\text{–}14) + 3(\text{Total Energy Consumption}) - 7{,}200 \pm \text{S.E. of } 3{,}700$$

Multiple $r = .993$; $r^2 = .986$

29. Charles Ramond, "The Strategy of Multinational Marketing Analysis: A Case History from the World Data Bank," in *Multinational Business Operations: Marketing Management,* ed. S. Prakash Sethi and Jagdish N. Sheth (Pacific Palisades, Calif.: Goodyear, 1973), vol. III, p. 50–72.

TABLE 7.4 Descriptor Variables

A. WEATHER VARIABLES
   Altitude above sea level
   Average monthly average temperature
   Latitude from equator
   Days without rainfall

B. POPULATION AGE GROUPS
   Population aged 10–14
   Population aged 15–24
   Population aged 25–34
   Population aged 35–44
   Population aged 45 and over
   Total population, mid-year

C. ECONOMIC, TRANSPORTATION, POWER, AND MEDIA VARIABLES
   Gross national product
   Total national income
   GNP per capita
   TNI per capita
   Passenger cars in use
   Telephones in use
   Total energy consumption per capita

Source: Charles Raymond, "The Strategy of Multinational Marketing Analysis: A Case History from World Data Bank," in *Multinational Business Operations: Marketing Management,* ed. S. Prakash Sethi and Jagdish N. Seth (Pacific Palisades, Calif.: Goodyear, 1973), p. 73.

Cluster 2: 9 poor Asian and Latin American countries:

Payoff = 16 (passenger cars in use) + 5,400 ± S.E. of 5,800

Multiple $r = .807$; $r^2 = .651$

The difference in variable relationship to payoff demonstrates the different effectiveness of marketing expenditure variables for each cluster. For countries in cluster one, funds could be reallocated from variables *B* and *C* to *A*, whereas for cluster two countries, funds could be shifted from *H* to either *C* or *E*.

This rather technical and intricate analysis of the effectiveness of various marketing variables under different environmental conditions is probably not available to every company. However, the results do indicate that managers should expect different response factors for their expenditure categories. The results also indicate that there are differences due to environmental circumstances that may require a differentiated approach in funding marketing expenditures. This World Bank study reflects a conceptual approach that international marketing managers can take without necessarily proceeding to a statistical analysis as just described.

TABLE 7.5 Country Clusters and Respective Factor Loadings

Rich European and Far Eastern		Poor Asian and Latin American		Richer Latin American	
Sweden	.99	India	.99	Mexico	.95
Switzerland	.98	Thailand	.99	Puerto Rico	.94
Denmark	.97	Pakistan	.98	Argentina	.91
France	.96	Malaysia	.94		
Netherlands	.94	Brazil	.91		
United Kingdom	.94	Turkey	.91		
Finland	.94	Peru	.88		
New Zealand	.92	Philippines	.82		
Belgium	.90	Colombia	.80		
Norway	.88				
Italy	.87				
West Germany	.86				
Australia	.86				
Japan	.81				
Austria	.80				

Source: Charles Raymond, "The Strategy of Multinational Marketing Analysis: A Case History from World Data Bank," in *Multinational Business Operations: Marketing Management,* ed. S. Prakash Sethi and Jagdish N. Seth (Pacific Palisades, Calif.: Goodyear, 1973), p. 73.

The Macro Survey Technique

The lack of market data has led to the use of a specially designed method for the identification of primary data: the *macro survey*. Developed for anthropological research, this method attempts to identify market potential of rural trading areas by observing the presence or absence of certain types of specialized institutions.[30] Such an approach was adapted in Thailand by the U.S. Department of Commerce that wanted to promote U.S. products in rural areas. The market potential was assessed by developing a macro survey scale consisting of five steps. Each step depended on the presence of certain public, religious, or commercial building(s), as shown in Table 7.6. Each next higher step naturally included the characteristics of the previous step. The scales were developed from the Commerce Department personnel's detailed knowledge of the region. Other scales could be developed based upon empirical data or research in a small

30. Richard P. Carr, Jr., "Identifying Trade Areas for Consumer Goods in Foreign Markets," *Journal of Marketing,* October 1978, pp. 76–80.

TABLE 7.6 Macro Survey for Rural Thailand

Step Number	Item Content	Population Estimate	Markets
1	Market Square	1,000 to 3,000	Piece-good cloth and light agricultural implements (shovels)
2	Fair ground agricultural support shops, food shops	3,000 to 8,000	Manufactured clothes, canned and dried foods, radios, bicycles, mopeds
3	Raimie fiber mill and pond, Buddhist temple, elementary school, urban support shops (auto repair shops)	5,000 to 10,000	Service for mopeds, hardware (e.g., hammers, saws, roofing material); school supplies; one-man motorized agricultural equipment (e.g., front end tiller)
4	Government administration building; ambulatory health care, secondary school, police services	7,000 to 10,000	Window/door screen material glass; social dresses, primitive plumbing equipment (e.g., lavatories, shower heads, etc., with support piping)
5	Raimie sack mill and water reservoir; high school and/or technical college; sewer and water purification systems	22,000 to 30,000	Light industrial machinery (welding, pipe threading equipment); air conditioning; cement; construction services; office supplies and equipment

Source: Richard P. Carr, Jr., ''Identifying Trade Areas for Consumer Goods in Foreign Markets.'' Reprinted from *Journal of Marketing,* October 1978, p. 79, published by the American Marketing Association.

sample area to be later extended to a much larger region. Once a scale exists, research only needs to identify the absence or presence of the indicated key items to conclude on the potential for a given product category.

The data collection on the presence of key items for a macro survey is as unconventional as the method itself. One important method is area photography to discern visible key items from the air, such as temples, schools, and so on. Aerial photography, even via satellite, is quick and relatively inexpensive. A second method for ascertaining the step or level of a given trade area is the use of yellow pages telephone directories. Available for purchase from many countries, yellow pages allow the researcher to check on the availability of commercial establishments and make analogies accordingly. Of course, a community visit would allow a more comprehensive check.

TOWARDS A WORLDWIDE MARKETING INFORMATION SYSTEM

To assist decision making about marketing on a global scale, researchers must provide more than data on strictly local factors within each country. All firms that market their products in overseas markets, particularly MNCs, require information that allows analysis across several countries or markets. However, leaving each local subsidiary or market to develop their own data base does not usually result in an integrated marketing information system (MIS). Instead, authority to develop a centrally managed MIS will have to be assigned to a central location, with reports given directly to the firm's chief international marketing officer. Jagdish Sheth made a very effective case for a centralized marketing research staff that would monitor buyer needs on a worldwide basis.[31] Sheth favors the establishment of a longitudinal panel in selected geographical areas encompassing all major markets, present and potential. By assessing client needs on a worldwide basis, the company would ensure that products and services are designed with all buyers in mind. This avoids the traditional pattern of initially designing products for the company's home market and looking at export or foreign opportunities only once a product has been designed.

A principal requirement for a worldwide MIS is a standardized set of data to be collected from each market or country. Though the actual data collection could be left to a firm's local units, they would do so according to central and uniform specifications.

CONCLUSIONS

In this chapter, we discussed the major challenges and difficulties in securing necessary data for international marketing. We have shown that effective marketing research is based on a conceptual framework combined with a thorough but flexible use of conventional marketing research practices. The major difficulties are the lack of basic data on many markets and the likelihood that research methods will have to be adapted to local environments. The final challenge of international marketing research is to provide managers with a uniform data base covering all the firm's present and potential market. This would allow for cross-country comparisons and analysis as well as the incorporation of worldwide consumer needs into the initial product design process. To achieve this interna-

---

31. Jagdish N. Sheth, "A Conceptual Model of Long-Range Multinational Marketing Planning," *Management International Review*, No. 4–5, 1971, pp. 3–10.

tional comparability of data, given the difficulties in data collection, is indeed a challenge for even the most experienced professionals.

Questions for Discussion

1. Why is it so difficult to do market research in multi-country settings?
2. Comparative marketing analysis is a powerful technique that provides the basis for the study of international marketing. What is the comparative approach and how do you apply it to multi-country environments?
3. What are the advantages and disadvantages of secondary and primary data in international marketing?
4. How would you protect against definitional, instrument, and frame error in international marketing research?
5. If you were estimating the demand for bathroom cleaners, what type of inference analysis would you use? Give a specific example.
6. If you headed Kodak, how would you monitor reactions around the world to a major competitor such as Fuji Film?
7. How would you conduct a marketing efficiency study of the countries your firm was present in?

For Further Reading

Davis, Harry L., Susan P. Douglas and Alvin J. Silk. "Measure Unreliability: Hidden Threat to Cross-National Marketing Research." *Journal of Marketing,* 45, No. 2 (Spring 1981), pp. 98–109.

Douglas, Susan P., and Samuel Craig. *International Marketing Research.* Englewood Cliffs, New Jersey: Prentice-Hall, 1983.

Green, Robert, and Philip D. White. "Methodological Considerations in Cross National Consumer Research." *Journal of International Business Studies* (Fall-Winter 1976), pp. 81–88.

Jaffee, E. D. "Multinational Marketing Intelligence: An Information Requirements Model." *Management International Review,* 19, No. 2 (1979), pp. 53–60.

Kracmar, John Z. *Marketing Research in the Developing Countries.* New York: Praeger, 1971.

Mayer, Charles S. "The Lessons of Multinational Marketing Research." *Business Horizons* (December 1978), pp. 7–13.

Moyer, Reed. "International Market Analysis." *Journal of Marketing Research* (November 1968), pp. 353–360.

Murray, J. Alex. "Intelligence Systems of the MNCs." *Columbia Journal of World Business* (September-October 1972), pp. 63–71.

Permut, Steven F. "The European View of Marketing Research." *Columbia Journal of World Business* (Fall 1977), p. 94.

Samli, A. Coskun. "An Approach to Estimating Market Potential in East Europe." *Journal of International Business Studies* (Fall-Winter 1977), pp. 49–55.

Wind, Yoram, and Susan Douglas. "International Market Segmentation." *European Journal of Marketing*, 6, No. 1 (1972), p. 18.

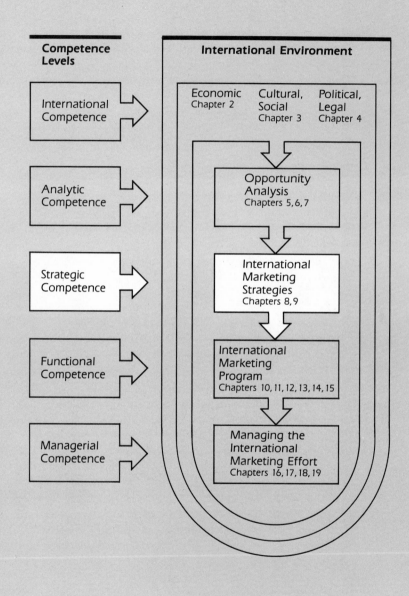

PART 4

INTERNATIONAL MARKETING STRATEGIES

8 ▪ **Global Marketing Strategies**

9 ▪ **Market Entry Strategies**

International companies increasingly will be asked to design their business strategies with a global point of view. Globalized business strategies require an ability to look at business and competitive developments all over the world and to digest often conflicting information into a workable plan. Global strategies require different skills and conceptual understanding than domestic strategies.

In this section, we concentrate on the global strategies international firms must be able to develop in order to be successful. No company can do all things to all people, and international managers have to learn to focus and build upon their company's strengths. Future international marketing managers will need to have the strategic competence necessary to develop global marketing programs that will ensure the success of their firms.

Chapter 8 concentrates on the major strategic decisions faced by firms active in international marketing. The chapter will introduce the most recent concepts on globalization of international marketing strategies. The various alternative entry strategies will be the subject of Chapter 9.

8.
GLOBAL MARKETING STRATEGIES

Companies will need to make a number of strategic decisions concerning their international marketing operations. At first, there is the decision to become an international company. Second, an international company will have to decide on the geographic concentration of its business, whether its business or operations should locate in developing or in industrialized countries. Third, a company will need to choose the particular countries to be entered. Closely related is the type of entry strategy a firm will adopt for each country selected. Another strategic decision concerns the marketing mix the firm intends to employ for its international operations. Finally, companies will have to address key organizational and planning issues. When designing strategy, companies will need to develop generic strategies in terms of geographic expansion, product or markets, and competitive strategies. The purpose of this chapter is to describe the nature of these strategic decisions with particular emphasis on the first three topics. The other topics will be introduced as they are treated in greater detail in separate chapters. Figure 8.1 shows the decision elements involved in international marketing.

REASONS FOR INTERNATIONALIZATION

Whether a company wants to compete internationally is a strategic decision that will fundamentally affect the firm, its operations, and its management. For many companies, the question as to why they should internationalize remains an important and difficult decision. Typically, there are many reasons or causes behind a company's decision to start to compete in foreign markets. For some

FIGURE 8.1 International Marketing Strategies

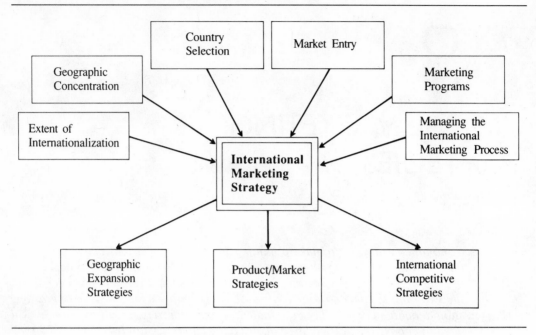

firms, going abroad is the result of a deliberate policy decision whereas for others it is a reaction to a specific business opportunity or a competitive challenge.

Opportunistic Development

Probably the most common reason for international expansion is recognition that opportunities exist in foreign markets. Many companies, particularly in the United States, promote their products in trade journals and through other media to their U.S. customers. Because these publications are also read by foreign business executives, orders are made that are initially unsolicited. Because these transactions are usually more complicated and more involved than a routine shipment to domestic customers, the firm will have to make a decision at this time whether or not to respond. The company can also adopt a more aggressive stance by actively pursuing foreign customers, moving beyond filling unsolicited orders. Thus, some firms have built sizable foreign businesses by first responding to orders and by taking a more proactive approach later on. Most of today's large internationally active companies were built initially around an opportunistic strategy, although today these firms have moved to a more orchestrated and deliberate strategy in their approach to international marketing.

Following Customers Abroad

For a company whose business is concentrated on a few large customers the decision to internationalize is usually made when one of its key customers moves abroad to pursue international opportunities. Many of the major U.S. automobile component suppliers are operating plants abroad to supply their customers in foreign locations. Similar trends can be observed as Japanese and European automobile manufacturers set up their own operations in the United States. These moves tend to be followed by a series of component suppliers who do not want to lose out on a new business opportunity.

The service sector has seen similar expansions triggered by client moves overseas. The establishment of international branch networks of major U.S. banks, such as Citibank or Chase Manhattan, was motivated by a desire to service key domestic clients overseas. Major U.S. advertising agencies and accounting firms have set up extensive networks of foreign offices for the same reasons. Thus, as a firm's customer base becomes international, so will the firm's own operations if it wants to maintain its business.

Pursuing Diversification

A need to diversify beyond a single country can also be behind moves to internationalize a company. Although this is less of a factor for United States–based companies, firms in other parts of the world often do not want their operations to be dominated or overdependent on the economies of one single country. Sometimes this may be caused by a long economic decline of a country, as was the case for the United Kingdom within the past ten years. Many U.K. firms pursued opportunities overseas because they saw their home operations decline. Firms in countries with considerable political risk, such as South Africa or Hong Kong, are diversifying into other parts of the world as a hedge against potentially negative domestic trends.

International Market Extension for Incremental Profit

A deliberate international expansion policy is pursued by firms who are motivated by profit potential through market extension. In industries where investment in research and development is high, companies often want to harvest past investment by introducing established products into other countries. Such a strategy is particularly profitable when additional market entries do not require substantial investments in product changes or additional research and development. This is the case for much of the computer industry where products are substantially standardized across the world.

Taking Advantage of Different Growth Rates of Economies

Growth rates among countries are subject to wide variations. In situations where a company is based in a low-growth country, the firm might suffer a competitive disadvantage and might want to expand into faster growing countries to take advantage of growth opportunities. For those reasons, many European companies looked for new business opportunities in the United States during the mid-1970s to 1980s. A similar rush of companies to the Middle East was noticeable during the time period following the first substantial oil price increase in 1973 and 1974. Currently, economies in the Pacific Basin, such as Korea, Taiwan, Hong Kong, and Japan, tend to experience high growth rates which in turn attract many foreign companies.

Exploiting Product Life Cycle Differences

When the market for a firm's product becomes saturated, a company can open new opportunities by entering into foreign markets where the product may not be very well known. Adding new markets thus works like an extension of the product's life cycle. Among U.S. firms following this strategy are many consumer goods marketers, such as Philip Morris, Coca-Cola Company, and PepsiCo. These companies often go into markets where the per capita consumption of their products is still relatively low. With economic expansion and the resulting improvement in personal incomes, these companies expect to experience substantial growth later on—though operations in the United States are showing little growth. Likewise, Yoplait, a French yogurt maker, moved into the U.S. market where per capita consumption of yogurt was less than one tenth of the French consumption. By moving into a low consumption market, the firm stood to gain substantially when consumption started to grow.

Pursuing Potential Abroad

Despite its size as the world's largest economy, the U.S. market accounts usually for little more than one half the business in many high technology product categories. For some of the more common product or industry categories such as food, the U.S. market represents a much smaller portion of the overall world market. As a result, many firms are attracted by the sheer size of the potential business abroad. For example, H. J. Heinz built a baby food factory in China. Dr. Anthony O'Reilly, President and CEO reasoned, "The U.S. produces 3.5 million babies per year. China produces 16 million."[1] With a population that is

---

1. Joseph O. Eastlack, Jr. and Roberta Lucker, "Is China Moving from Marx to Mastercard?" *The Journal of Consumer Marketing,* Summer 1986, pp. 9–10.

exceeding that in the United States, the European market, although fragmented into many countries, offers a market that is economically as large as the U.S. market. The Pacific Rim countries of Korea, Taiwan, Japan, and China have very large populations and are attracting many newcomers who want to go where they see new potential.

Internationalizing for Defensive Reasons

Sometimes, companies do not pursue new growth or potential abroad but decide to enter international business for largely defensive reasons. When a domestic company sees its markets invaded by foreign firms, that company may react by entering the foreign competitor's home market in return. As a result, the company can learn valuable information about the competitor which will help in its operations at home. A company may want to slow down a competitor by denying it the cash flow from its profitable domestic operation which could otherwise be invested into expansion abroad. As a result, companies who had not had to compete internationally find themselves suddenly forced to expand abroad.

Many U.S. companies opened operations in Japan because this allowed them to get closer to what was the most important competition for them. For example, major companies such as Xerox and IBM use their local subsidiaries in Japan to learn new ways to compete with the major Japanese firms in their field. Likewise, many European firms want to be represented in the U.S. market because they can learn about new opportunities more directly than if they waited in their home markets for U.S. firms to arrive with new products or technologies.

Leveraging Key Success Factors Abroad

Although many companies joining the ranks of internationally active firms still do so largely to search for new opportunities, there are also those companies that internationalize to achieve additional leverage for key resources or investments. Leveraging key success factors, or KSFs,[2] requires a firm to first become aware of the key functions it must concentrate on to beat both domestic and international competitors. Typically, to outdo competitors within these functions requires additional investment. Such investments can frequently be justified only if the market is large enough. Many times, a single domestic market cannot support the required outlays to stay competitive, forcing such firms to eye the international market from the very beginning.

In the late 1970s, Plessey PLC, a British telecommunications equipment manufacturer, needed to make a substantial investment for a new generation of public digital telephone switching equipment in order to remain competitive in its

---

2. Kenichi Ohmae, *The Mind of the Strategist* (New York: McGraw-Hill, 1982), p. 42.

domestic market. However, the research and development costs were such that the company needed a volume two times the U.K. market to justify its expenditures. As a result, Plessey PLC made additional investments in the United States with the idea of gaining additional volume to offset its substantial research investment. Unless Plessey PLC was prepared to become a large international company, a move to a new generation of switching equipment would not have been feasible. Similar challenges are faced by pharmaceutical firms whose research costs are rapidly increasing and cannot be justified unless the companies have the international reach to amortize research costs across many countries.

KSFs may not only be research and development. For a company that manufactures construction equipment, such as Caterpillar, an efficient dealer network with ample stocks of spare parts may be the key to success. In that case, the company would obtain more volume through its spare parts system by expanding internationally; and thus it could afford to maintain a more elaborate system than if it were based in only one market. Consequently, companies need to become keenly aware of their relevant KSFs so that appropriate strategies can be devised that will make them more competitive both at home and abroad. How leveraging KSFs will influence strategic decisions will be discussed in greater detail later in this chapter.

DETERMINING GEOGRAPHIC CONCENTRATION

Once a company has made a commitment to extending its business internationally, management will soon be confronted with the task of setting some geographic or regional emphasis. A company could decide to emphasize developed nations such as those of Europe, North America, or Japan. Alternatively, some companies might prefer to pursue primarily developing countries in Latin America, Africa, or Asia. Management must make a strategic decision to direct business development in such a way that the company's overall objectives are congruent with the particular geographic mix of its activities.

Concentrating on Developed Countries

Developed countries account for a disproportionate share of world GNP (68% in 1984) and thus tend to attract many companies.[3] In particular, firms with technology-intensive products have concentrated their activities in the developed world. Although competition is usually more intensive in those markets both from other international firms and local companies, doing business in developed countries is generally preferred over doing business in developing nations. This

---

3. *World Economic Survey 1986* (New York: United Nations, 1986), p. 16.

is primarily because the business environment is more predictable and the investment climate is more favorable.

Developed countries are located in North America (United States and Canada), Western Europe, and Asia (Japan, Australia, New Zealand). Although some very large multinational firms such as IBM have operations in all of these countries, many others may be represented in only one or two areas. United States multinational companies have very early in their development established strong business bases in Europe and more recently in Japan. Japanese firms tended to start their overseas operations in the United States and Canada and moved then into Europe.

Toshiba, a large Japanese electronics company, was widely considered the second most important producer of electronic chips worldwide. However, in Europe, where the firm was a late-comer, it ranked only fifteenth. As a result, Toshiba saw Europe as a major growth market and pursued the goal of becoming one of the top five semiconductor suppliers.[4] European multinationals have often pursued business in developing countries, and of course Europe, but they have only more recently expanded their operations in the United States and Japan. Philips, the large Dutch electric equipment company, is a major player in the consumer electronics area. During World War II, when the Netherlands was occupied by Germany, Philips reorganized its U.S. subsidiary as an independent trust with local control. As a result, the company never developed a fully integrated strategy for the U.S. market. With new electronics products such as compact disk players just around the corner, worldwide success depends largely on more expansion in the U.S. market.[5]

Emphasizing Developing Countries

Developing nations differ substantially from developed nations by geographic region and by the level of economic development. Markets in Latin America, Africa, the Middle East, and Asia are also characterized by a higher degree of risk than markets in the developed countries. Due to the less stable economic climates in those countries, a company's operation can be expected to be subject to greater uncertainty and fluctuation. Furthermore, the frequently changing political situations in developing countries often affect operating results negatively. As a result, some markets that may have experienced high growth for some years may suddenly experience drastic reductions in growth. Mexico and Brazil are good examples of countries that grew rapidly in the 1970s but whose economic expansion came to an abrupt halt with their sudden inability to service their extensive foreign debt. In many situations, the higher risks are compen-

4. "Toshiba Seeks a Bigger European Market Share with Megabit Chip," *Financial Times*, February 23, 1987, p. 10.
5. "How Far Can Philips Elbow Its Way into the U.S.?" *Business Week*, March 2, 1987, p. 46.

sated for by higher returns, largely because competition is often less intense in those markets. Consequently, companies need to balance the opportunity for future growth in the developing nations with the existence of higher risk.

However, there are also industries that will certainly profit from a move to developing countries. The tobacco industry, for one, is moving heavily into developing countries because it sees more growth there than in the developed world of North America and Europe.[6] The cigarette consumption of Third World countries amounts to about one third of world consumption and is rapidly rising. Whereas cigarette consumption in Europe's largest markets declined about 5 percent between 1979 and 1984, it grew more than 15 percent in Africa. Tobacco companies also meet less stringent laws in developing countries with respect to advertising and anti-smoking regulations; thus many of the leading tobacco firms have emphasized their business development efforts in those regions.

Balancing the Global Sales Mix

One firm that considered itself overexposed to Third-World countries was Nestlé. This Swiss-based multinational food company found itself with a substantial business volume in developing countries. To balance this risk, the company took specific steps to increase its business in North America, with special emphasis on the U.S. market. The company acquired several U.S. firms, including Stouffer Foods and Carnation, and thus achieved a more balanced distribution of its global sales as well as a corresponding decrease in its risk on investments in the Third World. Other European firms, such as Siemens of Germany and Alfa-Laval of Sweden, made it a policy to add to their sales in the U.S. because they found that, measured against the market potential for their industries, their U.S. sales were underperforming.

Although developing a regional or geographic concentration constitutes an important decision for a firm's international marketing strategy, policy decisions of this magnitude are not a daily occurrence. In fact, redirections may occur only occasionally, and companies would not be able to show any specific results for some time as these decisions are clearly of a long-term nature.

COUNTRY SELECTION

At some point, the development of an international marketing strategy will come down to selecting individual countries where a company intends to compete.

---

6. "Cigarette Companies Develop Third World as a Growth Market," *The Wall Street Journal*, July 5, 1985, p. 1.

There are about 150 members at the United Nations, which is some indication as to how many different countries companies have to select from. Very few international firms end up competing in all of these markets. The decision on where to compete is referred to as the country selection decision and is one of the components of developing an international marketing strategy. Selecting a country as part of a firm's portfolio only determines that a company has decided to build up a market presence or to market its products; it does not automatically require a particular form of presence such as a plant, or a sales office. This latter decision will be described separately under the entry strategy section of this chapter.

Why is country selection a strategic concern for international marketing management? Adding another country to a company's portfolio always requires some additional investment in management time and effort and capital. Although the opportunities for additional profits are usually the driving force, each additional country also represents a new business risk. It takes time to build up business in a country where the firm was not previously represented and profits may not show until later. For these reasons it may be preferable to invest in a country that belongs to an economic group, such as the EC or ANCOM. Once a firm is involved with one member of the group, it becomes easier to sell to other member countries. Furthermore, many firms do not like to withdraw from markets once success has not been achieved for fear of causing uncertainty among its clients. Consequently, companies will need to go through a careful analysis before they decide to move ahead.

Analyzing the Investment Climate

A complete understanding of the investment climate of a target country will help in making the country selection decision. The investment climate of a country is made up of its political situation, its legal structure, its foreign trade position, and its attitude towards foreign investment or the presence of foreign companies. In general, companies will try to avoid countries with uncertain political situations. The impact that political and legal forces can have on the operations of a foreign company abroad was described in detail in Chapter 4.

A country's foreign trade position can also determine the environment for foreign firms operating there. Countries with a strong balance of payments surplus or strong currencies that are fully convertible are favored as good places to invest. Countries with chronic balance of payments difficulties and those where there are great uncertainties about the transferability of funds are viewed as risky and as such are less favored by foreign investors. These aspects were described in greater detail in Chapter 2 and Chapter 4. Consequently, assessing a country's investment climate will require a thorough and skillful analysis. However, investment climate is not the only determinant for a country being selected for entry.

Determining Market Attractiveness

Before a country can be selected or targeted for addition to a firm's portfolio of countries, management needs to assess the overall attractiveness of that country with respect to the firm's products or services. Initially, this will require a clear indication of the country's market size. This could consist of analyzing existing patterns of demand. Also needed is some data on growth, both past and future, that would allow a firm to determine market size not only as it relates to the present situation but also with respect to the future potential of that country.

Analyzing demand patterns will allow a company to plot where on the product life cycle a given product or service can be located. Also, a firm may want to analyze potential competitors in that country to achieve an understanding as to how it could compete. Finally, companies entering a new country should get to know that market enough to make a determination if their way of competing and marketing is allowed in that country. Some markets might be very attractive but if the firm's key strength cannot be employed success is questionable.

The analytic approach required for an in-depth analysis of a country's market attractiveness was covered in great detail in Chapters 5 and 7. Analyzing international markets and the company's prospective international buyers—the ability to perform marketing research and analysis on an international scale—will be a prerequisite to sound country selection decisions.

Assembling a Country Portfolio

By combining the results of analyses on investment climate and market attractiveness, a company can move towards specific country selection. However, choices will most likely entail some tradeoffs among conflicting facts. Some countries with a very positive and secure investment climate might offer only small markets or disappointing growth opportunities. Alternatively, countries with a less than perfect investment climate could offer very attractive markets with substantial growth and profit opportunities. Consequently, companies will frequently have to choose between the two sets of indices that offer contradictory advice. Depending on the type of industry or the type of investment required, a company may favor one or the other factor in its country selection decision.

As a company starts to add a large number of countries where it competes, this collection of markets can be referred to as the *country portfolio*. Looking at the firm's entire country portfolio, management would want to be concerned about a balance and a distribution of risk factors. Ideally, the company would have countries with good investment climate but probably lower market attractiveness as well as other countries where the riskier investment climate was compensated for by a higher market attractiveness.

MARKET ENTRY DECISIONS

Once a company has decided to select a certain group of countries for further market development, the company will then be confronted with market entry decisions. In this phase, a company will face a series of options as to how it wants to enter the selected country. The options range from a very low level of involvement and investment, such as various forms of exporting, to more involved and investment intensive forms of entry, such as a company owned sales subsidiary or even a manufacturing base.

Entry strategies are of strategic importance because most companies often will not be able to quickly shift from one alternative to another following initial market feedback. Depending on the type of entry strategy selected, market success may differ substantially. Furthermore, some entry strategies require a substantial amount of initial investment and the results cannot be realized until much later. As a result, companies are very careful in finding the right amount of commitment combined with the expected results and the type of market they want to enter.

Representing a lower level of involvement are export strategies based on serving a given target country from a manufacturing base that is located elsewhere. These strategies do not include a new investment into fixed assets. The company can export to a foreign market through the use of domestic intermediaries or through direct contacts with wholesalers and distributors located in the foreign market. If deemed appropriate, a company may select an exporting strategy by relying on its own sales subsidiary in the foreign market.

Representing a greater level of involvement is the establishment of a local production facility combined with local sales efforts. A company may want to open an assembly operation for only partial manufacturing or may even proceed so far as to establish an integrated manufacturing unit. Local production calls for a greater level of capital expenditure and therefore a greater risk.

An intermediate level of involvement is also possible through licensing. In licensing, a company, called the licensor, grants to another firm, the licensee, located in the foreign market the right to exploit its technology, brand name, or trademark under specific circumstances. Typically, it is the local firm that will take the business risk for the venture with a prearranged licensing fee paid to the licensor.

Given the importance of managing entry strategies for success in international marketing, Chapter 9 is entirely devoted to this topic. The chapter will concentrate on documenting the various analytic steps companies go through in making entry strategy decisions for their foreign ventures while describing influencing factors such as costs, investments, market potential, and sales volume.

MARKETING PROGRAMS

Although companies face a host of important decisions when developing marketing programs for international markets, the most important strategic decision they face relates to the amount of standardization versus differentiation aimed for in the various target markets. As we explained in considerable detail in our first chapter, companies face many barriers that will prevent or make it very difficult to offer standardized marketing programs. Standardization is not only to be understood in terms of product hardware but includes the "software" of marketing programs such as distribution, pricing, and promotion strategies.

It will not always be clear whether a marketing program needs to be tailored to each individual market. Although local conditions might signal on the surface that such an approach might be advantageous, other concerns need to be considered. Substantial changes in a company's marketing program will naturally bring additional costs. Such cost increases might occur in the production of new or additional product models with corresponding research and engineering costs. Such incremental costs are not always justified by the incremental business volume expected. Consequently, in some cases a company may not be in a position to differentiate even though management believes the market would require it. Similar concerns apply for other marketing aspects such as advertising, distribution, or logistics.

Of equal concern is the extent to which a company's systems may be applied abroad. A marketing program doesn't only consist of products or services; it is embedded in the whole system or the way a firm does its business. The company's culture, or even its unwritten rules can become important to the competitive advantage of a company. Whether these are important planning systems, methods of working with advertising agencies, or firm rules on how to deal with marketing intermediaries with respect to pricing, companies are reluctant to make changes for fear of precedent. As a result, systems or methods of operation that are closely related to a firm's competitive advantage may not be changed even if a particular country's environment demanded it.

By preserving the key elements of a company's marketing program even when faced with different business environments, companies intuitively respond to obstacles preventing them from unfolding their strategies. When countries do not allow a firm to unfold its traditional marketing program, and therefore prevent it from working on the basis of its inherent competitive strength, a company is forced to choose between three alternatives: adapt its marketing program, insist on unfolding the existing program, or stay out of a market entirely.

Adaptation might be acceptable if the incremental costs of such a strategy outweigh the expected returns. Under such circumstances, a company could hope to get a relatively larger share of the market. Alternatively, the company could use its standardized strategy, though it would be less suitable to a local market than an adaption strategy, and accept a smaller market share as a result. Finally, a company could decide to avoid markets where its key strengths, as reflected in its marketing programs, could not be sufficiently applied.

MANAGING INTERNATIONAL MARKETING

How a company manages, organizes, and controls its operations greatly influences the direction it takes. Executives, both domestically and abroad, tend to adapt to a company's organizational systems, which makes the choice of organizational system important. Although the impact of the organization's design or planning and control systems are less obvious to an outside observer, these factors are nevertheless considered of strategic importance because the effect is often realized only years after such systems have been put in place.

Of major concern to a company are the organizational structure to be selected for its international operations, the location of decisions making authority with respect to international marketing, and the nature of its planning process as it impacts on international marketing. We will review each one of these aspects broadly since Chapters 16 and 17 are devoted entirely to these important concerns.

Organizing International Marketing

A company with strictly domestic operations faces the challenge of bringing together product knowledge, industry knowledge, market, and customer knowledge all under one umbrella. Firms with international operations face the additional problem of how they should deal with the international dimension present in their business. Because there are few managers with international experience in most companies, the organizational structures chosen are often geared towards conserving that scarce talent by concentrating international responsibilities under one or few key executives.

Thus, strategic organizational concerns result in a selection of either concentrated or diffused organizational designs. A company chooses a concentrated approach to international marketing when all of its international operations are organized under one division and kept separate from its other domestic divisions that might be product or functionally oriented. A company that has chosen a diffused approach to its international organization may give worldwide responsibility to all of its product divisions, thus creating in fact a number of international marketing departments. Many companies have learned that such choices can have a considerable impact on the growth of their international operations and consequently treat them with great care.

Allocating Decision-Making Authority

International organizations need to allocate decision-making authority for key decisions. Who decides, where the decisions are made, what is decided, and how much the decision makers can decide are the key questions to be addressed. In a strictly centralized organization, all the key decisions will be made by a few executives located at headquarters. Other companies prefer a decentralized decision-making approach where a considerable amount of the decision-making authority is delegated to the various country organizations. The extent of centralization versus decentralization can be expected to differ from company to company and tends to be affected by industry factors, market factors, and by the maturity of the international organization itself, as we will see in Chapters 16 and 17.

The Planning Process

Another aspect of strategic importance is the planning process in an international organization. Companies may elect to plan "top-down," which implies that the initiative in planning will come from headquarters and foreign market units will be expected to adjust their plans accordingly. "Bottom-up" planning means that the initiative is at the country level and higher organization units consolidate what are basically individual country plans. Whether a company elects top-down or bottom-up planning depends on a number of external and internal factors. Clearly, the company's own organizational structure and management style has an effect on the planning mode. Also, the diversity of a firm's markets can also impact on the planning cycle. Firms competing in very similar markets worldwide are more apt to use a headquarters-directed planning mode compared to firms whose operating conditions differ substantially from country to country. A substantial portion of Chapter 17 is devoted to a more complete discussion of these topics.

GENERIC INTERNATIONAL MARKETING STRATEGIES

Having explored some of the key strategic decisions faced by international marketing executives, our focus will now shift to the generic international marketing strategies companies can adopt. Generic strategies are general classifications used to organize a large number of possible individual strategies. This is done to highlight certain general principles—no company will neatly fall into any one of these categories. Instead, it is expected that most companies will fall somewhere in between categories, or they may use a combination of strategies from different categories. Furthermore, many companies actually pursue several kinds of strategies at once, varying them according to product line or business unit.

Generic international marketing strategies may be classified along two dimensions. The geographic dimension deals with the extent of international expansion, ranging from purely domestic, single-country strategy to a global, multi-country strategy. Secondly, we can distinguish strategies by the extent of market/product lines offered. This can range from a narrow line, or niche strategy, all the way to a broad or multi-segment line. For a graphical depiction of these dimensions, see Figure 8.2.

FIGURE 8.2 Generic International Marketing Strategies

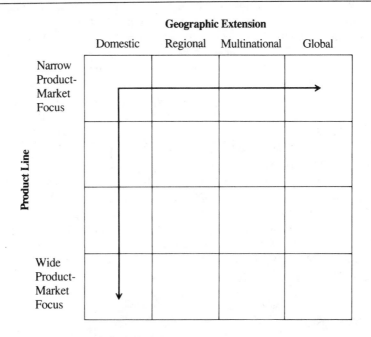

GEOGRAPHIC EXPANSION STRATEGIES

To succeed in international marketing competition, companies need to carefully look at their geographic expansion. To some extent, a firm makes a conscious decision about its extent of internationalization by choosing a posture that may range from entirely domestic without any international involvement to a global reach where the company devotes its entire marketing strategy to global competition. Each level of internationalization will profoundly change the way a company competes and will require different strategies with respect to marketing programs, planning, organization, and control of the international marketing effort.

Domestic Strategy

A company with a strictly domestic strategy has decided not to actively involve itself in any international marketing. To use our terminology from Chapter 1, such a firm will not develop globetrotting skills as no sales take place outside its domestic or home market. Clearly, such companies are not the main interest for our text but there are nevertheless situations where a company should not or cannot become an active participant in international marketing.

When a company has a very limited product range that only appeals to its own local market, international marketing would not be advisable unless the company were prepared to expand its product line. In many service oriented businesses, customer relations are such that business is only done within a narrow or limited geographic range. To expand to new business centers other affiliates would have to be built, again requiring considerable capital assets. Also, some industries are substantially domestic, with individual companies not directly competing beyond their own local markets. And newly started companies might not be in a position to expand abroad before their domestic market is satisfied.

What has become evident is that, over the past two decades, an ever increasing number of domestic industries have started to become international. These developments might have been triggered by a foreign company arriving on the scene and changing the competitive situation, or that new technological developments were invented abroad that affected the industry in the home market. When such situations become common, an industry clearly should move from being purely domestic to international in scope. Consequently, today fewer and fewer industries can view themselves from a purely domestic point of view and more and more companies must move on to some level of internationalization.

Regional Expansion Strategies

Mapping out a regional strategy implies that a company will concentrate its resources and marketing efforts on one or possibly two of the world's regions. Emphasizing North America or Europe could be the result of a regional strategy. Other regions a company might want to concentrate on are Latin America, the Pacific Basin, or Asia. In such a situation, the company has expanded beyond a domestic environment but, as we will see later, has not yet reached a multinational or global state.

There are a number of reasons that make companies pursue a regional expansion strategy. Such firms are competing in the region that is part of their home market. Neighboring markets within the same region are invaded because of market or product similarity requiring few adaptations. Regional strategies are also encouraged when the customer requirements in one region are substantially different from others. Under those circumstances, different sets of competitors and market structures might exist, and industry participants might not invade each other's regions or market territories. When such a fragmentation exists, a firm can compete on the basis of knowing its own region best by being closer to its customers.

Examples for regional strategies can be found in a number of industries including the automobile, home appliance, and telecommunications industries. Among some of the leading automobile manufacturers, both Chrysler and Fiat can be classified as pursuing regional strategies. Chrysler Corp. withdrew from most overseas markets in the mid-1970s as a result of poor performance and a need to retrench to its major market, the United States. By the mid-1980s, Chrysler Corporation was competing largely in the United States, Canada, and Mexico. Another regional manufacturer in the automobile industry is Fiat of Italy. This company competes primarily in Europe with a few small operations in Latin America. Fiat does not play a major role in the North American markets or in Asia. Fiat has been very successful in leveraging its strong position in Italy into a sufficient volume to compete primarily in the small car segments in European countries.

Other examples of regional strategies are found in the telecommunications and technological industries. ITT, a United States–based company, had very strong market positions in Europe and Latin America but only minor positions in the U.S. market. Olivetti of Italy, while pursuing a global strategy in technology, started with a regional base in Europe to compete in the office equipment industry. And Electrolux, a very large Swedish company in the home appliance industry, sold off its U.S. subsidiary years ago to retrench into the European markets where today it plays the dominant role.

Companies with regional strategies recently came under intense competitive pressure as their territories became invaded by other firms from North America and the Far East. As a result, many of these firms have undergone a transformation to break out of the regional limits and to broaden their bases into other regions. These efforts have not always been successful. Fiat failed in the North American market but was successful in Latin America, particularly in Brazil. Electrolux successfully re-entered the U.S. market, by purchasing another firm, Eureka; and it now finds itself competing against its former subsidiary, still a successful firm using the Electrolux name. ITT was unable to penetrate the U.S. market for large switching systems for regional telephone companies, which would have broadened its base beyond the regional presence it had in Europe and Latin America. However, ITT joined its telecommunications business in Europe with the leading French company, CGE, to form a large group with a chance to compete globally.[7]

Multinational Strategies

As we discussed in Chapter 1, multinational corporations tend to be represented in a large number of countries and the world's principal trading regions. The majority of today's large internationally active firms would therefore be classified as multinational corporations.

A large number of U.S. firms listed by Fortune Magazine in its Fortune 500 list are operating as MNCs. This includes such well-known firms as General Motors, Ford, IBM, Gillette, General Electric, Kodak, as well as major service businesses including Citibank or Chase Manhattan, two of the largest United

---

7. "The CGE-ITT Deal: It Looks Like a Turning Point," *Financial Times*, January 7, 1987, p. 16.

States–based finanical services organizations. Common to most of these firms is their very large percentage of sales and profits generated from overseas business. For IBM and Gillette more than half of their volume is generated overseas.

Overseas firms such as Unilever, Royal Dutch-Shell, and Nestle are foreign based MNCs with only a small portion of their sales coming from their domestic or home market. Because most foreign markets are smaller than the U.S. market, foreign MNCs show a larger percentage of their operations from business abroad due to their relative small domestic markets. The ranks of MNCs have also been joined by many Japanese firms, Hitachi, Matushita, Toyota, and Nissan among them, as well as firms from newly industrialized countries such as Korea, Taiwan, and some developing countries.

Although we will present organization issues in more detail in Chapter 16, some general principles of how MNCs are organized should be introduced at this point. To a large extent, MNCs have organized their businesses around countries or geographic regions. While some key strategic decisions with respect to products and technology are made at the central or head office, the initiative of implementating marketing strategies is largely left to local country subsidiaries. As a result, profit and loss responsibility tends to focus on each individual country. At the extreme, this leads to an organization that runs many different businesses in a number of countries. MNCs with large domestic markets, where new products tend to be introduced first, might see their subsidiaries largely as sales arms for the execution of an already proven marketing strategy. As a result, MNCs are often dominated by communications and directions from the single head office to its large number of country organizations. Each subsidiary represents a separate business that must be run profitably.

Global Strategies

To many readers the term *global strategy* will probably suggest a company represented everywhere and pursuing more or less the same strategy. However, global strategies are not to be equated with global standardization, although this may be the case in some situations. A global strategy represents an application of a common set of strategic principles across most world markets. It may include, but not require, similarity in products or in marketing processes. When a company pursues a global strategy, it looks at the world market as a whole rather than looking at markets on a country-by-country basis, which is more typical for the multinational firm.

Standardization deals with the amount of similarity companies want to achieve across many markets with respect to their marketing strategies and marketing mix. Standardization may also apply to general business policies or the modes of operation a company may want to pursue. Globalization, on the other hand, deals with the interconnection of the many country strategies and the subordination of these country strategies under one global framework. As a result, it is conceivable that one company might have a globalized approach to its marketing strategy but leave the details for many parts of the marketing plan to local subsidiaries. Few companies would want to globalize all of their marketing operations. The difficulty then becomes to establish which marketing operations would gain from globalization. Such a modular approach to globalization is likely to yield greater returns than a total globalization of a company's marketing strategy.[8]

Globalizing for Internal Efficiency

What are the advantages in pursuing a global strategy? Internal efficiency is one advantage. By coordinating its operations for maximum efficiency, a company reduces costs and thus becomes more competitive.[9] Some companies may encounter new technological breakthroughs that represent substantial costs. These up-front research and development costs cannot be paid off by one or a few markets alone; consequently, companies become global out of a need to gain more volume. As we already discussed earlier in this chapter, this need for more global volume triggered Plessey's move into the United States.

Globalizing to Compete in Homogeneous Markets

Another factor that encourages companies to pursue a global strategy is the homogenization of markets. In a much discussed article, Theodore Levitt encouraged companies to pursue globalization of products by looking at the similarities of their markets as opposed to differences. As a result, companies would gain economies of scale through cost reductions because the multitude of model variations used by many MNCs drove up costs and prevented internal efficiency from standardized volume. Levitt also pointed out that lower prices, which could be offered as a result of standardization, would often overcome the resistance of customers against products with unique features tailored at individual markets.[10]

Globalizing for Added Synergies

While the MNC tends to see its investments in each market as separate and nonconnected, the global company aims at managing the interdependence be-

---

8. John Quelch, "Customizing Global Marketing," *Harvard Business Review,* May–June 1986, pp. 59–68.

9. Thomas Hout, Michael E. Porter, and Eileen Rudden, "How Global Companies Win Out," *Harvard Business Review,* September–October 1982, pp. 98–108.

10. Theodore Levitt, "The Globalization of Markets," *Harvard Business Review,* May–June 1983, pp. 92–102.

tween various foreign subsidiaries. This managing for interdependency tries to leverage strong positions in one market to help shore up weak positions in another. If one company showing a strong market in Japan would bring about extra business in Europe, the global company would pursue such moves by looking at its total position in all markets rather than justifying additional market share in Japan with incremental profits from Japan only.[11]

Leveraging strong positions to help weaker markets, also called *cross-subsidization,* is a move away from the traditional principle that each subsidiary should financially stand on its own. Cross-subsidizing foreign subsidiaries would allow the global company to selectively slow a competitor's development in markets where it is most difficult for it to strike back. The global company will try to maximize its profits for the entire system of subsidiaries whereas the traditional MNC aims at maximizing profits for each subsidiary independently.[12]

Indicators for Globalization

Now that we have outlined the operating principles of the global firm and its differences compared to MNCs, let us turn to the conditions that must be met before a global strategy may be employed to the benefit of the firm. There are five key indicators that might signal benefits from globalization:

1. Interdependencies of market positions
2. Same set of customers
3. Same set of competitors
4. Similarity of market factors
5. Existence of lead markets

When a company's success or failure in one market creates a negative or positive impact in other markets, interdependencies exist. Under those circumstances, a company may not want to leave each market on its own but carefully monitor its relevant position and interfere before negative repercussions take place. For many foreign companies, the United States market is important because it accounts for anywhere between one-third to one-half of the volume in most industries. To do well globally will therefore require a strong showing in the United States, even if it entails less than satisfactory earnings. To the extent that a company can showcase its U.S. performance in order to get sales in other countries, market interdependence must exist.

Companies consistently encountering the same set of customers in most of their overseas markets may also benefit from globalization of marketing strategies. Morgan Guaranty Trust Company of New York is well known for the

11. Hout, Porter, and Rudden, "How Global Companies Win Out," pp. 98–108.
12. Gary Hamel and C. K. Prahalad, "Do You Really Have a Global Strategy?" *Harvard Business Review,* July–August 1985, pp. 139–148.

services it offers to the world's largest corporations. Although the bank operates offices in many financial markets of the world, its customers are always the same big international firms. Delegating strategy to its individual subsidiaries might at times result in decisions that are beneficial to one subsidiary but not to the service network of the entire bank. Thus the bank's strategy is to offer its target customers any financial services they may need, wherever they may need them.

Although some companies may deal with different sets of customers in each country, they may encounter the same competitors. Particularly with industrial products that require technical expertise and experience, many markets are dominated by the same set of players. In the construction and earth-moving equipment market, it is Caterpillar of the United States versus Komatsu of Japan; in film it is Kodak of the United States versus Fuji of Japan. Globalizing the marketing strategy makes sense under such circumstances.

When a company consistently encounters the same set of market factors or characteristics, it could gain from exploiting these factors on a global scale. Globalization of marketing is helped when the same key success factors apply to a company's business everywhere. To the extent that the company's business is subject to such similarities in market structure, the infrastructure encountered, or even customer need and demand, a larger part of the company's strategy can become globalized.

When an industry is driven by one or a few lead markets, which tends to signal developments encountered elsewhere in the world later on, a company may benefit by taking a global approach. A lead market is a particular country where new developments show up first. A company aware of such trends can capitalize on its lead market presence by leveraging that experience to its other markets or countries. The United States tends to be the lead market for new electronic office equipment including computers. For many years, Olivetti, an Italian office equipment company, operated a subsidiary in the United States but never achieved much market success. However, the operation was justified by the company's management in Italy on the grounds that it allows the company to learn first hand how to compete in the most advanced and sophisticated market of the world for the industry. By learning such lessons in the U.S. market, Olivetti was able to quickly apply them to Europe, its prime market. Consequently, the U.S. operation could be justified for the overall benefit of the company even if it did not become profitable. Companies are increasingly sensitive to lead markets and are taking actions to assure that they are adequately represented in such markets wherever they may be.[13]

The United States is no longer the only lead market in many key industries. When it comes to electronics or semiconductor manufacturing, Japan has captured the lead in a number of segments, as indicated in Table 8.1. As a result, a

---

13. Jean-Pierre Jeannet, "Lead Markets: A Concept for Designing Global Business Strategies," Working Paper, IMEDE, International Management Development Institute, Lausanne, Switzerland, May 1986.

TABLE 8.1 Japan's Technological Lead for Key Industries

Product or Processes	Japanese Lead	U.S./Japanese Parity	U.S. Lead
Silicon products			
D-RAM's	●		
S-RAM's	●		
Eproms		■	
Microprocessors			●
Custom logic			●
Bipolar	●		
Non-silicon products			
Memory	●		
Logic	●		
Linear			■
Opto-electronics	●		
Hetero-structures	●		
Materials			
Silicon	●		
Gallium arsenide	●		

Key: ● U.S. position declining. ■ U.S. position maintaining.

Source: From *The New York Times*, "Where Japan Has a Technological Lead," January 6, 1987. Copyright © 1987 by The New York Times Company. Adapted by permission.

number of U.S. semiconductor firms have looked for ties with Japanese companies. Other companies, such as Texas Instruments, are producing in Japan to keep in touch with that market.

PRODUCT/MARKET STRATEGIES

The previous section dealt primarily with the geographic extension of a company's international business. However, as outlined earlier in this chapter, geographic extension is one of two key dimensions in the strategy of an international company. The other dimension deals with the range of a firm's product and service offerings. To what extent should a company become a supplier of a wide range of products aimed at several or many market segments? Should a company become the global specialist in a certain area by satisfying one or a small number of target segments, doing this in most major markets around the world?

Even some of the largest companies cannot pursue all available initiatives. Resources for most companies are limited, often requiring a tradeoff between product expansion and geographic expansion strategies. Resolving this question is necessary to achieve a concentration of resources and efforts in areas where they will bring the most return. We can distinguish between two models: on the one hand, we have the broad-based firm marketing a wide range of products to many different customer groups, both domestic and overseas. On the other hand we have the narrow based firm marketing a limited range of products to a homogenous customer group around the world. Both types of companies can be successful in their respective markets.

Companies such as Procter & Gamble, Unilever, and Nestlé are all examples of consumer good firms practicing a broad-based product strategy. In most markets, these firms offer many brands and product lines. Among industrial marketers, General Electric follows a similar strategy. Some of these firms, however, are broken down into a large number of strategic business units, or divisions with a limited product range aimed at a limited market segment, and within each business unit the chosen strategy may be much more focused.

Firms with a narrow product range include Hertz or Avis, the U.S. car rental companies, and Rolex, the Swiss watch manufacturing company. These firms have in common a narrow and clearly focused product line with the intent of dominating their chosen market segment across many countries. Many specialty equipment manufacturers in the fields of machine tools, electronic testing equipment, and other production process equipment tend to fit this pattern of niche or focus marketing.

Two concepts will help explain why some companies manage to achieve dominance of one small segment worldwide. As is the case with domestic business, to be successful the firm must combine a relevant competitive advantage,

FIGURE 8.3 Focusing Key Skills for International Marketing Success

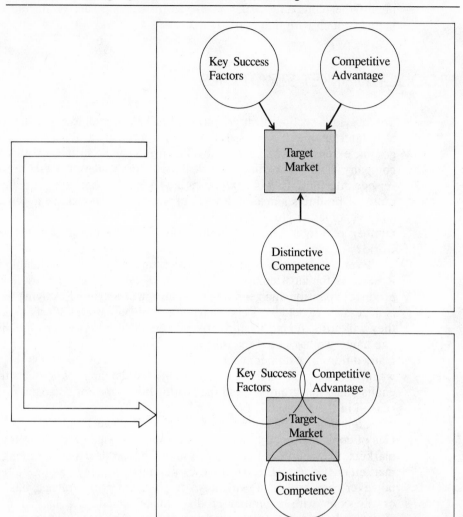

the mastery of key factors for success (KSF),[14] and the relationship between the target market and the firm's distinctive competence. To the extent that these three areas overlap and that the firm focuses them on its chosen target market, a much greater chance for success occurs (see Figure 8.3).

Competitive advantage includes the firm's relative advantage over other competitors. This may consist of an absolute advantage in technology or some

---

14. Ohmae, *The Mind of the Strategist*, p. 42.

other area, or a relative advantage where the firm is only relatively better. A competitive advantage may be based on marketing expertise, production technology, or better market contacts than competitors. The key factors for success, KSF, consist of those steps or business functions that a company must do well to survive in a given industry. KSF can consist of distribution, advertising, research, lower cost production, or other business steps. A company's distinctive competence consists of its acquired experience and usually covers a skill area where the firm has excelled over time. For one company, that may be managing mass production; for another, it may consist of innovation in a certain field or having served a certain customer group particularly well.

To stretch success geographically, companies must bring about an overlap of these three areas. Ideally, for any target segment the company brings together a competitive advantage, does well in the relevant key factors for success, and has a distinctive competence that is relevant for its market. As we extend this to other countries, firms that are active in markets where customer needs and market structures are relatively homogeneous can gain success with the same skill base and thus often find themselves dominating a certain segment worldwide. However, in markets where the KSF and the competitive advantage differ from country to country, it becomes much more difficult to leverage a company's experience base into other countries. This may either reduce the drawing range of the company to a limited number of markets or the company will have to acquire new skills to enter those more diverse markets. Such moves will increase risks because this adds greater uncertainty and requires more resources.

COMPETITIVE STRATEGIES FOR INTERNATIONAL MARKETING

The focus of this section will be the various competitive strategies firms can adopt in the international field. The examples given will show the impact of various geographic and product/market structures on a firm's competitive position. For our purposes, we will define competitive strategy "as the way in which a firm can compete more effectively to strengthen its market position."[15] When firms compete in the international market, their competitive strategies are likely to depend on their relevant resources and the type of competition they are meeting. At the country level, companies are apt to meet a variety of different players, ranging from local firms to multinational companies and even global firms. As we outlined in detail in the previous section of this chapter, these types of firms operate differently. Consequently, a company will have to be able to adjust to any differences in competition on a country-by-country basis. The purpose of this section is therefore to characterize some typical match-ups and

---

15. Michael E. Porter, *Competitive Strategy* (New York: The Free Press, 1980), p. x.

to make it clear to the reader how competitive dynamics differ depending on the players involved.

We will be looking at competitive strategy by examining three prototype players: the local, the multinational, and the global firm. By describing some real competitive battles between such companies, we will aim at distilling some general concepts as to what type of competitive strategy would work for each type of firm.

Local Company Versus Multinational Corporation

Generally, multinational corporations, MNCs, competing against local companies in any given market would be expected to walk away with the largest market share. MNCs, relying on substantial resources and considerable experience are often in a situation where they can out-spend the local firms in research and development, product design, and marketing funds. The following example should make clear to us that local firms can in fact compete effectively against much larger international companies if they compete wisely.

Ramlösa, the leading Swedish bottler of mineral water, is such a local firm that was able to compete effectively against Perrier of France, probably the most successful marketer of mineral water worldwide. Ramlösa sold its mineral water primarily in Sweden with some minor export business to Norway and Finland, two neighboring countries. Ramlösa executives had watched Perrier invade market after market in Europe and finally dominate the premium segment for mineral water worldwide.[16]

In the early 1980s, when Perrier was repeating its attack on the premium segment of Denmark, Ramlösa executives realized that it would not be long before Perrier would invade their market also. In Sweden, Ramlösa enjoyed a market share of close to 100 percent, and an aggressive new entrant like Perrier was feared to lower Ramlösa's share considerably. Having studied Perrier's strategy in other European markets, Ramlösa searched for a response and, in 1981, it finally decided to launch its own premium brand of mineral water. The company invested in expensive packaging and bottles, invested in advertising to obtain a premium image, and increased the price by almost 50 percent although the mineral water of the premium brand was identical to that sold under its regular label. The sales volume of the premium brand did end up decreasing the sales of the regular brand, but Ramlösa was not unhappy since the profitability of the premium brand per unit was substantially higher than its regular brand.

When Perrier finally entered the Swedish market in 1983, it followed its tried and proven strategy of aiming at the premium spot. However, with Ramlösa already owning the premium spot with its top brand, Perrier was forced to enter

---

16. For more details, see Jean-Pierre Jeannet, *Competitive Marketing Strategies in a European Context,* IMEDE, International Management Development Institute, Lausanne, Switzerland, 1987.

on a premium-premium strategy. This resulted in such a high price that Perrier gained very little market share over Ramlösa. By correctly spotting and predicting the Perrier strategy in advance, Ramlösa was able to design a response that prevented Perrier from unfolding the approach that had proven so successful elsewhere.

Although MNCs have superior resources, they often become inflexible after several successful market entries and tend to stay with standard approaches when flexibility is called for. In general, MNCs' strongest local competitors are those who watch the MNCs carefully and learn from their moves in other countries. With some MNCs requiring several years before a product is introduced in all markets, local competitors in some markets can take advantage of such advance notice by building defenses or launching a preemptive attack on the same segment.

Local Company Versus Global Firm

As we have learned, global firms are able to leverage their experience and market position in one market for the benefit of another. Consequently, the global firm is often a more potent competitor for a local company. The example of how Procter & Gamble dealt with two local competitors in the Swiss disposable diaper market will serve as an illustration of such a competitive dynamic.

In the mid-1970s, the Swiss market for baby diaper products consisted of cloth diapers, still the largest segment, and some disposable products such as inserts for traditional diapers.[17] Having observed the success of disposable diapers in the United States and in other larger markets, a Swiss company, Moltex, introduced its own version of the disposable diaper. Although a considerable habit change was needed, the company supported its product with little advertising and relied primarily on Switzerland's largest supermarket chain, Coop, for support. Moltex quickly gained a 35 market share.

When Procter & Gamble wanted to introduce its Pampers brand one year later, the large U.S. company found the channels blocked with Coop, its largest potential retail customer, unwilling to stock another brand. Moltex had strengthened its hand with the trade by offering larger discounts and higher margins. In an effort to outflank the blocked channel, Pampers were introduced through drug stores, department stores, and in hospitals through heavy sampling. Once initial distribution was attained, Pampers brand was supported with considerable advertising aimed at the consumer. Despite its distribution handicap, Pampers became the brand leader.

When the large supermarket chain realized the profitability of the disposable diaper market, the chain introduced its own store brand. Moltex, up to that time the only brand carried by this chain, lost its most important distribution over-

---

17. *Ibid.*

night. However, Procter & Gamble was able to continue to expand its market share and maintain dominance despite a substantial premium price because the company had continued to build its brand image with consumers by supporting it with advertising. In the end, the supermarket chain began to carry Pampers. Moltex, having lost distribution, was relegated to a minor brand.

Why was Procter & Gamble able to overcome substantial local competition despite a late entry into the Swiss market for disposable diapers? Moltex had learned from the considerable market potential in disposable diapers by observing market trends abroad. However, the company had adopted a marketing strategy that did not consider the marketing strength of its principal and most likely competitor, Procter & Gamble, though P&G was already on the Swiss market with other products and could be expected to follow suit soon. Local market connections to the retail trade were not sufficient to overcome the marketing expertise of a global firm.

Multinational Corporation Versus Multinational Corporation

When two multinational firms clash in a single market, the battles tend to be more expensive and more drawn out than when international firms compete against local competitors. This is largely so because MNCs have sufficient resources to fight it out. Such clashes take place in many markets. However, when multinational firms compete in a certain market, there is normally no spill-over into other markets since those firms view strategy mostly on a country-by-country basis.

How two multinationals, United States–based CPC International and Swiss-based Nestlé, clashed in Denmark in the 1980s serves as a typical example of a head-on collision between large multinational companies.[18] Both firms are large food companies operating subsidiaries in many countries. Aside from producing in Denmark for export, both companies operated two local marketing subsidiaries distributing a full line of products to the local retail trade. Nestlé marketed instant coffee, infant food products, and bouillons under its Maggi brand name. Maggi bouillons were Nestlé's most important product line in Denmark. Competing directly against Maggi was CPC's Knorr brand of dehydrated products, which included bouillon, but also soups and sauces. Nestlé controlled about 80 percent of the bouillon market compared to CPC's 20 percent. However, CPC's Knorr brand completely dominated the sauce and soup segments.

CPC's Knorr launched an attack in the bouillon segment by substantially underpricing Maggi. When Maggi realized that it suffered a disadvantage from a smaller shelf space area due to offering only one product in that category, it

---

18. See case series Nestlé Nordisk A/S (A) through (E), reprinted in Jean-Pierre Jeannet, *Competitive Marketing Strategies in a European Context,* IMEDE, International Management Development Institute, Lausanne, Switzerland, 1987.

countered by introducing a new dehydrated line of mixes that were not sold by Knorr in Denmark. This instantly gave Maggi more shelf space. Knorr followed suit, however. When Maggi realized that Knorr's funds for attacking in the bouillon segment came largely from its profitable sauce business, Maggi introduced a limited sauce line with low prices to reduce Knorr's cashflow. Although this payed for itself, Maggi was not able to impact on Knorr's profitability because the market grew due to higher competitive activity. In the end, Maggi also expanded into soups which enabled it to improve its position and to make up for lost profits in the bouillon segment, where price competition substantially lowered profit margins after several years.

Although both CPC International and Nestlé subsidiaries fought an intense marketing battle for several years, both subsidiaries relied largely on their own financial resources and had profit and loss responsibility on a local basis. Both multinationals made available to their subsidiaries the full product development resources of their international networks. The two companies offered full lines of dehydrated products in all major European markets including soups, sauces, mixes, and bouillons. As a result, the Danish subsidiaries could easily and quickly launch new products that were already marketed elsewhere. However, the two subsidiaries obviously had to bear all marketing costs on their own. At no time did this intensive battle spill over into other markets, nor was it a reflection of head-office strategy to expand certain product lines in Denmark.

Multinational Corporation Versus Global Firm

As was pointed out earlier, multinational firms tend to operate differently from global firms. Multinational companies operate their subsidiaries independently of each other; whereas global companies are actively looking for links and leverage opportunities wherever possible.

The development of the world color television industry serves as an excellent example of how the different operating approaches impact on direct competition. In the late 1950s, color TV systems became commercialized first in the United States. United States broadcasters were the first to switch transmission to color. To make the system feasible, U.S. TV manufacturers and broadcasters agreed on a single technical system with identical norms enabling TV sets to receive signals from all stations. When the market for color TVs expanded rapidly in the United States, European firms became interested in the same technology. The German and French industries both tried to come up with a system of even higher fidelity, which they promptly did; but the two systems were different. As the various European countries lined up behind either a French or German color TV system, the market became segmented and no single set could receive both signals simultaneously. The result was several smaller submarkets instead of a single market that could have rivalled the United States in size. European color TV manufacturers developed two different products and thus missed out on the advantages of economies of scale.

The Japanese broadcasting industry, by contrast, did not opt for a better system. Instead, the Japanese industry opted for the U.S. system. While technically inferior to the more recent European systems, it did allow the Japanese color TV manufacturers to produce sets for the Japanese and U.S. markets side by side and no substantial changes were necessary. Japanese TV set manufacturers were thus able to become the dominant suppliers in the large U.S. market. The European firms did not have the same chance because they would have had to invest into a third model variety. In the end, the manufacturing economies of scale also allowed the Japanese to enter Europe at a later date with sets that could receive both types of signals used in Europe. When the European color TV manufacturers began to pool their resources in the 1980s, the Japanese had already a substantial market share and had become the dominant competitors in all three key regions.

Global firms, by relentlessly leveraging strengths from one market into another, are usually better positioned to capitalize on new trends and developments. Global firms, by accepting occasional losses in one subsidiary or market with the intent of recouping them somewhere else, tend to have greater operating flexibility than traditional multinational firms that aim at balancing the results in each country separately. Today, many firms operating according to multinational principles are looking at ways to become global in outlook to obtain a competitive advantage.

Global Firm Versus Global Firm

In some industries, developments have already reached a point where most key competitors have attained some level of globalization. In such situations, the type of competitive behavior has changed and global companies go beyond the leveraging of key developments or new product trends. The detergent industry offers us a case in point.

The detergent industry is dominated by three global players: Procter & Gamble (U.S.), Unilever (U.K./Netherlands), and Colgate-Palmolive (U.S.). Procter & Gamble dominates in the United States whereas Unilever dominates in Europe. Colgate-Palmolive is a distant third in both areas. Some decisions these companies make are less aimed at the customer and more focused on the key competitor. Unilever, by bringing new products from its European operations into the United States, hoped to improve the efficiency of its U.S. subsidiary, Lever Brothers, and thus slow the profitability of Procter & Gamble, its prime competitor. Procter & Gamble, in return, has been able to make substantial inroads in the detergent market in the United Kingdom against Unilever, thus depressing Unilever's cash flow in that important market.[19] When another U.S. consumer goods company, Richardson-Vicks, became a target for acquisi-

---

19. "A Tough Three-Cornered Fight," *Financial Times*, September 24, 1985, p. 16.

tion, both firms competed directly, each wanting to deny the prize to the other. In the end, Procter & Gamble won out, giving it an important foothold in several new product segments and some overseas markets where Procter & Gamble had been weak.[20]

In some ways, global competition is like a global chess game with a few competitors blocking each other's moves in or around key markets. What a competitor might be doing in a given market becomes more important than what potential customers might desire. To do well in this kind of a game requires, however, that individual country aspirations and strategies become subordinated to the overall strategy directed from a central point.

CONCLUSIONS

Any company engaging in international marketing operations is faced with a number of very important strategic decisions. At the outset, a decision in principle needs to be made committing the company to some level of internationalization. Increasingly, firms will find that for competitive reasons international business must be pursued and that it is often not an optional strategy. Once committed, the company needs to decide where the international business should be pursued, both in terms of geographic region and specific countries. A firm's entry decision into each market and the selection of the international marketing program are additional strategic decisions.

During this decade, a changing competitive environment has considerably affected these choices. In the past, companies have moved from largely domestic or regional firms to become multinational. As multinational companies, these firms competed in many local markets and attempted to meet the local market requirements as best they could. Although many firms still approach their international marketing effort this way, an increasing number of firms are taking a global view of their marketplace. The global firm operates differently from the multinational or regional company. Pursuing a global strategy does not necessarily mean that the company is attempting to standardize all of its marketing programs on a global scale. Furthermore, a global strategy also does not imply that the company is represented in all markets of the world. Rather, global strategy is a new way of thinking about the business. Global companies are fully aware of their strengths across as many markets as possible. Consequently, the global company will build its strategy on the basis of its key skills and will enter markets where those skills are relevant.

A global company is also keenly aware of the value of global size and market share. As a result, a number of strategic decisions, such as which markets to enter, will become subject to the overall global strategy. Rather than making

---

20. "Unilever Fights Back in the US," *Fortune,* May 26, 1986, p. 32.

each market pay its way separately, a global firm might aim to break even in some markets if this will help its overall position by holding back a key competitor. As strategy begins to compare with that of a global chess game, companies will have to develop new skills and learn about new concepts to survive. Exploitation of the lead market principle and its understanding will become more important. The ability of building alliances on a global scale will also be necessary as fewer firms will be able to pursue all of their objectives on their own.

Globalization of many industries today is a fact. Some companies have no choice but to become globalized. Once key competitors in their industries are globalized, other firms must follow. This leads to a rethinking of the strategic choices and will inevitably lead to new priorities. Globalization is not simply a new term for something that had existed all along; it is a new competitive game requiring companies to adjust to and learn new ways of doing business. For many companies, survival depends on how well they learn this new game.

Questions for Discussion

1. Many companies have different reasons for internationalizing their operations. Contrast the reasons for a large firm, such as IBM, and a much smaller one, such as Apple or Compaq.
2. What reasons are there for small firms to pursue an international strategy? Should they do this at all?
3. Investigate the geographic portfolio of three large Fortune 500 companies. What differences do you see, and what do you think accounts for these differences?
4. Contrast global and other types of geographic expansion strategies. In particular, how does it differ from a multinational strategy?
5. Select three different industries you are interested in and compare them with regard to the factors for globalization. What implications are you making from your analysis?
6. How can a local company best compete against multinational or global concerns?

For Further Reading

Ayal, Igel, and Jehiel Zif. "Competitive Market Choice Strategies in Multinational Marketing." *Columbia Journal of World Business* (Fall 1978), pp. 72–81.

Ayal, Igal, and Jehiel Zif. "Market Expansion Strategies in Multinational Marketing." *Journal of Marketing,* vol. 43 (Spring 1979), pp. 84–94.

Boddewyn, J. J. "Standardization in International Marketing: Is Ted Levitt in Fact Right? *Business Horizons* (November–December, 1986).

Contractor, Farok J., and Peter Lorange, eds. *Cooperative Strategies in International Business*. Lexington, Mass.: D. C. Heath, 1987.

Hallen, Lars, and Jan Johanson. "Industrial Marketing Strategies in Different National Environments." *Journal of Business Research* (December 1985), pp. 495–509.

Harrell, Gilbert D., and Richard O. Kiefer. "Multinational Strategic Market Portfolios." *MSU Business Topics* (Winter 1981), pp. 5–16.

Kaynak, Erdener, ed. *Global Perspectives in Marketing*. New York: Praeger Publishers, 1985.

Ohmae, Kenichi. *The Mind of a Strategist*. New York: McGraw-Hill, 1982.

Rapp, William V. "Strategy Formulation and International Competition." *Columbia Journal of World Business* (Summer 1973), pp. 98–112.

Samiee, Saeed. "Elements of Marketing Strategy: A Comparative Study of U.S.- and Non-U.S.-Based Companies." *Journal of International Marketing,* No. 2 (1982), pp. 119–126.

9.
MARKET ENTRY STRATEGIES

MNCs must determine the type of presence they expect to maintain in every market where they compete. One major choice concerns the method of supplying the selected market. A company may want to export to the new market or may prefer to produce locally. A second major choice involves the amount of direct ownership desired. Should the company strive for full ownership of its local operation or is a joint venture preferable? These initial decisions on market entry tend to be of a medium- to long-term character, leaving little room for change once a commitment has been made. Therefore, it is important to treat these decisions with the utmost care. Not only is the financial return to the company at stake, but the extent to which the company's marketing strategy can be employed in the new market also depends on these decisions.

In this chapter, we concentrate on the major entry strategy alternatives by explaining each one in detail and citing relevant company experiences. We also treat the entry strategy from an integrative point of view and offer guidance as to how a specific strategy might be selected to suit a company's needs. For an overview of all chapter topics, see Figure 9.1.

EXPORTING AS AN ENTRY STRATEGY

Exporting to a foreign market is a strategy many companies follow for at least some of their markets. Since many countries do not offer a large enough opportunity to justify local production, exporting allows a company to centrally manufacture its products for several markets and therefore gain economies of scale. Furthermore, since exports represent incremental volume out of an existing

FIGURE 9.1 Market Entry Strategies

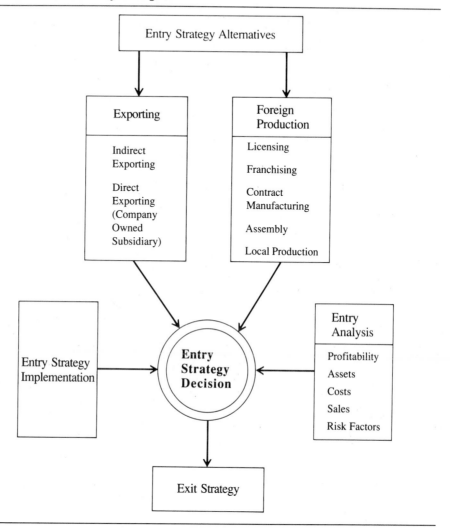

production operation located elsewhere, the marginal profitability of such exports tends to be high. A firm has two basic options in carrying out its export operations. Markets can be contacted through a domestically located middleman (located in the exporter's country of operation)—an approach called *indirect exporting*. Alternatively, markets can be reached through a middleman located in the foreign market—an approach termed *direct exporting*. The use of various types of export middlemen is described in detail in Chapter 12.

Indirect Exporting

Several types of middlemen located in the domestic market are ready to assist a manufacturer in contacting foreign markets or buyers. The major advantage for using a domestic middleman lies in the middleman's knowledge of foreign market conditions. Particularly for companies with little or no experience in exporting, the use of a domestic middleman provides the exporter with readily available expertise. The most common types of middlemen are brokers, combination export managers, and manufacturers' export agents. Group selling activities can also help individual manufacturers in their export operations.

The Broker

Brokers are middlemen who bring buyers and sellers together for a modest fee or commission. Brokers do not take ownership of the products, and they are normally paid by whoever engages them. Brokers are usually specialized by country or product group. For instance, specialized brokerage houses handle trade with certain countries when special skills are required, such as trade with countries in Eastern Europe or China. Also, many more brokers specialize in commodity trading than in manufactured goods.

A broker is typically used by companies that do not regularly or frequently engage in export activities. For the few and infrequent transactions, the exporter may depend on a broker for assistance. The commission paid would normally amount to less money than maintaining a specialist on a full-time basis. Brokers are less useful when a company is looking for a long-term relationship with a market or a particular buyer. Other forms of domestic middlemen would better suit such a permanent relationship with a foreign market.

Manufacturer's Export Agent (MEA)

The manufacturer's export agent (MEA) may be an individual or a firm providing a selling service for manufacturers. As in the case of the broker, the MEA does not take title to the products sold but arranges for the transfer or shipment to the buyer abroad. Acting on their own, MEAs usually obtain the right to sell a manufacturer's products in a limited area of the world, such as in two or three countries. Compensation is arranged on a straight commission basis. An MEA usually has long-term involvement with the exporter; this is the MEA's main advantage over a broker.

Combination Export Manager (CEM)

For companies in need of more services than a broker or MEA can provide, the CEM offers a particularly attractive alternative. The CEM virtually works as a manufacturer's export department in such a way that a foreign buyer often is not aware of the involvement of a middleman. The CEM runs the complete export operation of a domestic manufacturer on a commission basis. He or she acts in the name of the manufacturer and is responsible for contacting foreign buyers and negotiating terms of sale. Commissions vary, but they may range from 10 to 20 percent and are substantially higher than those for a broker or MEA. CEMs maintain a staff of foreign trade specialists. They are able to do this because they represent many smaller companies that do not produce directly competitive products, and they can therefore spread fixed costs over a larger export volume than what any individual firm might be able to achieve. Due to the CEM's dependence on commission income, involvement in longer-term market development tends to be limited. However, for additional fees or alternative compensation, the CEM may assume a larger role in a company's export business.

Group Export Activities

Exporters may engage in group activities to achieve better results than they would by engaging in independent exporting operations. The United States government has exempted such organizations from U.S. anti-trust legislation and has permitted some industries to pool their resources for exporting. Under the Webb-Pomerene Export Trade Act of 1918, U.S. companies may pursue exports as a group, provided the pooling of resources does not result in a restraint of trade in the United States. Very few such organizations exist today and their share of total exports is estimated at below 5 percent of total U.S. exports. Typical Webb-Pomerene groups include agricultural, forest, and rubber products.

Other Domestic Middlemen

Several other, less prominent types of domestic middlemen exist. Among these are merchant middlemen, who accept full ownership for the exported products. The most important of these are involved in trading companies with major activities in Japan and to a lesser extent in Europe. As a result, these middlemen are discussed in greater detail under *foreign middlemen.*

Company-Owned Export Department or Operations

In any of the circumstances described above, a manufacturer has the option of establishing a company-owned export department having the responsibility of contacting foreign buyers directly without the services of domestically located middlemen. Of course, such an operation represents a commitment to a staff and corresponding fixed costs. Only when there is a sufficient volume of export business can the company-owned department be justified.

The breakeven of such a department may be calculated by comparing the commission volume to be paid to prospective domestic middlemen with the fixed operating expenditures of the export department. For a small manufacturer contracting with a CEM for a 15 percent commission on export sales and estimated operating costs of $150,000 for an export department, the breakeven point would be reached when:

$$B - E = \frac{\text{Export Department Fixed Costs}}{\text{Commission Rate Middleman}} = \frac{\$150,000}{.15} = \$1,000,000.00$$

Consequently, a CEM would be advantageous for an anticipated export volume below the $1 million mark. For a volume above the $1 million mark, a company-owned export department would become profitable and more efficient than a CEM (given the above cost assumptions).

Direct Exporting

A company is engaged in direct exporting when it exports through intermediaries located in the foreign markets. Under direct exporting, an exporter would have to deal with a large number of foreign contacts, possibly one or more for each country the company plans to enter. While a direct exporting operation requires a larger degree of expertise, this method of market entry does provide the company with a greater degree of control over its distribution channels than would be the case under indirect exporting. The exporter may select from two major types of middlemen: agents or merchants. Also, the exporting company may establish its own sales subsidiary as an alternative to independent middlemen.

The Agent Middleman

Similar to agents who are domestically located and engaged in indirect exporting, agents abroad only facilitate the sale of products or services and do not become a party to the deal. The *broker* is one such agent. He or she performs services similar to those of a domestic broker. Brokers are more common for standardized products such as wood, agriculture, or mining products. In general, the role and market coverage by brokers abroad is not as highly developed as in the United States or some of the other developed countries. Brokers in the United States and abroad earn their compensation strictly on a commission basis.

A *manufacturer's representative* can also market a company's products abroad. Manufacturers' representatives sell within a predetermined territory— either within a country, a group of countries, or a region of a country. They also do not take title to the products sold but merely act as the exporter's sales force. The exporter is still responsible for shipping the goods directly to the final purchaser. Manufacturers' representatives, whose title may differ by country, act primarily as a substitute sales force in the assigned territory. Compensation is on a commission basis. Manufacturers' representatives typically carry several lines of noncompeting products.

Merchant Middlemen

Merchant middlemen are intermediaries in foreign markets who buy products on their own for resale to final users or buyers. They thus absorb all the risks associated with the transaction. Naturally, their margins tend to be substantially higher than the commissions paid to agents. The *distributor* is the most common type of merchant middleman. Usually, the distributor is assigned a particular territory—either a group of countries, a country, or a specific region. The distributor carries products that do not directly compete and maintains an inventory. Sales are made to buyers through the distributor's own sales force. Manufacturers develop longstanding relationships with such distributors and may achieve a high level of cooperation with respect to local marketing policy. Nevertheless, sales largely depend on the skills of the distributor and the extent to which they are motivated to perform. Agreement between exporting manufacturers and the foreign merchant middlemen may vary. If the sales rights are not for an exclusive territory, the middleman is called an *import jobber*. In the case in which the middleman's sales consist largely of one exporter's products, the middleman is called a *dealer*. This latter arrangement is typical of the equipment or truck industry, where major manufacturers maintain independent dealer networks all over the world.

The Company-Owned Sales Office (Foreign Sales Subsidiary)

Many companies export directly to their own sales subsidiaries abroad, sidestepping any independent middlemen. The sales subsidiary assumes the role of the independent distributor by stocking manufacturers' products, selling to buyers, and assuming the credit risk. The sales subsidiary offers the manufacturer full control of selling operations in a foreign market. This may be important if the company's products require the use of special marketing skills, such as advertising or selling. The exporter finds it possible to transfer or export not only the product but also the entire marketing program that often makes the product a success.

The operation of a subsidiary adds a new dimension to a company's international marketing operation. It requires the commitment of capital in a foreign country, primarily for the financing of accounts receivables and inventory. Also, the operation of a sales subsidiary entails a number of general administrative expenses that are essentially fixed in nature. As a result, a commitment to a sales subsidiary should not be made without careful evaluation of all the costs involved.

Independent Distributor Versus Sales Subsidiary

The independent distributor earns a margin on the selling price of the products. Although the independent distributor does not represent a direct cost to the exporter, the margin the distributor earns represents an opportunity that is lost to the exporter. By switching to a sales subsidiary, the exporter could earn the same margin by carrying out the distributor's tasks. For example, a manufacturer of electronic equipment exports products priced $7,500 each (at the factory in Boston). With air freight, tariffs, and taxes, the product's landed costs amount to $9,000 each. An independent distributor would have to price the products at $13,500 to earn a desired gross margin of 33 1/3 percent. Instead, the exporter could set up a wholly owned sales subsidiary, assumed in this case to consist of a manager, a sales manager, several salesmen, clerical staff, a warehousing operation, and the rental of both an office and a warehouse location. If the total estimated cost amounted to $450,000 annually, then the point at which the manufacturer could switch from an independent distributor to a company-owned sales subsidiary would be as follows:

$$\frac{\text{Operating costs subsidiary}}{\text{Distributor's gross profit per machine}} = \text{Unit breakeven volume}$$

$$\frac{\$450,000}{\$4,500} = 100 \text{ Pieces of equipment}$$

or

$$\frac{\text{Operating costs subsidiary}}{\text{Distributors' gross profit percentage}} = \text{Dollar sales breakeven volume}$$

$$\frac{\$450,000}{33\ 1/3\%} = \$1,350,000 \text{ breakeven volume}$$
$$\text{(ex. subsidiary prices)}$$

With increasing volume, the incentive to start a sales subsidiary grows. On the other hand, if the anticipated sales volume is small, the independent distributor will be more efficient since sales are channeled through a distributor who is maintaining the necessary staff for several product lines.

Exporting remains a very common entry strategy with many internationally active companies. Even some of the largest MNCs with production facilities in many countries find it uneconomical to produce and market for each country separately. Instead, companies locate production facilities in strategic locations, either on the basis of cost savings or transportation costs, and supply a network of sales subsidiaries and distributors from those sourcing points. However, research has shown that firms marketing products that require the development of special skills or special working relationships tend to have their own sales subsidiaries.[1]

1. Erin Anderson and Anne T. Coughlan, "International Market Entry and Expansion in Independent or Integrated Channels of Distribution," *Journal of Marketing,* vol. 51, January 1987, pp. 71–82.

LICENSING AS AN ENTRY STRATEGY

Under licensing, a company assigns the right to a *patent* (which protects a product, technology, or a process) or a *trademark* (which protects a product name) to another company for a fee or royalty. Using licensing as a method of market entry, a company can gain market presence without an equity investment. The foreign company, or licensee, gains the right to commercially exploit the patent or trademark either on an exclusive (exclusive right to a certain geographic region) or unrestricted basis.[2]

Licenses are signed for a variety of time periods. Depending on the investment needed to enter the market, the foreign licensee might insist on a longer licensing period to pay off the initial investment. Typically, the licensee will make all necessary capital investments, such as in machinery, inventory, and so on, and market the products in the assigned sales territories, which might consist of one or several countries. Licensing agreements are subject to negotiation and tend to vary considerably from company to company and from industry to industry.

Few companies rely exclusively on licensing as an entry strategy. Continental Can, the U.S. packaging manufacturer, started its international expansion in the 1930s by relying largely on licensing. First starting in Europe, the company licensed its technology to eighty-eight foreign firms. Wholly owned subsidiaries existed only in a very few countries. In later years, Continental Can did become a shareholder in about twenty-five of its licensees. In some important markets, Continental Can licensees achieved very high market shares. Metal Box, its British licensee, maintained a share of almost 85 percent of the U.K. market, and Continental Can's German and Dutch licensees have market shares of 40 percent and 60 percent respectively. Although Continental Can's earnings are restricted to royalties in these markets, it would be unlikely that the company would have achieved the same market dominance had it entered these countries with its own operations.[3]

Even today, licensing remains common in some industries. One company that is new to licensing is the largest brewer in the United States, Anheuser-Busch. As the first U.S. brewer to actively pursue foreign markets, Anheuser-Busch signed licensing agreements with several brewers in Canada, the United Kingdom, France, Germany, and Japan. The company's strategy is to enter a country through the leading brewer or beverage manufacturer rather than to export U.S. brewed beer. In Canada, the Anheuser-Busch brand Budweiser was licensed to Labatt Brewing Company and met with immediate success. In Japan, Budweiser is licensed to Suntory, the country's smallest brewer but a leader in the liquor business. Anheuser-Busch switched from exporting to licensing partly

---

2. For a thorough analysis of licensing among MNCs, see Piero Telesio, *Technology Licensing and Multinational Enterprises* (New York: Praeger Publishers, 1979).
3. "Continental Can's Intercontinental Tribulations," *Fortune*, August 1973, p. 74.

because it wanted to cut the retail price of its Budweiser brand in Japan in half. In Germany, the United Kingdom, and France, Budweiser was brewed by leading local brewing companies.[4]

Reasons for Licensing

Companies have used licensing for a number of reasons. The market potential of the target country might be too small to support a manufacturing operation. A licensee has the advantage of adding the licensed product's volume to an ongoing operation, thereby reducing the need for a large amount of investment in new fixed assets. For a company with limited resources, it can be advantageous to have a foreign partner market its products by signing a licensing contract. Licensing not only saves capital since no additional investment is necessary, but it also allows scarce managerial resources to be concentrated on more lucrative markets. Also, some smaller companies with a product in high demand might not be able to satisfy demand unless licenses are granted to other companies with sufficient manufacturing capacity.

In some countries where the political or economic situation appears uncertain, a licensing agreement will avoid the potential risk associated with investments in fixed facilities. Both commercial and political risks are absorbed by the licensee.

In some countries, governments favor the granting of licenses to independent local manufacturers as a means of building up an independent local industry. In such cases, a foreign manufacturer may prefer to team up with a capable licensee despite a large market size because other forms of entry may not be possible. The same applies for countries where trade restrictions prohibit the free import of products. A licensing agreement is ideal to overcome such barriers.

Competitive factors also influence the use of licensing. In industries with high visibility or national importance, local governments or buyers often prefer to purchase from local manufacturers. This might result in the formation of a "club" whereby foreign competitors find it difficult to gain any market share. In industries such as telecommunications, defense, or aerospace, where governments are the major buyers and often direct their purchases toward local firms, foreign competitors are forced to join such "clubs" via licensing to some of its members. Some companies use licensing as a means of preventing competitive technology from achieving market success, thereby assuring themselves of a larger market share. Such strategies were followed by Philips with its cassette recording technology, and Telefunken (Germany), with its PAL color TV system. In the case of Philips, the strategy quickly made the company's cassette

---

4. "Anheuser Tries Light Beer Again," *Business Week,* June 29, 1981, p. 138; and "International Trend May Resume," *Financial Times,* April 7, 1984, p. 30.

recorders the standard of the industry. From the company's point of view, a small percentage of the world market was preferable to a larger share of a market restricted to the Philips' system.

Advantages and Disadvantages of Licensing

The major advantage of licensing is the ability of a company to enter a foreign market without a substantial investment of its resources. Local market knowledge is provided by the foreign licensee who markets the products independently of the licensor. In cases where either exporting or local manufacturing fail to offer any long-term profitability, licensing may be the only entry strategy for gaining additional revenues from an already developed product.

A major disadvantage of licensing consists of a substantial dependence on the local licensee to produce revenues and thus royalties. Once a license is granted, royalties, usually paid as a percent on sales volume only, will only be paid if the licensee is capable of performing an effective marketing job. Since the local companies' marketing skills may be less developed, revenues from licensing may suffer accordingly. Another disadvantage is the resulting uncertainty of product quality. A foreign company's image may suffer if a local licensee markets a product of substandard quality. Insuring a uniform quality requires additional resources from the licensor that may reduce the profitability of the licensing activity.

To many companies, the possibility of nurturing a potential competitor is viewed as a disadvantage of licensing. With licenses usually limited to a specific time period, a company has to guard against the situation in which the local licensee will use the same technology independently after the license has expired and therefore turn into a competitor. Although there is a great variation according to industry, licensing fees in general are substantially lower than the profits that can be made by exporting or local manufacturing. Depending on the product, licensing fees may range anywhere between 1 percent to 20 percent of sales with 3 to 5 percent as more typical for industrial products.

Conceptually, licensing as an entry strategy should be pursued if the amount of licensing fees exceeds the incremental revenues of any other entry strategy, such as exporting or local manufacturing. A thorough investigation of the market potential is required to estimate potential revenues from any one of the entry strategies under consideration. Unfortunately, research has shown that many licensing decisions are made without a complete comparison of the respective incremental profitabilities.[5]

---

5. David B. Zenoff, "Licensing as a Means of Penetrating Foreign Markets," *Idea,* vol. 14, Summer 1970, p. 292.

Franchising

Franchising is a special form of licensing in which the franchisor makes a total marketing program available, including the brand name, logo, products, and method of operation. Usually, the franchise agreement is more comprehensive than a regular licensing agreement inasmuch as the total operation of the franchisee is prescribed.

Numerous companies that have successfully exploited franchising as a distribution form in their home market are exploiting opportunities abroad through foreign entrepreneurs.[6] Among these companies are McDonald's, Kentucky Fried Chicken, Burger King, and other U.S. fast-food chains with operations in Latin America, Asia, and Europe. Service companies such as Holiday Inns, Hertz, and Manpower, Inc. (a temporary employment agency) have also successfully used franchising to enter foreign markets. Some of the most extensive franchising networks are those maintained by the two leading soft drink manufacturers, Coca-Cola and Pepsi Cola.[7]

In 1985, about 25,600 foreign outlets were maintained by U.S. franchise operators compared to 3,300 in 1971.[8] Some 37 percent of U.S. franchisers were operating abroad in 1985 and another 27 percent planned to expand abroad in the near future. Among those starting to expand in 1985 were Tandy Corporation with its Radio Shack stores.

LOCAL MANUFACTURING AS AN ENTRY STRATEGY

A common and widely practiced form of entry is the local production of a company's products. Many companies find it to their advantage to manufacture locally instead of supplying the particular market with products produced elsewhere. Numerous factors such as local costs, market size, tariffs, laws, and political considerations may affect a choice to manufacture locally. The actual type of local production depends on the arrangements made; it may be contract manufacturing, assembly, or fully integrated production. Since local production represents a greater commitment to a market than other entry strategies, it deserves considerable attention before a final decision is made.

6. Donald W. Hackett, "The International Expansion of U.S. Franchise Systems: Status and Strategies," *Journal of International Business Studies,* Spring 1976, pp. 65–76.

7. Bruce Walker and Michael J. Etzel, "The Internationalization of U.S. Franchise Systems: Progress and Procedures," *Journal of Marketing,* April 1973 pp. 38–46.

8. "Franchising: Big Businesses Go Worldwide," *Financial Times,* October 7, 1985, p. 27.

Contract Manufacturing

Under contract manufacturing, a company arranges to have its products manufactured by an independent local company on a contractual basis. The manufacturer's responsibility is restricted to production. Afterwards, products are turned over to the international company, which usually assumes the marketing responsibilities of selling, promotion, and distribution. In a way, the international company "rents" the production capacity of the local firm to avoid establishing its own plant or to circumvent barriers set up to prevent the import of its products. Contract manufacturing differs from licensing with respect to the legal relationship of the firms involved. The local producer manufactures based upon orders from the international firm but the international firm gives virtually no commitment beyond the placement of orders. It is normal, however, to negotiate supply contracts over longer time periods specifying delivery terms such as volume, prices, and the timing of shipments. Contract manufacturing is less common as an entry strategy than exporting or local production since this type of arrangement is not always satisfactory to the foreign firm.

Typically, contract manufacturing is chosen for countries with a low volume market potential combined with high tariff protection. In such situations, local production appears advantageous to avoid the high tariffs but the local market does not support the volume necessary to justify the building of a single plant. These conditions tend to exist in the smaller countries of Central America, Africa, and Asia. Of course, whether an international company avails itself of this method of entry also depends on its products. Usually, contract manufacturing is employed where the production technology involved is widely available and where the marketing effort is of crucial importance in the success of the product.

Assembly

By moving to an assembly operation, the international firm locates a portion of the manufacturing process in the foreign country. Typically, assembly consists only of the last stages of manufacturing and depends on the ready supply of components or manufactured parts to be shipped in from another country. Assembly usually involves heavy use of labor rather than extensive investment in capital outlays or equipment.

Motor vehicle manufacturers have made extensive use of assembly operations in numerous countries. General Motors has maintained major integrated production units only in the United States, Germany, the United Kingdom, Brazil, and Australia. In many other countries, disassembled vehicles arrive in assembly operations that produce the final product on the spot. This method of shipping cars as CKDs (completely knocked-down) and assembling them in local markets is also used extensively by Ford Motor Company, American Motors' Jeep subsidiary, and most European and Japanese car manufacturers.

Often, the companies want to take advantage of lower wage costs by shifting the labor-intensive operation to the foreign market. This results in a lower final price of the products. In many cases, however, it is the local government that forces the setting-up of assembly operations by sometimes banning the import of fully assembled products or by charging excessive tariffs on imports. As a defensive move, foreign companies begin assembly operations to protect their markets. Some recent developments in Third-World countries are discussed in the following section.

Establishing Assembly Operations in Developing Countries

Hitachi Sales Corp., the marketing subsidiary of Hitachi Ltd., announced plans to replace exports of color TV sets from Japan to developing countries with local assembly operations.[9] Initially, small scale assembly operations were started in Kenya, Chile, and Guatemala, with other developing countries to be added to the list later on. The company expected to assemble in as many as twenty countries once the new program had been fully adopted. The company's strategy was to convert any sales subsidiary with monthly sales of U.S. $200,000 or more to an assembly operation. Any newly formed sales subsidiary would automatically have an assembly operation attached. Many of these plants were to have a capacity of only about 4,000 sets annually with most of the components supplied by Hitachi's worldwide network of production affiliates.

There were several reasons for Hitachi's complete shift from exporting to local assembly as its major entry strategy. Developing nations started to impose higher tariffs on color TV sets imported in assembled form. Furthermore, the sharp appreciation of the Japanese yen made it difficult to increase overseas sales of color TV sets shipped from Japan. Also, developing nations started to push Japanese companies to undertake local production. Consequently, Hitachi's strategy has to be viewed as a move to protect present markets that otherwise might be lost to competitors that might be more willing to open up local operations.

In 1981, Mexico announced that it would eventually require that all mini-computers sold domestically be assembled locally. Within just two years, several U.S. computer manufacturers moved to set up assembly operations in Mexico. IBM and Burroughs opened up assembly plants in 1983 in response to this government intention, joining Hewlett-Packard, NCR, and Mohawk Data Sciences that were already producing in Mexico. Many other companies had indicated their intention to follow. Mexico, strapped for foreign exchange, saw its computer imports increase rapidly. By requiring foreign companies to set up local operations, foreign exchange could be saved. Furthermore, within four years of start-up, a foreign company was expected to balance component im-

---

9. "Hitachi Sales Will Replace Exports with Local Output," *The Japan Economic Journal,* January 23, 1979, p. 9.

ports with exports from Mexican plants or face cutbacks in import licenses. NCR exported about half of its Mexican production and IBM intended to use Mexico as a production base for many of its Latin American markets.[10]

Integrated Local Production Operations

To establish a fully integrated local production unit represents the greatest commitment a company can make for a foreign market. Since the building of a plant involves a substantial outlay in capital, companies only do so where demand appears assured. Multinational companies may have any number of reasons for establishing factories in foreign countries. Often the primary reason is to take advantage of lower costs in a country, thus providing a better basis for competing with local firms or other foreign companies already present. Also, high transportation costs and tariffs may make imported goods uncompetitive.

Establishing Local Operations to Gain New Business

Some companies want to build a plant to gain new business and customers. Such an aggressive strategy is based upon the fact that a local production commitment represents a strong commitment and is often the only way to convince clients to switch suppliers. This is of particular importance in industrial markets where service and reliability of supply are main factors determining product or supplier choice. A typical example of such a strategy was the move made by a German manufacturer of diesel engines, Klockner-Humboldt-Deutz (KHD).[11] In December of 1979, the company decided to spend 50 million dollars on a new plant in the United States that could produce small diesels in the 40 hp to 160 hp range for the U.S. market. KHD was attracted by the substantial increase in fuel costs which was expected to increasingly favor diesel engines for applications such as industrial compressors or small- to medium-sized trucks where gasoline engines still dominated. The construction of its own plant was intended to enhance KHD's bargaining leverage with potential customers. Sales were expected to triple with the opening of its U.S. production site.

Following several years of studying, Volkswagen decided in 1976 to build a plant in the United States. The plant was intended for manufacture of the successor model to the old Beetle, the Rabbit. This bold move required an investment of about $600 million.

Several years later, Volkswagen's strategy for the United States did not work out as expected. Sales of its U.S. produced Rabbit models began to decline

---

10. "U.S. Computer Makers Are Feeling at Home," *Business Week,* November 14, 1983, p. 64; and "U.S. Computer Makers Rush to Set Up Plants," *Business Week,* May 17, 1982, p. 50.

11. "A German Salvo Starts a Small-Diesel Duel," *Business Week,* December 24, 1979, p. 49.

and exports from Germany began to assume a greater importance again. Again, this happened against the backdrop of changing currency values as the U.S. dollar increased against foreign currencies. Consumer tastes had changed as well. Volkswagen's difficult experience was cited by many Japanese car manufacturers as a reason for being cautious with the establishment of their own manufacturing plants in the United States.[12]

Although Volkswagen's problem with its U.S. business was primarily due to changes in the world's currency markets, other companies have moved to protect their markets when threatened by political forces. Japanese manufacturers in particular have come under pressure from local groups concerned about trade imbalance to embark upon local production for such diverse products as automobiles, consumer electronics, machine tools, and semiconductors. Honda Motor Co. was not only motivated by the pressing need for additional plant capacity. Honda was well aware of the mounting political pressure on Japanese companies to build cars in the United States.

Honda started production at its Marysville, Ohio plant in 1983.[13] One year later, Nissan started operations for a car line in Smyrna, Tennessee. In 1984, Toyota established a joint production company with General Motors in Fremont, California to manufacture a small car similar to its Corolla model based on largely imported components. Toyota decided to begin producing for its own dealers in the United States and Canada at some future point. Mazda, a company in which Ford is a major shareholder, planned to open a plant in 1987 in Flat Rock, Michigan. Mitsubishi will also set up a joint venture to produce cars with Chrysler which owns a substantial stake in the Japanese company. It is anticipated that, by 1990, Japanese automobile manufacturers will have the capacity to produce as many as 1.5 million units a year in the United States and Canada.[14]

The move into local production to protect export markets as a result of dumping charges has also prompted Komatsu, the leading Japanese manufacturer of construction equipment, to open up a plant in the United Kingdom. In July of 1985, the EEC had placed anti-dumping duties ranging from 2.9 percent to 31.9 percent on Japanese construction machinery. The duties for hydraulic excavators, one of Komatsu's key products, amounted to 26.6 percent. Komatsu, which up to now had largely relied on exports from Japan and did not have a production site in Europe, intended to supply all European markets from its new U.K. plant.[15]

---

12. "Tough Times for VW's Rabbit," *Financial Times,* July 2, 1982, p. 12.

13. "Home Sales War to Maintain Jobs," *Financial Times,* December 15, 1986, p. v.

14. "High-Tech Road to a Change of Image—Motor Industry," *Financial Times,* December 17, 1985, Japanese Industry—p. 5.

15. "Komatsu Plans First EEC Production Unit," *Financial Times,* December 17, 1985, p. 8.

Moving with an Established Customer

Moving with an established customer can also be a reason for setting up plants abroad. In many industries, important suppliers want to keep their relationship by establishing plants near customer locations; and when customers build new plants elsewhere, suppliers move too. The automobile industry, with its intricate networks of hundreds of component suppliers feeding into the assembly plants, is a good example of how companies follow customers. As Japanese car manufacturers build plants in the United States and in Canada, Japanese parts suppliers are becoming concerned that U.S. production will partially replace car shipments from Japan and that a reduction in parts volume will result. To counter this possibility, many of them are either building new plants or looking for joint ventures with U.S. companies. Bridgestone Tire Co., Japan's largest tire manufacturer, decided to set up shop in Tennessee only after Japanese automobile firms began to move manufacturing into the United States.[16] The Japanese parts suppliers also have a competitive advantage due to some Japanese industry practices. Japanese car manufacturers have long relied on parts suppliers for detailed manufacturing drawings and designs and have tended to provide these companies with only general designs. As a result, Japanese car manufacturers are reluctant to enter the same close relationship with U.S. suppliers that have close ties to U.S. competitors.[17]

In similar fashion, Detroit's major automotive parts and component suppliers, such as tire companies and battery manufacturers, have long ago opened manufacturing facilities abroad to supply General Motors' and Ford's various foreign facilities. With the arrival of Japanese car manufacturers in the United States, similar moves were expected on the part of their longstanding parts suppliers.

Shifting Production Abroad to Save Costs

The experience of Compaq Computer illustrates the complex decision making process involved in deciding on a foreign manufacturing plant and its location. This United States–based manufacturer of small personal computers was founded in 1982 and experienced rapid growth. The company entered the European market in 1984 and began to look for a plant location in 1985. Compaq researched many European countries for possible locations and was courted by many countries that wanted the company to set up the plant in their localities. Eventually, Compaq decided to locate in Scotland in an area dubbed "Silicon Glen" for its likeness to the famous Silicon Valley in California. The company justified its plant location with the prediction that the U.K. market was likely to

16. "A Different Kind of Tiremaker Rolls into Nashville," *Fortune*, March 22, 1982, p. 136.
17. "Yet Another Japanese Transplant Threat," *Financial Times*, September 16, 1986, p. 9.

become Compaq's most important and fastest growing single market in Europe, so it would make sense to be close to that market.[18]

MNCs with plants in Taiwan, Hong Kong, Singapore, and other foreign countries have little intention of penetrating these markets with the help of their new factories. Instead, they locate abroad to take advantage of favorable conditions that reduce manufacturing costs, and the products are slated for markets elsewhere. This cost savings strategy has been employed by many U.S. companies in the electronics industry and has more recently been adopted by Japanese and European MNCs as well. Less common is location in areas with lower raw material or energy costs. A large Japanese producer of *sake,* the traditional Japanese rice wine, built a plant in California to use the cheaper U.S. rice in its distillation process. The finished product was shipped to Japan.

The motivation behind the location of plants in foreign countries may therefore at times be related to cost-cutting rather than to entering new markets. Such decisions are of a sourcing or production nature and are not necessarily tied to a company's international marketing strategy.

JOINT VENTURES

Companies entering foreign markets not only have to decide on the most suitable entry strategy, they also need to arrange ownership either as a wholly owned subsidiary or as a joint venture. Under a joint venture (JV) arrangement, the foreign company invites an outside partner to share stock ownership in the new unit. The particular participation of the partners may vary with some companies accepting either a minority or majority position. In most cases, MNCs prefer wholly owned subsidiaries for reasons of control. Once a joint-venture partner secures part of the operation, the MNC can no longer function independently, which sometimes leads to inefficiencies and disputes over responsibility for the venture. If an MNC has strictly defined operating procedures such as for budgeting, planning, and marketing, it may become difficult to get the JV company to accept the same methods of operation. Problems may also arise when the JV partner would like to maximize dividend payout instead of reinvestment, or when the capital of the JV has to be increased and one side is unable to raise the required funds. Experience has shown that JVs can be successful if the partners share the same goals with one of them accepting primary responsibility for operations matters.

Reasons for Entering Joint Ventures

Despite the potential for problems, joint ventures are commonly used because they offer important advantages to the foreign firm. By bringing in a partner, the

---

18. "A Tactical Victory for Silicon Glen," *Financial Times,* January 5, 1987, p. 8.

company can share the risk for a new venture. Furthermore, the JV partner may have important skills or contacts of value to the MNC. Sometimes, the partner may be an important customer who is willing to contract for a portion of the new unit's output in return for an equity participation. In other cases, the partner may represent important local business interests with excellent contacts to the government. An MNC with advanced product technology may also gain market access through the JV route by teaming up with companies that would be prepared to distribute its products. In a 1980 survey by the Conference Board, an association of large U.S. industrial corporations, half of the respondent companies indicated they were involved with joint ventures abroad. According to Conference Board sources, 40 percent of industrial companies with sales of $100 million or more are involved in at least one joint venture.

A critical factor in many joint venture decisions is the local government's attitude. In many countries, the governments look more favorably upon JVs than upon wholly owned foreign subsidiaries. These governments fear a loss of control over their economies if a substantial sector of their industry became owned by foreign-based MNCs. For this reason, it was for many years impossible to own more than 50 percent of a subsidiary in Japan, a practice that was revised in the mid-1970s. In Japan, foreign MNCs typically used JVs to gain access to distribution channels, whereas the Japanese partners were primarily interested in a new technology. This difference in the partners' basic objectives has been the root cause for many joint venture failures.

Joint Ventures to Enter Government-Controlled Economies

Joint ventures are sometimes necessary to enter countries where the economy is largely under state control. In such countries, foreign investors are only allowed to take minority positions in conjunction with local firms. In the case of government-controlled economies, this often means a joint venture must be signed with a government-owned firm. Given the country's large economic potential, many foreign firms have been attracted to China. Within two years of the adoption of China's law on joint ventures in 1979, more than 400 joint-venture contracts had been signed between Chinese and foreign firms. Among those having made investments were American Motors Corp., with its Jeep vehicles, and several other United States–based multinational corporations. In one instance, 3M was able to obtain approval for a fully-owned operation to make products for communications and electric power distribution.[19]

Schindler, a Swiss-based firm and a leading elevator manufacturer, was the first foreign firm taking advantage of China's law on joint ventures in 1979.[20] The company took a 25 percent equity position with the goal of becoming both a

---

19. "3M Signs with China to Open Unit There That Will Be 100%-Owned by U.S. Firm," *The Wall Street Journal,* November 16, 1983, p. 18.
20. "Schindler Gives Chinese Business a Lift," *Financial Times,* August 29, 1986, p. 6.

major supplier of elevators in China and using the venture as a production base for its growing business in the Far East. Growth in output has averaged more than 20 percent during the first six years of operation. The venture has been profitable for Schindler. The company has been able to beat out Hitachi and Mitsubishi, its two leading Japanese competitors, as the leader of the Chinese market. Although Schindler has still not met its target of exporting some 25 percent of local production, due to quality problems of suppliers, Schindler executives believe that the venture was successful because it offered major advantages to both sides.

Joint Ventures to Overcome Import Limitations

Companies may at times opt for a JV even when no specific law exists against opening a wholly owned operation. Often firms give way to subtle political pressure. Japanese car manufacturers have been under strong pressure from European governments to restrict their penetration of European markets.

In 1978, their market share in the nine EC member countries reached 6 percent, and in 1979 even rose to 6.9 percent.[21] Since additional growth was likely to provoke action by the EC on behalf of its major car manufacturers in Italy, the United Kingdom, France, and Germany, Japanese car manufacturers opted for joint ventures or cooperation agreements to protect their volume of cars sold in the EC.

Despite all the potential difficulties, joint ventures can be expected to remain a viable entry option for many companies in a large number of important markets. The challenge for international companies is to make joint ventures work and to use the strengths of the local partners in combination with the international company's own inherent strengths.

The Constant Danger of Joint-Venture Divorce

Not all joint ventures are successful and fulfill their partners' expectations. One study cited that between 1972 and 1976 some 90 major ventures failed in Japan alone. Many of these ventures involved large United States–based firms such as General Mills, TRW, and Avis. Another study showed that 30 percent of investigated joint ventures formed before 1967 between American companies and partners in other industrialized countries failed. In most cases, the ventures were either liquidated or taken over by one of the original partners.[22]

Dow Chemical encountered considerable difficulties with a joint venture in South Korea. Dow owned a 70 percent stake in Korea Pacific Chemical Corpora-

---

21. "Europe-Japanese Exports Have Carmakers Quaking," *Business Week*, April 7, 1980, p. 44.
22. J. Peter Killing, "How to Make a Global Joint Venture Work," *Harvard Business Review*, May–June 1982, p. 121.

tion with a Korean holding company, Korea Pacific Chemical Holding, which had some 2,000 local shareholders subscribing to the rest. The venture was to become a major customer of Dow's wholly owned local subsidiary. Dow sold off its stake in 1982 because it could not agree with its JV partner on how to make the operation profitable. Although Dow was the majority owner, management was shared equally with a group of four directors appointed by the Korean partners. Dow claimed that these directors, some of them retired career military officers, did not have sufficient business background. When Dow wanted to take over the entire venture and merge it with its local subsidiary, the Korean partner refused. Eventually, the Korean government interceded, and Dow was able to sell its stake to another Korean company. Other companies who sold their JV stakes included Searle, the pharmaceutical company, Control Data, the computer manufacturer, and Gulf Oil—all U.S. companies. Cultural differences and misunderstandings between foreign management and local executives were blamed in most situations.[23]

STRATEGIC ALLIANCES

A more recent phenomenon is the development of a range of strategic alliances. Alliances are different from traditional joint ventures in which two partners contribute a fixed amount of resources and the venture develops on its own. In an alliance, two entire firms pool their resources directly in a collaboration that goes beyond the limits of a joint venture. Although a new entity might be formed, this is not a requirement. Sometimes, the alliance is supported by some equity acquisition of one or both of the partners. In an alliance, partners bring a particular skill or resource, usually one that is complementary, and by joining forces both are expected to profit from the other's experience. Typically, alliances involve either distribution access, technology transfers, or production technology.

Technology-Based Alliances

Exchanging technology for market access was the basis of the AT&T alliance with Olivetti of Italy. AT&T needed to enter the European computer market to obtain economies of scale for its U.S. operations, but it did not have any marketing contacts of its own. On the other hand, Olivetti was eager to add larger computers to its existing line. As a result, Olivetti marketed AT&T computers through its extensive distribution system in Europe. In return, Olivetti became the key supplier to AT&T for personal computers and was able to use AT&T as

---

23. "South Korea Acts on Joint-Venture Friction," *Financial Times,* October 13, 1982, p. 20.

its distribution arm in the U.S. market. Both companies are receiving the benefit of each other's market access and each other's production and technology resources.[24]

A similar alliance was struck between AT&T and Philips of the Netherlands. AT&T, following its divestiture in the United States, was looking for a way to market its large public-exchange switching technology abroad where it had never been sold. Philips, who had excellent market contacts in a number of countries, was in need of a digital public-exchange system that followed earlier generations of mechanical switching systems. By joining into an alliance and forming a joint venture, AT&T gained immediate market access in a number of countries, whereas Philips gained immediate access to digital technology and thus saved a considerable investment.

Production-Based Alliances

General Motors in the United States made an alliance with Toyota to obtain manufacturing know-how from Toyota on small cars and to help Toyota gain access to the U.S. market.[25] The two companies formed a venture, named New United Motor Mfg., Inc., to jointly run an assembly plant that would produce up to 200,000 small cars for both General Motors and Toyota. General Motors will get a chance to learn modern Japanese manufacturing technology, while Toyota will get a sourcing point for its U.S. market at a time when import restrictions are keeping Japanese cars out of the United States. GM entered another alliance with Fanuc of Japan, a leading robot manufacturer, to form GMF.[26] This company quickly became the world's largest robot manufacturer and is supplying most of GM's own robots. Through this venture, Fanuc of Japan received immediate access to one of the world's largest robot markets, the U.S. automobile industry, whereas General Motors was assured the necessary technology to build and install the large number of robots it needed to become more efficient.

Distribution-Based Alliances

Alliances with a special emphasis on distribution are becoming increasingly common. Furthermore, alliances are also struck between direct competitors, usually with an eye towards eliminating inefficiencies. The construction machinery industry had been plagued by volume reductions for years causing several

---

24. George Taucher, "Building Alliances (A)—The American Telephone and Telegraph Company, Case GM 351, and Building Alliances (B)—Ing. C. Olivetti & Co. S.p.A., Case GM 352, IMEDE International Management Development Institute, Lausanne, Switzerland, 1986.

25. "The GM-Toyota Linkup Could Change the Industry," *Business Week*, December 24, 1984, p. 71.

26. "Corporate Odd Couples," *Business Week*, July 21, 1986, p. 105.

firms to link up with each other.[27] Caterpillar of the United States and Mitsubishi of Japan are merging their hydraulic excavator lines into a joint venture in Japan. Both companies will share distribution networks in the Far East, and Caterpillar can supply its Australian market out of Japan and save in transportation costs. Komatsu of Japan will purchase, through Brown of the United Kingdom, Norwegian-made Moxy dump trucks to be sold through the Komatsu dealer network. This will give Komatsu a chance to round out its own line and will give Brown access to a wider distribution network for its specialized dump trucks.

Similarly, Hitachi agreed to an alliance with Fiatallis of Italy whereby Fiatallis will have the chance to eliminate its outdated line of hydraulic excavators by selling the superior Hitachi models. Hitachi will have the chance to use the Fiatallis network, which is important for this Japanese company producing only one type of earth-moving equipment. Increasingly, buyers have concentrated their purchases on a single distribution system to gain extra volume discounts. This change in the market makes it imperative for a manufacturer to be part of a large dealer network rather than have its own specialized dealers.

The Future of Alliances

This trend towards entering alliances is not unilaterally applauded, and many critics maintain that they tend to favor Japanese firms wherever they are involved. Recent research has found that two Japanese computer companies, Fujitsu and NEC, profited more from the partnerships they entered with a large number of U.S. and European firms than did their foreign partners.[28] As a matter of fact, NEC shifted from being a strict licensee of Honeywell in the 1960s to taking control of Honeywell's computer business through a cooperation with Bull, Honeywell's French partner. Boeing's recent agreement with a group of Japanese aerospace companies was criticized for giving away crucial technology in a still United States–dominated industry.[29]

But others argue that many firms will have no choice but to join forces with potential competitors. Cosmos, Inc., a small software development firm based in Seattle, Washington that had become successful with a special range of database programs, decided to cooperate with Japan Computer Science Co. (JCS). Through this cooperation, Cosmos gets its programs adapted to the Japanese market as well as immediate access to some 400 distributors. To launch such an effort on its own in Japan would have been impossible for a company the size of Cosmos.[30]

27. "Wary Friends Seek Survival," *Financial Times,* February 10, 1987, p. 17.

28. "How Japan Can Put a Spoke in the Wheels of the West," *Financial Times,* October 17, 1986, p. 9.

29. "A Faustian Bargain with the Japanese," *The New York Times,* April 6, 1986, p. 2F.

30. "Do the Japanese Make Good Partners?" *INC.,* March 1987, p. 30.

Although many existing alliances are still new and have to prove themselves over time, it does appear that alliances will remain a frequent way to penetrate new markets. For international companies to remain successful, their managers will have to learn to strike shrewd distribution alliances by leveraging their own company skills for market entry elsewhere. Most likely we will see an accelerating trend towards such alliances in the future.

ENTRY STRATEGY IMPLEMENTATION

As international companies face a myriad of entry operations for many markets, their ability to maximize the most effective strategy calls for greater skill at entry configuration. Companies will be challenged to find specific entry strategies that fit a given market. In some instances, these configurations will be tailor-made rather than off-the-shelf type strategies. Also, entry strategies will no longer fall into neat categories of exporting, local production, licensing, or joint ventures, but will increasingly become a mixture of a number of entry modes.

The biggest challenge to international firms will be the closed markets. Those are countries where normal entry through exporting is virtually prohibited and where access to local customers is limited either through outward prohibition or through customers and culture. Over the years, many foreign firms have found it very difficult to penetrate and enter the Japanese market. Japan could only be entered through exporting or through a joint venture with a local partner until the Japanese government relaxed its limitations on foreign ownership. Texas Instruments, one of the most successful foreign electronics companies in Japan, started out with a joint venture with Sony; but the understanding was that TI could buy back Sony's share some time later on when the regulatory environment had changed.[31]

The ability to switch from one mode of entry into another may be an important requirement of the initial arrangement. Data General of the United States was a company that was able to shift its entry strategy following the changes in the investment laws in Japan in 1978.[32] Data General had originally signed a licensing agreement with a consortium of seven Japanese companies in 1971 called Nippon Minicomputer. A few years later, Data General realized that most of its customers in Japan were other multinationals who wanted to make direct purchase agreements for buying Data General minicomputers with its head office in the United States. Since the company could not make a licensee obey such agreements, Data General negotiated first to buy a 50 percent stake in 1979 and

---

31. Vernon R. Alden, "Who Says You Can't Crack Japanese Markets?" *Harvard Business Review*, January–February 1987, p. 52.

32. "Data General Shows Friendly Takeovers Are Possible in Japan," *Business International*, August 6, 1982, p. 249.

finally up to 85 percent in 1982. The local organization was changed to Nippon Data General (NDG), but Japanese management was left in place. This stepwise approach to a integrated production and sales organization was very successful for Data General and the company was able to obtain a leadership position in the Japanese market.

Entry Through Acquisition

The outright acquisition of an existing company has become another important entry alternative. Frequently practiced by foreign companies in the United States and by U.S. firms in Europe, acquisitions have only recently become a possibility in some markets such as Japan. One of the first acquisitions was made by General Motors of Isuzu Motors in 1970.[33] Other U.S. companies who acquired what amounted to minority ownership stakes were Ford Motor Company in Toyo Kogyo (producer of Mazda automobiles) and Oscar Mayer in Prima Ham, Japan's third-largest meat processor. However, all of these acquisitions were minority ownerships of less than 50 percent.

The first international company to acquire a controlling interest in a large publicly owned, Tokyo Stock Exchange listed Japanese company was Merck & Co., the leading U.S. pharmaceutical company.[34] Merck bought a controlling interest in Banya Pharmaceutical with sales of more than $300 million. Merck had operated a small joint venture with Banya but its Japanese volume had never exceeded $140 million, a small amount for a company with global sales of $3.1 billion. This acquisition would give Merck both additional market penetration and a further ability to do research in Japan.

Entry Through Local Venture Capital

One of the more innovative new approaches to entry strategy in Japan was selected by LSI Logic, a new California manufacturer of custom-designed logic semiconductor chips. Rather than pursuing any of the many alternatives tried before by other firms, LSI Logic was able to convince a leading Japanese investment house to float 30 percent of the needed capital for the Japanese company to a number of local investors. The company raised $20 million for the 30 percent stake and began operations as Nihon LSI Logic under the leadership of a senior Japanese executive who had held important positions in Japanese electronics firms. Nihon LSI Logic opened two custom-chip design centers in Japan and formed another venture with Kawasaki Steel to build a $100 million electronic chip manufacturing plant to supply both the Japanese and European markets.

---

33. "Merck Finds a Formula for Success," *The New York Times*, October 30, 1983.
34. "Merck's Big Venture in Japan," *The New York Times*, October 13, 1983.

Following its success with venture capital funding, Nihon LSI Logic aspired to become listed on the Tokyo Stock Exchange. Its parent company would then reduce its holding to about 50 percent of total capital.[35]

PREPARING AN ENTRY STRATEGY ANALYSIS

Assembling the correct data is of course the cornerstone of any entry strategy analysis. The necessary sales projections have to be supplemented with detailed cost data and financial need projections on assets. The data need to be assembled for all entry strategies under consideration (see Figure 9.2). The financial data are collected not only on the proposed venture but also on its anticipated impact on the existing operations of the MNC. The combination of the two sets of financial data results in incremental financial data incorporating the net overall benefit of the proposed move on the total company structure.

For best results, the analyst must take a long-term view of the situation. Asset requirements, costs, and sales have to be evaluated over the planning horizon of the proposed venture, typically three to five years for an average company. Furthermore, a thorough sensitivity analysis is incorporated. This may consist of assuming several scenarios of international risk factors that may adversely affect the success of the proposed venture. For each scenario, the financial data can be adjusted to reflect the "new" set of circumstances. Possibly, one scenario may include a 20 percent devaluation in the host country combined with currency control and difficulty of receiving new supplies from foreign plants. Another situation may assume a change in political leadership less friendly to foreign investments. With the help of a sensitivity analysis approach, a company can quickly spot the key variables in the environment that determine the outcome of the proposed market entry. The MNC then has the opportunity to further add to its information on such key variables or at least closely monitor their development.

In the following section of this chapter we provide a general methodology for the analysis of entry decisions. It is assumed that any company approaching a new market is looking for profitability and growth. Consequently, the entry strategy must be subordinated to these goals. Each project has to be analyzed for the expected sales level, costs, and asset levels that will eventually determine profitability (see Table 9.1).

Sales

An accurate estimate of the market share or sales volume is of crucial importance for the entry strategy decision. Sales results will largely depend on the

---

35. Thomas Y. Miracle, "An End-Run Around by the Barricades: LSI Logic's Unique Entry into the Japanese Chip Market," *Pacific Basin Quarterly,* Spring 1986, p. 15.

FIGURE 9.2 Considerations for Market Entry Decisions

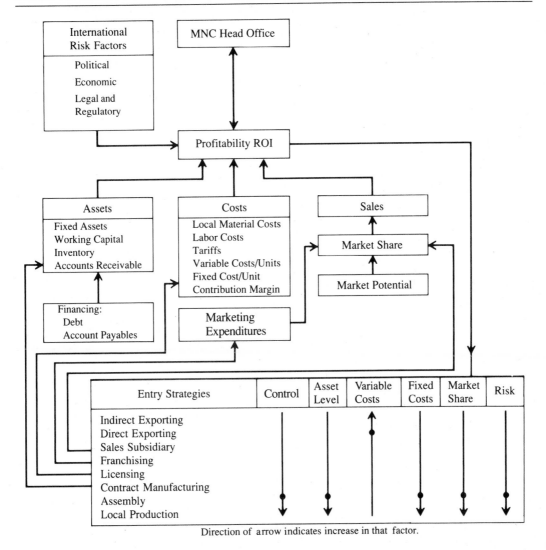

Direction of arrow indicates increase in that factor.

company's market share and the total size or potential of the market. The market share to be gained is primarily competitively determined. The foreign company can influence the market share through a strong marketing mix which in turn is also dependent on the level of financial commitment for marketing expenditures. The various types of entry strategies also allow a foreign firm to unfold its marketing strategy to varying degrees. Typically, direct or indirect exporting results in a lower market share than local sales subsidiaries or local production due to the founder's weaker market presence. This weaker presence causes a

TABLE 9.1 Financial Analysis for Entry Strategy

Financial Variables	*Local Values*
Assets	
Cash	New amount of assets needed to sustain chosen entry
Accounts Receivable	strategy in local market
Inventory	
Equipment	
Buildings	
Land	
Liabilities	
Accounts Payable	New amount of liabilities incurred due to entry
Debt	strategy
Net Assets	_____
Costs	
Unit Variable Costs (VC)	Amount of VC in newly selected operations
Material costs	
Labor costs	
Purchases	
Fixed and Semifixed Costs	Local fixed costs due to selected entry mode
Supervision	
Marketing	
General Administrative	
Expenses	
Total Unit Costs	_____
Sales	Local sales of chosen entry mode
Total Sales	

TABLE 9.1 *continued*

Decreases Elsewhere (*Due to new operation*)	*Incremental Value*
Assets liquidated or no longer needed due to shift of operation	Net new assets required
Reduction or change in liabilities due to shift in operation	Net new liabilities incurred
————————————	Net asset requirement
Diseconomies of scale due to volume loss by shifting production to new subsidiary	Net variable costs across all subsidiaries resulting from new entry mode
Lost contribution if production shifted elsewhere	Net fixed burden of new entry mode
————————————	Incremental total costs
Lost sales in other units of the MNC subsidiary network	Net additional sales of entry strategy

loss of control over local middlemen. Also, to some extent, independent firms have to be depended upon to carry out the company's marketing functions.

Leveraging the nature of its presence in the United States was the goal of Nixdorf, a leading German computer company. For effective sales and service, the company needed a presence in some 120 U.S. cities. Once the network was in place, the company could expect to make inroads in market share and start to gain volume. Nixdorf considered its investment into this service network a necessary price for becoming a player in the U.S. market.[36]

Market potential is of course not subject to the influence of the international firm seeking entry. The size of a local market combined with the expected market share often determines the outcome of an entry strategy analysis. Local assembly or production with correspondingly high levels of assets and fixed costs need large volumes to offset these costs, whereas exporting operations can usually be rendered profitable at much lower sales volumes than other entry strategies.

Particularly in markets with considerable growth potentials, it becomes essential to forecast sales over a longer period of time. A low expected volume right now might indicate little success for a new subsidiary, but data on expected volume later on could suggest a change in the future entry strategy. Since it is often impossible to shift quickly into another entry mode once a firm is established, special attention has to be focused on the need to ensure that the chosen entry strategy offers a long-term opportunity to maximize profits.

Costs

The MNC will have to determine the expected costs of its operation in a foreign country both with respect to manufacturing and general administrative costs. Unit variable costs may vary depending on local production, assembly, or exporting as the chosen strategy. To establish such costs, local material costs, local wage levels, and tariffs on imports will have to be taken into consideration. Again, unit variable costs should be expected to vary according to the entry strategy alternatives considered.

Necessary fixed costs represent another important element in the analysis. Administrative costs tend to be much smaller for a sales subsidiary compared to a local manufacturing unit. Through use of a contribution margin analysis, breakeven for several levels of entry strategies could be considered. Government regulations or laws may also affect local costs and substantially change costs over time.

Cost levels may differ substantially from country to country (see Table 9.2). Estimating and forecasting costs in the international environment requires a keen sense of awareness that environmental factors of a political, economic, or

---

36. "Nixdorf Takes on the Americans," *The New York Times,* September 15, 1984.

TABLE 9.2 International Comparison of 1987 Labor Costs (Average hourly compensation, including fringe benefits)

West Germany	$16.74
Switzerland	16.63
Sweden	14.72
United States	13.52
Italy	12.52
France	12.40
Japan	11.48
United Kingdom	8.96
Greece	4.86
South Korea	1.80

Source: Business Europe, Fortnightly Managers' Monitor, Geneva: Business International, June 15, 1987, pp. 1–2.

legal nature can render a careful analysis invalid. Consequently, such possibilities need to be considered from the outset.

Assets

The level of assets deployed greatly affects the profitability of any entry strategy. The assets may consist of any investments made in conjunction with the entrance (or exit, for that matter) into the new market. Such investments may comprise working capital in the form of cash, accounts receivables, or inventory, or it may include fixed assets such as land, buildings, machinery, and equipment. The amount of assets required depends to a great extent on the particular entry strategy chosen. Exporting or sales subsidiaries require an investment in working capital only with little additional funds for fixed facilities. Local assembly or production, however, demand substantial investments. Often it will be possible to use local financing to reduce the net investment amount of the international firm. For an adequate comparison of the various entry strategies, an asset budget should be established for each of the alternatives considered.

Profitability

Conceptually, a company should maximize the future stream of earnings discounted at its cost of capital. Other companies may prefer to concentrate on return on investment (ROI) as a more appropriate measurement of profitability. In either case, profitability is dependent on the level of assets, costs, or sales.

Several exogenous international risk factors influence profitability and therefore have to be included in the analysis. The outcome of such an analysis determines the selection of the entry strategy. In the following sections, each of these factors will be described and their possible impact on profitability will be indicated.

International Risk Factors

Aside from the normal business risk factors that every company also confronts in its home market, there are additional risks involved due to the existence of more than one single economy or country. Each country hosting a foreign subsidiary may take action of a political, economic, or regulatory nature that can completely obliterate any carefully drawn up business plan. As we discussed in Chapter 4, political turmoil in many parts of the world greatly affects business and investment conditions. Following the departure of the Shah of Iran, the country's political stability deteriorated to such an extent that business could not be conducted as usual. Many foreign operations were taken over by the government or just ceased to exist. Similar effects could be witnessed on business in other countries, particularly Nicaragua (in 1979), and Turkey (1978 to 1980).

As we discussed in Chapter 2, different economic systems add to uncertainties and are reflected in currency changes or diverging economic trends. Manufacturing costs are particularly sensitive to various changes. Many times, a company has shifted production from one country to another on the basis of the latest cost data just to find out a few years later that costs have changed due to fluctuations of macroeconomic variables beyond company control. Local labor costs over the years have fluctuated considerably and are very sensitive to local inflation and foreign currency changes.

Labor cost data shows that the U.S. labor cost disadvantage increased from 1981 to 1983, when the U.S. dollar increased in value compared to other currencies. From 1985 to 1987, the U.S. dollar declined substantially compared to other leading currencies. As a result, average hourly compensation in Switzerland and Germany surpassed U.S. wage levels (see Table 9.2).

Since 1982, Caterpillar has increased its overseas production from 19 percent to 25 percent of total sales as a response to higher production costs in the United States. However, as the value of the U.S. dollar declined, so have Caterpillar's margins in its overseas units in the United Kingdom and France, whereas some of its U.S. competitors now have an advantage by producing in the United States. Capterpillar's largest competitor, Japan's Komatsu, however, had to absorb even larger cost increases in its Japanese production as a result of the rapidly rising yen.[37]

37. "Weaker Dollar Isn't a Boon for Caterpillar," *The Wall Street Journal*, February 20, 1987, p. 6.

MNC Head Office

Once profitability on a local level has been established and the relevant international risk factors included, the proper analysis has to turn to the MNC as a whole. The expected profits of the new market entry have to be analyzed along with the overall impact on the total organization. Replacing imports with local production may cause a loss of sales or output at the existing facility which may counterbalance the new profits gained from the plant opening. Consequently, such an impact may exist with respect to assets, costs, and sales depending on the entry strategy. As a result, the MNC aims at maximizing incremental profits achieved on incremental assets and sales. A promising opportunity abroad may suddenly appear less attractive when allowances are made for displacement in other parts of an MNC.

EXIT STRATEGIES

Circumstances can arise when companies decide to leave a country or market. Other than failure to achieve marketing objectives, there may be political, economic, or legal reasons to dissolve or sell an operation. MNCs have to be aware of the high costs attached to the liquidation of foreign operations; substantial amounts of severance pay may have to be paid to employees.

Exiting Markets for Consolidation Purposes

Consolidation of foreign subsidiary operations may be a reason for closing down some operations. Overcapacity and small production units were causing problems for U.S. tire manufacturers in Europe. Some tried to increase productivity by closing marginally profitable plants but were only partially successful. In 1976, Goodyear Tire & Rubber Company was evaluating the closing of its Swedish factory in Norrkoping. The thirty-six-year-old operation had been profitable until the previous year and employed some 1,000 workers. The company claimed that its Swedish plant was losing money despite a strong market for cars in Sweden. Losses were caused by the high local wage levels and low-price imports from other European countries. Nearly 50 percent of the Swedish demand was supplied by imports, so that even Sweden's largest tire maker, Trelleborg AG, switched from local production to importing from the United Kingdom. Other local producers, Firestone-Vishafors and Gislaved, however, were both operating in the black, leading to accusations that Goodyear's subsidiary was in the red largely due to mismanagement. In fact, the two leading domestic producers even exported a substantial portion of their output despite high Swedish labor costs. The rumors about the impending closing triggered a debate in the Parliament over the role of the MNCs. Goodyear was accused of milking its Swedish plant by engaging in questionable practices. Given the adverse publicity, Goodyear at that time dropped its plans to close the plant.[38]

In 1978, the situation was different for Firestone in Switzerland. Its plant was thirty-four years old and produced one million tires annually. The company's market share had steadily declined from 50 percent after World War II to 20 percent in 1978. Exports had suffered a steep decline due to the strong revaluation of the Swiss franc and cheap import competition. But plant closings were politically unacceptable in Switzerland despite its microscopic unemployment rate of only 0.4 percent. The 600 laid-off employees went on a protest strike causing a public uproar against Firestone. Despite this resistance, the company insisted on closing the plant and satisfying the Swiss market from lower cost production centers in other European countries.[39] Uniroyal Inc. and B. F. Goodrich withdrew from Europe entirely.[40]

Since the laying off of excess workers is not an acceptable practice in many countries, the costs of an actual closing could be very high. Employees have to be paid up to 150 percent of their annual wages in some parts of Europe and often more in Latin America.[41] As a result, operations are often sold rather than closed down.

Exiting Markets for Political Reasons

Changing political situations have at times forced companies to leave markets. Procter & Gamble, the giant United States–based consumer goods manufacturer, sold its Cuban subsidiary in 1958, one year before Fidel Castro won the Civil War. It also disposed of its Chilean subsidiary shortly before the election victory of Allende in Chile in 1970. Had the company insisted on staying in those markets, the subsidiaries would most likely have been expropriated.

Changing government regulations can at times pose problems prompting some companies to leave a country. India is a case in point.[42] There, the government adopted its Exchange Regulation Act in 1973 to require most foreign companies to divest themselves of 60 percent of their subsidiaries by the end of 1977. Companies that manufactured substantially for export or whose operations comprised advanced technology were exempted. Since IBM's Indian operation did little exporting and sold mostly older computer models, the computer manufacturer was asked to sell 60 percent of its equity to Indian citizens. IBM, which operated a small manufacturing facility and several data services and sales offices, made a counter-proposal to the government to retain 100 percent owner-

---

38. "Sweden: Goodyear Thinking about Leaving," *Business Week,* March 8, 1976, p. 38.
39. "Trouble in Baselland: Firestone Wants Out," *Business Week,* May 1, 1978, p. 30.
40. "Troubles Hit Europe's Tire Makers," *The Wall Street Journal,* March 11, 1981, p. 3.
41. "U.S. Firms Dissatisfied with Earnings Abroad," *The Wall Street Journal,* September 23, 1977.
42. "IBM to Leave India and Avoid Loss of Control," *The New York Times,* November 16, 1977.

ship in one subsidiary but to sell 60 percent in another; but this was rejected by the Indian government. Since the company was unwilling to lose control of its subsidiary, IBM decided to close it down and lay off the work force. IBM was believed to have about 180 computers installed in India with sales of less than $100 million annually. The work force had reached 800 in 1977.

Also, IBM stopped accepting orders in Nigeria and Indonesia pending the outcome of negotiations on new laws in these countries that required IBM to sell some part of its equity to local nationals. IBM's policy was to protect its technological base and not to give in to any country's attempt to gain partial control; it was feared that other countries might be encouraged to follow suit. Since IBM's business was primarily with developed nations, it could afford to leave some of the developing markets.

The situation with South Africa shows that exit strategies can also be the result of negative reactions in a firm's home market. With the political situation in South Africa open to challenge on moral grounds, many multinational corporations have exited that country by abandoning or selling their local subsidiaries. In 1984, some 325 U.S. companies were maintaining operations in South Africa. Two years later, this number had decreased to 265. The total amount of U.S. direct foreign investment was estimated at U.S. $1.3 billion.[43] One of the U.S. firms leaving was Coca-Cola, the soft-drink bottler.[44] Other U.S. firms that have exited South Africa include General Motors, IBM, Motorola, and General Electric. Some European firms have withdrawn from that country also: Alfa-Romeo of Italy, Barclays Bank of the United Kingdom, and Renault of France among them.[45]

CONCLUSIONS

The world comprises more than 150 individual countries or markets. Thus, entry decisions are the strategy decisions international companies make most frequently. Since the type of entry strategy can be clearly related to the later market success, such decisions need to be made with careful analysis. Companies often find that it is very difficult to break out of an initial arrangement, which is another reason that special attention must be given to this type of decision. In some of the more difficult markets, such as Japan, making the correct entry decision can become a key competitive advantage for a firm and can unlock markets otherwise not accessible to a foreign company.

To survive in the coming global battles for market dominance, companies

---

43. "South Africa: Time to Stay—or Go?" *Fortune*, August 4, 1986, p. 45.
44. "If Coke Has Its Way, Blacks Will Soon Own 'The Real Thing,'" *Business Week*, March 27, 1987, p. 56.
45. "High Risks and Low Returns," *Financial Times*, November 25, 1986, p. 10.

have to become increasingly bolder and more creative in their entry strategy choices. Long gone are the days when entry was restricted to exporting, licensing, foreign manufacturing, and joint ventures. New concepts such as global alliances have become common, and international firms will have to include acquisitions, venture capital financing, and complex government partnerships as integral elements in entry strategy configurations. The myriad new entry alternatives have raised the level of complexity in international marketing and will remain an important challenge for managers.

This added complexity will make detailed analysis of entry strategy alternatives and their comparisons more difficult. For adequate analysis, companies will have to take into consideration not only present cost structures but the ever changing economic and political environment. Rapidly changing foreign exchange rates have changed the costs of various entry alternatives and have forced companies to shift their approach. These economic changes are likely to remain and companies will be forced to reevaluate their entry strategy decisions on an ongoing basis. Entry strategies will rarely be made on a permanent basis but will have to be adapted to the most recent situation.

Although most companies will have preferences as to which entry strategy they would like to pursue given no objections, firms will be increasingly adopting a flexible approach. Establishing a sales subsidiary may be the best alternative for entering some countries, whereas joint ventures may be necessary to enter other countries. Managers will be forced to learn to manage with a variety of entry strategies, and they will be less able to repeat the same entry patterns all over the world. A great amount of managerial flexibility will thus be required of international companies and their executives. We can also expect that the future will bring other types of entry strategies that will challenge international managers anew.

Questions for Discussion

1. Contrast the entry strategies practiced by Boeing and IBM. What differences do you find and what explains these differences?
2. Would entry strategies differ for companies considering to enter Germany, Japan, or China? If so, in what way and for what reasons?
3. How would the entry strategy differ for a new start-up firm versus a mature multinational company?
4. What difficulties and special problems would you expect from a firm practicing only franchising as an entry strategy.
5. Perform a literature search on alliances and try to determine the reasons particular alliances were made.
6. It has been speculated that alliances between Japanese and Western firms work primarily to the benefit of Japanese companies. Comment.

For Further Reading

Brasch, John J. "Using Export Specialists to Develop Overseas Sales." *Harvard Business Review* (May–June 1981), pp. 6–8.

Cannon, T. "Managing International and Export Marketing." *European Journal of Marketing*, No. 1 (1980), pp. 34–49.

Cavusgil Tamer S., and John R. Nevin. "Internal Determinants of Export Marketing Behavior: An Empirical Investigation." *Journal of Marketing Research* (February 1981), pp. 114–119.

Hackett, Donald W. "The International Expansion of U.S. Franchise Systems: Status and Strategies." *Journal of International Business Studies* (Spring 1976), pp. 65–75.

Harrigan, Kathryn Rudie. "Joint Ventures and Global Strategies." *The Columbia Journal of World Business,* 19 (Summer 1984), p. 7.

Killing, J. Peter. "How to Make a Global Joint Venture Work." *Harvard Business Review* (May–June 1982), pp. 120–127.

Killing, J. Peter. *Strategies for Joint Venture Success.* New York: Praeger, 1983.

Piercy, Nigel. "Export Strategy: Key Markets vs. Market Spreading." *Journal of International Marketing,* No. 1 (1981), pp. 56–67.

Reid, Stan D. "The Decision-Maker and Export Entry and Expansion." *Journal of International Business Studies* (Fall 1981), pp. 101–112.

Root, Franklin R. *Entry Strategies for International Markets.* Lexington, Mass.: D.C. Heath, 1987.

Townsend, James B. "Forms of International Involvement." In *Contemporary Perspectives in International Business.* Ed. Harold W. Berkman and Ivan R. Vernon. Chicago: Rand McNally College Publishing Company, 1979, pp. 151–161.

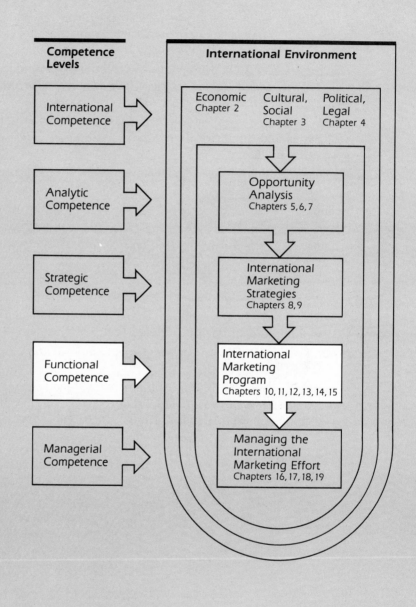

Competence Levels

International Competence

Analytic Competence

Strategic Competence

Functional Competence

Managerial Competence

International Environment

Economic
Chapter 2

Cultural, Social
Chapter 3

Political, Legal
Chapter 4

Opportunity Analysis
Chapters 5, 6, 7

International Marketing Strategies
Chapters 8, 9

International Marketing Program
Chapters 10, 11, 12, 13, 14, 15

Managing the International Marketing Effort
Chapters 16, 17, 18, 19

PART 5

INTERNATIONAL MARKETING PROGRAMS

Assembling an international marketing program requires an analysis of how the international environment will impact the four major marketing mix elements: product, distribution, pricing, and communications. In this section, we focus on how companies adapt to different marketing environments by adjusting certain elements of their marketing programs to ensure market acceptance. In concentrating on these issues, our aim is to help you increase functional competence. Marketing managers must not only be knowledgeable about the international environment, they must also possess the solid, functional skills necessary to successfully compete in the international marketplace.

In Chapter 10 we concentrate on product strategy issues in international markets. In Chapter 11, we discuss how to manage the new product development process in an international environment. Important distribution and channel decisions are discussed in Chapter 12. Chapter 13 outlines the differences between domestic and international pricing and how companies can deal with problems arising from different prices in different markets. In Chapter 14, we give an overview of communications strategies, sales force management, and promotion policies for international companies. The final chapter in this section, Chapter 15, focuses on international advertising and the challenges faced by companies running different advertising programs simultaneously in many countries.

10
INTERNATIONAL PRODUCT STRATEGIES

This chapter focuses on the strategies companies can pursue to adapt their products to international markets. (Figure 10.1 highlights the elements involved in product strategy decisions.) The chapter discussion first centers on the many possible environmental factors that tend to prevent the marketing of uniform and standardized products across a multitude of markets. Our attention then shifts to the various implications of selecting brand names for international markets. MNCs are concerned not only with determining appropriate brand names but also with protecting those names against abuse and piracy. The following sections focus on international packaging and managing product lines and support services. The chapter concludes with a section on the marketing of services on a global scale. We also highlight the enormous opportunities in the service industry and explain how various companies are pursuing such challenges.

PRODUCT DESIGN IN AN INTERNATIONAL ENVIRONMENT

One of the principal questions in international marketing concerns the types of products that can be sold abroad. With respect to existing products, the international firm will want to know whether these products have to be adapted or whether they can be shipped in their present form. For new products, the firm will have to select the particular features their products should incorporate and determine the desired function and performance of these features. The major elements of product design are explained in the following sections, with an emphasis on the effect of international complexities.

FIGURE 10.1 International Product Strategies

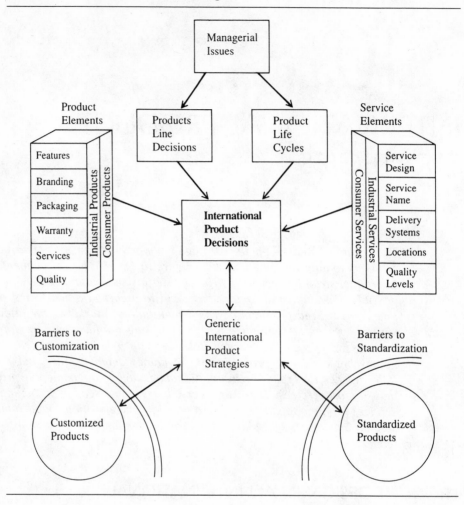

To select the most desirable product features is an involved decision for international marketers. The approach taken should include a thorough check on all the environmental factors that may impact product use (see Table 10.1). Furthermore, a thorough analysis should include the relative physical success factors developed in detail in Chapter 7. In all cases, however, a firm will have to picture its products in the targeted foreign market and ask the question: "How would our product be used in that country?" In some situations it may be necessary to send some units to the foreign market for testing purposes.

TABLE 10.1 Environmental Factors Requiring Product Design Changes

Environmental Factors	*Design Changes*
Level of technical skills	Product simplification
Level of labor costs	Automation or manualization of product
Level of literacy	Remaking and simplification of product
Level of income	Quality and price change
Level of interest rates	Quality and price change (investment in high quality may not be financially desirable)
Level of maintenance	Change in tolerances
Climatic differences	Product adaption
Isolation (heavy repair; difficult and expensive)	Product simplification and reliability improvement
Difference in standards	Recalibration of product and resizing
Availability of other products	Greater or lesser product integration
Availability of materials	Change in product structure and fuel
Power availability	Resizing of product
Special conditions	Product redesign or invention

Source: Richard D. Robinson, *International Business Management* (Hinesdale, Ill.: The Dryden Press, 1978), pp. 41–42. Reprinted by permission of Holt, Rinehart & Winston.

Product Dimensions for International Use

Dimensions as expressed by size, capacity, or volume are subject to market and environmental influences that often require different approaches to any given market. One important factor, particularly for U.S. firms, is the selection of a metric versus a nonmetric scale. The firm must go beyond a single translation of nonmetric into metric sizes to help users or consumers understand the design of products. Simple translations do not lead to round standardized numbers, forcing companies actually to change the physical sizes of their products to conform to new standards. The U.S. market is the only remaining major nonmetric market, with Europe and Japan operating on the metric standard. It is therefore less of an issue for foreign firms than for United States–based companies that normally operate on a nonmetric basis at home.

Many U.S. multinationals that have operated on a metric basis abroad have announced their intention to switch home plants to metric standards in order to achieve cost advantages through standardization. General Motors built North

America's first metrically designed car, the 1976 model Chevette.[1] Before the car could be assembled, some 47,300 suppliers had to be notified of the intended switch. Most of these suppliers also had to convert from a strictly nonmetric operation to a mixed operation often requiring new tooling and machinery. By converting its U.S. operations to metric dimensions, GM intended to integrate foreign and U.S. operations and to organize spare parts manufacturing on an international level. The company expected to save more over the years than the original conversion cost. Savings were estimated at about 1 percent of gross sales over a ten-year period.

Many other environmental factors can influence the size of products. Swiss watch manufacturers have learned over the years to adapt their watch cases to different wrist sizes: the Japanese have smaller wrists than Americans, thus design changes are required that do not necessarily change the function or look of the watch. A leading Italian shoe manufacturer had a similar experience exporting shoes to the United States. Research revealed that feet were not the same in every country. Americans were found to have longer toes than Italians, and their feet had a smaller instep.[2] Also, the company learned that Americans have thicker ankles and narrower, flatter feet. To produce a properly fitting shoe, the Italian company decided to make appropriate changes in its design to achieve the necessary comfort for American customers. Edmont, a division of Becton Dickinson, asked Japanese factory workers to test their new work gloves. They found that Japanese workers have smaller hands and and shorter fingers than their counterparts in Europe and the United States.[3]

Size is often affected by the physical surroundings of product use or space. In some countries living space is limited, necessitating home appliances that are substantially smaller than those found in a country such as the United States where people live in relatively larger dwellings. In many countries, customers have come to expect certain products in certain sizes, and thus MNCs are forced to adapt to meet these expectations.

Matching Product Design Features with International Markets

Invariably international firms find they must alter some components or parts of a product because of local circumstances. One worldwide manufacturer of industrial abrasives has had to adjust to different raw material supply situations by varying the raw material input according to country while maintaining abrasive performance standards. Aerospatiale, the large French aerospace company, de-

---

1. "Multinationals Lead as U.S. Slowly Turns to the Metric System," *The Wall Street Journal,* August 20, 1976, pp. 1, 21.

2. "Three Scientists Seek U.S. Data on Genetic Engineering, *The New York Times,* March 8, 1978, p. A-19.

3. Robert Thomas, Vice President, Edmont Division of Becton Dickinson. Discussion with authors on July 13, 1987.

cided to make its helicopters more acceptable to the U.S. market by using engines from Avco Corp.'s Lycoming Stratford Division, an engine supplier well-known to potential U.S. clients.[4] To please U.S. pilots, navigation and communication equipment was bought from local suppliers. There was considerable risk in this move; while orders were pouring in, Avco had technical problems with the engines. Thus delivery of about sixty helicopters was delayed in 1980, causing an estimated $18 million in lost sales opportunities.

Researchers have considered the U.S. customer to be particularly feature-conscious.[5] Consequently, features considered necessary in the United States may not be required abroad, although others may be in greater demand. Adding the desired features can strengthen a company's marketing effort and offset the added engineering and production costs. In some local markets customers may even expect a product to perform a function different from the one originally intended. One U.S. exporter of gardening tools found that its battery-operated trimmers were used by the Japanese as lawn mowers on their small lawns. As a result, the batteries and motors did not last as long as they would have under ordinary use. Because of the different function desired by Japanese customers, eventually a design change was required.

Adapting Performance Standards

Manufacturers typically design products to meet domestic performance standards. As we've seen, such standards do not always apply in other countries, and product changes are required in some circumstances. Products designed in highly developed countries often exceed the performance needed in developing Third World countries. These customers prefer products of greater simplicity, not only to save costs but to assure better service over a product lifetime. MNCs have been criticized for selling excess performance where simpler products would do. Stepping into this market gap are companies from some of the less developed countries whose present technology levels are more in line with those in the Third World. In the computer industry, an East German firm has begun to ship medium-sized computers to India, Brazil, and Iraq, with sales to Syria and Libya in the offing.[6] Though less sophisticated than current Western products, machines from Eastern European companies have been more than adequate to handle data processing needs of Third World countries where much less sophistication is demanded. Different strategies have been pursued by Ford Motor Company and General Motors. Both companies have designed special vehicles for

4. "France: Aérospatiale's Raid on U.S. Helicopters," *Business Week,* December 22, 1980, pp. 34–36.

5. Montrose Sommers and Jerome Kernan, "Why Products Flourish Here, Fizzle There," *Columbia Journal of World Business,* vol. 2, March–April 1967, pp. 89–97.

6. "Communists Gain in Computer Sales," *The Wall Street Journal,* December 15, 1975, p. 6.

Third World countries that are less expensive than standard cars and offer less comfort and fewer features.[7]

The need for different product standards was behind a foreign acquisition by the Westinghouse Electric Corporation.[8] Standards for electrical equipment in the United States differed from those adopted by many foreign countries; relevant standards abroad were often set by the International Electrical Committee (IEC). Equipment based upon IEC standards tended to be smaller and less costly than standard U.S. equipment. This led to a preference for IEC standard products among many developing countries. Rather than rebuilding United States–made controls, Westinghouse decided to acquire a German firm specializing in IEC standard controls for use in its equipment.

Of course manufacturers from the Third World would face the opposite challenge, requiring companies to increase the performance of their products to meet the standards of industrialized countries. In general, the necessity to increase performance tends to be more apparent as the need arises, whereas the opportunities for product simplification are frequently less obvious to the observer.

Sometimes manufacturers have to build design changes into products for overseas sales that are not apparent to the buyer. These internal design changes can increase product use or performance or adapt it to a new environment. As we have seen in the case of Westinghouse, different electrical standards require product adaptation. In TV broadcasting, the prevalent U.S. system was not adapted worldwide. In Europe, countries installed either a French or a German-designed system, each requiring specially equipped TV receivers. RCA offered only its standard models in Asia, disregarding the fact that both Singapore and Malaysia, two neighboring countries, had different broadcasting systems. With the RCA model the buyer could receive only a picture but not sound. RCA distributors in Singapore had to wait several years for the company to make the necessary adaptations.[9]

Adjusting Quality to International Requirements

The quality of a product reflects the intended function and the circumstances of product use. Consequently, as these circumstances change it is sometimes necessary to adjust quality accordingly. Products that receive less service or care in a given country have to be reengineered to live up to the added stress. At times there may be an opportunity to lower product cost by reducing the built-in quality and in turn reducing price to customary purchase levels of the local

7. "Detroit Finds New Routes Across The Pacific," *Fortune,* October 1973, p. 164.
8. "Westinghouse's Gutsy Expansion Plans," *Business Week,* December 28, 1981, p. 61.
9. "RCA's New Vista: The Bottom Line," *Business Week,* July 4, 1977, p. 44.

market. However, this may be dangerous if company reputation could suffer in the process. It may be preferable not to market a product at all.

Some companies go to great lengths to live up to different quality standards in foreign markets. The experience of German firms exporting to Japan serves as an excellent example of the extra efforts frequently involved.[10] BMW, the German automaker, found that its customers in Japan expected the very finest quality. Typically, cars shipped to Japan had to be completely repainted. Even very small mistakes were not tolerated by customers. When a service call was made, the car was picked up at the customer's home and returned when completed. The German electronic company Semikron required extensive quality tests for its modules used with robots. But shipments to Japan had to go through additional tests beyond those of products distributed to German or U.S. clients. Billerbeck, a German maker of blankets and bed covers, submits each product shipped to Japan to an additional test. In case of a customer complaint, a letter of apology is sent from the German plant to the customer. These companies have experienced substantial success in Japan and believe that their strict quality has given them a competitive advantage in the market.

Adapting High Technology Products

Quite unique was the problem faced by Japanese computer manufacturers who made their first export attempts in the mid-seventies.[11] For their domestic clients Japanese manufacturers had long built machines similar to the standard U.S. machines offered by IBM, but they had their machines with special software packages. These programs were geared to the often unique needs of Japanese clients and written in a mixture of Japanese and English. The programs were not subject to easy translation. To write entirely new software packages for export markets would have been not only expensive but also extremely difficult for Japanese programmers. Under those circumstances, Hitachi, after repeated requests from its U.S. sales partner, Intel, finally accepted the idea of producing computers that were plug-compatible with IBM machines and that could also run with IBM software packages. Neither Hitachi nor other leading Japanese computer manufacturers sold machines domestically that were plug-compatible with IBM at that time. To achieve the necessary economies of scale, some Japanese manufacturers announced that they would also offer plug-compatible models to their domestic clients in the near future. Producing two entirely different lines would have been too expensive. In this case the requirements of the export markets outweighed those of the domestic market.

---

10. "Das braucht Zeit und Starke Nerven," *Der Spiegel,* no. 1, 1983, p. 83.

11. Bro Uttal, "Exports Won't Come Easy for Japan's Computer Industry," *Fortune,* October 9, 1978, p. 138.

United States computer manufacturers also learned that success in Japan depended on adapting their products. Apple Computer initially introduced its famous Apple model in 1977 with standard U.S. software written in the English language. It failed to gain any significant market share in Japan.[12] On the other hand, IBM was immediately successful in 1983 when it introduced the IBM 5550 model because it came equipped with a built-in Japanese language capability. It was the first such microcomputer offered by a foreign manufacturer.[13]

Changing Proven Products to Meet Foreign Requirements

One of the most difficult decisions for international companies is whether or not to change a proven product that has sold well in the past. Sometimes, a company may be in a position to change a proven design to gain a competitive advantage because other more tradition-bound firms declined.

Prior to 1974, French wines accounted for the largest volume of imported wines, with Italian suppliers a distant second. Since then, Italian vintners in the U.S. market have far surpassed their French competitors who concentrated on more expensive wines. In 1979, Italian vintners even outsold their French competitors in dollar volume. This remarkable upset of the world's most renowned wine producers was achieved by shrewd marketing and product adaptations that catered to specific preferences of the American consumer. Whereas Italians preferred their Lambrusco wine dry, light, and fruity, the U.S. population, according to data supplied by the American importer, preferred a wine that was bubbly and slightly sweet, similar to popular drinks consumed with meals, such as soda. The Italians adjusted their fermentation process to produce such a wine significantly below the cost of French wines. This cost advantage was achieved with efficient bottling plants. Also, the Lambrusco wine was ready for consumption immediately upon fermentation, thus eliminating the customary two-to-four-year aging process of more expensive wines. Lambrusco soon accounted for two-thirds of all Italian wines imported into the United States.[14]

Adapting Products to Cultural Preferences

To the extent that fashion and tastes differ by country, companies often change their styling. Color, for example, should reflect the values of each country.[15] For

---

12. "In Japan, Software and Distribution Are Ways to Success," *Business Marketing,* November 1983, p. 74.

13. Ibid., p. 74.

14. "Creating a Mass Market for Wine," *Business Week,* March 15, 1982, p. 108; and "The Toyota of the Wine Trade," *Fortune,* November 30, 1981, p. 155.

15. *International Marketing Management,* ed. Michael J. Thomas (Boston: Houghton Mifflin, 1969), p. 35.

Japan, red and white have happy associations, whereas black and white indicate mourning. Green is an unpopular color in Malaysia since it is associated with the jungle and illness. Green is also the national color of Egypt and should therefore not be used for packaging purposes there. United States textile manufacturers who have started to expand their export business have consciously used color to suit local needs.[16] The Lowenstein Corporation has successfully used brighter colors for fabrics exported to Africa.

Scent is also subject to change from one country to another. S.C. Johnson & Son, a manufacturer of furniture polish products, encountered resistance to its Lemon Pledge furniture polish among older consumers in Japan. Careful market research revealed that the polish smelled similar to a latrine disinfectant used widely in Japan in the 1940s. Sales rose sharply after the scent was adjusted.[17]

INTERNATIONAL BRANDING DECISIONS

Selecting appropriate brand names on an international basis is substantially more complex than having to decide on a brand name for just one country. Typically a brand name is rooted in a given language and, if used elsewhere, may have either a different meaning or none at all. Ideally marketers look for brand names that evoke similar emotions or associations around the world. By past learning experience, people around the world have come to expect the same thing from such brand names as Coca-Cola, IBM, Marlboro, or Kodak. However, it has become increasingly difficult for new entrants to become recognized unless the name has some meaning for the prospective customer. Language problems are particularly difficult to overcome. One simple example is the English term *mist* that is associated with many consumer products for a romantic connotation. In German however, that same word—with the exact same spelling—means cow manure. This is just one indication of the difficulty of picking a name with positive associations in most major languages.

Brand Name Selection Procedures

Given almost unlimited possibilities of names and the restricted opportunities to find and register a desirable one, international companies spend considerable effort on the selection procedure. One well-known consulting company specializes in finding brand names with worldwide application. The company brings

16. Herbert E. Meyer, "How U.S. Textiles Got to Be Winners in the Export Game," *Fortune*, May 5, 1980, p. 260.
17. Vernon R. Alden, "Who Says You Can't Crack Japanese Markets?" *Harvard Business Review*, January–February 1987, pp. 52–56.

citizens of many countries together in Paris where, under the guidance of a specialist, they are asked to state names in their particular language that would combine well with the product to be named.[18] Speakers of other languages can immediately react if a name comes up that does not sound well in their language. After a few such sessions, the company may accumulate as many as 1,000 names that will later be reduced to 500 by a company linguist. The client company then is asked to select 50 to 100 names for further consideration. At this point, the names are subjected to a search procedure to determine which ones have not been registered in any of the countries under consideration. In the end only about 10 names may survive this process, and from these the company will have to make the final selection. Although this process may be expensive, it is generally considered a small cost compared with the advertising expenditures invested in the brand name over many years.

When confronted with a search for a brand name with international applications, a company can use the following sources:

1. An arbitrary or invented word not to be found in any standard English (or other language) dictionary.
2. A recognizable English (or foreign language) word but one that is totally unrelated to the product in question.
3. An English (or other language) word that merely suggests some characteristic or purpose of the product.
4. A word that is evidently descriptive of the product, although the word may have no meaning to persons unacquainted with English (or the other language).
5. Within one or more of these categories, a geographical place or a common surname.
6. A device, design, number, or some other element that is not a word or a combination of words.[19]

Selection of a brand name based upon these six approaches is also closely related to another key issue in international branding: should the company use one brand name worldwide or should it use different names in different countries?

Single-Country Versus Universal Brand Names

International marketers are constantly confronted with the decision of whether the brand name needs to be universal. Brands such as Coca-Cola or Kodak have universal use and lend themselves to an integrated international marketing strat-

---

18. "Trademarks Are a Global Business These Days, But Finding Registrable Ones Is a Big Problem," *The Wall Street Journal*, September 4, 1975, p. 28.
19. George W. Cooper, "On Your 'Mark,' " *Columbia Journal of World Business*, March–April 1970, pp. 67–76.

egy. With worldwide travel a common occurrence, many MNCs do not think they should accept a brand name unless it can be used universally. Many product brands originated, however, in one single market, typically the company's home market; and they were given a brand name that reflected the home market's cultural background. Later extensions of such a brand name internationally can pose problems. When Bank Americard Inc. changed its logo and name to VISA in 1977, a primary consideration was bringing the card, which had been issued in over 20 countries with as many names, under the umbrella of a single meaningful brand name.[20] The resulting name change, though expensive, nevertheless led to such strong growth that VISA surpassed Mastercard to become the most widely used card in the world. This was largely because the latter did not create such unified worldwide image.

Of course it is not always possible to use the same name elsewhere, and a change in the home market might jeopardize the positive feelings for the original name gained after years of marketing efforts. In such instances different names have to be found. Procter & Gamble had successfully marketed its household cleaner, Mr. Clean, in the United States for some time. This name, however, had no meaning outside of countries using the English language. This prompted the company to arrive at several adaptations abroad, such as *Monsieur Propre* in France and *Meister Proper* in Germany. In all cases, however, the symbol of the genie with gleaming eyes was retained since it evoked responses abroad that were similar to those in the United States.

Car manufacturers have traditionally followed a strategy of tailoring their product names to individual countries or areas.[21] When Volkswagen designed successor products to its successful Beetle model, the company decided to base the names on famous winds. This brought about Golf (the German word for the Gulf Wind), Scirocco (the Italian word for a hot wind that brings desert dust from the Libyan desert to Italy), and Passat (the German word for trade wind). Since the German translations of wind names were inappropriate in their original form, Volkswagen completely renamed two of its major models for the United States. The Golf became the Rabbit, and the Passat was named Dasher. The Golf model kept its name throughout Europe, Asia, and Africa, but was adapted to the Spanish name Caribe in Latin America. To avoid any brand name limitations in foreign expansion, companies are increasingly making the original brand name decision based on international considerations, even though the new product introduction may be limited to the domestic market at first.

Trademarks

Because brand names or trademarks are usually backed with substantial advertising funds, it makes sense to register such brands for the exclusive use of the

---

20. *Business Week,* July 14, 1980, p. 109.
21. *Small World* (Magazine for Volkswagen Owners), vol. 19, 1980, pp. 12–13.

sponsoring firm.[22] However, registration abroad is often hampered by a number of factors.

Different interpretations exist in different countries and may affect filing. In some countries, registration authorities may object that the name lacks the inherent distinctiveness needed for registration or that the chosen word is too common to be essential to the promotion of the product, thus allowing other firms to continue to use the name in a descriptive manner. Other countries allow registration of trademarks and renewals for actual or intended use, thus increasing the possibility that some other firm may already have registered the name. In countries where the first applicant always obtains exclusive rights, companies risk the possibility of having their brand names pirated by outsiders who apply for a new name first. The foreign company is then forced to buy back its own trademark. When a country does not allow registrations until all objections are settled, registration may be postponed for years.

Trademark Protection

Violations of trademarks have been an ever-present problem in international marketing. Many companies have found themselves subject to violations by people who use either the protected name or a very similar one. Deliberate violations can usually be fought in court, though often at great expense. A rather unusual case occurred in Mexico, where the French company Cartier de Paris saw its name used by a local businessman as Cartier de Mexico.[23] A Mexican businessman who for years had represented foreign luxury watch manufacturers had by chance noticed that Cartier's trademark registration expired in 1946, thus allowing him to register with the Cartier name in 1968. He then proceeded to open Cartier stores in expensive hotels that were complete copies of the famous French stores. Cartier watches and jewelry were copied with cheaper materials, but lighters were bought from the original company. As a result, Cartier de Mexico was able to sell look-alike products at one third the Paris retail price and still achieve high profitability. The French company filed suit and won twenty-three decisions in Mexican courts, but there always existed a chance for appeal, allowing Cartier de Mexico to continue operation. The French company refused to repurchase the Mexican trademark, supposedly offered for several million dollars, or to engage in a joint venture with the local firm. The Mexican government issued an import license in 1980 to allow Cartier de Paris to open its own operation just twenty yards from the Mexican look-alike store. The experience of Cartier de Paris demonstrates the need for trademark protection and the necessity to monitor trademark status continuously in major markets.

---

22. The information in this section is based upon George W. Cooper, "On Your 'Mark,' " *Columbia Journal of World Business,* March–April 1970, pp. 67–76.
23. "The Big Couture Rip-Off," *The New York Times Magazine,* March 1, 1981, p. 62.

Counterfeiting has been injurious to both businesses and consumers alike. A specialist agency in London estimated the total volume of counterfeit in world trade at $60 billion annually.[24] The U.S. Commerce Department estimates that some 750,000 jobs have been lost to the U.S. economy due to forgeries. Abuses of trademarks and patents are particularly acute in these ten developing countries: Taiwan, South Korea, Thailand, Singapore, Malaysia, Indonesia, the Philippines, Mexico, Brazil, and India.[25] Although many industries have suffered from the effect of counterfeiters, expensive consumer goods, automobile parts, and pharmaceuticals have encountered particular problems.

In Thailand, patent laws do not apply to pharmaceutical products. As a result, many local companies freely copy the drugs of international firms without having to pay royalties to the patent holder abroad. Smithkline Beckman Corp., the producer of Tagament, an ulcer drug accounting for one of the largest volumes for any drug worldwide, sold only $2.4 million for Tagament in Thailand in 1984. Without any domestic copiers selling a generic version of this drug, the company would have had sales of $7.6 million in Thailand. In fact, the company faced some twenty-five local generic competitors. This intensive competition also tends to depress the prices for international drugs substantially below levels elsewhere.[26]

Copyrights for music differ by country. In Japan, record companies are limited to twenty years of protection after initial release, whereas U.S. companies receive seventy-five years of protection. With the recent introduction of compact disks, some Japanese firms have copied old popular songs, such as Beatle songs from 1960, without paying royalties to the original record company.[27]

International companies have been going on the offensive to defend themselves against counterfeiting. The United States passed the Trademark Counterfeiting Act of 1984 which makes counterfeiting punishable by either fines of up to $250,000 and prison terms of up to five years.[28] Ford Motor Company launched a counterattack in 1984 collaborating with various government agencies. The company was able to confiscate more than one million illegal parts suing many of the companies in the process. The U.S. government has also put pressure on some foreign governments, particularly on Taiwan, to prosecute its own counterfeiters more aggressively.[29] However, given the difficulty of tracking counterfeiters and the obvious opportunities for making quick profits, counterfeiting is a

---

24. "The Counterfeit Trade," *Business Week,* December 16, 1985, p. 64.

25. "Intellectual Property: Foreign Pirates Worry U.S. Firms," *Chemical & Engineering News,* September 1, 1986, p. 8.

26. "Thailand's Drug-Copying Companies Keep Prices Down, Upset Foreign Firms," *The Wall Street Journal,* December 1, 1986, p. 25.

27. "A Cruel Cut for Sergeant Pepper," *Business Week,* June 27, 1987, p. 62.

28. "The Counterfeit Trade," p. 64.

29. "Taiwan Curbs Its Counterfeiters," *The New York Times,* March 30, 1986, p. 74.

problem that international companies will have to deal with for some time to come.

Private Branding As an International Marketing Strategy

The practice of private branding or supplying products to a third party for sale under its brand name has become quite common in many domestic markets. Similar opportunities exist on an international scale and may be used to the manufacturer's advantage. Private branding offers particular advantages to a company with strong manufacturing skills but little access to foreign markets. Arranging for distribution of the firm's product through local distributors or companies with already existing distribution networks reduces the risk of failure and provides for rapid volume growth via instant market access. Some Japanese companies have used the private branding approach to gain market access in Europe and the United States. Ricoh serves as one of many examples.[30] Known as a manufacturer of cameras, Ricoh entered the market for small plain paper copiers (PPC) in the early 1970s. Supply contracts were signed with Savin for the U.S. market, with Nashua of New Hampshire for Canada and Europe, and with Kalle of West Germany for Europe. With the help of these three firms, Ricoh gained 9 percent of the worldwide copier market within five years.[31]

These private branding arrangements are also called OEM contracts, short for original equipment manufacturer, in which the foreign manufacturer assumes the role of the OEM. As the market grows, they have become difficult to manage from the manufacturer's point of view. Nevertheless, these arrangements have opened markets more quickly and at much lower investment cost than would have been required for the Japanese firms to develop these markets on their own. Similar private branding or OEM strategies were pursued by Japanese manufacturers of video recorders (VCRs) in Europe, where Japanese companies were battling Philips of the Netherlands and Grundig of Germany for market dominance.[32] Japanese companies were supplying VCRs to European home electronic manufacturers with established distribution systems who did not want to invest research and funds to produce their own systems. Victor of Japan concluded long-term agreements with Saba, Nordmende, and Telefunken, all of West Germany, with Thorn Consumer Electronics of the United Kingdom, and with Thomson-Brandt of France. Matsushita Electric had similar arrangements with Blaupunkt Werke Gmbh of West Germany, whereas Hitachi had an OEM arrangement with Granada TV Rental of the United Kingdom. The latest entrant, Toshiba, signed a long-term OEM contract with Rank Radio International

---

30. "PPC Marketers Take Over American Distribution," *The Japan Economic Journal*, May 22, 1979, p. 7.
31. "Competition Heats Up in Copiers," *Business Week*, November 5, 1979, p. 115.
32. "Sony and Philips Seal Tie-up," *The Japan Economic Journal*, October 16, 1979, p. 8.

of the United Kingdom. In all of these cases, the European companies placed their own labels on the VCRs imported from Japan.

Private branding or OEM contracts are not without drawbacks for the manufacturer. With control over marketing in the hands of the distributor, the manufacturer remains dependent and can only indirectly influence marketing. For long-term profitability, companies often find that they need to sell products under their own names, even where the OEM has achieved substantial marketing success. Such partnerships often end because of conflicting interests. The Japanese copier manufacturer Ricoh, which successfully used OEM arrangements to carve out a large market share in the United States for its plain copiers, reportedly paid Savin $14.5 million in compensatory royalties to obtain the right to sell copiers under its own name, Ricoh, as early as July 1981.[33]

PACKAGING FOR INTERNATIONAL MARKETS

Differences in the marketing environment may require special adaptation in product packaging. Changed climatic conditions often demand a change in the package to ensure sufficient protection or shelf life. The role a package assumes in promotion also depends on the market retailing structure. In countries with a substantial degree of self-service merchandising, a package with strong promotional appeal is desirable for consumer products. These requirements may be substantially scaled down in areas where over-the-counter service still dominates. In addition, distribution handling requirements are not identical the world over. In high-wage countries of the developed world, products tend to be packaged to reduce further handling by retailing employees. For consumer products, all mass merchandisers have to do is place products on shelves. In countries with lower wages and less developed retailing structures, individual orders may be filled from larger packaged units, entailing extra labor by the retailer.

R. J. Reynolds of Winston-Salem, North Carolina exported cigarettes to 160 countries and territories.[34] The company observed more than 1,400 different product codes covering its various brands in all markets. For its leading brand, Winston, the company needed more than 250 different packages to satisfy different brand styles and foreign government requirements. The U.S. package design was used for fewer than six markets. Differences were due to various regulations on health warnings. In Australia the number of cigarettes contained in a package had to be printed on the package front. Some countries such as Canada require bilingual text. To avoid errors in the printing process when working with alpha-

33. "PPC Marketers Take Over American Distribution," p. 7.

34. "Tobacco Companies Face Special International Packaging Obstacles," *Marketing News,* February 4, 1984, p. 20.

bets as diverse as Greek, Arabic, or Japanese, replicas of the original package were prepared in the foreign market and forwarded for production to the United States.

Specific decisions affected by packaging are size, shape, materials, color, and text.[35] Size may differ by custom, or by existing standards such as metric and nonmetric requirements. Higher income countries tend to require larger unit sizes, since these populations shop less frequently and can afford to buy larger quantities each time. In countries with lower income levels, consumers buy smaller quantities, and more often. Gillette, the world's largest producer of razor blades, sells products in packages of five or ten in the United States and Europe, whereas singles are sold in some developing countries. Packages can assume almost any shape largely depending on customs and traditions of each market. Materials used for packaging can also differ widely. Whereas Americans prefer to buy mayonnaise and mustard in glass containers, consumers in Germany and Switzerland buy these same products in tin tubes. Cans are the customary material to package beer in the United States, whereas most European countries still prefer glass bottles. The color and text of a package have to be integrated into a company's promotional strategy; and therefore they may be subject to specific tailoring by country. The promotional effect is of great importance for consumer goods and has led some companies to attempt to standardize their packaging in color and layout. In areas such as Europe or Latin America where the consumers frequently travel to other countries, standardized colors help identify a product quickly. This strategy is naturally dependent on a set of colors or a layout with an appeal beyond one single culture or market. An example of a company pursuing a standardized package color is Procter & Gamble, the U.S. manufacturer of the leading detergent, Tide. The orange and white box familiar to millions of U.S. consumers can be found in many foreign markets, even though the package text may appear in the language or print of the given country.

MANAGING A PRODUCT LINE FOR INTERNATIONAL MARKETS

In the early sections of this chapter, we covered decisions about individual products in detail. Most companies, however, manufacture or sell a multitude of products; some, such as General Electric, produce as many as 200,000 items. To facilitate marketing operations, companies group these items into product groups consisting of several product lines. Each product line is made up of several individual items of close similarity. A company with several product lines is faced with the decision to select those most appropriate for international

---

35. Philip Kotler, *Marketing Management,* 5th ed. (Englewood Cliffs, N.J.: Prentice-Hall, 1984), pp. 490–492.

marketing. As with each individual product or decision, the firm can either offer an identical line in its home market and abroad or, if circumstances demand, make appropriate changes.

In most cases, a firm would look at the individual items within a product line and assess marketability on a product-by-product basis. As a result, the product lines abroad are frequently characterized by a narrower width than those found in a company's domestic market. The circumstances for deletions from product lines vary, but some reasons dominate. Lack of sufficient market size is a frequently mentioned reason. Companies with their home base in large markets such as the United States, Japan, or Germany will find sufficient demand in their home markets for even the smallest market segments, justifying additional product variations and greater depth in their lines. Abroad, opportunities for such segmentation strategies may not exist because the individual segments may be too small to warrant commercial exploitation. Lack of market sophistication is another factor in product line variation. Aside from the top twenty developed markets, many markets are less sophisticated and their stage of development may not demand some of the most advanced items in a product line. And finally, new product introduction strategies can impact product lines abroad. For most companies, new products are first introduced in their home markets and introduced abroad only after the product has proved successful at home. As a result, the lag in extending new products to foreign markets also contributes toward a product line configuration that differs from that of the firm's domestic market.

Firms confronted with deletions in their product lines sometimes add specialized offerings to fill the gap in the line, either by producing a more suitable product or by developing an entirely new product that may not have any application outside a specific market. Such a strategy can only be pursued by a firm with adequate research and development strength in its foreign subsidiaries. An excellent example of a company with variations in its product line is the German automobile manufacturer Volkswagen.[36] Its 1980 product line included more than 20 individual models manufactured in five different countries, with assembly operations in another three. As could be expected, Volkswagen's product line in Germany was the most complete. The company's three assembly plants in Nigeria, Yugoslavia, and Belgium assembled cars shipped from any of the five major manufacturing plants in Germany, Brazil, Mexico, South Africa, and the United States. Important components such as engines and transmissions were only produced in German factories. The United States factory manufactured only the Rabbit, and the other models were shipped from abroad to complete the company's product line. The Volkswagen Polo and Derby and the Audi Avant were small models not sold in the U.S. market. Volkswagen's large factory in Brazil still produced the famous Beetle model, which was no longer produced in Germany. Two other models produced in Brazil, the Brasilia and the Variant, were developed locally and were not available in the United States or Europe.

---

36. *Small World* (Magazine for Volkswagen Owners), vol. 19, 1980, pp. 20–21.

The Mexican factory also produced three of five Volkswagen products not in the German product line.

Exploiting Product Life Cycles in International Marketing

The existence of product life cycles immediately opens opportunities to the international firm but, on the other hand, poses additional hurdles that may complicate product strategy. Experience has shown that products do not always occupy the same position on the product life cycle curve in different countries.

New products receiving initial introduction in the world's developed markets tend to move into later life cycle stages before those in countries which receive the product at a later date. As shown in Figure 10.2, it is possible for a product to be in different stages of the product life cycle for different countries. Other countries follow, usually according to their own stage of economic development. Consequently, although a product may be offered and produced worldwide, it is common for a product to range over several stages in the product life cycle. The principal opportunity offered to the firm is the chance to extend product growth by expanding into new markets to compensate for declining growth rates in mature markets. A risk arises when a company enters new markets or countries too fast, before the local market is ready to absorb the new product. To avoid such pitfalls and to take advantage of long-term opportunities, international companies may follow several strategies.

During the introductory phase, a product may have to be debugged and refined. This job can best be handled in the originating market or in a country close to company research and development centers. Also, the marketing approach will have to be refined. At this stage, the market in even the more advanced countries is relatively small, and demand in countries with lower levels of economic development will hardly be commercially exploitable. The introductory stage will therefore be limited to the most advanced markets, often the company's home or domestic market.

Once the product has been fully developed and a larger group of buyers has become interested, volume will increase substantially. Domestic marketing policies foresee price decreases due to volume gains and to the entry of new competitors with an expansion of the entire market beyond early innovators. It is at this stage that many firms start to investigate opportunities elsewhere by introducing the product in selective markets where it would be in the introductory phase. This requires some adaptation of communication strategy to parallel earlier efforts in the home market, as the approach designed for the second phase, the growth stage, cannot be used.

A product facing life cycle decline may be withdrawn in stages, similar to its introduction. The most advanced countries will see such a withdrawal earlier than some of the less developed markets. Volkswagen has withdrawn its popular Beetle model from European and American markets, though it remains in production in Brazil and Mexico. In the meantime, Volkswagen has introduced

FIGURE 10.2 Possible Product Life Cycle for a Product in Different Countries

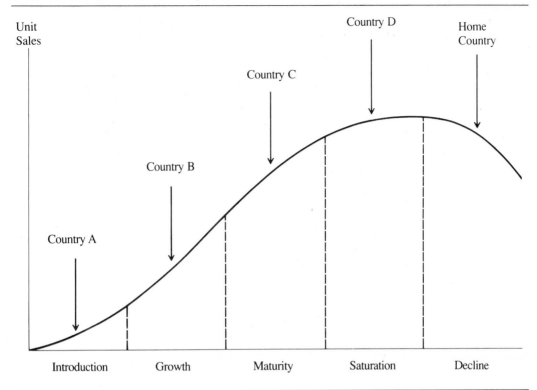

several newer models in Europe and the United States that have yet to be introduced elsewhere.

As we have seen, a product cannot automatically be assumed to reach the various stages in its life cycle simultaneously in all countries, thus requiring flexibility in marketing strategy. To introduce a product abroad in stages represents a strategic decision in itself, as described later in this chapter. Though typical, the phased introduction to foreign markets may not always be in the best interest of the firm, as it may offer competitors a chance to expand locally.

INTERNATIONAL WARRANTY AND SERVICE POLICIES

Buyers around the world, like domestic consumers, expect more than just the physical benefits of a product. Clients purchase products with certain performance expectations and will consider company policies for backing promises.

As a result, warranties and service policies have to be considered as an integral aspect of a company's international product strategy. Companies interested in doing business abroad frequently find themselves at a disadvantage with local competitors when competing on warranties and service. With the supplier's plant often thousands of miles away, foreign buyers sometimes want extra assurance that the supplier will back the product. A comprehensive warranty and service policy thus can become a very important marketing tool for international companies.

Product Warranties

A company must address its warranty policy for international markets either by declaring its domestic warranty valid worldwide or by instituting a policy of tailoring warranties to specific countries or markets. Although it would be administratively simple to declare a worldwide warranty with uniform performance standards, local market conditions often dictate a differentiated approach. Aside from the two technical decisions as to what standards should be covered under a warranty and for how long, a company would be well advised to consider the type of actual product use. If buyers in a foreign market subject the product to more stress or abuse, some shortening of the warranty period may become necessary. A company might be able to change product design to allow for different performance standard requirements. In developing countries, where technical sophistication is below North American or European standards, maintenance may not be adequate, causing more frequent equipment breakdowns. Another important factor is local competition. Since an attractive warranty policy can be helpful in obtaining sales, a firm's warranty policy should be in line with that of other firms competing in the local market. But no warranty will be believable unless backed with an effective service organization, the subject of the following section.

Product Service

Although important to the individual buyer, service is even more crucial to the industrial buyer, since any breakdown of equipment or product is liable to cause substantial economic loss. This risk has led industrial buyers to be conservative in their choice of products, always carefully analyzing the supplier's ability to provide service in case of need. To provide this required level of service outside the company's home base poses special problems for international companies. The selection of an organization to perform the service is an important decision. Ideally, company personnel would be preferable since they tend to be better trained. This can only be organized economically if the installed base of the market is large enough to justify such an investment. In cases where a company does not maintain its own sales subsidiary, it will generally be more efficient to turn to an independent service company or to a local distributor. To have adequate services via independent distributors requires extra training for the service technician, usually at the manufacturer's expense. In any case, the selection of an appropriate service organization should be made so that fully trained service personnel are readily available within the customary time frame for the particular market.

Closely related to any satisfactory service policy is an adequate inventory for spare parts. Because service often means replacing some parts, the company must place sufficient inventory of spare parts within reach of its markets. Whether this inventory is maintained in regional warehouses or through sales subsidiaries and distributors depends on volume and the required reaction time for service calls. Buyers will generally want to know how the manufacturer plans to organize service before making substantial commitments. Firms that demonstrate serious interest in a market by committing to their own sales subsidiaries are often at an advantage over other firms using distributors. One German truck manufacturer that recently entered the U.S. market advertised the fact that "97 percent of all spare parts are kept in local inventory," thus assuring prospective buyers that they could get spares readily. In some instances, the difficulty with service outlets may even influence a company's market entry strategy. This was the case with Fujitsu, a Japanese manufacturer of electronic office equipment. By combining forces with TRW Inc., a United States–based company, Fujitsu was able to sell its office equipment in the U.S. market with the extensive service organization of TRW.

Since the guarantee of reliable and efficient service is such an important aspect of a firm's entire product strategy, at times investment in service centers must be made before any sales can take place. In this case, service costs must be viewed as an investment in future volume rather than as a recurring expense.

MARKETING SERVICES GLOBALLY

Marketing services on an international scale have assumed an increasingly important role for many service firms. Decisions about marketing services are related to the structure of the service itself. A firm has to decide which services to sell or offer and how the service should be designed. Again the issue of standardization needs to be addressed, although there are fewer opportunities for economies of scale by standardizing services worldwide. A company needs to decide on the content of the service it wants to offer and the manner in which the service is performed or consumed. Business services tend to be more standardized, and more in demand worldwide, since the needs of companies are more uniform than those of individual consumers. Personal services are to a much greater degree subject to cultural and social influences and exhibit a greater need for tailoring to local circumstances.

Business Services

The services aimed at business buyers that are most likely to be exported are those that have already met with success. The experience of United States–based service companies can be used as an example. Some of the services most successfully marketed abroad include financial services. United States commercial banks such as Citibank, Chase Manhattan, and Bank of America have built extensive branch networks around the world, to the extent that foreign deposits and profits make up nearly half of business volume. United States advertising agencies have also expanded overseas either by building branch networks or by merging with local agencies.[37] Similar strategies were followed by accounting firms and management consultants. More recently, many United States–based marketing research firms have expanded into foreign countries.

Opportunities for New Service Firms

A great many opportunities exist for service companies abroad. Just as the U.S. economy is slowly moving to become a service economy, similar trends can be found in the economies of other developed countries in Western Europe and in Japan. Some examples will demonstrate the many types of services that are in great demand abroad. In 1976, United Parcel Service opened its first foreign operation in West Germany following an exhaustive internal company analysis. The initial investment for four sorting centers and twenty operating centers, together with 120 vans, did not provide instant profitability.[38] Volume, however, grew from 15,000 parcels a day to 75,000 parcels, and the first profit was expected in 1980.[39] This was still only a very small percentage of the total German market, where UPS was consistently confused with the much better known American news agency United Press International, or UPI. As in the United States, UPS marketing strategy was to provide faster delivery than the official postal operations at a lower rate.

More recently, several United States–based air courier companies have also extended their services abroad. United States–based DHL Worldwide Express had dominated the United States, originating international courier service for several years before Federal Express decided to enter the foreign segment also. In 1985, Federal Express committed to build a European operations center in Brussels. Imitating its hub system in Memphis, Tennessee for the U.S. market, Federal Express planned to run nightly flights from several countries into Brus-

---

37. Arnold K. Weinstein, "The International Expansion of U.S. Multinational Advertising Agencies," *MSU Business Topics,* Summer 1974, pp. 29–35.

38. "West Germany: UPS Starts Driving an Overseas Route," *Business Week,* September 6, 1976, p. 39.

39. "UPS's Challenge in Germany," *The New York Times,* December 9, 1980, p. D-4.

sels and to send the planes back with another load early in the morning. Federal Express hoped that the knowledge of running such a large system acquired in the United States would give them a competitive advantage.[40] Differences existed, however, due to different customs systems. In Europe, customs officials would have to clear each system upon arrival. DHL traditionally used couriers that flew with the plane, treating their shipments as personal baggage. This ensured that the shipments would be cleared right away as the couriers passed through customs.

Health care has suddenly become an export item demanded from U.S. companies, particularly those specializing in hospital management.[41] American Medical International (AMI) expected to earn 25 percent of its revenues from foreign contracts by 1983. Whittaker Corporation won a $100 million contract in 1974 to run three hospitals in Saudi Arabia for three years. Though the costs of keeping U.S. personnel at foreign locations caused sales costs to triple compared to those of domestic sales, profit margins were often twice those achieved in the United States. Demand for such services is expected to grow, as many governments in developing countries can now begin to afford Western or modern health care.

Selling Technology Overseas

Some companies have switched from selling products to selling technology. One company that has achieved considerable success in this area is Kawasaki Steel, one of the largest steel producers in Japan.[42] Faced with a stagnant market at home and with growing reluctance by foreign governments to increase Japanese steel imports, Kawasaki turned to its 800 scientists and engineers to produce better steel more efficiently. This effort led to substantial cost savings at Japanese plants while tempting foreign steel operators to purchase the technology. A specially organized division composed of engineering and marketing experts began exporting this know-how. The company had engineers who could engage in a one-shot technical consulting assignment or furnish an entire turnkey plant. Other engineers were available to help important steel users, such as builders of pipelines, off-shore platforms, and shipping berths around the world. Kawasaki was not concerned about exporting technology as long as its own engineers and scientists continued to develop the new techniques. Since it took years to bring a new steel mill on stream, its own scientists were expected to have advanced beyond currently installed technology. Similar opportunities were pursued by other Japanese steel manufacturers and by other companies all over the world.

40. "Air Couriers Outdo Each Other Sparring for Global Markets," *International Management*, July 1985, p. 30.

41. "Health Care Industry Becomes a Hot Export Item," *Business Week*, December 18, 1978, p. 94.

42. "Kawasaki Steel: Using Technology as a Tool to Bolster Exports," *Business Week*, January 29, 1979, p. 119.

United Breweries of Denmark, brewers of Carlsberg and Tuborg beer, started to exploit opportunities for selling brewing technology to those markets where the company would have had great difficulty exporting beer.[43] The company formed Danbrew Consult Ltd. in 1970 to sell its brewing process know-how around the world. Even large U.S. breweries, such as Philip Morris's Miller brewery, have availed themselves of Danbrew services. The company believed that in some markets it could make more money selling services and technology than marketing beer.

Services for Consumers and Individual Households

Marketing services to consumers turns out to be more difficult than selling to industrial users. Since consumer purchasing and usage patterns between countries differ to a greater degree than industry usage patterns many services have to be adapted to local conditions to make them successful. United States–based fast-food chains were some of the first consumer service companies to pursue foreign opportunities. McDonald's, Kentucky Fried Chicken, Dairy Queen, and many others opened restaurants in Europe and Asia in large numbers.[44] Though eventually successful, initial results were disappointing for McDonald's in Europe. The company had anticipated differences in taste by serving wine in France, beer in Munich and Stockholm, and tea in England, where the company also lowered the sugar content of its buns by 4 percent.[45] But McDonald's based its first store locations on U.S. criteria and moved into the suburbs and along highways. When volume did not develop according to expectations, McDonald's quickly moved into the inner cities. Once this initial problem had been overcome, McDonald's grew very quickly abroad. In 1985, international revenue accounted for 24 percent of revenue. Although some local food variations have been allowed, the company operated using the same standardized manual worldwide indoctrinating all of its franchise operations abroad with the same type of operating culture.[46]

The success of United States–based restaurant chains has encouraged foreign companies to venture abroad. Yoshinoya & Co., a Japanese restaurant chain, started its U.S. operations in 1973.[47] The company planned to set up some sixty beef-bowl shops around Los Angeles and another forty around San Francisco by 1981. Yoshinoya was originally motivated to move abroad because of

43. "Denmark's United Breweries Prospers by Selling Its Expertise as Well as Beer," *The Wall Street Journal*, February 16, 1984, p. 40.

44. Donald Hackett, "The International Expansion of the U.S. Franchise Systems: Status and Strategies," *Journal of International Business Studies*, Spring 1976, pp. 65–76.

45. *The New York Times*, April 13, 1979.

46. "McWorld?" *Business Week*, December 13, 1986, p. 78.

47. "Yoshinoya Eyes Beef Bowl Chain Operation on U.S. West Coast," *The Japan Economic Journal*, April 10, 1979, p. 14.

Japanese restrictions on beef imports. The United States was selected because beef prices were lower than those in Japan, and beef was widely available. The food served in the United States is virtually the same in taste and menu. However, Yoshinoya did adjust the size of portions by serving between 30 to 50 percent more beef per bowl than was served in Japan, where beef was two to three times more expensive.[48] American consumers, unlike the Japanese, were found to be dissatisfied unless they were served food in quantity.

Even producers of films for American television have come to court foreign food buyers.[49] In 1970, exports of American-made television movies, serials, and full-length motion pictures shown on television amounted to $97 million. By 1980 sales had reached $365 million, an increase of more than 300 percent. Britain, Canada, Japan, Australia, and Brazil were believed to be the major customers. The only hurdle so far has been government quotas. In England, only 14 percent of daily air time could go to imports; and other countries enforced similar limitations. However, as governments abroad have begun to tolerate more competition, independently owned stations are being opened in many countries. This greatly increases the demand for imported programming. In Italy for instance, independent commercial television was not allowed until recently. Suddenly fifty stations opened in Rome alone, all looking for attractive programming.

CONCLUSIONS

To be successful in foreign markets requires that companies be flexible in product and service offerings. Although a given product may have been very successful in a firm's home market, environmental differences can often force the company to make unexpected or costly changes. While a small group of products may be marketed worldwide without significant changes, most companies will find success abroad to be dependent on a willingness to adapt to local market requirements. Additional efforts are also frequently required in product support services to assure foreign clients that the company will stand behind its products. For those companies that successfully master the additional international difficulties while showing a commitment to foreign clients, success abroad can lead to increased profits and more secure market positions domestically.

Questions for Discussion

1. Generalize about the overall need for product adaptations for consumer products versus high technology industrial products. What differences exist. Why?

---

48. *The Japan Economic Journal,* April 10, 1979, p. 14.
49. "American T.V. Abroad," *The New York Times,* January 18, 1981, p. 18F.

2. Which one of the factors in Table 10.1 would be of particular importance for a company such as GMC (trucks) as opposed to Atari (electronics)?
3. What are the major reasons for a company to have a worldwide brand name?
4. Under what circumstances would it be advisable to use different brand names in different countries?
5. Are there any differences between the international marketing of services versus the international marketing of products?

For Further Reading

Ayal, Igal. "International Product Life Cycle: A Reassessment and Product Implications." *Journal of Marketing,* 45, No. 4 (Fall 1981), pp. 91–96.

Bartels, Robert. "Are Domestic and International Marketing Dissimilar?" *Journal of Marketing* (July 1968), pp. 56–61.

Britt, Stewart H. "Standardizing Marketing for the International Market." *Columbia Journal of World Business* (Winter 1974), pp. 39–45.

Buzzell, Robert D. "Can You Standardize Multinational Marketing?" *Harvard Business Review* (November–December 1968), pp. 1, 2, 113.

Davidson, William H., and Richard Harrigan. "Key Decisions in International Marketing: Introducing New Products Abroad." *Columbia Journal of World Business* (Winter 1977), pp. 15–23.

Hill, John S., and Richard R. Still. "Adapting Products to LDC Tastes." *Harvard Business Review* (March–April 1984), pp. 92–101.

Keegan, Warren J. "Multinational Product Planning: Strategic Alternatives." *Journal of Marketing* (January 1969), pp. 58–62.

Levitt, Theodore. "Globalization of Markets." *Harvard Business Review* (May–June 1983), pp. 92–102.

Samli, A. Coskun, and Rustan Kosanko. "Support Service Is the Key for Technology Transfer to China." *Industrial Marketing Management* (April 1982), pp. 95–103.

Sorenson, Ralph Z. II. "U.S. Marketers Can Learn from European Innovators." *Harvard Business Review* (September–October 1972), pp. 89–99.

Sorenson, Ralph Z., and Ulrich E. Wiechmann. "How Multinationals View Marketing Standardization." *Harvard Business Review* (May–June 1975).

Ward, James J. *The European Approach to U.S. Markets: Product and Promotion Adaptation.* New York: Praeger, 1973. Chapter 4.

11.

NEW PRODUCT DEVELOPMENT STRATEGIES

In the previous chapter, we focused on individual product decisions. In this chapter, we concentrate on the strategic issues of product design and development for international markets (see Figure 11.1). Following an in-depth analysis of the standardization versus adaptation issue, the first segment of this chapter covers a series of alternatives involving product extension, adaptation, and innovation strategies. This leads into a segment on global products which deals with the complexities of designing products for many markets simultaneously. This part of the chapter is devoted to a discussion of product development strategies for international companies. Emphasis is on the organizational issues, sources, and approaches that will enhance a firm's ability to innovate in a changing marketplace. The chapter concludes with a section on the process of new product introductions.

INTERNATIONAL PRODUCT STRATEGIES[1]

The purpose of this section is to outline the basic product strategies a firm may select and to demonstrate their close relationship with a company's communication policy, particularly with respect to advertising. A company's decision to pursue a specific product strategy depends primarily on three factors: first, whether the product function or the need satisfied is the same or different in a new market; second, whether particular conditions surrounding product use can

---

1. This section is based upon Warren J. Keegan, "Multinational Product Planning: Strategic Alternatives," *Journal of Marketing,* vol. 33, January 1969, pp. 58–62.

FIGURE 11.1 International Product Development Strategies

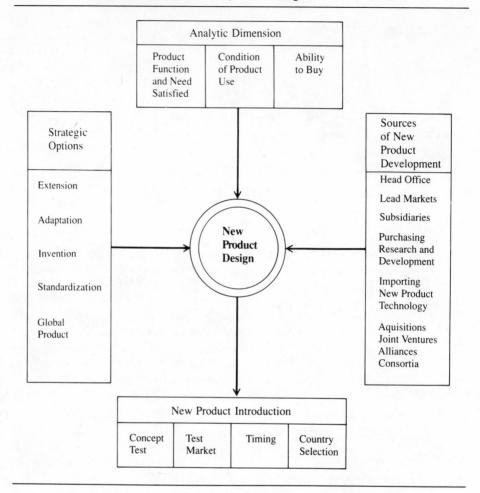

affect company strategy; and third, whether target market customers are financially able to buy the product. These three factors greatly influence the product strategy chosen. Before we turn to a company's strategic options, we first will examine the three elements in some detail.

Product Function/Satisfied Need

The key to this factor is the role the product plays in a given market. Although certain kinds of products may be consumed by individuals in many countries, a company cannot automatically assume that the underlying purchase motivation is identical. One example is the difference between Americans and Russians with respect to purchasing and wearing T-shirts and blue jeans (which we discussed earlier in Chapter 3).[2] In the United States, people who wear this kind of clothing convey an attitude of informality and a lack of interest in status. In fact, by dressing in T-shirts and jeans, they give the appearance of wanting to be ordinary rather than standing out. This is not the case in Russia. Because real blue jeans and T-shirts are in short supply, those who wear such clothing signal society that they are aware of current fashions and are highly status conscious. This type of clothing clearly separates the individual from the rest of society. Consequently, the rationale for buying an identical product in the two countries appears quite contradictory.

On the other hand, products for industrial use, such as plant machinery, are purchased the world over for the same intention or reason. Therefore, very little difference in product function or satisfied need is expected. But even among consumer goods, examples can be found where the need to be satisfied is identical. For example, the motivation behind the purchase of razor blades is quite homogeneous across countries and cultures.

Differences in product function or satisfied need, even when present, do not necessarily call for a change in product design or features. The primary focus here is the buyer and the motivation that triggers a purchase. As a psychological concept, motivation requires a corresponding response. Therefore, dissimilar motives for purchase require unique communications responses, or a change in a firm's advertising, to relate the product to these different motives.

Conditions of Product Use

Physical-environmental variables combine into a physical event that determines the salient factors surrounding a product's actual use. To the extent that these events are identical within any two countries, a product may be marketed without any changes or alterations. The use conditions reflect the actual use or consumption of a product regardless of the motivation that triggered its purchase. In seeking opportunities for product standardization, marketers must consider the physical events surrounding product use that substantially determine the viability of the strategy.

The Ability to Buy

Although purchasing power is generally not an issue in the developed countries of Europe, North America, and Asia, there are nevertheless hundreds of millions of potential customers in countries that simply do not have the economic re-

---

2. Heard on "All Things Considered," a news program of NPR, August 7, 1979.

sources found in more affluent countries. The motivation to purchase a product and actual use conditions may be identical to those in affluent societies, but the products used to satisfy these demands are beyond the price that buyers in developing countries can afford. Consequently, such situations may require an entirely different strategy. The product can be changed so that it can be made available at a substantially lower price. Thus, substantial differences in the nature of the economic event can have a significant influence on international product strategy. General Motors' attempt to market its Basic Transportation Vehicle (BTV) in developing countries serves as an excellent example. The BTV was designed at costs substantially below those of traditional cars by sacrificing comfort, style, and performance.[3]

Three Strategic Choices: Extension, Adaptation, Invention

A company can follow one of three basic strategies when moving into a foreign market. With respect to both its product and its communications policy, the firm can opt for an *extension* strategy, basically adopting the same approach as in its home market. The strategy of *adaptation* requires some changes to fit the new market requirements. When an entirely new approach is required, the company would adopt the strategy of *invention*. These three basic strategies can be further refined into five strategies as shown in Table 11.1. These five strategies are explained in the following sections.

Strategy One: Product Extension— Communications Extension

This extension strategy calls for marketing a standardized product with the same communications strategy across the globe. Although this strategy has considerable attraction because of its cost effectiveness, it is rarely realizable for consumer products. The few exceptions include companies in the soft drink industry and some luxury goods firms. Industrial products, with a greater homogeneity of buyers internationally, offer a somewhat greater opportunity for this strategy, but again the extension strategy is far from the norm.

The cost effectiveness of this strategy should not be underestimated, however. Product adaptations entail additional research and development expenses and tooling costs and do not allow economies of scale to the extent possible under an extension strategy. Though less substantial, savings from the creation of only one communications strategy should also be considered. In any case, a

---

3. Harvard Business School, *"General Motors Malaysia Adm. Bhd.,"* HBS Case Services, Boston, Mass., 9-574-065, 1974/1981.

TABLE 11.1 International Product Strategies

Strategy	Product Function or Need Satisfied	Conditions of Product Use	Ability to Buy Product	Recommended Product Strategy	Recommended Communications Strategy	Relative Cost of Adjustments	Product Examples
1	Same	Same	Yes	Extension	Extension	1	Soft drinks
2	Different	Same	Yes	Extension	Adaptation	2	Bicycles, Motorscooters
3	Same	Different	Yes	Adaptation	Extension	3	Gasoline, Detergents
4	Different	Different	Yes	Adaptation	Adaptation	4	Clothing, Greeting cards
5	Same	—	No	Invention	Develop New Communications	5	Hand-powered washing machine

Source: From Warren J. Keegan: "Multinational Product Planning: Strategic Alternatives." Reprinted from *Journal of Marketing,* vol. 33, January 1969, pp. 58–62, published by the American Marketing Association.

decision should consider the anticipated impact on demand in the foreign market if the product is not fully suited to local tastes or preferences, as well as the potential savings. Past experience shows that rigidly enforcing a product and communication extension policy can lead to disaster and therefore should only be adopted if all requirements with respect to product function, need, use condition, and ability to buy are met.

Strategy Two: Product Extension— Communications Adaptations

When the sociocultural event surrounding product consumption differs from country to country, but the use conditions as part of the physical event are identical, the same product can be marketed with a change in the communication strategy. Examples can be found among bicycle and motorcycle manufacturers. In the developing countries of Asia, Africa, and Latin America, a bicycle or motorcycle is primarily a means of transportation, whereas the same products are used in sports or for recreation purposes in the United States. This strategy is still quite cost effective, since communications adaptation represents a low-cost approach to tailoring a product to a local market.

Strategy Three: Product Adaptation— Communications Extension

This strategy is appropriate when the physical event surrounding product use varies but the sociocultural event is the same as in the company's home market. Although changes in a product are substantially more costly than changes in the communications approach, a company will follow this course when the product might not sell otherwise in a foreign market. In some cases product formulations may be changed without the consumer knowing it, as with detergents and gasoline, so that the product can function under different environmental circumstances.

Strategy Four: Product Adaptation— Communications Adaptation

When both the physical and sociocultural events vary, a strategy of dual adaptation is generally favored. To make this strategy profitable, however, the foreign market or markets need to be of sufficient volume to justify the costs of dual adaptation. Nike, Inc., a leading U.S. manufacturer of running shoes, soon found that its continued growth in Europe could not be built on jogging shoes alone. In Europe jogging never developed to the extent it did in the United States. By far the largest sports-shoe category in Europe was soccer, prompting Nike to develop a shoe specifically designed for that market. To market the new product, Nike developed a unique promotional campaign that took into consideration the dominating positions of Adidas and Puma in the soccer shoe segment.[4]

Strategy Five: Product Invention

When the ability to purchase a product is generally missing, some companies have elected to invent an entirely new product, usually by redesigning the original product to a lower level of complexity. As a result, a substantially cheaper product leads to more purchases. As previously mentioned, this approach was followed by General Motors in designing a Basic Transportation Vehicle (BTV) for sale in developing countries. The new vehicle did not have all the comforts and equipment of a typical GM car produced in the United States. Instead the buyer bought only a shell, and the BTV could be equipped with a flatbed or any other structure at the buyer's option. The car was offered only in developing nations. Another example was the strategy followed by Philips, the Dutch MNC.[5] In response to the desire of many developing countries to own their own televi-

---

4. "Fitting the World in Sports Shoes," *Business Week,* January 25, 1982, p. 73.
5. *The Wall Street Journal,* February 27, 1981.

sion manufacturing plants, the Dutch company redesigned its equipment and tools to suit the volume requirements of some of the world's poorest countries. The molding machines used in its European plants to produce TV cabinets cost about $150,000, an amount justified by a factory output of about 100,000 units per year. But many African countries could only support plants with an average annual output of 3,000 to 5,000 sets. By borrowing from existing technology found in automobile dashboard manufacture, Philips eventually invented a press that cost only $2,150.

Advantages of Product Standardization

Complete standardization of product design results in a substantial saving of production and research and development costs and will allow a company to take full advantage of economies of scale. Often, several markets can be supplied from a regional or central manufacturing plant with efficient and long production runs. Aside from these obvious advantages, production sharing and simultaneously supplying markets from several plants are important factors that support standardized output. Managers in the U.S. subsidiary of Liebherr, a large German company producing construction machinery, decided to make some changes in the basic design of an excavator that was made to identical specifications elsewhere in Europe and Latin America.[6] To make the excavator more acceptable to U.S. customers, the Virginia-based subsidiary enlarged the fuel tank and strengthened the undercarriage. When U.S. sales dropped in the recession of 1974–1975, the company accumulated a substantial inventory of excavators. However, it could not help its European plants, filled with back-orders, because of the difference in design. Obviously the advantages gained from adaptation have to be compared to the overall loss in manufacturing flexibility.

Farell, a unit of Emhart, pursued complete standardization with its subsidiaries in Italy and England in order to build in flexibility in production allocation. Farell manufactured heavy machinery such as presses and molding machines used for tire manufacturing, among other things. For many of its international orders, credit terms were a crucial factor in obtaining a sale. Farell's major credit sources were export-import banks of various governments, though not all governments provided the same extensive services or low-interest rates. The company placed an individual order with that plant which was best suited for the requested financing. Orders shifted between the United States, Italy, and the United Kingdom, and also varied according to available plant capacity. The buyer, however, was not concerned, since specifications and performance standards were kept identical. Of course this strategy could only work if production equipment was standardized across all company plants. To accom-

---

6. "It's Tough Digging in the U.S.," *Fortune,* August 11, 1980, p. 146.

plish this, Farell developed a system to keep all engineering drawings updated simultaneously in its three manufacturing centers.

Despite the advantages of economies of scale, there are few companies that can fully standardize their products for the many markets they serve. To bridge the gap between various local adaptations and the need to standardize some components, some MNCs have moved to a new breed of products, the global product, which we will discuss in the following section.

GLOBAL PRODUCTS

In response to the pressure for cost reduction, and considering the relatively few opportunities for producing completely standardized products, many MNCs have moved to the creation of a *global product*. The global product, based upon the acknowledged fact that only a portion of the final design can be standardized, builds on flexibility to tailor the end product to the needs of individual markets. This represents a move to standardize as much as possible those areas involving common components or parts. This modularized approach has become of particular importance in the automobile industry, where both U.S. and European manufacturers are moving toward the creation of "world components"[7] to combat growing Japanese competitiveness.

Although both the Ford Model T and the original Volkswagen Beetle could be considered world cars, General Motors was the first to produce a car of this type within the last ten years as part of a concerted strategy. In response to the first gasoline supply crisis in 1973–1974, GM management decided to build a small fuel-efficient car in the United States. Rather than create an entirely new model, U.S. engineers borrowed from their colleagues at GM's Opel subsidiary in Germany. Designers at Opel had already planned a basic car by compiling statistics and information on local modifications for each of the eleven countries where the car might be introduced.[8]

These variations included a strengthened suspension system for use on South American roads, front-end styling, and safety and emission standards. The product, called the T-car by GM engineers, was introduced as the Opel Kadette by the German subsidiary in 1973. The Brazilian version was introduced the same year under the name Chevette, and it incorporated about 75 percent of the original Opel model. Introduced as the Gemini model in Japan by Isuzu Motors and in Australia by GM-Holden, this version retained about 35 percent of the original plan. Argentina's GM unit introduced the T-car as Opel K-180, retaining 60 percent of the original version; and GM's U.K. Vauxhall subsidiary launched the T-car under the Chevette name, containing 40 percent of the basic

7. "Renault Takes Its Hit Show on the Road," *Fortune,* May 4, 1981, p. 275.
8. *The New York Times,* May 12, 1975.

Opel Kadette design. The introduction of the T-car, while based on a single design, did not include a coordinated strategy with respect to component design or sourcing. Nevertheless it represented a step forward from first producing cars for home markets and secondly looking for export opportunities.

Local market adaptation for automobiles is still necessary for a number of geographical, regulatory, and taste reasons. France is the only country in the world to require yellow headlights. Japan demanded a protective shield under the catalytic converter and a sensor in the dash to warn about converter over-heating. Australia required a thermal reactor for emissions control, rather than a catalytic converter, because of the continued use of leaded gasoline. Ride and handling qualities also differ among markets.[9]

An example of a first step in achieving economies of scale for components can be seen in the single basic design of Ford European Fiesta. Designing the Fiesta for simultaneous production by Ford plants in Spain, the United Kingdom, and West Germany, the company developed a high degree of flexibility, assigning wherever possible the production of one component to a single plant, thus reaching greater economies of scale. The Fiesta could best be called a hemisphere car, since only Ford's European operations were involved.[10] Nevertheless it represented a substantial step toward greater standardization of components.

The first real world cars were introduced by Ford and GM during the 1981 model year. Ford's Escort model was simultaneously assembled in the United States, Great Britain, and Germany from parts produced in ten countries. The United States–assembled Escort contained parts made in Japan, Spain, Brazil, Britain, Italy, France, Mexico, Taiwan, and West Germany.[11] The European assembly plants in return bought automatic transmissions from a U.S. plant. Ford was estimated to have saved engineering and development costs amounting to hundreds of millions of dollars because the design standardized engines, transmissions, and ancillary systems for heating, air conditioning, wheels, and seats.[12]

Ford's global product development strategy has evolved into a search for "doing everything only once." The company realized that it was no longer possible for each region to develop their own models. On the other hand, market realities were also such that completely standardized models were not market-able. As a result, Ford moved towards a structure that would allow for the use of more and more commonly engineered components. (See Figure 11.2.) Such key components were transmissions, engines, body panels, platforms for trucks, among others. The company created a high executive position dealing exclu-sively with the coordination of technical resources on a worldwide scale with the

9. "What's Good for the World Should Be Good for GM," *Fortune,* May 7, 1979, p. 134.

10. Ibid.

11. *The New York Times,* November 9, 1980.

12. "Ford's Financial Hurdle," *Business Week,* February 2, 1981, p. 66.

FIGURE 11.2 Ford's Global Product Design Approach

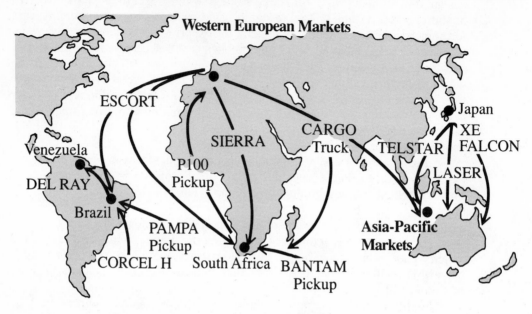

Source: Financial Times, November 16, 1984. Reprinted by permission.

main goal of achieving as much simplicity as possible. As a result, although the outside of a product may appear tailor-made to the customer, the nonvisible parts underneath are the same as those used in a wide variety of models to achieve economics of scale in component manufacturing and engineering.[13]

The challenge faced by Ford or other automobile manufacturers is largely similar to that faced by manufacturers and marketers of both industrial and consumer products all over the world. Cost pressures force them to standardize while market pressures require more customization. Conceptually, these companies will gain from increasing the standardized components in their products while maintaining the ability to customize the product at the end for each market segment. International firms will have to respond by achieving economies of scale on the core of their products, or the key portion offered as a standard across all markets. This core will be built upon a series of standardized components resulting in economies of scale. Different firms will have different levels of standardization, but they will rarely be able to standardize the product 100 percent. For one company, moving from a global core representing 15 percent of

13. "Ford's 'Do it Only Once' Approach," *Financial Times*, November 16, 1984.

the total product to 20 percent of the total product might result in a considerable cost improvement; and this might be the maximum level of standardization desirable. For another firm, the core might have to represent some 80 percent of the total product to achieve the same effect. These levels will depend on the market characteristics faced by the company or industry.

NEW PRODUCT DEVELOPMENT FOR INTERNATIONAL MARKETS

To develop new products or services for international markets offers unique challenges to a firm. In contrast to the strictly domestic company, MNCs must assign development responsibilities to any one of their often numerous international subsidiaries. Aside from the question of who should perform development work, there are organizational problems to be overcome that pertain to participation by experts in many subsidiaries. There is no doubt that the future success of international firms will to a substantial degree depend on how well firms marshal their resources on a global scale to develop new products for foreign markets.

The Organization of Head-Office-Sponsored Research and Development

Most companies currently engaged in research and development on a global scale originally conducted their development efforts strictly in centralized facilities in the firm's domestic market. Even today, the largest portion of research and development monies spent by MNCs is for efforts in domestically located facilities.[14] As a result, new product ideas are first developed in the context of the domestic market, with initial introduction at home, followed by a phase-in introduction in the company's foreign markets.

There are several reasons for this traditional approach to research and development. First, it must be integrated into a firm's overall marketing strategy. This requires frequent contacts and interfacing between research and development facilities and the company's main offices. Such contacts are maintained more easily with close proximity. The argument for a centralization of research and development is based on concern that a duplication of efforts will result if this responsibility were spread over several subsidiaries. Centralized research and development is felt to maximize results from scarce research funds. A final important reason for centralization is the company's experience in its home or domestic markets. Typically the domestic market is very important to the com-

14. Vern Terpstra, "International Product Policy: The Role of Foreign R&D," *Columbia Journal of World Business,* Winter, 1977.

pany; and, in the case of MNCs based in the United States, West Germany, and Japan, it is often the largest market as well. As a result, new products are developed with special emphasis on these domestic markets, and research and development facilities should be therefore close by.

International Lead Markets and Research and Development[15]

Prior to 1960, new developments in industry, marketing, or management tended to emerge primarily in the United States. Such developments, once accepted in the United States, were apt to be adopted later in other countries. As a result, the United States market served as the lead market for much of the rest of the world. In general, a lead market is a market whose level of development exceeds that of the market in other countries worldwide and whose developments tend to set a pattern for other countries.

Lead markets are not restricted to technological developments as embodied in product hardware. The concept covers developments in design, production processes, patterns in consumer demand, or methods of marketing. Virtually every phase of a company's operation is therefore subject to lead market influences, although those focusing on technological developments are of special importance.

During the first half of the twentieth century, the United States achieved a position of virtual dominance as a lead market. Not only were U.S. products the most advanced with respect to features, function, and quality, but they also tended to be marketed to the most sophisticated and advanced consumers and industrial buyers. This U.S. advantage was partially based upon superior production methods, with the pioneering of mass production in the form of the assembly line. The U.S. advantage extended to management methods in general, and particularly to access to new consumers. The rapid development of United States–based MNCs was to a considerable degree based upon the exploitation of these advantages in applying new U.S. developments abroad and in creating extensive networks of subsidiaries across a large number of countries.

But the U.S. lead over other countries did not last. Foreign competitors from Europe and Japan eroded the U.S. MNC advantages, and as a result no single country or market now unilaterally dominates the world economy. Though the United States may have lost its lead in steel, television, radios, shoes, textiles, and automobiles, it still leads the world in electronics, the biosciences, computers, and aerospace.

The fragmentation of lead markets led to a proliferation of centers, substantially complicating the task of keeping abreast of the latest developments in market demands, products design, and production techniques. However, to

---

15. This section is based upon: Jean-Pierre Jeannet, "Lead Markets: A Concept for Designing Global Business Strategies," Working Paper, IMEDE, 1986.

prosper in today's increasingly internationalized business climate, corporations must keep track of evolving lead markets as major sources for new product ideas. New product ideas can stem from influences in demand, processes of manufacture, and scientific discoveries; and no single country should expect to play a lead role in all facets of a firm's business. This means any corporate research and development effort must look for new developments abroad rather than solely in the domestic market. Foreign-based MNCs adjusted long ago to this fact and organized research and development with the U.S. lead market role partially in mind. United States–based MNCs, however, conduct about 90 percent of research and development in their home market and thus run the risk of excluding themselves from important developments in foreign markets unless provisions are made.[16]

The rapid expansion of United States–based MNCs depended to a large extent on their capacity to take advantage of lessons learned in the U.S. market. This strategy was characterized by centralized research and development functions and initial product introductions in the United States. Naturally the success of this strategy depends to a large degree on the inputs the central research and development staff derives from its own market environment. Should any part of a company's market become subject to foreign lead market influences, the organization of a firm's research and development function will have to be adjusted. United States steel companies and manufacturers of automobiles, shoes, and textiles cannot disregard developments elsewhere in the world, since the lead market for those industries is no longer the United States. To expose itself to lead market developments, Kodak has invested $65 million in a research and development center in Japan. It is to be completed in 1988 and will employ a staff of about 200 people.[17]

The Role of Foreign Subsidiaries in Research and Development

Foreign subsidiaries of MNCs rarely play an active role in research and development unless they have manufacturing responsibilities. Sales subsidiaries may provide feedback to the central organization on product adjustments or adaptation, but generally this participation does not go beyond the generation of ideas. Past research has shown that subsidiaries may assume some research and development functions if the products require some adaptation to the local market.[18] The ensuing research and development capability is often extended to other applications unique to the local market. In many instances, however, the new

---

16. D. B. Creamer, *Overseas Research and Developments by U.S. Multinationals, 1966–1975* (New York: The Conference Board, 1975).

17. "Kodak Invades Japan to Fight Fuji—and Learn," *Providence Sunday Journal,* December 21, 1986, p. 71.

18. Jean-Pierre Jeannet, *Transfer of Technology Within Multinational Corporations* (New York: Arno Press, 1980).

product may prove to have potential in other markets; and as a result, these developments get transferred to other subsidiaries and to the central research and development staff.

Hewlett-Packard, a United States–based electronics company, assigned substantial autonomy to its European subsidiaries, including authority to engage in locally sponsored research and development.[19] This strategy paid off particularly well in West Germany, which generally is not considered a center for high technology electronics products. But Hewlett-Packard's German subsidiary was able to tap some unique local talent and developed new products as a result. The subsidiary supported the development of a fetal heart monitoring system and a number of related monitoring instruments by a local gynecologist. By attracting engineers from the University of Stuttgart, a university with a strong reputation in the field of electronic pulse research, the German subsidiary spearheaded this important area of instrument testing for the parent company. Also, the German subsidiary acquired a local firm with strong capabilities in liquid chromatograph instruments used in food and pharmaceutical research. As a result, Hewlett-Packard's German subsidiary was assigned worldwide responsibility for this product line by its parent company.

MNCs' subsidiaries assume special positions when lead markets change from one country to another. Countries that can assume lead market status tend to be among the most advanced industrial nations of North America, Europe, and Asia. Larger MNCs quite often have subsidiaries in all these markets. A subsidiary located in a lead market is usually in a better position to observe developments and to accommodate to new demands. Consequently, MNCs with subsidiaries in lead markets are in a unique position to turn such units into effective "listening posts."[20] For quite some time now, United States–based MNCs have profited from technological advances made by their European subsidiaries, leading to a reverse flow of technology.[21] Much of this flow however has occurred on an ad hoc basis without any attempts to exploit deliberately the capabilities of foreign subsidiaries in newly emerging lead markets.

In the future, international companies will have to make better use of the talents of local subsidiaries in the development of new products. Increasingly, the role of the subsidiary as a selling arm or production arm of the company will have to be abandoned and companies will have to find innovative ways to involve their foreign affiliates into the product development process. This involvement can be patterned around several role models.[22] The strategic leader role for developing a new range of products to be used by the entire company may be

19. *Business Week,* July 7, 1980, p. 32.

20. Raymond Vernon, "Gone Are the Cash Cows of Yesteryear," *Harvard Business Review,* November–December 1980, p. 150.

21. Jeannet, *Transfer of Technology Within Multinational Corporations.*

22. Christopher A. Bartlett and Sumantra Ghoshal, "Tap Your Subsidiaries for Global Reach," *Harvard Business Review,* November–December 1986, p. 67.

assigned to a highly competent subsidiary in a market of strategic importance. Another subsidiary with competence in a distinct area may be assigned the role of contributor by adapting some products in smaller but nevertheless important markets. Most subsidiaries, being of smaller size and located in less strategic markets, would be expected to implement the overall strategy and contribute less either technologically or strategically.

Purchasing Research and Development from Foreign Countries

Instead of developing new products through its own research and development personnel, a company may acquire such material or information from independent outside sources. These sources are usually located in foreign countries that have acquired lead market status. Managers commonly read literature published by lead markets. Also, through regular visits to foreign countries and trade fairs, managers maintain close contact with their lead markets. Increasingly, however, these ad hoc measures are becoming insufficient for maintaining the necessary flow of information in rapidly changing markets.

For companies without immediate access to new technology embodied in new products, the licensing avenue has been the traditional approach to gain new developments from lead markets. United States technology has been tapped through many independent licensing arrangements. Japanese companies have made extensive use of the licensing alternative to acquire technologies developed in countries that were lead markets from Japan's point of view. In the early 1960s, several Japanese manufacturers of earth-moving equipment signed licensing agreements with U.S. manufacturers to obtain expertise in hydraulic power shovels.[23] Though some Japanese companies attempted to develop a new product line from their own internal resources, it was Komatsu which, based upon a licensing agreement with a U.S. company, achieved leadership in Japan. Though the advantage of licensing lies in its potential to teach new product technologies, there are typically some restrictions attached, such as limiting the sale of such products to specific geographic regions or countries.

A variation of the licensing agreement is the technology assistance contract with a foreign company, allowing a constant flow of information to the firm seeking assistance. Such agreements have been signed by several U.S. steel companies. Japanese steel makers have achieved world leadership. Consequently steel companies all over the world, Americans among them, have tapped the former's knowledge and experience. Sumitomo Metal signed contracts with clients in nineteen countries, including U.S. Steel, for steel making, plate rolling, and pipe manufacturing. Other U.S. companies purchasing from Japanese com-

---

23. *The Japan Economic Journal,* issues of October 2, 1979 and August 5, 1980.

panies included Armco, from Nippon Steel; Inland Steel, from Nippon Kokan; and Bethlehem Steel, from Kawasaki Steel.[24]

The Korean firm Lucky-Gold Star is an example of a company that aggressively buys technology abroad to assist in the development of its technologically advanced products. Over the years, the company has formed some twenty joint ventures and maintained technology cooperation agreements with more than fifty foreign firms. Lucky-Gold Star linked up with United States–based AT&T to manufacture electronic telephone switching gear, fiber-optic cables and semiconductors. Entering such agreements offered the Korean firm quick access to modern technologies while allowing AT&T to build contacts within a new market.[25]

Importing As a Source of New Product Technology

Some corporations have decided to forego internally sponsored research and development, importing finished products directly from a foreign firm. Sometimes the importer assumes the role of an original equipment manufacturer (OEM) by marketing products under its own name. Some recent agreements have been made between Japanese suppliers and European and U.S. manufacturers and will serve to illustrate this strategy.

Siemens, a large MNC based in West Germany, had been marketing numerical controls (NCs) for machine tools, but the line was missing some smaller models. Rather than developing a new line of smaller numerical controls, the company decided to import products made by Fanuc, a Japanese company generally believed to be the world leader in NCs and industrial robots.[26] This new product line was to be marketed under a common brand name, Sinumerik. Similar captive agreements existed between several U.S. machine tool manufacturers and Japanese suppliers.[27] When IBM was looking for a small desk-top copier to fill a gap in its product line, the company turned to a Japanese supplier, Minolta Camera Co. Ltd., instead of developing its own machine.[28] IBM's product line included photocopying machines ranging from $6,000 to $40,000, after it dropped an older model that had sold for $4,000. But in 1980 the company opened its first retail outlets, which were targeted at small businesses. The need for a small desk-top model became apparent and had to be filled quickly. The Minolta-supplied model was sold as the IBM Model 102 and resembled the

24. *The New York Times,* October 28, 1980.

25. "Lucky-Gold Star: Using Joint Ventures to Spring Ahead in the High-Tech Race," *Business Week,* July 9, 1984, p. 94.

26. *Business Week,* November 19, 1980, p. 36.

27. "Making Machine Tools Increasingly Requires Ties to Foreign Firms," *The Wall Street Journal,* September 4, 1984, p. 1.

28. *The Wall Street Journal,* February 18, 1981; *The New York Times,* February 18, 1981.

Model EP-310, which was marketed by Minolta in the United States through a network of independent dealers.

Though the importing method gives a firm quick access to new products without incurring any research and development expenditures, a company could become dependent and lose the capacity to innovate on its own in the future. As was the case with General Electric's color TV production, economic changes can lead to reversals later on. GE had stopped production of color TV sets in the United States in the mid-1970s and sourced all such products from Matsushita in Japan. When the value of the yen rose to record levels in 1986, GE switched back to U.S. sourcing. This move was made possible because the company had earlier acquired RCA which still operated a color TV plant in the United States.[29] Consequently, such a strategy of importing new products should be pursued with great care and possibly only in areas that do not represent the core of the firm's business and technology.

Acquisitions As a Route to New Products

To acquire a company for its new technology or products is a strategy many firms have followed in domestic markets. To make international acquisitions for the purpose of gaining a window on emerging technologies or products is developing into an acceptable strategy for many firms. Several European firms have acquired United States–based electronics companies for that purpose. Siemens of West Germany bought into Advanced Micro Devices, Inc.[30] Robert Bosch, another German MNC, acquired an interest in American Microsystems, Inc.; and Philips of Holland purchased Signetics. In all these cases, the foreign firms had to pay substantial premiums over the market value of the stock as a price for access to new product development.

Whereas the major purpose of the above mentioned acquisitions was access to state-of-the-art technologies, other MNCs sought access to products to be marketed abroad. In the 1960s, CPC International acquired Knorr, a leading European manufacturer of dehydrated soups, and subsequently made a major effort to market these products on a broader scale in the United States. Though that effort failed, another United States–based MNC was more successful. Litton substantially increased sales of Sweda cash registers in the United States following acquisition of the Swedish company. But foreign MNCs have also taken advantage of opportunities in the United States. Schloemann-Siemag, a unit of the large West German GHH company, acquired Gloucester Engineering Co., located in Massachusetts. The German company then began marketing

29. "GE Will Resume Some US Production of Color TVs Instead of Buying Abroad," *The Wall Street Journal,* February 13, 1987, p. 6.
30. *Business Week,* October 17, 1977.

plastics machinery produced by Gloucester in Europe.[31] GHH's MAN subsidiary acquired Wood Industries, Inc., a New Jersey based manufacturer of printing presses. Although selling MAN presses in the United States was a major factor in the move, the German company planned to sell United States–built Wood presses in Germany and other foreign markets as well.[32]

The Joint Venture Route to New Product Development

Forming a joint venture with a technologically advanced foreign company can also lead to new product development, often at lower costs. In the 1960s and 1970s, it was largely Japanese companies that sought to attract foreign technology for the manufacture of advanced products in Japan. Many of these Japanese companies can be found in the front ranks of their industries today. Typically, these joint ventures were set up as separate entities, with their own manufacturing and marketing functions.

Recent examples of this strategy can be found in France, where two French firms, Saint-Gobain-Pont-a-Mousson and Matra, entered into joint ventures with two American semiconductor manufacturers, National Semiconductor and Harris Corp., with the goal of manufacturing chips in France.[33] In a similar move, the French manufacturer of machine tools, Ernault-Somur, agreed to enter a joint venture with Toyoda Machine Works of Japan, a major machine tool supplier for Toyota.[34] The French company is a major supplier of machine tools to the French automobile industry and hopes to gain access to Tyoda's experience with industrial robots, an area where Japan has assumed the lead position.

United States car manufacturers have also acquired parts of Japanese and other Asian firms to participate in the development of new small cars. General Motors owns 34 percent of Isuzu Motors, Ford owns 25 percent of Mazda, and Chrysler owns 15 percent of Mitsubishi.[35]

More recently, GM also entered into joint ventures with Daewoo, a large Korean conglomerate, to build cars to GM's specifications. In the United States, GM jointly operated a plant with Toyota for the production of subcompact cars.[36]

More recently, joint ventures have taken the form of alliances in which entire companies pool their resources for competitive advantage. Although in the more traditional joint venture the cooperation restricted the legal entity of the venture, in an alliance the cooperation goes beyond a joint venture company.

31. "West Germany: Buying into U.S. Trucks and Machinery," *Business Week,* March 5, 1979, pp. 39–41.

32. *Ibid.*

33. "Europe's Wild Swing at the Silicon Giants," *Fortune,* July 28, 1980, p. 76.

34. *The Japan Economic Journal,* September 2, 1980.

35. "Detroit's New Asian Strategy," *Fortune,* December 10, 1984, p. 172.

36. *Business Week,* July 16, 1984.

In some instances the agreement is made directly between two large firms without even forming a new legal entity. The strategic importance of alliances has already been discussed in Chapter 9. Our concern here is on the ability to develop new products and how an alliance can help an international firm to accomplish this objective better, faster, and with less investment funds.

When Motorola of the U.S. and Toshiba of Japan decided to pool their resources by swapping technology and creating a joint venture in Japan, both firms had important strategic objectives in mind. Motorola was to get access to Toshiba's production technology for mass-produced memory chips with a chance to get back eventually into producing both one mega and four mega ram chips in large numbers—a production segment that Motorola had to abandon under intense price pressure from Japanese competitors. In return, Motorola was to give Toshiba access to its logic chips, particularly the large 32-bit microprocessors that are key components for the production of computers.[37]

Toshiba was no newcomer to such alliances. The Japanese company, which is a major force in electronics, concluded other deals with Olivetti of Italy (by buying into Olivetti's Japanese subsidiary), with AT&T of the United States, and with LSI Logic Corp. of the United States (to develop and sell specialized chips). Other development contracts were concluded with General Electric and Siemens of Germany. To strengthen its competitive position compared to other Japanese electronics firms, Toshiba needed access to the most advanced technology. By working with foreign partners the company expected to save both valuable time and development costs.[38]

Alliances can sometimes be formed by firms for some part of their business while they remain competitors in other segments. Olivetti of Italy and Canon of Japan decided to join forces for the development and marketing of office equipment in Europe. The companies created a new joint company in Italy consisting of Olivetti production and research facilities for copiers and an infusion of capital and technology from Canon. With access to Canon's latest technology, particularly in the laser printing and electronic publishing area, Olivetti managers hoped that the new company would triple present volume—supplying both Olivetti and Canon distribution channels in Europe. Despite this cooperation, the two firms would remain competitors in the typewriter market.[39]

The Consortium Approach

To share the huge cost of developing new products, some companies have established or joined consortia to share in new product development. Under the consortium approach, member firms join in a working relationship without form-

---

37. "Toshiba's Motorola Tie-Up Is Latest Bid to Bolster Its Semiconductors Business," *The Wall Street Journal,* December 5, 1986, p. 35.
38. *Ibid.*
39. "Olivetti and Canon Form Venture for Office Equipment Production," *Financial Times,* January 20, 1987, p. 1.

ing a new entity. Upon completion of the assigned task, member firms are free to seek other relationships with different firms. Consortia have been used for some time in marketing entire factories or plants, or in the banking industry, but they are a relatively new approach to new product research and development.

Since the development of new aircraft is a particularly cost-intensive business, the aircraft industry offers several examples of the consortium approach to product development. The high development costs require that large passenger aircraft must be built in series of 200 or 300 units just to break even. Under these circumstances, several companies form a consortium to share the risk. One of the first highly successful efforts was the European Airbus, developed and produced by French, British, and German manufacturers.

Several new consortia involve Japanese aerospace firms joined with American or European companies. Kawasaki Heavy Industries combined with Messerschmitt-Bölkow-Blohm GmbH of West Germany to develop and produce a multipurpose helicopter BK-1177.[40] Fuji Heavy Industries developed an executive aircraft together with Rockwell International, a U.S. firm.[41] And three Japanese companies, Ishikawajima-Harima Heavy Industries, Kawasaki Heavy Industries, and Mitsubishi Heavy Industries, planned to form a consortium to develop a new jet engine with Rolls Royce Motors, Ltd. of Britain.[42]

Even U.S. firms have joined the consortium approach. Boeing planned to develop a new generation of jet models, the 767 and 777 jetliners, with Aaeritalia S.A. of Italy and three Japanese firms, Mitsubishi Heavy Industries, Kawasaki Heavy Industries, and Fuji Heavy Industries. Each consortium member would assume the responsibility of some parts of the aircraft, and Boeing would also be in charge of final assembly.[43]

The advantage of a consortium approach also lies in sales. The widespread participation of companies from the United States, Europe, and Japan gives partial reassurance for future sales, thus further reducing the risk to each participating company.

The consortium approach is becoming increasingly popular in several technology-intensive industries.[44] Companies in the automobile, computer, and biotechnology industries have formed cooperative agreements to share in the development and exploitation of technology. What is new to this trend is that sometime competitors will become partners, whereas previously no cooperation would have been possible. For another example of such a consortium, see Figure 11.3.

---

40. *The Wall Street Journal,* June 24, 1980.

41. *The Japan Economic Journal,* November 13, 1979.

42. *Ibid.*

43. *Ibid.*

44. Kenichi Ohmae, *Triad Power: The Coming Shape of Global Competition* (New York: The Free Press, 1985), pp. 125–148.

FIGURE 11.3 International Aircraft Consortium

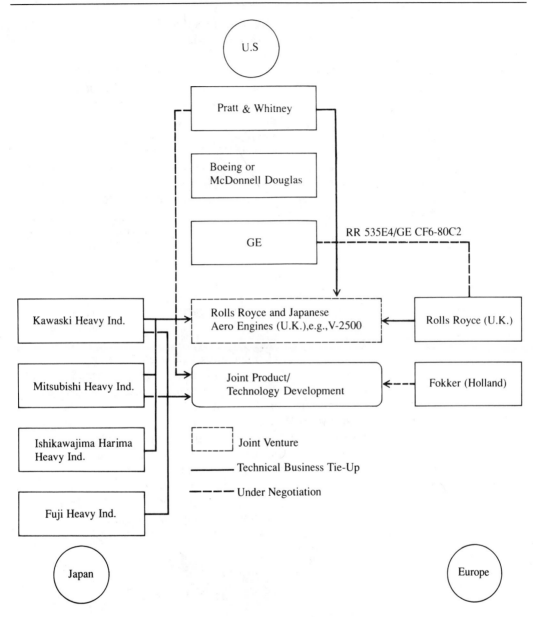

Source: Adapted with permission of The Free Press, a division of Macmillan, Inc. from *Triad Power: The Coming Shape of Global Competition* by Kenichi Ohmae. Copyright © 1985 by Kinichi Ohmae and McKinsey & Company.

The Internationalization of the Product Development Process

The previous sections dealt primarily with the sources of product development. To bring about a total integration of the product development process for a multinational enterprise often requires adoption of new organizational forms and restructuring the development process as a whole. The challenge in multinational product development is finding a way to combine domestic and foreign expertise so that truly international or global products can result.

The latest approach to new product development is best described by an executive of Fiat, the Italian car manufacturer. "Fifteen years ago we designed cars for the Italian market. Ten years ago we began designing 'European' cars. Now we develop them for the country with the biggest market—the U.S.—and scale them down for the others."[45] This shift from localized to worldwide development requires that the unique or special concerns for major markets be considered from the outset of the process, rather than attempting to make various adaptations on the initial model or prototype. This early introduction of global considerations not only ensures that the product will achieve wide acceptance, but also aims at maximizing the commonality of models to achieve economies in component manufacturing. A global product then is not identical in all countries. Instead, a world product is engineered from the outset with the goal of maximizing the percentage of identical components, design, or parts, to the point where local needs can be met with a minimum of additional costs in tooling, engineering, and development.

To develop a global product also demands a different organizational setup. Changes instituted by General Motors are an indication of moves made by other MNCs. With the advent of world cars, GM realized that the company needed closer coordination between its domestic units and its overseas subsidiaries. GM moved its overseas staff from New York to Detroit in 1978 in order to speed up communication between domestic and international staffs.[46] GM adopted the "project center" concept to manage its engineering effort. Each division or subsidiary involved in a new car design would lend engineers to a centrally organized project center, which would design, develop, and introduce the new model. Upon introduction of the model, the project center is disbanded. Of course, not every firm will find a project center approach feasible. Other alternatives include assigning primary responsibility to a subsidiary with special capability in the new product field.

INTRODUCING NEW PRODUCTS TO THE MARKET

Once a product has been developed for commercial introduction, a number of complex decisions still need to be made. Aside from the question of whether to

---

45. "To a Global Car," *Business Week*, November 20, 1978, p. 102.
46. "GM Plans an Offensive for Growth Overseas," *Business Week*, March 27, 1978, p. 46.

introduce the product abroad, the firm will have to decide on a desirable test marketing procedure, select target countries for introduction, and decide on the timing or sequence of the introduction. With the large number of alternatives due to numerous possible markets, decisions surrounding new product introduction often attain strategic significance.

The determination of which product to introduce abroad would of course depend upon the sales potential. Following a careful analysis, a list of target countries can be developed. A company would then have to determine the next steps leading to actual introduction in the target countries.

Concept Tests

Once a prototype or sample product has been developed, a company may decide to subject its new creation to a series of tests to determine commercial feasibility. It is particularly important to subject a new product to actual use conditions. When the development process takes place outside the country of actual use, a practical field test can be crucial. The test should include all necessary usage steps to provide complete information. When CPC International tested the U.S. market for dehydrated soups made by its newly acquired Knorr subsidiary, the company concentrated primarily on taste tests to assure that the final product suited U.S. consumers. Extensive testing led to soups different in formulation from those sold in Europe. CPC, however, had neglected to have consumers actually try out the product at home as part of their regular cooking activities. Such a test would have revealed consumers' discontent with the relatively long cooking time of up to 20 minutes, compared to 3 minutes for comparable canned soups. The company realized these difficulties only after a national introduction had been completed and sales results fell short of original expectations.

The concept testing stage would be incomplete if the product were only tested in the company's domestic market. A full test in several major markets is essential so that any shortcomings can be alleviated at an early stage before costly adaptations for individual countries are made. Such an approach would be particularly important in cases where product development occurred on a multinational basis, with simultaneous inputs from several foreign subsidiaries. When Volkswagen tested its original Rabbit models, test vehicles were made available to all principal subsidiaries in order to insure that each market's requirements were met by the otherwise standardized car.

There may be some differences between concept testing for consumer products and for industrial products. Industrial products tend to be used worldwide for the same purposes under very similar circumstances. Factories for textile machinery are relatively standardized across the world so that a test in one country might be quite adequate for most others. As a result, single country market testing would be more appropriate for industrial products.

Test Marketing

Just as there are good reasons to test market a product in a domestic market, an international test can give the firm valuable insights into potential future success. A key question is where should the test market be held? United States companies have largely pioneered test marketing procedures because it has been possible to isolate a given market in terms of media and distribution. This may not always be possible in smaller countries, and even less so in countries where most of the media are national rather than local. If a test market were considered in a country with national TV only, and print media were substituted for TV for the purpose of the test, the test would not be a true replication of the actual full-scale introduction. As a result, the opportunities for small local test markets are substantially reduced outside the United States.

To overcome the shortage of test market possibilities, MNCs often have substituted the experience in one country for a test market in another. Although test markets were typical for many United States–based firms before full-scale introduction in the U.S. market, subsidiaries tended to use these early U.S. results as a basis for analysis. Such a strategy requires that at least one subsidiary of the MNC have actual commercial experience with a product or any given aspect of the marketing strategy before introducing the product elsewhere.

Use of the U.S. market as a test market depends on the market situation and the degree to which results can be extrapolated to other countries. Since circumstances are rarely exactly the same, early U.S. results must be regarded with caution. Also, extrapolation may only be appropriate for other advanced countries in Europe and Asia.

For MNCs with extensive foreign networks of subsidiaries, test markets can be used beyond the traditional mode. Gillette used its Australian subsidiary as a distribution test for its facing-edge double-blade razor.[47] Since market characteristics faced by Gillette in Australia were judged similar to those in the United States, results were used to make a final determination on the U.S. distribution strategy. Another approach to test marketing is to use a foreign country as a first introduction and proving ground before other markets are entered. In Europe, smaller markets such as the Netherlands, Belgium, Austria, or Switzerland may be used to launch a new product. Because of their size, a test would include national introduction with results applicable in other countries. When Toyota started its European sales drive, Switzerland was used as a test, and the strategy developed by its independent Swiss distributor, Jean Frey AG, was later adopted elsewhere.

Special attention should be given to the lead market as a potential test market. Any new product that succeeds in its lead market could be judged to have good potential elsewhere as other markets mature. Philips, the Dutch elec-

---

47. Douglas G. Norvell, "Eleven Reasons for Firms to Go International," *Marketing News,* October 17, 1980, pp. 1–2.

tronics company, intends to use the United States market as its proving ground for consumer electronics products.[48] Though new products may be developed in the Netherlands, U.S. subsidiaries would market them first. Having to compete with major Japanese and U.S. manufacturers in the largest market for consumer electronics should provide input for European markets. European markets are believed to follow ultimately the consumption patterns set by U.S. consumers.

Timing of New Product Introductions

Very early in the introduction process a company will be faced with a decision to establish the timing and sequence of its introduction. Timing determines when a product should be introduced in a foreign market. Sequencing becomes an issue when a firm deals with several countries and must decide on a phased or simultaneous entry approach. Traditionally, MNCs have introduced new products first in their domestic markets to gain experience in production, marketing, and service. Foreign market introductions have been attempted only after a product has proven itself in the domestic market. Research has shown, however, that the time lag between domestic and initial foreign market introduction has substantially declined (see Table 11.2).[49] From 1945 to 1950, only 5.6 percent of investigated firms introduced new products abroad within one year. By 1975, the percentage had increased to 38.7 percent, and about two-thirds were introduced abroad within five years. This time lag reduction reflects the increased capability by U.S. firms to introduce products abroad rapidly. It also reflects the rapid economic development of many advanced countries, to the point where the United States no longer leads in a number of fields. It can be safely assumed that the average time lag will continue to decline.

Some companies are now in a position to introduce products simultaneously in several countries. Data General, the small computer manufacturer, held simultaneous press conferences in New York and Paris, the location of its European regional head office, whenever a new product was introduced. Many other electronics manufacturers follow the same practice. Simultaneous introduction depends on the company's foreign market development stage and the ability to satisfy demand. When the primary function of foreign subsidiaries is the sale of products shipped from one or a small number of central manufacturing centers, simultaneous introduction is possible, as long as marketing efforts can be coordinated. This structure is typical for electronics firms. Other companies produce in many markets; thus the manufacturing function would be strained if simultaneous introduction was attempted. Gillette produced most of its own machinery

---

48. "In Consumer Electronics The U.S. Is a Top Target," *Business Week,* March 30, 1981, pp. 97–100.
49. William H. Davidson and Richard Harrigan, "Key Decisions in International Marketing: Introducing New Products Abroad," *Columbia Journal of World Business,* Winter 1977, p. 15.

TABLE 11.2 Frequency of First Foreign Introduction Within One and Five Years of U.S. Introduction (By period of U.S. innovation)

Period of U.S. Innovation	Number of Innovations	Percent introduced in foreign markets	
		Within 1 year of U.S. Introduction	Within 5 years of U.S. Introduction
1945–1950	161	5.6%	22.0%
1951–1955	115	2.6%	29.6%
1956–1960	134	10.4%	36.6%
1961–1965	133	24.1%	55.6%
1966–1970	115	37.4%	60.1%
1971–1975	75	38.7%	64.0%

Source: From William H. Davidson and Richard Harrigan, ''Key Decisions in International Marketing: Introducing New Products Abroad.'' *Columbia Journal of World Business,* Winter 1977, p. 15. Reprinted by permission.

for blade production and therefore scheduled markets according to its marketing output, though the time lag was only a few months between first and last introduction.

Country Selection

Although MNCs have subsidiaries in numerous countries, initial product introductions have always been limited to the industrialized nations. William Davidson and Richard Harrigan documented that for the forty-four United States–based MNCs investigated, 83.5 percent of first introductions took place in developed countries for the 1945–1976 time period.[50] Leading target countries for the 1965–1975 period were the United Kingdom, Japan, Australia, France, and West Germany.[51] Other research has shown that some companies use a two-step approach to new product introduction. At first products are introduced in the most advanced markets, with developing countries following in a second stage.[52] Many United States–based MNCs have used their European subsidiaries as stepping stones to Latin America or Eastern Europe. One electronics

50. *Ibid.* p. 17
51. *Ibid.*
52. Jeannet, *Transfer of Technology Within Multinational Corporations.*

manufacturer transferred an innovation first to its Italian subsidiary; the Italian subsidiary then introduced it in Spain through another subsidiary there. The same company has also used its Dutch subsidiary to transfer innovations to Poland.

A firm's competitive situation abroad influences its country selection. Major subsidiaries tend to get new products first, and manufacturing subsidiaries are usually favored over sales subsidiaries. Also, each local market expects to face different competitors. This often means that the MNC first will choose a country where the firm is well entrenched over a market where competitive pressures make operating results less favorable.

CONCLUSIONS

When companies search for new markets for their products, they face the difficult choice of adapting their products to new environments. Such adaptations are frequently expensive when done after the fact. In the future, companies will increasingly consider international opportunities early in the development cycle of a new product. Incorporating international requirements early will allow new products to be immediately usable in many markets. Such a move toward internationalization of the product development cycle will result in the development of more world products. These products will be produced in modularized forms to include as many world components as possible, and they will incorporate a set of unique components to fit the product needs of individual markets. The challenge for international marketers will be to find the best tradeoffs between the standardized world components of a product and the tailor-made components designed for specific markets.

Questions for Discussion

1. Analyze three different products (freezers, compact disks, and contact eye lenses) according to Table 11.1. What general marketing strategy recommendations do you arrive at?
2. What, in your opinion, is the future for global products?
3. How should MNCs organize their new product development efforts today and in the future?
4. What is the impact of a loss of lead market position in several industries for United States–based multinational corporations?
5. If you were to test market a new consumer product today for worldwide introduction, how would you select test countries for Europe, Asia, and Latin America?

For Further Reading

Afriyie, Koti. "International Technology Transfers." In *Cooperative Strategies in International Business*. Ed. Farok Contractor and Peter Lorange. Lexington, Mass.: D.C. Heath 1987.

Behrman, J. N., and W. A. Fischer. "Transnational Corporation: Market Orientations and R&D Abroad." *Columbia Journal of World Business* (Fall 1980), pp. 55–60.

Crawford, Merle C. *New Products Management*. Homewood, Ill.: Irwin 1983.

Gerstenfeld, Arthur, and Lawrence H. Wortzel. "Strategies for Innovation in Developing Countries." *Sloan Management Review* (Fall 1977), pp. 57–68.

Hill, John S., and Richard R. Still. "Cultural Effects of Technology Transfer by Multinational Corporations in Lesser Developed Countries." *Columbia Journal of World Business* (Summer 1980), pp. 40–50.

Kaikati, Jack G. "Domestically Banned Products: For Export Only." *Journal of Public Policy and Marketing* 3, (1984), pp. 125–133.

Leroy, Georges. *Multinational Product Strategy*. New York: Praeger, 1976.

Ronstadt, Robert. "The Establishment and Evolution of R&D Abroad." *Journal of International Business Studies* (Spring–Summer 1978), pp. 7–24.

Terpstra, Vern. "International Product Policy: The role of Foreign R&D." *Columbia Journal of World Business* (Winter 1977), pp. 24–32.

Wind, Yoram. "The Myth of Globalization." *The Journal of Marketing,* 3, No. 4 (Spring 1986), pp. 23–26.

12.
MANAGING INTERNATIONAL CHANNELS

Distribution decisions in international marketing are similar to those in a domestic setting. What differs, of course, are the environmental influences that in the end may lead to substantially different policies and channel options. The international marketer needs to understand how environmental influences may affect these distribution policies and options. Using this knowledge, the marketer must structure an efficient channel for products on a country by country basis. These environmental differences are related to the culture, physical environment, and legal/political system.

With a focus on these environmental influences, this chapter discusses the structure of international distribution systems; developing a distribution strategy; and selecting, locating, and managing channel members (see Figure 12.1). We will also explain the issues of international logistics, gaining access to channels, and worldwide trends in international distribution.

THE STRUCTURE OF INTERNATIONAL DISTRIBUTION SYSTEMS

The structure of the distribution systems available in a country is affected by the economic development of the country, the personal disposable income of consumers, the quality of the infrastructure, as well as environmental factors such as the culture, the physical environment, and the legal/political system. Marketers who develop a distribution strategy must decide how to transport the goods from the manufacturing locations to the consumer. Although the distribution of goods can be handled completely by the manufacturer, often the goods are moved through middlemen, such as agents, distributors, and retailers. An under-

FIGURE 12.1 International Distribution

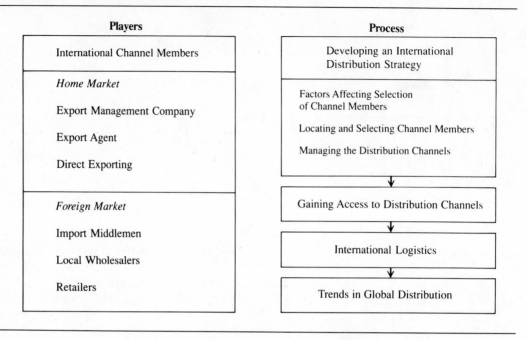

standing of the structure of the available distribution systems is extremely important in the development of a strategy. The various channels available to a manufacturer are shown in Figure 12.2.

There are two major categories of channel members: (1) home country middlemen and (2) foreign middlemen. In the home country, a manufacturer can utilize the services of an export management company or an export agent, or it can export the products using company personnel. In Chapter 9, we discussed whether or not any of these channel members should be used. In this chapter, our focus is on how to locate, select, use, and manage channel members.

Home Market Channel Members

Export Management Company

The Export Management Company (EMC) is a firm that provides a variety of sales and marketing services to a manufacturer.[1] The EMC will normally take responsibility for the promotion of goods, marketing research, credit, physical handling of the product, patents, and licensing. The population of EMCs is

---

1. John J. Brasdy, "Using Export Specialists to Develop Overseas Sales," *Harvard Business Review,* May–June 1981, pp. 6–8.

FIGURE 12.2 International Marketing Channel Alternatives

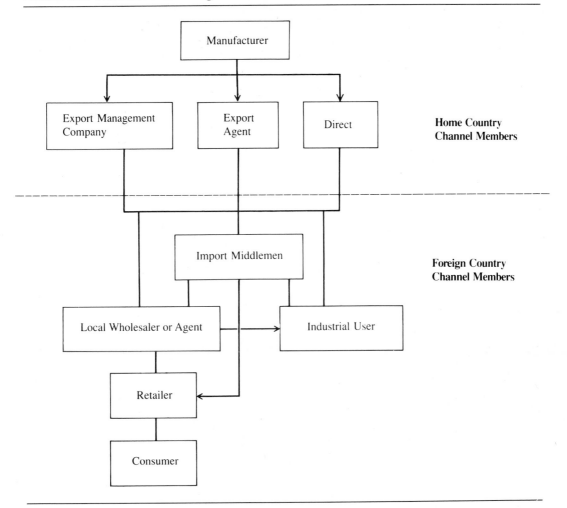

estimated to be 1,200 firms, which represent some 10,000 manufacturers and account for 10 percent of U.S.–manufactured exports.[2] The arrangement between an EMC and manufacturer will vary, depending on the services offered and the volume expected. The advantages of an EMC are that (1) little or no investment is required to enter the international marketplace; (2) no company personnel are required; and (3) the EMC will have an established network of sales offices and international market and distribution knowledge. One disadvantage is that the manufacturer gives up direct control of the international sales and marketing effort. Also, if the product has a long purchase cycle and requires a

2. Franklin R. Root, *Entry Strategies for International Markets* (Lexington, Mass.: D.C. Heath, 1987), p. 78.

large amount of market development and education, then the EMC may not devote the necessary effort to penetrate a new market.

Export Agents

Export agents are individuals or firms that assist manufacturers in exporting goods. Export agents are similar to EMCs, except that they tend to provide limited services and focus on one country or one part of the world. Export agents understand all the requirements for moving goods through the customs process. Export agents do not provide the marketing skills that an EMC does; these agents focus more on the sale and handling of goods. The advantage of using an export agent is that the firm does not need to have an export manager to handle all the documentation and shipping tasks. One disadvantage is the export agent's limited market coverage, which requires the use of numerous export agents to cover different parts of the world.

Direct Exporting

Instead of using an EMC or export agent, a firm can export its goods directly, through in-house company personnel. Due to the complexity of trade regulations, customs documentation, insurance requirements, and worldwide transportation alternatives, people with special training and experience are necessary to handle these tasks. Also, the current or expected volume must be sufficient to support the in-house staff.

Foreign Market Channel Members

As shown in Figure 12.2, once the goods have left the home market, there's a variety of channel alternatives in the international marketplace. These are import middlemen, local wholesalers or agents, and retailers.

Import Middlemen

Import middlemen identify needs in their local market and find products from the world market to satisfy these needs. The import middlemen will normally purchase goods in their own name and act independently of the manufacturers. As independent middlemen, these channel members will use their own marketing strategies and will keep in close contact with the markets they serve. A manufacturer desiring distribution in an independent middleman's market area should investigate this channel partner as one of the ways to get its product to wholesalers and retailers in that area.

TABLE 12.1 Wholesale Patterns in Selected Countries

	Number of Wholesalers (thousands)	Employees per Wholesaler	Retailers per Wholesaler	Population per Wholesaler
United States	370	11	4	549
Japan	369	10	5	303
Brazil	45	6	13	2,052
Belgium	56	3	4	172
Turkey	23	1	8	1,754
Republic of Korea	20	5	18	1,734
Philippines	12	9	27	3,486
Sweden	21	9	3	391
New Zealand	6	9	4	489
Puerto Rico	2	12	14	1,232
USSR	1	120	481	174,922
Kenya	1	11	4	10,944
Yugoslavia	1	115	77	18,657
Panama	6	18	2	2,559

Source: Statistical Yearbook 1979–1980 (New York: United Nations, 1981), Table 134, pp. 404–420. Reprinted by permission.

Local Wholesalers or Agents

In each country, there will be a series of possible channel members who move manufacturers' products to retailers, industrial firms, or in some cases other wholesalers. Local wholesalers will take title to the products, while local agents will not take title. Local wholesalers are also called distributors or dealers. In many cases the local wholesaler has exclusive distribution rights for a specific geographic area or country.

The structure of the wholesale distribution varies greatly from country to country, as shown in Table 12.1. The number of wholesalers, the number of retailers per wholesaler, and the number of people per wholesaler varies according to the distribution structure and wholesale pattern of the country. For example, although the United States and Japan have approximately the same number of wholesalers having an average number of ten employees, the U.S. wholesaler will indirectly serve 549 people, whereas in Japan a wholesaler will serve only 303—or 45 percent fewer people. In state-controlled economies, the wholesalers employed a much larger group of people—over 100 employees—and served a larger number of retailers and consumers.

The functions of wholesalers can vary by country. In some countries, wholesalers provide a warehouse function, taking orders from retailers and shipping

TABLE 12.2 Retail Patterns in Selected Countries

Country	Population (millions)	Number of Retailers	Population per Retailer
Belgium	10	128,989	78
Colombia	23	547,000	42
France	53	569,000	93
West Germany	61	344,752	177
Hungary	10	35,346	283
India	548	3,760,000	146
Iran	34	214,063	159
Italy	54	927,372	58
Japan	112	1,548,000	72
Kenya	15	4,756	3,154
Republic of Korea	35	320,471	109
Malaysia	10	7,036	1,421
Philippines	42	320,400	131
United Kingdom	56	262,501	213
United States	203	1,855,018	109

Source: Statistical Yearbook 1979–1980 (New York: United Nations, 1981), Table 165, pp. 705–706; Table 18, pp. 69–74; Table 134, pp. 404–415. Reprinted by permission.

them appropriate quantities. Wholesalers in Japan provide the basic wholesale functions but also share risk with retailers by providing financing, product development, and even occasional managerial and marketing skills.[3]

Retailers

Retailers are the last member of the consumer distribution channel. Retailers will purchase products for resale to consumers. The size and accessibility of retail channels varies greatly by country, as shown in Table 12.2. The population per retailer varies from a low of only 42 people per retailer in Colombia to 72 people in Japan, to 109 people in the United States, and to 3,154 people in Kenya. Although this data gives a general picture of the number of retailers and the population served per retailer, the data also varies by type of retailer. For example, a country may have an extremely large number of electronics retailers, but few bookstore retailers. Table 12.2 shows that there is a great diversity in retailer

3. "Why Japanese Shoppers Are Lost in a Maze," *The Economist,* January 31, 1987, p. 62.

distribution systems from country to country. Until recently, all retailing in China was through state-owned stores. By the end of 1985, however, there were about 60,000 free-market retailers, and a rapid increase was expected.[4] The international marketer must evaluate the available retailers in a country and develop a strategy around that structure.

DEVELOPING AN INTERNATIONAL DISTRIBUTION STRATEGY

The environmental variables of culture, physical environment, and the legal/political system combined with the unique structure of wholesale and retail distribution systems complicate the development of an international distribution strategy. A distribution strategy is one part of the marketing mix, and it needs to be consistent with other aspects of the marketing strategy. The distribution strategy must be consistent with product policies, pricing strategy, and communications strategy (see Figure 12.3).

Within the structure of the marketing mix, the international marketer makes the following distribution decisions:

1. *Distribution Density*. Density refers to the amount of exposure or coverage desired for a product, particularly the number of sales outlets required to provide for adequate coverage of the entire market.
2. *Channel Length*. The concept of channel length involves the number of intermediaries involved in bringing a given product to the market.
3. *Channel Alignment and Leadership*. The area of alignment deals with the structure of the chosen channel members to achieve a unified strategy.
4. *Distribution Logistics*. Logistics involves the physical flow of products as they move through the channel.

These four major decision areas cannot be approached independently. The decisions are interrelated, and they need to be consistent with other aspects of the marketing strategy. The following sections deal primarily with a company's distribution policies, their dependency on distribution-specific variables, and their relationship to the other elements of the marketing strategy.

Distribution Density

The number of sales outlets or distribution points required for the efficient marketing of a firm's products is referred to as the density of distribution. The

---

4. Heidi Vernon-Wortzel and Lawrence H. Wortzel, "The Emergence of Free Market Retailing in China," *California Management Review,* Spring 1987, pp. 59–76.

FIGURE 12.3 Distribution Policies

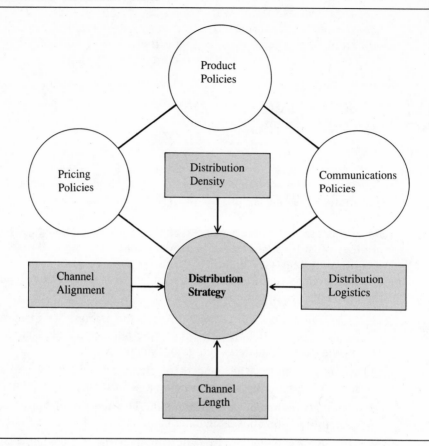

density is dependent on the shopping or buying habits of the average customer. For consumer goods, an extensive or wide distribution is required if the consumer is not likely to exert much shopping effort. Such products, also called convenience goods, are bought frequently in nearby outlets. Other products, such as appliances or clothing, are shopped for by visiting two or more stores; and these require a more limited or selective distribution, with fewer outlets per market area. For products that inspire consumer loyalty to specific brands, called specialty goods, a very limited or *exclusive* distribution is required. It is assumed that the customer will search for the product desired and is willing to stop at several places until the item is located.

The key to distribution density then is the consumer's shopping behavior, the expended effort to locate a desired item. This behavior, however, may vary substantially from country to country. In the United States, for example, where per capita income is much higher than in many other countries, consumers shop for many regular-use items in supermarkets and other widely accessible outlets, such as drugstores. In other countries, particularly for some with a much lower per-capita income, the purchase of such items may be a less routine affair, causing consumers to exert more effort to locate such items. This would lead to a less extensive distribution of products. It is therefore necessary for the international marketer to assess the shopping behavior of various countries' consumers.

In the industrial sector, differences in buyer behavior or the use of a particular product may require changes in distribution density. Since industrial products applications are more uniform around the world due to the similarity in application and use conditions, what constitutes capital equipment in one country typically is also classified as capital equipment in another nation. Differences might exist, however, among the decision makers. In the United States, for instance, radiology supply products are sold directly to hospitals and radiology departments through hospital supply distributors. In France, however, patients must pick up radiology supplies, by prescription, from a pharmacy before visiting the radiology department at the hospital. In this latter case, radiology supplies have to be presold to physicians and stocked with pharmacies to be successful. This is the same strategy pursued by pharmaceutical firms. Of course, when selling to both physicians and pharmacies, the necessary distribution in France is much more extensive than it is in the United States where only hospitals need to be contacted.[5]

Channel Length

The number of intermediaries directly involved in the physical and/or ownership path of a product from the manufacturer to the customer is indicative of the channel length. Long channels have several intermediaries, whereas short or direct channels have few or no intermediaries. Channel length is usually influenced by three factors: (1) a product's distribution density, (2) the average order quantities, and (3) the availability of channel members. Products with extensive distribution, or large numbers of final sales points, tend to have longer channels of distribution. Similarly, as the average order quantity decreases, products move through longer channels to add to the distribution efficiency.

Since distribution density does affect channel length, it is clear that the same factors that influence distribution density influence channel length; namely, the shopping behaviors of customers. The average order quantity often depends on the purchase power or income level of a given customer group. In countries with lower income levels, people often buy food on a daily basis at nearby small stores. This contrasts substantially with more affluent consumers who can afford to buy food or staples for one week, or even a month, and who don't mind

5. Warren J. Keegan, *Multinational Marketing Management* (Englewood Cliffs, N.J.: Prentice-Hall, 1974), p. 175.

traveling some distance to do this more infrequent type of shopping. In the first case, a longer channel would be required, whereas a shorter channel would be adequate in the latter case. The type of distributors available in a country will affect the channel length. Also, the culture may demand a specific type of channel member.

Channel Alignment

One of the most difficult tasks of marketing is to get various channel members to coordinate their actions so that a unified approach can be achieved. The longer the channel, the more difficult it becomes to maintain a coordinated and integrated approach. On an international level, the coordinating task is made all the more difficult since the company organizing the channel may be removed by large distances from the distribution system, with little influence over the local scene. In each country, the strongest channel member will be able to dictate policies to the other channel members, though situations will vary by country. The MNC will find it much easier to control the distribution channel if a local subsidiary with a strong sales force exists. In countries where the MNC has no local presence and depends on independent distributors, control is likely to slip to the independent distributor. This loss of control may be further aggravated if the international company's sales volume represents only a small fraction of the local distributor's business. Of course, the opposite would be true when a high percentage of the volume consists of the international corporation's products.

To achieve maximum efficiency in a channel of distribution, one participant emerges as the channel captain, or dominating member. Differences exist among countries as to who typically emerges as the dominating member. In the United States, for example, the originally strong wholesalers have become less influential, with manufacturers playing the dominant role in many channels. In Japan, on the other hand, wholesalers continue to dominate the channel structure. In many developing countries, independent distributors are very strong because they are the only authorized importers.

The structuring of the channel relationships is a key issue and of particular concern to marketers. The relationships are usually structured to form an integrated unit, a vertical marketing system (VMS), by selecting any of three major organizational forms: a corporate VMS under one single ownership, an administered VMS under the dominating channel captain, and a contractual VMS through formal cooperation agreements by the independent channel members. The international marketer will analyze each country with respect to the best operating mode, recognizing that it may be impossible to pursue the same strategy in all countries.

The international company used to its usual distribution arrangements in the domestic market often faces the problem of how to adapt the channel to foreign market situations. One U.S. company that abandoned its customary arrangement when entering Japan was the cosmetic firm Max Factor. Franchised corners were opened in large department stores or specialty shops with generous advertising and sales help from the company. The use of a multistage Japanese wholesale channel supported this strategy, which was patterned after the leading Japanese competitors Shiseido and Kanebo.[6] This strategy allowed Max Factor to far outdistance any foreign competitors in Japan. A different approach was chosen by Caterpillar, the large U.S. manufacturer of earth-moving equipment, for its entry into Japan. At first, the company's joint venture partner, Mitsubishi, suggested marketing equipment through existing channels. (In Japan, the manufacturers sell through large trading houses who resell and provide financing to dealers. The dealers are relatively small and leave parts inventory and service to independent repair shops.) Caterpillar preferred to market its equipment through large independent dealers who not only sell but also service the equipment and maintain a sufficient parts inventory. Caterpillar thus implemented their traditional strategy in Japan, which turned out to be successful, and the operation quickly emerged as one of the leading earth-moving equipment manufacturers in Japan.

Distribution Logistics

Distribution logistics focuses on the physical movement of goods through the channels. An extremely important part of the distribution system, logistics will be discussed in detail later in the chapter.

FACTORS INFLUENCING THE SELECTION OF CHANNEL MEMBERS

After developing a distribution strategy, a marketer then needs to identify and select appropriate distribution partners who support the overall distribution strategy. This selection of distribution partners is an extremely important decision because often the partner will assume a portion or the entire marketing responsibility for a set of markets. Also the distribution partner will usually be involved in the physical movement (logistics) of products to the customers. Therefore, the success of a firm's international efforts are dependent on the partners it selects. A number of factors influence the selection of distribution partners. The factors that significantly affect selection are the following:

1. Cost
2. Capital Requirement
3. Product and Product Line
4. Control
5. Coverage

---

6. "Shiseido Will Set Up French Cosmetics Venture," *The Japan Economic Journal*, October 23, 1979, p. 12.

Cost

Channel costs fall into three categories, initial costs, maintenance costs, and logistics costs. The initial costs include all the costs of locating and setting up the channel, such as executive time and travel to locate and select channel members, cost of negotiating an agreement with channel members, and the capital cost of setting up the channel. The capital cost will be discussed separately in the next segment of this chapter. The maintenance cost of the channel includes the cost of the company's salespeople, sales managers, travel expenses, and the cost of auditing and controlling channel operations, local advertising expenses, and the profit margin of the middlemen. The logistical costs include the transportation cost, storage costs, breaking bulk shipments into smaller lot sizes, and customs paper work.

Although it is often difficult to predict all of these various costs when selecting different channel members, it is necessary to estimate the cost of various alternatives. High distribution costs usually result in higher prices at the consumer level, which may hamper entry into a new market. Companies often will establish direct channels, hoping to reduce distribution cost. Unfortunately, most of the functions of the channel cannot be eliminated, so these costs show up later. A study of five different international channels of distribution found that the least profitable was exporting directly to the retailers in the host country. The most profitable channel was selling to a distributor in a country that had its own marketing channels.[7]

Capital Cost

The capital cost of different channel alternatives can be very high. The capital costs include the cost for inventories, cost of goods in transit, accounts receivable, and inventories on consignment. The capital costs will be offset by the cash flow patterns from a channel alternative. For example, an import distributor will often pay for the goods when received, before they are sold to the retailer or industrial firm. On the other hand, an agent may not receive payment until the goods reach the industrial customer or retailer. This is also true of direct sales efforts. The establishment of a direct sales channel often requires the maximum investment, whereas use of distributors often reduces the investment required. Capital costs of various distribution channels will affect the company's return on investment.

7. Warren J. Bilkey, "Variables Associated with Export Profitability," presented at the 1980 Academy of International Business Conference, New Orleans, October 23, 1980.

Product and Product Line

The nature of a product can affect channel selection. If the product is perishable or has a short shelf life, then the manufacturer will be forced to use shorter channels to get the product to the consumer quicker. A technical product will often require direct sales or highly technical channel partners. For example, a manufacturer of technologically advanced equipment to test silicon chips may use its own salespeople or use an agent with advanced electronics training. Nonperishable or generic, unsophisticated products that are available in many types of retail stores, such as batteries, may be distributed through a long channel that reaches many different types of retailers.

The size of the product line will also affect selection of channel members. A broader product line is more desirable for channel members. A distributor or dealer is more likely to stock a broad product line than a single item. Limited product lines often must be sold through agents. If a manufacturer has a very broad, complete line, it is easier to justify the cost of a more direct channel. With more products to sell, it is easier to generate a high average order on each sales call. With a limited product line, an agent or distributor will group your product together with products from other companies to increase the average order size.

Control

Each type of channel arrangement offers a different level of control by the manufacturer. With a direct sales force a manufacturer can control price, promotion, the amount of effort, and the type of retail outlet used. If these are important, the increased level of control may offset the increased cost of a direct sales force. Longer channels, particularly with distributors who take title to goods, often result in little or no control. In many cases, a company may not know who is ultimately buying the product.

Limited control is not necessarily bad, however. If the volume of sales is adequate, the manufacturer may not necessarily care where the product is being used. Also, a manufacturer can increase its level of market knowledge, its influence on channel members, and its channel control by increasing its presence in the market. For example, the manager of international sales and marketing may be located in Europe and spend all of his or her time traveling with distributor salespeople.

Coverage

Coverage refers to the geographic coverage that a manufacturer desires. Though it is usually easy to get coverage in major metropolitan areas, it can be difficult to gain adequate coverage of smaller cities or sparsely populated areas. Selection of one channel member over another may be influenced by the respective market coverage. To determine an agent, broker, or distributor's coverage the following must be determined: (1) location of sales offices, (2) salespersons' home base, and (3) last year's sales by geographic location. The location of sales offices will indicate where efforts are focused. Salespeople generally have the best penetration near their homes. Past sales clearly indicate the channel member's success in each geographic area.

LOCATING AND SELECTING CHANNEL PARTNERS

The process of building an international distribution system will normally take one to three years. The process involves a series of steps shown in Table 12.3. The critical aspect of developing a successful system is locating and selecting channel partners.

The development of an international distribution strategy in terms of distribution density, channel length, channel alignment, and distribution logistics will establish a framework for the "ideal" distribution partners. The company's preference regarding key factors that influence selection of channel partners (cost, capital requirements, product, control, and coverage) will be used with the distribution strategy to establish criteria for the selection of partners. The strategy will normally focus the selection on one or two types of channel partners; for example, export manager's company and import distributors.

Selection criteria will include geographic coverage, managerial ability, financial stability, annual volume, reputation, and so on. The following sources can be used to locate possible distribution partners:

1. *U.S. Department of Commerce.* The Agent/Distributor service is a customized service of the Department of Commerce that locates distributors and agents interested in a certain product line. Also, the Commerce Department's Export Marketing Service can be used to locate distribution partners.

2. *Banks.* If the firm's bank has foreign branches, they may be happy to help locate distributors.

3. *Directories.* Country directories of distributors or specialized directories, such as those listing computer distributors, can be helpful.

4. *Trade Shows.* Exhibiting at an international trade show or just attending will expose managers to a large number of distributors and their salespeople.

5. *Competitors' Distribution Partners.* Sometimes a competitor's distributor may be interested in switching product lines.

6. *Consultants.* Some international marketing consultants specialize in locating distributors.

7. *Associations.* There are associations of international middlemen or country associations of middlemen. For example, Japan has numerous industry associations.

TABLE 12.3 Process of Establishing an International Distribution System

1. Develop distribution strategy.
2. Establish criteria for selecting distribution partners.
3. Locate potential distribution partners.
4. Solicit the interest of distributors.
5. Screen and select distribution partners.
6. Negotiate agreements.

8. *Foreign Consulates.* Most countries have a commercial attaché at their embassies or a separate consulate, both of which are helpful in locating agents/distributors in their country.

After compiling a list of possible distribution partners, a letter might be sent to each with product literature and distribution requirements. The prospective distributors could be asked to respond if they have an interest in the firm's product line, with relevant information such as lines currently carried, annual volume, number of salespeople, geographic territory covered, credit and bank references, physical facilities, relationship with local government, and knowledge of English or other relevant languages.[8] The firms that respond should be checked against the selection criteria. Before making a final decision, a manufacturer's representative should go to the country and talk to the industrial end-users or retailers to determine the best two or three distributors.[9] Also, while in the country, the manufacturer's representative should meet and evaluate the possible distribution partners before making a final decision.

MANAGING THE DISTRIBUTION SYSTEM

Selecting the most suitable channel participants and gaining access to the market are extremely important steps in achieving an integrated and responsive distribution channel. However, without proper motivation and control over that channel, sales may remain unsatisfactory to the foreign marketer. The following sections discuss the steps that must be taken to ensure the flow of the firm's products through the channel by gaining the full cooperation of all channel members.

---

8. Root, *Entry Strategies for International Markets*, pp. 63–65.
9. G. Beeth, "Distributors—Finding and Keeping Good Ones," in *International Marketing Strategy*, ed. Hans Thorelli and Helmut Becker (New York: Pergamon Press, 1980), p. 261.

Motivating Channel Participants

Keeping channel participants motivated is an important aspect of international distribution policies. Financial incentives in the form of higher-than-average gross margins can be a very powerful inducement, particularly for the management of independent distributors, wholesalers, or retailers. The expected gross margins will be influenced by the cultural history of that channel. For example, if a certain type of retailer usually gets a 50 percent margin and the firm offers 40 percent, the effort may be less than expected. Inviting channel members to annual conferences and introductions of new products is also effective. By extending help to the management of distributorships in areas such as inventory control, collections, advertising, and so on, goodwill can be gained that will later be of advantage to the international firm. Special programs may also be instituted to train or motivate the channel members' sales forces.

Programs to motivate foreign independent middlemen are likely to succeed if monetary incentives are considered along with efforts that help make the channel members more efficient and competitive. To have prosperous middlemen is, of course, in the interest of the international firm as well. These programs or policies are particularly important in the case of independent middlemen who distribute products on a nonexclusive basis. Often these middlemen are beleaguered by the principals of other products they carry; everyone is attempting to get the greatest possible attention from the distributor for their own purposes. The international firm must therefore have policies that make sure the channel members devote sufficient effort to its products.

The motivation of channel partners and the amount of effort devoted to the firm's product line is enhanced by a continuous flow of two-way information between the manufacturer and distributor. The amount of effort an MNC will need to expend will depend on the marketing strategy for that market. For example, if the MNC is using extensive advertising to pull products through a channel, the middleman may be expected only to take orders and deliver the product with no real sales effort. If the marketing strategy is dependent on the channel member developing the market and/or pushing the product through the channel, then a significant sales effort will be required. As much as possible, the manufacturer should send letters, public relations releases, product news, and so on to encourage attention to its product line and reduce conflict. A study of manufacturer-distributor relationships found that more intense contact between the export manufacturer and the distributor resulted in better performance by the distributor.[10]

In addition to telephone and mail communication, periodic visits to distribution partners can have a positive effect on their motivation and control. Visits

---

10. Philip J. Rosson and I. David Ford, *Manufacturer-Overseas Distributor Relations and Export Performance,* presented at the 1980 Academy of International Business Conference, New Orleans, October 1980, p. 10.

can provide other benefits as well. By visiting the distribution partner, any difficulties can be resolved. Also, sales volumes can be reviewed and emphasis placed on the most important products and/or types of customers. Often it is helpful to travel with a channel member salesperson to gain knowledge of the marketplace and to evaluate the skills of the salesperson. The most important benefit of a visit to the channel member is that it gives a clear message that the member's performance is important to the firm. Visits strengthen the personal relationship between the manufacturer and the channel member.

During these personal visits, the manufacturer can identify other ways to help and support the channel member. Strong advertising support either through national advertising or cooperative advertising can help strengthen the manufacturer's consumer franchise. Effective advertising will make it easier for the channel member to sell the manufacturer's products, which leads to increased sales and often more attention devoted to the product line.

The training of the channel partners' managers, salespeople, and service personnel can also lead to obtaining increased cooperation. For example, an international firm with distributors throughout Latin America can hold a Latin-American regional meeting to train the distributors, introduce new products, confirm pricing policies, and build overall distributor-manufacturer relations.

Controlling Channel Participants

Although motivated middlemen will expend the necessary effort on a international company's products, there is generally no assurance that these efforts will be channeled in the right direction. The company will, therefore, want to exert enough control over its channel members to help guarantee that they interpret and execute the company's marketing strategies. The firm wants to be sure that the local middlemen price the products according to the company's policies. The same could be said for sales, advertising, or service policies. Since the company's reputation in a local market could be tarnished due to the ineffective handling of local distribution by independent middlemen, international companies closely monitor the performance of local channel members.

One way to exert influence over the international channel members is to spell out the specific responsibilities of the middleman, including minimum annual sales, in the distribution agreement. Attainment of the sales goal would be required for renewal of the contract. Also, the awarding of exclusive distribution rights can be used to increase control over middlemen. Typically, the firm's business will be channeled through one middleman in a given geographic area only, raising its importance to the middleman. Frequently, such exclusive rights are coupled with a prohibition to carry directly competing products. Thus, a dependence is created on the part of the local middleman that tends to increase the leverage enjoyed by the firm. Ultimately, the firm could withdraw distribution rights, causing financial losses to the local agent or middleman. Many international companies limit the distribution rights to short time periods with periodic renewal. Caution is advised, however, since cancellation of distribution rights is frequently subject to local laws that do not allow a sudden termination.

Although termination of a distributor or agent for nonperformance is a relatively simple action in the United States, termination of international channel members can be very costly in many parts of the world. For example, in Honduras, termination of an agent can cost up to five times the annual gross profits plus the value of the agent's investment, plus all kinds of additional payments. In Belgium, termination compensation for agents and distributors includes the value of any goodwill, plus expenses in developing the business, plus the amount of compensation claimed by discharged employees who worked on the product line. The minimum termination notice is three months.[11] As you can see, the termination of a channel member can be a costly, painful process, which in almost all cases is governed by local laws that tend to protect and compensate the channel member.

GAINING ACCESS TO DISTRIBUTION CHANNELS

To actually gain access to distribution channels may well be the most formidable challenge in international marketing. Decisions on product designs, communications strategies, or pricing can be very complex and pose difficult choices at times. But once a company has made those choices, the implementation is more a question of diligence and follow-through. With respect to the access to distribution channels, any decisions taken by managers require the tacit agreement and cooperation of channel members. This poses some special challenges to international marketers that differ from the situations faced in other areas of marketing. This section is, therefore, aimed at illustrating alternatives to companies that, while offering an excellent product or service, encounter difficulties in convincing channel members to carry their products.

The "Locked-up" Channel

A channel is considered locked up when a newcomer cannot easily convince any channel member to participate despite the fact that both market and economic reasons would suggest otherwise. In the United States, channel members customarily decide on a case-by-case basis what products should be added or dropped from their line. Retailers typically select products that they expect to sell easily and in volume, and they can be expected to switch sources when better opportunities arise. Similarly, wholesalers and distributors compete for retail accounts or industrial users on economic terms. They can expect to entice

---

11. "Guidelines for Terminating Agents and Distributors." *The Export Advisor,* November 1981.

a prospective client to switch by buying from a new source if they can offer a better deal. Likewise, U.S. manufacturers compete for wholesale accounts with the expectation that channel members can be convinced to purchase from any given manufacturer if the offer exceeds those made by competitors. Consequently, the distribution system in the United States is characterized by open access to anyone. Decision making is based on economic considerations.

The U.S. experience, however, cannot necessarily be extended to other countries. In general, distribution systems elsewhere are less likely to make decisions on economic terms alone, and elements such as past association or personal contacts may surpass other considerations in the decision making process. This is particularly pronounced in Japan where relationships between manufacturers, wholesalers, and retailers are of a long-standing nature and do not allow channel participants to change allegiance quickly to another source because of a superior product or price. In Japan, channel members develop strong personal ties, and a sense of economic dependence develops. These close ties make it very difficult for any participant to break the long-standing relationship. In some cases, most existing wholesale or retail outlets may be committed in such a way that a newcomer to the market may not find qualified channel participants.

These cultural forces may not be the only influence in blocking a channel of distribution. Competitors, domestic or foreign, may try to obstruct the entry of a new company; or the members of a channel may not be willing to take any risks by pioneering unknown products. In all of these instances, the result is a locked-up channel that severely limits access to markets.

Not that U.S. manufacturers are entirely new to the situation of the locked-up channel. Marketers of consumer goods developed the pull-type communication strategy to circumvent nonresponsive channel members by concentrating advertising directly on consumers. Manufacturers of industrial products could usually make use of independent manufacturers' representatives or agents to gain quick access to users. To use the same strategies abroad requires equally free access to communications channels in other countries. However, this access is often restricted due to government regulations that forbid TV or radio advertising or allow only limited availability of these media to consumers. In the case of industrial markets, the frequent entry of new entrepreneurs as independent agents is also considerably less prevalent. With fewer chances to outflank nonresponsive channels abroad, international marketers have developed new approaches to the difficult situation of gaining access to distribution channels.

Piggybacking

When a company does not find any channel partners with sufficient interest to pioneer new products, the practice of piggybacking may offer a way out of the situation. Piggybacking is an arrangement with another company that sells to the same customer segment to take on the new products as if it were the manufacturer. The products retain the name of the manufacturer, and both partners normally sign a multi-year contract to provide for continuity. The new company is in essence "piggybacking" its products on the "shoulders" of the established company's sales force.

A Japanese manufacturer of soy sauce, Kikkoman, decided to piggyback on Del Monte's sales force for its entry into Mexico. The two companies had signed an earlier technical agreement allowing Kikkoman to sell Del Monte's tomato juice in Japan. Following Kikkoman's successful entry into the U.S. market, the company planned to enter several South American countries. The company also wanted to use Del Monte's existing strong retail sales network.[12] As a result of this move, Kikkoman was in a position to gain immediate distribution, a process that would have taken years to develop on its own.

Under a piggyback arrangement, the manufacturer retains control over marketing strategy, particularly pricing, positioning, and advertising. The partner acts as a "rented" sales force only. This is of course quite different from the private label strategy in which the manufacturer supplies a marketer who places its own brand name on the product.

Joint Ventures

As we discussed in Chapter 9, when two companies agree jointly to form a new legal entity, this is called a joint venture. Such operations have been quite common in the area of joint production. Our interest here is restricted to joint ventures in which distribution is the primary objective. Normally, such companies are formed between a local firm with existing market access and a foreign firm that would like to market its products in a country where it has no existing market access. One of the best ways to enter the Japanese market is a joint venture with a Japanese partner that is in a similar but not competitive field.[13] Many such joint ventures have been signed between Japanese firms and foreign companies eager to enter the Japanese market. Through access to the distribution channel, the Japanese partner either acted as a sales agent or opened the doors for the joint venture's sales force. Many such joint ventures expanded into production, though the original intention on the part of the foreign partner was clearly to gain access to the distribution system. The largest Japanese computer company, Fujitsu Ltd., chose the joint-venture route to expand its marketing operation. The company joined forces with the U.S. multinational, TRW, which had the largest independent network of electronic equipment service personnel available in the United States. The joint-venture company, TRW-Fujitsu Co., was 51 percent owned by Fujitsu and would market Fujitsu computers in the

---

12. "Kikkoman Is Due Actively to Sell Soy Sauce in Mexico in January," *The Japan Economic Journal,* November 6, 1979, p. 14.

13. "Beating the System," *The Economist,* January 31, 1987, p. 63.

United States. Using the joint-venture tie, Fujitsu got immediate access to a large service network.[14]

Original Equipment Manufacturers (OEM)

In a situation in which the international manufacturer signs a supply agreement with a domestic or local firm to sell the international manufacturer's products but under the established brand name of the local firm, the arrangement is termed an OEM agreement or private labeling (for consumer products). The foreign company uses the already existing distribution network of the local company, whereas the local company gains a chance to broaden its product lines.

The French automobile manufacturer Renault signed an OEM agreement with the U.S. truck builder Mack. The agreement provided that medium-duty diesel trucks built by Renault would be sold under the Mack name through Mack's more than 300 dealers. Due to fuel prices, U.S. truck operators have shown a preference for the diesel trucks that always were very popular in Europe. Recognizing the opportunity, Renault signed the agreement and got immediate access to a well-entrenched distribution system. This was much easier than building one from scratch. Furthermore, selecting a well-known U.S. partner was viewed as less costly than joining a foreign company attempting to enter the same segment. The agreement was solidified by Renault's purchase of 20 percent of Mack's equity. Mack, of course, received an already proven line of medium-duty diesel trucks, thus saving the costs that it would have taken to develop its own line.[15]

Japanese companies have been particularly adept in using the OEM strategy to build whole alliances of captive markets. Matsushita, for example, marketed a substantial portion of its video tape recorders (VTRs) through OEM arrangements with RCA, Magnavox, Sylvania, Curtis Mathes, and General Electric—all U.S. companies. Likewise, another Japanese VTR-producer, joint venture company distributed its products in Europe through Thorn (UK), Thompson-Brandt (France), Saba, Normende, and Telefunken (Germany). All of these OEMs sold joint venture company products under their own brand names.[16]

In the computer field, Japanese companies have adopted strategies that differ from those customarily chosen by computer manufacturers in the United States. Hitachi Ltd. entered the United States market as an OEM supplier to Intel Corp., which sold Hitachi's computers under Intel's own name. Following Intel Corp.'s financial difficulties in the late 1970s, Hitachi found a new sales ally in National Semiconductor Corp. and signed similar OEM agreements

14. "TRW: Fujitsu's Key to the U.S.," *Business Week,* May 19, 1980, p. 118.
15. "Signal Unit Plans to Sell Trucks of Renault Unit," *The Wall Street Journal,* July 27, 1978, p. 7.
16. Ibid.

with Olivetti of Italy, and Great Britain's International Computers Limited (ICL).[17]

Japan's largest computer manufacturer, Fujitsu Ltd., also entered the United States market in 1972 under an OEM contract with Amdahl Corp. by buying a minority equity interest in the U.S. company.[18] Though the company had signed a joint-venture agreement with TRW, Fujitsu continued to market its larger machines through Amdahl.[19] In Europe, Fujitsu's large computers were sold through Siemans A.G., a German multinational corporation that used the Fujitsu line to round out its own line of computers.

Distributing in foreign markets under OEM agreements has its dangers also. Since the local OEM will put its own label on the imported product, the international company does not get any access to local customers and therefore will find it difficult to achieve a strong identity in the market. This reliance on the local OEM can pose problems when the local company's performance declines. An excellent example is the situation faced by Mitsubishi International Corporation, a large Japanese automobile manufacturer that supplied Chrysler Corporation with small cars under an OEM agreement. With Chrysler's weak financial situation in 1983 to 1985, Mitsubishi would have preferred to sell its cars directly to the U.S. market under Mitsubishi's brand name. As long as the present agreement was in effect, Mitsubishi was prohibited from doing that and its fortune in the U.S. market would continue to depend on Chrysler's efforts. The OEM tie-up allows a company to reach a high volume more quickly by sacrificing independence and control over its own distribution system. Of course, a company selecting this route is partially motivated by the corresponding savings of expenses by not building its own distribution system.

Acquisitions

The acquisition of an existing company can give a foreign entrant immediate access to a distribution system. Although it requires a substantial amount of capital, operating results tend to be better than starting a new venture that often brings initial losses. It is often less important to find an acquisition candidate with a healthy financial outlook or top products than one with a good relationship to wholesale and retail outlets. A good example of the acquisition strategy to gain access to distribution channels was the purchase of General Motors Corp.'s Terex unit by IBH Holding, a German concern. IBH Holding was a conglomerate of ten construction equipment companies from Germany, Britain, and France.

---

17. "Hitachi and Fujitsu Step Up Their Computer Exports." *The Japan Economic Journal*, May 6, 1980, p. 9.

18. "Computers: Here Comes Fujitsu," *The New York Times*, November 16, 1980, Section 3, p. 1.

19. "TRW: Fujitsu's Key to the U.S.," p. 118.

While on the lookout for additional plant capacity, IBH Holding was primarily attracted to Terex for its worldwide distribution network of independent dealers. The German company sold the products of its European units through Terex's U.S. dealers. It also has attempted to have Terex's overseas distributors, whose sales consisted of only 50 percent of Terex products, drop competing lines to get additional distribution for its European products worldwide.[20]

Starting New Ventures

To build its own distribution system is not only costly but also requires patience and time. Aware of these risks, IVECO, a European truck manufacturer jointly owned by Italy's Fiat and Germany's Klockner-Humboldt-Deutz, first attempted to enter the U.S. market with an arrangement with a U.S. truck manufacturer. But an agreement could not be reached because IVECO refused to have its vehicles sold under an OEM contract allowing the U.S. company to put its own name on the trucks. When it started out on its own, the company began to realize the difficulty ahead. Each individual dealer had to be separately recruited and sales had to be limited to the eastern and southern part of the United States. To overcome its low profile, IVECO budgeted $2 million for an advertising campaign. The company accepted the fact that break-even volume would be at least two years away with the actual outcome uncertain.[21] Though this strategy is higher in initial risk, it offers a company the chance to eventually control its own distribution system.

A substantially different strategy was selected by the German cosmetics firm, Wella, in Japan. Confronted with a limited number of wholesalers that had long-standing ties to existing manufacturers and traditional retail outlets, the company decided to circumvent the established channels and to create its own access to the market. Instead of the traditional methods of selling cosmetics through department stores and specialized retailers, the German company concentrated on the large number of hairdressers and barbershops that bought cosmetics for their own use. Interested in expanding their income, these shop owners could be convinced to sell the cosmetics to their clients who would normally buy such products elsewhere. Backed by the image of manufacturing "the profession's" cosmetics, the company was able to build a distribution system independent of the competition. While such tactics may not always be applicable, there is no doubt that a creative or innovative approach can at times achieve better results than following traditional channels dominated by competitors.

20. "German Pursues Cachet in G.M. Deal," *The New York Times,* October 6, 1980, p. D4.
21. "A New Challenge in Trucks," *Business Week,* July 3, 1978, p. 88.

INTERNATIONAL LOGISTICS

The logistics system, also called physical distribution, involves planning, implementing, and controlling the physical flow of materials and final goods from points of origin to points of use to meet customer needs at a profit.[22] On an international scale, the task becomes more complex since so many external variables have an impact on that flow of materials or products. As geographical distances to foreign markets grow, competitive advantages are often derived from a more effective structuring of the logistics system, by either saving time, costs, or increasing a firm's reliability. The following sections deal with the objectives of an international logistics system and the individual organizational operations that have to be managed into an efficient system.

Determining Service Levels

The principal objective of the logistics system is to provide the service of dependable and efficient movement of materials and/or products to the user. Since any combination of logistics arrangements involve expenditures, the firm is urged to first determine the level of service desired before any implementation is made. The determination of these service levels is marketing management's responsibility and requires attention in four areas:

1. *To maximize the number of orders shipped compared to the number of orders received.* For most firms it is important to be able to ship products for orders received. It is generally accepted that a level of 100 percent is unrealistic since it would require the company to be prepared for all eventualities and would most likely result in high inventories. Marketing managers have to decide on an appropriate percentage given the existing competition, both here and abroad, and taking into consideration the delivery systems in the particular foreign market.

   Since it is not possible to fill all orders received, managers have to balance the costs of maintaining a sufficient inventory with the cost of lost business since clients may place orders elsewhere if delivery is not forthcoming immediately.

2. *To minimize the time between order submission and actual order shipment.* Aside from having the products physically on hand, the firm must reduce its reaction or order-filling time; there should be speedy delivery to customers. Any reduction of this order processing time results in a reduction of the client's inventory needs and can, therefore, be turned into a competitive

---

22. Philip Kotler, *Marketing Management,* 5th ed. (Englewood Cliffs: N.J.: Prentice-Hall, 1984), p. 591.

advantage. On an international level, it is unlikely that customers in all countries have the same expectation of this reaction time. Consequently, management has to pay special attention to local requirements or, where necessary, to ensure that orders submitted to one regional distribution center from different markets receive the necessary attention. It may not be feasible to have a unified or single policy for all markets.

3. *To minimize the variance between promised delivery and actual delivery.* Once a customer has been promised delivery by a set date, the customer will draw down on inventory in anticipation of the new delivery. Consequently, a delay could substantially affect the client's operation, maybe even cause a loss of orders. Minimizing the variance between promised and actual delivery does not always require the fastest mode of transportation. Reliability is the key. International logistics often involves various modes of transportation subject to unexpected occurrences that upset delivery schedules. The firm that manages to insulate its clients from such unexpected events can gain a substantial advantage over competitors.

4. *To minimize damage in transit.* Any shipment that reaches its destination in damaged form represents an opportunity loss to the buyer who planned for the arrival of the product. Even if an insurance settlement replaces the actual value of products damaged, the loss of business due to the absence of additional inventory cannot be replaced. International shipments are often subject to numerous adverse physical stresses due to long transit times, changes in climate, or numerous handling at ports for transshipments. Adequate protective packaging is therefore required and may far exceed standards for domestic shipments.[23]

Logistics Decision Areas

The total task of logistics management consists of five separate, though interrelated, jobs. The areas include

1. Traffic or transportation management
2. Inventory control
3. Order processing
4. Materials handling and warehousing
5. Fixed facilities location management

Each of these five jobs or decision areas offers unique challenges to the international marketer and is described below in more detail.

---

23. John F. Magee, "The Logistics of Distribution," *Harvard Business Review,* vol. 28, July–August 1960, pp. 89–101.

Traffic or Transportation Management

Traffic management deals primarily with the mode of transportation. Principal choices are air, sea, rail, or truck, or some combination thereof. Since transportation costs contribute substantially to the costs of marketing products internationally, special attention has to be given to the selection of the transportation mode. Such choices are made by considering three principal factors: lead times, transit times, and costs. Companies operating with long lead times tend to use slower, and therefore low-cost transportation modes such as sea or freight. For short lead-time situations, faster modes of transportation such as air or truck are used. Also important are transit times. Long transit times require higher financial costs since payments arrive later, and there are normally higher average inventories at either the point of origin or destination. Modes of transportation with long transit times are of course sea or rail, whereas air and truck transportation result in much shorter transit times. Costs are the third factor considered for the decision of a mode of transport. Typically, air and truck transportation are more expensive than either sea or rail for any given distance.

In order to obtain the best results, traffic managers will weigh all three factors of lead time, transit time, and costs. The choice of a given transportation method depends not only on the actual freight charges but also on the working capital tied up in the process. To ensure that the most economical approach is adopted, alternative transportation routes have to be fully costed out and compared. The cost advantage enjoyed by any given method of transportation can change over time due to changes in transportation rates, government regulations, and containerization technology.

In recent years, the job of a traffic manager in an international or multinational corporation requires dealing with what sometimes may appear as insurmountable problems. Strikes, revolutions, or the outbreak of war can cause severe bottlenecks with badly needed products blocked for long periods of time. Even more common are large traffic tie-ups that cause monumental delays in shipments. In 1975, Nigerian authorities had ordered large quantities of cement from overseas suppliers to be used for the country's large development needs.[24] With its ports unable to handle this traffic efficiently, huge tie-ups developed, with some 400 ships reportedly awaiting unloading. The delay in unloading was estimated at 450 days, causing shippers excessive additional demurrage charges for vessels waiting to be unloaded. Similar chronic problems occurred in the mid-1970s at Saudi Arabia's main port Jiddah.[25] Delays in Middle Eastern ports were caused by the massive boom in imports of materials used in the drive for industrial development by these countries. To avoid such delays, some compa-

---

24. "Nigeria Setting Its Own Rules for Banking and Trade," *Business Week,* November 3, 1975, p. 40.
25. "Easing the Jam-Up in Arabian Ports," *Business Week,* January 10, 1977, p. 27.

nies have switched to more expensive air freight or overland truck routes for Europe to Persian Gulf ports.

Problems with overloaded ports or transportation facilities can be found even in such developed countries as the United States. With coal again in great demand worldwide, U.S. coal exporters were restricted in their export shipments by bottlenecks in major ports.[26] With volumes of 90 million tons in 1980 and 110 million tons in 1985, U.S. coal exporters decided it was in their own best interest to expand port facilities. In 1980 alone, foreign customers paid about $1 million for waiting charges to foreign vessels waiting to load coal. At the beginning of 1981, about 150 coal transport vessels waited at one Virginia port for an average delay of 60 to 70 days. If U.S. producers cannot guarantee speedier unloading, foreign customers may turn to other suppliers in Canada, South Africa, or Australia.

Inventory Control

The level of inventory on hand substantially affects the service level of a firm's logistics system. Due to the substantial costs of tied-up capital, inventory is reduced to the minimum level needed. In international operations, adequate inventories are needed as insurance against unexpected breakdowns in the logistics system. As a result, these inventory levels often exceed requirements for domestic operations.

Order Processing

Since rapid processing of orders shortens the order cycle and allows for lower safety stocks on the part of the client, this area becomes a central concern for logistics management. The available communications technology greatly influences the time it takes to process an order. Managers cannot expect to find perfectly working mail, telephones, or telex systems everywhere. Aside from the United States, Europe, and Japan, the communications systems are inferior and tend to delay order processing. In Europe, however, order processing tends to rely substantially on telex due to the greater difficulty of placing telephone calls across borders. To offer an efficient order processing system worldwide represents a considerable challenge to any company today. However, doing this can be turned to a competitive advantage since customers would reap added benefits from such a system.

---

26. "Inadequacy of U.S. Coal-Export Terminals Sparks Oil Money Push to Expand Capacity," *The Wall Street Journal,* February 27, 1981, p. 25.

Materials Handling and Warehousing

Throughout the logistics cycle, materials and products will have to be stored and prepared for moving or transportation. How these products are stored or moved is the principal concern of materials handling management. For international shipments, the shipping technology or quantities may be different, causing firms to adjust domestic policies to the circumstances. Warehousing in foreign countries involves dealing with different climatic situations, and longer average storage periods may require changing warehousing practices. In general, international shipments often move through different transportation modes than domestic shipments. Substantial logistics costs can be saved if the firm adjusts shipping arrangements according to the prevalent handling procedures abroad.

Fixed Facilities Location Management

The crucial facilities to the logistics flow are, of course, production facilities and warehouses. To serve customers worldwide and to maximize the efficiency of the total logistics system, production facilities may have to be placed in several countries. In doing this, there is a tradeoff between economies of scale and savings in logistics costs. At times, an advantage can be gained from shipping raw materials or semiprocessed products to a market for further processing and manufacture instead of supplying the finished product. These advantages arise from varying transportation costs for given freight modes or from different rates for each product category. Some companies compare the costs for several operational alternatives before making a final decision. The location of warehousing facilities greatly affects the company's ability to respond to orders once received or processed. A company with warehouses in every country where it does business would have a natural advantage in delivery, but such a system would greatly increase the costs of warehousing and, most likely, the required level of inventory systemwide. A balance is thus sought that still satisfies the customer's requirements on delivery and at the same time reduces overall logistics costs.

Managing the International Logistics System

The objectives of a firm's international logistics system are to meet the company's service levels at the lowest cost. Costs are understood as total costs covering all five decision areas. Consequently, a company has to combine cost information into one overall budget typically involving many departments from several countries. The key to effective management is coordination. A situation in which managers all try to reduce costs in their individual areas would either reduce the service levels provided or force other areas to make up for the initial reduction by possibly spending more than the original savings. Consequently, companies have to look carefully at opportunities to save in one area by comparing additional costs accruing in another. This process of comparison has caused some managers to call logistics tradeoff management.

With markets becoming more scattered and dispersed over numerous countries, the opportunities for competitive advantages in international logistics grow. The firms that manage to combine the various logistics areas under the responsibility of one manager have a chance at achieving either substantial cost savings or an enhancement of their marketing position by increasing service levels at minimum costs.

WORLD TRENDS IN DISTRIBUTION SYSTEMS

Distribution systems throughout the world are continually changing due to economic and social change. As a manager develops a worldwide distribution strategy he or she must consider not only the current state of distribution but also the expected state of distribution systems in the future. Five major trends seem dominant throughout the world: (1) the growth of larger scale retailers, (2) an increased number of international retailers, (3) the growth of direct marketing, (4) the spread of discounting, and (5) the development of strategic alliances to support a distribution strategy.

Growth of Larger Scale Retailers

There is a trend toward fewer and larger scale retailers. As countries become more economically developed, they seem to follow the pattern of the United States with fewer, larger stores. Three factors that contribute toward this trend are increased car ownership, increased number of households with refrigerators and freezers, and the growth in the number of working wives.[27] Although the European housewife twenty years ago may have shopped two or three times per day in local stores, the transportation capacity, refrigerator capacity, cash flow, and reduced availability of shopping time have increased one-stop shopping in supermarkets. The reduction in the number of grocery stores per 1,000 people is shown in Table 12.4.

With the exception of Brazil and Japan, the number of grocery stores per person declined between 1970 and 1979. The increased size of retailers, along with the reduction of the number of small retailers, reduces the cost of distribution and increases the sophistication of retailers.

---

27. Stanley R. Hill, ''Distribution in Britain—The Next Ten Years,'' *Journal of Retailing,* Summer 1974, pp. 23–30.

TABLE 12.4 Number of Grocery Stores per 1,000 Inhabitants in Different Countries

Country	1970	1979
Australia	1.2	.7
United States	1.1	.8
South Africa	1.3	1.0
Netherlands, The	1.3	1.0
Sweden	1.7	1.1
Canada	1.7	1.3
Great Britain	2.1	1.3
New Zealand	1.7	1.4
Switzerland	2.4	1.5
Germany, Federal Republic of	2.8	1.6
France	2.7	1.8
Austria	2.7	1.9
Brazil	1.9	2.0
Belgium	3.6	2.1
Japan	1.4	2.2
Ireland	5.9	2.6
Mexico	3.2	3.1
Spain	3.9	3.2
Portugal	5.7	4.5

Source: E. Dichtl and G. Finck, "Public Policy Towards Distribution in the Federal Republic of Germany," Institut fur Marketing, Universitat Mannheim, 1982, p. 6. Reprinted by permission.

Retail concentration is increasing in most countries. Between 1980 and 1984, chains and cooperatives increased their total share of grocery trade from 75 percent to 81 percent in Britain, from 58 percent to 67 percent in West Germany, and from 44 percent to 60 percent in Holland. During the same period, the chains and cooperatives stayed at 69 percent in the United States and 43 percent in Japan.[28]

International Retailers

There has been a growth in the number of international retailers. Most of these international retailers originate in advanced industrial countries and spread to the developed countries of the world. For example, Sears, Roebuck

28. "Retailing: Grocer Power," The Economist, January 10, 1987, p. 56.

and Company is now in Mexico, South America, Spain, and Japan; Walgreen Co. is in Mexico; Tandy Corporation is in Belgium, the Netherlands, Germany, the United Kingdom, and France. The internationalization of retailing includes firms originating in the United States, Canada, France, Germany, and Japan. This trend toward international retailers allows manufacturers to build relationships with retailers who are active in a number of markets.

Direct Marketing

Selling directly to the consumer by telephone, mail, or door-to-door grew to a $150 billion industry in 1985, almost triple the $60 billion it made in 1975 in the United States. There is also a growth of direct marketing around the world. Direct marketing generated $10 billion in West Germany, $3 billion in France, $3 billion in the United Kingdom, and $2.4 billion in Japan.[29] Avon had an Asian sales force of 10,000 salespeople in 1981, selling more than $200 million in cosmetics directly to the consumer.[30] The increased affluence of consumers in developed countries, a reduction in the amount of time devoted to shopping, changing lifestyles, increased acceptance of credit cards, and improved postal and telephone services have all contributed to the growth in direct marketing.

Discounting

The growth of international brands having strong consumer support due to advertising has helped discounting become a major international force. Also, the elimination of required list prices has contributed to a growth in discounting. Innovative retailers have used price reductions with limited high volume assortments to develop successful discount stores.

CONCLUSIONS

To be successful in the marketplace, a company needs market acceptance among buyers and market access via distribution channels. Companies entering foreign markets often do so without substantial acceptance initially. Consequently, the company must guarantee some degree of market access either through effective marketing programs or sheer financial strength. To achieve access the firm must select the most suitable members or actors of a channel, keeping in mind that

29. "Direct Marketing Is Gaining Impetus for a Number of Reasons," *Business International,* July 17, 1981, pp. 225–228.
30. "Business Briefs," *World Press Review,* February 1981, p. 55.

substantial differences exist among countries both on the wholesale and retail levels. Proper distribution policies have to allow for the local market's buying or shopping habits. A company should not expect to be able to use the same distribution density, channel alignment, or channel length in all its markets. The logistics system must reflect both local market situations and additional difficulties due to longer distances. To actually find willing and suitable channel members may be extremely difficult; access might only be achieved by forging special alliances with present channel members or local companies with access to them. Once the distribution system has been designed, participants still have to be motivated and controlled to assure that the firm's marketing strategy is properly executed.

Questions for Discussion

1. Your firm is just beginning to export printing equipment. How would you assess the decision to use an export management company or an export agent versus direct exporting?
2. What are the key elements of a distribution strategy?
3. If you enter a new marketplace and decide to distribute the product directly to the consumer, what are the types of costs you will incur?
4. You have been assigned the task of selecting distributors to handle your firm's line of car batteries. What criteria will you use to select among the twenty possible distributors?
5. The performance of your agents and distributors in South America has been poor over the past three years. How will you improve the management of these agents and distributors?
6. What are the elements of an international logistics system, and how will they differ from a domestic logistics system?
7. Your firm has just entered the South Korean market for automobile parts. The major distributor is owned by a competitive manufacturer of automobile parts. What strategies could you use to gain access to this market?
8. Given the trends in distribution, what distribution strategies should a world-wide manufacturer of women's clothing consider?

For Further Reading

Bagley, Barbara J. "Packaging Goods for International Shipment." *Traffic Management* (April 1977), p. 56.

Bello, Daniel C., and Lee D. Dahringer. "The Influence of Country and Product on Retailer Practices." *International Marketing Review* (Summer 1985), pp. 45–52.

Brasch, John J. "Export Management Companies." *Journal of International Business Studies* (Spring-Summer 1978), pp. 59–72.

Czinkota, Michael R. "Distribution of Consumer Products in Japan." *International Marketing Review* (Autumn 1985), pp. 39–51.

Dholakia, Nikhilesh, and R. R. Dholakia. "A Comparative View of Public Policy Toward Distribution." *European Journal of Marketing,* 12, No. 8 (1978), pp. 541–552.

Hall, R. Duane, and Ralph J. Gilbert. *Multinational Distribution: Channel, Tax and Legal Strategies.* New York: Praeger, 1985.

Kacker, Madhav P. *Transatlantic Trends in Retailing.* Westport, Conn.: Quorum Books, 1985.

Kaynak, Edener. "The Global Spread of Supermarkets: The Case of Turkey." In *Global Perspectives in Marketing.* Ed. Edener Kaynak. New York: Praeger, 1985.

"Law and Rulings." *Modern Packaging* (July 1975), p. 55.

McIntyre, David R. "Your Overseas Distributor Action Plan." *Journal of Marketing* (April 1977), pp. 88–90.

Perlmutter, Howard W., and David A. Heenan. "Cooperate to Compete Globally." *Harvard Business Review* (March-April 1986), pp. 136–152.

Rosson, Philip J., and I. David Ford. "Manufacturer-Overseas Distributor Relations and Export Performance." *Journal of International Business Studies* (Fall 1982), pp. 57–72.

Samli, A. Coskun. "Wholesaling in an Economy of Scarcity: Turkey." *Journal of Marketing* (July 1964), pp. 55–61.

"Selecting Sales and Distribution Channels." In *International Marketing: Managerial Perspectives* Ed. Subhash C. Jain and Lewis R. Tucker, Jr. Boston: CBI Publishing Co., 1979, p. 302.

Shimaguchi, Mitysuaki, and Larry J. Rosenberg. "Demystifying Japanese Distribution." *Columbia Journal of World Business* (Spring 1979), pp. 32–41.

Stock, James R., and Douglas M. Lambert. "Physical Distribution Management in International Marketing." *International Marketing Review* (Autumn 1983), pp. 28–41.

13.
PRICING FOR INTERNATIONAL MARKETS

The purpose of this chapter is to give an overview of the key factors that affect pricing policies in an international environment. We assume that you are already aware of the basic pricing decisions that companies must make in a single-country or domestic environment. In this chapter we concentrate exclusively on the unique aspects of international pricing. (See Figure 13.1 for a chapter overview.)

The material is organized around four major issues. First we look at internal factors and company policies as they impact on international pricing policies. Key concerns will be costs and how they affect price determination. The second section is devoted to the market factors companies must consider in setting prices, such as competition and the income levels of various countries. The third segment focuses on the environmental variables, such as foreign exchange rates, inflation, and legal constraints, that are not controlled by individual firms but that play an important role in shaping pricing policies. The chapter ends with a section on managerial issues, such as transfer pricing and price arbitrage—issues of great concern to companies active internationally.

COMPANY INTERNAL FACTORS

Most companies begin pricing deliberations based on their own internal cost structure. It therefore makes sense to look first at internal cost before considering other issues. Included under internal factors are profits, and the requirement for profits, as they impact internal pricing procedures. Also of concern to us are international transfer costs, such as tariffs, transportation, insurance, taxes, and local channel costs.

FIGURE 13.1 International Pricing Strategies

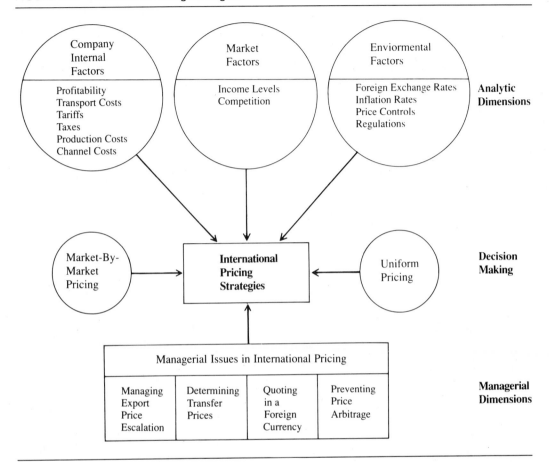

Such costs frequently make exported products more expensive than domestic ones; and this fact must be taken into consideration if a company wants to compete effectively. However, such costs do not have to be taken as given. Companies can, through various actions, affect the level of these costs. It is the purpose of this section to point out the options available to companies in managing their international costs.

Profit and Cost Factors

The basis for any effective pricing policy is a clear understanding of the cost and profit variables involved. Experience shows that a clear definition of relevant costs or of profits is often difficult to achieve. On the other hand, the field of

TABLE 13.1 Profit and Cost Calculation for Western Machine Tool, Inc.

Selling price (per unit)		$60,000	
Direct manufacturing costs			
Labor	10,000		
Material	15,000		
Energy	1,000	$26,000	
Indirect manufacturing costs			
Supervision	5,000		
Research and development contribution	3,000		
Factory overhead	5,000	$13,000	
General administrative cost			
Sales and administrative overhead	10,000		
Marketing	5,000	$15,000	
Full costs			54,000
Net profit before tax			6,000

international marketing offers many examples of firms that have achieved substantial profits through flexible or nonconventional costing approaches. Understanding the various cost elements can therefore be considered a prerequisite for a successful international pricing strategy.

According to standard accounting practice, costs are divided into two categories: fixed and variable. Fixed costs do not vary over a given range of output, whereas variable costs change directly with output. The relationship of these variables is shown in Table 13.1 using a fictitious example, Western Machine Tool, Inc., a manufacturer of machine tools selling at $60,000 per unit in the U.S. market.

The total cost of a machine tool is $54,000. If it were sold at $60,000, the company would achieve a profit of $6,000 before taxes from the sale of each unit. However, if one additional unit were sold (or not sold), the marginal impact would not only amount to an additional profit of $6,000 (or loss of the same amount). Rather, the extra cost of an additional unit would be limited to its variable costs only, or $31,000, as shown in Table 13.2. For any additional unit sold, the marginal profit would be $29,000, or the amount in excess of the variable costs. This amount may also be referred to as the contribution margin.

An example may be used to illustrate the relationships between variable costs, fixed costs, and contribution margin. Our company, Western Machine Tool, Inc., had a chance to export a unit to a foreign country, but the maximum price the foreign buyer was willing to pay was $50,000. Machine Tool, Inc., using the full cost pricing method, might argue that the company would incur a loss of $4,000 if the deal were accepted. However, since only $31,000 of additional variable cost would be incurred for a new machine because all fixed costs are

TABLE 13.2 Marginal Profit Calculation for Western Machine Tool, Inc.

Selling Price (per unit)			$60,000
Variable costs			
Direct manufacturing costs			
Labor	10,000		
Material	15,000		
Energy	1,000	$26,000	
General administrative costs			
Marketing	5,000	5,000	
Total variable costs			$31,000
Contribution margin			$29,000
(Selling price minus Variable costs)			

incurred anyway and are covered by all prior units sold, the company could go ahead with the sale and claim a marginal profit of $19,000, using a contribution margin approach. In such a situation, a profitable sale might easily be turned down unless a company is fully informed about its cost composition.

Cost components are subject to change. By adding new output to a plant, such as new export volume, a company may achieve economies of scale that allow operation at lower costs, both domestically and abroad. Furthermore, as the experience curve indicates, companies with rapidly rising cumulative production may reap overall unit cost reductions at an increasing rate due to the higher output caused by exporting.[1]

Transportation Costs

International marketing often requires the shipment of products over longer distances than for purely domestic operations. Since all modes of transportation, rail, truck, air, or ocean, depend on a considerable amount of energy, the total cost of transportation has become an issue of growing concern to international companies. High technology products are less sensitive to transportation costs than standardized consumer products or commodities. In the latter case, the seller with the lowest transportation costs often has the advantage.

The following example demonstrates how the development of ocean freight rates affected the U.S. coal industry. In the late 1970s, a rush of orders from Europe sparked an increase in U.S. coal exports. United States producers wor-

---

1. For a detailed discussion of the experience curve concept, see Derek F. Abell and John S. Harmon, *Strategic Market Planning* (Englewood Cliffs, N.J.: Prentice-Hall, 1979), Chapter 3.

ried that the world coal trade, fueled by skyrocketing oil prices, would pass them by. The demand for Polish coal in the Soviet Union and to other Communist bloc nations forced coal-hungry Western European nations to look elsewhere for supplies. Coal from Australian mines had an edge in Western Europe. But a doubling of ocean freight rates hit Australian producers especially hard. Prices of Australian coal in Europe rose by more than 20 percent in six months to $48 per ton. Much to the delight of U.S. companies, this turned the Australian $5 to $6 per ton advantage over the U.S. coal price into a $3 to $4 per ton disadvantage. This was a major reason for the European rush to order U.S. coal.[2]

For commodities, low transportation costs can decide who gets an order. For expensive products, such as computers or sophisticated electronic instruments, transportation costs usually represent only a small fraction of total costs and rarely influence pricing decisions. For products between the two extremes, companies can substantially affect unit transportation costs by selecting new transportation methods. The introduction of container ocean vessels has made large scale shipment of many products possible. Roll-on-roll-off ships (ro-ro carriers) have reduced ocean freight for cars and trucks to very low levels, making exporters more competitive vis-à-vis local manufacturers. The international firm must thus continuously search for new transportation technologies to reduce unit transportation costs and thus enhance competitiveness.

Tariffs

When products are transported across national borders, tariffs have to be paid unless a special arrangement exists between the countries involved. Tariffs are usually levied on the landed costs of a product, which includes shipping to the importing country. Tariffs are usually assessed as a percentage of the value.

Tariff costs can have a rippling effect and increase prices considerably for the end-user. Middlemen, whether they are sales subsidiaries or independent distributors, tend to include any tariff costs in their costs of goods sold and add any operating margin on this amount. As a result, the impact on the final end-user price can be substantial whenever tariff rates are high.

Although tariffs have declined over recent years, they still influence pricing decisions in some countries. As we have seen in Chapter 9, to avoid paying high duties, companies have shipped components only and established local assembly operations because tariffs on components are frequently lower than on finished products. The automobile industry is a good example with the shipment of knocked-down cars to be assembled on the spot. Companies can reduce overall tariff costs by shifting the place of production. Such a move may be called for when tariffs are especially high.

---

2. "The New International Strategy for U.S. Coal," *Business Week,* October 29, 1979, p. 91.

TABLE 13.3 Rates for Value-Added Taxes (VAT) for Countries of the European Community

	VAT Rate	Percent
United Kingdom	Standard rate	0
	Luxury rate for nonessential goods	15.0
West Germany	Standard rate	13
	Reduced rate (some services and food products)	6.5
France	Standard rate	18.6
	Luxury rate (cars, jewelry, tobacco, etc.)	33.3
	Reduced rate (food, books, fertilizers, etc.)	5.5
Ireland	Standard rate	0
	Luxury rate (cars, radios, TVs)	23–35
	Reduced rate (foodstuffs, agricultural products)	0
	Reduced rate (fuel, services)	5
Italy	Standard rate	14
	Luxury rate	38
	Reduced rate (mass consumption goods, foodstuffs, pharmaceuticals, and other necessities)	8
Belgium	Standard rate	19
	Luxury rate	25
	Reduced rate (necessities)	6
	Intermediate rate (many services)	6–17
Luxembourg	Standard rate	12
	Reduced rate	3–6
Netherlands	Standard rate	19
	Reduced rate (necessities)	5

Source: Price Waterhouse Inc., *Country Publications*, January 1, 1984. Reprinted by permission.

Taxes

Local taxes imposed on imported products can also affect their landed cost. A variety of taxes may be imposed. One of the most common ones is the tax on value added (VAT) used by member countries of the European Community.

Each EC country sets its own value-added tax structure (see Table 13.3). Common to all, however, is a zero tax rate (or exemption) on exported goods. A company exporting from the Netherlands to Belgium would thus not have to pay any tax on the value added in the Netherlands. However, Belgian authorities would collect a tax on products shipped from the Netherlands at the Belgium rate. Merchandise shipped to any EC member country from a nonmember country, such as from the United States or Japan, will be assessed the VAT rate on landed costs in addition to any customs duties that may apply to those products.

Local Production Costs

Up to this point we have assumed that a company has only one production location, exporting from there to all other markets. However, most international firms manufacture products in several countries. In such cases, operating costs for raw materials, wages, energy, or financing may differ widely from country to country, allowing a firm to ship from a particularly advantageous location to reduce prices or costs. Increasingly, companies produce in a location that gives them an advantage in freight, tariffs, or other transfer costs. Consequently, judicious management of sourcing points may reduce product costs and thus result in added pricing flexibility.

Channel Costs

Channel costs are a function of channel length, gross margin, and logistics. Many countries operate with longer distribution channels than the United States, causing higher total costs and end-user prices because of additional layers of middlemen. Also, gross margins at the retail level tend to be higher outside the United States. Since the logistics system in a large number of countries is also less developed than that in the United States, logistics costs are also higher on a per unit basis. All of these factors add additional costs to a product marketed internationally.

Campbell Soup Company, a United States–based MNC, found that its retailers in the United Kingdom purchased soup in small quantities of twenty-four-can cases of assorted soups, requiring each can to be hand-picked for shipment. In the United States, the company sold to retailers in forty-eight-can cases of one variety purchased by the dozens or hundreds. To handle small purchases in England, the company had to add an additional level of distribution and new facilities. As a result, distribution costs were 30 percent higher than they were in the United States.[3]

3. Philip R. Cateora, *International Marketing,* 6th ed. (Homewood, Ill.: Irwin, 1987), p. 489.

MARKET FACTORS AFFECTING PRICING

Companies cannot establish pricing policies in a vacuum. Although cost information is essential, prices also have to reflect the realities of the marketplace. The challenge of pricing for international markets is the large number of local economic situations to be considered. Two factors stand out and must be analyzed in greater detail: income levels and competition.

Income Levels

The income level of a country's population determines the amount and type of goods and services bought. When detailed income data is not available, incomes are expressed by Gross National Product (GNP) divided by the total population. This measure, *GNP per capita,* is a surrogate measure for personal income and is used to compare income levels among countries. To do so, all GNPs have to be converted to the same currency. If you look back at Table 5.7, you'll see that GNP per capita figures for key countries were expressed in U.S. dollars. Since the U.S. dollar has fluctuated substantially over the years, GNP per capita figures of countries such as Switzerland, Germany, and Japan have fluctuated correspondingly when translated into U.S. currency, placing these countries at times ahead of the United States on a per capita income basis.

As a result of widely differing income and price levels, elasticity of demand for any given product can be expected to vary greatly. Countries with high income levels often display lower price elasticities for necessities such as food, shelter, or medical care. These lower elasticities in part reflect a lack of alternatives such as "doing it yourself," which forces buyers in these countries to purchase such goods even at higher prices. For example, in many countries with low income levels, a considerable part of the population has the additional alternatives of providing their own food or building their own shelters should they not have sufficient money to purchase products or services on a cash basis. Availability of such options increases price elasticity, as these consumers can more easily opt out of the cash economy than consumers in developed economies. International companies would theoretically set product price by considering the price elasticity in each country. However, there are forces at work that will not always allow this practice because prices might vary widely across several countries. The danger of disparate price levels is examined later in the pricing issues segment of this section.

Competition

The nature and size of competition can significantly affect price levels in any given market. A firm acting as the sole supplier of a product in a given market enjoys greater pricing flexibility. The opposite would be true if that same company had to compete against several other local or international firms. The number and type of competitors therefore greatly influence pricing strategy in any market.

Also important is the nature of the competition. Local competitors may have different cost structures from those of foreign MNCs, resulting in different prices. On the other hand, if all major competitors are MNCs based in the United States, cost similarities might equalize pricing policies. Market prices for the same product may vary from country to country, based on the competitive situation. Volkswagen in the 1970s priced cars shipped from Germany to the United States according to the prices of its U.S. competitors: General Motors, Ford, and Chrysler. As a result, the VW Rabbit sold in the United States for some time at a lower price than in Germany, despite the extra transportation and duty costs. This reversed after the dollar rose against the German mark in the early 1980s. Japanese automakers followed the same strategy by pricing their products relative to local competition.

Occasionally, price levels are manipulated by cartels or other agreements among local competitors. Cartels are forbidden under United States law, but many foreign governments allow cartels provided they do not injure the consumer. Cartels might be officially recognized by a local government or might consist of competitors following similar pricing practices. In general, new market entrants must decide whether to accept current price levels or to set price levels different from those of the established competition.

The cartel formed by Swiss chocolate manufacturers provides an excellent example of the type of arrangement that companies can legally enter abroad. Established in 1945 by the leading manufacturers of quality chocolate in Switzerland, the cartel specified rules to be followed by each member. Chocolate could not be sold to the trade below a mutually accepted minimum price. Retail margins and volume discounts were standardized. Maximum marketing expenditures as a percent of sales were also specified. The cartel was registered with the Swiss government, which considered the benefits of maintaining a sound chocolate industry more important than the resulting adverse impact on competition.[4]

The U.S. government has a very strict approach to cartels, and any similar cartel would be clearly against existing U.S. laws. Furthermore, U.S. companies might find themselves in violation of U.S. laws if they actively participated in any foreign cartel.

ENVIRONMENTAL FACTORS AFFECTING PRICE

We have thus far treated pricing as a matter of cost and market factors. A number of environmental factors also influence pricing on an international level.

---

4. John R. Kennedy, "Chocolate Division, Nestlé," IMEDE, Management Development Institute, Lausanne, Switzerland, 1977.

These external variables, uncontrolled by any individual company, include the general economic environment, foreign exchange, inflation, and government price controls. These factors restrict company decision-making authority and can become dominant concerns for country managers.

Exchange Rate Fluctuations

One of the most unpredictable factors affecting prices is foreign exchange rate movement. As the past decade has shown, world currencies can fluctuate over a short period of time. Major currencies such as the deutsche mark (Germany), yen (Japan), and franc (Switzerland) appreciated against the dollar between 1973 and 1980, followed by the opposite development in the early 1980s. In 1986 and 1987, the U.S. dollar declined again to reach record lows compared to other major trading currencies. First, products made in the U.S. became cheaper than those manufactured in other countries. In the early 1980s, however, U.S. products increased again in price because of the changed value of the dollar. Then, the steep decline of the U.S. dollar in 1986 made U.S. products more competitive again. In Chapter 2 we explained the reasons behind these foreign currency fluctuations.

Changing currency values widen existing price gaps among countries. When the British pound dropped rapidly against major European currencies, many Europeans, particularly the French, traveled to England to take advantage of price differentials of up to 40 percent.[5] Similar developments occurred in Latin America, particularly Buenos Aires, and in New York, where major department stores increased business with foreign tourists when the local currency dropped in value.

Though foreign exchange fluctuations can present new opportunities, they may also make operations more difficult, particularly for companies operating in countries with appreciating currencies. Retailers in Switzerland, where many consumer goods are imported from neighboring countries, found this to be true. When the Swiss franc increased in value by 20 to 50 percent against neighboring currencies in the late 1970s, Swiss consumers found they could buy German-made cars at lower prices in Germany than in Switzerland. Swiss car dealers continued to quote the same prices in Swiss francs, despite the much lower value of the German mark. Buying cars in Germany, Swiss consumers could get the full value of the currency change. Such *arbitrage,* the practice of taking advantage of different market prices for the same financial instrument in two different markets, usually causes a price decrease in the high-price country. This eventually was the case with automobile prices in Switzerland. How companies face these problems will be dealt with more specifically at the end of this chapter.

---

5. "Weakness of Pound Lures Tourists to England on One-Day Trips to Buy Inexpensive Products," *The Wall Street Journal,* August 26, 1976, p. 28.

Between 1981 and 1985, the dollar appreciated against foreign currencies, causing problems in terms of higher prices for some United States–based companies. The German mark traded at DM 2.15 per U.S. dollar in early 1981, as opposed to DM 3.30 in early 1985. Even if a U.S. exporter had kept prices stable in dollar terms, a German buyer would have experienced a price increase of about 50 percent. As a result, export volume for many U.S. companies dropped, as experienced by Mack Trucks when it competed against Mercedes trucks in several overseas markets.[6]

In order not to suffer reduced sales volumes, Millipore Corp. of Bedford, Massachusetts, a maker of equipment for chemical and electrical industries, decreased the export price of some of its United States–produced products, thus cutting its own profit margin. Millipore executives considered the future value of market share more important than the temporary reduction in profits.[7] On the other side of the Atlantic, Jaguar, the British maker of luxury cars, maintained U.S. dollar prices to U.S. customers and enjoyed a profit increase. This was because its costs were in British pounds, which had depreciated against the U.S. dollar over the same period.[8]

Since February of 1985, when the U.S. dollar had reached its highest level in years, U.S. currency has declined sharply changing the cost basis of many international firms. The decline of the U.S. dollar had been particularly steep against the currencies of the major European trading partners and Japan (see Table 13.4). Foreign companies selling in the United States have had to raise prices, although the price increases have averaged only about 5 percent across all imports (see Table 13.5).[9] United States exporters are eventually expected to profit from the lower value of the U.S. dollar.

Inflation Rates

The rate of inflation can affect product cost and may force a company to take specific action. Inflation rates have traditionally fluctuated over time and, more importantly, differ from country to country. In some cases, inflation rates have reached several hundred percent (see Table 13.6). When this happens, payment for products may be delayed for months, harming the economy because of the local currency's rapid loss of purchasing power. A company would have to use a LIFO (last-in-first-out) method of costing or, in the extreme, a FIFO (first-in-first-out) approach to protect itself from eroding purchasing power. A company can usually protect itself from rapid inflation if operating margins (gross margin,

---

6. "Strong U.S. Currency Gives Companies Here Competitive Problems," *The Wall Street Journal*, January 18, 1984, p. 1.

7. Ibid.

8. Ibid.

9. "Import Price Surge Foreseen," *The New York Times*, January 16, 1987, p. D1.

TABLE 13.4 United States Dollar Depreciation, February 1985–March 1986

Country	Change of Local Currency Versus the U.S. Dollar
Switzerland	+53%
W. Germany	+52%
France	+50%
Japan	+47%
UK	+42%
Italy	+39%
Sweden	+34%
Spain	+32%
Kuwait	+8%
Singapore	+5%
Australia	+2%
Taiwan	+1%
Hong Kong	0%
South Korea	−5%
Philippines	−12%
Nigeria	−14%
Israel	−49%
Mexico	−53%
Brazil	−72%

Source: "Economic Financial Indicators," The Economist, March 29, 1986, p. 90. © The Economist, distributed by Special Features. Reprinted by permission.

gross profit, net margin) remain constant combined with constant price adjustments, sometimes on a monthly basis.

In countries with extremely high inflation, companies may price in a stable currency, such as the U.S. dollar, and translate prices into local currencies on a daily basis.

Price Controls

In many countries government and regulatory agencies influence prices of products and services. Controls might be applied to an entire economy to combat inflation; or regulations may be applied only to specific industries, such as the Civil Aeronautics Board regulations for air fares in the United States (although they were phased out in the early 1980s). Cases in which price controls apply equally to all industries are often temporary or, as was the case in the United

TABLE 13.5 Prices of Imported Products in the United States

Product	January 1986	January 1987	Percent Change
BMW 528e	$26,280	$28,330	+7.8%
Toyota Camry	$ 9,378	$10,648	+13.5%
Seiko Man's Watch Model SPF-048	$ 115	$ 135	+17.4%
Seiko Woman's Watch Model STE-125	$ 150	$ 175	+16.7%
Canon Camera Sure Shot	$ 240	$ 275	+14.6%
Panasonic VCR	$ 299	$ 299	—
Sony Walkman WMF-100	$ 149.95	$ 179.95	+20%
French Wine Beaujolais Villages	$ 4.29	$ 4.99	+16.3%
French Cheese Roquefort	$ 7.49	$ 8.49	+13.4%

INDEX CHANGES FOR SAME PERIOD

Value of US$ vs. Deutsche Mark	−25%
Value of US$ vs. Japanese Yen	−24%

Source: From *The New York Times,* "Prices Rise as Dollar Falls," from January 16, 1987, p. D1. Copyright © 1987 by The New York Times Company. Adapted by permission.

States, of a voluntary nature. In other cases, price increases might only be permitted when a real improvement in a product or its quality has taken place.

Other measures may be taken to prevent excessive pricing by individual companies. One such case involved Hoffmann-LaRoche & Co., A.G., a large producer of drugs and vitamins located in Switzerland. The company had a monopoly in tranquilizers known under the brand names Valium and Librium. As a result, the British Monopolies Commission ordered the company in 1973 to reduce prices by 35 to 40 percent. Similar action was brought against Hoffmann-LaRoche by the German cartel office and by the Danish and Dutch governments. After years of litigation, Hoffmann-LaRoche was forced to reduce prices, even though the reductions were smaller than originally demanded. Higher courts, however, later rolled back all price concessions in these countries after Hoffmann-LaRoche filed suit. The Hoffmann-LaRoche experience indicates that MNCs cannot always make independent pricing decisions in each country.[10]

10. "The EEC Cracks Down on Price Discrimination," *Business Week,* December 7, 1981.

TABLE 13.6 Inflation Rates 1981–1982

North and South America	
United States	7.3%
Venezuela	11.5%
Mexico	76.6%
Brazil	202.0%
Chile	12.0%
Argentina	337.0%
Asia and Middle East	
Israel	261.0%
Iran	23.2%
Japan	3.2%
Singapore	4.2%
Thailand	14.0%
Korea (South)	5.3%
Africa	
Egypt	16.4%
Ghana	120.0%
Nigeria	23.0%
South Africa	16.9%
Europe	
Belgium	9.4%
Czechoslovakia	1.0%
Denmark	11.3%
Spain	16.5%
France	14.4%
West Germany	5.6%
Switzerland	6.0%
Yugoslavia	46.0%
United Kingdom	9.6%
Soviet Union	2.1%

Source: Euromonitor: European Marketing Data and Statistics, 1984; *Euromonitor: International Marketing Data and Statistics,* 1984; and *EIU: Quarterly Economic Review of USSR,* no. 3, 1984, p. 8.

Even in the European Community, where many aspects of the countries' economies are coordinated, methods of controlling prices for drugs may vary considerably. In the United Kingdom, drug prices are established through the Pharmaceutical Price Regulation Scheme (PPRS). Though companies are allowed to set prices for individual drugs, the government limits their overall profitability. However, company profit targets are established through confidential negotiations and are set differently for each company. Furthermore, the British National Health Service recently introduced price limits for drugs that qualify for customer reimbursement. In Italy, a similar restrictive list is used combined with price controls and varying levels of reimbursements. France uses a method of strict price controls to contain overall health costs, and West Germany also maintains a restrictive list for some drugs but otherwise lets the companies set their own prices. In the United States, by contrast, prices for some drugs are established through negotiations between the drug company, the federal government Medicare program, and several private insurance companies that reimburse their customers for drug costs. Otherwise, prices are set by the pharmaceutical companies, with most U.S. consumers paying out-of-pocket for their own drugs.[11]

As a result of widely differing pricing controls, wholesale pharmaceutical prices may vary by a factor of three among some European countries. In general, prices tend to be higher in countries with large pharmaceutical industries, such as Great Britain and West Germany, and lower in other countries, such as France or Italy. Due to the substantial price difference for some pharmaceuticals, some wholesalers of drugs have taken to the practice of buying some drugs in countries with low price levels and selling in countries with a higher level.[12]

Price controls are of special concern in countries with high inflation rates. To compensate for inflation, companies must raise prices periodically. In Brazil, the government publishes a consumer price index quarterly, and companies try to increase prices quarterly with the rate of inflation. With rates of inflation over 100 percent in 1984–1985, pricing flexibility is of great importance.

In Venezuela, prices on most products were strictly controlled until 1979. Controls were later relaxed except for essentials such as food and pharmaceuticals. Given Venezuela's 30 percent inflation at that time, some foreign companies had difficulties with this policy. Heinz de Venezuela, a subsidiary of H. J. Heinz Co., decided to hold back on a major expansion of its baby food business until it was allowed to raise prices again. Another U.S. firm, Wm. Underwood Co. of Westwood, Massachusetts, had not been able to raise prices on its popular Deviled Ham for ten years.[13]

---

11. "Schools Brief: A Regulatory Overdose," *The Economist,* October 18, 1986, p. 78.
12. Ibid.
13. "Venezuela Beckons Foreign Investors, But Credibility Gap Obstructs Reentry," *The Wall Street Journal,* December 31, 1980, p. 10.

Regulatory Factors: Dumping Regulations

The practice of selling a product at a price below actual costs is referred to as *dumping*. Most governments have adopted regulations that prevent dumping because of potential injuries to domestic manufacturers. Anti-dumping actions are allowed under Article 6 of the GATT as long as two criteria are met: "sales at less than fair value" and "material injury" to a domestic industry.[14] The first criterion is usually interpreted as selling abroad at prices below those in the country of origin. However, the GATT rules adopted in 1968 prohibit assessment of retroactive punitive duties and require all procedures to be open. The United States differs from GATT in its dumping regulations, determining "fair market value" and "material injury" sequentially rather than simultaneously. Also, the U.S. government will assess any duty retroactively and has on numerous occasions acted to prevent anti-dumping practices from injuring domestic manufacturers.

The U.S. government has taken anti-dumping actions on numerous occasions over the past decade. In 1978, the U.S. Treasury Department assessed $46 million in retroactive penalties against importers of Japanese TV sets for 1971 and 1972. Japanese exporters responded quickly by establishing their own manufacturing operations in the United States. Additional action was undertaken to protect the U.S. steel industry against dumping from foreign competitors.[15]

In July of 1986, the U.S. government signed a trade pact on semiconductor components covering the tiny electronic chips that are part of most electronic products. As a result of strong indications that the Japanese semiconductor manufacturers were selling in the United States at market prices below those applicable to Japan, the U.S. Commerce Department was empowered to determine for each type of memory chip a "fair market value" (FMV) based upon Japanese manufacturing prices. Each Japanese manufacturer was assigned such FMVs for its products on quarterly prices. This has led to immediate and substantial price increases for memory chips sold in the United States to levels that are now above those of Europe or Japan.[16] This action was undertaken because the U.S. government was concerned about the survival of the U.S. semiconductor industry—an industry of strategic importance in the world of high technology.

The United States is not alone in taking anti-dumping action. Numerous European governments have also initiated anti-dumping duties for steel and other low-priced imports. International marketers have to be aware of anti-dumping legislation that sets a floor under export prices, limiting pricing flexibil-

---

14. Franklin R. Root, *International Trade and Investment*, 3rd ed. (Cincinnati: Southwestern, 1973), p. 296.

15. Robert W. Crandall, "Competition and 'Dumping' in the U.S. Steel Market," *Challenge*, July–August 1978, p. 17.

16. "Is a Big Federal Role the Way to Revitalize Semiconductor Firms?" *The Wall Street Journal*, February 17, 1987, p. 1.

ity even in the event of overcapacity or industry slowdown. On the other hand, anti-dumping legislation can work to a company's advantage, protecting it from unfair competition.

MANAGERIAL ISSUES IN INTERNATIONAL PRICING

Now that we have given you a general overview of the context of international pricing, we would like to turn our attention to managerial issues. These issues are recurring and require constant management attention as they are never really considered solved. The issues are export price escalation, transfer pricing, quoting in foreign currencies, and price arbitrage.

Determining Transfer Prices

A substantial amount of international business takes place between subsidiaries of the same company. It was estimated that among the world's largest 800 multinational companies in 1983, accounting for about 90 percent of world trade, in-house trading between subsidiaries accounted for 34 percent of those companies' volume. In 1985, Digital Equipment Corporation alone had worldwide sales of $6.7 billion, of which intercompany transfers accounted for $2 billion. As a result, the cost to the importing or buying subsidiary depends on the negotiated transfer price agreed on by the two involved units of the MNC.[17]

How these prices are set continues to be a major issue for international companies and governments alike. Because negotiations on transfer prices do not represent arms-length negotiations between independent participants, the resulting prices frequently differ from free market prices.[18]

Companies may deviate from arms-length prices for two reasons. They may want to (1) maximize profits or (2) minimize risk and uncertainty.[19] To pursue a strategy of profit maximization, a company might lower transfer prices for products shipped from some subsidiaries while increasing prices for products shipped to others. The company would then try to accumulate profits in subsidiaries where it was advantageous and keep profits low in other subsidiaries.

17. "The World's In-House Traders," *The Economist,* March 1, 1986, p. 61.

18. For a thorough conceptual treatment, see Jeffrey S. Arpan, *International Intracorporate Pricing,* (New York: Praeger Publishing, 1972).

19. Sanjaya Lall, "Transfer-Pricing by Multinational Manufacturing Firms," *Oxford Bulletin of Economics and Statistics,* August 1973, pp. 173–175.

Impact of Tax Structure on Transfer Pricing

Different tax, tariff, or subsidy structures by country frequently invite such practices. By accumulating more profits in a low-tax country, a company lowers its overall tax bill and thus increases profit. Likewise, tariff duties can be reduced by quoting low transfer prices to countries with high tariffs. In cases where countries use different exchange rates for the transfer of goods as opposed to the transfer of capital or profits, advantages can be gained by increasing transfer prices rather than transferring profits at less advantageous rates. The same is true for countries with restrictions on profit repatriation. Furthermore, a company may want to accumulate profits in a wholly owned subsidiary rather than in one that is minority owned; by using the transfer price mechanism, it can thus avoid sharing profits with local partners.

Puerto Rico's tax exemption law for corporations has attracted many international firms. Income tax exemptions for periods of ten to thirty years are granted on the payment of U.S. federal and local taxes, provided such tax-free earnings are not transferred to the United States before the exemption runs out. Several hundred corporations have taken advantage of this situation, accumulating earnings of close to 1 billion dollars annually, especially U.S. pharmaceutical companies. For a number of them, tax-free Puerto Rican earnings accounted for almost half of their entire corporate after-tax income. These companies produced their highest margin drugs in Puerto Rico and transferred them to sales operations in the United States and elsewhere. However, the U.S. Internal Revenue Service challenged their practices and charged the companies with artificially increasing transfer prices to depress taxable income in the United States while increasing tax-free earnings in Puerto Rico.[20]

Companies may also use the transfer price mechanism to minimize risk or uncertainty by moving profits or assets out of a country with chronic balance-of-payment problems and frequent devaluations. Since regular profit remittances are strictly controlled in such countries, many firms see high transfer prices as the only way to repatriate funds and thus reduce the amount of assets at risk. The same practice might be employed if a company anticipates political or social disturbances or a direct threat to profits through government intervention.

In actual practice, companies choose a number of approaches to transfer pricing. Market-based prices are equal to those negotiated by independent companies or at arms length. Of thirty United States–based MNCs, 46 percent were reported to use market-based systems.[21] Another 35 percent used cost-based systems to determine the transfer price. Costs were based on a predetermined formula, which might include a standard markup for profits.

20. "Closing in on Puerto Rico's Tax Haven," *Business Week,* May 22, 1978, p. 154.
21. Scott S. Cowen, Lawrence C. Phillips, and Linda Stillabower, "Multinational Transfer Pricing," *Management Accounting,* January 1979, pp. 7–22.

Internal Considerations for Transfer Pricing

Rigorous use of the transfer pricing mechanism to reduce a company's income taxes and duties and to maximize profits in strong currency areas can create difficulties for subsidiary managers whose profits are artificially reduced. In such cases, managers may be subject to motivational problems when the direct profit incentive is removed. Furthermore, company resource allocation may become inefficient since funds are appropriated to units whose profits are artificially increased; conversely, resources may be denied to subsidiaries whose income statement was subject to transfer-price-induced reductions. It is generally agreed that a transfer price mechanism should not seriously impair either morale or resource allocations, since gains incurred through tax savings may easily be lost through other inefficiencies.

External Problems with Transfer Pricing

Governments do not look favorably upon transfer pricing mechanisms aimed at reducing their tax revenues. United States government policy on transfer pricing is governed by tax law, particularly Section 482 of the United States Revenue Act of 1962.[22] The act is designed to provide an accurate allocation of costs, income, and capital among related enterprises to protect United States tax revenue. The U.S. Internal Revenue Service accepts the following transfer price methods:

> Market prices are generally preferred by the IRS, either based on a comparable uncontrolled price method or a resale price method. As far as cost-plus pricing is concerned, the IRS will accept cost-plus markup if market prices are not available, and economic circumstances warrant such use. Not acceptable are, however, actual cost methods. Other methods, such as negotiated prices, are acceptable as long as the transfer price is comparable to a price charged to an unrelated party.[23]

Other governments have also taken measures to control tax avoidance through transfer pricing mechanisms. The British government created a separate inland revenue unit that has greatly increased tax revenues from MNCs.[24] Pharmaceutical companies such as Roche Products, Ciba-Geigy, and Glaxo were investigated and ended up paying additional taxes. European Community members would also like to make tax havens such as Luxembourg, Gibraltar, and

---

22. Cowen, Phillips, and Stillabower, "Multinational Transfer Pricing," p. 18; and Larry J. Merville and T. William Petty: "Transfer Pricing for the Multinational Firm," *The Accounting Review*, vol. LIII, October 1978, pp. 935–951.

23. Cowen, Phillips, and Stillabower, "Multinational Transfer Pricing," p. 19.

24. "Transfer Pricing: Fiddlers Beware," *The Economist*, November 11, 1978, p. 113.

Liechtenstein more difficult to use.[25] More recently international bodies, such as the United Nations' Center for Transnational Corporations, are advocating stiffer rules on abusive transfer pricing practices.

Quoting in a Foreign Currency

For many international marketing transactions, it is not always feasible to quote in a company's domestic currency to sell or purchase merchandise. Although the majority of U.S. exporters quote prices in dollars, there are situations when customers might prefer quotes in their own national currency. For most import transactions, sellers usually quote the currency of their own country. When two currencies are involved, there is the risk that a change in exchange rates may occur between the invoicing date and the settlement date for the transaction. This risk, the foreign exchange risk, is an inherent factor in international marketing and clearly separates domestic from international business. Situations occur in which an exporter is able to sign an order only if the buyer's currency is used. In such circumstances special techniques are available to protect the seller from the foreign exchange risk.

The tools used to cover a company's foreign exchange risk are either (a) hedging in the forward market or (b) covering through money markets. Foreign exchange futures or options are also available but still represent only a small fraction of total volume. These alternatives are given because of the nature of foreign exchange. As we discussed in Chapter 2, for most major currencies, international foreign exchange dealers located at major banks quote a spot price and a forward price. The *spot price* determines the number of dollars to be paid for a particular foreign currency if purchased or sold today. The *forward price* quotes the number of dollars to be paid for a foreign currency bought or sold 30, 90, or 180 days from today. The forward price, however, is not necessarily the market's speculation as to what the spot price will be in the future. Instead, the forward price reflects interest rate differentials between two currencies for maturities of 30, 90, or 180 days. Consequently there are no firm indications as to what the spot price will be for any given currency in the future. For a review of foreign exchange markets, please see Chapter 2.

A company quoting in foreign currency for purchase or sale could simply leave settlement until the due date and pay whatever spot price prevails at the time. Such an uncovered position might be chosen when exchange rates are not expected to shift, or if any shift in the near future would result in a gain for the company. With exchange rates fluctuating widely on a daily basis, even among major trading nations such as the United States, Japan, Germany, and the United Kingdom, a company would expose itself to substantial foreign exchange risks. Since many MNCs are in business to make a profit from the sale of goods

25. "Multinational Versus the Tax," *Dun's Review*, February 1976, pp. 68–69.

rather than from speculation in the foreign exchange markets, managements generally protect themselves from unexpected fluctuations.

One such protection lies in the forward market. Instead of accepting whatever spot market rate exists on the settlement in 30 or 90 days, the corporation can opt to contract for future delivery of foreign currency at a firm price, regardless of the spot price actually paid at that time. This allows the seller to incorporate a firm exchange rate into the price determination. Of course, if a company wishes to predict the spot price in 90 days and is reasonably certain about the accuracy of its prediction, a choice may be made between the more advantageous of the two: the expected spot or the present forward rate. However, such predictions should only be made under the guidance of experts familiar with foreign exchange rates.

An alternative strategy, called covering through the money market, involves borrowing funds to be converted into the currency at risk for the time until settlement. In this case, a company would owe and hold the same amount of foreign currency, resulting in a corresponding loss or gain when settling at the time of payment. As an example, an exporter holding accounts receivable in deutsch marks (DM), and unwilling to absorb the related currency risk until payment is received, might borrow DM for working capital purposes. When the customer pays in the foreign currency, the loan, also denominated in that same currency, would be paid off. Any fluctuations would be cancelled, therefore resulting in neither loss nor gain.

How to Incorporate a Foreign Exchange Rate into a Selling Price Quote

To illustrate the incorporation of a foreign exchange rate into a price quote for export, let's assume the following: a U.S. company needs to determine a price quote for its plastic extrusion machinery sold to a Canadian customer. The customer requested billing in Canadian dollars. The exporter, with a list price of U.S. $12,000, does not want to absorb any exchange risk. The daily foreign exchange rates on January 23, 1987 are U.S. $.7361 spot price for one Canadian dollar, or $.7331 in the 90 days forward market.[26] The exporter could directly figure the Canadian dollar price by using the forward rate, resulting in an export price of $16,368 in Canadian currency. Upon shipping, the exporter would sell at $16,368 (in Canadian money) forward with 90 days delivery and, with the rate of $.7331 per Canadian dollar, receive U.S. $12,000. Consequently, wherever possible, quotes in foreign currencies should be made based on forward rates, with respective foreign currency amounts sold in the forward market.

---

26. "Foreign Exchange," *The Wall Street Journal*, January 26, 1987, p. 38.

Selection of a Hedging Procedure

To illustrate the selection of a hedging procedure, let's assume the following situation: A U.S. exporter of packaging machinery sells one machine valued at $24,000.00 to a client in the United Kingdom. The client will pay in British pounds quoted at the current (spot) rate (January 23, 1987) of $1.5245, or £15,743. This amount will be paid in three months (90 days). As a result, the U.S. exporter will have to determine how to protect such an incoming amount against foreign exchange risk. Although uncertain about the outcome, the exporter's bank indicates that there is an equal chance for the British pound spot rate to remain at $1.5245 (Scenario A), to devalue to $1.3721 (Scenario B), or to appreciate to $1.6770 (Scenario C). As a result, the exporter has the option of selling the amount forward in the 90 days forward market, at $1.5070.

	A	B	C
Spot rate as of January 23, 1987	$1.5245	$1.5245	$1.5245
Spot rate as of April 23, 1987 (estimate)	$1.5245	$1.3721	$1.6770
U.S. dollar equivalent of £15,743 at spot rates on April 23, 1987	$24,000.00	$21,600.00	$26,400.00
Exchange gain (loss) with hedging	–0–	($2,400.00)	$2,400.00

The alternative available to the exporter is to sell forward the invoice amount of U.K. £15,743 at $1.5070 to obtain a sure $23,724, a loss of $276 on the transaction. In anticipation of a devaluation of the pound, such a hedging strategy would be advisable. Consequently the $276 represents a premium to insure against any larger loss. However, a company would also forego any gain as indicated under Scenario C. Acceptance for hedging through the forward market depends on the expected spot rate at the time the foreign payment is due. Again, it should be kept in mind that the forward rate is not an estimate of the spot rate in the future.

Dealing with Parallel Imports

One of the most perplexing problems international companies face is the phenomenon of different prices between countries. When such price differentials become large, individual buyers or independent entrepreneurs step in and buy products in low-price countries to re-export to high-price countries while profiting from the price differential. This arbitrage behavior creates what experts call the "gray market" or "parallel imports" because these imports take place outside of the regular trade channels controlled by distributors or company-owned sales subsidiaries. Such price differences can occur as a result of company price strategy, margin differences, or currency fluctuations.

FIGURE 13.2 Price Comparisons for BL Cars in Europe

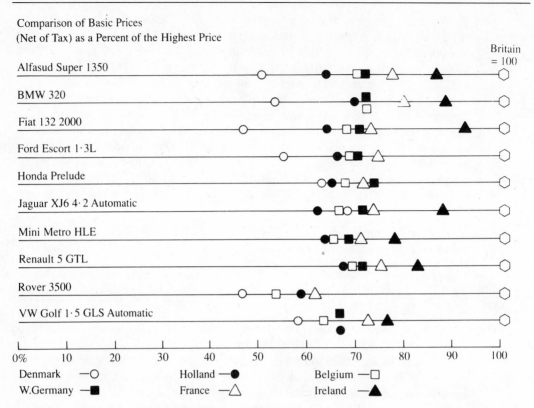

Comparison of Basic Prices
(Net of Tax) as a Percent of the Highest Price

Britain = 100

Denmark —○   Holland —●   Belgium —□
W.Germany —■   France —△   Ireland —▲

Source: From *The Economist,* October 3, 1981. © 1981 The Economist, distributed by Special Features. Reprinted by permission.

Pricing differently for its domestic market and export markets, the U.K. car manufacturer BL created a price gap that caused an active parallel import market. During the late 1970s, prices for BL cars in the United Kingdom were increased in line with the relatively high inflation. However, BL was not in a position to pass on these increases in European export markets, thus resulting in very high car prices in the United Kingdom.[27] As shown in Figure 13.2, U.K. car prices were almost twice those of the lowest country (Denmark) when adjusted for local taxes.

In response to this difference, British buyers started to go to Belgium to purchase their cars. When BL and other U.K. car manufacturers tried to contain the flow of parallel imports, or gray market cars, the British government stepped

27. "Car Prices: What Common Market?" *The Economist,* May 3, 1980, p. 75.

in to protect the private consumer.[28] As a result, car companies could not take direct measures against these practices other than lowering prices in their domestic market or increasing prices abroad.

The effect of different channel margins on end-user price was felt by most Japanese camera producers. Although prices ex-factory in Japan vary little by country, camera manufacturers market their products through wholly owned distributors in the United States and Europe. These distributing companies add a substantial margin because they also invest heavily in consumer-oriented advertising. The same cameras are sold in Singapore or Hong Kong through independent importers who charge very low margins. As a result, retail customers in the United States and Europe have bought cameras directly from Far East wholesalers at prices below those of regular distributors. For example, one Vivitar lens is sold at $229 in the United States as opposed to $179 in Singapore, both prices at wholesale levels.[29] This practice hurts the established distributor, who loses the contribution toward high advertising expenditures.

Fluctuating currency values can also create opportunities for parallel imports as we have observed earlier in this chapter. This can affect even U.S. companies, as experienced by Duracell, the U.S. battery producer.[30] This company maintained a manufacturing facility in Belgium as well as in the United States. When the dollar began to appreciate against European currencies, some U.S. retailers and wholesalers realized they could profit by importing Belgian-made batteries. Such purchases turned out to be at least 20 percent below those of Duracell's list price in the United States. Duracell saw its profitability threatened because it earned more on United States–produced batteries. Although the company tried to have this practice ruled illegal, in most countries parallel imports are not against the law.

Spot shortages in one market can also generate parallel imports. Corton Trading Co., located in Tokyo, specialized in buying surplus semiconductor chips from Japanese companies and selling them to U.S. companies that could not get sufficient local supplies. During the chip shortage in 1984, the price differential between Japan and the United States amounted to 100 percent, with Corton Trading earning as much as one dollar per chip.[31]

To stop parallel imports, international companies have tried a series of steps, although not always with great success. To prohibit distributors or wholesalers in low-price countries from exporting their products is effective only where it can be enforced. The Japanese home electronics manufacturer, Pioneer, tried to prevent such imports into France by requiring its German and Belgian

---

28. "The Coming Car Price Crash," *The Economist,* December 12, 1981, p. 62.

29. "Photo Equipment Manufacturers Try to Stamp Out Gray Market," *Marketing News,* April 2, 1982, p. 13.

30. "Duracell Attacks U.S. Gray Market," *Financial Times,* February 23, 1984, p. 6.

31. "The $7 Billion Gray Market: Where It Stops, Nobody Knows," *Business Week,* April 15, 1985, p. 86.

importers to agree to a no-export policy. However, this was found by EC authorities to be against competition regulations, and Pioneer had to pay a hefty fine. Other companies that ran afoul of the same legislation included BMW and Kawasaki Motors.[32]

For the United States alone, parallel or gray market volume was estimated to be $6 billion at retail level in 1984.[33] However, parallel imports are not restricted to consumer products.

With the legal situation in the United States favoring the official importer or distributor, companies have used other methods in the United States. Vivitar began to code all of its products according to the intended market. The company notified its distributors that agreements would be terminated if parallel export products were traced to them. Other camera producers changed their names on products or did not extend warranty coverage to parallel exports. The British whiskey distiller, National Distillers, went as far as to withdraw its number-one brand, Johnny Walker Red Label from the U.K. market, because parallel exports originating from the United Kingdom were undermining its distribution system throughout Europe. The company has since re-introduced the product in the United Kingdom but at much higher prices.

Product arbitrage will always occur when price differentials get too large and when transport costs are low in relation to product value. International companies will have to match price differentials more closely for standardized products in particular. Products that are highly differentiated from country to country are also less likely to become parallel traded.

Managing Export Price Escalation

The additional costs described earlier may raise the end-user price of an exported product substantially above its domestic price. This phenomenon, called export price escalation (see Table 13.7 for an example), may force a company to adopt any one of two strategic patterns. First, a company may realize its price disadvantage and adjust the marketing mix to account for its "luxury" status. By adopting such a strategy, a company sacrifices volume to keep a high unit price. Alternatively, a company may grant a "discount" on the standard domestic price to bring the end-user price more in line with prices paid by domestic customers. Such discounts may be justified under marginal contribution pricing methods. Because of reduced marketing costs at the manufacturer's level, particularly when a foreign distributor is used, an export price equal to a domestic price is often not justified. Legal limits such as anti-dumping regulations prevent price reductions below a certain point.

---

32. "Car Prices: What Common Market?" p. 75.
33. "The Assault on the Right to Buy Cheap Imports," *Fortune*, January 7, 1985, p. 89.

TABLE 13.7 Export Price Escalation

E-Z-EM Company, a manufacturer of radiology supplies located in Westbury, New York, experienced export price escalation with a sample order for a typical product:

Sample order: 12 dozen #314 pre-filled kits, at $14.20 doz. domestic and $11.20 doz. export

	Domestic	*Export*
Price FOB Westbury	$170.40	$134.40
Freight:		
$0.05/lb. via truck	9.00	
$0.25/lb. via air		$ 45.00
Export broker handling fee		20.00
Insurance		2.00
Duty (16% CIF)		32.22
Value added tax (25% of landed cost)		58.40
Cost delivered to buyer	$179.40	$292.02
Terms	net 30 days	sight draft
Distributor markup (20%), only for export	—	40.28
Cost to end-user (hospitals, etc.)	$179.40	$332.30

Source: Warren J. Keegan, *Multinational Marketing Management,* © 1974, p. 175. Adapted by permission of Prentice-Hall, Inc., Englewood Cliffs, New Jersey.

Customary margins, both wholesale and retail, may differ considerably among countries. Table 13.8 illustrates such differences for a packaged food product exported to France and Germany.

International Pricing Strategies

As international companies deal with market and environmental factors, they are facing two major strategic pricing alternatives. Essentially, the choice is between the global, single-price strategy and the individualized country strategy.

To maximize a company's revenues it would appear to be logical to set prices on a market-by-market basis, looking in each market for the best combination of revenue versus volume yielding maximum profit. This strategy had been common for many firms in the early part of their international development. For many products, however, noticeable price differences between markets are taken advantage of by independent companies or channel members who see a profit from buying in lower-price markets and export products to high-price

TABLE 13.8 Distribution Margin Differences for Same Channel in Different Countries

	Importer	*Wholesaler*	*Retailer*
France	12%	15%	31%
Germany	23%	12.5%	10%

Source: From *International Marketing,* 2nd ed. by Vern Terpsta. Copyright 1978 by The Dryden Press. Reprinted by permission of Holt, Rinehart & Winston, Inc.

markets. For products that are relatively similar in many markets, and where transportation costs are not significant, substantial price differences would quickly result in such an emergence of the gray market. As a result, fewer companies have the possibility of pricing on a market-by-market basis. As the markets become more transparent, the information flows more efficiently; and as products become more similar, the trend away from market-by-market pricing is likely to continue.

Employing a uniform pricing strategy on a global scale would require that a company determine its prices in local currency but, when translated into a base currency, would always charge the same price everywhere. In reality, this will become very difficult to achieve whenever different taxes, trade margins, and customs duties are involved. As a result, there are likely to be price differences resulting from those factors not under control by the company. Keeping prices identical aside from those noncontrollable factors would be a challenge nevertheless. Firms might start out with identical prices in various countries but soon find that prices would have to change in line with often substantial currency fluctuations.

Although it is becoming increasingly clear for many companies that market-by-market pricing strategies will cause difficulties, many firms have experienced that moving to a uniform pricing policy is rather like pursuing a moving target. Even when a global pricing policy is adopted, a company must carefully monitor price levels in each country and avoid large gaps that can then cause problems when independent or gray market forces move in and take advantage of large price differentials.

CONCLUSIONS

Managing pricing policies for an international firm is an especially challenging task. The international marketer is confronted with a number of noncontrollable factors out of the economic, legal, and regulatory environment that all have an impact on how prices are established in various countries. Though these influences are usually quite manageable in any given country, the difficulty for pricing across many markets arises from the price differentials that evolve out of environmental factors working in various combinations in different countries. Managing these price differentials and keeping them within some tolerable limits is a major task in international pricing.

One of the most critical values affecting price levels are foreign exchange rates. Foreign exchange rates have been subject to substantial fluctuations over the past fifteen years compared to previous periods when they were either stable or moved in very predictable directions. Today, managers find currencies moving both up or down, and the swings have assumed magnitudes that may substantially affect the competitiveness of a company. Understanding the factors that shape the directions of the foreign exchange market and mastering the technical tools that protect firms against large swings have become required skills for the international marketer. To the extent that a company can make itself less vulnerable from exchange rate movements compared to its competitors, it may be able to gain additional competitive advantage.

Because the relevant factors that impact on price levels on an international scale are always fluctuating, the international pricing task is a never-ending process in which each day may bring new problems to be resolved. Whenever a company is slow to adapt or makes a wrong judgment, the market is very quick at adapting and at taking advantage of any weaknesses. As long as noncontrollable factors such as currency rate and inflation are subject to considerable fluctuations, the pricing strategies of international companies will have to remain under constant review. The ultimate goal is to minimize the gap between the price levels of various markets.

Questions for Discussion

1. Discuss the difficulty or desirability of having a standardized price for a company's products across all countries.
2. Why should a company not go ahead and price its products in each market according to local factors?
3. You are an exporter of industrial installations and have received an order for $100,000 from a Japanese customer. The job would take six months to complete and would be paid in full at that time. Now your Japanese customer has called you and also wants a price quote in Yen. What would you quote him?
4. What strategies, other than through pricing, do companies have to combat parallel imports?
5. What should be the government's position on the issue of parallel imports? Should the government take any particular actions?

For Further Reading

Arpan, Jeffrey S. "International Intracorporate Pricing." *Journal of International Business Studies* (Spring 1972), pp. 1–18.

Baker, James C., and John K. Ryans, Jr. "International Pricing Policies of Industrial Product Manufacturers." *Journal of International Marketing,* 1, No. 3 (1982), pp. 127–133.

Baker, James C., and John K. Ryans, Jr. "Some Aspects of International Pricing: A Neglected Area of Management Policy." *Management Decisions* (Summer 1973), pp. 177–182.

Farley, John U., James M. Hulbert, and David Weinstein. "Price Setting and Volume Planning by Two European Industrial Companies: A Study and Comparison of Decision Processes." *Journal of Marketing,* 44, No. 1 (Winter 1980), pp. 46–54.

Burns, Jane O. "Transfer Pricing Decisions in U.S. Multinationals." *Journal of International Business Studies* (Fall 1980), pp. 21–39.

Frank, Victor H., Jr. "Living With Price Control Abroad." *Harvard Business Review,* (March–April 1984), pp. 137–142.

Ghoshal, Animesh. "Flexible Exchange Rates and International Trade." *International Trade Journal,* 1, No. 1 (Fall 1986), pp. 27–66.

Kaikati, Jack G. "The Reincarnation of Barter Trade." *Journal of Marketing* (April 1975), pp. 17–24.

Kressler, Peter R. "Is Uniform Pricing Desirable in Multinational Markets?" In *International Marketing: Managerial Perspectives* Ed. Subhash C. Jain and Lewis R. Tucker, Jr. Boston: CBI Publishing Company, Inc., 1979.

Leff, Nathaniel H. "Multinational Corporate Pricing Strategy in the Developing Countries." *Journal of International Business Studies* (Fall 1975), p. 55.

Lecraw, Donald J. "Pricing Strategies of Transnational Corporations." *Asia Pacific Journal of Management* (January 1984), pp. 112–119.

O'Burns, Jane. "Transfer Pricing Decisions in U.S. Multinational Corporations." *Journal of International Business Studies* (Fall 1980), pp. 23–39.

Kim, Seung H., and Stephen W. Miller. "Constituents of the International Transfer Pricing Decision." *Columbia Journal of World Business* (Spring 1979), p. 71.

Solnik, Bruno H. "The International Pricing of Risk: An Empirical Investigation of the World Capital Market Structure." *Journal of Finance* (May 1974), pp. 305–379.

14

COMMUNICATIONS STRATEGIES

To manage a communications process in one single market is no easy task. International marketers, however, have to communicate to prospective customers in many markets. In the process, they struggle with different cultures, habits, and languages.

In this chapter, we describe how the communications process differs when more than one country is involved and how a company structures its international communications mix. Advertising, a key element of the promotional mix, will be covered in detail in our next chapter (Chapter 15). After a closer look at the differences between a single-country versus a multi-country communications process, we will turn to the challenge of developing a personal selling effort on an international level. Various methods of sales promotion are analyzed, and special problems involving the selling of industrial goods are highlighted. (See Figure 14.1.)

THE SINGLE-COUNTRY COMMUNICATIONS PROCESS

Before we embark on a detailed discussion of the various tools available to firms in the international communications area, we first need to discuss the international dimension of the communications process. From studying basic marketing, you should be familiar with the generalized single-country communications process. Communications flow from a source, in this case the company, through several types of channels to the receiver, in this case the customer. Channels are the mass media, both print or electronic, and the company's sales force. Communication takes place when intended content is received as the perceived content by the receiver or customer. Through a feedback mechanism, the communi-

FIGURE 14.1 International Communications Strategies

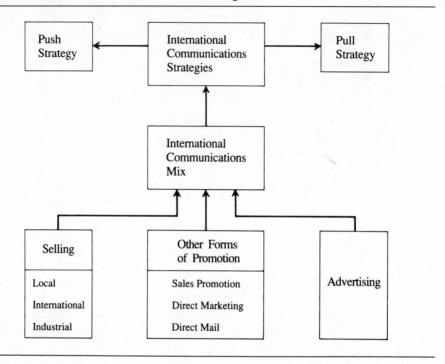

cations sender will be able to verify that the intended and perceived content were in fact identical.

This communications process is typically hindered by three potentially critical variables. A *source effect* exists when the receiver evaluates the received messages based on the status or image of the sender. Secondly, the level of noise caused by other messages being transmitted simultaneously tends to reduce the chances of effective communication. Finally, the messages have to pass through the receiver's, or target's, perceptional filter, which keeps out any messages that are not relevant to the receiver's experience. Consequently, effective communications require that the source, or sender, overcome the source effect, noise level, and perceptional filter. This is the communications process that most students of marketing are familiar with, involving a domestic, or single-country, situation.

THE MULTI-COUNTRY COMMUNICATIONS PROCESS

Research evidence and experience have demonstrated that the communications model adopted for the single-country or domestic situation is applied to con-

FIGURE 14.2 Barriers in the Multi-Country Communications Process

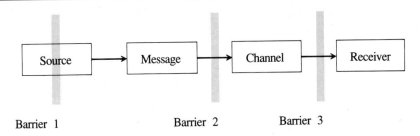

Barrier 1   Head office outside target country;
             messages devised in target country

Barrier 2   Messages created by company outside
             target country and disseminated by
             local channels

Barrier 3   Company, message creation, and channel
             outside target country, directed at Local
             Consumers

sumers in other countries as well. Consequently, the communications model covering international situations is the same as discussed above. What we do find, however, are some additional barriers to overcome: the cultural barrier, different source effects, and different noise levels. Figure 14.2 contains a multi-country communications model with the cultural barrier arising at different times or steps in the process.

What is meant by a cultural barrier? In any multi-country communications flow, the source and the receiver are located in different countries and thus they have different cultural environments. The kind of influence culture can have on the marketing environment has already been discussed at length in Chapter 3. The difficulty of communicating across cultural barriers, however, lies in the danger of substituting, or falling back on, one's own self-reference criteria in situations in which no particular information exists. This danger is particularly acute for executives who are physically removed from the target country. By moving additional decision-making responsibility into the local market, the cultural barrier will have to be overcome at a point closer to the source.

Even in situations where a local subsidiary has substantial decision-making authority, there will be some input from a regional or corporate head office operation. For most firms, then, some effort of overcoming this cultural barrier will have to be made. This means that in virtually all cases some executives will be involved in bridging two cultures. The result of not successfully bridging this gap can be failure and substantial losses.

Multi-country communications may also have an impact on the source effect. A foreign company's communications may trigger different reactions than the communications of a local firm. In cases where a positive reference group effect exists, a multinational corporation (MNC) might want to exploit the situation. Frequently, however, the reaction to MNCs is negative, forcing companies to de-emphasize their foreign origins.

The noise level may differ due to different economic and competitive circumstances. In highly developed countries such as the United States, "noise" from competing companies for the attention of target customers is extremely high. In some developing countries, fewer companies might vie for the attention of prospective clients. With media availability differing widely from country to country, the nature of channels used to reach target customers tends to vary accordingly. And finally, the feedback mechanisms are subject to additional delays due to the distances involved.

Consequently, we can characterize the multi-country communications process as similar to the single-country process, though subject to considerable additional difficulties that make this a highly challenging task. The purpose of this chapter is to develop strategies that international companies can employ to overcome these additional difficulties and barriers. We will thus begin our analysis by concentrating first on the different elements of the communications mix.

THE INTERNATIONAL COMMUNICATIONS MIX

How to manage the communications mix internationally is a critical question for many companies. Most firms are used to doing business in a certain way and do not have to rethink their communications mix regularly. International marketers, however, cannot take the full availability of all communications elements for granted. As a result, many companies find themselves in countries or situations that require an adjustment or a substantial change in their communications mix. This section is therefore devoted to understanding how different international environments impact on communications mix decisions (see Figure 14.1).

Elements of the Communications Mix

The communications mix, sometimes referred to as the promotion mix, includes the following key elements: advertising, sales promotions, personal selling, and publicity. It is the responsibility of marketing management to maximize these elements in such a way as to obtain the best possible mix. In a domestic or single-country environment, companies achieve a balance in their communications mix on the basis of experience, costs, and effectiveness. For most companies, communications mix decisions require the selection of an appropriate balance between advertising and personal selling. This translates into a push versus pull strategies decision. How different is the company's approach to marketing its products internationally?

Push-Oriented Strategies

Companies that have adopted push-oriented marketing strategies have tended to emphasize personal selling rather than advertising in their communications mix. Although very effective as a communications tool, personal selling, which requires intensive use of a sales force, is relatively costly. Companies marketing industrial or other complex products to other firms or governmental agencies have relied on personal selling. Personal selling is usually more effective when a company is faced with a short channel. International marketers basically look at the personal selling requirements in the same way that marketers do in a domestic situation. However, some of the key inputs into the decision-making process need to be reviewed.

The complexity of a product usually influences how extensively personal selling is used. Although most companies market products of equal or less complexity abroad, the level of complexity will have to be compared to the readiness level of the clients. Consequently, a U.S. company selling the same products abroad as those sold domestically might find that more personal selling might be necessary abroad because some foreign clients are less sophisticated than domestic clients. A U.S. company might use the same amount of personal selling in Europe as it does in the United States, but may need to put forth a greater personal selling effort in developing countries.

How a firm's products are purchased abroad could also lead to adjustments in the push policy. When a company markets industrial equipment, push policies will usually be employed both domestically and abroad. There are some product categories, however, where buying might not be the same. What might be minor equipment or supplies purchased on a limited-involvement basis in one country, such as the United States, might be considered major equipment for smaller firms abroad and thus require a more involved personal selling effort.

Many U.S. companies, though preferring personal selling as a communications mix, are using increasingly more advertising due to the high cost of maintaining a personal sales force. These costs, which are estimated to have passed $200 for a typical sales call, have motivated some companies to shift a part of the selling job to advertising. In foreign markets where salary levels may be lower than in the United States, companies might gain by making more use of personal selling.

Channel length can also be an important factor determining the amount of personal selling or push strategy to be used. To the extent that a company faces the same channel length abroad as it does in the United States, no change is needed in the push strategy. However, when a company does face a longer channel because other intermediaries such as local distributors are added, the firm might be better off shifting to a pull campaign.

Pull-Oriented Strategies

Pull strategies are characterized by a relatively greater dependence on advertising directed at the end-user for a product or service. Pull campaigns are typical for consumer goods firms that need to approach a large segment of the market. For such companies, the economies of using mass communications such as advertising have dictated a reliance on pulling the product through the distribution channel. Pull campaigns are usually advisable when the product is widely used by consumers, when the channel is long, when the product is not very complex, and when self-service is the predominant shopping behavior.

Increased or decreased reliance on pull campaigns for international marketers depend on a number of factors. Most important are access to advertising media, channel length, and the leverage the company has with the distribution channel.

Marketers accustomed to the large number of media available, such as in the U.S. market, will find that in overseas markets the choice may be substantially limited. For many products, pull campaigns work only if access to electronic media, particularly TV, is guaranteed. This is the case in Japan and in some developing countries where radio and TV stations tend to be commercially operated. However, in many European countries, advertising is restricted to print media only. In Scandinavia, no commercial television or radio stations were in existence in 1987.[1] In many other countries, access to those media is restricted through a limit on time imposed by governments. Consequently, companies will find it difficult to duplicate their strategies when moving from a free environment such as the United States to the more restricted environment in Europe. Although in many countries a company might be able to shift advertising from one media into another, it is nevertheless true that the unfolding of a full-blown push campaign as practiced in the United States is usually much more difficult if not impossible.

Channel length is a major determinant of the use of a pull campaign. Companies in markets such as the United States often face long channels in consumer goods and thus try to overcome channel inertia by directing their advertising directly to end-users. When a company markets overseas, it may face an even

---

1. "Media Fact Europe," *Focus*, January 1987, p. 21.

longer channel because local distribution arrangements are different. In the case of a country such as Japan, channels tend to be very long compared to those in the United States. As a result, a greater reliance on a pull strategy might be advisable or necessary in such countries.

Distribution leverage is also different for each company from market to market. Getting cooperation from local selling points, particularly in the retail sector, is often more difficult than it is in the domestic market. The fight for shelf space may be very intensive; shelf space in most markets is more limited than it is in the United States where it is customary to carry several competing brands of a product category. Under these more difficult situations, the reliance on a push campaign becomes more important. If consumers are demanding the company's product, retailers will make sure they carry it.

Push Versus Pull Strategies

In selecting the best balance between advertising and personal selling for the push versus pull decision, companies have to analyze the markets to determine the need for these two major communications mix elements. However, as we have seen, the availability or access to any one of them may be limited. This is particularly the case for firms depending a great deal on pull policies. Many such companies find themselves limited in the use of the most powerful communications tool. How shall a company adjust its communications policy under such circumstances?

When access to advertising media makes the pull strategy less effective, a company may have to resort to a greater use of personal selling. In some instances, this may already be the case when access to television advertising forces a company to use less effective media forms such as print advertising. In such circumstances, a company will be employing a larger sales force to compensate for the lesser efficiency of consumer-directed promotions.

Limited ability to unfold a pull strategy from a company's home market has other effects on the company's marketing strategy. Limited advertising tends to slow the product adoption process in new markets, thus forcing the firm to accept slower growth. In markets crowded with existing competitors, newcomers will find it difficult to establish themselves when access to pull campaigns is limited.

Consequently, a company entering a new market may want to consider such situations for its planning and adjust expected results accordingly. A company accustomed to a given type of communications mix usually develops an expertise or a distinctive competence in that use. When suddenly faced with a situation in which that competence cannot be fully applied, the risk of failure or underachievement is increased. This could even affect entry strategies or the market selection process.

PERSONAL SELLING

Personal selling takes place whenever a customer is met in person by a representative of the marketing company. When doing business internationally, companies will have to meet customers from different countries. These customers may be used to different business customs and may speak in a different language. Personal selling in an international context is therefore extremely complex and requires some very special skills on the part of the salesperson.

In this section, we will differentiate between international selling and local selling. When a company's sales force travels across countries and meets directly with clients abroad, it is practicing international selling. This kind of selling requires the special skill of being able to manage within several cultures. Much more often, however, companies engage in local selling; they organize and staff a local sales force made up of local nationals to do the selling in only one country. Managing and operating a local sales force involves different problems from those encountered by international salespersons.

International Selling (Multicountry Sales Force)

The job of the international salesperson seems glamorous. We imagine a professional who frequently travels abroad, visiting a large number of countries and meeting a large number of different businesspeople with various backgrounds. However, this type of work is quite demanding, and becoming a globetrotter (see Chapter 1 for our definition) requires a special set of skills.

International salespersons are needed only when companies deal directly with their clients abroad. This is usually the case for industrial equipment or business services and rarely for consumer products or services. Consequently, for our purposes, international sales will be described in the context of industrial selling.

Purchasing Behavior

In industrial selling, one of the most important parts of the job consists of finding the right decision maker in the client company. The seller must locate the key decision makers which may differ from company to company or from country to country.[2] In some countries, the purchasing manager may have different responsibilities or engineers may play a greater role. The international salesperson thus must be able to deal effectively with buying units that differ by country.

---

2. Thomas V. Bonoma, "Major Sales: Who Really Does the Buying?" *Harvard Business Review*, May–June 1982, p. 112.

FIGURE 14.3 Organizational Buying Behavior in Japan: Packaging Machine
Purchase Process

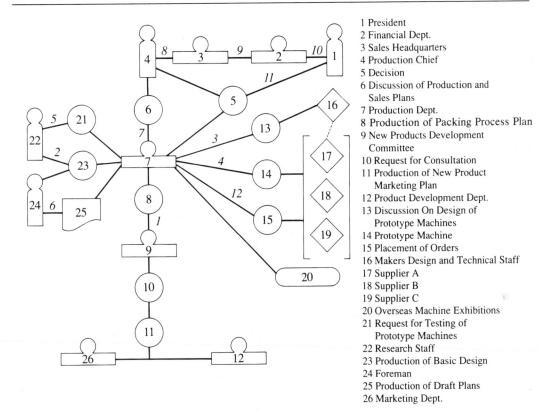

1 President
2 Financial Dept.
3 Sales Headquarters
4 Production Chief
5 Decision
6 Discussion of Production and
  Sales Plans
7 Production Dept.
8 Production of Packing Process Plan
9 New Products Development
  Committee
10 Request for Consultation
11 Production of New Product
  Marketing Plan
12 Product Development Dept.
13 Discussion On Design of
  Prototype Machines
14 Prototype Machine
15 Placement of Orders
16 Makers Design and Technical Staff
17 Supplier A
18 Supplier B
19 Supplier C
20 Overseas Machine Exhibitions
21 Request for Testing of
  Prototype Machines
22 Research Staff
23 Production of Basic Design
24 Foreman
25 Production of Draft Plans
26 Marketing Dept.

Source: "Japanese Firms Use Unique Buying Behavior," *The Japan Economic Journal,* December 23, 1980,
p. 29. Reprinted by permission.

A Japanese study investigated the purchasing process of a large corporation
for packaging machinery.[3] The entire decision-making process took 121 days and
involved 20 people from the purchasing company. In Japan, middle management
is given considerable authority for purchasing. However, the staff departments
responsible for the purchasing process will involve all interested and affected
departments in the decision-making process. In the case of the company pur-

3. "Japanese Firms Use Unique Buying Behavior," *The Japan Economic Journal,* December 23,
1980, p. 29.

TABLE 14.1 Languages Spoken in European Households

	Belgium	Denmark	France	Germany	Ireland	Italy	Netherlds.	Norway	Spain	Switzld.	UK
Households (m)	3.6	2.1	20.3	25.3	0.85	18.5	5.3	1.55	10.3	2.5	21.03
Adults who speak:											
English (%)	26	51	26	30	99	13	50	80	n.a.	26	100
French (%)	71	5	100	12	12	27	16	10	n.a.	55	16
German (%)	22	48	11	100	2	6	61	20	n.a.	81	9
Italian (%)	4	1	8	2	1	100	2	4	n.a.	17	2
Spanish (%)	3	1	13	2	1	5	2	2	100	3	3
Flemish-Dutch (%)	68	1	1	3	—	—	100	—	—	—	1

Source: Data from a Gallup survey, as published in "European Satellite Battle Looms," *Financial Times*, September 16, 1985. Reprinted by permission.

chasing packaging machinery, the process involved the production manager and the entire production department staff, the new product committee, the laboratory of the company, the marketing department, and the department for market development. For a detailed chart see Figure 14.3.

Buying Criteria

Aside from the different purchasing patterns found, the international salesperson may have to deal with different decision criteria or objectives on the part of the purchaser. Buyers or users of industrial products in different countries may expect to maximize different goals. However, it should be pointed out that for standardized uses for specific industries, relatively little difference between countries applies. Particularly for high technology products, such as production equipment for semiconductor components used in the electronics industry, the applications are virtually identical regardless of whether the factory is located in Korea or in the United States.

Language

Overcoming the language barrier is an especially difficult task for the international salesperson. The personal selling effort is substantially enhanced if the salesperson speaks the language of the customer. A summary of languages spoken in European countries is shown in Table 14.1. For some of the products marketed by an international sales force today, two trends are evident. First, the dependency on the local language for many industries is not as strong today as it was just one or two decades ago. For many new and highly sophisticated products, such as in the electronics or aerospace industry, English is the language spoken by most customers. Consequently, with more and more executives speaking English in many countries, more firms have been in a position to actually market their products directly, without local intermediaries. English is widely spoken in Scandinavia and in Europe, just as it is the leading second language in Asia and Latin America. Consequently, we now see a trend in which the ability to speak a number of foreign languages is less of a necessity. More important is an ability to appreciate the foreign cultural context, which is helped by understanding a language but which can also be gained by better understanding the foreign culture itself.

In industries where knowledge of the local language is important, companies tend to assign sales territories to salespersons on the basis of language skills. A European multinational manufacturer of textile equipment assigns countries to its salespersons according to the languages they speak, such as French, Spanish, German, Italian, or English. This is more important in the traditional industries such as textile manufacturing, where businesses are more local in orientation and where English is not spoken that well by management.

Even executives who speak fairly good English may not understand all the details of product descriptions or specifications. As a result, a company can make an excellent impression by having its sales brochures translated into some of the key languages. European companies routinely produce company publications in several languages. Such translations may not be needed for Scandinavia, but might go a long way in other parts of the world where the level of English-language skills is not that high.

Business Etiquette

International marketers selling to overseas markets are likely to encounter a diverse set of business practices as they move from one country to another. Since interpersonal behavior is intensely culture bound, this part of the salesperson's job will vary by country. Many differences exist in how an appointment is made, how (and whether) an introduction is made, and how much lead time is needed for making appointments. The salesperson must also know whether or not gifts are expected or desired. When a salesperson is traveling to the same area repeatedly, familiarity with local customs can be expected. But for newcomers or experienced executives traveling to a new area, finding out the correct information is necessary.

For example, visiting businesspersons must attend long banquets when engaging in negotiations with the Chinese. These banquets may start in the late morning or early in the evening. Sitting mostly at a round table, the visitors will normally be seated next to the host who is expected to fill the visitor's plate at regular intervals. Foreign businesspersons are cautioned that frequent toasts are the norm and that many Chinese business hosts expect that the guest should become drunk; otherwise, the guest is believed not to have had a good time.[4] Business etiquettes can change from one country to another. While it is acceptable for visitors to arrive late in China, India, or Indonesia, arriving late in Hong Kong is not. Lateness causes the visitor to "lose face," which is an extremely serious matter among Hong Kong businesspersons.[5]

Important information can be obtained from special sources, since no manager can be expected to know the business customs of every country. For one, the company's own foreign market representatives or sales subsidiary can provide important information or suggestions. Also, when such access is not available, governments tend to collect data on business practices through their commercial officers posted abroad. For example, the United States Department of Commerce (DOC) publishes a regular series, "Doing Business in . . ." with a wealth of helpful suggestions. Some business service companies, such as accounting firms or international banks, also provide customers with profiles of business practices in foreign countries.

---

4. "Chemicals in China: Capacity for Enjoyment," *Financial Times*, September 30, 1986, p. VI.
5. "Hong Kong: Executive Guide to the Territory," *Financial Times*, June 27, 1986, p. XV.

Foreign businesspersons receiving visitors from the United States or any other foreign country rarely expect the foreign visitor to be familiar with all local customs. However, it is always appreciated when the visitor can indicate familiarity with the most common practices and some willingness to try to conform. Learning some foreign customs will help generate goodwill towards the company and can therefore enhance the chance of doing business.

Negotiations Strategies

Negotiations in the international arena are complicated because the negotiating partners frequently come from different cultural backgrounds. As a result, misunderstandings or misjudgments can occur leading to failure. To maximize the outcome in often difficult, long, and protracted negotiations, international sales personnel must be in tune with the cultural differences.

Although a myriad of negotiation strategies exist, concentrating on the mutual needs rather than the issues is a much practiced approach. In international marketing, the salesperson, or negotiator, must first determine the true objectives and needs of the other party. When negotiating within an unknown cultural setting, this is often a challenging task. Careful assessment of the negotiating party's needs can, however, enhance the chance for success.

For successful negotiation, understanding the *mindscape* of the counterpart can be very important.[6] Wenlee Ting, a noted anthropologist, defined mindscapes as "a structure of reasoning, cognition, perception, design, planning, and decision making that may vary from individual to individual and from culture to culture." Ting developed mindscape models based upon earlier work by another anthropologist, Maruyama. Building on Maruyama's work, Ting identified three common mindscapes for Hong Kong executives. Executives with an H-type mindscape tended to be interested in structured competition and the scientific organization of business. The tendency of executives with the I-type mindscape was to see separation of individual efforts as a key to higher efficiency. The G-type mindscape considered heterogeneity as a basis for mutually beneficial competition and tended to encourage differences among units. I-type mindscapes were said to be predominant among players in international finance or real estate; H-type mindscapes were predominant in family businesses; and G-type mindscapes were typical in international trading and business.[7]

The evidence further suggested that Hong Kong businesspersons negotiate well in Eastern and Western cultures. Skilled Hong Kong negotiators are able to

6. Alf H. Walle, "Conceptualizing Personal Selling for International Business: A Continuum of Exchange Perspective," *Journal of Personal Selling and Sales Management*, November 1986, pp. 9–17.

7. Wenlee Ting, *Business and Technological Dynamics in Newly Industrialized Asia* (Greenwood, 1985); and Magorah Maruyama, "Mindscapes and Social Theories," *Current Anthropology*, 1980, pp. 589–608.

engage in reasoning with Western counterparts while simultaneously employing other reasoning and negotiation techniques when dealing with local groups, family members, and other business associates.[8] This suggests that successful negotiation may depend on the foreign businessperson's ability to scout out the mindscape of his or her foreign counterpart's mindscape. Careful preparation of the cultural norms prevalent in the foreign country would be a starting point to successful negotiations and selling.

Timing is also an important aspect for negotiating abroad. In some countries, such as China, negotiations tend to take much more time than in the United States or some other Western countries. One European company that operated a joint venture in China observed that during one annual meeting, two weeks were spent in a discussion that elsewhere might have only taken a few hours. In this situation, however, much of the time was used for interdepartmental negotiations among various Chinese agencies rather than for face-to-face negotiations with the European company.

In another instance, a European firm negotiated with a Middle Eastern country over several months for the delivery of several hundred machines. When the company representatives went into that country for the final round of negotiations, they found that the competing firm had already been there several weeks before their arrival. The European firm's representatives decided to prepare themselves for long negotiations and refused to make concessions, figuring that the competitor had most likely been worn out in the prior weeks. As it turned out, that assessment was correct and the European company won the order by outstaying its competitor in a rather difficult negotiating environment. Obviously, unprepared sales executives might lose out to competitors if they do not understand the negotiation customs of a foreign country as they relate to the amount of time necessary to conclude a deal.

International Selling at Soudronic[9]

The sales function at Soudronic AG, a medium-sized manufacturer of welding equipment used primarily in the can-making industry, offers a good example of how an international sales force is organized and operated. Located in Switzerland, where all of its machines were produced, the company sold to can-makers in some eighty countries. The selling of these machines, which welded the bodies of metal cans at very high speeds, rested with a small sales force of seven sales managers. These managers reported to two regional sales managers, who in turn reported to the manager for sales and marketing. The entire world territory had been divided into seven parts in such a way that made travel schedules more

---

8. Walle, "Conceptualizing Personal Selling for International Business," pp. 9–17.
9. Jean-Pierre Jeannet, *Soudronic AG,* Case, IMEDE, International Management Development Institute, Lausanne, Switzerland, 1983.

efficient, that maximized the language competency of the sales force, and that balanced overall workloads.

Each sales manager was responsible for all client contact in his territory. In the assigned countries, the sales manager usually worked with local agents who indicated when a prospective client needed to be visited. The sales manager scheduled a visit on the next trip to that country and visited the client along with the local agent. The sales manager was technically trained to the extent that most questions could be answered on the spot. The sales manager also negotiated with the client for delivery and price terms within limits. Once a contract had been negotiated, the sales manager turned the client contact over to the service technician; although in many cases, the sales manager remained in contact with the client who preferred to deal primarily with one person.

Sales managers were expected to spend 50 percent of their time with clients either in the form of local contact, telephone contact, or correspondence. As a result, the Soudronic salespersons traveled a good percentage of their time. The availability of sales managers for such positions was limited. The company preferred to hire people who had a technical or engineering background together with several years of sales experience in the capital goods sector, not necessarily in the can-making industry. Prospective sales managers were also expected to have good first-hand knowledge of their assigned region, preferably through one or more years of work experience and to have acquired the language locally. Compensation was partially on a commission and incentive basis.

Local Selling (Single Country Sales Force)

When a company is able to maintain a local sales force in the countries where it does business, many of the difficulties of bridging the cultural gap with its clients will be minimized. The local sales force can be expected to understand the local customs, and the international company typically gains additional acceptance in the market. This is primarily because local sales forces are usually staffed with local nationals. However, many challenges remain, and the management of a local sales force often requires different strategies from those used in running a sales force in the company's domestic market.

Role of Local Sales Force and Control

When a company has decided to build up a local sales force, the decision has already been made for forward integration in its distribution effort. As we learned in Chapter 9, establishing a sales force means that the company has moved to assume the full role of a local sales subsidiary, sidestepping the independent distributor. Depending on the distribution strategy adopted, the company might sell directly, as might be the case for many industrial products or business services, or indirectly through local wholesalers, as would be the case for many consumer products and services. Although international companies will not make such a move unless present business volume justifies it, there are substantial benefits for a company in having its own sales force.

Control over a firm's sales activities is a frequently cited advantage for operating a company-owned local sales force. With its own sales force, the company can emphasize the products it wants to market at any time; and the company has better control over the way it is represented. In many cases, price negotiations, in the forms of discounts or rebates, are handled uniformly rather than leaving these decisions to an independent distributor with different interests. Having a company sales force also ensures that the personnel is of the necessary level and qualification. Control over all of these parameters usually means higher sales compared to using a distributor sales force.

Also, the local sales force can represent an important bridge with the local business community. For industries where the buying process is local rather than international, the sales force speaks the language of the local customer, can be expected to understand the local business customs, and can thus bring the international firm closer to its end-users. In many instances, local customers, though not objecting to buying from a foreign firm, may prefer to deal with local representatives of that firm. As a result, the ability of the international company to make its case heard with prospective customers is substantially enhanced.

However, local sales forces are single-country, or single-culture, by nature. While they do speak the language of the local customers they often do not speak any other language. As many U.S. firms have experienced, the local sales force abroad may have a very limited understanding of English, and its understanding of the head-office language is, in general, not sufficient to conduct business in that language. Furthermore, a local sales force cannot be expected to speak the languages of neighboring countries sufficiently in order to deal directly with such customers. In Europe, where this problem is particularly acute, language competency usually precludes a German firm from sending its sales force into France, or a French firm from sending its sales force into Italy or Spain. In some countries, there are several different languages spoken and this tends to further reduce the mobility of a sales force.

Local Sales Job

The type and extent of local sales effort a company will need is dependent on its own distribution effort and the relationship to the other communications mix elements. For firms who still use distributor sales forces to a large extent, a missionary sales force with limited responsibilities may suffice. This missionary sales force would concentrate on visiting clients together with the local distributor's sales force. If the international company's sales force needs to do the entire job, a much larger sales force will be necessary. As for the international firm's domestic market, the size of the local sales force depends to a large extent on the number of clients and the desired frequency of visits. This frequency may differ from country to country, which means that the size of the sales force would differ from country to country.

The role of the local sales force needs to be coordinated with the communications mix selected for each market. As many companies have learned, advertising or other forms of promotion can be used to make the role of the sales force more efficient. In many consumer goods industries, companies prefer a pull strategy concentrating their communications budget on the final consumer. In such cases, the role of the sales force is restricted to gain distribution access. However, as we've mentioned previously, there are countries where access to communications media is severely restricted. As a result, companies might place greater emphasis on the local sales force, thus affecting both role definition and size.

Foreign Sales Practices

Although sales forces are employed virtually everywhere, the nature of their interaction with the local customer is unique and may affect local sales operations. For most Westerners, Japanese practices seem substantially different. Here is an example reported by Masaaki Imai, President of Cambridge Corporation in Tokyo, a management consulting and recruiting firm.

Wnen Bausch & Lomb Japan introduced its then new soft lense line into Japan, the company had targeted influential eye doctors in each sales territory for its introductory launch. The assumption was that once these leading practitioners signed up for the new product, marketing to the majority of eye doctors would be easier. One salesperson was quickly dismissed by a key customer. The doctor said that he thought very highly of Bausch & Lomb equipment but preferred regular lenses for his patients. The salesperson did not even have a chance to respond; but he decided, since it was his first visit to this clinic, to stay around for awhile. He talked to several assistants at the clinic and talked to the doctor's wife who was, as was typical for Japan, handling the administration of the practice.

The next morning, the salesman returned to the clinic and observed that the doctor was very busy. He talked again with the assistants and joined the doctor's wife when she was cooking and talked with her about food. When the couple's young son returned from kindergarten, the salesman played with him and even went out to buy him a toy. The wife was very pleased with the well-intentioned babysitter. She later explained to the salesman that her husband had very little time to listen to any sales presentations during the day, so she invited him to come to their home in the evening. The doctor, obviously primed by his wife, received the salesman very warmly and they enjoyed *sake* together. The doctor listened patiently to the sales presentation and responded that he did not want to use the soft lenses on his patients right away. However, he suggested that the salesman try them on his assistants the next day. So on the third day, the salesman returned to the clinic and fitted soft lenses on several of the clinic's assistants. The reaction was very favorable, and the doctor placed an order on the third day of his sales call.[10]

It is probably fair to say that salespersons in many countries would have taken the initial negative response as the final answer from the doctor and would have tried elsewhere for success. In the context of Japan, however, the customer expects a different reaction from the salesperson. Japanese customers often judge from the frequency of the sales calls they receive whether the company really wants to do business. When the salesperson of one company makes more frequent calls to a potential customer than the competition, he or she may be regarded as more sincere.

This also means that companies doing business in Japan have to make frequent sales calls to their top customers often only for courtesy reasons. Customers get visited twice a year, usually in June and December, without necessarily discussing any business. Although this may occasionally be only a telephone call, the high frequency of visits significantly affects the staffing levels of the company-owned sales force.

Recruiting

Many foreign companies have found recruiting sales professionals quite challenging in many overseas markets. Although the availability of qualified sales personnel is a problem even in such countries as the United States, the scarcity of skilled personnel is even more acute in developing countries. Multinational companies, used to having salespersons with certain standard qualifications, may not find it easy to locate the necessary salespersons in a short period of time. One factor limiting their availability in many countries is the local economic situation. Depending on the economic cycle, the level of unemployment may be an excellent indicator as to the difficulty of finding prospects. This will limit the number of people a company can expect to hire away from existing firms unless a substantial increase over present compensation is offered.

More importantly, the image sales positions hold in a society may differ substantially. Typically, sales as an occupation or career has a relatively high image in the United States. This allows companies to recruit excellent talent, usually fresh from universities, for sales careers. These university recruits can usually consider sales as a career path toward middle-management positions. Such an image of selling is hardly found elsewhere in the world. In Europe, many companies continue to find it difficult to recruit university graduates into their sales forces, except in such highly technical fields such as computers, where the

---

10. "Salesmen Need to Make More Calls Than Competitors to Be Accepted," *The Japan Economic Journal,* June 26, 1979, p. 30.

recruits are typically engineers. When sales is a less desirable occupation, the quality of the sales force may suffer. If the company wants to insist on top quality, the time it will take to fill sales positions can be expected to increase dramatically.

How then can a company approach its formation of a company-owned sales force in a local market? When the firm already operates a limited-function sales subsidiary with responsibility to deal with local distributors, existing local executives can be entrusted with the recruiting function. Where such a beachhead does not exist, the company might want to find an international sales executive presently active in one of its other markets who knows the situation and cultural context of the new market. That executive, sometimes called *expatriate* because he or she is living outside of his or her own country, can be expected to build up the sales force step by step. Alternatively, executive recruiting firms have now sprung up in many countries, and these could be contacted to find the necessary personnel.

Compensation

In their home markets where they usually employ large sales forces, multinational companies become accustomed to handling and motivating their sales force in a given way. In the United States, typical motivation programs include some form of commission or bonus for meeting volume or budget projections as well as vacation prizes for top performers. When an international company manages local sales forces in various countries, the company is challenged to determine the best way to motivate them. Not all cultures may respond the same way, and motivating practices may differ from country to country. For example, Fiat produces trucks in Yugoslavia under an agreement with Zavodi Crvena Zastava. At a recent training session, the idea of paying salespeople an incentive based on profit margins was met with laughter.[11]

One of the frequently discussed topics in motivating salespersons is the value of the commission or bonus structure. In particular, U.S. companies have tended to use some form of commission structure for their sales force. Although this may fluctuate from industry to industry, U.S. firms tend to use more of a flexible and volume-dependent compensation structure than European firms. Japanese firms more often use a straight-salary type of compensation. To motivate the sales force to achieve superior performance, the international company may be faced with using different compensation practices depending on the local customs.

11. "American Abroad: IVECO's Man in Yugoslavia," *Sales & Marketing Management,* June 1987, p. 77.

Local Sales Force Examples

Selling in Brazil[12]

Ericsson do Brasil was the Brazilian affiliate of L. M. Ericsson, a Swedish multinational firm with a strong position in the telecommunications industry. The company marketed both central switching equipment for telephone companies and private exchanges (PBXs) to individual firms. The sales force for the PBX business numbered about one hundred persons and was organized geographically. In the southern sector of Brazil where industry was concentrated, the sales force was divided into specialists for either large PBXs, with up to two hundred external lines and several thousand internal lines, or for smaller systems called key systems, which could accommodate up to 25 incoming lines or up to 50 internal lines. In the northern, more rural part of Brazil, this specialization could not be achieved due to fewer accounts. As a result, the northern sales offices had sales representatives that sold both large and small systems.

Ericsson's sales force was compensated partially with a fixed salary and partially through commissions. Fixed monthly salaries amounted to about $400. A good salesperson could earn about $2,000 per month when the 4 percent sales commission was added to the base salary. Special government regulations required that each salesperson be assigned an exclusive territory. If a salesperson were reassigned, the company was then liable to maintain his or her income for another twelve months. As a result, changes in sales territory had to be considered carefully. When Ericsson do Brasil was faced with the introduction of a new paging system that was to be sold to corporate clients, most of whom also bought telephone equipment, the company found it difficult to assign territories to each of its present salespersons. If it wanted to reassign territories later on once it became clear who was good at selling paging systems over and above the telephone systems, the company would not be able to easily reassign territories without incurring compensation costs. In the end, Ericsson decided to assign the new paging system to its salespersons on a temporary basis only, thus preserving the chance to make other assignments later on without extra costs.

Wiltech India[13]

Selling in India is very different from selling in other countries. India, with the second-largest population in the world, is an example of a typical developing country. Wiltech, a venture between the British company Wilkinson and a large

---

12. Jean-Pierre Jeannet, "Ericsson Do Brasil: Ericall System," IMEDE, International Management Development Institute, Lausanne, Switzerland, M-296, 1983.
13. Jean-Pierre Jeannet, *Wiltech India,* case in progress, Babson College, 1987.

Indian conglomerate, was founded to market razor blades in India based upon Wilkinson technology. Founded in the early 1980s, the company needed to build up its sales force to compete against local competition. In India, there are more than 400,000 retailers or distributors of razor blades, and about 20 percent of them carry Wiltech blades.

The sales force of sixty persons primarily concentrates on urban markets. The sales representative working in a big metropolitan city directly handles one distributor and about 600 to 700 retail outlets. He or she is expected to visit the distributor every day and to make another 40 to 60 sales calls per day. The sales representative accomplishes this largely on foot because the sales outlets are relatively small and are clustered close to each other. The goal is to see important retailers at least twice per month and smaller retailers once a month. The sales representative working in smaller cities might cover about a dozen distributors and some 800 to 1,000 outlets. He or she would see distributors once or twice per month and see from 35 to 40 outlets per day. Travel would be by railway or by bus, whichever is more convenient.

Wiltech sales representatives are paid a fixed salary of 800 rupees to 1,200 rupees per month (about U.S. $70 to U.S. $100). Sales representatives that achieve their quotas and productivity targets can earn another 400 to 500 rupees per month in bonus. Expenses are paid on the basis of daily allowances for transport, lunch, and hotel stays when necessary. For sales representatives selling from a fixed location, this daily allowance amounts to 30 rupees per day. When travelling away from home, the daily allowance amounts to 50 rupees plus the actual transportation costs for first-class train fare or bus fare. Although these costs might appear very low compared to typical salaries and travel expenses paid for in a developed country, they nevertheless represent a very good income in India where per capita GNP cost of living is very low by Western standards.

Alternatives to a Local Sales Force

Because the building up of a local sales force is both a costly and time-consuming task, some companies have looked for alternatives without necessarily falling back on independent distributors. When competitive pressures require a rapid access to a sales force, piggybacking has been practiced by some companies.

Recently, companies have joined into a wide variety of international distribution alliances. The sales alliance format differs from other ventures because the two firms who join forces do so as independent firms and not necessarily in the form of a limited joint venture. In an alliance, two companies might swap products, with one company carrying the other firm's products in one market and vice versa. Such swaps have been used extensively in the pharmaceutical industry. The short period of time left for marketing once the products have been approved and before the patents expire has called for a very rapid product roll-out in as many countries as possible.

INDUSTRIAL PROMOTION

Many of the communications approaches discussed so far were geared toward the marketing of consumer goods and industrial goods. However, there are some specific promotional methods that are geared largely for the industrial market and that play an important role in the international marketing of such products. The use of international trade fairs, bidding procedures for international projects, and consortium selling all have to be understood if an investment or industrial products company wants to succeed in international markets.

International Trade Fairs

Participation in international trade fairs has become an important aspect for companies marketing industrial products abroad. Trade fairs are ideal for exposing new customers and potential distributors to a company's product range and have been used extensively both by newcomers and established firms. In the United States, industrial customers can be reached through a wide range of media, such as specialized magazines with a particular industry focus. In many overseas countries, the markets are too small to allow for the publication of such trade magazines in only one country. As a result, prospective customers usually attend these trade fairs on a regular basis. Trade fairs also offer companies a chance to meet with prospective customers in a less formalized atmosphere. For a company that is new to a certain market and does not yet have any established contacts, participation in a trade fair may be the only way to reach potential customers.

Companies have a large number of fairs to select from. International shows of general orientation include the Hanover Fair of West Germany, usually held in April each year. More than 500,000 visitors attend the fair coming from all industry sectors and representing many European countries. Many U.S. firms exhibit at the fair each year, both small and large. More companies are represented through their European offices or distributors. The Hanover Fair is considered the largest industrial fair in the world.[14] Other large general fairs include the Leipzig Fair in East Germany, the Canton Fair in China, and the Milan Fair in Italy.

Specialized trade fairs concentrate on a certain segment of the industry or user group. Such fairs usually attract limited participation both in terms of exhibitors and visitors. Typically, they are more technical in nature. Some of the specialized trade fairs may not take place every year. One of the leading specialized fairs is the Achema for the chemical industry in Germany held every three

---

14. "World's Biggest Industrial Trade Fair Lures 500 U.S. Firms," *Industrial Marketing*, February 1981, p. 24.

years. Annual fairs having an international reputation are the air shows of Farn-borough, England, or Paris where aerospace products are displayed.

Participation in trade fairs can save both time and effort for a company that wants to break into a new market and does not yet have any contacts. For new product announcements or demonstrations, the trade fair offers an ideal forum for display. Trade fairs are also used by competitors to check on each other's most recent developments. They can give a newcomer an idea of the potential competition in some foreign markets before actual market entry. Consequently, trade fairs are both a means of selling products and of gathering important and useful market intelligence. Marketers with international aspirations would there-fore do well to search out the relevant trade fairs that are directed at their industry or customer segment and to schedule regular attendance.

The Bidding Process

The bidding process for industrial products tends to be more complicated, partic-ularly when major industrial equipment is involved. For companies competing for such major projects, a number of stages have to be passed before negotiations for a specific purchase can ever take place. Typically, companies go through a search process for new projects, then move on to prequalify for the particular project before a formal project bid or tender is submitted. Each phase requires careful management and the appropriate allocation of resources.

During the search phase, companies want to make sure that they are in-formed of any project worth their interest that is related to their product lines. For particularly large projects that are government sponsored, full-page adver-tisements may appear in leading international newspapers. More likely, compa-nies have to have a network of agents, contacts, or former customers who will inform them of any project being considered.

In the prequalifying phase, the purchaser will frequently ask for documenta-tion from interested companies who would like to make a formal tender. At this phase, no formal bidding or tender documents are submitted. Instead, more general company background will be required that might describe other or simi-lar projects the company has finished in the past. At this stage, the company will have to sell itself and its capabilities. A large number of companies can be expected to pursue prequalification.

In the next phase, the customer will select the companies to be invited to submit a formal bid. Usually, these may be only three to four companies. Formal bids consist of a proposal of how to solve the specific client problem at hand. For industrial equipment, this usually requires personal visits on location, special design of some components, and preparing full documentation including engi-neering drawings for the client. The costs can be substantial and can range from a few hundred thousand dollars to several million for some very large projects. The customer will select the winner from among those submitting formal pro-posals. Normally, it is not just the lowest bidder who will obtain the order.

Technology, the type of solution proposed, and the financing arrangements all play a role.

Once an order is obtained, the supplying company may be expected to ensure its own performance. For that purpose, the company may be asked to post a performance bond which is a guarantee that the company would pay certain specified damages to the customer if the job was not completed within the pre-agreed specifications. Performance bonds are usually issued by banks on behalf of the supplier. The entire process, from finding out about a new prospect until the order is actually received in hand, may take from several months to several years depending on the project size or industry.

Consortium Selling

Because of the high stakes involved in marketing equipment or turn-key projects (a plant, system, or project in which the buyer acquires a complete solution so that the entire operation can commence at the turn of a key), companies have frequently banded together to form a consortium. A consortium is a group of firms that share in a certain contract or project on a pre-agreed basis but act almost like one company towards the customers. Joining together in a consortium can help share the risk in some very large projects. A consortium can enhance the competitiveness of the members by offering a turn-key solution to the customer.

Most consortiums are formed on an ad-hoc basis. For the supply of a major steel mill, for example, companies supplying individual components may combine into a group and offer a single tender to the customer. The consortium members have agreed to share all marketing costs and can help each other with design and engineering questions. The customer gets a chance to deal with one supplier only, which substantially simplifies the process. Ad-hoc consortiums can be found for some very large projects that require unique skills from their members. The consortium members frequently come from the same country and thus expect to have a greater change to get the contract than if they operated on their own. In situations where the same set of skills or products are in frequent demand, companies may form a permanent consortium. Whenever a chance for a deal arises, the consortium members will immediately prepare to qualify for the bidding.

Companies that market equipment that represents only a small part of a much larger project may find the consortium approach helpful because marketing costs can be shared. Preparation of bid documents is expensive and a time-consuming process. Participating in a consortium may be the only chance for a company that is faced with a client demanding a turn-key project. The selection of appropriate partners is important in this context, and chances for overseas orders may be improved if the foreign firms participating in the consortium understand the foreign buying environment.

OTHER FORMS OF PROMOTION

So far, our discussion has been concentrated on personal selling as one key element of the communications mix. However, next to advertising, various forms of promotion play a key role in international marketing. Usually combined under the generic title of promotions, they may include such elements as in-store retail promotions or coupons. Many of these tools are consumer goods oriented and are used less often in industrial goods marketing. In this section, we will look at sales promotion activities, as well as sports promotions and sponsorships.

Sales Promotion

In many ways, the area of sales promotion has largely a local focus. Although some form of promotions, such as coupons, gifts, or various types of reduced-price labels, are in use in most countries, strict government regulations and different retailing practices tend to limit the options for international firms (see Table 14.2).

In the United States, coupons are the leading form of sales promotion. Consumers bring product coupons to the retail store and obtain a reduced price for the product. Second in importance are refund offers. Consumers who send a proof of purchase to the manufacturer will receive a refund in the form of a check. Also used, but less frequently, are cents-off labels or factory-bonus packs, which induce consumers to buy large quantities due to the price incentive. Marketers of consumer goods in the United States, who are the primary users of these types of sales promotion, find a full array of services available to run their promotions. Companies such as A. C. Nielsen Company specialize in managing coupon redemption centers centrally so that all handling of promotions can be turned over to an outside contractor.

In other countries, the primary sales promotion tools tend to be different. Coupons, the most frequently used tool in the United States, are frequently prohibited in such countries as Germany or Greece. Where they are being used, they tend to play a minor role, such as in Sweden or the United Kingdom. In most overseas markets, price reductions in the store are usually the most important promotional tool, followed by reductions to the trade, such as wholesalers and retailers. Also of importance in some countries are free goods, double-pack promotions, and in-store displays.

Most countries have restrictions against some forms of promotions. Frequently regulated are any games of chance, but games in which some type of skill is required are usually allowed. When reductions are made available, they often are not allowed to exceed a certain percentage of the product's purchase price. As a result, international firms will encounter a series of regulations and restric-

TABLE 14.2 Concise Guide to Sales Promotion

	Austria	Australia	Belgium	Brazil	Canada	Switzerland	Germany	Spain	Ireland	France
Top 3 sales promotion techniques	Reduced price in store	Reduced price in store	Reduced price in store	Gift Banded pack	Reduced price in store	Reduced price in store	Reduced price in store	Coupons	Reduced price in store	Reduced price in store
	Open competitions	Trade discounts	Trade discounts	Extra product free	Trade discounts	Trade discounts	Displays	Free goods	Trade discounts	Trade discounts
	Trade discounts	Promotional pack sizes with extra free product	Extra product free	Reduced price in store	Coupons	Merchandising contribution by manufacturers to trade	Trade discounts	Reduced price in store	Extra product free	Free samples
Restrictions on sales promotion techniques	No coupons, restrictions for on-pack deals.	Individual state coupons restrictions. Promotions and trade support must be available for all stores. Lotteries and games of chance subject to government authorization. Some restrictions on proof of purchase.		Distribution of prizes via vouchers, contests etc. is subject to government authorization. Ethical products, alcoholic beverages, cigarettes, cigars, not permitted any type of sales promotion.	Promotions must be offered to all stores. No promotions of pharmaceuticals except as samples to doctors. Competitions require skill testing questions.	Laws against unfair competition exist.	No coupons. Free goods restricted to value of about 0.10 DM.		Below cost selling. License required for competitions which must inspire a degree of skill.	Games of chance are usually forbidden. Premiums and gifts are limited to 5% of product value and no more than 1% off.

	Great Britain	Greece	Italy	Japan	Mexico	Netherlands	New Zealand	Portugal	Argentina	Sweden	United States	South Africa
Top 3 sales promotion techniques	Reduced price in store; Trade discounts; Coupons	Trade discounts; Special offers; Reduced price in store	Reduced price in store; Banded packs; Coupons	Reduced price in store; Trade discounts; Premiums	Reduced price in store; Bonus packs; On-pack premiums	Trade discounts; Reduced price in store; Display promotions, premiums	Reduced price in store; Banded packs; Coupons	Trade discounts; Reduced price in store; Competitions	Reduced price in store; Trade discounts; In-store displays, promotions	Co-op advertising and money-off; Local activities; Coupons	Coupons; Refund offers; Cents-off label, factory packs, bonus packs	Reduced price in store; Trade discounts; In-store coupons, promotions
Restrictions on sales promotion techniques	Legislation on bargain offers, lotteries, sweepstakes. Competitions must include a degree of skill. No price promotion on categories like pharmaceuticals.	No coupons. Gifts limited to 5% of product value.	No coupons on butter, oil, coffee. No self-liquidating offer or contest or gifts. Gifts limited to 8% of product value.	Some regulations regarding lotteries. Some regulations on excessive gifts or premiums.	Government authorization required. No promotions based on collecting a series of labels etc. No promotions of alcohol, tobacco products.	Legislation on gift schemes, pharmaceuticals, tobacco, games of chance.	No pyramid selling. No trading stamps. Coupons redeemable for cash only. Competitions require a degree of skill. Legislation on Christmas Club funds.	Some rules regarding lotteries and sweepstakes.	Rules regarding lotteries, special prizes. Products like pharmaceuticals cannot be promoted through prices.	No premium redemption plans. Competitions must include a degree of skill. Mixed offers are restricted. Cross-coupons "in-" or "on-pack" not allowed.	All promotion & trade support must be equally available to all retailers. Restrictions on frequency of use of "cents-off" and special packs. Numerous voluntary industry standards.	No lotteries or games of chance. Restrictions on coupons, especially no conditional purchase. No comparative advertising.

Source: From William J. Hawkes' Presentation to the International Marketing Workshop AMA/MSI, March 1983, of A. C. Nielsen Company material. Reprinted by permission of A. C. Nielsen Company.

tions on promotions that differ among countries. Consequently, there is little opportunity to standardize sales promotion techniques across many markets. This has caused most companies to make sales promotions the responsibility of local management who are expected to understand the local customs and restrictions.

Sports Promotions and Sponsorships

With major sports events becoming increasingly covered by the mass media, television in particular, the commercial value of these events has increased tremendously over the last decade. Today, large sports events, such as the Olympics or world championships in other sports, could not exist in their present form without funding by companies who do this either through advertising or through different types of sponsorships.

In the United States, companies have for some time purchased TV advertising space for such events as regularly broadcasted baseball, basketball, or football events. Gillette was one company that regularly used sponsorship of the World Series to introduce new products. This was just another extension of the company's media strategy to air television and radio commercials at times when its prime target group could be found in large numbers watching TV or listening to the radio. More recently, companies have purchased similar time slots for the Olympics when they are broadcast in the United States.

In many foreign countries where commercial television advertising was restricted or not even allowed, companies did not have the opportunity to purchase air time. A U.S. firm that had invested heavily in U.S. television time for the Olympics would find itself unable to do the same in Germany, where TV advertising was shown only during some very limited time blocks during the day and not interspersed during sports shows. Therefore, companies that still wanted to expose their products to the large audience of these sports shows needed to use different methods.

In order to circumvent restrictions on commercial television during sports programs, companies have purchased space for signs along the stadiums or the arenas where sports events take place. When the event is covered on television, the cameras will automatically take in the signs as part of the regular coverage. No mention of the company's product is made in any way either by the announcer or in the form of commercials.

It is the visual identification that the firms are looking for. For the 1982 Soccer World Championship held in Spain, four Japanese companies (JVC, Seiko, Canon, and Fuji) paid a reported $9 million for the privilege of having their names posted along stadiums. An estimated one billion people watched parts of that event which extended over several weeks involving 16 teams from all over the world.[15] In the case of the 1986 Soccer World Cup in Mexico, the

---

15. "Japanese Play the Sponsor Game," *Financial Times,* September 24, 1982, p. 24.

event extended over almost four weeks and involved some twenty-four national teams. It was estimated that nine billion viewers watched either all the games or parts of them on television, which meant nine billion exposures for any company that had managed to obtain sign space along the playing field. Most of this was delivered in countries where it was from the very beginning difficult to get TV space and thus of great importance to the firm. Although contracts between sponsors and FIFA (the world football association) are confidential, it is believed that a company would have to pay about U.S. $7 million for two signs along the field for all the 117 preliminary and final games played by the 24 national team finalists.[16]

To take advantage of such global sports events, a company should have a logo or brand name that is worth exposing to a global audience. It is not surprising to find that the most common sponsors are companies producing consumer goods with a global appeal, such as soft drink manufacturers, consumer electronics producers, or film companies. To purchase sign space a firm would have to take into consideration the popularity of certain sports. Few sports have global appeal. Soccer, which is the number one spectator sport in much of the world, still has little commercial value in the United States or in Canada. In contrast, baseball and American football have little appeal in Europe or parts of Asia and Africa. Many other sports have also only local or regional character, which requires a company to know its market and the interests of its target audience very well.

Aside from sponsoring sporting events, companies have also moved more aggressively into sponsoring direct competitors or teams. Manufacturers of sports equipment have for some time concentrated on getting leading athletes to use their equipment. For sports that have achieved international or even global reach, such as tennis, skiing, or soccer, such endorsement of sports products by leading athletes can be a key to success. Manufacturers of sports equipment have therefore always attempted to get their equipment used by world class athletes.

Adidas, the German manufacturer of athletic footwear has used such sponsorships in the past. To succeed, companies must first get the athlete to use its products and then try to commercialize that success. This can take some ingenious planning. In World Cup skiing, where winning athletes can impact on the fortune of ski manufacturers, winners are usually photographed with their skis in hand. Manufacturers will try to get their names on the bottom of the skis so that in the winning skier's photograph, which receives wide circulation, their names can be easily read and the positive identification with the winner is made. How various running shoe manufacturers fared in the 1985 London Marathon is shown in Table 14.3.

To exploit the media coverage of spectator sports, many non-sporting goods manufacturers have joined the sponsoring of specific athletes or teams. These are firms who intended to exploit the visual identification created by the media

---

16. "The Selling of the Biggest Game on Earth," *Business Week,* June 9, 1986, p. 102.

TABLE 14.3 Market Shares of Running Shoes in 1985 London Marathon (in percentages)

	Under 2 hrs. 30 min	2·30–3·00	3·00–3·30	3·30–4·00
Adidas	20	14	15	16
Brooks	4	4	3	3
Hi-Tech	1	7	14	19
New Balance	12	14	17	16
Nike	42	45	33	30
Reebok	4	9	10	10
Tiger	9	1	3	2
Others	9	6	5	4

Source: "Trials of a Long Distance Runner," Financial Times, April 14, 1986, p. 14. Reprinted by permission.

coverage. Many will remember the pictures of winning race car drivers with all the various corporation names or logos on their uniforms. Although these promotions once tended to be mostly related to sports products, now sponsors are increasingly unrelated to the sports. A well-known example is Marlboro's sponsoring of formula one race car driving. In Europe, companies that sponsor soccer teams may place the company name or logo on the jersey of each player. Companies have also become involved in bicycle racing. The U.S. convenience store chain, 7-Eleven, sponsored a team of U.S. professional riders during the 1986 and 1987 Tour de France. Although the race took place in France, the company had intended to exploit its sponsorship in the U.S. through extensive coverage of the race in the U.S. news media.

Puma AG, a large West German manufacturer of sports shoes and other sports accessories, having a worldwide revenue of about $2.2 billion, was caught by surprise when the U.S. market, accounting for half its worldwide sales, began to favor soft-leather walking shoes. The company's sales declined and its market share slipped from 12 percent to 7 percent in the United States. To help, Puma signed West German tennis star Boris Becker to a six-year contract valued at around $29 million, the largest such agreement at that time. Becker was to wear Puma tennis shoes and the company planned to open as many as 1,000 U.S. retail sports shops under the name "Boris Becker Shops." The company hoped to more than recoup its considerable investment in the tennis star and believed that Becker accounted in 1987 for about $55 million in annual sales. Puma hoped that Becker could do the same for its other lines as he did for its tennis racket business. In 1984, Puma sold only 15,000 tennis rackets a year. In 1985, following Becker's first victory in Wimbledon and his backing of Puma's rackets, sales jumped to 150,000 rackets. Following Becker's second Wimbledon victory in 1986, Puma expected sales to grow again.[17]

Through the intensive coverage of sports in the news media all over the world, many companies will continue to use the sponsorship of sporting events as an important element in their international communications programs. Successful companies will have to track both the interest of various countries in the many types of sports and exhibit both flexibility and ingenuity in the selection of available events or participants. In many parts of the world, sports sponsoring may continue to be the only available way to reach large numbers of prospective customers.

DIRECT MARKETING

Direct marketing includes a number of marketing approaches that involve direct access to the customer. Direct mail, door-to-door selling, and telemarketing are the primary direct marketing tools used in the United States. Some companies have been able to achieve considerable success in their fields through aggressive direct marketing. Many of these firms realize that not all markets respond equally well to direct marketing. For the most part, the United States has the most developed direct marketing field.

Direct marketing, including both industrial- and consumer-directed promotions, is growing rapidly worldwide and is considered a significant marketing tool in more than thirty countries. Direct marketing grew 140 percent in Japan between 1977 and 1979, with some $760 million in advertising-related expenditures. However, in the United States, media spending estimates for 1979 amounted to more than $22 billion by comparison. Total direct marketing expenditures outside the United States were estimated to have amounted to $6 billion. West Germany, the United Kingdom, and Japan are the most important markets for direct marketing. Direct marketing is much less common in Latin America, Africa, and the Middle East.[18]

Direct Mail

Direct mail, largely pioneered in the United States by catalogue houses such as Sears, Roebuck and Montgomery Ward, is being used extensively in other countries. For mail order sales to be successful, it takes an efficient postal system and an effective collection system for the shipped products. In countries where these

---

17. "Puma Hopes Superstar Will Help End U.S. Slump, Narrow Gap with Adidas," *The Wall Street Journal,* February 6, 1987, p. 24.
18. "Focus: Direct Response," *Industrial Marketing,* August 1981, p. 84.

preconditions exist, direct mail is being used extensively by retail organizations and other service organizations such as *Reader's Digest* or credit card suppliers.

Companies who may want to engage in direct mail will have to ensure that their mail pieces or catalogues are translated into the respective foreign language. Obtaining accurate mailing lists may also be difficult, although list brokers exist in many countries as they do in the United States. Direct mail offers an opportunity for companies that want to extend their business beyond a limited location and even into foreign countries. Stockman, the leading Finnish department store located in Helsinki, has been doing an extensive mail order business with foreigners who live in Eastern European countries and who have difficulty purchasing modern or Western consumer goods. In general, however, mailing of packages abroad always involves the receiver country's custom system, which tends to delay parcels considerably.

Door-to-Door Sales

Companies such as Avon or Mary Kay Cosmetics have met with considerable success in the United States.[19] These and other firms have grown entirely by the use of door-to-door selling techniques and by employing large numbers of part-time salespersons. Some of the cosmetics firms employ women who sell through organized home "party" demonstrations or by contacting friends in their own neighborhoods or at work. Expansion of these and other companies into foreign markets has been met with mixed success.

The concept of door-to-door selling is not equally accepted in all countries. Moreover, it may also not be equally accepted to make a profit from selling to a friend, colleague at work, or neighbors. The willingness to find suitable sales persons on a part-time basis may also be limited because in some countries women or even students are not necessarily expected to work. As a result, the type of door-to-door selling that is the hallmark of a number of successful U.S. firms may be largely limited to the cultural background of the United States.

Telemarketing

Telemarketing is the most recent technique in direct marketing and has enjoyed explosive growth in the United States. Selling by telephone allows companies to quickly access large numbers of target customers in a short period of time, something that could not be done personally. Furthermore, the high cost of personal selling has motivated many firms to augment their sales effort through telephone sales to save costs.

---

19. "Mary Kay Cosmetics: Looking Beyond Direct Sales to Keep the Party Going," *Business Week,* March 28, 1983, p. 130.

To make telephone sales effective abroad, an efficient telephone system is a requirement. Telephone sales for individual households might become practical when a large number of subscribers exist and when their telephone numbers can be easily obtained. However, not all countries accept the practice of soliciting business directly at home. Yet, in Western Europe where the economic pressures on selling are the same as they are in the United States, companies could expect to gain if telemarketing were used appropriately. Because of the language problems involved, companies would be advised to make sure their telemarketing sales forces not only speak the language of the local customer but do so fluently and with the correct local or regional accent. British Telecommunications, the British company operating most telephone systems in that country, maintained a telephone sales force of some 300 operators, which was believed to be the largest telephone sales operation in Europe. Other countries with substantial telephone selling activities include the Netherlands, France, Scandinavia, and West Germany (a country where this practice is heavily restricted).[20]

On an international level, telephone sales might be helpful for business-to-business marketing when decision makers can be contacted quickly and when they can be identified from available directories. Travel costs for overseas travel are considerable; and since direct dialing is now possible for international calls in many countries, telemarketing on a cross-country or international basis might become possible.

CONCLUSIONS

Communications in an international context are particularly challenging because managers are constantly faced with communicating to customers with different cultural backgrounds. This tends to add to the complexity of the communications task, which demands a particular sensitivity to culture, habits, and at times even different types of rational reasoning.

Aside from the cultural differences that largely affect the content and form of the communications, international firms will encounter a different set of cost constraints for the principal communications mix elements, such as selling or advertising. Given such large differences from country to country with respect to sales force costs or media costs, international firms will have to carefully design their communications mix to fit each individual market. Furthermore, the availability of any one individual communications mix element cannot be taken for granted. The absence of one or the other, either due to legal or economic development considerations, will force the international firm to compensate with a greater use of other mix elements.

---

20. "Cold Calls Seek a Warmer Welcome," *Financial Times*, June 26, 1986, p. 6.

When designing effective sales forces for local markets, international marketers need to take into consideration the challenge of international sales and the requirements for doing well. Such international sales efforts can usually be maintained for companies selling highly differentiated and complex products to a clearly defined target market. In most other situations, in which the products are targeted at a broader type of industrial or consumer customer group, international firms will typically have to engage a local sales force for each market. Local sales forces are usually very effective in reaching their own market or country, but they are not always able to transfer to another country because of language limitations. Building up and managing a local sales force is a challenging task in most foreign markets and requires managers with a special sensitivity to local laws, regulations, and trade practices.

Questions for Discussion

1. What factors appear to affect the extension of push or pull policies in international markets?
2. Under what circumstances should a company pursue an international versus a local selling effort?
3. What factors most often appear to make local selling different from country to country?
4. What patterns can you detect in the use of sales promotion tools across many countries?
5. To what type of companies would you suggest sponsorship in the next Olympic Games; and what sports would you suggest to them? How would such firms profit from any kind of association with the Olympic Games?

For Further Reading

"Advertising Jingle-Jangles Through the Slump." *The Economist* (September 20, 1980), pp. 85–86.

Behrman, J. N., J. J. Boddewyn, and Askok Kapoor. *International Business—Government Communications.* Lexington, Mass.: D. C. Heath, 1975.

Blake, David H., and Vita Toros. "The Global Image Makers." *Public Relations Journal* (June 1976), pp. 10–16.

Davidson, Robert E. "Pan Am Soars into International Direct Mail." *The International Advertiser,* 11, No. 1 (1970), pp. 17–20.

Dunn, S. Watson. "Effect of National Identity on Multinational Promotional Strategy in Europe." *Journal of Marketing* (October 1976), pp. 50–57.

Ferguson, Henry. "International Exhibit Marketing: A Management Approach" *Dimensions* (1986).

Hoke, Peter. "Wunderman's View of Global Direct Marketing." *Direct Marketing* 48 (March 1986), pp. 76–88, 153.

Japan External Trade Organization. *Sales Promotion in the Japanese Market.* Tokyo: Jetro, 1980.

Ordolis, C. N. "Standardization versus Adaption of the Communication Process: A Diagnostic Approach to International Advertising and the Dilemma of Major Marketing Organizations Operating in Western Europe." Unpublished research paper. Concordia University, Montreal, August 1980.

Still, Richard R. "Sales Management: Some Cross-Cultural Aspects." *Journal of Personal Selling and Sales Management* (Spring-Summer 1981), pp. 6–9.

Thomas, L. R. "Trade Fairs: Gateways to European Markets." Business American (April 20, 1981), pp. 7–10.

Tung, Rosalie L. "Selection and Training of Personnel for Overseas Assignments." *Columbia Journal of World Business* (Spring 1981), pp. 68–78.

Wills, James R., Jr., and John K. Ryans, Jr. "An Analysis of Headquarters' Executive Involvement in International Advertising." *European Journal of Marketing,* No. 8 (1977), pp. 577–583.

15.

MANAGING INTERNATIONAL ADVERTISING

At the outset of this book we defined international marketing as those marketing activities that applied simultaneously to more than one country. In the case of advertising, the volume that is directed simultaneously towards targets in several countries is actually very small. The majority of advertising activity tends to be directed toward one country only. Despite the "local" nature of international advertising, it is important to recognize that the initial input, either in terms of the product idea or the basic communications strategy, largely originates in another country. Consequently, although there is a largely local aspect to most international advertising, there is also an international aspect to consider. Therefore, there are two important decisions to be made in international advertising: (1) how much of a local versus an international emphasis should there be, and (2) what should be the nature and content of the advertising itself. The first part of the chapter is organized around the explanation of key external factors and their influence on international advertising. The second part of the chapter focuses on the major advertising decisions and helps to explain how external factors affect specific advertising areas. Special emphasis is given to advertising in Japan, where the advertising environment differs considerably from that in the United States or Europe. (For a chapter overview, see Figure 15.1.)

CHALLENGES IN INTERNATIONAL ADVERTISING

Probably no other aspect of international marketing has received as much attention as international advertising. Consider the following examples:

- In Italy, "Schweppes Tonic Water" had to be reduced to "Schweppes Tonica" because "il water" turned out to be the idiom for a bathroom.

FIGURE 15.1 International Advertising

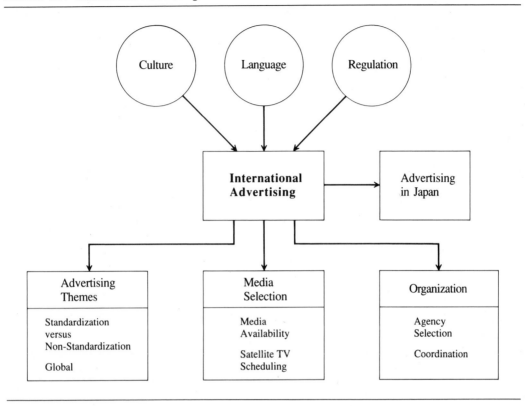

- General Motors, translating its slogan "Body by Fisher" into Flemish for its Belgium campaign, found out belatedly that the meaning was the equivalent of "Corpse by Fisher."[1]

These are only a few of many examples where mistakes were made in translating advertising copy from one language into another. Most of these mistakes, however, occurred in the 1960s, a time when international advertising was in its infancy. Today, most companies and advertising agencies have reached a level of sophistication that has reduced the chances of translation errors. This does not mean that language is not a factor to consider in today's international communications strategy. However, we have moved from a primary concern about translation to concerns about ways to be more efficient.

---

1. David A. Ricks, Jeffrey S. Arpan and Marilyn Y. Fu, "Pitfalls in Advertising Overseas," *Journal of Advertising Research,* December 1974, p. 48.

A second major cause of international advertising mistakes has traditionally been the neglect of cultural attitudes of consumers in foreign countries. Here are two examples:

- To penetrate the British market in breakfast cereals, General Mills, a United States–based MNC, pictured on its package an appealing, red-haired, freckle-faced boy saying: "See kids, it's great!" This very attractive design, which was effective in the United States, contributed little towards moving the products off the supermarket shelf. The British homemaker was not attracted by what appeared to be a meaningless expression by a child, given the British preference for more formality and a less child-oriented society.
- A manufacturer of eyeglasses ran into troubles with its advertising campaign in Thailand. To promote a line of glasses, ads and billboards were used depicting cute pictures of animals wearing glasses. The campaign failed to catch on despite its charm because, as was found out later, Thai regarded animals as a lower level of creation and so they were thus unmoved by the advertising.[2]

These and other examples we've cited point out that, even when the language or translation hurdle is correctly overcome, there still remains the need to consider the cultural and social background of the target market. Mistakes based on a misinterpretation of cultural habits are more difficult to avoid, though substantial progress has been made by international marketers to stay away from the most obvious violations. However, the avoidance of either translation or cultural errors will not be enough to produce an effective advertising campaign. Although we will initially concentrate on approaches to overcome such cultural difficulties, we will eventually emphasize critical issues around organizing campaigns internationally.

Overcoming the Language Barrier

Most of the translation blunders referred to in the previous section were due to literal translations performed outside of the target country. The translators, not always in contact with the culture of the target country, were unable to judge the actual meaning of the translated copy for the target audience. Furthermore, the faulty translation could not be checked by the executives involved since they too were from a different culture and did not possess any foreign language skills.

Today, the traps of faulty translations can be avoided through the involvement of local nationals or language experts. Typically, international marketers have any translations checked by either a local advertising agency, its own local subsidiary, or an independent distributor located in the target country. Because MNCs are active in a large number of countries and thus require the use of many

---

2. *Ibid.*

languages, today's international marketers can find an organizational solution to the translation errors of the past. Many errors can still occur, however, if the foreign language copy is typeset incorrectly or by inexperienced typesetters. This is particularly true for non-Roman letters.[3]

Overcoming the Cultural Barrier

When international marketers fail due to misinterpretation of the local culture, they usually do so because they advocated an action that was inconsistent with the local culture or because the appeal chosen was inconsistent with the motivational pattern of the target culture. Advocating the purchase of a product whose use is inconsistent with the local culture will result in failure, even if the appeal chosen did not violate that culture per se. However, companies can also fail if only the appeal, or message employed, is inconsistent with the local culture, even if the action promoted is not. Consequently, a foreign country entering a new market has to be aware of both cultural aspects: the product's use and the message employed.

To ensure that a message is in line with the existing cultural beliefs of the target market, an MNC can use resources similar to those used to overcome the translation barriers. Local subsidiary personnel or local distributors can judge the cultural content of the message. Also helpful are advertising agencies with local offices. The international marketer could not possibly know enough about all the cultures he or she will come into contact with. However, it is the responsibility of the international executive to make sure that knowledgeable local nationals have given enough input so as to avoid the mistake of using an inappropriate appeal with respect to the local culture.

For successful advertising in Nigeria, Africa's largest and most populous nation, the standard advertising patterns used in other countries would not necessarily work.[4] Gulda beer ads showed a large, roughhewn man in a blue-jean jacket based upon the U.S. movie character Shaft. The person was shown holding a mug, and the brown glass bottle of Gulda beer was on the table. The slogan "Gulda man, Gulda man, sure of his taste, proud to be different" was used. However, this ad did not appear to promote the brand. Research showed that Nigerian consumers of beer felt that good beer came only in green bottles. They noted that the person in the Gulda ad was always drinking alone. For many Nigerians, drinking beer was a social activity. The ad was finally changed. Gulda was presented in a green bottle, and the theme was changed to "Gulda makes you feel real fine," and the setting was changed to show elegant people drinking together. Sales volume increased dramatically.

---

3. "A Not-So-Funny Thing Happened on the Way to the Printer," *Business Marketing*, February 1987, p. 113.
4. "Of Ads and Elders: Selling to Nigerians," *The New York Times*, April 20, 1987, p. D10.

The experience of Nigerian advertisers with black models also showed interesting cultural traits.[5] Black models from the United States were only acceptable to the upper class Nigerian, but most middle and lower class Nigerians reacted negatively to the dress and speech of U.S. models, although they could pass otherwise for Nigerian. In contrast, the experience with models in Mexico turned out to be the opposite.[6] Despite the fact that most Mexicans have dark hair and brown eyes, most models shown in posters are blond. According to many Mexican advertising specialists, Mexicans relate more positively to blond models because they are a reminder of the lifestyle in the United States.

The judgment on the appropriateness of a product or service for a culture is substantially more difficult than making a judgment only on the type of advertising to be employed. In Chapter 3 we discussed the nature of cultural and social forces, and in Chapter 7, we covered the evaluation of market potential for products. Here we have therefore restricted ourselves to a discussion of the advertising aspects of cultural analysis.

Selecting an Advertising Theme

For international marketers with products sold in many countries, the basic decision tends to center around the appropriate level of standardization for the advertising theme and its creative execution. As a result of early failures by inexperienced MNCs in the early 1950s that employed a totally standardized approach, companies shifted to the other extreme by allowing each market to design its own campaign. In the mid-1960s, European-based advertising executives started to discuss the possibility of greater standardization. Erik Elinder has been among the first to advocate the benefits of a more standardized approach.[7] Elinder argues that European consumers are increasingly "living under similar conditions although they read and speak different languages."[8]

Elinder has also pointed out that much of the European consumption has become international and that mass media coverage in several areas overlaps national boundaries. With people thinking and living more and more similarly, why should advertising be different for each market?

Some of the barriers to standardized advertising were pointed out by Illmar Roostal, who indicated that many structural and organizational problems existed that could prevent companies from selecting a more standardized approach.[9]

---

5. *Ibid.*

6. "Amid Dark-Haired Mexicans, Blonds Really Have More Fun," *The Wall Street Journal,* February 18, 1987, p. 30.

7. Erik Elinder, "How International Can Advertising Be?" *The International Advertiser,* vol. 2, December 1961, pp. 12–16; "How International Can European Advertising Be?" *Journal of Marketing,* vol. 29, April 1965, pp. 7–11.

8. "How International Can European Advertising Be?" p. 9.

9. Illmar Roostal, "Standardization of Advertising for Western Europe," *Journal of Marketing,* October 1963, pp. 15–20.

Among the factors preventing standardization were the absence of international advertising agencies with offices in many countries, the lack of interest among some companies to impose stricter controls over their local operations, the proliferation of languages, and the diversity of media characteristics by country.

What are the advantages of, or even the needs for, standardizing more of the MNC's international advertising? First, there is the concern that *creative* talent is scarce and that one effort to develop a campaign would produce better results than 40 or 50 efforts. This would particularly apply to countries where the marketing or advertising experience was limited. A second advantage centers around the economics of a global campaign. To create an individual campaign in many countries creates costs for photographs, layouts, and the production of television commercials. In a standardized approach, these production costs could be reduced and more funds could be spent on purchasing space in the media. A third reason for a standardized approach is found in global brand names. Many companies market products under one single brand name in several countries within the same region. With the substantial amount of international travel occurring today and the considerable overlap in media across national borders, companies are interested in creating a single image to avoid any confusion caused through local campaigns that might be in conflict with each other.

One of the best recent examples of a successful standardized campaign was Philip Morris' Marlboro campaign in Europe, particularly in Germany. Until 1970, Marlboro had been marketed by a German company, Brinkmann, with little success.[10] Philip Morris used the expiration of the licensing agreement to take over the marketing of Marlboro cigarettes in Germany. Simultaneously, the bland European-designed advertising of the licensee was discontinued and replaced by the ''Marlboro Country'' ads used in the United States. The new theme, ''The taste of freedom and adventure,'' caught on immediately and propelled the brand into second place by 1979, with a market share of about 13 percent.[11] Over the same period of time, the leading German brands declined. In fact, Philip Morris was so successful that the leading German tobacco company, Reemtsma, started a new brand, West, in 1981 to counter the inroads made by Marlboro. There is a definite reason for Marlboro's success in Germany and in other countries where that same ''Marlboro Country'' theme was used. The cowboy has become a symbol of freedom and evokes the same feelings among Americans, Brazilians, or Germans. (This phenomenon was discussed earlier in Chapter 3 under the subject of reference groups.) Consequently, the cowboy is a relevant reference group for the German smoker, causing a positive identification.

---

10. ''Freier Geist,'' *Der Spiegel,* no. 34, 1979, p. 63.

11. ''New German Cigarette, West, Saddles Up for Showdown With U.S. Competitors,'' *The Wall Street Journal,* March 12, 1981, p. 35; ''U.S. Cigarettes Gain in Europe,'' *The New York Times,* February 18, 1980, p. D1.

The difficulty of extending a domestic advertising campaign abroad was experienced by 7UP with the famous "Uncola" campaign.[12] The company's international division had tended to use 7UP's U.S. campaigns abroad. When the company realized it had an image problem in the United States because the product was not perceived as a soft drink, the "Uncola" campaign was launched to make U.S. consumers view 7UP as appropriate for use whenever colas were used. At the same time, the "Uncola" term indicated to the prospective consumer that 7UP after all was not a cola. Despite the campaign's success in the United States, the international division found it impossible to translate the term "Uncola" into other languages without a loss of its meaning. As a result, an entirely different campaign was created featuring an unusual character living in a little green box. The voice-over copy lines made a simple statement about 7UP that could be easily translated into any of the languages used to advertise 7UP.

As these examples show us, there are some specific factors that either allow or prevent some or parts of an advertising campaign to be standardized. The nature of these factors will be the topic of the following section.

Requirements for Standardized Campaigns

For a company to launch a worldwide standardized campaign, some requirements will first have to be met. These requirements center around the name, packaging, awareness, competitive situation, and consumer or customer attitudes.

The need for a standardized brand name or trademark is viewed as a prerequisite to a standardized campaign by many companies. Not only should the name be written in identical format, but it should also be pronounced identically. The major product 7UP, which is sold in about 80 markets worldwide, is consistently pronounced in the English language in all countries.[13]

Trademarks or corporate logos can also help in achieving greater standardization of corporate campaigns. Such well known logos as Kodak's or General Electric's are used the world over. The Japanese automobile manufacturer, Nissan Motor Co., had been selling automobiles outside Japan under the Datsun name. In 1981, it announced its decision to change the name of future models from Datsun to Nissan. Apparently, the Datsun name had been used abroad because it appeared less Japanese at a time when Japanese products did not have the excellent reputation they enjoy today. But the company found it difficult to project a unified corporate image, and thus it decided to change the product name to obtain a better awareness for the company. The change in the United States alone was expected to cost the company in excess of $150 million.[14]

---

12. "Man in the Green Box Sells 7UP in World Markets," *Advertising Age,* May 19, 1975, p. 25.
13. *Ibid.*
14. "A Worldwide Brand for Nissan," *Business Week,* August 24, 1981, p. 104.

To aid the prospective customer in identifying the advertised product with the actual one placed in retail stores, consumer products manufacturers in particular aim at packages that are of standardized appearance. Despite differences in sizes, these packages carry the same design in terms of color, layout, and name. Nonstandardized packages could not be featured in a standardized campaign, of course. Naturally, this concern is of much greater interest to consumer products companies since the package has to double both as a protective and a promotional device.

As products may be at different stages of their product life cycle in some countries, a need for different types of advertising may emerge due to the various levels of awareness customers have. Typically, a campaign during the earlier stages of the product life cycle concentrates on the product category since many prospective customers may not have heard about it. In later stages, with more intensive competition, the nature of the campaign tends to shift towards emphasizing the product's advantages over competitive products.

Consider the experience of Black & Decker, the United States–based manufacturer of power tools, in Japan. When the company started to sell its line in Japan, it found out that many average consumers simply did not understand the functioning of a power tool. Its cordless lawn trimmer had been returned for mechanical failures because many Japanese used it as a lawn mower thus overtaxing the battery.[15] In such circumstances, companies have to adapt their communications programs to reflect the different awareness stage. Among industrial companies, the major concern is frequently awareness of the company rather than the service or the product. Companies that might be well-known in their home markets will suddenly have to engage in advertising that raises the market's level of awareness for the company before products or services can be sold.

As companies enter new markets, they can expect to find different competitive situations that require an adjustment in the advertising campaign. Competing with a different group of companies and being placed in the position of an outsider often demands a change from the advertising policy used in the domestic market where these firms tend to have a strong position. The French company, Source Perrier, entered the U.S. market with its Perrier mineral water using a snob appeal. Emphasizing the product's noncaloric attributes, Perrier was positioned as an alternative to soft drinks or alcoholic beverages. With a premium price, Perrier was geared towards the more affluent adults.[16] In European markets where Perrier was well entrenched and the drinking of mineral water accepted by a vast number of consumers, such an approach would not have yielded the same results.

---

15. "Japan: A Developing Taste for U.S. Power Tools," *Business Week,* January 17, 1977, p. 38.

16. "Perrier: The Astonishing Success of an Appeal to Affluent Adults," *Business Week,* January 22, 1979, p. 64.

Suntory, the leading Japanese whiskey distiller, dominates its domestic market with about a 60 percent market share. When entering the United States, however, the company also chose the snobbish appeal for people who looked for something special. Suntory's print advertising promoted its whiskey as "slightly east of Scotch." This campaign was specifically created for the U.S. market and differed substantially from Suntory's Japanese advertising that included a substantial amount of television commercials.[17]

A U.S. company that found itself in the role of an outsider in foreign markets was Anheuser-Busch. The largest U.S. beer brewer started to invade several foreign markets with tailor-made campaigns. In both Germany and France, the company promotes its beer as "The beer for the men of the West."[18] This campaign took into account the company's situation as a newcomer competing against highly reputed local brewers.

These three examples show companies with solid leadership positions at home entering foreign markets as outsiders. They were forced by this circumstance to develop advertising programs that were substantially different from those used in their home markets.

The Impact of Regulations on International Advertising

Although there are many situations where different customer needs require tailor-made advertising campaigns, in many instances it is the particular regulations of a country that prevent firms from using standardized approaches, even when they would appear desirable. When Coca-Cola internationally launched its theme, "Coke adds life," in the late 1970s, Scandinavian countries and Thailand refused the slogan because it was considered an overclaim. Eventually, the company was able to overturn the countries' prohibition after some considerable lobbying effort.[19] In countries such as Malaysia, regulations are a direct outgrowth of changing political circumstances. Following the growing influence of Moslem fundamentalists in many parts of the world, Malaysia, a country with a large Moslem population, outlawed ads showing women in sleeveless dresses and pictures showing underarms. These were considered offensive by strict Moslem standards. Obviously, this caused considerable problems to marketers of deodorant products.[20]

Advertising for cigarettes and tobacco products are under strict regulations in many countries. In France, R. J. Reynolds, the manufacturer of Camel brand cigarettes, was prohibited from showing humans smoking cigarettes. The com-

---

17. "The Liquor Industry's Aggressive New Ad Blitz," *Business Week*, March 20, 1978, p. 174.
18. "Anheuser Tries Light Beer Again," *Business Week*, June 29, 1981, p. 136.
19. "Curbs on Ads Increase Abroad as Nations Apply Standards of Fairness and Decency," *The Wall Street Journal*, November 25, 1980, p. 56.
20. *Ibid.*

pany finally overcame the restrictions by showing a smiling camel smoking a Camel cigarette.[21] On the other hand, cigarette advertising is permitted in Greece, the only member of the Economic Community to do so. Although a ban exists on cigarette ads for television and radio, no limits exist for print advertising and posters.[22]

Advertising to children is also an area facing considerable regulation. General Mills, when marketing its Action Man soldiers in Germany, could not simply translate its copy into German. The company was forced to produce a very different television commercial by reducing tone of voice and violence. Instead of showing the toy soldiers holding machine guns and driving tanks, they were shown unarmed and driving a jeep.[23] Kellogg could not use a commercial produced in the United Kingdom for its Continental European business. The reference to Kellogg's cereals' iron and vitamin contents would not have been permissible in the Netherlands. The child wearing the Kellogg T-shirt in the original commercial would have had to be edited out for use in France, where children are forbidden to endorse a product. And the key line ''Kellogg's makes their cornflakes the best they have ever been'' would have been disallowed in Germany because of a prohibition against making competitive claims.[24]

Other regulations companies might encounter cover the production of advertising material. Some countries require all advertising, particularly television and radio, to be produced locally. As a result, it has become a real challenge for international advertisers to find campaigns that can be used in as many countries as possible to save on the production costs. Such campaigns are, however, only possible if a company has sufficient input from the very beginning on the applicable legislation so this can be taken into account.

Advertising in the Japanese Market

Given different cultural backgrounds, it is quite normal to expect differences in advertising appeals due to varying consumer attitudes. Japan offers us several examples that can be contrasted with experiences in the United States or Europe. In Japan, consumers tend to be moved more by emotion than by logic compared to North Americans or Europeans.[25] According to Gregory Clark, a European teaching at Sophia University in Tokyo, the Japanese are culturally oriented to consider the mood, style, and sincerity demonstrated by a deed more

---

21. *Ibid.*

22. ''Greece: No Limits on Ads for Cigarettes,'' *International Herald Tribune*, October 1, 1984, p. 15.

23. ''Countries' Different Ad Rules Are Problem for Global Firms,'' *The Wall Street Journal*, September 27, 1984, p. 33.

24. *Ibid.*

25. ''Emotion, Not Logic, Sways the Japanese Consumer,'' *The Japan Economic Journal*, April 22, 1980, p. 24.

important than its content. Consequently, consumers are searching for ways to be emotionally convinced about a product. This leads to advertising that rarely mentions price, occasionally even omits the actual features or qualities of a product, and shies away from competitive advertising aimed at competing firms. This type of advertising is further supported by the Japanese language, which even has a verb (*kawasarern*) to describe the process of being convinced to buy a product contrary to one's own rational judgment.

Some differences were further elaborated by James Herendeen, an American executive working for one of the largest Japanese advertising agencies, Dai-Ichi Kikaku.[26] Japanese advertising has a strong nonverbal component, uses a contemporary Japanese language, frequently shows man-woman, mother-child, or even father-daughter relationships, demonstrates Japanese humor, and above all stresses long-term relationships. There is also some evidence of the individual's place in Japanese society in the use of evocative pictures or events to indicate individual values. With respect to the emotional tendency, Herendeen suggests the use of nonverbal communication or things that lead to inference rather than direct understanding. Also important is the product origin and the need to present the product as being right for the Japanese. This requires a strong corporate identity program to establish a firm's credibility in the Japanese market.

Research conducted for the Nikkei Advertising Research Institute in Japan on advertising expressions used in Japan, Korea, Taiwan, the United States, and France showed the high degree of nonverbal communication in Japan.[27] The study found that sentences of less than four phrases or words appeared in 50.1 percent of Japanese ads, 81.6 percent in Korea, 80.6 percent in Taiwan, but only 22.6 percent in the United States and 21.3 percent in France. The same study also compared the number of foreign words appearing in advertising headlines. Japan, with 39.2 percent, used the highest amount of foreign words, followed by Taiwan with 32.1 percent, by Korea with 15.7 percent, and by France with 9.1 percent. The United States used foreign words in only 1.8 percent of the headlines investigated. This underlines the strong Japanese interest in foreign countries and words, particularly those of the English language. A more recent study has confirmed the Japanese preference for less wordy advertising copy and a greater reliance on mood or symbolism.[28]

The need for a strong corporate image was emphasized in an annual survey of leading Japanese and foreign firms.[29] Table 15.1 contains the ratings for both domestic- and foreign-based food manufacturers active in the Japanese market.

---

26. James Herendeen, "How to Japanize Your Creative," *International Advertiser,* September/October 1980, p. 22.

27. *The Japan Economic Journal,* December 23, 1980, p. 33.

28. Jae W. Hong, Aydin Muderrisoglu, and George M. Zinkhan, "Cultural Differences and Advertising Expression: A Comparative Content Analysis of Japanese and U.S. Magazine Advertising," to be published in *Journal of Advertising* (1987).

29. *The Japan Economic Journal,* December 23, 1980, pp. 33, 34.

TABLE 15.1 Ratings of Food Manufacturers in Japan (Percentage of Respondents Rating Companies as Excellent)

Foreign-affiliated companies		Japanese makers	
1 Coca-Cola (Japan)	66.4	1 Ajinomoto	83.7
2 Ajinomoto General Foods	56.7	2 Snow Brand Milk Products	83.5
3 Lipton Japan	46.5	3 Suntory	82.2
4 Twinings	45.0	4 Kirin Brewery	81.6
5 Nestlé Japan	43.9	5 Morinaga Milk Ind.	80.7
6 PepsiCo (Japan)	30.7	6 Kikkoman Shoyu	77.3
7 McDonald's	29.9	7 Taiyo Fishery	71.0
8 Brookbond	27.5	8 Nippon Suisan	68.2
9 Kirin-Seagram	20.8	9 Lotte	62.8
10 Yamazaki Nabisco	20.8	10 Calpis	61.3

Source: The Japan Economic Journal, December 23, 1980, p. 33. Reprinted by permission.

The Japanese firms with high ratings tended to be of long standing, technologically superior, diversified, and employing high quality personnel. Japanese consumers tended to buy these companies' products even if prices were high. The products were also used as gifts. The need for a strong corporate image also exists in the Japanese industrial goods market. Table 15.2 ranks the corporate images of top computer manufacturers by management stability, technology, and advertising. Compared to consumer goods firms, foreign industrial goods companies have a better corporate image. But Japanese firms have been catching up fast and now surpass foreign subsidiaries in sales and market share.

Although you might now conclude that anything American might not sell in Japan, the reality shows that this is not necessarily so. Japanese television commercials are full of U.S. themes, use many of the U.S. stars or heroes, and are frequently using U.S. landscapes or backgrounds. By using U.S. stars in their commercials, Japanese companies give the impression that these products are very popular in the United States. Given the Japanese interest and positive attitudes towards many American cultural themes, such strategies have worked out well for Japanese advertisers. This is why Nissan asked Paul Newman to drive its new car, Skyline, in its ads, and why John Travolta was asked to appear in an ad sipping a new semi-alcoholic fruit juice.[30] When Mitsubishi Electric paid rock-singer Madonna a reported $650,000 for the right to use fragments of a rock tour, the company's VCR sales doubled in three months while competitors experienced only a 15 percent increase.[31] Actress Faye Dunaway was paid some

30. "U.S. Sets the Pace Despite Growing Pride in Things Japanese," *International Herald Tribune,* October 1, 1984, p. 12.
31. "Madonna in Japan," *Fortune,* September 15, 1986, p. 9.

TABLE 15.2 Corporate Images of Top Computer Manufacturers in Japan (Percentage of Computer Buyers Rating Companies as Excellent)

	Stable management		Good technologies		Excellent AD	
1.	IBM Japan	66.2	IBM Japan	70.3	Fujitsu	34.9
2.	Fujitsu	50.2	Fujitsu	53.4	IBM Japan	33.3
3.	Hitachi	49.7	Hitachi	48.4	NEC	14.5
4.	NEC	31.9	NEC	35.5	Ricoh	10.7
5.	Mitsubishi	22.1	Univac	24.3	Sharp	10.5
6.	Univac	17.4	Burroughs	23.7	Canon	9.3
7.	Toshiba	15.4	Mitsubishi	16.1	Olivetti	8.9
8.	NCR	13.7	NCR	13.2	Mitsubishi	8.8

Note: Based on 878 samples in Tokyo as of December, 1979.

Source: "Foreign Computer Makers Take Lead in Industrial Advertising," *The Japan Economic Journal,* December 23, 1980, p. 34. Reprinted by permission.

$900,000 by the Tokyo Department store Parco for saying only, "This is an ad for Parco.[32]" In contrast to U.S. testimonials, however, Japanese advertisers tend to use foreign stars as actors using the product but not openly endorsing it.

Sometimes, the use of U.S. symbols borders on the comical. In one television commercial for mayonnaise, a group of U.S. cowboys is pictured with the subtitle, "It tastes like a river, not like a pool." This approach is part of a Japanese tendency to strive for product awareness only; advertisements are devoid of any mention of the product itself. As a result, comparative advertising rarely exists in Japan; and before and after claims are also seldom used. According to some experts, Western advertising is designed to make the product look superior, whereas Japanese advertising is aimed at making it desirable.[33]

GLOBAL ADVERTISING

Global advertising has received a considerable amount of attention in the 1980s and can now be considered the most controversial topic in international advertising. The debate was triggered by Professor Theodore Levitt who argued in an article and in his recent book, *The Marketing Imagination,* that markets are becoming increasingly alike worldwide and that this new trend of convergence

32. *Ibid.*
33. "Advertising: Upping a Youthful Image," *Financial Times,* October 22, 1986, p. VI.

would call for a global approach to marketing.[34] Levitt's ideas were applied to the field of international advertising, where Saatchi & Saatchi, a new British advertising agency, had risen to prominence on the basis of its global campaigns.[35] Saatchi & Saatchi claimed that worldwide brands would soon become the norm and that such an advertising challenge could only be handled by worldwide agencies. One such advertising campaign is Procter & Gamble's Pampers' campaign—used successfully throughout the world.

The proponents of global advertising cite several trends as indicators of what the future of international advertising will be.[36] Consumer tastes, needs, and purchasing patterns are said to be converging. This can be supported by the converging trends in demographics across many countries. At the forefront of these trends has been the decline of the nuclear family, both in the United States and in many countries around the globe. In most countries, more women are working. Similarly, divorce trends are increasingly pointing in the same direction in both the United States, Europe, and other developed countries. This has changed the role of women in society almost everywhere. Standards of living have risen in many countries and earlier differences among nations have been reduced. In addition to these demographic trends, common media such as films, television, and music are creating cultural convergence as well. These developments are said to reduce cultural barriers among countries; and these barriers are expected to be reduced even more through satellite television networks covering many countries with identical programs.

Many marketing professionals remain skeptical about the claims for gobal advertising.[37] Although many observers agree that for products aimed at the very affluent market in many countries, global marketing might be an advantage since these highly affluent and mobile consumers could be thought of as living in a global village.[38] Products included might be diamonds, some brands of whiskey, or some very expensive watches. Because of the many local differences that become evident in making up a global advertising campaign, many advertising agency executives remain dubious about the prospect for large-scale global advertising. Instead, indications are that more regionalized approaches, such as for Europe or for Asia, might be more appropriate at this time than going directly to a global approach.[39]

What might be more likely to happen is a modularized approach to international advertising. A company might select some features as standard for all its

34. Theodore Levitt, "The Globalization of Markets," *Harvard Business Review,* May–June 1983, p. 92; *The Marketing Imagination* (New York: Free Press, 1983); and *International Herald Tribune,* October 1, 1984, p. 7 (interview with Theodore Levitt).

35. "Saatchi & Saatchi Will Keep Gobbling," *Fortune,* June 23, 1986, p. 36.

36. "Advertising by Saatchi & Saatchi Compton," *The New York Times,* January 22, 1984, p. 87.

37. "Global Marketing Debated," *The New York Times,* November 13, 1985, p. D21.

38. Rena Bartos, "And What About the Consumer Who Brushes His Teeth With Shampoo?" *International Herald Tribune,* October 1, 1984, p. 8.

39. "Prof. Real World's Lesson for Levitt," *Advertising Age,* January 6, 1986, p. 17.

advertising while localizing some others. Pepsi Cola chose this approach in its 1986 international campaign. The company wanted to use modern music in connection with its products while still using some local identification. As a result, with the assistance of Ogilvy and Mather, its advertising agency, Pepsi Cola hired the U.S. singer, Tina Turner, who teamed up in a big concert setting with local rock stars from six countries singing and performing the Pepsi Cola theme song. In the commercials, the local rock stars will be shown together with Tina Turner. Except for the footage of the local stars, all the commercials are identical. For other countries, local rock stars will be spliced into the footage so that they also appear to be on stage with Tina Turner. By shooting the commercials all at once the company saved in production costs. The overall concept of the campaign could be extended to some thirty countries without forcing local subsidiaries or bottlers to come up with their own campaigns.[40]

MEDIA SELECTIONS

Across the world, the international marketer is faced with a large variety of different media. Difficulties arise because not all media are available in all countries; or if they are available, their technical quality or capability to deliver to the required audience may be limited. International media decisions are therefore influenced, aside from the considerations that concern domestic operations, by the availability or accessibility of various media for advertisers and the media habits of the target country.

Media Availability

Advertisers in the United States have become accustomed to the availability of a full range of media for advertising purposes. Aside from the traditional print media consisting of newspapers and magazines, the U.S. advertiser has access to radio and television as well as billboards and cinemas. In addition, there is the availability of direct mail to any prospective client group.

Aside from the socialist and communist countries of the Eastern Bloc, commercial radio is still not available in Norway, Denmark, Sweden, Finland, Switzerland, and Saudi Arabia. In Norway, Denmark, Sweden, and Saudi Arabia not even commercial television is available for advertisers.[41] Consequently, a company marketing its products in several countries might find itself unable to apply

---

40. "Advertising: Tina Turner Helping Pepsi's Global Effort," *The New York Times,* March 10, 1986, p. D13.

41. *Fifteenth Survey of Advertising Expenditures in 1983,* by International Advertising Research Associates (INRA), New York, 1985.

the same media mix in all markets. Even when some media are available, access might be partially restricted. The use of commercials interspersed through programs on radio or television is common in the United States, Japan, and Latin America among others, but less so in Europe. In Germany, advertisers have access to commercial television only during a few blocks of several minutes at several time slots.[42] Because the commercials are not shown during frequent intervals as interruptions to TV programming, viewership of these pre-announced commercial blocks tends to be very low. In addition, the time available for commercials is limited to twenty minutes daily. For the most preferred block on German television, the evening program, less than half of the firms applying will ever be able to obtain media time. Some firms have therefore avoided television altogether because they were unable to obtain frequent showings, which are necessary for a successful campaign. Similar restrictions exist in several other European countries. Difficulties also exist for companies with existing television schedules. In some countries, the available time for commercials is allocated for various product groups, often regardless of the number of competitors or products on the market. For some competitive product categories, new products may only be launched by reallocating a company's television time among its existing products. This lack of flexibility inhibits new product introduction in some consumer product categories where television would be the most efficient advertising media.

Existing government regulations have also had a substantial impact on how much television advertising is used. In Europe, television time is freely available in the United Kingdom, Greece, Ireland, Portugal, Spain, and Italy.[43] In Italy, the breakup of the state monopoly in 1976 resulted in the creation of several hundred commercial television stations alone.[44] In those countries, television advertising equals 30 to 50 percent of the print advertising volume. In European countries with restricted or limited access, television advertising amounts to about 5 to 20 percent of the total amount spent on print advertising. In Sweden, television advertising is not allowed and all advertising is in print (see Table 15.3).

Availability of media may also be limited by law. Most countries do not allow advertising for cigarettes or alcoholic beverages on television or radio, though they are usually permitted in print media. When the leading Japanese whiskey distiller Suntory entered the United States market, the company had to do without its preferred medium of television.[45] In Japan, Suntory was estimated to have spent about $50 million annually on television advertising because no restrictions existed with respect to alcoholic beverages there.

---

42. "Werbung: Bis Zum Spaten Abend," *Der Spiegel,* November 22, 1981, p. 81.

43. "European Ads' Potential 'Vast'," *Financial Times,* March 24, 1983, p. 10.

44. "U.S. Style TV Turns on Europe," *Fortune,* April 13, 1987, p. 95.

45. "The Liquor Industry's Aggressive New Ad Blitz," *Business Week,* March 20, 1978, p. 174.

TABLE 15.3 Concise Guide to Advertising in Twenty-Two Countries

	Austria	Australia	Belgium	Brazil
Total advertising expenditure 1979 Local Currency	7,900 Million A.S.	1,482 Million Dollars	9,500 Million Francs	50,700 Million Cruzeiros
Total expressed as a % of Gross National Product	0.88%	1.46%	0.3%	0.95%
Breakdown of Advertising Expenditure by principal media. %				
TV	16.5	30.3	12.8	42.0
National Press		10.6	31.0	
Regional Press	25.3	29.4	10.8	22.5
Magazines/Periodicals		7.6	28.7	
Trade & Technical	In Other	2.6		9.5
Radio	6.5	8.8	1.2	16.0
Cinema	0.3	1.6	1.2	0.5
Outdoor	4.2	9.1	14.3	3.5
Other	47.2	NA	NA	6.0
Proportion of households with TV sets	91%	96%	93%	54%
Proportion of households with color TVs	44%	75%	50%	30%
Number of TV channels accepting advertising/sponsorship	2	50	None but RTL Luxembourg is received	89
Advertising time in 24 hour period. Approximate minutes	20	154	62 (RTL)	360
Restrictions on TV advertising	No tobacco, hard liquor; regulated drugs and foods. Restrictions on children's advertising	No cigarettes	No tobacco, alcohol	No alcohol, cigarettes, cigars, until 9 PM
	+DM, −AC, PC	−DM, PC, PC	−DM, PC, +AC	+DM, AC, PC

Note: NA = not available. * = insignificant amount. O = medium not used. DM = direct mail. AC = agency commission. PC = production cost.

Source: From William J. Hawkes' presentation at the International Marketing Workshop AMA/MSI, March 1983, of A.C. Nielson Company material. Reprinted by permission of A.C. Nielson Company.

Canada	Switzerland	Germany	Spain	Ireland	France
3.008 Million Dollars	981 Million Francs	10,786 Million D. Marks	64,800 Million Pesetas	45.1 Million Punts	17,400 Million Francs
1.16%	0.6%	0.8%	0.5%	0.6%	0.83%
16.6	12.1	9.6	33.0	32.1	9.5
*	55.9	48.1	29.4	32.6	17.5
28.6	NA			7.9	
17.9	32.0	18.4	16.9	1.5	21.1
19.1	NA	*		*	
11.4	0	3.3	12.3	9.9	6.5
O	NA	0.8	1.9	*	1.0
6.4	NA	3.6	6.5	6.0	9.3
*	NA	16.2	NA	*	35.2
97%	84%	85%	95%	85%	92%
81%	53%	62%	30%	32%	33%
95	3	2	2	2	2
216 Per Channel	60	40	85	85	48
No cigarettes, liquor. Regional restrictions on beer and children's advertising.	No alcohol, tobacco, drugs, politics, religion.	No cigarettes, religion, charities, narcotics, prescription drugs, children's advertising, cures.	No tobacco, hard drinks.	No tobacco, contraceptives, religion, politics.	Many categories are excluded, alcohol, margarine, slimming products, tobacco products, etc.
+DM, PC, −AC	−DM, AC, PC	+DM, −AC, PC	−DM, AC, PC	−DM, AC, PC	+DM, AC, −PC

TABLE 15.3 Concise Guide to Advertising in Twenty-Two Countries (*cont.*)

	Great Britain	Greece	Italy	Japan	Mexico
Total advertising expenditure 1979 Local Currency	2,219 Million Pounds	3735.6 Million Drachmas	1,186 Billion Liras	2,113 Billion Yen	9,660 Million Pesos
Total expressed as a % of Gross National Product	1.34%	0.32%	0.35%	0.95%	0.36%
Breakdown of Advertising Expenditure by principal media. %					
TV	22.1	46.4	19	35.5	65.0
National Press	48.0	27.8	24	31.0	8.0
Regional Press					NA
Magazines/Periodicals	22.3	20.0	53	5.3	4.0
Trade & Technical			NA	In "other"	1.0
Radio	2.4	4.6	4	5.0	15.0
Cinema	0.8	NA	NA	In "other"	4.0
Outdoor	4.4	1.1	NA	In "other"	2.5
Other	NA	NA	NA	23.1	0.5
Proportion of households with TV sets	94%	95%	96%	98%	43.8%
Proportion of households with color TVs	65%	5%	27%	96%	None
Number of TV channels accepting advertising/sponsorship	1	2	2+ Many private stations	93	15
Advertising time in 24 hour period. Approximate minutes	80	120	27 excluding private stations	230	12 Hour/station
Restrictions on TV advertising	No contraceptives, cigarettes, politics, gambling, religion or charities	No cigarettes, ethical drugs	No jewels, furs, newspapers, magazines, cigarettes, gambling, clinics & hospitals	No overstatement comparison with competitors, sensual messages on commercial films	No liquor before 10 PM
	−DM, +AC, PC	−DM, PC, +AC	−DM, PC, +AC	+DM, AC, PC	−DM, PC, +AC

Netherlands	New Zealand	Portugal	Argentina	Sweden	United States	South Africa
3,825 Million Florins	195.5 Million Dollars	1462.5 Million Escudos	1,028 Billion Pesos	2,004 Million Kronor	49,690 Million Dollars	290 Million Rands
1.29%	1.12%	0.2%	1.27%	0.46%	2.1%	1.8% (G.D.P.)
5.0	25.4	55	24.6	0	20.5	19.3
46.9	0			36	4.2	35.3
	48.1	29	42.3	41	25.1	4.1
8.7	6.6			16	5.9	16.3
3.6	NA		15.7		3.4	6.5
0.7	8.2	16	9.0	0	6.6	12.0
0.3	1.2	NA	1.4	1	0	2.1
6.1	0.3	NA	6.1	5	1.1	4.4
28.7	10.2	NA	0.9	NA	33.2	NA
97%	95%	NA	86%	93%	98%	26.5%
65%	70%	NA	18%	71%	83%	18.4%
2	2	2	38	None	728	1
30	260	30	10 Hour/channel	—	Voluntary code: hour/station	24
No tobacco, political, religion. Special legislation for pharmaceuticals, sweets, alcohol	No cigarettes, alcohol, feminine hygiene products, contraceptives, politics	No tobacco, gambling, liquor only after 9 P.M. Restrictions on medicines	No use of foreign words or slang. No attitudes against morals. No misuse of country symbols	—	No tobacco, contraceptives, fortune tellers	No Sunday advertising, no spirits, wine, beer, cigarettes after 9 PM except Saturday. No "sensitive" products
+DM, AC, −PC	+DM, AC, +PC	−DM, PC, +AC		−DM	+DM, AC, PC	−DM, AC, PC

These examples demonstrate that, on an international basis, companies have to remain flexible with respect to their media plans. A company cannot expect to be able to use its preferred media to the fullest extent everywhere. Consequently, international advertising campaigns will have to be designed with delivery over several media in mind.

Credibility of Advertising

Great differences exist with how various countries view the value of advertising. In the United States, about two-thirds of the population felt abused by advertising.[46] In the United Kingdom, approval amounted to about 77 percent. In Germany, where television commercials are bunched up in a few blocks of about 10 minutes each, viewership is very low. The viewership rates have been steadily decreasing and have dropped below 20 percent. Observers believe that this low rate is a direct result of the German's critical opinion of advertising in general and the television medium specifically.[47]

In other countries, particularly those of the developing world, advertising tends to be held in much higher regard. Advertised products have more prestige and those advertised on television are viewed by consumers as the most prestigious. Experts believe that the Japanese basically believe in the message of an advertisement, quite the opposite from U.S. consumers.

Differences in the credibility of advertising in general, and some media in particular, will have to be taken into consideration by the international firm. Companies may want to place a greater reliance on advertising in countries where its credibility is very high. In other countries, the use of alternative forms of communication may be stressed.

Media Habits

As the experienced media buyer for any domestic market knows, the media habits of the target market is a major factor in deciding which media to use. The same applies on an international level. However, substantial differences in media habits exist due to a number of factors that are of little importance to the domestic or single-country operation. First of all, the penetration of various media differs substantially from one country to another. Secondly, we encounter radically different literacy rates in many parts of the world. And finally, we may find different cultural habits or traits that favor one media over another regardless of the penetration ratios or literacy rates.

Ownership or usage of television, radio, newspapers, or magazines varies substantially from one country to another. Whereas the developed industrial

---

46. "Are Ads Your Favorite Reading?" *The Economist,* September 5, 1981, p. 31.
47. "Werbung: Bis Zum Späten Abend," p. 81.

nations show high penetration ratios for all three major media carriers, other countries of the Third World have few radio and television receivers or low newspaper circulation (see Table 15.3). In general, the use or penetration of all of these media increases with the average income of a country. In most countries, the higher income classes avail themselves first of the electronic media and newspapers. International marketers have to be aware that some media, though generally accessible for the advertiser, may be only of limited use since they reach only a small part of the country's target population.

The literacy of a country's population is an important factor influencing media decisions. Though this is less of a concern for industrial products companies, it is a crucial factor in consumer goods advertising. In countries where large portions of the population are illiterate, the use of print media is of limited value. (Please see Table 3.2 for literacy rates of selected countries.) Both radio and television have been used by companies to circumvent the literacy problem. Other media that are occasionally used for this purpose are billboards or cinemas. The absence of a high level of literacy has forced consumer goods companies to translate their advertising campaigns into media and messages that communicate strictly by sound or demonstration. Television and radio have been used most successfully to overcome this problem, but they cannot be used in areas where the penetration of such receivers is limited. Frequently, this applies particularly to countries that have low electronic media penetration and low literacy rates.

In most developed countries, detailed statistics are available to advertisers documenting the time people spend in contact with any given medium. A survey conducted by the A. C. Nielsen Co. in 1980 determined that the average family in Tokyo, Japan used a television set for 8 hours and 12 minutes a day.[48] The corresponding figure for the United States amounted to 6 hours and 4 minutes. The difference between the U.S. and Japanese attitudes becomes even more apparent in a poll conducted in both countries.[49] People were asked which of the following items they would keep if they had to make due with all but one: television, newspapers, telephone, automobile, and refrigerator. The answers were as follows:

Japan		United States
31%	Television	3%
23%	Newspapers	6%
16%	Telephone	9%
15%	Automobile	39%
13%	Refrigerator	42%

---

48. *International Herald Tribune,* July 26, 1982.
49. *Ibid.*

Consequently, 31 percent of the polled Japanese would rather give up all other four items to keep their television, whereas only 3 percent of the Americans felt that way.

In both the United States and Europe, viewership of television appears on the decline. This has caused some companies to make adjustments in the media mix for those areas. In other countries, particularly those of the Third World, media habits are rapidly shifting towards electronic media as ownership of radio and television receivers is becoming more common. For a more detailed summary of media habits in various countries, see Table 15.4.

Satellite Television

Only recently available, satellite television channels not subject to government regulations are about to revolutionize television in many parts of the world. The impact of satellite television channels is nowhere felt more directly than in Europe.

The leader in this field of privately owned channels is Sky Channel owned by Rupert Murdoch, who also has substantial media interests in many countries. Sky Channel had reached 4.7 million homes in 13 countries by the end of 1985, and it transmitted a maximum of 17 hours per day. Sky claimed that about 10 percent of all TV viewers served watched its channel. About one-third of all advertising revenue is generated from U.S. companies, another one-third from Japanese, and some 20 percent from Continental Europe. Advertisers include such well-known companies as Canon, Digital, NEC, Kodak, Mattel, Nikon, Panasonic, Ford, Toyota, Xerox, Remington, Siemens, and Unilever.[50]

Sky Channel offers English language general entertainment programs that are now available in more than 7 million homes connected to cable television networks throughout Europe.[51] Growth is expected because only about 10 million of Western Europe's 125 million households are connected to cable television. Within the next ten years, this number is expected to triple to more than 30 million. At the same time, advertising revenue is expected to grow from only $20 million in 1985 to about $1 billion in 1995.[52] Sky Channel has been particularly successful in Scandinavia where it achieved a 44 percent share among 16 to 24 year olds, the largest group of English speakers in Europe.[53]

The presently existing satellite networks have not yet attracted a large number of advertisers. Companies still prefer an entire national audience, such as all of Germany, to a small segment throughout Western Europe. However, a recent deal arranged between Gillette and the Murdoch group of broadcasting channels

50. "Advertising Potential Elevated by Satellite," *Financial Times*, November 14, 1985, p. 12.
51. "Advertising: Direct Route to the Young," *Financial Times*, October 22, 1986, p. VI.
52. "European Satellite Battle Looms," *Financial Times*, September 16, 1985, p. 12.
53. "Murdoch's Sky Channel Is Turning Advertisers On," *Business Week*, March 31, 1986, p. 82.

TABLE 15.4 1985 Population, Advertising Expenditures by Type, and Per Capita
Advertising Expenditures

| Country | 1985 Population (Millions) | 1985 Advertising Expenditures (In U.S. Millions of Dollars) | | | | 1985 Per Capita Expenditures (In U.S. Dollars) |
		Print	Radio	Television	Total*	
Argentina	30.7	146	52	126	446	$ 14.52
Australia	15.6	1,125	213	789	2,318	148.56
Austria	7.5	188	40	95	347	46.25
Belgium	9.9	251	3	55	534	53.93
Bahrain	.4	2	—	5	7	17.76
Brazil	140.0	782	153	1,439	2,453	17.52
Canada	25.4	1,711	418	766	4,465	175.79
Chile	12.0	50	12	57	123	10.21
Columbia	29.3	74	96	183	352	12.02
Cyprus	.7	3	1	6	10	14.05
Finland	4.9	771	2	92	1,122	228.91
France	55.0	1,352	301	563	3,292	59.86
Greece	9.9	46	7	58	112	11.26
Guatemala	8.3	14	13	35	61	7.40
Hong Kong	5.4	94	4	117	231	42.82
India	767.7	410	15	51	512	.67
Israel	4.1	132	15	7	206	50.29
Italy	57.1	801	78	960	1,951	34.16
Japan	120.7	4,515	669	4,510	12,890	106.13
S. Korea	42.6	371	51	320	867	20.34
Nepal	17.0	1	.3	—	1	.06
Netherlands	14.5	979	29	97	2,027	139.79
Norway	4.2	499	—	—	783	186.43
Peru	19.7	15	14	179	208	10.55
Philippines	56.8	27	18	46	92	1.62
Portugal	10.0	15	10	32	56	5.64
Saudi Arabia	11.2	46	—	—	46	4.08
South Africa	32.5	280	37	135	576	17.73
Spain	38.8	724	168	446	1,671	43.07
Sweden	8.3	668	—	—	1,134	136.65
Switzerland	6.4	755	13	63	1,486	235.14
Turkey	50.7	55	5	77	147	2.90
United Kingdom	56.4	3,686	108	1,811	6,442	114.22
United States	238.6	30,325	6,490	20,770	94,750	397.11
Venezuela	17.3	75	12	191	286	16.54
West Germany	61.0	3,539	184	511	5,430	89.02

* Includes Print, Radio, T.V., Cinema, Outdoor, Direct Advertising.

Source: World Advertising Expenditures, 20th Edition (Mamaroneck, N.Y.: Starch INRA Hooper, Inc., 1986), pp. 7, 13, 15, 17. Reprinted by permission.

might be an indication as to what companies might be able to do in the future. In October 1986, Gillette began to air through Sky Channel in Europe. The same advertisement had been carried earlier by Murdoch's Fox Broadcasting System in the United States and Network Ten, the group's Australian system. This arrangement allowed Gillette to show the same commercial in all three continents.[54]

Music Box, another commercially organized satellite television network operating in Europe, attracts mostly 15 to 25 year olds with its pop music, but it also has a good coverage of ages 8 through 35.[55] The channels show ads in regular breaks for six minutes per hour, thus generating 100 minutes of new commercial airtime each day. Companies who have used it include Swatch of Switzerland, Benetton of Italy, Mars and Coca Cola of the United States, and Sony of Japan. Launched in 1984, the channel claimed to have reached over 3 million homes in 11 countries by the end of 1985.

Different firms are using satellite television for different purposes. Polaroid used it to advertise its sunglasses on Super Channel, an English language channel, to reach mostly younger people in the Netherlands. Polaroid found that the domestic Dutch TV channel reached an older audience, which was less appropriate for its products. On the other hand, Nissan used Super Channel to promote its corporate image in Europe. Nissan executives believed that the English language channel would get superior results for the unification of its image.[56]

For satellite-shown commercials to be effective, companies would have to be able to profit from a global brand name and a uniform logo. Also, language remains a problem, with English being the only language of the majority of satellite channels. But most observers admit that the availability of satellite commercial networks has already had an impact on the national regulatory boards of countries that have tended to restrict or limit commercial air time (see Figure 15.2). It is now expected that even in Scandinavia commercial television might be allowed in the near future. In other parts of Europe, existing commercial television time is expected to avoid losses to other channels. This could substantially enlarge the TV advertising market in Europe.

According to industry data, Europeans spend about .75 percent of GNP on advertising compared to 1 percent for Japan and 1.5 percent for the United States. In 1983, TV advertising amounted to $4.3 billion or only 20 percent of total European advertising expenditures. This compares to some $16.2 billion for the United States (32.5 percent of all advertising expenditures). If Europeans increased TV advertising to 1 percent of GNP and spent 30 percent of all advertising on TV, instead of only 20%, TV revenue could double and would require much more airtime to accommodate the new demand.[57]

54. "Advertising: Global Network Beams Nearer," *Financial Times,* October 22, 1986, p. IV.

55. "Advertising Potential Elevated by Satellite," *Financial Times,* November 14, 1985, p. 8.

56. "Super Channel: A Test for the Global Concept," *Financial Times,* February 17, 1987, p. 11.

57. "Pan-European Television: The Sky's Limit for Broadcasters," *The Economist,* February 8, 1986, p. 71.

FIGURE 15.2 Commercial TV Advertising Time in European Countries in Minutes per Day

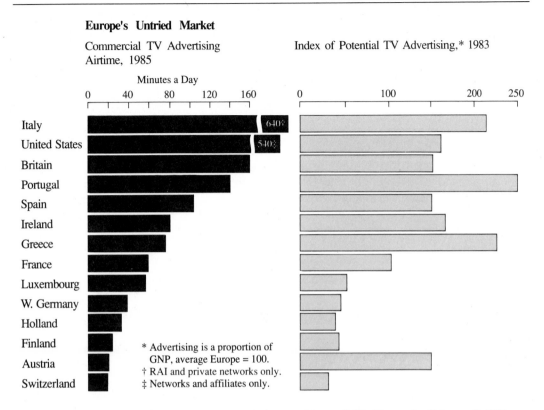

Europe's Untried Market

Commercial TV Advertising Airtime, 1985

Index of Potential TV Advertising,* 1983

Minutes a Day

* Advertising is a proportion of GNP, average Europe = 100.
† RAI and private networks only.
‡ Networks and affiliates only.

Source: "Pan-European Television: The Sky's Limit for Broadcasters," *The Economist,* February 8, 1986, p. 71. © 1986 The Economist, distributed by Special Features. Reprinted by permission.

SCHEDULING INTERNATIONAL ADVERTISING

The general rule in scheduling advertising suggests that the company more or less duplicate the sales curve or seasonality of its product. Furthermore, depending on the complexity of the buying decision or the deliberation time, the media expenditures tend to peak before the actual sales peak. This practice, though somewhat generalized here, applies as well to foreign or international markets. Differences may exist, however, due to different sales peaks in the year, vacations, or religious holidays, and differences in the deliberation time regarding purchases.

Sales peaks are influenced both by climatic seasons or by customs and traditions. Winter months in the United States or Europe are summer months in some countries of the southern hemisphere; namely Australia, New Zealand, South Africa, or Argentina. This substantially influences the purchase for many consumer goods such as clothing, vacation services, travel, and so on. Vacations are particularly important for some European countries. In Europe, summer school vacations tend to be shorter than in the United States, but employees are granted typically four to five weeks, which is more than those granted to the average employee in the United States. With vacations concentrated in a few weeks during the summer, this can have substantial impact on the advertising scheduling. A company would not want to engage in a major media campaign when a substantial amount of the population is traveling away from home. In Sweden, many public places are closed in July; and Italy and France concentrate their holidays in August. In Germany, vacations are staggered by region over the period of July and August. There are also religious holidays that may affect the placement or timing of advertising. During the Islamic Ramadan, usually celebrated over a month during July, many Moslem countries do not allow the placement of any advertising.

For industrial products, the timing of advertising in support of sales efforts may be affected by the budgetary cycles prevailing in a given country. For countries with large state-controlled sectors, heavy emphasis needs to be placed on the period before a new national or sector plan is developed. Private sector companies tend to be more influenced by their own budgetary cycles usually coinciding with their fiscal years. In Japan, many companies begin their fiscal year in June rather than on January 1. To the extent that capital budgets are completed before the new fiscal year commences, products that require budgetary approval will need advertising support in advance of the budget completion.

The time needed to think about a purchase has been cited as a primary factor in deciding on the appropriate time by which the advertising peak is to precede the sales peak. In its domestic market, a company might have become accustomed to a given purchase deliberation time by its customers. Since the deliberation might be determined by income levels or other environmental factors, other markets might show different patterns. The purchase or replacement of a small electrical household appliance might be a routine decision for a U.S. household, and the purchase might occur whenever the need arises. In another country with lower income levels, such a purchase might be planned several weeks or even months ahead. Consequently, a company engaged in international advertising needs to carefully evaluate the underlying assumptions of its domestic advertising policies and not automatically assume that they apply elsewhere.

REACH VERSUS FREQUENCY

Invariably, an advertiser will be forced to make a tradeoff between the number of target customers to be reached and the number of messages placed through the media. This reach versus frequency tradeoff is created by advertising budget limitations existing even in the largest organizations. Typically, consumer interest in the product is used as a guide to determine the frequency needed. This interest in any given product category may vary from country to country. Furthermore, in countries with otherwise extensive advertising, the existing "noise" might require a step-up in the frequency to ensure that the messages actually get through to the targets. Consequently, international advertisers should not assume that the reach versus frequency tradeoff would be the same in different countries.

ORGANIZING THE INTERNATIONAL ADVERTISING EFFORT

A major concern for international marketing executives centers around the organization of their company's international advertising effort. Key concerns are the role of centralization at the head office versus the roles subsidiaries and the advertising agency should play. Marketers are aware that a more harmonious approach to the international advertising effort might enhance both the quality and efficiency of the total effort. Thus, organizing the effort deserves as much time as individual advertising decisions about individual products or campaigns. Thus, in this section, we will look in greater detail at advertising agency selection and the managerial issues of running an international advertising effort in a multinational corporation.

Agency Selection

International companies face a number of options with respect to working with a given advertising agency. Many companies first develop an agency relationship domestically and have to decide at one point if they expect that domestic agency to handle their international advertising business as well. In some foreign markets, companies will need to select foreign agencies to work with them—a decision that might be left to the local subsidiaries or might be made by the head office alone. Recently, some agencies have banded together to form international networks to attract more international business.

Working with Domestic Agencies

When a company starts to grow internationally, it is not unusual for the domestic advertising agency to handle the international business as well. However, that is only possible when the domestic agency has international experience and international capability. Many smaller domestic agencies do not have that type of experience. Thus the companies are forced to make other arrangements. Frequently, the international company starts to appoint individual agencies in each of the various foreign markets where it is operating. This might be done with the help of the local subsidiaries or through the company's head office staff. Before long, the company will end up with a series of agency relationships that might make international or global coordination very difficult.

PPG Industries' Automotive Finishes Group had been using a domestic agency for ten years when the company was anticipating a substantial growth in its international business. PPG was looking to acquire several companies in Europe in addition to the two plants already in place. The company therefore switched all of its business from the domestic agency to Campbell-Ewald, which was organized as a network with its many affiliates overseas.[58] To better coordinate its U.S. and international advertising campaigns, Goodyear requested that its domestic agency, J. Walter Thompson, closely work with its international agency, McCann-Erickson, on a global campaign even though the advertising would not be identical.[59] By having the two agencies work together, Goodyear would be assured that the resulting campaign would be coordinated and that the company would speak with the same voice worldwide.

Working with Local Agencies

The local agency relationship offers some specific advantages. First of all, the local advertising agency is expected to fully understand the local environment and is in a position to create advertising targeted to the local market. However, many firms question the expertise and professionalism of local agencies, particularly in countries where advertising is not as developed as in the major markets of North America and Europe.

Jaguar had some interesting experiences in penetrating the Saudi Arabian market.[60] Jaguar had its own advertising in the Middle East handled through a British agency. The Saudi audience reacted negatively towards the Lebanese Arabic used in the copy. They also noticed that the visuals must have been shot in the United Arab Emirates, because the drivers in the pictures were wearing black bands with long black strings at the back that weighted down the Arabian headdress. This type of headdress was typical for that part of the Arabian Gulf region but not for Saudi Arabia. When the Jaguar importer in Saudi Arabia complained about the advertising, Jaguar looked for a local agency run by American and British expatriates. However, this attempt was also a failure and the account was finally shifted to a local agency run largely by Saudi managers. This

58. "PPG Finishes Switches Shops Citing New International Needs," *Industrial Marketing,* August 1981, p. 25.
59. "Goodyear Pulls Back From Print," *The New York Times,* November 5, 1986, p. D19.
60. "The Sleek Cat Springs into the Saudi Market," *Financial Times,* November 2, 1985, p. 14.

agency heavily relied on high quality visuals from Jaguar in the United Kingdom but wrote all of its own copy.[61]

Working with International Advertising Networks

Many companies with extensive international operations find it too difficult and cumbersome to deal simultaneously with a large number of agencies, both domestically and internationally. For that reason, multinational firms have tended to concentrate their accounts with some large advertising agencies that operate their own networks. Among the leaders are Saatchi & Saatchi, now the world's largest advertising agency measured in client billings, McCann-Erickson, Young & Rubicam, J. Walter Thompson, and Ogilvy & Mather.[62]

When Texas Instruments was looking for a different advertising approach for its international business, it centralized all of its accounts with McCann-Erickson, replacing some twenty-six domestic and foreign agencies.[63] McCann already had accounts worldwide from other large companies including Coca-Cola, Exxon, Johnson & Johnson, and Levi Strauss. Kodak centralized all of its worldwide advertising in 1983 with just three international agencies (Young & Rubicam, McCann-Erickson, and J. Walter Thompson) which resulted in the replacement of fifty-three local agencies around the world.[64]

International advertising networks are sought after because of their ability to quickly spread the globe with one single campaign. Usually, only one set of advertisements will be made and then circulated among the local agencies. Working within the same agency guarantees consistency and a certain willingness to accept direction from a central location. If a company were to coordinate a global effort alone without the help of an international network, the burden of coordination would largely rest with the company itself. Not all firms are geared or equipped for such an effort. The international network is therefore a convenience to multinational firms. International agency networks handled 20 percent of world advertising in 1986 compared to 13 percent ten years earlier. This signals a strong trend towards these new types of agencies.[65] For a list of leading world advertising agencies, see Table 15.5.

Not all companies find a network a necessity. Some advertisers argue that a company might profit from a single strategy but that the execution of this strategy in the various markets should be left to local agencies that are willing to work in an ad-hoc network geared only to the company's needs. Acorn, a British

61. *Ibid.*
62. "The Saatchis Hit a Pocket of Turbulence," *Financial Times,* October 2, 1986, p. 14.
63. "McCann Overseas Buildup," *Business Week,* February 23, 1981, p. 148.
64. "Europe Sorts Out Alignments," *Financial Times,* October 13, 1983, p. VIII.
65. "Advertising's Bigger Than Ever," *The Economist,* March 9, 1985, p. 72.

TABLE 15.5 World's Top 50 Ad Agency Groups in 1986

Rank	Agency	Gross Income*	Billings*
1.	Dentsu Inc.	$681.0	$5.31 bill.
2.	Young & Rubicam	628.4	4.19 bill.
3.	Saatchi & Saatchi Compton Worldwide	490.5	3.32 bill.
4.	Ted Bates Worldwide	486.0	3.26 bill.
5.	J. Walter Thompson Co.	471.0	3.14 bill.
6.	Ogilvy & Mather Worldwide	459.6	3.15 bill.
7.	BBDO Worldwide	445.1	3.26 bill.
8.	McCann-Erickson Worldwide	427.7	2.85 bill.
9.	DDB Needham Worldwide	375.0	2.56 bill.
10.	DMB&B	336.3	2.26 bill.
11.	Foote, Cone & Belding Communications	323.0	2.15 bill.
12.	Hakuhodo International	309.6	2.27 bill.
13.	Grey Advertising	309.1	2.06 bill.
14.	Leo Burnett Co.	292.3	2.06 bill.
15.	SSC&B:Lintas Worldwide	237.0	1.65 bill.
16.	Bozell, Jacobs, Kenyon & Eckhardt	175.6	1.25 bill.
17.	DFS Dorland Worldwide	165.1	1.21 bill.
18.	N W Ayer	125.5	901.3
19.	Publicis International	119.6	792.4
20.	HCM	106.0	723.0
21.	Wells, Rich, Greene	99.7	665.2
22.	Dai Ichi Kikaku	98.7	724.3
23.	Campbell-Ewald Worldwide	87.6	584.2
24.	Tokyu Advertising Agency	83.8	647.0
25.	Daiko	82.0	693.7
26.	Roux, Seguela, Cayzac & Goudard	80.3	552.2
27.	Scali, McCabe, Sloves	77.5	556.6
28.	Ketchum Communications	75.3	528.5
29.	William Esty Advertising	75.0	510.0
30.	Belier Group	72.7	484.6
31.	Ogilvy & Mather Direct Response	68.0	454.0
32.	Backer & Spielvogel	68.0	453.3
33.	TBWA	65.7	453.5
34.	Ross Roy Inc.	62.4	416.0
35.	Lowe Marschalk Worldwide	57.8	400.4
36.	Campbell-Mithun	57.1	380.2
37.	I&S Corp.	51.8	398.6
38.	Asatsu	51.1	400.7
39.	DYR Worldwide	50.7	347.1
40.	Wunderman Ricotta & Kline	49.1	327.5
41.	Yomiko	48.9	361.8
42.	GGK	47.9	337.3
43.	Chiat/Day Advertising	47.1	314.1
44.	Tracy-Locke	46.2	316.5
45.	Asahi Advertising	44.6	280.5
46.	HBM/Creamer	40.1	267.0
47.	Laurence, Charles, Free & Lawson	39.4	287.0
48.	Hill, Holliday, Connors, Cosmopulos	39.4	262.5
49.	C&W Group	38.4	274.3
50.	W.B. Doner	36.3	238.2

* Figures are in millions, unless otherwise noted.

Source: "Agency Income Report," *Advertising Age,* May 17, 1987, p. 60. Reprinted with permission. Copyright Crain Communications Inc., 1987.

manufacturer of minicomputers, had its U.K. agency develop a campaign with independent agencies in Germany and in New York. Acorn had a clear strategy for attacking the educational segment in all markets. However, because of the differences in each market, the company did not opt for a standardized advertising campaign. In the United Kingdom, where the company faced a very high penetration of households with personal computers, Acorn capitalized on the fact that it was chosen by the BBC, the leading broadcasting network. Major targets were parents, but opinion leaders in schools were also addressed. In the United States, Acorn targeted mostly decision makers in schools and did not advertise to individual households. In Germany, the emphasis was more on creating a strong corporate identity. As a result, the company had three different campaigns, but all three of them aimed at the educational market segment that remained the cornerstone of Acorn's international marketing strategy.[66]

Coordinating International Advertising

The role the international marketing executive plays in a company's international advertising effort may differ from firm to firm and depend on several factors. Outside factors, such as the nature of the market or competition, and company internal factors, such as company culture or philosophy, may lead some firms to adopt a more centralized approach in international advertising. Other firms, for different reasons, may prefer to delegate more authority to local subsidiaries and local agencies. The purpose of this final section is to review the key factors that might cause a firm to either centralize or decentralize decision making for international advertising.

External Factors Affecting Advertising Coordination

One of the most important factors influencing how companies allocate decision making for international advertising is market diversity. For products or services where customer needs and interests are homogeneous across many countries, greater opportunities for standardization exist. For companies with relatively standardized products, pressures also point in the direction of centralized decision making. Consequently, companies that face markets with very different customer needs or market systems and structures will work more towards de-

---

66. "A Dichotomy in Campaign Style," *Financial Times,* January 26, 1984, p. 12.

centralizing their international advertising decision making. Local knowledge would be more important to the success of these firms.

The nature of the competition can also impact on how an international firm plans for advertising decision making. Firms that essentially face local competition or different sets of competitors from country to country will find it more logical to delegate international advertising to local subsidiaries. On the other hand, if a company is competing everywhere with a few sets of firms, which are essentially global firms using a similar type of advertising, the need to centralize will be apparent.

Internal Factors Affecting Advertising Coordination

A company's own internal structure and organization can also greatly influence its options of either centralizing or decentralizing international advertising decision making. The opportunities for centralizing are few when a company follows an approach of customizing advertising for each local market. However, when a company follows a standardized advertising format, a more centralized approach will be possible and probably even desirable.

Skill levels and efficiency concerns can also determine the level of centralization. Decentralization requires that the advertising skills of local subsidiaries and local agencies be sufficient to perform successfully. On the other hand, international advertising might not be centralized successfully in companies where the head office staff does not possess a good appreciation of the international dimension of the firm's business. Decentralization is often believed to result in inefficiencies or decreased quality because a firm's budget might be spread over too many individual agencies. Instead of having a large budget in one agency, the firm has split-up minibudgets that may not be sufficient to obtain the best creative talent to work on its products. Centralization will often give access to better talent, though knowledge of the local markets may be sacrificed. See Figure 15.3 for an example of how international campaign planning develops at one U.S. multinational corporation.

The managerial style of the international company may affect the centralization decision in advertising as well. Some companies pride themselves on giving a considerable amount of freedom to local subsidiary managers. Under such circumstances, centralizing advertising decisions would only be counterproductive. It has been observed with many multinational firms that the general approach taken by the company's top management towards international markets relates closely to its desire to centralize or decentralize international advertising. However, since the company's internal and external factors are subject to change over time, it can be expected that the decision to centralize or decentralize will never be a permanent one. These different levels of head office involvement are outlined in Figure 15.4.

FIGURE 15.3 International Advertising Campaign Development at Goodyear (1976)

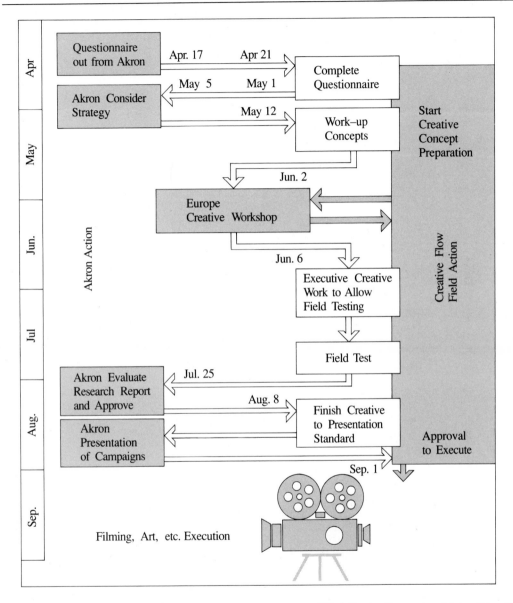

Source: Dean M. Peebles, John K. Ryans, Jr., and Ivan R. Vernon, "Coordinating International Advertising." Reprinted from *Journal of Marketing*, January 1978, p. 32, published by the American Marketing Association.

FIGURE 15.4 Headquarters Involvement in International Advertising Strategy

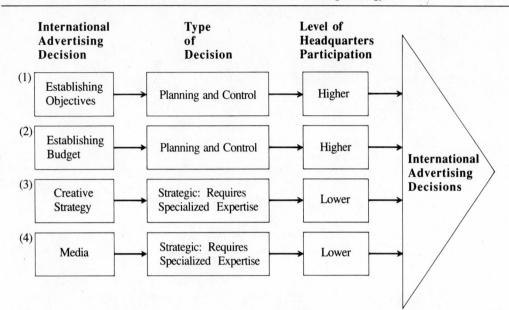

Source: J. R. Wills and J. K. Ryans, Jr., "An Analysis of Headquarters Executive Involvement in International Advertising," *European Journal of Marketing,* vol. 11, 1977, p. 579.

CONCLUSIONS

Few areas of international marketing are subject to hotter debate than international advertising. The complexity of dealing simultaneously with a large number of different customers in many countries, all speaking their own languages and subject to their own cultural heritage, offers a real challenge to the international marketer. International executives must find the common ground within these diverse influences so that coherent campaigns can still be possible.

The debate in the field has recently shifted from one of standardization versus customization to one of global versus nonglobal advertising. Proponents of global advertising point to the convergence of customer needs and the emergence of the "world consumer," a person who is becoming ever more homogeneous whether he or she lives in Paris, London, New York or Tokyo. However, many aspects of the advertising environment remain considerably diverse. Although English is rapidly becoming a global language, most messages still have to be translated into local languages. Regulations in many countries on the execution, content, and format of advertisements still make it very difficult to offer standardized solutions to advertising problems. Also, media availability to advertisers is substantially different in many parts of the world, so many companies still have to adapt their media mix to the local situation. Many executives thus believe that considerable local content is necessary. They will therefore give the local country organizations substantial responsibility for input and decision making.

Most marketers realize that total customization is not desirable because it would require that each market create and implement its own advertising strategies. Top creative talent is scarce everywhere, and better creative solutions tend to be the costlier ones. As a result, companies appear to be moving towards modularization, in which some elements of the advertising message are common to all advertisements while other elements are tailored to local requirements. To make customization work, however, companies cannot simply design one set of advertisements and later expect to adapt the content. Successful modularization requires that companies, from the very outset, plan for such a process by including and considering the full range of possibilities and requirements to be satisfied. This offers a considerable challenge to international marketing executives and their advertising partners.

Questions for Discussion

1. What are the major factors that impact on the extension of an international advertising campaign into several countries?
2. How do you explain that some companies appear to be successful with very similar campaigns worldwide while others fail with the same strategy?
3. What advice would you give to a U.S. firm interested in advertising in Japan, and what would you suggest to a Japanese firm interested in advertising in the United States?
4. What future do you see for global advertising?
5. What would be the impact of increased commercial satellite television on international advertising, both in the United States and abroad?
6. How will the advertising industry need to react to the new trends in international marketing?

For Further Reading

"Advertising Regulations, Self-Regulations and Self-Discipline Around the World: Some Facts, Trends, and Observations." *Journal of International Marketing,* No. 1 (1981), pp. 46–55.

"A Survey of the Advertising Industry." *The Economist* (November 14, 1981), pp. 6–7.

Aydin, Nizam, Vern Terpstra, and Attila Yaprak. "The American Challenge in International Advertising." *Journal of Advertising* 13, No. 4 (1984), pp. 49–57.

Boddewyn, J.J. "The Global Spread of Advertising Regulation." *MSU Business Topics* (Spring 1981), pp. 5–13.

Colvin, Michael, Roger Heeler, and Jim Thorpe. "Developing International Advertising Strategy." *Journal of Marketing,* 44, No. 4 (Fall 1980), pp. 73–79.

Crunch, A. Graeme. "The Changing Faces of International Advertising." *The International Advertiser,* 13, No. 2 (1972), pp. 4–6.

Donnelly, James H. Jr., and John K. Ryans, Jr. "Standardized Global Advertising, A Call As Yet Unanswered." *Journal of Marketing* (April 1969), pp. 57–60.

Dunn, S. Watson, and E.S. Lorimor. *International Advertising and Marketing.* Columbus, Ohio: Grid, 1979.

Harper, Malcolm. "Advertising in a Developing Economy: Opportunity and Responsibility." *European Journal of Marketing,* No. 3, (1975), pp. 215–223.

Killough, James. "Improved Payoffs from Transnational Advertising." *Harvard Business Review* (July-August 1978), pp. 102–110.

Neelankavil, J.P., and Albert B. Stridsberg. *Advertising Self-Regulation: A Global Perspective.* New York: Hastings House, 1980.

Peebles, Dean M., and John K. Ryans, Jr. *Management of International Advertising.* Boston: Allyn and Bacon, 1984.

Peebles, Dean M., and John K. Ryans, Jr. "Advertising as a Positive Force." *Journal of Advertising* (Spring 1978), pp. 48–52.

Peebles, Dean M., John K. Ryans, Jr., and Ivan R. Vernon. "Coordinating International Advertising." *Journal of Marketing* (January 1978), pp. 28–34.

Ryans, John K., Jr. "Is It Too Soon to Put a Tiger in Every Tank? *Columbia Journal of World Business* (March 1969), pp. 69–75.

Stridsberg, Albert. "Can Advertising Benefit Developing Countries?" *Business and Society Review* (Autumn 1974), pp. 76–77.

Weinstein, Arnold K. "The International Expansion of U.S. Advertising Agencies." *MSU Business Topics* (Summer 1974), pp. 29–35.

Wills, James R., and John K. Ryans. "Headquarters Involvement in International Advertising." *European Journal of Marketing,* 11, No. 8 (1977), pp. 577–584.

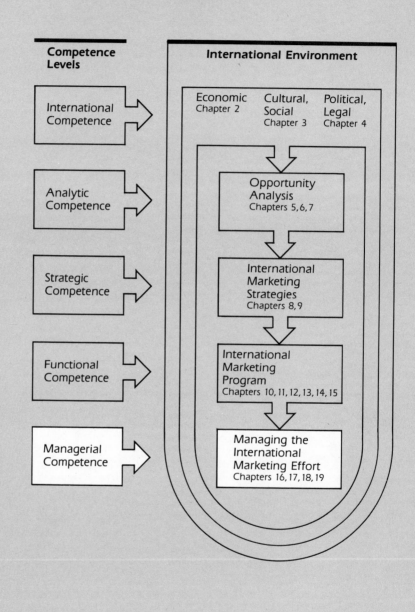

PART 6

MANAGING THE INTERNATIONAL MARKETING EFFORT

16 ORGANIZING INTERNATIONAL MARKETING

17 PLANNING AND CONTROLLING INTERNATIONAL MARKETING

18 FINANCING INTERNATIONAL MARKETING OPERATIONS

19 THE EXPORT AND IMPORT TRADE PROCESS

For a company to become successful in international marketing, it must do more than analyze markets and devise marketing programs. Increasingly, international companies are running complex organizations with operating units in many different countries. The managerial challenges of running such diverse organizations are substantial and require skills that are far different from those required by largely domestic or single-country organizations. This final part of our text is devoted to issues involving the managerial competence of international marketing managers. The goal is to show how managers can guide their operations more effectively in this very competitive global marketplace.

In Chapter 16, we will concentrate on organizational design issues for international firms and on where the decision-making process should be concentrated. Chapter 17 focuses on how international firms should control their operations and marketing programs. In the next two chapters, we deal with two specific issues that are very important in the success of an international firm. How to use financing as a competitive tool in international marketing will be the focus of Chapter 18. The final chapter, Chapter 19, covers the various exporting and importing procedures faced by international marketing managers.

16.

ORGANIZING INTERNATIONAL MARKETING

An important aspect of international marketing is the establishment of an appropriate organization. The organization must be able to formulate and implement strategies for each market. The objective of an international marketing organization is to develop a structure that will allow the firm to respond to distinct variations in each market while utilizing the company's appropriate experience from other markets and products. The key issue in establishing an international organization is deciding where to locate the international responsibility in the firm. The major dilemma facing international marketers involves the tradeoff between the need for an individual response to the local environment and the value of centralized knowledge and control. For companies to be successful, it is necessary to find a proper balance between these two extremes.

There are a number of various organizational structures that are best suited for different internal and external environmental factors. No one structure is best. In this chapter, we will examine the elements that affect the international marketing organization, the alternative organizational structures, the common stages through which organizations evolve, the elements that affect the international marketing organization, the location of corporate global responsibility in an organization, and the recent trends in international organization design. (The elements of organizational design are shown in Figure 16.1.)

ORGANIZING: THE KEY TO STRATEGY IMPLEMENTATION

The global marketplace offers numerous opportunities for the astute marketer. To take advantage of these opportunities, the marketer will develop strategies to fit the needs of diverse markets while capitalizing on economies of scale in centralized operations, centralized control, and experience in other markets. These strategies will be adapted to the internal and external environment so that they will prevail over the competition.[1] The final success of the strategy will be determined by the selection of an appropriate organization.

The structure of an international organization should be congruent with the tasks to be performed, the need for product knowledge, and the need for market knowledge. It is difficult to select an organizational structure that can effectively and efficiently implement a marketing strategy while responding to the diverse needs of customers and the corporate staff. Chapter 17, "Planning and Controlling International Marketing Operations," examines the simultaneous pressures for greater integration and greater diversity which also create a significant tension in the development of an ideal organizational structure.

ELEMENTS AFFECTING THE INTERNATIONAL MARKETING ORGANIZATION

The ideal structure of an organization should be a function of the product(s) or service(s) to be sold in the marketplace and the external/internal environment. Theoretically, the approach to developing such an organization would be to analyze the specific tasks to be accomplished within an environment and subsequently design a structure that would complete these tasks most effectively. There are a number of other factors that complicate the selection of an appropriate organization. The diagram shown in Figure 16.1 reflects the elements that affect organizational design. We will discuss each of these elements individually.

External Forces

Geographic Distance

Technological innovations have somewhat eased the problem associated with physical distance. Companies, primarily in the United States and other developed countries, enjoy such conveniences as next-day mail, facsimile machines, teleconferencing, and rapid transportation. These benefits, however, cannot be taken for granted. Distance becomes a distinct barrier when operations are established in less-developed countries, where a simple phone call can take hours

---

1. Alfred D. Chandler, *Strategy and Structure* (Cambridge, Mass.: M.I.T. Press, 1962).

FIGURE 16.1 Factors Affecting Organizational Design

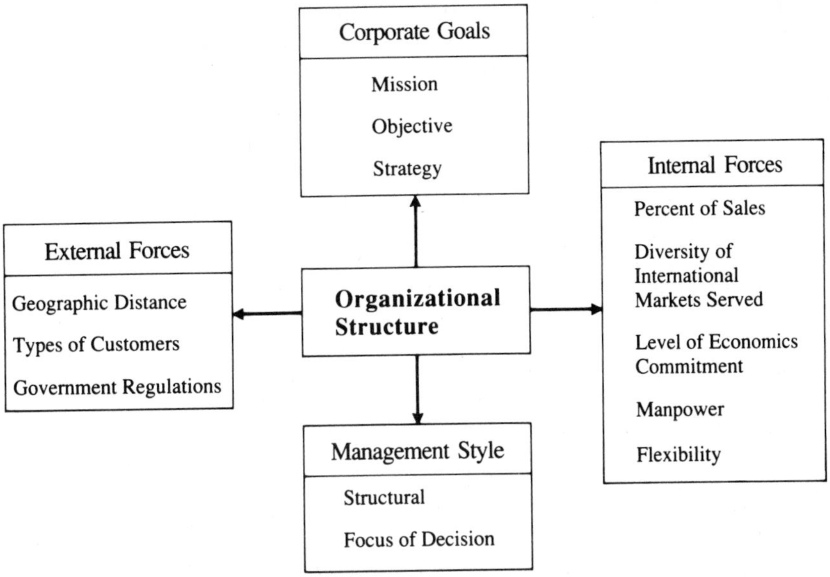

if not a few days to place. Even in developed countries, postal systems can be slow and telephone connections weak.

Geographic distance results in communication barriers; and one problem that even high technology cannot solve is the time differentials. Managers in New York who reach an agreement over lunch will have a hard time finalizing the deal with their headquarters in London until the following day, as most executives will be on their way home for the evening. The five-hour difference results in lost communication time, which impedes rapid results in a divisional structure. However, the time difference would not affect a geographic organization with a regional management center in the United States.

Types of Customers

A complete evaluation and understanding of the consumers within the marketplace will enable companies to structure their organization appropriately. The more homogeneous the consumers with respect to the product or service, the easier it will be for a firm to consolidate its efforts. For example, bicycles are used primarily for recreation in both the United States and Canada, so a bicycle company could use a similar marketing approach in both countries, and a centralized organization would be adequate. On the other hand, in China, bicycles are used as a primary means of transportation, so the marketing approach would be significantly different from that used in the United States and Canada. This requires a geographic organization that can respond to differences in local product use.

Government Regulations

How various countries attract or repel foreign operations can affect the structure of the organization. Laws involving imports, exports, taxes, hiring, and so on differ from country to country. Many developing countries require a firm that establishes plants on their territory to hire, train, and develop local employees and to share ownership with the government or local citizens. These requirements for local investment and ownership may require an organization with a local decision-making group.

Internal Forces

Percent of International Sales

The amount of international sales will affect the type of organization. If only a small percent of sales (1% to 10%) are international, a company will tend to have a simple organization, such as an export department. As the amount of international sales increases relative to total sales, a company would tend to change from an export department to an international division to a worldwide organization.

Diversity of International Markets Served

The number and diversity of international markets served will affect the choice of international organization. As the number and diversity of markets increase, the organization necessary to manage the marketing effort will become more complex. It will require a larger number of people to understand the markets.

Level of Economic Commitment

A company unwilling or unable to allocate adequate financial resources to its international efforts will not be able to sustain a complex or costly international structure. The less expensive organizational approaches to international marketing usually result in less control by the company on the local level. It is extremely important to build an organization that will provide the flexibility and resources to achieve the corporation's long-term goals for international markets.

Manpower

Available and capable manpower is just as vital to a firm as financial resources. Some companies send top domestic executives to foreign operations and then find that they do not understand the nation's culture. According to statistics compiled on U.S. corporations, 30 percent of the executives sent on overseas assignments have not worked out.[2] The hiring of local executives is also difficult because in many countries competition for such people is extremely intense. Because people are such an important resource in international organizations, many companies structure their organization based on the availability of internationally trained executive talent. Also, more companies are developing cross-cultural training programs to help prepare executives for new environments.[3]

Flexibility

Although a rigid structure enables a firm to gain more control over operations, it also restricts adaptability. When a company devises an organization structure, it must build in some flexibility, especially in the event of the need for future reorganization. Companies that establish a perfect design for the present find themselves in trouble when the firm grows or dissolves.

Management Style

Structural Basis

There are three basic dimensions to the structure of an organization. These dimensions provide the foundation on which to design an organization. Figure 16.2 depicts the direction each company can take once it decides on the basic framework.

American Standard restructured its company from a geographic organization to a product-based organization. The purpose of the change was to encourage cross-fertilization of management skills and technology. Additionally, American Standard's corporate philosophy was to promote the best person. This policy meant that non-Americans not only ran most of the overseas divisions, but were moving into senior U.S. and global jobs. This philosophy enabled American Standard to shed its reputation as a United States–based company.[4]

A multimillion-dollar MNC, a manufacturer of consumer nondurables, changed its management structure from a decentralized, regional format. Under

2. Edwin R. Henry, "What Business Can Learn from Peace Corp's Selection and Training," *Personnel,* vol. 41, July–August 1965.

3. Mark Mendenhall and Gary Oddow, "Acculturation Profiles of Expatriate Managers: Implications for Cross-Cultural Training Programs," *Columbia Journal of World Business,* Winter 1986, p. 73.

4. Hugh D. Menzies, "Happy Days at American Standard," *Fortune,* September 22, 1980, p. 136.

FIGURE 16.2 Basis for Organizational Design

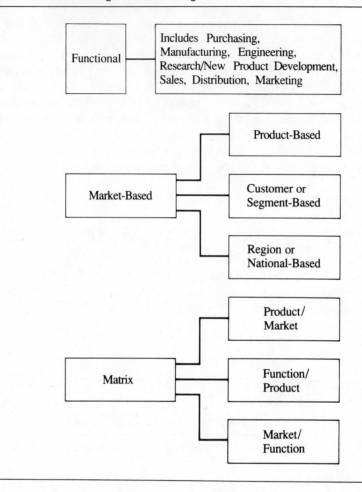

the old system, four regional divisions reported to the CEO. The new structure has eight product divisions reporting directly to the president and CEO. The reasons for the change were several:

1. The widened scope of business increased the jobs of senior divisional managers.
2. Expanded geographic territories made travel between divisional headquarters and regional departments difficult.
3. The diverse economic level of various markets created an imbalance in strategic planning.

4. The benefit of decentralization had run its course as staff functions of all corporate levels had expanded and resulted in duplication of efforts.[5]

Focus of Decision

Who makes what decisions provides an orientation for the organizational design. If all decision-making responsibility is in the hands of headquarters, then the international operations should reflect this. There are many layers or types of decisions to be made from the purchasing of paper clips to the acquisition of a product line or a company. The focus of decision is very much a function of the CEO's management style. Texaco reorganized its structure to reflect the management style. August Long, the past CEO, made decisions on even minor expenditures and the company's success (or lack of success) reflected his authoritarian style. His successor, Maurice Granville, allowed the president, John McKinley, to make all the decisions; and subsequently Texaco was restructured to provide more authority and responsibility to lower levels of management.[6]

Corporate Goals

No company should begin establishing an international organization until it has reviewed and established its strategies and subsequent objectives. If the company anticipates future growth in international markets, then it must establish a structure that can evolve into a larger operation effectively and efficiently. Too often, short-sighted executives establish international operations that do not enable the managers to grow with the company when markets begin to expand. These managers are not equipped to take on added responsibility. Additionally, headquarters fail to communicate short-term goals, long-range objectives, and sometimes even the total mission of the company. Inadequate communications result in an ambiguous corporate image and the inability to facilitate coordination of all marketing elements.

TYPES OF INTERNATIONAL ORGANIZATIONS

The international marketplace offers many opportunities. To take advantage of these opportunities, a company must evaluate the options, develop a strategy,

---

5. "Corporate Organization: Why One Firm Chose to Change a Textbook Setup," *Business International,* March 16, 1984, pp. 81–82.
6. "Texaco Restoring Luster to the Star," *Business Week,* December 22, 1980, pp. 54–61.

and establish an organization to implement the strategy. The organization should take into account all the factors affecting organizational design shown in Figure 16.1. In the following segment of the chapter, we review the various types of international organization structure.

Companies Without International Specialists

Many companies first begin selling products to foreign markets without a separate international organization or an international specialist. A domestically oriented company may begin to receive inquiries from foreign buyers who saw an advertisement in a trade magazine or attended a domestic trade show. The domestic staff will respond to the inquiry in the same fashion as it does other inquiries. Product brochures would be sent to the potential buyer for review. If sufficient interest exists on the part of both the buyer and seller, then more communication (telex, air mail, telephone, personal visits) may transpire. With no specific individual designated to handle international business, it may be directed to a sales manager, an inside salesperson, a product manager, or an outside salesperson.

Companies without an international organization will obviously have limited costs. Of course with no one responsible for international business, there will probably be little or no sales and profit from it. Also, when the firm attempts to respond to the occasional inquiry, no one will understand the difficulties of translation into another language, the particular needs of the customer, transfer of funds, fluctuating exchange rates, shipping, legal liabilities, or many of the other differences between domestic and international business. As the number of international inquiries grows and/or management recognizes the potential international markets, international specialists will be added to the domestic organization.

International Specialists/Export Department

The complexities of selling a product to a variety of different countries encourages most domestically oriented firms to establish an international expertise. This can vary from having a part-time international specialist to a full staff of specialists organized into an export department or international department. Figure 16.3 illustrates an organization with an international specialist.

The international specialist/export department is primarily a sales function. They will respond to inquiries, exhibit at international trade shows, handle export documentation, shipping, insurance, and financial matters. Also, the international specialist(s) would maintain contact with embassies, export financing agencies, and the Department of Commerce. All of these groups regularly publish requests for bid quotations from other countries.

FIGURE 16.3 Organization with an International Specialist

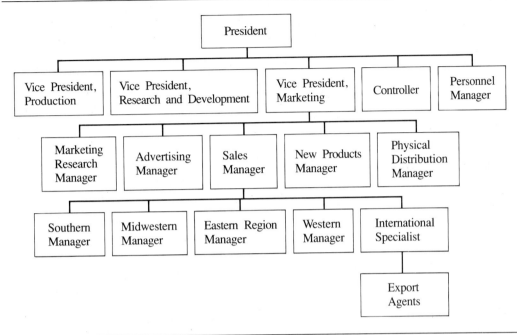

The advantage of hiring the international specialist(s) is that the firm will have the ability to respond, bid for, and process foreign business. The size of this type of organization will be directly related to the amount of international business that is handled. The costs should be minor compared to the potential.

The international specialist/export department is often reactive, rather than proactive, in nature. The specialist does not usually evaluate the worldwide demand for a product or service, identify pockets of opportunities, develop a strategy to infiltrate these opportunities, or reap the rewards; he or she basically responds to inquiries. Also, the international specialist may have little opportunity to modify the current products/services to meet international market needs because the international sales are so small. In most cases the products are sold as is, with no modification.

International Division

As the sales to foreign markets become more important to the company and the complexity of coordinating the directing of the international effort extends beyond a specialist or a single department, a company may establish an international division. The international division would normally report to the presi-

FIGURE 16.4 Organization with an International Division

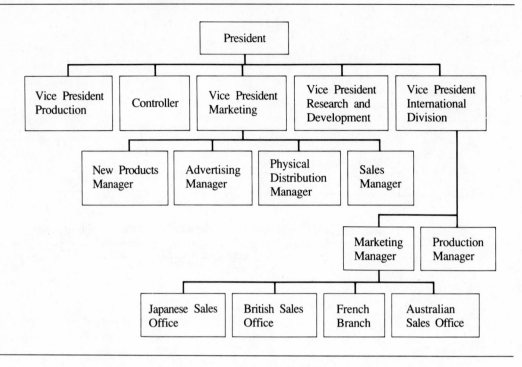

dent, thus having an equal status with other functions such as marketing, finance, and production. Figure 16.4 illustrates the organization design of a firm using an international division.

The international division will be directly involved in the development and implementation of an international strategy. The head of the international division would have marketing, sales, and possibly production managers reporting to him or her. These individuals would focus their entire efforts on the international markets. It has been suggested that the international division is the best organizational alternative when international business represents 10 to 15 percent of the total business.[7]

The advantage of an international division is that it focuses on the international market at a high enough level in the organization to directly influence strategy. Also the international division will begin to actively seek out market opportunities in foreign companies. The sales and marketing efforts in each country would be supported through a regional or local office. This office would be able to understand the local environment, including legal requirements, cus-

---

7. "Leaving the Rules for Global Selling," *Business Abroad,* November 1969, pp. 43–44.

tomer needs, competition, and so on. This close contact with the marketplace improves the organization's ability to perform successfully. The international division is obviously more expensive than having either no international focus or a specialist. However, the increased cost would be offset by increased sales. An international division can be the transition stage between a domestically oriented and a globally oriented company. As a company begins to adopt a worldwide focus, the international organization will evolve into a broader entity.

Worldwide Organizations

As a firm recognizes the potential size of the international market, it begins to change from a domestic company doing some business overseas to a worldwide company doing business in a number of countries. A worldwide focus will normally result in a worldwide organizational design. There are four dimensions that a company can choose to organize: (1) geography, (2) function, (3) product, and (4) business unit. We will discuss and illustrate each organizational alternative. The matrix organization, another type of worldwide organization which combines two or more of the four dimensions, will also be discussed.

Geographic Organizational Structures

Geographic organizational designs focus on the need for an intimate knowledge of the customer and his/her environment. A geographic organization will allow a company the opportunity to understand local culture, economy, politics, law, and the competitive situation. There are two general types of geographic organizations, a regional management center and a country-based organization. In many cases, the regional management center and country-based organizations are combined.

Regional Management Centers

Regional management centers form a worldwide organization that focuses on a particular region of the world, such as Europe, the Middle East, Latin America, the Caribbean, or the Far East. Figure 16.5 illustrates the regional management structure of a worldwide geographic organization.

The reason for a regional geographic approach to organizational design is twofold. First, there is the pressure of size. Once a market reaches a certain size, the firm must have a staff focused on that region to maximize revenues from that area of the world and to protect the firm's assets. The second reason for a regional focus is the regional nature of markets. A group of countries located close together, having similar social and cultural histories, climates, resources, and often languages, will have many similar needs for products. In many cases,

FIGURE 16.5 Regional Management Centers

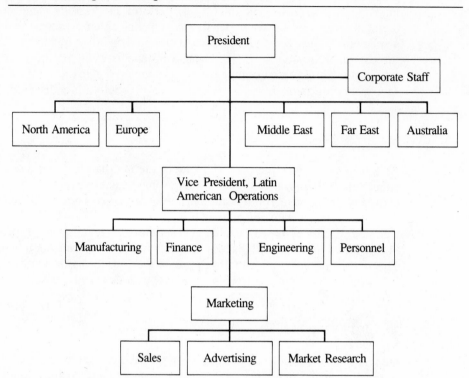

these regional country groups have unified themselves for political and economic reasons; for example, the European Community is a regional group.

The regional approach to a worldwide organization has a number of benefits. It allows a company to locate marketing and manufacturing efforts to take advantage of regional agreements such as the EC or EFTA. Also, the regional approach puts the company in close contact with the distributors, customers, and subsidiaries. The regional management will be able to respond to local conditions and react more quickly than a totally centralized organization, in which all decisions would be made at headquarters.

One of the disadvantages of a regional management center is cost. In general the cost of overseas offices are expensive due to the following: international moving costs are high; executives living abroad usually receive additional compensation; and manpower, office space, communication, and travel expenses all result in increased costs. The increased costs of a regional office must be offset by increased organizational effectiveness, such as generating sales and/or controlling costs.

FIGURE 16.6 Country-Based Geographic Organization

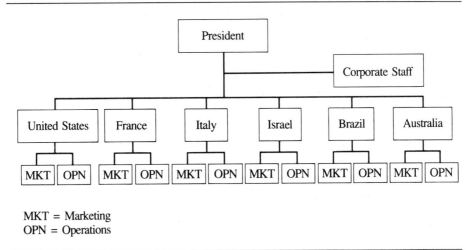

MKT = Marketing
OPN = Operations

Country-Based Organizations

The second type of geographic organization is a country-based organization. This type of organization utilizes a separate organizational unit for each country. Figure 16.6 illustrates a simple country-based geographic organization.

A country-based organization is very similar to a regional management center, except that the focus is on a single country rather than a group of countries. For example, instead of having a regional management center in Brussels overseeing all European sales and operations, there would be an organizational unit in each country. The country-based organization can be extremely sensitive to local customs, laws, and needs, which may be different even though the countries participate in a regional organization like the EC.

One of the difficulties of a country-based organization is its higher cost, so the benefit of a local organization must offset its cost. The second difficulty is coordination with headquarters. If a company is involved in forty countries, it is difficult and cumbersome to have all forty country-based organizational units reporting to one or more people in the company's headquarters. The third problem of a country-based unit is that it may not take advantage of the regional groupings of countries discussed in Chapter 5. The regional trading agreements such as the EC make it valuable to coordinate activities in EC countries. Also, there are regional media that often cut across country boundaries, such as television and print media, and require coordination. To deal with the shortcomings of a country-based organization, many firms combine the concept of a regional management center and a country-based unit, as shown in Figure 16.7.

FIGURE 16.7 Organization Using Both Country-Based Units and Regional Management Centers

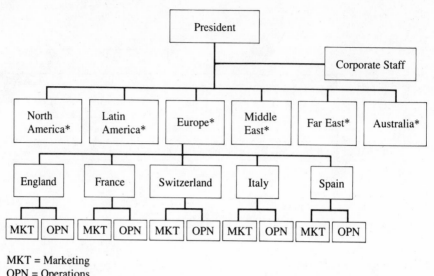

MKT = Marketing
OPN = Operations

* Under these regional offices would be country organizations similar to the European offices.

The combination of a regional and country approach minimizes many of the limitations of both designs, but it also adds an additional layer of management. Some executives think that the regional headquarters' additional layer reduces the country-level implementation of strategy rather than improving it. In order to receive benefits from a regional center, there must be a value in a regional strategy. Each company must reach its own decision regarding the organization design, its cost, and its benefits.

Worldwide Functional Organizations

A second way of organizing a worldwide organization is by function. In a function organization, the top executives in marketing, finance, production, accounting, and research and development all have worldwide responsibilities. For international companies this type of organization is most suitable for narrow or homogeneous product lines, with little variation between products or geographic markets. As shown in Figure 16.8, the functional organization is a simple struc-

FIGURE 16.8 Functional Worldwide Organization

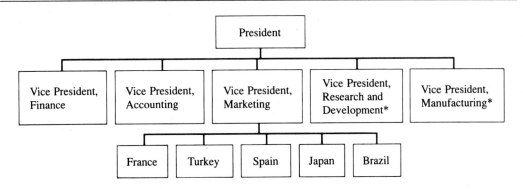

* Each functional vice president would have managers of that function in the countries served reporting to him/her as illustrated with the Vice President, Marketing.

ture. Each functional manager would have worldwide responsibility for that function. Usually the manager would have people responsible for the function in regions and/or countries around the world.

The functional organization, though common in domestic companies, is less common in international companies since few companies sell narrow homogeneous product lines with little region to region variations. The functional executives in American firms who do have international responsibilities usually work through a product or regional organization.

Worldwide Product Organizations

A third type of worldwide marketing organization is based on the product line rather than on the function or geographic area. The product group becomes responsible for the performance of their organizational unit, which incorporates marketing, sales, planning, and in some cases production. Other functions, such as legal, accounting, and finance, could be included in the product group or performed by the corporate staff. Structuring by product line is common for companies with several unrelated product lines. The rationale for selecting a product versus a regional focus is that the differences between the marketing of the products is greater than the differences between the geographic markets. Typically, the end-users for a product organization will vary by product line, so that there is no advantage to having the marketing for the different product lines done by the same group. The product is the focus of the organizational structure shown in Figure 16.9.

FIGURE 16.9 Worldwide Product Organizations

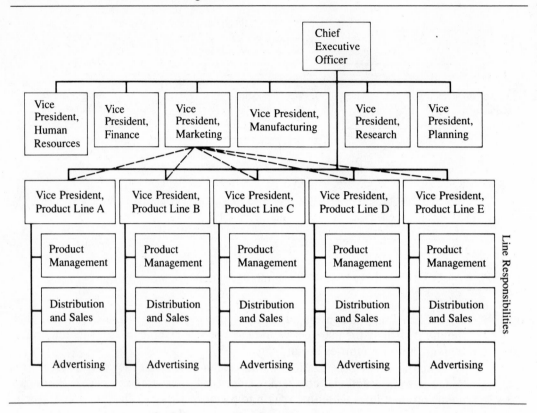

A product organization concentrates management on the product line, which is an advantage when the product line constantly changes due to technology. The product focus also gives the organization excellent flexibility. Within a product group the management can control the product life cycle, adding and deleting products with a marginal effect on overall operations. Also, the firm can add new product groups as they add new unrelated products through acquisition.

The product organization has its limitations.[8] Knowledge of specific areas may be limited, since each product group cannot afford a local organization. This lack of knowledge may cause the company to miss market opportunities. The managers of international product divisions can also be a problem. They can be ethnocentric and relatively disinterested or uneasy with the international side of the business. Another limitation of a product organization is the lack of coordi-

---

8. For a detailed discussion of a product organization, see William H. Davidson and Philippe Haspeslagh, "Shaping a Global Product Organization," *Harvard Business Review,* July–August 1982, pp. 125–132.

nation in international markets. If each product group goes its own way, the company's international development may result in inefficiencies. For example, two product divisions may be purchasing advertising space in the same magazine, which would be less expensive if the purchases were combined. To offset the inefficiencies of a worldwide product organization, the organization must provide for global coordination of activities such as advertising, customer service, and government relations.

Matrix Organization

Companies have become frustrated with the limitations of the one-dimensional geographic, product, or functional organization structures. In response to the limitation of single dimension organizations, the matrix organization was developed. As shown in Figure 16.10, the matrix organization allows two dimensions of equal weight (here, geographic and product dimensions) in the organization structure and in decision making responsibility. A matrix organization structure has a dual, rather than a single chain of command, which means that many individuals will have two superiors. Firms tend to adopt matrix organizations when it is necessary to be highly responsive to two dimensions, such as product and geography; when there are stringent constraints on financial and/or human resources; and when uncertainties generate very high informational processing requirements.[9]

A matrix organization can include both the product and geographic management components. Product management would have worldwide responsibility for a specific product line, while geographic management would be responsible for all product lines in a specific geographic area. Both of these management structures would overlap at the national product/market level.

The matrix organization includes approximately 38 different combinations of functional, product, and geographic dimensions.[10] The combination of different organization objectives and dual reporting relationships fosters conflict and complexity. Power struggles are a common problem when a matrix organization is first established. The power struggle is the result of the dual reporting relationship. The power limits of the two relationships are tested as each side attempts to identify their place in the organization.

The key to successful matrix management is the degree to which managers in an organization can resolve conflict and achieve the successful implementation of plans and programs. The matrix organization requires a change in management behavior from traditional authority to an influence system based on technical competence, interpersonal sensitivity, and leadership.

---

9. Paul R. Lawrence, Harvey F. Kolodny, and Stanley M. David, ''The Human Side of the Matrix,'' *Organization Dynamics,* Summer 1979, pp. 43–47.

10. ''New Directions in Multinational Corporate Organization,'' *Business International,* 1981, p. 2.

FIGURE 16.10 Matrix Organization

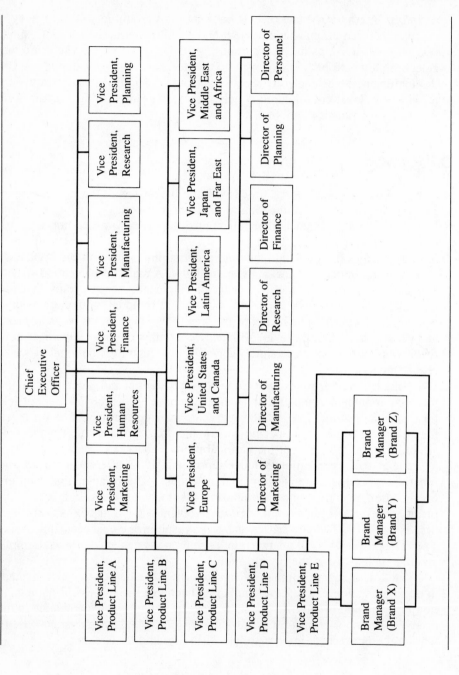

The advantages of a matrix or hybrid structure are that it:

- Permits an organization to function better in an uncertain and changing environment
- Increases potential for control and coordination
- Gives more individuals the chance to develop from technical or functional specialists to generalists

There are problems with matrix organizations; G.E., Citibank, Ciba-Geigy and Texas Instruments realized the limitations of pure matrix organizations and switched to simplified structures. The main problem with matrix organizations is that it assumes that product and geographic consideration are evenly balanced; but in reality few large diversified companies have such a balance. A United States–based consumer goods firm with two major businesses, ethical drugs and local brand candy bars, found that the matrix organization did not work for these two products. The company therefore reorganized, putting its billion dollar ethical drug division on a worldwide basis with close ties to headquarters and retaining the matrix organization for the over-the-counter drugs and toiletries divisions.[11]

The matrix organization requires a substantial investment in dual budgeting, accounting, transfer pricing, and personnel evaluation systems. The additional complexity and cost of a matrix organization should be offset by the benefit of the dual focus, increased flexibility and sales, and economies of scale.

Research shows that most firms have complex organizations with some form of matrix structure. The most typical matrix includes a product/market dimension on one axis and the geographic dimension on the other axis.[12]

Strategic Business Units

One of the most recent forms of organizational design is the *strategic business unit (SBU)*. An SBU is an organizational group of people supporting products and technologies that serve an identified market and compete with identified competitors. The SBU may either be a separate organizational design, similar to a product organization, or could be an organizational unit that is used only for the purpose of developing a business strategy for many products in a geographic area.

The increased penetration of global competition has forced many firms to set up SBUs to address the global markets and assess competition in developing a global business strategy. For example, both Coors (beer) and Norton Company (grinding wheels) have set up separate business units to explore the markets for

11. J. Quincy Hunsicker, "The Matrix in Retreat," *Financial Times,* October 25, 1982, p. 16.

12. Milton Halman, "Organization and Staffing of Foreign Operations of Multinational Corporations," Academy of International Business Meeting, New Orleans, October 25, 1980.

ceramic products based on new high performance ceramic technologies. These business units are particularly alert to the efforts of Japanese manufacturers such as Yokoyana, Sumatoms, and many others who are engaged in ceramics research, as well as the Japanese Ministry of International Trade and Industry that sponsors long-term ceramics research and development.

LIFE CYCLE OF INTERNATIONAL ORGANIZATIONS

Companies evolve into different organizations over time. As their international involvement expands, the degree of organizational complexity increases and firms reorganize accordingly. When a firm moves from exporting a few goods to a worldwide organization, it finds that the company has gone through organizational changes with differing structures and focus. The following diagram (Figure 16.11) depicts the typical progress of the international organizational life cycle. Because this is a dynamic and integrative process, most companies do not follow this life cycle exactly; but the framework does provide a method to evaluate the degree of focus and responsibility.

Export

When the domestic market becomes saturated or a need is identified in foreign markets, companies begin exporting their product and/or services. The export department is still a function of the company and normally reports and follows company procedures and strategies. Often, companies will first begin to receive inquiries from foreign companies about their products. Then, an export person or department is established to process and respond to the foreign inquiries.

Foreign Sales Office

If the demand for the product increases and there appears to be a need to establish an office either to ease administrative procedures or to investigate new markets or refine old markets, then a company will normally establish an office in a foreign country. Normally this office is under headquarters' control and acts according to home office directions.

Regional Market Center

Regional market centers act as filters between the headquarters and various country organizations. Regional market centers coordinate the marketing function of the branches so that they remain in line with corporate objectives. Re-

FIGURE 16.11 Life Cycle of International Organizations

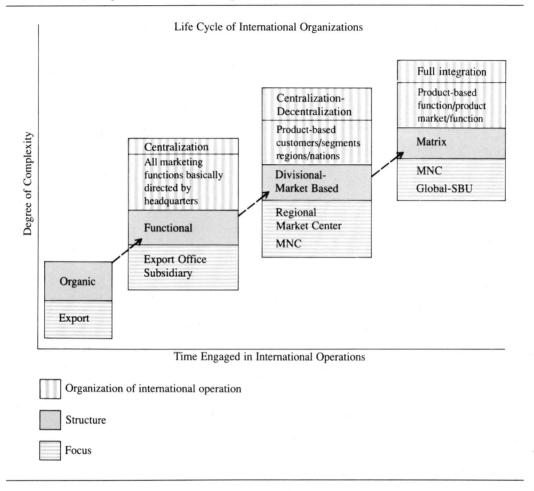

Life Cycle of International Organizations

gional market centers are normally organized along geographic lines; however, these centers might be organized along product groups and/or similar target markets.

Matrix Organizations

The matrix organization is the most complex and sophisticated structure. It requires a firm to be fully competent in:

1. Geographic knowledge
2. Product knowledge

3. Functional aspects, such as finance, production, and marketing
4. Customer/Industry knowledge

Instead of choosing which one to adopt—a national organization or a product organization—the matrix incorporates both and each operate as profit centers. Matrix organizations allow low levels to have substantial authority; however, they require an open and flexible "corporate culture/orientation" for successful implementation.

Global Integration—Strategic Business Units

Fully advanced MNCs with complete integration have begun to establish strategic business units. An SBU acts as a separate business and contains a group of products and/or technologies directed at a specific target market. SBUs are part of a formal structure but act primarily to determine strategies.

CONCLUSIONS

Organizing the marketing efforts of a company across a number of countries is a difficult process. As the scope of a company's international business changes, its organizational structure must be modified in accordance with the internal and external environment. As the number of countries a company is marketing in increases, as product line expands and objectives change, so will the organizations. In this chapter, we have reviewed the various organizations commonly used, showing the benefits of each. The dynamic nature of business requires a constant re-evaluation of organizational structure with necessary modifications to meet the objectives of the firm.

Questions for Discussion

1. What aspects of the external environment cause multi-country marketing organizations to be different from single-country marketing organizations?
2. What effect will the marketing strategy have on an international marketing organization? For example, if the key aspect of a computer manufacturer's strategy is to focus on three industries worldwide—banks, stockbrokers, and educational institutions—will the organization be different from that of another company that decides to focus on end-users who require mainframe computers?
3. How does a single-country organization evolve into an international organization? What type of international organization is likely to develop first? Second? Why?

4. What actions will cause a company to develop an international marketing organization?
5. What are the pros and cons of a regional management center versus a product organization?
6. A country-based geographic structure responds well to the local culture and marketing. What would cause a company to switch from a country structure to a worldwide product organization?
7. Matrix organizations can be very costly and complex. What are the advantages of a matrix organization?

For Further Reading

Bartlett, Christopher A. "MNCs: Get Off the Reorganization Merry-Go-Round." *Harvard Business Review* (March–April 1983), pp. 138–146.

Brandt, William K., and James M. Hulbert. "Headquarters Guidance in Marketing Strategy in the Multinational Subsidiary." *Columbia Journal of World Business* (Winter 1972), pp. 7–14.

Business International. *Designing the International Corporate Organization.* New York: Business International Corporation, 1976.

"Corporate Organization: Where in the World Is It Going?" *Business International* (August 15, 1980), pp. 257, 258.

David, Stanley M. "Trends in the Organization of Multinational Corporations." *Columbia Journal of World Business* (Summer 1976), pp. 59–70.

David, Stanley M., and Paul R. Lawrence. "Problems of Matrix Organization." *Harvard Business Review* (May–June 1978), pp. 134–136.

Davidson, William H., and Phillippe Haspeslagh. "Shaping a Global Product Organization." *Harvard Business Review* (July–August 1982), pp. 125–132.

Drake, Rodman, and Lee M. Caudill. "Management of the Large Multinational: Trends and Future Changes." *Business Horizons* (May–June 1981), pp. 88–90.

Goggin, William C. "How the Multinational Structure Works at Dow Corning." *Harvard Business Review* (January–February 1974), pp. 64–65.

Holmen, Milton G. "Organizing and Staffing of Foreign Operations of Multinational Corporations." Paper presented at the Academy of International Business Meeting in New Orleans, October 25, 1980.

Hutchinson, J. "Evolving Organizational Forms." *Columbia Journal of World Business* (Summer 1976), pp. 49–50.

Parker, Herbert S. "Restructuring the Corporation." *Planning Review* (January–February 1987), pp. 46–48.

Perlmutter, Howard V. "The Tortuous Evolution of the Multinational Corporation." *Columbia Journal of World Business* (January–February 1969), pp. 9–18.

Picard, Jacques. "Determinants of Centralization of Marketing Decision Making in Multinational Corporations." In *Marketing in the 80's,* Proceedings of the Educators' Conference. Chicago: American Marketing Association, 1980, pp. 259–261.

Shetty, Y. K. "Managing the MNC: European and American Styles." *Management International Review,* No. 3 (1979), pp. 39–48.

17

PLANNING AND CONTROLLING INTERNATIONAL MARKETING

The processes of planning and controlling are interrelated. Planning allows a company to understand the environment and develop a strategy. Controlling is the process of evaluating strategy implementation and managing the efforts of those people responsible for the strategy. The processes of planning and controlling will also be related to the specific organization (see Chapter 16), because the processes are completed within the organizational structure. As the environment changes and new strategies are developed, the organization may change, which may affect the planning and control process. For example, if a company changes from a functional organization, with all marketing decisions made at the headquarters in New York, to a geographic organization, with regional management centers in Paris, Tokyo, New York, and Sao Paulo, the planning and control processes will change. Figure 17.1 shows how the planning and control processes relate to strategy implementation and to the organizational structure of the firm.

THE PLANNING PROCESS

Planning in the international environment is difficult because of the number of extraneous elements involved. Table 17.1 illustrates the differences between planning in a domestic setting and planning in the international sector.

As shown in Table 17.1, there are numerous factors that increase the complexity of international planning, such as language, political differences, currency fluctuations, and a lack of market data. These differences increase the difficulty of developing international plans as well as the difficulty of implementing these plans.

FIGURE 17.1 Planning and Controlling International Marketing

Planning Methods	Boston Consulting Group	General Electric/ McKinsey	Profit Impact of Marketing Strategy	Scenario Planning

Planning Process	Selecting Markets	Coordinating Planning Efforts	Decision Making	Centralized Versus Decentralized

Control Process	Standards	Measurements and Evaluation	Correcting Deviations

As businesses move into international markets, the decision makers are faced with increasingly complex alternatives.[1] Should we license in Brazil, export to South Africa, establish a joint venture in Kuwait, or set up a wholly owned subsidiary in Hong Kong? Which project or combination of projects will

---

1. Noel Capon et al., "Comparison of Corporate Planning Practice in American and Australian Manufacturing Companies," *The Journal of International Business Studies,* Summer 1985, pp. 41–54.

TABLE 17.1 Domestic Versus International Planning

Domestic Planning	*International Planning*
1. Single language and nationality	1. Multilingual/multinational/multicultural factors
2. Relatively homogeneous market	2. Fragmented and diverse markets
3. Data available, usually accurate and collection easy	3. Data collection a formidable task, requiring significantly higher budgets and personnel allocation
4. Political factors relatively unimportant	4. Political factors frequently vital
5. Relative freedom from government interference	5. Involvement in national economic plans; government influences business decisions
6. Individual corporation has little effect on environment	6. "Gravitational" distortion by large companies
7. Chauvinism helps	7. Chauvinism hinders
8. Relatively stable business environment	8. Multiple environments, many of which are highly unstable (but may be highly profitable)
9. Uniform financial climate	9. Variety of financial climates ranging from overconservative to wildly inflationary
10. Single currency	10. Currencies differing in stability and real value
11. Business "rules of the game" mature and understood	11. Rules diverse, changeable, and unclear
12. Management generally accustomed to sharing responsibilities and using financial controls	12. Management frequently autonomous and unfamiliar with budgets and controls

Source: William W. Cain, "International Planning: Mission Impossible?" *Columbia Journal of World Business,* July–August 1970, p. 58. Reprinted by permission.

meet our corporate objectives? The two dimensions that differentiate international from domestic strategic planning are the multiple countries that businesses market to and the modes of entry into those markets.

This chapter will review the various types of planning processes being used, their application to the international market, and the advantages and disadvantages of each procedure when used with the international markets. The most widely used approaches to planning are the following:

- Boston Consulting Group Approach (BCG)
- General Electric/McKinsey Approach (GE)

- Profit Impact of Market Strategy (PIMS)
- Scenario Planning[2]

There are numerous articles and papers that review and compare the various planning models as they apply to domestic markets. Using these domestic systems as a base, each approach will be examined as it is used for international markets.

At any point in time, a firm really consists of a number of businesses, such as divisions, products, or brands. When these businesses were established, each of them was expected to grow. The firm would encourage growth by expanding research and development, advertising, and promotional budgets for all but the declining products. In recent years, the cost and availability of capital have caused corporations to be much more selective in the financing of their businesses. The tendency has been for a firm to look at its individual businesses and decide which ones to build, maintain, phase down, or close down. Therefore, the job of planning has become one of evaluating current businesses and searching out new opportunities so that the mixture of businesses within the firm will provide the necessary growth and cash flow for growth. For international markets, the breakdown of a firm's activities into the different businesses, usually referred to as strategic business units (SBUs), is normally done on a product-by-country basis. Once the firm is broken down into SBUs, planning must classify the firms based on expected future potential. One of the original classification schemes was developed by the Boston Consulting Group.

The Boston Consulting Group[3]

The Boston Consulting Group (BCG) approach classifies all current strategic business units into a business portfolio matrix shown in Figure 17.2. This includes both current SBUs as well as potential or proposed opportunities. The proposed opportunities are normally an extension of the current business via expansion into a new country or new product. BCG's methodology classifies these businesses based on market growth rate and market share. The market growth rate is the expected total market demand growth on an annualized basis. The market share is the company's relative share compared to the largest competitor. For example, a rate of 1.0 means the SBU has the same share as the next competitor, a 0.5 means it has one-half the share of the next largest competitor, and a 3.0 means the SBU has a three times larger share than the next largest competitor.

---

2. Richard G. Hamermesh, "Making Planning Strategic," *Harvard Business Review,* July–August 1986, p. 115.

3. Bruce D. Henderson, "The Experience Curve Reviewed: IV. The Growth Share Matrix or the Product Portfolio," (Boston: The Boston Consulting Group, Inc., 1973), Perspectives No. 135.

FIGURE 17.2 Boston Consulting Group Matrix

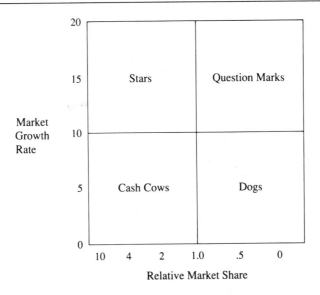

A firm's SBUs are evaluated and classified based on this approach. Market growth rate relates to the stage of the product life cycle and relative market share is based on the concept of market dominance. According to their positioning, products are classified as follows:

Dogs: Low market share and low growth. Should break even. Not a source of cash.

Question Marks: Low market share and high market growth. These SBUs are cash users. Money must be spent to maintain market position. They could become either stars or dogs.

Stars: High growth and high share. May break even or use cash to support high growth rate. Eventually growth will slow down and they will become cash cows.

Cash Cows: High market share and low market growth. As expected, these SBUs throw off cash to support other SBUs.[4]

To survive in the long term, a firm needs the proper balance of businesses in each area. Over time, businesses will change their positions. Many SBUs start as problem children, then become stars, then cash cows, and finally dogs. The

4. Bruce D. Henderson, *Henderson on Corporate Strategy* (Cambridge, Mass.: Abt Associates, 1979).

corporate planning function must work with the managers of each SBU to fore-cast the future mix of businesses in each area. Then, resources must be allocated based on this forecast as well as on the corporate objectives. Firms will use one of the following four strategies.

- First, Build—invest for the future, forego short-term earning while improv-ing market position.
- Second, Hold—maintain the current position.
- Third, Harvest—generate short-term cash flow regardless of the long-term effect.
- Fourth, Divest—sell or liquidate.

The most difficult part of using the BCG method is determining which level or unit of analysis to examine. For example, a firm may only have 5 percent of the world industrial pipe market, but it has 35 percent of the world industrial pipe market over 15 inches in diameter and 58 percent of the Spanish industrial pipe market over 12 inches in diameter.

The method used most often when applying the BCG approach in interna-tional planning is to use one product compared by country, as shown in Figure 17.3.

The suggested procedure is to develop the market portfolio material for the firm's own products and for those of major competitors. Then, the analysis should be repeated in five years. This will assist management in deciding which countries to build, hold, harvest, or divest.

The major advantages of the BCG approach in international planning are the following:

1. It requires a global view of the firm's business and its competition.
2. The approach provides a framework for analysis and comparison of busi-ness.
3. The procedure is a good basis for the formulation of marketing objectives for specific international markets.
4. The methodology allows a convenient graphical form which is easily under-stood by executives.

Although the BCG approach has had wide acceptance, it has also received criticism. The main criticisms are oriented toward the oversimplification of the process. The BCG approach assumes that high market share and high growth rate will result in success. Obviously other internal and external factors also affect the success of a business. Even if you accept the basic premise of the BCG approach, there are still problems defining the product, defining the market, measuring market growth, and measuring market dominance. These limitations apply to both international and domestic applications.

When using the BCG method for international markets with one product compared in several countries, the following four problems arise. First, the elements chosen for analysis are the countries. This may be wrong. Instead of looking at the countries by country market growth and market share for hair

FIGURE 17.3 Industrial Pipe—Market Portfolio

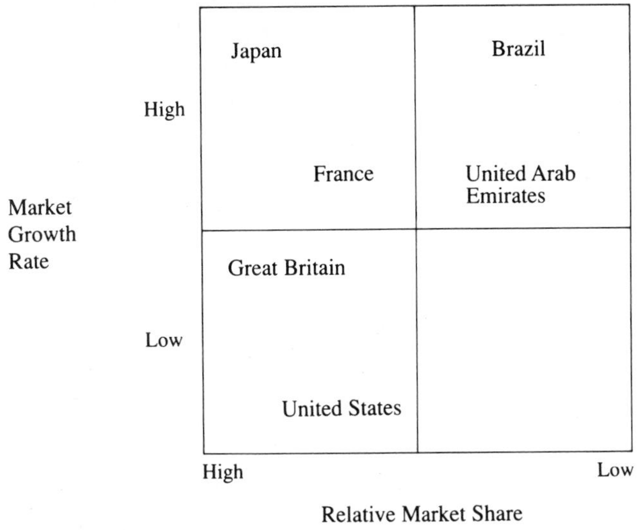

shampoo, maybe we should be analyzing the world portfolio for hair shampoo, by product market. For example, the men's expensive shampoo market, children's shampoo market, young women's shampoo market, and so on. The original BCG model ignores the interdependence of international markets. While our Paris operation may be a dog, using Paris as a production point for Greece, Italy, Spain, Portugal, and France may result in a cash cow or star.

Second, the BCG approach assumes a firm has extended experience with a product. Therefore, a high market share and more production experience will result in decreased costs. This concept becomes very gray when we start to examine possible variations in input costs, such as capital, manpower, material, tariffs, inflation, exchange rates, and transportation for different countries.

Third, the BCG method assumes the motivations of international firms to be similar, that is, profits, return on investment, and so on. This is not always true. Different countries emphasize different things. For some it's full employment and a favorable balance of payments. Others may desire low inflation. A country's economic or social policies will affect implementation of the BCG method.

Finally, the individual firm may have other objectives besides the generation of cash, for example, gaining technical information, preventing competition, or establishing good relations with a local government.

The General Electric/McKinsey Approach[5]

General Electric and McKinsey management consultants worked together to develop the GE business screen—a multifactor assessment based on an analysis of factors relating to profitability. The approach is an extension of the BCG approach.

The GE screen uses the following factors to evaluate SBUs:

Industry Attractiveness
- Market Size
- Market Growth
- Market Diversity
- Profit Margins
- Competitive Structure
- Technical Role
- Cyclicality
- Environment
- Legal, human, social

Business Strength
- Relative Market Share
- Price Competitiveness
- Size, Growth
- Product Quality
- Profitability
- Technological Position
- Strengths and Weaknesses
- Knowledge of Customers/Market
- Image, pollution, people

The GE approach rates each SBU based on these factors for industry attractiveness and business strength.[6] Each of the factors is given a certain weight. A procedure of aggregating various executives' opinions on these weights results in a high, medium, or low attractiveness and business strength.[7] Each SBU is then located on GE's nine-cell business screen, shown in Figure 17.4.

As shown in the screen, the GE approach results in strategic decisions similar to those in the BCG approach. The three cells in the upper left show the SBUs in favorable industries with good business strengths. The firm should invest and grow with these cells. The three diagonal cells are in the middle. The firm needs to decide whether to maintain, improve, or harvest these SBUs. The three cells in the lower right are those SBUs with an overall low attractiveness; this makes them candidates for harvesting or divesting.

The principles of the GE approach have been modified and used in the international environment. As we mentioned in Chapter 7, Ford Motor Company's Tractor Division has developed a strategic market portfolio evaluation system that focuses on country attractiveness and competitive strengths.[8]

The GE approach has the same limitations as the BCG method. However, the GE method is more adaptable to international markets. Each firm can determine which factors are important to their success in an international market and

---

5. Information in this section is drawn from *Managing Strategies for the Future Through Current Crises* (Fairfield, Conn.: General Electric Company, 1975).

6. Francis J. Aguilar and Richard Hamermesh, "General Electric: Strategic Position: 1981," Harvard Business School Case 9-381-174, p. 25.

7. Derek F. Abell and John S. Hammond, *Strategic Market Planning* (Englewood Cliffs, N.J.: Prentice-Hall, 1979), pp. 211–227.

8. Gilbert D. Harrell and Richard O'Kiefer, "Multinational Strategic Market Portfolios," *MSU Business Topics*, Winter 1981, p. 12.

FIGURE 17.4 GE's Business Screen for Evaluating SBUs

Industry Attractiveness

		High	Medium	Low
	High	Invest and Grow	Selective growth	Selectivity
Business Strengths **Medium**		Selective Growth	Selectivity	Divest or Harvest
	Low	Selectivity	Divest or Harvest	Divest or Harvest

evaluate SBUs based on these factors. Unfortunately, little empirical work has been done on either approach in the international market. The GE approach is still two dimensional, using only the factors of country attractiveness and business strength. This ignores the form of entry. For example, the importance of political stability varies greatly depending on whether a firm is exporting or involved in direct foreign investment. In conclusion, the GE approach is useful for multinationals. It provides more flexibility than the BCG approach, but its limitations should not be ignored.

Profit Impact of Marketing Strategy (PIMS)[9]

The PIMS project was started in 1960 at General Electric. Over the years the model was developed at the Harvard Business School, The Marketing Science

9. Information in this section is drawn from Sidney Schoeffler, Robert D. Buzzell, and Donald F. Henry, "Impact of Strategic Planning on Profit Performance," *Harvard Business Review,* March–April 1974, pp. 137–145.

Institute, and finally at The Strategic Planning Institute. The PIMS model data base includes the history and performance of over 450 companies and 3,000 businesses.[10] The model includes a computer-based regression model that utilizes the experience of the data base to determine what explains (or drives) profitability.

Each business is described in terms of thirty-seven factors such as growth rate, market share, product quality, investment intensity, and so on. The PIMS model uses multivariate regression equations to establish relationships between these different factors and two separate measures of performance, specifically, ROI and cash flow. PIMS research indicates that these performance measures are explained by general factors such as the following:

- Market growth rate
- Market share of business
- Market share divided by share of three largest competitors
- Degree of vertical integration
- Working capital requirements per dollars of sales
- Plant and equipment requirements per dollars of sales
- Relative product quality

The PIMS model uses many more variables than either the BCG or GE approach. Using the thirty-seven factors the model explains over 80 percent of the observed variation in profitability of the 1,000 businesses in the data base. The general opinion of business planners is that while the PIMS model has limitations, it is far superior to the other approaches. There are three major criticisms of the PIMS model. First, since the model uses variables related to each other, multicollinearity results. Therefore, the impact of individual factors on performance cannot be clearly identified. Second, most of the data was collected during the 1970s, which was an unusual economic period not indicative of a "normal" period. Third, the technical procedure for eliminating extreme values of data input tends to bias the results and improve the model's appearance. Although all these criticisms are valid, the methodology of the PIMS approach is one of the best approaches available to domestic planning.

To date, the PIMS model has had limited use in the international market. The complexity and secrecy of multinational corporations have hampered data collection. The data already collected have been run with the domestic data base, but the explained variance in ROI is too low.

Though the outlook for an international PIMS model is optimistic, there will still be limitations. The PIMS model should analyze performance based on the traditional criteria as well as by mode of entry. The form that a multinational business takes has a significant impact on costs, profitability, risks, and so on. Also the PIMS model will probably be limited to product-by-country analysis.

---

10. Robert D. Buzzell and Bradley T. Gale, *The PIMS Principles: Linking Strategy to Performance* (New York: The Free Press, 1987).

Although the data will be helpful, many products need to be analyzed on a product-by-market segment. Also, with the regional trade groups that have formed, such as ANCOM, CACM, EC, EFTA, LAFTA, and OPEC, many markets are becoming regionalized. This will also be an obstacle for the international PIMS model. Finally, although the PIMS model has been successful domestically, the political instability of many governments may reduce the explanatory power of the model.

However, despite these limitations, the PIMS model may become one of the key international strategic planning models in the future. With the utilization of a multinational data base, the PIMS model will be able to assist planners in deciding how to allocate resources to meet corporate objectives.

Scenario Planning[11]

The three strategic planning models discussed so far are referred to as portfolio models. These models do not take into consideration the impact of various external factors such as economic growth, energy costs, inflation, East/West relations, war, and economic fluctuations.

Scenario planning is a unique approach to strategic planning. With scenario planning, the multinational's business is broken down into business/country segments. Then a central or most probable scenario is developed regarding significant external variables such as energy costs, world politics, inflation, and so on. Possible variants of this central scenario are also developed. Then, the business/country segments are evaluated based on the central scenario and the variant scenarios. Ideally, investment decisions could be made based on this analysis.

The limitations of scenario planning are as follows. First, development of a central scenario and variants will be difficult. There will be many inputs to this scenario with limited agreement. Second, analysis of the effect of each scenario will also be complex. For example, if a firm is selling pipe to the United Kingdom and the central scenario predicts oil prices will go up 10 percent per year, how would the firm evaluate the U.K. pipe market? Increased oil prices mean more tax revenues from North Sea oil, an increase in exports, favorable impact on the balance of trade, strengthening of the pound sterling, an increase in imports, and a decrease in the ability of the remaining U.K. industries to export.

Although the scenario planning or contingency planning are useful techniques, they should be used to augment the portfolio methods—BCG, GE, and PIMS.

---

11. Information in this section is drawn from Harold F. Klein and Robert E. Linneman, ''The Use of Scenarios in Corporate Planning—Eight Case Histories,'' *Long Range Planning,* October 1981, pp. 69–77.

International Business Planning—A Look to the Future

Strategic planning for the multinational firm is a complex process. We have already reviewed four of the most widely accepted methods of international strategic planning. Each form has limitations. Now we will describe a hybrid planning system that deals with all the complexities of the multinational marketplace. This system is specifically designed for resource allocation decisions. A review of the problems and limitations of the current strategic planning systems will clarify the requirements for this hybrid system:

Level of Analysis: The level of analysis should include products by country and products by market segment for a region. Although a firm may be using market segments instead of countries for a unit of analysis, in most cases the market segment will still have some geographic areas like Latin America, the EC or the Middle East.

Mode of Entry: Each opportunity should be judged based on the mode of entry. Sources of inputs differ for each form of entry. Quality, availability, and costs of sources of inputs should also be evaluated.

Risk: The level of risk should be quantified as it relates to the form of entry.

Maximization: Traditional models are driven by market growth, market share, and profitability—ROI or cash flow. On an international level this is shortsighted. Jean-Claude Larreche suggested in a recent paper that "the relationship between market share and profitability may be blurred by a number of factors in the international environment." He suggests redeployment of resources away from mature markets to developing markets.[12] Therefore, on an international basis, the maximization will vary according to the firm's objectives.

Scenarios: Markets should be evaluated based on the present situations as well as the future scenarios.

The operation of a multinational business system (an SBU) is a function of two critical sets of items: the uses of the output and the sources of inputs. Depending on the form of entry, the uses of the outputs would include demand for the particular goods, demand for wages by the country, ability to repatriate profits, need for the profits, and so on. The sources of inputs would include the availability of domestic production capacity (for export), sources of local labor, sources of capital, sources of raw material, and so forth. The sources and uses of a multinational business system should be the critical elements of determining resource allocation. The steps to be used in this hybrid model are shown in Table 17.2.

---

12. Jean-Claude Larreche, "The International Product Market Portfolio," *Instead,* Fontainbleau, France, 1979.

TABLE 17.2 Recommended Steps for Use of a Hybrid Model

Step 1: Continue collection of international PIMS data, based on sources and uses of an operation by mode of entry. Use the PIMS multivariate regression technique to determine which sources and uses empirically explain the variation of performance by mode of entry. This will assist in determining critical factors and assigning weights to these factors.

Step 2: Determine the central scenario and variant scenarios. This will be integrated into the model based on positive or negative or minimal impact of the future scenario on an investment decision.

Step 3: Use a preliminary macro screen to reduce the number of countries and data collection process and costs.

Step 4: Construct an evaluation model for each mode of entry based on the sources and uses of the business. Weigh the importance of each factor. Remember, the use of the organization will be part optimalization process, therefore, the weight put on profits vs. market share or technological exchange is critical.

Step 5: Develop a bonus system to reward operations or combinations of operations which will receive benefits from joint marketing, i.e., standardization or economics of scale.

Step 6: Develop a weighting scale to evaluate the level risk. The risk should include factors of political stability, exchange rate risk, expropriation risk, etc. The importance of risk will vary by mode of entry.

Step 7: Collect data for product by country and by market segment for each region (where applicable).

Step 8: Run model, allocate resources based on ranking of opportunities.

The initial development of this model will be complex. Once the model is developed, it can be easily applied to different multinational corporations. However, there will be operational challenges. First, it is dependent on more international PIMS data. Second, the weight of various factors will require advanced analytical techniques. While more research is required, some form of decision utility and sharing or scholastic dominance methodology will also be required. Third, the collection of data will be a large and costly task. A firm may decide to limit the modes of entry it will consider and/or the number of countries to reduce data collection costs. Finally, the exact ranking of alternatives is unclear at this time. Although the PIMS methodology seems appropriate, it may have to be expanded to quantitatively differentiate the various rankings on a large number of countries and possible modes of entry.

The International Marketing Planning Process

The complexity of international markets requires a structured approach to the planning process. The heterogeneous nature of international markets and the

FIGURE 17.5 International Marketing Planning Matrix

International Decisions	Marketing Planning Variables					
	Situation Analysis	Problems-Opportunity Analysis	Objectives	Marketing Program	Marketing Budgets	Sales Vol. Cost/Profit Estimate
A. Commitment Decision						
B. Country Selection						
C. Mode of Entry						
D. Marketing Strategy						
E. Marketing Organization						

Source: Reprinted with permission from Helmut Becker and Hans B. Thorelli: *International Marketing Strategy,* copyright © 1980, Pergamon Books Ltd.

difficulty of data collection require that the marketer take an organized approach to evaluating opportunities and preparing plans. Figure 17.5 illustrates an international marketing planning matrix.

The planning matrix is an organized approach to evaluating international opportunities. The matrix requires that the marketer evaluate the marketing planning variables at each level of decision making. The levels of decision making, which are located on the vertical axis, begin with the commitment decision. This first decision is whether or not to enter foreign markets; and this is based on the firm's objectives, its resources, and the opportunities available in international versus domestic markets. After making the commitment decision, a company will select the country it wishes to enter. The country decision is based on evaluation of the environment, the demand, the corporate resources, and the financial projections. The mode of entering the selected country will be based on the firm's commitment decision, the country selection, and the cost/benefit evaluation of different modes of entry. As discussed in Chapter 9, the mode of entry will also be affected by a variety of other factors, such as risk assessment, laws of foreign ownership, and so on. The marketing strategy will flow logically from the firm's objective in a market, which will include the marketing mix required to differentiate products in that environment. The market organization decision is related to the objective and strategy for each market. The organization structure will determine which people will be where, how decisions will be made, what information and services will go back and forth between the organizational unit and headquarters, and the budgeting control process.

Selecting Markets

Only the largest multinational company with a product that appeals to all types of people in all environments can afford to be in all the countries of the world. Given the limited employee and financial resources of most companies, international activities must be limited to a selective set of countries. Given that most companies desire to be profitable in each market served, and profitability will be determined by the level of resources required to meet the competitive demands of the marketplace, it is important to maintain a critical mass of marketing resources. These resources include the costs of modifying the product to be competitive, the distribution coverage, and the advertising and direct sales coverage required to be competitive. This set of marketing resources must reach a critical mass in order to be effective and profitable. Figure 17.6 shows a grid for evaluating new foreign markets. The horizontal axis measures the market attractiveness of each country and the vertical axis describes the company's position in each market with respect to the critical mass of marketing resources.

Using the grid for selecting new markets will focus a company's resources on the opportunities with the greatest profitability. It will also tend to concentrate market expansion in markets that are geographically close to current markets.

Coordinating the Planning Process[13]

Coordinating the strategic planning process between the product marketing functions and the country managers is a challenging process. There is a natural tendency to emphasize the product element that shortchanges the geographic element. To improve coordination of product management and country management while utilizing the expertise of each, General Electric has each *country* executive develop a comprehensive country opportunity plan that covers all products and strategies. The country executive's plan is compared to the plans of G.E.'s individual strategic business units for that market. The combination of the two different organizations provides a rich pool of information on tactics and opportunities. The final plan will be an integration of the product and country point of view, with conflicts identified and solutions proposed.

---

13. Information in this section is drawn from ''Many Subs in One Country? Getting More Coordination Without Stifling Initiative,'' *Business International*, January 15, 1982, pp. 17–19.

FIGURE 17.6 A Grid for Evaluating Foreign Markets

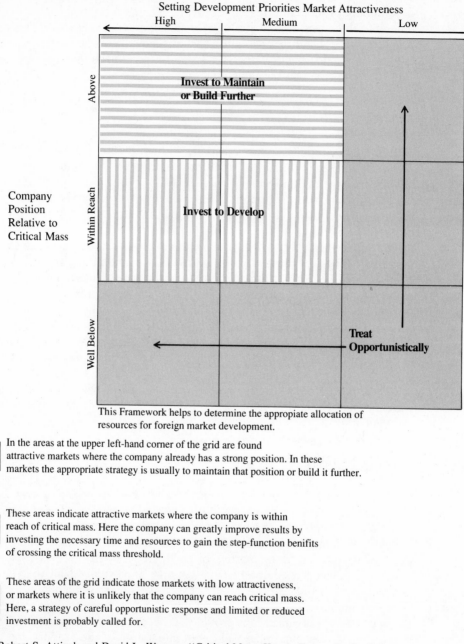

Setting Development Priorities Market Attractiveness

This Framework helps to determine the appropiate allocation of resources for foreign market development.

In the areas at the upper left-hand corner of the grid are found attractive markets where the company already has a strong position. In these markets the appropriate strategy is usually to maintain that position or build it further.

These areas indicate attractive markets where the company is within reach of critical mass. Here the company can greatly improve results by investing the necessary time and resources to gain the step-function benifits of crossing the critical mass threshold.

These areas of the grid indicate those markets with low attractiveness, or markets where it is unlikely that the company can reach critical mass. Here, a strategy of careful opportunistic response and limited or reduced investment is probably called for.

Source: Robert S. Attiyeh and David L. Wenner, "Critical Mass: Key to Export Profits," *Business Horizons,* December 1979, p. 32. Redrawn and used with permission.

Siemens, the world's fifth-largest electrical and electronics equipment maker, has a formalized communication phase between the product groups and the geographic structures. During this formal communications phase of the planning process, the product and country management meet to establish an understanding of each other's position. Eaton Corporation, which is organized around a worldwide product structure, found it necessary to inform managers of methods to respond to common environmental issues such as political conditions, taxes, inflation, and joint ownership. To share information and experience, regional coordinating committees that meet monthly were set up in Latin America and Europe.

Who Makes the Decisions?

Decision making responsibility is dependent upon several internal and external factors. What decisions are made within each line of command differs from firm to firm.

Table 17.3 summarizes a study of eighty-six separate marketing programs in nine United States–based multinationals that determined the degree of local management autonomy with respect to various marketing decisions. Aylmer found that primary authority for the advertising, pricing, and distribution decisions were with local management. Only the product design decision was controlled primarily by headquarters and imposed on local management.

Standardized Versus Decentralized Planning

When perspective markets can be grouped together as a result of homogeneous characteristics, then marketing decisions can often be standardized and applied to the markets. There are, however, certain marketing functions that cannot be complete standardized. A survey of one hundred senior executives in twenty-seven leading packaged-goods multinationals was conducted to determine the level of standardization for each of the elements in the marketing process. The results of this study are shown in Figure 17.7.

The annual operating plan is the most widely used process in most multinational firms.[14] Most firms combine their annual operating plan with a five-year plan. The planning process should be a major force for increasing the degree of integration and coordination between different entities of a global enterprise. According to James Hulbert and William Brandt, most of the problems with multinational planning lie with people, not with the planning systems.[15]

---

14. James M. Hulbert and William K. Brandt, *Managing the Multinational Subsidiary* (New York: Holt, Rinehart and Winston, 1980), pp. 35–64.

15. *Ibid.*

TABLE 17.3 Degree of Local Management Autonomy According to Type of Marketing Decision

	Local Marketing Decision			
Degree of Local Management Autonomy	Product Design	Advertising Approach	Retail Price	Distribution Outlets/1000 Population
Primary authority rested with local management	30%	86%	74%	61%
Local management shared authority with other levels in organization	15%	8%	20%	38%
Decision primarily imposed upon local management	55%	6%	6%	1%
	100%	100%	100%	100%
N (Marketing programs observed)	N = 86	N = 84*	N = 84*	N = 86

* Classification information not available in two cases.

Source: R.J. Aylmer, "Who Makes Marketing Decisions in the Multinational Firm?" Reprinted from *Journal of Marketing,* October 1970, p. 26, published by the American Marketing Association.

CONTROLLING INTERNATIONAL MARKETING OPERATIONS

Control of international operations is a growing concern in light of the increasing trends toward global companies. As a company becomes larger, it faces more critical decisions, and control over operations tends to dissipate. A company's planning process is usually based on a number of assumptions about country environments, competitors, pricing, government regulations, and so on. As a plan is implemented, the company must monitor its success as well as monitor the variables that were used to develop the plan. As the environment changes, so will the plan; therefore a critical part of planning is control. Establishment of a system to control marketing activities in numerous markets is not an easy job. But if companies expect to achieve the goals they have set, then a control system must be established to regulate the activities for achieving the desired goals.

Variables that Affect Control

There are several variables that affect the degree and effectiveness of a control system for international operations.

FIGURE 17.7 Standardization of Marketing Decisions Among European Subsidiaries of Selected Multinational Enterprises

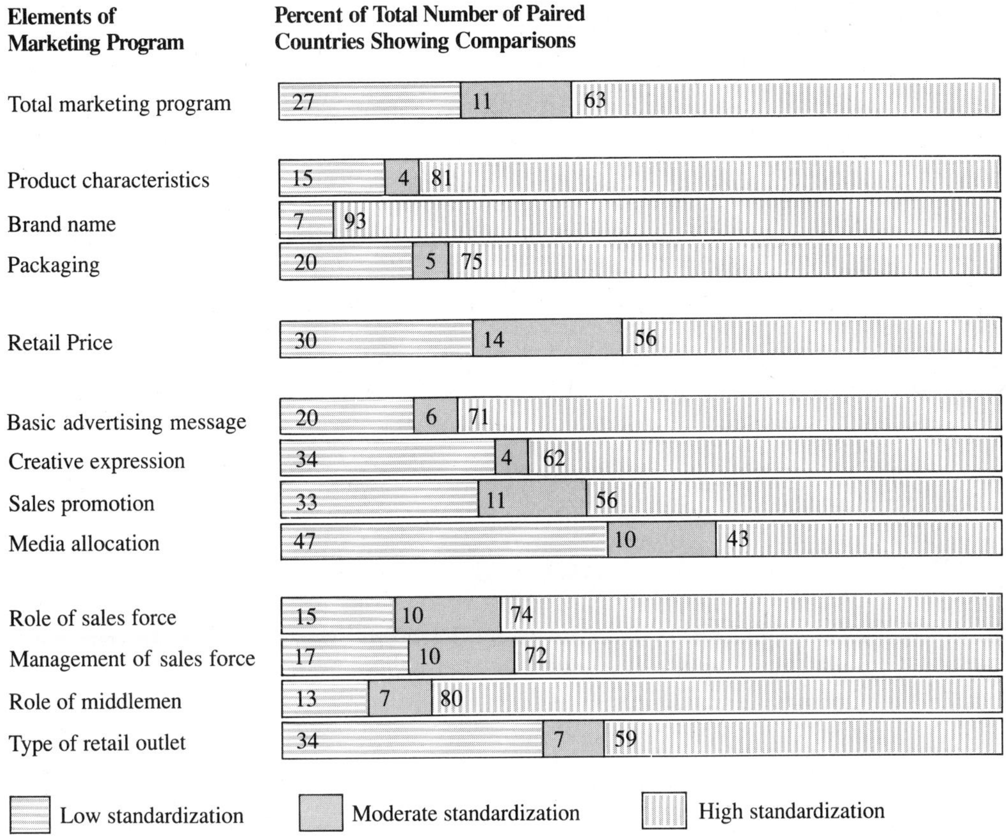

Elements of Marketing Program	Percent of Total Number of Paired Countries Showing Comparisons		
Total marketing program	27	11	63
Product characteristics	15	4	81
Brand name	7		93
Packaging	20	5	75
Retail Price	30	14	56
Basic advertising message	20	6	71
Creative expression	34	4	62
Sales promotion	33	11	56
Media allocation	47	10	43
Role of sales force	15	10	74
Management of sales force	17	10	72
Role of middlemen	13	7	80
Type of retail outlet	34	7	59

Low standardization   Moderate standardization   High standardization

Source: Reprinted by permission of the *Harvard Business Review.* An exhibit from ''How Multinationals View Marketing Standardization'' by R. Z. Sorenson and V. E. Weichmann (May/June 1975). Copyright © 1975 by the President and Fellows of Harvard College; all rights reserved.

Communication Systems

Effective communication systems will facilitate control. Physical communication methods, such as the phone, mail, and personal visits, are greatly affected by both distance and location. The more sophisticated a country's telecommunications are, the easier the communication process is.

Likewise, the closer the subdivision is to headquarters, the less chance there is of lost control. As physical distances separating headquarters and operating divisions increase, the time, expense, and potential for error increase. The physical distance also affects the speed with which changes can be implemented and problems can be detected.

Adequacy of Data

The accuracy and lack of complete economic, industrial, and consumer data affect control. If the marketing plan and the goals for a particular country are based on inadequate data, then the ability to control and modify the marketing activities will be affected. For example, let's examine the goal of selling washing machines to Iran, maybe to achieve a 30 percent share of last year's market, which was estimated to be 100,000 units. Therefore, the goal would be 30,000 units. But if the actual sales were only 70,000 units because the government had exaggerated its report to indicate economic prosperity, then the goal of 30,000 units will be too high. It may also be difficult to get timely and accurate statistics, such as the level of inflation and disposable income, which would influence the marketing strategy.

Diversity of Environments

Currency values, legal structures, political systems, advertising options, and cultural factors all influence the task of developing and controlling a marketing program. Due to this diversity of the local environments there are continuous conflicts between the needs of the local situation and overall corporate goals. The issue of diversity must be reflected in the control system.

Management Philosophy

The management philosophy about whether the company should be centralized or decentralized will affect the development of a control system. A highly centralized management control system will require an effective communication system so that the headquarters staff has timely and accurate local input that may affect decision making. The communication system must also allow decisions to be made quickly and transmitted to the local management for quick implementation. A decentralized management control system may not require the same type of communication system for day-to-day decision making, but it will require a well-documented and communicated set of objectives for each autonomous unit. These objectives will help guide local decision making and control so that the corporate goals are achieved.

Size of International Operations

As the size of the international operation increases as a percentage of total sales, top management becomes more active in decision making. One author found that as the size of a local affiliate grew, the frequency of decisions imposed by headquarters declined and the frequency of decisions shared with headquarters increased.[16]

Elements of a Control Strategy

Control is the cornerstone of management. Control provides the means to direct, regulate, and manage business operations. The implementation of a marketing program requires a significant amount of interaction between the individual areas of marketing (product development, advertising, sales) as well as the other functional areas (production, research and development, finance). The control system is used to measure these business activities, competitive reaction, and market reaction. Deviations from the planned activities and results are analyzed and reported so that corrective action can be taken.

A control system has three basic elements: (1) the establishment of standards, (2) the measure of performance against standards, and (3) the analysis and correction of any deviations from the standards. Although it seems that control is a conceptually simple aspect of the management process, there are a wide variety of problems that arise in international situations which result in inefficiencies and intracompany conflicts. Table 17.4 reveals many of the control-related problems that arise in the international environment.

Developing Standards

Setting standards is an extremely important part of the control process because standards will direct the efforts of individual managers. To effectively influence the behavior of the managers who direct the international marketing programs, the standards must be clearly defined, accepted, and understood by these managers. Standard setting is driven by the corporate goals. The corporate goals are achieved through the effective and efficient implementation of a marketing strategy, on a local country level. Control standards must be specifically tied to the strategy and based on the desired behavior of the local marketing people. The desired behavior should reflect the actions to be taken to implement the strategy as well as performance standards that indicate the success of the strategy, such as increased market share or sales. Examples of behavioral standards include the type and amount of advertising, the distribution coverage, market research to be performed, and expected price levels. Performance standards could include trial rates by customers or sales by product line.

---

16. R. J. Aylmer, "Who Makes the Decisions in the Multinational Firm?" *Journal of Marketing,* October 1970, p. 26.

TABLE 17.4 Control Problems

Indicators	*Characteristics*
• Conflicts among divisions or subsidiaries over territories or customers in the field.	• Most common when a company is expanding into new geographic areas. Also caused by the introduction of new products abroad and acquisitions or mergers.
• Failure of foreign operations to grow in accordance with plans and expectations.	• May only apply to overall sales in a particular area, or to a particular product line. Obviously more acute if one's share of the marketing is falling even when sales are increasing.
• Lack of financial control over operations abroad.	• Related to the company's philosophy of centralization versus decentralization and the degree to which authority is delegated to managers overseas. Further complicated by foreign tax laws and accounting conventions.
• Duplication of administrative personnel and services.	• Most common when product lines go abroad as extensions of independent domestic divisions, or when major acquisitions are made.
• Underutilization of manufacturing or distribution facilities abroad.	• Often occurs when various product lines extend operations abroad independent of each other, or when consolidation does not take place after a merger.
• Duplication of sales offices and specialized field salesmen.	• Common within corporations selling technical products such as specialty chemicals or electronic equipment.
• A proliferation of relatively small legal entities and/or operating units within a country or geographical area.	• Often results from establishing a new subsidiary each time a domestic division enters a new foreign country, until five, six, or even more function side by side.
• A proliferation of distributors.	• Overlapping coverage and conflicting interests.
• An increase in complaints relating to customer service abroad.	• Often a symptom that field marketing personnel do not have a coordinated approach to handling a common customer.

The standards should be set through a joint process with corporate head-quarters personnel and the local marketing organization. Normally the standard setting will be done annually, when the operational business plan is established.

Measuring and Evaluating Performance

After the standards are set, a process is required to monitor performance. In order to monitor performance against standards, management must be able to observe current performance. Observation in the international environment is often impersonal through mail, cable, or telex; but it also can be personal through telephone, travel, or meetings. Much of the numerical information will be reported through the accounting system, such as sales, expenses, and so on. Other items such as the implementation of an advertising program would be communicated through a report. The reporting system may be weekly, monthly, or quarterly.

Analyzing and Correcting Deviations from the Standards

The purpose of establishing standards and reporting performance is to assure achievement of the corporate goals. In order to achieve these goals, management must evaluate performance versus the standards and initiate actions where performance is below the standards set. The control process can be difficult in the international setting due to distance, communication, and cultural differences issues. Control strategy can be related to the principle of the carrot and the stick, using both positive and negative incentives. On the positive side, outstanding performance may result in increased independence, more marketing dollars, and salary increases and/or bonuses for the managers. On the negative side, unsatisfactory performance can lead to reduction of all the items mentioned for satisfactory performance as well as the threat of firing the managers responsible. The key to correcting deviations is to get the managers to understand and agree with the standards, then give them the ability to correct these deficiencies. This will often mean that the managers will be given some flexibility with resources. For example, if sales are down 10 percent, the ability to increase advertising or reduce prices may be necessary to offset the sales decline.

CONFLICT BETWEEN HEADQUARTERS AND SUBSIDIARIES

A universal problem facing international marketing executives is the internal conflicts between headquarters and subsidiaries. A study of 109 large U.S. and European multinationals and their worldwide subsidiaries found that this conflict

TABLE 17.5 Key Problems Identified by Large U.S. and European Multinationals

Key Problems Identified by Headquarters Executives

- Lack of qualified personnel
- Lack of strategic thinking and long-range planning at subsidiary level
- Lack of marketing expertise at the subsidiary level
- Too little relevant communication between headquarters and subsidiaries
- Insufficient utilization of multinational marketing experience
- Restricted headquarters control of the subsidiaries

Key Problems Identified by Subsidiary Executives

- Excessive headquarters control procedures
- Excessive financial and marketing constraints
- Insufficient participation of subsidiaries in product decisions
- Insensitivity of headquarters to local market differences
- Shortage of useful information from headquarters
- Lack of multinational orientation at headquarters

Source: Reprinted by permission of the *Harvard Business Review*. An exhibit from ''Problems That Plague Multinational Marketers'' by V. E. Weichman and L. G. Pringle (July/August 1979). Copyright © 1979 by the President and Fellows of Harvard College; all rights reserved.

was a bigger problem than competition, political instability, or many of the other challenges of international marketing. Table 17.5 summarizes the results of the study.

Conflicts between two parts of a corporation are inevitable due to the natural differences in orientation and perception between the two groups. The subsidiary manager usually wants less control, more authority, and more local differentiation, whereas headquarters wants more detailed reporting and greater unification of geographically dispersed operations. This expected conflict is not bad. In fact, the conflict causes constant dialogue between different organizational levels during the planning and implementation of strategies. This dialogue will result in a balance between headquarters versus subsidiary authority, global versus local perspective, and standardization versus differentiation of the international marketing mix.[17]

Some of the problems in planning and controlling international marketing operations can be reduced or eliminated. Common problems such as deficiencies in the communications process, overemphasis on short-term issues, and failure to take full advantage of an organization's international experience, require open discussions between headquarters and subsidiary executives.

17. Ulrich E. Wiechmann and Lewis G. Pringle, ''Problems That Plague Multinational Marketers,'' *Harvard Business Review*, vol. 57, July–August 1979, p. 124.

Retaining Talented Country Managers

Many companies are shifting to a global marketing orientation, with standardized products, packaging, advertising themes, and pricing. To successfully manage this shift to global marketing, companies must successfully utilize and integrate the talents of country managers. Five suggestions on how to motivate and retain talented country managers when making the shift to global marketing follow:

1. Encourage field managers to generate ideas and give them recognition for those ideas. R. J. Reynolds revitalized the Camel brand after a German subsidiary came up with a new positioning and copy strategy.
2. Include the country managers in the development of marketing strategies and programs. When Procter & Gamble introduced a sanitary napkin as a global product, local managers were encouraged to suggest changes in the global marketing program. Also, local managers could develop their own coupon and sales promotion programs.
3. Maintain a product portfolio of regional and global brands.
4. Allow country managers control of their marketing budgets, so they can respond to local consumer needs and competition.
5. Emphasize the general management responsibilities of country managers that extend beyond the marketing function. Country managers who have risen through the marketing function often do not spend enough time on local manufacturing, industrial relations, and government affairs. Global marketing can free them to focus on and develop their skills in these other areas.[18]

CONCLUSIONS

The processes of planning marketing programs and controlling their implementation are the first and last steps in international marketing. Marketers must first evaluate the global environment and select opportunities using one of the planning approaches. This process will lead to a strategy that is implemented by the organization. Sometimes the organization will be changed in order to effectively implement the strategy. Finally, a system must be put in place to evaluate the implementation and measure the progress toward the desired effect of the strategy.

The planning and controlling processes are critical parts of the marketing process that require communication and agreement from different parts of the organization. This is difficult. It is no surprise that the planning and controlling processes lead to conflict. However, it also promotes understanding the world

---

18. John A. Quelch and Edward J. Hoff, "Customizing Global Marketing," *Harvard Business Review*, vol. 64, May–June 1986, p. 68.

market, developing effective strategies, and successfully implementing the strategies with excellent results.

Questions for Discussion

1. You have recently been transferred from a domestic marketing division to the international marketing staff. Part of your new job is to review the planning process of each geographic marketing group—Europe, Asia, and South America. What differences could you expect from domestic planning?
2. What are the advantages and disadvantages of the Boston Consulting Group planning method when applied to international markets?
3. What are the advantages and disadvantages of the PIMS model over other planning methods that could be used for international planning?
4. What types of marketing decisions are usually left up to the local management? Why?
5. What is the purpose of a control system? How would you differentiate a good control system from a poor one?
6. Recent feedback for sales, profit, and market share indicate that your subsidiary in Japan had not implemented the strategy that was developed. How would you influence the management to focus more effort on successful strategy implementation?
7. Recently you have lost four key international marketing people to other companies. You suspect that these losses indicate that the morale of your international executives is poor? What could be done to improve morale?

For Further Reading

Aylmer, R. J. "Who Makes Marketing Decisions in the Multinational Firm?" *Journal of Marketing* (October 1970), pp. 25–30.

Becker, Helmut, and Hans B. Thorelli. "Strategic Planning in International Marketing." In *International Marketing Strategy*. Ed. Hans Thorelli and Helmut Becker. New York: Pergamon Press, 1982, pp. 367–378.

Brandt, William K., and James M. Hulbert. "Headquarters Guidance in Marketing Strategy in the Multinational Subsidiary." *Columbia Journal of World Business* (Winter 1977), pp. 7–14.

Chakravarthy, Balaji S., and Howard V. Perlmutter. "Strategic Planning for a Global Business." *Columbia Journal of World Business* (Summer 1985), pp. 3–10.

Dymsza, William A. "Global Strategic Planning," *Journal of International Business Studies,* 15, No. 2 (Summer 1985), pp. 169–183.

Hamel, Gary, and C. K. Prahalad. "Managing Strategic Responsibility in the MNC." *Strategic Management Journal,* 4 (1983), pp. 341–351.

Hulbert, James M., William K. Brandt, and Raimar Richers. "Marketing Planning in the Multinational Subsidiary: Practices and Problems." *Journal of Marketing,* 44, No. 3 (Summer 1980), pp. 7–15.

Lorange, Peter, and Richard F. Vancil. "How to Design a Strategic Planning System." *Harvard Business Review* (September–October 1976), pp. 75–81.

Michman, Ronald D. "Linking Futuristics With Marketing Planning, Forcasting and Strategy." *The Journal of Business and Industrial Marketing,* 2, No. 2 (Spring 1987), pp. 61–67.

Nowakoski, Christopher A. "International Performance Measurement." *Columbia Journal of World Business* (Summer 1982), pp. 53–57.

O'Connell, Jeremiah J., and John W. Zimmerman. "Scanning the International Environment." *California Management Review* (Winter 1979), pp. 15–22.

Porter, Michael E., ed. *Competition in Global Industries.* Boston: Harvard Business School Press, 1986.

Sim, A. B. "Decentralized Management of Subsidiaries and Their Performance." *Management International Review,* No. 2 (1977), pp. 45–51.

Wiechmann, Ulrich. "Integrating Multinational Marketing Activities." *Columbia Journal of World Business* (Winter 1974), p. 12.

Wind, Yoram, and Susan Douglas. "International Portfolio Analysis and Strategy: The Challenge of the 80's. *Journal of International Business Studies* (Fall 1981), p. 7.

Wind, Yoram, Susan P. Douglas, and Howard V. Perlmutter. "Guidelines for Developing International Marketing Strategies." *Journal of Marketing* (April 1973), pp. 14–23.

18.
FINANCING INTERNATIONAL MARKETING OPERATIONS

As many international marketers have observed, the ability to make financing available at low cost can become the deciding factor that beats competitors. In the context of international marketing, financing should be understood in its broadest sense (see Figure 18.1). Not only does it consist of direct credits to the buyer, but it also includes a range of activities that enable the customer to afford the purchase. In this chapter we examine financing provided by the selling company, as well as financing through the financial community and government-sponsored agencies. The chapter concludes with a section on counter-trade, which covers all types of barter deals that allow a hard-currency-restricted buyer to purchase products or services without a cash outlay. In including this material here, we continue our focus on international marketing, treating financing as a marketing tool.

INTERNATIONAL FINANCING RISKS

Financing international marketing transactions involves a host of risks over and above those encountered by strictly domestic operations. International companies have to be aware of these risks and understand the methods available for reducing risk to an acceptable level. The four major risks include commercial risk, foreign currency risk, transfer risk, and political risk.

Commercial risk refers to buyer ability to pay for the products or services ordered. This risk is also typical for a domestic operation. As a result, companies are accustomed to checking the financial stability of their customers and may even have internally approved credit limits. Although checking credit references in a domestic environment poses no great difficulty, such information is not

FIGURE 18.1 *Financing International Marketing Operations*

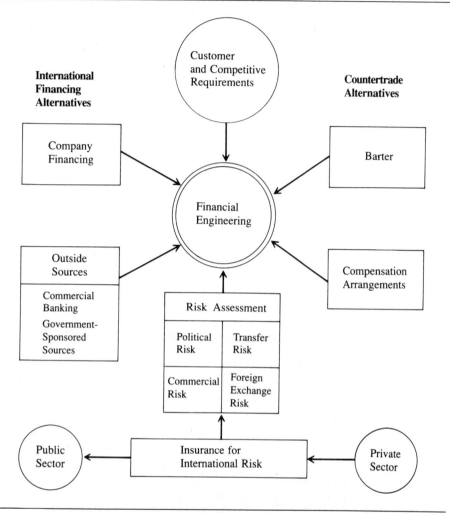

always readily available in many overseas markets. Companies can rely on their banks or on foreign credit reporting agencies where such organizations exist. Past experience with a commercial customer abroad may frequently be the only indicator of a firm's financial stability.

Foreign currency risk exists whenever a company bills in a currency other than its own.[1] For U.S. companies billing in Japanese yen, a currency risk exists

---

1. Chuck C. Y. Kwok, "Hedging Foreign Exchange Exposures: Independent Versus Integrative Approaches," *Journal of International Business Studies*, Summer 1987, p. 33.

because the value of the yen versus the dollar is subject to market fluctuations and therefore cannot be determined at the outset. Foreign currency risk grows with the length of credit terms and with the instability of a foreign currency. Suppliers can insure themselves against foreign currency fluctuations, as was described in more detail in Chapter 13.

Invoicing in their own currency, suppliers shift the currency risk to the customer. The customer may not be in a position to cover that risk, as is the case in many countries with unsophisticated financial markets. In such a case, the exporting company frequently must choose between selling in a foreign currency or no deal at all.

Although the customer may be able to pay, payments often get delayed by bureaucracies, creating a *transfer risk*. Transfer delays prevail in countries where the foreign exchange market is controlled and where the customer has to apply for the purchase of foreign currency before payment takes place. Delays of up to 180 days beyond the credit terms agreed upon are not unusual and add to the costs of exporter or supplier. In countries where a foreign exchange shortage prevents immediate payment of all foreign currency denominated debts, complex debt restructuring negotiations may take place, causing additional delays. Many countries have had to negotiate such extensions, including Brazil, Mexico, Argentina, Turkey, and Zaire.

Financing for international marketing operations is also subject to *political risk,* which includes the occurrence of war, revolutions, insurgencies, or civil unrest, any of which may result in nonpayment of accounts receivable. In some instances, civil unrest may demand rescheduling of foreign trade debt, as was the case in Poland in the early 1980s. In other situations, political unrest may bring about a new government that cancels foreign debt, as was the case in Iran following the downfall of the shah.

The international marketer needs to understand the risks of providing financing to customers. In cases where the supplier shoulders all international risks, companies may want to build extra costs into their prices. Smaller price adjustments may be required when only a portion of the international credit risk is carried.

CUSTOMER VERSUS SUPPLIER-ARRANGED FINANCING

As discussed in this section, financing arranged by suppliers goes beyond the open account practices that will be described in the next chapter. In this context, supplier financing is viewed as any term beyond the usual 30 to 90 days customary for open account shipment.

Because credit risks are higher for clients abroad, companies have a preference for shorter payment terms with foreign clients. However, many customers might not be able to purchase under shortened credit terms. Consequently, companies might charge an interest rate on the outstanding amount. When companies cannot get at least market interest rates, they might try to capture the additional cash through higher prices. However, most clients today are adept at comparing total costs to themselves, and opportunities for hiding interest cost behind higher list prices are limited.

Since most companies do not consider themselves to be in the business of financing their customers, they prefer to assist clients in finding suitable financing opportunities. One such exception is financing without recourse, a relatively new method for financing shipments abroad, which is explained below.

SOURCES OF FINANCING

Companies can choose from a wide selection of alternatives to finance international marketing transactions: traditional financing through commercial banks, government-sponsored loans, or countertrade. The international marketer is increasingly expected to be knowledgeable about complicated financial arrangements. As buyers compare acquisition costs, including any necessary financing, providing such financing becomes a matter for international marketing management to handle. The following sections are intended to offer you a general background on the most common financing alternatives practiced by many international companies today.

Financing Through Commercial Banks

Commercial banks, whether domestic or foreign, are usually willing to finance transactions only to first-rate credit risks. This fact makes financing unavailable to any but the largest companies. Furthermore, commercial banks avoid long-term financing and prefer short maturities. Commercial banks that have loaned heavily to developing countries have recently experienced difficulties with repayment and interest payments on outstanding loan portfolios. Banks located in developed countries have therefore hesitated to loan further to developing countries, forcing exporters to look elsewhere to finance their clients.

Clients outside the developed countries of Europe and Asia have also found local financing difficult. Especially for purchases in currencies other than their own, foreign buyers in developing countries are increasingly dependent on financing from abroad. For larger industrial projects, this is now almost the rule. With commercial banks only partially able to close the gap, both buyers and suppliers are availing themselves of other financing sources.

Forfaiting: Financing Without Recourse[2]

Forfaiting or financing without recourse (see Table 18.1) means that the seller of merchandise can transfer a claim, resulting from a transaction in the form of a bill of exchange, to a forfaiting house by including the term ''without recourse''

---

2. This section is based upon *Forfaiting,* Finanz A. G., Zurich, Switzerland, 1986, p. 6.

TABLE 18.1 Typical Forfait Discount Rates*

	Debtor Country (Importer's Territory)	Final Maturity (Half-Yearly Instalments)	Commitment Fee (Until Pay-out)	SFr Forfait Rates (Approx. Disc. %pa)	U.S. $ Forfait Rates (Approx. Disc. %pa)	DM Forfait Rates (Approx. Disc. %pa)
Europe	Austria	5	0.75% pa	4½	8½	4⅜
	Belgium	5	0.75% pa	4½	8½	4⅝
	Denmark	5	1% pa	4⅝	8½	4¾
	Finland	5	1% pa	4½	8½	4⅝
	France	5	0.75% pa	4½	8½	4⅝
	W. Germany	NL	0.5% pa	4¼	8¼	4⅜
	Great Britain	NL	0.75% pa	4⅙	8⅜	4⅜
	Greece	3	0.1% pm	5¼	9⅛	5⅜
	Iceland	4	0.1% pm	5	9	5⅛
	Ireland	4	1% pa	4¾	8¼	5
	Italy	5	0.75	4½	8½	4¾
	Netherlands	NL	0.5% pa	4⅜	8⅜	4½
	Norway	5	0.75% pa	4½	8½	4⅝
	Portugal	4	1% pa	4¾	8¼	5
	Spain	5	1% pa	4¾	8½	4¾
	Sweden	5	0.75% pa	4½	8½	4⅝
	Switzerland	NL	0.5% pa	4¼	8¼	4⅜
Comecon	Bulgaria	3	0.1% pm	5¼	9⅛	5⅛
	E. Germany	3	1% pa	4⅝	8½	4¼
	Hungary	5	1% pa	4⅝	8½	4¾
	USSR	5	0.75	4⅜	8⅜	4⅛
	Czechoslovakia	5	1% pa	4⅝	8½	4¾
Americas	Canada	NL	0.5% pa	4⅛	8¾	4⅜
	Colombia	2	0.1% pm	6¼	10	6¼
	Trinidad & Tobago	2	0.1% pm	5½	9½	5¼
	USA	NL	0.5% pa	4¼	8¼	4⅜

Africa and Middle East	Bahrain	3	0.1% pm	5	9	5⅛
	Israel	2	0.1% pm	6¼	10	6⅛
	Tunisia	3	0.1% pm	5⅜	9¼	5½
	Jordan	2	0.1% pm	5½	9½	5¾
	Kuwait	2	0.1% pm	5	9	5⅛
	Saudi Arabia	2	0.1% pm	4¾	8½	4¾
	United Arab Emirates	2	0.1% pm	5	9	5⅛
Far East	Australia	5	0.75% pa	4⅝	8½	4¾
	China	5	0.75% pa	4½	8½	4⅝
	Hong Kong	3	0.75% pa	4¾	8⅝	4⅞
	India	3	1% pa	4⅞	8⅞	5
	Indonesia	3	0.1% pm	5⅛	9¼	5½
	Japan	NL	0.5% pa	4¼	8¼	4⅜
	Korea (South)	3	1% pa	5¼	9⅛	5⅜
	Malaysia	5	1% pa	4¾	8¼	5
	New Zealand	5	1% pa	4⅝	8½	4¾
	Singapore	5	0.75% pa	4½	8½	4⅝
	Taiwan	5	0.75% pa	4½	8½	4⅝
	Thailand	3	1% pa	5½	9⅛	5¼

* These figures provide a rough guide to discount rates on paper (promissory notes or bills of exchange) issued by an importer and guaranteed by a reputable bank. However, rates move quickly to reflect country risk and the availability of paper and investors. Exporters should therefore obtain immediate quotations from individual forfaiters.

NL = No Limit

For comparison purposes all rates are based on average credit life of 2¾ years (10 six-monthly instalments). The rates are based on end May LIBOR quotations: if LIBOR rates move forfait rates move with them.

Source: Finanz A.G., Zurich, as published in *Euromoney*, June 1987, p. 47.

as part of the endorsement. The collection risk is thus transferred to the forfait-ing house, and the seller receives upon presentation of documents the full amount minus a discount for the entire credit period. The discount varies with the country risk and the currency chosen for financing. Typical maturities range from six months to several years.

Nonrecourse financing offers the advantage of selling products over medium terms at market rates. Such transactions are not possible through commercial banks. An exporter may obtain a firm quote on a given business deal ahead of time, allowing inclusion of the discount rate into the price calculation. This assures that the net payout meets normal profitability standards. For capital equipment exporting countries such as Germany and Switzerland, approxi-mately 5 to 10 percent of exports are arranged through this financing technique. However, there are limitations to this financing method. For countries that are poor credit risks, forfait transactions are not possible. Transaction size is usually under ten million dollars, although larger amounts may be financed through several institutions that together form an ad-hoc consortium or syndicate.

Government-Sponsored Financing

With ability to assemble the best financing package often determining the sale of capital equipment or other large volume transactions, governments all over the world have realized that government-sponsored banks can foster exports and therefore employment. Government-subsidized financing now exceeds that which commercial banks and exporters formerly provided. For this purpose the United States created its Export-Import Bank (Exim for short) in 1934. Other countries, particularly members of the Organization for Economic Cooperation and Development (OECD), have established their own export banks also aimed at assisting their respective exporters with the financing of large transactions. Tables 18.2 and 18.3 are designed to give some background on the government-sponsored financing programs offered by leading exporting nations.

Japan committed $7.9 billion in 1987 to provide export insurance for devel-oping countries and political risk insurance for Japanese companies investing overseas. The export insurance plan will cover up to 97.5 percent of the value for prepaid contracts.[3]

The Export-Import Bank[4]

The Export-Import Bank and its affiliated institutions, the Foreign Credit Insur-ance Association (FCIA), and the Private Export Funding Corporation

---

3. "Japan to Commit Almost $8 Billion to Trade Insurance," *The Wall Street Journal*, March 31, 1987, p. 48.

4. This segment draws heavily from official publications of the Export-Import Bank of the United States, Washington, D.C., 1979.

TABLE 18.2 Export Insurance Premiums as a Percent of Insured Exports
for Selected Countries

	1982	1983		1982	1983
Sweden	2.50	3.40	France	1.00	1.10
Italy	1.60	2.30	Britain	1.80	1.00
W. Germany	1.85	1.70	Netherlands	1.00	0.90
Norway	2.40	1.70	Canada	0.70	0.60
Spain	2.46	1.64	Australia	0.50	0.45
Switzerland	3.70	1.60	New Zealand	0.40	0.43
Austria	1.30	1.44	Denmark	0.30	0.34
Finland	0.97	1.20	Japan	0.27	0.30
Belgium	0.85	1.17	United States	0.30	0.20

Source: Der Monat, Swiss Bank Corporation, April 1985, p. 10. Reprinted by permission.

(PEFCO), make a number of services available to U.S. exporters. Exim has special services for short-term, medium-term, and long-term financing requirements. See Figure 18.2 for a depiction of the financing process.

Short-Term Financing

Financing requirements of 180 days or less are considered short-term. For such commitments Eximbank does not make direct financing available. Instead, through the Foreign Credit Insurance Association (FCIA), Eximbank offers export credit insurance to the U.S. exporter. This insurance covers the exporter for commercial risk, such as nonpayment by the foreign buyer; political risk, such as war, revolution, insurrection, expropriation; and currency inconvertibility. The cost of such insurance averages less than one-half of 1 percent per $100 of gross invoice value. With such insurance in force, the exporter has the choice of carrying accounts receivable on the company records or refinancing with a commercial bank at domestic interest rates, provided the transaction is insured. In general, commercial risks are insured up to 90 percent of the invoiced value. Political risks are covered for up to 100 percent of the merchandise value, depending on the type of policy selected.

In 1983, about 7.5 billion dollars or 3.8 percent of U.S. exports were insured by FCIA.[5] Total premium costs were about 0.2 percent of the insured volume. In the same year, FCIA paid out $193 million to exporters or banks financing such trade. For the past few years, U.S. firms have enjoyed lower export insurance

---

5. Der Monat, publication of Swiss Bank Corporation, Basle, Switzerland, April 1985.

TABLE 18.3 Export Credit Insurance Programs of Selected Countries

	Year	Premium Income (In Millions of U.S. Dollars)	Collections on Defaulted Debt (In Millions of U.S. Dollars)	Paid Out to Insured Companies (In Millions of U.S. Dollars)	Profit (+) or Loss (−) (In Millions of U.S. Dollars)	Insured Exports (In Millions of U.S. Dollars)	Percent Exports Insured
Australia	1979	7.0	4.7	5.0	+6.7	1.364	7.3
	1980	11.3	3.0	3.0	−7.6	2.380	10.8
	1981	12.9	3.1	8.1	+7.9	2.362	13
	1982	11.6	6.2	6.0	+11.8	2.250	11.6
	1983	10.4	7.9	13.9	+4.4	2.301	12.2
West Germany	1979	206.4	20.8	234.3	−8.1	13.708	8.0
	1980	258.9	26.66	380.4	−94.85	15.702	8.1
	1981	247.2	25.7	340.9	−67.8	16.106	9.2
	1982	299.2	106.9	332.1	−74	16.152	9.2
	1983	222.8	40.8	611.0	−347.4	13.043	7.7
France	1979	348.4	253.3	823.6	−239.9	25.467	30
	1980	372.6	353.7	904.2	−198.8	37.775	31
	1981	369.4	524.7	737.9	−155.5	39.392	32
	1982	360.0	272.4	1.013	−380.6	35.122	33
	1983	416.4	381.3	1.240	−42.3	35.310	34
UK	1979	222.3	209.3	560.1	−28.5	34.469	33.5
	1980	350.2	187.4	675.6	−138	39.646	35.3
	1981	475.3	160.0	609.4	+25.9	35.145	36.2
	1982	608.7	181.1	1021.2	−231.4	33.374	33.9
	1983	268.9	205.8	1011.2	+536.5	26.930	29.6
Italy	1979	102.3	—	110.0	—	8.423	11.7
	1980	115.9	14.6	119.1	−11.4	8.889	11.4
	1981	133.4	33.2	185.6	−19	10.818	14.3
	1982	142.6	140.6	374.7	−91.6	9.017	12.3
	1983	111.2	50.7	436.6	−273.7	4.872	6.7
Japan	1979	124.7	27.1	126.7	+25.1	46.242	40.9
	1980	132.2	20.1	97.7	+54.6	61.694	38.3
	1981	148.9	24.7	170.7	−2.9	61.155	38.5
	1982	150.0	49.5	251.9	+52.4	53.601	38.4
	1983	143.4	63.9	338.8	−131.5	46.740	30.3
Canada	1979	10.0	5.0	3.2	+11.8	1.780	2.6
	1980	10.5	1.5	8.9	+3.1	2.305	2.9
	1981	12.3	0.2	6.0	+6.5	2.661	3.1
	1982	12.7	1.7	7.4	+7.0	1.853	2.2
	1983	17.9	4.5	23.7	−1.3	3.157	3.5
Netherlands	1979	59.1	13.6	110.6	−37.9	8.569	13.5
	1980	94.7	31.3	94.9	+31.1	9.406	12.6
	1981	79.6	24.4	58.2	+45.8	7.078	10.3
	1982	76.2	28.1	95.5	+8.8	7.624	11.8
	1983	69.7	57.5	268.0	−140.8	7.849	12.0
Austria	1979	51.6	12.5	140.8	−76.7	6.342	32
	1980	55.3	16.6	98.6	−26.7	6.351	40
	1981	64.4	14.0	14.9	−63.5	7.099	45
	1982	81.9	48.6	174.3	−43.8	6.266	40
	1983	72.2	55.5	154.2	−26.5	5.020	35
Sweden	1979	25.9	15.6	74.7	+33.2	1.866	6.8
	1980	36.9	14.9	63.7	−11.9	2.815	9.1
	1981	43.6	21.2	126.3	−61.3	2.113	7.4
	1982	41.6	29.4	131.7	−60.7	1.639	6.1
	1983	41.5	38.2	115.3	−35.6	1.213	4.4
Switzerland	1979	104.4	18.5	210.3	−87.4	4.630	17.4
	1980	101.1	5.6	148.7	−42.0	5.260	17.7
	1981	69.8	21.2	163.6	−62.6	3.208	11.2
	1982	59.6	14.2	177.3	−103.5	1.626	6.4
	1983	42.6	19.86	186.16	+123.7	2.668	10.4
USA	1979	—	—	—	—	—	—
	1980	25.4	5.4	22.0	+8.8	8.118	3.7
	1981	25.0	4.7	19.6	+10.1	8.221	3.5
	1982	26.3	7.0	34.3	+1.0	6.841	3.0
	1983	20.3	69.9	193.0	+102.8	7.523	3.75

Insurance System Status			Services Offered							
					Maximum Coverage Percentage					
Gov. Owned	Mixed	Private	Exports Credits	Garan-tees	Political Risks	Currency Risks	Commer-cial Risks	Short-Term	Middle-Term	Long-Term
					100		85			
					90	85	85			
					90	90	90			
					95		90			
					90	90	90			
					97½		90			
					90		90			
					96		95			
					100	90	90			
					90		90			
					95	80				
					100		90			

Source: Swiss Bank Corporation, ''Pleite der Exportförderer?'' *Der Monat,* April 1985, p. 9. Reprinted by permission.

FIGURE 18.2 Export Import Bank Financing

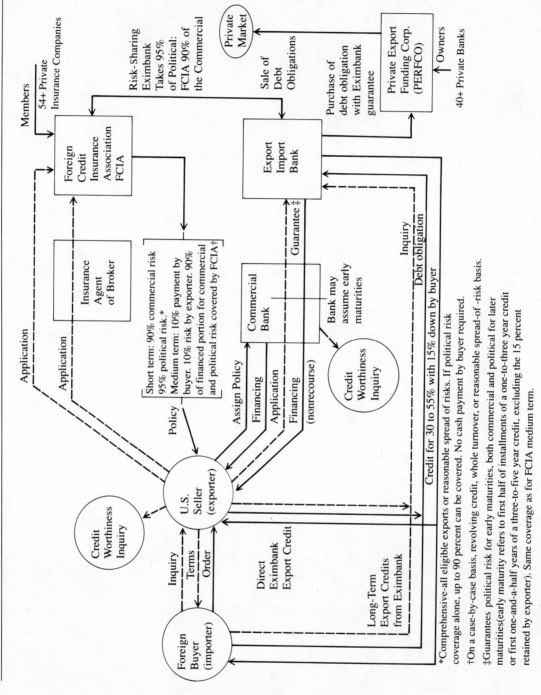

*Comprehensive-all eligible exports or reasonable spread of risks. If political risk coverage alone, up to 90 percent can be covered. No cash payment by buyer required.

†On a case-by-case basis, revolving credit, whole turnover, or reasonable spread-of -risk basis.

‡Guarantees political risk for early maturities, both commercial and political for later maturities(early maturity refers to first half of installments of a one-to-three year credit or first one-and-a-half years of a three-to-five year credit, excluding the 15 percent retained by exporter). Same coverage as for FCIA medium term.

Source: Richard D. Robinson, *International Business Management,* 2nd edition (Hinsdale, Ill.: Dryden Press, 1978), p. 536. Reprinted by permission of Holt, Rinehart & Winston.

rates than those available in other countries. Companies in Sweden and Western Germany paid 3.4 and 2.3 percent respectively.

Medium-Term Financing

Eximbank classifies terms ranging from 181 days to 5 years as medium-term. To serve exporters, four special programs exist: the medium-term export credit insurance (FCIA) programs, the U.S. Commercial Bank Guarantee program, the Discount Loan Program, and the Cooperative Financing Facility.

Several insurance alternatives are available through FCIA. Provided the foreign buyer makes a cash payment of 15 percent on or before delivery, and subject to a deductible of 10 percent, Eximbank will insure each specific transaction. Through the cooperation of nearly 300 U.S. commercial banks, Eximbank organized the U.S. Commercial Bank Guarantee Program. Under this program, Eximbank offers protection against commercial and political risks on debts acquired by U.S. banks from U.S. exporters. This coverage is now extended to more than 140 countries. Conditions for the guarantee program include a cash payment of 15 percent by the foreign buyer, a deductible of 10 percent, and passing credit checks imposed by Eximbank and the participating commercial bank. The interest rate is set by the commercial bank according to prevailing domestic market conditions.

A special program to increase the capacity of U.S. commercial banks to grant credit on exports is the Discount Loan Program. Under this program, U.S. banks may refinance fixed-rate export credits with Eximbank at rates lower than the prevailing market rates. The Cooperative Financing Facility also helps foreign banks finance U.S. exports to foreign customers. Again, the foreign buyer is required to pay 15 percent cash before delivery, and Eximbank will extend a loan of up to 50 percent of the shipment to the foreign participating bank, which must assume the full commercial risk.

A special version of medium-term financing is the *switch-over* feature for foreign distributors. Since many exports reach the final buyer only through a foreign distributor, this feature allows an export transaction to a distributor to be covered by Eximbank financing and to be switched over to the end-user within 270 days of delivery. This feature applies to all four medium-term programs. Wholly owned U.S. subsidiaries abroad may also use the switch-over service.

Long-Term Financing

Long-term financing by Eximbank extends from five to ten years. Under special circumstances, as in the case of conventional or nuclear power plants, financing may be arranged for longer periods. Financing may occur either by direct credit to the foreign buyer or by a guarantee assuring repayment of private financing arranged by the buyer. Eximbank requires a 15 percent downpayment by the foreign buyer and assurance that private financing is not possible on similar terms. In the past, foreign airlines and utilities have made frequent use of such facilities to finance purchases of aircraft and power-generating equipment.

In general, Eximbank programs do not extend direct financing to the U.S. exporter. Rather, the bank closes the gap between commercial bank financing and foreign buyer needs by guarantees or financing for the foreign buyer.

The Value of Eximbank Loans to U.S. Exporters

Although less than 10 percent of U.S. exports are financed through Eximbank, loans at lower than market rates are crucial to exporters of many products. In 1980, about $3 billion of Boeing Company's $5 billion in exports were financed by Eximbank.[6] In 1981, more than 2,600 firms used the services of Eximbank.[7] Researchers estimated that Eximbank operations in 1980 supported about 570,000 U.S. jobs.

Another U.S. company that has relied heavily on Eximbank financing is J.I. Case, one of the nation's leading farm equipment manufacturers. With foreign sales accounting for nearly half of company business, Eximbank credit helps it compete with European and Japanese manufacturers that can profit from low-cost government export financing. In 1980, a $10.4 million contract with the Dominican Republic was facilitated by an 8 percent loan for $3.5 million to the buyers. Also in 1980, a five-year loan at 7.75 percent helped clinch a deal with Israel.[8]

Eximbank support of U.S. exporters depends on funding from the U.S. government. United States exporters have in the past lobbied heavily to expand Eximbank funding, hoping to receive more loans at more favorable rates. However, many critics argue that Eximbank serves large MNCs that are already profitable. It is expected that the political debate surrounding Eximbank will continue and that its lending authority will vary as Congress appropriates differing fund levels from year to year.

For smaller companies, access to the full range of government-sponsored export financing is still difficult. Large commercial banks with the sophistication to help do not like to make small loans. On the other hand, the small local banks who handle the banking business for small companies do not have the resources and experience to assist in international export financing. As a result, several U.S. states, California among them, have set up their own state-sponsored export financing schemes for transactions of about $500,000 or less. California guarantees 85 percent repayment on loans used to finance working capital or

---

6. "U.S. Firms Already Cut Back Work As Result of Ex-Im Bank Restraints," *The Wall Street Journal,* March 31, 1981, p. 35.

7. "U.S. Companies and Unions Fight to Save Exim Bank from Budget Knife," *Business International,* May 14, 1982, p. 153.

8. "Banking on Ex-Im," *Time,* March 2, 1981, p. 28.

TABLE 18.4 Minimum Rates Charged by National Export Credit Programs*

EXPORT CREDITS' CONSENSUS
New Interest Rates

Borrowing country	Criteria	Length of loan (years)		Maximum credit term (years)	Minimum cash payment (%)
		2–5	Over 5		
Category 1 Relatively rich	GNP per capita $4,000 (1979)	9.55	9.80	5†	15
Category 2 Middle income	Not in categories 1 or 3	8.25	8.75	8.5	15
Category 3 Relatively poor	GNP per capita under $624 (1978)	7.4	7.40	10	15

* The following rates have been approved by the Arrangement on Guidelines for Officially Supported Export Credit entered by twenty-two nations under the umbrella of the OECD.
† 8.5 years exceptionally
Source: Euromoney, June 1987, p. 47. Reprinted by permission.

accounts receivable tied to export orders. Illinois will even lend the bank of the small firm up to 90 percent of the funds needed to make export-related loans. More than 10 U.S. states have started similar programs.[9]

COMPETING AGAINST EXPORT CREDIT BANKS OF FOREIGN NATIONS

Most developed nations of North America, Europe, and Asia maintain programs to finance exports from their own countries. To the extent that internal loan conditions differ from those offered by other countries, an exporter from a given country might have an advantage. United States Eximbank rates are usually higher than those offered by other export banks in other countries. To prevent an interest rate "war" from developing, leading industrial nations have agreed to minimum rates and loans for various groups of countries. Such agreements are renegotiated periodically, and the U.S. government has taken a lead in such negotiations.[10] See Table 18.4 for minimum rates charged by OECD countries.

9. "States Launch Efforts to Make Small Firms Better Exporters," *The Wall Street Journal,* February 2, 1987, p. 25.
10. "U.S. Overcomes EEC Resistance," *Financial Times,* July 5, 1982, p. 4.

The Eximbank has an active intermediary program to loan money to banks at 150 basis points below OECO concensus rates (see Table 18.4) for loans valued at less than one million dollars. These funds are designated to finance medium and small exporters for small transactions.[11]

FINANCIAL ENGINEERING: A NEW MARKETING TOOL

With financing costs becoming ever more important for capital goods, many companies have moved toward exploiting the best financial deal from bases around the world. A company with manufacturing bases in several countries might bid on a contract from several subsidiaries to let the client select the most advantageous package, or it might pre-select the subsidiary that will bid based on available financing. Devising such financial packages is known as financial engineering. It is practiced by independent specialists located in leading financial centers and by international banks that have developed expertise in this field.

An example of financial engineering is offered by Massey-Ferguson, Ltd., a Canadian farm machinery manufacturer.[12] Massey-Ferguson had traditionally supplied tractors to Turkey from its U.K. plants. Turkey experienced balance of payments difficulty, and the company met problems obtaining credit for the country. Massey-Ferguson looked to its other manufacturing bases for new sources of financing. The best deal was offered by Brazil, a country eager to expand its exports. Brazilians helped convince the Turkish customer Mafer to buy Brazilian-made equipment in U.S. dollars.

Massey sold 7,200 tractors worth $53 million to a Brazillian agency which in turn sold to the Turkish buyer. Massey was to be paid cash and a Brazilian state agency guaranteed payment. Brazil was thus able to attract business of about 20,000 tractors annually from the United Kingdom because it assumed all risk for Massey-Ferguson.

Other companies are now institutionalizing financial engineering in their global operations. Sulzer Brothers, Ltd., a Swiss heavy equipment manufacturer, maintains in its international division a full-time specialist prepared to advise all operating divisions on financial engineering opportunities in bidding. One division of the company with manufacturing operations in several countries frequently submits bids from several of its plants and lets the customer select the most desirable package. This strategy works best if products are highly standardized and quality differences between the various plants are minimal.

---

11. Business International, "What's New at Eximbank and Why U.S. Exporters Should Take Another Look, *Weekly Report to Managers of Worldwide Operations,* March 30, 1987, pp. 98–99.
12. "How Massey-Ferguson Uses Brazil for Export Financing," *Business Week,* March 17, 1978 p. 86.

Noncash Pricing: Countertrade

International marketers are likely to find many situations in which an interested customer will not be able to find any hard currency financing at all. In such circumstances, the customer might offer a product or commodity in return. The supplier must then turn the product offered into hard currency. Such transactions, known as countertrade, are estimated to have accounted for 8 to 10 percent of world trade or more than $200 billion in 1985. Other private sources have estimated countertrade as high as 30 percent of world trade and expect it to climb steadily in the near future.[13]

The U.S. International Trade Commission surveyed 500 of the largest U.S. companies accounting for some 60 percent of U.S. exports on their use of countertrade. For 1984, the survey found that 5.6 percent of those firms' exports were covered by some part of a countertrade arrangement, totaling U.S. $7.1 billion. About 80 percent of this volume was accounted for by military equipment sales. Nonmilitary countertrade grew from $285 million in 1980 to $1.4 billion in 1984.[14]

Forms of countertrade have always been popular between Comecon countries (U.S.S.R. and Eastern Europe) and Western countries. For that region, countertrade was estimated to represent about 15 percent of international trade, twice the average for the rest of the world.[15] A study by a private research firm reported that in the early 1970s some fifteen countries insisted on countertrade in some circumstances. By the end of the 1970s, this number had doubled, and by 1985 it had risen to more than 50 countries.[16] To respond to this challenge, international marketers have developed several forms of countertrade (see Figure 18.3). The purpose of the following sections is to explain each one and then examine the problems associated with each.[17]

Barter

Barter, one of the most basic types of countertrade, consists of a direct exchange of goods between two partners. In most cases, these transactions take place between two or more nations (three in case of triangular barter). Barter involves no currency and is concluded without the help of intermediaries. Barter has become less common while other forms of countertrade have become more popular.[18].

---

13. "Beleaguered Third World Leads the Barter Boom," *Financial Times,* February 28, 1984, p. 6.

14. "Countertrade Comes Out of the Closet," *The Economist,* December 20, 1986, p. 89.

15. David B. Yoffie, "Barter: Looking Beyond the Short-Term Payoffs and Long-Term Threat," *International Management,* August 1984, p. 36.

16. "Countertrade Comes Out of the Closet," p. 89.

17. The terminology used in this section is based upon *Barter, Compensation and Cooperation,* Credit Suisse, Publication No. 47 IV, Zurich, Switzerland, 1978.

18. See Henry Ferguson, "Tomorrow's Global Manager Will Use Countertrade," *Corporate Barter and Countertrade,* July 1987.

FIGURE 18.3 Forms of Countertrade

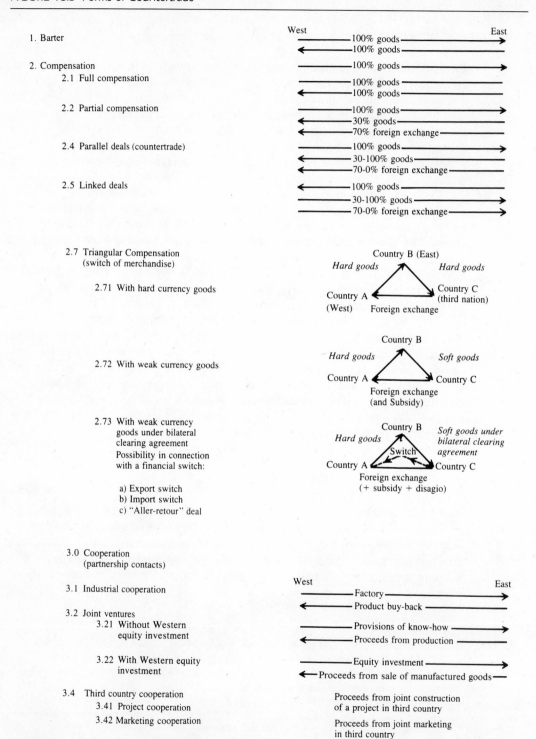

1. Barter

2. Compensation
   2.1 Full compensation

   2.2 Partial compensation

   2.4 Parallel deals (countertrade)

   2.5 Linked deals

   2.7 Triangular Compensation
       (switch of merchandise)

       2.71 With hard currency goods

       2.72 With weak currency goods

       2.73 With weak currency
            goods under bilateral
            clearing agreement
            Possibility in connection
            with a financial switch:

            a) Export switch
            b) Import switch
            c) "Aller-retour" deal

3.0 Cooperation
    (partnership contacts)

3.1 Industrial cooperation

3.2 Joint ventures
    3.21 Without Western
         equity investment

    3.22 With Western equity
         investment

3.4 Third country cooperation
    3.41 Project cooperation
    3.42 Marketing cooperation

Source: Barter, Compensation and Cooperation, Credit Suisse, Zurich, Switzerland, Vol. 47, IV, 1978, pp. 8–9.

One of the largest known barter deals involved Boeing Co. of the United States, Rolls-Royce of the United Kingdom and the Saudi Arabian government. Boeing sold to Saudi Arabia ten 747 jumbo jets equipped with British-made Rolls-Royce engines. The total value of the contract, estimated at $1 billion, was paid for with 34 million barrels of oil sold on the spot market by Boeing. When this barter deal was entered into by Boeing, which had traditionally maintained a policy of not engaging in such trading, it signaled the increase of such activities.[19]

Compensation Arrangements

Compensation arrangements are transactions that include payment in merchandise and/or foreign exchange. Depending on the type of arrangement, the method or structure of the compensation transaction may change. One usually speaks of compensation transaction when the value of an export delivery is offset by an import transaction or vice versa. Compensation transactions may be classified into several categories as described below.

Full Compensation

Full compensation is similar to barter in that a 100 percent mutual transfer of goods takes place. However, deliveries are made and paid for separately. Upon signing the sales agreement, the exporter commits to purchase products or services at an amount equal to that specified in the export contract. An option exists to sell such a commitment to a third party who may take over the commitment from the exporter for a fee.

Partial Compensation

Under partial compensation, the exporter receives a portion of the purchase price in hard currency and the remainder in merchandise. The exporter will actually not be able to convert such merchandise into cash until a buyer can be found, and even then only at a discount.

A partial compensation transaction was concluded in 1981 by Honda, a Japanese car manufacturer, and the Algerian government to cover 15,000 passenger cars valued at $50 million. When Algeria could not pay in hard currency as a result of depressed crude oil volumes, Algeria offered to pay the entire value in oil. However, Algeria's official export price of $37.50 per barrel was above the valid spot price of $33. This would have resulted in a price discount of about 10

19. "Countertrade Wins a Stamp of Respectability," *Financial Times*, October 25, 1984, p. 5.

percent by Honda. The parties eventually agreed to compensate 40 percent of the contract value of Algeria's official export price for crude oil with the rest paid in hard currency. This was the first such deal for Honda.[20]

Parallel Deals

In a parallel deal the exporter agrees to accept the merchandise equivalent of a given percentage of the export amount. Payment is received on delivery. This arrangement is intended to offset the outflow of wealth from the country when a very large purchase has been made. Within a given amount of time, the exporter searches for a specific amount of merchandise which can be bought from the country or the company that purchased the products originally. Eastern European countries often include a penalty fee in case the Western exporter defaults on the countertrade portion of the arrangement. Offset arrangements are a type of parallel deal gaining popularity today. In 1980, Lockheed, a U.S. aerospace manufacturer, sold wide-bodied passenger airplanes to Portugal's state airline, TAP. As partial compensation to offset the $250 million deal, Lockheed agreed to purchase $65 million worth of Portuguese products over a 10-year period. In case of failure, Lockheed would pay a fine of $4.5 million.[21]

McDonnell Douglas has a similar deal with Yugoslavia for the sale of DC-10 planes. Over the past twenty years, McDonnell Douglas has exceeded its takeback commitment of $90 million by $10 million through the Yugoslav Foreign Trade Organization (the state trading company). The $10 million credit has opened sales opportunities for McDonnell Douglas. The firm has recently registered similar agreements with China and Korea.[22]

Linked Deals

Linked deals, sometimes called junction, are a form of countertrade not frequently used. A Western importer finds a Western exporter willing to deliver merchandise to a country in Eastern Europe or the Third World. At the same time, the importer is released from a counter-purchase agreement by paying a premium to the importer, who in turn organizes the counter-purchase. This transaction requires agreement of the state-controlled trading nation.

---

20. *Ibid.*

21. "How Lockheed Copes with Countertrade in Portugal," *Business Europe,* October 8, 1982, p. 321.

22. Business International, "Countertrade Watch: Benefits and Pitfalls of Evidence Accounts," *Weekly Report to Managers of Worldwide Operations,* March 23, 1987, p. 94.

Triangular Compensation

Triangular compensation arrangements, also called switch trades, involve three countries. The Western exporter delivers hard goods (saleable merchandise) to an importing country, typically in Eastern Europe. As payment, the importing country may transfer hard goods (easily saleable merchandise) or soft goods (heavily discounted merchandise) to a third country in the West or in Eastern Europe, which then reimburses the Western exporter for the goods received. Such negotiations may become complex and time consuming. Often the assistance of skilled traders, switch traders, is required to assure profitable participation by the Western exporter.

Offset Deals

One of the fastest growing types of countertrade is offset. In an offset transaction, the selling company guarantees to use some products or services from the buying country in the final product. These transactions are particularly common when large purchases from government-type agencies are involved, such as public utilities or defense-related equipment. To land the large order for its airborne early radar system (AWACS) from the United Kingdom, the Seattle-based Boeing company offered to offset the purchase by 130 percent. This would commit the Boeing company to spend 130 percent of the purchase value on U.K. products to offset the purchase, which was competed for by a British company as well. These types of transactions were first popularized by Canada and Belgium some twenty years ago and are now common for very large defense contracts in Western Europe, Australia, and New Zealand. This technique is now also spreading to orders involving state railways or state airlines.[23]

Cooperation Agreements

Cooperation agreements are special types of compensation deals extending over longer periods of time. They may be called product purchase transactions, buy-back deals, or pay-as-you-earn deals. Compensation usually refers to an exchange of unrelated merchandise, such as coal for machine tools. Cooperation usually involves related goods, such as payment for new textile machinery by the output produced by these machines.

   Although sale of large equipment or of a whole factory can sometimes only be clinched by a cooperation agreement involving buy-back of plant output, long-term negative effects must be considered before any deal is concluded. In industries such as steel or chemicals, the effect of high volume buy-back ar-

23. "Countertrade Comes Out of the Closet," p. 89.

rangements between Western exporters of manufacturing technology and Eastern European importers has been devastating. Western countries, especially Europe, have been flooded with surplus products. Negotiations among European Community members are aimed at drafting a general policy on such arrangements to avoid further disruption of their domestic industries.

International Harvester is one U.S. company with experience in buy-back arrangements.[24] In 1973, the company sold the basic design and technology for a tractor crawler to Poland. At the same time, International Harvester agreed to buy back tractor components manufactured by the Polish plant. These components were shipped to a subassembly plant in the United Kingdom which served the European market. In 1976, the company sold Hungary the design for an axle. To offset this sale, the company agreed to purchase complete axles for highway trucks.

Dangers in Compensation Deals

The greatest danger in compensation arrangements stems from the difficulty of finding a buyer of the merchandise accepted as part of the transaction. Often such transactions are concluded with organizations of countries where industry is under government control. Since prices for goods in these countries are not determined by the supply and demand forces of a free market economy, merchandise transferred under compensation arrangements is often overvalued compared to open market products. In addition, such merchandise, obviously not saleable on its own, may be of low quality. As a result, the exporter may be able to sell the merchandise only at a discount. The size of these discounts may vary considerably, ranging from 10 percent to 33 percent of its value.[25] The astute exporter will raise the price of the export contract to cover such potential discounts on the compensating transaction.

Precautions for Countertrade

A study of 57 British companies involved in countertrade reported that the most difficult problems with countertrade were that there was no in-house use for the goods offered and the negotiations were complex and time consuming.[26]

At the conclusion of the sales agreement, the exporter should obtain a clear notion of the merchandise offered for countertrade. The description, origin,

24. "Countertrade," *Commerce America,* June 19, 1978, p. 1.

25. "Algeria: When Barter Is Battery," *The Economist,* October 3, 1981, p. 80.

26. David Shipley and Bill Neale, "Industrial Barter and Countertrade," *Industrial Marketing Management,* February 1987, p. 6.

quality, quantity, delivery schedules, price, and purchasing currency in local or hard currency should be determined. With a detailed description given to a specialized trader, an estimate on the applicable discount may be rendered. The sale price of merchandise offered may be structured to include the difference between purchase amount and actual cash value. It is paramount that the Western exporter not agree on any price before these other items are determined. Maintaining flexibility in negotiation requires skill and patience.

Organizing for Countertrade[27]

International companies are moving toward organizing countertrade for higher leverage. Many larger firms have established specialized units whose single purpose is to engage in countertrade. Many independent trading companies offer countertrading services. Recently, several large U.S. banks have formed their own countertrade units.

Daihatsu, a Japanese automobile manufacturer, offers a good example of how a willingness to engage in countertrade can lead to a competitive advantage. Although the company is the smallest Japanese automobile manufacturer, Daihatsu has managed to become the market leader for imported cars in Comecon countries such as Poland or Hungary. In Hungary, the company went as far as to schedule its parties for retiring Japanese workers through Hungary, allowing that country to earn additional foreign exchange, which resulted in the sale of another forty cars.[28]

CONCLUSIONS

In this chapter we have examined the rather technical aspects of trade financing, foreign exchange transactions, and countertrade. Many executives have realized that they cannot leave these trade forms to the occasional specialist but must use them as a competitive weapon against aggressive competition. If knowledge of financial engineering and countertrade is to become a competitive advantage, marketing executives negotiating such transactions must master these techniques. International companies will be forced to expose and train their executives in these aspects of trade. We can expect an increasing world trade to be attached to one or the other of these techniques.

---

27. See also Christopher M. Korth, *International Countertrade* (Westport, Conn.: Quorum Books, 1987).

28. "Daihatsu Sets Sights on Europe," *Financial Times,* March 5, 1986, p. 4.

As competition in many industries increases, companies that have maintained a policy of "cash or no deal" must often face a situation of "countertrade or no deal." Companies established in industrialized countries have seen that expansion into state-controlled economies or Third World countries requires willingness to engage in countertrade. Understanding countertrade is now part of the background of an international marketing executive.

Questions for Discussion

1. What is meant by the term *financial engineering?*
2. Assume the position of a turn-key supplier for complete hospitals. For a client in Saudi Arabia that desires financing over five years, what kind of alternatives does the exporter have to arrange for the financing? How would you include this in the quoted price?
3. How should a firm approach the decision on whether or not its exports should be insured?
4. Explain the major forms of countertrade? Under what circumstances should a company enter into such transactions?
5. What are the major risks to a firm engaging in countertrade?

For Further Reading

Allan, Ian. "Return and Risk in International Capital Markets." *Columbia Journal of World Business* (Summer 1982), pp. 3–21.

Briggs, J. A. "Back to Barter?" *Forbes* (March 12, 1984), pp. 42–44.

Ferguson, Henry. "Tomorrow's Global Manager Will Use Countertrade." *Corporate Barter and Countertrade,* 1, No. 6 (July 1987).

"Friends Again, But the Money Would Flow Anyway." *The Economist* (August 13, 1983), pp. 17–18.

Gut, Rainer E. "Ten Principles of International Financing." In *The International Essays for Business Decision Makers.* Vol. V. Ed. Mark B. Winchester. The Center for International Business and Amacom, A Division of American Management Association, 1980, pp. 217–225.

Kindleberger, Charles P. "Lessons of Floating Exchange Rates." *Journal of Monetary Economics* (January 1976), pp. 51–76.

Korth, Christopher M. *International Countertrade.* Wesport, Conn.: Quorum Books, 1987.

Jacque, L. *Management of Foreign Exchange Rates.* Lexington, Mass.: Lexington Books, 1978.

Springate, David J. "International Cash Management and Foreign Exchange Exposure Management: Separate But Interlocking Concepts." In *The International Essays for Business Decision Makers*. Vol. V. Ed. Mark B. Winchester. The Center for International Business and Amacom, A Division of American Management Association, 1980, pp. 217–225.

Weigand, Robert E. "International Trade Without Money." *Harvard Business Review* (November–December 1977) p. 28.

19

THE EXPORT AND IMPORT TRADE PROCESS

Throughout the previous chapters we have maintained that exporting and importing are subsets of international marketing. We have also indicated that international marketing may take place without any physical movement of products across country borders, thereby taking an even broader view of international marketing. However, most companies will, as part of their international marketing activities, engage in some form of exporting or importing. This could take place in the form of shipments from the headquarters location to a foreign market or through cross-shipments among various subsidiaries. Invariably, such export or import shipments cause specific problems that have not been discussed in the previous chapters and that can best be handled in the form of a specialized section such as this one.

To deal with all specific rules and regulations that can be found in today's complex international business environments is not possible or necessary for our purposes. In this chapter, we will view export and import mechanics from the point of view of a United States–based firm. However, many aspects of the export section, such as those related to pricing, are of universal application and would be of interest to all readers. The structure and components of the chapter are depicted in Figure 19.1.

FIGURE 19.1 Export and Import Trading Process

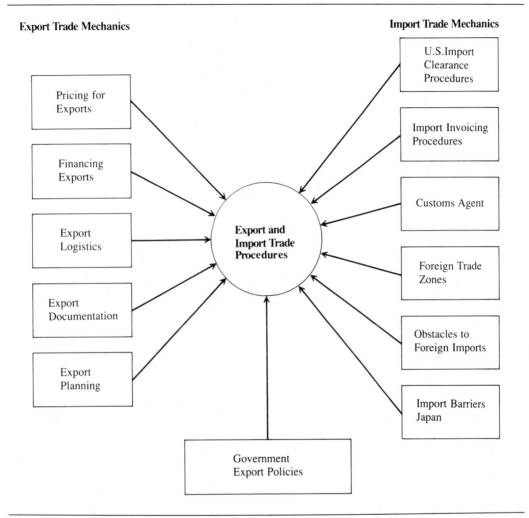

Export Trade Mechanics

Pricing for Exports

Financing Exports

Export Logistics

Export Documentation

Export Planning

Import Trade Mechanics

U.S.Import Clearance Procedures

Import Invoicing Procedures

Customs Agent

Foreign Trade Zones

Obstacles to Foreign Imports

Import Barriers Japan

Export and Import Trade Procedures

Government Export Policies

EXPORT TRADE MECHANICS[1]

Any successful export activity of a firm should be based upon a careful analysis of a company's export potential, as has been discussed in Chapter 9 on entry strategies. Potential techniques and approaches for such an analysis were cov-

1. This section has been adapted and based upon *A Basic Guide to Exporting,* U.S. Department of Commerce, International Trade Administration, September, 1986.

ered in Chapters 7 and 8. Consequently, we start our discussion of export trade mechanics with the assumption that a potential market has been defined, measured, and located, and that the company has made the decision to exploit the opportunity through exporting. Our focus will be on the execution of a firm's export operation, paying special attention to pricing, logistics, information, planning, and present government policies that affect the individual firm.

Pricing for Export

In Chapter 13, we described in detail the process by which companies may determine prices for products to be shipped abroad. These methods of internal costing, profit analyses, and demand analyses can be applied to the export process. What is peculiar to exporting, however, is the method of quoting prices. Foreign buyers need to know precisely where they will take over responsibility for the product—or what shipping costs the exporter is willing to assume. In the United States, it is customary to ship f.o.b. factory, freight collect, prepaid, charge, or C.O.D. However, in export marketing, different terms are used worldwide.

Figure 19.2 depicts commonly used export quotations for a hypothetical shipment by a Peoria, Illinois company to a client in Bogota, Colombia. The shipment is to go via truck to the railroad depot in Peoria and by rail to a New York pier. The products will then be shipped by sea to Barranquilla, Colombia. Following customs clearance, the shipment will go on by rail and truck to eventually reach the client's warehouse. In international trade, nearly twenty different alternatives exist to quote the price of the merchandise, all indicating different responsibilities for the U.S. company or its Colombian client.

The most common terms used in quoting prices in international trade are these:

c.i.f.: (Cost, insurance, freight) to a named port of import. Under this term, the seller quotes a price that includes the product, all transportation, and insurance to the point of unloading from the vessel or aircraft at the named destination.

c. & f.: (Cost and freight) is similar to the above term c.i.f. except that insurance of the shipment is not included.

f.a.s.: (Free alongside) at a named port in the exporter's country. Under this term, the exporter quotes a price that includes the goods and any service and delivery charges to get the shipment alongside the vessel used for further transportation, but now at the buyer's expense.

f.o.b.: (Free on board) includes the price of placing the shipment on to a specified vessel or aircraft, but further transportation will be the buyer's responsibility.

Ex (*named point of origin*): Applies to a price for products at the point of origin and requires that the buyer assumes all transportation charges.

FIGURE 19.2 Exporting Example

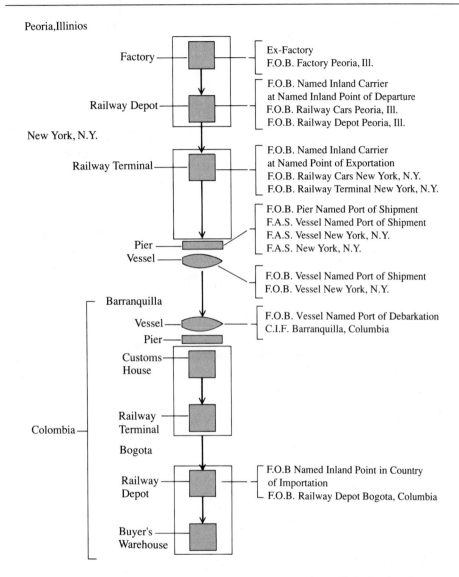

Source: Gerald R. Richter, "Basic Principles of Foreign Trade," in Leslie L. Lewis, ed., *International Trade Handbook* (Chicago: Dartnell Corporation, prepared in cooperation with The American Institute for Foreign Trade, 1965), p. 32.

Incoterms is a booklet of terms and their definitions. These are the internationally agreed upon terms used by international freight forwarders all over the world. The incorrect use of a delivery term can cause significant problems between the exporter and the buyer. (*Incoterms* can be obtained from the International Chamber of Commerce, 801 Second Avenue, Suite 1204, New York, New York 10017.)

When asked by a foreign buyer to quote a price, the exporter will have to quote a price that takes into consideration the methods of freight payment. In quoting a price, the company is advised to stipulate a price that easily allows the buyer to figure out total costs for the shipment. Usually, this means quoting a price c.i.f. foreign port. The foreign buyer can then estimate additional transportation charges for the final distance under known circumstances. In the case of our example in Figure 19.2, the most meaningful quote for the Colombian buyer would be c.i.f. Bogota. Quoting a price ex factory would place the burden of estimating transportation entirely on the foreign buyer. But, as one might imagine, the estimation of costs could be quite difficult to do from abroad. However, an exporter can do a great service to the buyer by quoting prices that reflect the final destination charges based upon information from freight forwarders with experience shipping to the foreign country.

The computed freight, transportation, and insurance charges may also depend on the leverage the exporter or importer has with freight forwarders. To use the example shown in Figure 19.2 again, the U.S. exporter may only have this one shipment going to Bogota, Colombia. The added costs are therefore relatively high. Should the importer have several shipments that could be combined, average freight costs from New York to Colombia might be less. The exporter can facilitate the process by quoting several prices at various points along the shipment route and then leave the choice to the buyer who will select the best method. Exporters should not underestimate the possibility of turning the export price process into a selling tool, particularly when there are similar products to choose from other manufacturers.

Financing Exports

The previous chapter contained several sections on financing international marketing operations through, among others, export banks of various countries. Also discussed were noncash transactions such as barter. These types of arrangements will not be repeated in this chapter. This section will focus on the various arrangements exporters can make to ensure payment for their merchandise and credit methods that can be offered to foreign clients.

Although cash transactions can be desirable, payments in this form are rarely used. The shipment may be in transit for weeks or even months at a time, thus tying up the importer's capital. Also, the importer does not really know what was shipped until the products are in the importer's possession. Consequently, most forms of payment are designed to protect both parties, even though credit extension may shift between participants, depending on the situation. When an exporter knows the foreign clients and fully trusts their financial integrity, shipments on *open account* may be arranged. Usually, the terms are arranged such that the foreign client can wait with payment until the goods have arrived at their final destination. However, in this case, the exporter will have risked capital in the transaction. *Consignment sales* is the method whereby credit is extended by the exporter. The exporter is not compensated until the products are physically sold by the importer. In short, the entire risk is absorbed by the exporter. Those companies which are considering this method should consider carefully the client's political and economic environment and, where necessary, get political risk insurance in addition to the normal coverage against property damage or loss.

To control both ownership and payment terms for international shipments, traders have developed the *draft* or bill of exchange.[2] The draft is a formal order issued by the exporter to the importer specifying when the sum is to be paid to the third party, usually the exporter's bank. A triangular relationship is established with the issuer of the draft, or exporter, as drawer, the importer as drawee, and the payee as the recipient of the payment. Since the draft is a negotiable instrument, it can be sold, transferred, and discounted, and the exporter can use it to finance the shipment.

Exporters may use either a *sight draft* or a *time draft*. Sight drafts are used when the exporter desires to control the shipment beyond the point of original shipment, usually to assure payment. In practice, the exporter endorses the bill of lading (B/L) and adds a sight draft on the correspondent bank of the exporter's bank. Along with the bill of lading and sight draft, other documents will be provided such as the packing list, invoice, consular invoices, and certificate of insurance. Once the documents have arrived, a transfer by way of endorsement to the importer will be made upon payment in full at that bank. Consequently, the importer cannot take possession of the goods until payment has been made (on sight of documents). Yet, the importer is assured that the goods have actually been shipped as indicated by the accompanying documents.

Alternatively, transactions can be made in time drafts. This method specifies the period in which the payment is to be made. The payment period beginning upon receiving the documents may be 30, 60, 90 days, or longer. Drafts will not only allow the exporter to control the shipment until proper payment occurs, but they also allow further financing by having the properly signed draft discounted with a bank before the payment term agreed to expires. In such a case, the banking system assumes the role of the creditor, thus reducing the capital risks of the exporter.

Also used quite frequently is a financial instrument called a *letter of credit*. With a letter of credit the importer, or foreign buyer, finances the transaction,

---

2. Endel J. Kolde, *International Business Enterprise,* 2nd ed. (Englewood Cliffs, N.J.: Prentice-Hall, 1973), pp. 289–290.

thus alleviating the credit burden on the exporter. With a letter of credit, the responsibility is in the hands of the importer. Once informed that the exporter will ship with a letter of credit (L/C), the importer will ask the bank to write an irrevocable L/C with a bank specified by the exporter on the latter's behalf. The importer will usually instruct the bank on the conditions of payment, typically against submission of all necessary documents including a bill of lading (B/L). When the exporter has placed the shipment on the appropriate vessel, the company will go to the bank and turn over all documents associated with the transaction. When satisfied, the exporter's bank will pay out the funds and debit the importer's bank who will in turn debit the importing company. Overall, the irrevocable L/C has distinct advantages for the exporter since it represents a firm order that, once issued by the bank, cannot be cancelled or revoked. For example, a firm that sells machinery that is built to order can use the irrevocable L/C to guarantee that payment will be made. Time limits are placed on the L/C that protect the importer against an open-ended transaction. Should the exporter fail to ship and submit documents before the expiration date, the L/C would expire without any further responsibility on the part of the importer to finance the transaction. Any bank charges associated with the transaction are usually paid by the buyer.

Letters of credit are a widely used instrument that have developed into several specialized forms over and above the standard irrevocable L/C described above. The following additional forms exist:

Revolving or Periodic Letters of Credit allow for a repetition of the same transaction as soon as the previous amount has been paid by the bank that originated the L/C.

Cumulative Letters of Credit are opened to cover payments of partial shipments and/or the use of the unused portion of the L/C for another transaction between the same parties.

Red Clause Letters of Credit are used to permit partial cash payments to the beneficiary, or exporter, as an advance on the shipment without any documentation. Final payments are made only against full documentation, however.

Back-to-Back Letters of Credit are issued based upon an earlier L/C. This might be done if an exporter, in whose favor an L/C was opened by a foreign client, would use the original L/C as a basis or security to issue a second L/C in favor of a supplier for materials connected with that particular transaction.

Circular Letters of Credit are issued without designating any particular bank. The exporter may send documents to the issuing bank or present them to any bank who will send them on for collection.

Performance Letters of Credit are used to guarantee the completion of a contract undertaken abroad. They can be drawn upon if the exporter fails to meet performance requirements and are therefore also known under the term *performance bonds*.[3]

As we have seen, there are numerous options available to arrange for payment in export transactions. The exporting company can, of course, select the particular type of transaction, always keeping in mind the needs and requirements of the buyer who might, if offered better credit terms elsewhere, decide to place an order with a different company. The payment process is an important part of the transaction between the buyer and seller in an export situation; it can minimize the risks of exchange rate fluctuations and the process of dealing with a distant buyer or seller.

Export Logistics

The requirements of export logistics differ substantially from domestic operations requiring special care on the part of the exporting firm. Practices must ensure that the shipment arrives in the best possible condition and at the lowest possible cost.

To ensure that the products arrive in usable condition, export packages will have to be prepared to avoid four typical problems: breakage, weight, moisture, and pilferage. Export shipments often are subject to additional handling procedures including the use of a sling for loading onto a vessel, nets to combine various items for loading, or conveyors, chutes, and other methods that put added stress and strain on the shipment and are frequently the cause of breakage. Once on board a vessel, the weight or other cargo placed on top of the shipment could also be hazardous. At the overseas destination, handling facilities are frequently less sophisticated than those in the United States. Consequently, the cargo may be even dragged, pushed, or rolled during unloading, causing damage to the goods.

While on a voyage, moisture is a constant problem due to condensation in the hold of a ship. This may even be so for vessels equipped with air conditioning and dehumidifiers. At the point of arrival, unloading may take place in the rain and many foreign ports do not have covered storage facilities. Furthermore, without adequate protection, theft or pilferage is common.

To avoid these problems, exporters are encouraged to add extra packaging to protect their cargo. However, overpacking should be avoided since both freight and customs are frequently assessed on the gross weight of the merchandise, resulting in unneeded charges for extra packaging. Air freight usually requires less packaging than ocean freight, and container shipments can be used to provide added protection for the goods. Exporters are encouraged to check with

---

3. *Ibid.,* p. 294.

carriers or marine insurance companies for advice on proper packaging. For companies that are not equipped to do export packaging, professional companies exist that provide this service for a moderate fee.

Equally important is the proper marking of the shipment. Although the destination should be marked clearly and in large stenciled letters of black water-proof ink, experienced exporters advise that no additional facts be provided on the content of the packages to avoid pilferage or theft. Where necessary, special handling instructions should be added in the language of the port of destination.

Arrangements for the actual shipping of a company's products can be made through the services of an international freight forwarder. In general, a freight forwarder licensed by the Federal Maritime Administration should be used because these agents are familiar with foreign import regulations, methods of shipping, and the requirements of U.S. export documentations. Not only will freight forwarders advise on freight costs and other related fees, but they can also make recommendations on packaging. Since the cost for their services is a legitimate export cost, exporters can add such costs to their prices charged to foreign customers. Aside from advising exporters, forwarders also make the necessary arrangements to clear shipments through customs, arrange for the actual shipping, and check for the necessary documents as described in the section below.

Export Documentation

To facilitate the transfer of goods out of the United States and through a foreign country's procedures, a series of export documents have to be prepared. Exporters prepare such documents with care since frequently the export documents have been used as a basis for obtaining trade credit from banks or collection from the buyer.

One requirement is a detailed export packing list usually containing substantially more details about weight and volume than those used for domestic commerce. This packing list is used by shippers to reserve or book the necessary space on the vessel. Furthermore, port officials at the dock use this list to determine whether the correct cargo has been received. In addition, customs officials both in the United States and abroad use the packing list; and ultimately, the buyer will want to check the goods against the list to verify that the entire shipment was received. To satisfy all these users, the packing list must contain not only a detailed description of the products for each packaging unit but also weights, volume, and dimensions in both metric and nonmetric terms.

The U.S. government requires that all export shipments be subject to a licensing procedure. Basically, there exist two types of export licenses. The *validated export license* must be secured for each individual order from the Office of Export Administration in Washington, D.C. Several types of products and commodities may fall into this category, such as chemicals, special types of plastic, advanced electronic and communications equipment, and scarce materials including petroleum. For defense products, licenses are issued by the Department of State. The requirement for a validated export license may apply for shipments of certain commodities to all countries or only for a limited number of countries. The entire mechanism was instituted to protect the United States' strategic position for reasons of foreign policy, national security, or to regulate supply for select scarce products. Regulations are also subject to frequent changes depending on the political or economic climate prevailing at the time of decision.

All other products are subject to several types of *general licenses*. These are published general authorizations, each with a specific license symbol that is dependent on product category. Exporters must inquire at the Department of Commerce to obtain the correct general license symbol. Exporters usually check with the Department of Commerce before an order is accepted to determine the type of license required. For validated licenses, the buyer frequently must submit several forms himself in support of the request. These forms should be requested in advance to avoid delays. The government, however, usually only issues licenses upon receipt of an order. The average processing time for a license is 14 days, which can be checked through a sophisticated system called Status Tracking Export License Applications (STELA).[4]

The exporter's *shipper's export declaration* has to be added to all shipments and requires a declaration of the products in terms of the U.S. Customs Service definitions and classifications. In this form, the exporter must note the applicable license for the shipment. A sample of the shipper's export declaration is shown in Figure 19.3.

Most exporters also submit a series of documents to their customers to facilitate additional financing and/or handling at the point of destination. These documents may vary by country, method of payment, mode of transportation, and even by customer. The following documents may be required:

Commercial Invoices. In addition to the customary content, the invoice should indicate the origin of the products and export marks. Also needed is an antidiversion clause, such as "United States law prohibits disposition of these commodities to North Korea, North and South Vietnam, Cambodia, or Cuba." When payment is against a letter of credit, the invoice should contain all necessary numbers and bank names. Some countries require even special certification, at times in the language of that country; and a few countries may need signed invoices with notarization. The Commerce Department keeps a current list of all requirements by country.

Consular Invoices. Some countries, particularly those of Latin America, require a special invoice in addition to the commercial invoice prepared in the language of the country and issued on official forms by the consulate. The forms are typically prepared by the forwarding agent.

---

4. "Commerce Simplifiers Export Licensing," *Business America,* June 8, 1987, p. 3.

FIGURE 19.3 Shipper's Export Declaration

U.S. DEPARTMENT OF COMMERCE — BUREAU OF THE CENSUS — INTERNATIONAL TRADE ADMINISTRATION

FORM **7525-V** (3-19-85) **SHIPPER'S EXPORT DECLARATION** OMB No. 0607-0018

1a. EXPORTER *(Name and address including ZIP code)*

ZIP CODE

2. DATE OF EXPORTATION

3. BILL OF LADING/AIR WAYBILL NO.

b. EXPORTER EIN NO.

c. PARTIES TO TRANSACTION
☐ Related ☐ Non-related

4a. ULTIMATE CONSIGNEE

b. INTERMEDIATE CONSIGNEE

5. FORWARDING AGENT

6. POINT (STATE) OF ORIGIN OR FTZ NO.

7. COUNTRY OF ULTIMATE DESTINATION

8. LOADING PIER/TERMINAL

9. MODE OF TRANSPORT *(Specify)*

10. EXPORTING CARRIER

11. PORT OF EXPORT

12. FOREIGN PORT OF UNLOADING

13. CONTAINERIZED *(Vessel only)*
☐ Yes ☐ No

14. SCHEDULE B DESCRIPTION OF COMMODITIES, *(Use columns 15–19)*

MARKS, NOS., AND KINDS OF PKGS. (15)	D/F (16)	SCHEDULE B NUMBER (17)	QUANTITY — SCHEDULE B UNIT(S) (18)	SHIPPING WEIGHT *(Pounds)* (19)	VALUE (U.S. dollars, omit cents) *(Selling price or cost if not sold)* (20)

21. VALIDATED LICENSE NO./GENERAL LICENSE SYMBOL

22. ECCN *(When required)*

23. Duly authorized officer or employee

The exporter authorizes the forwarder named above to act as forwarding agent for export control and customs purposes.

24. I certify that all statements made and all information contained herein are true and correct and that I have read and understand the instructions for preparation of this document, set forth in the **"Correct Way to Fill Out the Shipper's Export Declaration."** I understand that civil and criminal penalties, including forfeiture and sale, may be imposed for making false or fraudulent statements herein, failing to provide the requested information or for violation of U.S. laws on exportation (13 U.S.C. Sec. 305; 22 U.S.C. Sec. 401; 18 U.S.C. Sec. 1001; 50 U.S.C. App. 2410).

Signature

Confidential – For use solely for official purposes authorized by the Secretary of Commerce (13 U.S.C. 301 (g)).

Title

Export shipments are subject to inspection by U.S. Customs Service and/or Office of Export Enforcement.

Date

25. AUTHENTICATION *(When required)*

This form may be printed by private parties provided it conforms to the official form. For sale by the Superintendent of Documents, Government Printing Office, Washington, D.C. 20402, and local Customs District Directors. The **"Correct Way to Fill Out the Shipper's Export Declaration"** is available from the Bureau of the Census, Washington, D.C. 20233.

Source: U.S. Department of Commerce.

Certificates of Origin. Some countries may require a specific and separate statement that is normally countersigned by a recognized Chamber of Commerce. Based upon this statement, import duties are assessed; and if preferential rates are claimed, the inclusion of the certificate of origin is often necessary.

Inspection Certificate. A foreign buyer may request that the products be inspected, typically by an independent inspection firm, with respect to quality, quantity, and conformity of goods as stated in the order and invoice.

Bill of Lading. Bills of lading are issued in various forms depending on the mode of transportation. The exporter endorses the B/L in favor of either the buyer or the bank financing the transaction. The B/L identifies the owner of the shipment and is needed to claim the products at the point of destination. The bill of lading provides *three* functions: (1) receipt for goods; (2) content for shipment; and (3) title to the goods, if consigned ''to the order of.''

Dock Receipts or Warehouse Receipts. In cases in which the shipper or exporter is not responsible for moving the goods to the foreign destination but only to the U.S. port instead, a dock or warehouse receipt is usually required confirming that the shipment was actually received at the port for further shipment.

Certificate of Manufacture. Such a certificate may be issued for cases in which the buyer intends to pay for the order before shipment. The certificate may be presented, combined with a commercial invoice, to a bank appointed by the buyer for early payment. More typical is to pay only against a B/L indicating that the merchandise has actually been shipped.

Insurance Certificates. Particularly where the exporter is required to arrange for insurance, such certificates are usually necessary. They are negotiable instruments and must be endorsed accordingly.

Exporters pay careful attention to the specifications attached to letters of credit with respect to the required set of documents. The paying bank will only effect payment if all submitted documents fully conform to the specifications determined by the buyer. Mistakes can cause lengthy delays that can be costly to the exporter.

The Export Planning Process

The plan for a firm's export operations is central to any successful exporting effort. The planning activities are designed as a guideline for the future instead of depending on chance to pursue export business. The export plan ensures that all activities are directed towards the achievement of preformulated objectives that are selected to ensure the long-term profitability of the firm. Planning allows a firm to develop its export business on its own terms instead of having it be dictated by foreign clients' demands.

Several aspects are part of a successful export plan. Initially, the company will have to select an appropriate time horizon for its planning process.[5] Root suggests that the planning horizon be chosen so that the firm will be forced to raise fundamental and basic questions about the future direction and extent of the firm's export business.[5] Secondly, planning horizons should be long enough to project the effects of the firm's decisions. The normal plan is three to five years, though for some it may be as short as one year or as long as ten years.

The planning unit would target specific countries for each product. The combination of the various country and/or product plans is the corporate export plan. However, the effort will almost always start at the country and/or product level. Viewing export planning as a process, one can identify three major steps as shown in Figure 19.4: identifying and measuring market opportunities, developing an export strategy, and making the export strategy operational.

The process and analysis of identifying and measuring market opportunities has been described in detail in Chapter 7, International Marketing Research and Analysis. Essentially, the plan has to start with a preliminary screening of the great many export markets that exist to identify those that might be pursued. The preliminary screening prevents any unnecessary effort spent on markets that do not warrant any resources at this time. For the targeted markets, the market potentials will be estimated always keeping in mind that the potential may be measured at various levels (see Figure 7.4). As a next step, an estimate of the firm's sales potential for each market will determine the best possible outcome given the firm's competitive position. Where appropriate, market segments may be analyzed separately if the marketing strategy would require changes for each segment.

The development of the export strategy includes the setting of some objectives. Naturally, these objectives must be in line with the firm's capabilities and reflect the realities of the marketplace as derived from the analysis of the market opportunities. The specific objectives will differ by company. The objectives could include sales volume, market share, and profit expectations. The export plan should consider the potential market reaction to the firm's action and should recognize that competitors may adapt their marketing activities to planned changes.

Once export objectives have been clearly defined, the firm can go about planning the individual elements of the marketing mix. The product offering, including service, must be prepared, and allowances will have to be made for any adjustments if required. Prices will be predetermined based upon both the internal price structure and the demand situation. The export plan will include a detailed promotional plan outlining all the steps to be undertaken to promote the product in the target market. Finally, the plans for the distribution strategy will have to be included as well, containing both entry and local distribution approaches. The key to a successful plan is the relationship between the objectives

5. Franklin R. Root, *Strategic Planning for Export Marketing* (Scranton, Penn.: International Textbook Company, 1966), pp. 4–7.

FIGURE 19.4 Export Planning Process

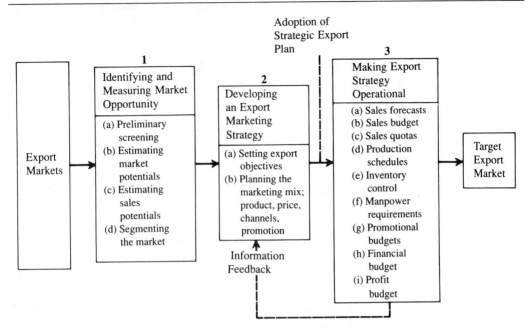

Source: Franklin R. Root, *Strategic Planning for Export Marketing* (Scranton, Penn.: International Textbook Company, 1966), p. 5.

and the planned action. Management will have to ensure that the desired objectives can in fact be reached with the planned marketing mix.

Based upon the detailed marketing mix plans, operational budgets have to be established. These budgets include:

1. Sales forecasts (in monetary and unit terms)
2. Sales budget (all planned sales-related expenditures)
3. Sales quotas (in monetary and unit terms)
4. Production schedules
5. Inventory control (including the requirements for inventories, both in domestic and foreign warehouse locations)
6. Employee requirements (the hiring of all necessary personnel to achieve the objectives set earlier)
7. Promotional budgets (with all expenses for advertising, exhibitions, and sales material)
8. Financial budget (for the capital requirements to carry out the planned effort)
9. Profit budget (as the final criterion and measuring device of the export operation)

Under ideal situations, operational budgets might be prepared for a number of alternative plans, with the final selection depending on the profitability of each of the scenarios. In a world where the present situation is constantly subject to new developments, a plan or the export effort over a period of three to five years might appear unnecessary or unwise. But even under rapidly changing situations, executives cannot avoid making some assumptions about the future. The export plan will bring discipline and cohesion to the process. Once the assumptions originally made have had to be changed, modifications in the plan may have to be made as well. However, as with any planning process, the export plan forces the company to think about its future in an organized fashion.

GOVERNMENT EXPORT POLICIES AND LEGISLATION

There is no doubt that exports can greatly enhance the economy of any nation. Thus, governments frequently try to influence their country's export volume through legislation or direct government supports. To outline the export policies of all major countries would be too difficult. Consequently, this section will concentrate on the United States as the country of particular interest to most of our readers. Though the respective export policies of other countries may vary by specific objective or by approach, understanding the U.S. export policies will nevertheless give you some conceptual background for the understanding of the policies of all countries and an appreciation for the important role governments can play.

Organization of U.S. Export Policies

The execution of the U.S. government's export policies lies with the Department of Commerce, whereas negotiations and policy advisement to the president are the responsibilities of the Trade Representative, a cabinet position. Also part of the U.S. export policymaking is the Export-Import Bank, an independent agency whose activities were described in Chapter 18.

The U.S. Department of Commerce coordinates the activities of 162 commercial attachés in 65 countries.[6] Involved with U.S. embassies abroad, these attachés provide U.S. business with support at the local level. Also available are about 150 international trade specialists in 32 U.S. cities.[7] An important aspect of the Commerce Department's activities are trade promotion programs that include permanent overseas trade fairs and seminars on exporting for U.S. businesspersons in the United States. With a budget of several million dollars,

---

6. "The New Export Policy Works Like the Old—Badly," *Business Week*, July 21, 1980, p. 89.
7. *Ibid.*, p. 90.

the Department is now developing an Automated Information System that is expected to serve up to 50,000 subscribers in the United States.[8] The office of the U.S. Trade Representative (USTR) has major responsibility for both multilateral and bilateral trade negotiations that of course include exports. Under the USTR falls the negotiation of the GATT agreements, any international commodity agreements, and many of the negotiations that take place within international organizations.[9] To provide for some coordination between the USTR office and the Department of Commerce leading government officials participate in the Trade Policy Committee. In 1987, 36 states maintained offices abroad and programs at home to encourage export trade, particularly with smaller companies.[10]

In addition to federal government programs, many states have established organizations and agencies to assist U.S. companies in their exporting efforts. For example, C. M. Magnetics, a three-year-old company in Santa Fe Springs, California recently received a $2.7 million order from China. This order was the direct result of efforts by the state of California's World Trade Commission. "Without their help," company president J. Carlos Macrel said of the agency, "we probably wouldn't be in business today."[11]

Though the resources committed on behalf of U.S. exports may appear substantial, the $30.5 million spent on the export development program for fiscal 1981 is substantially less than the corresponding budget of the Japan External Trade Organization (JETRO). JETRO is endowed with a budget of $48 million and is able to maintain a staff of about 600 in Japan and another 650 persons overseas.[12] This discrepancy in budget is despite the fact that U.S. exports are almost twice the volume of Japan's exports. For many U.S. businesspersons, this difference in funding export programs is symbolic of a lack of interest on the part of many government officials and legislators who have accumulated a substantial amount of legislation that actually hinders U.S. exports. In the following section, we explore the various legislative and regulative disincentives that the United States and some other countries have accumulated.

Obstacles to U.S. Exports

The policies mentioned in this section are generally viewed as hindrances to commercial activity that ultimately affects domestic exports. Consequently, U.S. exports are below potential. These policies typically have been enacted by Congress to achieve other political goals such as environmental conservation.

---

8. *Ibid.*, p. 89.
9. "Service Exporters Spell Relief GATT," *Business Marketing,* January 1987, p. 58.
10. "Big Plans for Small Business: Firm Try to Boost Exports," *Insight,* July 13, 1987, p. 40.
11. "States Launch Efforts to Make Small Firms Better Exporters," *The Wall Street Journal,* February 2, 1987, p. 25.
12. "The New Export Policy Works Like the Old—Badly," p. 90.

The Foreign Corrupt Practices Act of 1977 was enacted as a result of published reports on corporate bribery of foreign nationals, initially triggered by the "United Brands Affair" in Honduras. The company reportedly paid funds to that country's president to get favorable tax treatment on banana exports. Subsequent investigations by the Securities and Exchange Commission (SEC) and the U.S. government found scores of other U.S. companies guilty of the same practices. The resulting "Act of 1977" places stringent restrictions on the type of payments that third party agents can receive. Consequently, some U.S. companies have the expense accounts of their foreign representatives certified by American consular officers. However, competitors from other major trading nations are not subject to such legislation, a fact that many U.S. businesspersons consider a disadvantage.

The U.S. government's tax policy for citizens living abroad is also considered a hindrance to the expansion of U.S. exports. In recent years, taxes on U.S. personnel abroad substantially increased the costs of U.S. MNCs' operations. Aside from their local taxes, U.S. citizens remain taxable in the United States on their worldwide income despite some local tax credit. In countries where the local taxes are substantially below U.S. rates, the citizen will have to pay the difference to the U.S. authorities, thus placing him or her at a disadvantage compared to other foreign nationals who do not have this extra burden. Thus, U.S. executives had lower take-home earnings than their foreign colleagues working for identical salaries. United States MNCs usually compensate their employees with additional salary adjustments, thus substantially raising company personnel costs. One U.S. company found that to provide an American employee in Saudi Arabia with a $40,000 salary (net) the company had to pay that employee about $140,000.[13] To keep up with foreign competitors, U.S. MNCs have hired fewer American employees and have replaced those who leave with foreign nationals to whom no such adjustments have to be paid.

With respect to this U.S. tax policy, changes have been voted by the U.S. Congress in 1981 that substantially increase the tax-free limit on earned income abroad. For 1982, this limit was set at $75,000 and by 1986 the amount of foreign earned income not subject to U.S. income tax was $80,000. However, the Tax Reform Act of 1986 reduced the tax-free limit on earned income to $70,000 for 1987. Although the new policy represents a substantial liberalization compared to the earlier policies, it still does not remove all restrictions from U.S. citizens abroad.

The policy instituted under the Carter Administration on nuclear power plant exports illustrates the effect of a political decision on foreign trade. The U.S. passed the Nuclear Non-Proliferation Act of 1978 requiring all governments that use enriched uranium from U.S. sources to obtain the U.S. government's permission in advance if the uranium is to be sent anywhere for reprocessing.[14]

---

13. *Ibid.*, p. 92.
14. "How Carter's Nuclear Policy Backfired Abroad," *Fortune,* October 23, 1978, p. 124.

The retroactive law applied to most of the twenty-six loyal and trusted foreign customers who would face a cutoff in supplies if this new feature was not approved by them.

The U.S. Nuclear Non-Proliferation Act was enacted to enhance existing controls administered by the International Atomic Energy Agency (IAEA) based in Vienna, Austria. An international nonproliferation treaty had been in effect since 1970 and was signed by over one hundred governments, including those who had purchased uranium under U.S. contracts. The act reflects the U.S. government's position that existing controls were not strict enough to prevent further proliferation of atomic weapons to nations that were on the verge of attaining such capabilities (Brazil, Argentina, Iran, Pakistan, and India among them).

Even before the enactment of the 1978 Act, U.S. export sales of nuclear reactors had been declining since 1974 due to a tremendous overbooking of orders.[15] In 1971, U.S. manufacturers supplied all eight foreign orders for nuclear reactors, but supplied only one of ten in 1976 and none of the seven ordered in 1977. Foreign orders went to suppliers in Germany, France, and other countries that did not insist on rules such as those of the U.S. government. The loss of foreign orders for such nuclear reactors was further influenced by the U.S. government's decision to stop the development of the breeder reactor that allowed for reprocessing of spent uranium and would reduce the world's demand for raw uranium. However, other foreign governments, such as the French government, have continued to develop this new breeder technology and consequently are at an advantage over U.S. companies such as Westinghouse or General Electric who must compete with the older and simpler design. With each nuclear installation worth nearly one billion dollars, the effect on U.S. exports must be considered substantial.

The U.S. government has also affected exports through politically motivated actions. Unilaterally, the United States has employed trade embargoes against Cuba, Vietnam, and the Soviet Union. Most of these actions were imposed by the U.S. government alone and were not followed by other nations, thus giving the clear advantage to foreign countries.

One of the most interesting examples of the effect of embargoes is seen in the trade relationship between the Soviet Union and the United States. Following the era of detente in the late 1960s and early 1970s, trade between the United States and the Soviet Union expanded considerably, as did trade between Europe and the Soviet Bloc and trade between the United States and the Soviet Union's allies, the Comecon countries. But the situation changed drastically with the Soviet invasion of Afghanistan in December of 1979. The U.S. government quickly imposed an embargo that covered both grain shipments and strategic shipments. Besides the embargo of 17 million tons of grain, restrictions were placed on the export of high-technology items over and above those that always

---

15. "Why the Nuclear Power Race Worries the U.S.," *Business Week,* August 23, 1976, pp. 68–69.

existed for military hardware.[16] Export licenses that had already been granted were suspended, which meant that U.S. companies could not ship products they had already contracted for. Some export license applications were denied, such as the one requested by Western Electric to supply $1 billion worth of telecommunications equipment and related technology to the Soviet Union.

The impact of the U.S. government's embargo on trade with the Soviet Union was severe.[17] United States agricultural exports declined from $2.9 billion in 1979 to $1.1 billion in 1980, and the total embargo was lifted in 1981. Nonagricultural exports suffered also. They declined from $750 million in 1979 to $360 million in 1980, depriving many United States–based companies of profitable business opportunities (see Figure 19.5) Many opportunities denied to U.S. corporations are grabbed up by foreign-based companies whose governments may not enforce the same regulations or embargoes.

Sometimes, regulations that prevent exports are pushed by special interest groups. Exports of U.S. lumber in the form of logs were severely hurt by a rule that prohibited exports of logs cut on U.S. government land in raw form. Congress prevented such sales to satisfy U.S. sawmill owners and their workers who saw too many logs shipped to Japan where they were cut to Japanese specifications that differed from those used in the United States. Since the majority of U.S. logs are cut on government land, each year several hundred million dollars worth of export sales were lost. The Japanese simply bought logs elsewhere rather than buying cut timber in the United States.[18]

Many business and political leaders have recognized the considerable negative effect of such rules for U.S. exports, and recent changes indicate a move towards fewer such restrictions. Occasionally, U.S. companies have diverted export orders to their foreign subsidiaries where such restrictions do not apply. In general, however, any company that depends on exports as a source of income is well-advised to carefully monitor government legislations and acts, both domestically and abroad, since the potential effect can be either to create new opportunities or to prevent the exploitation of existing ones.

IMPORT TRADE MECHANICS

In many ways, the importer is concerned with the same trade mechanics as the exporter. Communications with foreign suppliers can be difficult due to distances involved, time changes, and cultural differences. Import trade makes use of the same price quoting vocabulary as exporting does, and the payment mechanism is the same with respect to the use of letters of credit or open accounts.

---

16. "What Trade Sanctions Will Cost," *Business Week,* January 28, 1980, p. 34.
17. "Russian Trade—Credit Where It Is Due," *The Economist,* June 6, 1981, p. 78.
18. Lee Smith, "The Neglected Promise of Our Forests," *Fortune,* November 5, 1979, p. 112.

FIGURE 19.5 Primary Western Trading Partners of the Soviet Union

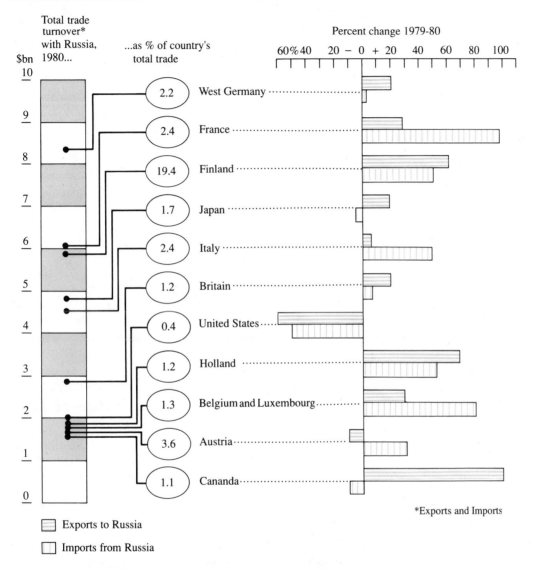

*Exports and Imports

☐ Exports to Russia

☐ Imports from Russia

Source: Data from the Office of Economic Cooperation and Development, as published in
"Russian Trade—Disenchanted but Trapped in a Marriage of Convenience," *The Economist,*
June 6, 1981, p. 75. © 1981 The Economist, distributed by Special Features. Reprinted by
permission.

Finally, the logistic concerns of the importer are identical to those of the exporter, so that many of the points covered in the earlier portion of this chapter need not be repeated.

A substantial amount of effort is expended by importers to bring products through local customs. Not surprisingly, import requirements vary by nation and are numerous. In this section, we concentrate solely on the major import procedures as they apply to the United States. However, these procedures are indicative of the type of procedures employed in other countries.

United States Import Clearance Procedures[19]

Upon reaching the United States, the recipient, or consignee, of the shipment will have to file an entry for the products or goods with U.S. Customs. The importer has the choice of filing for consumption or filing for storage. Under the second alternative, imported products may be stored for some time before they are officially entered for consumption in the United States, or they may be re-exported.

Since the proper declaration of imported products requires some specific knowledge, many importers use the services of licensed customs brokers. A broker is empowered by the firm to act on its behalf at the customs and file the necessary forms. To determine the customs status of a shipment, an examination is typically performed to check the following:

1. The value of the shipment to assess customs
2. The verification of required marking and labelling
3. Shipment of prohibited merchandise
4. Verification of invoicing and determination of either shortages or excess compared to the invoice

The importer will have to prepare all necessary forms to allow the U.S. Customs officials to make these determinations. Failure to meet these requirements may result in lengthy delays in clearing any shipment, unnecessary expenses on behalf of the importer, and higher fees charged by customs brokers.

1. *Valuation of Shipments.* U.S. Customs officers are required by law to find the value of the imported merchandise. Basically, customs value is determined by selecting the higher of either foreign value or export value. *Foreign value* is based upon the prices at which the imported merchandise is freely placed for sale in the country of origin in the usual wholesale quantities. The *export value* is the price at which the merchandise is freely offered

---

19. The section on import trade mechanics was written based upon a publication *Exporting to the United States* by the U.S. Customs Service, Department of the Treasury. Since these regulations are subject to frequent revisions, the interested reader is advised to obtain the latest information directly from the Customs Service.

for sale as an export to the United States in the major markets of the country of origin. When neither a foreign value nor export value can be found, the merchandise may be entered at the corresponding U.S. value at which such or similar merchandise is freely offered in the United States less the necessary allowance for bringing the products into the country. If a corresponding U.S. value does not exist, valuation can be based upon the cost of production. In a few cases, valuation can be based upon the U.S. selling price, which is based upon the typical price for the same product offered in the United States.

Products that are subject to duty are assessed either *ad valorem* (a percentage of the established value), with a *specific duty* (a specific amount per unit of measurement), or with a *compound duty* (combination of ad valorem and specific duty). Though the U.S. Customs Office publishes a list of the various duties by type of product, an importer can find out by contacting the U.S. Customs Office with the following information:

a. Complete description of the imported item
b. Method of manufacture
c. Specifications and analyses
d. Quantities and costs of component materials
e. Commercial designation of the product in the United States and identification of the primary use of the product

Given sufficient material as described above, the U.S. Customs Service can provide importers with a binding assessment on import duties that make it possible to assess the entire landed cost for the importer for later use in pricing. No binding information is available via telephone or based upon incomplete information.

2. *Marking and Labelling.* Unless otherwise stated, each product or article imported into the United States must be legibly marked in a conspicuous place with the name of the country of origin stated in English so that the U.S. purchaser can easily determine the country of origin. In some cases, markings may be made on the containers rather than the articles themselves. Importers are advised to obtain the particular regulations or exemptions from the U.S. Customs Service. In case of a lack of proper markings, the U.S. Customs Service can assess a special marking duty unless the imported products are marked under customs supervision. In either case, the lack or absence of the required markings can cause costly delays to the importer.

3. *Prohibited or Restricted Merchandise.* The importation of certain articles is either prohibited or restricted. It is impractical to list all the prohibited or restricted items. However, the major classes of items are shown in Table 19.1. Restricted items can be imported with proper clearance.

4. *Import Invoicing Procedures.* For some special categories of merchandise, only a commercial invoice prepared in the same manner typical for commer-

TABLE 19.1 Classes of Products That Are Prohibited or Restricted for Import into the United States

- Alcoholic Beverages: Require a permit from Bureau of Alcohol, Tobacco and Firearms
- Arms, Ammunition, Explosives: Require a permit from Bureau of Alcohol, Tobacco and Firearms
- Automobiles: Must conform to Federal Motor Vehicle Safety Standards
- Coins, Currencies and Stamps: No replicas of U.S. or foreign items permitted
- Eggs and Egg Products: Subject to the Egg Products Inspection Act
- Animals and Plants: Subject to regulations of the Animal or Plant Health Inspection Service
- Electronic Products: Subject to the Radiation Control Act
- Food, Drugs, Devices, Cosmetics: Subject to the federal Food, Drug and Cosmetics Act
- Narcotic Drugs: Prohibited
- Nuclear Reactors and Radioactive Material: Subject to the U.S. Atomic Energy Commission
- Obscene, Immoral, Seditious Matter: Prohibited
- Pesticides: Subject to the federal Environment Control Act
- Wool, Fur, Textiles and Fabric Products: Subject to the Wool Products Labeling Act, the Textile Fiber Products Identification Act, the Flammable Fabrics Act, and the Fur Products Labeling Act

cial transactions is sufficient for U.S. Customs clearance. Quite frequently, either a special invoice or a commercial invoice is not available at the time of entry. In such instances, the importer can prepare a pro forma invoice (see Figure 19.6) by promising to deliver final invoices within six months of the date of entry. Also, a bond must usually be posted to cover the value of the estimated duties.

Inaccurate information can cause costly delays to both the importer and exporter. To provide for smooth clearance through customs the U.S. importer should assume the responsibility of properly informing the foreign supplier. The Journal of Commerce, a private company, has a service called PIERS, which is a data base of all imports and exports reported to the U.S. Customs in the largest 47 U.S. ports. The data is helpful for competitive and market research analysis.

The Role of the Customs Agent

Since the handling of shipments through customs requires specialized knowledge, most companies employ outside specialized firms that are registered with U.S. Customs. These agents will not only prepare the necessary invoices from

FIGURE 19.6 Pro Forma Invoice

PRO FORMA INVOICE

Importers Statement of Value or the Price Paid in the Form of an Invoice (Sec. 484(b), Tariff Act of 1930)

Not being in possession of a customs or commercial sellers or shippers invoice I request that you accept under authority of section 484(b), Tariff Act of 1930, the statement of value or the price paid in the form of an invoice submitted below.

Name of shipper................ address............   Name of consignee.............. address............
Name of seller.................. address............   Name of purchaser.............. address............

The merchandise (has) (has not) been purchased or agreed to be purchased by me. The prices, or in the case of consigned goods the values, given below are true and correct to the best of my knowledge and belief, and are based upon (check basis with an "X"):

(*a*) The prices paid or agreed to be paid ( ) as per order dated...............
(*b*) Advices from exporter by letter ( ) by cable ( ) dated...........................
(*c*) Comparative values of shipments previously received ( ) dated...........................

(*d*) Knowledge of the market in the country of exportation ( )
(*e*) Knowledge of the market in the United States (if U.S. value) ( )
(*f*) Information as to value obtained from U.S. Customs pursuant section 14.4, CR. ( )

Check which of the charges below are, and which are not included in the prices listed in columns "D" and "E":

	Amount	Included	Not included		Amount	Included	Not included
Packing....................	......	......	......	Lighterage..............	......	......	......
Cartage....................	......	......	......	Ocean freight..........	......	......	......
Inland freight.............	......	......	......	U.S. duties............	......	......	......
Wharfage and loading abroad....................	......	......	......	Total..............			

A	B	C	D	E	F	G
Case marks numbers	Manufacturer's item number symbol or brand	Quantities and full description	Unit purchase price in .... currency	Total purchase price currency	Unit foreign value in	Total foreign value
....						
....						
....						

Country of origin

IF ANY OTHER INVOICE IS RECEIVED, I WILL IMMEDIATELY FILE IT WITH THE DISTRICT OR PORT DIRECTOR OF CUSTOMS.

Signature of person making invoice........................

Title and firm name........................

Date.................

Source: Reprinted by permission of the United States Customs Service.

information supplied by the importer, but they will also arrange for clearance through customs, inspection where necessary, payment of duties, and transport to the final destination. Frequently, such customs agents are also international freight forwarders, or freight forwarding firms with a specialized customs section. To allow the customs agent to act on behalf of the importer, a special power of attorney is granted that then identifies the customs agent as a legally empowered actor.

Free Trade Zones or Foreign Trade Zones

Within the United States and elsewhere in the world, zones have been established where merchandise can be placed for unlimited time periods without the payment of duties. Duty will be assessed, however, as soon as the merchandise is transferred from the free trade zone.

Such zones offer many advantages to both exporters or importers. For one, duty payable can tie up a substantial amount of working capital. The use of a free trade zone allows a firm to keep an inventory close by without prepaying duty. In addition, many importers may later want to re-export products to other countries and would thus prefer to temporarily store the merchandise in a place where no duties have to be paid until the final destination is determined.

Free trade zones are also valuable as manufacturing sites. Any merchandise brought into such zones may be broken up, repackaged, assembled, sorted, graded, cleaned, or used in the manufacturing process with domestic material. The latter can be brought duty free into trade zones and reimported, again duty free, into the United States. Duty will only have to be paid on components or parts subject to duty, rather than on the entire value.

Free trade zones exist in most countries and are typically attached to ports or airports. In some countries with low labor costs, free trade zones were established to allow for the further processing of semimanufactured goods originating from developed countries. These goods are later re-exported into the country of origin. Malaysia is one country that has allowed many foreign electronics companies to bring components for further assembly to Malaysian foreign trade zones. As a result, the foreign trade zones have ceased as a strictly distribution- or transportation-related phenomenon and are now incorporated by many MNCs in their production or sourcing strategy.

Obstacles to Foreign Imports

Recently, there has been extensive political debate over protectionist measures for certain key U.S. industries. The trade law known as the "escape clause" authorizes the president to file a protecting grant for any industry that can prove that it is being hurt by imports.[20] The law dates back to the New Deal and FDR.

Nowhere have imports made a bigger impression than in the steel industry. In 1983, the United States imported roughly 20 percent of all our steel needs. United States companies claim that the steel is being "dumped" in our country at artificially low costs. Domestic companies blame foreign government subsi-

---

20. Clyde H. Farnsworth, "Industry's New Assault on Imports," *The New York Times,* January 27, 1984, p. D1.

dies for the low import cost. Hence, the steel workers and their companies are pushing government to protect U.S. markets against unreasonable foreign competition.

Yet, consumers are the main beneficiaries of these imports. They are able to purchase quality at low cost. In addition, there are countless numbers of jobs involved with trade firms in imports. A recent estimate states that 194,000 jobs are related to auto imports alone.[21] Quotas have been the recent political answer to the conflict. However, a 15 percent import quota on steel is estimated to have the effect of raising consumer prices over 20 percent.[22] The conflict boils down to lower prices versus jobs.

Japanese Import Barriers

Alternatively, the Japanese have been criticized for not allowing enough imports into their country. The United States is a leader in the fight to ease barriers that prevent U.S. goods from entering Japan. Japan's trade surplus has averaged 30 billion dollars.[23] Many foreign countries insist that trade is a two-way street. Countries can't expect to export unless they allow free and easy access to imports. Although the Japanese have been criticized for unfair trade practices, a recent survey indicated that 70 percent of Japanese consumers do not discriminate against imports.[24]

Japan has, recently, greatly simplified import procedures under a four-point plan.

1. Establishment or changes of specifications or standards with the aim of conforming to foreign standards.
2. The nature and aim of such establishment or changes will be made public in advance.
3. The views of those affected both at home and abroad will be sought. Efforts will be made to reflect these views in improving procedures as soon as possible.
4. Foreign inspection standards will be recognized as soon as possible and domestic inspection simplified.

These four points are hoped to increase harmony among trading nations. How-

---

21. "Imports, Often Blamed for Killing U.S. Jobs, Create New Ones Too," *The Wall Street Journal,* February 29, 1984, p. 1.

22. "Jobless Rate Off Despite Slowing of the Economy," *The Wall Street Journal,* February 6, 1984, p. 5.

23. "Japan—Headaches in the Labyrinth," *Financial Times,* September 19, 1983, Special Section—Japan, p. I.

24. "New Emphasis on Import Promotion," *Financial Times,* September 19, 1983, Special Section—Japan, p. VI.

ever, if trade figures do not improve, one can predict more negotiations in the future.[25]

CONCLUSIONS

This chapter has dealt with some of the procedural aspects of international marketing. Thorough knowledge of these trade mechanics is often a prerequisite for international marketers. All too frequently, an international strategy fails because some of these mechanics have been neglected.

You should be aware, however, that this text could not and did not specify all the regulations in force for any particular product category or country. We have provided a general background, listing the factors that might have to be investigated before a strategy can be implemented. The regulations described are also subject to change. Consequently, we suggest that close contact with specialists in this area be maintained so that executives responsible for international marketing activities can be kept abreast of new developments.

Questions for Discussion

1. Your company manufactures telephones at your plant in Scranton, Pennsylvania. South Korea would like a quote on 10,000 telephones. How should you quote so that it is convenient for the buyer?
2. Irrevocable letters of credit have become very popular. How do they protect the buyer and the seller?
3. When calculating the cost of a shipment of machinery for export, what additional costs will the exporter be faced with in addition to shipping and insurance?
4. Explain the possible uses of export documentation on a shipment of pipe from Los Angeles to Bolivia?
5. What are the critical elements of the export planning process? If you were asked to develop a plan for exporting gloves to South America, how would you do it?
6. What are the advantages and disadvantages of import limits in the United States; for example, the import quotas on Japanese automobiles into the United States?
7. How can free trade zones be used by U.S. manufacturers?

25. *Japanese Economic Journal,* June 26, 1979.

For Further Reading

Attiyeh, Robert S., and David L. Wenner. "Critical Mass: Key to Exports." *Business Horizons* (December, 1979), pp. 28–38.

Ayal, Igal. "Industry Export Performance: Assessment and Prediction." *Journal of Marketing* (Summer 1982), pp. 54–61.

Brasch, J. "Using Export Specialists to Develop Overseas Sales." *Harvard Business Review* (May–June), pp. 6–8.

Fitzpatrick, Peter B., and Alan S. Zimmerman. *Essentials of Export Marketing.* New York: American Management Association, 1985.

Fox, Harold W. "Export Pricing Entails Extra Planning." *Managerial Planning* (July–August 1973), pp. 26–28.

"Export Activity in Developing Nations," *Journals of International Business Studies* (Spring–Summer 1978), pp. 95–102.

Mandato, Joseph, Thomas J. Skola, and Kenneth L. Wyne. "Counterpurchase Sales in the German Democratic Republic." *Columbia Journal of World Business* (Spring 1978), pp. 82–89.

McGuinness, Norman W., and Blair Little. "The Influence of Product Characteristics on the Export Performance of New Industrial Products." 45. No. 2 (Spring 1981), pp. 110–122.

Rabino, Samuel. *Journal of Marketing,* "Tax Incentives to Export: Some Implications for Policy Makers." *Journal of International Business Studies* (Spring–Summer 1980), pp. 74–85.

Root, Franklin R. *Entry Strategies for International Markets* Lexington, Mass.: D. C. Heath, 1987.

Weiss, Kenneth D. *Building an Import-Export Business.* New York: John Wiley & Sons, 1987.

Yorio V., *Adapting Products for Export.* New York: The Conference Board, 1983.

CASES

CASE 1 ▪ Medical Equipment Company*

In 1981, Medical Equipment Comany (MEC) faced a perplexing problem in its Latin American markets. Sales for its blood gas and electrolyte product lines in four countries typical of the Latin American market, Brazil, Argentina, Venezuela, and the Dominican Republic, were subject to substantial annual fluctuations. As an example, sales were increasing as much as 100% in one year in Argentina (1979–80) while sales in Venezuela consistently moved in the opposite direction from the previous year's sales (see Exhibit 1). The marketing department was very concerned with these fluctuations and inconsistencies and sought to find reasons to explain the behavior of these markets. The regional management also wondered whether the markets were of sufficient interest, or whether they should be abandoned. What they could expect from these markets in the future was of particular interest to management.

COMPANY HISTORY

Medical Equipment, whose headquarters were located in the Greater Boston area, was a company manufacturing 60 different instruments marketed through four different divisions. Each major product line was organized around a particular division, namely the Biomedical Division, the Analytical Instruments Division, the

Micro Chemical Division, and the Sensorlab Division. The company's most recognized line was the blood gas line of the Biomedical Division.

The Biomedical Division included electrolyte, blood gas and chemistry analyzers for laboratory medicine, as well as parts, reagents and other expendables for these instruments. The electrolyte product line consisted of flame photometers which were among the most widely used instruments throughout clinical medicine. By measuring sodium and potassium, two elements vital to health, they provided valuable diagnostic information. Also measured were lithium levels which were important for the treatment of manic depressive patients (see Exhibit 2). The blood gas line included blood gas analyzers which measured blood parameters that were useful in critical care medicine and for the treatment of pulmonary diseases. MEC was one of the world's leading producers of blood gas analyzers, the company's first and original product line (see Exhibit 3).

The Micro Chemical Division manufactured a special instrument which was one of the most flexible chemistry analyzers on the market. It could be used in a hospital room or a doctor's office and could be operated by both paraprofessionals and highly skilled professionals. A cassette-programmable minicomputer made it possible to perform 120-350 tests per hour. Its disposable test motors and low reagents requirements helped hospitals combat rising costs.

The Analytical Instrument Division designed and manufactured atomic absorption

---

* Names and some facts are disguised.

This case was prepared by Visiting Professor Jean-Pierre Jeannet as a basis for class discussion rather than to illustrate either effective or ineffective handling of an administrative situation. Copyright 1981 by IMEDE (International Management Development Institute), Lausanne, Switzerland. Reproduced by permission.

609

EXHIBIT 1 Total MEC Exports of Electrolyte and Blood Gas Product Lines

	1980	1979	1978	1977	1976
Argentina	$ 208,833	$ 91,812	$ 16,530	$ 3,448	$ 6,861
Dom. Rep.	65,060	16,142	9,324	12,367	17,892
Brazil	255,099	131,400	175,527	297,657	205,213
Venezuela	98,478	243,367	197,628	473,293	137,254
Total*	$2,675,000	$2,280,000	$1,372,000		

* Export sales from U.S. to unaffiliated customers.

EXHIBIT 2 Spectrophotometers

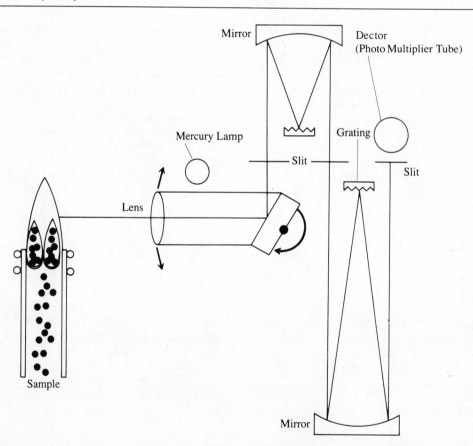

The optical system of this instrument had an innovative design which incorporated a double mono-chromator system to minimize errors due to stray light. Also included was an automatic wavelength-scanning system, internally calibrated mercury source, to ensure accurate wavelength selection.

EXHIBIT 3 Blood Gas Analyzer

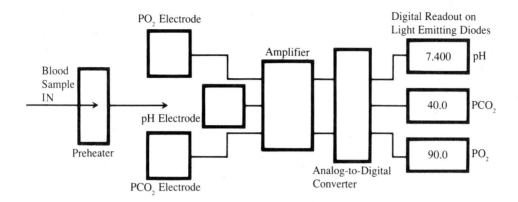

The blood gas analyzer heated blood samples up to body temperature. At this point an electrical charge built up and the electrodes were activated to measure the pH unit, carbon dioxide tension, and oxygen tension. This happened as blood gases transferred across the membrane.

spectrophotometers and inductively coupled plasma emission spectrophotometers. These instruments were used extensively to monitor the purity of water supplies. They were of great value to industries where parts-per-billion purity of materials, finished products and effluent were critical.

The Sensorlab Division technologies were also of great value to critical care medicine, as well as of use in food, beverage and drug processing industries. Among the instruments in this division, the MEC 501 System measured cardiac output and pulmonary artery pressure; the 200 CDE Monitor measured carbon dioxide; and the MEC 300 measured oxygen delivered during anesthesia. The industrial products group included, among others, instruments to monitor the beer brewing process or the fermentation process in cheese manufacturing.

INTERNATIONAL SALES

MEC's international sales accounted for some 40% of total 1980 sales of 99.1 million dollars, i.e., 39.6 million dollars. This represented an increase of 2% over the 38% of total 1979 sales figures (see Exhibits 4 and 5 for financial data). Sales growth in Latin America and Mexico was attributed to products in the biomedical line, specifically blood gas analyzers and flame photometers. The two were considered to meet basic needs of health care facilities which were being upgraded to include sophisticated diagnostic instrumentation where none had existed before. In Mexico the increase was significant for all products, however, including those of the Analytical Instruments and Sensorlab Division.

MEC's international markets, besides Europe and Latin America, included Canada, Asia, Australia/New Zealand, the Middle East, Africa, and the People's Republic of China since 1980. MEC's International Division was comprised of two separate areas. Latin America, Asia Pacific and Canadian operations were managed through an area headquarters located in MEC's home office (see Exhibit 6 for an organization chart). MEC's international operations had just been reorganized toward the end of 1980. Its markets in Canada, Central and South America were now being served by an area division separate from the one in Europe. MEC ex-

EXHIBIT 4 Price List

Model	Domestic Retail	International Retail*
Blood Gas 570	U.S.$ 9,900	10,395
Blood Gas 670	15,200	15,960
Electrolyte 290	6,700	7,035
390	4,900	5,145
590	9,500	9,975

* International prices were net 5% higher than domestic.

pected continuing growth in the upcoming years although they realized that oil-importing countries had to restrict their purchases somewhat. Still, the fact that health care remained a high priority for all of these countries was recognized by their political leaders.

DOMESTIC MARKETING POLICIES

In the U.S. market, MEC granted exclusive distribution rights to Scientific Products, a division of American Hospital Supply Corporation. MEC still had its own sales force organized geographically with specific salesmen reporting to their respective area managers, who in turn reported to the National Sales Manager. Also reporting to the Sales Managers were three Government/National Account Managers. The Area Technical Directors were included in another group which formed a part of the sales force.

The entire direct sales force constituted a personnel of 65 and covered 30 sales territories. Besides the traditional duties attached to most sales positions, MEC's sales force was expected to coordinate dealer activities. Depending on the territory, each MEC representative worked with approximately 8–10 Scientific Product representatives. Their efficiency in communicating with their respective dealers helped them reach their individual sales quotas. The Area Technical Directors did not have direct sales responsibilities but provided customers with services through

consulting about their problems and rendering technical assistance.

MEC's various divisions utilized "education" as a marketing tool. For its major customers the Biomedical Division held three-day training seminars in applications, operations, routine maintenance and trouble shooting. In the past year about 600 laboratory professionals attended these seminars. Biomedical also provided Continu-ED audiovisual programs which were used to teach the theory and practice of clinical analysis in laboratories in the schools where technologists were being trained. The Analtyical Instruments Division also held regular training sessions in its field laboratories. The division sponsored one-day seminars for chemists in major cities around the country. Over 5,000 current and potential users of spectrophotometers attended these seminars during the past year. Sensorlab conducted critical care symposia for respiratory therapists, anesthesiologists, cardio-pulmonary technicians and critical care nurses throughout the United States. These symposia included lectures and discussions on the theory and operation of the equipment as used to monitor the critically ill, plus hands-on demonstration of equipment.

LATIN AMERICAN OPERATIONS

In three of the four Latin American countries in question, i.e., Argentina, Venezuela, and the Dominican Republic, MEC marketed its products through independent agents. Only in Brazil did MEC have its own sales force. The agents in the other three countries underwent the same educational process given in the seminars and symposia to domestic clients. The end users in these countries were therefore not given this information and instruction by MEC personnel but by the respective sales agents. (See Exhibits 7 to 17 for some background data on the Latin American market.)

The independent agents also carried the products of MEC's competitors, as MEC didn't have the same exclusive distribution system that they employed domestically. MEC, a leader in blood gas instruments, had the same competition internationally as domestically. This consisted of Beckman Instruments in California, Technicon Instruments of New York; Corning, Instrumentation Laboratories, Nova, Radiometer, and MCA, all located in the greater Boston area. While no data on market share was available, it was recognized that MEC was among the leaders in the blood gas analyzer line domestically and internationally. On an international level the extent of leadership might vary from country to country, however.

Although MEC could not identify who actually made the final decision in the purchasing process, it was believed to occur in a "ladder" type form. Initially, a group of laboratory managers would evaluate the product and then send their recommendations up to higher level management and eventually perhaps to a hospital administrator. How much influence any one group had, or who actually made the purchase decision, was unknown to MEC.

THE ARGENTINIAN MARKET

Argentina was a country with about 27 million people, growing at a rate of 2.9 percent. One third of the population lived in or around Buenos Aires, the nation's capital, and 72 percent lived in urban areas.

Argentina had been a republic since 1816. The Constitution of 1853, largely patterned after the U.S. model, remained in force for most of the time, though subject to alterations depending on the political situation. The country experienced its first military coup in 1930. A second coup by the military prepared the way for General Peron who assumed power in 1946. Assisted by his immensely popular wife, Evita, Peron formed a coalition of workers and the urban poor. He attempted to develop a modern welfare state and pursued extremely nationalistic policies. Overthrown in 1955, he went into exile in Spain but continued to play an important politi-

EXHIBIT 5 MEC Consolidated Statement of Income for the Years Ended March 31, 1980 and 1979 Medical Equipment Company and Subsidiaries

	1980	1979
NET SALES	$ 99,082,000	$ 87,866,000
COST AND EXPENSES:		
Cost of sales	50,311,000	45,112,000
Research and development	9,910,000	7,856,000
Marketing	21,305,000	16,718,000
General and Administrative	8,713,000	6,677,000
	90,239,000	76,363,000
INCOME FROM OPERATIONS	8,843,000	11,503,000
OTHER INCOME (EXPENSE):		
Interest	(2,450,000)	(1,501,000)
Foreign exchange adjustments	272,000	119,000
Other, net	(90,000)	(34,000)
	(2,268,000)	(1,416,000)
INCOME BEFORE PROVISION FOR INCOME TAXES	6,575,000	10,087,000
PROVISION FOR INCOME TAXES (note 2)	2,478,000	4,577,000
NET INCOME	4,097,000	5,510,000
EARNINGS PER SHARE	$ 1.39	$ 1.87

EXHIBIT 5 (cont.) MEC Consolidated Balance Sheet for March 31, 1980 and 1979 Medical Equipment Company and Subsidiaries

ASSETS	1980	1979
CURRENT ASSETS:		
Cash, including time deposits of $350,000 in 1980	$ 2,059,000	$ 1,009,000
Accounts receivable, less allowances of $315,000 in 1980 and $189,000 in 1979	24,002,000	20,997,000
Inventories:		
Finished goods	8,499,000	8,425,000
Work-in-Process	4,854,000	5,003,000
Raw materials	9,389,000	7,595,000
	22,742,000	21,023,000
Prepaid expenses and other	1,395,000	1,004,000
Total current assets	50,198,000	44,033,000
PROPERTY, PLANT AND EQUIPMENT		
Land	1,780,000	758,000
Buildings and leasehold improvements	10,333,000	4,598,000
Laboratory and manufacturing equipment	11,640,000	9,902,000
Office and other equipment	2,082,000	1,856,000
	25,835,000	17,114,000
Less – Accumulated depreciation and amortization	8,880,000	7,123,000
	16,955,000	9,991,000
Construction in progress	2,152,000	2,102,000
Property under capital leases, less accumulated amortization	2,100,000	2,176,000
OTHER ASSETS	1,072,000	929,000
	$72,477,000	$59,231,000

cal role from abroad. In 1966, the military again overthrew the civilian administration and ruled for seven years. In 1973, Dr. Campora, a member of the Peronist party, won the elections, only to resign 3 months later to allow for another election won by General Peron as President and his second wife, Maria, as Vice-President (Evita Peron had died in 1952). When General Peron died in 1974 he was succeeded by Maria who 'd not control the increasing urban unrest and terrorism originally emanating from the Montenero guerilla group but later practiced by other political groups as well. In 1976, Maria Peron was overthrown by the armed forces under General Videla who was named President.

The Argentinian military continued to rule the country, and in October of 1980 General Viola was named successor to President Videla to assume power in spring of 1981. The military had made several important changes in the Constitution of 1853. Most power was centered in the hand of the Junta consisting of the leaders of the army, air force, and navy. It was this Junta that named the president, usually for three

EXHIBIT 5 (cont.) MEC Consolidated Balance Sheet for March 31, 1980 and 1979 Medical Equipment Company and Subsidiaries

LIABILITIES AND STOCKHOLDERS' INVESTMENT	1980	1979
CURRENT LIABILITIES:		
Notes payable to banks	$ 6,141,000	$ 8,085,000
Current maturities of long-term debt	523,000	487,000
Accounts payable	7,108,000	6,228,000
Accrued expenses	7,967,000	6,292,000
Accrued Federal and foreign income taxes	2,219,000	1,906,000
Total current liabilities	23,958,000	22,998,000
DEFERRED FEDERAL AND FOREIGN INCOME TAXES	2,239,000	1,654,000
LONG-TERM DEBT		
Notes payable to insurance companies	8,000,000	—
Bank term loan	7,000,000	7,000,000
Obligations under capital leases, less current maturities	2,112,000	2,208,000
Other	319,000	382,000
	17,431,000	9,590,000
COMMITMENTS AND CONTINGENCY		
STOCKHOLDERS' INVESTMENT		
Common Stock, $1 per value:		
Authorized 8,000,000 shares:		
Outstanding 2,926,888 shares in 1980 and 2,897,856 shares in 1979	2,927,000	2,898,000
Capital in excess of par value	6,230,000	6,030,000
Retained earnings	19,692,000	16,061,000
	28,849,000	24,989,000
	$72,477,000	$59,231,000

years, who must be a retired military officer. At the present time, a return to civilian rules was not planned.

The Argentinian economy was traditionally based upon agriculture with livestock and grains accounting for the majority of its output. In 1979, agriculture accounted for 12 percent of GNP and represented the largest export item.

At the time of Maria Peron's overthrow in 1976, the economic scene was rapidly deteriorating. Production was declining, inflation was accelerating rapidly, and Argentina was facing a moratorium on its foreign debt. Under the leadership of the Minister of the Economy, Martinez de Hoz, the government attempted to get to the root of these problems. In place of the Peronist populist programs designed to redistribute income and expand state activities, the government sought to establish more of a free market economy. The government emphasized an export-oriented growth strategy built around an improved agricultural sector. Major objectives were the reduction of the chronic fiscal deficit, rationalization of all public sector activities,

EXHIBIT 6 MEC International Division

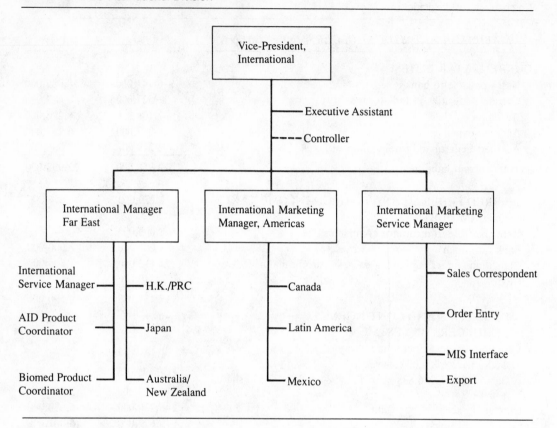

monetary discipline, and the expansion of domestic and foreign private investment.

The peso was initially devalued in March of 1976 to 140 per one U.S. dollar, down from 109 previously, in an attempt to achieve these objectives. In May, further devaluations were announced. Now, exports could be financed with 65% of currency through the "official" market rate of 140 per U.S. dollar and 35% through the "free market" rate of 245–250 pesos per U.S. dollar. Free market pesos could be obtained outside the channels provided by the Central Bank of Argentina. A further devaluation occurred in July when 69% of exports could be financed in the "free market" and 31% in the "official" market. By November of 1976 the financing was set at 85% at the free rate and 15% official. Al-

though GNP declined 3% in 1976, economic indicators at the end of the year were showing an upward trend. Despite the recession the government managed to keep unemployment at relatively low levels, but at the cost of keeping wages low. The government reduced its budget deficit from 12.8% of GNP in 1975 to 7.8% in 1976. The Central Bank's reserves had increased by December of 1976 to 2.2 billion dollars, the highest level in Argentina's history. In 1976 Argentina's balance of trade showed a surplus of about $800 million. Inflation decelerated considerably in the second half of 1976 with an announced goal for 1977 to keep the rate of inflation below 100%.

By 1978, the rate of inflation was still at 170 percent, still not better than 1977's 160 percent

EXHIBIT 7 Population (in millions)

	1975	1976	1977	1978	1979	1980
Argentina	25.38	25.72	26.06	26.39	26.73	27.1
Brazil	106.23	109.18	112.24	115.4	118.65	119.0
Dom. Rep.	4.7	4.84	4.98	5.12	5.28	5.3
Venezuela	11.99	12.36	12.74	12.98	13.12	13.52

rate. The budget deficit in 1978 could be financed for the first time without printing money, a common practice under earlier regimes.

In an effort to reduce inflation the government reduced some tariff barriers and thus hoped to cut the sizeable trade surpluses. Because authorities maintained a managed exchange rate, and determined in advance the dollar-peso exchange rate, the country suffered from an excess of dollars caused by the resulting surplus in the current account and government borrowing. Thus, the government decided to encourage imports in an effort to reduce the money supply. By early 1980 the Argentinian economic policy displayed strong liberal and classical tendencies. Price controls, interest rate ceilings, foreign exchange controls, credit controls, rent controls, state monopoly on exports, and import quotas had all been abolished. By now, real growth, fixed investments, and exports were rising at a healthy rate. Inflation was down to 45% from 900% just four years earlier. Whereas in earlier times the government had printed money to pay for its expenses, 80% of expenditures were now met by government revenues. Tax collections used to be a problem as people would delay payments in an attempt to pay in devalued pesos. By 1980, the peso's value was thought to be restored. The flight from real currency was no longer a necessity. Contrary to economic theories and the Phillips curve principle, unemployment had fallen together with the rate of inflation.

By the end of 1980 the liberal economic policies had come under fire. The number of bankruptcies of small businesses and the failure of the banks that had financed them had risen dramatically. Businessmen accused the government of setting the value of the peso at an artificially high level, making life easy for importers

EXHIBIT 8 Gross National Product (billion US $) and GNP Per Capita (in US $)

	1975	1976	1977	1978
Argentina	44.257	42.972	44.788	42.939
(per capita)			(1,719)	(1,627)
Brazil	108.007	117.690	123.178	130.568
			(1,088)	(1,122)
Dom. Rep.	3.354	3.570	3.728	3.862
			(749)	(753)
Venezuela	22.826	24.603	26.277	27.985
			(2,063)	(2,127)

EXHIBIT 9 Growth Rates of GNP and GNP Per Capita

	1975	1976	1977	1978
Argentina	−1.3	−3.0	4.4	−4.1
(per capita)	(−2.6)	(−4.2)	(3.0)	(−5.3)
Brazil	5.7	9.2	4.7	5.9
	(2.7)	(6.1)	(1.8)	(3.1)
Dom. Rep.	5.0	5.9	3.3	3.6
	(1.6)	(2.4)	(− .1)	(.5)
Venezuela	5.2	7.4	8.1	6.5
	(1.7)	(3.9)	(4.6)	(3.1)

and causing great difficulties for domestic industries. In addition, considerable lines of short term subsidized credits to affected businesses were cut off by the government. In 1981, Martinez de Hoz admitted that his program had fallen short of expectations. Government expenses were viewed to be at the root of the problem as huge deficits still continued to exist. It was admitted that the exchange rate had been deliberately set to favor the importers.

With a new regime under General Viola to take power in March of 1981, a new economic team was appointed under the leadership of a new Minister of the Economy, Mr. Sigaut. It was believed that Mr. Sigaut would most likely take the "Japanese" approach which would include an all-out drive to promote exports, with subsidies, tariff barriers, and multi-tiered exchange rates likely to return. This would represent a return to the practices of the past. Many critics complained such a course should not be adopted, lest they ended up in the economic nightmare they had experienced in the past.

THE BRAZILIAN MARKET

In terms of land area, Brazil was the fifth largest nation of the world and had an estimated population of about 118 million. There had been a growing trend towards urbanization with over 50 percent of the population currently living in urban areas.

Politically, the country had long been dominated by military leaders who last staged a coup in 1964 and had remained in power ever since. According to the present constitution, promulgated in 1967, Brazil was organized as a federal republic with broad powers granted to the federal government. At the national level, the constitution established a presidential system with three "independent and harmonious powers"— the executive, the legislative and the judicial. The president was elected for a six year term by an electoral college composed of members of the congress and representatives of state legislatures and municipalities.

Despite the superficial similarities between the governments of Brazil and the U.S., the Brazilian president played a more prominent role in national affairs than did his U.S. counterpart. For example, the constitution gave the president the power to intervene in individual states and municipalities if he determined that conditions warranted such action. He could also issue decrees in matters concerning national security and public finance. In 1968, the president was given expanded powers, including the power to declare a state of siege for an unlimited time. He could also suspend the writ of habeas corpus in cases involving national security and was empowered to restrict traditional civil liberties. Furthermore, all actions carried out under this special authority were removed from judicial review. In April of 1979 these powers were exercised when then President Geisel closed the na-

EXHIBIT 10 Exchange Rates (Local Currency per U.S. Dollar)

	1976	1977	1978	1979
Argentina				
(end of period	274.5	597.5	1,003.5	1,618.5
period average)	140	407.6	795.8	1,317.0
(pesos/$)				
Brazil	12.345	16.050	20.920	42.530
(cruz./$)	10.675	14.144	18.070	26.955
Dom. Rep.	1.0000			→
(peso/$)				
Venezuela	4,2925			→
(bolivars/$)	4,2899	4.2925		→

tional congress and the country returned to a virtual dictatorship. This threatened the existence of civilian political participation in the government. This occurred because the opposition party in congress gained enough seats to block Geisel's control over the judicial system. Geisel had not anticipated that the "token" opposition would exercise their power in this manner. As a result, he took these actions to appease hard liners in the military who weren't keen about the recent liberalization policy.

General Baptista Figueiredo became President in 1979, winning in the electoral college by a vote of 355–266 over the opposition party candidate. Figueiredo had been hand picked to represent the ruling party of a group of military officers. He promised to continue the political opening process, allowing students the right to demonstrate and also granting their right to strike.

As a result of the military inspired revolution, the Brazilian government had focused on the following economic policy objectives: (1) maintenance of a high rate of growth, (2) control of inflation, and (3) gradual improvement of the welfare system. The years 1968–1973 were excellent ones for the Brazilian economy with the growth rate averaging 10% annually. In 1973, President Geisel announced a plan to equal the growth rates of these earlier years for the period 1975–1979. Investments in basic industries, sciences and technology, as well as economic infrastructure during the five-year plan were projected at about $100 billion. The priority industries in the plan included steel, fertilizer, non-metallic minerals, petrochemicals, paper and cellulose, pharmaceuticals, and all types of capital goods. A major reason why the economy was in need of adjustments stemmed from the pressure that the price of petroleum created on the balance of payments due to Brazil's position as a heavy oil importer. Underlining the nation's need to earn more foreign exchange, the government promoted a rapid growth of exports. Renewed efforts were made at strengthening domestic industries with special emphasis on import substitution, both as a means of conserving foreign exchange and as a step towards developing a modern industrial society.

EXHIBIT 11 Balance of Payments (in million US$)

	1975	1976	1977
Argentina	−679	121	2,479
Brazil	−964	2,312	460
Dom. Rep.	28	−11	57
Venezuela	2,711	69	−79

EXHIBIT 12 Inhabitants Per Physician

Argentina	450 (1973)
Brazil	2,025 (1972)
Dom. Rep.	1,866 (1973)
Venezuela	921 (1976)

Brazil's very recent international financial policy had also been aimed at its very large and increasing foreign debt. Brazil had been following a policy of frequently adjusting its exchange rates by small percentages to reconcile its own inflation rate with that of its major trading partners, which allowed it to maintain its international competitiveness.

Late in 1979, however, President Figueiredo saw the need for change as inflation rapidly approached 80% compared to 1977's rate of 30% or 1976's rate of 46%. Thus, he devalued the Cruzeiro 30%, departing from the system of mini-devaluations to prevent serious financial disruptions. He also weaned the private sector from over-generous subsidies and controls and ended export subsidies. Domestic concerns also lost import protection when the "law of similarity" was repealed which required that a domestically produced product be purchased over an imported one if the two products were similar. These actions, in essence, called for a gradual return to a free market economy.

Late 1980 saw another shift in emphasis as the Brazilian government tried to come to grips with 113% inflation and the deficit in its international payments account. The plan called for a more restrictive monetary policy with extremely heavy support for exports and priority treatment for agricultural developments. The goal was an inflation rate of 70% and to boost exports from 20 to 25 billion dollars. Domestic credit and the monetary base were supposed to increase by 50% in 1981.

Although Planning Minister Delfim had been criticized for abandoning the more classical economic approach in solving Brazil's problems, he viewed Brazil's case as unique because the young people in Brazil accounted for a very large percentage of its population. Substantial unemployment and underemployment existed in Brazil and trying to fight inflation and other problems with the classic tools of fiscal and monetary controls could provoke a recession, Delfim argued. This would be very detrimental to Brazil because of its low income levels and general impoverishment.

THE MARKET OF THE DOMINICAN REPUBLIC

The Dominican Republic was located on the eastern part of the island of Hispaniola which lay between Cuba and Puerto Rico. The western part of the island was occupied by the State of Haiti. About 70 percent of the country's population of 5.2 million lived in rural areas. The annual population growth rate was about 3 percent.

After a long period of control under General Trujillo, the country had entered a period of instability in the early 1960's followed by several terms of popularly elected governments. Under the constitution of 1966 the Dominican Republic was constituted as a representative democracy whose national powers were divided among the executive, legislative, and judicial branches of government. The president was directly elected for a four year term. In May of 1978, then President Balaguer was defeated in his try for a fourth consecutive term by Antonio Guzman of the Partido Revolucionario Dominicano (PRD). These elections were generally acknowledged to have been free and fair. Many parties, including the communist party, participated in an open and hard fought campaign. The inauguration of

EXHIBIT 13 Average Number of Hospital Beds Per Thousand Inhabitants

Argentina	5.7 (1971)
Brazil	3.8 (1970)
Dom. Rep.	1.5 (1975)
Venezuela	2.9 (1976)

President Guzman was significant in that it represented the country's first peaceful transfer of power from one freely elected president to another in this century. President Guzman pledged that his administration would promote democratic institutionalization, economic development, and social justice, along with focusing public resources on the education, health, energy, and agricultural sectors of the Dominican economy.

The PRD participated for the first time in elections since 1966 and also gained a majority in the senate, but Balaguer's Partido Reformista retained control of the lower house. In 1980, the PRD claimed that President Guzman had deviated from party policies and disassociated itself from him.

In the early 1970's the Dominican Republic enjoyed one of the highest economic growth rates in Latin America. More recently the country had experienced an economic slowdown brought on by a fall in sugar prices and a rise in petroleum costs. Real GNP growth in 1977 was 3.3%, following increases of 2.9% in 1976, and 5% in 1975. Total real GNP for 1977 was 2.1 billion dollars, with real per capita income of $433.

Inflation, which had declined from a previous average of 14% to 7.8% in 1976, jumped to 16.4% in 1977. Its balance of payments rebounded from a $30 million deficit in 1976 to a $59.2 million surplus in 1977, thanks to increased coffee and cacao earnings and high capital inflows. Although the hurricanes Frederick and David devastated the country in 1979, the long term economic outlook was promising.

Agriculture continued to dominate foreign trade. In 1977, the Dominicans exported 1.4 million metric tons of sugar accounting for 32% of

EXHIBIT 14 Hospitals Per Country

Argentina	2,864 (1971)
Brazil	4,067 (1971)
Dom. Rep.	306 (1972)
Venezuela	340 (1972)

EXHIBIT 15 Total Imports of Complete Electro-Medical Equipment (in US$)

	1980	1979	1978
Argentina	$2,287,000	$647,000	$462,000
Brazil	584,000	408,000	528,000
Dom. Rep.	N.A.	N.A.	73,443
Venezuela	462,000	646,000	819,000

foreign exchange earnings. More than 80% of Dominican exports went to the U.S., and more than 50% of Dominican imports came from the U.S. The Dominican government was promoting foreign investment in industrial free-trade zones to foster employment. Free-trade zone firms were allowed to import and re-export goods duty-free, in addition to enjoying certain tax advantages such as tax holidays.

THE VENEZUELAN MARKET

Venezuela's population of about 14 million grew at an annual rate of 3 percent resulting in a doubling of its entire population every 20 years. Venezuela's mostly oil based wealth was distributed very unevenly and a large segment of the population suffered from inadequate nutrition, housing, clothing, and education. These problems were aggravated by the rapidly growing population and an increasing number of illegal aliens, primarily from Colombia, who were attracted to Venezuela's booming labor market.

Though an independent state since 1830, Venezuela was governed primarily by dictators until 1958 when Romulo Betancourt became the country's first elected president to finish his term of office. In 1969, Caldera became the first Christian-democratic president, followed by Perez in 1974, who belonged to the opposition party, Accion Democratica. Since 1979, Herrera, again a Christian-democrat, had been president.

The present constitution guaranteed freedom of speech, religion, and assembly, and

EXHIBIT 16   Total Central Gov. Expenditure on Health*

	1972	1973	1974	1975	1976	1977
Argentina		.3%		.1%		.3%
Brazil	.2%			.8%		.23%
Dom. Rep.			1.7%	.9%		2.3%
Venezuela				2.7%		.9%

* Expressed as a percentage of Gross National Product.

assigned substantial economic development responsibilities to the federal government. National elections were held every five years in which the president and members of congress, the state legislature, and the city councils were directly elected. The president could not be reelected until ten years after his most recent term. The executive, legislative, and judicial branches were separate. The president had extensive powers that included the power to appoint the council of ministers (the cabinet) and the state and territorial governors, by decree. The Democratic Republic Union (URD) and the Social-Christian Party (COPEI) were the two major parties in this democratic system although there were many smaller ones. The objectives of the Venezuelan government included the preservation and protection of free and democratic institutions and to maintain public order; promote, expand, and diversify agricultural and industrial production; to create new jobs, to carry out agrarian reforms, and to expand education, housing, public health, social welfare and community services. Venezuela's petroleum revenues provided excellent prospects for the country's continuing political, social, and economic development.

Venezuela's economy was totally dominated by its petroleum industry. Until 1970, the country was the world's third largest petroleum producer, and the leading exporter. Since 1971, the country had remained in fifth place with respect to production and third on exports. Petroleum had reached a peak of 3.7 million barrels a day in 1970 and averaged slightly over 2 million for the last 3 years. Petroleum accounted for 96 percent of Venezuela's export earnings in 1979. As a result of this over-dependency on oil, industrial diversification was a high government priority. Huge investments were made in agriculture, steel, and aluminum industries, and the latter had replaced iron ore as the second export earner.

Venezuela's historically positive balance of payments turned negative for the first time in 1977. The deficit had reached $5.7 billion in 1978 due to enormous public expenditures on ambitious development programs, and later fell to $228 million in 1978. Higher oil prices returned the balance of payments into surplus in 1979. When President Herrera assumed power in 1979, he pledged to place his emphasis on the development of agriculture and social services rather than on heavy industry as was done by his predecessor. The present 5-year plan aimed at economic expansion while placing renewed emphasis on social priorities. It anticipated an average annual growth rate of 6 percent, continued oil production at a level of 2.2 million barrels per day, and an annual increase of 15 percent in oil revenues.

MANAGEMENT APPRAISAL

As in most Latin American countries, MEC's management had identified three health care systems that existed in most countries. One system consisted of "social security" type hospi-

EXHIBIT 17 Total U.S. Exports*

	1979	1978	1977	1976
Argentina	$4,159,113	$2,094,951	$ 888,218	$ 330,764
Brazil	7,058,969	7,079,688	2,554,142	1,468,369
Dom. Rep.	184,437	109,989	none reported	none reported
Venezuela	2,908,793	3,235,966	1,281,688	1,728,350

* Figures from U.S. Department of Commerce include only blood gases and electrolyte equipment, products which often took priority in developing countries.

tals catering to citizens who could not afford private hospitals, which represented the second system. A third system, also government funded, consisted of hospitals for military personnel and government employees. The two public systems and the private hospitals each contributed about equally to MEC sales. Among the public systems, the ones organized for military and government employees were always better funded than the social security hospitals.

MEC's management believed that politics and balance of payments played a major role in medical equipment sales. Also of importance was the country of education for medical doctors. And next to the official market always existed a parallel market of unauthorized imports representing about 15 percent of sales for each market. These sales were undocumented with products usually "smuggled" into the country.

MEC found independent agents of considerable importance in securing foreign currency under tight monetary situations. Particularly for private hospitals such agents had been able to occasionally arrange for creative financing to sell MEC instruments.

Over the past decade, only Mexico had shown a consistently increasing sales volume for MEC products. Though the Latin American market was considered to be growing overall, the considerable fluctuations were nevertheless cause for concern for MEC's regional management. A task force was formed that had collected the attached data. It was now up to the task force's members to form some conclusions on the reasons for this erratic sales pattern and to attempt to forecast future volume. Eventually, the task force would also have to make a recommendation to the company as to whether MEC should continue to serve these markets.

CASE 2 ▪ American Electronics Company*

In January of 1977, the management of American Electronics Company's Communications Product Division decided that the recent experience gained with turnkey plants in a Middle Eastern country was positive enough to look at opportunities in other developing countries. Since the division's management wanted to present its preliminary assessment to the company's board at its March meeting, time was of the essence. A preliminary in-house study selected four possible target countries out of a list of 25 (see Exhibit 1). A major consulting firm was hired to collect relevant data in just 4 weeks. At the end of February, it was now up to the division's management to analyze the opportunities offered in Venezuela, Nigeria, Egypt, and the People's Republic of China.

COMPANY BACKGROUND

American Electronics Company was one of the world's largest manufacturers of communications and electrical products and was based in the United States. In 1976, total worldwide revenues exceeded 7 billion dollars with total assets of about 14 billion. The company was divided into three major divisions: communications products, lighting products, and the consumer electronics division. American Electronics Company (AEC) has traditionally been a major

competitor in the European and American markets for telecommunications systems and equipment, and more recently had made significant gains in the consumer electronics and lighting product areas.

TURNKEY FACTORY GROUP

In the early 1970's, AEC won a contract to build a turnkey or product-in-hand factory for communications equipment destined for a major Middle Eastern country market which was rapidly expanding its communication network. A turnkey plant meant that AEC not only built the factory to produce the specified communication network, but also was to recruit and train the workers and managers from the Middle Eastern country to operate the plant eventually without AEC's day-to-day involvement. AEC was contractually bound to maintain a presence in the country until the factory had reached 85% operating capacity. AEC was successfully completing this project in 1977 when it was asked by the same government to prepare a bid for a similar contract to build a consumer electronics products factory in the same country.

The company's management had also discovered during these years that the traditional export markets were becoming increasingly competitive and that there was a growing market in developing nations that was not adequately served by the industry at present. Most of these developing countries were facing balance of

---

* Some names and facts disguised.

This case was prepared by Maricel Blum under the supervision of Visiting Professor Jean-Pierre Jeannet as a basis for class discussion rather than to illustrate either effective or ineffective handling of an administrative situation. Copyright © 1981 by IMEDE (International Management Development Institute), Lausanne, Switzerland. Reproduced by permission.

payment problems and were looking for means to reduce imports and also to increase domestic production and gain technology transfers to their country. Management felt that the experience gained in the Middle Eastern country was worth being repeated and in January of 1977 made the decision to explore the market for turnkey factories in less developed countries.

A preliminary in-house study chose four countries for an in-depth study. The four countries were chosen from a list of twenty-five divided into six major groupings.

The following four countries were chosen:

- Venezuela
- Nigeria
- Egypt
- The People's Republic of China

The major findings for each of these countries are summarized below.

THE MARKET FOR COMMUNICATIONS EQUIPMENT IN EGYPT

Egypt's economic growth had been modest to date. From 1960 to 1965, her national income increased by an average of about 10% annually. Following the 1967 Middle Eastern war, however, this average fell to below 5% annually, which resulted in virtually no growth in real terms on a per capita basis. Egypt's economic plan from 1965 to 1970 was ambitious, but economic difficulties—due to a heavy military defense burden and a widening trade gap—led to its abandonment. Another five-year plan was to be implemented in the summer of 1970, but because of the uncertainties posed by the then still warlike situation with Israel, it was not even published.

The latest five-year plan (1976–1980) emphasized the completion of unfinished projects left from the previous period. It concentrated on the petroleum and tourist sectors, the Suez Canal area and the ports. Its objective was to prepare the country for a major drive to industrialize over the next five years. Egypt's economic infrastructure was also due for some improve-

ments helped by loans of $250 million for extending the electricity grid into new areas.

Egypt's economic problems traditionally centered around a lack of capital. In the war period between 1967 and 1973, Egypt's heavy defense spending had risen to 20 and 30% of her GNP, draining funds away from investments in upkeep and renewal of the industrial base. Egypt's military spending continued to be far above what it could afford, and amounted to 23% of the 1975–1976 GNP. For an economic profile of Egypt see Exhibit 2.

Egypt's balance of payments had suffered heavy deficits in recent years. Her deficit in the current account more than doubled in 1974 rising to $1.3 billion, and doubled again in 1975, increasing to $3 billion. However, her future did look a little more encouraging as industrial activities showed some healthy growth rates. Furthermore, the oil fields in the Sinai would make Egypt a consistent exporter of petroleum, and the reopened Suez Canal would also provide Egypt with some foreign exchange. However, Egypt's trade deficit continued to be a problem with total imports of $3.75 billion in 1975 and exports of only $1.40 billion.

Regardless of Egypt's poor economic performance in the past there was a general feeling that over the next 15 years Egypt's real GNP would experience an average annual increase of around 6%. The government's official target of a 10% growth rate in GNP was considered to be very optimistic, though. Her "open-door" policy on investment was also expected to keep the inflation rate above 20%. On the more positive side from AEC/TFG's point of view, Egypt had a large population which was far from fully employed. In addition, its workforce contained many well trained or trainable men and women.

In recent years, OECD countries overtook the Soviet Bloc as major suppliers of Egyptian imports. In 1975, of Egypt's total imports of $3.75 billion, the United States provided 20.1%; EEC countries 49.1%; and Japan about 6.2%.

Egypt's communications system was the second largest on the African Continent with about 355,000 main line telephones in use in 1975. This gave the country a density of about

EXHIBIT 1 Major Markets for Telecommunications Equipment

	Population 1975 Millions*	% Population in Major Cities	Population Annual Growth 1975–1980	G.D.P. 1975 Billions*	Per Capita Income* 1975
Latin America					
Brazil	109.7	25.2	2.9	109.2	940
Venezuela	12.2	42.9	2.9	28.7	1,910
Mexico	59.2	37.9	3.4	79.0	1,201
Ecuador	7.1	28.7	3.2	4.3	547
Colombia	25.9	37.7	3.1	13.4	467
Far East					
South Korea	33.9	40.3	2.0	19.1	500
Taiwan	16.1	51.3	1.6	14.4	698
Philippines	44.4	8.8	3.3	15.7	312
Indonesia	136.0	11.1	2.6	28.9	184
Thailand	42.1	14.4	3.3	14.3	320
Europe					
Spain	35.4	32.4	1.0	102.4	2,596
Portugal	8.8	17.5	0.5	14.6	1,608
Greece	8.9	—	0.4	21.0	2,244
Centrally Planned					
U.S.S.R.	254.4	9.8	1.1	486.5	1,912
People's Republic of China	935.0	—	—	299.0	320
Africa					
Nigeria	62.9	—	2.9	27.2	216
Ghana	9.9	—	2.9	4.1	381
Egypt	37.5	—	2.3	10.3	268
Algeria	16.8	17.0	—	13.1	772
Tanzania	15.2	3.6	—	2.2	139
Middle East					
Iran	32.9	32.7	3.2	52.7	1,534
Saudi Arabia	7.0	—	2.9	32.7	2,701
Abu Dhabi	.3	75.0	—	7.0	23,300
Kuwait	1.1	—	4.9	9.1	8,620
Iraq	11.1	39.7	3.4	13.6	778

* In U.S. dollars.

G.D.P. Annual Growth	% Mfc. of G.D.P.	International Liquidity June 1976 Millions*	Total Imports 1975 Millions*	% Imported from U.S. 1974	Imports of Communication Electronics from U.S. Millions*
9.3	19.2	3,716	13,558	23.6	13.6
4.4	17.6	7,791	5,359	42.1	11.4
5.7	23.2	1,501	6,581	82.1	35.5
10.2	15.5	338	943	37.9	1.4
5.7	20.4	784	1,495	54.7	4.1
10.1	26.0	2,044	7,274	24.9	42.7
7.6	25.6	1,394	5,915	24.1	13.2
6.1	17.4	1,679	3,774	24.1	17.0
8.0	8.6	953	4,800	15.6	43.5
6.2	17.1	1,896	3,075	13.1	5.1
5.5	28.2	5,298	16,266	15.5	23.7
4.7	30.6	1,291	3,841	8.9	2.1
4.6	18.2	870	5,321	9.2	3.4
4.7	51.3	—	17,492	5.4	0.8
5.6	38.8	—	5,915	12.7	0.1
4.7	5.1	5,885	6,035	11.5	34.9
4.5	10.3	161	805	10.7	0.01
0.7	19.3	448	3,750	21.3	2.6
—	12.7	1,538	5,861	8.6	2.3
—	8.2	92	772	6.7	0.3
13.7	29.5	6,821	10,962	33.6	67.0
12.2	6.0	24,662	7,260	26.4	26.5
—	2.0	—	—	—	—
—	3.2	1,823	2,263	15.1	3.6
—	10.0	2,884	4,204	6.9	4.4

EXHIBIT 1 (cont.)

	Total Private Consumption Billion* 1974	% Increase Past 5 Yrs.	% Consumption Spent on Household Durables 1974	Telephones 1975 Thousands	% Annual Growth Past 3 Yrs.
Latin America					
Brazil	71.08	64.0	—	3,371	15.5
Venezuela	10.47	—	8.5	650	11.3
Mexico	45.51	33.6	—	2,915	14.2
Ecuador	2.11	33.7	—	193	17.8
Colombia	8.16	34.2	—	1,286	8.3
Far East					
South Korea	11.66	49.3	3.2	1,400	—
Taiwan	7.54	46.3	23.5	1,118	23.3
Philippines	10.39	25.7	7.0	490	7.8
Indonesia	14.65	45.4	—	305	8.3
Thailand	8.64	36.6	5.6	312	9.9
Europe					
Spain	58.24	34.3	8.6	7,836	11.1
Portugal	10.88	52.8	—	1,066	6.8
Greece	13.57	32.1	9.3	2,009	11.8
Centrally Planned					
U.S.S.R.	289.34	—	—	16,129	6.9
People's Republic of China	—	—	—	—	—
Africa					
Nigeria	10.00	—	—	111	—
Ghana	1.54	—	—	61	—
Egypt	5.98	1.6	—	—	—
Algeria	5.17	—	—	250	5.8
Tanzania	1.69	—	—	63	—
Middle East					
Iran	14.2	55.9	—	688	15.5
Saudi Arabia	2.92	—	—	—	—
Abu Dhabi	—	—	—	16	—
Kuwait	1.24	—	—	129	14.9
Iraq	—	—	—	185	15.0

* In U.S. dollars.

Telephones per 100 Population 1975	Radios 1975 Thousands	T.V.'s 1975 Thousands	Electricity Production 1975 Billion KWH	% Increase Past 5 Yrs.	Energy Consumption 1974 % of U.S. Per Capita
3.08	6,300	9,530	70.73	55	5.5
5.34	2,050	1,284	18.40	—	24.8
4.76	—	4,020	43.86	53	11.2
2.94	—	252	1.27	—	3.2
5.45	2,808	1,200	11.97	36	5.3
4.03	—	—	19.84	106	8.4
6.92	1,700	2,500	—	—	10.6
1.17	1,850	470	10.11	16	2.6
0.23	5,010	300	—	—	1.3
0.74	5,500	658	—	—	2.6
21.98	8,075	6,525	81.56	44	18.0
12.30	1,581	575	10.48	30	8.9
22.12	3,250	1,140	14.63	55	17.9
6.63	—	57,700	10.38	40	45.6
—	—	—	—	—	4.8
0.16	5,000	100	3.36	116	0.8
0.64	1,060	33	3.65	25	1.6
—	5,120	620	—	—	2.8
1.46	1,010	500	8.22	44	4.4
0.42	232	7	0.50	41	0.6
2.00	—	1,700	—	—	11.1
—	255	124	—	—	8.5
6.86	—	—	—	—	—
12.49	500	135	—	—	88.0
1.69	1,252	—	—	—	7.9

EXHIBIT 2 Egypt Summary

Population	37.5 million
Population Annual Growth Rate	2.3%
GNP	$10.3 billion
GNP Real Annual Growth Rate	0.7%
Percentage Manufacturing in GNP	19.3%
Per Capita Income	$268
Total Exports	$1,402 million
Total Imports	$3,750 million
Percentage Imports from U.S.	20.1%
International Liquidity (1976)	$448 million
Telephones per 100 population	1.4
Number of Radios	5.12 million
Number of TV sets	620,000
Energy Consumption as a Percentage of U.S. Per Capita Energy Consumption	2.8%

1975 data. All figures expressed in U.S. dollars.

1.4 phones per 100 population. However, the system was generally in a poor state of repair.

The government's priorities were changing and communication was receiving renewed emphasis with indications that some 360,000 telephones were to be added over the next five years with $275 million in estimated expenditures for local subscriber loop plant installations as well. Continental Telephone, a U.S. corporation, was conducting a major study in order to define specific requirements and recommend plans for implementation. Thus, new large programs ought to develop over the next few years.

The Masara Company for Telephones was a government controlled manufacturing organization producing telephone sets, public exchange equipment, and PABX's. The company currently had a technical assistance agreement with L.M. Ericsson of Sweden which extended through 1980. Present government policy re-

quired the UAR Telecommunications Organization (UARTO) of Egypt to purchase from Masara any equipment that was within the company's capabilities. Masara's current annual single-shift capacity appeared to exceed likely requirements in the following areas:

Telephone sets: 60–75,000 units/year
Public exchanges: 35–40,000 lines/year
PABX's: 3–4,000 lines/year

Egypt also imported communications equipment from European and U.S. sources. Her 1976 imports from the United States amounted to $2,573,000. Egyptian imports had come from the following other sources:

L.M. Ericsson (Sweden), switching equipment and cable systems
STC (U.K.), cable systems and switching equipment
G.E.C. Marconi (U.K.), radio systems
Siemens (Germany), teleprinters
Olivetti (Italy), teleprinters

Egypt had not enjoyed a healthy balance of trade position and therefore was quite dependent on long-term credit to finance her communications plans. Recently, the government had changed its position and was encouraging more free enterprise and foreign investment and had loosened some of its import restrictions.

Egypt, like some other Middle East countries, could also provide an opportunity for AEC/TGF consumer electronics and lighting products. Egypt's move away from Russia toward the United States and the West was one very favorable indicator for such opportunities. While there was no indication that the large nationalized companies were to be broken up, there was strong indication that private enterprise and participation with foreign companies would be accepted in the near future.

During the recent past, much of Egypt's energy and resources had been diverted to strategic requirements of defense spending. This posture, coupled with the recent worldwide economic situation had not allowed Egypt to achieve its full potential in industrial, electrical, and electronics manufacturing industries.

It was estimated that more than 620,000 TV sets were in use in Egypt in 1975, an estimated 60,000 set increase between 1970 and 1975. Factors which contributed to that low growth of set population were expected to be relieved in the near future. In a similar fashion, it was estimated that 5,120,000 radios were in use in 1975, a 3.1% increase over the 4,400,000 estimated for 1970. Earlier studies indicated that the income elasticity[1] of product ownership for television sets was very often 1.0 or slightly above. Radios, on the other hand, had an income elasticity for product ownership in the range of 0.82. Thus, it can be understood that the demand for these products in a country where private consumption had increased at a rate of only 1.6% for the past five years did not create a rapidly expanding market.

THE NIGERIAN MARKET FOR TELECOMMUNICATIONS EQUIPMENT

Nigeria's Third National Development Plan (1976–1980) called for expenditures of nearly $50 billion. However, some Nigerians were skeptical that this amount could be spent due to delays attributable to transportation bottlenecks and skilled manpower shortages. In the plan, a total of $2 billion had been budgeted for communications and $1.7 billion for power projects.

The government expected the GNP to increase from $23 billion in the 1974–75 period to $36 billion in the 1979–80 period amounting to an annual growth rate of 9.4%. The government was trying to promote a faster growth rate in manufacturing, infrastructure, and social service sectors of the economy to lessen Nigeria's dependence on petroleum and agriculture. The

---

1. *Income elasticity* is defined as the change in demand as a result of changes in income. Mathematically, it is computed by dividing the percentage change in quantity demanded by the percentage change in income. An income elasticity less than 1, as in the case of radios, means that demand will not increase as fast as a rise in income, which in Egypt has been very low in the past five years.

agricultural sector employed 70% of the work force. Only one-fifth of all Nigerians were estimated to have moved from a barter to a money economy so far. An economic profile of Nigeria is presented in Exhibit 3.

Nigerian imports rose 117% to 5.9 billion in 1975, from $2.8 billion the previous year. Machinery and transport equipment, manufactured goods, chemicals and foodstuffs together comprised 90% of all the imports. Due to its large oil reserves and production, Nigerian exports were substantial and exceeded $8 billion. However, due to the rise in imports in 1975, Nigeria's foreign exchange reserves rose only by $259 million as compared to the $5 billion increase which was reported in 1974.

Severe shortages occurred in the country over the past year or so due to the large increase in demand. This was reflected in the rate of infla-

EXHIBIT 3 Nigeria Summary

Population	80 million
Annual Population Growth Rate	2.9%
GNP	$27.2 billion
GNP Real Annual Growth Rate	9.4%
Percentage Manufacturing in GNP	5.1%
Per Capita Income	$216
Total Exports	$8,096 million
Total Imports	$6,035 million
Percentage Imports from U.S.	11.0%
International Liquidity (June 1976)	$5,885 million
Telephones per 100 population	0.16
Number of Radios	5 million
Number of TV Sets	100,000
Energy Consumption as a Percentage of U.S. Per Capita Energy Consumption	.8%

1975 data. All figures expressed in U.S. dollars.

tion which approached 50% in 1975 and continued at that rate in 1976. Inflation was caused by pressures precipitated by a short supply of goods, by high prices for imports due to increases in foreign costs, by higher freight rate surcharges for notorious port congestions, and by domestic wage increases combined with low productivity. To combat inflation the government implemented some recommendations. They included, among others, bank credit controls, selected tariff reductions, and price controls on automobiles and beverages.

On February 13, 1976, Nigeria's Military Head of State was assassinated in an attempted coup which was quickly crushed by loyalist military forces. The coup had a detrimental effect on the self-confidence of the nation, reflected by the fact that the economic pace of the nation temporarily slowed down. However, the new administration stated that Nigeria was moving ahead with the economic plans previously developed.

The Nigerian government continued to offer a number of incentives to encourage private sector industrial developments. The most important was a tax holiday of 2–5 years for companies in "pioneer" industries. The government aimed at stimulating greater participation from the private sector and many government decisions reflected the federal policy of distributing the benefits of development evenly throughout the country even if this did not prove to be the most economical option.

Much of the foreign investment made in Nigeria took the form of joint ventures with states or the federal government. Twenty-two types of enterprises were reserved exclusively for Nigerians; among them were the assembly of radios, record turntables, television sets, tape recorders and other domestic appliances not combined with the manufacture of components. Thirty three types of enterprises, forming a second category, were reserved for at least 40% Nigerian participation.

The formalities involved in getting established in Nigeria were time consuming. These included company registration, expatriate quota/residence permits, and "indigenization."

The purpose of these formalities was to secure greater local participation and to preclude conflicts of interest which could arise from foreign investments in certain areas of the economy.

American products and services are well appreciated by Nigerians, but European manufacturers managed to capture a large share of the market for communications apparatus and electric power transmission and distribution equipment. The United States was the third largest supplier to the country with 12% of all imports in 1974; the United Kingdom was first with 23%, followed by West Germany with 15%. American technology was highly valued by the Nigerian consumer.

A major problem within Nigeria was the lack of skilled manpower at all levels. As a result, the government was particularly interested in attracting industries which would bring in new technologies, utilize local materials, and allow Nigerians to move quickly into upper-level technical and managerial positions. The training component of any project under consideration in Nigeria, especially by the government, is therefore extremely important.

With regard to the transportation problem, as many as 400 ships at a time were waiting to get into Lagos Harbor throughout 1975. By mid-1976, however, the government had successfully reduced this volume by more than half. The government had acquired additional cargo-unloading equipment, extended wharf areas, and introduced new techniques for unloading. Nigerian-bound ships were now required to receive full clearance two months before their anticipated arrival, and clearance was only given to ships in conference lines using a priority base and precleared schedules. However, the basic problem was still a lack of warehouses and dock facilities. Internally, there were limitations with respect to the highways and other infrastructure, and in many parts of the country there was a total absence of electrical power. One-fifth of the Third National Plan ($12 billion) was programmed for transportation improvement, $7 billion of which was planned to go toward highway construction.

As noted above, a portion of Nigeria's Third National Development Plan entailed the expenditure of $2 billion for over 70 communications projects. There were at present about 109,000 main line telephones installed. This number had been expected to grow to 600,000 lines over the next five years, bringing the telephone density up from 0.16 in 1975 to about 0.8 in the early 1980's.

For the foreseeable future, Nigeria was heavily dependent upon foreign communications equipment, engineering and management skills, but the country was most anxious to establish plants and build up its own domestic manufacturing capability, wherever possible, to meet its future internal needs. As early as 1971, the Nigerian P&T indicated its intentions to call for tenders for construction of a communications manufacturing facility in Nigeria. To date, no action had been taken towards this objective. The U.S. exports of communications equipment to Nigeria in 1976 totalled about $35 million.

Many manufacturers throughout the world recognized Nigeria as an attractive future market and established subsidiaries—mostly shell organizations—for the purpose of giving the appearance of doing business locally. These companies, which had not yet set up significant operations, included besides AEC:

ITT (U.S.)
Plessey (U.K.)
L.M. Ericsson (Sweden)
Siemens (Germany)
GEC TELECOMMUNICATIONS (U.K.)
Marubeni (Japan)
GTE (U.S.)

It was reported that 5,000,000 radios were in use in 1975, an increase from 1,275,000 in 1970. This represented an annual compound growth rate in excess of 31% in the population of radios over the period. Television had not expanded as rapidly. It was estimated that the number of television sets amounted to 100,000 in 1975, up from 75,000 in 1970. This represented an annual compound growth rate of only 6%.

THE MARKET FOR TELECOMMUNICATIONS EQUIPMENT IN THE PEOPLE'S REPUBLIC OF CHINA

In the People's Republic of China (PRC), the potential market for goods and services, such as turnkey plants, or the products which they might produce, was extremely difficult to assess in spite of the fact that there were a number of reasons which suggested a long-term market potential. The Chinese did not publish their five-year plans or otherwise provide information on equipment and technology of particular interest to them.

China's economy was centrally planned and the level or composition of imports were programmed to support the overall economic plan. Thus trade was not an independent economic activity with its own growth pattern, but instead reflected changes in the level of domestic investment and production dictated by the national plan. These changes could be rather large and sudden, creating or foreclosing major opportunities for potential foreign suppliers. Exhibit 4 presents an economic summary of the PRC.

China had used imports as a means of introducing many of those technological innovations which were often provided by foreign investors in developing economies. China's import requirements and export programs were developed through a long process involving many different national and local government agencies. On the demand side, end-users presented their requirements to the various ministries in charge of the industries concerned. If the product could not be supplied domestically, a list of goods to be imported was forwarded to a state planning commission for approval. The commission's list was to be sent to the Ministry of Foreign Trade for implementation and for further refinement. The government drew up three major import requirement plans:

1. Long-range import requirements in line with the objectives of the relevant five-year plan,
2. Annual plans, and
3. Revisions which were made during each

EXHIBIT 4 The People's Republic of
China Summary

Population	935 million
Percentage in Major Cities	15%
Labor Force	476 million
GNP	$299 billion
GNP Real Annual Growth Rate	5.6%
Percentage Manufacturing in GNP	38.8%
Per Capita Income	$320
Total Exports	$5,292 million
Total Imports	$5,915 million
Percentage Imports from U.S.	5.6%
Number of Radios	46,750,000
Number of TV Sets	500,000
Energy Consumption as a Percentage of U.S. Per Capita Energy Consumption	4.8%

1975 data. All figures expressed in U.S. dollars.

quarter to reflect actual changes in the annual plan.

Annual U.S. exports to China during the 1971–1976 period were $5, $96, $804, $934, $350 millions, respectively. U.S. exports to China and other communist countries were subject to a control exercised by the Export Administration Act of 1969 and amended by the Equal Export Opportunity Act of 1972. One purpose of this legislation was to authorize controls over the export of goods and technology that would contribute to the military potential of these countries, thus possibly jeopardizing U.S. national security. This legislation also declared that it was the policy of the United States to encourage trade in non-sensitive items with all nations, including China, with which the U.S. maintained diplomatic or trading relations. The United States did not have diplomatic but did have trading relations with the People's Republic of China.

For the most part, China had concentrated on purchasing "complete plants" which could contribute directly to increased productivity, more export capacity, or reduced imports. Over the 18-month period preceding June 1974, China had contracted for nearly $1.9 billion in "complete plants." The plants were purchased for the following industrial sectors: electric power, iron and steel, petroleum exploration and production, petroleum, refining and petrochemicals, chemicals fertilizer plants, metal-working equipment, mining equipment, communications equipment and transportation equipment (aircraft only).

It was likely that U.S.-China Trade would expand over the years ahead, with China's purchases of machinery, equipment, and completed factories probably increasing as a percentage of total imports. The Chinese were more likely to continue to buy completed factories until they had learned how to construct such plants on their own. Finally, China would be unable to produce some machinery and equipment at all, for an indefinite period, or would be able to produce it only at prohibitive costs; such examples were commercial jet aircraft and computers. It was in this category of technology-intensive machinery that United States manufacturers could be expected to enjoy their greatest advantage.

One difficulty in selling turnkey plants to the Chinese was their reluctance to have foreign technicians in their country over an extended period of time. There were currently, approximately, 200 U.S. technicians in China.

In 1975, it was estimated that there were less than 5 million telephones in China with only about 1 million lines. Clearly, if China was to become a modern industrial state, a more modern communications systems was required. The Electronic Industries Association delegation, which visited the PRC in 1975, concluded that the Chinese had not yet decided on the extent or direction of their communications development, but were assessing technology and equipment from sources throughout the world in an attempt to put together their next Five-Year Plan. The delegation further concluded that if the PRC chose to invest heavily in a communications network, it could represent a significant market for U.S. manufacturers and systems planners.

About 85% of the PRC's 935 people lived in rural areas, while the rest lived in just a few cities along China's eastern border. A breakdown of urban population concentrations is presented below.

	Estimated Population (millions)
Peking	7.6
Shanghai	11.0
Tientsin	4.0
Shen Yang	3.0
Wuhan	2.7
Kwang Chow	3.0
Total	31.3

Of the 1 million main telephone lines in use in China today, almost all were located in the cities listed above. It seemed that there were no plans to greatly expand telephone service to the general public for at least another decade, nor to increase telephone density to levels that were comparable to the more highly developed countries of the world. To date, most of the expenditures for communications had been for governmental, military, and international applications such as an international satellite earth station installed two years ago.

The PRC's manufacturing facilities, visited by an EIA trade commission group during July 1975, were described as being quite old and almost totally dependent on manual labor. At present, their production skills were limited to manufacturing radio and TV transmitters, teleprinters, carrier equipment, and rather simple digital computers. They seemed almost entirely dependent on imports to meet the rest of their communications needs and these came largely from Japan, Russia, and Eastern Europe. In 1976, communications imports from the United States totalled only $123,000.

Recent studies by the U.S. Department of Commerce revealed that communications and photographic equipment imports into China from non-Communist countries amounted to less than 1% of total machinery and transportation equipment imports over the past 20 years. This import level indicates the relatively low priority attributed to communications programs in the country.

The PRC today had approximately 50 radios for every 1,000 people, as compared to 200 or 2,000 radios for every 1,000 people in the Soviet Union and the United States, respectively. Production of radios was estimated to be 12 million units per year, and they were manufactured in 150 factories distributed throughout the PRC's 29 provinces. Like many other consumer goods, radios had to be considered luxury items since their cost, ranging between $10 and $50, was high in comparison to the average urban wage of $25 per month.

It was estimated that the population of television sets was now 500,000 and growing at approximately 100,000 sets per year. These sets were produced locally in 35 different plants.

THE VENEZUELAN MARKET FOR TELECOMMUNICATIONS EQUIPMENT

Venezuela's current Five-Year Plan reflected the government's intention to guide the industrial development of the country toward a greater processing of local materials, to diversify the economy away from petroleum, and thus make Venezuela a more self-sufficient country. The government's economic program was mainly based on six elements:

1. A more equitable distribution of wealth.
2. State ownership of extractive industries.
3. Regulation of foreign investments according to Decision 24 of the Cartagena Agreement (Andean Pact regulations).
4. Utilization of petroleum-generated revenues to finance the development of a balanced economy.
5. Promotion of non-traditional exports.
6. Support of world oil prices to ensure that

revenues from that sector were sufficient to finance Venezuela's ambitious development plans.

Even though Venezuela's foreign exchange revenues increased dramatically in the past five years (foreign exchange reserves were almost $8 billion in February of 1976), the balance of payments surpluses had been declining. This decline was expected to continue as imports increased faster than exports. The government had also taken deliberate actions to reduce production of oil to decrease the country's dependency on petroleum exports. The fall in world petroleum demand resulting from higher oil prices had also enabled Venezuela to preserve more of her resources for future use. Against the decline in petroleum production there had been a very rapid growth of the non-petroleum sectors of the economy.

Recent government actions with respect to the movement towards the nationalization of some companies, the changes in the investment regulations, the limitations on profit remittances, as well as those regulations affecting the transfer of technology, had caused some uneasiness among foreign investors. Venezuela had published regulations for foreign investors and established deadlines for compliance. Some of the stricter deadlines had been extended to allow foreign investors sufficient time to comply. Basic industries, such as petroleum and mining, were to be totally owned by nationals, and certain sensitive industries such as domestic transport, radio, and television were required to be at least 80% owned by Venezuelans. Exhibit 5 presents an economic profile of Venezuela in 1975. Venezuela's rate of inflation was very low in the 1968–1972 period, but the country was now experiencing inflation ranging from 15% to 20%. The government had taken some steps, such as the restriction of credit and some alterations of the price structure, to help reduce the rate of inflation.

The United States presently occupied a favored position as a supplier of goods to the Venezuelan market and relationships with Venezuela had been good. In 1975, 40% of the goods imported by Venezuela were supplied by the United States, and it was believed that the United States' share would remain high.

EXHIBIT 5 Venezuela Summary

Population	12.2 million
Percentage in Major Cities	25.2%
Annual Population Growth Rate	2.9%
Labor Force	3.7 million
GNP	$28.7 billion
GNP Annual Growth Rate	7.5%
Percentage Manufacturing in GNP	17.6%
Per Capita Income	$1,910
Total Exports	$11,150 million
Total Imports	$5,359 million
Percentage Imports from U.S.	41.9%
International Liquidity (June 1976)	$7,791 million
Telephones per 100 Population	5.34
Number of Radios	2,050 million
Number of TV Sets	1,284 million
Energy Consumption as a Percentage of U.S. Per Capita Energy Consumption	24.8%

1975 data. All figures expressed in U.S. dollars.

The labor force in Venezuela in 1976 was estimated to be somewhat less than 4 million. However, skilled workers were in very short supply and productivity was considered to be quite low. High labor turnover was a major problem for a firm's operation in that country. Training of local labor was considered to be an important factor in any bid for a project in Venezuela. The government in Venezuela had mounted a large effort on training programs, both locally through the government Manpower Training Institute, and abroad.

As in many other petroleum-exporting nations, Venezuela's existing infrastructure had been strained. A large demand for imports had caused major congestions at ports, and delays of up to 48 days had occurred. The 1976–1980 national plan called for improving the infrastructure with investments of about $20 billion. The plan estimated an investment of $3.1 billion for transportation and communication systems, $3 billion for social infrastructure, and $2.7 billion for electrification. It was hoped that the nation's power-generating capacity would double in this five-year period and that the transportation and communication network would be upgraded to reduce the problems that were afflicting the country today.

For new projects in the country it had become common for the government to limit bid requests to firms which were already on selected prequalification lists. The prequalification process would start six months or more before the bids for specific projects were issued and the process included a review of the firm's reputation for meeting time limit, quality of its product, servicing capability, and performance. A firm which produced a given type of equipment would not always be asked to bid on a turnkey project. Requests for turnkey jobs were fairly common.

In the communications area, Venezuela represented one of the more forward-looking and well planned situations uncovered in this international survey. The current five-year plan called for an expansion of the telephone service by increasing telephone density from 5.2 telephones per 100 population to a figure of 10 by 1981 through investments in communications of about $1.2 billion. This would entail a doubling of telephones in use throughout the entire country from the 1975 level of about 650,000.

Because of its favorable international trade position, Venezuela, through its national telephone company CANTV, had been able to finance its expansions through internal resources, credit from international banks, and at times through supplier credits.

To increase the country's industrial base, CANTV would participate in the production of equipment required for its expansion. Such capabilities would usually take the form of joint ventures with private firms.

Initially, almost all of the equipment needed for the planned expansion of the telephone and telex systems would be imported. Due to the long lead times required for the delivery of telephone equipment, a substantial amount of

equipment to be installed during the six-year period was already on order, mostly from Japan and Europe. U.S. equipment was at a disadvantage since the original telephone systems installed were European and the present system was based on CCITT standards.

The principal suppliers of equipment were Ericsson of Sweden; ITT supplying through Belgium and Spain; Hitachi and Nippon Electric from Japan; Siemens from Germany; and American Electronics Company (AEC) supplying through Italy. Ericsson and ITT had been sharing the market for central office switching equipment on a 60/40 basis. Both companies did some local assembly of imported components. Hitachi and AEC were the main suppliers to the microwave market.

Siemens had a contract running through 1978 to expand the telex system. Three local manufacturers supplied most of CANTV's cable requirements. However, these companies did not yet produce stalpeth insulated cable, and CANTV had been importing this type of cable.

CANTV had been negotiating with Ericsson and others on the possibility of manufacturing mechanical switching equipment in Venezuela.

There was only one local company that manufactured telephone sets: Maplatex. Foreign firms continued to sell telephone sets since Maplatex was new in this business and could not satisfy the entire demand. However, once Maplatex was to reach a production level approaching domestic demand, the company would be able to obtain tariff protection, effectively curtailing other sources of supply.

PABXs were currently manufactured in limited numbers in Venezuela by a local company based upon its own design. The import market for PABXs was dominated by Siemens with an estimated 45% share. Tele Norma, another German firm, took around 25%, ITT 15%, AEC 10%, and Ericsson 5%. Siemens assembled PABXs in Venezuela, and planned to begin more extensive local manufacture in 1976. The company was to accommodate about 15,000 extensions a year with their initial production. They also planned to assemble telephone sets in Venezuela.

Telex units were not manufactured in Venezuela. Siemens supplied 100% of CANTV's need and was expected to continue to do so through 1978. About 60% of the private market was also controlled by Siemens. The rest of the private market was shared by ITT and Olivetti, with 15% each, AEC 7%, and Sagem, a French firm, with 3% of the market.

Venezuela was a participant in the Andean Common market along with Ecuador, Colombia, Peru, and Bolivia. Should this regional arrangement become operative within the next few years, Venezuela was to be given responsibility for the manufacture of various consumer electronics and lighting products to serve the entire regional area.

Between 1970 and 1975, the population of television sets in Venezuela rose from 720,000 to 1,284,000, an annual increase of 12.3%. Local production of television sets began in 1967 with the assembly of 28,000 sets and in the early years increased at the rate of nearly 50% per year.

The population of radios was estimated to be 2,050,000 in 1975, a rise from 1,700,000 in 1970, which meant over this period the population of radios rose at a rate of 3.8% per year. Radios, like television sets, were also assembled locally and the first meaningful production began in 1960 with the assembly of 10,000 units. Recent figures indicated assemblies of more than 100,000 units per year. Between 1971 and 1974, imports of radios rose from $11,398,000 to $16,026,000 per year, which reflected a 12% growth rate in the import market for radios.

As had been the pattern throughout Latin America, the Japanese and some European firms had set up assembly projects for the manufacture of consumer electronic products. Barely qualifying as manufacturing, some projects began by simply installing completed imported chassis into imported cabinets and relabeling of shipping cartons in which the cabinet components were shipped. The next level of integration was often the local manufacturing of cabinets, followed by board stuffing and higher levels of assembly. Notably Brazil, Argentina, Chile, and Mexico manufactured electronic components, but in Venezuela component manufacturing was limited to transformers and yokes for TV sets, along with some other easily manufactured components.

PRIORITY LIST

Given this general information about the four target countries, the TFG of the Communications Product Division had to establish a priority list to be presented to the upcoming board meeting. Since the development of such projects took an enormous amount of time and consumed substantial amounts of resources, it would not be possible to pursue all opportunities. Instead, the TFG management issued a priority list of the four countries for guidance to its own planning. There was no time left for additional studies and a decision had to be made with the information at hand.

CASE 3 ▪ New England Nuclear

INTRODUCTION

In April of 1980, Paul Green, International Marketing Planning Manager of New England Nuclear (NEN), was asked by the company's management to develop some estimates of market potential for the company's line of radiopharmaceuticals in Asia with special emphasis on Singapore, Hong Kong, the Philippines, Taiwan, South Korea, and Thailand. Following NEN's successful introduction of its radiopharmaceuticals into the United States, Canada, Western Europe, South and Central America, and most recently Australia and New Zealand, the Pacific Rim countries represented the next major opportunity for NEN. The largest Asian market, however, Japan, was a special case and would not be included in this next phase of market expansion.

COMPANY BACKGROUND

The nuclear age produced many high technology companies, among them New England Nuclear Corp. (NEN). The firm was formed in 1956 to transfer the knowledge of atomic research to biological and medical sciences. The Boston based company found a growing market in research institutes, hospitals and clinics. Operating primarily in North America and Western Europe, NEN went public in 1978, selling on the New York Stock Exchange. In 1979 sales were US $65.8 million with 22% in the international division (Exhibit 1).

RESEARCH PRODUCTS

To understand both normal body functions and disease processes, research scientists followed (or traced) the movement of chemicals in the body. However, the chemical compounds and the atoms from which they were built were extremely small and could not be seen. To overcome this problem NEN applied the technology of radioactivity.

In nature some atoms were unstable, and the nuclei of the atoms released particles or waves of energy, i.e., "radiation." These unstable atoms were said to be "radioactive." Nonradioactive atoms could be made unstable, or radioactive, by bombarding them with energy in a cyclotron, a machine used to accelerate atomic particles to great speeds.

As the radioactive isotopes (atoms) released their excess energy they became cold, i.e., nonradioactive. This process of releasing radiation (decay) often caused the atom to change into another type of atom, e.g., Molybdenum →

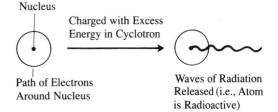

Nucleus

Charged with Excess Energy in Cyclotron

Path of Electrons Around Nucleus

Waves of Radiation Released (i.e., Atom is Radioactive)

This case was prepared by Jean-Pierre Jeannet, Professor of Marketing at Babson College based upon research conducted by Gary Silva. This case was designed for classroom purposes only and not to illustrate either effective or ineffective handling of a business situation. Copyright © 1980 Jean-Pierre Jeannet.

Technetium. For each type of atom there was a specific time for the process of decay from radioactivity to nonactivity (or decay to another radioactive atom). The time could range from thousands of years to just a few hours.

Whether natural or man-made, the radioactivity of the atoms could be detected by film or electronic devices:

More than 1,200 radioactive compounds were now available for genetic research, basic cell physiology, and the study of diseases, such as diabetes, hormone disturbances, and cancer. In 1979, such products for basic research accounted for 47% of NEN's sales.

Other radioactive compounds were devel-

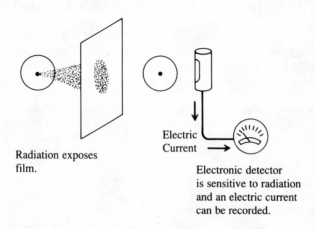

Radiation exposes
film.

Electric
Current

Electronic detector
is sensitive to radiation
and an electric current
can be recorded.

Since the atomic radiation passed through solid objects the presence of a radioactive atom could be detected even though the atom is in a cell or within the body. The process of passing a detector over the body to detect radiation was called "scanning." By scanning, the physician could obtain a "picture" of the organs, or the cells.

Very few *natural* chemical compounds were radioactive. To follow the movement of specific chemicals in cells, or in the body, NEN developed techniques to make one or more of the atoms in a chemical radioactive.

$$C^* + OXYGEN \rightarrow C^*O_2$$
$$C^*O_2 + WATER \rightarrow HC^*O_3 \ (CARBONATE)$$

C = CARBON
C* = RADIOACTIVE CARBON
H = HYDROGEN
O = OXYGEN

oped to be used in the diagnosis of disease. These compounds are called "radiopharmaceuticals," i.e., radioactive drugs.

RADIOPHARMACEUTICAL PRODUCT LINE

The second major product line, radiopharmaceuticals, accounted for approximately 48 percent of NEN's corporate sales. It was this relatively new but rapidly growing group of products for which Mr. Green had to determine the market potential for selected Asian countries. NEN actually decided to enter the radiopharmaceutical field in the mid-60s by aiming at introducing products better than its competition, consisting of Abbott, Squibb, and Mallinckrodt.

When the radioactive atom Technetium was injected into the body it collected in the brain tissues. By passing a radiation detector over the skull differences in the intensity of radiation (hot spots and cold spots) could be detected. In this way a physician could make a picture of the brain and locate the tumor (Exhibit 2). Since Technetium remained radioactive for only a few days and could not be made at the hospital, several firms sold Technetium generators (Exhibit 3). The name was a misnomer. The product was not a generator; it was not a machine at all. Like the competitors, NEN produced a radioactive metal Molybdenum and put it in a container which prevented the radiation from escaping (excessive radiation could cause radiation sickness and cancer). The Molybdenum decayed and produced a second radioactive atom, Technetium 99. These "so-called" Technetium generators were delivered to hospitals weekly. The

Technetium was then withdrawn for injection in patients so that scans of the brain could be made.

It was also possible to combine Technetium with other chemicals which collected in certain organs such as the kidney or the liver. Thus, scans or pictures of the liver could be made. Different chemicals were developed for carrying the Technetium to different organs and were sold as "kits." This technique represented a major breakthrough in medical diagnosis. Some of these kits currently produced by NEN for use in conjunction with TECHNETIUM 99M included a lung-imaging kit, PULMOLITE™, to assist in the diagnosis of diseases such as pulmonary embolism and emphysema, a bone imaging kit, OSTEOLITE™, to aid in the detection of fine

EXHIBIT 1 Consolidated Statement of Income and Retained Earnings

	Year Ended February 28	
	1979	1978
Net sales	$65,826,000	$50,687,000
Costs and expenses		
Cost of goods sold	26,515,000	22,515,000
Selling, general, and administrative	19,705,000	14,717,000
Research and development	5,198,000	3,003,000
	51,418,000	40,235,000
Operating income	14,408,000	10,452,000
Interest and dividend income (expense), net	314,000	(98,000)
Income before income taxes	14,722,000	10,354,000
Income taxes	6,698,000	5,131,000
Net income	8,024,000	5,223,000
Retained earnings at beginning of year	22,335,000	17,890,000
	30,359,000	23,113,000
Cash dividends: per share—$.38 in 1979 $.2675 in 1978	1,187,000	778,000
Retained earnings at end of year	$29,172,000	$22,335,000
Net income per common and common equivalent shares	3,182,158	2,949,776

EXHIBIT 1 Consolidated Balance Sheet (*cont.*)

	February 28	
ASSETS	1979	1978
Current Assets		
Cash	$ 2,756,000	$ 804,000
Short-term marketable securities	10,600,000	2,600,000
Accounts receivable, less allowances (1979—$317,000, 1978—$263,000)	13,174,000	10,928,000
Inventories	5,289,000	4,094,000
Other current assets	2,599,000	1,664,000
Total Current Assets	34,418,000	20,090,000
Property, Plant, and Equipment		
Land	1,111,000	1,111,000
Buildings and improvements	19,947,000	15,671,000
Laboratory and other equipment	16,753,000	12,605,000
	37,811,000	29,387,000
Less accumulated depreciation	7,348,000	5,658,000
Net Property, Plant, and Equipment	30,463,000	23,729,000
Other Assets	169,000	201,000
	$65,050,000	$44,020,000
LIABILITIES AND STOCK-HOLDERS' EQUITY		
Current Liabilities		
Accounts payable	$ 5,173,000	$ 4,003,000
Payroll and other accrued liabilities	1,391,000	1,331,000
Income taxes	2,170,000	1,769,000
Current portion of long-term debt	68,000	62,000
Total Current Liabilities	8,802,000	7,165,000
Long-Term Debt	4,372,000	4,404,000
Deferred Income Taxes	2,302,000	1,807,000
Stockholders' Equity		
Common Stock, par value $1.00 per share: authorized 8,000,000 shares in 1979 and 4,000,000 in 1978; issued 3,275,000 in 1979 and 1,474,000 in 1978	3,275,000	1,474,000
Capital in excess of par value	17,127,000	6,835,000
Retained earnings	29,172,000	22,335,000
Total Stockholders' Equity	49,574,000	30,644,000
	$65,050,000	$44,020,000

EXHIBIT 2

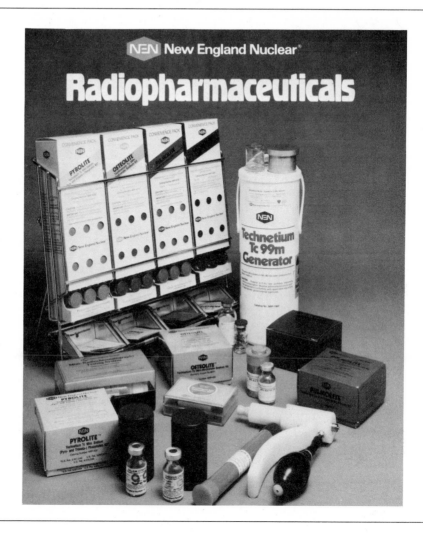

fractures and small metastases, and GLUCON-SAM™, used for brain imaging (Exhibit 2).

In extending the research NEN produced Gallium Citrate (Ga 67), which concentrated in specific types of cancer cells. With this product operations were no longer necessary to locate cancers. The physician was able to determine the progress of cancers such as Hodgkin's dis-

ease, and to select more appropriate therapy. Moreover, the new product Ga 67 produced a radiation without Beta-particles. Since Beta-particles tended to pose side-effects with repeated use, this was a clear advantage.

In 1978 NEN introduced Thallous Chloride 201 more commonly called Thallium 201. It was used to measure blood flow through coronary

EXHIBIT 3

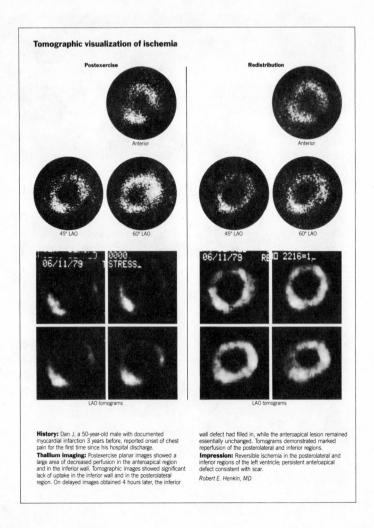

Tomographic visualization of ischemia

Postexercise

Anterior

45° LAO   60° LAO

Redistribution

Anterior

45° LAO   60° LAO

LAO tomograms

LAO tomograms

History: Dan J, a 50-year-old male with documented myocardial infarction 3 years before, reported onset of chest pain for the first time since his hospital discharge.

Thallium imaging: Postexercise planar images showed a large area of decreased perfusion in the anteroapical region and in the inferior wall. Tomographic images showed significant lack of uptake in the inferior wall and in the posterolateral region. On delayed images obtained 4 hours later, the inferior wall defect had filled in, while the anteroapical lesion remained essentially unchanged. Tomograms demonstrated marked reperfusion of the posterolateral and inferior regions.

Impression: Reversible ischemia in the posterolateral and inferior regions of the left ventricle; persistent anteroapical defect consistent with scar.

Robert E. Henkin, MD

arteries into the heart. With partial blockage of one of the coronary arteries less blood entered the heart muscle. Exercise and stress then caused pain (angina). Additional stress or a total blockage of a coronary artery could kill the heart tissue, producing a heart attack or infarct. Thallium 201 was attracted to healthy heart muscle with normal blood perfusion. Areas of the heart not receiving adequate blood flow picked up less Thallium 201 and appeared as cold spots on the scan (Exhibit 3). Prior to Thallium 201, the physician had to obtain an arteriogram, a painful and sometimes fatal surgical procedure for introducing dyes into arteries of the heart. While the new technique with Thallium 201 did not fully replace the arteriogram, it did reduce the number that had to be done, and reduced the cost from 2,000 US$ to 300 US$.

The third new product was a gas, Xenon 133. This gas was inhaled by the patient and a scan of the lungs was made. In conjunction with other tests, the physician was better able to diagnose respiratory diseases such as emphysema and chronic bronchitis. Lung dysfunction or the existence of blood clots could also be detected. Xenon 133 could be used in conjunction with the NEN lung kit, to test for both functional and pulmonary diseases at the same time.

MEDICAL APPLICATION OF RADIOPHARMACEUTICALS

Radiopharmaceuticals were essentially a tool for the physician to help with the diagnosis of various diseases. Any of these tests using NEN's radiopharmaceuticals had to be specifically ordered by a physician, cardiologist, or internist. The specialist in charge of nuclear medicine in a hospital would not use such a procedure if it was not specifically requested by the referring physician. Once a test had been requested, it was the nuclear technician who decided on the particular brand of isotope to be used.

The procedure of a typical test was as follows. The radioactive isotope was taken from the generator and mixed with the chemicals of the particular diagnostic kit. Approximately 10 min later the chemical was injected into the patient's blood stream and flowed to specific organs. Scans or pictures were then taken with a gama-camera (an electronic detector) either as a single scan or a series of scans. From the radiation picture made by the gama-camera the physician could diagnose abnormalities or locate tumors. In the past scans had also been taken with linear scanners but the modern gama-camera was much more sophisticated and detected a wider range of isotopes.

THE U.S. MARKET FOR RADIOPHARMACEUTICALS

The market for Technetium Generators in the United States was estimated to have reached about $35 million for 1978 with future growth rates estimated at 7.5 percent annually. Sales for kits used with Technetium were expected to grow considerably faster having achieved an estimated volume of $26.3 million in 1978. Growth rates through 1983 were estimated at 14.7 percent annually (see Exhibits 4 and 5). Substantially higher growth rates were expected in the areas of isotopes, particularly Thallium. This product group was expected to grow from $22.2 million in 1978 to $71.4 million in 1983. Thallium would account for the greatest amount of this growth, reaching growth rates of 40 percent annually. Thallium was used primarily to diagnose heart disease which accounted for approximately two million patient hospitalizations annually. It had been estimated that some 4 million Americans had some evidence of coronary heart disease with an even greater number seeking medical attention for symptoms similar to heart disease. While it appeared unrealistic to consider all these patients with any of these symptoms of heart disease likely candidates for Thallium scanning, it did appear that a Thallium test would be particularly useful in cases where the initial diagnosis was equivocal. For patients with chest pains but normal EKG or abnormal EKG but no other symptoms, thallium scanning appeared to be the logical next step.

Presently, approximately 500 hospitals were using thallium scanning, or only 20 percent of the 3,000 institutions with nuclear medicine capability. The percentage among teaching institutions was considered to be much higher, however. It was estimated that in 1979 90,000 to 100,000 thallium scans were to be performed. Within the next 5 years, it was believed that thallium tests will surpass 700,000 annually in the United States alone. Overseas use represented still no more than 10 to 15 percent of present U.S. usage. It should be kept in mind that for bone and perfusion lung scans alone more than 1 million were performed annually.

EXHIBIT 4 Growth of the Domestic Radiopharmaceutical Market ($ Millions)

	1976(E)	1978(E)	% Change	1983(E)	Compound Growth Rate 1978-1983E
Technetium 99M	$30.0	$35.0	+16.7%	$ 50.0	7.5%
Kits used with technetium					
Lung Agents	7.6	8.5	+11.8	10.8	5.0
Bone Agents	5.8	8.1	+39.7	14.7	13.0
Liver Agents	3.5	4.2	+20.0	8.6	15.4
Other Kits	3.5	5.5	+57.1	18.0	26.6
	$20.4	$26.3	+28.9	$ 52.1	14.7
Isotopes					
Gallium 67	$ 5.5	$ 8.6	+56.4	$ 18.9	17.0
Thallium 201	1.2	7.4	+516.7	40.0	40.1
Xenon 133	4.0	6.2	+55.0	12.5	15.0
	$10.7	$22.2	+107.5	$ 71.4	26.2
Other	$ 8.9	$12.5	+40.4	$ 31.5	20.2
Total U.S. Market	$70.0	$96.0	+37.1	$205.0	16.4

(*E*) Estimates from independent sources.

COMPETITION

NEN was the market leader in virtually all areas of radiopharmaceuticals. (See Exhibit for sales by product item.) NEN's major competitors were, by order of importance, Mallinckrodt, Inc. ($392 million sales), Abbott Laboratories ($1,445 million sales in 1978), Squibb Corporation ($1,515 million sales in 1978), Medi-Physics (a fully owned subsidiary of Hofmann-LaRoche, a very large pharmaceutical producer) and the Radiochemical Center Limited of U.K. with annual sales of about $80 million in 1979.

Most of these competitors were larger than NEN or were subsidiaries of very large pharmaceutical producers. Abbott had concentrated lately on the in vitro area, or the use of radiopharmaceuticals for test tube analysis, and was no longer a major factor in NEN's market segments. Because isotopes (Thallium was one

of them) were not directly processed from nuclear reactors such as technetium, only companies with knowledge of the complicated manufacturing process could actually enter the market. Isotopes were produced in a cyclotron, a circular accelerator, that cost several million dollars to install. NEN in fact operated the first commercial cyclotron and now had three installed. Mallinckrodt had acquired a Dutch company with a cyclotron but its capacity was largely used to satisfy the European market. Medi-Physics was now installing its own cyclotron in the United States.

MARKETING OPERATIONS IN THE U.S.

NEN maintained a sales force of 59 product specialists with support from home office staff and

EXHIBIT 5 New England Nuclear Radiopharmaceutical Product Line ($ Millions)

Product Group	Applications	Fiscal 1976 Revs. (E)	Fiscal 1977 Revs. (E)	Fiscal 1978 Revs. (E)	Fiscal 1979 Revs. (E)	Fiscal 1980 Revs. (E)	3–5 Year Growth Rate (E)
Specialty Isotopes							
Gallium 67	Diagnosis of Hodgkin's Disease, lymphomas, bronchogenic carcinoma	$ 3.40	$ 5.10	$ 8.30	$14.70	$21.70	25–30%
Thallium 201	Diagnosis of coronary artery disease and myocardial infarctions						
Xenon 133	Pulmonary function studies						
Ruthenium 97	Developmental						
Technetium		$ 5.40	$ 5.50	$ 5.80	$ 6.20	$ 6.60	6–8%
Technetium 99 M generator	Brain imaging, imaging of other organs in conjunction with kits						
Kits		$ 3.50	$ 5.20	$ 6.80	$ 8.60	$10.20	15–20%
Osteolite	Bone imaging						
Pyrolite	Bone and cardiac infarct imaging						
Pulmolite	Detection of pulmonary embolisms						
Glucoscan	Kidney and brain imaging						
DTPA	Kidney and brain imaging						
Cardiolite	Cardiac wall motion and ejection fraction studies						
Microlite	Liver scanning						
Other		$ 0.35	$ 0.41	$ 0.50	$ 0.60	$ 0.70	20–25%
Total		$12.65A	$16.21A	$21.40	$30.10	$39.20	

(E) Estimates from independent sources.
(A) Actual

service departments. About 40 of these specialists worked mostly for the radiopharmaceutical product line calling on technicians, doctors, radiologists, and scientists who specialized in nuclear medicine.

The logistic aspect of the product's distribution was extremely important due to short shelf-life for many items. The isotopes were shipped by air freight specially packed in shielded lead containers to the nearest airport of the destination. The products were then shipped by truck for immediate use at the hospital. Isotopes were produced so that the calibrated radiation was above the necessary level to do the intended test. So when the chemical's radioactivity decayed during shipping time, the chemical would still have the necessary radioactivity at the time of its actual use.

Besides regular advertising in the *Journal of Nuclear Medicine*, NEN made heavy use of educational programs. Seminars were held all over the United States with doctors in attendance.

INTERNATIONAL OPERATIONS

Approximately 22 percent of NEN's business was done overseas, mostly in Canada, Europe, and Japan. In most countries, NEN has to work through agents licensed to handle radioactive materials. For some markets such as Japan, entry had proved to be very difficult. NEN had been very successful in South America, and lately in Australia and New Zealand. But all of these countries belonged to the most developed nations of the world.

According to Mr. Green, the potential for NEN's product in the country depended on predominant disease states and medical technology, particularly on the availability of the new gamma cameras for scanning. The following data were his personal estimates on gamma cameras in operation:

- Hongkong   2–4
- Singapore   2–4
- South Korea   2
- Thailand   unknown
- Taiwan   10–15
- Philippines   10–15

Additional information on population, income, and various diseases and medical statistics had been provided by a student from Babson College, a nearby business school (see Exhibits 6–15). It was now up to Mr. Green to make a market potential forecast to be used to plan NEN's future radiopharmaceutical business in the Pacific Basin Area.

EXHIBIT 6 Population Statistics

	Mid-Year Population Estimates	Annual Rate of Increase
Hong Kong (1977)	4,514,000	1.9%
South Korea (1977)	36,437,000	1.8%
Philippines (1977)	45,028,000	2.9%
Singapore (1977)	2,308,000	1.5%
Thailand (1977)	44,039,000	2.8%
Taiwan (1970)	13,800,000	2.8%
United States (1980)	230,000,000	—

EXHIBIT 7 Income Statistics

	National Income	Per Capita Income
Hong Kong (1975)	$ 7,035,000,000	$ 1,599
South Korea (1977)	31,549,000,000	866
Philippines (1977)	18,566,000,000	412
Singapore (1975)	5,156,000,000	2,292
Thailand (1977)	16,698,000,000	379
Taiwan (1970)	3,726,000,000	270
United States	—	$10,000 (est.)

EXHIBIT 8 Medical Statistics

	Hospitals	Physicians	Population Per Physician
Hong Kong	91	3,127	1,444
South Korea	187	17,848	2,042
Philippines	813	13,480	3,341
Singapore	14	1,705	1,354
Thailand	315	5,000	8,808
Taiwan	28	4,353	3,170

EXHIBIT 9 Hong Kong

Cause of Death	Absolute Number	% of Total
1. Infective and Papasitic Diseases	1,281	5.8
Tuberculosis of Respiratory System	895	4.1
2. Neoplasms	4,710	21.4
Malignant Neoplasm of Trachea, Bronchus, and Lung	1,073	4.9
3. Endocrine, Nutritional, and Metabolic Diseases	218	.9
4. Diseases of Blood and Bloodforming Organs	46	.2
5. Mental Disorders	26	.1
6. Diseases of the Nervous System and Sense Organs	176	.8
7. Diseases of the Circulatory System	5,604	25.4
Hypertensive Disease	698	3.2
Ischaemic Heart Disease	1,265	5.7
Cerebrovascular Disease	2,105	9.6
8. Disease of the Respiratory System	3,795	17.2
Pneumonia	2,557	11.6
Bronchitis, Emphysema and Asthma	937	4.2
9. Diseases of the Digestive System	1,115	5.1
10. Diseases of Genito-Urinary System	373	1.7
11. Complications of Pregnancy, Childbirth, etc.	13	.1
12. Diseases of the Skin Subcutaneous Tissue	32	.2
13. Diseases of the Musculoskeletal System and Connective Tissue	35	.2
14. Congenital Anomalies	398	1.8
15. Certain Causes of Perinatal Mortality	552	2.5
16. Symptoms and Ill-Defined Conditions	1,921	8.7
17. External Causes	1,748	7.9

EXHIBIT 10 Philippines

Cause of Death	Absolute Number	% of Total
1. Infective and Papasitic Diseases	66,086	23.3
Enteritis and Other Diarphoeal Diseases	18,106	6.4
Tuberculosis of Respiratory System	26,011	9.2
Measles	4,866	1.7
2. Neoplasms	11,897	4.2
3. Endocrine, Nutritional and Metabolic Diseases	15,040	5.3
Avitaminoses and Other Nutritional Deficiency	13,850	4.9
4. Diseases of Blood and Blood forming Organs	1,924	.7
5. Mental Disorders	364	.1
6. Diseases of the Nervous System Sense Organs	4,329	1.5
7. Diseases of the Circulatory System	33,119	11.7
Hypertensive Disease	7,294	2.6
Ischaemic Heart Disease	8,499	3.0
Other forms of Heart Disease	8,096	2.9
Cerebrovascular Disease	4,569	1.6
8. Diseases of the Respiratory System	64,802	22.9
Pneumonia	48,058	17.0
9. Diseases of the Digestive System	10,656	3.8
10. Diseases of Genito-Urinary System	5,061	1.8
11. Complications of Pregnancy, Childbirth, etc.	1,488	1.2
12. Diseases of the Skin and Subcutaneous Tissue	623	.2
13. Diseases of the Musculoskeletal System and Connective Tissue	609	.2
14. Congenital Anomalies	5,524	2.0
15. Certain Causes of Perinatal Mortality	14,501	5.1
16. Symptoms and Ill-Defined Conditions	32,193	11.4
17. Accidents, Poisonings, and Violence	15,259	5.4

EXHIBIT 11   Singapore

Cause of Death	Absolute Number	% of Total
1. Infective and Papasitic Diseases	714	6.1
Tuberculosis of Respiratory System	401	3.4
2. Neoplasms	2,002	17.2
Malignant Neoplasm of Stomach	326	2.7
Malignant Neoplasm of Trachea, Bronchus, and Lung	412	3.5
3. Endocrine, Nutritional, and Metabolic Diseases	377	3.2
Diabetes Mellitus	257	2.2
4. Diseases of Blood and Blood-forming Organs	60	.5
5. Mental Disorders	16	.1
6. Diseases of the Nervous System Sense Organs	149	1.3
7. Diseases of the Circulatory System	3,295	28.2
Hypertensive Disease	333	2.8
Ischaemic Heart Disease	1,155	9.9
Other forms of Heart Disease	420	3.6
Cerebrovascular Disease	1,213	10.4
8. Disease of the Respiratory System	1,631	14.0
Pneumonia	958	8.2
9. Disease of the Digestive System	451	3.9
10. Disease of Genito-Urinary System	320	2.7
11. Complications of Pregnancy, Childbirth, etc.	8	.2
12. Disease of the Skin and Subcutaneous Tissue	19	.2
13. Diseases of the Musculoskeletal System and Connective Tissue	21	.2
14. Congenital Anomalies	177	1.5
15. Certain Causes of Perinatal Mortality	322	2.0
16. Symptoms and Ill-Defined Conditions	1,218	10.4
17. Accidents, Poisonings, and Violence	894	7.7

EXHIBIT 12 Taiwan

Cause of Death	Absolute Number	% of Total
1. Cholera	3,871	5.7
2. Avitaminoses and other Nutritional Deficiency	9,605	14.1
3. Chronic Rheumatic Heart Disease	1,684	2.5
4. Hypertensive Disease	2,731	4.0
5. Influenza	4,474	6.6
6. Pneumonia	2,083	3.1
7. Bronchitis, Emphysema, and Asthma	1,109	1.6
8. Intestinal Obstruction and Hernia	1,657	2.4
9. Cirrhosis of Liver	1,919	2.8
10. Nephritis and Nephrosis	1,917	2.8
11. External Causes	8,551	15.5

EXHIBIT 13 Thailand

Cause of Death	Absolute Number	% of Total
1. Infective and Parasitic Diseases	25,245	10.6
Enteritis and Other Diarphoeal Disease	7,174	3.0
Tuberculosis, Other Forms	6,415	2.7
Malaria	3,350	2.2
2. Neoplasms	1,164	2.6
3. Endocrine, Nutritional and Metabolic Diseases	3,237	1.4
4. Diseases of Blood and Blood-forming Organs	515	.2
5. Mental Disorders	360	.2
6. Diseases of the Nervous System Sense Organs	4,077	1.7
7. Disease of the Circulatory System	11,291	4.7
Cerebrovascular	3,185	1.3
8. Diseases of the Respiratory System	23,254	9.7
Acute Respiratory Infections	14,169	5.9
Pneumonia	6,190	2.6
9. Diseases of the Digestive System	10,918	4.6
10. Diseases of Genito-Urinary System	2,111	.9
11. Complications of Pregnancy, Childbirth, etc.	2,154	2.1
12. Disease of the Skin and Subcutaneous Tissue	185	.1
13. Diseases of the Musculoskeletal System and Connective Tissue	31	—
14. Congenital Anomalies	545	.2
15. Certain Causes of Perinatal Mortality	2,679	1.1
16. Symptoms and Ill-Defined Conditions	126,532	52.9
17. External Causes	19,853	8.3

EXHIBIT 14 Korea, Republic of

Disease	Cases	Deaths
Cholera	206	12
Typhoid Fever	4,222	40
Paratyphoid Fever	42	—
Amoebiasis	72	1
Bacillary Dysentery	814	13
Tuberculosis, Total	103,398	6,428
Leprosy	2,372	313
Diphtheria	568	18
Whooping Cough	3,818	3
Scarlet Fever	1	—
Meningococcal Infection	4	2
Poliomyelitis, Acute	176	—
Measles	4,867	7
Viral (Infect.) Encephalitis	126	10
Mumps	2,039	—
Malaria	15,926	—
Syphilis and Sequelae	3,129	—
Gynococcal Infections	35,997	—

EXHIBIT 15 Causes of Death in the United States (All Ages)*

Cardiovascular disease	52%
Cancer	20%
Accidents	5%
Pneumonia and influenza	3%
Diabetes	2%
Other Causes	18%

* Reproduced with permission. © 1988 HEART FACTS American Heart Association.

CASE 4 ▪ Nippon Vicks K.K.

In March of 1983, Mr. Masahiro Horita, product manager for Nippon Vicks' acne care business, was uncertain what to recommend to further grow the "Clearasil" business in Japan. "Clearasil" had been introduced nationally in 1979 and quickly reached a volume of 2.5 million packages. Nippon Vicks K.K. had been unable to expand volume beyond that point despite a general expansion of the market. Sales volume had recently dropped to a rate of 2.0 million packages per year. Horita felt under increasing pressure to remedy the situation, particularly given a period of intense competitive activity in early 1983.

During the last 12 months, Horita had held several discussions with head office executives on Clearasil strategy for Japan. He was expected to come up with a final proposal to be presented at the marketing strategy review meeting to be held at the end of this month. Despite extensive consultations, there still existed a substantial disagreement between Horita's views and those held by division head office personnel.

COMPANY BACKGROUND

Richardson-Vicks

Richardson-Vicks was a leading worldwide marketer of branded consumer products in the areas of health care, personal care, nutritional care, and home care. Corporate sales amounted to $1,115 million for the fiscal year ending June 30, 1982.

The Vicks name was recognized around the world for treatment of the common cold. In the United States, 25 percent of all consumer expenditures in this category went to purchase Vicks products. Abroad, Vicks cough drops were market leaders from Germany to Japan. VapoRub, originally introduced in 1906, was marketed in more than 100 countries. Cold care provided for the original base of Richardson-Vicks, and in 1983 the company continued to add new products to that segment. The company had recently moved to expand its non-cold health care products by adding an antacid, "Tempo," and acquiring "Percogesic" from DuPont's Endo Laboratories as an entry into the analgesic market.

Richardson-Vicks had been in the personal care business since 1958 and expanded this segment through product development and acquisitions. "Oil of Olay" was the leading adult skin care product in the world with sales of more than $150 million. The company marketed several teenage skin care products. Clearasil was the leading acne product in the United States, Germany, and Japan. Topex, another entry in the acne care category, was the leader in the benzoyl peroxide segment in many international markets. The company also sold several shampoo brands, toothpaste, and denture care products in many non-U.S. markets.

International Division

International operations accounted for slightly more than half of Richardson-Vicks' sales in 1982. With $303.8 million in sales for 1982,

This case was prepared by Visiting Professor Jean-Pierre Jeannet, as a basis for class discussion rather than to illustrate either effective or ineffective handling of an administrative situation. Copyright 1986 by IMEDE (International Management Development Institute), Lausanne, Switzerland. Reproduced by permission.

Vicks International Europe/Africa Division represented more than half of the company's foreign sales. Headquartered in Paris, the division's leading brands were Kukident denture care products, Vicks cough drops, Oil of Olay beauty fluid, and Clearasil acne care products.

The Vicks International Americas/Far East Division included Canada, Latin America, and the Far East. Sales for the Western Hemisphere (Americas) amounted to $136.9 million and other areas (mostly Far East) totalled $137.9 million. Headquartered in Westport, Connecticut, leading products of this division included "Choco Milk," a powdered chocolate nutritional supplement. Clearasil acne care products, Larin candy products, Oil of Olay beauty fluid, Colac laxative, Vicks cold products, and a line of insecticides.

Nippon Vicks K.K.

Nippon Vicks K.K. (NVKK) was a wholly owned subsidiary of Richardson-Vicks, Inc. The Japanese subsidiary was incorporated in 1964 and had experienced rapid growth. Sales grew from 1.8 billion yen in 1972/1973 to 11 billion yen in 1981/1982 and were expected to reach 13 billion yen in 1983/1984.[1] NVKK maintained its corporate offices in Osaka and operated a manufacturing plant near Nagoya, where about half of NVKK's staff was employed.

NVKK's leading product was "Colac," accounting for about one-half of the company's sales. "Colac" was the leading laxative in Japan with a market share of about 40 percent. Other products marketed were Vicks Cough Drops, Vicks VapoRub, and two infant care products, Milton and Milgard. With about 15 percent of NVKK's sales, Clearasil was an important contributor to the company's profitability. NVKK was one of the most successful foreign subsidiaries operating in Japan and its brands enjoyed a leadership position in their market segments. NVKK had been particularly successful in introducing consumer products in Japan for which domestic products did not exist.

---

1. yen 250 = 1 U.S. dollar.
    1 billion yen = U.S. $4 million.

THE U.S. MARKET FOR SKIN CARE PRODUCTS

When the Clearasil business was acquired by Richardson-Vicks in 1960, total value amounted to U.S. $2.3 million. By 1980, Clearasil sales represented about U.S. $30 million and consisted of Clearasil Regular Tinted Cream, Clearasil Soap, Clearasil Stick, Clearasil Vanishing Formula, Clearasil Medicated Cleanser, Clearasil Antibacterial Acne Lotion, and most recently New Super Strength Clearasil Creams and Clearasil Antibacterial Soap.

The target audience for acne care products were almost all teenagers. The most typical skin problems faced by this group were pimples, oily skin, and blackheads. It was estimated that about 20 percent of the target audience represented new users each year. Although this was a teenage product, mothers were believed to make the selection in six out of ten occasions for boys and three out of ten for girls.

About 50 percent of the target population used treatment products, up from 35 percent in 1975. Of the 50 million teenagers, only 25 million were users of treatment products, 10 percent had clear skin, and 40 percent represented potential new users. Clearasil was the market leader with Clearasil creams accounting for about 25 percent of dollar value and 30 percent of unit value.

The treatment market in the U.S. had undergone substantial changes in the 1970's. Prior to 1975, sulfur and resourcinol, used in Clearasil, was the only approved treatment agent for creams. In 1975, the Federal Drug Administration cleared benzoyl peroxide in strength of up to 10 percent. This provided an opportunity for a new brand, Oxy 5, and later Oxy 10 (indicating the percentage of benzoyl peroxide) marketed by Norcliff-Thayer, a unit of Revlon. Oxy began to erode Clearasil's market share, a trend that was stopped only when Richardson-Vicks launched New Super Strength Clearasil Cream with 10 percent benzoyl peroxide in 1979. Clearasil's market share as a result rebounded and the brand continued to dominate the acne treatment segment.

In the U.S., Clearasil was heavily supported by advertising. Budgeted expenditures in 1980

EXHIBIT 1 Japanese Skin Care Industry: Segmentation

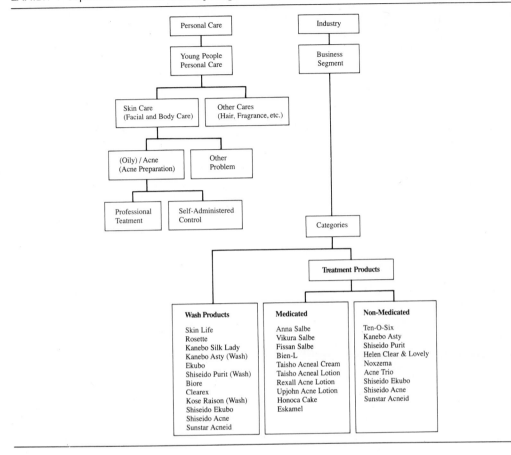

accounted for about U.S. $5 million, or 25 percent of all advertising expenditures for the category. Richardson-Vicks employed a strategy in the U.S. that was closer to a two-way action benefit.

THE SKIN CARE MARKET IN JAPAN

In Japan skin care products were a part of the personal care industry. Since acne products were targeted for people in their teens and early twenties, the acne products were part of the young people's personal care segment. Two principal categories were offered: skin care, including facial and body care; and "other" cares,

consisting of hair care, fragrances, etc. See Exhibit 1.

The youth skin care market included 21.6 million consumers between the ages of 12 and 24, both male and female. Some 77 percent, or 16.6 million young people, suffered some type of skin problems. About 51 percent or 11.0 million suffered from acne, or pimples. There was no difference between male or female populations when it came to acne suffering. See Exhibit 2.

About the remaining 47 percent, or about 5.2 million of acne sufferers, were characterized as treaters. A very small percentage of these would search out professional help. Treaters were described as acne sufferers using a specific acne product other than ordinary bar soap.

EXHIBIT 2 Japanese Skin Care Market: Young People

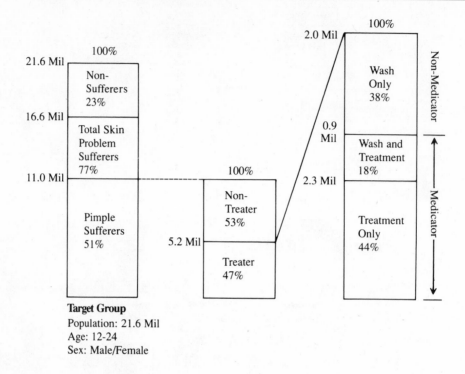

Target Group
Population: 21.6 Mil
Age: 12-24
Sex: Male/Female

Source: Post 24 A&U Tokyo (July, 1981).

Some 53 percent of Japanese acne sufferers fell into the category of non-treaters. "Pimples are the symbol of youth" was a common saying in Japan according to Horita. "Japanese in general consider that the time will be coming for everyone to have pimples, and that they will disappear automatically. It was just a matter of time until they would disappear." Non-treaters used only ordinary bar soap to wash their face.

About 38 percent of treaters used "wash products" only, such as toiletry facial wash products, toiletry bar soaps, and cosmetic facial soaps. The wash-only group was 60 percent female. Wash products were marketed as preventatives.

About 44 percent of treaters used treatment products only. Of those, 70 percent were Cleara-sil users. Users of treatment products were about equally divided between male and female users.

The third and smallest group of treaters, 18 percent of all treaters, were simultaneous users of treatment products and wash products.

Products for Acne Treatment

"Before Clearasil's re-launch in 1978, there was no product on the market advertised exclusively for acne treatment. NVKK and Clearasil created this market," explained Horita.

Treatment products were classified either as drug or quasi-drug. The difference between the two categories depended on the product's ingredients and its registration with the Japanese

Drug Administration. Clearasil was drug registered.[2]

Competitors in this category included a number of domestic and foreign brands including Upjohn Acne Lotion, Rexall Acne Lotion, Taisho Acneal Cream, Taisho Acneal Lotion. None of these products was actively supported by promotional campaigns and all were priced between 700 yen to 1200 yen per unit. Most of the manufacturers were pharmaceutical companies that tended to concentrate on ethical drugs that required promotion directed at the medical profession and distribution through drug store outlets.

The quasi-drug acne treatment products consisted of a number of products positioned largely for acne prevention. These products were licensed under a different procedure and were prevented by law to be positioned for treatment. Major competitors were Kanebo Asty, Shiseido Purit, Helene Curtis, Clear and Lovely, Noxema, and Acne Trio. These included some of the largest Japanese cosmetic companies. Prices for these products ranged from 500 to 1,500 yen.

There was a difference between the two product categories with respect to product claims and distribution. Drug registered products could claim to treat and cure acne. Quasi-drug products at most could claim to prevent acne from occurring. If a company decided to license a product as a drug, that product's distribution was restricted to drug stores only. Quasi-drug products could be sold through a variety of outlets including drug stores, supermarkets, and department stores.

"Wash" Products

On a unit basis, "wash" products accounted for the largest share of the acne market in Japan. That share had been expanding and was estimated at more than 50 percent for the most recent two-month Nielsen period. There were

seven subcategories in this wash market. See Exhibit 3.

Major competitors included Gyunyu Sekken with its Skin Life soap priced at 150 yen for a 46 gram bar, and Kao Sekken Biore cleansing foam (300 yen for a 60 gram tube). Kao was Japan's leading soap and detergent company.

The wash category had consistently gained in market share compared to the drug and quasi-drug categories. However, the leading brands—Ekubo and Biore—had not been exclusively positioned as acne products. These three leading wash brands were supported by mass media and marketed for general skin care. It was in the "wash" products category that competitive activity was particularly strong. This category had witnessed several new product entries in the past two months. See Exhibit 4.

MARKET CHANNELS

All of NVKK's products fell into the proprietary drug category. Consequently, distribution was standardized for all products. About 2,000 companies competed in the proprietary trade but only about 175 employed 100 or more people. Proprietary drugs (OTC) accounted for 15 percent of all drug sales in Japan compared to ethical drugs with 85 percent.

NVKK used the same channels as its Japanese competitors. Sales were made from the factory to a group of primary wholesalers. Some of these in turn sold to a number of sub-wholesalers. The sub-wholesalers distributed NVKK's products through a large number of retail outlets which included general drugstores and various types of chain drugstores. Because NVKK products could only be sold through drug stores, the company did not maintain contacts with discount stores, department stores and convenience stores that did not have drug corners.

Wholesale Drug Distribution

NVKK used about 60 primary wholesalers which, together with their branches, maintained about 250 sales offices. Primary wholesalers

---

2. The term *drug-registered* is identical with medicated product, and *quasi-drug* with non-medicated, as used elsewhere in this case.

EXHIBIT 3 Japan Wash Market

Segment	Target	Benefits
Cosmetic cleansing (lotion, cream, gel)	Female adults use make up user	Remove make-up and dirt thoroughly Refreshing Dirts free
Cosmetic facial soap (Honey cake, moon drops)	All females Normal/dry skin, primarily	After washing, leave skin smooth and moist Less irritation
Toiletry bar soap by cosmetic company	Female	Keep skin smooth and moist Leave refreshing
Toiletry facial wash (Biore, Silk Lady)	All females Normal/dry skin primarily	After washing, leave skin smooth and moist Less irritation Good for preventing pimples (secondary) Good for delicate skin
Specialized facial soap	Female for delicate skin	Good for face washing for very delicate/sensitive skin
Medicated soap	Male/female Younger	Sterilize skin Good for preventing pimples Treatment for skin disease
Medicated soap for sterilization	Specifically for treating skin problem	Sterilize skin

were granted non-exclusive sales territories which resulted in at times very keen competition among various branch offices. "For this kind of trade, 60 primary wholesalers is probably a moderate figure," explained Mr. Nagata, NVKK's national sales manager. A large Japanese competitor would maintain up to 200 primary wholesalers. NVKK's top 5 primary wholesalers accounted for about 57 percent of NVKK's total sales volume, the next 5 for 14 percent, while the smallest 25 were responsible for only 8 percent of NVKK sales. See Exhibit 5.

The role of the primary wholesaler was to distribute the products both directly and through smaller sub-wholesalers. In the Japanese drug

EXHIBIT 3 Japan Wash Market (cont.)

Support	Price/size/Form	Distribution	Others
Deep cleansing After feeling by product foam	Wide range of product forms	Cosmetic store	Use as part of daily make up routine Personal use only Double usage with facial soap
Ingredients (honey, lemon, etc.) Appearance Perfume Company image	Transparant bar soap Premium price (1,000–1,500)	Cosmetic store (Chain store)	Personal use
Product line by skin type	Medium price bar soap	All distribution channel	Personal–family
Special ingredient (MFP) Company image	Mainly cream type Several size Medium price (300–600)	All distribution channel	Quasi drug Personal use–family use
No perfume No coloring No irritants Weak acidity same as skin Ingredients	Premium price 1,000–2,000	Cosmetic/drug store (specialized)	Only for sensitive skin
Antibacterial ingredients Drying effects	Low–medium	Drugstore–Cosmetic	Specialized purpose only (pimple–allergy)
Ingredients	Small size Medium–High	Drugstore only	

trade existed about 2700 wholesalers of all types. Of those, about 500 carried ethical products only and 2200 carried both ethical and proprietary drugs or only the latter category. Among the top 100 wholesalers, 25 specialized in ethical products only. The rest carried both proprietary and ethical lines. Some of these also carried toiletry products. "Of the about 1000 wholesalers involved in proprietary drugs, we cover about 160," said Mr. Nagata, "and they maintain another 96 sales branches among themselves."

Of NVKK's primary wholesalers, only one concentrated in proprietary products accounting for 5 percent of NVKK's volume. Another eight primary wholesalers, accounting for 59 percent

EXHIBIT 4 Competitive Actions

Acne Preparations
Trend of Consumer Sales (units)

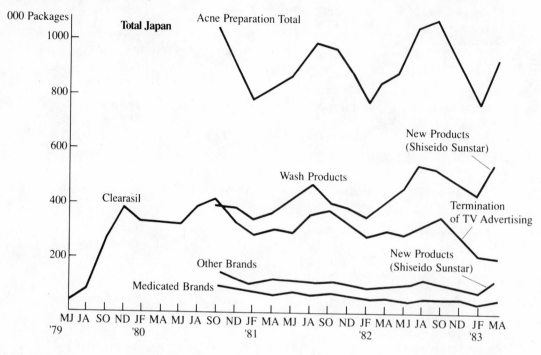

of sales, carried both proprietary and toiletry products. The remainder of its volume was accounted for by primary wholesalers carrying both drug categories.

Retail Drug Distribution

"NVKK has achieved virtually 100 percent penetration of the drug-related retail trade" declared Mr. Nagata. General drug stores were the most important retail segment, accounting for 70 percent of NVKK's volume. There were about 51,500 such stores in Japan. Most of these stores were small and had less than 6 employees. Two-thirds of all stores had only one or two employees. They accounted for 40 percent market share. In Japan, only 1 percent of all drugstores

had more than 6 employees. These larger stores accounted for only 7 percent of the general drug-store sales volume.

The second most important group was the national and local chain drugstores. This category included about 2800 drugstores. They accounted for 20 percent of NVKK's volume. The local chains numbered about 1500 stores. Another 1300 outlets in this segment were accounted for by national chain stores, e.g., Kokumin and Higuchi, or supermarkets with drug corners such as Daiei or Jusco. These chains maintained drug corners and employed a licensed pharmacist.

With about 300 outlets, local discount drug-stores were small in numbers but accounted for 5 percent of NVKK's volume. These were indi-

EXHIBIT 5 Distribution Channels

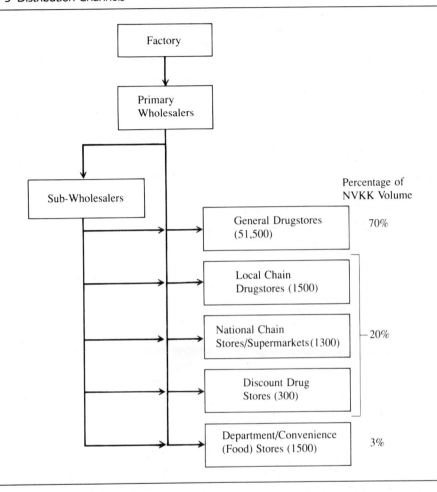

vidually managed stores operated on a discount basis. The department store and convenience store segment included about 1500 outlets and accounted for only 3 percent of NVKK's volume. This last segment included 1000 drugstore corners in department stores and about 500 in convenience food stores. Most convenience food stores did not have drug sections.

In 1980, the typical drugstore's retail sales consisted of the following product categories:

drugs	51%
cosmetics	12%
toiletries	9%
medical supplies	9%
other	19%

Drug sales were further sub-divided into the following categories:

nutritional and tonic drugs	30.8%
psychotropic drugs (includes cold remedies and sleeping pills)	19.0%
gastro-intestinal drugs	16.2%
external skin drugs	15.8%
respiratory tract drugs	4.3%
others	13.9%

NVKK's Sales Organization

NVKK's sales force consisted of 5 branch managers and 25 salesmen. They focused their activities on NVKK's primary wholesalers, the sub-wholesalers, and NVKK's largest 1500 retail customers. In urban areas, primary wholesalers were visited weekly, and twice per month in rural areas. Both sub-wholesalers and top retailers were visited once per month.

NVKK's sales force was responsible for distributing all of the company's eight products in national distribution, as well as any test markets the company might run. For its size, NVKK maintained a small sales force. In accordance with NVKK's reliance on a pull strategy that included heavy use of consumer advertising, NVKK's sales force was primarily used to maintain good relationships with wholesalers and to solve minor problems. Almost all orders were telephoned to NVKK by its wholesalers. In contrast, NVKK's Japanese competitors in the drug market tended to follow more of a "push" campaign with a greater reliance on personal selling.

NVKK's price structure offered the average retailer a 30 percent gross margin. Sub-wholesalers bought at 64 percent of list, and the average primary wholesaler's purchase price was 60 percent of list. Although retailer margins for NVKK products were the same as for competitor products, NVKK wholesale margins were 3 to 4 percent below those of other major advertised brands. "NVKK follows much more of a pull strategy than other Japanese competitors in this field who tend to emphasize more of a push strategy," commented Mr. Nagata.

RECENT COMPETITIVE DEVELOPMENTS

Starting in February 1983, competition in the acne preparation market had been very active. This activity was largely concentrated on the quasi-drug and "wash" segments of the acne market. In February, Shiseido added "Acne Wash Foam" as a line extension to its Ekubo "wash" product line. Also in February, Sunstar launched a set of "wash" products and a quasi-drug spot lotion under the brand name "Acneid." In March, Shiseido introduced a series of six wash products, including both wash and quasi-drug lotions, under the "Acne" brand name. That same month Kanebo added a drug registered acne cream "Mydate Acne Fresh" as an extension of its Mydate lotion and moisturizer wash products.

These new entries differed from existing cosmetic products insofar as they were exclusively positioned as acne products. Previously, products were either integrated into an existing line of cosmetics or represented a complete acne cosmetic line. These new wash products were registered as quasi-drug cosmetics with acne prevention as the key benefit. The new entries were distributed through a wide range of channels typical of cosmetic products.

The Ekubo line was produced and distributed by Shiseido, Japan's largest cosmetics company. The line included Ekubo Washing Foam, Milky Cream, Lemon Fresh, Milky Fresh, Milky Cream Soft, and Deodorant. The Ekubo Acne Foam came in two sizes of 20 grams and 80 grams, priced at 180 yen and 460 yen, respectively. The key benefit was "washing with it prevents acne." The line was supported by advertising in TV, magazines, outdoors, and informational leaflets and brochures.

Shiseido's later entry, Acne, was an entirely new line of six products consisting of:

Acne Soap	75 grams	600 yen
Acne Washing Foam	75 grams	1,000 yen (equals U.S. $4.00)
Acne Pack	75 grams	1,200 yen
Acne Lotion	75 grams	1,200 yen
Acne Skin Milk	75 grams	1,200 yen
Acne Spot Touch	10 ml	1,000 yen

These products appeared to be primarily targeted at consumers aged 15 to 17, both male and female, with the age group 18 to 24 as a secondary target. The introduction was supported with heavy TV, magazine, newspaper, and outdoor advertising.

Sunstar, Japan's leading market of toothpaste, introduced "Acneid," its first entry into the acne preparation market:

Acneid Washing Foam	60 grams	600 yen
Acneid Washing Foam S	60 grams	600 yen
Acneid Soap	60 grams	600 yen
Acneid Lotion	30 ml	700 yen

These products were fully supported with advertising in TV, magazine, outdoor, and point-of-purchase brochures.

Kanebo, Japan's second largest cosmetics company, introduced a medicated cream, Mydate Acne Fresh (30 grams at 600 yen) as a line extension for its Mydate series that included Clean Fresh cream, Milky Moist moisturizer, and Lotion Fresh.

CLEARASIL'S PERFORMANCE IN JAPAN

Skin toned Clearasil had been marketed without advertising support in Japan from mid 1961 until early 1974. It had reached a unit volume of only 44,500 units at a consumer price of 300 yen. It was taken off the market together with other small volume items in conjunction with a reorganization of NVKK's sales efforts.

Test Market Experience

NVKK decided to test market a reformulated version of Clearasil acne skin cream in 1978. The reformulated product was a "vanishing spot cream" that could be applied to acne on a person's face. Given its effective medicated ingredients, the product was designed to open the acne pimple head, drain the pimple without the need for squeezing, and finally to dry the acne pimples. The reformulated Clearasil was virtually identical to the product sold in the United States at that time. It did not contain benzoyl peroxide as it was not an approved ingredient in Japan. It was packaged in an 18 gram tube wrapped in a carton.

NVKK tested Clearasil in two test markets between July 1978 and June 1979. The two markets, Hiroshima and Shizuoka, represented about 4.5 percent of the total Japanese market and were supported with spot television advertising. Clearasil was priced at 700 yen per package at the consumer level and was distributed through drugstores only. Given Clearasil's registration as an OTC proprietary product, NVKK was restricted to the drugstore channel. "We choose to register Clearasil as a proprietary (OTC) drug product because we believe it was a marketing advantage," explained Horita.

The test market results were very encouraging. Factor shipments amounted to about 122,000 packages over a twelve-month period. National roll-out was commenced in July 1979 and was completed by October. It was supported by TV advertisement exclusively and the consumer price was increased to 900 yen. Factory shipments for the first twelve months after national introduction amounted to 2,560,000 packages. The company had not expected to reach this sales level for at least another year. Factory shipments remained at about the same level for the 1980/1981 fiscal year but began to decrease to 2,308,000 packages in 1981/1982 and 2,031,000 packages for the 1982/1983 fiscal year. For a detailed history of Clearasil's performance over the period 1979–1983, see Exhibit 6.

Throughout this time, NVKK supported Clearasil heavily with advertising. Advertising expenditures averaged about 70 percent of sales for the first three years after the national launch.

Dane Battiato, NVKK's marketing director, commented: "In our business it is typical to spend lots of money on advertising. When we first launch a new brand in a market, we are prepared to investment-spend beyond the normal level of advertising for a certain period. At Richardson-Vicks, we use a hurdle rate of 18 percent ROI for investment projects. With Clearasil, we can only reach normal product contribution if we cut marketing expenditures back to about 40 percent of the current level while holding sales."

EXHIBIT 6 Clearasil Product Performance

		Sales Units		Value (000) yen	
		Clearasil	Clearasil Share %	Clearasil	Clearsail Share %
1979	S/O	261,400	9.9	190,097	14.3
	N/D	373,380	11.0	271,092	17.0
1980	J/F	334,060	9.8	242,297	14.4
	M/A	314,280	10.9	228,591	15.0
	M/J	312,520	54.9	227,290	53.8
	J/A	385,340	45.3	298,146	45.9
	S/O	403,720	39.4	339,445	42.4
	N/D	325,870	36.2	227,498	40.6
1981	J/F	278,430	36.1	239,166	40.7
	M/A	295,680	36.1	251,942	39.9
	M/J	287,290	33.3	244,303	37.1
	J/A	358,610	36.2	306,242	41.1
	S/O	380,030	39.7	324,731	43.5
	N/D	320,350	37.0	273,877	41.9
1982	J/F	284,670	37.5	243,623	42.7
	M/A	305,290	36.0	260,285	40.2
	M/J	296,540	33.6	253,132	37.4
	J/A	333,300	31.8	283,883	35.8
	S/O	356,500	33.6	303,375	38.1
	N/D	300,210	32.2	252,702	36.7
1983	J/F	216,300	28.7	182,790	33.0
	M/A*	212,410	22.9	108,447	26.5

* Estimated by NVKK executives for period March/April 1983.

Strategic Decisions on Clearasil

Horita believed NVKK management had reached a point where some critical decisions had to be made with respect to Clearasil's direction in Japan. "It bothers me that we cannot expand volume beyond the earlier reached levels of 2.5 million packages while the rest of the market is expanding rapidly."

In reviewing Clearasil's progress to date, management concluded that neither pricing nor product formulation were at the root of the problem. Horita pointed to indications that Clearasil's advertising was not communicating as well as it should. In order to restore Clearasil's volume growth, the advertising strategy might have to be changed.

Another opportunity for Clearasil was to expand into the "wash" segment by launching a Clearasil soap. This would give NVKK a chance to participate in the fastest growing acne preparation segment, the "wash" products, with the possibility of launching additional line extensions at a later time.

CLEARASIL ADVERTISING IN JAPAN

Clearasil's advertising was centered around the theme used worldwide by Richardson-Vicks. The key component was the documentation of Clearasil's three-way action:

1. Clearasil opens the acne/pimple head.
2. Clearasil drains the inside of the acne pimple without squeezing.
3. Clearasil dries the acne pimple.

From the outset, Clearasil was positioned as a unique and highly effective medicated cream with a special three-way action unsurpassed in its ability to clear up acne and thereby improve the appearance and social confidence of acne sufferers.

For the test market and the first year of national launch, NVKK used two TV commercials produced locally, both in a 30-second and 15-second version around two themes, "High School" and "Date." The same themes were used until mid-1980 when a revised version, "Adolescence," was introduced. Starting January 1981, a new commercial titled "Testimonial" was used in 30-second and 15-second versions to be followed a year later by still another new campaign titled "Disarming." See Exhibit 7.

The "High School" and "Date" Campaigns

The "High School" and "Date" versions of Clearasil were the initial commercials aired during both the test market period and during the first 12 months of national distribution. The campaign was designed to position Clearasil as *the* specific acne treatment product in a market where specific acne treatment products had never been actively marketed. See Exhibit 8.

The copy objectives were to make the point that Clearasil was specifically formulated to deal with acne, was a serious medicated product for treatment of acne, and would contribute to the improvement of the complexion of users. The advertising had to communicate Clearasil's three-way action and that it was suitable for all ages of the primary target audience, and to imply that it provided some form of social reward.

Change to the "Adolescence" Campaign

By the end of 1979, Horita concluded that the "High School" and "Date" campaigns worked well as introductory campaigns to build brand awareness. In fact, the campaigns had surpassed all NVKK objectives. However, Horita believed that the two commercials used did not wear very well over time. The commercials were too similar to each other because they both relied on the 3-way-action demonstration. Furthermore, low interest scores were indications of problems with the commercials.

Drawing on unused footage from the "High School" commercials, a new commercial entitled "Adolescence" was produced. There was, of course, little difference in copy compared to the earlier version. The major differences were new visuals on other aspects of school life. See Exhibit 9.

The "Testimonial" Campaign

Successive research indicated that the previous campaigns successfully communicated with and generated trial among the sufferer/treater segment. The campaign failed to generate sufficient trial among the sufferer–non-treater segment because Clearasil was perceived as a very serious and specific product, possibly too medical, due to the overall serious tone of the commercials and the continuous use of the 3-way-action demonstration.

The "Testimonial" campaign was produced to increase trial among the non-treater segment which was identified as the key source for future volume growth for the brand. A documentary approach similar to Australian and Mexican testimonial commercials was used. These commercials featured testimonial comments in quick cut sequences depicting teenagers who suffered from acne and who shared their various ideas on remedies and their advice with the television audience in a frank and natural way. The 3-way-action of earlier commercials was made slightly shorter and lighter in tone but NVKK retained

EXHIBIT 7 Clearasil TV Campaign History

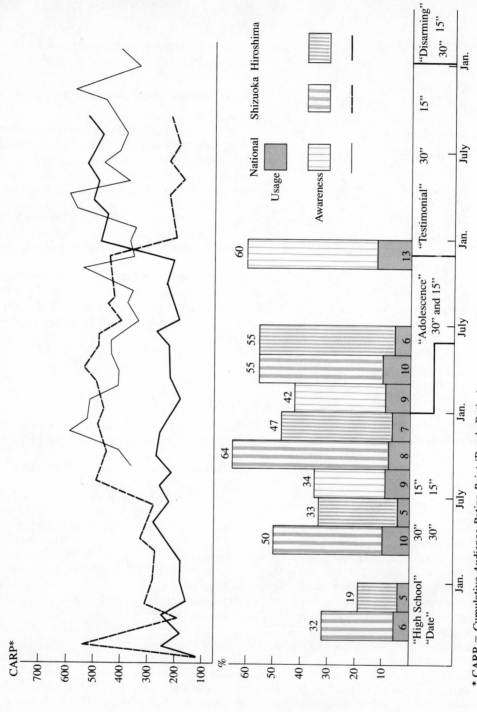

* CARP = Cumulative Audience Rating Point (People Rating)
  Shows Gross Coverage over the total people or each target ar

EXHIBIT 8 Story Board for "Date" Campaign, 1978/1979, June 14, 1978

1.

Isn't it a little too late to start doing something about acne pimples when you already have a boyfriend?

オーイ、ドートってくらべる さみし きょも 見えまけんかが キョニニキビワイ門衆。

2.

3.

Now, use CLEARASIL, the acne pimple treatment cream.

これ、ニキビにお薬 クリーム クレアシルを 使ってみせしげ。

4.

CLEARASIL has the following 3-way action which helps:

クレアシルは プスの 3つの 作用を うながします。

5. (1)

1. to open the acne pimple head.

オーバー、ニキビ 内部を 別く 作用。

6. (2)

2. to drain the in-side of the acne pimple without squeezing.

オニに、アラ・さ ぎ に ニキビ 内部を 出ぐ 作用。

7. (3)

3. to dry up the acne pimples.

オミに、ニキビを 乾かす 作用。て。

8.

Have your face at its best for that date!

デートには 一番いい 頗して

9.

And now, go to it.

サァ ごかり ましよう

10.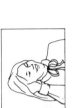

The acne pimple treatment cream, CLEARASIL. Newly on sale.

ニキビ治療薬 クリーム クレアシル 新発売！

EXHIBIT 8 (cont.)

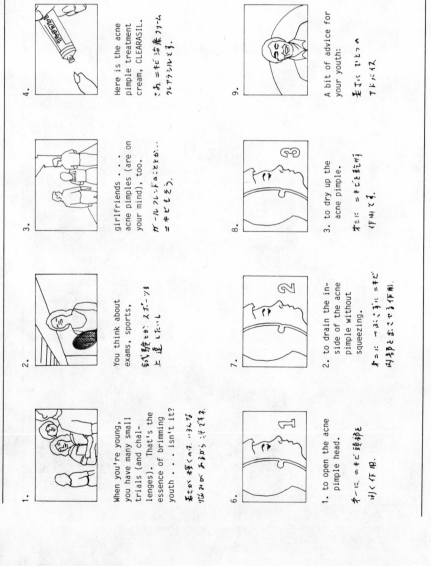

1.

When you're young, you have many small trials (and challenges). That's the essence of brimming youth . . . isn't it?

若さが輝くって、いろいろ
悩みも あるから 浮て当ろえ.

2.

You think about exams, sports,

試験とか、スポーツ
と違しない

3.

girlfriends . . . acne pimples (are on your mind), too.

ガール フレンド…ときどき…
ニキビ ときどう.

4.

Here is the acne pimple treatment cream, CLEARASIL.

さあ、ニキビ 治療 クリーム
クレアランシルです.

5.

CLEARASIL has the following 3-way action which helps:

クレアランシルは、ツギの こ3ヲ
作用を うながかし ます.

6.

1. to open the acne pimple head.

ナーに、ニキビ 頭部を
ひらく 作用.

7.

2. to drain the inside of the acne pimple without squeezing.

ナニに、一ぶさずに ニキビ
内部を 出にてくる 作用.

8.

3. to dry up the acne pimple.

ナミに ニキビ まわりヲ
作用です.

9.

A bit of advice for your youth:

若さに いっとつ
アドバイス

10.

The acne pimple treatment cream, CLEARASIL. Newly on sale.

ニキビ治療クリーム
クレアランシル
新発売

EXHIBIT 9 Story Board for "Adolescence" Campaign, 1980, August 27, 1980

1.

When you're young, you have many small trials (and challenges). That's the essence of brimming youth . . . isn't it?

若さが輝やくのは
いろんな問がが
あるからこそですね

2.

You think about your studies, your future . . .

勉強のこと.
将来のこと.

3.

girlfriends . . .

ガールフレンドのこと…

4.

and acne pimples (are also on your mind) . . .

そして. ニキビのこと.

5.

Here is the acne pimple treatment cream, CLEARASIL.

さあ ニキビ治療クリーム
クレアラシル です.

6.

CLEARASIL has the following 3-way action which helps:

クレアラシルの3っの
3っの作用を
うながします.

7.

1. to open the acne pimple head.

アーに. ニキビ
幹部を司く作用.

8.

2. to drain the inside of the acne pimple without squeezing.

ヤニに. つぶさず
ニキビ中部を
そう作用.

9.

3. to dry up the acne pimple.

ヤニに. ニキビ
を乾かす作用
です.

10.

A bit of advise for your youth.

若ニに. ひとつの
アドバイス

11.

The acne pimple treatment cream, CLEARASIL.

ニキビ治療クリーム
クレアラシル

---

the basic copy points and animation flow. NVKK added a new end benefit "clear and smooth" and dropped the reference to "acne treatment cream." Both a spring and summer version of the "Testimonial" campaign was produced. The media mix strategy remained unchanged. See Exhibit 10.

Testing of the "Testimonial" commercials against the earlier campaigns showed little improvement in interest, involvement and effectiveness. In those categories, the "Testimonial" campaign was rated in the fourth, or lowest, quartile compared to average scores achieved by Japanese commercials.

The poor results of pre/post test among non-treaters despite high copy comprehension convinced NVKK executives that the "Testimonial" campaign could not live up to their expectations. An earlier study had shown that almost 70 percent of acne sufferers in the past year did not treat their acne other than washing with regular soap. It was increasingly clear that Clearasil could only grow as expected if an effective way to reach non-treaters could be found. Past campaigns were found amateurish (61%), dull (45%). A low interest test score of 480 was observed with a sharp drop during the explanation of the 3-way action. By comparison, for pharmaceutical products interest scores of 510 to 520 were considered average; 550 or more was viewed as very good. Many commercials on the air scored in the 525 to 530 range. See Exhibit 11.

The Change to the "Disarming" Campaign

To more effectively communicate with non-treaters, a new "Disarming" commercial was produced. A new format for expressing the 3-way action was considered necessary. The previous approach created the impression that the product worked very quickly, i.e., overnight,

EXHIBIT 10 Story Board for "Testimonial" Campaign

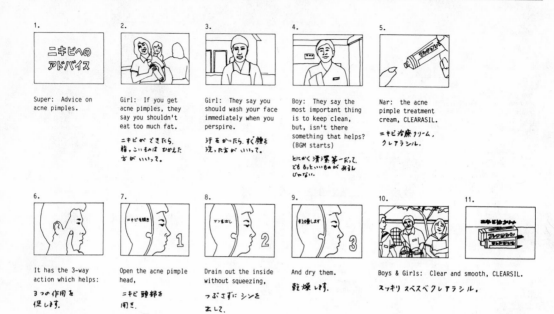

1.
Super: Advice on acne pimples.

2.
Girl: If you get acne pimples, they say you shouldn't eat too much fat.

ニキビが できたら、 脂、こいものは ひかえた 方が いいって。

3.
Girl: They say you should wash your face immediately when you perspire.

汗を かいたら、すぐ 顔を 洗った方が いいって。

4.
Boy: They say the most important thing is to keep clean, but, isn't there something that helps? (BGM starts)

とにかく 清潔第一だって。 でも もっといいものが あるん じゃない。

5.
Nar: the acne pimple treatment cream, CLEARASIL.

ニキビ 治療 クリーム、 クレアラシル。

6.
It has the 3-way action which helps:

3つの 作用を 促します。

7.
Open the acne pimple head,

ニキビ 頭部を 開き、

8.
Drain out the inside without squeezing,

つぶさずに シンを 出して、

9.
And dry them.

乾燥 します。

10.
Boys & Girls: Clear and smooth, CLEARSIL.

スッキリ スベスベ クレアラシル。

11.

---

which was not the case. Furthermore, the 3-way action was perceived as having been worn out. However, the 3-way action was perceived to be the most impressive and important aspect of Clearasil. See Exhibit 12.

The new campaign also had to address the impression that Clearasil was for serious sufferers only and was not appropriate for light sufferers. The product was perceived as too strong for people with sensitive skin and was not "fashionable" because its image was inconsistent with that of a serious medicine. The previous execution of the "social reward" aspect was felt to be obvious, forced, and thus unpleasant to the viewer. While the concept of teenagers giving advice to other teenagers was acceptable, its execution was judged to be "preachy" in tone.

With respect to tone and image, the commercials were considered to be dark, gloomy, boring, repetitious, not lively, and lacking a modern contemporary "feeling." Contributing to this was the absence of music, the use of a

male narrator, the execution of the 3-way action with its worn-out image and the fixed pattern of setting up the acne problem, on to 3-way action explanation, and then to end-benefit. Furthermore, some of the characters in the commercials were not felt to be typical of contemporary teenagers.

A serious and direct approach to acne problems by highlighting disadvantages of acne sufferers was not responsive to non-treaters. Research showed that non-treaters were not seriously concerned about acne. "Do not worry about it" was the most often mentioned reason among non-treaters for not treating acne.

Dissatisfaction with Past Advertising Campaigns

During the first twelve months of the national campaign, Clearasil achieved an advertising intensity of about 14,700 GRP's in the two key regions of Japan, Kanto and Kansai, compared

EXHIBIT 11 Clearasil TV Commercials Test Ratings for "Testimonial" Campaign

	"HIGH SCHOOL"	"DATE"	"TESTIMONIAL" Summer Version	
	30 Sec Score	30 Sec Score	30 Sec	
			Score	Quartile
INTEREST				
Profile Curve Score	479	466	438	(4)
INVOLVEMENT				
Commercial Image Index	15%	12%	8%	(4)
COMMUNICATION				
A) Comprehension of Copy Point	48%	64%	42%	(2)
Comprehension of Sales Message	77	78	50	(1)
B) Recall of Brand Name	57	35	95	(1)
Recall of Copy Point	24	32	19	(2)
EFFECTIVENESS				
Pre/Post Score	+8%	+4%	+3%	(4)
			+5	(4)
Persuasion Score	37	30	25	(4)

to a total of 18,888 GRP's and 19,947 GRP's respectively for all acne preparation products.[3] In March of 1980, Ekubo and Biore entered the market with budgets two to three times larger than Clearasil's for the March/June period of 1980. During the 1980/1981 period, Clearasil maintained its advertising at the same earlier level while Ekubo spent about 60% less and Biore maintained a level of slightly less than half of Clearasil's GRP's. During both years, Clearasil was the most advertised brand with a 45.9 percent share of GRP's. For more details, see Exhibit 13.

Horita, who had been off the brand between the end of 1979 due to an 18 months stay at the division's head office, became concerned about Clearasil's advertising in July of 1981. In his new position as creative development coordinator for all of NVKK's new products, he supervised some tests on Clearasil's advertising effectiveness on the "Adolescent" campaign. Interviewed teenagers connected the commercials with "dassai," a slang word used for a crumpled looking middle manager, somebody who was neither chic nor sophisticated. "In terms of U.S. equivalent, this comes close to the 'Columbo' role played by Peter Falk in the U.S. detective movie series," explained Brian Taylor, one of the U.S. expatriate managers at NVKK. What Horita was concerned about was that the teenagers believed only a "dassai" could create such a commercial. Even worse was the connection between "dassai" and "kusai," the Japanese equivalent of "something disgusting."

3. GRP = Gross Rating Point. GRP equals the sum of all airings of the program or spot announcement during a given time period. For example, a once-a-week program constantly recording a 15 percent rating (or 15 percent of TV homes covered) results in 60 GRP's for a 4-week period.

EXHIBIT 12 Story Board for "Disarming" Campaign, Jan. 22, 1982

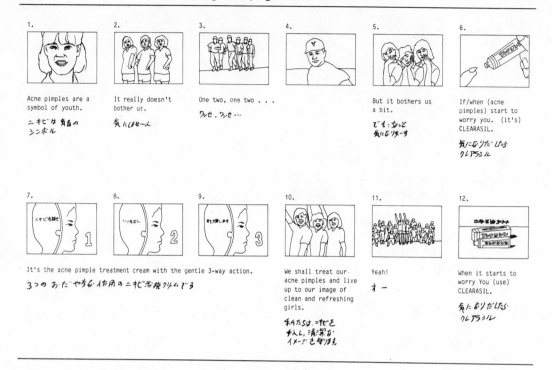

1. Acne pimples are a symbol of youth.
ニキビは 青春の シンボル

2. It really doesn't bother us.
気にしせーん

3. One two, one two . . .
ワセ、ワセ・・・

4.

5. But it bothers us a bit.
でも ちょっと 気になります

6. If/when (acne pimples) start to worry you. (it's) CLEARASIL.
気になりだしたら クレアラシル

7–9. It's the acne pimple treatment cream with the gentle 3-way action.
3つの あたやさし 作用の ニキビ治療クリムです

10. We shall treat our acne pimples and live up to our image of clean and refreshing girls.
私たちは ニキビを 直し、清潔な イメージ を守ります

11. Yeah!
オ ー

12. When it starts to worry You (use) CLEARASIL.
気になりだしたら クレアラシル

Throughout this time period, NVKK had regularly measured consumer attitudes. Testing was done in the Tokyo area and in both of Clearasil's test markets. The results of the tests are shown in Exhibit 14.

"The data indicates a significant decrease in the satisfaction of Clearasil users," commented Mr. Horita, the brand manager. "At the same time, our brand awareness was ahead of objective. In our test markets, we expected a brand awareness of 50 to 60 percent after 12 months; instead, we achieved figures at 80 percent."

"Obviously, we are not getting our message across as effectively as we wanted. Our interest scores for both commercials were below average compared to the typical Japanese commercial. Where we did very well was in the comprehension of copy points, sales message, and copy point recall. However, despite the excellent comprehension scores, the Clearasil commercials scored low on pre-post effectiveness and persuasion." See Exhibit 11.

Withdrawal of Advertising Support in November 1982

In the fall of 1982, it became clear that Vicks' latest campaign, "Disarming," was no more successful than previous ones. Interest curves in theater testing dropped even more. "As it did not make sense to support Clearasil with a campaign that did not meet our communications objective, we decided to withdraw all advertising support in November 1982. For the last 5 months, we have not put any advertising expenditures behind Clearasil," explained Horita.

The impact of the advertising withdrawal was felt almost immediately in figures on consumer off-take collected regularly for NVKK. Market share for Clearasil dropped to a low of 23 percent as compared to more than one-third in earlier periods. The biggest winners were the wash products. The share of wash products reached 57 percent for the most recent period. See Exhibit 15.

EXHIBIT 13 Acne Preparation Advertising Expenditures (in GRPs), 1979–1981

	Total	'79 July	Aug.	Sept.	Oct.	Nov.	Dec.	'80 Jan.	Feb.	Mar.	Apr.	May	June
Kanto													
Clearasil (7/79)	7,308	278	649	709	895	752	738	558	560	600	590	463	516
Ekubo (3/80)	4,847	—	—	—	—	—	—	—	—	1,805	1,185	1,271	588
Biore (3/80)	2,058	—	—	—	—	—	—	—	—	216	1,571	159	112
Skin Life	653	73	95	49	—	4	130	109	75	62	56	—	—
Noxema	1,113	256	635	—	—	—	91	—	18	16	20	77	—
Asty	1,104	—	—	—	—	—	—	—	—	1,104	—	—	—
Clearex	60	—	—	—	—	—	—	—	—	—	—	—	60
Jelleje	—	—	—	—	—	—	—	—	—	—	—	—	—
Silk Lady	1,745	—	—	—	—	—	—	—	—	—	1,068	237	440
Total	18,888	607	1,379	758	895	756	959	667	653	3,801	4,490	2,207	1,716
Kansai													
Clearasil	7,447	262	682	671	848	626	626	611	474	574	941	560	572
Ekubo	4,741	—	—	—	—	—	—	—	—	1,605	1,195	1,354	587
Biore	2,164	—	—	—	—	—	—	—	—	68	1,781	183	129
Skin Life	612	59	97	28	—	7	132	110	54	68	57	—	—
Noxema	973	181	601	—	—	—	67	—	18	15	23	68	—
Asty	1,072	—	—	—	—	—	—	—	—	1,072	—	—	—
Clearex	78	—	—	—	—	—	—	—	—	—	—	—	78
Jelleje	—	—	—	—	—	—	—	—	—	—	—	—	—
Silk Lady	2,860	—	—	—	—	—	—	—	—	—	1,819	526	515
Total	19,947	502	1,380	699	848	633	825	721	546	3,402	5,819	2,691	1,881

Source: MEH.

EXHIBIT 13 Acne Preparation Advertising Expenditures (in GRPs), 1979–1981 (cont.)

	Total	'80 July	Aug.	Sept.	Oct.	Nov.	Dec.	'81 Jan.	Feb.	Mar.	Apr.	May	June
Kanto													
Clearasil	7,089	513	812	456	468	442	812	848	509	625	569	478	557
Ekubo	4,197	1,574	916	443	255	284	212	105	80	93	80	94	61
Biore	3,138	674	170	83	208	614	109	260	46	71	558	165	180
Skin Life	736	35	15	27	16	7	100	166	95	137	116	22	—
Noxema	1,865	121	260	212	156	170	128	3	—	125	126	415	149
Asty	—	—	—	—	—	—	—	—	—	—	—	—	—
Clearex	79	79	—	—	—	—	—	—	—	—	—	—	—
Acne Trio	515	—	—	—	—	—	—	—	—	—	—	—	515
Jelleje	—	—	—	—	—	—	—	—	—	—	—	—	—
Silk Lady	1,445	—	—	—	—	—	—	—	—	—	922	523	—
Total	19,064	2,996	2,173	1,221	1,103	1,517	1,361	1,382	730	1,051	2,371	1,697	1,462
Kansai													
Clearasil	7,492	553	857	536	452	477	825	941	518	725	605	509	494
Ekubo	4,561	1,690	1,000	479	320	305	264	125	83	76	75	85	59
Biore	3,427	752	234	83	249	666	116	278	77	101	517	216	138
Skin Life	934	33	19	29	16	6	120	216	141	180	151	23	—
Noxema	1,876	275	266	236	—	190	100	5	—	125	124	400	155
Asty	—	—	—	—	—	—	—	—	—	—	—	—	—
Clearex	99	99	—	—	—	—	—	—	—	—	—	—	—
Acne Trio	—	—	—	—	—	—	—	—	—	—	—	—	—
Silk Lady	1,729	—	—	—	—	—	—	—	—	—	1,002	727	—
Total	20,118	3,402	2,376	1,363	1,037	1,644	1,425	1,565	819	1,207	2,474	1,960	846

Source: MEH.

EXHIBIT 14 Attribute Ratings on Clearasil (Among Clearasil Users)

Base	Tokyo			Shizuoka				Hiroshima			
	Post 6	Post 12	Post 24	Post 6	Post 12	Post 18	Post 24	Post 6	Post 12	Post 18	Post 24
	153 %	75 %	85 %	142 %	155 %	150 %	98 %	111 %	148 %	155 %	115 %
Leaves skin feeling clean	23	23	13	20	13	14	15	17	28	25	25
Leaves skin smooth	22	15	15	12	12	6	10	10	21	18	16
Not greasy	37	36	23	28	23	26	17	32	42	37	35
Does not irritate skin	34	33	20	19	19	20	21	24	37	29	38
Fast working	44	33	19	22	24	41	34	27	30	37	37
Dries up oily skin	37	29	22	25	21	47	28	26	34	37	38
Helps open pimples	35	35	23	22	20	34	33	20	28	31	46
Can use with assurance	NA	36	26	NA	NA	NA	23	NA	NA	NA	44
Disappears into skin	25	19	14	17	12	13	11	18	27	32	25
Helps prevent pimples	30	28	19	21	13	18	14	31	36	39	38
Improves appearance of facial skin	NA	15	14	NA	NA	NA	11	NA	NA	NA	21
Helps clear up pimples	47	36	23	24	21	35	28	32	37	41	45
Helps drain pimples	43	32	21	24	19	37	33	26	39	36	43
Is a medicine	NA	24	20	NA	NA	NA	15	NA	NA	NA	25
Is a product that suits me	NA	24	21	NA	NA	NA	18	NA	NA	NA	24
Is a contemporary product	NA	21	19	NA	NA	NA	10	NA	NA	NA	27
Is a cosmetic	NA	6	2	NA	NA	NA	4	NA	NA	NA	6

EXHIBIT 15 Clearasil Consumer Off-Take, Spring 1983

	80/81	81/82	82/83	MAT	'83 J/F
Total Market	5,226	5,301	5,695	6,064	753
% Change Y/A		+1.4%	+7.4%	+6.5%	
Clearasil	1,973	1,943	1,642	1,660	216
% Change Y/A		+19.0%	−15.5%	+1.1%	
% Share	37.8%	36.7%	28.8%	27.4%	28.7
Medicated Brands	354*	338	280	276	36
% Change Y/A		−4.5%	−17.2%	−1.4%	
% Share	6.8%	6.4%	4.9%	4.6%	4.9
Other Brands	594*	567	661	702	84
% Change Y/A		−4.5%	+16.6%	+6.2%	
% Share	11.4%	10.7%	11.6%	11.6%	11.2
Wash Products	1,831*	2,445	3,104	3,417	415
% Change Y/A		+33.5%	+27.0%	+10.1%	
% Share	35.0%	46.1%	54.5%	56.3%	55.2

* These data '80 S/O–'81 M/J.
Units: In thousands.

Advertising in Japan

A specialist in Japanese advertising gave the following explanation: "When a Western businessman enters his hotel room in Japan and turns on the switch of his TV and watches the Japanese commercials, he invariably complains that they seem to be heavy on mood elements and often difficult to even understand what they were selling. On the other hand, Japanese businessmen complain on returning from the U.S. about the heavy verbiage in the U.S. commercials. How could the viewer, they would ask, stand being talked at so incessantly?"

When tested in Japan, U.S. and Japanese commercials ranked differently. Japanese commercials tended to score higher in "execution interest" whereas U.S. commercials scored higher on the "image index." The key difference was "copy recall" where Japanese commercials ranked overwhelmingly lower than U.S. commercials. There was little difference in brand recall, pre/post attitude shift, and product interest.

McCann-Erickson, NVKK's advertising agency in Japan, described the Japanese style of advertising as "understated" or "non-linear." There was a saying that in Japan "you don't go into somebody's living room without first taking your shoes off." Consequently, Japanese advertising showed more "respect" for the consumer by being less direct.

Japanese consumers perceived little difference in the quality or technical superiority of various products. Often they were not knowledgeable about product details such as ingredients in medicine. Because most products were in general believed to be equal, no comparative advertising was used in Japan. In the opinion of one of the executives, "you sell your product by becoming your consumer's friend."

For OTC products, word-of-mouth communications were very important and, together with store recommendations, outranked advertising as a source for product decisions. For both drug and cosmetics buyers, store recommendations are frequently solicited. Some 90 percent of buyers asked "always" or "sometimes" before purchasing.

THE OPPORTUNITY FOR LINE EXTENSION

As Horita was working on a solution for Clearasil's advertising problem he also investigated opportunities to participate in the rapidly growing wash segment. "With most of the competitive activities right now taking place in the wash category, we should definitely consider entering with our own wash product," explained Horita. "Growth in the wash-only segment has outpaced growth in the treatment-only segment."

During the past few months, NVKK had a bar soap under test that could be marketed as Clearasil Soap. "We should see the Clearasil franchise as a business on its own with opportunities to expand into various categories, but all under the Clearasil franchise." The soap had been marketed by Richardson-Vicks in other countries under the Clearasil name and was thus available to NVKK. However, corporate policy did not allow a "prevents acne" claim which the Japanese government allowed as a claim for medicated soaps.

Product concept tests had already been carried out. Results indicated that a price of about yen 450 per package would be appropriate. The soap would be classified as a drug registered bar soap. Product usage tests indicated that treaters evaluated the product more positively than the general population. In general, test scores on Clearasil soap were equal to or better than those for Clearasil Cream a few years ago. However, since NVKK had no prior experience with a drug-registered soap in Japan, there was no control group to compare its soap against.

Distribution Requirements for Entering Wash Category

Several options existed for NVKK's entry into the wash segment. Horita had to consider not only whether NVKK should enter this segment but also how this might be done. In addition, any initiative needed to be coordinated with actions for Clearasil cream.

"Entry into the wash product segment has some important consequences for distribution," commented Mr. Nagata, the sales manager. In Japan, bar soaps were sold primarily through supermarkets and department stores. Only cosmetic soaps were sold in important volumes through drug and cosmetic stores. Bar soap for bath use was a very popular gift item among Japanese with about 90 percent of the volume sold through department stores. Cosmetic soap was sold 75 percent through cosmetic stores or the cosmetic section in supermarkets, with drug stores accounting for 25 percent. "For us to be successful with a soap, we have to open more channels into the cosmetic stores, supermarkets, and department store segment. Right now, we don't have these channels."

"To appreciate the buying environment at the store level, you have to understand that soaps are treated as a toiletry product category. Although we may be selling to the same store, wholesaler and buyer choices are different from OTC products."

Japanese drugstores were notorious for their small size and crowded conditions. A typical drugstore was about 300 square feet in size. Arrangements included a U-shaped main counter and one or two middle aisles. Drug products, including Clearasil, were displayed behind the main counter and had to be specifically requested by the customer. Toiletries were typically displayed in one of the center aisles. In many instances, the wholesaler supplying toiletry products to a drug store would differ from a wholesaler supplying drug products. In the case of chain drugstores, the buyer for toiletries was not identical to the buyer of drug products.

In cosmetic stores, a similar arrangement with a U-shaped main counter existed. Soaps would typically be displayed in one of the center aisles as a separate category with another aisle reserved for other toiletry products. Frequently, the supplying wholesalers for those categories were not identical, making it difficult, e.g., for a drug wholesaler supplying a cosmetics store to add a product category that had traditionally been supplied by another wholesaler. Supermarkets and department stores typically bought from wholesalers that combined cosmetic and toiletry lines.

"Right now, only 5 of our primary wholesalers and 60 sub-wholesalers carry both proprietary drugs and toiletries" remarked Mr. Nagata, the sales manager. "To develop the same network in toiletries takes time. Ideally, we need other toiletry products and/or an entire new line to accomplish this. To give us adequate coverage in toiletries we need 60 to 70 primary and another 80 to 100 sub-wholesalers."

Competition in the Toiletry Sector

Japanese competitors in the toiletry segment employed various distribution and sales strategies. Sunstar, Japan's largest marketer of toothpaste, made non-exclusive use of primary wholesalers as did NVKK. Kao, the largest Japanese detergent and toiletry company, often referred to as the "Procter & Gamble of Japan," had its own sales company. This firm maintained numerous local joint-ventures with wholesalers. For Tokyo, the company operated under Tokyo Kao Sales Co. and was owned fifty percent by Kao. These joint-venture sales companies sold directly to retailers. Yet another approach was followed by Lion, a large toiletry company, whose major products were detergents, toiletry, and toothpaste. Lion also employed primary wholesalers but had its own sales groups inside each primary wholesaler that gave exclusive attention to its own products. Although Mr. Nagata was unsure, he believed that these sections were funded by Lion. Both Kanebo and Shiseido were classified as "affiliated chains." "Chain" products were marketed directly to retailers. The Kanebo "chain" included about 15,000 cosmetic stores. Kanebo's salesforce numbered 250 salesmen. The Shiseido "chain" consisted of 28,000 stores. Shiseido employed about 1,800 salesmen and about 10,000 demonstrators-merchandisers.

SEARCHING FOR A NEW ADVERTISING APPROACH

"Our original approach to advertising Clearasil in Japan has been to follow quite closely the approaches used around the world for this brand. The three-way action is the basic product support that has become the cornerstone to Clearasil advertising worldwide. It worked everywhere, and it certainly also worked in the early campaign in Japan," explained Mr. Horita. "Typical advertising in Japan is much more subtle than advertising used in the United States. There is clearly a soft-sell approach, and frequently the product is mentioned only briefly at the end."

Mr. Robert Whelan, the product manager for Vicks cough drops in Japan, explained Richardson-Vicks' advertising approach as follows: "In the United States, we believe that the advertising message should explain the benefit of a product, supply some rationale or reason for saying it, and offer some opportunity to distinguish the product from the competition with some credibility about the claimed advantages. To give up any of these elements would be a major change from past practices."

Mr. Harold Todd, President of NVKK, commented, "The Clearasil situation is very complex. Here we are with a commercial that scores very high on recall but low on interest. Horita would like to eliminate the three-way action part that has been the key to the product's success worldwide. Maybe it is true. But originally, we were successful with just that approach. Maybe we are simply telling the story the wrong way? There are pro's and con's on both sides. But certainly at this point I don't have enough confidence to simply take the 3-way action out."

NVKK's Advertising Approach for Other Products

With the exception of Colac, a laxative sold only in Japan, NVKK followed an advertising policy that was similar to the one used by other Richardson-Vicks subsidiaries. The TV commercials, while produced in Japan, followed the usual approach of product benefit and support claim. Virtually in all other product areas NVKK was the market leader by a wide margin.

Colac, the laxative, was different since it was only marketed in Japan. Accounting for almost half of NVKK's sales, Colac was a success story. Colac's advertising focused entirely on brand personality with no defined, rational exposition of support. Imagery and mood were used extensively in the earlier part of all Colac commercials to symbolize some of the key benefits promised. Later in the commercials, what would appear to most observers to be just a conventional product introduction shot, is in fact the "clincher" in the eyes of the Japanese consumers.

Division Views

When the decision was made to relaunch Clearasil in Japan, the division argued strongly for the 3-way action approach which had proved successful in Brazil and Australia. Already at that time, Horita had felt uncomfortable with that approach. Although NVKK's top executives shared Horita's concern, they went along with the division's arguments of "why don't you try it." As a result, the Japanese campaign was built on the extensive documentation supplied by the division which included advertising strategy, logo, packaging, lay-outs, etc.

Following Horita's transfer to the divisional head office in Westport, Connecticut, NVKK followed the original strategy. Although Horita returned to Japan in mid-1981, he was not put back on Clearasil until spring of 1982. In the meantime, divisional management had changed and Horita, convinced that the existing policies would lead nowhere, tried again to get the division to accept a change. Two major meetings were held in Japan. "So far, the division has not accepted our point of view yet," said Horita, "perhaps they felt that I did not listen to anyone and that I was stubborn. After all, other countries work with the 3-way action. Why should Japan be an exception?"

Mr. Horita's Views

Mr. Horita himself was uncertain as to what approach he should suggest. "We started out with a largely U.S. approach with emphasis on the three-way action argument. When our scores turned out low, we reduced the three-way action component by making it shorter or lighter, thus moving more into the direction of a Japanese approach. However, our scores got worse, not better. Now I am no longer convinced that moving to an even more typical Japanese style advertising would actually improve the situation. On the other hand, I have all along felt that the three-way action argument was kind of obvious to the Japanese consumer and it encouraged over-expectation of product performance. Its constant repetition just does not help."

For the upcoming meeting on Clearasil marketing strategy in Japan, Horita wanted to take an integrated approach to his business in Japan. "I don't see the Clearasil cream or the possibility of a Clearasil soap as two distinctly different issues. Instead, I would like to present an overall strategy for our Clearasil business in Japan and integrate both cream and soap under this umbrella."

CASE 5 ▪ Interactive Computer Systems, Corp.[1]

In September 1980, Mr. Peter Mark, Marketing Manager of Interactive Computer Systems Corporation, was faced with a perplexing conflict between his company's USA sales group and the European subsidiaries. The USA sales group had begun to sell a display controller which had been developed in Europe. The product had been selling in Europe for several years and sales were relatively strong. Now, however, several major European customers had begun to purchase the product through their USA offices and shipped it back to Europe. The Europeans were complaining that the US pricing was undercutting theirs and that they were losing sales volume which was rightfully theirs. Both the US and European groups claimed that their pricing practices followed corporate guidelines and met the profit objectives set for them.

INTERACTIVE COMPUTER SYSTEMS, CORP.

Interactive Computer Systems Corporation (ICS), headquartered in Stamford, Connecticut, was a large multinational manufacturer of computer systems and equipment. The company made a range of computer systems and was best known for its small or "mini" computers. ICS was considered one of the industry leaders in that segment of the computer industry which in-

cluded such companies as Data General, Digital Equipment, Prime Computer, Masscomp, and Hewlett-Packard.

The company was primarily a US based corporation with the majority of its engineering and manufacturing facilities located in the eastern United States. In addition, ICS had manufacturing facilities in Canada, Singapore, West Germany, Brazil, and a joint venture in South Korea.

Sales were conducted throughout most of the non-Communist world by means of a number of sales subsidiaries with sales offices located in Canada, Mexico, Brazil, Argentina, Chile, Japan, Australia, and several European countries. Elsewhere, sales were conducted through a network of independent agents and distributors.

PRODUCT LINE

The ICS line of products was centered around a family of 16-bit mini computer systems. "Mini computer" was the popular term referring to small to medium sized computer systems which were used in a wide variety of applications including industrial control, telecommunications systems, laboratory applications, and small business systems. "16-bit" refers to the size of the computer "word" or unit of data. These systems were different from the large computer systems of IBM, Univac, and Honeywell which had word sizes of 32-36 bits.

In addition to the computer central processing units (CPU) and memory units, ICS pro-

1. Names and data are disguised.
All prices and costs are stated in US $.

This case was prepared by Visiting Professor Jean-Pierre Jeannet as a basis for class discussion rather than to illustrate either effective or ineffective handling of an administrative situation. Copyright 1981 by IMEDE (International Management Development Institute), Lausanne, Switzerland. Reproduced by permission.

duced a line of peripheral devices required for making complete computer systems. These included devices such as magnetic tape units, disk storage units, line printers, card readers, video and hard copy terminals, display units, and laboratory and industrial instrumentation interface units. These various peripherals were used as appropriate and combined with the final computer systems to meet the specific customer's requirements. ICS produced most of these products in-house but some, such as line printers and card readers, were purchased to ICS specifications from companies specializing in those products such as Data Products and Documentation.

ICS manufactured several central processing units (CPU) which were positioned in price and performance to form a product family. They all had similarity of design, accepted (executed) the same computer instructions, and ran on the same operating system (master control programs). The difference was in speed, complexity and cost. The purchaser was able to select the model which economically met the performance requirements of the intended application.

This family of CPUs, together with the wide range of available peripheral devices, formed a family of computer systems offering a considerable range of price and performance but with compatible characteristics and programming.

COMMUNICATIONS INTERFACES

A communications interface was a peripheral device used for transmitting data to or from the computer system. This could either be:

- a terminal on which a user could enter data, for example on a typewriter-like "keyboard," and have data displayed, typically on either a video screen, or "hard copy" on a typewriter-like printer.
- for other computers, either of the same type or from a different manufacturer.

These connections were made by direct wire, if the distance involved was short (50–100 feet). In cases where the distance was longer, the connection was made via telephone lines or special high speed "data lines" which were specially treated telephone lines.

The communications interface operated under control of the program running in the computer to take data, either as presented to it by the program or itself directly from the computer's memory (depending on the specific interface) and to send the data out on the "communication line" transformed as a string of digital pulses. When the computer received data, the interface worked in the reverse manner. If telephone or data lines were used, the connection was made through a special adapter called modulator-demodulator, or "modem," suitable for transmission on a telephone line. Modems followed industry standards and were available from a large number of modem vendors.

The pieces of data being sent (or received) were usually referred to as "characters" since they most often consisted of alphanumerics (letters and numbers) or special characters such as punctuations, brackets, etc. There existed several common systems for constructing the digital pulse sequence representing the characters, ranging from 5 to 8 bits in length (a bit was a single digit in the binary number system of 0 and 1). The most common was "8 bit ASCII" as specified by the American Standard Code for Information Interchange.

In addition to being organized as strings of characters, the data could be sent to another computer or a more sophisticated terminal often organized into a message or "packet" using one of a variety of protocols. A protocol was simply a definition of the orderly rule or format by which data could be exchanged. The protocol aided this data transfer process by including in the message a header with a message of identification, length count, and sometimes source and destination codes or other information depending on the protocol used. In addition, more information could be included to aid in the detection and sometimes correction of errors in the data received.

A number of protocols have been devised, each with its own relative advantages and proponents. Some of the more common protocols were:

BSC or BI Sync—IBM, dated

    HDLC—CCITT (European Standards Organization)

    SDLC—IBM, similar to HDLC

      2780—IBM, remote batch station protocol

      3271—IBM, display terminal protocol

      X.25—CCITT packet switch networks protocol, gaining wide acceptance

MODEL 431 COMMUNICATIONS INTERFACE

The specific product in question was the model 431 communications interface, a 4 line programmable multiplexer.

The 431 consisted of one electronic circuit module which plugged into the I/O (input/output) "bus" of the computer (a bus was an electrical cable or wiring on which data signals flowed in some organized manner). It provided the interface for four separate communications lines which were connected by means of specially designed connectors on the module. Such multi-line interfaces were typically called multiplexers after the manner in which they worked internally. They offered the advantages of more efficient space utilization and lower per-line costs compared with the normal alternative of a separate single line interface per line. Depending on the computer vendor, multiplexers come in various sizes such as 2, 4, 6, 8, 16, 32, and 64 lines.

ICS already has 4, 8, and 16 line multiplexers in its line of high volume standard products. The specified advantage of the 431 was its programmable nature. It could be loaded with software to handle any of several different protocols directly in the interface using its own microprocessor on the module. It also performed error checking and moved data directly to or from the main computer memory. Since these functions had previously all been performed by a program running in the computer, the 431 relieved the computer of this load and freed it up to do other work. The result was a net improvement in system speed and power.

EXHIBIT 1 Model 431 Sales Volume (Units), Selected Countries

	1977	1978	1979	1980 (*forecast*)
Germany	30	100	110	100
UK	5	40	60	70
France	10	20	50	40
Canada	—	—	5	5
Switzerland	3	20	30	15
Australia	—	—	10	30
USA	—	2	80	200

The model 431 was designed in 1977 at ICS's small European engineering facility assigned to its German subsidiary, Interactive Computers GmbH, in Frankfurt and was manufactured there for shipment world-wide to those ICS subsidiaries who were selling the 431. Sales had initially started in Europe and then spread to other areas. Sales volumes are given in Exhibit 1.

INTER-SUBSIDIARY TRANSACTIONS

With the exception of the Korean joint venture, all of ICS's subsidiaries were wholly owned and products moved freely between them. ICS had set up its procedures and accounting systems in line with the fact that it was basically a US based company manufacturing a uniform line of products for sales world-wide through various sales subsidiaries. For the major product lines, the only differences by countries were line voltages and some minor adaptations to comply with local government regulations.

Although the subsidiaries in the various countries were essentially sales subsidiaries functioning as sales offices to sell products in those countries, they were separately incorporated entities and wholly owned subsidiaries, operating under the laws of that particular country. Careful accounting of all transactions between the parent company and the subsidiaries had to be maintained for the purpose of import duties and local taxes.

When a customer ordered a computer system, the order was processed in the subsidiary and then transmitted back to the parent company (ICS) in the US to have the system built. The order paperwork listed the specific hardware items (CPU, memory size, tape and disk units, etc.) wanted by the customer and each system was built specifically to order. The component pieces were built by ICS in volume to meet the requirements of these specific customer systems orders. Like most companies, ICS expended a great amount of effort attempting to accurately forecast the mix of products it would need to meet customer orders.

When the customer's system, or any product, was shipped to the subsidiary, the subsidiary "bought" it from the parent at an intercompany discounted price or "transfer price" of list minus 20%. The level of subsidiary transfer price discount was established with two factors in mind:

- It was the primary mechanism by which Interactive repatriated profits to the US parent corporation.
- The 20% subsidiary margin was designed to give the subsidiaries positive cash flow to meet their local expenses such as salaries, facilities, benefits, travel, supplies, etc.

Import duties were paid on the discounted (list minus 20%) transfer price value according to the customs regulations of the importing country. Some typical import duties for computer equipment are shown in Exhibit 2.

Most countries were quite strict on import/export and customs duties and required consistency in all transactions. Therefore, all shipments were made at the same discounted transfer price, including shipments among subsidiaries and shipments back to the United States.

PRICING

ICS set prices world-wide based on US price lists which were referred to as "Master Price Lists" or MPLs. Prices in each country were

EXHIBIT 2 Import Duties for Computer Equipment for Selected Countries[1]

USA	5.1%
Canada	8.8%
Japan	9.8%
Australia	2%
EEC[2]	None between EEC countries; 6.7% from outside EEC countries

1. These are typical amounts only. The topic of customs duties is quite complex. It varies with the type of goods, even within an industry (computer systems may be one rate while computer terminals may be another, higher rate and parts a third rate), and by country of origin.
2. European Economic Community (Common Market) consisting of the UK, France, Germany, Italy, Belgium, Netherlands, Ireland, Denmark, and Luxemburg.
NOTE: Duty calculated on a "C.I.F." basis—cost of the product plus insurance and freight.

based on the MPL plus an uplift factor to cover the increased cost of doing business in those countries. Some of these extra costs were:

- Freight and duty: in those countries where it was included in the price (in some countries duties were paid for separately by the customer).
- Extended warranty: in some countries, the customary warranty periods were longer than in the US, e.g., one year vs. 90 days.
- Cost of subsidiary operations and sales costs: to the extent that they exceed the normal selling costs in the US.
- Cost of currency hedging: in order to be able to publish a price list in local currency, ICS bought US dollars in the money futures market.

Uplift factors were periodically reviewed and adjusted if needed to reflect changes in the relative cost of doing business in each country. Typical uplift factors for some selected countries are shown in Exhibit 3.

Each subsidiary published its own price list in local currency. The list was generated quar-

EXHIBIT 3 Typical Country Uplift Factors: Local
Price = Master Price List + Uplift %

UK	8%
Germany	15%
France	12%
Switzerland	17%
Sweden	15%
Australia	12%
Brazil	20%
Canada	5%

terly by use of a computer program which took a tape of all the MPL entries and applied the uplift and a fixed currency exchange rate which has been set for the fiscal year. This price list was used by all salespeople in the subsidiary as the official listing of products offered and their prices.

SPECIAL PRODUCTS

In addition to its standard line of products which were sold world-wide in volume, ICS had a number of lower volume or specialized products. The model 431 communications interface was considered one of these. Specialized products were typically not on the MPL and prices were set locally by each subsidiary wherever they were sold. They were either quoted especially on request for quote basis or added to a special price list supplement produced by each country. This was a common procedure in the computer industry. IBM, for example, had several products "available on a RPQ basis" (Request Product Quotation) only.

To support the sales of the specialized products, ICS had a separate team of specialists with one or more specialists in each subsidiary. They were responsible for the pricing of their products and had a high degree of independence in setting prices in each subsidiary. The specialist or team in each subsidiary was responsible for all aspects of the sales of their assigned products and essentially ran a business within a business.

For the purposes of internal reporting to management, the specialists were measured on achieving a profit before tax, or PBT, of 15% which was the ICS goal. The results were shown on a set of internal reports which were separate from the legal books of the subsidiary. The purpose of the internal reports was to give ICS management more information on the profitability of its various product lines. These reports took the form of a series of profit and loss statements of operation by line of product with overhead and indirect costs allocated on a percentage of revenue basis. For these internal P&L reports, the cost of goods was the actual cost of manufacture (internal cost) plus related direct costs instead of the discounted price paid by subsidiaries and shown on their official statements of operation.

"431" SALES IN EUROPE

The model 431 communications interface was designed in 1977 by the European engineering group in Frankfurt as a follow on to some special engineering contracts for European customers. It was introduced in the European market in 1978 where it had grown in popularity.

The 431 was produced in Frankfurt only on a low volume production line. The manufacturing and other direct costs amounted to US $1500 per unit. Because there were no tariffs within the EEC and shipping costs were covered by allocated fixed costs, there were no other direct costs. The allocated fixed costs in Europe were running at 47% of revenue. Thus, a contribution margin of 62% was required to achieve a 15% PBT. Based on these costs, a list price of US $3,900 had been set within the EEC. The resulting P&L is shown in Exhibit 4.

Because of the popularity of this product, it had been listed on the special products price list in most European countries. Within the EEC, the price had been set at the same level with any variation only due to local currency conversions. In European countries outside the EEC, the price was increased to cover import duties.

At the above price, the 431 had gained market acceptance and had grown in popularity, especially in Germany, the UK, and France. Its

EXHIBIT 4 Model 431 European Profit Analysis (in U.S. dollars)

European List Price	US $3,900
Manufacturing and Other Direct Costs	1,500
Contribution Margin	2,400
	62%
Allocated Fixed Costs (47%)	1,833
PBT	US $ 567
	14.5%

EXHIBIT 5 Model 431 USA Profit Analysis

USA List Price	$3,000
Manufacturing Cost	$1,500
Contribution Margin	$1,500
	50%
Allocated Fixed Costs (35%)	$1,050
PBT	$ 450
	15%

customers included several large European based multinational companies who were of major importance to ICS in Europe. These customers designed specific system configurations and added programming to perform specified applications and shipped the systems to other countries, either to their own subsidiaries for internal use (e.g., a factory) or to customers abroad.

"431" SALES IN USA

The 431 was brought to the attention of the US sales group in two different ways. In sales contacts with US operations of some European customers, ICS was told of the "431" and asked to submit price and availability schedules for local purchase in the USA. US customers expressed irritation at being told that the model was not available in the US.

Secondly, the US sales force also heard of the "431" from their European counterparts at sales meetings where the Europeans explained how the "431" had been important in gaining large accounts.

As a result of this pressure from customers and the sales force, the US special products specialists obtained several units for evaluation and in 1979 made the "431" available for sale in the US.

Originally, the US specialists set the price equal to the European price of $3,900. However, it became obvious that the market in the US was more advanced and more competitive with customers expecting more performance at that price. As a result the price had to be reexamined.

The "431" was obtained from Frankfurt at the internal cost of $1,500. Transportation costs were estimated at $200. In the USA accounting system, import duties and transportation are not charged directly and were absorbed by general overhead. This came about because ICS was primarily an exporter from the US with very little importing taking place. Consequently, it was felt that import costs were negligible. Thus, the only direct cost was the $1,500 internal cost. Overhead and allocated fixed expenses in the US averaged 35%.

The result was, as shown in Exhibit 5, a revised price of $3,000 with a contribution margin of 50% and a PBT of 15%—the ICS goal. Following this analysis, the US price was reduced to $3,000. The "431" was not listed on the main USA price list but was quoted only on a RPQ basis. Subsequently, this price had also been listed on special products price list supplements which were prepared by the US product specialists and handed out to the sales force in each district.

CURRENT SITUATION

The repricing of the "431" to $3,000 was instrumental in boosting US sales. The sales volume continued to grow and some large customers were captured. These customers included existing ICS customers who previously used other, lower performance, communications interfaces, or had bought somewhat equivalent devices from other companies who made "plug compatible" products for use with ICS computers. Also, a good volume of sales was being obtained from the US operations of European multinationals who were already familiar with the product. ICS's US group, who had first viewed the European designed product with suspicion, was now more confident about it.

But the Europeans were not entirely happy with the situation. Recently, they started complaining to ICS management that the US pricing of the "431" was undercutting the European price. This was causing pressure on the European subsidiaries to reduce their price for the "431" below the $3,900 they needed to meet their profitability goals. Pressure was coming from customers who knew the US price and from European sales people who, as a result of travel to the US or discussions with US colleagues knew the US price and what the uplifted European price "was supposed to be."

The price difference had also been noticed by several of ICS's larger European multinational customers. They started buying the "431" through their US offices and reexported it, both back to Europe and to other countries.

So far, three customers had done this, two German firms and one French customer. Several additional customers were showing definite signs of "shopping around."

This loss of customers to the US was particularly painful to the Europeans. They had invested considerable amounts of effort into cultivating these customers.

In addition, the customers still expected to receive technical and pre-sales support from their local ICS office (i.e., European) as well as warranty and service support, regardless of where they placed the purchase order. Attempts to discuss this with the customers or persuade them to purchase in Europe had not been successful. Typical reactions had been "that's ICS's problem" (UK customer) and "but are you not one company?" (German customer).

In brief, the ICS European subsidiaries were complaining that they were "being denied the profitable results of their own work" by the unfair pricing practices of the US parent company.

In the eyes of the US team, however, they were pricing in accordance with corporate guidelines to achieve a 15% PBT. They also maintained that the market did not allow them to price the "431" any higher. Furthermore, they felt that they were simply exercising their right to set their own country prices to maximize profits within their specific country market.

The US group was so pleased with the market acceptance of the "431" in the US that they wanted to begin an aggressive promotion. As an important part of this, they were now planning to add the "431" on the official ICS US price list. This was viewed as a key to higher sales since, especially in the US, products tended to be sold from the regular price list and the sales force tended to lose or ignore special price list supplements.

At this point, both the European and US specialists were upset with each other. Both sides maintained that they were following the rules but that the actions of "the other side" were harming their success and profitability.

It had been a long day and it was time to go home. As he turned his car out into the traffic on High Ridge Road, Mr. Mark was still feeling confused about the issues and wondering what should be done.

CASE 6 ■ P.T. Food Specialties—Indonesia (FSI)

On Tuesday morning, January 21, 1981, Ian Souter, Marketing Manager of FSI, was congratulating himself on having gotten an early start, as the Jakarta traffic seemed even worse than normal. He had allowed himself some extra time in order to prepare the agenda for a 10 o'clock meeting with his staff. On the way to the office he asked the driver radio in order to catch the beginning of the English language news. One block from the office he was reeling with shock as he learned that the Indonesian government was banning all TV advertising as of April 1, 1981. As the car pulled into his parking space it occured to him that his entire organization, his marketing strategies and campaigns, and his own job structure had become obsolete in one single day.

P.T. FOOD SPECIALTIES (FSI)

FSI was owned jointly by Nestlé S.A., a large multinational food products company, and a group of Indonesian investors. Nestlé S.A. had been founded in Vevey, Switzerland in 1867 by Henri Nestlé as a small producer of milk products. In 1905, it merged with the Anglo-Swiss Condensed Milk Co. Between 1905 and 1980 this merged unit expanded rapidly, becoming Switzerland's largest multinational company and the largest company in the food industry in the world. In 1905, Nestlé already had 80 factories, 300 sales offices and 12 subsidiaries worldwide. By 1980, the Nestlé group produced revenues of almost SFr. 24.5 billion through its sales offices and factories in more than 100 countries worldwide. Prior to 1972, Nestlé operated under the name Indonepro Distributors Inc. as the importer and distributor of Nestlé's products to Indonesia. In 1972, it began operating as a manufacturer and marketer of food products. It had discontinued its distribution operations after the introduction of an Indonesian law that restricted distribution activities to companies that were wholly owned by Indonesians. Since 1972, FSI had lost the right to sell its products directly to retailers or consumers.[1]

In 1981, FSI produced and marketed six products in Indonesia. The most important of these was MILKMAID SWEETENED CONDENSED MILK. Introduced in 1972 after a long history of importation, MILK MAID accounted for roughly 40 percent of FSI's annual turnover. It was perhaps the least profitable of its six products. The Indonesian sweetened condensed milk market was both very large and competitive. It was dominated by three large organizations, Frisian Flag (with 50 percent of the market), Indo Milk, in conjunction with the Australian Dairy Board, (with 34 percent of the market) and FSI (with 15 percent of the market). A 14 oz can of MILKMAID had a selling price of approximately 400 Rupiah in 1981.[2]

---

1. In 1981, \$1 = Sfr. 2.
2. In 1981, 300 Rupiah = Sfr. 1.-, 625 Rupiah = \$1.-.

This case was prepared by Barbara Priovolos under the supervision of Visiting Professor Jean-Pierre Jeannet as a basis for class discussion rather than to illustrate either effective or ineffective handling of an administrative situation. Copyright 1982 by IMEDE (International Management Development Institute), Lausanne, Switzerland. Reproduced by permission.

DANCOW powdered milk had also been introduced in 1972. It was sold in two forms, regular and instant. In 1981 DANCOW accounted for approximately 30 percent of FSI's total revenue. It was also one of FSI's most profitable products. The Indonesian powdered milk market was dominated by two large organizations. FSI had a 45 percent market share, and Frisian Flag had a 52 percent market share. The balance of the market was held by several imported brands. A 454 gram package (about one pound) of DANCOW regular carried a suggested retail price of 1,200 Rupiah in 1981.

In 1978, FSI had introduced two infant cereals into Indonesia. Neither of these products were to be used as breast milk substitutes. CERELAC contained powdered milk, whereas NESTUM did not. These had become two of FSI's most profitable products and accounted for approximately 10 percent of FSI's annual revenue. The infant cereal market was fairly small, but FSI controlled almost 63 percent of it. The balance of the branded cereals were supplied largely by one local producer P.T. Sari Husada, whose brand SNM had a 31 percent share of the market. All other brands, most of them imported, shared the remaining 6 percent of the market. Homemade cereals were very popular, and although little firm data was available on the subject, FSI executives believed that the vast majority of the children's cereal consumed in Indonesia was homemade. A 400 gram box of CERELAC and a 250 gram box of NESTUM had 1981 retail prices of 1000 Rupiah and 750 Rupiah, respectively.

MILO, a chocolate-malted powder that was mixed with milk to produce a high energy drink, accounted for eight percent of FSI's revenue. It was a moderately profitable product that had been introduced in 1974. The market for MILO was thought to be fairly small. It consisted primarily of children who used MILO as a "growing up" high nutrition drink and sports conscious adults who used it as a high energy drink. FSI had approximately 45 percent of this market segment. It shared the market with the Ovaltine brand which had a 47 percent market share and the Malcoa brand which had an eight percent

market share. In 1981, the retail price for MILO was 100 Rupiah for a 350 gram box.

PRODUCT DISTRIBUTION

Products found their way from the factory to the consumer's cupboard through a rather intricate series of distributors and wholesalers. SFI itself had only two customers. It sold all of its output to one of two main distributors, a Chinese-Indonesian company, and a Pribumi, or native Indonesian, company. These two main distributors sold FSI's products to subdistributors, or to agents for subdistributors. The approximately 45 subdistributors then sold the products to wholesalers or directly to small shops. As a result FSI's products changed hands a minimum of four times, and often as many as six times on their way from the factory to the consumer. See Exhibit 1 for a diagram of this distribution network.

FSI suggested price levels for both the retail and the wholesale outlets and paid for, although did not arrange, product transportation from the factory to the retailer. It also employed marketing personnel who served as advisors to the subdistributors and the retailers. Twenty area supervisors advised the subdistributors with regard to stock hygiene, merchandising and promotional activities. They also trained subdistributor sales personnel to set up in-store displays, point-of-sale selling materials and on-the-shelf product arrangement for maximum consumer impact. This type of support was considered by FSI executives as crucial. Many Indonesian retailers saw little difference between having a product in the store and making a product available to, or even attractive to, the customer. Many retailers ordered products that were left in cartons behind desks, in storage rooms, or in similar areas well out of reach of the consumer. This marketing support was also consistent with the marketing advice of businessmen based in Indonesia who believed that personalized attention was an effective marketing tool in Indonesia.

In most cases, the subdistributors were grateful for the help provided by the area super-

EXHIBIT 1 Product Distribution

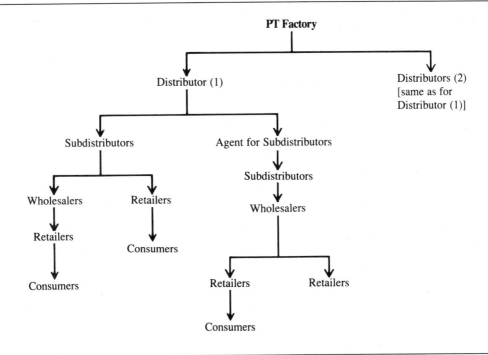

visors. Some conflicts of interest did occasionally occur. The subdistributors had a short-term view of business. They were generally most interested in products that were currently selling in large volumes. The area supervisor was interested in marketing every product and in building the market for new products, thus ensuring that the FSI brand was associated with goodwill and confidence in the mind of the extremely brand loyal Indonesian consumer. See Exhibit 2 for retail distribution data for FSI's products and its competitors' products.

The FSI marketing office also included one national sales coordinator to whom all of the area supervisors reported, and one product executive for each FSI product group. The product executives were responsible for developing and implementing supplemental promotional activities for their products, both trade oriented and consumer oriented, and for monitoring their

products in the Indonesian market. See Exhibit 3 for the FSI Marketing Department organization chart.

THE INDONESIAN BUSINESS CLIMATE

In 1981 Indonesia was the fifth largest country in the world in terms of population, behind China, India, the USSR and the USA. Its 150 million people lived on approximately 6,000 of the roughly 13,000 islands that, straddling 5000 km (3000 miles) of Equator, made up Indonesia. It was a country of uncharted jungles and densely populated cities. Twenty percent of all Indonesians were city dwellers and two thirds of them lived on the islands of Java, Madura and Bali. These islands contained only 7 percent of Indonesia's land mass and were among the most

EXHIBIT 2 Retail Distribution—P.T.

MILKMAID
- Distribution largely urban
- 80% Supermarkets, 16% Independent Shops, 20% Bazaar Shops stock product
- Sweetened condensed milk as a product category sells
  0.5% volume through Supermarkets
  30% volume through Independent Shops
  70.5% volume through Bazaar Shops

DANCOW
- Distribution largely urban

	Standard	Instant	
Supermarkets	97%	90%	} stock product
Independent Shops	15%	10%	
Bazaar Shops	30%	20%	

- Full cream powdered milk as a product category sells
  2% volume through Supermarkets
  35% volume through Independent Shops
  63% volume through Bazaar Shops

CERELAC/NESTUM
- Exclusively urban distribution

	CERELAC	NESTUM	
Supermarkets	95%	94%	} stock product
Independent Shops	10%	10%	
Bazaar Shops	20%	27%	

MILO
- Exclusively urban distribution with concentration in 5 or 6 main Towns
- 98% of Supermarkets, 12% of Independent Shops, 37% of Bazaar Shops stock product
- Tonic food beverages sell
  5% volume through Supermarkets
  32% volume through Independent Shops
  64% volume through Bazaar Shops

---

densely populated areas on earth. Indonesia's capital city of Jakarta was home to seven million people. See Exhibit 4 for a map of Indonesia.

The Indonesian people were of more than 300 different ethnic groups, most of them of Malaysian origin. More than 90 percent of the population were followers of Islam giving Indonesia the world's largest Moslem population. Although more than 300 languages and dialects were in regional use, the national language of Bahasa Indonesia was believed to be understood by all but the most remote village dwellers.

Indonesia had been under Dutch colonial rule for almost 300 years prior to its occupation by the Japanese between 1942 and 1945. In 1945, two days after the surrender of the Japanese, Indonesia made a unilateral declaration of independence. In 1949, the Netherlands unconditionally recognized the Sovereignty of Indonesia. The political climate of Indonesia was

EXHIBIT 2 (*cont.*) Retail Distribution—Competitors

Competition to MILKMAID

Frisian Flag	91% of supermarkets 60% of independent shops 60% of bazaar shops	} stock product
Indomilk	91% of supermarkets 31% of independent shops 39% of bazaar shops	} stock product
Respective market shares	Frisian Flag 50% Indomilk 34% MILKMAID 16%	

Competition to DANCOW

Frisian Flag Standard	97% of all supermarkets 27% of independent shops 46% of bazaar shops	} stock product
Frisian Flag Instant	98% of all supermarkets 14% of independent shops 22% of bazaar shops	} stock product
Respective market shares	DANCOW Std. 27% DANCOW Inst. 18.3% Frisian Flag Std. 43.2% Frisian Flag Inst. 8.6%	

Competition to NESTUM/CERELAC

SNM	84% of all supermarkets 11% of independent shops 22% of bazaar shops	} stock product
Nutricia	91% of all supermarkets 3.5% of independent shops 4.3% of bazaar shops	} stock product
Respective market shares	NESTUM 22% CERELAC 41% SNM 31% All Others 6%	

Competition to MILO

Ovaltine	98% of all supermarkets 10.7% of independent shops 24.7% of bazaar shops	} stock product
Malcoa	91% of all supermarkets 4% of independent shops 10% of bazaar shops	} stock product
Respective market shares	MILO 45.0% Ovaltine 47.0% Malcoa 8.0%	

EXHIBIT 3 P.T. Food Specialties Marketing Department

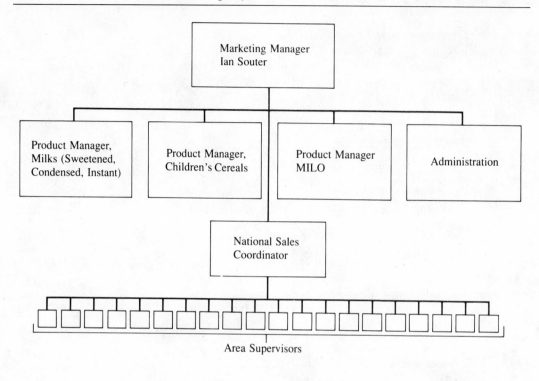

stable. Its President, Suharto, had been in power since 1965. Although he was considered by many to be slow in initiating reforms that would stimulate economic growth, his leadership had been credited with reducing inflation from over 200 percent in the mid-1960's to under 10 percent in 1981, opening up Indonesia to some private and foreign investment, reducing the rate of its population growth and bringing the country to the brink of self sufficiency in rice production, after having been the world's largest rice importer for many years. Indonesia was a country very rich in natural resources, but with a very poor population. It was a country that

was deeply preindustrial, but one with a pocket of high technology industries.

Indonesia was a member of OPEC and the largest oil producer in South-East Asia. It had proven reserves of 14 billion barrels, and an estimated 50 billion barrels of reserves yet to be officially confirmed. Oil export earnings accounted for 75 percent of its foreign income in 1981. Oil was not the only important natural resource in Indonesia. Indonesia was the world's second largest producer of liquified natural gas and largest producer of tin. It also produced significant quantities of bauxite, nickel, coal, iron, manganese, gold, silver, copper, phosphates

EXHIBIT 4 Map of Indonesia

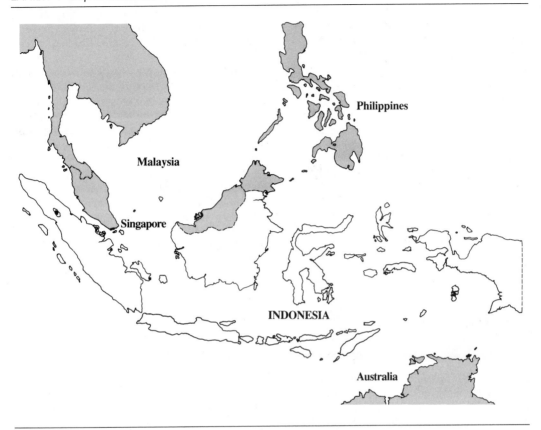

and sulphur. Nevertheless, the Indonesian economy was primarily agricultural. Agriculture, forestry and fishing employed two thirds of the Indonesian labor force and accounted for almost one third of GNP. Small farms produced food for domestic consumption as well as natural rubber, coffee, pepper and tobacco for export. Large plantations, holdovers from its colonial days, produced Indonesia's most important agricultural exports: timber, rubber, coffee, tea, palm oil and sugar.

The Indonesian manufacturing sector was very small, accounting for less than 5 percent of exports and only 7 percent of GNP. The trading sector of the economy, wholesale and retail, ac-

counted for approximately 16 percent of the GNP and was dominated by Indonesia's Chinese minority. Until 1965, Indonesia's five million Chinese had had a virtual monopoly of business and manufacturing activities within the country, and their influence in 1981 was still considerable.

In 1981, Indonesia had at least US$ 10 billion in hard currency reserves that did not benefit the economy due to an underdeveloped banking and financial services sector. Poverty was acute in Indonesia, and many of its income statistics were misleading. Although the per capita income was about $370 per year, the concentration of wealth was such that certain economists estimated that 40 percent of the population existed on less than $90 per year.

The Indonesian population could be classified into five separate economic classes in terms of disposable household income.[3]

Economic segment	Percentage of population	Monthly disposable income (in Rupiahs)
A	3%–5%	100,000
B	13%–18%	75,000–100,000
C	25%–30%	50,000– 75,000
D	29%–30%	30,000– 50,000
E	34%	30,000

FSI'S MARKETING MIX

As Marketing Manager, Ian Souter had generally emphasized developing customized campaigns for each of FSI's six products. The campaign budgets were divided between "above the line" mass media activities and "below the line" consumer promotion and trade promotion activities. In line with Nestlé and FSI company policy, which called for mass media promotion in order to build long term brand loyalty and confidence in their products, 60 percent to 90 percent of a campaign's budget was spent on mass media advertising. FSI executives felt that price promotions produced customers who only used the product while it was selling for the reduced price. These customers were likely to change brands again as soon as other manufacturers lowered their own prices. See Exhibit 5 for media spend data, Exhibit 6 for media cost data and Exhibit 7 for some magazine advertisement samples.

Mr. Souter felt that the 1980 MILKMAID campaign had been especially important. Mr.

3. Each household contained approximately 7 people. This classification was based on the best estimates of foreign businessmen operating in Indonesia during 1981.

Souter had, in an effort to increase market share, attempted to reposition MILKMAID from a "growing up" children's drink to an "energy" drink for all ages. In 1980 FSI had for the first time created its own TV campaign for MILKMAID rather than adopting a campaign that had been developed by the Nestlé subsidiaries in Malaysia or the Philippines. This change in direction was seen by Mr. Souter as very important. Developing his own campaign had been both a lengthy and at times frustrating process. However it had given him the ability to adapt his campaign to the Indonesian market by using Indonesian actors, actresses and locations.

All of FSI's advertisements required approval by the Nestlé home office staff in Switzerland. In addition, working with the relatively inexperienced Indonesian film and creative personnel was frustrating even at the best of times. Thus the process of creating an Indonesian campaign required almost six months versus the two to three months that were required when already approved Malaysian or Philippine ads were adapted for use in Indonesia.

DANCOW powdered milk was promoted in two versions. The instant version received 90 percent of the promotional funds. DANCOW instant, or "the 4 second milk" had been the first locally produced instant milk in Indonesia. It had been a huge success. The instant form had, since its introduction, been advertised on TV and in women's magazines. Because the brand name was the same for both the instant and standard varieties it was believed that the standard form also benefitted from the advertisements for the instant form. The ad budget for the standard form was used for newspaper and cinema slide advertisements.

FSI's two infant cereals were both mass marketed and promoted to the medical profession with the help of samples and literature. CERELAC, the milk based cereal, had been introduced using TV ads that had been developed in Malaysia. This reliance on Malaysian TV advertisements had continued, as had the product's success in the market place. NESTUM, a non-milk cereal, had been introduced with magazine advertisements and had experienced very moderate initial sales. In mid-1979, a TV cam-

EXHIBIT 5 Media Spending—Per Product 1979 to 1981 (planned)

1979, In Million Rupiah

MEDIA / PRODUCT	T.V.	RADIO	NEWSPAPER	MAGAZINE	CINEMA	OUTDOOR (form & amount)	TRADE PROMOTION (form & amount)	CONSUMER PROMOTION (form & amount)	TOTAL
Sweetened Condensed Milk (MILKMAID)	40.55	7.73	—	7.66	0.01	—	0.60	—	56.55
DANCOW Instant	37.43	—	0.83	17.04	—	—	0.85	—	56.15
DANCOW Standard	22.46	—	8.69	—	11.90	—	0.52	—	43.57
NESTUM	29.82	—	—	—	—	—	—	3.87	33.69
CERELAC	42.97	—	—	—	—	—	—	3.59	46.56
MILO	33.07	—	—	—	—	2.00	0.07	0.45	35.59
TOTAL	206.30	7.73	9.52	24.70	11.91	2.00	2.04	7.91	272.11

EXHIBIT 5 Media Spending—Per Product 1979 to 1981 (planned) (cont.)

1980, *In Million Rupiah*

MEDIA / PRODUCT	T.V.	RADIO	NEWSPAPER	MAGAZINE	CINEMA	OUTDOOR (form & amount)	TRADE PROMOTION (form & amount)	CONSUMER PROMOTION (form & amount)	TOTAL
Sweetened Condensed Milk (MILKMAID)	65.14	12.91	—	12.23	0.03	—	0.50	0.07	90.88
DANCOW Instant	65.71	—	—	26.82	—	—	0.77	—	93.30
DANCOW Standard	36.97	—	13.19	—	11.40	—	0.65	—	62.21
NESTUM	72.90	—	—	—	—	—	0.11	2.40	75.41
CERELAC	51.73	—	—	—	—	—	0.11	2.24	54.08
MILO	90.82	—	6.29	21.21	—	0.24	2.79	2.04	123.39
TOTAL	383.27	12.91	19.48	60.26	11.43	0.24	4.93	6.75	499.27

EXHIBIT 5 Media Spending—Per Product 1979 to 1981 (planned) (cont.)

1981, (*planned as of January 20, 1981*), *In Million Rupiah*

MEDIA / PRODUCT	T.V.	RADIO	NEWSPAPER	MAGAZINE	CINEMA	OUTDOOR (form & amount)	TRADE PROMOTION (form & amount)	CONSUMER PROMOTION (form & amount)	TOTAL
Sweetened Condensed Milk (MILKMAID)	120.0	20.1	—	17.6	2.3	—	18.0	3.0	181.0
DANCOW Instant	124.0	—	—	66.0	—	—	13.0	30.0	233.0
DANCOW Standard	50.0	—	—	38.8	11.2	—	18.0	4.0	122.0
NESTUM	91.0	—	—	29.0	—	—	5.5	5.5	131.0
CERELAC	90.0	—	—	—	—	—	5.5	6.0	101.5
MILO	120.0	—	—	30.0	—	—	20.0	28.0	198.0
TOTAL	595.0	20.1	—	184.4	13.5	—	80.0	76.5	966.5

EXHIBIT 6 January 20, 1981 Media Costs—Development and Production

In Thousands of Rupiah

Media	Cost to Develop One Spot	Cost to Broadcast One Spot	
TV		476.7	75.7
Radio	287.0	2.0	0.05
Newspaper	102.0	217.3	52.1
Magazine	2,300.0	1,358.9	

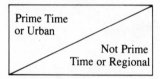

Prime Time or Urban / Not Prime Time or Regional

Outdoor Media	Cost	Fixed Investment/Unit*	
A-Boards	20,000		15,000
Billboards	25,000		15,000
Foot Bridges	140,000		

A-Boards: In Stadium/Outside

Bill Board: Strategic Location/Ordinary

*All Quotes Include Taxes and Annual Maintainance

paign for NESTUM was introduced, and sales increased dramatically. The TV campaign and the impressive sales results had both continued throughout 1980.

MILO was advertised primarily on television with some back up advertisements in women's magazines and children's comic books. It was also the only FSI product advertised in outdoor media. At selected sports events MILO had been advertised using A-boards (wooden signs placed back to back to form an A shape) around the entrance area to the event. Occasionally, these A-boards had also been used along parade routes.

EXHIBIT 7 Ad Sample for MILKMAID

TELEVISION ADVERTISING IN INDONESIA

Mr. Souter believed that:

There is no substitute for television. Without television my job, the job of marketing these products, would be nearly impossible, and the job of introducing a new product would be entirely impossible. There is no other marketing tool in Indonesia that can ever come close to reaching exactly my market with exactly my message, the message that FSI products are consistently high quality products, products that one ought to use.

There were approximately two million television sets in Indonesia in 1981. They could tune into one government owned network, Televisi Republik, Indonesia (TVRI). Television advertisements were carried during two "blocks" per

EXHIBIT 7 *(cont.)* Ad Sample for CERELAC

Cerelac, bubur bergizi lengkap untuk bayi anda

Sebagai ibu, anda ingin agar bayi anda mendapatkan makanan bergizi lengkap. Berilah **Cerelac**, karena **Cerelac** sudah mengandung susu dan 11 vitamin utama serta mineral yang diperlukan untuk pertumbuhan bayi anda. Bayi anda pasti menyukai rasa biskuit dari **Cerelac**, yang merupakan variasi makanan bayi anda. Cerelac dapat diberikan mulai umur 4 bulan atau menurut nasehat dokter.

easy to prepare, add water and stir
Mudah menyiabkannya, hanya tambahkan **Cerelac** pada air

Didihkanlah air.   Tuangkan air masak ke dalam mangkuk yang bersih.   Taburkanlah **Cerelac** di atas permukaan air, sesuai petunjuk pada kaleng.   Aduk hingga rata dan Cerelac siap untuk makanan bayi.

NESTLÉ®

Cerelac, lengkap gizinya - agar sehat bayinya

As a mother you want your baby to have nutritious food. CERELAC already contains milk, 11 vitamins and minerals necessary for good health. Your baby will love CERELAC with its biscuit base. CERELAC can be given to babies 4 months old and older, or according to the advice of your doctor.

day, as well as before, during and at the end of programs or sports events that the advertiser itself had sponsored. The early evening advertising block, from 17:30 to 18:00, was for regionally based commercials. The late evening block, from 21:00 to 21:30, was immediately before the late evening news break and carried national advertisements.

Some Western businessmen operating in Indonesia believed that television advertising in Indonesia, thanks to a happy and rare coincidence of business need and cultural forces working together, pleased just about everyone. Indonesia's television audience seemed to eagerly await the televised signals that one of the twice daily commercial breaks was about to begin.

EXHIBIT 7 (*cont.*) Ad Sample for NESTUM

NESTUM—rice cereal which is ideal for your baby. If milk is no longer enough for your baby, give NESTUM rice cereal as a first solid food. NESTUM rice cereal contains many of the vitamins and minerals necessary for the health of your baby. NESTUM is for babies 4 months old and older or according to the advice of your doctor.

Cartoon type drawings of consumer product packages bearing generic names such as coffee, soap or milk lined up on the screen and a butterfly flew into view to alight briefly on several packages, as if to select them for its own use. Many marketing executives felt that the television appearance of a commercial product was as appealing to the Indonesian consumer as those packages were to that butterfly. To the Indonesian consumer it was the sign that the product was of high quality, dependable, "real" and deserving of their confidence and trust.

Although firm statistics on television viewership did not exist, FSI executives believed that Indonesia's two million television sets were located almost entirely in urban areas.

EXHIBIT 7 (*cont.*) Ad Sample for DANCOW

The best milk for growth. Every child wants to grow healthy and strong. DANCOW Instant is the best milk for growth. DANCOW Instant is enriched with vitamins, is easy to prepare and is delicious.

Beginning in the late 1970's, the Indonesian government supported a program to put a television set in every village for educational purposes. The number of sets involved in this program was never made clear. FSI executives also estimated that 11 percent of the televisions were in use during the early evening advertising break and that 24 percent were in use during the late evening advertising break. They were not sure who was watching. They felt that during the early break it was primarily children and domestic household help. Mr. Souter continued:

> I can control television advertising. I know, roughly, who sees it, and when they see it, I know what they see and I can judge how they interpret it because the visuals are so

EXHIBIT 7 *(cont.)* Ad Sample for MILO

MILO is full of nutrition and rich in energy because it is full of nutrients like malt, sugar, milk, the main vitamins and the main minerals. Your family needs MILO energy. Everyone uses energy every day, especially healthy, active children. This energy needs to be replaced. Chocolate flavored MILO gives this energy every day—at school, at home, and while exercising—to help one grow healthy and strong.

powerful. I can produce a TV campaign 1000 times more efficiently than any other mass media campaign. Or, for that matter, any other marketing or promotion effort whatsoever. That is not to say that producing a TV campaign is easy. It's not! But other campaigns are much more difficult to create—and much, much, much more difficult to implement.

When a television campaign was employed for a FSI product it was used to create the themes that were repeated and reflected by advertisements in other media. Mr. Souter believed that every product's ad campaign needed to be cohesive and self-reinforcing. To insure this, he always developed TV campaigns first, and then designed the radio, magazine, cinema, outdoor and point of sale advertisements to reinforce and support the initially designed television message.

Not only FSI, but all its competitors as well, felt that television advertising was the most important factor in a product's marketing success. Competition for the 40 to 60 second advertising "spots" was breathtaking. Advertising spots were distributed by the government bureaucracy specifically charged with this mission. Simply filing a request for a spot entailed making one's way around an obstacle course of problems that governmental bureaucrats throughout the world seemed so skilled in designing. At this point, simple arithmetic brought the real scope of this situation into focus. FSI's experience, which they believed to be similar to that of most other advertisers as well, was that roughly one in every ten requests was granted. On average, FSI was granted three national and five regional spots per month. In order to increase their television presence, FSI sponsored each year eight to ten nationally televised series, 12 to 15 nationally televised sports events, and several regionally televised programs.

Television campaigns were also costly. One hundred million Rupiahs per year per product was required for an effective television campaign. Each regional spot cost about 300,000 Rupiahs to broadcast and each national spot cost about 750,000 Rupiah to broadcast. In addition, the production costs for one spot, in both a 60 second and a 40 second version, were about ten million Rupiahs.

Two phrases highlighted both the advantages television advertising provided for a marketing manager operating in Indonesia in 1981 and the relative disadvantages of other media forms and promotional efforts: "ability to control" and "not labor intensive."

The production and broadcast of a television ad required the management and cooperation of a small team of professionals. Production required more people than might have been required in a country with a more experienced tel-

evision establishment. However, one could identify fairly easily who was needed and what they needed to do. Similarly, to broadcast an advertisement was not a difficult task. Once permission had been granted, the result was available for all to see and to monitor. In addition to the ability to self-monitor a TV campaign, both TVRI and the advertising agencies provided certificates of broadcast for each broadcasted spot.

INDONESIA'S OTHER MASS MEDIA

Radio networks, in contrast with television, were operated only regionally. There was one government owned station that serviced major cities and many private stations that served both cities and rural areas. The radio networks were characterized by their variety in format, location and language. A radio campaign with national coverage cost 40 to 50 million Rupiahs and required the participation of 70 to 80 different radio stations. Local radio spots were arranged through local advertising agents. Neither the station nor the agents provided certificates to confirm that the ad had actually been broadcast. It was extremely difficult for FSI head office personnel to insure or confirm that the radio ads that they had paid for had been aired.

Obtaining the translations for the regional stations posed another problem when using radio advertisements. According to Mr. Souter "no two Indonesians will ever agree on an exact translation." The translation of only three advertisements into three dialects had recently required "months and months" to complete. The Indonesian radio "population" was believed to be many times that of its TV population, so that, theoretically at least, radio could have had as much, if not more, penetration value as TV.

Radio advertising could be booked throughout the day. The times most in demand, though, were early morning (workdays began around 7:00) and early evening before the TV was tuned in. During the Moslem fasting month in June or July advertisements for food and drink could be carried only after sunset.

Advertising in cinemas was fairly common in Indonesia. Most cinema advertising was in the form of slides that were shown before the start of the film. FSI had advertised MILK-MAID in cinemas in smaller towns, but had not been very satisfied with the effectiveness of this media. Indonesian cinemas were of two classes. Class A cinemas were in major cities and were very expensive to attend, especially when good or well-known films were being shown. Class B cinemas were in smaller towns. They were less expensive to attend and were often rather shabby in appearance. Operational problems plagued both classes of cinema. In FSI's experience the slides, when they were shown at all, were often presented out of sequence or upside down.

FSI used some of Indonesia's magazines having national circulations for full page color advertisements that reflected their television advertisements. In magazine advertising their strategy was to cluster together several ads in several magazines in order to create an impact. They would then use these advertisements in cycles. For two months the clustered ads would appear in several different magazines and then, for one month, no magazine advertisements would be employed. When magazine advertising was the only mass medium used for a product as had been initially the case for NESTUM, a yearly ad budget of 56 million Rupiahs was required to obtain what they felt was an effective penetration.

High caliber magazines were costly to the consumer. They had newsstand prices of between 800 and 1000 Rupiahs per issue and were generally issued bimonthly. This high cost led to very high readership figures per issue. Advertising agency personnel multiplied circulation estimates by eight to compute actual readership. For its market, FSI executives felt that a multiple of five was more realistic. It was, however, very difficult, if not impossible, to estimate readership at all due to the very poor circulation figures that were available. Audited circulation figures were virtually unavailable and some FSI executives believed that the only way to really know who read which magazines was to survey the market by themselves.

Indonesia had six general interest magazines. Three of these were women's magazines

which reported on fashion, decorating and cooking. These had very impressive European formats. "Femina" and "Kartini" were aimed at the upper class housewife and "Gadis" was designed for younger women. Research figures seemed to indicate that readership duplication was approximately 60 percent within this category. "Intisari," a Readers Digest style monthly, Tempo, a Time style magazine, and "Executif," for high level business executives had not been used often by FSI. However these magazines were very popular among Indonesia's elite.

FSI used newspaper advertising primarily for special promotions and as a signal to the trade that FSI was very interested in supporting a given product. Mr. Souter felt that newspaper advertising was of strategic importance in dealing with the trade. Newspaper market penetration seemed to be fairly low. It was also a medium that was more effective in reaching a male audience than a female audience. Agency figures indicated that total readership was five times circulation figures. Although again circulation figures were considered to be very unreliable. FSI executives accepted a multiple of three in terms of their own market. New ads needed to be created for all newspaper campaigns because magazine artwork did not reproduce effectively in black and white. Mr. Souter estimated that 40 million Rupiahs were required, over a three month period, for an effective newspaper campaign.

The range of newspapers was very wide. Probably the most important ones were the two Jakarta based nationals "Kompas" and "Sinar Harapan." Their primary circulation was in Jakarta. In other important regional markets they were very often second in circulation after the local newspaper. There were two rather low circulation English language newspapers, the "Observer" and the "Indonesian Times"; these were not cited by FSI. In addition, a Chinese newspaper with a small but very influential readership was available. The advertising rates for the national and Chinese newspapers were much higher than those of the other newspapers.

Outdoor advertising was very popular in Indonesia, although FSI had rarely employed it.

Billboards in shimmering or plain versions, foot-bridges, bus stop shelters and A-boards were all used for advertising purposes. Mr. Souter believed that few of the outdoor advertising opportunities were appropriate for FSI because of the nature of their products. Outdoor locations soon became dirty, especially those in crowded cities. He did not feel that a dirty environment was appropriate for food products. Nevertheless, many of FSI's competitors did make use of outdoor advertisements. A second problem with outdoor advertisements was the negotiations involved in arranging them. Various "fees" and taxes were often imposed on the advertisers for which no receipt was ever given.

Outdoor advertisements were not inexpensive and each form had its own particular drawbacks. Billboards needed to be leased for three to five years at a time, payable in advance. Bus stop shelters advertising different brands of the same products tended to line up one after the other. A similar problem arose with A-boards. These were often used temporarily at the entrance to sports events or along parade routes. They would often be massed so close together that the impact of each board was substantially reduced.

Pedestrian footbridges were an expensive, but popular, advertising medium. A company could build, for approximately 15 million Rupiahs, a pedestrian footbridge over a crowded street. The company would become liable for all maintenance charges and the ever popular annually negotiated tax. In return, advertisements could be painted on the bridge for five years. At one time FSI executives had considered building such a bridge but had decided against it on the basis of cost and their reluctance to negotiate the "taxes."

TRADE BASED PROMOTION

Indonesia's wholesalers and retailers always welcomed trade based promotions that involved distributing premiums such as drinking glasses, which were a particular favorite, or product samples. These were promotions that they could easily participate in. To them, the immediate nature of the reward was a tremendous allure. They disliked coupon type promotions that required them to give up something first by accepting less money for a product or accepting only a coupon for a product in anticipation of later reimbursement by the company sponsoring the promotion. The concept of a monetary society was new to some retailers, who were far more comfortable being barter traders.

TUESDAY AFTERNOON

It was late in the afternoon of Tuesday, January 21, 1981 and Ian Souter had spent the day reviewing the marketing campaigns for each of the six products FSI manufactured and marketed in Indonesia. He now had less than ten weeks to redesign and implement a "non-TV" campaign for each of those products. The campaigns needed to be finalized by mid-March for their April introductions. He needed to meet those deadlines despite the delays and interruptions that he had come to expect during his three years in Indonesia. He felt that his list of campaign and promotion ideas would serve as the basis of a very intensive review meeting the next day with the staff of the Fortune Advertising Agency, who had served FSI for 22 years, and his own superiors.

CASE 7 ▪ American Hospital Supply— Japan Corporation

INTRODUCTION

In the spring of 1975, executives of AHS-Japan, under the direction of Mr. F. Nakamoto, the company president, met to discuss the possible method of entering the Japanese dental equipment market. The company was a subsidiary of American Hospital Supply, Inc., and had introduced two of its parent company's product lines very successfully during the last 5 years. It was now up to the executive team to select a strategy and to submit the proposal to its parent company for endorsement. The selection process was made particularly difficult by the nature of the distribution system and the strength of AHS-Japan's potential competitors.

AHS-JAPAN CORPORATION

AHS-Japan Corporation was originally established in 1968 as a branch of the American Hospital Supply Corporation. Just recently, its status had been changed to a subsidiary following the liberalization of the Japanese investment regulations that earlier had not allowed a foreign company to own the majority of the share capital of a subsidiary in Japan. The original mission of the branches was to sell a product line similar to the parent company's with a possibility for local production later on. At the outset, the company carried only medical equipment, such as surgical equipment for operating rooms, intensive-care or critical-care units. In 1971, diagnostic reagents were introduced as the second major product line. The planned introduction of dental equipment would represent the third major product line for AHS-Japan with further additions planned every 1 to 2 years. The company had been successful practically from its inception growing from originally 3 employees in 1968 to about 50 at the present time. Sales had shown a growth pattern of 50 percent compounded annually.

AMERICAN HOSPITAL SUPPLY CORPORATION BACKGROUND

American Hospital Supply was formed in 1922 as the first distributor specializing solely on products for hospitals. The company had concentrated on this segment for many years before introducing other product lines such as dental equipment and materials or scientific instruments. Today, the original hospital supply business accounted for about 50 percent of total sales of US $1,002 million in 1974. The other major segments were science (32 percent of sales), medical and dental specialties (11%), and pharmaceuticals (7%). (See Exhibits 1, 2, and 3.) The company had integrated backwards over the years producing approximately 45 percent of its sales through its own manufacturing subsidiaries. The approximately 24,100 employees serviced more than 140 countries through about 50 production centers and 120 sales or distribution centers. The product line comprised about 100,000 items.

This case was prepared by Jean-Pierre Jeannet, Professor of Marketing and International Business at Babson College, while teaching as Visiting Lecturer at Keio University Graduate School of Business in Tokyo. This case was prepared for the sole purpose of class discussion rather than to illustrate either effective or ineffective handling of an administrative situation.

EXHIBIT 1 Group Net Sales and Net Earnings

Net Sales
($ in millions)

	1975		1974		1973		1972		1971	
Hospital	$ 323.2	29%	$268.7	27%	$213.7	26%	$181.7	26%	$168.7	28%
Science Specialties	355.9	31	312.6	32	300.2	36	242.9	35	197.7	33
Medical Specialties	72.4	6	67.5	7	52.7	6	44.1	6	39.1	6
Pharmaceutical	91.1	8	74.8	8	62.0	7	54.9	8	51.0	9
Capital Goods	60.0	5	55.9	6	49.4	6	43.8	6	42.4	7
Dental	46.9	4	41.7	4	34.3	4	30.9	4	25.2	4
Dietary	43.8	4	39.6	4	30.0	4	24.0	4	21.2	4
Services	92.1	8	79.3	8	57.9	7	46.0	7	34.9	6
International	81.8	7	71.2	7	53.7	6	38.1	6	28.4	5
Unallocated eliminations and adjustments	(23.8)	(2)	(25.4)	(3)	(16.5)	(2)	(12.7)	(2)	(12.4)	(2)
	$1143.4	100%	$985.9	100%	$837.4	100%	$693.7	100%	$596.2	100%
Total international sales	$ 202.9	18%	$168.8	17%	$125.2	15%	$ 97.4	14%	$ 81.0	14%

Net Earnings
($ in millions)

	1975		1974		1973		1972		1971	
Hospital	$ 19.3	35%	$ 13.7	29%	$ 10.0	25%	$ 7.5	21%	$ 6.1	21%
Science Specialties	16.5	30	14.6	31	13.6	33	12.3	34	10.7	35
Medical Specialties	6.8	12	5.9	13	3.7	9	3.4	10	2.6	8
Pharmaceutical	6.3	12	5.0	11	4.9	12	5.1	14	5.4	18
Capital Goods	3.0	6	2.3	5	2.2	5	2.0	6	2.1	7
Dental	2.4	4	2.6	6	1.8	4	1.5	4	0.4	1
Dietary	2.3	4	1.5	3	0.8	2	0.5	1	0.1	—
Services	1.8	3	3.0	6	1.6	4	0.9	3	0.6	2
International	.2	—	2.4	5	3.1	8	1.9	5	2.3	8
Unallocated interest, eliminations and adjustments	(3.4)	(6)	(4.4)	(9)	(0.7)	(2)	0.6	2	(0.1)	—
	$ 55.2	100%	$ 46.6	100%	$ 41.0	100%	$ 35.7	100%	$ 30.2	100%
Total international earnings	$ 10.5	19%	$ 10.9	23%	$ 7.9	19%	$ 4.9	14%	$ 3.2	10%

Sales and earnings for each market group include their respective export and Canadian operations. Appropriate eliminations have been made to reflect group results on a consolidated basis. Normal income tax provisions, less tax incentives and adjustments, are reflected within reported group earnings.

The International Group has responsibility for coordination of all domestic export shipments as well as direct responsibility for foreign-based operations. Total international net sales and net earnings shown as separate amounts include Canadian operations and United States exports, royalties from foreign sources, income from foreign investments, and foreign exchange gains and losses in addition to the International Group foreign-based operations.

Unallocated eliminations and adjustments reflect transactions between groups as well as corporate interest income and expense and other miscellaneous adjustments. Such unallocated interest expense after taxes amounted to $3.2 million in 1975 and $3.6 million in 1974. Other corporate office expenses have been allocated to group operations on the basis of sales and number of employees in each group.

EXHIBIT 2 Statement of Earnings

$ and shares in thousands	Year ended December 31				
	1974	1973	1972	1971	1970
Net sales	$981,788	$834,336	$691,550	$594,687	$523,784
Cost of products and services	653,709	565,404	459,248	392,282	347,380
	328,079	268,932	232,302	202,405	176,404
Selling, shipping, warehousing and administrative expenses	238,816	193,434	167,629	146,658	127,503
	89,263	75,498	64,673	55,747	48,901
Other income	2,557	1,994	3,123	3,867	3,833
Interest expense	(8,444)	(2,756)	(1,576)	(1,642)	(1,503)
Earnings before income taxes	83,376	74,736	66,220	57,972	51,231
Income taxes	37,049	33,926	30,617	27,801	25,328
Net earnings	$ 46,327	$ 40,810	$ 35,603	$ 30,171	$ 25,903
Net earnings per share	$1.28	$1.13	$.99	$.84	$.72
Average shares and equivalents	36,337	36,134	36,088	35,845	35,745

See notes to financial statements.

Financial and Operating Statistics

	1974	1973	1972	1971	1970
Ratios to net sales:					
Gross profit	33.4%	32.2%	33.6%	34.0%	33.7%
Operating expenses	24.3	23.2	24.2	24.7	24.3
Operating earnings	9.1	9.0	9.4	9.4	9.4
Earnings before income taxes	8.5	9.0	9.6	9.7	9.8
Net earnings	4.7	4.9	5.1	5.1	4.9
Effective income tax rate	44.4%	45.4%	46.2%	47.9%	49.4%
Days of sales:					
Accounts receivable	64	63	70	69	74
Inventory	112	106	111	115	120
Working capital:					
Amount in thousands	$287,912	$223,828	$228,027	$213,400	$202,324
Current ratio	3.2 to 1	2.8 to 1	3.9 to 1	3.9 to 1	4.5 to 1
Dividends:					
Amount paid in thousands	$ 10,749	$9,799	$9,372	$8,880	$8,332
Percent of earnings paid	23.2%	24.0%	26.3%	29.4%	32.2%
Paid per share	$ .300	$ .280	$ .270	$ .260	$ .245
Shareholders investment:					
Amount per share—year end	$11.36	$10.37	$ 9.47	$ 8.74	$ 8.13
Return on average	11.8%	11.4%	10.9%	10.0%	9.3%
Number of employees	23,500	21,800	19,400	15,700	14,900
Number of shareholders	43,076	44,095	45,494	47,804	52,132

AHS INTERNATIONAL OPERATIONS

AHS organized its international operations as a separate corporate group directed by a president. For 1974, net sales amounted to $104.2 million of which $33 million represented exports by U.S. subsidiaries to AHS companies and clients outside the U.S. and Canada. Net earnings amounted to $2.4 million on international group companies and another $6.1 million on the ex-port transactions. The International Group had the responsibility for coordination of all domestic export shipments as well as direct responsibility for foreign-based operations. It has always been the strategy of AHS to concentrate on major markets with a sufficiently high level of health care to justify local operations. As a result, the group operated its 23 operations concentrated on just 14 markets (see Exhibit 4 for details).

EXHIBIT 3 Balance Sheet

		December 31
$ in thousands	1974	1973
Current Assets:		
Cash	$ 9,145	$ 8,025
Marketable securities, at cost (approximates market)	4,055	32
Receivables, less allowances—$3,851 (1974); $3,842 (1973)	184,116	162,712
Inventories	209,817	169,726
Prepaid expenses	10,405	6,874
Total current assets	417,538	347,369
Other Assets:		
Investments in and advances to affiliates	5,313	4,842
Miscellaneous investments, receivables due after one year and other	9,345	5,953
	14,658	10,795
Property, Plant and Equipment, at cost:		
Land	11,131	10,257
Buildings	140,931	113,128
Machinery and equipment	111,567	90,489
Furniture and fixtures	16,444	12,835
	280,073	226,709
Less accumulated depreciation	77,813	68,215
	202,260	158,494
Intangibles, at cost less amortization	6,151	5,369
	$640,607	$522,027

EXHIBIT 3 Balance Sheet (*cont.*)

$ in thousands	December 31	
	1974	1973
Current Liabilities:		
Notes payable to banks	$ 4,549	$ 23,469
Commercial paper	7,265	—
Current maturities on long-term obligations	1,420	1,049
Accounts payable	83,640	72,772
Commissions, salaries and withholdings	15,892	11,199
Retirement and profit-sharing plans	5,221	4,981
Taxes other than federal income taxes	5,837	4,833
Federal income taxes	5,802	5,238
Total current liabilities	129,626	123,541
Long-Term Obligations, less current maturities:		
5% Notes payable	11,800	12,600
7½% Notes payable	5,325	4,973
Real estate mortgages and notes	1,159	1,422
5¾% Convertible subordinated debentures	75,000	—
	93,284	18,995
Deferred Income Taxes	7,086	4,877
Shareholders' Investment:		
Common stock	158,059	157,640
Earnings reinvested in the business	252,552	216,974
	410,611	374,614
	$640,607	$522,027

EXHIBIT 4 Directory of Operations

AMERICAN HOSPITAL SUPPLY CORPORATION
Executive Offices
1740 Ridge Avenue
Evanston, Illinois

HOSPITAL GROUP

Manufactures and markets supplies and equipment to hospitals and other health care institutions.

American Hospital Supply Division
McGaw Park, Illinois

American Hospital Supply Division*
Toronto, Canada

Convertors Division
Evanston, Illinois

Pharmaseal Division
Glendale, California

Texpack Division*
Brantford, Canada

Pharmaseal Division*
Brantford, Canada

CAPITAL GOODS GROUP

Manufactures and markets specialized wood and metal products for health care institutions, laboratories, schools and industry.

EXHIBIT 4 Directory of Operations (cont.)

Hamilton Industries Division
Two Rivers, Wisconsin

DIETARY GROUP

Distributes supplies and equipment used in the storage, preparation and serving of food in health care institutions.

Dietary Products Division
McGaw Park, Illinois

SCIENCE SPECIALTIES GROUP

Manufactures and markets supplies and equipment used in surgical, educational, industrial and government laboratory facilities.

Canlab Division*
Toronto, Canada

Dade Division
Miami, Florida

Harleco Division
Gibbstown, New Jersey

Scientific Products Division
McGaw Park, Illinois

MEDICAL SPECIALTIES GROUP

Manufactures and distributes medical devices, instruments and equipment used by physicians surgeons or medical specialists.

Edwards Laboratories Division
Santa Ana, California

Heyer-Schulte Corporation
Goieta, California

V. Mueller Division
Niles, Illinois

PHARMACEUTICAL GROUP

Manufactures and distributes intravenous and irrigating solutions and ethical pharmaceutical specialties to physicians, hospitals and other health care institutions.

Arnar-Stone Laboratories, Inc.
Mount Prospect, Illinois

McGaw Laboratories Division
Glendale, California

SERVICES GROUP

Provides non-medical support services to health care institutions.

American Health Facilities Division
Winnetka, Illinois

Information Systems Division
Evanston, Illinois

Red Top, Inc.
Denver, Colorado

Wells National Services Corporation
New York, New York

DENTAL GROUP

Manufactures and markets equipment, supplies and prosthetics used by dentists.

Midwest American Dental Division
Melrose Park, Illinois

Denticon, Inc.
Evanston, Illinois

Denco Division*
Toronto, Canada

Beavers Dental Products, Ltd.
Morrisburg, Canada

INTERNATIONAL GROUP

Manufactures and distributes a variety of health care products.

AHS/Mexico, S.A. de C.V.
Cuernavaca, Mexico

American Hospital Supply (U.K.) Ltd.
Didcot, England

American Hospital Supply Corporation de Puerto Rico, S.A.
San Juan, Puerto Rico

American Hospital Supply Corporation de Venezuela, C.A.
Caracas, Venezuela

AHS/Belgium, S.A.
Brussels, Belgium

AHS/France, S.A.
Saint-Quen l'Aumore, France

Merz & Dade, A.G.
Berne, Switzerland

Merz & Dade, G.m.b.H.
Munich, West Germany

Pharmaseal Laboratories, G.m.b.H.
Gemering, West Germany

McGaw Baxter Laboratories, Inc.
Rizal, Philippines

McGaw Ethicals Ltd.
Auckland, New Zealand

AHSC/South Africa (Pty.) Ltd.
Johannesburg, South Africa

EXHIBIT 4   Directory of Operations (cont.)

AHS/Australia Pty. Ltd.
Sydney, Australia
Scientific Products, Inc. (Japan Branch)
Tokyo, Japan

AHS/Japan, k.k.
Tokyo, Japan
AHS/International, Inc. (Branch Office)
Seoul, Korea

PRODUCT LINES IN JAPAN

AHS-Japan's first product introduction consisted of a portion of the parent company's medical equipment line. Due to the competitive nature of the Japanese market, special emphasis was put on sophisticated products, particularly those with a focus on cardiac disease applications. As a result, the product line consisted of heart valves, pacers, bypass or intra-aortic balloon pumps, and surgical instruments for open heart surgery.

As a newcomer to the market, the company found the distribution problem particularly vexing. The market for medical instruments consisted of hospitals and clinical laboratories and some general practitioners. The larger hospitals and clinics sought their equipment directly from domestic manufacturers, importing companies, or foreign affiliated subsidiaries in Japan. All three of the above sources for medical equipment, however, also sold through a group of 27 specialized wholesalers who partially sold directly to smaller hospitals and clinics or resold to about 150 regional dealers. As it turned out, the 27 specialized primary wholesalers had strong ties to already established importers or domestic manufacturers and were therefore not willing to adopt a product line that was competing with one of their established suppliers. Furthermore, AHS-Japan's cardiac equipment was of the highest sophistication that required the sales force to be fully trained in and knowledgeable about heart surgery, something that trade salesmen of both primary and regional wholesalers could not be expected to be. This situation

led to AHS-Japan's decision to sell directly to end-users (see Exhibit 5).

Following the introductory period, AHS-Japan continued to monitor the activities of medical equipment wholesalers in Japan. The company discovered that operating margins were relatively low with net earnings averaging about 1 percent compared to 5.5 percent for AHS-US or 5 to 10 percent for typical US dealers. While gross margins tended to be similar to those of the United States, Japanese intermediaries engaged in many additional activities and services of value to both suppliers and customers that were normally not performed by a wholesaler in the United States. Besides shipping goods to the customers, wholesalers gave general service, maintained excellent customer relations before and after the sale, collected valuable market information, sold repeat orders, and collected funds from their customers. Despite their gross margins,[1] these service functions tended to reduce the net profit margin below a level typical for the United States. AHS-Japan also noted that wholesalers in Japan were able to carry out all of these functions at a lesser cost than a US subsidiary due to their lower wages.

---

1. Gross margins for medical products varied substantially and depended on individual products. Items with low unit value and a large volume in repeat orders might carry margins of as low as 15 percent. For equipment that required sophisticated service, long lead times, and relatively high unit value, the gross margins might be as high as 30 percent.

EXHIBIT 5 Distribution Channels for Medical Equipment and Devices

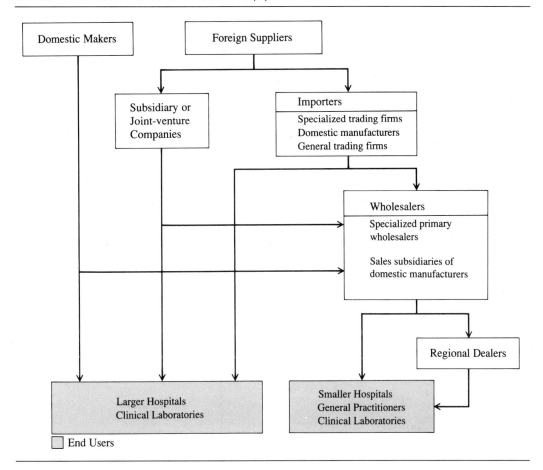

As a result, AHS-Japan decided later to include wholesalers in its distribution effort for medical equipment. The resulting savings in manpower, particularly since salesmen did not have to make monthly collection calls, added to AHS-Japan's sales productivity. Today, close to 80 percent of its sales were transacted through wholesalers or distributors. But the company believed these wholesalers to remain weak in promotion and technical after sales service. Consequently, these two aspects continued to be supplied by AHS-Japan. As a result, AHS-Japan has been very successful competing with medical equipment in Japan.

Following the successful introduction of medical equipment, American Hospital Supply Corporation (AHSC) introduced clinical and diagnostic reagents. This product of the pharmaceutical industry was sold to the same targets as the medical equipment: hospitals, clinics, and general practitioners. Domestic producers only shipped about 30 percent of reagents directly, mostly to large hospitals or clinics; 70 percent was sold to 188 specialized primary wholesalers who partially sold directly to hospitals or supplied small regional wholesalers. These latter ones were not really necessary except that local governments preferred to deal with regional wholesalers. Foreign competitors could either sell through independent importers or distributors or could form a joint venture company in partnership with a Japanese company. Since

EXHIBIT 6 Distribution Channels for Clinical Diagnostic Reagents

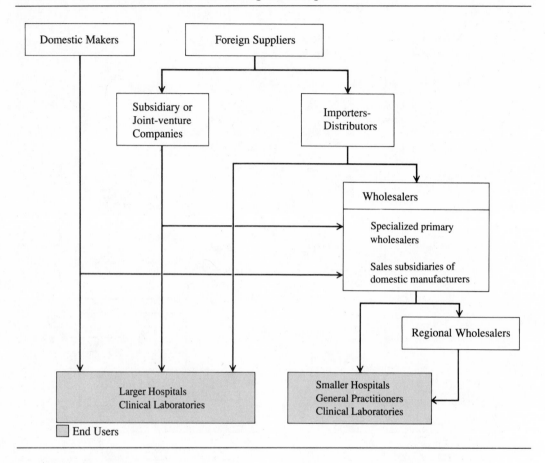

clinical reagents had to be kept under refrigeration with special equipment, AHSC had to find a way to obtain cooperation of some of these primary wholesalers who supplied the largest market segment. Since it was very difficult to obtain their cooperation as a newcomer, AHS-Japan decided on a production joint-venture with Green Cross Co., a highly respected drug manufacturer who also marketed whole blood. International Reagents Corporation, the JV manufacturing company, was then able to distribute its reagents through 50 of the primary wholesalers with the help of Green Cross Co. (See Exhibit 6 for marketing channels.) Again, the product introduction was successful.

OPPORTUNITIES IN THE DENTAL EQUIPMENT MARKET

The market for dental equipment and materials in Japan was one of the largest in the world. There were approximately 40,000 dentists in Japan, and about 2,000 entered the field each year. They spent approximately $500 million in 1975 for both equipment and materials. Materials included all items that were actually used up or consumed by the dentist in his practice, or about $300 million annually. This amount was very high because it included precious metals, particularly gold, which accounted for 60 percent of the total used for fillings or tooth repair. Dental equipment, consisting of items such as chairs, lighting, handpieces, drills, etc., amounted to about $200 million annually. It was this latter segment of the market that was of prime interest to AHS-Japan Corporation. Japan's 40,000 practicing dentists were trained in the country's 27 dental colleges. Their income was relatively secure, because Japan's National Health Insurance Plan limited the amounts to be charged for a typical service. As a result, Japanese dentists had a tendency to see many more patients than their colleagues in Western countries—often 40 to 50 per day. Since the equipment of a dental practice represented a very large outlay, Japanese dentists turned to the equipment manufacturers for help to finance their initial costs.

The market for dental equipment was essentially dominated by three firms: Yoshida, Morita, and Osada. Together they accounted for 80 percent of the market. Yoshida, with a market share of 30 percent, was selling equipment manufactured by itself. Morita, also with a market share of 30 percent, had a licensing arrangement with Ritter, a major dental company in the United States. In contrast to the United States where a dentist might combine equipment from several manufacturers into a total package, the Japanese dentist only chose one manufacturer who then provided the total service. To attract dental college graduates, the leading companies even assisted in the planning, locating, and renting suitable buildings for dental practices and, in addition, provided the loans directly to the dentists to purchase or finance the practice. In the United States, the dentist typically received loans from a bank on his own without involving the dental equipment manufacturer. Of course, the Japanese system provided for a very strong tie between the dentists and the major manufacturers. To assist in the servicing of their equipment, each manufacturer provided expert repair service through an extensive servicing network. It was believed that the "new" market to dental college graduates represented about 60 percent of the equipment market.

The remainder of the market consisted of replacement sales to established dentists, or expansion of dental practices. This included most of the 40,000 practicing dentists. This segment of the market was dominated by 20 large wholesalers with strong contacts to the many retailers, or dealers, who were in almost daily contact with their dentists to supply them not only with replacement equipment but primarily with dental materials. The leading equipment manufacturers also used these intermediaries to sell in the replacement market.

Sharing the same distribution channel were the manufacturers of dental materials. This $300 million market consisted to 60 percent of precious metals, primarily gold and silver. The market had been growing at a rate of 10 to 15 percent. The market for materials in Japan was dominated by a few large firms, with the top three alone accounting for 70 percent of the market. G.C. Dental Industries was the leader with 28 percent, followed by Sankin with 22 percent and Shofu with 20 percent of the market. These manufacturers made extensive use of the 800 to 900 large and small retailers by selling to them either directly or through primary wholesalers (see Exhibit 7 for more details).

Sales to dentists took place almost on a daily basis. A retailer carrying one of the leading lines typically called the dentist in the morning and asked for the needs of the day. Orders were then accepted and shipped almost immediately. Contrary to equipment purchases, dentists sought materials from a number of manufacturers "cherry picking" each line for its best products.

AHS-JAPAN'S LINE OF DENTAL EQUIPMENT

It was planned to introduce primarily handpieces, or "drills," and dental units (see Exhibits 8 and 9) made by American Hospital Supplies' Midwest Subsidiary.[2] The handpieces and dental units were generally regarded as the best in the industry, both in the United States and in Japan. While more expensive than competitive

---

2. Midwest did not produce any other dental equipment such as chairs, lamps, etc.

EXHIBIT 7 Distribution Channels for Dental Industry

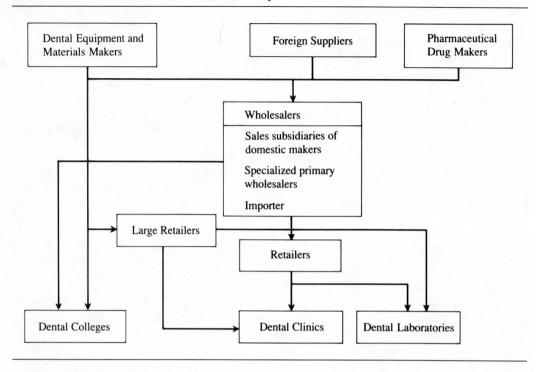

products by about 25 percent, they offered considerable benefits compared to other handpieces. Drill speeds were as high as 450,000 R.P.M., though some local competitors' products achieved even higher speeds. The speed could be gradually adjusted from zero to top speed with a foot pedal, whereas local competitors had no adjustable speed or foot pedal. And finally, AHS units were generally considered to be superior to competitors in styling.

Japanese dentists were considering accuracy, quality, and high speed as the primary criteria in selecting handpieces. In general, American equipment was highly regarded among Japanese dentists, many of whom knew Midwest equipment from their trips to conferences in the United States and Europe. In fact, some of them had purchased Midwest handpieces abroad or wrote directly to the factory in the United States. In the past, Midwest had filled these orders despite the absence of a servicing network to assist the dentists.

The dental units were to sell at about yen 4.5 million[3] compared to simpler ones available for as little as 2.5 million. Due to the expensive nature of AHS-Japan's equipment, the company considered the top 5–10% of practicing dentists as its main target market. Such a dentist typically had been in business for several years and achieved a relatively high income. When replacing equipment, he was more interested in status and willing to pay a premium price for what was considered the "Cadillac" of the industry. Of course, the products had to be adjusted to the Japanese environment. Because Japanese dentists were smaller than their American col-

---

3. 250 yen = 1 US $.

EXHIBIT 8 Midwest Handpieces

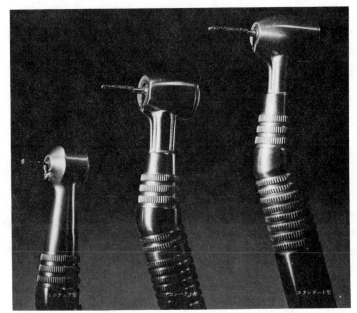

《エアータービン コントラアングル》
クワイエットエアー
スタンダード型
コンパクト型
ミニチュア型

回転ブレが無く、長寿命
磨耗の少ない特殊ボールベアリングと独特のメタルチャックシステムの採用により、バーのセンターリングは抜群。回転ブレが無いだけでなく、耐久性も連続回転試験で延べ800時間と、他社製品の2倍以上です。

強力で安定したトルク特性
高効率タービンと独自の軸受機構により、低速回転や加圧操作中においても安定した強いトルクを発揮します。

冷却効果の大きいスプレー
ヘッド先端のノズルからは冷却水が霧状になって噴出。形成歯牙を直接、効果的に冷やします。

ミッドウェスト社独自の4ホール方式
コントラ内には4本の（ドライブエアー用、エキゾーストエアー用、チップエアー用、水用）が独立して組込まれていますので──

❶●2ホール式よりさらに音が低くなります。
❷●スプレーの他にチップエアーだけ独立して使えます。
❸●排気をユニットに回収するので清潔です。
①水 ②ドライブエアー ③エキゾーストエアー ④チップエアー

leagues, they preferred somewhat smaller chairs and lighter handpieces. Also, electricity in Japan was not everywhere the same: the Western part used 60 cycles and Eastern part 50 cycles. Some adjustment to the dental units was required, since in rural areas Japanese dentists worked on the traditional tatami (straw) mats and it was not possible to screw the equipment to the floor as was the case in urban areas or in the United States.

To facilitate such local adjustments, AHS-Japan planned to import the equipment initially from Midwest, and later to move into local assembly with local production as the ultimate goal. However, such adjustments to both dental units and equipment for an otherwise standardized product line would only be possible if AHS-Japan could guarantee sufficient sales volume to make the changes profitable.

SELECTION OF DISTRIBUTION CHANNEL

There were four basic options for AHS-Japan's entry into the dental equipment field. The company could (a) go directly to dentists with its

EXHIBIT 8 Midwest Handpieces (cont.)

《エアータービン ハンドピース》

ツルートルクショーティ I型 II型

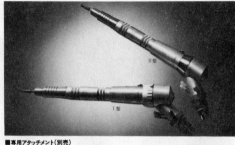

低速使用時にも充分なトルク
エアータービンの高速回転を強力なトルクに変える画期的な伝達装置。これが「粘り強く安定した低速回転を実現しました。

優れた耐久性
回転部分の軸受けには特殊ボールベアリングを使用。長時間にわたる苛酷なご使用に耐えます。またエアーを動力源としますから電気的なトラブルなどに悩まされることなく、ほとんど故障知らずです。

振動のないスムーズな回転
ボールベアリングの使用に加えて、ミッドウエスト社独自のメタルチャック方式の採用がバーの回転ブレを皆無にしました。ドリオット型のアタッチメント装置の場合もシッカリと安定します。

コントラ型の専用アタッチメントも用意
強力なトルクをそのままコントラアングルとしても使用できる専用アタッチメントを用意しました。特にバランスを重視。交換操作はワンタッチです。

回転速度が自由にコントロールできる
ミッドウエストアメリカン社のユニットと組合せれば回転数をフットペダルで自由にコントロール。どの回転領域でも有効な力を発揮します。

チップエアー、スプレーが使用可能
必要に応じてスプレーホースを取付けることにより、チップエアー及びスプレーが使えます。

●I型
変速リングを切換えることにより、低速(200〜6,000rpm)から高速(6,000〜25,000rpm)まで自由に回転スピードをコントロールできます。

●II型
200〜6,000rpmの低速領域で高性能を発揮。回転スピードのコントロールは自在です。

■専用アタッチメント（別売）

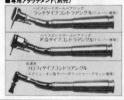

own distribution set-up, or (b) AHS-Japan could use existing wholesalers and retailers to go to the market. The next two alternatives involved (c) some form of cooperation with one of the leading dental equipment manufacturers or (d) align themselves with a leading dental material supply manufacturer.

AHS-Japan had set several objectives for the introduction. The company wanted to become an important factor in the market with a goal of a 10 percent market share for handpieces and 5 percent for dental units. Also, it was important to portray reliability and, if some form of arrangement were to be negotiated, it would have to be with a first-class company. And, finally, AHS-Japan wanted to open up channels for additional dental product introductions at a later time, both in the equipment and the materials segments of the market.

ALTERNATIVE A: GOING DIRECT

This would require AHS-J to sell directly to dentists, either to new graduates of dental colleges or established dentists, by use of a specially trained sales force. At this time, AHS-J did not have sufficient manpower to handle such a task, but additional personnel with sufficient qualifications could be hired and trained. AHS-J would also have to provide an extensive service network that could back up its selling effort. This was the option chosen for introduction of its medical equipment line.

EXHIBIT 9 Midwest Dental Unit

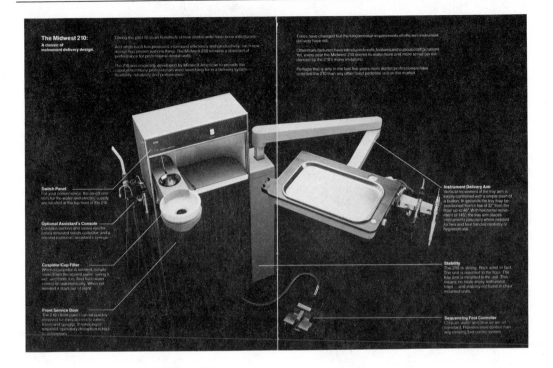

210 Dental Unit

Basic Unit	610090	Three Handpiece AUTOMATIC Activation and Syringe
(Right or Left		Two Handpiece AUTOMATIC Activation and Syringe
Handed versions)		Two Handpiece MANUAL Activation and Syringe

Basic Unit Includes:

Midwest Tri-Clear® Syringe and Hose
Counter Balanced Tray Arm with:
    a. Height adjustment button
    b. Spray control knob
    c. Water for handpiece cooling
    d. Stainless steel tray
    e. Warm water for 3-way Tri-Clear Syringe
    f. Air pressure gauge
Concealed Cuspidor with Automatic Flush and Gravity Drain
Concealed Cup Filler
Master Electric Switch
Flat Working Top
Variable Speed Foot Controller with Chip Air
Light Adapter Opening and Bracket

EXHIBIT 9 Midwest Dental Unit (*cont.*)

(Light Post Must be Obtained from Light Manufacturer)
Duplex Electrical Outlet in Unit Base
Air Line Filter with Automatic Moisture Drain
Fused Electrical Service
Counter Balanced Accent Panel
Hydrocolloid and Drain Connection with Flow Adjustment
Dual Water Filtration System
Straight handpiece tubing with Midwest or Borden back end

210 Dental Unit Accessories

Evacuation System	611467	Fittings for Central Suction Hi Volume Evacuation. Includes Solids Collector with Remote Switch for Central Pump and Saliva Ejector
	611472	Self-Contained Air Venturi Hi Volume Evacuation System with Fittings
Burner	303795	Bunsen Burner with Fittings
Syringe	611476	Tri-Clear® Syringe with Fittings (Auxiliary Syringe on Assistant's Console and Custom Installations)
Hoses	611328	Coiled Midwest 4-Hole Tubing (When Purchased with Unit) Also available with Borden 2 and 3 hole Tubing.
	611329	Coiled Syringe Hose (When Purchased with Unit)
	731074	Fiber Optic Hose Installed 5' Straight Hose with 10' Fiber Optic Bundle
	731075	Coiled Fiber Optic Hose Installed
Oraluminator	731076	Oraluminator III Light Source with Remote Control Unit. Mounting Holes Predrilled in 210 Side Panel and Tray Bottom
HVE Hose	611481	Second HVE Hose (Central Vacuum only)
Syringe	280022	Tri-Clear® Syringe
Installation Kit	610117	Kit for Field Installation of Assistant's Tri-Clear Syringe on 210 Unit. (Does Not Include Syringe)
Tray Arm Lock	611494	U.S. Navy Tray Arm Locking Mechanism

ALTERNATIVE B: USING EXISTING INTERMEDIARIES

AHS-J had the option of selling to its targets through the 29 primary wholesalers and 800 to 900 large and small retailers. Essentially, this was the channel used by the leading manufacturers for the replacement portion of their business. It would be necessary to gain the cooperation of a number of the primary wholesalers, so that, in combination with their respective retail accounts, satisfactory coverage of the market could be established.

Using these intermediaries, however, would entail for AHS-J to assist in the sales task by training the distributor sales personnel. Technical service, however, would have to be provided by AHS-J, since wholesalers and retailers were historically weak in that area. To some extent, this was the alternative selected for the medical equipment line, following its successful initial introduction.

ALTERNATIVE C: COOPERATION WITH A DENTAL EQUIPMENT MANUFACTURER

The Japanese equipment manufacturers, which were now selling their own handpieces and dental units, were believed to be interested in using AHS-J's line as a new, top-of-the-line addition for dentists who were willing to pay for the added performance of Midwest equipment. Management believed that any one of the three leading manufacturers would be interested in carrying the line. Service could of course be handled by the Japanese manufacturer. However, management expected that whichever would be chosen as a distributor would require an exclusive arrangement with the Japanese market.

ALTERNATIVE D: COOPERATION WITH A DENTAL MATERIALS MANUFACTURER

Over the past few years, manufacturers of dental materials had made attempts to invade the equipment market with their own products. Management therefore believed that any of the leading three materials manufacturers would be willing to carry the Midwest line as its entry into the dental equipment market. Sales would take place primarily through wholesalers and retailers which was the customary channel for the material segment of the dental market. Service would have to be provided in conjunction with AHS-J, since that was an important factor in the market.

THE REALITIES OF THE JAPANESE DISTRIBUTION SYSTEM

The choice of any of these basic alternatives greatly depended on AHS-J's objectives for its dental line in the Japanese market and on the "realities" of the Japanese distribution system, both in general and with respect to dental equipment and material.

One of the overriding factors in any Japanese distribution or business arrangement was the nature of the personal contact with one's business partners. In general, the Japanese did not like to conduct business with strangers, be that an unknown company or an unknown salesman. This often required that a businessman who wanted to see a particular person had to have an appropriate introduction. At best, this would be a good personal friend of the person to be visited, maybe even someone the latter was beholden to. Also, the higher the status of the person making an introduction, the better for later business. When no one could be found to give an introduction, sometimes a bank could serve as a reference. In any case, it was extremely difficult to see someone without an introduction, particularly when both the company and the person were unknown.

Another reality of business relationships was the loyalty displayed to existing contacts or associates. This was particularly strong in the channel structure. Over the years, manufacturers had become very close to their distributors and wholesalers, making it difficult for some to enact policies that would harm the other. Manufacturers would, whenever possible, tie wholesalers to their operations by granting liberal trade credit. Wholesalers in turn would likewise with "their" retailers. As a result, a retailer would often be hesitant to carry a new, or even competitive, product from another wholesaler for fear of alienating his established supplier, and hence endanger his source of financing. Such ties also existed between retailers and customers. In the extreme, a market could at times be virtually "locked up" through existing relationships making it extremely difficult for a newcomer to enter.

With respect to trends in the dental market, one important factor was the attempt by both the equipment manufacturers and material producers to invade each other's territory. Both groups maintained strong controls with "their" loyal group of wholesalers and retailers, ensuring the "Big Three" of each group coverage of the entire Japanese market.

It was these general factors, combined with AHS-J's intermediate and long-term objectives, that the company's management had to consider. Whatever the company decided, it would also have to gain the support of its parent organization.

CASE 8 ▪ Biral International (A)

INTRODUCTION

In the fall of 1979, the executive committee of Bieri Pumpenbau AG Biral International, located in Muensignen near Berne, Switzerland, met to discuss the implications of entering into a cooperation agreement with a Hungarian manufacturer to produce Bieri pumps. The committee had to decide if the company should pursue this opportunity along the lines negotiated by Mr. Vacano, the coordinator for sales to the COMECON area.[1] Negotiations had stretched over the better part of the last two years and had reached a critical point. A final decision on the part of Bieri's executive committee was required before the formal blessing of Hungary's Ministry of Foreign Trade could be obtained.

COMPANY HISTORY

The company was formed in 1919 by Bieri to produce a number of different pumps. In later years, the founder's two sons, Franz and Werner Bieri, took over management of the company. Under their direction, the company's manufacturing facilities were expanded in 1953 and 1961, and an entirely new factory was

---

1. COMECON is an abbreviation for "Council of Mutual Economic Assistance" comprising the Soviet Union, East Germany, Poland, Hungary, Rumania, Bulgaria, Czechoslovakia, Cuba, North Korea, and a few associated members in Asia and Africa.

opened in 1971. The company's sales had reached a record of about 52 million francs by 1978, not including sales of the principal supplier of many of Bieri's electrical motors whose equity was partially owned by the principals of Bieri. In total, the company employed about 400 persons and, since 1978, had been under the direction of the third generation, Ueli and Peter Bieri, the two sons of Franz Bieri, and Hansrudolf, the son of Werner Bieri.

Bieri had been affected negatively during the recessionary period of 1974–1976 when residential construction, a major user of Bieri's products, went into a sharp decline in Switzerland. This happened at a time when the value of the Swiss franc moved up sharply against other currencies increasing the price of Bieri products in its major export markets while these countries also went through a recessionary period. Net profits (computed after funding of various reserves and depreciation) significantly dropped in 1975 but they had since recovered. For 1979, Bieri expected its profits to reach levels of the early '70s. (See Exhibit 1 for sales and profit history.) The name Biral International had just been added to the company name. Originally, the Biral brand name applied only to a portion of the company's product line but now described all of Bieri's products.

PRODUCT LINES

Bieri had four major product lines: circulating pumps, general pumps, swimming pool pumps

This case was prepared by Visiting Professor Jean-Pierre Jeannet as a basis for class discussion rather than to illustrate either effective or ineffective handling of an administrative situation. Copyright 1985 by IMEDE (International Management Development Institute), Lausanne, Switzerland. Reproduced by permission.

EXHIBIT 1 Biral's Sales and Profit History

Year	Sales (S. Fr.)	Profit (S. Fr.)	Profit Margin
1970	37,647,500	NA	NA
1971	42,165,200	191,600	0.4%
1972	49,284,000	82,140	0.1
1973	51,225,242	164,280	0.3
1974	51,474,400	10,952	0.2
1975	44,508,928	(39,701)	(0.08)
1976	53,527,900	(12,514)	(0.02)
1977	50,195,754	31,007	0.06
1978	51,917,486	100,518	0.19

and filters, and control systems. Circulating pumps accounted for 54.8 percent of 1978 sales. These pumps, traditionally marketed under the brand name Biral, were sold both in Switzerland, where Bieri was the undisputed market leader, and in other countries of Western Europe. Negotiations with the Hungarian cooperation partner covered exclusively circulating pumps, but the other product lines had also to be taken into consideration as additional orders could be expected if the agreement went into effect.

The second major product line, general pumps, or APB for "Allgemeiner Pumpenbau," accounted for 33.3 percent of sales. Included were pumps for water supply systems, irrigation systems, and wastewater pumps. These products were produced according to specifications submitted by the client. Sales were strongest in Switzerland with exports accounting for only about 10 percent of the output.

Bieri had two additional product lines of lesser importance. The swimming pool pumps, or SBF, accounted for 10.4 percent of 1978 sales. More than 90 percent of these sales were to customers in Switzerland. Control systems, Bieri's smallest product line, represented an extension of the company's efforts in the area of general pump construction. Control systems were suited for controlling large pump systems and had been manufactured in-house for several

years. This capacity and knowledge was then also made available to other companies for different control applications. But volume never exceeded 1.5 percent of sales and amounted to only 0.3 percent in 1978.

BIRAL CIRCULATING PUMPS

Bieri company had for many years dominated the market in Switzerland with its circulating pumps. The pumps were used to circulate the water of heating systems in both commercial and residential buildings. Biral pumps, while more expensive than competitive products, were considered of the highest quality requiring minimal service. Also, their unique construction with the separating shell ensured that the pumps were effectively protected from penetrating water which could cause short circuits. While the separating shell was, by itself, an easily understood concept, competitors had been unable to produce such a part for their own use. Bieri had developed a special 400-ton press to mass produce these separating shells with high precision.

Other advantages of Biral pumps were their highly efficient electric motors which ran with a minimum of noise and required lower electricity. The electric motors were produced by RCB Elektro-Apparate AG, a small company about 50 miles from the Bieri plant. Bieri was RCB's largest customer and, through the Bieri family, owned a substantial portion of RCB's share capital. Final assembly of Biral pumps took place at Bieri's plant in Muensingen. In 1979, Bieri expected to produce 200,000 to 250,000 units.

The separating shell technology was the property of RCB. Bieri had the shells produced by an outside contractor who used RCB's technology on an exclusive basis. All other parts were sourced by Bieri from independent contractors. At Bieri's plant in Muensingen, the circulating pumps were simply assembled from these purchased parts. Depending on product mix, output could be expanded by 100 to 200 percent on the part of Bieri without any substantial investments.

THE MARKETS FOR BIERI PUMPS

Circulating pumps were primarily sold in Europe under the Biral brand name. Forty-seven percent of the pumps were sold on the Swiss market, with the remainder exported to a few European countries with strong sales' networks such as Austria, Belgium, Germany, France, UK, Italy, and the Netherlands (see Exhibit 2). These Biral pumps were primarily used for heating systems, but could also be installed in connection with climate control systems and hot water supply systems. The pumps were generally bought by plumbing contractors who installed a heating system in a house. The pumps, valued at an average of between Fr. 50 to Fr.

EXHIBIT 2 Total Sales 1978 (in S. Fr.)

Country	Circulating Pumps	General Pumps 'APB'	Swimming Pool 'SBF'	Controls	Total
Switzerland	13,463,780	15,620,291	5,214,850	545,294	34,844,215
Algeria	—	42,475	7,803	—	50,278
Australia	56,681	—	—	—	56,681
Austria	2,650,860	5,742	38,295	236,522	2,931,419
Belgium	609,094	457	—	—	609,551
Denmark	5,282	11,187	—	—	16,469
W. Germany	3,623,573	167,315	5,899	9,108	3,805,895
France	1,121,639	3,313	—	—	1,124,952
Gt. Britain	1,627,906	63,747	11,579	—	1,703,232
Iraq	—	855,696	64,340	—	920,036
Ireland	—	79,261	—	—	79,261
Italy	2,813,158	2,097	30,527	—	2,845,782
Morocco	—	3,793	—	—	3,793
Netherlands	2,436,754	57,076	—	—	2,493,830
Norway	14,404	45,118	—	—	59,522
Poland	6,448	—	—	—	6,448
Singapore	—	1,512	—	—	1,512
So. Africa	—	13,936	—	—	13,936
Sw. Africa	22,794	—	—	—	22,794
USSR	—	20,890	—	—	20,890
Hungary	—	306,990	—	—	306,990
Total	28,452,373	17,300,896	5,373,293	790,924	51,917,486
As % of Sales	54.8%	33.3%	10.3%	1.5%	100.0%
Total Export	14,988,593	1,680,605	158,443	245,630	17,073,271
As a % of Exports	87.8%	9.8%	.9%	1.4%	100.0%

EXHIBIT 3 Geographic Sales Distribution

Where Bieri products were sold in 1977 and 1978

	26,933,706	28,452,373
	Others	Others
	Switzerland 46, 4%	Switzerland 47, 3%
	W. Europe 52, 9%	W. Europe 52, 4%
	CIRCULATING PUMPS	
	BIRAL	

	15,701,061	17,300,896
	E. Europe 1	E. Europe 2
	W. Europe 5	W. Europe 3
	Other 5	Other 5
	Switzerland 89%	Switzerland 90%
	1977	1978
	APB	

	5,988,006	5,373,293
	Europe 2, 1	Europe 1, 6
	Other 3, 5	Other 1, 3
	Switzerland 94, 4%	Switzerland 97, 1%
	1977	1978
	S B F	

	599,622	790,924
	Europe 39	Europe 31
	Switzerland 61%	Switzerland 69%
	1977	1978
	CONTROLS	

1400, represented only a small portion of the approximately Fr. 10,000 to Fr. 20,000 for a complete system.[2] However, the pumps represented a crucial part since the proper circulation of the heated water throughout the pipe system of a building had a major influence on the efficiency of the heating plant. Plumbing contractors were particularly interested in trouble-free pumps that required little servicing. Should the pump fail, it was usually the plumber who was asked to service it.

Bieri offered Biral pumps in a large variety of sizes. Depending on the height of a building and the amount of water to be circulated, the plumber could determine exactly what pump was most appropriate. The correct selection was important since the right pump could run on lower rpms, resulting in lower energy costs and lower noise levels. Since circulating pumps had to run continuously during heating periods, energy consumption and noise level were important considerations for building owners.

Biral pumps were marketed directly by Bieri only to a few selected plumbing contractors in the canton of Berne, the particular area of Switzerland where the company was located, and to manufacturers of heating furnaces (OEMs). In the rest of Switzerland, as well as in France, Italy, UK, Netherlands, Austria and Belgium, Bieri had an exclusive sales agreement with Hoval. Hoval was a well-known manufacturer of furnaces with a technological advantage. Since furnaces were sold to plumbing and heating contractors, Hoval was in an excellent position to carry the Biral pumps as an addition to its own product line. Hoval had its own sales force in Switzerland, and operated sales subsidiaries in various European countries. Bieri, however, had an individual sales agreement with each Hoval subsidiary. This very close relationship was further enhanced through a small stock ownership of Hoval in both Bieri and the producer of the pumps' electrical motors, RCB

_____
2. In 1979 1 Fr. (Swiss Franc) equalled U.S. $.60.

EXHIBIT 4 Sales Distribution by Region and by Product Line

What the markets bought in 1977 and 1978

	32,435,667	34,844,215
	Controls 1	Controls 1
	BIRAL 38% Circulators	BIRAL 39% Circulators
	APB 44%	APB 45%
	1977	1978
	DOMESTIC (100%)	

	15,240,255	15,669,913
	SBF 1	SBF 0,6
	Controls 1,5	Controls 1,5
	APB 4%	APB 2,8%
	BIRAL 93,5%	BIRAL 95,7%
	1977	1978
	W. EUROPE (100%)	

	1,397,384	1,068,414
	BIRAL 15	BIRAL 7
	SBF 19	SBF 7
	APB 66%	APB 86%
	1977	1978
	OTHER (100%)	

	149,084	334,994
		BIRAL 2
	BIRAL 8	
	APB 92%	APB 98%
	1977	1978
	E.EUROPE (100%)	

Elektro-Apparate AG. Hoval was also represented on the boards of both of these companies. Hoval's management has made it clear that it considered the Hungarian proposal to be Bieri's decision.

MARKET FORCES IN THE CIRCULATING PUMP MARKET

Sales of Biral pumps depended largely on building activity and Bieri's competitive advantage. Each new house or building in Bieri's market area required a heating system, and this usually meant an oil- or gas-heated furnace with hot water pumped throughout the house. Any such installation required a circulating pump. Electric heat, more popular in the United States, was not widely accepted, and in Switzerland a permit issued by the electric company was required to install it. Since electric generating capacity was barely sufficient to cover present demand, few such permits were granted. In other European countries, the situation was not much different from that in Switzerland.

The competitive situation, however, was quite dynamic and subject to rapid changes. Over the past eight years, currencies had fluctuated widely in the world markets. The free float of the Swiss franc had resulted in a marked appreciation against other European currencies. Against the Italian lira, the French franc, and the British pound, the Swiss franc had more than doubled in value. While this was partially offset in these countries by inflation rates of 5 to 10 percent above the Swiss rate, Swiss production costs had increased relative to competitors located in those countries. Against the DM and the Dutch guilder, the Swiss franc appreciated about 25 percent, but these two latter countries had experienced an inflation rate similar to that of Switzerland. These currency changes left Bieri's prices 20 to 40 percent above those of its competitors. This had a particularly strong effect on Bieri's export markets where the company did not profit from the same strong brand loyalty that it enjoyed in Switzerland.

While Bieri had no significant competition in the circulating pump market in Switzerland, there were several European companies with substantially larger output and well entrenched positions in specific countries. The largest one, Grundfos, a Danish company, had operations in all major European countries and a total volume of more than 2.5 million circulating pumps annually. Grundfos was able to sell its pumps at prices of 20 to 30 percent below Bieri's due to its very large output. Next to Grundfos, there were three other major producers—Wilo in Germany, Euramo in France, and Myson in the UK. These manufacturers had an annual output of about twice Bieri's volume and maintained strong positions in their home markets with only spotty coverage of the rest of Europe.

In its latest move, Grundfos started sales operations in Switzerland in 1978. This represented a major competitive threat to Bieri since Switzerland was its major market absorbing almost half of its Biral output at prices substantially above prevailing levels in other European markets. Grundfos pumps were not produced in Switzerland, resulting in greater price flexibility for the Danish company. Bieri believed that the Swiss plumbing and heating contractors were unlikely to buy an inferior product even at a very low price. This forced Grundfos to price higher than in other European markets, but still substantially below Bieri's prices. With Biral's reputation for quality and longevity, Bieri executives believed that the threat emanating from Grundfos was real but not critical.

From a long-term point of view, it was of importance to Bieri to increase its own annual output to obtain economies of scale and, as a result, to lower its unit costs. Combined with the already existing technological advantage, the company could look forward to a promising future.

BACKGROUND TO THE HUNGARIAN COOPERATION PROPOSAL

For several years, Bieri had employed a Marketing Manager for the Comecon Area, a position occupied by Mr. Vacano. He had made numerous trips to Eastern Europe to contact the various buying organizations. While each country in Eastern Europe had a somewhat different set-up, all had from 4 to 25 foreign trade organizations which bought and/or sold merchandise, as ordered by their "clients," all state-run manufacturing or trading companies. Typically, these foreign trade organizations would compete against each other for the same clients or business in their country. During the first phase of Bieri's marketing offensive in Eastern Europe, it was Mr. Vacano's task to make contact with these organizations. Sales were never quite large, but had been steadily increasing as shown below:

Sales of Bieri Products to Comecon Countries

Year	Volume (SFR)	% BIRAL	% APB
1976	225,923	—	—
1977	145,272	8	92
1978	334,173	2	98
1979 (estimate)	520,220	—	—

General pumps (APB) accounted for the bulk of the business. Sales also tended to be concentrated by countries. In 1976 all sales were to Hungary, and Czechoslovakia accounted for 91 percent of 1977 sales. Hungary again absorbed 92 percent of sales to Eastern Europe in 1978. Bieri's had grown at about 50 percent per year despite strong competition from other European pump manufacturers. Direct annual marketing costs were relatively low averaging 40,000 francs and consisted mostly of trips by Bieri executives to the area and participation in trade shows.

Early in 1977, Bieri was approached by a Hungarian foreign trade corporation, Magyarexport (MAGEX) to open negotiations for a cooperative agreement with one of MAGEX's clients, Villamos.[3] The interest centered from the very beginning around Biral circulating pumps. Biral pumps were to be produced in cooperation with Villamos but payment for manufacturing

---

3. All Hungarian names are disguised.

know-how and licensing fees was, in part, to be made with output from the plant, either in the form of finished pumps or parts. Most Eastern European countries, and Hungary was no exception, were in need of western products and technology but they were usually unable to pay in convertible currency. To alleviate the problem, these countries imported technologies and preferred to pay primarily in merchandise.

Bieri's management quickly realized that such a cooperation agreement could offer an attractive way of entering the Hungarian or Comecon market provided the conditions were favorable. Mr. Vacano was authorized to commence negotiations, and, by 1979, he had gone through 8 revisions of the original proposal.

Villamos, the manufacturing enterprise, had no experience in producing pumps. It was a relatively small company operating about 15 workshops. In 1979, a new factory was built allowing the company to centralize its operation just outside Budapest, Hungary's capital. The company's operations included an aluminum foundry and manufacturing of garden furniture and camping equipment. The negotiations were carried out by MAGEX on behalf of Villamos.

An abridged form of the latest version of the proposal is shown in the Appendix. The contract could be summarized as follows:

Cooperation Agreement:

Bieri was to deliver to MAGEX-Villamos the documentation and know-how to produce a specified number of Biral pumps. Included were all rights to the patents including those related to the electric motors with an additional responsibility of Bieri to provide 45 man-days of training at Bieri and a further possible 30 man-days at the Hungarian plant. Villamos was obligated to produce a minimum of 30,000 pumps over the 5 years the contract was to be in force plus pay an additional royalty fee of 3 percent for every pump produced. The fee could be paid in hard currency or parts shipment.

MAGEX and/or Villamos were prepared to buy pumps and parts from Bieri over the life of the contract and had a contractual obliga-

tion to give Bieri preference on such purchases. In return, Bieri would be obligated to buy back an equivalent value from the Hungarian companies. This obligation would remain in effect until termination of the contract. All money transfers were to take place in hard currency and values would be calculated according to Bieri's price list.

PRELIMINARY EVALUATION OF THE AGREEMENT

For Bieri's executive committee's final evaluation, Mr. Vacano estimated that the direct costs arising from the agreement, such as training, would amount to about 50,000 francs. While it was difficult to estimate the size of the market for circulator pumps in Hungary, Mr. Vacano believed that 20,000 pumps annually was a "good figure." Sales of other pumps to Hungary had been very slow this year despite the fact that Bieri had submitted quotes for several installations totaling more than 1 million francs. Just this April, Bieri submitted a bid for a large project but all the orders went to the traditional suppliers. Sales so far had amounted to less than 20,000 francs for 1979.

Negotiations had stretched over 2 years and were now at a point where he felt that Bieri could not obtain better terms. If Bieri would not go ahead with the contract, Villamos was certain to enter into an agreement with another European manufacturer, possibly even Grundfos.

As far as Mr. Vacano could determine, COMECON countries had for some time bought limited amounts of circulating pumps from Western sources. The major producer of circulating pumps was Czechoslovakia, but in amounts insufficient to satisfy domestic or COMECON demand. Once Villamos was in a situation to sell circulators, it would have to market its pumps through Szerelvenyertekesito, a Hungarian trading company that alone had the right to market such pumps in Hungary. With respect to those pumps covered in the corporation agreement, no competition existed in Hungary for those pumps covered in the corporation agreement. Once production started such pumps could be obtained only through Villamos. For larger circulating pumps, Hungarian foreign trade companies would continue to buy from western firms, including competitors of Bieri.

Under the proposed agreement Bieri would first supply the parts for the production of the pumps. Within two years, it was planned to reduce these supplies to zero. The pumps covered by the contract ranged in price from Fr. 57.65 to Fr. 161.70 ex factory Muensingen. Contribution margin (covering variable costs of purchases, direct labor, but excluding factory overhead, depreciation, marketing, sales, and servicing costs) was approximately 50 percent. Consequently, the sales volume of the 30,000 pumps amounted to about Fr. 3 million based on going Bieri ex factory-prices. For a detailed price list, see Exhibit 5.

THE HUNGARIAN BUSINESS CLIMATE

Ever since the end of World War II, Hungary had been under the influence of the Soviet Union. A member of COMECON, Hungary had a state-operated industry similar to those in other communist countries in Eastern Europe. The present political leadership, installed after the 1956 revolution, had over the years liberalized much of the economic activities. With a per capita income of approximately $2,500, Hungarians enjoyed a standard of living that surpassed those of other COMECON members except East Germany. The country's population amounted to about 11 million. Exports had reached a level of about 8 billion dollars but were still exceeded by imports amounting to $10 billion.

EXHIBIT 5 Prices and Delivery Conditions for Biral Pump Parts

| Number | Part | Pump Types | | |
		NRB 12 S-1 V	NRB 13 S-2 V	NRB 15 S V
	Completely assembled	Fr. 57.65	Fr. 76.75	Fr. 161.70
	Motor (complete)	Fr. 41.09	58.17	132.47
1	Separating Shell (unfinished)	4.20	6.50	15.40
12, 13	Carbon bearing	1.81	3.50	3.50
15	Tolerance ring	.42	.50	.67
19/20	Impeller	1.22	1.91	8.14
8	Packing between pump motor	.32	.50	.92
23	Pump casing	7.08	8.47	10.66
7	Screw	.11	.11	.11
27	Control knob for pump settings	.38	.38	.49
26, 28, 31, 36, 53	O-Ring	.15	.15	.15
	Screwed Plug	.09	.17	.36
35	Name Plate	.32	.49	.78
56	Label	.03	.03	.03
	Connecting parts	2.63	2.63	3.81

All prices are valid for deliveries up to December 12, 1980 and do not include packaging or freight. Packaging and freight will be billed separately after each shipment. These conditions are subject to the agreement as covered in Article 12.

EXHIBIT 6 Biral Circulating Pump (Cross Section)

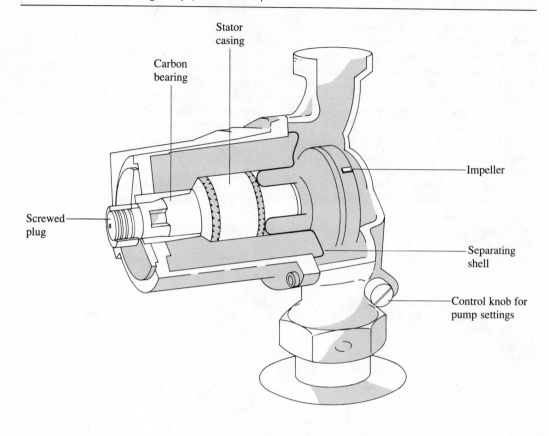

The negative balance of trade prompted the Hungarian government to take corrective action in 1972. Hungary became the second COMECON government after Rumania to allow for joint ventures with western companies. However, due to restrictions and what western businessmen considered still unclear practices, only three ventures were formed. Since 1974, the Swedish firm Volvo produced a 4-wheel drive vehicle with the Csepel Company in Budapest that sold abroad through the Volvo organization.

Siemens of Germany established the second venture and, since 1975, Corning Medical of the United States produced medical equipment jointly with the Hungarian firm Radelhis. More activity could be found among strict licensing agreements. It was estimated that over the past few years alone, the Hungarian machinery industry had concluded more than 300 licensing agreements with Western firms. Moreover, Hungary had taken the leadership among COMECON countries for cooperation agreements. So far, it was estimated that Hungarian enterprises had concluded more than 500 such agreements.

Over the past few years, Switzerland had been an important trading partner for Hungary. Among the countries outside the COMECON area, Switzerland was Hungary's fourth important trading partner. Switzerland exported goods worth Fr. 268 million to Hungary in 1976, up from only Fr. 157 million in 1973. Imports from Hungary grew from Fr. 155 million to Fr. 170 million over the same time period. During the past few years, Swiss companies had signed many licensing agreements and cooperation arrangements. At the beginning of 1977, a total of 55 cooperation and 10 licensing agreements were in effect, and, by April 1978, it was reported that another 52 cooperation agreements were being negotiated. These agreements, however, still represented only 1.4 percent of Swiss-Hungarian trade compared to 5.3 percent for German-Hungarian trade and 7.5 percent for Swedish-Hungarian trade. The majority of these agreements were signed by machinery and chemical companies. Among others, there existed an agreement by Hermes Company to have its typewriters produced in Hungary; Sibir for the production of refrigerators; and Brown Boveri & Cie for the construction of steam turbines. Despite several attempts on the part of Mr. Vacano, Bieri had not been able to learn details of the experiences of these Swiss companies' operations in Hungary.

CONCLUSION

The latest version of the agreement had been made available to members of the executive committee. It was Mr. Vacano's strong belief that he had negotiated the best possible contract, particularly when considering the improvements over earlier versions. Should Bieri accept this agreement, it was then up to the Hungarian partners to have it ratified by the Hungarian Ministry of Foreign Trade. Only then would it become available for signature. It was now up to Bieri's management to decide if they wanted to proceed.

APPENDIX I Licensing Agreement (Abridged)

Article I: Introduction

Bieri Pumpenbau AG, located in Muensingen, Switzerland, to be named "BIERI," and MAGEX Hungarian Export Commercial Enterprise, to be called "MAGEX," located in Budapest, Hungary, conclude a cooperation agreement for the manufacture, use and sale of BIRAL[1] circulating pumps and decide to engage in technical and commercial relations as follows:

- MAGEX will acquire from BIERI the know-how for the manufacture, use and sale of BIRAL circulating pumps type RB12S, RF12S, RB155, and RF15S. This know-how will be turned over to Villamos in Budapest, a Hungarian manufacturing company, and includes the know-how for the electric motors.
- BIERI is prepared to deliver to MAGEX the technical documentation and manufacturing know-how for the above pumps including the use of all relative industrial patents and rights. The only exception are rights related to the separating shell.
- Within the scope of this agreement, MAGEX is interested in obtaining a yet to be determined amount of components from BIERI.
- BIERI is prepared to accept from MAGEX a like amount of finished pumps, subassemblies, or individual parts manufactured by MAGEX in Hungary based upon the technical documentation of BIERI and provided they meet BIERI's requirements for quality, price, and delivery terms.

Article II: Purpose of Contract

It is the purpose of the cooperation between the partners of this contract to enable MAGEX to manufacture in Hungary the circulating pumps with the same characteristics and the same parameters of performance as those manufactured by BIERI in Switzerland and to sell these pumps

---

1. The Biral brand name was not part of this agreement.

in Hungary and some other countries specified later on.

Article III: Object of Contract

BIERI grants MAGEX the following rights:

- the right to manufacture in Hungary the circulating pumps BIRAL RB/RF 12 S/15S including all replacement parts and the electric motor with the exception of the separating shell that is not part of this agreement.
- the right to all new changes and developments with respect to the pumps under consideration for the duration of this cooperation agreement.
- the right to all industrial protective rights (patents, trademarks, etc.) granted to BIERI in relation to the pumps covered by this agreement.
- the right to sell these circulating pumps in all countries according to special stipulations set forth below.

Article IV: Sales and Export Rights

BIERI grants herewith MAGEX the unlimited non-exclusive right to offer and to sell the pumps in Hungary as well as the following countries:

To sell without any restrictions:

COMECON Territory: USSR, Poland, East Germany, Czechoslovakia, Hungary, Rumania, Bulgaria, Cuba

People's Republic of China, Yemen, Korea, Khmer Republic, (Cambodia), as well as Laos and Burma

To sell upon consultation with BIERI and after determination of the relative range of export prices in the following countries in the world:

Afghanistan	Libya
Albania	Malaysia
Angola	Malta
Bangladesh	Morocco
Ceylon	Nepal
Egypt	Pakistan
Finland	Philippines

Greece	Portugal
Iceland	Sweden
India	Tunesia
Indonesia	Turkey
Iraq	Yugoslavia

plus in all states of Central and South America as well as in the remaining countries of the world, with the exception of those listed below where MAGEX has the right to export the subject matter upon consultation and solely through the existing sales organization of BIERI to the following countries:

Algeria	Netherlands
Australia	Norway
Belgium	Saudi Arabia
Canada	Singapore
Denmark	South Africa
Emirates of Persian Gulf	Spain
France	Syria
Great Britain	Thailand
Kuwait	USA
Luxemburg	West Germany

Pumps installed as a part of a turnkey plant may be exported by MAGEX without any restrictions. In the future, BIERI is prepared to enter an agreement about territorial expansion under consideration of the interest of the parties to this contract.

The contract parties will vote upon prices and conditions on the export markets at their regular biannual meetings.

As long as the contract is in force, Villamos may place a label on each pump indicating "Produced under license of Bieri Pump BIRAL International."

Article V: Technical Data

BIERI will turn over to MAGEX the entire technical documentation on the subject matter within 3 months of the signing of the contract. The total documentation passes into the possession of MAGEX which may dispose of it at liberty but with the restrictions of Article IX.

Article VI: Technical Assistance

BIERI will render technical assistance to MAGEX with respect to manufacturing the subject matter. BIERI will specifically instruct specialists of MAGEX at its manufacturing plant in Switzerland for the maximum of 45 man-days. The group of specialists is never to exceed 3 men and will have sufficient knowledge of the German language. BIERI will make one of its own specialists available to MAGEX at its Hungarian plant for a period not exceeding 30 mandays. The entire costs of traveling, lodging, and board for both the Hungarian and Swiss specialists will be paid for by MAGEX. BIERI will pay the Hungarian specialists a daily flat fee, according to Hungarian norms in effect at that time.

For any man-hours requested by MAGEX in excess of those specified, BIERI will supply the necessary personnel at the typical rates in force in Switzerland for the level of specialists made available. The partners agree to form a group of experts which is to meet twice annually, once in Hungary and once in Switzerland, to treat technical and commercial questions. The group should not exceed 3 experts on either side.

Article VII: Delivery of Components and Finished Products

MAGEX obligates itself to purchase during the course of the contract and, according to its requirements, pumps, subassemblies, or separate parts on the subject matter entirely from BIERI should MAGEX not be in a position to manufacture the subject matter itself. BIERI, in return, will undertake deliveries of entire pumps or parts and subassemblies, in order to assure the sufficient supply of MAGEX with the subject matter of this contract.

Article VIII: Guarantees

Provided that suitable manufacturing shops and equipment for the manufacturing of the subject matter of the contract are existing, and provided that all instructions, statements, and directions contained in the technical documents are strictly adhered to, BIERI guarantees that MAGEX will be in a position to produce the subject matter of the contract in the identical quality and with the same performance parameters as produced by BIERI.

In the case of difficulties, BIERI will indicate suitable measures to be taken by MAGEX to produce as indicated above.

Article IX: Secrecy

MAGEX obligates itself to treat the manufacturing know-how confidentially during the duration of the contract and for an additional period of 10 years after its expiration. Exempt from this are the manufacturing company in Hungary and Hungarian export trade enterprises with respect to information normally delivered to clients for quotations or orders. MAGEX will assure that the manufacturing company complies with the same rules of confidentiality.

Article XI: Licensing Fee

As compensation, MAGEX will pay BIERI 3% of the sales price for the pumps and parts manufactured in Hungary. MAGEX obligates itself to produce a minimum of 30,000 pumps within the 5 years of the contract. The basis for computing the licensing fee is the effective transfer price for fully assembled pumps as per Exhibit 5.

BIERI is prepared to purchase from MAGEX, up to the expiration of the contract, pump parts in compensation of the licensing fee at repurchase prices equal to 30 percent below list prices as per Exhibit 5.

In case MAGEX will produce less than the guaranteed minimum quantity, MAGEX will pay the 3% fee on the deficient quantity in Swiss Francs. The first payments will be made at the end of the second year of the contract, and then annually at the end of each calendar year until the contract expires.

Article XII: Compensation

BIERI is prepared to accept from MAGEX for the duration of the contract pump parts at the same value as MAGEX bought from BIERI, provided that MAGEX can actually effect delivery. The purchases by BIERI and the sales by MAGEX should be equalized annually as much as possible. Again, MAGEX will purchase parts at the full transfer price as per Exhibit 5 whereas BIERI would repurchase parts at 30 percent below these list prices.

To cover any goods delivered by BIERI, MAGEX will have opened irrevocable letters of credit through a large Swiss bank with payments due upon presentation of shipping documents. To guarantee its purchases, BIERI will establish a bank guarantee for 10% of the minimum sales agreed upon. MAGEX may cash the guaranteed amount should BIERI not make any purchases from MAGEX.

Article XIII: Priority as a Supplier

MAGEX will invite BIERI to tender offers when importing other pumps which are also contained in the manufacturing program of BIERI. MAGEX will exert its entire influence to insure that these pumps be bought from BIERI, provided that BIERI's quotes are competitive with regard to quality, price, and delivery terms. However, these transactions are on a cash basis and are not included in this cooperation agreement.

Article XIV: Higher Power (Acts of God)

The contract allows for cancellation given certain acts of God beyond the control of the partners. Any final dissolution, however, is subject to the court of arbitration.

Article XV: Court of Arbitration

Any disputes that cannot be settled by the parties is to be brought before the court of arbitration in Munich, West Germany. Each party nominates one member to the 3-person court, with the two selected members agreeing on a third person who is a citizen of Germany. In case an agreement on that 3rd person cannot be reached within 30 days, the chairman of the International Chamber of Commerce in Paris will be asked to nominate the 3rd member. The arbitrators decide by majority vote and their decision is final. The contractual relationship of this agreement is subject to the law of the Federal Republic of Germany. The court of arbitration decides on its own procedures.

Article XVI: Duration of Contract

This contract will be in force for 5 years. It will be prolonged automatically for one year at a time, provided that neither party gives notice by registered letter within six months prior to expiration of the contract.

After expiration of the contract, MAGEX will be authorized to continue to manufacture, use, and sell the products in Hungary according to Article II. However, Villamos is not allowed to use any labels on its exported pumps that may infer any relationship with BIERI.

Article XVII: Servicing

MAGEX assumes the entire servicing duties of customers and obligations of attendance as well as the entire servicing of replacement parts during the course of the contract, for pumps sold by itself. If MAGEX so desires, BIERI is prepared to offer suggestions and proposals free of charge for creation of a suitable service organization.

CASE 9 ▪ Soudronic AG

Our sales and marketing department must be able to handle a range of responses to some new and growing competitive threats. We do not know yet exactly how we are going to deal with them, but we do know that we must put together an organization that will be effective under a range of product line compositions. Our present product line revenue ratio of 90 percent body welders and 10 percent specialty welding equipment might stay the same indefinitely. It is very likely, though, that in five years the ratio will be more like 50–50, or even 10–90. We therefore need to organize our sales and distribution systems to maximize our sales potential with different, and even changing, product line compositions.

Mr. Dieter Hanusek, Director of Marketing and Sales for Soudronic AG, was describing the issues he felt would be most important for him, and for Soudronic AG, over the next one to five years.

During Mr. Hanusek's first two years at Soudronic he had completely reorganized the sales and marketing functions in order to solve some of the more pressing issues of coordination among Soudronic Sales Managers, technical experts and production personnel. He was now shifting his sights to the longer range issues that he felt needed to be evaluated in order to further develop Soudronic's sales and marketing efforts.

We, at Soudronic, have done so much right up until now, and in some sense our success seems to have taken control of us. At the moment we are reevaluating where we are and where we want to go. How we are going to get there is the issue we now face in Germany.

THE DEVELOPMENT OF SOUDRONIC AG

Soudronic AG was located at Berg-Dietikon near Zürich, Switzerland. The company was founded in 1953 by Mr. Paul Opprecht, an electrical engineer who had wanted to implement his own ideas for improving the design and production of resistance welding and seam welding machines. Resistance welding was a technique that used electrical current passing from one electrode through the two pieces to be welded to a second electrode. The heat created by the resistance melted the surrounding metal to produce the weld. Other welding techniques in use were gas welding and electrical welding.

Soudronic's first products were electronic controls for resistance welding machines. Their product line was soon expanded to include the production of three phase[1] spot and seam welding machines. These machines performed specialty welding functions in the production of in-

---

1. Three phase welding is resistance welding using electrical current that is applied in phases of build up, full force, and reduced levels of power.

dustrial goods such as radiators, machinery, aircraft and railroad cars and most were "one of a kind" machines that had been designed to respond to a manufacturer's specific and well-defined need. In March 1959 Soudronic engineers made an important technological breakthrough that changed the direction of the company. They developed a semi-automatic tinplate[2] seam welding machine that used copper wire electrodes at the weld. The use of copper wire as an intermediate electrode resulted in near faultless welds on plated sheet metal (tin, zinc, lead, etc.) to produce consistently high quality products. In 1964, this first generation copper-electrode based seam welding system was used in the first fully automatic tinplate welding machine for medium and large sized sheet metal containers.

Soudronic's "body forming" machines rolled and welded pieces of tinplate or blackplate[3] to form the bodies of three piece cans and three piece drums and barrels. These machines did not make or place can tops or bottoms or fill the cans, they simply made the can bodies. The essential technology in this process was the technology of the seam weld. In the area of seam welding for three piece cans Soudronic AG soon became the acknowledged world leader.

Sales of body welding machines had fueled Soudronic's growth. Annual revenue increased from Sfr. one million in 1953 to Sfr. 12 million in 1969. By 1973 it had reached Sfr. 30 million and in 1978 it reached Sfr. 60 million. In 1982, less than 30 years after its founding, Soudronic had sales of about Sfr. 130 million. Ninety percent of machine sales were based on the sale of body makers and 10 percent of machine sales came from the sale of specialty welding machines. Spare part sales had increased greatly in recent years due to the increased importance of high speed machines in the product line. In 1982 spare part sales accounted for 15 percent of total sales revenue. Total employment, which had been five in 1953, was 450 in 1982. Soudronic

had increased its international representation from 10 countries in 1964 to 80 countries in 1982.

Approximately 70 percent of each piece of equipment that Soudronic produced was built using parts that were manufactured to Soudronic specifications by outside suppliers. Approximately 30 percent of each piece of equipment was built using Soudronic-produced parts. Assembly took place in a large company owned building that served as Soudronic's factory, research and product testing center. This installation was immediately adjacent to the company's five story headquarters building. Employees had easy access to each other, but also had space for their own work because, as company literature pointed out "precision requires concentration." A well planned work environment was one employee benefit offered by Soudronic. Other benefits included a fully paid and comprehensive insurance program, subsidized housing and subsidized lunches at the headquarters restaurant.

Soudronic had become the technology leader in creating welding processes for industry, in particular for the metal container industry. It planned to expand its leadership position by the continued reinvestment of a considerable share of its profits into research and development. Of particular interest were the areas of fully automated production processes and increased output rates that would provide even higher degrees of efficiency and quality.

RECENT DEVELOPMENTS IN RESISTANCE WELDING TECHNOLOGY AT SOUDRONIC

In 1970 Soudronic's second generation seam welding machines made their appearance in the form of high speed fully automatic welding machines for the manufacture of aerosol containers. These machines used the then newly developed ELLIPTIC-MONOFIL welding system. In the ELLIPTIC-MONOFIL process standard round copper wire was shaped into an elliptical form in the machine and was used as the basis of a broad weld. The broad weld reduced both the

---

2. Tinplate is steel sheet coated with a thin layer of tin.
3. Blackplate is blank steel sheet.

size of loose ends at the seam and the required overlap at the weld, thus producing significant material savings. It also permitted the can body to be "ridged" and/or "necked" easily. Ridging gave a can additional strength and necking improved the appearance of a can as well as permitting cans to be packed more closely together. Necked cans could be packed body to body rather than folded over top to folded over top. Cans welded with the ELLIPTIC-MONOFIL welding system could be used for aerosol products, oil, paint, cleaning products, coffee and powdered chemicals.

In 1975, the development of the third generation of Soudronic welding systems opened the door to the use of Soudronic welding equipment in the fabrication of cans for the food and beverage industry. Historically this industry consumed 80 to 85 percent of total world metal container production. The WIMA, or wire mash, welding system completely eliminated loose ends from the welded seam, had a very narrow non-printable weld area and produced some additional material saving thanks to an even smaller overlap. Most importantly, it could be adapted for use in the food beverage industry by lacquering the weld's inside seam.

In 1978 the WIMA process was improved even further. The SUPER WIMA process eliminated the sharp corner that had been present in the WIMA weld, and made after weld lacquering or seam striping easier and safer for food and beverage cans. Seam striping provided a layer of paint, lacquer, or coating powder along the inside and/or outside of the weld seam to prevent the contents from corroding the copper and sheet metal at the can's weld. The body maker could be adapted to provide the additional inside seam striping.

The SUPER WIMA weld's strength was equal to that of the metal plate being used. The extent to which the can body could be ridged, necked, and expanded was a function only of the quality of the metal plate itself. Nonetheless, the non-printable width of the seam was only two to three millimeters so virtually the entire surface area of the can was available for graphics. See Exhibit 1 for further details concerning these welding advances.

THE 1983 SOUDRONIC PRODUCT LINE

The 1983 Soudronic metal container body maker product line consisted of 16 different models. These 16 different machines were of four basic families: semi automatic equipment for drums and barrels which used simple crushed seam welding technology, fully automatic equipment for drums and barrels which used Soudronic's first generation resistance welding technology, semi automatic equipment for cans and containers which used the ELLIPTIC-MONOFIL welding technology and fully automated equipment for cans and containers which used SUPER WIMA welding technology.

Semi automatic tinplate machines welded can body seams. The pre cut pre roll-formed body needed to be placed on a welding arm manually, but all other aspects of the seam welding process such as body clamping, feeding, switching on and off the welding current, body release and carriage return to the starting position, were performed automatically.

Basic fully automatic body makers performed four functions, they destacked the sheet metal, flexed it, in preparation for the rolling operation, roll formed it, and welded the seam. The basic machine could also be equipped to lacquer the inner and/or outer seam, to make tapered can bodies, to score the metal sheets in order to make smaller can bodies and to make oxide free, metal colored, seams. In 1982 very high speed fully automatic machines were introduced. These machines produced can bodies at rates of up to 500 can bodies per minutes, with production speed largely a function of can body size.

Soudronic SUPER WIMA body makers offered many advantages to the can producer. They could be designed to use almost all of the different types of metal plate that was then available for use in the metal packaging industry. The welding process they used was an ecologically non-harmful process that complied with strict environmental regulations. All lead, solder, flux and fumes had been eliminated from the seam forming process. The energy consumption of the SUPER WIMA body maker was minimal and

EXHIBIT 1

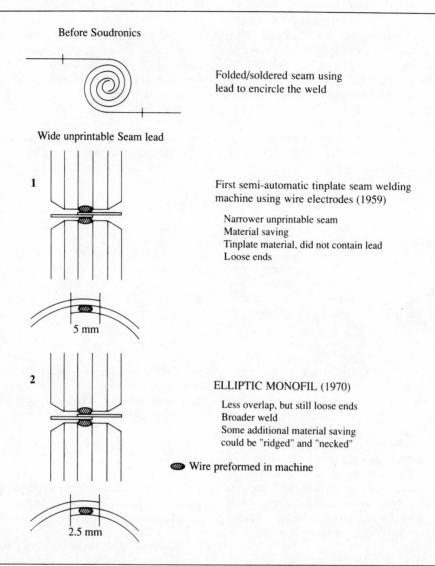

Before Soudronics

Folded/soldered seam using
lead to encircle the weld

Wide unprintable Seam lead

1

First semi-automatic tinplate seam welding
machine using wire electrodes (1959)

    Narrower unprintable seam
    Material saving
    Tinplate material, did not contain lead
    Loose ends

5 mm

2

ELLIPTIC MONOFIL (1970)

    Less overlap, but still loose ends
    Broader weld
    Some additional material saving
    could be "ridged" and "necked"

◖ Wire preformed in machine

2.5 mm

the air and water consumption of the machines was negligible. The machines were extremely compact, very easy to install, required very little maintenance, and produced even small lots economically. A fully automatic welding machine could be put in operation with the push of a button. It could also be retooled to work on different can body diameters within an hour. If the machine had been equipped with an optional scoring unit[4] production output could be in-

4. Scoring units made it possible to, in effect, weld two or three cans at the same time and then to separate them at a later stage.

EXHIBIT 1 (*cont.*)

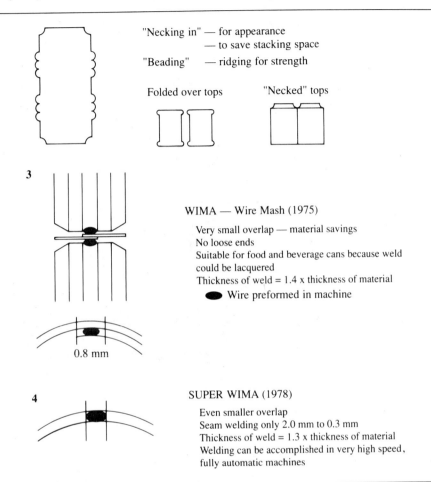

"Necking in" — for appearance
— to save stacking space

"Beading"   — ridging for strength

Folded over tops   "Necked" tops

3

WIMA — Wire Mash (1975)

Very small overlap — material savings
No loose ends
Suitable for food and beverage cans because weld
could be lacquered
Thickness of weld = 1.4 x thickness of material
⬤ Wire preformed in machine

0.8 mm

4

SUPER WIMA (1978)

Even smaller overlap
Seam welding only 2.0 mm to 0.3 mm
Thickness of weld = 1.3 x thickness of material
Welding can be accomplished in very high speed,
fully automatic machines

creased dramatically. Fully automatic machines already in service had been attaining efficiency rates of 90–97 percent. As were all Soudronic machines, SUPER WIMA welders were factory tested for three full weeks before being shipped, in almost assembled form, to the customer. See Exhibit 3 for more details concerning Soudronic's 1983 product line, Exhibit 2 for a picture of a SUPER WIMA welding unit, and Exhibit 4 for sales data concerning the product line.

SOUDRONIC'S CUSTOM MADE WELDING MACHINES

To respond to the special welding needs of a manufacturer one needed, according to Mr. Hanusek, "four people sitting around a table bending over a blueprint." It was an exacting business where one was obligated to commit both financial and human resources to the solution of a problem with a machine that was, for the moment, only lines on paper. The price of a

EXHIBIT 2

The FBB bodymaker has been kept as small as possible but as large as necessary.

Money and show do not guarantee success – but the right idea does.

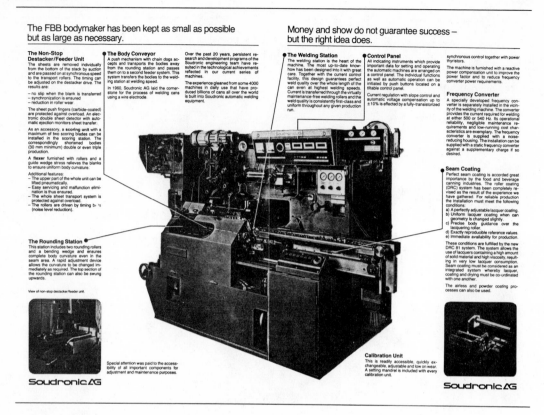

The Non-Stop Destacker/Feeder Unit
The sheets are removed individually from the bottom of the stack by suction and are passed on at synchronous speed to the transport rollers. The timing can be adjusted on the destacker drive. The results are:
– no slip when the blank is transferred
– synchronization is ensured
– reduction in roller wear.
The sheet push fingers (carbide-coated) are protected against overload. An electronic double sheet detector with automatic ejection monitors sheet transfer.
As an accessory, a **scoring unit** with a maximum of two scoring blades can be installed in the scoring station. The correspondingly shortened bodies (30 mm minimum) double or even triple production.
A **flexer** furnished with rollers and a guide wedge stress relieves the blanks to ensure uniform body curvature.
Additional features:
– The upper part of the whole unit can be lifted pneumatically.
– Easy servicing and malfunction elimination is thus ensured.
– The whole sheet transport system is protected against overload.
– The rollers are driven by timing belts (noise level reduction).

The Rounding Station
This station includes two rounding rollers and a bending wedge and ensures complete body curvature even in the seam area. A rapid adjustment device allows the curvature to be changed immediately as required. The top section of the rounding station can also be swung upwards.

View of non-stop destacker/feeder unit.

Special attention was paid to the accessibility of all important components for adjustment and maintenance purposes.

Soudronic AG

The Body Conveyor
A push mechanism with chain dogs accepts and transports the bodies away from the rounding station and passes them on to a second feeder system. This system transfers the bodies to the welding station at welding speed.
In 1960, Soudronic AG laid the cornerstone for the process of welding cans using a wire electrode.

Over the past 20 years, persistent research and development programs of the Soudronic engineering team have resulted in the technological achievements reflected in our current series of machines.
The experience gleaned from some 4000 machines in daily use that have produced billions of cans all over the world is built into Soudronic automatic welding equipment.

The Welding Station
The welding station is the heart of the machine. The most up-to-date know-how has been designed into it with great care. Together with the current control facility, this design guarantees perfect weld quality over the whole length of the can even at highest welding speeds. Current is transferred through the virtually maintenance-free welding rollers and the weld quality is consistently first-class and uniform throughout any given production run.

Control Panel
All indicating instruments which provide important data for setting and operating the automatic machines are arranged on a control panel. The individual functions as well as automatic operation can be initiated by push buttons located on a tiltable control panel.
Current regulation with slope control and automatic voltage compensation up to ±10% is effected by a fully-transistorized

synchronous control together with power thyristors.
The machine is furnished with a reactive power compensation unit to improve the power factor and to reduce frequency converter power requirements.

Frequency Converter
A specially developed frequency converter is separately installed in the vicinity of the welding machine. The converter provides the current required for welding at either 500 or 540 Hz. Its operational reliability, negligible maintenance requirements and low-running cost characteristics are exemplary. The frequency converter is supplied with a noise-reducing housing. The installation can be supplied with a static frequency converter against a supplementary charge if so desired.

Seam Coating
Perfect seam coating is accorded great importance by the food and beverage canning industries. The roller coating (DRC) system has been completely revised as the result of the experience we have gathered. For reliable production the installation must meet the following conditions:
a) A perfectly adjustable lacquer coating.
b) Uniform lacquer coating when can geometry is changed slightly.
c) Precise body guidance over the lacquering roller.
d) Exactly reproducible reference values.
e) Immediate availability for production.
These conditions are fulfilled by the new DRC 81 system. The system allows the use of lacquers containing a high amount of solid material and high viscosity, resulting in very low lacquer consumption. Seam coating must be considered as an integrated system whereby lacquer, coating and drying must be co-ordinated with one another.
The airless and powder coating processes can also be used.

Calibration Unit
This is readily accessible, quickly exchangeable, adjustable and low on wear. A setting mandrel is included with every calibration unit.

Soudronic AG

---

custom designed machine was set before the machine was built—so the risk of error was absorbed by Soudronic.

Soudronic built custom designed three-phase frequency converter machines, spot welding machines, seam welding machines, and projection welding machines. All of these were equipped with Soudronic's own "state of the art" electronic controls. Soudronic's electronic controls contributed to the very high reliability that was expected of automatic manufacturing processes. Some control systems provided programmed heat-control and pressure cycle control for spot and seam welding. Other systems combined process control with power control for spot, seam, and pulsation welding and automatic voltage control. These electronic control systems were sold only as part of a Soudronic

welding machine. They were not sold as individual units.

Three phase frequency converter machines eliminated the high voltage diodes that were required by direct current machines to convert AC current to DC current. As a result, they provided significant reductions in power consumption, cooling water use, and power regulation and installation costs for the operator.

Custom built spot welding machines for single and three phase connections responded to a variety of production requirements in terms of the material to be welded, the welding quality, the shape of the workpiece and the available public electrical supply system. For example, machines for the bilateral welding of radiator ribs on to convectors and three phase spot welding machines for welding steel, stainless steel,

EXHIBIT 3 The Soudronic AG 1983 Product Line—Metal Container Body Makers

	Body Diameter	Body Height	Prod/Min.	Price* (00's SFr.)
Semi-automatic (*tinplate*)				
Series B	99–350 mm	60– 510 mm	20–25	70–110
Series C	52– 99 mm	50– 325 mm	20–25	70–110
Series D	135–400 mm	100– 700 mm	20–25	70–110
Fully automatic (*tinplate*)				
Series E	52–100 mm	90– 140 mm	500	450–600
Series F	52–115 mm	96– 315 mm	300	450–600
Series G	52–108 mm	65– 280 mm	150	450–600
Series H	99–200 mm	95– 320 mm	280	450–600
Series I	99–330 mm	80– 515 mm	80	200–250
Series J	150–400 mm	150– 600 mm	80	200–250
Series K	260–600 mm	260–1000 mm	25	450–600
Semi-automatic for drums and barrels			*Prod/hr.*	
Series L	230–450 mm	300– 700 mm	350	200–250
Series M	300–630 mm	300–1000 mm	180/250	200–250
Series N	450–600 mm	300–1050 mm	65	200–250
Fully automatic for drums and barrels (*blackplate*)				
Series O	450–600 mm	450–1050 mm	400	350–450
Series P	450–600 mm	450–1050 mm	720	350–450
Series Q	for standard drum sizes		150–600	350–450

* The customer's price could be 15% to 50% higher based on the options, accessories, spare parts inventory and testing equipment ordered, as well as on whether or not the customer had special utility requirements for the unit.

EXHIBIT 4 Sheet Metal Container Machines—Yearly Volume by Category

	1975	1976	1977	1978	1979	1980	1981	1982
Category								
Semi-automatic tinplate	40	40	42	45	48	50	60	65
Fully automatic tinplate	45	58	71	89	147	189	209	216
Semi-automatic barrels and drums	3	2	7	6	5	4	6	7
Fully automatic barrels and drums	—	—	—	—	—	7	5	7
Total number of machines	90	100	120	140	200	250	280	295

highly heat resistant steel and light alloys for building railroad cars and aircraft were in use worldwide. Specialty seam welding machines were designed for straight-line and contoured welding with overlapped or mashed seams using blank or surface treated metal. Custom designed seam welding machines were used primarily in the fabrication of vehicles and industrial equipment.

Projection welding machines permitted four or more projections to be welded simultaneously during one work cycle. These machines had short work cycles, low power consumption and installation costs, excellent reliability, long useful lives and countless applications. They had been already adapted for use in cooking utensil, motor vehicle, television, and brake cylinder production.

BODY WELDER AND SPECIALTY WELDER USERS

Mr. Hanusek segmented the body welder machine market in terms of size and profession. Size was a function of the number of metal container manufacturing "lines" using a Soudronic's body welder, that a client had in operation. A large multinational client typically had between 10 and 200 lines, a medium sized client typically had three to 10 lines and a small client had one to three lines. Sixty percent of Soudronic sales revenue came from medium sized clients, 20 percent came from the large multinationals, and 20 percent came from the small clients. These figures had changed over time. In years past 80 percent of sales revenue had come from the large multinationals, the balance having come from medium sized companies.

Market segmentation in terms of profession was determined by how the client *used* the machine. Here there were basically four segments. *Can makers* produced and sold cans and other metal containers as their primary businesses. Metal Box, Crown Cork and Seal and American Can were typical of this group. *Canners or fillers* produced the cans that they used themselves. Their primary businesses were the production and distribution of the can's contents. Campbell

Soup, Del Monte, Libby, and Green Giant were typical of this group. *Original equipment manufacturers,* or OEM's, produced most of the machines required for can making lines. They seldom produced the welding units, however, and purchased these from Soudronic. *Contractors* sold can making operating know-how. They served as consultants to can makers. In this capacity they would occasionally contract for a welding unit.

It was much harder to segment the specialty welding machine user. These clients came from a wide range of industries and were from very large industrial plants as well as small factories. Mr. Hanusek believed, though, that the largest potential markets for specialty resistance welding machines were large industrial groups that produced automobiles or other vehicles, household goods such as pots, pans, and small appliances, and producers of metal products for the construction industry.

SALES AND MARKETING AT SOUDRONIC

Effective January 1, 1983 Soudronic AG started operating within a new structure. The new structure had been designed in order to redefine certain workflows and to emphasize the sales aspect of the marketing effort. Mr. Hanusek wanted to encourage the development of sales personnel, where there once had been order takers. See Exhibit 5 for the organization chart of Soudronic AG. See Exhibit 6 for the 1982 organization chart of the Soudronic Marketing Department, and see Exhibits 7 and 8 for the organization chart of the Soudronic's Marketing Department as of January 1, 1983.

Historically, sales and order processing had been one department. Sales personnel had been responsible for every aspect of the customers' relationship with Soudronic. Upon Mr. Hanusek's arrival he had conducted a workflow analysis and discovered that only 20 percent of the department's efforts had been sales oriented and that 80 percent of the department's efforts had been spent in various administrative functions. This had been consistent with Soudronics re-

EXHIBIT 5 Organization Chart—Soudronic AG, January 1, 1983

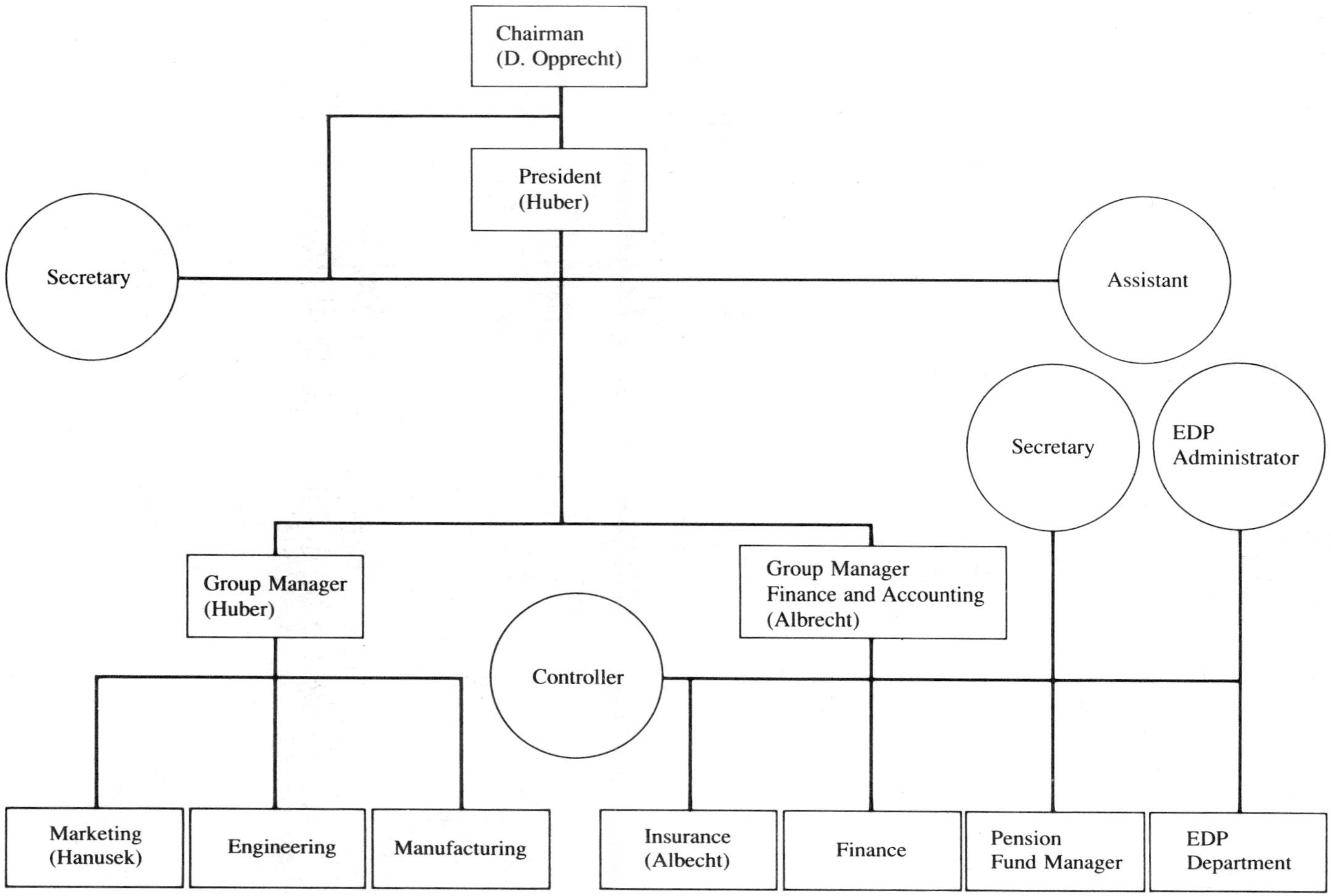

EXHIBIT 6 Organization Chart—Soudronic Marketing Department 1982/1983

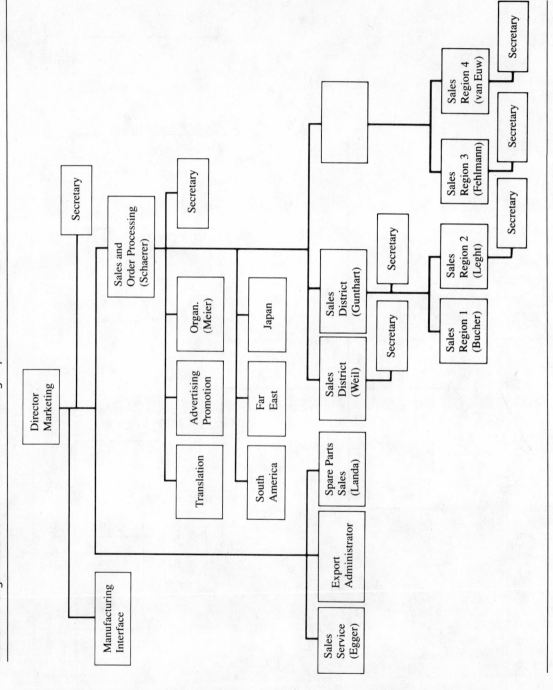

EXHIBIT 7 Soudronic Marketing Department, January 1, 1983

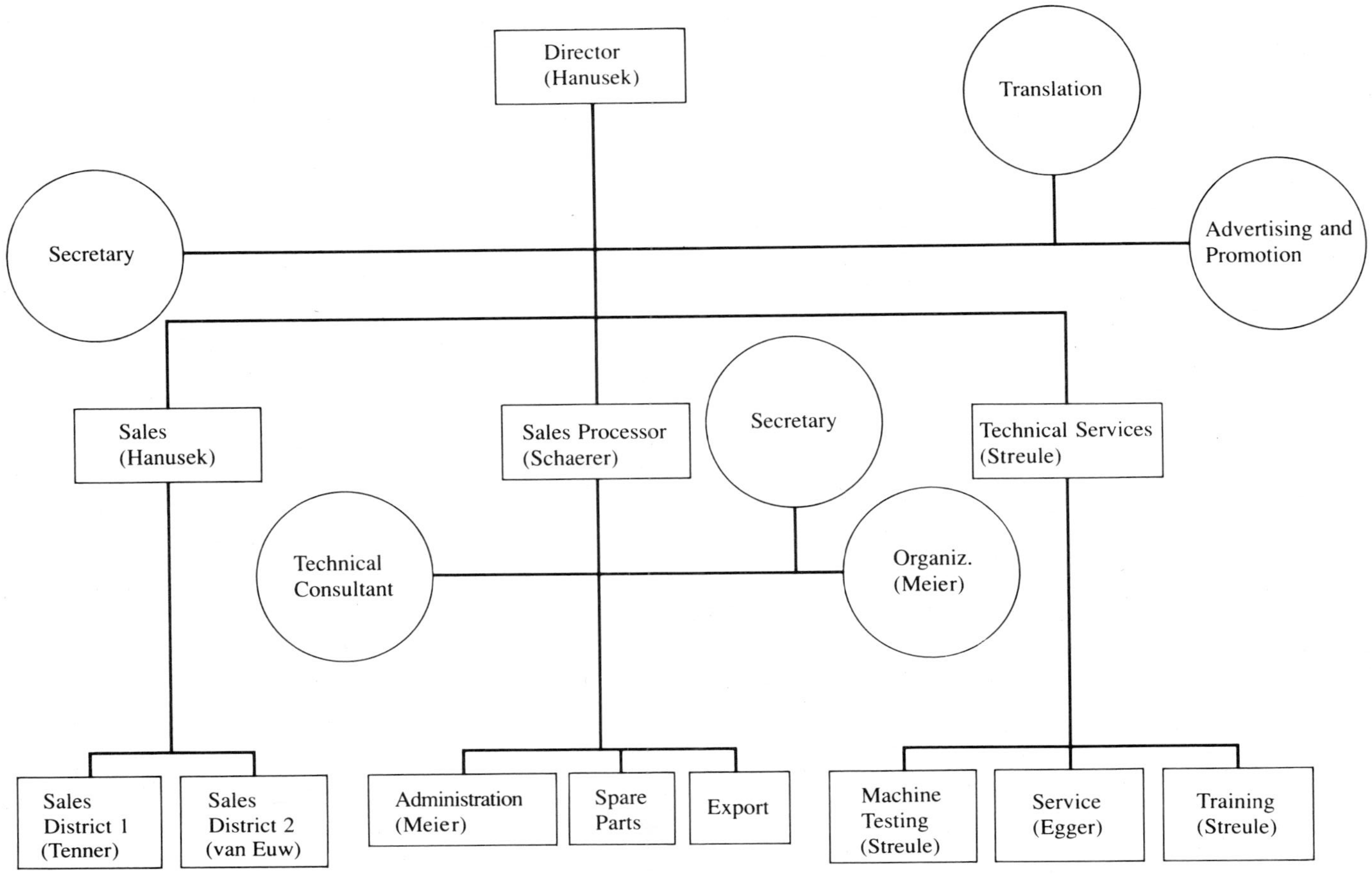

EXHIBIT 8 Soudronic's Sales Organization, January 1, 1983

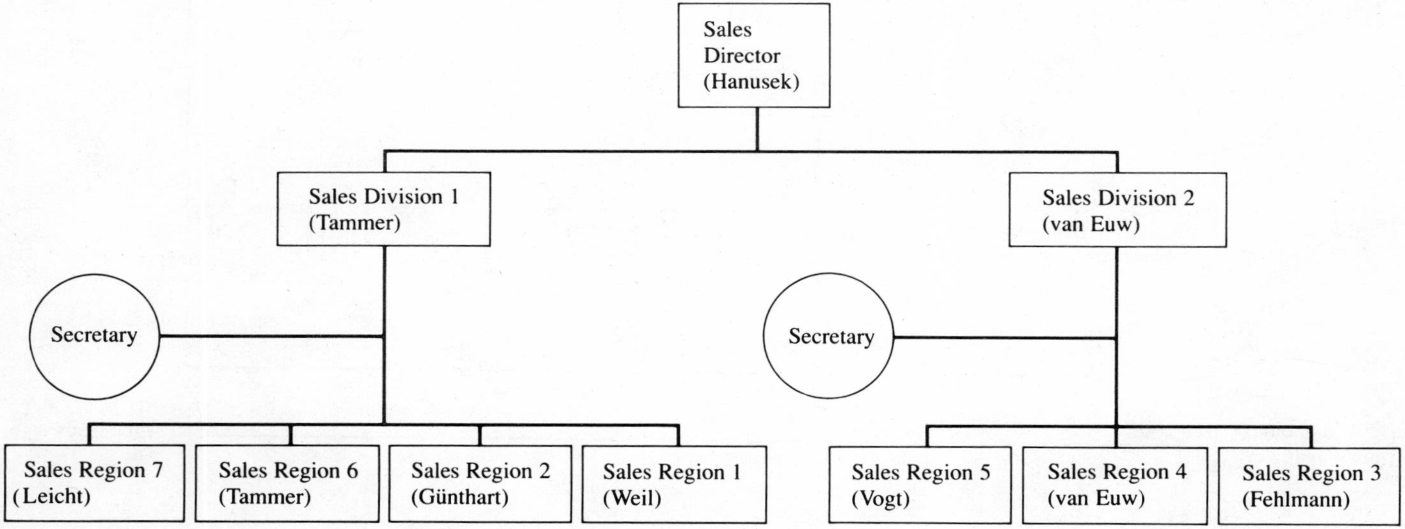

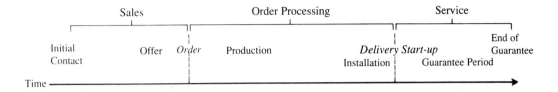

quirements between the mid-1960's and the mid-to late 1970's. During that time clients called Soudronic with orders for all of the machines that it could produce. Soudronic's products seemed to literally "sell themselves." The only serious negotiations into which Soudronic entered during that period concerned delivery time. One of the most important goals of the reorganization, according to Mr. Hanusek, was to increase the time Sales Managers spent on selling activities to 50 percent of their time, and to give the administrative tasks to someone else. It was still a little early to see if these targets were actually being met.

Before Mr. Hanusek's reorganization of the Sales and Marketing department every contact between Soudronic and its customers had been coordinated by one department. The needs of the client, and the Soudronic specialist required, varied over time. It had been the intention of Mr. Hanusek to create departments and department heads that were consistent with the function actually performed at the different times.

The new Marketing Department was divided into three departments: Sales, Sales Administration and Technical Services. Mr. Hanusek was serving as the Sales Director as well as the Marketing Director on a temporary basis. It was expected that it would take Mr. Schaerer 12 to 18 months to fully organize the Sales Administration Department, and that he would then train a successor for his position and accept the position of Sales Director.

The Sales Department contained two sales regions, one region had three Sales Managers and one had four Sales Managers. The Sales Administration Department had three separate departments: Order Processing, Spare Parts and Shipping. It also had a technical consultant, a newly created position, whose function was to serve as the "go-between" and/or coordinator between the Sales Managers and the various technical departments. The Technical Services section had three departments: Testing, Customer Service, and Training. In addition to these functional departments the staff positions of Translation and Public Relations also reported to Mr. Hanusek.

Not yet solved by the reorganization was the problem of gathering information about the industries, customers, potential customers, and competitors that affected Soudronic's business. Sales Managers were now expected to be in contact with the customers 50 percent of their time and were aware of their responsibilities in terms of gathering and transmitting environmental data. Other Soudronic personnel, such as service technicians, were also in contact with clients and industry personnel at least 50 percent of their time. They were, however, often unaware of how important their opportunities to gather information, and the information itself, were to Soudronic. As a result they did not take advantage of the opportunities that were available to them and did not transmit to home office personnel the information that they acquired. Technical personnel often had a narrow view of their job functions and responsibilities. They saw their role as one of solving technical problems only and not as a "boundary spanner" with an information processing function as well. Mr. Hanusek felt that he and other Soudronic executives were probably not receiving all of the market based information that was potentially available to them. He believed that this lack of information, while not a serious problem at the moment, could develop into one as the rates of technological and environmental change in the metal container and specialty welding industries accelerated.

THE ROLE OF THE SALES MANAGER

Soudronic Sales Managers were responsible for the sale of Soudronic body welding machines and replacement parts. The Sales Managers were all based at Soudronics headquarters, but traveled between 10 and 30 percent of the time. One of Mr. Hanusek's goals was to increase this travel time to 30 percent to 50 percent of the time. Their role was to represent Soudronic to both sales agents and customers. As envisioned by the new organization structure, 50 percent of their time was to be spent making customer contacts and 50 percent was to be spent performing "desk" work. Customer contact was considered to be meeting with customers at their plants and/or at Soudronic, telephone calls with customers, participating in industrial exhibitions and promoting Soudronic equipment in lectures given at institutes, universities, and meetings for metal container suppliers. Desk work consisted of staff meetings, report preparation, correspondence, budgeting, strategic planning and, most importantly, responding to customers' questions and needs.

Sales Managers were paid a fixed salary plus a commission that represented 10–20 percent of the fixed salary. The sales commission percentages were individually determined by Mr. Hanusek. They were lower for geographic areas where it was considered to be easier to make sales, such as the U.S., and higher for areas where it was considered to be more difficult to sell, such as developing countries. All of the Sales Managers had technical and commercial backgrounds and were given extensive on the job training. They ranged in ages from 30 to 62, although most were under 45. The number of years each had spent with Soudronic ranged from one and one-half to more than ten, the average being about five. It was the responsibility of the Sales Managers to coordinate and plan their travel schedules one year in advance. They were also responsible for insuring that one of the other Sales Managers covered for them in responding to the needs and questions of the agents and customers within their geographic area while they were traveling. It was extremely difficult to find qualified applicants for the position of Sales Manager. Recently Mr. Hanusek had spent six months looking for one additional Sales Manager for Latin America. Although he had had many applications, none had had the right background. He wanted Sales Managers to have five to ten years experience in industrial sales in the geographic areas under consideration, appropriate language capabilities, a technical background and a familiarity with the commercial areas of shipping and finance. The chances of locating, for example three qualified Sales Managers within three to six months, were considered to be extremely small.

The Sales Manager entered the selling process after the sales agent had made the initial client contact and had determined that the client was a serious prospect. At that point the sales agent and the Sales Manager visited the client together. In fact, almost all client visits made by the Sales Manager were made in the company of the sales agent who was responsible for the account. About 95 percent of the technical questions a customer had concerning the specifications of the machine, a machine's installation requirements and its operating characteristics and requirements were answered by either the sales agent or the Sales Manager. A Soudronic-based technical consultant served as the interface between the Sales Managers and Soudronic's technical and production staffs. He was contacted by the Sales Managers and was responsible for providing the more detailed information that a customer might require.

THE NEGOTIATION/SALES PROCESS

As recently as 1980 Soudronic very rarely negotiated any of the terms of a sale, with the occasional exception of the delivery date. In 1983, "exceptions" were still rare; only 10 percent of the 300 body welders that Soudronic shipped each year were sold under "exceptional" terms. These exceptions were, for the most part, negotiated by the customer and the Sales Manager, within the confines of limits that had been set by Mr. Hanusek. In permitting the Sales Manager to negotiate with the customer Mr. Hanusek hoped to instill confidence in the Sales Manager; he wanted the Sales Manager to feel and to be seen as one who had the authority to negotiate.

Exceptions were negotiated for price, financing terms, guarantee periods, and, most commonly, delivery dates. The demand for food and beverage cans was somewhat seasonal. Beverage cans were in high demand for the summer months and food cans were in very high demand during harvesting seasons. In order to prepare for that demand most can suppliers wanted their machines in April and May. The required delivery times for the most popular machines were well known to the Sales Managers. Exceptions in terms of delivery time could sometimes be negotiated through Soudronic's computerized business planning system. This system had up-to-date information on work-in-process and equipment inventories as well as on order backlog. In combination with meetings with the production staff, some flexibility in delivery dates could sometimes be negotiated.

After a sale was concluded Sales Managers made arrangements for the operating personnel of the customer to attend one of the five-day in-house training workshops that Soudronic held at its Berg-Dietikon factory throughout the year. These training sessions were offered for each body welder series and were given in several languages. The Sales Managers coordinated the training program schedule with the training needs of the customer's operating personnel and the expected delivery date for the equipment. The purchase of one body welder entitled the purchaser to send two people through the appropriate five-day course without charge. Living and transportation expenses, however, were paid by the purchaser.

After the sale, delivery and installation of a body welder the client's contact with Soudronic should, Mr. Hanusek felt, be shifted to the service department. The client's questions and needs, at that point, were more the responsibility of the service department than of the Sales Manager. This shift, however, was proving to be very difficult to manage. During the process of buying a machine, which was a considerable investment for many purchasers, clients often came to depend on the Sales Manager for infor-

mation and even reassurance concerning the machine. Soudronic exported virtually 100 percent of its machines. Many of these customers were located very far from Switzerland. The Sales Managers spoke their language, knew their plants and knew their problems. Customers did not want to speak with someone they did not know and who did not know them. Interestingly, the Sales Managers themselves were often reluctant to sever the relationship with the client as well. They wanted to maintain close client contacts in order to insure that subsequent replacement or capacity expansion sales would be made through them. Mr. Hanusek estimated that 10 percent to 20 percent of a Sales Manager's time was spent dealing with after sales issues that should have been handled by the service department, and the reduction of this figure was a top priority item for him.

Mr. Hanusek had divided the world into seven geographic areas and each Sales Manager was responsible for the sales effort within one of these seven areas. The "fit" between the geographic area and the Sales Manager was based on a variety of criteria. The most important criteria were the Sales Manager's language capabilities and his having had field experience within the geographic area. Mr. Hanusek also wanted to try to balance the revenue potential of each area, and when that was not possible, create a balanced workload among the areas.

The geographic sales regions were:

1. German speaking countries (Germany, Austria, Holland) and Eastern European Countries. These areas represented about 20 percent of annual turnover.
2. North and South America. These areas represented about 25 percent of annual turnover.
3. A "Potpourri" of the Scandinavian countries (Norway, Finland, Sweden and Denmark), Greece, Turkey, India, Pakistan, Australia, and New Zealand. These areas represented about 10 percent of annual turnover.
4. The Near and Middle East (except Israel), Libya, Egypt, Iraq and Iran and the Far East, Japan, and South Korea. These areas

represented about 12 percent of annual turn-over.

5. South East Asia, Thailand, Indonesia, Malaysia, Singapore, the Philippines, China, and Taiwan. These areas represented about 10 percent of annual turnover.

6. The United Kingdom, Ireland, Africa (including South Africa, but not including French-speaking Northern Africa). These areas represented about 12 percent of annual turnover.

7. Belgium, France, Spain, Portugal, Italy, and French-speaking Northern Africa and Libya. These areas represented about 12 percent of annual turnover.

THE ROLE OF THE SALES AGENT

Soudronic body welders were distributed in 80 countries. The bulk of these sales were initiated by sales agents that were based in the country where the customer operated. These sales agents kept in close contact with the Soudronic customer and potential customers within their areas. Certain of them even maintained their own sales engineers, technical experts, and replacement parts inventories. The metal container industry was not large in terms of the number of participants so a relatively small number of people could effectively keep "tabs" on the market. Sales agents were expected to keep themselves informed about the capacity expansions of clients and potential clients alike.

Sales agents did not buy the machines themselves. They put the client and the Soudronic Sales Manager in touch with one another, aided the negotiations, maintained client contacts, and received a commission for the machines and spare parts that were sold in their regions. These commissions were between 6 percent and 12 percent, depending on the price of the part or machine sold. The more expensive the equipment, the lower the percentage commission. There were three different categories of sales agent: the very small one man or one family operation, the medium sized company that employed 10 to 20 people and operated within one country and the very large trading house which had branch offices in several countries and handled a variety of goods.

THE SMALL FAMILY OWNED SALES AGENCY

Twenty-five percent of Soudronic sales agents were small family owned operations. These agents tended to focus on one or two sectors of the metal container industry. They were generally very loyal distributors who were dependent on their Soudronic based business for survival. These small agents had virtually no financial resources and many had what might be considered a "hand to mouth" existence. In order to reduce expenses they sometimes did not visit customers, or invest in customers, to the extent Mr. Hanusek would have liked.

The sales agent for France was representative of this type of sales agent. He derived 70 percent to 80 percent of his income from Soudronic based sales and did all of his own selling. From his Paris office, where about 70 percent of his contacts took place, he worked from a list of current and potential customers in France and Northern Africa. These customers were large, medium, and small users with whom he maintained contact through phone calls and plant visits. When he felt that he had located a customer who was likely to purchase a machine he called the Soudronic Sales Manager for France and arranged for a joint visit to the client.

He handled between 10 and 24 actual and potential customers in France, and about six each in both Belgium and Northern Africa. As was the case for most agents of this type, Mr. Hanusek believed that he could effectively monitor and serve all of the potential customers for Soudronic's automatic body welders. There were approximately twice as many potential customers for semi-automatic equipment, and Mr. Hanusek believed that he had a difficult time monitoring all of those.

Sales agents of this type also served Scandinavia, Italy, Greece, the Middle East, Brazil, Argentina, South Africa, Australia, and New Zealand.

THE MEDIUM SIZED SALES AGENCY

About 40 percent of Soudronic's sales agents were medium sized companies whose Soudronic based income represented 20 percent to 50 percent of their total annual income. These sales agents tended to have a small workshop or service facility, a spare parts inventory, moderate financial resources and good communication facilities, including telex facilities and secretarial assistance. They usually specialized in groups of industries and employed sales engineers that were familiar with the needs and requirements of their industries. The company owners typically did not do any selling themselves.

The Soudronic sales agent for Spain was fairly representative of this type of agent, although his company was somewhat larger than most of the medium sized firms. The Spanish agent was headquartered in Madrid and had three or four branch offices throughout Spain. This sales agent employed 30 people, including two sales engineers. One of the sales engineers dealt only with Soudronic equipment. The company also employed a service engineer who was qualified to do Soudronic installations. This firm specialized in machine tool machinery and packaging machinery and its line of Soudronic machines represented about 10 percent of its annual turnover.

Companies in the Spanish metal container industry tended to be both users and marketers of the metal containers that they produced. In 1983 there were 12 large user/suppliers, 10 medium user/suppliers and some small user/suppliers. The Spanish sales agent was able to stay in fairly constant contact with its 12 largest clients. Mr. Hanusek felt that he could probably use more sales assistance in Spain. Soudronic's Sales Managers for Spain spent one week to ten days every quarter there, but even this failed to meet the needs of the Spanish market.

Medium sized companies also served as Soudronic sales agents in Holland, Austria, the United Kingdom, the Philippines, Colombia, Ecuador, Central America, the Caribbean, Kenya, Nigeria and Japan.

THE LARGE TRADING COMPANIES AS SALES AGENTS

About 35 percent of Soudronic's sales agents were large trading companies whose Soudronic income ranged from less than one percent to about 30 percent of their total annual income. These companies generally had European based headquarters and branch offices in several other countries. They tended to have a lot of financial power, would occasionally buy machines and assume the risk of resale themselves, employed their own sales and service engineers and maintained significant spare parts inventories. Soudronic liked to use large trading houses that either specialized in packaging machinery or had a lot of experience handling industrial goods. Because these firms were so large, and their Soudronic business was such a small percentage of their total business, Mr. Hanusek encouraged his Sales Managers to keep in close contact with them in order to insure that Soudronic equipment was being given as much attention as possible.

The German trading company, G. Melchers & Co. was typical of this type of sales agent. G. Melchers & Co. was an established trading company that had been doing business in the Far East and South East Asia for 175 years. Through its 11 departments it handled goods that ranged from complete factories to consumer products. It had its own sales and service engineers, a considerable spare parts inventory, excellent communications facilities and huge financial resources. G. Melchers' Soudronic equipment sales represented only one half to 1 percent of its total annual turnover. Even the most expensive of Soudronic's body welders were rather small sales for them. G. Melchers & Co. serviced almost 90 Soudronic clients through its branch offices in Sri Lanka (three customers), Singapore (24 customers), Malaysia (12 customers), Indonesia (12 customers), Taiwan (24 customers) and South Korea (12 customers).

Other large trading houses served as sales agents in Thailand, Hong Kong, China, and Chile for body welders, and in Brazil and Japan for specialty welding machines.

DISTRIBUTION IN JAPAN

Japan was one of Soudronic's largest markets for body welders. The Japanese market was served by an independent distributor who owned a medium sized business that employed about 20 people and whose Soudronic based sales accounted for approximately 60 percent of annual turnover. This was the only Soudronic sales agent who bought machines himself from Soudronic and who did not rely on the Soudronic's Sales Managers for customer negotiations. Mr. Matsumoto had founded his business in Osaka. As his firm's leading salesman as well as its owner he made all of his firm's important decisions. He employed a sales engineer and a service engineer and maintained a workshop that produced auxiliary transportation and heating equipment for Soudronic equipment. He also maintained a spare parts inventory valued at about Sfr. 300,000.

The Japanese metal container industry was rather unusual for an industrialized country because there was a very clear segmentation between can producers and can fillers. For the most part can fillers did not make any of the cans that they used.

In Japan, Soudronic's most severe competition came from a competitive technology that consisted of gluing metal containers together. Glued seams were fairly narrow in appearance but had overlaps of 5 mm. compared with 0.4 mm. for SUPER WIMA seams. Glued seams were very attractive, but they had two major drawbacks for the Japanese market. They could be heated to only 160° C and they could not be "expanded," or made to take a barrel-like shape. These were drawbacks because the Japanese seemed to like cans that were shaped like barrels and because vendor machines that dispensed coffee in Japan dispensed the drinks in cans, as soft drinks were dispensed in the U.S. and Europe. In the winter, these cans needed to be heated very quickly once a customer made his selection at the machine, so heating coils that reached temperatures of up to 200° C were used. Welded seams could withstand such temperatures but glued seams disintegrated under them.

Three producers, together, accounted for 80 percent to 85 percent of the metal containers used in Japan. Ten other companies, together, produced about 10 percent of the Japanese metal container and another 25 companies produced the remaining 5 percent. Soudronic's decision to use a medium size sales agent in Japan was, in part, based on this segmentation of the metal container producers, and in part due to the diffi-

culty all foreigners experienced doing business in Japan. Doing business in Japan was very much a function of the informal relationships that existed between businesses. These relationships were very often exclusive. If one did business with one firm, one did not do business with another in the same industry. If Soudronic had engaged, for example, a large trading concern, there was a high probability that this trading concern would have already had established business relationships with one or two of the major metal container producers, and that these previously established relationships would have prevented it from dealing with other metal container producers.

Engaging a medium sized agent, which was very small by Japanese standards, gave Soudronic a neutral position in the market place and the industry. From this neutral position it was able to deal with all of the participants in Japan's metal container industry.

DISTRIBUTION IN THE U.S.

Soudronic Limited, based in Scarsdale, New York was Soudronic AG's only subsidiary. Its staff of 15, including seven service engineers, operated out of a newly built company owned 15,000 sq. ft building. It used 10,000 sq. ft of the building and leased 5,000 sq. ft to other businesses. The suburban New York headquarters housed a sales department, a service department, a spare parts inventory and a training and demonstration center. Mr. Hanusek estimated that the cost of operating the U.S. subsidiary was approximately one million U.S. dollars per year. This figure included real estate costs, salaries, traveling expenses, interest expense and taxes.

Soudronic Limited was the importer, dealer and distributor for the U.S., Canada and Puerto Rico. U.S. based customers had the option of being billed in U.S. dollars, making those who so chose the only Soudronic customers who were not billed in Swiss Francs. The subsidiary bought in Swiss Francs and sold in dollars and exchange rate fluctuations caused changes in the dollar price only if those fluctuations exceeded predetermined limits. Since its establishment the manager of the subsidiary had always as-

EXHIBIT 9 Major Geographic Markets for Sheet Metal Container Body Welders*

	1975	1976	1977	1978	1979	1980	1981	1982
Market								
USA	11%	17%	22%	29%	29%	16%	19%	15%
Japan	9%	9%	8%	6%	13%	1%	4%	8%
United Kingdom	3%	12%	7%	5%	7%	7%	10%	9%
Far East	5%	6%	12%	13%	4%	8%	9%	10%
Spain	1%	3%	3%	1%	2%	6%	8%	2%
France	3%	4%	13%	10%	16%	7%	1%	6%
West Germany	13%	8%	7%	9%	4%	5%	11%	7%
Others	55%	41%	28%	27%	25%	50%	38%	43%
	100%	100%	100%	100%	100%	100%	100%	100%

* The figures are the percentages of total Soudronic body welder revenues that derive from sales made in the given market in the given year.

sumed the selling responsibility as well. In July 1983 this was expected to change due to the arrival of a new Sales Manager. Please see Exhibit 9 for sales data by geographic market.

The U.S. market differed from every market, except perhaps Japan, in two areas. First, prices in the U.S. were high. These high prices reflected not only additional expenses for duties, shipping and door to door delivery, packaging and insurance but also reflected American demand for 24 hour a day service. Second, there was a trend in the U.S. for even very large canners and fillers to close their company owned can manufacturing plants in favor of purchasing cans from can manufacturers. Can manufacturing was such a competitive industry in the U.S. that buying cans from the large scale producers was often cheaper than producing them in house, even for the largest users.

DIRECT DISTRIBUTION

There were three groups of customers to whom Soudronic AG sold directly. These were "original equipment manufacturers" (OEM's), contractors and major customers. OEM's designed complete can making lines using equipment that they manufactured themselves, with the exception of certain units like Soudronic's body

welder. They then sold the entire system to a third party. The OEM's traditional customers had been can manufacturers in developing countries. More recently their customers were small processors and fillers in the developed countries who had decided to manufacture the cans they used themselves. Because these processors and fillers lacked the expertise to put together the systems they needed, dealing with an OEM greatly simplified the purchase and installation process for them.

Mr. Hanusek distinguished between OEM's and contractors in the following way: OEMs built and sold machine systems but not know-how while contractors sold know-how. Contractors taught companies how to run a metal container manufacturing operation. As such they provided advice and recommendations to their clients concerning the machines that were on the market, but did not build or distribute the machines themselves. They acted as advisers and business consultants. Some even advised metal container manufacturers with regard to marketing strategies.

Some major customers had bought up to 30 body welders in any given year. Most of these were large metal container suppliers who regularly updated their equipment and occasionally expanded their capacity. It was not uncommon for them to also put together canning systems, as an OEM would do, to sell to third parties. Clearly there was some overlap between these two groups, but not all OEM's and contractors were major customers, and vice versa.

Soudronics directly managed the OEM's, contractors, and major customers who contacted them. Soudronic's practice was to insist that they reveal where the final customer for the machine was located. When that information was provided the Soudronic's Sales Manager for the appropriate region was assigned to the account. In addition, all major customers, like Nestlé, Metal Box and Crown Cork and Seal had client coordinators. This system simplified the customers' contacts with Soudronic, while at the same time maintained the internal consistency of Soudronic's Sales Manager system. At any one time, one client could have had sales being negotiated with three or more Sales Managers. The client coordinator served to intermediate between the client and the respective Sales Managers.

1982 Sales volume by type of sales agent was as indicated in Table 1.

TABLE 1

	1982 Turnover in Percent Terms
1. One Man Operations	20%
2. Medium Sized Sales Agents	25%
3. Large Trading Companies	18%
4. OEM's	10%
5. Major Customers	12%
6. Sales Subsidiary	15%
	100%

This ranking had been fairly consistent over time, and with no major changes on the part of Soudronic, was expected to continue.

Changing a sales agent was considered to be a drastic decision. Customers became very concerned about such a change and generally wanted to know why such a change was required. Further, it was very important to sever such relationships carefully and to remain on good terms with the former agent. The pool of potential sales agents was very small and finding qualified replacements was extremely difficult. In Mr. Hanusek's first one and one-half years at Soudronic he had found it necessary to replace two sales agents, the agents for Brazil and for Hong Kong.

THE SALES PROCESS—SPECIALTY MACHINES

The business of selling the specialty machine had evolved around the Soudronic network of Sales Agents and Sales Managers. There were many important similarities, as well as differences, between the two sales processes. Soudronic did not market their capabilities in terms of designing specialty resistance welding machines as actively as they marketed their standard metal container body welders. They were generally "known" by those who needed to know of their expertise in this area and had most often been approached by users in Central and Southern Europe, Scandinavia and the Benelux countries.

Soudronics exhibited examples of their specialty machines at industrial fairs, and some of their Sales Agents actively marketed the service. For the most part, when discussing specialty machine clients, Mr. Hanusek felt that "they found us."

Once specialty machine clients "found" Soudronic they either contacted their own regional Sales Agent or the Soudronic office. The Sales Agent screened the contact and, if it was a serious request, the request was passed on to the Sales Manager for the region. A letter or call to Soudronic headquarters was, likewise, referred to the Sales Manager who was in charge of the region where the request had originated. The Sales Manager further screened the request, and if he felt that it was reasonable and consistent with Soudronic specialty machine business he passed the request on to the appropriate technical personnel. The sales commission for a specialty machine was the same as for a body welder of comparable price.

The specialty machine customer was seen by Soudronic executives as being a more deliberate prospect than the potential body welder client. He really needed Soudronic services and his attitude was often one of "if you can do it, I'll definitely buy it," as compared with the body welder client who often had more options or alternatives available to him. The "time line" of a specialty machine sale was also different than that of a body welder sale. Here the negotiation, technical service, production, and testing periods were longer.

Soudronic executives felt that they had much more competition in this business than they did in their body welder business. Most of this competition was from firms in Switzerland, Germany, and France. In response to both the number of competitors and their own marketing strengths Soudronic had developed a special philosophy for its specialty machine business. This philosophy was that if the machine that it was being asked to develop had, in fact, only one potential user, then it was not to their benefit to accept that contract. They were most interested in pursuing ideas that, although they responded to special welding needs, would be useful to other manufacturers as well as the one making the original order. They wanted to pursue products or product ideas that, as concepts, could be adapted to serve the needs of other manufacturing processes or systems as well.

This was one way to spread the risks and costs of development. It also created potential for eventual diversification, and established boundaries for what could have developed into a rather fragmented business that would have been very difficult to control.

An example of the type of development Soudronic most liked to pursue was the creation of a one-machine one-man production-unit that could weld both sides of an "elbow" shaped piece of tubing. This process had originally been created for one manufacturer to replace a two-machine two-man system and was now used by others in the same industry. It had also been adapted for use in other industries. See Exhibit 10 for sales data comparing metal container body welder sales and specialty machine sales.

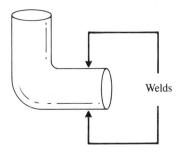

COMPETITORS AND COMPETITIVE TECHNOLOGIES

In terms of welded seam technology Soudronic's main competitors were small companies that copied their machines using less expensive labor and production processes. Typically

EXHIBIT 10 Percent of Yearly Revenue by Product Line

	1975	1976	1977	1978	1979	1980	1981	1982
Category								
Metal Container Body Welders	88%	96%	94%	96%	95%	92%	92%	97%
Specialty Welding Machines	12%	4%	6%	4%	5%	8%	8%	3%
	100%	100%	100%	100%	100%	100%	100%	100%

these companies did not support any research and development, and this combination of low labor costs and low R&D budgets resulted in very low prices for their machines. Because the quality of these machines tended to be low as well, the small market share they took was less a problem for Soudronic than was combating the impression, when these low quality machines developed problems, that the basic technology was not good. One growing problem was the appearance of several high quality manufacturers who were also copying the body welders, despite Soudronic's patents and their own lack of licensing arrangements. Soudronic company policy was to file suit in such cases, but the suits were still pending, and the producers were still manufacturing. In certain markets there was also established, or establishing, competition for semi-automatic machinery. This local competition was most in evidence in India, Taiwan and Brazil.

Specifically, Mr. Hanusek was concerned about the strategies of four companies. Generally these were well-established firms that had tended to copy the Soudronic body welder, while adapting their versions to the extent necessary to circumvent Soudronic patents. Fael and Schweiss-maschinen AG were small Swiss companies that had entered the metal container body welder machine market after having hired former Soudronic employees. In the case of Fael its only known customer, Continental Can, had recently moved its body welder order from Fael to Soudronic. Schuler, a West German company, was a much larger company than were the Swiss-based competitors. It employed about 2,000 people, including some former Soudronic employees. Schuler was famous for making presses that were used in the automobile industry. It had "presented" its high speed body welder in 1981, although as of early 1983 it was still not available for delivery. The size and financial resources of Schuler made it an important threat to Soudronic's position in the metal container welder market.

Fuji, Japan represented a different type of threat. Fuji was a small company by Japanese standards, but it was backed by a very large firm, Kawasaki Steel. In 1982 it had attempted to introduce its machines in the U.S. Soudronic

had brought a patent infringement suit in the Federal District Court in Chicago, Illinois, and although the suit was still pending Fuji withdrew its products from the U.S. market immediately after the suit was filed. Fuji was a real threat to Soudronic in areas where Soudronic would have had difficulty enforcing its patent rights, such as in Southeast Asia and Japan.

Competitive technologies were of two types. First, there were competitive technologies among different metal container technologies. Secondly, there were packaging material alternatives to metal container packaging. In the area of three piece metal containers, there were two techniques for joining the metal that were in large scale use: the welding technique that had been developed at Soudronic and the lead-based soldering process it had been designed to replace. Mr. Hanusek believed that Soudronic's largest markets were to be found in replacing metal container soldering capacity with welding capacity. In 1982 almost all of the metal containers produced in the USSR and Latin America were still soldered. In contrast, in the U.S. about 50 percent of all metal containers were welded. Mr. Hanusek considered this 50 percent figure to be very high. In Japan the figure was 5 percent to 10 percent. The Swiss, thanks to some obvious special circumstances, welded more than 80 percent of their metal containers.

The two-piece aluminum can was the product of a metal container technology that Soudronic executives had studied years earlier. Two piece cans were "punched" out of aluminum sheet metal. The resulting cup-shaped can was very thin and very light. It took graphics very well and was very clean, attractive and modern in appearance. Fully automatic two-piece can makers produced 250 to 600 cans per minute. The two piece cans needed to be washed and printed with graphics after they were formed.

Soudronic executives had decided against pursuing this two piece technology for several reasons. They had felt that the market for such equipment would be very limited due to the high cost and inflexibility of the production process. When comparing the two-piece process to the Soudronic welding process, the two-piece can process required an investment that was three times as high as was required for a Soudronic based system of equal capacity. In order to reach efficient production levels, the two-piece systems needed to operate twenty-four hours per day. The two-piece process had very high set up costs, and produced only one sized container per line. Further, changing the graphics that were printed on the can after production was a very time consuming and costly operation. The two piece can was growing in popularity in certain large markets such as the U.S., Germany, and Japan. In these markets it was used primarily for the most popular, and widely distributed, brands of beer and soft drinks.

Rumors had been circulating within the metal container industry concerning the development of a new laser welding technology. Soudronic executives were aware that commercially made cans were not yet on the market, but that laser joined cans and can making machinery were in the testing stage in some firms.

In Mr. Hanusek's view the biggest threat to the metal container industry was not going to come from new metal container technologies, but from new non-metal packaging alternatives. He believed that growth in the metal container industry was going to stagnate in the next ten years and that growth in the packaging industry as a whole would come from increasing the applications of new materials. New packaging such as the "composite" can with a paperboard wall and a metal or plastic bottom and top, was expected to become very popular. Plastic containers, glass containers, coated paper containers for noncarbonated beverages such as milk, plastic pouches for deep frozen vegetables and prepared foods all had impressive growth potential. In addition, the process of freezing foods rather than canning foods was increasing in popularity in developed countries.

MARKET SATURATION

Another type of threat was also seen as having potential significance for Soudronic—the possible saturation of the metal container body welder market. As of 1983 the development of even faster fully automatic machines guaranteed a certain volume in machine replacements because, according to Mr. Hanusek, "can making is a penny business and can suppliers cannot afford to manufacture using anything other than the fastest, most efficient and least expensive process." The economic life of a semi-automatic body welder was about 10 years, for an automatic body welder it was five to 10 years, and the economic life of a high speed body welder was only three to five years.

Soudronic's experience in New Zealand had revealed that even replacement had its limits. When Soudronic first entered the New Zealand market New Zealand had had one metal container manufacturer who sold cans to a fruit and vegetable canner, a dairy, and a beverage "bottler." The can maker was quickly convinced about the advantages of Soudronic welded seam technology and incorporated it into his can production plant. The New Zealand market was saturated. Next, Soudronic Sales Managers approached the fruit and vegetable canner, the dairy, and the bottler, all of whom then saw the advantages of producing their own welded cans. They each installed can producing equipment, including Soudronic body welders, and the New Zealand market was again saturated and was showing every indication of remaining so for quite some time.

Markets could close for other reasons as well. On August 2, 1982, the Mexican peso collapsed, and so did what had been considered as a market of very high potential. This type of risk seemed to indicate to Soudronic executives that they needed to diversify. One option was to go back to what Soudronic had started out to do—to build specially designed machines that solved unique problems for manufacturers. One possible solution was to emphasize the special machine business to the extent that it would increase its revenue contribution to 50 percent of total Soudronic revenues within 5 years.

Soudronic could also keep its concentration in body welders, and make sure that it participated in the development of the newest welding technologies. Or, it could search for new welding applications and develop the machines that would open up new markets for them as it had already done with applying welding technology to metal food and beverage containers. These areas were all being investigated, and the decisions concerning these possibilities were not expected to be made within the near future.

THE WEST GERMAN MARKET

Soudronic executives considered the West German market to be an ideal market for both of their product lines. It had become their number one market for specialty welding equipment, thanks to its large automotive and household products industries. West Germany also was a very big market for metal container body welders. There was high demand for metal containers, and a range of financially healthy small, medium and large sized metal container manufacturing installations. Since Soudronic had never had a sales agent for Germany, all sales to the country had always been handled directly by the Soudronic Sales Manager responsible for Germany. In 1983 this Sales Manager was one of Soudronic's most experienced, and valued, employees.

Mr. Hanusek felt that the West German market's enormous potential had never been fully developed by Soudronic. Even with the important advantages of a common language and geographic proximity, Mr. Hanusek felt an acute lack of the right kind of information concerning how the West German specialty welding equipment business really operated. The market, he felt sure, was tremendous, but the competition was, he was equally sure, much more severe there than in almost any other country. Representation in Germany could take many forms. Soudronic could follow their sales agents format and engage one of the three types of sales agents or it could seek out joint venture: a partner to establish a larger office, one that could be staffed with sales engineers and technical experts. This would reduce both the expense and the risk of entering the German market with a substantial operation. Finally, it could establish a U.S. style subsidiary or a branch office there and fund the unit itself.

In establishing branch office or subsidiary representation in Germany, and elsewhere, Mr. Hanusek wanted the office to meet four specific criteria. It needed to have long-term viability and an excellent ROI, that is to be less expensive than a sales agent. It also needed to be able to absorb product line changes and to show superb marketing results.

The Sales and Marketing organization, as a whole, also needed to be consistent with Soudronic's "Major Business Goals," as they were published in a booklet about the company that was furnished to customers and other interested parties. They were:

- "[The] development and construction of resistance welding machines and controls of high quality and performance.
- Sales and distribution to users throughout the world and the provision of necessary maintenance and support facilities.
- Research commensurate with the needs of the market and the development of new technologies.
- [To maintain both a] leadership position within the field and independence.
- The promotion and social security of our employees and the maintenance and creation of job opportunities.
- [The] maintenance of a sound financial basis in the interest of the country and the economy."

Germany has always been an important market for us in both of our product areas. It has also always been a market we have served from headquarters. We have never had a sales agent or representative there. We are now approaching what we feel is a threshold annual sales level of Sfr. five to ten million (being approximately 80 percent body welders and 20 percent specialty machines) and need to establish our physical presence in the market. Further, because of Germany's geographic proximity to us and its high concentration of heavy industry it is a good place for us to create a prototype of our sales office "of the future." We need to be in place there within six months to one year, and the operation we install in Germany needs to be something that we can expand with globally.

CASE 10 ∎ Alfa-Laval Filters Product Center

In December 1980, Rune Glimenius, General Manager of the product center for Alfa-Laval filters, and David Webster, Marketing Manager, were reviewing marketing options. All year they had collected information on the world market for ultrafiltration. Management intention was to secure a worldwide lead position in this market which was growing at 20 percent annually. Glimenius and Webster were uncertain which of many possible applications to select for emphasis. Other pending decisions were which countries to target and what channels to use. The new product center had to be organized either by product, by geographic area, or by application. Glimenius struggled to resolve these issues before detailing a plan for group management.

COMPANY BACKGROUND

Alfa-Laval, a diversified manufacturer of industrial equipment with applications in many fields, was a leading Swedish multinational with annual sales of 6.5 billion Swedish Krona (SEK).* Founded under the name AB Separator in 1878 by Gustav de Laval and Oscar Lamm, it produced the first continuously operating cream separator, invented by de Laval and used to separate cream from milk. Alfa-Laval became one of the first multinational companies when it established a subsidiary in the United States in

_____
* 1 SEK = U.S. $0.25 = SFr 0.40.

1883 and constructed a plant in Poughkeepsie, N.Y., in 1892. It formed sales subsidiaries in several European countries at about the same time. Although all foreign subsidiaries had operated under the name Alfa-Laval, the parent company in Sweden did not adopt that same name until 1963. In 1980 Alfa-Laval employed 18,000 persons in 140 countries. Alfa-Laval included 140 companies, subsidiaries, or units with 40 factories located in 35 countries. Sales were worldwide with 15 percent in Sweden, 55 percent elsewhere in Europe, 15 percent in North and South America, and the remainder spread throughout Asia and Africa (Exhibit 1).

PRODUCT LINES

Product lines had evolved from the cream separator to include separators for oil and water purification, for yeast, and for many other applications. Alfa-Laval was the lead company worldwide for centrifugal separators. In the 1920's Alfa-Laval had added milking machines to its product line. With growing popularity of automated milking machines in the 1950's, this product gained importance and Alfa-Laval became a household word among farmers worldwide. Alfa-Laval was also a leading manufacturer of heat exchangers and separation equipment. Company technical expertise included separation and thermal technology, liquid handling, and continuous processes with plants for both separation and thermal technology. Alfa-Laval had in-depth knowledge of milk-

EXHIBIT 1 Activities in Summary*

	1980	1979	1978	1977	1976	1975	1974	1973	1972
Net sales by business group									
Agri-group	1 922	1 805	1 530	1 329	1 127	1 023	960	842	652
Industrial group	3 135	2 562	2 443	1 899	1 795	1 701	1 506	1 091	881
Other companies	1 445	1 119	1 013	980	834	817	708	521	372
Income Data									
Net sales	6 502	5 486	4 986	4 208	3 756	3 541	3 174	2 454	1 905
Income after net financial items	477	391	321	305	303	264	249	207	122
As percentage of net sales	7.3	7.1	6.4	7.3	8.0	7.5	7.8	8.4	6.4
Adjusted income per share	22.9	18.8	15.4	14.7	14.6	14.1	13.4	11.1	6.5
Income before taxes	297	275	212	172	153	139	124	154	107
Provision for taxes	102	108	114	90	89	77	68	78	52
Balance Sheet Data									
Liquid assets	1 056	1 138	1 278	1 228	935	572	334	358	314
Inventories	2 313	2 023	1 790	1 656	1 486	1 295	1 108	850	685
Other current assets	1 833	1 754	1 677	1 309	1 139	1 131	1 048	853	786
Long-term assets	1 485	1 350	1 175	996	855	564	456	395	351
Current liabilities	2 754	2 666	2 587	2 230	1 678	1 440	1 200	971	769
Long-term liabilities	1 010	978	954	821	694	645	515	390	356
Untaxed reserves	1 464	1 282	1 151	1 034	910	544	431	325	271
Equity capital	1 459	1 339	1 228	1 104	1 133	933	800	770	740
Total assets	6 687	6 265	5 920	5 189	4 415	3 562	2 946	2 456	2 136

Number of employees								
Sweden	7 363	7 081	6 875	6 895	6 781	6 739	6 464	6 152	5 202
Outside Sweden	10 711	10 815	10 888	10 890	11 039	11 269	11 258	10 157	9 635
Profitability									
Return:									
On average operating capital before taxes	14.0	12.3	11.4	12.2	13.3	15.1	16.4	14.8	9.9
On equity capital after taxes	11.4	10.3	9.4	9.5	10.2	11.9	12.8	11.5	7.1
Ratios									
Current assets to current liabilities	1.9	1.8	1.8	1.9	2.1	2.1	2.1	2.1	2.3
Solidity ratio	32.8	31.6	30.5	31.2	36.0	33.8	34.5	38.0	41.0
Interest coverage	4.3	4.3	4.3	4.4	4.7	4.2	4.8	5.5	4.9
Other data									
Dividend									
As per cent of earnings	26.3	25.5	31.2	27.3	27.4	25.2	21.3	25.6	43.6
SEK per share	6.0	4.8	4.8	4.0	4.0	3.6	2.9	2.9	2.9
Capital stock, December 31	521	417	417	417	417	333	267	267	213
Share price, December 31 (SEK)	137	98	115	118	122	106	79	79	71
Price/earnings ratio, per share	6	5	7	8	8	8	6	7	11

* As originally stated except for 1976, which is restated in accordance with accounting principles adopted in 1977. (Amounts in MSEK)

ing, milk refrigeration, feeding, and all activities centered around cattle farming and barns.

ALFA-LAVAL WORLDWIDE ORGANIZATION

Alfa-Laval was structured to meet the needs of a multi-application product line with worldwide manufacturing and sales. Corporate staff was located in Tumba near Stockholm. Three business groups and the marketing companies were located in over 140 countries.

Eight executives directed the corporate staff group, in turn supported by 20 departments. The three business groups, a unit called "Regional Management," and the larger composite marketing companies all reported to the executive group. Regional Management was a central unit recently formed to coordinate marketing activities in controlled-economy and developing countries. Composite marketing companies were sales companies marketing both agricultural and industrial equipment. They were relatively large units assigned to report directly to certain members of the executive group (Exhibit 2).

Alfa-Laval had segmented into three units, each with its own business group. The Agri unit had three product divisions: milk production, barn equipment, and farm supplies. Milk production manufactured milking and feeding equipment. Barn equipment manufactured equipment to cool milk, milking parlours, and equipment for manure handling. Farm supplies produced accessories, other equipment, and spare parts. Agri had two sales divisions. The farm supplies unit delivered entire projects such as the SAADCO project in Saudi Arabia, a farming and dairy complex to house 10,000 milk cows and 15,000 young stock. The export unit handled sales to state-controlled economies and to countries where Agri was represented only by agents. Ten local marketing subsidiaries selling Agri products exclusively reported to the export unit. Exports conducted its own research worldwide, employed 5000 people, and accounted for one third of sales.

Eight independent companies produced specialized products unrelated to the three main units. These eight contributed 20 percent of sales. Based in Nordic countries, these eight produced electric steam boilers, marine refrigeration plants, heat pumps, products for animal feeding and fish breeding, rotary machines, and heat exchangers.

ALFA-LAVAL INDUSTRIAL GROUP

The industrial group with nearly half of worldwide sales volume was Alfa-Laval's largest. Each of its four product divisions had worldwide responsibilities. The separation engineering division manufactured centrifugal separators, decanter centrifuges, and filters. The thermal engineering division made plate heat exchangers. The flow equipment division produced pumps, control valves, and fittings. The automation division made electronic products.

The industrial group also had three application divisions responsible for sales of the four product divisions in certain target markets worldwide. The marine and power engineering division marketed equipment for ships and for the power industry: separators, heat exchangers, and fresh-water distillers. The dairy and food engineering division sold process equipment to dairies and food processing plants. The food technology division marketed components, equipment, and complete installations for fish processing, starch production and vegetable oil processing. Also in the industrial group were 13 sales companies which specialized exclusively in product lines for their countries or areas. The newly formed filters product center was part of the separation engineering division of the industrial products group. The separation engineering division had three product centers: high speed separators, decanters, and filters.

Alfa-Laval had a complex international structure. Product groups had worldwide responsibility for manufacturing and sales. In countries where marketing companies existed, customer contacts were limited to the marketing company for that geographic area. Marketing was the responsibility of the applications divisions except where local marketing companies existed. Transfer prices were set so that product

EXHIBIT 2 Worldwide Organization

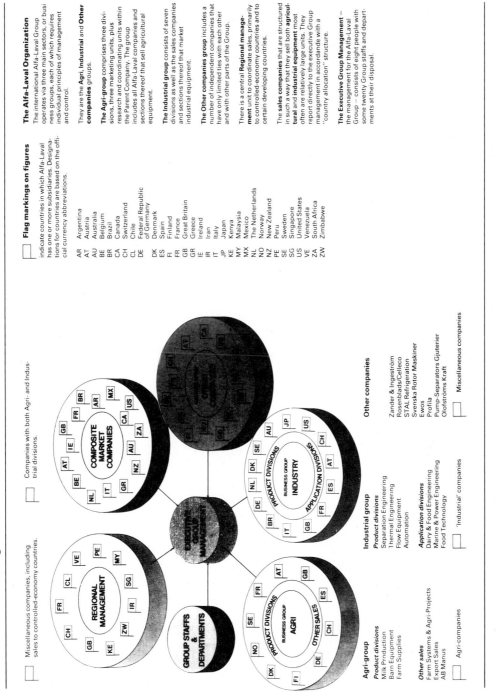

☐ Miscellaneous companies, including sales to controlled-economy countries.

☐ Companies with both Agri- and Industrial divisions.

The Alfa-Laval Organization

The international Alfa-Laval Group operates via three main sectors, or business groups, each of which requires individual principles of management and control.

They are the **Agri, Industrial** and **Other companies** groups.

The Agri-group comprises three divisions, three marketing units, plus research and coordinating units within the Parent Company. The group includes all Alfa-Laval companies and sections thereof that sell agricultural equipment.

The Industrial group consists of seven divisions as well as the sales companies and sections thereof that market industrial equipment.

The Other companies group includes a number of independent companies that have only limited ties with each other and with other parts of the Group.

There is a central **Regional management** unit to coordinate sales, primarily to controlled-economy countries and to certain developing countries.

The **sales companies** that are structured in such a way that they sell both **agricultural** and **industrial equipment** most often are relatively large units. They report directly to the executive Group management in accordande with a "country allocation" structure.

The Executive Group Management – the management for the Alfa-Laval Group – consists of eight people with some twenty Group staffs and departments at their disposal.

Flag markings on figures

indicate countries in which Alfa-Laval has one or more subsidiaries. Designations for countries are based on the official currency abbreviations.

AR	Argentina
AT	Austria
AU	Australia
BE	Belgium
BR	Brazil
CA	Canada
CH	Switzerland
CL	Chile
DE	Federal Republic of Germany
DK	Denmark
ES	Spain
FI	Finland
FR	France
GB	Great Britain
GR	Greece
IE	Ireland
IR	Iran
IT	Italy
JP	Japan
KE	Kenya
MY	Malaysia
MX	Mexico
NL	The Netherlands
NO	Norway
NZ	New Zealand
PE	Peru
SE	Sweden
SG	Singapore
US	United States
VE	Venezuela
ZA	South Africa
ZW	Zimbabwe

Agri-group

Product divisions
Milk Production
Barn Equipment
Farm Supplies

Other sales
Farm Systems & Agri-Projects
Export Sales
AB Manus

☐ Agri-companies

Industrial group

Product divisions
Separation Engineering
Thermal Engineering
Flow Equipment
Automation

Application divisions
Dairy & Food Engineering
Marine & Power Engineering
Food Technology

☐ 'Industrial' companies

Other companies

Zander & Ingström
Rosenblads/Celleco
STAL Refrigeration
Svenska Rotor Maskiner
Ewos
Profila
Pump-Separators Gjuterier
Olofströms Kraft

☐ Miscellaneous companies

divisions would show balanced results. Consequently, profits were usually realized in applications divisions or in marketing companies. Alfa-Laval was a federation of companies. This loose federation had been enhanced during both world wars when communications with the parent company were extremely difficult. As a result, unit independence was an important characteristic of Alfa Laval.

THE FILTERS PRODUCT CENTER

Before 1978, filter activities had been spread throughout the industrial group. The new product center was formed to concentrate filter activities into one unit. A broad product line had formerly concentrated around filter centrifuges, a low technology item sold to another company. Management decided to eliminate half the product line by selling, licensing, and discontinuing operations. Traditionally Alfa-Laval had emphasized high margin products within a limited product range. Product line reorganization allowed the filters center to benefit from global operations with high market shares in some applications. The company enjoyed an excellent reputation and was known for its service. To foster a high technology image, the center emphasized new filtration methods. High speed separators, the major product of the separation division, had existed for 100 years. Alfa-Laval held a strong market share in high speed separation. With the total world market growing slowly, and with new competitors entering the market, this segment was viewed as mature and saturated. Alfa-Laval had long regarded high speed separators as subject to considerable substitution risk from new technologies and processes. The filters product center was intended to gain a strong position in new technology as a hedge against obsolescence of traditional lines.

SEPARATION TECHNOLOGY

Separation was any process whereby particles were separated from a liquid. Different separation methods were employed depending on par-

ticle size. The following techniques were used at each level:

Particle Size

Particle size (in microns)

	100	
		Conventional filters
	10	High speed separators
Bacteria	1	Microfiltration
Microemulsions	0.1	Ultrafiltration (UF)
Macromolecules	0.01	
Sugar	0.001	Reverse Osmosis (RO)
Salts		

Conventional filters were used for solid/liquid filtration and high speed separators for liquid/liquid and liquid/solid. Other methods employed membrane technology. For microfiltration, ultrafiltration, and reverse osmosis, pressure was combined with cross-flow. Ultrafiltration and reverse osmosis depended on the availability of efficient membranes, which lasted for about 10 years. Industrial processes fell within one category, and no substitution occurred among filtration technologies.

Alfa-Laval separation had concentrated on high speed separators for a wide range of applications. Industry increasingly demanded new processes for separation of ever smaller particles. Of five technologies for separation, ultrafiltration was the most recently developed. The new product center was therefore directed to concentrate on membrane technology and ultrafiltration.

ULTRAFILTRATION TECHNOLOGY

Ultrafiltration (UF) was a pressure-driven membrane process to separate and fractionate components of liquids. Separation was performed by a porous membrane allowing water and other low molecular substances to pass. Larger molecules, micro-emulsion droplets, and suspended solids were held back. Ultrafiltration could selectively concentrate solutes, particles, colloids, and emulsions. Separation problems previously requiring expensive and complicated methods could now be solved using ultrafiltration, at low pressure and without heat or chemical additives. Process and waste liquids could be treated at a fraction of the cost of traditional evaporation.

Alfa-Laval membranes were hollow fibers of slightly over 1 mm inner diameter. Inside each fiber was a thin skin with small pores uniform in size. The inner skin was surrounded by a highly permeable sponge-like support structure, thicker and with larger open pores. The process liquid was pumped into one end of the fiber. Smaller molecules such as water and salts were forced radially outward through the membrane skin and support structure and discharged as ultrafiltrate or "permeate." Pore size was chosen so that molecules with different weights and micro-emulsions could not follow the same path through the fiber. Some molecules thus continued with the flow inside the fiber. This crossflow prevented build-up of the material retained inside the fiber. Without the crossflow, the flow rate of the ultrafiltrate would be reduced. This method allowed high flow rate even under low pressure (Exhibit 3).

The frame of reference used to measure ultrafiltration ability was the capacity of the membrane to retain a given macromolecule of known molecular weight. A "cut-off" was the molecular weight of the test macromolecule used because molecular shape and other factors could affect membrane performance.

The concept of ultrafiltration had existed for some time. Alfa-Laval had sold its first installations in 1973/74 to pharmaceutical companies processing human albumin. The new company strategy called for marketing ultrafiltration equipment outside a laboratory environment, targeting companies already using expensive methods of filtration. Technology had to be reengineered to fit industrial processes and capacity requirements.

THE ALFA-LAVAL UF SYSTEM

The Alfa-Laval ultrafiltration system was modular in design. All system elements were included, and it was adaptable to individual client needs. Hollow fiber cartridges were available with different characteristics depending on the applications desired. To accommodate either batch or continuous-flow operations, the system could be equipped with a batch tank or a feed inlet. All systems were equipped with feed pump, circulation pump, strainer, ultrafilter cartridges, and a collector for the permeate and the end concentrate (Exhibit 4). Permeate from cartridges was collected in a common outlet manifold and continuously discharged.

Alfa-Laval's system had several important characteristics. Permanent parts such as piping, pumps, strainers, valves, fittings, and control panels, were manufactured by Alfa-Laval, simplifying service and spare-part requirements. Cartridges had to be cleaned at regular intervals, but the optimum operating period between cleanings varied according to application. Circulating a detergent solution usually sufficed. Alfa-Laval offered a back-flush system using a hollow fiber cartridge. This process prevented membrane fouling and concentration polarization. Hollow fiber cartridges required lower material consumption and lower plant pressure. The technology permitted a short residence time for treated fluids and gave higher product yields. Romicon, a subsidiary of the U.S.-based chemical company Rohm & Haas, manufactured the cartridge from durable polymers. After several years of experience in this field, Alfa-Laval enjoyed in-house expertise and knowledge of all UF and RO applications.

Alfa-Laval offered four plant configurations. The UFP I was designed as a pilot plant with only one membrane cartridge, at SEK 60,000. The UFS 4 was designed for batch processing with four membranes, SEK 100,000. Two larger configurations, the UFS 14 with 14 membranes and the UFS 30 with 30 membranes, cost SEK 150–200,000 and SEK 200–300,000 respectively. Any of these single units could be combined into a "cascade" of units to achieve higher purification, or as parallel units to obtain more capacity (Exhibit 5).

EXHIBIT 3 Membrane Technology

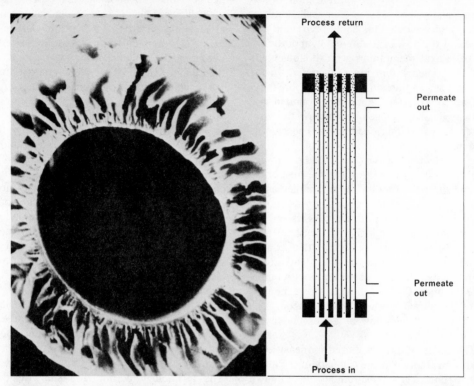

The Hollow Fiber consists of a thin inner skin surrounded by a porous "sponge-like" outer support. The inner skin is the separating membrane surface. The pore size in this skin determines the size of molecules which can pass through the membrane. Larger molecules are retained on the inside of the fiber.

A large number of Hollow Fibers is imbedded on both ends in epoxy resin. The cartridge shell and adapters are made of inert clear polysulfone.

Shipping data

	Long type cartridges	Short type cartridges
Height	180 mm	180 mm
Length	1 170 mm	710 mm
Width	205 mm	205 mm
Weight	4.6 kg	2.5 kg

EXHIBIT 4 The Ultrafiltration Process

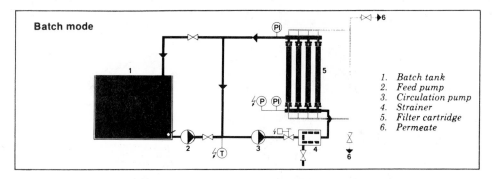

Batch mode

1. Batch tank
2. Feed pump
3. Circulation pump
4. Strainer
5. Filter cartridge
6. Permeate

The plant can be designed for batch or continuous operation in relation to concentrate production. In the batch mode the process liquid is recirculated through the cartridges until the desired level of concentration is achieved in the batch tank.

In continuous operation process liquid is continuously fed into the circulation loop. The concentrated liquid is constantly discharged. As in the batch mode, permeate production is continuous during the process.

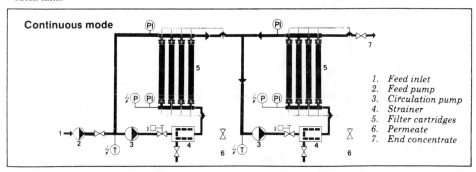

Continuous mode

1. Feed inlet
2. Feed pump
3. Circulation pump
4. Strainer
5. Filter cartridges
6. Permeate
7. End concentrate

THE WORLD MARKET FOR ULTRAFILTRATION

When the filters product center was formed, Alfa-Laval had estimated the 1980 market for ultrafiltration, microfiltration, and original equipment as follows:

Dairy	SEK	55 million
Electrophoretic paint		55
Oil/water		30
Pharmaceutical & biotechnology		20
Process water		15
Others		15
Total		190 million
		(at customer prices)

Given the 20 percent annual growth rate, the total market was expected to grow as follows:

1980	SEK 190 million
1981	225
1982	270
1983	325
1984	390
1985	470
1986	560

Potential applications existed in pulp and paper production, foods, chemicals, sewage treatment, and farming.

EXHIBIT 5 Membrane Separator Ultrafiltration Unit, UFS-14

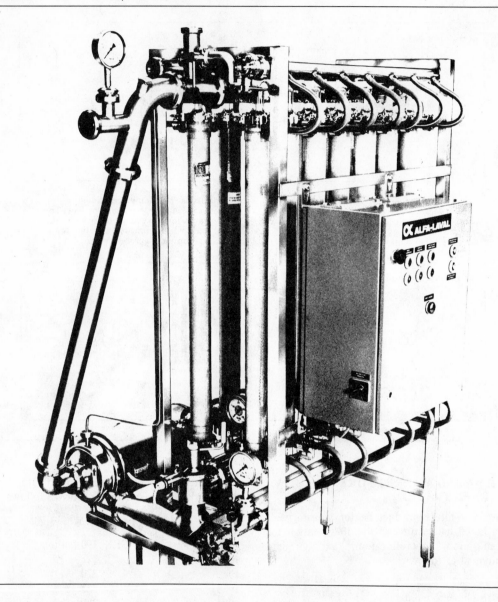

DAIRY APPLICATIONS

The dairy industry offered opportunities to use ultrafiltration for two purposes: concentration of whey to recover protein, and preconcentration of milk for subsequent production of dairy products. Market size in 1980 for these applications was estimated at SEK 55 million.

Whey, a by-product of cheese, had high protein content. Protein recovery using traditional filtration methods was difficult, and therefore whey had been generally discharged as waste. UF preconcentration of milk offered applications for cheese making. Ymer in Denmark was a very popular fermented milk product similar to sour milk and high in protein. Ymer producers converted to UF for a top-grade product with yields 18 percent above those from standard methods. UF could achieve similar results for cheeses such as Camembert, cream cheese, ricotta, and feta. Although the final product had different composition and structure, consumers could discern no difference in taste.

Alfa-Laval executives believed UF provided substantial advantages: higher yield, increased nutritional value, simpler product composition, reduced space requirements, capability to produce sweet permeate, and ease of continuing processing.

Two customer groups used UF in the dairy industry: newly built cheese operations and dairies adding a UF system to an already existing plant. Installation at an existing plant required changes often discouraging to the customer. Newly built plants offered greater promise. Addition of UF whey processing to existing or new cheese plants was much easier.

Buying habits differed by size of cheese producers. Small dairies were likely to buy new equipment for prestige purposes and could easily be talked into buying. Large dominant producers such as Sweden's two coops showed little interest in new technology or new products. Multinationals such as part of Kraft in the U.S. purchased according to engineering specifications.

Cheeses most likely to benefit from UF were produced in small plants, particularly common in France. Fewer than 50 cheese plants were built annually worldwide, and the trend was to larger, more centralized operations.

ELECTROPHORETIC PAINT PROCESSES

Electrophoretic processes, a market of SEK 55 million, deposited paint by electrolysis. A painted part had to be rinsed to give it an acceptable finish. Using water to rinse created waste that could not be re-used. A UF recycling loop could rinse and recover the paint, allowing the customer to use more expensive paint because of reduced losses.

Fifty percent of all users in this segment, automobile manufacturers maintained extensive paint operations. Automobile manufacturers hesitated to install UF without approval of their paint suppliers and manufacturers. Installation of a UF system could be viewed as an equipment change invalidating a paint supplier's guarantee. Dürr, one of the largest paint suppliers, had integrated UF systems made by Abcor, a U.S. company, into its paint systems. If automobile manufacturers specified UF equipment when ordering a new paint line, UF might account for 5 to 10 percent of the cost of an entire paint unit.

Non-automotive users composed the other half of the paint segment. Producers of consumer durable goods and furniture parts were more likely to adopt UF if contacted directly. Alfa-Laval's UF system offered reduced investment need, operating costs, down-time, and maintenance costs.

Approximately 100 paint systems of varying sizes were installed annually. Car manufacturers especially in the U.S. could be persuaded to install UF systems on the basis of cost savings. Manufacturers would often adopt UF systems when switching from older anionic paint to newer catiodic paint.

Glimenius considered this segment the most price sensitive. Having a similar company already using a UF system in the same country was an important reassurance for the prospective customer.

THE OIL/WATER SEGMENT

UF could be used to treat oil waste or to recover oils from soluble oil waste produced by mechanical engineering. Wherever cutting or lubrication fluids were needed, companies faced a disposal problem. Users could either contract for the collection of effluent and return usable oil for a fee, or install their own treatment systems. Some types of oil/water emulsions used for cooling and lubrication in metal and mechanical industries could not be split with a high speed separator unless chemical splitting agents were added and the emulsion heated. Such separation was often used before UF to remove "tramp" oil that had contaminated the emulsion and was present in unemulsified form. Tramp oil could adversely affect UF performance but could be removed by paper band filters or a simple settling tank.

The advantage of UF was its ability to concentrate oil into less than one tenth of the original volume. For example, if 100 liters of water with 3 percent oil content were subjected to UF, the 3 liters of oil could be concentrated into 5 liters of emulsion, returning 95 liters of water in pure form. The concentrated oil emulsion could be re-used. UF functioned mechanically and required no chemical substances which were often a greater environmental hazard than the effluent.

Oil-water applications were evenly split between factory and commercial contractors. Purchase of a UF system depended on cost comparison between in-house treatment and outside collector services. In Sweden 20 to 25 plants could justify an in-house UF system, and in France, 50 to 100. Commercial collectors needed efficiency and flexibility for a variety of effluents and sold extracted material for additional income.

Commercial collectors and their organizational structures varied from country to country. In Sweden there was one government-owned collector agency. In the U.K. there were two or three large collectors and 10 of medium size. In Germany a fully developed system existed. In some countries waste could be dumped in old mines leaving little demand for UF. However, worldwide attitudes were quickly changing with regard to waste treatment.

THE PHARMACEUTICAL AND BIOCHEMICAL SEGMENT

The pharmaceutical industry held potential for UF in the areas of enzyme processing, human blood, antibiotics, process water, and biochemistry. Most enzyme processing companies already had or were considering UF. Ten companies with worldwide operations produced 80 percent of total enzyme output. Enzymes were used for bulk chemicals, detergent additives, and in the U.S., corn syrup. The industry leader by volume was Novo of Denmark, followed by Gist Brocard in Holland, and Miles Laboratories and Pfizer in the U.S. UF's advantage was that it reduced the need for purification and spray drying because the process concentrated and purified simultaneously.

UF advantages in human blood processing were less marked than in enzyme processing. UF lowered salt and ethanol concentration in albumin and other products during a complicated fractioning process. Major customers were blood collection centers, depending on size and volume. Germany, France, and the U.K. had three or four blood centers with enough volume to consider UF plants. U.K. centers got blood for free and were less interested in economics.

UF could also be used to produce animal blood albumin and blood plasma for processing into concentrated or dried products. UF was an alternative to concentration by evaporation or a pre-treatment before drying. UF offered lower operating costs and improved quality. It also minimized the time that plasma or albumin were kept at temperatures capable of supporting bacterial growth. Whereas many industrial products did not have a high enough market value to justify a UF process, pharmaceutical products were of sufficient value to make UF attractive.

Many companies used UF to process antibiotics. A major advantage of UF was the simultaneous removal of undesirable low-molecular compounds and salts during concentration. The cost of one more step in producing a high-value antibiotic was minimal. Since national drug control agencies licensed the composition and application of a drug and also its production process, introducing UF into an existing plant required reapproval by the local drug administration agency. UF increased yield and resulted in higher return, necessitating custom designed systems and engineering advice. Margins were highest where development work was done concurrent with new process introduction. Potential customers were 50 well-known pharmaceutical manufacturers with a few hundred installations worldwide. Decision makers were difficult to find.

UF was also suited for the production of high quality water, used to remove microorganisms, bacteria, toxins, and pyrogens from water for final washing and rinsing of pharmaceutical product containers. Such processed water was required by both antibiotics manufacturers and "pill makers," which bought raw materials from pharmaceutical companies and packaged them into pills. Several thousand such companies existed worldwide. Similar potential applications existed for cosmetics manufacturers.

Biochemistry offered opportunities for UF applications in downstream processing, an area currently in development. Biotech companies existed in the U.S., Japan, and Europe. An unknown company could become a leader tomorrow.

SMALLER SEGMENTS

The process water segment with volume estimated at SEK 15 million was the smallest application segment. Two sub-segments were the electronics industry, needing high resistivity 18 Mega Ohm water to rinse electronic components or chips, and the water treatment industry.

A limited number of large plants could be equipped for a specific application, such as indigo recovery or vinegar processing. UF sales depended on knowledge of the existence of these unique opportunities, which were difficult to identify.

POTENTIAL UF APPLICATIONS

Alfa-Laval executives had identified four areas where UF was not currently used but might have a bright future. The pulp and paper industry had five projects expected to be built over the next five years in the U.S., Canada, and Scandinavia.

In the food industry, starch, vinegar or fish production, and waste recovery were possible applications. In the fruit juice industry, UF could be used for juice clarification and recovery of citrus oil. UF also had applications for production of wine, beer, and soft drinks.

Individual dairy farms could become buyers of UF systems to separate, concentrate, or filter milk. Although farm-based UF plants were not economical for fewer than 100 cows, France, New Zealand, the U.S., and Canada offered excellent potential. The great distances between farm and dairy in these countries made attractive the potential to reduce the number of times products had to be transported. Sewage treatment was believed to have the largest number of potential UF users.

COMPETITION

Ten competitors including Alfa-Laval marketed UF systems, three from the U.S., four from Europe, and two from Japan. All 10 competed worldwide, but only two or three competed directly in any given country.

Abcor, located in Wilmington, Massachusetts, was the largest U.S. competitor. Abcor was owned by Koch Industries, a diversified company, and employed 200 persons. Abcor dominated the segment for electro-coat industrial applications and had a tie-in with Dürr of Germany, the leading supplier of large paint systems to the car industry. Oil-water applications were another Abcor strength, with 60 percent of sales in replacement membranes. Abcor was market leader in the U.S. and also sold systems in Europe, Australia, and Comecon countries. Except for the U.K., where Abcor sold through a subsidiary, the company relied on agents or distributors. Abcor appointed several agents in one country, each specializing in a different application. Alfa-Laval management considered Abcor its most aggressive price competitor.

Another U.S. competitor, and a unit of the chemical company Rohm & Haas, Romicon had 60 employees and specialized in supplying membranes. It also competed for entire UF systems. Outside the U.S. Romicon was active in Japan and Europe, using distributors for local contacts and a small subsidiary in Holland to coordinate European business. A specialist in the production of hollow fibre cartridges, Romicon supplied cartridges for Alfa-Laval UF systems and for other UF systems on an OEM basis.

Millipore was the third U.S. firm, a leading supplier of filtration equipment for food and beverage manufacturers and laboratories. Millipore was very profitable and had considerable financial resources. UF was small compared to its total operations. The company was strong in laboratory size UF equipment but weak in industrial scale systems. Millipore had concentrated on UF applications in the pharmaceutical and beverage industries and in potable water, marketing worldwide through its own subsidiaries.

The Danish Sugar Company (DDS) was the largest European competitor. With ample financial resources, this company sought new growth opportunities. There was only low growth potential in sugar refining. DDS marketed UF equipment through two subsidiaries, Pasilac and Niro Atomisor. Similar to Alfa-Laval, Pasilac had concentrated on buying components, on contracting, and on turnkey plants. It was one of Alfa-Laval's principal competitors for plate heat exchangers. DDS employed 150 people in its membrane business and concentrated in hygienics, food and dairy, and pharmaceuticals. DDS was not in paint or water-oil applications. Strong in Europe, it also competed in the U.S., Japan, and Australia, selling through subsidiaries and agents.

Paterson Candy International, PCI, was the second largest European competitor. PCI employed 1200 persons, of which 70 were in separation technology. PCI concentrated on nondesalination applications and was the world leader in reverse osmosis. Only 15 persons worked in UF membranes. The company competed in the dairy and food industries for reverse osmosis but had not concentrated on any given UF application. PCI sold UF in Europe through sales subsidiaries or agents.

Two other European firms were both French. Rhone-Poulenc, a very large multinational chemical company, had no other filtration activity. Twenty people composed its membrane unit. In France the company was strong in dairy applications because of the French cheese industry. Rhone-Poulenc sales outside France were relatively small. The company had an agreement with Eisenmann of Germany, a paint specialist and major competitor of Dürr. The other French company, SFEC, was state-owned and associated with the French Atomic Energy Commission. SFEC had acquired UF technology from Union Carbide, a U.S. chemical company. Its new UF unit was still small and as yet had no commerical opportunities.

Activities of the two Japanese companies marketing UF systems remained unknown to Alfa-Laval executives. Both Nitto and Toray concentrated in Japan and were believed to be in the system-perfecting stage.

ACCEPTANCE OF UF BY REGION

Various parts of the world showed different levels of acceptance for UF. The U.S., Australia, New Zealand, and parts of Europe showed high acceptance. High acceptance occurred in the U.K., France, Germany, and Italy. Scandinavian countries showed average acceptance. Spain had low acceptance. Knowledge and use of UF was low in Latin America and Africa, with the exception of South Africa. Glimenius knew too little about Japan to assess penetration.

The U.S. and Canada had one half of world UF capacity. Europe had 35 percent, Japan 10 percent, and Australia and New Zealand combined, 5 percent. Installed capacity in Europe had not been broken down by country. Current sales were believed to approximate the distribution of installed capacity, with Europe holding a somewhat higher share due to faster growth in this region.

Glimenius was concerned about selection of a geographic area for future concentration. He preferred proximity to his unit, expecting a need for close contacts until his product center gained sufficient experience.

SELLING THROUGH ALFA-LAVAL SUBSIDIARIES

Utilizing Alfa-Laval subsidiaries was a major question for Glimenius and Webster. Each subsidiary was an independent marketing company responsible for all sales within its country. Product divisions marketed through the marketing companies. Although Glimenius was not forced to utilize the marketing companies, he did not know where else to turn. He knew the flow equipment division used non-Alfa-Laval channels to market valves and fittings. If he chose to utilize the marketing companies, he had to recognize their strengths and weaknesses.

The marketing companies had varying structures, depending on applications. Divisions corresponded to the industrial groups used by Alfa-Laval in Sweden. Each division had product departments. The regional organization included the salesforce. The number and size of divisions and departments depended on sales volume. Regional agents were sometimes used instead of company salesmen.

Department financial results were the performance measure. Training new people showed no short-term results. It was likely that one or two specialists would be selected to be trained in UF while keeping other responsibilities. Engineers were excited about the prospects in UF, as were executives at the division level in various marketing companies.

The regional salesforce was familiar with only one type of product. UF was not among them because of its recent introduction. The salesforce did not quote prices but handed specifications to the product department which concluded deals. The salesforce consisted of technical people recruited and trained as salesmen. Despite their title as area sales engineers, there was a natural product specialization. Training for a new UF line would take time and reduce sales in other applications. An obstacle to UF was the need to train both the salesforce and the service division for selling and servicing UF equipment.

MARKETING COMPANY STRUCTURES

In the U.K., the marketing company had six divisions: separation and thermal, food and dairy, marine and power, farming, contracting, and service. The service division was responsible for all after-sales service. The separation and thermal division consisted of two departments: separation and thermal. The separation department employed 12 engineers, each specializing by product line. There was no UF specialist in the department. Regional sales were the responsibility of six sales engineers. Four specialized in separation machines and two sold the entire division product range. In France, the salesforce specialized by division and operated out of the head office in Paris.

The German company resembled the U.K. company. The separation department employed 12 specialists by application. Regional sales offices were located in 10 cities. The salesforce was organized by types of customers or industries and reported to a separate division head for field sales. A salesman's strength was his knowledge of individual customers and his personal contacts. A salesman could not know more than one or two product lines in depth and therefore required support from the head office in Hamburg, which if necessary could contact the respective product center in Sweden.

German high speed separator salesmen had good contacts with the dairy industry and also for applications such as chemicals and oil/water where high speed separators were easiest to sell. Separator salesmen did not visit paint application customers, although thermal heat exchanger salesmen did. No contacts existed in process water applications. The high speed separation division had lost control of pharmaceutical and biochemical applications. The German salesforce exerted strong influence which might conflict with corporate planning.

The U.S. salesforce operated from regional offices. Salesmen of all divisions were combined into one regional center while remaining under division control. The separation division salesforce specialized by customer type. High salesforce turnover was a problem. Selling separation equipment was more an art than a science. Experience was essential, and it took three or four years to learn. With greater job mobility in the U.S. than elsewhere, the salesforce was constantly changing. Consequently, most salesmen did not even have knowledge of all Alfa-Laval older separation products.

The special unit selling Alfa-Laval products to government trading countries was a staff group paid by the corporate units. With no P&L responsibility, this unit had good connections in COMECON countries and operated an office in Moscow. There was a possibility of using this government trading unit as a means for geographical concentration. It would take time to show results. No short-term arrangements were possible through this channel.

ORGANIZATIONAL ISSUES FOR THE FILTERS PRODUCT CENTER

When the filters product center was formed as S-5 in the separation division, it included four other product ranges. Three of these, sieve band presses, foam scrubbers, and rotoshears, were dropped. Rotary vacuum filters was targeted for harvesting. Only UF was selected for further investment. The product center had no manufacturing facilities and sourced all components from Sweden or from outside vendors when necessary.

The filters product center had a small administrative unit, an R+D unit, a marketing department, and an engineering department. Marketing under David Webster included one assistant and one secretary. Glimenius had to decide whether to organize the marketing department by application or by geographical area. The engineering department could be organized by function, such as service, design, purchasing, and procurement, or by application, by geographic area, or by product line. There were three engineers and a department head. Growth was expected.

In marketing Glimenius had been limited by availability of qualified personnel with sufficient background. Two different postures were possible for the marketing department. It could assist the marketing companies in quoting for UF plants and projects, or it could employ its own sales engineers who would contact prospective

clients. A new salesman would require 3 months to start finding customers and another 9 months to generate orders. For UF lines, negotiation time was 3 to 6 months, with delivery and invoicing 6 months later. Volume for a good sales engineer would be SEK 3 million, possibly only after one or two years.

FINANCIAL CONSIDERATIONS

Glimenius had full profit and loss responsibility for his product center. Costs averaged SEK 300,000 per person, including fringe expenditures. The company charged 18 percent on capital. SEK 200,000 in capital were required for every 1 million in sales. Average A/R turnover of 45 days was standard for Alfa-Laval marketing companies, which earned 25 percent margins on prices. Product center gross margin was one third.* Glimenius could ask for a supplemental budget, but he would have to demonstrate need.

DEVELOPMENT OF A BUSINESS PLAN

Glimenius knew that Alfa-Laval would look at the long-term perspective. The option was for rapid growth in volume or smaller growth with emphasis on profits. The company expected him to raise UF market share from less than 5 percent to one third of the worldwide market while earning at least the company average of 7 percent return on sales. Organizational issues had to be resolved for the product center. (For a listing of existing Alfa-Laval U.S. installations, see Exhibits 6–8.)

Given the present competitive and market situation, Glimenius had to chart a strategy for presentation to management. He knew that such a presentation would entail both general strategy and financial forecasts. He wondered which industry applications he should emphasize. Looking at the structure of Alfa-Laval marketing companies, he was unsure how to market the UF product line and which geographic areas to select for concentration.

---

* Estimates by case writer.

EXHIBIT 6 Ultrafiltration—Dairy Applications

Customer	Type of application		Product	Commissioning
Denmark				
CM, Århus	UFS-14	35 m²	Skimmilk	1977
Dan-Maelk, Århus (includes the CM, Århus, installation)	3 × UFS-14	105 m²	Skimmilk	1978
Esbjerg	UFS-14	35 m²	Skimmilk	1978
Fynsk Maelk, Odense	UFS-14	35 m²	Skimmilk	1978
Randers	UFS-14	35 m²	Skimmilk	1978
Plumrose A/S Alka-Assens	UFS-4	10 m²	Skimmilk	1978
Jaegersborg	UFS-4	10 m²	Skimmilk	1978
Snejbjerg	UFS-14	35 m²	Skimmilk	1979
Horsens	UFS-6	15 m²	Skimmilk	1979
Hilleröd Research Dairy	3 × UFS-4	25 m²	Milk, Whey	1979
*	3 × UFS-4	25 m²	Cheese	1981
France				
Laiterie Mont St Michel	UFS-14	12 × 35 m²	Lactic Acid Casein Whey	1976–80 (Expansion from 3 × 35 m²)
Montfaucon	UFS-10 UFS-20	53 m²	Whole milk Camembert	
*	3 × UFS-30	281 m²	Feta	1981
Switzerland				
Nestle	UFS-4	10 m²		1978
Germany				
	UFS-14	35 m²	Acid Whey	1980

* Confidential.

EXHIBIT 7 Alfa-Laval Ultrafiltration Plants for Soluble Oil Wastes

Customer	Year Commissioned	Address	Type of plant	Membrane Surface m²	Pretreatment	Application	Average plant capacity l/h
BELGIUM							
Fabrique National		Herstal	UFO-4	7.5	Separator WSB 104B-74	Washing liquid	
Fabrique National		Herstal	UFO-4	7.4	Separator WSB 104B-74	Washing liquid	
Fabrique National	1976–1978	Hauts-Sarts	UFO-4	7.5	Separator WSB 104B-74	Emulsions	
Fabrique National		Harze	UFO-4	10	Separator WSB 104B-74	Washing liquid	450
FRANCE							
Citroen	1977–79	Various factories	Pilot unit UFO-1	2.5	MAB 103	Test on various fluids	—
Le Compresseur Frigorifique		Montluel	UFO-4	7.5	Settling tank	Emulsions / Wash water	120 / 180
Recyclage Industriel Chimique (RIC)		Beynes	UFO-12	30.0	Separator FUVPX 207	Emulsions / Wash water	800 / 1 500
Poly Oil Chemie		Bassens	UFS-14/8	20.0	Separator FUVPX 207	Mixture of emulsions and wash water	950
Glanzer-Spicer	1980	Le Mans	UFS-14/8	20.0	Separator WSPX 204	Emulsions / Wash water	500 / 900
Gaz de France	1980	St Clair Sur Epte	UFS-4/5	12.5	—	Oily water from air compressor	400
UNITED KINGDOM							
Lanstar	1980	Manchester	UFS-14N	35	Separator WSPX 213	Emulsions	1 000

EXHIBIT 8 Alfa-Laval Ultrafiltration Plants for Pharmaceutical and Biochemical Applications

Customer	Country	Application	Membrane surface (m^2)	Start-up year
Merck, Sharp & Dohme	France	Vaccine manufacturing	25	1979
*	Scandinavia	*	40	1980
*	Scandinavia	*	40	1981
*	Denmark	Enzyme processing	10	1981
*	UK	Pilot	3	1981
*	Asia	Enzyme processing	10	1981

* Denotes confidential.

CASE 11 ▪ General Concepts

INTRODUCTION

During Spring of 1977, Mr. William P. Edwards, Director of Corporate Marketing Communications of General Concepts, was conducting a review of his company's approach to international advertising. During the last four years, the European subsidiaries had become more independent in their approach to advertising causing General Concepts to present a sometimes different image to its worldwide clientele. It was up to Mr. Edwards to choose from several possible alternatives a workable structure for General Concepts' international advertising keeping in mind General Concepts' corporate goals and the realities of the marketplace.

COMPANY HISTORY

General Concepts was incorporated in 1966 as a manufacturer of small and medium sized general purpose digital computers. The company grew very quickly from sales of 2 million dollars in 1969 to sales of over 180 million dollars for fiscal year 1976 (see Exhibits 1 and 2) for financial summaries. At the same time, the company expanded its product line to include peripheral computer equipment, software and software services, and maintenance and training services for its clients.

Traditionally, the electronic data processing industry had been characterized by a rapid tech-nological progress and price reductions. Some of the company's competitors, such as Digital Equipment Corporation, were long established companies with substantially greater resources than General Concepts. There were, however, also a number of competitors smaller than General Concepts. Since small and medium scale general purpose digital computers were usually sold outright rather than leased, manufacturers were attracted by the relative ease of entry into this market segment compared to large computers where leasing terms required substantial financial resources on the part of the seller. Despite this tough competitive climate, and without benefit of exact industry statistics, General Concepts' management felt the company was one of the major manufacturers of small and medium scale general purpose digital computers for industrial and scientific applications. By the end of fiscal year 1976, a total of 33,900 units had been shipped to customers, compared with 3150 units just 4 years ago.

PRODUCT LINES

The company's product line consists of three basic segments: central processors, software, and peripheral equipment.

Central processors were marketed under the trademarks of *Orion, MicroOrion,* and *Satellite.* From a design point of view, all *Orion* line computers used the same central processor and pe-

This case was prepared by John Bleh, Research Assistant, under the direction of Jean-Pierre Jeannet, Professor of Marketing and International Business at Babson College, as a basis for class discussion rather than to illustrate either effective or ineffective handling of an administrative situation. All names and confidential data were disguised.

EXHIBIT 1 Financial Summary ($'s in 000's)

	1976	1975	1974	1973	1972	1971	1970	1969
Expenditures for property, plant, and equipment	15,277	7,344	6,458	6,674	3,897	770	456	102
Current assets	137,523	102,865	61,137	41,227	30,232	23,020	5,225	854
Current liabilities	50,337	25,721	26,595	14,152	7,600	2,677	1,175	523
Working capital	87,186	77,144	34,542	27,075	22,632	20,343	4,050	331
Stockholders' equity	114,787	92,224	48,809	37,245	27,080	21,446	4,377	429
Per share data:								
Outstanding shares (000)	9,839	8,787	8,386	8,421	7,980	6,976	5,946	4,841
Net income	$2.11	1.53	1.21	.81	.49	.22	.11	(.06)
Return on average assets	14.4%	13.6%	16.0%	15.4%				
Return on average equity	20.1%	19.1%	23.5%	20.8%				
Cumulative computers shipped	33,900	25,500	19,300	11,000	4,170	1,710	690	110
Employees at year end	6,190	3,610	3,650	1,910	840	480	240	90

Fiscal Year Ended (000's)

	1977 (estimate)	1976	1975	1974	1973	1972	1971	1970	1969
Net Sales	250,000	180,000	119,611	92,952	59,558	30,324	15,341	7,035	2,000
Costs and Expenses		141,104	94,659	73,910	47,491				
Income from Operations		37,649	24,952	19,042	12,067	3,897	1,561	433	(300)
Other Income, principally interest		2,832	1,368	889	1,145			200	32
Interest Expense		(406)	(365)	(437)	(141)				
Income before Income Taxes		40,075	25,955	19,494	13,071				
Provisions for Income Taxes		19,295	12,479	9,368	6,220				
Net Income		22,780	13,476	10,126	6,851	3,897	1,561	633	(268)

ripheral equipment, although performance and price of each model was different. All *Orion* computers were 16-bit binary computers using medium and large-scale integration, with four accumulators, two of which could be used as index registers. Parts, service, and additional equipment for old and new models were continuously kept available. *Orion* computers were mostly sold to Original Equipment Manufacturers (OEM's) to be added to machines or systems for controlling discrete assembly line operations, monitoring continuous production processes, testing, production planning, inventory management, and environmental surveillance.

EXHIBIT 2 Consolidated Balance Sheet

	September 25, 1976
ASSETS	
Current assets:	
Cash	$ 597,000
Short-term investments, at cost and accrued interest which approximates market	35,716,000
Accounts receivable, less allowance for doubtful accounts of $2,500,000 in 1977 and $2,200,000 in 1976	46,853,000
Inventories	54,009,000
Prepaid expenses	348,000
Total current assets	137,523,000
Property, plant and equipment, at cost	39,676,000
Less-accumulated depreciation	12,075,000
Total property, plant and equipment, net	27,601,000
	$165,124,000
LIABILITIES AND STOCKHOLDERS' EQUITY	
Current liabilities:	
Notes payable, including accrued interest	$ 5,466,000
Accounts payable	19,576,000
Accrued payroll and commissions	2,685,000
Federal, state and foreign income taxes	15,665,000
Deferred income taxes	4,515,000
Other accrued expenses	2,430,000
Total current liabilities	50,337,000
Stockholders' equity:	
Common stock, $.01 par value:	
Authorized—20,000,000 shares	
Issued—	
9,574,000 shares at September 24, 1977	
9,474,000 shares at September 25, 1976	95,000
Capital in excess of par value	58,245,000
Retained earnings	56,488,000
	114,828,000
Less: Treasury stock at cost (48,000 shares)	1,000
Note receivable from sale of stock	40,000
Deferred compensation	—
Total stockholders' equity	114,787,000
	$165,124,000

EXHIBIT 3 Chart of Computer Families

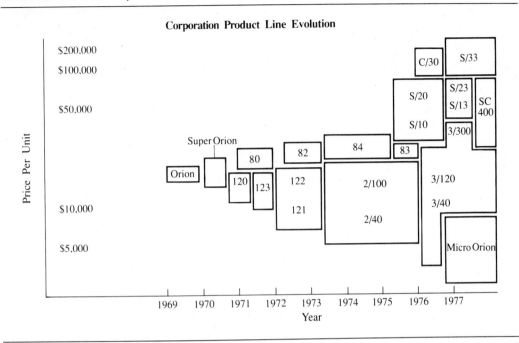

Corporation Product Line Evolution

Furthermore, *Orion* computers had been successfully employed in scientific and engineering problem solving, medical and scientific laboratory analysis, and education. Orion models were marketed under model number Orion 120/121/122, Orion 80/82, Orion 84, ORION 2, ORION 83, ORION 3/300 and SC/400 (see Exhibit 3).

As a more powerful extension of the Orion models, the *SATELLITE* line was developed in 1975. The three models S/10, S/20, and C/30 were aimed at large and complex applications in both general scientific and business operations. For this latter segment, the C/30 was equipped with a commercial instruction set, Report Generating Program, and a data file management system. Within the first 12 months of introduction, over 1000 SATELLITE systems had been installed at an average value of about $60,000 per system.

The *MicroORION,* introduced in 1976, was a family of microprocessors, but also available as a fully equipped computer with software and peripheral equipment.

General Concepts also marketed a number of peripheral equipment to satisfy the needs of clients who preferred to purchase systems as complete packages. Produced and sold were teletypewriters, paper tape readers and punches, cathode ray tube terminals, magnetic disc memories, magnetic tape equipment, line printers, plotters, card readers, communications controllers, multiplexors, and analog-to-digital as well as digital-to-analog converters.

In conjunction with its central processors, General Concepts developed and offered an extensive list of *software products* to be used with its ORION, SATELLITE, and microORION lines. Such software systems could be sought on a prepared basis, or, if contracted by the customer, developed to fit special needs.

Not yet on sale, but planned for introduction within the next few months, was a new family of small business computers, the SC/400 family. The product family was designed for business information processing for small to medium sized companies with sales ranging from $500,000 to $20 million. Also, the SC/400 computers could be used by departments or regional offices at large corporations as part of a distributed processing network. Operated on a transaction-by-transaction basis rather than batch process, and with as many as 9 stations operating simultaneously and independently, the system offered advantages not presently available in other small business systems. The SC/400 family, made up of three models, was priced from $30,000 to $90,000 per system.

SALES AND DISTRIBUTION

While manufacturers of large computer systems, such as IBM, sold their products directly to end users, small computers were generally sold through intermediaries. General Concepts was typical of such small computer manufacturers selling about 30 percent of its products directly to end users and 70 percent through 4 major types of intermediaries: Original Equipment Manufacturers (OEMs), systems integrators, industrial distributors, and retail stores or dealers (see Exhibit 4).

Direct sales were made by more than 420 sales engineers and 220 systems engineers operating from various sales offices in the United States and abroad. With the increase in direct sales activities, General Concepts developed a more specialized sales force such as for micro products, technical systems, or commercial systems. In some cases, sales representatives were targeted at special industry segments such as medicine, banking, or government.

OEMs had long been the most important segment for small computer manufacturers. These companies combined computer hardware (central processors, terminals, storage equipment, etc.) with other equipment to produce products such as electronic cash registers, body scanning equipment, microfiche developers, or numerically controlled machine tools to be sold under the OEM's own name. The small computer was actually "buried" inside the OEM's product. In many instances, the end user of the product was not aware of the supplier of the computer portion contained in the end product.

Systems Integrators (SI's) and Small Business Systems Suppliers formed the fastest growing segment in the distribution of small computers. Unlike OEM's, SI's bought their computers already assembled into a system from a single computer vendor, such as General Concepts. SI's added value to the product they resold in the form of application software designed to do a specific job: inventory control, order entry, accounting, etc. Many SI's were originally service bureaus that had accepted data processing work for clients who had insufficient in-house information processing capacity or capabilities. Some SI's also offered installation assistance, diagnostic help, and field maintenance. Since the demand for application software and support had exceeded the capabilities of both the traditional and minicomputer vendors, this segment could be expected to continue its rapid development and growth.

Industrial Distributors were an important distribution channel for all those computer products sold in large numbers approaching the sale of a commodity. Microprocessors (also called computer on a chip) or operator terminals were bought by users on that basis as components for their own products. The strength of the industrial distributor was to offer an immediate local supply of the components to the OEM.

Retail distributors formed the latest distribution segment. The "computer store" displayed small computer systems or microprocessors of several manufacturers for purchase by individuals. Originally frequented by hobbyists, computer stores increasingly served small businesses by assisting them in selecting computers on the basis of ease-of-use, pricing, and overall capability.

Service and maintenance of General Concepts' products was supported by about 800 field engineers, both to fulfill product warranty service and to service installed machines on a service contract basis.

EXHIBIT 4 Channels of Distribution

Product Families

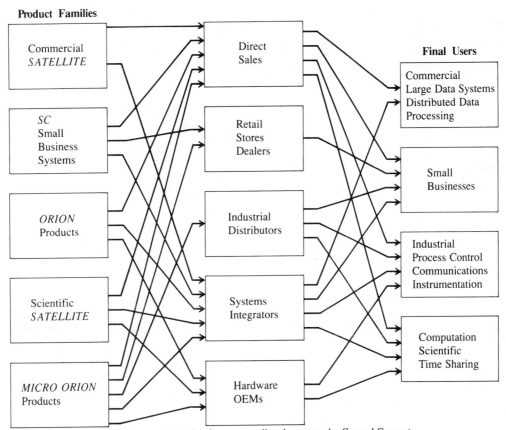

As can be seen in the graph above, while sale of computers directly to users by General Concept has increased substantially the systems integrators, distributors, and retail channels have become increasingly important. Many of the product and service developments described in this section should stimulate this rapid growth further in the year ahead.

GC'S ADVERTISING STRATEGY

GC's communication strategy was dominated by the existence of three primary customer groups: OEM's, Systems Houses, and Direct End-Users. GC's advertising was primarily directed at this latter group, the clients that bought GC equipment directly from the manufacturer and, to a smaller degree, from Systems Houses. These customers again could be divided into two main user groups: clients for business data service processing and clients who used GC products primarily for science, industrial computing, and process control of manufacturing operations. GC had to communicate its products' features to these prospective clients.

GC believed that there was a difference in target group for computers for business use vs. scientific or manufacturing control use. The main target group for computers with application for business data processing were corporate managers, particularly presidents, VP of finance, and chief operating officers, in addition to data processing executives. The important aspect was to justify a choice of acquiring little known GC computers instead of machines manufactured by larger main frame companies such as IBM, Honeywell, etc. GC's strategy was to reduce the risk as perceived by company executives for such a decision by using a message that was essentially non-technical. This approach was selected since non-technical executives, or generalists, had to make a technical, or data processing, decision with little knowledge of the hardware aspects of the computers to be chosen.

GC therefore occupied the position of a newcomer or outsider in the market for small computers. To compete against its better known competitors such as Digital Equipment Company or Hewlett-Packard, GC selected a communications strategy that depicted the company as unique, often bizarre, a company with a chip on its shoulder, using advertising copy that paid little attention to plain facts. Recognizing that technical or line managers paid greater attention to the products themselves whereas corporate officers were primarily risk averse, GC often chose testimonials of successful applications of its computers as a basis for its message development.

With respect to the scientific and industrial applications, corporate managers were involved to a lesser extent. Technical managers such as manufacturing managers, research directors, senior systems engineers, and scientists had a somewhat greater influence on the selection process. These technical managers were more likely to select a piece of equipment on its technical merit alone. As a result, technical or product oriented copy played a somewhat larger role for this market segment than for business data processing applications.

GC advertising in the United States was almost exclusively in print. Due to the fact that corporate management was the primary audience, about 75 percent of the advertising expenditures was concentrated on the *Wall Street Journal* and *Business Week*. Additional space was bought in other leading executive magazines such as *Forbes, Dun's,* and *Fortune*.

GENERAL CONCEPTS' INTERNATIONAL OPERATIONS

From its early existence, General Concepts had been selling abroad. Total international sales as a percent of total corporate sales grew from 23 percent in 1971 to 41 percent in 1976. This rapid growth brought about the formation of many subsidiaries, particularly in Europe, and the establishment of production units in South Korea and Hong Kong. General Concepts' international sales developed as follows for 1971–1977.

	Sales $	Percent of Consolidated Sales
1971	3.4M	23%
1972	7.8	26%
1973	17.2	29%
1974	25.1	27%
1975	42.8	39%
1976	72.3	41%
1977 (est.)	80.0	—

General Concepts had 17 wholly owned foreign sales subsidiaries and two production subsidiaries. Aside from European sales subsidiaries, General Concepts maintained subsidiaries in Canada, Australia, New Zealand, Brazil, Venezuela, and Israel. Japan was served through a licensing agreement with Nippon Computer Corp. since 1971. Whenever new products were introduced, they were made available to all the sales subsidiaries simultaneously, both in the U.S. and abroad.

GENERAL CONCEPTS' EUROPEAN OPERATIONS

General Concepts maintained 11 wholly owned sales subsidiaries in each of the following countries.

	Year Formed
United Kingdom	1971
Germany	1971
Spain	1971
France	1972
Netherlands	1972
Austria	1972
Italy	1973
Sweden	1974
Switzerland	1974
Denmark	1975
Belgium	1975

European sales had shown the same rapid development as sales in the domestic market or other international sales, quickly growing from about 1 million dollars or 7% of corporate sales in 1971 to about 50 million dollars or about 30 percent of corporate sales in 1976. In general, European area sales represented 70 percent of General Concepts' international sales. The bulk of these European sales was accounted for by the subsidiaries in the U.K., Germany, and Spain, in that order of importance.

As a result of General Concepts' rapid growth in Europe, several changes in its operational set-up had to be made. The most important move came in 1972 when General Concepts consolidated under the direction of Mr. Bailey, since succeeded by Mr. Blair, all its European subsidiaries into General Concepts Europe, Inc., with operations headquartered in Paris. Mr. Blair, Vice-President Europe for General Concepts, controlled the European subsidiaries through four area managers, each of whom had three to four subsidiaries assigned. A special-

ized group of staff personnel was maintained at the office of General Concepts Europe in Paris. (See Exhibit 5.)

The managers of the local subsidiaries maintained a considerable degree of autonomy over their operations inasmuch as each subsidiary was a separate profit center. In line with their P&L responsibility, subsidiary managers decided which products to carry in their product line, and how to budget for their marketing expenditures, including advertising.

INTERNATIONAL ADVERTISING AT GENERAL CONCEPTS THROUGH 1976

In its early stages of market development, all advertising for Europe was done in the United States by Henderson, Sloan, Williams, Inc., New York, one of the leading advertising agencies in the United States. Henderson also made all media purchases in New York. With the formation of General Concepts Europe in 1972, the newly appointed Vice President Europe had a communications manager reporting to himself, located in Paris. This communications manager also worked on PR assignments. Essentially, all creative work, however, was done by Henderson and then sent to Europe. No clearcut advertising policy existed, and Europe's largest subsidiary, General Concepts Limited in the U.K., had about 10 advertisements produced locally by a small technically oriented advertising agency.

In 1973, Mr. William P. Edwards was hired as Director, Corporate Communications. During his first trip to Paris that same year, Mr. Edwards hired Alain Ray to fill the recently vacated position of communications manager. Ray had come to General Concepts from Hewlett-Packard's European headquarters in Geneva, Switzerland.

While in Paris, Mr. Edwards made a number of changes in the reporting structure as well. He decided to centralize all advertising for Europe under Ray. Each major subsidiary hired its own marketing communications expert, called MCE,

EXHIBIT 5 Organization Chart

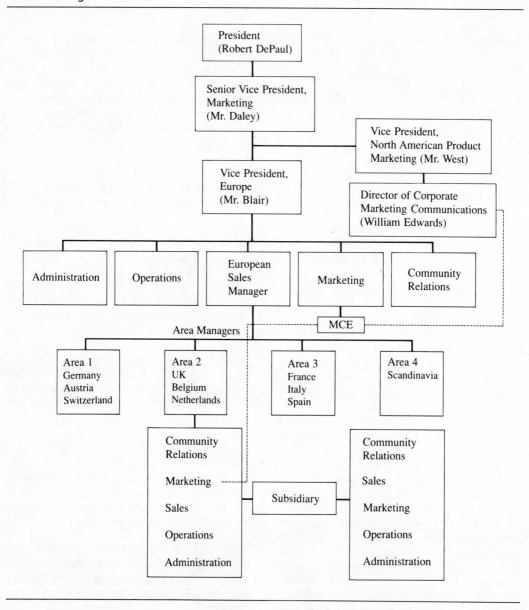

responsible to Ray in Paris who in turn reported directly to Mr. Edwards in General Concepts' headquarters in Connecticut.

Creative work continued to be done by Henderson in New York for the U.S. market. This material was sent to Ray in Paris who, together with his MCE's for the various countries, made suggestions as to how the advertising could be adapted to each individual market. All space purchased for print media continued to be handled in New York by Henderson, Sloan, Williams.

In 1973, Henderson introduced an independent agency "network" to better control the series of changes made in the various countries' advertising. These agencies, selected by Henderson in Germany, Spain, and the U.K., allowed the adaptations to be made with the same degree of continuity or oneness throughout all markets but with changes for each local market as needed. This additional measure of decentralization was felt necessary to allow local changes while continuing to project the same image in all European countries. So by 1974, Ray had about 7 MCE's reporting to himself, but continued to report to Mr. Edwards.

In 1975, two important events substantially affected General Concepts' approach to international advertising. First, Mr. Edwards left the company (to return about two years later to assume the same position). In the same year still, Henderson, Sloan, Williams, General Concepts' advertising agency for several years, was fired and the account was assigned to Nazzaro Associates, Inc., in Los Angeles, with Mr. E. Richard Steele as Account Executive. Since Nazzaro was not asked initially to handle European advertising, Ray at General Concepts Europe assumed greater control continuing to work with each local agency. Local subsidiaries were allowed to appoint and/or continue with their own local advertising agencies to either adapt U.S. creative from Nazzaro's or to create their own material. Only after the creation of the advertising did it have to be submitted to Ray in Paris. As a result, General Concepts' advertising began to assume a different look in each country with Nazzaro in Los Angeles essentially used

for General Concepts' North American business only. By 1976, General Concepts Europe had, in the eyes of the U.S. parent company, become sufficiently mature to handle its advertising more independently. As a result, Ray reported now directly to the new V.P. in Europe, Mr. Larry J. Bailey. Any adaptations made in Europe were only checked by Mr. William P. Edwards who had returned to General Concepts in 1977, with the title of Corporate Director of Marketing Communications.

PROBLEMS WITH GENERAL CONCEPTS' EUROPEAN ADVERTISING

Ever since its entry into the European market General Concepts had to face situations that at times differed significantly from its U.S. environment. General Concepts' approach of being unique, at times even bizarre, led to the creation of advertisements that in the eyes of General Concepts' European subsidiaries were ill suited for their markets and could not be adapted.

General Concepts had experienced three basic difficulties with the extension of all its ads to Europe. First, General Concepts in the U.S. used minority groups in its advertisements. European subsidiaries were opposed to using such pictures with minority members on the grounds that Europeans could not identify with black computer specialists since many companies had no blacks in such positions. Secondly, the direct naming of a competitor, a practice often used by General Concepts, was only accepted in the U.K. and against the law in most other countries. For all other European subsidiaries a different message had to be created. And finally, the sweepstake campaigns so successful in the U.S. were outlawed in many European countries, Germany among them, and were eventually only instituted in the U.K. and Sweden.

The difficulty of General Concepts' advertising situation was best expressed by three very successful U.S. ads that all were either substantially changed or not run at all in Europe. General Concept used one ad with "Hillbillies" capitalizing on the wide knowledge and positive general attitude towards such persons in the U.S. However, when General Concepts tried to run the same ad in Europe its subsidiaries objected since such "Hillbillies" did not exist as a separate identifiable group in Europe nor was there an appropriate concept to express it therefore completely losing the desirable message of the ad.

A similar reaction was found towards General Concepts' "Redneck" ad depicting General Concepts' computers as breaking the speed barrier without paying the price. Hence identification with the "Redneck" sheriff as a folk hero. But this image did not exist in Europe, and the ad would have lost its punch line. Furthermore, the Italian subsidiary objected since in Italy nobody wearing a uniform, either police, military or otherwise, could be depicted in advertising. And one ad, showing a picture of a man hanging by his thumbs to visualize the result of "One test of a computer company is the kind of support you get after the sale," was rejected by General Concepts' German subsidiary since the meaning of the ad conveyed a sense of terrorism in Germany. Another successful U.S. ad with the slogan "With some computer companies you can end up paying for more company than computer," showed a steak with a lot of fat indicating the overhead associated with General Concepts' bigger competitors. However, when translating the message for German customers, the meaning communicated by the picture turned out to be just the opposite one, since the steak with fat had a positive connotation to Germans. And finally, General Concepts had some problems with the ad "When your business expands and your computer can't, where does that leave you?" combined with the picture of a single hand holding a bag. In the U.K., the same meaning was expressed by the phrase "don't get left holding the baby" while in France the expression centered around "being in a basket of crabs."

In general, General Concepts' creative philosophy did not always translate very well since the U.S. idiom both in terms of copy and visual could not be extended abroad. These problems were most extreme with Germany, somewhat less with Italy and France, while both Scandinavia and particularly the U.K. offered greater opportunities for General Concepts' U.S. approach.

An additional problem was created by General Concepts' U.S. advertising emphasizing products only and therefore not developing any company image ads as requested by its subsidiaries. Since in many European countries General Concepts was not very well known, some subsidiaries, notably the Italian unit, were authorized to create special advertisements to improve their markets' awareness of General Concepts as a small computer manufacturer. In 1976, Nazzaro had recommended that each area develop testimonial ads for its area. That program was ongoing and apparently successful.

ALTERNATIVES TO GENERAL CONCEPTS' APPROACH TO ADVERTISING IN EUROPE

Upon his return to General Concepts, Mr. Edwards and Nazzaro felt that General Concepts' advertising in Europe had to be revised to follow general corporate philosophy and present a uniform image to all customers, both domestic and foreign. Over the last two years, General Concepts' advertising in the various European countries had become fragmented and did not offer the uniform image it once had.

General Concepts aimed at presenting a unified look to all its customers all over the world, and this goal was presently not achieved in Europe. This desire for a unified look had already resulted in a corporate identity program to cover the corporate mark, stationery, business cards, printed sales promotion material, personal identifications, product identification, and signage. The program was put forward in a manual with a cover letter written by Mr. dePaul, General Concepts' President (see Exhibit 6). The program did not pertain to the company's worldwide advertising effort. Furthermore, Mr. Edwards felt he lacked leverage with Ray reporting to Blair to exercise any kind of control or influence over Europe's advertising. While the mechanics of the advertising side were well taken care of, General Concepts Europe depended largely on these small local agencies for creative input as well as for marketing expertise.

In Mr. Edwards' view, leverage, mechanics, creative input, and marketing expertise combined with people relationships among different ad agencies and subsidiaries substantially affected productivity and advertising quality. Since the subsidiaries had selected their own agencies, people relationships were likely to be good. However, Mr. Edwards believed that without additional control he could not significantly influence the European subsidiaries' advertising approach. In his words, "control does not necessarily mean direct control. It means a method to project a better understanding of what General Concepts wants in all of its communication endeavors."

As he approached the decision, Mr. Edwards believed he had four basic alternatives to improve General Concepts' present set-up in Europe: (a) assign authority to Nazzaro Associates for both domestic and European advertising; (b) have General Concepts create a "network" of European different advertising agencies selected by Mr. Edwards for better control and assigned to each subsidiary; (c) keep present European agencies but coordinate their efforts through General Concepts in Southern California; and finally (d) assign the creative strategy and execution of the international advertising program to a large New York agency with its own network of international affiliates in place.

At about the same time as Mr. Edwards was reviewing his alternatives in Europe, Nazzaro Associates also became dissatisfied with General Concepts' setup and proposed its own solution to the problem. Nazzaro wanted the responsibility to create advertising for General Concepts' domestic and international business

---

EXHIBIT 6

A CORPORATE IDENTITY PROGRAM
FOR GENERAL CONCEPTS CORPORATION

General Concepts is one of the world's fastest growing organizations, in one of the fastest growing industries.

As we continue to expand worldwide, it is essential that the company maintain a clear and consistent visual identity with customers, employees, and other important audiences.

The enclosed is an interim guideline that covers the major aspects of General Concepts' corporate identity program.

The elements of the program reflect the "face" of the company—progressive, experimental, innovative, fast moving.

Through these elements, we hope to create a thread of graphic continuity woven into our worldwide corporate identity program in all areas whether it be brochure, sending a bill, plus all of the numerous other ways you influence and communicate with our public.

I urge everyone to use this manual as the standard for corporate identity.

Robert DePaul
President

---

which meant that it was Nazzaro who supplied the creative work for all General Concepts ads. However, Nazzaro did not have any foreign affiliates to carry out this proposal on its own. To compensate for this lack of foreign contacts, Mr. E. Richard Steele proposed that Nazzaro affiliate with Ed Hopkins Europe, a large and well known international advertising agency headquartered in New York, who would supply the foreign expertise to Nazzaro. Ed Hopkins had its European headquarters in Paris and subsidiaries in European countries where General Concepts' own subsidiaries were located. Under Mr. Steele's plan, Nazzaro would supply drafts of all creative work to Ed Hopkins in Paris. Ed Hopkins' people would review the potential need for changes by contacting their own locally affiliated agencies who would discuss each proposed advertisement with General Concepts' local MCE's. The reviewed proposals would then be returned to Nazzaro with any changes indicated. Proposed concept changes would also be added. The final result would be advertising concepts and copy that could be adopted by all subsidiaries with only local translation done under the supervision of the local Ed Hopkins affiliate. Advertising media space would be purchased by Ed Hopkins Europe under coordination with local subsidiaries.

Of course, as an alternative General Concepts could create its own network of affiliated advertising agencies. Such a network would be coordinated through General Concepts Europe in Paris. General Concepts would select in each country an appropriate agency who would be assigned to work with its local subsidiary. Nazzaro creative work would be circulated to each advertising agency who would discuss the proposal with its assigned General Concepts subsidiary and review the creative necessary changes. These comments would be sent to John Clarke, (who reported to Ray) at General Concepts Europe who in turn would confer with Richard Steele at Nazzaro. Mr. Edwards believed it would not be easy to select good agencies in each country. At the present time, he had no particular agencies in mind. Besides, Nazzaro had worked with the present network and found

it wholly lacking. In production requirements alone (film screens for publication, etc.) the problems were monumental when you added the language barrier and the constant need to convert to metric measures.

A third alternative for Mr. Edwards was to work with those agencies already selected by each subsidiary but to attempt to control their creative output. He felt that if each agency were required to execute its creative work locally under the guidance of General Concepts' general advertising directives, and if each agency were required to submit all creative to General Concepts Southern California office for approval, some measure of common approach to General Concepts' image in Europe could be achieved. In fact, it would be up to Mr. Edwards and his office to coordinate Nazzaro creative strategy with the proposals from Europe to provide for the common image desired by General Concepts.

A fourth alternative available to Mr. Edwards was the selection of a large New York based advertising agency with good connections in Europe through either affiliates or subsidiaries. This agency would be given authority to execute General Concepts' advertising strategy outside the U.S. based upon Nazzaro's initial creative proposals. This move meant to revert to the pre-1974/75 policy. While no serious discussions had taken place, Mr. Edwards thought that Marsteller might be a possibility to take charge under this alternative.

POTENTIAL REACTION BY AFFECTED PARTIES

In Mr. Edwards' view, all four alternative proposals reflected a considerable improvement over status quo. The adaptation of any of the alternatives would present General Concepts with additional leverage over the execution of its advertising in Europe, improve the creative input, and add some additional marketing expertise for the subsidiaries. While all four alternatives increased General Concepts' control over its European advertising, the four proposals of course did so to varying degrees, with Nazzaro's alternative or the big New York agency approach to be favored over the other alternatives.

An important consideration was also the views and possible reaction among General Concepts' European subsidiaries. Mr. Edwards knew that personal chemistry played a very important role in advertising and that the imposition of any agency selection in General Concepts' local subsidiaries might create tensions along that way. If the four proposals were presented to the subsidiaries for a free vote, he was convinced that the subsidiaries would prefer to continue to work with their own agencies over any other choice.

Mr. Edwards knew it was up to him to determine the direction of General Concepts' advertising approach in Europe. With present European measured media expenditures for 1977 at $500,000 and European budget expenditures for the next fiscal year of about $700,000, he was determined to reach a decision that could be acceptable to most parties concerned.

CASE 12 ▪ Puritan-Bennett Corporation Boston Division

As he stepped into the elevator at the Skyline Hotel in London, John Sweeney, Vice President and General Manager of the Boston Division of Puritan-Bennett Corporation, reflected on his problems and frustrations with the British market. He had been with Ray Oglethorpe, Vice President for Sales and Marketing, and Bob Taylor, Vice President for International Operations, since early morning. It was a typical day for London in late November of 1983. They had been trying to determine the best distribution for Puritan-Bennett medical products in Europe for next year. John Sweeney suspected that some parent company current channels did not meet Division needs.

Earlier that day they had met with Adamson and Carr Ltd., Puritan-Bennett's British distributor, to discuss plans and forecasts for Division and corporate product lines. The three vice presidents had then reviewed the situation in the U.K. and the rest of Europe.

PURITAN-BENNETT CORPORATION

Puritan-Bennett Corporation was founded in 1913 as the Puritan Company, a welding supply manufacturer and distributor. The company emphasized the manufacture and supply of medical gas and equipment. It had pioneered development of oxygen as a medicinal agent. The company manufactured and sold three product lines: medical, aviation, and industrial, with medical products accounting for the largest percentage of sales (Exhibit 1).

In 1956, acquisition of the Bennett Company accelerated corporate growth in the United States and abroad. The company, now known as Puritan-Bennett, had sales offices worldwide for medical, aviation, and industrial product lines. Expansion continued in the late 1970's and early 1980's through acquisition and research and development. In 1978 the medical line was extended by purchase of the Foregger Company, a manufacturer of operating room equipment. The Boston Division was acquired in 1981 (Exhibit 2).

DEVELOPMENT OF THE BOSTON DIVISION

In 1978, John Sweeney acquired the assets of a bankrupt company and started LSE Corporation. The firm initially employed a total of four people, including Sweeney. LSE had a small manufacturing facility. Included in the purchase was a line of screening spirometers in process of development. The company specialized in developing and selling a full line of spirometers, used in doctors' offices and industrial clinics as screening devices to diagnose lung dysfunction (Exhibit 3). Until this time most spirometry had been done in hospitals. While the test took only a few minutes of a patient's time, evaluation of test results was time-consuming (about 30 minutes) and cumbersome. When a physician suspected a patient might be suffering from COPD (Chronic Obstructive Pulmonary Disease), he or

This case was prepared by Susan Nye under the direction of Visiting Professor Jean-Pierre Jeannet as a basis for class discussion rather than to illustrate either effective or ineffective handling of an administrative situation. Copyright 1984 by IMEDE (International Management Development Institute), Lausanne, Switzerland. Reproduced by permission.

EXHIBIT 1 Five-Year Financial Summary, Corporate and Subsidiaries

(All dollar amounts in thousands, except common share data and number of employees)	1983	1982	1981	1980	1979
Operating Results					
Net Sales					
Bennett Division	$ 48,525	$ 47,505	$ 53,382	$ 47,464	$ 40,817
Puritan Division	37,944	35,859	33,889	29,431	26,903
Boston Division	5,614	5,208	1,282	—	—
Total Medical	92,083	88,572	88,553	76,895	67,720
Aviation Division	12,772	14,161	18,437	17,863	14,764
Industrial Division	4,890	4,424	5,562	5,361	5,262
Total Net Sales	109,745	107,157	112,552	100,119	87,746
Gross Profit	45,551	40,757	47,748	38,910	34,289
Percent of Sales	41.5%	38.0%	42.4%	38.9%	39.1%
Marketing, Research & Administrative Expense	41,348	40,877	37,401	30,517	26,425
Operating Profit (Loss)	4,203	(120)	10,347	8,393	7,864
Other Income (Expense)	(407)	(6,551)	540	20	(81)
Income (Loss) Before Income Taxes	3,796	(6,671)	10,887	8,413	7,783
Percent of Sales	3.4%	—	9.7%	8.4%	8.9%
Provision for (Benefit from) Income Taxes	1,220	(4,412)	4,335	3,628	3,118
Effective Tax Rate	32.1%	(66.1)%	39.8%	43.1%	40.1%
Net Income (Loss)	2,576	(2,259)	6,552	4,785	4,665
Percent of Sales	2.3%	—	5.8%	4.8%	5.3%
Financial Data					
Net Working Capital	$ 39,126	$ 36,037	$ 39,079	$ 37,789	$ 34,761
Current Ratio	2.5	3.3	3.9	4.6	4.3
Long-Term Debt	9,131	6,089	7,599	7,327	8,813
Debt/Equity Ratio	13.0%	9.4%	10.9%	11.5%	14.3%
Stockholders' Equity	60,922	58,622	61,932	56,464	52,805
Return on Average Stockholders' Equity	4.3%	—	11.1%	8.8%	9.1%
Common Share Data					
Earnings (Loss)	$ .87	$ (.78)	$ 2.27	$ 1.66	$ 1.62
Dividends Declared	.40	.40	.40	.40	.40
Net Book Value	20.62	20.28	21.45	19.62	18.37
Average Number of Shares Outstanding	2,947,652	2,889,444	2,883,588	2,876,471	2,873,084
Other Data					
Depreciation and Amortization	$ 4,677	$ 4,865	$ 4,672	$ 4,197	$ 4,305
Capital Expenditures	7,287	6,415	7,057	3,933	4,851
Plant and Equipment, Net	30,710	27,996	28,666	26,682	27,087
Total Assets	99,894	83,204	86,241	77,015	74,479
Number of Employees	1,893	1,869	2,080	1,978	1,837

EXHIBIT 2 Corporate Organization Chart

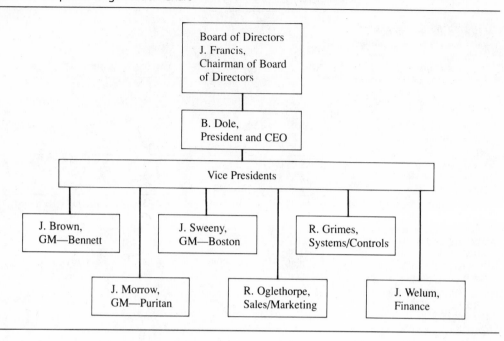

she would recommend the patient be tested at a hospital.

A pioneer in the field, LSE offered within three years a broad range of microprocessing spirometers which allowed a doctor or nurse to evaluate test results in only five minutes. Improvements in technology led to a competitive price. In 1979 the top-of-the-line spirometer sold for $7,000 in the U.S., and in 1981 for $4,500. John Sweeney's small company had grown to $3 million in sales and to an approximate 30 percent market share in the U.S.

Puritan-Bennett acquired LSE Corporation in 1981 as part of an expansion program to increase the number of product lines and to upgrade the level of its microprocessing technology. An innovator in microprocessing spirometers, LSE met the parent company's need. Shortly after the merger, the re-named Boston Division joined another Puritan-Bennett acquisition, a firm manufacturing noninvasive blood pressure monitors. Noninvasive blood pressure monitors measured blood pressure during sur-

gery, during stress testing, and for chronically or critically ill patients (Exhibit 4). The newly organized Boston Division developed, coordinated, and manufactured spirometers and monitoring devices. Sales and responsibilities were divided between the Division, which sold to individual physicians, and the company, which sold to hospitals and clinics. The Boston Division manufactured all spirometers in-house. Some monitoring devices were assembled from a combination of in-house product parts and purchased components. Others were imported through an arrangement with a Finnish company.

The Boston Division had recently moved to a larger manufacturing and sales facility in Wilmington, Massachusetts. The Division employed seventy people to manufacture and sell spirometers and other Division products. Three engineers researched and developed innovative pulmonary diagnostic and monitoring products.

The Boston Division was most closely aligned with the Bennett Division, one of several

EXHIBIT 3 PS600 Spirometer

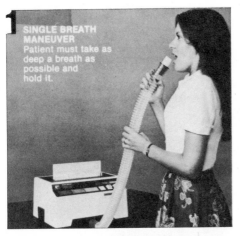

1 SINGLE BREATH MANEUVER Patient must take as deep a breath as possible and hold it.

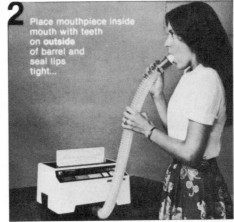

2 Place mouthpiece inside mouth with teeth on **outside** of barrel and seal lips tight...

3 Exhale the air as **force-fully** as possible from the beginning and keep exhaling until all the air is emptied out...

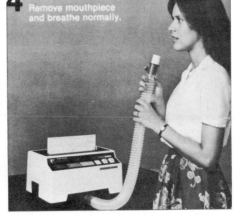

4 Remove mouthpiece and breathe normally.

MVV MANEUVER (Page 21 in Manual)

CAUTION: The MVV (Maximum Breathing Capacity) is a breathing stress test and should not be performed on patients with heart problems unless supervised by a physician.

1. Subject should take a deep breath before placing mouthpiece inside mouth with teeth on outside of barrel and lips sealed tight.

2. Instruct the subject to then breathe out and in as **rapidly** and **deeply** as possible.

3. Encourage the subject to continue to breathe in and out for a minimum of 10-12 seconds before telling them to stop.

FEF$_{25-75}$

This is the Forced Expiratory Flow during the middle 50% of the FVC curve.**

FEF$_{200-1200}$

This is the Forced Expiratory Flow between 0.2 liters and 1.2 liters.**

**If desired, this parameter may be calculated using the technique described on page 19 of the VS400 Operating Manual.

 PURITAN-BENNETT CORPORATION

PURITAN-BENNETT CORPORATION OF MASSACHUSETTS
BOSTON DIVISION
265 BALLARDVALE STREET, WILMINGTON, MA 01887
(617) 657-8650 (800) 225-5344 TELEX 94-9467

EXHIBIT 4 D4000 Noninvasive Blood Pressure Monitor

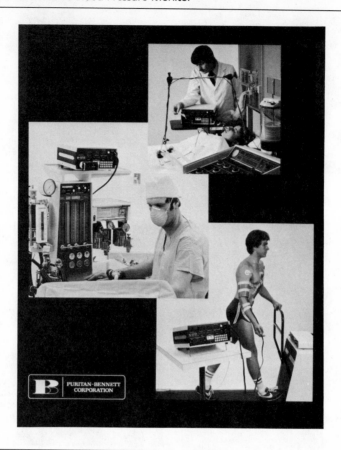

Puritan-Bennett units. The Bennett Division sold life supporting medical equipment, primarily ventilators, to hospitals. Ventilators assumed respiratory function, either short term for patients under anesthesia in the recovery room or in intensive care, or long term for terminally ill patients.

The Bennett Division had succeeded with its newest product, the 7200 Microprocesser Ventilator, which had sold well in the U.S. since introduction in 1983. Benefits of the new product included increased breathing ease for the patient, better operator control over ventilatory parameters, and lower operating costs. Products were competitively priced in the U.S. at $10,000 to $12,000 (Exhibit 5).

BACKGROUND ON SPIROMETRY

Spirometers were used to measure lung capacity and to diagnose lung dysfunctions. Lung dysfunctions could be categorized as restrictive, reducing volume (vital lung capacity), or obstructive, reducing flow through the airways, or a combination of both.

Spirometers were used in early diagnosis of chronic obstructive pulmonary disease (COPD), the sixth leading cause of death in the United States in 1980. Grouped under COPD were bronchitis, asthma, and emphysema. Leading causes of COPD were smoking, air pollution, occupational pollution, infection, heredity, aging, and allergies.

EXHIBIT 5 7200 Microprocessor Ventilator

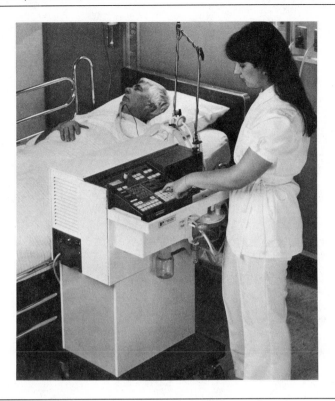

As depicted in Exhibit 6, air initially enters the body through the nose and mouth, then passes through the pharynx, larynx, trachea, bronchi, and bronchioles. At the chest cavity the trachea branches into two bronchi. Each bronchus subdivides forming tiny tubes called bronchioles which open into small air sacks called alveoli. The alveoli form clusters around the bronchioles and unite into lobes. Each alveolus contains a mesh-like network of capillaries, or tiny blood cells. The lungs carry oxygen to the body by the air passage to the thin walls of the alveoli. Blood then absorbs the oxygen. The average office worker inhales 400 cubic feet of air each day, and the body absorbs an average of 20 cubic feet of oxygen.

Spirometer manufacturers had benefited in 1979 when U.S. health officials mandated spi-rometry for certain high risk groups. High risk groups included textile industry employees exposed to cotton dust, miners susceptible to black lung, and asbestos industry employees. A voluntary medical group had determined standards for spirometry, and government regulations later incorporated these standards. Some spirometer manufacturers were temporarily forced out of the market when their products failed to meet the new standards.

BOSTON DIVISION SPIROMETRY PRODUCT LINE

Puritan-Bennett spirometers analyzed volume displacement and rate of airflow. The VS400 and the PS600 measured the volume of air inspired

EXHIBIT 6 The Respiratory System

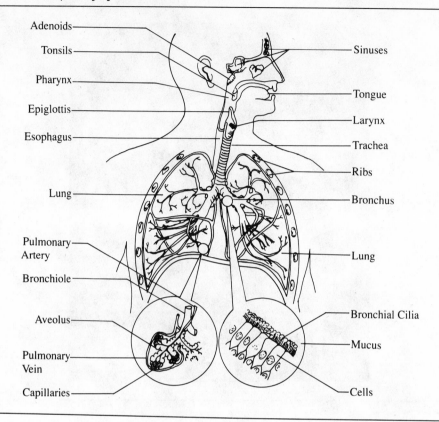

Adenoids
Tonsils
Pharynx
Epiglottis
Esophagus
Lung
Pulmonary Artery
Bronchiole
Aveolus
Pulmonary Vein
Capillaries

Sinuses
Tongue
Larynx
Trachea
Ribs
Bronchus
Lung
Bronchial Cilia
Mucus
Cells

and expired and calculated flow. The DS705 and the ES800 measured the flow of air expired and calculated volume based on expiration speed and time (Exhibit 7). To perform the test a patient inhaled deeply and exhaled forcefully into a tube connected to the spirometer. The test was repeated three times.

The VS400 and the PS600 produced tracings of individual single breaths and maximum voluntary ventilation (MVV). While the VS400 still required hand calculations of pulmonary function parameters, the more advanced PS600 included a microprocessor to compute test results automatically. This innovation was considered key to the Division's continued growth. The Boston Division was also working on an Apple

software package allowing a physician to automate storage and retrieval of patient records on an Apple personal computer.

MONITORING PRODUCT LINE

Puritan-Bennett's Boston Division also manufactured monitors. Noninvasive blood pressure monitors were the only line of monitors produced in-house. Other monitors were imported from Europe for sale throughout the Western Hemisphere.

Blood pressure monitors measured the pressure blood exerted on arteries throughout the body. Blood pressure level depended on the rate

EXHIBIT 7 Spirometers

of heart contraction, the amount of blood in the circulatory system, and the elasticity of arteries. Blood pressure was continuously monitored during surgery. Patients with chronic diseases and those convalescing from acute diseases also required monitoring. Serious illness and surgery could alter blood pressure and thus needed to be controlled. A regular part of health checks, blood pressure screenings were particularly important for older people because blood pressure may rise with age.

Blood pressure was measured by pumping air into a bag or cuff fastened around the arm. Inflation continued until blood flow stopped. This measure, called systolic pressure, represented blood pressure when the heart contracted. Pressure when the heart relaxed between beats was called diastolic pressure.

The Puritan-Bennett D4000 and D4001 monitors could be used anywhere in a hospital and provided automatic inflation and deflation. The devices employed a patented infrasonde technique to monitor blood pressure continuously. Digital display of the blood pressure reading facilitated use by physicians or nurses. The product was designed for continuous monitoring rather than one-time screening.

THE U.S. MARKET FOR SPIROMETERS

The Boston Division, particularly strong in the U.S., enjoyed a 25 percent market share. Spirometer sales had reached $4 million in 1983 and were expected to account for 50 percent of Boston Division sales in 1984. There were 467,000

practicing physicians in the U.S. Spirometers were used in doctors' offices, hospitals, and clinics. Boston Division strength lay in the doctors' office segment which included more than 100,000 physicians. The U.S. medical profession had begun to emphasize preventive health care, and John Sweeney believed that approximately 38 percent of practicing physicians could benefit from owning a spirometer. He estimated that only 30 percent of respiratory specialists or general practitioners currently employed spirometers in office. Spirometers were Puritan-Bennett's only medical product marketed to physicians' offices.

Physicians used spirometers primarily as a screening device. Lung screening was common in a variety of medical situations in the U.S. Hospital admissions, pre-operative checks, and annual checkups for senior citizens and smokers required lung screening as a part of regular test procedure. Many industries such as asbestos and mining regularly screened employees for lung dysfunction due to inhalation of dust or chemicals.

Most U.S. hospitals maintained respiratory therapy departments and pulmonary laboratories. Respiratory therapy departments treated lung problems early and monitored changes in patient progress during therapy. The spirometer was used for a five minute simple screening test of patients undergoing therapy before and after medication. The pulmonary laboratory evaluated chronically ill patients. Large pulmonary laboratory equipment cost from $50,000 to $75,000. Tests using such equipment were more extensive than those using spirometers and took longer to perform. The spirometer quickly screened large numbers of people, while the pulmonary laboratory equipment was used to evaluate treatment of patients identified as already having a lung dysfunction.

PURITAN-BENNETT CORPORATE MARKETING EFFORT IN THE U.S.

Puritan-Bennett employed 55 salespersons to sell medical products to all operating divisions of a hospital. This salesforce accounted for approximately $80 million in sales in 1983. Until 1983 Puritan-Bennett had sold through distributors in the U.S. market, with a trained salesforce giving missionary support for all product lines. In early 1983 Puritan-Bennett began to sell equipment directly to hospitals. The decision to develop a direct salesforce was based on two criteria. First, many distributors were not expanding sales volume according to company expectations. Second, the company expansion program was creating conflict. As Puritan-Bennett added new products to its line, it found that some dealers already carried similar competitive products. Furthermore, Puritan-Bennett's new technology for its 7200 microprocessing ventilator required extensive training for a highly technical sale. As the company continued to expand, these problems were expected to continue. Puritan-Bennett also used the cost savings on distribution margins to lower its prices. Selling costs now averaged 20 percent of sales.

BOSTON DIVISION U.S. MARKETING EFFORTS

Three segments composed Division spirometry sales: hospitals accounting for 20 percent of total volume, industry with 20 percent, and physicians with 60 percent. Hospital sales were made by Puritan-Bennett's corporate salesforce. The Boston Division had sole responsibility for marketing spirometers to private physicians and industrial users through 100 dealers. Most Division volume came from the top 40 percent of these dealers. Dealers ranged from highly specialized ones to others carrying a broad line of medical equipment, accessories, and disposables. The best distributors were specialized either by area of medical expertise, such as cardiac or respiratory, or by end-user, such as hospitals or physicians' offices. Dealers were supported by a 10 person missionary salesforce reporting to the Division office in Wilmington, MA. Three area managers representing East, Central, and West regions reported to sales manager Bob Glinski. The missionary salesforce was divided among the three regions. Bob Conley, one of the original employees at LSE, acted as marketing manager. Sales were strong in regions of the U.S. where environmental or industrial influences created respiratory problems.

John Sweeney liked the combination of dealers and support sales staff and felt they had been key to Division success in the U.S., particularly in the physician segment.

The physician's office spirometry market was still developing. The selling approach was less technical but required that the salesperson be able to stimulate primary demand by identifying potential users and key customers and by offering creative financial plans. Key customers were doctors or researchers who, through speeches and/or publications, were influential within their professions.

Monitor equipment sales were expected to grow to 50 percent of Division sales. Noninvasive blood pressure monitors were to account for one third of this volume. Noninvasive blood pressure monitors represented a rapidly growing market and required a highly technical sale. Unlike spirometers, monitors did not represent a new concept in medicine, but successful selling required a thorough technical understanding of the product. These products were sold directly to hospital users. John Sweeney estimated market share worldwide at 5 percent.

The U.S. represented about 50 percent of the world market for spirometers. Major industrial nations composed the remaining 50 percent. Sweeney estimated the spirometry market in Europe at $25 million, including hospital sales, which accounted for 80 percent of the spirometry market abroad.

Puritan-Bennett and the Boston Division sold medical products through dealers at 25 percent off list price. Division gross margin was 55 percent, with selling costs averaging 20 percent of sales.

BOSTON DIVISION INTERNATIONAL MARKETING EFFORT

John Sweeney believed that to survive in today's medical equipment industry a company must have an international sales base. The bankrupt company Sweeney acquired in 1978 had sold nearly $1 million in spirometers in Europe in 1977. Reorganization of that company into LSE Corporation had left ill feelings with its German distributor, prompting Sweeney to seek a new distribution network. In 1979 he visited trade shows and signed on new distributors.

In spite of John Sweeney's efforts, initial attempts at European sales for LSE were not successful. Sweeney feared the small size of his organization was a major drawback in dealing with European distributors. LSE merged with Puritan-Bennett in 1981, partially in the hope that as part of a larger company the new division would gain greater leverage with distributors. Continual spirometer improvements had been made, and Sweeney was convinced that spirometers would sell in the European market if distributors paid more attention to his products. Special sourcing was required, however, to overcome limitations caused by the relative strength of the U.S. dollar versus other currencies.

Marketing spirometers in Europe required changing electrical wires and switches and programming for "normal" reference values by country. These changes had already been made for the U.K., and the Division was working on changes for other countries as well.

Whereas in Europe pulmonary laboratories existed for treatment of chronically ill patients, there were no respiratory therapy departments. Furthermore, little screening occurred for hospital admission and preparation for operations. Screening in physician offices was developing at a slower rate than in the U.S. John Sweeney

believed this market had potential. Rising cost of hospital care worldwide evoked interest in products for use in doctor's office or at home. European and Japanese participants at conventions of the American Lung Association, as well as other pulmonary specialists, voiced growing interest in nonhospital screening and treatment techniques.

PURITAN-BENNETT INTERNATIONAL SALES ORGANIZATION

Following the merger, the Boston Division depended upon Puritan-Bennett's international sales division for overseas sales.

The International Division channeled all sales through independent distributors. International sales reached $20 million in 1983. The vice president of international sales, Bob Taylor, was based at the head office in Kansas City. International operations were divided into three geographical areas. Les Fuller was area manager for Europe and the Middle East. The other divisions were Latin America, smallest of the three in terms of sales, and the Far East, largest in sales but employing fewer people than the European division.

There were three European area sales representatives. One representative based in Germany covered German speaking countries, including Germany, Austria, and Switzerland, as well as Eastern Europe. Another representative based in France covered France, Italy, Belgium, and Spain. A third representative in the U.K. covered the U.K. and Scandinavia. A fourth representative responded for the Middle East.

Puritan-Bennett had entered Europe before 1970 on an export basis. In the mid-1970's, the company had expanded its international commitment by forming a service organization in England. Puritan-Bennett's International Division had sold only ventilators, marketing directly to hospitals. Hospital doctors and nurses were the key decision makers in the purchase decision.

Puritan-Bennett U.K. Limited was the company's only wholly owned sales and distribution subsidiary. Based in Chichester, England, it imported and sold medical equipment to European distributors and performed technical service for distributors. Contact with end users was restricted to key customers or new product introductions. The U.K. operation employed 10 people.

In Europe, Puritan-Bennett's larger distributors carried a full line of medical equipment and supplies. Smaller distributors concentrated on a specific medical expertise. It was very difficult to find distributors which fit the entire product line but were not already carrying a competitor's product.

Spirometers were sold to Puritan-Bennett U.K. Ltd. at 25 percent off U.S. list price. Duty and freight added 11 percent to landed costs. Puritan-Bennett U.K. Ltd. used a markup of 20 percent. Average transportation costs of 10 percent within the European marketplace were paid by the final distributor. The local distributor expected a 50 percent gross margin.

Stiff price competition threatened any U.S. company operating in Europe. The strong U.S. dollar, as well as transportation and tariff costs, made price competition difficult. Puritan-Bennett relied on technical superiority of its products. Continued strength of the U.S. dollar intensified the price differential between U.S. and European or Japanese products.

EXPERIENCE IN THE U.K.

Puritan-Bennett's U.K. distributor for 10 years, Adamson and Carr was owned by a larger firm which manufactured cardiac care equipment. Adamson and Carr distributed products not only for its parent company but also for other medical equipment manufacturers. Following their visit earlier this day, Messrs. Sweeney, Taylor, and Oglethorpe worried about low 1984 forecasts for ventilators, projected by A&C at five to eight units. When pressured, A&C revised to 10 to 20 units, still far below the estimate of 50 to 100 units predicted for Germany by Puritan-Bennett's German distributor. John Sweeney believed that sales in the U.K. should be similar to those in Germany. Touring the A&C plant,

Sweeney noticed what appeared to be inventory build-up of A&C parent company products. Parent company cardiac care equipment had an average price of $3,000 to $12,000.

With A&C, Puritan-Bennett benefited from an installed sales base. Sales management, sales training, order processing, accounting, and inventory management adequately met the needs of both Puritan-Bennett and A&C's parent.

The distributor employed twelve salespeople who had established key contacts at hospitals with recovery rooms (RR), intensive care units (ICU), and critical care units (CCU), all important in marketing A&C cardiac care line. These contacts provided access to anesthesiology departments which were major users of monitoring and support equipment.

A&C had recently sold few noninvasive blood pressure monitors or spirometers and hesitated to expand that part of its product line. Prior to this time, A&C had carried Vitalograph spirometers. Vitalograph, a major European competitor of Puritan-Bennett, had now decided to sell direct in the U.K.

Under socialized medicine the government provided almost all health care. This meant that most testing and screening, including spirometry, was done in hospitals.

Previously the International Division had enjoyed good sales results with Bennett ventilators in the U.K. Price increases and greater sophistication lowered late generation sales. The International Division had experienced similar distribution problems in other European countries. Ventilators sold well in the Middle East, Japan, and Germany. Sales in Spain were building, and sales in Italy held promise.

EXPERIENCE IN GERMANY

Strong ventilator sales in Germany had reached $3 million, 10 percent of U.S. sales. Puritan-Bennett Corporation used Carl A. Hoyer G.m.b.H. as its independent distributor. The International Division had enjoyed a good relationship with Hoyer for many years. Hoyer specialized in ventilation and respiratory products. Hoyer distributed for several companies, and

Puritan-Bennett ventilator sales represented 50 percent of volume. Hoyer had a strong technical orientation and employed 10 salespersons for Germany and Switzerland.

Hoyer was a good source of new product information for Puritan-Bennett. Because of their technical orientation, Hoyer salespeople helped Puritan-Bennett define new needs in the medical equipment market and identified new products in development by Puritan-Bennett competitors. Hoyer desired to expand its product line but only within the hospital segment. Already Hoyer carried a competitor's noninvasive blood pressure equipment. Germany had a large industrial base, making spirometry viable. Spirometry and blood pressure monitoring were both reimbursable through public and private health insurance programs.

The Puritan-Bennett U.K. subsidiary supported Hoyer activities. As in other European countries, this support included active missionary sales work. Puritan-Bennett participated in medical conventions, sponsored direct mailings, sought and referred dealer leads from other regions, and supported medical research using papers mentioning Puritan-Bennett products. Almost all missionary efforts in Europe centered on ventilators.

EXPERIENCE IN JAPAN

Amco Japan Ltd. was Puritan-Bennett's Japanese distributor. Amco Japan distributed throughout Japan, emphasizing high tech medical equipment. The medical equipment industry consisted of two segments: instruments and accessories or added features, and disposables. Disposables were those products which were consumed or would wear out and had to be thrown away. They included patient circuits, tubes, and mouthpieces. Amco Japan had emphasized technical equipment sales, featuring disposables and accessories as incremental business.

The Japanese distributor had no manufacturing facility. Amco Japan had begun with kidney dialysis equipment and broadened its product line to high tech medical equipment as the

industry matured. Amco was second only to Hoyer in international sales volume for Puritan-Bennett. Twelve to 15 salespeople, organized by specialty in terms of product function, called almost exclusively on hospitals. Amco Japan carried products from several different companies and desired to maintain a broad product line.

Most other Japanese distributors were large firms with internal specialization, either by end user or by area of medical specialty, such as respiratory or cardiac care.

Amco Japan was Boston Division's largest distributor of noninvasive blood pressure monitors. Introducing the Boston Division spirometer, Amco would face strong domestic competition. Heavy industry and heavy smoking habits created a viable market for spirometry, a reimbursable medical expense.

Mr. Bream headed sales for the Far East. The International Division maintained two offices to serve the Far East, one in Hong Kong and one on the U.S. West Coast. Puritan-Bennett had no representative based in Japan. Amco provided warehouses.

COMPETITION FOR VENTILATORS, SPIROMETERS, AND MONITORS

Puritan-Bennett was one of three leading competitors in the worldwide ventilation market. The others were Siemens and Bourns. Based in Germany, Siemens sold direct throughout Europe and the U.S. Bourns Ltd., a British company, sold its Bear ventilator direct in the U.S. and the U.K. Bourns was less active on the continent than Puritan-Bennett or Siemens.

Siemens ventilators had microprocessors and cost $15,000. The Bourns Bear 20 ventilator at $10,000 had no microprocessor.

Noninvasive blood pressure monitoring was rapidly expanding and attracting new entrants. First in the market with its Dinamap monitor, Critikon became world leader and marketed direct in the U.S. and Europe, selling elsewhere via distributor. John Sweeney counted eight international competitors selling noninvasive blood pressure monitors. Most used a mix of direct sales and distributors. Many, like Datascope, were between one and two years old, rapidly gaining sales volume.

Competition in spirometry existed in countries where industry, pollution, and smoking prevailed and where government or private medical insurance reimbursed spirometry.

Puritan-Bennett dominated U.S. office spirometry with 30 percent market share but held only a negligible share of the non-U.S. market. Tariffs and duties impeded manufacturers in this price competitive market. These extra costs resulted in end user prices sometimes 50 percent above prices of European manufactured spirometers.

Vitalograph, Ltd., a British company and Puritan-Bennett's largest competitor, dominated the European spirometer market. Vitalograph sold direct in the U.K. but used distributors throughout the rest of Europe.

Before technological developments by LSE and later by the Boston Division, Vitalograph had sold the most widely used spirometer in the U.S. Vitalograph European prices ranged from $1,150 for the basic model to $5,000 for the top-of-the-line model. Vitalograph offered no spirometer with microprocessing but had designed personal computer software to sell with the spirometer. A physician or nurse would connect the volume mechanism with a computer.

Puritan-Bennett's International Division and Vitalograph shared many European distributors, notably in Italy, Austria, and the Netherlands. Vitalograph was not represented in Japan, and its U.S. market share had declined. Vitalograph did all manufacturing in the U.K. Its sales volume equalled that of the Boston Division.

Litton Industries operated two subsidiaries, Hellig A.G. in Germany and Mijnhardt A.G. in the Netherlands. Both produced spirometers under the name Vicatest. Vicatest, a small part of this very large company, was fighting to gain a stronger position in the spirometry market. Vicatest sold direct in the Netherlands and Germany but used distributors throughout the rest of Europe. Vicatest had entered neither Japanese nor U.S. markets. The product line included Vicatest 3 with microprocessing. Vicatest priced items 33–35 percent below those of the Boston Division.

The Chest Co., a Japanese firm new to the European market, sold spirometers priced below Puritan-Bennett by 50 percent in Europe and 25 percent in the U.S.

The Warren E. Collins Company of Braintree, Massachusetts, sold in both the U.S. and Europe but had not substantially dented the spirometry market in Europe. Jones Medical Instrument Company competed primarily in the U.S. but had begun to compete overseas. Other U.S. companies attempted to enter the international market as industrialized countries increased concern for preventive health care. A U.S. National Health Institute study showed strong correlation between lung capacity and heart disease. Early detection of reduced lung capacity might decrease patient risk if followed by early treatment or behavior change.

Spirometer manufacturers faced a new group of competitors. With technological breakthroughs leading to cost and time savings, manufacturers of large pulmonary laboratory systems showed interest in the screening market. System manufacturers included Warren E. Collins and the Gould Company in the U.S., and Jaeger A.G. in Germany.

CORPORATE STRATEGY

The late 1970's and early 1980's marked significant change for Puritan-Bennett. Through acquisitions and intensified R&D activities, the company adopted a more innovative position in the marketplace, incorporating electronics and microprocessing into its products. Puritan-Bennett also broadened its product line. This dual positioning strategy of broad and innovative product lines increasingly mandated international rather than domestic focus.

In the past decade European and Japanese competitors had entered the U.S. market. Entry into foreign markets would allow Puritan-Bennett to know foreign competitors before they entered the U.S. John Sweeney felt that presence in a foreign market could buy time for an American firm. By competing well on foreign soil, Puritan-Bennett could instill reluctance by European or Japanese firms to enter the U.S.

International presence supported the company desire to maintain a leading edge in technology. "This allows us a window on technology," said John Sweeney. "U.S. doctors do not have all the answers. We need worldwide contacts with doctors and researchers." An example of new techniques developed outside the U.S., high frequency ventilation was most widely used in Germany, and therefore the German market provided the best place for feedback.

Different regulatory environments confirmed the importance of an international base. The U.S. Federal Drug Administration (FDA) could inhibit rapid introduction of new technologies. If Puritan-Bennett introduced a product in its foreign markets first, it would begin earlier pay-back of the initial investment. Puritan-Bennett discovered that despite approvals required, the process was fast in the U.K. and in Germany. In France, the process known as "homolugation" was cumbersome and difficult. The "Koseisho" procedure in Japan was well defined and predictable within a clear time frame.

With greater emphasis on innovation, Puritan-Bennett rapidly increased its R&D investment. Seeking a larger sales base would allow the company to spread initial investment cost over larger unit sales. This was true for all medical products, both hospital and physician office segments.

U.S. firms were at a cost disadvantage in many international markets because of labor, tariffs, transportation, and the strong U.S. dollar. Product quality and differentiation were therefore essential for success in Europe or Japan.

INTERNATIONAL PARTNERSHIP WITH A FINNISH FIRM

In 1981 Puritan-Bennett entered a partnership with the Datex Division of Instrumentarium, a Finnish company manufacturing hospital monitoring products. Instrumentarium had sought U.S. market entry as a first step to expansion throughout the Western Hemisphere.

The initial agreement focused on one product, a carbon dioxide monitor that measured carbon dioxide [CO_2] level of patients in surgery or patients under ventilation in respiratory therapy. The monitor measured carbon dioxide levels breath to breath, providing continuous feedback on the oxygen-carbon dioxide exchange.

Because John Sweeney's division marketed all monitoring products, he was asked to oversee the partnership. Monitors were produced in Finland and sold by Puritan-Bennett in the U.S. through its distribution network. In 1983 when Puritan-Bennett began direct sales to hospitals, Finnish products were handled by the Kansas City based corporate sales group. The Boston Division continued to coordinate all activities with the Finnish company.

Since conclusion of the original agreement, the two companies had broadened their cooperation, expanding the product line to include an anesthesia brain monitor. This equipment monitored the brain waves of a patient under anesthesia and functioned with other Puritan-Bennett products. The two companies were in negotiation to add monitoring devices to both Instrumentarium and Puritan-Bennett product lines. Further agreement gave Puritan-Bennett responsibility for the entire Western Hemisphere by adding sales to Canada and Latin America.

Puritan-Bennett and Instrumentarium had entered joint product development projects. Instrumentarium was to develop specific products to fit the Puritan-Bennett line, either by complementing it or working in conjunction with an existing Puritan-Bennett product.

Elsewhere Instrumentarium sold monitors through dealers. In Germany and Switzerland it had used Carl A. Hoyer G.m.b.H. The Finnish company used a different dealer in the U.K. and enjoyed strong sales there.

Both Puritan-Bennett and Instrumentarium were pleased with the relationship to date. They considered the possibility of a marketing joint-venture in one or two key markets. The joint-venture could market both the current line and any new products. Both companies felt that a joint-venture could maximize their effectiveness. They were still in the early stages of target identification.

ALTERNATIVE DISTRIBUTION CHANNELS

As Messrs. Taylor, Sweeney, and Oglethorpe reviewed distribution channels at their meeting in the Skyline lobby, they recognized several viable alternatives. Considering the U.K. as an example, they knew they could keep their current distributor, seek a new distributor, or use a direct salesforce.

All three gentlemen agreed that ventilator sales projected by Mr. Grant at A&C were unacceptably low. The new generation 7200 model had sold well in the U.S. Previous experience with A&C had been satisfactory, and Puritan-Bennett did not want to create tensions in its European distribution chain by dropping an established distributor after an extended relationship.

Puritan-Bennett could seek a new distributor. Bob Taylor was concerned about the time it would take to establish and to train a new distributor. He believed it might require two or three years to reach adequate volume.

A direct salesforce was also possible. Puritan-Bennett currently sold $500,000 in disposables for ventilators already installed in the U.K. Bob Taylor considered this to be "captive" business regardless of any change in channels. Disposables revenue would adequately cover the cost of adding salespeople to Puritan-Bennett U.K. Ltd. John Sweeney estimated that the cost of maintaining a sales force approached $70,000 per salesman.

CONCLUSION

Growing product lines and innovations were important for the three vice presidents to consider when examining distribution channels. Training a new distributor and subsequent high volume could take two or three years, particularly for ventilators because this equipment required a highly technical approach. Medical equipment sales demanded commitment from a sales organization, and finding a strong distributor could be difficult. A direct salesforce guaranteed early commitment but might not have immediate access to necessary channels. Hard feelings by distributors already providing good volume and service should not be risked.

John Sweeney considered how his division's products could and should fit with Bennett Division ventilators. One reason LSE had joined Puritan-Bennett was to improve international distribution by better access to European distributors. Another consideration was future broadening of Boston Division product line. Expansion was expected to continue in all medical product lines. Sweeney wanted to determine which channels could best accommodate expansion.

CASE 13 ▪ The SWATCH Project

"This watch is the product which will reintroduce Switzerland to the low and middle price market. It is the first step of our campaign to regain dominance of the world watch industry," said Dr. Ernst Thomke, President of ETA SA, a subsidiary of Asuag and Switzerland's largest watch company. Ernst Thomke had made this confident declaration about SWATCH to Franz Sprecher, Project Marketing Consultant, in late spring 1981. Sprecher had accepted a consulting assignment to help ETA launch the watch, which was, at that time, still in the handmade prototype phase and as yet unnamed. This new watch would come in a variety of colored plastic cases and bracelets with an analog face. ETA had designed an entire production process exclusively for SWATCH. This new process was completely automated and built the quartz movement directly into the watch case. Sprecher's key concern was how to determine a viable proposal for moving this remarkable new product from the factory in Grenchen, Switzerland into the hands of consumers all over the world.

COMPANY BACKGROUND: ETA, EBAUCHES AND ASUAG

SWATCH was only one brand within a large consortium of holding companies and manufacturing units controlled by Allgemeine Schweizer Uhrenindustrie (Asuag, or General Company of Swiss Watchmaking). SWATCH was to be pro-

duced by ETA, a movement manufacturer, which was part of Ebauches SA, the subsidiary company overseeing watch movement production within the Asuag organization (Exhibits 1 and 2).

Asuag was founded in 1931 when the Swiss government orchestrated the consolidation of a wide variety of small watchmakers. The major purpose of this consolidation was to begin rationalization of a highly fragmented, but vital, industry suffering the effects of one world war and a global depression. By 1981 Asuag had become the largest Swiss producer of watches and watch components. Asuag was the third largest watchmaker in the world behind two Japanese firms, Seiko and Citizen. Asuag had a total of 14,499 employees, 83 percent of whom worked within Switzerland. Asuag accounted for about one third of all Swiss watch exports, which were estimated at Sfr. 3.1 billion in 1980.* Major activities were movement manufacture and watch assembly. Bracelets, cases, dials and crystals were sourced from independent suppliers.

Ebauches SA, a wholly owned subsidiary of Asuag, controlled the various movement manufacturers. The Swiss government played an important role in encouraging and funding Ebauches' formation in 1932. An "Ebauche" was the base upon which the movement was built and Ebauches companies produced almost all of the movements used in watches produced

---

* 1 US$ = SFR 2.00/1 SFR = US $0.50

This case was prepared by Susan W. Nye and Barbara Priovolos under the direction of Visiting Professor Jean-Pierre Jeannet as a basis for class discussion rather than to illustrate either effective or ineffective handling of an administrative situation.
Copyright © 1985 by IMEDE (International Management Development Institute), Lausanne, Switzerland. Reproduced by permission.

EXHIBIT 1 Asuag Organization

Subsidiaries	Movements	Components	Industr. Components Equip./Measure Tools/Services
Ebauches SA, Neuchatel (ESA)	x	x	x
ETA, Fabriques d'Ebauches SA, Grenchen	x	x	
Les Fabriques d'Assortiments Reunies SA, Le Locle (FAR)		x	x
Nivarox SA, La Chaux-de-Fonds (NIV)		x	x
Pierres Holding SA, Bienne (PH)		x	x
General Watch Co. Ltd., Bienne	x	x	x
Eterna SA, Grenchen Eterna	x	x	
Compagnie des Montres Longines, Francillon SA, St. Imier Longines	x	x	x
Montres Rado SA, Longeau Rado	x	x	
Mido, G. Schaeren & Co. SA, Bienne Mido	x	x	
Fabrique de Montres Rotary SA, La Chaux-de-Fonds Rotary		x	
Era Watch Co. Ltd., Bienne Edox	x		
Certina, Kurth Frères SA, Grenchen Certina	x	x	
Gunzinger SA, Fabrique d'Horlogerie Technos, Bienne Technos		x	
Endura SA, Bienne Microma, Dynasty	x		
Diantus Watch SA, Castel San Pietro Dafnis, Diantus	x		
Oris Watch Co. SA, Hölstein Oris	x	x	x

EXHIBIT 1 Asuag Organization (cont.)

Number of employees at the end of December 1980 by subsidiary:

Industries	Switzerland	Abroad	Total
Ebauches SA	6739	719	7458
Fabriques d'Assortiments Reunies SA	1573	39	1612
Nivarox SA	383	—	383
Pierres Holding SA	880	571	1451
Societe du Produit Termine (GWC, ARSA et ATLANTIC)	2733	435	3168
ASU Components SA/Statek Corp.	194	978	1172
DG Asuag, Asam SA, Asulab SA	330	—	330
Total:	12832	2742	15574

EXHIBIT 2 Summary of Financial Activity for Asuag (in million SFR)

ASUAG GROUP/31 DECEMBER	1972	1973	1974	1975	1976	1977	1978	1979	1980
Consolidated Sales	1081	1264	1404	1073	1041	1169	1195	1212	1332
Number of employees	19350	19720	20230	17205	15725	16351	16195	15289	15574
Current Assets	696	761	878	786	786	813	782	761	788
Longterm Assets	263	272	287	309	319	341	338	324	390
Debt	443	479	589	542	418	483	552	580	680
Equity	1352	1384	1436	1372	1364	1352	1063	998	979

	1980/1981 Fr.	1979/1980 Fr.
INCOME STATEMENT		
Dividends from subsidiaries	4,507,001.65	4,938,768.43
Remittances from affiliates	14,225,219.10	10,604,457.95
Interest income	9,910,303.23	10,517,844.92
	28,642,523.98	26,061,071.30
EXPENSES		
General Administrative Costs	6,296,053.53	5,404,093.33
Research and Development	1,809,858.13	2,050,212.05
Information and Promotion	3,550,406.81	3,943,119.75
Taxes	692,994.85	698,932.00
Amortization	2,539,096.00	1,622,761.80
Interest Paid	8,985,565.05	7,872,187.46
Profit	4,768,549.61	4,469,764.91
	28,642,523.98	26,061,071.30

EXHIBIT 2 Summary of Financial Activity for Asuag (in million SFR) *(cont.)*

Companies or Groups of Companies	Sales 1st Half 1981 Francs Millions	Difference 1st Half 1981/1980	Sales 1980 Francs Millions	Difference 1980/1979
SALES DEVELOPMENT OF AFFILIATED COMPANIES				
Ebauches SA	389.2	+18.7%	670.7	+16.2%
Fabriques d'Assortiments Reunies SA	61.0	+ 4.4%	109.8	+ 9.9%
Nivarox SA	13.3	− 2.8%	25.8	+ 4.1%
Pierres Holding SA	38.4	+11.1%	66.8	+ 4.1%
Soc. du Produit Termine (GWC, ARSA, Atlantic)	282.1	+23.2%	569.9	+ 6.7%
ASU Components SA, Statek Corp.	39.8	+31.4%	62.4	+44.4%

by Asuag group companies. Sixty-five percent of Ebauches production was used by Asuag group companies, and the rest was sold to other Swiss watch manufacturers. Ebauches SA recorded sales of Sfr. 675.0 million in 1980, a 3.1 percent increase over the previous year. Ebauches companies employed a total of 6,860 people, 90 percent of them in Switzerland.

ETA SA, the manufacturer of SWATCH, produced a full range of watch movements and was known as the creator of the ultra-thin movements used in expensive watches. The quality of ETA movements was so renowned that some watches were marked with "ETA Swiss Quartz" as well as the name brand. ETA movements were distributed on a virtual quota basis to a select group of watch manufacturers. The demand for its movements had always equalled or exceeded its production capacity. In 1980 ETA employed over 2000 people and produced more than 14 million watch movements for revenues of approximately Sfr. 362 million and profits of about Sfr. 20 million.

Dr. Ernst Thomke had joined ETA as president in 1978. Early in his career, he had worked as an apprentice in production at ETA. He left the watch industry to pursue university degrees

in chemistry and cancer research earning both a Ph.D. and a medical degree. He then moved on to a career in research at British-owned Beecham Pharmaceutical. Thomke did not stay in the lab for long. He moved into the marketing department where he boosted Beecham sales with ski trips and concerts for physicians and their families. His unorthodox selling techniques led to skyrocketing sales. He looked for a new challenge when faced with a transfer to another country. His colleagues at Asuag and throughout the watch industry described Thomke as a tough negotiator and as iron willed. After joining ETA he agreed to provide advertising and support allowances to movement customers. However, these agreements stated that ETA only provided aid if it had a role in product planning and strategy formulation.

THE GLOBAL WATCH INDUSTRY

To understand the global watch industry three key variables were considered: watch technology, watch price and the watch's country of origin.

Watch Movement Technology

Watch design underwent a revolutionary change in the early 1970's when traditional mechanical movement technology was replaced with electronics. A mechanical watch's energy source came from a tightened mainspring which was wound by the user. As the spring unwound it drove a series of gears to which the watch hands were attached, the hands moved around the analog (or numerical) face of the watch to indicate the time. Highly skilled workers were required to produce and assemble the movements in accurate mechanical watches and the Swiss were world renowned in this area.

The first electronic watch was built by a Swiss engineer, Max Hetzel, in 1954, but it was U.S. and Japanese companies that first commercialized electronic technology. Bulova, a U.S. company, was the first to bring an electronic watch to market in the early 1960's, based upon tuning-fork technology. A vibrating tuning-fork stimulated the gears movements and moved the hands on a traditional analog face. At the end of the decade, quartz crystal technology began to appear in the market place. An electric current was passed through a quartz crystal to stimulate high frequency vibration. This oscillation could be converted to precise time increments with a step motor. Quartz technology was used to drive the hands on traditional analog watches and led to an innovation: digital displays. Digital watches had no moving parts and the conventional face and hands were replaced with digital readouts. Electronic watches revolutionized the industry because for the first time consumers could purchase an inexpensive watch with accuracy within 1 second per day or less.

Ebauches owned companies had been involved in electronic watch technology since its pioneering stages. In 1962, Ebauches was among a number of Swiss component manufacturers and watch assembly firms which established the "Centre Electronique Horlogère" (CEH). The center's immediate goal had been to develop a movement which could compete with Bulova's tuning-fork movement. CEH was never able to successfully produce a tuning-fork movement which did not violate Bulova's patents. In 1968 Ebauches entered into a licensing agreement with Bulova to manufacture and sell watches using Bulova's tuning-fork technology. In 1969 CEH introduced its first quartz crystal models and Ebauches subsequently took over manufacture and marketing for the new movement, introducing its first quartz line in 1972.

Ebauches also worked with the U.S. electronics firm, Texas Instruments, and FASEC (1) in the early 1970's to pursue integrated circuit and display technology. By 1973 Ebauches was producing movements or watches for three generations of electronic technology: tuning-fork, quartz analog and digital. Ebauches did not stay in the assembled watch market for long, and returned to its first mission of producing and supplying watch movements to Asuag companies. Between 1974 and 1980 the Swiss watch industry as a whole spent Sfr. 1 billion towards investment in new technology and Asuag accounted for half the expenditure. Ebauches Electronique on Lake Neuchâtel was a major use of investment funds and was created to produce electronic components.

Price

Price was the traditional means of segmenting the watch market into three categories. "AA" and "A" watches were sold at prices above Sfr. 1200 and accounted for 42 percent of the total value of watches sold and 2 percent of total volume. "B" watches priced at Sfr. 120–1200 made up 25 percent of the market in value and 12 percent in units. "C" watches were priced under Sfr. 120 and accounted for 33 percent of the market in value and 86 percent of total units.

PLAYERS IN THE GLOBAL WATCH INDUSTRY

Japan, Hong Kong and Switzerland, together accounted for almost 75 percent of total world

---

(1) FASEC was a laboratory for joint research in semiconductors, integrated circuits and lasers. It was formed in 1966 by the Swiss Watch Federation (FHS), Brown Boveri, Landis & Gyr and Philips of the Netherlands.

watch production. In 1980 watch producers worldwide were faced with inventory buildups at factory warehouses and retail stores. A worldwide recession had slowed demand for watches and overproduction compounded the problem. 1980 projections were not being met, and factory-based price cutting, particularly by large producers, was becoming common as a substitute for production cuts.

The Swiss Watch Industry

The Swiss watchmakers' position was viewed by many industry observers as being more precarious than others. Since 1970, when the Swiss accounted for 80 percent, their share of the world watch market in units had declined to 25 percent of the world's watch exports. The Swiss ranked third in unit production but remained first in the value of watches sold. Twenty-five percent of all Swiss watch factories were permanently shut down during the 1970's and 30,000 workers lost their jobs.

Despite extensive factory and company shut-downs within the Swiss industry, in 1981 the Swiss still owned the rights to 10,000 registered brand names, although less than 3,000 were actively marketed. Most Swiss watches were priced in the mid- to expensive price ranges, above Sfr. 100 ex-factory and Sfr. 400 retail. In 1981, industry analysts were congratulating the Swiss for their adherence to the upper price segments, as the low-price segments were beginning to turn weak. Industry observers noted that the Swiss seemed to be emerging from a decade of uncertainty and confusion and were focusing on higher quality segments of the watch market. Swiss component manufacturers had been supplying their inexpensive components to Far East assemblers and it was felt that this practice would continue.

Swiss watch manufacturers generally fell into one of three categories. First, there were the well established, privately owned companies which produced expensive, handmade watches. These firms included Rolex, Patek-Philippe, Vacheron Constantin, Audemars-Piguet and Piaget. For the most part, these firms were in good health financially. Stressing high quality as

the key selling point, these manufacturers maintained tight control through vertical integration of the entire production and marketing processes from movement and component production through assembly and out into the market. The recession had cost them some customers, but these had been replaced by new Middle Eastern clients.

Second, there were a number of relatively small privately owned companies that concentrated on watch components—bracelets, crystals, faces, hands or movements. This group included an ETA competitor Ronda SA. The financial health of these companies was mixed.

The third sector of the industry were the largest participants, Asuag and Société Suisse pour l'Industrie Horlogère (SSIH). SSIH was an organization similar to, but smaller than Asuag, producing 10 percent of all Swiss watch and movements output. Its most famous brand, Omega, had for years been synonymous with high quality. Omega had recently run into trouble and had been surpassed by the Asuag brand Rado as Switzerland's best selling watch. In June 1981, SSIH announced a loss of Sfr. 142 million for the fiscal year ending March 31, 1981. This loss gave SSIH a negative net worth of Sfr. 27.4 million. A consortium of Swiss banks and the Zurich trading group Siber Hegner & Co., AG were brought together to save the company.

In the late 1970's Asuag and SSIH began working in a cooperative effort to cut costs through the use of common components. However, this effort did not affect individual brand identities or brand names. Industry analysts did not rule out the eventual possibility of a full merger. Asuag was noted for its strength in production and quality, but was reported to have a weakness in the marketing function. SSIH was noted for strong marketing skills, but had recently been faced with a slippage in product quality. It was believed that both companies would stand to gain from closer ties in research and production.

The watch industry played a significant role in Switzerland's economy. The banks and the government took a serious interest in its operations and the performance of individual companies. Between 1934 and 1971 the Swiss government made it illegal to open, enlarge, transform or transfer any watch manufacturing plant without government permission. This action was justified as a defensive move to combat potential unemployment due to foreign competition. It was also illegal to export watch components and watch making technology without a government issued permit. The government essentially froze the industry by dictating both prices and the supplier-manufacturer relationship. These constraints were gradually removed, beginning in 1971, and by 1981 were no longer in effect.

The Japanese Watch Industry

Japan was the world's second largest watch producer in 1980 with approximately 67.5 million pieces, up from 12.2 million pieces in 1970. The growth of the watch industry in Japan was attributed to the Japanese watchmakers' ability to commercialize the electronic watch. K. Hattori, which marketed the Seiko, Alba and Pulsar brands, was Japan's largest watchmaker, and responsible for approximately 42 million units. Selling under 3 different brand names allowed Hattori to compete across a broad price range. Seiko watches fell into the "B" category. Alba and Pulsar competed in the "C" range.

Casio entered the watch market in 1975 selling low cost digital watches. Philip Thwaites, the U.K. marketing manager, described Casio as follows: "Casio's strategy is simple, we aim to win market share by cutting prices to the bone." Casio's product line was exclusively digital. The company was noted for adding "gadgetry" to its watches, such as timers, stop watches and calculators. In Casio's view the watch was no longer just a time piece but a "wrist instrument."

In contrast to Switzerland, Japan's "big 3" watch producers: the Hattori group, Casio and Citizen, had a combined product line of fewer than 12 brands. All three firms were fully integrated: producing movements, most components, assembling and distributing worldwide through wholly owned distribution subsidiaries. These watchmakers made extensive use of automated equipment and assembly line production techniques.

The Watch Industry in Hong Kong

Hong Kong manufacturers had only entered the market in 1976 but by 1980 unit output had reached 126 million units. Ten major producers accounted for an estimated 70 percent of total volume. Watch design costs were minimized by copying Swiss and Japanese products. As many as 800 "loft workshops" were in operation in the late 1970's. These facilities could be started at low cost and ran with minimum overheads. The expanded capacity led to the rapid fall of Hong Kong watch prices; prices of simple watches in the Sfr. 15–20 range in 1978 and dropped to Sfr. 10 the next year with margins of less than Sfr. 1. Hong Kong watches were sold under private label in minimum lot sizes of 1000–2000 units with average ex-factory costs of Sfr. 20 for mechanical watches and Sfr. 50 for quartz analog and Sfr. 10 for electronic digitals. Most watchmaking activity in Hong Kong was concentrated on assembly. The colony had become Switzerland's largest client for watch components and movements. Swiss movement exports to Hong Kong had grown from 13.3 million pieces in 1977 to 38.5 million pieces in 1980.

THE "POPULARIUS" PROJECT

The SWATCH project began under the code name "Popularius." Thomke's goal had been to discover what the market wanted and then to supply it. He told his engineers that he wanted a plastic, analog watch that could be produced at less than Sfr. 10 and sold ex-factory at Sfr. 15. He also wanted to use the technology which ETA had developed for its high priced, ultra-thin "Delirium" movements to enter the low priced watch segment. Thomke was convinced that ETA's long term viability and profitability depended on increasing the company's volume and integrating downstream into fully assembled watch production and marketing. Thomke had seen the demand for ETA movements dwindle when exports of finished Swiss watches declined from 48 million pieces in 1970 to 28.5 million in 1980. The mass market "C" watch all but disappeared from Swiss production and was replaced by inexpensive Japanese and Hong Kong models. The Swiss manufacturers pushed their products up-market and sales value of exports moved from Sfr. 2,383.7 million in 1970 to Sfr. 3,106.7 million in 1980.

With electronic technology, movements were no longer a major cost factor in the end price of a watch. The average price of an ETA movement was Sfr. 18 and applied whether the watch sold ex-factory at Sfr. 80 or Sfr. 500. Thomke wanted to increase ETA volume output and knew that Asuag transfer pricing policies made this difficult. Asuag was a loose consortium of companies, each operating as an independent profit center. Transfer pricing reflected this fact. At each point of production and sales: movements, components, assembly and through the distribution channels, a profit was taken by the individual unit. Thomke believed that this system weakened the Swiss brands' competitive position for the volume business which his movement business needed to be profitable. Thomke believed that if he wanted to introduce a successful new product, he would need to sell it to 1 percent of the world's population, which amounted to about 10 percent of the "C" market segment. He knew that the Japanese companies were fully integrated and that the Hong Kong assemblers, which already operated with low overheads, were moving increasingly towards full integration (Exhibit 3).

Thomke knew he could turn over the "Popularius" project to another Asuag unit, but he did not have a great deal of confidence in the production and marketing capabilities of Asuag branded watch assemblers. ETA was the only company within the Asuag group which had extensive experience in automated manufacturing. If the "Popularius" was to succeed as the latest entry in the low price market, it would have to be produced in an automated environment. Furthermore, Thomke had watched many of the finished watch companies steadily lose market share to Japanese and Hong Kong competitors over the last decade and he had little confidence in their marketing capabilities. ETA currently sold 65 percent of its output to Asuag companies

and Thomke wanted to reduce this dependence. He planned to use the "Popularius" as ETA's own entry into the finished watch market (Exhibit 4).

ETA engineers and technicians, responding to Thomke's specifications, developed the "Popularius." To meet the low unit ex-factory price was no small accomplishment. A cost analysis at that time showed that the required components without assembly would have cost Sfr. 20. Quartz technology provided accuracy within one second per day, and the watch was waterproof, shock resistant and powered by a readily available and inexpensive 3 year battery. The watch weighed 20 grams and was 8mm thick with an analog face. The face and strap were made of durable mat finished plastic and the strap was attached with a special hinge that was flush with the face. It was considered stylish and attractive. Further aesthetic enhancements could be made with the careful selection of color and face design. Ultrasonic welding produced a finished product which would not be reopened after it left the assembly line. In the event of failure, designers believed that the watch was essentially unrepairable and would be replaced rather than repaired. Batteries were replaceable by the owner and inserted in the back of the watch (Exhibit 5).

The product line was, at that time, limited to one size, a large "man's" watch, which could be produced in a number of solid colors with several designs or patterns on the face. Although a 25 percent smaller version for women and children was being considered, no definite introduction plans had as yet been developed. Management believed that the young were a potentially strong secondary market for the new product. A number of ideas were in development for "novelty" watches with special functions, a button watch and special colors and motifs. A day/date calendar with a quick reset feature was available. The production system was designed for strict quality control conditions to produce highly reliable watches. The movement was designed with a theoretical life of 30 years and "Popularius" would be sold with a one year guarantee.

EXHIBIT 3 Breakdown of Costs and Margins for Traditional "B" Watches (By Country of Origin)

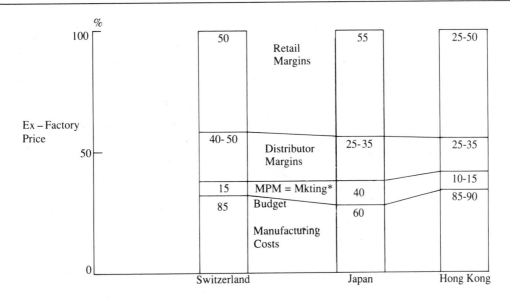

*Manufacturing and Profit Margins

Manufacturing Systems for "Popularius"

The ability to produce and sell a watch with the "Popularius" features, for a low price, was largely dependent upon unique production technology developed at ETA. ETA's product development staff was respected throughout the watch industry for its technical abilities in mass production. Its production technology was considered by industry observers to be equal to that of the best Japanese companies. In the early stages of electronic movement production, even with high priced luxury movements, automated assembly was not only possible but a practical means of production. The production equipment planned for "Popularius" was entirely Swiss made, and would in its final form consist of a fully automated production line that consumed raw materials at one end and delivered complete watches at the other.

ETA technology built the movement right into the base of the watch and required only 51 parts versus the 90 to 150 parts found in most electronic and mechanical watches. ETA had already used this technology to create the "Delirium," the world's thinnest movement measuring .98 mm at its thickest point. These movements were used in high precision, luxury watches measuring 2.4mm at their thickest point and selling at retail for Sfr. 40,000.

The "Popularius" production process and the equipment that made the technology possible were protected by seven patents. The ETA technical staff felt that it would be impossible for a competitor to duplicate "Popularius," especially at a low ex-factory price, because the watch was closely linked to its unique production process. ETA engineers had already invested nearly two years on this project, including the efforts of 200 employees and more than Sfr. 10 million in research and development funds.

EXHIBIT 4 Comparison of Ebauches SA Sales to World Market

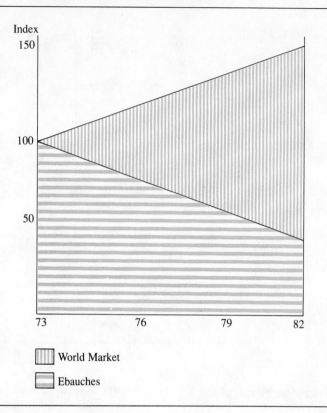

Production was still limited to hand production of prototype watches and watches for test marketing purposes. ETA expected the line to have semi- but not full automation with forecasted production levels of 600,000 men's watches and 150,000 smaller versions for women or children in the first year. Fully automated lines which would produce 2 million units per year were targeted for the second year. Production goals of 3 million units had been set for the third year. Production quotas for later years had not yet been finalized. Management expressed the desire to reach production and sales levels of 5 million units after 3 years.

Initially it was expected that full unit cost could go as high as Sfr. 16. As volume increased the per unit cost would drop and the full unit cost was expected to be less than Sfr. 10 at pro-

duction levels of 5 million watches per annum. The project was not considered technically feasible at annual production levels below 5 million, and higher volume was expected to drive the unit price just below Sfr. 7. Asuag pricing and costing policy suggested that individual projects should reach contribution margins of 60 percent for marketing, sales and administrative expenses, fixed costs and profits. Each size model would require a separate production line. Within each line economic order runs were 10,000 units for each color and 2,000 units for each face style. Maximum annual production per line was 2 million units and the initial cost of installing a line was Sfr. 5 million, including engineering costs of Sfr. 2 million. Additional assembly lines could be installed at an estimated cost of Sfr. 3 million. Production costs included

EXHIBIT 5 Photograph of the Product

SWATCH.
THE REVOLUTIONARY NEW TECHNOLOGY.

swatch ✚
SWATCH. THE NEW WAVE IN SWISS WATCHES.

depreciation of this equipment over 4 years. The equipment occupied space which was already available and no additional real estate investments were expected.

ETA had applied for special financing packages with local authorities. No response had as yet been received. However, obtaining the necessary financing was not viewed as a problem.

Initial plans suggested a marketing budget of Sfr. 5 per unit. The brand was expected to break even in the third year and begin earning profits for ETA in the fourth year. Per unit marketing costs were expected to decline as volume increased. Decisions as to how the budgeted marketing funds would be distributed had not been finalized. It was expected that they would be divided between ETA and its distributors, but

on what basis and how the "campaigns" would be coordinated could not be decided until distribution agreements had been finalized. Thomke was a firm believer in joint ventures and wanted to develop 50/50 relationships with distributors.

Still to be decided were questions of packaging, advertising, production line composition and distribution. Packaging alternatives centered around who should do it. ETA needed to decide if the product would leave the factory prepackaged and ready to hang or display, or shipped in bulk and packaged by the distributor or retailer or even sold "as is." Advertising budgets and campaigns had not been finalized. The size of the budgets and the question of whether or not advertising costs would be shared between ETA and the distributors were still open. The advertising agencies had not yet been chosen and no media decisions had been finalized.

DISTRIBUTING "POPULARIUS"

Sprecher felt that distribution was the most important and problematic of the issues still outstanding. Discussions at ETA on developing an introduction strategy were confined to five industrial markets. Although, it was not as yet definitive, the emerging consensus seemed to be that distribution would begin in Switzerland, the U.S., the U.K., France and West Germany. Distribution in Japan, other industrialized countries and certain developing countries was also being discussed for a later date.

Market and Country Selection

A major motivation in choosing the target entry markets would be the probability of gaining high volume sales and meeting Thomke's goal of selling a watch to 1 percent of the world population. The U.S. would be an important market for "Popularius" success. It was the world's single largest watch market and success with a product in the U.S. often signaled global success. Thomke planned to keep the watch priced below $30 in the U.S. Germany and the U.K. were significantly large in terms of population, but

FIGURE 1 Projected Marketing Costs and Profits for SWATCH

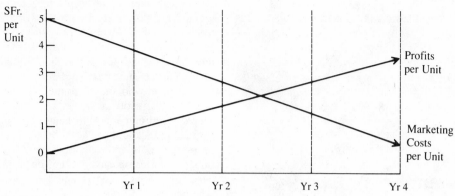

Per Unit:
Full Cost to Produce = SFr. 10 (with long range target of less than SFr. 7
                                including depreciation for production machinery)
Ex-factory Price = SFr. 15
Contribution Margin for Marketing Costs and Profit = SFr. 5

could be difficult markets to enter because they were known to be particularly price sensitive. Germany was also noted as being particularly slow in accepting new innovations in consumer goods. Switzerland was chosen because it was the home market. ETA management assumed that their next move would be into Canada and the rest of Europe. If ETA decided to enter Japan and the LCDs, management would have some special considerations. Japan would be a particularly difficult market to crack because almost all "B" and "C" class watches sold in Japan were produced domestically. Furthermore, Sprecher had heard that Seiko was considering plans for introducing a new quartz analog watch which would be priced under Sfr. 50. The LCDs of Africa and Latin America provided ETA with opportunities for volume sales. Sprecher expected that consumers in these markets would use price as the only criteria for choosing a watch. Selling the "Popularius" to LCDs would put ETA in competition with the Hong Kong producers' inexpensive digital watches.

Selecting Distributing Organizations

Within each market there was a range of distribution alternatives. But a fundamental need was a central marketing, sales and distribution unit within ETA with sole responsibility for "Popularius." However, at that time, there was no marketing or sales department within the ETA organization. ETA's products, watch movements, had always been distributed to a select and consistent group of users. Distribution at ETA had essentially been a question of arranging "best way" shipping, letters of credit and insurance. The annual costs of establishing a central marketing division within ETA was estimated at Sfr. 1–1.5 million. This figure would cover management and administrative salaries for a marketing manager, regional managers, product managers, service, sales planning and advertising and promotion planning. Sprecher believed that 8 to 10 people would be required for adequate staffing of the department. Furthermore, he estimated that wholly owned subsidiaries in any of the major target markets could be staffed and run at a similar cost.

Contracting individual, independent marketing organizations in each country and then coordinating the marketing, sales and distribution from the Grenchen office would, Sprecher believed, allow ETA to retain a much greater degree of control over the product. He felt that this type of organization would allow ETA to enter the market slowly and to learn about it gradually without having to relinquish control.

Following Thomke's suggestion, throughout the summer of 1981 Sprecher took a number of trips to the U.S. to determine possible solutions to this and other marketing problems. Sprecher's agenda included visits to a number of distributors, advertising agencies and retail stores. Sprecher completed his investigation with visits to some of the multinational advertising agencies' Zurich offices. Sprecher made his rounds with a maquette which he described as an "ugly, little black strap." The "Popularius" prototype still had a number of bugs to iron out and Sprecher could only make promises of the variety of colors and patterns which were planned.

The U.S. would be essential to "Popularius" success because it was the world's largest watch market. Thomke and Sprecher also believed that the U.S. market would be more open to this new idea and felt they would gain the best advice from U.S. distributors and advertising agencies (Exhibit 6).

Retailer and Wholesaler Reactions

Sprecher began his first U.S. trip with a visit to Zales Corporation. The Zales organization included both a large jewelry and watch wholesale business and a chain of jewelry stores. Sprecher met with a high level marketing manager who responded positively to the product, but said that Zales could not seriously consider it at this early stage. He invited Sprecher to return when the project was further along. Zales management did advise Sprecher that if ETA decided to go ahead with the project and start production and sales, then "do it right." Doing it "right" meant heavy spending on advertising, point-of-purchase displays, merchandising and aggressive pricing.

Sprecher also paid a visit to Gluck and Company. Gluck was a jewelry, watch and accessory wholesaler operating in the low price end of the market. An aggressive trader, Gluck operated mainly on price and much of its business involved single lots or short term arrangements to catalogue and discount houses. Gluck executives told Sprecher that they did not believe in advertising, but relied on low prices to push goods through the distribution chain and into the hands of the customer. If Gluck agreed to take on "Popularius" it would have to be sold with a retail price of under Sfr. 40. Sprecher attempted to discuss the possibility of a long term relationship between ETA and Gluck, but the wholesaler did not appear particularly interested.

Sprecher's reception at Bulova's New York offices was very different from Gluck. Andrew Tisch's, president of the company, first reaction was that the "Popularius" should be packaged as a fashion watch. Tisch had had substantial experience in consumer goods marketing and believed that "Popularius" should be heavily advertised and promoted, suggesting a budget of Sfr. 20 million. He was sufficiently impressed with the project, and voiced some interest in establishing a separate company with ETA to market the watch.

Considering OEM Arrangements

Sprecher was concerned that he might be taking a "hit-or-miss" approach to his investigation and decided to pay a visit to Arthur Young and Company. Arthur Young was among the largest accounting firms in the world, one of the "Big Eight," and was noted for its industry analysis and consulting. Sprecher visited Arthur Young to see if their consultants might have some suggestions on potential partners for ETA. The accounting firm put together a proposal on how to attack the problem of finding a distribution partner. Sprecher was well aware that his investigation was still incomplete, and he returned to Switzerland with the Arthur Young proposal to work out a new agenda of visits.

Included in the Arthur Young proposal was the possibility of turning all marketing responsibilities of "Popularius" over to an independent company. Sprecher investigated this possibility and entered into negotiations with two well-known multinational consumer good companies:

EXHIBIT 6A Retail Watch Purchases in the U.S. (Summary of Market Research)

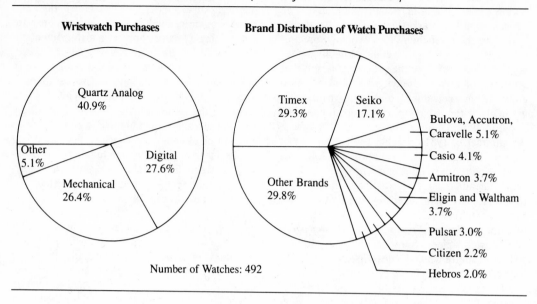

Wristwatch Purchases

Quartz Analog 40.9%

Other 5.1%

Digital 27.6%

Mechanical 26.4%

Number of Watches: 492

Brand Distribution of Watch Purchases

Timex 29.3%

Seiko 17.1%

Bulova, Accutron, Caravelle 5.1%

Casio 4.1%

Armitron 3.7%

Eligin and Waltham 3.7%

Pulsar 3.0%

Citizen 2.2%

Hebros 2.0%

Other Brands 29.8%

EXHIBIT 6B Watch Purchases by Retail Price (Sample size = 465)

	% Quartz Analog	% Digital	% Mechanical
(Number of watches)	(200)	(135)	(130)
Price categories			
$1,000 or more	.5	.7	1.5
$300 to $999	4.0	.7	1.5
$100 to $299	38.0	8.9	14.6
$50 to $99	33.5	31.9	35.4
$30 to $49	24.0	57.8	47.0

Note: 46.6 percent of all watches are purchased on sale or discount.

EXHIBIT 6C Retail Watch Purchases in the U.S. (Watch Purchases by Outlet Type [Sample Size = 485])

	% Watches (All)	% Analog Quartz	% Digital
(Number of items)	(485)	(198)	(134)
Jewelry Store	27.6	34.3	12.0
Department Store	26.2	26.3	27.6
Discount Store	16.7	14.7	23.1
Catalog Showroom	10.3	14.7	10.4
Mail Order	5.4		11.2
Wholesaler	2.1		1.5
Drug Store	5.1		6.0
Flea Market	0.4		
Other Outlets	6.2		7.5

EXHIBIT 6D Distribution of Watch and Jewelry Purchase Prices by Age of Purchaser

	18–24 yrs	25–34 yrs	35–54 yrs	55 and over
(Number of customers)	(150)	(419)	(821)	(431)
$25 to $49	39.4%	39.6%	35.7%	32.3%
$50 to $99				
$100 to $299	20.7%	24.8%	25.3%	28.5%
$300 to $999	27.3%	25.3%	26.7%	27.6%
$1,000 or more	11.3%	8.8%	9.0%	10.4%

Timex and Duracell. Both of these companies had their own extensive and established distribution channels. ETA executives believed that an agreement with either of these two firms might provide "Popularius" with a virtual guarantee of high volume sales due to the extensive and intensive marketing resources at both.

The Duracell Proposal

Duracell produced and distributed high quality batteries worldwide and was interested in becoming the exclusive distributor of "Popularius." Contact was initiated with the U.S. battery company's general manager in Zurich and followed up with a visit at Duracell's U.S. headquarters. The company had a distribution system in place which covered the entire globe. Duracell batteries were sold through drug stores, supermarkets and hardware stores. Duracell made batteries for watches as well and therefore had some contacts in the retail watch trade. The company employed an experienced and well trained sales force and had a wealth of marketing knowledge. Duracell had unused distribution capacity and its management was looking for extensions to the product line and felt that an electronic watch could be complementary to and a logical extension of Duracell batteries.

Sprecher felt that an agreement with Duracell could be interesting but was concerned that ETA was being relegated to the role of product supplier with little or no impact on marketing decisions. Duracell wanted to establish itself in an original equipment manufacture relationship with ETA. Duracell would buy the watch from ETA and then control the product's marketing strategy. ETA would be supplying the product, the product's name and some marketing funds, but would be left out of most mass marketing decisions. Furthermore, while Duracell continued to express interest, they were proceeding at what ETA executives considered to be a snail's pace. In late summer, Duracell management informed ETA that they were continuing their evaluation of "Popularius" as a product and that their investigation of its potential market was still incomplete.

The Timex Organization

Timex was known for producing durable, inexpensive watches. The U.S.–based company had become famous in the late 1950's and 1960's for circumventing traditional watch outlets, jewelry stores and distributing through mass outlets such as drug, department and hardware stores and even cigar stands. At its peak, Timex had sold watches through an estimated 2.5 million retail outlets. In 1982 Timex had an estimated 100,000 to 150,000 worldwide. Timex and ETA were considering the possibility of ETA production of a limited range of watches under the Timex name. The Timex "Popularius" would be produced in black with a different, but ETA approved, design. The hinge which attached the plastic strap to the watch case would be different and "Swiss Made" would not be stamped on the face. Timex was willing to guarantee a minimum annual order of 600,000 units, at Sfr. 10 ex-factory price.

Sprecher knew that ETA executives considered private label production as a viable option which could be implemented in either the introductory phase of distribution or later when the brand was well established. However, they felt that the Timex arrangement had some drawbacks. First, they perceived the Timex organiza-

tion as somewhat stodgy and bureaucratic and ETA executives were unsure as to how close a working relationship they could establish with Timex management. Second, Timex seemed to want "Popularius" for "nothing." Sprecher did not think that they could keep "Popularius" to a Sfr. 50 retail price and gain a profit in the Timex agreement. Sprecher considered the Timex distribution system very costly. Sprecher estimated that Timex watches were distributed with a retail price of 4 to 4.5 times the ex-factory watch price. ETA wanted to maintain a 3 to 3.5 ex-factory ratio. Sprecher believed that the Timex system was costly because it used a direct sales force as well as two middlemen (distributor and broker) to get watches into the retail store. Finally, ETA management was also concerned with Timex's most recent performance. The company had been steadily losing market share.

Positioning Options

Towards the end of his second trip to the States, Sprecher hit upon the "perfect" name for the new product—SWATCH. He had arranged to spend two weeks with the advertising agency Lintas SSC&B to work on developing a possible product and advertising strategy. This arrangement initiated a quasi-partnership between the two firms; Lintas invested its time and talent in the "Popularius" project and would receive payment later if they were to get the advertising account.

Lintas had been influenced by their work with another client, Monet, a producer of costume jewelry. Monet supported its products with heavy point of sale promotion activities. Lintas believed that this kind of promotion would be beneficial to "Popularius."

Lintas saw a number of positioning options for the "Popularius," a (new) Swiss watch, a second watch, an activity watch, a fashion watch or a combination of images. The agency had suggested approaching the "Popularius" positioning with a combination of a fashion and sports image while emphasizing the watch's Swiss origin. The copy staff was excited about stressing the Swiss watch concept and the contraction S'watches was repeated throughout their notes. Sprecher looked at the abbreviation and was struck by the idea of taking it one step further to SWATCH and the "Popularius" finally had a name.

Considering Direct Mail

Back in Switzerland, Sprecher continued interviewing advertising agencies. He visited the Zurich office of McCann-Erickson, a large multinational advertising agency to discuss advertising strategy and to look into the mail order market. McCann-Erickson made an investigation of the mail order market for the SWATCH in West Germany. The purpose of this study was to demonstrate what a mail-order approach might accomplish for SWATCH.

McCann-Erickson's proposal suggested using mail order as an initial entry strategy for SWATCH. This arrangement would later be expanded into a mail-order business through specialized companies with a full range of watches and jewelry. Target group would be young men and women between 20 and 29 years as well as people who "stay young." The target group would be motivated and interested in fashion, pop culture, and modern style.

To achieve sufficient penetration of the target market which the agency estimated at 12.5 million, advertising support of about Sfr. 1 million would have to be spent. Orders were estimated anywhere from 50,000 units to 190,000. This estimate included volume of 4,500 to 18,000 for a test market with total advertising costs of about Sfr. 150,000. The effort would be organized in two waves, one in spring and a second in the fall.

Additional costs to be considered were mailing at Sfr. 2.50 per unit sold as well as an unknown amount for coupon handling. Furthermore, experience indicated that about 10 percent of all orders would not be paid.

Considering an Exclusive Distributorship

Zales had suggested that Sprecher contact Ben Hammond, a former Seiko distributor for the southwestern region of the U.S. Sprecher was unable to make this contact, but Thomke followed up on this lead on a separate visit to the U.S. in late summer. Ben Hammond, president of Bhamco, was interested in the exclusive distribution rights for North America for SWATCH and a second Asuag brand, Certina. Bamhco was a gem stone firm and Hammond had been in the jewelry and watch business in the southwest for several years. Up until the recent past he had been the southwest distributor for Seiko. Hammond reported that he and Seiko had had a falling out when the Japanese manufacturer opened a parallel distribution system, selling its watches through new distributors to mass merchandise and discounters in direct competition to its traditional outlets and "exclusive" distributors. He proposed to start a new company, Swiss Watch Distribution Center (SWDC) and wanted an agreement for three years. Hammond was very enthusiastic about the SWATCH and told Thomke that he could "sell it by the ton." Hammond projected first year sales of 500,000 units growing to 1.2 million and 1.8–2 million in years two and three and then leveling off at 2.5 million.

Hammond felt that the watch should be positioned as a fashion item and sold through jewelry and fine department stores. He believed that a heavy advertising and point of sale budget would be important to gaining large volume sales and felt that a Sfr. 5 per watch was a reasonable figure. Furthermore, after his experience at Seiko, he promised a careful monitoring of consumer take-off and a close relationship with retail buyers to avoid discounting and to give service support. Based in Texas, Hammond had substantial financial backing from a group of wealthy investors. He planned to begin initial efforts in the southwest and then promised to spread rapidly to all major U.S. cities and Canada.

Next Week's Meeting

Thomke had just returned from the U.S. and briefed Sprecher on his meeting with Ben Hammond. Thomke was anxious to get moving on the project and planned to make a proposal to Pierre Renggli, the president of Asuag in mid-

September, less than three weeks away. At the end of the briefing they had scheduled a strategy planning session for the next week. Sprecher now had less than one week to evaluate his information and to prepare his proposals for Thomke in preparation for their final presentation to Renggli. Sprecher knew that Thomke expected to receive approval for ETA production and marketing of SWATCH at that presentation. Sprecher knew that his proposals to Thomke needed to be operationally feasible, and with target launch date of 1 January 1982, available implementation time was short. Sprecher knew that they could pursue negotiations with some of the companies which he had visited or "go it alone" with a direct sales force. Sprecher needed to balance the economic restraints which required minimum annual sales volume of 5 million with Thomke's desire to keep strategic control of the product within ETA. Sprecher needed to consider ETA's lack of marketing experience and what that would mean in the international marketplace.

CASE 14 ▪ Tissot: Competing in the Global Watch Industry

INTRODUCTION

One sunny afternoon in May 1985 Dr. Ernst Thomke drove his Porsche through the Jura mountains; he was on his way to Bienne for a Tissot strategy session. After more than a decade of declining sales, layoffs and factory closings the popular business press was proclaiming the return of the Swiss watch industry. Much of the credit for the resurrection had been given to Thomke, president of Ebauches SA, one of the Asuag-SSIH companies, and initiator of a new, low priced Swiss fashion watch: the SWATCH. Thomke believed that the predictions of a revived Swiss watch industry were premature. He had accepted the considerable task of giving the Asuag brands, and particularly Tissot, a hard look to formulate new strategies to bring the Asuag group profitability in the second half of the 1980's and beyond. Specifically, his goal was to increase Asuag-SSIH total volume from 7 million to 50 million units. As his Porsche sped through the countryside he considered the past and future trends for the global watch industry and he asked himself, "How can Tissot grow and profit?"

In 1985, the future trends for the global watch industry were anything but clear. Over the past 15 years, the industry had experienced radical changes. Innovation in products, production and marketing were all key factors in the volatility which marked a period of rapid entry (often followed by rapid exit) of new competitors and the departure of some established producers.

In 1970 the global watch industry was dominated by Swiss watch manufacturers. By 1975 the competitive field had expanded and key players came from Switzerland, Japan and the U.S. By the early 1980's the U.S. had all but disappeared as a contender and Hong Kong was the world's largest exporter in units in the industry with 326.4 million watches and movements in 1984. Japan ranked second in number and value of units produced. Between 1970 and 1984, the Swiss dropped to third place in unit volume as their assembled watch exports dwindled from 48 million to 17 million pieces. However, Switzerland continued to rank first in value of watch exports, Sfr. 3.4 billion in 1984 (Exhibit 1).

THE WATCH INDUSTRY IN SWITZERLAND

The Swiss watch industry was concentrated in the Jura along the western border of Switzerland. The Swiss had conquered the world market with mechanical watches and had developed a reputation for fine craftsmanship, elegance and style. Swiss companies produced 80 percent of the watches selling for Sfr. 1,200 or more and virtually all top priced watches. A large portion of these watches were still mechanical.

Until the early 1970's, Swiss watchmaking was intensely specialized and fragmented, with

This case was prepared by Susan W. Nye under the supervision of Visiting Professor Jean-Pierre Jeannet as a basis for class discussion rather than to illustrate either effective or ineffective handling of an administrative situation. Copyright 1985 by IMEDE (International Management Development Institute), Lausanne, Switzerland. Reproduced by permission.

EXHIBIT 1A Total Production of Watches and Watch Movements Worldwide 1960–1984 (million pieces)[1]

1960	1970	1975	1980	1982	1983	1984
98.0	174.0	220.0	300.0	330.0	370.0	n.a.

[1] Without other timepieces as penwatches, and so on.

Source: Swiss Watch Federation.

EXHIBIT 1B Watch Production by Country 1960–1983 (Percentage of Worldwide Unit Production)

	1960	1970	1975	1980	1982	1983
Switzerland	43.0%	42.0%	32.0%	18.4%	10.8%	9.3%
Japan	7.2	13.7	14.0	22.5	24.7	26.1
Hong Kong	—	—	—	18.5	30.0	35.0
USA	9.7	11.5	12.5	4.0	—	—
E. Ger.	20.5	14.5	16.7	15.7	14.8	13.2
France	5.6	6.3	7.6	3.3	2.9	2.2
W. Ger.	8.0	4.7	4.3	2.2	1.2	1.1

Source: Swiss Watch Federation.

EXHIBIT 1C Watch Exports—Watches and Movements 1960–1984 (in million of frs)

	1960	1970	1975	1980	1982	1984
Switz.*	1159.2	2383.7	2764.3	3106.7	3091.9	3397.3
Japan	16.4	399.3	835.1	1911.1	1908.5	2876.2
Hong Kong	—	63.1	246.1	1855.6	1779.0	2091.2
France	26.2	78.1	209.3	265.0	218.3	233.7
Germany	83.6	129.6	140.2	171.7	175.4	231.4

* Including nonassembled movements.

Source: Swiss Watch Federation.

EXHIBIT 1D Watch Exports—Watches and Movements
1960–1984 (million pieces)

	1960	1970	1975	1980	1982	1984
Switz.*	42.6	73.4	71.2	51.0	45.7	46.9
Japan	0.1	11.4	17.1	48.3	63.6	94.7
Hong Kong	—	5.7	16.1	126.1	213.7	326.4
France	1.3	4.4	9.5	9.8	8.4	6.2
Germany	3.8	4.1	9.5	4.5	4.7	5.5

* Including nonassembled movements.

Source: Swiss Watch Federation.

EXHIBIT 1E Exports As a Percentage of Total Pieces Produced
1960–1984

	1960	1970	1975	1980	1982	1984
Switz. (E)	97%	97%	97%	97%	97%	97%
Japan	2	48	57	72	80	n.a.
Hong Kong	—	100	100	100	100	100
France	24	40	57	*	*	*
W. Ger.	48	50	*	*	*	*

(E) = Estimation.
n.a. = not available.
* Not available; because of reexports, exports are larger than production.

Source: Swiss Watch Federation.

EXHIBIT 1F Assembled Watches As a Percentage of Watches and
Movements Exported (value)

	1960	1970	1975	1980	1982	1984
Switz.	81.3%	86.1%	87.9%	85.9%	91.5%	92.9%
Japan	51.6	83.6	92.1	90.6	87.6	85.0
Hong Kong	97.1	100.0	96.6	95.4	96.9	96.7
France	87.7	93.8	93.8	88.7	91.5	94.4
Germany	91.1	88.7	90.6	89.0	92.0	94.8

Source: Swiss Watch Federation.

EXHIBIT 1G Assembled Watches As a Percentage of Watches and Movements Exported (pieces)

	1960	1970	1975	1980	1982	1984
Switz.	73.7%	73.6%	71.7%	55.9%	59.3%	55.2%
Japan	29.0	64.8	78.1	75.5	67.5	60.6
Hong Kong	98.2	100.0	98.1	94.4	95.6	92.1
France	n.a.	89.5	90.4	81.6	79.0	94.4
Germany	89.3	88.9	85.5	69.0	74.4	72.6

n.a. = not available.

Source: Swiss Watch Federation.

a rigid structure which had remained unchanged for centuries. Major changes began in the 1970's with several mergers involving sizeable firms and important initiatives in both horizontal and vertical integration.

The Swiss watch industry was essentially a group of industries. Traditionally, the Swiss had operated on a two tier system: components manufacturing and assembly. In 1934 the Swiss government had instituted laws that made it illegal to open, enlarge, transfer or transform any watchmaking facilities without government permission. Exports of components and movements were also illegal without permission, as was the export of watchmaking machinery. These regulations were instituted to protect the Swiss watch industry against foreign competition. The government began de-regulating the industry in 1971 and in 1985 these laws were no longer in effect.

Swiss watch firms generally fell into one of three categories. First, there had been a large number of "one-man-and-a-boy" and other small enterprises which produced components, movements or put purchased parts into cases. These firms marketed on the basis of long-established personal contacts. Included in this category were the piece work assemblers. A significant portion of inexpensive mechanical watches were assembled by Jura farmers during the winter as in-home piece work. Second were the well-established, privately owned watchmakers which produced expensive, handmade watches.

And finally, there was the Asuag-SSIH organization which was a group of companies representing approximately 35 percent of total Swiss exports of watches and movements.

Watches and movements declined from 11.9 percent to 7.2 of total Swiss exports from 1970 to 1980. At the start of the 1970's there were 1,618 watchmaking firms in the industry; this figure had fallen to 634 by 1984. Between 1970 and 1984 the full-time labor force producing watches shrank from 89,500 to 31,000. Lay-offs due to the shrinking demand for mechanical watches were exacerbated by automation, rationalization and concentration initiated throughout the Swiss watch industry.

ASUAG-SSIH*

Company Background

In an effort to resuscitate the industry, a consortium of seven Swiss banks orchestrated a merger between SSIH and Asuag in 1982. They provided the merger with a capital and cash infusion totaling more than Sfr. 700 million. In return the bank gained 97 percent ownership of the combine and planned to sell shares to the public when it returned to profitability, estimated at 5 to 10 years. Turn around began in 1984 with sales totaling Sfr. 1,582.4 million and after tax

_____

* The company has since changed its name to SMH.

profits of Sfr. 26.5 million. In February 1985, it was announced that control would be returned to private investors (see Exhibit 2).

Asuag, short for Allgemeine Schweizer Uhrenindustrie, had been the largest producer of watches and watch components in Switzerland, accounting for about one-third of total Swiss watch exports and 25 percent of production in Switzerland. Asuag had been founded in 1931 when the Swiss government orchestrated the consolidation of a wide variety of small watchmakers to strengthen the industry during the worldwide depression.

Movements were produced by the twelve subsidiaries of Ebauches SA, including ETA. ETA was the largest Swiss movement manufacturer. ETA produced a full range of movements, but was best known as a producer of high quality, expensive ultra-thin watch movements used for luxury watches. Ebauches companies sold 65 percent of their production volume to the Asuag-SSIH brands. Ebauches' sales had dropped from 51.1 million to 32.1 million pieces between 1973 and 1984. During this period the world market for movements had grown from 215 million to 350 units. Ebauches world market share dropped from 23.8 to 9.2 percent.

Asuag's brands of finished watches included: Longines, Eterna, Certina, and Rado. Rado was the largest selling mid priced Swiss watch with annual sales of about 1 million units. Fifty-five percent of Asuag's production was in finished watches. Asuag began losing money in 1977, reporting an accumulated net loss of Sfr. 129 million in 1982.

Société Suisse de l'Industrie Horlogère (SSIH) had been the second largest watch company in Switzerland, responsible for 10 percent of total output. SSIH was made up of a diverse group of companies producing watches and movements in all price categories. SSIH group companies included Omega, Tissot and Economic Time.

SSIH had encountered severe financial problems in the late 1970's. In 1977 the Zurich-based trading group Siber Hegner & Co. AG, a major international distributor of Swiss watches, including Omega and Tissot provided SSIH with a capital infusion of Sfr. 32.5 million. A rescue plan was devised which de-emphasized the lower price end of the market. Siber Hegner management concentrated on electronic quartz models which sold at prices above Sfr. 235. Tissot watch prices were pushed upwards and Tissot models were sold in the Sfr. 235 to 1500 range. Omega watches were priced above Sfr. 600 at retail. Companies producing at the low price end of the market were sold off and inexpensive watch production was reduced from 69.2 to 19.7 percent of total. At the same time, the product mix was shifted and electronic watches increased from 8.9 percent of total in 1976 to 47.9 percent of total sales in 1980. Siber Hegner provided a cash infusion for research and development and a worldwide advertising campaign. Acquisitions and joint ventures were arranged to improve integration, although management, production, marketing and sales remained decentralized.

Initially, turn-around was successful with profits in 1979 allowing for the first dividend payment since 1974. Profitability was short lived and in June 1981, SSIH announced a loss of Sfr. 142 million for the year ending March 31, 1981, giving the company a net loss of Sfr. 27.4 million. A consortium of Swiss banks in an effort to bail out the company provided cash and credit valued at almost Sfr. 230 million in return for 96.5 percent equity in the recapitalized company.

Tissot SA

Thomke described Tissot, and most Asuag-SSIH watches, as a "branded commodity." The individual companies produced their products under recognized brand names, but Thomke felt that the watches had been poorly developed in terms of brand image and personality. Thomke believed the weak image had led to the decline in Tissot sales (Exhibit 3). His goal was to create a workable brand strategy and identity for Tissot. In May 1985, Thomke believed that Tissot had gained the reputation of an "inexpensive" Omega.

The company produced about 400,000 watches in 1984, for watch sales of Sfr. 42 million. The average retail price for a Tissot watch was about Sfr. 375. Strongest sales volume was from watches in the Sfr. 300–700 range. Retail

EXHIBIT 2 Asuag-SSIH ORGANIZATION 1983

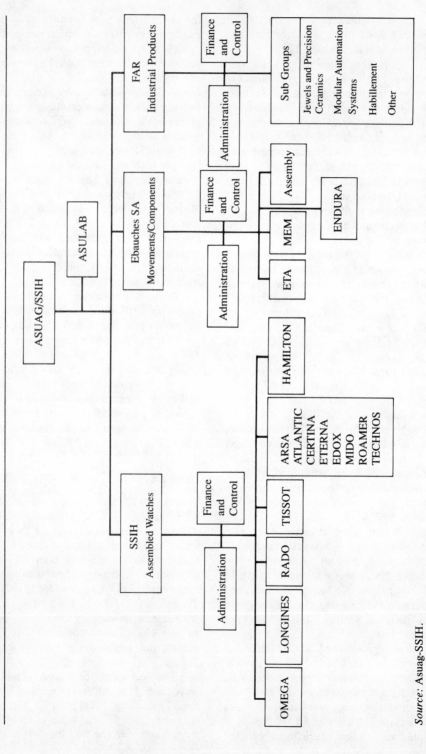

EXHIBIT 3 Tissot World Sales 1981–1984

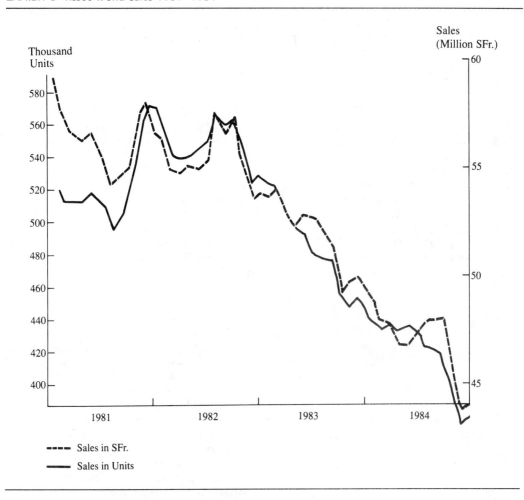

----- Sales in SFr.

——— Sales in Units

prices ranged from Sfr. 175 to 800 for stainless steel and gold plated watches. A second smaller line of gold watches sold for between Sfr. 1000 and 5000. Tissot watches were sold in Europe: Switzerland, West Germany, Italy, Scandinavia and the U.K. Tissot was also sold in Brazil, South Africa, Hong Kong, Singapore and Japan. Tissot had been withdrawn from the U.S. market in the 1970's but Thomke wanted to re-introduce it to the U.S. as soon as possible.

Tissot production was limited to assembly. Employment at the factory had declined from a

high of 1200 to 200. All components and movements were purchased from Asuag-SSIH or independent companies. At the start of 1985 Tissot workers were assembling a product line of some 300 styles, each produced in a woman's and man's model and in a number of different metals and combinations. Thomke had already assigned ten engineers at Tissot to review the product line and production process.

Tissot shared Omega's distribution at both the wholesale and retail level. Almost all Omega wholesalers were independent distributors. A total of 12,000 retail stores, mostly jewelry stores and a few "high class" department stores carried Tissot watches. The majority of its watch sales came from the top 3,000 stores. Ex-factory prices ranged from Sfr. 60 to 2,000. Both wholesalers and retailers provided advertising and promotion support, but all promotion activities had to be initiated by Tissot.

Thomke was aware that if he wanted to build up a strong image for Tissot, he would have to increase his marketing and promotion expenditure. Asuag-SSIH set targets for marketing and profit margins (MPM) for each brand. Thomke felt that a 50 percent margin would give a brand adequate funds for marketing and profit. Only his latest product, SWATCH, came close to that figure, followed by Rado with almost 30 percent. A target MPM* of 15 percent had been set for Tissot for 1984, but Thomke had learned that the actual margin had been closer to 10 percent.

Thomke believed that the MPM had been squeezed by wholesalers because of the slow turnover for Tissot watches. Wholesalers demanded a margin of 28 to 45 percent for Tissot watches. Explaining the situation, Thomke said, "Tissot has never recovered the sales and market share it lost to Seiko and Citizen in the 1970's. Sales to retailers have slowed considerably and consumer demand is down. To encourage wholesalers to keep Tissot in inventory, the company granted more liberal wholesaler margins, at the expense of marketing funds and profits."

Thomke felt that it was still possible to build up the brand and re-establish a strong wholesale network. However, he realized that this was an expensive proposition. He was prepared to invest 18 to 20 percent of sales in promotion, but to have any effect he needed a promotion budget of Sfr. 12 million for Europe alone. Thomke estimated that the company could spend Sfr. 6–8 million in Germany, Tissot's largest market in 1985. This figure would be divided with one half targeted for media advertising and the rest for point-of-sale promotion. If handled correctly,

promotion activities would give Tissot the strong image which Thomke felt was essential to successful watch sales.

WATCHMAKING TECHNOLOGY

Designing a Watch Collection

Watches covered a broad spectrum in terms of style and price, ranging from sport watches for informal or daytime wear, to luxury dress watches which were pieces of jewelry. It could take 3 years to bring a watch from the drawing board to the market. A watch collection was made up of as many as 30 to 40 lines. Each line had up to 1000 models. A watch line was differentiated by case shape, design and the movement. The differences between models were cosmetic variations in color and types of materials or due to slight variations in technology, such as day/date calendars or self-winding mechanisms.

Watch cases were made in precious metals, standard steel, brass and plastic. The cases of many expensive luxury watches were decorated with semi-precious and precious stones, such as lapis lazuli, diamonds and sapphires. Watch cases were made in 2 or 3 pieces. Two pieces, the back and front, were standard and held the watch together. For better watches a separate rim held the crystal in place. The rim provided designers with more flexibility when developing new models and gave the watches a finer finish.

Watch crystals were pieces of thin glass or plastic which protected the hands and dial and came in three types. The most inexpensive were plastic, followed by mineral glass and sapphire glass. Sapphire glass was very hard and could not be scratched or chipped.

Straps or bracelets held the watch on the wrist and came in a variety of materials. Straps came in leather, plastic and cloth ribbons. Bracelets were made from precious metals, standard steel, brass and plastic. Precious and semi-precious stones were often set into the bracelets of luxury watches. Up until the 1970's most watches were sold with leather straps. In the past 15 years fashion had changed and most watches were purchased with bracelets.

---

* MPM = Marketing and Profit Margin

Timekeeping Technology

Every watch was composed of four basic elements: a time base, a source of energy, a transmission and a display. The movement was the watch's time base. Movements came in two major categories: mechanical and electronic. Mechanical movements were driven by the release of energy from an unwinding spring. Electronic watches ran on an electric battery. Energy was transmitted through a series of gears, a motor or integrated circuits to the hands of analog watches. These hands moved around the dial to display time. Integrated circuits were used to transmit time to digital watches, and time was displayed numerically in a frame on the watch case (Exhibit 4).

Mechanical Watch Movements

The movement was a complex set of 100 or more tiny parts. While all mechanical watch movements operated on the same principle, there was a great deal of variety in watch quality. Friction and wear had to be minimized to insure long term accuracy of the tiny moving parts. To minimize friction, jewels were placed at all the movement's critical pivot and contact points. Fifteen was the standard number of jewels but high-quality movements might contain as many as thirty. Contrary to popular belief, adding more jewels did not necessarily indicate increased quality, or cost to production. These internal jewels were synthetic and relatively inexpensive. It was the overall care and craftsmanship that went into the watches that created the expense and not the jewels themselves.

The precision and accuracy found in high quality jewel-lever watches required micromechanical engineering expertise. A variety of modifications could be made to a spring-powered watch which added to the complexity of the interior design but not the basic mechanism. Refinements, such as improved accuracy, miniaturization, water resistance and self-wind technology, rather than radical new developments had occurred. Calendars and chronographs, as well as watches with start/stop mechanisms were also possible.

Pin-lever watches, also called "Roskopfs" after their inventor, had metal pins instead of jewels on the escapement mechanism gear teeth. Roskopf's original goal in inventing this watch had been to make the movement so simple that watches could be made affordable to everyone (Exhibit 5).

Electronic Movements

A Swiss engineer, Max Hetzel, invented the first electronic watch in 1954. This development was largely possible due to advances in miniature batteries and electric motors during World War II. Initially, electronics did not represent a big departure from mechanical technology, nor offer substantially better accuracy. While the energy source was replaced with electronics, the transmission and regulating components remained unchanged.

The tuning-fork watch, developed in the 1960's, represented a significant change to the traditional principles of determining time. A small battery in the watch sent an electric current to the tuning-fork and stimulated it to vibrate at 360 cycles per second. The vibrations were transmitted to a set of gears which drove the hands on the watch face. Tuning-fork watches if properly adjusted were accurate to within one minute per month.

The quartz crystal watch began appearing in the marketplace at the end of the 1960's. An electric current was passed through a quartz crystal to stimulate high frequency vibration which could be converted into precise time increments. Microcircuitry subdivided the crystal's frequency into an electric pulse which drove the watch. The pulse operated a tiny electric stepping motor or was transmitted through conductors and integrated circuits to drive the gears and watch hands.

In 1972, digital watches appeared for the first time. These watches had no moving parts and the conventional face and hands were replaced with digital readouts. Early digital watches used light emitting diodes (LED) to show the time. With this technology, users pressed a button for time display. LED watches required a great deal of power and batteries

EXHIBIT 4 Watchmaking Technologies

Inside a mechanical watch

the time base is composed of a spiral balance wheel whose movement back and forth recurs, for instance 4 times per second;

the source of energy is a taut spring;

the transmission consists of a train of pinions and wheels;

the display consists of hands moving around a dial.

The components of a mechanical watch

The movement-blank

The Ebauche, the key part of the watch, serves to carry the main spring, the wheel pins and the regulating parts. The cocks provide the support at the other end of the pins and pinions.

Finally, the wheels and pinions intermesh to provide the transmission moving the hands.

The plate, the cocks, the wheels together make up the movement-bland of a watch in its unassembled stage.

In addition, the movement of a watch includes the regulating pieces. The whole assembly is inserted into a watch case with glass, dial and crown for winding up the watch and setting the time, the whole thus constituting the finished product.

Despite the minute dimensions and the finishing and precision required for each unit, mass production reaches a rate of as much as 4,000 to 10,000 complete movement-blanks (depending on calibre) per day and per assembly line.

The regulating parts

The regulating parts carry out the function of time base. They include the balance-wheels, the hairspring and the assortment. These parts regulate the working of the watch, keeping constant control of the amount of energy provided by the main spring and transmitted to the display by the wheel assembly.

Their production calls for extreme precision to micrometer* standards and a high degree of know-how for handling the tiny delicate pieces.

The jewels

The jewels, synthetic rubies, are used to support the pins of the wheel and thus diminish friction and wear. Shaping them with the aid of a diamond paste has taken centuries to develop and achieve precision to a scale of a tenth of a micrometer. A new technology for doing this using laser beams has made it possible to speed up the pre-drilling of the holes in the jewels.

Inside an electronic watch
(analogical or digital),

the time base is composed of a quartz crystal vibrating at, for instance, 32,768 times per second;

the source of energy is an electric battery;

the transmission is provided by conductors and integrated circuits (analogical and digital watches), a motor synchronized with a train of pinions and wheels (analogical watches);

the display is provided by:

hands moving around a dial in the case of analogical watches;

figures appearing in a frame in the case of digital watches.

EXHIBIT 4 Watchmaking Technologies *(cont.)*

Mechanical Watch

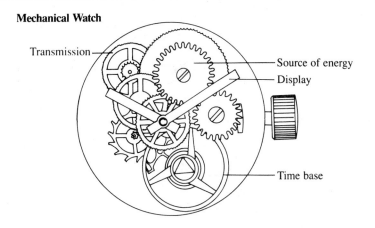

Electronic Analogue

Electronic Digital

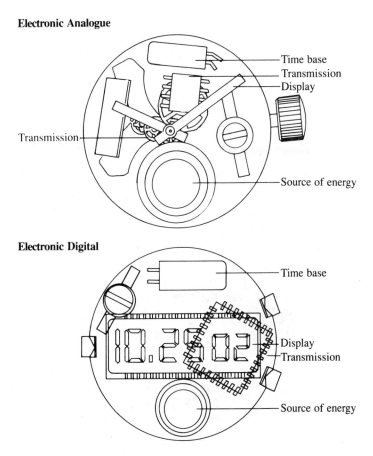

* 1 micrometer, or micron, is equal to a thousand of millimeter.

Source: Asuag-SSIH.

EXHIBIT 5A Mechanical Watch and Movement Exports
(Percentage of Total Units Exported 1960–1984)

	1960	1970	1975	1980	1982	1984
Switz.	100.0	99.6	98.1	80.4	50.8	29.4
Japan	100.0	n.a.	n.a.	33.6	16.5	8.5
Hong Kong	—	n.a.	n.a.	28.7	15.1	7.6
France	100.0	94.4	98.2	75.5	60.7	45.1
Germany	100.0	85.8	84.7	50.7	29.2	16.8

n.a. = not available.

Source: Swiss Watch Federation.

EXHIBIT 5B Electronic Watch and Movement Exports
(Percentage of Total Pieces Exported 1960–1984)

	1960	1970	1975	1980	1982	1984
Switz.	—	0.4	1.9	19.6	49.2	70.6
Japan	—	n.a.	n.a.	66.4	83.5	91.5
Hong Kong	—	n.a.	n.a.	71.3	84.9	92.4
France	—	5.6	1.8	24.5	39.3	54.9
Germany	—	14.2	15.3	49.3	70.8	83.2

n.a. = not available.

Source: Swiss Watch Federation.

EXHIBIT 5C Mechanical Watch and Movement Exports
(Percentage of Total Value Exported 1960–1984)

	1960	1970	1975	1980	1982	1984
Switz.	100.0	98.5	94.0	69.2	51.1	46.6
Japan	100.0	n.a.	n.a.	22.2	11.4	9.8
Hong Kong	—	n.a.	n.a.	32.0	28.2	16.9
France	100.0	91.1	96.2	56.2	34.3	24.0
Germany	100.0	85.1	84.4	51.8	26.4	15.2

n.a. = not available.

Source: Swiss Watch Federation.

EXHIBIT 5D Electronic Watch and Movement Exports
(Percentage of Total Value Exported 1960–1984)

	1960	1970	1975	1980	1982	1984
Switz.	—	1.5	6.0	30.8	48.9	53.4
Japan	—	n.a.	n.a.	77.8	88.6	90.2
Hong Kong	—	n.a.	n.a.	68.0	71.8	83.1
France	—	8.9	3.8	43.8	65.7	76.0
Germany	—	14.9	15.6	48.2	73.6	84.8

n.a. = not available.

Source: Swiss Watch Federation.

EXHIBIT 5E Wristwatch Purchases in the U.S.

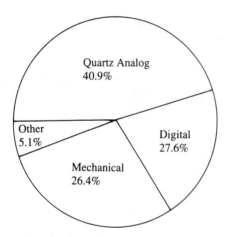

Number of Watches: 492
(Total number of surveyed buyers: 492)

Source: National Jewelers/HTI.
Consumer Survey 1983.

lasted no longer than one year. Liquid crystal diodes (LCD) came on the market in 1972; these watches displayed the time continually. These watches were considerably more conservative in energy usage, and batteries lasted from 3–5 years or longer.

Early electronic watches were not fully water and shock proofed and the batteries often malfunctioned in hot, humid climates. However, within a short period of time, technological advances led to electronic watches which were water proof to depths of 30 meters, shock proofed and able to withstand tropical climates.

Designing electronic watches for women had initially created problems, as well as opportunities. To create models which fit a woman's smaller wrist required considerable miniaturization of the movement and battery. Creating smaller movements led to increased design flexibility. Improvements in miniaturization and advancement in large-scale integrated circuits (LSI) and battery technology allowed manufacturers to add special functions without excessive bulk. Watches began to take on the appearance of multifunction instruments. Runners, skin divers, sailors, and other sports enthusiasts bought watches which would provide them with waterproofing and sophisticated chronograph functions. Travelers were afforded the opportunity to buy watches with multi-time zone functions and alarms. Watches were also available with calculators and radios, and progress was being made toward a television watch (Exhibit 5).

Producing Watches

Movements, hands, cases and bracelets were assembled to produce a complete watch. Mechanical watch quality was dependent on the care taken in assembly as well as the quality of the individual components. High quality mechanical movements were made by hand and a combination of semi- and highly skilled craftsmen was needed. Mechanical watch assembly was done in batches. Highly skilled workers were essential at the final stages of production, for finishing and adjusting to produce high quality, finely finished, accurate movements and watches.

While the term *pin-lever* refers specifically to the replacement of jewels with metal pins, roskopfs were made from lower quality grade materials. Labor requirements for roskopfs were reduced with semi- or unskilled labor working in batch production.

Electronic movements for analog watches combined micro-mechanical and electronic engineering. The electronic regulating mechanism simplified the production process which could be run in an automated setting with semi-skilled labor. Movements for digital watches were radically different from analog watches. These watches had no moving parts and time was programmed onto a silicon chip. Unskilled labor could be used to assemble digital watches which were assembled in batches and on automated assembly lines.

Both mechanical and electronic watch reliability was tied to the number of inspections the manufacturer made. For mid-priced and expensive watches 100 percent inspection occurred at several points during the process. Tests were made for water- and shock-proofing as well as accuracy.

Costs of production were a function of a company's degree of integration and automation, material costs and the local wage rates. Material costs were based on the quality of the watch produced. With roskopf watches labor constituted a significant portion of variable costs, but as the watches moved up-market the materials, fine stainless steel, sapphire crystals and eventually precious metals and decorative jewels played the major role in the watch's ex-factory price. Watchmakers could improve their variable costs by assembling at volumes above 10,000 pieces. Assemblers producing 100,000–500,000 units per year could benefit from com-

ponent supplier discounts which were as high as 20–25 percent. Beyond this point, cost improvements could only be realized with new production processes, automation and robotics. Wages for the Swiss watch industry averaged Sfr. 12 per hour. Most Swiss watchmakers sought a 30 percent gross margin. In Japan average hourly' wages for factory workers were Sfr. 7.20. Japanese producers had an average gross margin of 40 percent. In Hong Kong manufacturers kept their ex-factory prices low with inexpensive, but highly productive piece-work labor, averaging under Sfr. 10 per day, fewer inspections and cheaper materials. Gross margins of approximately 10–15 percent were typical for Hong Kong manufacturers (Exhibit 6).

SEGMENTING THE GLOBAL WATCH INDUSTRY

Price Segments

Price has been a traditional means of segmenting the watch market into three categories. The first group were low price, "C," watches and included all watches sold at retail for under Sfr. 120. Roskopf watches and inexpensive digitals competed in this market. These watches accounted for 33 percent of total value of global watch sales and 86 percent of unit volume. The mid-price or "B" watches ranged from Sfr. 120–700 at retail. This sector represented 25 percent of sales in Swiss francs and 12 percent of total units for 1984. Electronic watches dominated both the "C" and the "B" price segments.

The third category were the top priced watches. The retail price of "A" watches ranged from Sfr. 700–5,000. Manufacturers of luxury watches "AA" class, sold to a small exclusive group willing to pay several thousand Swiss francs for a special custom design jeweled watch. Precious stones and/or metal used in the watch face and bracelet accounted for the major portion of the "A" and "AA" watch prices. This was particularly true for electronic watches where movements averaged Sfr. 18. About 27 percent of the value of total watches and 2 percent of pieces sold worldwide were from the

EXHIBIT 6 Breakdown of Production Costs

For a Swiss watch with an ex-factory price of Sfr. 390
variable cost breakdown was estimated as follows:

case	70
bracelet	90
dial	50
crystal	18
movement	18 (50 for mechanical)
hands	5
Total materials costs	251
Assembly and quality control	25
Margin	114
Ex-factory	390
Wholesalers' margin	260
Retailers' margin	650
Consumer price	1300

For Japanese watchmakers producing a watch with ex-
factory of Sfr. 250 breakdown of costs and margins as
follows:

Total variable costs	150
Margin	100
Ex-factory	250
Wholesalers' margin	60–90
Retailers' margin	310–340
Consumer price	630–700

For Hong Kong makers producing a watch with ex-factory
cost of Sfr. 80 break-down of variable costs were as follows:

case and dial	15
bracelet	15
crystal	15
movement	18
hands	2
Total materials costs	65
Assembly and quality control	6
Manufacturer's margin 10%	8
Ex-factory	80
Wholesalers' margin	30
Retailers' margin	55–110
Consumer price	165–220

Source: Asuag-SSIH and interviews with industry experts.

EXHIBIT 7 Watch Purchases in the U.S. at Retail Prices

No. of items	% Watches (490)*	% Quartz Analog (200)	% Digital (135)	% Mechanical (130)
$1,000 or more	.8	.5	.7	1.5
$300 to $999	2.4	4.0	.7	1.5
$100 to $299	23.5	38.0	8.9	14.6
$50 to $99	33.5	33.5	31.9	35.4
$25 to $49	39.8	24.0	57.8	47.0

* Total 490 responses for consumer survey.

Source: National Jeweler/HTI.
Consumer Survey 1983.

"A" tier. "AA" watches accounted for 16 percent of global watch sales in Swiss francs, but less than .5 percent of total units. Mechanical watches still dominated the high priced segments (Exhibit 7).

Evaluating timekeeping technology was difficult for consumers. When shopping for watches, consumers chose a particular price level and expected a certain level of technical proficiency, style, and intangibles such as prestige. Quartz technology had changed the price/accuracy ratio. Before the electronic watch, accuracy was bought with expensive, finely engineered jewel-lever watches. With the introduction of electronics, watches with accuracy of plus or minus 15 seconds per month could be purchased for as little as $9.95.

Geographic Segments

Technologies and price have had an impact on the world markets for watches. Historically, the U.S. has been the major importer of finished watches. The U.S. was often the launching ground for new products and success in this market indicated strong possibility of global success. The strong dollar and improving U.S. economy in 1984–85 had had a positive impact on the sales and profits of Swiss and Japanese watch companies. Europe and Japan were also strong markets for watches in all price categories. However, throughout the 1960's and

1970's, new opportunities for watch sales opened up in the oil producing countries in the Middle East and in less developed countries (LDC).

In the 1960's watch producers began to move into the LDC with inexpensive roskopf watches. This market was taken over by inexpensive digitals in the early 1970's. However, the initial success of the cheap digital in this market was short-lived and consumers returned to mechanical watches. The miniature batteries in the quartz watch were very expensive in these regions, sometimes more than the original cost of the watch. By 1984, this problem had been solved and inexpensive electric watches again dominated the LDC market.

A new opportunity for watch manufacturers developed in industrialized countries with young children providing a new and growing market for inexpensive watches. Until the 1960's most children received their first watch in their mid- to late teens, often as a gift. Roskopf watches opened up the market to children in the 7 to 10 year range. A significant portion of these purchases were novelty watches, with cartoon and storybook characters which were sold as gifts for young children (Exhibit 8).

The market for expensive watches moved to the Middle East in the early 1970's. The rest of the world was caught in a recession, largely due to escalating oil and gas prices, and demand for high price luxury items fell off. Buyers in the oil

EXHIBIT 8A Total Jewelry
and Watch Purchases by Age
Group (1,852 items)

Age	Percentage
55 + years	23.6%
35–54	45.0
25–34	23.0
18–24	8.4

Source: National Jeweler/HTI.
Consumer Survey 1983.

EXHIBIT 8B Distribution of Watch and Jewelry Purchase Prices by
Age of Purchaser

No. of items	18–24 yrs	25–34 yrs	35–54 yrs	55 + yrs
	(150)	(419)	(821)	(431)
$1000 and more	1.3%	1.5%	3.3%	1.2%
$300 to $999	11.3	8.8	9.0	10.4
$100 to $299	27.3	25.3	26.7	27.6
$50 to $99	20.7	24.8	25.3	28.5
$25 to $49	39.4	39.6	35.7	32.3

Source: National Jeweler/HTI.
Consumer Survey 1983.

producing countries had both the money and the interest to purchase luxury goods. The Swiss were particularly adept at meeting the changing fashions and tastes of this new luxury segment and provided expensive, luxury watches with lapis-lazuli, coral, diamonds and turquoise (Exhibit 9).

TRENDS IN WATCHES DISTRIBUTION

Wholesale Distributors

Watch distributors played an essential role in linking the manufacturer to the retailer. Distributors generally sold one or perhaps two non-competing brands. Wholesalers expected exclusive distribution rights for the brand for a given region. Distributors maintained a sales force to sell to and service retailers. They purchased watches outright and maintained a local inventory.

Manufacturers expected their distributors to participate in promotion activities. Distributors attended trade fairs and contributed to advertising, mailing expenses and point-of-purchase display materials.

The distributor was responsible to find and oversee adequate watch repair services. Watch repair was a key issue for watches in the "B," "A" and "AA" categories. This service need had led to a close working relationship between

EXHIBIT 9A Major Importers of Swiss Watches and Movements
(million pieces)

	1960	1970	1975	1980	1982	1984
Hong Kong	1.9	10.0	11.3	12.5	4.1	4.9
United States	12.4	19.2	12.0	5.9	3.6	4.6
Germany	1.3	2.9	5.0	4.9	3.6	4.0
Italy	1.2	2.6	2.6	2.5	2.3	3.0
France	0.2	0.7	0.8	1.6	1.9	2.2
Japan	0.2	1.0	1.6	0.7	0.7	2.0
United Kingdom	1.7	6.1	6.3	3.2	1.9	1.9
Saudi Arabia	0.2	3.4	1.1	1.0	1.2	0.9
Arab Emirates			1.4	1.9	1.3	0.8
Spain	0.8	2.5	1.9	1.3	1.1	0.8
Total 10 largest markets	19.9	48.4	44.0	35.5	21.7	25.1
Total worldwide	41.0	71.4	65.8	51.0	31.3	32.2

Source: Swiss Watch Federation.

EXHIBIT 9B Major Importers of Swiss Watches and Movements (million Sfr)

	1960	1970	1975	1980	1982	1984
United States	250.6	482.2	348.6	379.7	407.8	598.7
Hong Kong	76.6	242.6	257.6	401.6	344.1	351.5
Italy	70.1	153.9	194.0	256.4	287.7	300.3
Germany	48.2	135.3	195.6	241.7	212.4	246.6
Saudi Arabia*	12.2	92.0	84.0	201.9	271.9	233.1
France	10.6	38.6	75.6	123.3	152.0	169.8
Japan	14.1	88.0	172.5	109.0	120.3	167.1
Singapore	38.3	45.1	58.3	79.7	106.2	150.3
United Kingdom	43.1	131.3	176.6	125.3	127.2	139.9
Arab Emirates*	—	—	59.4	71.7	94.9	82.1
Total 10 largest markets	563.8	1,409.0	1,622.2	1,990.3	2,124.5	2,439.4
Total worldwide	1,146.3	2,362.2	2,720.3	2,917.5	3,011.0	3,298.8

* Saudi Arabia with Arab Emirates in 1960 and 1970.

Source: Swiss Watch Federation.

EXHIBIT 9C Major Importers of Japanese
Watches and Movements (million pieces)

		1980	1982	1983
Hong Kong		14.2	23.0	28.3
United States	7.5	10.3	11.8	
Germany		3.4	2.7	3.1
Italy		0.8	0.8	1.1
France		1.1	1.9	2.6
Canada		0.8	0.7	1.0
United Kingdom	1.1	1.7	2.2	
Saudi Arabia	2.1	2.8	3.9	
Arab Emirates	0.6	1.3	1.4	
Spain		0.5	2.0	2.1
Total 10 largest markets		32.1	47.2	57.5
Total worldwide		48.3	63.6	76.0

Source: Swiss Watch Federation.

EXHIBIT 9D Major Importers of Japanese Watches and
Movements (million Sfr.)

		1980	1982	1983
United States	316.9	372.9	403.4	
Hong Kong		383.7	471.0	580.8
Italy		40.9	33.3	47.6
Germany		142.4	94.4	88.0
Saudi Arabia	107.3	94.8	158.3	
France		72.0	73.0	95.5
Canada		44.6	39.6	51.1
Singapore		18.3	29.9	23.0
United Kingdom	54.3	56.0	56.7	
Arab Emirates	24.5	42.4	58.9	
Total 10 largest markets		1205.0	1306.4	1563.2
Total worldwide		1918.5	1925.4	2224.7

Source: Swiss Watch Federation.

EXHIBIT 9E Major Importers of Watches and Movements from Hong Kong (million pieces)

	1980	1982	1983
Canada	2.9	8.6	10.2
United States	32.6	81.7	119.2
Germany	11.5	15.6	20.5
Italy	4.6	5.2	8.0
France	6.6	4.8	4.2
Japan	5.9	8.2	12.4
United Kingdom	9.7	10.4	12.6
Saudi Arabia	2.4	6.4	7.1
Arab Emirates	1.4	3.9	6.2
Spain	4.2	9.5	14.8
Total 10 largest markets	81.8	154.3	215.2
Total worldwide	126.1	213.7	284.1

Source: Swiss Watch Federation.

EXHIBIT 9F Major Importers of Watches and Movements from Hong Kong (million Sfr.)

	1980	1982	1984
United States	469.4	591.3	671.7
Canada	56.7	63.3	57.8
Italy	62.7	34.9	40.8
Germany	194.9	129.4	145.9
Saudi Arabia	58.9	102.3	100.5
France	88.5	34.2	22.8
Japan	69.5	65.1	84.7
Singapore	43.8	46.8	34.2
United Kingdom	139.0	82.6	76.3
Arab Emirates	25.7	59.6	57.0
Total 10 largest markets	1209.0	1209.4	1291.5
Total worldwide	1859.7	1779.6	1915.3

Source: Swiss Watch Federation.

the producer, distributor and retailer. The distributor found and licensed watch repair services and jewelers with watch repair capabilities. For especially difficult repairs the distributor helped arrange for work to be sent back to the factory. With inexpensive, "throw-a-way" watches repairs were less critical or non-existent. Importers of "C" level watches had greater freedom in channel selection. Mass merchandisers, drug stores and even supermarkets were used to distribute watches to end users. Some of these watches were sold with a guarantee, and rather than repair, a replacement was offered.

Most watch manufacturers had agreements with independent distributors. The Japanese and some of the private Swiss firms operated wholly or partially owned marketing and sales subsidiaries in their foreign markets. Twenty-five to 35 percent was the standard markup granted wholesalers and importers of Japanese and Hong Kongese watches. This figure increased to 40 percent or more for importers of most Swiss watches.

Retailers

A wide variety of retailers sold watches to the end user, including jewelry and department stores, mass merchandisers and mail order catalogues.

An estimated 40 percent of worldwide watch sales came from jewelry stores. Watch manufacturers benefitted from the jeweler's selling expertise and personal interaction with consumers. Watches sold in exclusive jewelry and department stores benefitted from the store's deluxe or fashion image. Fine gold, mechanical watches were a natural extension of the jeweler's product line and most were capable of minor watch repairs and cleaning. When electronics were initially introduced, some jewelry stores resisted the new technology. Electronics were not within the jeweler's extensive training. Within a short period of time, however, customer demand and refinements to the technology moved quartz watches into jewelry stores worldwide.

Jewelry stores had been the traditional outlet for watch sales until the mid-1950's. The rapid growth in roskopf and later in inexpensive digital watch sales was accompanied by channel diversification and watches moved into new outlets: drug stores, department stores and supermarkets. Retail watch sales in the U.S. had been influenced by channel diversification and in 1983 less than 30 percent of watches sold in the U.S. were purchased in jewelry stores (Exhibit 10).

Stock turn for a "B", "A" or "AA" watch could be as low as two times per year at retail and phasing out older models and cleaning out the pipeline could take 2 to 3 years. "C" watches generally moved more quickly, with 4 to 6 stock turns per year.

Jewelry stores and department stores were accustomed to a 50–55 percent markup. Mass merchandisers' margins varied and went as low as 25 percent.

COMPETITORS IN THE GLOBAL WATCH INDUSTRY

Timex

Timex, a U.S. company, began selling inexpensive, mechanical watches in the late 1950's. Most Timex watches fell into the "C" range, with prices ranging from under Sfr 15 to just over Sfr 250.

The company developed into a manufacturer of mass-produced, hard alloy pin-lever watches. Manufacturing was mechanized, simplified and standardized. When the company's pricing plan called for a 30 percent markup at the retail level, jewelry stores refused to carry the watches. Timex moved into mass outlets such as drug, department and hardware stores, and even cigar stands. The number of outlets for Timex watches in 1985 was estimated between 100,000 and 150,000. This figure was down from a high of 2.5 million in the 1960's. By the late 1960's, 50 percent of all watches sold in the U.S. were Timex. In 1985 Timex had capacity to produce 15 million watches.

Timex had an advertising budget of approximately Sfr. 20 million, most of which was spent on television sports events. Timex produced a large number of styles, but did not promote any single model or style. The company was known

EXHIBIT 10A Watch Purchases by Outlet Type in the U.S.

Number of items	% Analog	% Digital	% Watches (485)
Jewelry store	34.3	12.0	27.6
Department store	26.3	27.6	26.2
Discount store	14.7	23.1	16.7
Catalog showroom	14.7	10.4	10.3
Mail order	14.7	11.2	5.4
Wholesaler	2.5	1.5	3.1
Drug store	2.0	6.0	5.1
Flea market*			2.4
Other outlets	3.0	7.5	6.2

* Flea markets accounted for less than 1% of all categories

EXHIBIT 10B Cost of Purchases in Main Outlets

Number of items	$1000+ (40)	$300–999 (173)	$100–299 (485)	$50–99 (466)	$25–49 (657)
Jewelry store	70.0%	69.4%	49.1%	34.6%	27.2%
Department Store		6.9	16.7	22.5	27.9
Discount Store	2.5	1.7	5.8	9.7	10.5
Catalog Showroom	5.0	5.2	8.9	9.4	7.3
Other outlets	22.5	16.8	19.5	23.8	27.1

for its "takes a licking and keeps on ticking" slogan, promoting Timex durability.

Timex began limited production of digital watches in 1972. By the mid-1970's the company was feeling pressure from new entrants from Japan and the U.S. Sales support for mechanical watches was withdrawn and Timex attempted to increase its digital capacity and to gain electronics capabilities rapidly. As a mechanical watch manufacturer Timex had been fully integrated, but used outside sources for electronic components. The company's initial entries to the digital market were poorly received and sales declined to Sfr. 1 billion in 1979. During the 1970's the company faced significant losses which amounted to Sfr. 260 million by the end of 1982. These losses were expected to escalate.

In the 1980's Timex moved into consumer electronics, computers, home health care products and refocused its watch business to try to halt its profit slide and plant closings. In 1981

EXHIBIT 10C Brand Distribution of Watch Purchases in the U.S.

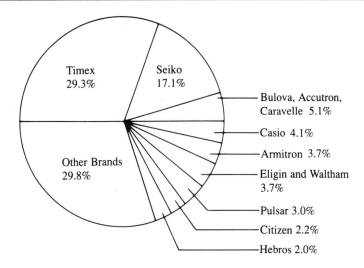

Source: National Jeweler/HTI.
Consumer Survey 1983.

Timex invested in a British home-computer company founded by inventor Clive Sinclair. The computer had little capacity but had the lowest price on the market. In 1982, fierce price competition in the home-computer market squeezed margins and the price was cut in half to approximately Sfr. 100. The company also lost sales to competitors such as Commodore which offered more power for about Sfr. 180. Timex management viewed the watch industry as splitting into two parts: jewelry and wrist instruments. Timex reported that its development plans would emphasize the wrist-instrument business with multi-function watches.

Texas Instruments, Inc.

In 1975 a number of U.S. electronics companies entered the industry with digital watches and circuits for electronic movements. Finding themselves with excess capacity an estimated 100 chip producers entered the watch market. Most started as suppliers of movements and components and integrated forward into produc-

tion and assembly of complete watches. In the early days of digital watch sales, demand far outstripped capacity. In spite of this fact, the electronics companies continually pushed price down in a market share war which eventually destroyed this attempted entry into the watch business.

Texas Instruments (TI) was the largest of the semi-conductor and computer companies to enter the watch industry. Its consumer electronics division began in the early 1970's with hand-held calculators. The company then broadened this line with watches, home computers and educational products.

Watch manufacturing at TI began in 1976, when its first LED, plastic-cased watch with a Sfr. 40 price tag was introduced. One month later the price was cut in half. TI developed a digital watch that could be made from TI built parts on automated equipment. Prices were set to undercut the mechanical watch competition with a goal to gain a large piece of both the U.S. and global market. Prices were set to reflect budgeted, future volumes.

While TI had surprised the competition with reduced prices, it was caught off-guard with advances in digital display readouts. To provide a full line of products the company imported 7 out of 13 of its basic lines from Hong Kong, including its multifunction watches. The corporation reported Sfr. 6.4 billion in sales in 1979, Sfr. 800 million of which came from consumer goods. The division showed a pre-tax profit of Sfr. 4 million down from pre-tax $28 million in 1978. Profits continued to slide and TI moved out of the watch industry in 1982.

Casio Computer Company

In 1974 Casio, a Japanese computer company entered the market and claimed 12 percent share of all Japanese watches sold within 5 years. Casio watches were sold in the "C" price range. Casio manufactured its watches in highly automated factories. Its product line was limited to digital watches, many of them multi-functional with stop watches, timers and calculators. Casio management has been quoted as saying: "People should own at least 3 watches." In 1985 Casio was selling an estimated 30 million watches per year. The Casio name was clearly linked worldwide with multifunction watches.

Casio's first entry into the digital market was priced at Sfr. 180 and initial sales were weak. As the company's watch prices began to fall, sales doubled annually from 1974–80.

Casio was among the first electronic watch producers to determine that the electronic watch's greatest appeal was technical rather than aesthetic. The company urged its department and mass merchandise store retailers to display its watches in the camera, calculator or stereo department, rather than the jewelry department. Casio management felt that sales personnel at these counters understood electronic equipment better than jewelry salespeople and could therefore answer customer questions.

The Hong Kong Watchmakers

Hong Kong entered the watch market in a major way in 1976, specializing in inexpensive electronic and mechanical watches. Hong Kong watch manufacturers did not sell under their own company or brand name. Private label watches were produced and sold in minimum lots of 1000–2000 pieces per model.

Ten major producers accounted for an estimated 70 percent of total volume, but as many as 800 "loft workshops" were also operating. These production facilities could be started at low cost and run with minimum overheads. Hong Kong was the world's largest watch exporter, and was responsible for 326.4 million units in 1984; total value was Sfr. 2,091.2 million.

Most watch production in Hong Kong was limited to assembly. Inexpensive components and movements were purchased in large lot sizes. Hong Kong manufacturers kept their design costs minimal or non-existent by producing copies and near-copies of watches displayed at trade fairs and in jewelry stores. Average ex-factory prices were Sfr. 25 for a mechanical, Sfr. 60 for quartz analog and Sfr. 12 for electronic digitals. Hong Kong watch prices began to fall rapidly in the late 1970's. Simple watches selling for Sfr. 18–20 in 1978 dropped to Sfr. 12 in one year and margins shrunk to less than Sfr. 1.

Counterfeiting was a fairly common practice among small Hong Kong manufacturers. A counterfeit copied the original watch design and was marked with the brand name. This practice was generally avoided by the large producers who beginning in the early 1980's were seeking entry into the international watch establishment. Counterfeiting was a significant problem faced by European and Japanese producers. Unlike technological innovations, it was very difficult to establish patents or copyrights on designs. Firms could begin to protect their brand name by establishing a company or joint-venture within Hong Kong.

SWATCH Watch SA

SWATCH was a plastic, quartz analog watch. SWATCH was sold at Sfr 15 ex-factory and Sfr 50 at retail in Switzerland. Prices outside of Switzerland were slightly higher and the top price was $30 in the U.S. The product was available in 12 styles, which changed twice per year, in a woman's and a man's model.

SWATCH WATCH was an Asuag-SSIH company under the direction of Ernst Thomke. It was founded in 1985 when it was split off from its original producer ETA. SWATCH WATCH remained within the Ebauches group of Asuag-SSIH. Within two years of its introduction in 1982, the brand had hit sales of 3.5 million units. Sales for 1985 were expected to reach 7.5 million units. In 1985 SWATCH management was concerned that the company's already constrained capacity could become an increasingly significant problem over the next few years. The product was produced on a fully automated and robotized assembly line and the hands were the only component purchased from an outside source. The company had enjoyed rapid decline in production costs per watch. Thomke had met and surpassed his original target production cost of Sfr. 10 per watch.

From introduction it had been positioned for active people, a sport or fashion accessory and not as a time piece. The watch sold in jewelry and department stores. The company had spent heavily on promotion and advertising, budgeting approximately Sfr. 5 per watch for marketing expense and profits.

SWATCH invested Sfr 20 million in marketing efforts and was expected to spend Sfr 30 million in 1985. SWATCH was sold in 19 industrial countries and approximately 50 percent of all SWATCHes were sold in the U.S. In the majority of markets independent distributors were employed. However, SWATCH WATCH USA was a wholly owned subsidiary which controlled distribution in the U.S. SWATCH WATCH USA played a significant role in the creation of marketing strategy and planning for the watch.

Seiko

Seiko, part of the K. Hattori Company, began marketing an electronic, quartz watch in 1969 and emerged as the market volume leader in the global watch industry within ten years. In 1984 the company reported annual sales of Sfr. 3.8 billion for watches and clocks. Seiko brand

watches fell within the "B" category. But the company competed in the "C" segment watches with the Alba and Larus labels; high "C" or low "B" segment with the Pulsar label and "A" segment with the Jean Lassale brand. In 1984 the company sold 55 million watches, 22 million under the Seiko brand.

Seiko had been using assembly line production since the mid-1950's. Following the example of the Detroit automobile factories, its engineers designed assembly lines and unskilled laborers were employed in most production. The firm was fully integrated: manufacturing key components, jewels and even watchmaking machinery. Seiko was among the first to initiate large scale production and sales of electronic watches.

Seiko had been protected from foreign competitors in its domestic market. Only expensive watches, about 5 percent of total units and 20 percent of total value of Japanese purchases, were imported. Almost all of the low- to mid-price watches purchased in Japan were produced by Seiko or one of its two domestic competitors, Citizen and Casio. Japanese companies produced some low priced movements for Hong Kong manufacturers. However, movements for "B" watch production were not exported to Hong Kong.

Seiko used the U.S. as a market for initial entry, where they gained a reputation which they then sold worldwide. The company offered fewer than 400 quartz and mechanical models in the U.S., but over 2,300 worldwide. These models included analog, digital and multifunctions watches. Plans called for an expansion of the number of styles sold in the U.S. and a broadening of the price range at the upper and lower ends of the market.

Seiko owned sales subsidiaries in all of its major markets. Seiko watches were sold in jewelry and department stores. It had also established service centers in all of its major markets. This service allowed the customer to bring or mail a repair problem directly to the company, by-passing the jeweler. Seiko spent as much as Sfr. 80–100 million annually in worldwide advertising, mostly television, to sell its quartz watches. Seiko had created a strong brand image based on its quartz technology and accuracy.

While Seiko was a formidable competitor for the Swiss watch industry, Japanese consumers were a major market for Swiss luxury watches. Throughout the 1970's and 1980's Swiss luxury watches were considered a status symbol in Japan. In 1981 Seiko moved into the luxury market, at home and abroad, when it purchased a small Swiss watch producer Jean Lassale. The company's plan was to combine Swiss design and elegance with Japanese engineering and technical skill in electronics.

By 1970 both Seiko and its Japanese competitor Citizen had diversified into new businesses with internal development, mergers and acquisitions. Included in the expanded product line were: consumer electronic products such as computers, software, calculators, high-speed printers, miniature industrial robots, office equipment and machine tools and even fashion department stores. As Seiko faced the 1990's, these product lines were expected to become an increasingly important part of the company's total sales and profits. In 1970 clocks and watches represented 99 percent of Seiko sales; but by 1983 that share had dropped to 40 percent. Top executives at Seiko expected this figure to continue to decline to 30 percent by 1990.

Longines SA

Longines was well-known internationally but losing money when it was acquired by Asuag in 1974. Longines was developed into the group's premiere, or top-priced, brand and began contributing to profits in 1976.

After joining ASUAG, Longines' prices began to climb, as the company edged its way into the high-priced "A" watch segment. The first Swiss manufacturer to produce electronic watches in 1969, Longines' product mix was 50 percent electronic. In 1985 average ex-factory price for Longines watches was Sfr 450 to 500.

Longines produced at levels of about 500,000 watches per year. Investments were made in more efficient machines to reduce dependence on skilled labor and the number of different types of movements and other precision

parts was cut back. Longines continued to make about 30 lines, each with many variations.

Longines put all of its promotion money behind its leader model, the "Conquest." Management felt that the top priced "Conquest" best represented the overall style of the collection. "The Longines Style" campaign was supported with an advertising and promotion budget of 10 percent of total sales and this sum was matched by Longines agents. Advertisements were placed in international and local media.

In 1984 Longines introduced a new watch line, the Conquest VHP. VHP stood for "very high precision" and the watch promised accuracy within 1 second per month. The gun metal-colored titanium and gold watch contained two quartz crystals. The first was the timekeeper and the second compensated for vibrations and effects of the weather. The watch sold for Sfr. 1,650 at retail and initial response from the marketplace was very positive. Advertising for the new line stressed the watch's Swiss origin with the heading "Swiss Achievement."

Rolex

Rolex, with its prestigious "Oyster" line was perhaps the best known of the Swiss luxury watch manufacturers. Rolex was a private company, owned by a foundation. The company was responsible for about 5.5 percent of Switzerland's watch exports by volume, with estimated annual export of 400,000 units, valued at Sfr. 700–800 million. Rolex did not disclose its domestic sales.

Ninety percent of all Rolex watches were produced with mechanical movements housed in gold or platinum cases. The "Oyster" line was described as a premium sports watch. Retail "Oyster" watch prices ranged from Sfr. 800 for stainless steel watches to Sfr. 14,000 for solid gold watches. Production was semi-automated and Geneva housewives made up a large part of the semi-skilled labor. Skilled workers were required for hand-assembly in the final stages of production. The company always allowed production to lag slightly behind demand.

Throughout the turbulent 1970's, the company had stayed consistently with the luxury sport watch market. Rolex limited advertising to the higher-priced "Oyster" line. Rolex also had a second line: "Cellini," of high priced luxury dress watches. The company resisted entry into the electronic age; only 10 percent of the Rolex line was electronic. There was some speculation that in the next 3 to 5 years quartz watches would rise to 30 percent of total output. In 1983, quartz production was limited to watches under the Tudor brand, at the low end of Rolex's market and were priced below Sfr. 1200. The Tudor watches were not advertised and did not bear the Rolex name. In 1985, Rolex catalogue included 3 "Oysterquartz" models.

Rolex employed wholly owned, marketing subsidiaries in 19 countries. The Geneva headquarters worked through the subsidiaries to license jewelers to sell and service its watches. The subsidiaries provided sales and service support to local retailers and watch repairers. Maintaining adequate service coverage was important in an era of throw-away watches. For example, the New York subsidiary licensed 70 watch repairers to service Rolex watches. Distribution to retail outlets was based on a quota system. Subsidiaries were also used to maintain tight control over retail prices; Rolex did not permit any discounting. Promotion and advertising expenditures were estimated at 10 percent of sales. This expenditure was matched by the wholesalers and retailers.

Piaget SA

Piaget SA was founded by George Piaget in 1874, and in 1985 was still a family business directed by the founder's grandsons and great-grandsons. The company's workshops produced approximately 15,000 handmade watches each year at prices ranging from Sfr. 4,000 to 400,000. The company carried a large collection of luxury watches for both men and women, producing approximately 1200 models.

Only gold and/or platinum were used to encase the watch movements, and many of the watches were decorated with precious stones. Both mechanical and quartz models were included in the Piaget's collection. Piaget was the only producer of luxury dress watches which was fully integrated. The company produced the world's thinnest mechanical watches: 1.2mm for a hand wind model, and 2mm for an automatic. Historically, the Piaget line was limited to dress watches, but the company entered the sports watch market in 1980.

Worldwide, Piaget watches were carried by 400 retailers. They tended to be the most prestigious stores in their areas and were located to be accessible to potential luxury watch buyers. Whenever possible, the watchmaker preferred retailers to carry only Piaget in their luxury dress watch line. Annual advertising expenditure for Piaget was estimated at Sfr. 3 million, excluding the U.S. About 55 percent of this expense was paid for by Piaget, and the rest was contribution from distributors and retailers.

Other Swiss manufacturers producing luxury dress watches included: Audemars-Piguet, Patek-Philippe and Vacheron & Constantin. All three were smaller than Piaget, producing less than 15,000 watches per year and followed similar strategies.

Ebel

Ebel was founded in 1911 by Eugene Blum. The company described its transition in the 1970's as a renaissance.

In 1974 the third generation of Blums, Pierre-Alain, took over the company. When Pierre-Alain Blum became president Ebel's 50 employees were making private label watches. With new management, Ebel began to take a closer look at the customers of its chief client Cartier. Within a short period of time, Ebel began branded watch production and employment grew to 500 people. 1984 sales were estimated between Sfr. 150 and 170 million.

The company's growth came about with the development of a unique one piece watch case and bracelet construction which became the base for the Ebel collection. Ebel's goal was to design and maintain a "classic," timeless collection and the company did not plan to make major annual changes to its line. Ebel watches sold at retail Sfr. 1,000 to 15,000. The company had five models and realized 90 percent of its sales from the top three. The company's goal was to create a strong brand image. Using its leader model, Ebel promoted its watch lines with the slogan "architects of time."

Ebel moved into electronic movements in 1978. With that change in technology the company enjoyed a boost in sales. In 1985 Ebel was assembling 300,000 units per year. The company maintained tight control over its suppliers. Ebel had production and development contracts with its movement suppliers and partial ownership of its case and bracelet manufacturer. The company still assembled private label watches for Cartier. In 1975 sales to Cartier had represented 90 percent of sales, 10 years later these sales represented less than 50 percent of total. It was estimated that Cartier sales provided about 25 percent of Ebel's profits in 1984.

Blum maintained close personal contact with the end customer with frequent visits to jewelry stores. His goal was to keep a close eye on stock levels at jewelry stores and avoid a build up of stocks in the distribution channels. He also wanted to insure that the jewelry store's image was in line with the Ebel image.

In addition to its "architects of time" media advertising, Ebel also used sports sponsorship as a means of building an image with the public. Ebel became one of the first watch companies to actively use sporting events for its watches' promotion. Ebel sponsorships included a soccer team in Geneva and tennis and golf matches.

In the 1980's Ebel was broadening its business activities. It expanded its product line by becoming the distributor for Schaeffer pens. Ebel also entered the clothing business with the American firm, Fenn, Wright and Manson. They opened a boutique in Geneva and others were in the planning stages. Finally, Ebel was the agent for Olivetti computers for the French speaking part of Switzerland. The distribution company employed 12 people including programmers.

Recent Entrants in the Watch Industry

A new group of "outsiders" and "newcomers" has entered the global watch industry. Many of these companies (or current ownership) have been operating for 10 years or less. With few exceptions, these "watchmakers" subcon-

tracted all production and assembly, mostly in Switzerland. The watches were then positioned in the market as high fashion pieces.

Included in this group were Raymond Weil, founded in 1976. Within 10 years the company had reached annual sales levels of approximately 300,000 quartz watches, at prices ranging from Sfr. 500 to 1700. All work was subcontracted to companies and individual component manufacturers and assemblers in the Jura region of Switzerland. The company employed 15 people for design, marketing and sales and administration. One-third of all wholesale activities were captively held.

Weil's success in the watch industry was attributed to the company's sense of style and fashion. A new collection was introduced each year with six woman's and six man's watches. Weil was constantly responding to changes in consumer tastes and the latest trend. His 1985 spring collection was named for a hit movie, *Amadeus,* a biography of the life of Mozart. Raymond Weil had a limited budget for its advertising and promotion expenditures, relying on a few well-placed messages and style to sell its products.

Cartier watches were classic in design and limited to 15 different models. Cartier subcontracted its watches from Ebel. The Cartier watch lines did include models which sold for as much as Sfr. 100,000. Most Cartier watches sold at prices ranging from Sfr. 1,200–25,000. Most Cartier watches were quartz. Selling at a level of 450,000 units per year, the watch was an addition to the company's collection of accessories and jewelry. The watches were sold through the company's specialized retail stores and independent boutiques, jewelry and fashionable department stores all over the world. Watch advertising and promotion expenses were minimized because the company's name was well recognized in the market place and the watch fell under the umbrella of the company's other accessories.

Gucci watches were sold by an independent entrepreneur who licensed the Gucci name. These "A" watches were sold at Gucci shops and by independent jewelers and high fashion department stores and boutiques. Annual volumes for Gucci watches were estimated at 400,000 units. The company did not advertise heavily and relied on the Gucci name for prestigious name brand identity.

SUMMARY

Thomke knew that there were a number of options open to him to bring Tissot from its current status of a "branded commodity." He estimated that relaunch in Europe would be a minimum of Sfr. 12 million. Costs for reintroducing Tissot to the U.S. would be even greater. To afford these marketing expenses, Tissot marketing and profit margins would have to improve and sales volumes would have to grow. Thomke knew he could shift prices and was considering pushing Tissot prices downward to the bottom of the "B" group. A downward price shift would require a considerable increase in volume if the Tissot brand was to be profitable. The producer's margin decreased as watches moved down market to the "B" and "C" segments. Thomke knew that producers of expensive watches which had a strong positive image with consumers could command high ex-factory prices. This provided the luxury watch firms with considerable margins for marketing expenditures and profit.

Thomke believed that to operate profitably a watch had to capture at least 10 percent of its market segment. He wanted to produce a workable brand strategy which would allow Tissot to gain at least 10 percent of its segment. Thomke had several key factors to consider. The fast paced technological changes of the 1970's had slowed and the traditional watch buying market was maturing. However, he saw that nontraditional approaches in the industry had allowed new entrants such as Raymond Weil and SWATCH to successfully gain footholds and profits in the global watch industry.

INDEX